SOMETHING ABOUT THE AUTHOR®

Something about
the Author *was named
an "Outstanding
Reference Source,"
the highest honor given
by the American
Library Association
Reference and Adult
Services Division.*

ISSN 0276-816X

something
ABOUT THE
AUTHOR®

**Facts and Pictures about Authors
and Illustrators of Books for Young People**

volume 231

GALE
CENGAGE Learning®

Detroit • New York • San Francisco • New Haven, Conn • Waterville, Maine • London

Something about the Author, Volume 231

Project Editor: Lisa Kumar

Permissions: Leitha Etheridge-Sims

Imaging and Multimedia: Leitha Etheridge-Sims, John Watkins

Composition and Electronic Capture: Amy Darga

Manufacturing: Rhonda Dover

Product Manager: Mary Onorato

© 2012 Gale, Cengage Learning

For product information and technology assistance, contact us at **Gale Customer Support, 1-800-877-4253.**
For permission to use material from this text or product, submit all requests online at **www.cengage.com/permissions.**
Further permissions questions can be emailed to **permissionrequest@cengage.com**

Gale, Cengage Learning
27500 Drake Rd.
Farmington Hills, MI, 48331-3535

LIBRARY OF CONGRESS CATALOG CARD NUMBER 62-52046

ISBN-13: 978-1-4144-6134-2
ISBN-10: 1-4144-6134-8

ISSN 0276-816X

This title is also available as an e-book.
ISBN-13: 978-1-4144-6463-3
ISBN-10: 1-4144-6463-0
Contact your Gale, Cengage Learning sales representative for ordering information.

Printed in Mexico
1 2 3 4 5 6 7 15 14 13 12 11

Contents

Authors in Forthcoming Volumes vii

Introduction ix

SATA Product Advisory Board xi

Illustrations Index 197

Author Index 233

A

Adam, Paul 1958- 1

Adler, David A. 1947- 3

Albee, Sarah 1962- 14

Allen, Constance
   See Albee, Sarah 14

Avasthi, Swati 1971- 19

B

Bachem, Paul 21

Bancks, Tristan 1974- 22

Bennett, Kelly 1958- 24

Bennett, Kelly Goldman
   See Bennett, Kelly 24

Birdsall, Jeanne 1951- 26

Blackall, Sophie 29

Bright, Paul 1949- 33

C

Callen, Liz 1951- 36

Cardinale, Christopher 37

Carter, Scott William 39

Cole, Joanna 1944- 41

Cooke, Ann
   See Cole, Joanna 41

Corriveau, Art 50

Cusick, Richie Tankersley 1952- 52

D

Day, Susie 1975- 56

Derting, Kimberly 1968- 57

E

Emond, Stephen 1979(?)- 58

Engel, Christiane 60

Engle, Margarita 1951- 62

F

Falcone, L.M. 1951- 66

Falcone, Lucy M.
   See Falcone, L.M. 66

Ford, A.G. 68

Fromental, Jean-Luc 1950- 71

G

Gilani, Fawzia
   See Gilani-Williams, Fawzia 74

Gilani-Williams, Fawzia 1967- 74

González, Christina Díaz 1969- 75

Gray, Steve 1950- 77

H

Harris, Maria Guadalupe
   See Harris, M.G. 79

Harris, M.G. 79

Hewitt, Sally 1949- 80

Houston, Dick 1943- 88

Houtman, Jacqueline 1960- 89

Houtman, Jacqueline Jaeger
   See Houtman, Jacqueline 89

Hoxter, Holly Nicole 1983- 90

J

Jay, Stacey 1978(?)- 92

Jennings, Sharon 1954- 94

Johnson, Dianne
   See Johnson, Dinah 99

Johnson, Dinah 1960- 99

Jutte, Jan 1953- 101

K

Katz, Alan 106

Kelley, J.A.
 See Kelley, Jane 109

Kelley, Jane 1954- 109

Khan, Rukhsana 1962- 111

Kurilla, Renée 1981- 116

L

Lacy, Rick 118

Lagos, Joseph 118

Larbalestier, Justine 120

Lloyd, Alison 1966- 123

Lukas, Catherine
 See Albee, Sarah 14

M

Mackler, Carolyn 1973- 124

Marino, Gianna 127

Max, Jill
 See Bennett, Kelly 24

McGhee, Alison 1960- 128

Messer, Stephen 1972- 132

Montalbano, Andrea 133

N

Na, Il Sung 135

Nolte, Jack
 See Carter, Scott William 39

O

Offermann, Andrea 137

Olander, Johan 1967- 138

P

Palmer, Gary 140

Patt, Beverly 140

Paulsen, Gary 1939- 141

Pogue, David 1963- 152

R

Rave, Friederike 1970- 155

Rockwell, Thomas 1933- 156

Ross, Sylvia 1937- 159

S

Salerni, Dianne K. 160

Schertle, Alice 1941- 161

Schmid, Paul 168

Shea, Bob 169

Smith Hernández, Duncan Tonatiuh
 See Tonatiuh, Duncan 180

Smith, Jim W.W. 172

Stone, Mary Hanlon 172

Swinburne, Stephen R. 1952- 173

T

Teplin, Scott 179

Tonatiuh, Duncan 180

Townsend, Michael 1981- 182

V

Vogel, Carole Garbuny 1951- 185

W

Waber, Paulis 188

Wiewandt, Thomas 1945- 189

Wildish, Lee 191

Willson, Sarah
 See Albee, Sarah 14

Wrongo, I.B.
 See Katz, Alan 106

Y

Yue, Stephanie 1984- 193

Z

Zakanitch, Robert Rahway 1935- 194

Zakanitch, Robert S.
 See Zakanitch, Robert Rahway 194

Authors in Forthcoming Volumes

Below are some of the authors and illustrators that will be featured in upcoming volumes of *SATA*. These include new entries on the swiftly rising stars of the field, as well as completely revised and updated entries (indicated with *) on some of the most notable and best-loved creators of books for children.

Barnholdt, Lauren ▌A Massachusetts-based writer, Barnholdt is the author of more than a dozen books, including novels for young adults and preteens and chapter books for apprentice readers. In addition to her fantasy series featuring the whimsically named second grader Hailey Twitch, Barnholdt entertains older readers with novels such as *Reality Chick, Two-way Street, One Night That Changes Everything,* and *Watch Me.*

*Bottner, Barbara ▌An accomplished writer and illustrator as well as a filmmaker and teacher, Bottner is the author of such popular children's books as *Bootsie Barker Bites* and its sequel as well as *Wallace's Lists, Raymond and Nelda,* and *Miss Brooks Loves Books! (and I Don't).* Often featuring animal characters and illustrated by artists that include Denise Brunkus, G. Brian Karas, and Victoria Chess as well as Bottner herself, her stories pair humorous narratives with endearing characters. In addition to her work as a writer, Bottner is also an acclaimed writing instructor, having worked with such individuals as Lane Smith, April Halprin Wayland, and Bruce Degen.

Córdova, Amy ▌A respected artist and educator, Córdova creates artwork for numerous picture books, among them stories by such authors as Carmen Tafolla and Rudolfo Anaya, in addition to illustrating several original stories of her own. Córdova has earned recognition for her vivid, brightly colored paintings which focus on the people and landscape of New Mexico, where she lives and works. Among her honors, she is the recipient of Pura Belpré Illustrator Award Honor Book citations for *What Can You Do with a Rebozo?* and *Fiesta Babies,* both which feature text by Tafolla.

*Katz, Karen ▌Katz is a former costume designer and quilt maker who now writes and illustrates picture books and lift-the-flap books for young readers. She earned her degree at the Yale School of Art and Architecture and then set about establishing her career, which has been highlighted by such critically acclaimed works as *Over the Moon: An Adoption Tale, Mommy Hugs, Princess Baby,* and *Babies on the Bus.* For her efforts, she has earned several National Parenting Publications awards among other honors.

Levy, Debbie ▌A former newspaper editor and attorney, Levy has established a second career as the author of nonfiction books that include *Richard Wright: A Biography, The Berlin Air Lift,* and *Bigotry.* She has also authored the verse novel *The Year of Goodbyes,* a Sydney Taylor Award Notable Book that recounts her mother's experiences as a young girl living in Nazi Germany. Although her law training strengthened her research skills and made her most comfortable telling true tales rather than spinning stories, Levy also indulges her whimsical side in *Maybe I'll Sleep in the Bathtub Tonight, and Other Funny Bedtime Poems.*

*Mora, Pat ▌One of the most distinguished Hispanic writers working in the United States, Mora is also an advocate working to advance cultural appreciation and literacy as well as conservation. In books such as *Pablo's Tree, Adobe Odes, Book Fiesta!,* and *Dizzy in Your Eyes,* Mora tries to instill in young Latinos pride in their heritage, mixing Spanish words into English texts as a way of advancing the recognition and preservation of Mexican-American culture.

Peirce, Lincoln ▌Peirce is a cartoonist and creator of the "Big Nate" comic strip, which is syndicated to over 250 U.S. newspapers, posted on *Comics.com,* and collected in the books *Big Nate from the Top* and *Big Nate Out Loud.* The eleven-year-old braniac who stars in Peirce's popular strip has also made appearances in several well-illustrated chapter books, among them *Big Nate: In a Class by Himself, Big Nate Strikes Again,* and *Big Nate: On a Roll.* In chronicling the preteen's comic exploits, Peirce draws on memories of his own childhood and his experience as a high-school art teacher.

*Schlitz, Laura Amy ▌Schlitz made a name for herself in 2006, when her first two books were published to widespread critical acclaim. A librarian at privately run Park School in Baltimore, Maryland, she had been writing for many years when Candlewick Press decided to release her middle-grade melodrama *A Drowned Maiden's Hair* as well as her nonfiction title *The Hero Schleimann: The Dreamer Who Dug for Troy.* Two years later, she made the news again, this time when her play anthology *Good Masters! Sweet Ladies! Voices from a Medieval Village* was honored with the prestigious Newbery Award.

Wright, Simeon ▌Wright shares the intersection between his own life and history in *Simeon's Story: An Eyewitness Account of the Kidnaping of Emmett Till,* a memoir coauthored by Herb Boyd. The cousin of Till, the teenaged victim of a tragic abduction and lynching that became a touchstone of the civil rights movement due to its violence and injustice, Wright helps new generations of Americans understand what life was like in 1944 Mississippi. He also shows that the horrors of racism did not stop brave people from speaking up during Till's murder trial and in the years since in their search for justice.

*Yelchin, Eugene ▌Born in the former USSR, Yelchin worked in Russian theatre before trading life under communism for a new life in the United States. In addition to winning respect for his work in advertising art and film—he designed the first polar-bear advertisements used by Coca Cola—Yelchin has become a widely exhibited fine-art painter who has also found an outlet for his creativity in children's picture books, where his work appears alongside stories by Candace Fleming, Ann Hodgman, Lee Wardlaw, Ann Redisch Stampler, Barbara Joosse, and his own wife, author Mary Kuryla. In 2011 he also added "author" to his list of credits with a self-illustrated story that draws on his memories of growing up in the USSR: *Breaking Stalin's Nose.*

Introduction

Something about the Author (*SATA*) is an ongoing reference series that examines the lives and works of authors and illustrators of books for children. *SATA* includes not only well-known writers and artists but also less prominent individuals whose works are just coming to be recognized. This series is often the only readily available information source on emerging authors and illustrators. You'll find *SATA* informative and entertaining, whether you are a student, a librarian, an English teacher, a parent, or simply an adult who enjoys children's literature.

What's Inside *SATA*

SATA provides detailed information about authors and illustrators who span the full time range of children's literature, from early figures like John Newbery and L. Frank Baum to contemporary figures like Judy Blume and Richard Peck. Authors in the series represent primarily English-speaking countries, particularly the United States, Canada, and the United Kingdom. Also included, however, are authors from around the world whose works are available in English translation. The writings represented in *SATA* include those created intentionally for children and young adults as well as those written for a general audience and known to interest younger readers. These writings cover the entire spectrum of children's literature, including picture books, humor, folk and fairy tales, animal stories, mystery and adventure, science fiction and fantasy, historical fiction, poetry and nonsense verse, drama, biography, and nonfiction. Obituaries are also included in *SATA* and are intended not only as death notices but also as concise overviews of people's lives and work. Additionally, each edition features newly revised and updated entries for a selection of *SATA* listees who remain of interest to today's readers and who have been active enough to require extensive revisions of their earlier biographies.

Autobiography Feature

Beginning with Volume 103, many volumes of *SATA* feature one or more specially commissioned autobiographical essays. These unique essays, averaging about ten thousand words in length and illustrated with an abundance of personal photos, present an entertaining and informative first-person perspective on the lives and careers of prominent authors and illustrators profiled in *SATA*.

Two Convenient Indexes

In response to suggestions from librarians, *SATA* indexes no longer appear in every volume but are included in alternate (odd-numbered) volumes of the series, beginning with Volume 57.

SATA continues to include two indexes that cumulate with each alternate volume: the Illustrations Index, arranged by the name of the illustrator, gives the number of the volume and page where the illustrator's work appears in the current volume as well as all preceding volumes in the series; the Author Index gives the number of the volume in which a person's biographical sketch, autobiographical essay, or obituary appears in the current volume as well as all preceding volumes in the series.

These indexes also include references to authors and illustrators who appear in *Gale's Yesterday's Authors of Books for Children, Children's Literature Review,* and *Something about the Author Autobiography Series.*

Easy-to-Use Entry Format

Whether you're already familiar with the *SATA* series or just getting acquainted, you will want to be aware of the kind of information that an entry provides. In every *SATA* entry the editors attempt to give as complete a picture of the person's life and work as possible. A typical entry in *SATA* includes the following clearly labeled information sections:

PERSONAL: date and place of birth and death, parents' names and occupations, name of spouse, date of marriage, names of children, educational institutions attended, degrees received, religious and political affiliations, hobbies and other interests.

ADDRESSES: complete home, office, electronic mail, and agent addresses, whenever available.

CAREER: name of employer, position, and dates for each career post; art exhibitions; military service; memberships and offices held in professional and civic organizations.

MEMBER: professional, civic, and other association memberships and any official posts held.

AWARDS, HONORS: literary and professional awards received.

WRITINGS: title-by-title chronological bibliography of books written and/or illustrated, listed by genre when known; lists of other notable publications, such as plays, screenplays, and periodical contributions.

ADAPTATIONS: a list of films, television programs, plays, CD-ROMs, recordings, and other media presentations that have been adapted from the author's work.

WORK IN PROGRESS: description of projects in progress.

SIDELIGHTS: a biographical portrait of the author or illustrator's development, either directly from the biographee—and often written specifically for the *SATA* entry—or gathered from diaries, letters, interviews, or other published sources.

BIOGRAPHICAL AND CRITICAL SOURCES: cites sources quoted in "Sidelights" along with references for further reading.

EXTENSIVE ILLUSTRATIONS: photographs, movie stills, book illustrations, and other interesting visual materials supplement the text.

How a *SATA* Entry Is Compiled

SATA editors examine a wide variety of published sources to gather information for an entry. Biographical and bibliographic sources are consulted, as are book reviews, feature articles, published interviews, and material sometimes obtained from the biographee's family, publishers, agent, or other associates. Whenever possible, the author or illustrator is sent a copy of the entry to check for accuracy and completeness.

Entries that have not been verified by the biographees or their representatives are marked with an asterisk (*).

Contact the Editor

We encourage our readers to examine the entire *SATA* series. Please write and tell us if we can make *SATA* even more helpful to you. Give your comments and suggestions to the editor:

Editor
Something about the Author
Gale, Cengage Learning
27500 Drake Rd.
Farmington Hills MI 48331-3535

Toll-free: 800-877-GALE
Fax: 248-699-8070

Something about the Author Product Advisory Board

The editors of *Something about the Author* are dedicated to maintaining a high standard of excellence by publishing comprehensive, accurate, and highly readable entries on a wide array of writers for children and young adults. In addition to the quality of the content, the editors take pride in the graphic design of the series, which is intended to be orderly yet inviting, allowing readers to utilize the pages of *SATA* easily and with efficiency. Despite the longevity of the *SATA* print series, and the success of its format, we are mindful that the vitality of a literary reference product is dependent on its ability to serve its users over time. As literature, and attitudes about literature, constantly evolve, so do the reference needs of students, teachers, scholars, journalists, researchers, and book club members. To be certain that we continue to keep pace with the expectations of our customers, the editors of *SATA* listen carefully to their comments regarding the value, utility, and quality of the series. Librarians, who have firsthand knowledge of the needs of library users, are a valuable resource for us. The *Something about the Author* Product Advisory Board, made up of school, public, and academic librarians, is a forum to promote focused feedback about *SATA* on a regular basis. The nine-member advisory board includes the following individuals, whom the editors wish to thank for sharing their expertise:

Eva M. Davis
Director,
Canton Public Library,
Canton, Michigan

Joan B. Eisenberg
Lower School Librarian,
Milton Academy,
Milton, Massachusetts

Francisca Goldsmith
Teen Services Librarian,
Berkeley Public Library,
Berkeley, California

Susan Dove Lempke
Children's Services Supervisor,
Niles Public Library District,
Niles, Illinois

Robyn Lupa
Head of Children's Services,
Jefferson County Public Library,
Lakewood, Colorado

Victor L. Schill
Assistant Branch Librarian/Children's Librarian,
Harris County Public Library/Fairbanks Branch,
Houston, Texas

Caryn Sipos
Community Librarian,
Three Creeks Community Library,
Vancouver, Washington

Steven Weiner
Director,
Maynard Public Library,
Maynard, Massachusetts

SOMETHING ABOUT THE AUTHOR

ADAM, Paul 1958-

Personal

Born 1958, in Sheffield, England; married; children: two sons. *Education:* Studied law at Nottingham University.

Addresses

Home—Sheffield, England. *Agent*—Zoe Pagnamenta Agency, LLC, 30 Bond St., New York, NY 10012; United Agents, 12-26 Lexington St., London W1F 0LE, England.

Career

Writer. Has worked as a journalist and as a writer for television and film.

Awards, Honors

Salford Children's Book Award, 2010, for *Escape from Shadow Island.*

Writings

ADULT MYSTERY NOVELS

An Exceptional Corpse, Crime Club (London, England), 1993.
Toxin, HarperCollins (London, England), 1994.

A Nasty Dose of Death, Crime Club (London, England), 1994.
Unholy Trinity (also see below), Little, Brown (London, England), 1999, Arcade (New York, NY), 2000.
Shadow Chasers (also see below), Little, Brown (London, England), 2000.
Genesis II, Little, Brown (London, England), 2001.
Flash Point, Time Warner (London, England), 2003, published as *Oracle Lake,* St. Martin's Minotaur (New York, NY), 2007.
Sleeper, Time Warner (London, England), 2004, published as *The Rainaldi Quartet,* Thomas Dunne Books (New York, NY), 2006.
Enemy Within, Time Warner (London, England), 2005.
Paul Adams Omnibus (includes *Unholy Trinity* and *Shadow Chasers*), Time Warner (London, England), 2006.
Knife Edge, Endeavour Publishing (Sheffield, England), 2008.
Paganini's Ghost, Time Warner (London, England), 2009, Minotaur (New York, NY), 2010.

"MAX CASSIDY ADVENTURE" SERIES

Escape from Shadow Island, Corgi (London, England), 2009, Walden Pond Press (New York, NY), 2010.
Jaws of Death, Random House UK (London, England), 2011.

Sidelights

British author Paul Adam established himself in journalism and television before launching a successful career as a mystery writer. In addition to popular adult novels that include *Shadow Chasers, The Rainaldi Quartet, Enemy Within,* and *Paganini's Ghost,* Adam also entertains middle-grade readers with his "Max Cassidy" novels, high-energy stories about a fourteen year old whose work as a modern-day Houdini is sidelined during a series of challenging adventures.

Adam's first work of fiction, the adult mystery *Unholy Trinity,* focuses on the murder of a controversial priest who has openly criticized corruption within the Vatican and takes readers along a trail of clues leading back to the final days of World War II. Reviewing *Unholy Trinity* in *Booklist,* Mary Carroll noted that while the implications against the Vatican are controversial, the novel treats readers to a "lively, fast-paced thriller." In a review of Adams' debut, a *Publishers Weekly* reviewer wrote that in "unraveling a fascinating tapestry of pious deceit, Adams explores carnal frailty, broken vows and religious genocide."

Sleeper—published in the United States as *The Rainaldi Quartet*—takes readers to Italy and an investigation into the death of a violin maker and music teacher. Tomaso Rainaldi disappeared sometime after playing music with his friends, parish priest Father Arrighi, detective Antonio Guastafeste, and violin maker Gianni Castiglione. After learning of his murder, Rainaldi's friends discover that he was obsessed with locating a legendary Stradivarius violin called the "Messiah's Sister," and they decide that to locate his killer they must first discover the instrument's whereabouts. Adam revisits this mix of mystery, musicianship, and an Italian setting steeped in history in *Paganini's Ghost,* which finds Detective Guastafeste rejoining Castiglione to ascertain how the contents of a locked box can be used to track down the murderer of a violin dealer with a questionable past. According to *Booklist* critic David Pitt, *The Rainaldi Quartet* utilizes "masterpieces and mayhem in nicely balanced proportions." A *Kirkus Reviews* writer noted that Adam's "leisurely, rococo storytelling perfectly suits the subtle pleasures of the tale," while in *Publishers Weekly* a critic cited the "fascinating historical and musical detail" in *The Rainaldi Quartet.* Adam's "story and style are of a piece" in *Paganini's Ghost,* noted another *Kirkus Reviews* writer, calling them "elegantly layered and intricately detailed." Praising the sequel in *Booklist,* Michele Leber deemed it "an intriguing puzzle [that] combines with an enthralling mix of Italian ambience, history, and—most of all—music."

Adam treats readers to another characteristically fast-paced page-turner in *Enemy Within,* as college lecturer Tom Whitehead is framed and arrested for possession of child pornography. *Oracle Lake* (first released in the United Kingdom as *Flash Point*) follows British photojournalist Maggie Walsh after she receives a tip that the fourteenth Dalai Lama is dying. After the death of the spiritual leader is announced to the world, Maggie joins forces with three monks who are determined to find the Dalai Lama's newborn successor and help him leave Tibet and the country's Chinese oppressors. Another novel, *Knife Edge,* follows investigative reporter Joe Verdi into a world of human smuggling and illegal migrant labor after a murder inquiry takes him undercover into Britain's agribusiness industry. A *Kirkus Reviews* critic called *Oracle Lake* "surprisingly effective in capturing the rigors of mountainous Tibet and the gentility of the Buddhist spirit," while a *Publishers Weekly* critic noted that Adam's inclusion of "numerous hairbreadth escapes" adds to the story's tension.

When readers meet Max Cassidy in *Escape from Shadow Island,* the teenaged Londoner is dealing with more pressures than the average adolescent: Max's job as an escape artist known as the "Half-Pint Houdini" presents constant challenges and opportunities to be innovative; his escape-artist dad, Alexander Cassidy, is missing and presumed dead; and his mom is serving a long prison term for her husband's presumed murder. When a stranger hints that Alexander may be alive, Max follows a lead to Santo Domingo where his professional skills may be the only thing that saves him from a terrible fate. His search moves to Sweden and Borneo in *Jaws of Death,* as the determined Max continues to dedicate his efforts to reuniting with his absent parents. A fast-moving story, *Escape from Shadow Island* is "made more interesting by its insider insights into escapology," noted *School Library Journal* critic Jeffrey Hastings, and a *Kirkus Reviews* critic predicted of the novel that "literate thriller readers . . . will enjoy and likely ask for the next installment" in the "Max Cassidy" series.

Biographical and Critical Sources

PERIODICALS

Booklist, May 15, 2000, Mary Carroll, review of *Unholy Trinity,* p. 1732; February 1, 2006, David Pitt, review of *The Rainaldi Quartet,* p. 35; January 1, 2010, Michele Leber, review of *Paganini's Ghost,* p. 52.

Bulletin of the Center for Children's Books, May, 2010, Elizabeth Bush, review of *Max Cassidy: Escape from Shadow Island,* p. 368.

Entertainment Weekly, March 3, 2006, Tina Jordan, review of *The Rainaldi Quartet,* p. 107.

Kirkus Reviews, May 15, 2004, review of *Flash Point,* p. 455; January 1, 2006, review of *The Rainaldi Quartet,* p. 17; June 15, 2007, review of *Oracle Lake;* November 1, 2009, review of *Paganini's Ghost*; January 1, 2010, review of *Max Cassidy: Escape from Shadow Island.*

Publishers Weekly, April 24, 2000, review of *Unholy Trinity,* p. 63; December 12, 2005, review of *The Rainaldi Quartet,* p. 42; May 21, 2007, review of *Oracle Lake,* p. 34; November 2, 2009, review of *Paganini's Ghost,* p. 38.

School Library Journal, April, 2010, Jeffrey Hastings, review of *Max Cassidy: Escape from Shadow Island,* p. 150.

Tribune Books (Chicago, IL), March 19, 2006, Dick Adler, review of *The Rainaldi Quartet*, p. 8.

Voice of Youth Advocates, January 7, 2011, review of *Max Cassidy: Escape from Shadow Island,* p. 53.

Washington Post Book World, March 26, 2006, Richard Lipez, review of *The Rainaldi Quartet,* p. 13.

ONLINE

Crime Time Web site, http://www.crimetime.co.uk/ (November 3, 2006), Michael Carlson, review of *Enemy Within.*

Paul Adam Home Page, http://pauladam.com (June 26, 2011).*

*   *   *

ADLER, David A. 1947-

Personal

Born April 10, 1947, in New York, NY; son of Sidney G. (a teacher) and Betty (a psychiatric social worker) Adler; married Renée Hamada (a psychologist), April 8, 1973; children: Michael, Edward, Etian. *Education:* Queens College of the City University of New York, B.A., 1968; New York University, M.B.A., 1971; doctoral study, 1971-72. *Religion:* Jewish. *Hobbies and other interests:* Travel, reading, photography, political memorabilia, baseball, art, old-time radio broadcasts.

Addresses

Office—P.O. Box 66, Hewlett, NY 11557. *Agent*—Writers House, 21 W. 26th St., New York, NY 10010. *E-mail*—CAMJ563@aol.com.

Career

Writer, editor, and illustrator. Math teacher in New York, NY, 1968-77; children's author, beginning 1972; Jewish Publication Society, Philadelphia, PA, senior editor of books for young readers, 1979-91. Professional artist whose drawings and cartoons have appeared in magazines and newspapers.

Member

Society of Children's Book Writers and Illustrators, PEN, Authors Guild, Mystery Writers of America.

Awards, Honors

Outstanding Science Trade Book for Children designation, National Science Teachers Association/Children's Book Council (NSTA/CBC), 1976, for *3D, 2D, 1D;* Children's Book Showcase, CBC, 1977, for *A Little at a Time;* Notable Book designation, American Library Association (ALA), 1981, for *A Picture Book of Jewish Holidays;* Pick of the List selection, American Booksellers Association, 1982, for *Cam Jansen and the Mys-*

David A. Adler (Reproduced by permission.)

tery of the Gold Coins, 1984, for *Cam Jansen and the Mystery of the Monster Movie* and *Cam Jansen and the Mystery of the Carnival Prize,* 1985, for *The Fourth Floor Twins and the Fish Snitch Mystery* and *The Fourth Floor Twins and the Fortune Cookie Chase,* 1989, for *A Picture Book of Abraham Lincoln* and *A Picture Book of George Washington,* and 1991, for *Happy Thanksgiving Rebus;* Best Books designation, New York Public Library, 1983, for *Bunny Rabbit Rebus;* Carter G. Woodson Award Honor Book citation, National Council for the Social Studies/CBC, 1984, for *A Picture Book of Sojourner Truth,* 1985, for *Our Golda,* 1986, for *Martin Luther King, Jr.: Free at Last,* 1989, both for *We Remember the Holocaust* and *A Picture Book of Martin Luther King, Jr.,* 1991, for *A Picture Book of Eleanor Roosevelt,* 1993, for *A Picture Book of Anne Frank,* 1994, for *Hilde and Eli, Children of the Holocaust,* and 1995, for both *One Yellow Daffodil* and *Child of the Warsaw Ghetto;* Sydney Taylor Book Award, Association of Jewish Libraries, 1987, for *The Number on My Grandfather's Arm;* Children's Book of the Year designation, Child Study Book Committee, 1987, for *Thomas Jefferson: Father of Our Democracy,* 1988, for *Cam Jansen and the Triceratops Pops Mystery,* and 1989, for *Jackie Robinson: He Was the First;* Best Books designation, Society of School Librarians

International, 1989, for *A Picture Book of Abraham Lincoln, Jackie Robinson: He Was the First,* and *A Picture Book of Martin Luther King, Jr.;* Best Books designation, Child Study Children's Book Committee at Bank Street College, 1984, for *Jackie Robinson,* and 1992, for *Cam Jansen and the Mystery at the Haunted House;* Best Books designation, *Parents* magazine, 1989, for *Happy Hanukkah Rebus,* and 1990, for *A Picture Book of Helen Keller;* ALA Notable Book designation, and 100 Titles for Reading and Sharing designation, New York Public Library, both 1997, Lemme Book Award, and Patterson Award, both 1998, *Boston Globe/Horn Book* Honor Book designation, Gold Medal Book citation, *Parents* magazine, and Garden State Children's Book Award for Younger Nonfiction, all 2000, and Best Books designation, *New York Times,* all for *Lou Gehrig: The Luckiest Man;* Parents' Choice Picture Book Award, 1998, for *Shape Up!;* Parents' Choice Honor Book designation, 1998, for *A Picture Book of Amelia Earhart;* Notable Book for a Global Society designation, IRA, for *One Yellow Daffodil;* Outstanding Children's Books citation, ALA, 1984, for *Our Golda;* Helen Keating Ott Award, Church and Synagogue Library Association, for promoting high moral and ethical values through children's literature; Golden Kite Honor Book designation, 1999, and Kentucky Bluegrass Award, 2001, both for *The Babe and I;* Orbis Pictus Honor Book selection, National Council of Teachers of English, 2001, for *America's Champion Swimmer: Gertrude Ederle; Storytelling World* Award, 2005, for *Joe Louis.*

Writings

PICTURE BOOKS

A Little at a Time, illustrated by N.M. Bodecker, Random House (New York, NY), 1976, illustrated by Paul Tong, Holiday House (New York, NY), 2010.

The House on the Roof, illustrated by Marilyn Hirsh, Bonim (New York, NY), 1976.

The Children of Chelm, illustrated by Arthur Friedman, Bonim (New York, NY), 1979.

You Think It's Fun to Be a Clown!, illustrated by Ray Cruz, Doubleday (New York, NY), 1980.

My Dog and the Key Mystery, illustrated by Byron Barton, F. Watts (New York, NY), 1982.

Bunny Rabbit Rebus, illustrated by Madelaine Gill Linden, Crowell (New York, NY), 1983.

My Dog and the Knock Knock Mystery, illustrated by Marsha Winborn, Holiday House (New York, NY), 1985.

My Dog and the Green Sock Mystery, illustrated by Dick Gackenbach, Holiday House (New York, NY), 1986.

My Dog and the Birthday Mystery, illustrated by Dick Gackenbach, Holiday House (New York, NY), 1987.

I Know I'm a Witch, illustrated by Suçie Stevenson, Holt (New York, NY), 1988.

Malke's Secret Recipe: A Hanukkah Story, illustrated by Joan Halpern, Viking (New York, NY), 1989.

One Yellow Daffodil: A Hanukkah Story, illustrated by Lloyd Bloom, Harcourt (San Diego, CA), 1995.

Chanukah in Chelm, illustrated by Kevin O'Malley, Lothrop, Lee & Shepard (New York, NY), 1997.

The Babe and I, illustrated by Terry Widener, Harcourt (San Diego, CA), 1999.

Mama Played Baseball, illustrated by Chris O'Leary, Harcourt (San Diego, CA), 2003.

It's Time to Sleep, It's Time to Dream, illustrated by Kay Chorao, Holiday House (New York, NY), 2008.

RIDDLE AND PUZZLE BOOKS

Hanukkah Fun Book: Puzzles, Riddles, Magic, and More, Bonim (New York, NY), 1976.

Passover Fun Book: Puzzles, Riddles, Magic, and More, Bonim (New York, NY), 1978.

Hanukkah Game Book: Games, Riddles, Puzzles, and More, Bonim (New York, NY), 1978.

Bible Fun Book: Puzzles, Riddles, Magic, and More, Bonim (New York, NY), 1979.

Fingerspelling Fun Book, F. Watts (New York, NY), 1981.

The Carsick Zebra and Other Animal Riddles, illustrated by Tomie dePaola, Holiday House (New York, NY), 1983.

The Twisted Witch and Other Spooky Riddles, illustrated by Victoria Chess, Holiday House (New York, NY), 1985.

The Purple Turkey and Other Thanksgiving Riddles, illustrated by Marylin Hafner, Holiday House (New York, NY), 1986.

Jewish Holiday Fun, Kar-Ben (Rockville, MD), 1987.

Remember Betsy Floss and Other Colonial American Riddles, illustrated by John Wallner, Holiday House (New York, NY), 1987.

Wild Pill Hickok and Other Old West Riddles, illustrated by Glen Rounds, Holiday House (New York, NY), 1988.

The Dinosaur Princess and Other Prehistoric Riddles, illustrated by Loreen Leedy, Holiday House (New York, NY), 1988.

Happy Hanukkah Rebus, illustrated by Jan Palmer, Viking (New York, NY), 1989.

A Teacher on Roller Skates, and Other School Riddles, illustrated by John Wallner, Holiday House (New York, NY), 1989.

Happy Thanksgiving Rebus, illustrated by Jan Palmer, Viking (New York, NY), 1991.

Calculator Riddles, illustrated by Cynthia Fisher, Holiday House (New York, NY), 1995.

Easy Math Puzzles, illustrated by Cynthia Fisher, Holiday House (New York, NY), 1997.

BIOGRAPHIES

Our Golda: The Story of Golda Meir, illustrated by Donna Ruff, Viking (New York, NY), 1984.

Martin Luther King, Jr.: Free at Last, illustrated by Robert Casilla, Holiday House (New York, NY), 1986.

Thomas Jefferson: Father of Our Democracy, illustrated by Jacqueline Garrick, Holiday House (New York, NY), 1987.

George Washington: Father of Our Country, illustrated by Jacqueline Garrick, Holiday House (New York, NY), 1988.

Jackie Robinson: He Was the First, illustrated by Robert Casilla, Holiday House (New York, NY), 1989.

Thomas Alva Edison: Great Inventor, illustrated by Lyle Miller, Holiday House (New York, NY), 1990.

Christopher Columbus: Great Explorer, illustrated by Lyle Miller, Holiday House (New York, NY), 1991.

Benjamin Franklin: Inventor, Statesman, Printer, illustrated by Lyle Miller, Holiday House (New York, NY), 1992.

Lou Gehrig: The Luckiest Man, illustrated by Terry Widener, Harcourt (San Diego, CA), 1996.

America's Champion Swimmer: Gertrude Ederle, illustrated by Terry Widener, Harcourt (San Diego, CA), 2000.

B. Franklin, Printer, Holiday House (New York, NY), 2001.

Dr. Martin Luther King, Jr., illustrated by Colin Bootman, Holiday House (New York, NY), 2001.

Heroes of the Revolution, illustrated by Peter Fiore, Holiday House (New York, NY), 2002.

A Hero and the Holocaust: Januscz Korczak and His Children, illustrated by Ben Farsworth, Holiday House (New York, NY), 2002.

Hellen Keller, illustrated by John Wallner, Holiday House (New York, NY), 2003.

Enemies of Slavery, illustrated by Donald A. Smith, Holiday House (New York, NY), 2004.

George Washington: An Illustrated Biography, Holiday House (New York, NY), 2004.

Joe Louis: America's Fighter, illustrated by Terry Widener, Harcourt (Orlando, FL), 2005.

President George Washington, illustrated by John Wallner, Holiday House (New York, NY), 2005.

Campy: The Story of Roy Campanella, illustrated by Gordon C. James, Viking (New York, NY), 2006.

Satchel Paige: Don't Look Back, illustrated by Terry Widener, Harcourt (San Diego, CA), 2007.

Heroes for Civil Rights, illustrated by Bill Farnsworth, Holiday House (New York, NY), 2008.

Honest Abe Lincoln: Easy-to-Read Stories about Abraham Lincoln, illustrated by John Wallner, Holiday House (New York, NY), 2009.

Frederick Douglass: A Noble Life, Holiday House (New York, NY), 2010.

"PICTURE BOOK" BIOGRAPHY SERIES

A Picture Book of Martin Luther King, Jr., illustrated by Robert Casilla, Holiday House (New York, NY), 1989.

A Picture Book of Abraham Lincoln, illustrated by John and Alexandra Wallner, Holiday House (New York, NY), 1989.

A Picture Book of George Washington, illustrated by John and Alexandra Wallner, Holiday House (New York, NY), 1989.

A Picture Book of Helen Keller, illustrated by John and Alexandra Wallner, Holiday House (New York, NY), 1990.

A Picture Book of Thomas Jefferson, illustrated by John and Alexandra Wallner, Holiday House (New York, NY), 1990.

A Picture Book of Benjamin Franklin, illustrated by John and Alexandra Wallner, Holiday House (New York, NY), 1990.

A Picture Book of Eleanor Roosevelt, illustrated by Robert Casilla, Holiday House (New York, NY), 1991.

A Picture Book of John F. Kennedy, illustrated by Robert Casilla, Holiday House (New York, NY), 1991.

A Picture Book of Christopher Columbus, illustrated by John and Alexandra Wallner, Holiday House (New York, NY), 1991.

A Picture Book of Harriet Tubman, illustrated by Samuel Byrd, Holiday House (New York, NY), 1992.

A Picture Book of Simón Bolivar, illustrated by Robert Casilla, Holiday House (New York, NY), 1992.

A Picture Book of Florence Nightingale, illustrated by John and Alexandra Wallner, Holiday House (New York, NY), 1992.

A Picture Book of Jesse Owens, illustrated by Robert Casilla, Holiday House (New York, NY), 1992.

A Picture Book of Frederick Douglass, illustrated by Samuel Byrd, Holiday House (New York, NY), 1993.

A Picture Book of Anne Frank, illustrated by Karen Ritz, Holiday House (New York, NY), 1993.

A Picture Book of Rosa Parks, illustrated by Robert Casilla, Holiday House (New York, NY), 1993.

A Picture Book of Sitting Bull, illustrated by Samuel Byrd, Holiday House (New York, NY), 1993.

A Picture Book of Sojourner Truth, illustrated by Gershom Griffith, Holiday House (New York, NY), 1994.

A Picture Book of Robert E. Lee, illustrated by John and Alexandra Wallner, Holiday House (New York, NY), 1994.

A Picture Book of Jackie Robinson, illustrated by Robert Casilla, Holiday House (New York, NY), 1994.

A Picture Book of Paul Revere, illustrated by John and Alexandra Wallner, Holiday House (New York, NY), 1995.

A Picture Book of Patrick Henry, illustrated by John and Alexandra Wallner, Holiday House (New York, NY), 1995.

A Picture Book of Davy Crockett, illustrated by John and Alexandra Wallner, Holiday House (New York, NY), 1996.

A Picture Book of Thomas Alva Edison, illustrated by John and Alexandra Wallner, Holiday House (New York, NY), 1996.

A Picture Book of Thurgood Marshall, illustrated by Robert Casilla, Holiday House (New York, NY), 1996.

A Picture Book of Louis Braille, illustrated by John and Alexandra Wallner, Holiday House (New York, NY), 1996.

A Picture Book of Amelia Earhart, illustrated by Jeff Fisher, Holiday House (New York, NY), 1998.

A Picture Book of George Washington Carver, illustrated by Dan Brown, Holiday House (New York, NY), 1999.

A Picture Book of Sacagawea, illustrated by Dan Brown, Holiday House (New York, NY), 2000.

A Picture Book of Dwight David Eisenhower, Holiday House (New York, NY), 2002.

A Picture Book of Lewis and Clark, illustrated by Ron Himmler, Holiday House (New York, NY), 2003.

A Picture Book of Harriet Beecher Stowe, illustrated by Colin Bootman, Holiday House (New York, NY), 2003.

(With son, Michael S. Adler) *A Picture Book of Samuel Adams,* illustrated by Ronald Himler, Holiday House (New York, NY), 2005.

(With Michael S. Adler) *A Picture Book of John Hancock,* illustrated by Ronald Himler, Holiday House (New York, NY), 2006.

(With Michael S. Adler) *A Picture Book of John and Abigail Adams,* illustrated by Ronald Himler, Holiday House (New York, NY), 2007.

(With Michael S. Adler) *A Picture Book of Dolley and James Madison,* illustrated by Ronald Himler, Holiday House (New York, NY), 2009.

(With Michael S. Adler) *A Picture Book of Harry Houdini,* illustrated by Matt Collins, Holiday House (New York, NY), 2009.

(With Michael S. Adler) *A Picture Book of Cesar Chavez,* illustrated by Marie Olofsdotter, Holiday House (New York, NY), 2010.

"CAM JANSEN" MYSTERY SERIES

Cam Jansen and the Mystery of the Stolen Diamonds, illustrated by Susanna Natti, Viking (New York, NY), 1980, reprinted, 2004.

Cam Jansen and the Mystery of the UFO, illustrated by Susanna Natti, Viking (New York, NY), 1980, reprinted, 2004.

Cam Jansen and the Mystery of the Dinosaur Bones, illustrated by Susanna Natti, Viking (New York, NY), 1981, reprinted, 2004.

Cam Jansen and the Mystery of the Television Dog, illustrated by Susanna Natti, Viking (New York, NY), 1981, reprinted, 2004.

Cam Jansen and the Mystery of the Gold Coins, illustrated by Susanna Natti, Viking (New York, NY), 1982, reprinted, 2004.

Cam Jansen and the Mystery of the Babe Ruth Baseball, illustrated by Susanna Natti, Viking (New York, NY), 1982, reprinted, 2004.

Cam Jansen and the Mystery of the Circus Clown, illustrated by Susanna Natti, Viking (New York, NY), 1983, reprinted, 2004.

Cam Jansen and the Mystery of the Monster Movie, illustrated by Susanna Natti, Viking (New York, NY), 1984, reprinted, 2004.

Cam Jansen and the Mystery of the Carnival Prize, illustrated by Susanna Natti, Viking (New York, NY), 1984, reprinted, 2004.

Cam Jansen and the Mystery at the Monkey House, illustrated by Susanna Natti, Viking (New York, NY), 1985.

Cam Jansen and the Mystery of the Stolen Corn Popper, illustrated by Susanna Natti, Viking (New York, NY), 1986, reprinted, 2004.

Cam Jansen and the Mystery of Flight Fifty-four, illustrated by Susanna Natti, Viking (New York, NY), 1989, reprinted, 2004.

Cam Jansen and the Mystery at the Haunted House, illustrated by Susanna Natti, Viking (New York, NY), 1992.

Cam Jansen Activity Book, illustrated by Susanna Natti, Viking (New York, NY), 1992.

Cam Jansen and the Chocolate Fudge Mystery, illustrated by Susanna Natti, Viking (New York, NY), 1993.

Cam Jansen and the Triceratops Pops Mystery, illustrated by Susanna Natti, Viking (New York, NY), 1995.

Cam Jansen and the Ghostly Mystery, illustrated by Susanna Natti, Viking (New York, NY), 1996.

Cam Jansen and the Scary Snake Mystery, illustrated by Susanna Natti, Viking (New York, NY), 1997.

Cam Jansen and the Catnapping Mystery, illustrated by Susanna Natti, Viking (New York, NY), 1998.

Cam Jansen and the Barking Treasure Mystery, illustrated by Susanna Natti, Viking (New York, NY), 1999.

Cam Jansen and the Birthday Mystery, illustrated by Susanna Natti, Viking (New York, NY), 2000.

Cam Jansen and the School Play Mystery, illustrated by Susanna Natti, Viking (New York, NY), 2001.

Cam Jansen and the First Day of School Mystery, illustrated by Susanna Natti, Viking (New York, NY), 2002.

Cam Jansen and the Tennis Trophy Mystery, illustrated by Susanna Natti, Viking (New York, NY), 2003.

Cam Jansen and the Snowy Day Mystery, illustrated by Susanna Natti, Viking (New York, NY), 2004.

Cam Jansen and the Valentine Baby Mystery, illustrated by Susanna Natti, Viking (New York, NY), 2005.

Cam Jansen and the Secret Service Mystery, illustrated by Susanna Natti, Viking (New York, NY), 2006.

Cam Jansen and the Summer Camp Mysteries: A Special, illustrated by Susanna Natti, Viking (New York, NY), 2007.

Cam Jansen and the Lions' Lunch Mystery, illustrated by Susanna Natti, Viking (New York, NY), 2007.

Cam Jansen and the Green School Mystery, illustrated by Joy Allen, Viking (New York, NY), 2008.

Cam Jansen and the Basketball Mystery, illustrated by Joy Allen, Viking (New York, NY), 2009.

Cam Jansen: The Sports Day Mysteries: A Super Special, illustrated by Joy Allen, Puffin Books (New York, NY), 2009.

Cam Jansen and the Wedding Cake Mystery, illustrated by Joy Allen, Viking Childrens Books (New York, NY), 2010.

Cam Jansen and the Graduation Day Mystery, illustrated by Joy Allen, Viking Childrens Books (New York, NY), 2011.

Cam Jansen and the Millionaire Mystery, illustrated by Joy Allen, Viking Childrens Books (New York, NY), 2012.

"YOUNG CAM JANSEN" MYSTERY SERIES

Young Cam Jansen's Chocolate Chip Mystery, illustrated by Susanna Natti, Viking (New York, NY), 1996.

Young Cam Jansen's Dinosaur Count, illustrated by Susanna Natti, Viking (New York, NY), 1996.

Young Cam Jansen and the Lost Tooth, illustrated by Susanna Natti, Viking (New York, NY), 1997.

Young Cam Jansen and the Ice Skate Mystery, illustrated by Susanna Natti, Viking (New York, NY), 1998.

Young Cam Jansen and the Baseball Mystery, illustrated by Susanna Natti, Viking (New York, NY), 1999.

Young Cam Jansen and the Pizza Shop Mystery, illustrated by Susanna Natti, Viking (New York, NY), 2000.

Young Cam Jansen and the Library Mystery, illustrated by Susanna Natti, Viking (New York, NY), 2001.

Young Cam Jansen and the Double Beach Mystery, illustrated by Susanna Natti, Viking (New York, NY), 2002.

Young Cam Jansen and the Zoo Note Mystery, illustrated by Susanna Natti, Viking (New York, NY), 2003.

Young Cam Jansen and the New Girl Mystery, illustrated by Susanna Natti, Viking (New York, NY), 2004.

Young Cam Jansen and the Substitute Mystery, illustrated by Susanna Natti, Viking (New York, NY), 2005.

Young Cam Jansen and the Spotted Cat Mystery, illustrated by Susanna Natti, Viking (New York, NY), 2006.

Young Cam Jansen and the Lion's Lunch Mystery, illustrated by Susanna Natti, Viking (New York, NY), 2007.

Young Cam Jansen and the Molly Shoe Mystery, illustrated by Susanna Natti, Viking (New York, NY), 2008.

Young Cam Jansen and the 100th Day of School Mystery, illustrated by Susanna Natti, Viking (New York, NY), 2009.

Young Cam Jansen and the Speedy Car Mystery, illustrated by Susanna Natti, Viking (New York, NY), 2010.

Young Cam Jansen and the Circus Mystery, illustrated by Susanna Natti, Viking (New York, NY), 2011.

Young Cam Jansen and the Magic Bird Mystery, illustrated by Susanna Natti, Viking (New York, NY), 2012.

"JEFFREY'S GHOST" ADVENTURE SERIES

Jeffrey's Ghost and the Leftover Baseball Team, illustrated by Jean Jenkins, Holt (New York, NY), 1984.

Jeffrey's Ghost and the Fifth-Grade Dragon, illustrated by Jean Jenkins, Holt (New York, NY), 1985.

Jeffrey's Ghost and the Ziffel Fair Mystery, illustrated by Jean Jenkins, Holt (New York, NY), 1987.

"FOURTH FLOOR TWINS" ADVENTURE SERIES

The Fourth Floor Twins and the Fortune Cookie Chase, illustrated by Irene Trivas, Viking (New York, NY), 1985.

The Fourth Floor Twins and the Fish Snitch Mystery, illustrated by Irene Trivas, Viking (New York, NY), 1985.

The Fourth Floor Twins and the Talking Bird Trick, illustrated by Irene Trivas, Viking (New York, NY), 1986.

The Fourth Floor Twins and the Silver Ghost Express, illustrated by Irene Trivas, Viking (New York, NY), 1986.

The Fourth Floor Twins and the Skyscraper Parade, illustrated by Irene Trivas, Viking (New York, NY), 1987.

The Fourth Floor Twins and the Sand Castle Contest, illustrated by Irene Trivas, Viking (New York, NY), 1988.

"T.F. BENSON" MYSTERY SERIES

T.F. Benson and the Funny Money Mystery, Bantam (New York, NY), 1992.

T.F. Benson and the Dinosaur Madness Mystery, Bantam (New York, NY), 1992.

T.F. Benson and the Jewelry Spy Mystery, Bantam (New York, NY), 1992.

T.F. Benson and the Detective Dog Mystery, Bantam (New York, NY), 1993.

"HOUDINI CLUB MAGIC MYSTERY" SERIES

Onion Sundaes, illustrated by Heather Harms Maione, Random House (New York, NY), 1994.

Wacky Jacks, illustrated by Heather Harms Maione, Random House (New York, NY), 1994.

Lucky Stars, illustrated by Heather Harms Maione, Random House (New York, NY), 1996.

Magic Money, illustrated by Heather Harms Maione, Random House (New York, NY), 1997.

"ANDY RUSSELL" SERIES

The Many Troubles of Andy Russell, illustrated by Will Hillenbrand, Harcourt (San Diego, CA), 1998.

Andy and Tamika, illustrated by Will Hillenbrand, Harcourt (San Diego, CA), 1999.

School Trouble for Andy Russell, illustrated by Will Hillenbrand, Harcourt (San Diego, CA), 1999.

Parachuting Hamsters and Andy Russell, illustrated by Will Hillenbrand, Harcourt (San Diego, CA), 2000.

Andy Russell, NOT Wanted by the Police, illustrated by Leanne Franson, Harcourt (San Diego, CA), 2001.

It's a Baby, Andy Russell, illustrated by Leanne Franson, Harcourt (San Diego, CA), 2006.

"JEFFREY BONES" BEGINNING-READER MYSTERY SERIES

Bones and the Big Yellow Mystery, Viking (New York, NY), 2004.

Bones and the Dog Gone Mystery, illustrated by Barbara Johansen Newman, Viking (New York, NY), 2004.

Bones and the Cupcake Mystery, illustrated by Barbara Johansen Newman, Viking (New York, NY), 2005.

Bones and the Dinosaur Mystery, illustrated by Barbara Johansen Newman, Viking (New York, NY), 2005.

Bones and the Birthday Mystery, illustrated by Barbara Johansen Newman, Viking (New York, NY), 2006.

Bones and the Math Test Mystery, illustrated by Barbara Johansen Newman, Viking (New York, NY), 2008.

Bones and the Roller Coaster Mystery, illustrated by Barbara Johansen Newman, Viking (New York, NY), 2009.

Bones and the Clown Mix-up Mystery, illustrated by Barbara Johansen Newman, Viking (New York, NY), 2010.

Bones and the Football Mystery, illustrated by Barbara Johansen Newman, Viking (New York, NY), 2012.

NONFICTION

Base Five, illustrated by Larry Rose, Crowell (New York, NY), 1975.

3D, 2D, 1D, illustrated by Harvey Weiss, Crowell (New York, NY), 1975.

Roman Numerals, illustrated by B. Barton, Crowell (New York, NY), 1977.

Redwoods Are the Tallest Trees in the World, illustrated by Kazue Mizumura, Crowell (New York, NY), 1978.

3-2-1 Number Fun, Doubleday (New York, NY), 1981.

A Picture Book of Jewish Holidays, illustrated by Linda Heller, Holiday House (New York, NY), 1981.

A Picture Book of Passover, illustrated by Linda Heller, Holiday House (New York, NY), 1982.

A Picture Book of Hanukkah, illustrated by Linda Heller, Holiday House (New York, NY), 1982.

Calculator Fun Book, illustrated by Arline and Marvin Oberman, F. Watts (New York, NY), 1982.

Hyperspace! Facts and Fun from All over the Universe, illustrated by Fred Winkowski, Viking (New York, NY), 1982.

Our Amazing Ocean, illustrated by Joseph Veno, Troll Publications (Mahwah, NJ), 1983.

All about the Moon, illustrated by Raymond Burns, Troll Publications (Mahwah, NJ), 1983.

World of Weather, illustrated by Raymond Burns, Troll Publications (Mahwah, NJ), 1983.

Wonders of Energy, illustrated by Raymond Burns, Troll Publications (Mahwah, NJ), 1983.

Amazing Magnets, illustrated by Dan Lawler, Troll Publications (Mahwah, NJ), 1983.

All Kinds of Money, illustrated by Tom Huffman, F. Watts (New York, NY), 1984.

Prices Go up, Prices Go Down: The Laws of Supply and Demand, illustrated by Tom Huffman, F. Watts (New York, NY), 1984.

Inflation: When Prices Go up, up, Up, illustrated by Tom Huffman, F. Watts (New York, NY), 1985.

Banks: Where the Money Is, illustrated by Tom Huffman, F. Watts (New York, NY), 1985.

The Number on My Grandfather's Arm, photographs by Rose Eichenbaum, Union of American Hebrew Congregations (New York, NY), 1987.

The Children's Book of Jewish Holidays, illustrated by Dovid Sears, Mesorah (Brooklyn, NY), 1987.

We Remember the Holocaust, Holt (New York, NY), 1989.

Breathe in, Breathe Out: All about Your Lungs, illustrated by Diane Paterson, F. Watts (New York, NY), 1991.

Hilde and Eli, Children of the Holocaust, illustrated by Karen Ritz, Holiday House (New York, NY), 1994.

Child of the Warsaw Ghetto, illustrated by Karen Ritz, Holiday House (New York, NY), 1995.

Fraction Fun, illustrated by Nancy Tobin, Holiday House (New York, NY), 1996.

(Editor) *The Kids' Catalog of Jewish Holidays,* Jewish Publication Society (Philadelphia, PA), 1996.

Hiding from the Nazis, illustrated by Karen Ritz, Holiday House (New York, NY), 1997.

Shape Up! Fun with Triangles and Other Polygons, illustrated by Nancy Tobin, Holiday House (New York, NY), 1998.

How Tall, How Short, How Far Away, illustrated by Nancy Tobin, Holiday House (New York, NY), 1999.

You Can, Toucan, Math: Word Problem-Solving, illustrated by Edward Miller, Holiday House (New York, NY), 2006.

Working with Fractions, illustrated by Edward Miller, Holiday House (New York, NY), 2007.

Fun with Roman Numerals, illustrated by Edward Miller, Holiday House (New York, NY), 2008.

Money Madness, illustrated by Edward Miller, Holiday House (New York, NY), 2009.

Fractions, Decimals, and Percents, illustrated by Edward Miller, Holiday House (New York, NY), 2010.

Time Zones, illustrated by Edward Miller, Holiday House (New York, NY), 2010.

Mystery Math: A First Book of Algebra, illustrated by Edward Miller, Holiday House (New York, NY), 2011.

The Hanukkah Story, illustrated by Jill Weber, Holiday House (New York, NY), 2011.

Perimeter, Area, and Volume: A Monster Book of Dimensions, illustrated by Edward Miller, Holiday House (New York, NY), 2012.

OTHER

A Children's Treasure of Chassidic Tales, illustrated by Arie Haas, Mesorah (Brooklyn, NY), 1983.

Eaton Stanley and the Mind Control Experiment (young-adult fiction), illustrated by Joan Drescher, Dutton (New York, NY), 1985.

Benny, Benny, Baseball Nut (young-adult fiction), Scholastic (New York, NY), 1987.

Rabbit Trouble and the Green Magician (young-adult fiction), illustrated by Giora Carmi, Weekly Reader Books (Stamford, CT), 1987.

Brothers in Egypt, Dreamworks (Los Angeles, CA), 1988.

My Writing Day, photographs by Nina Crews, R.C. Owen (Katonah, NY), 1999.

The Kids' Catalog of Hanukkah, Jewish Publication Society (Philadelphia, PA), 2004.

Don't Talk to Me about the War (young-adult fiction), Viking (New York, NY), 2008.

The House on the Roof: A Sukkot Story, illustrated by Marilyn Hirsh, Holiday House (New York, NY), 2009.

Contributor to anthologies, including *The Day I Lost My Hamster, and Other True School Stories,* Scholastic, 2006.

Sidelights

A prolific author as well as an artist and editor, David A. Adler shares his wide-ranging interests in books for children that range from picture books and juvenile adventure stories to biographies and nonfiction volumes.

Science, history, math, biography, and cultural traditions have each received Adler's attention, as have everyday humor and the fascination with mystery and adventure that are shared by most children. "Because of the diversity of the things I write," Adler once revealed, "I am able to vary my work even in a single day, from doing research on a nonfiction book to writing fiction to creating a silly riddle or poem." Among Adler's many works are the award-winning biographies *Our Golda: The Story of Golda Meir* and *Joe Louis: America's Fighter* as well as the award-winning Holocaust-themed *The Number on My Grandfather's Arm;* histories such as *Heroes of the Revolution* and *Heroes for Civil Rights;* picture books like *It's Time to Sleep, It's Time to Dream;* books introducing basic math concepts; and easy-reading mysteries in the "Cam Jansen," and "Young Cam Jansen," and "Jeffrey Bones" series.

"I am the second of six children, all very close in age," Adler once explained to *SATA.* "My parents encouraged each of us to be an individual. It was their way of lessening the competition between us. As a child I was known as the family artist. Paintings and drawings I did when I was as young as twelve still hang in my parents' home. And I was creative. I drew funny signs that I taped around the house. I made up stories to entertain my younger brothers and sisters. I'm still making up stories.

"We lived in a large house with a whole unused third floor, unused except for storage for our extended family. For thirty years my parents kept unwanted wedding gifts belonging to a relative who had moved overseas: an electric fan, dishes with a strange bird pattern, luggage, pots, and lots of cups and glasses. When the relative returned to the states, he was surprised my parents had kept all that, and he and his wife still didn't want all those gifts. But what a wonderful room to crawl between the boxes and suitcases and write stories!

"I was a math teacher in 1971 when my three-year-old nephew came to my house and asked me a question. And he kept asking questions. That led to my very first story, *A Little at a Time.* I sent it to Random House, my first story and my first submission, and after six months of consideration, it was accepted for publication." The original edition of *A Little at a Time* was published with artwork by N.M. Bodecker; a new edition was released in 2010 with illustrations by Paul Tong.

Adler's talent for making mathematical themes such as Roman numerals, fractions, and dimensions understandable to young readers has inspired him to write math-themed books such as *Base Five, How Tall, How Short, How Far Away,* and *You Can, Toucan, Math: Word-Problem Solving.* In 1977, after Adler and his wife had their first child, he made a career move that was viewed

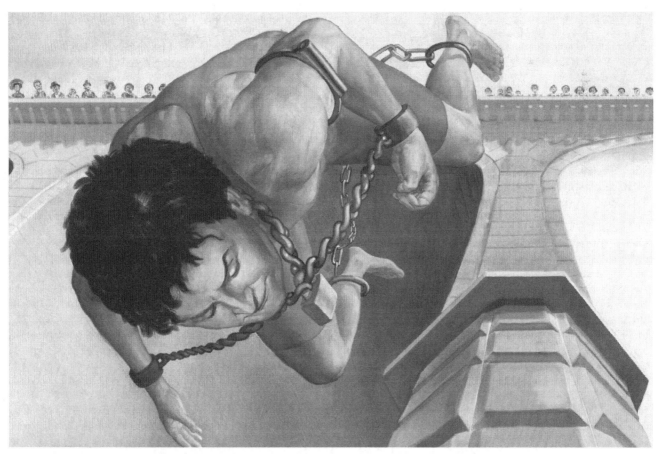

Adler profiles the life of one of the most famous daredevils of the twentieth century in **A Picture Book of Harry Houdini,** *featuring artwork by Matt Collins.* (Illustration copyright © 2009 by Matt Collins. Reproduced with permission of Holiday House.)

I needed to take so much along and that brought me to the clue and the great idea that became my very first Cam. THANK YOU, MICHAEL!"

Over the years, Adler's "Cam Jansen" novels have entertained beginning chapter-book readers with the humorous adventures of Cam and her best friend Eric. In each installment, a mystery presents itself and the clever Cam ultimately finds a solution through her superior memory. In *The Summer Camp Mysteries,* for example, a stay at Camp Eagle Lake is spoiled when campers' snack money goes missing, while the tragic disappearance of a packed lunch during a school field trip to the zoo provides the drama in *Young Cam Jansen and the Lion's Lunch Mystery,* part of the "Young Cam Jansen" spin-off series geared for budding readers. In *Young Cam Jansen and the Molly Shoe Mystery,* which *Booklist* critic Carolyn Phelan praised as "a short but satisfying mystery," Adler also features memory skill-builders that involve the "cheerful" full-color drawings contributed to the series by Susanna Natti. Reviewing *The Summer Camp Mysteries* in *School Library Journal,* Shelle Rosenfeld noted that Adler's "lively story features humor, familiar camp activities, and diverse . . . characters" that most readers will find likeable.

Although Adler's "Cam Jansen" novels number in the dozens, they are easily overshadowed by his lengthy list of biographies, some of which have been coathored with his son, Michael S. Adler. Frequently adopting a picture-book format, Adler's biographies introduce students to a wide range of men and women: sports heroes such as Lou Gehrig, Jackie Robinson, Joe Louis, and Gertrude Ederle; U.S. presidents George Washington, John Adams, Thomas Jefferson, Abraham Lincoln, and John F. Kennedy; political and social activists Martin Luther King, Jr., Cesar Chavez, Rosa Parks, and Sojourner Truth; inventor Thomas Alva Edison; and explorers Lewis and Clark and Christopher Columbus. Each biography requires Adler to do in-depth research. As he explained of his work for the middle-grade biography *B. Franklin, Printer:* "I read hundreds of issues of colonial newspapers. I found them fascinating. I included in the book many excerpts from those newspapers including first-hand accounts of the first shots of the [American] Revolution."

Discussing *President George Washington: An Illustrated Biography,* Margaret A. Bush described Adler's book as a "well-researched and thoughtfully structured account of the man and his time," *A Picture Book of James and Dolly Madison,* a father-and-son collaboration, pairs what a *Publishers Weekly* critic described as a "concise and accurate" text with "softly sketched illustrations" by artist Ronald Himler. *Frederick Douglas: A Noble Life,* Adler's biography of the noted former slave and abolitionists, was praised by *Booklist* critic Michael Cart as both "thoroughly researched" and "lucidly written," the critic adding that the biography benefits from a "generous use of quotations from Douglass' own writings." Other inspiring Americans are profiled in *A Pic-*

Adler entertains younger readers with chapter books such as Young Cam Jansen and the Zoo Note Mystery, *part of a series about a young sleuth that features art by Susanna Natti.*

as unusual at the time: he decided to work on a freelance writing career so he could remain at home and raise his son, Michael. "I was shunned in the playground," Adler later recalled, "and even yelled at by an older woman I didn't know. She told me I should be at work and my wife should be at home. But I was at work, and working very hard."

The year 1977 was significant for another reason. In addition to marking the birth of Adler's son, it was also the year he gave birth to one of his most popular characters: Cam Jansen. "The idea to write a book about a girl with a photographic memory who solves mysteries came to me from a classmate of mine, a boy, in elementary school who was said to have such a memory. In fact, the first few drafts were not about a girl, but a boy with a great memory. And his nickname was not Cam—short for "The Camera"—but the name of a famous camera company. The company denied me permission to use its name, so the nickname Cam was invented. My editor asked me to change Cam from a boy to a girl and I readily agreed. The first series installment, *Cam Jansen and the Mystery of the Stolen Diamonds,* was inspired by experiences I had while caring for my infant son. It wasn't easy taking him for a walk.

ture Book of Cesar Chavez and *Heroes for Civil Rights,* the latter which serves as a companion to *Heroes of the Revolution* and *Enemies of Slavery* in its focus on the individuals who steered the course of the United States during pivotal epochs. Also coauthored by Michael S. Adler, *A Picture Book of Cesar Chavez* was characterized by *School Library Journal* critic Grace Oliff as "another respectable edition to the [long-running] biography series," while in *Booklist* Daniel Kraus deemed the Adlers' "tempered and lucid" profile of the life of farmworker activist Chavez "an elegant introduction to a man who inspired thousands."

Reviewing Adler's *America's Champion Swimmer: Gertrude Ederle,* a *Publishers Weekly* critic dubbed the biography "an exciting story, well told," while another reviewer for that magazine wrote that in profiling a well-known African-American pitcher in *Satchel Paige: Don't Look Back* Adler and illustrator Terry Widener create a "multidimensional portrait of an . . . athlete worthy of the spotlight." Another sports star is the focus of *Campy: The Story of Roy Campanella,* which focuses on the African-American baseball player who joined the Brooklyn Dodgers in 1948 and became one of the greatest catchers in the history of the game until a car crash left him tragically injured. In *Campy* Adler "capably reprises Campy's on-field triumphs," noted *Booklist* critic Bill Ott, while *School Library Journal* critic Marilyn Taniguchi wrote that Gordon C. James' oil paintings combine with Adler's text to produce "an accessible introduction to this inspiring athlete's story."

One subject particularly close to Adler's heart is the plight of the Jewish people of Europe in the years leading up to and including World War II. He deals with the Holocaust in books such as *Hilde and Eli, Children of* the Holocaust, *Child of the Warsaw Ghetto, A Hero and the Holocaust: The Story of Janusz Korczak and His Children,* and *A Picture Book of Anne Frank.* It is also central to two of his best-known books: the poignant *The Number on My Grandfather's Arm* and *We Remember the Holocaust,* the latter a work of nonfiction that is composed of historical commentary, photographs, and interviews and recollections from survivors of the Nazi death camps. A *Publishers Weekly* reviewer noted that Adler's biography of well-known Dutch diarist Anne Frank "balances candor with discretion" and allows Frank's tragic story to "emerge . . . poignantly." Discussing *A Picture Book of Anne Frank,* Adler explained the challenge his subject presented. "I needed to write about Germany's problems following the First World War, the rise of Adolf Hitler and Nazism, the refusal of the world to accept refugees of extreme persecution, vital information about the Second World War, and the horrible truth about the death camps. I needed to do all that and still keep the book focused on the life and diary of Anne Frank, all for relatively young children, and all within 1,500 words."

While most of Adler's works are geared for younger reader, he has occasionally produced longer stories for young-adult readers, such as *Eaton Stanley and the Mind Control Experiment, Benny, Benny, Baseball Nut,* and *Don't Talk to Me about the War.* Combining Adler's interest in baseball with his interest in the holocaust, *Don't Talk to Me about the War* takes place in 1940. Thirteen-year-old Bronx native Tommy Duncan is mostly interested in baseball and the popular radio broadcasts of the day. His friend Beth is obsessed with war news from Europe. "Don't talk to me about the war," the teen announces at the beginning of his first-person account, but he trusts that Beth will keep him

Noted illustrator Ronald Himler brings to life one of North America's most remarkable treks, the exploration of the Northwest Territory, in Adler's **A Picture Book of Lewis and Clark.** (Holiday House, 2003. Illustration © 2003 by Ronald Himler. Reproduced by permission of Holiday House.)

Adler teams up with artist Terry Widener to capture the life of a baseball hero in the picture-book biography **Lou Gehrig: The Luckiest Man.** (Illustration copyright © 1997 by Terry Widener. Reproduced by permission of Houghton Mifflin Harcourt Publishing Company.)

informed of anything overseas that will actually affect him. Later, a friendship with Sarah, a Jewish girl who recently emigrated from Germany with her family, helps Tommy understand the realities of life in Europe. When his mother begins to exhibit the early symptoms of multiple sclerosis, the young teen is able to deal with the added responsibility for the family, a responsibility that only deepens when the reality of war hits tragically close to home. Recommending Adler's story to fans of history, *Kliatt* critic Paula Rohrlick described *Don't Talk to Me about the War* as a "warm, old-fashioned tale [that] extols the virtues of persisting through difficulties." In *Booklist* Phelan commented in particular on Adler's ability to evoke his story's 1940s setting in "an engaging and very accessible historical novel."

As is the case with many adults who write for children, the events within his own family often make their way into Adler's books; in fact, "the main character in the book *Benny, Benny Baseball Nut* is based on one of my sons," the author admitted. "The characters in the 'Andy Russell' books [are based on] another son. He is an interesting boy with interesting questions such as, 'Daddy, what if the Wright brothers had been Siamese twins, what would the cockpit of an airplane look like now?' The other members of the family in the 'Andy Russell' books are based on our family. The baby born in *It's a Baby, Andy Russell* is based on my youngest son."

Regarding his habit of splitting his time between nonfiction and fiction, Adler once commented: "I find fiction-writing to be a wonderful release from all the painstaking research I must do for nonfiction, which is why I try to alternate between [the two]." As busy as his work has kept him, he continues to make time for his top priority: his family. Such flexibility has not been the writing life's only attraction, however. "I love my work," Adler once stated. "It allows me to pursue my many interests." In short, he explained, "I feel very fortunate that I can indulge my interests and call it work."

Biographical and Critical Sources

BOOKS

Adler, David A., *My Writing Day,* photographs by Nina Crews, R.C. Owen (Katonah, NY), 1999.
Wyatt, Flora R., Margaret Coggins, and Jane Hunter Imber, *Popular Nonfiction Authors for Children,* Libraries Unlimited (Englewood, CO), 1998.

PERIODICALS

Booklist, November 1, 1995, Kay Weisman, review of *One Yellow Daffodil: A Hanukkah Story,* p. 476; August, 1996, Carolyn Phelan, reviews of *Young Cam Jansen and the Dinosaur Game* and *Young Cam Jansen and the Missing Cookie,* both pp. 1909-1910; May 15,

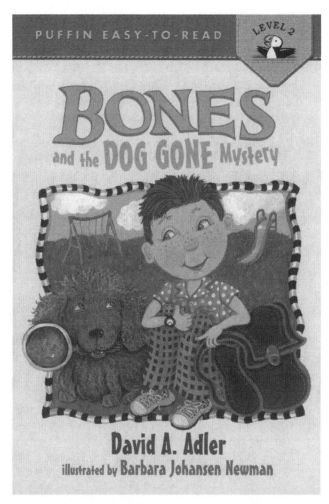

Adler entertains beginning readers with Bones and the Dog Gone Mystery, *a story featuring cartoon art by Barbara Johansen Newman.* (Illustration copyright © 2004 by Barbara Johansen Newman. Used by permission of Viking Children's Books, a division of Penguin Young Readers Group, a member of Penguin Group (USA) Inc., 345 Hudson St., New York, NY 10014. All rights reserved.)

1997, Ilene Cooper, review of *Lou Gehrig: The Luckiest Man,* p. 1575; April 15, 1998, Carolyn Phelan, review of *A Picture Book of Amelia Earhart,* p. 1447; August, 1998, Shelle Rosenfeld, review of *The Many Troubles of Andy Russell,* p. 2002; July, 2001, Carolyn Phelan, review of *Dr. Martin Luther King, Jr.,* p. 2002; January 1, 2002, review of *America's Champion Swimmer: Gertrude Ederle,* p. 864; January 1, 2002, Carolyn Phelan, review of *B. Franklin Printer,* p. 851, and Helen Rosenberg, review of *Andy Russell, NOT Wanted by the Police,* p. 855; December 1, 2002, Hazel Rochman, review of *A Hero and the Holocaust: The Story of Janusz Korczak and His Children,* p. 658; May 1, 2003, Hazel Rochman, review of *Young Cam Jansen and the Zoo Note Mystery,* p. 1530; February 15, 2005, Ilene Cooper, review of *Bones and the Cupcake Mystery,* p. 1082; May 15, 2005, Carolyn Phelan, review of *It's a Baby, Andy Russell,* p. 1656; September 1, 2005, Jennifer Mattson, review of *Joe Louis: America's Fighter,* p. 116; January 1, 2006, Carolyn Phelan, review of *Cam Jansen and the Valentine Baby Mystery,* p. 108; August 1, 2006, Carolyn Phelan, review of *You Can, Toucan, Math: Word Problem-solving Fun,* p. 80; October 15, 2006, Carolyn Phelan, review of *Cam Jansen and the Secret Service Mystery*, p. 44; January 1, 2007, GraceAnne A. DeCandido, review of *Satchel Paige: Don't Look Back*, p. 107; February 1, 2007, Bill Ott, review of *Campy: The Story of Roy Campanella*, p. 59; May 1, 2007, Carolyn Phelan, review of *Bones and the Birthday Mystery*, p. 49; May 15, 2007, Shelle Rosenfeld, review of *The Summer Camp Mysteries*, p. 45; February 1, 2008, Stephanie Zvirin, review of *Heroes for Civil Rights*, p. 55; April 15, 2008, Carolyn Phelan, review of *Don't Talk to Me about the War*, p. 53; January 1, 2009, Carolyn Phelan, review of *Money Madness*, p. 88; March 1, 2009, Julie Cummins, review of *It's Time to Sleep, It's Time to Dream*, p. 50; July 1, 2009, Diane Foote, review of *A Picture Book of Harry Houdini*, p. 64; March 1, 2010, Carolyn Phelan, review of *Fractions, Decimals, and Percents*, p. 66; June 1, 2010, Michael Cart, review of *Frederick Douglass: A Noble Life*, p. 94; July 1, 2010, Daniel Kraus, review of *A Picture Book of Cesar Chavez*, p. 54, and Shelle Rosenfeld, review of *A Little at a Time*, p. 66.

Bulletin of the Center for Children's Books, April, 1997, Janice M. Del Negro, review of *Lou Gehrig*, p. 270; March, 1993, Betsy Hearne, review of *A Picture Book of Anne Frank*, p. 204; November, 1994, Roger Sutton, review of *Hilde and Eli, Children of the Holocaust*, p. 79; November, 2004, Timnah Card, review of *Bones and the Big Yellow Mystery*, p. 112; December, 2005, review of *Joe Louis*, p. 169.

Horn Book, September-October, 1997, Susan Bloom, review of *Chanukah in Chelm*, p. 584; January-February, Margaret A. Bush, review of *President George Washington: An Illustrated Biography*, p. 105; January-February, 2006, Betty Carter, review of *Joe Louis*, p. 95; May-June, 2009, Tanya D. Auger, review of *Money Madness*, p. 317.

Kirkus Reviews, November 15, 1994, review of *Hilde and Eli, Children of the Holocaust*, p. 1521, review of *A Picture Book of Jackie Robinson*, pp. 1521-1522; October 15, 1997, review of *Hiding from the Nazis*, p. 1578; September 15, 2002, review of *A Hero and the Holocaust: The Story of Janusz Korczak and His Children*, p. 1382; February 15, 2003, review of *Mama Played Baseball*, p. 298; March 15, 2003, review of *A Picture Book of Lewis and Clark*, p. 458; October 1, 2003, review of *Heroes of the Revolution*, p. 1219; August 15, 2004, review of *Bones and the Big Yellow Mystery*, p. 801; August 1, 2006, review of *You Can, Toucan, Math*, p. 779; February 1, 2007, review of *Campy*, p. 119; December 1, 2007, review of *Heroes for Civil Rights*; September 1, 2008, review of *Fun with Roman Numerals*; January 1, 2009, review of *Money Madness*; January 15, 2010, review of *Fractions, Decimals, and Percents*.

Publishers Weekly, April 5, 1993, review of *A Picture Book of Anne Frank*, p. 76; February 24, 1997, review of *Lou Gehrig*, p. 91; October 20, 1997, review of *Hiding from the Nazis*, p. 76; August 17, 1998, review of *The Many Troubles of Andy Russell*, p. 73; May 10, 1999, review of *The Babe and I*, p. 67; March 6, 2000, review of *America's Champion Swimmer*, p. 111; December 11, 2006, review of *Satchel Paige*, p. 68; February 2, 2009, review of *A Picture Book of Dolley and James Madison*, p. 49.

School Library Journal, May, 1993, Cheryl Cufari, review of *A Picture Book of Anne Frank*, pp. 92-93; December, 1994, Tom S. Hurlburt, review of *A Picture Book of Jackie Robinson*, p. 94; October, 1995, Jane Marino, review of *One Yellow Daffodil*, p. 34; February, 1998, Lesley McKinstry, review of *Wacky Jacks*, p. 96; April, 1998, Cheryl Cufari, review of *A Picture Book of Amelia Earhart*, p. 112; January, 1999, Kit Vaughan, review of *Cam Jansen and the Catnapping Mystery*, p. 79; January, 2001, Wendy S. Carroll, review of *Cam Jansen and the Birthday Mystery*, p. 91; June, 2002, Kay Bowes, review of *Young Cam Jansen and the Double Beach Mystery*, p. 80; April, 2003, Steven Engelfried, review of *Mama Played Baseball*, p. 114; December, 2004, Corrina Austin, review of *Bones and the Dog Gone Mystery*, p. 96; March, 2005, Jennifer Cogan, review of *It's a Baby, Andy Russell*, p. 164, and Ellen Loughran, review of *Enemies of Slavery*, p. 190; June, 2005, Suzanne Myers Harold, review of *A Picture Book of Samuel Adams*, p. 132; October, 2005, Be Astengo, review of *Bones and the Dinosaur Mystery*, p. 102; November, 2005, Jennifer Cogan, review of *President George Washington*, p. 111; December, 2005, Barbara Auerbach, review of *Joe Louis*, p. 122; October, 2006, Jill Heritage Maza, review of *You Can, Toucan, Math*, p. 132; April, 2007, Marilyn Taniguchi, review of *Campy*, p. 118; May, 2007, Erika Qualls, review of *Bones and the Birthday Mystery*, p. 84; March, 2008, Rita Soltan, review of *Don't Talk to Me about the War*, p. 193; November, 2008, Erlene Bishop Killeen, review of *Fun with Roman Numerals*, p. 104; March, 2009, Sarah O'Holla, review of *A Picture Book of Dolly and James Madison*, p. 130; April, 2009, Laura Butler, review of *It's Time to Sleep, It's Time to Dream*, p. 99; August, 2009, Lucinda Snyder Whitehurst, review of *A Picture Book of Harry Houdini*, p. 88; August, 2010, Grace Oliff, review of *A Picture Book of Cesar Chavez*, p. 89; September, 2010, Suzanne Myers Harold, review of *A Little at a Time*, p. 117.

Tribune Books (Chicago, IL), February 5, 2006, Mary Harris Russell, review of *Joe Louis*, p. 7.

Voice of Youth Advocates, June, 1995, Charlene Strickland, "Chapter One," pp. 116-117.

ONLINE

David A. Adler Home Page, http://www.DavidAAdler.com (May 20, 2011).

Cam Jansen Web Site, http://www.CamJansen.com/ (May 20, 2011).

*   *   *

ALBEE, Sarah 1962-
(Constance Allen, Catherine Lukas, Sarah Willson)

Personal

Born 1962, in Cleveland, OH; married Jonathan C. Wilson (an educator and administrator); children: Sam, Cassie, Luke. *Education:* Harvard University, B.A., 1984.

Addresses

Home—Watertown, CT. *E-mail*—albee@taftschool.org.

Career

Writer for books and television. Formerly worked as a cartoonist, fashion model, and semi-professional athlete. Presenter at schools.

Member

Society of Children's Book Writers and Illustrators.

Writings

(As Constance Allen) *Bert's Beautiful Sights,* illustrated by Maggie Swanson, Western Pub. Co. (Racine, WI), 1990.

(As Constance Allen) *Ernie Follows His Nose,* illustrated by Maggie Swanson, Western Pub. (Racine, WI), 1990.

(As Constance Allen) *Grover's Book of Cute Things to Touch,* illustrated by Tom Cooke, Western Pub. Co. (Racine, WI), 1990.

(As Constance Allen) *Oscar's Grouchy Sounds,* illustrated by Tom Cooke, Western Pub. Co. (Racine, WI), 1990.

(As Constance Allen) *Sleep Tight!,* illustrated by David Prebenna, Western Pub. Co. (Racine, WI), 1991.

(As Constance Allen) *Grover's Guide to Good Manners,* illustrated by David Prebenna, Western Pub. Co. (Racine, WI), 1992.

(As Constance Allen) *Happy and Sad, Grouchy and Glad,* illustrated by Tom Brannon, Western Pub. Co. (Racine, WI), 1992.

(As Constance Allen) *My Name Is Big Bird,* illustrated by Maggie Swanson, Western Pub. Co. (Racine, WI), 1992.

(As Constance Allen) *Big Bird's Animal Game,* illustrated by Tom Cooke, Western Pub. (Racine, WI), 1993.

(As Constance Allen) *Elmo's Guessing Game,* illustrated by Tom Brannon, Western Pub. Co. (Racine, WI), 1993.

Halloween ABC, illustrated by Paul Meisel, Western Pub. Co. (Racine WI), 1993.

(As Constance Allen) *Merry Christmas, Everybody!,* illustrated by David Prebenna, Western Pub. Co. (Racine, WI), 1993.

(As Constance Allen) *My Name Is Elmo,* illustrated by Maggie Swanson, Western Pub. Co. (Racine, WI), 1993.

(As Constance Allen) *Natasha's Daddy: Featuring Jim Henson's Sesame Street Muppets,* illustrated by Lauren Attinello, Western Pub. Co. (Racine, WI), 1993.

(As Constance Allen) *Sesame Street's Mother Goose Rhymes,* illustrated by Maggie Swanson, Western Pub. Co. (Racine, WI), 1993.

(As Constance Allen) *I Am a Bird,* illustrated by Tom Brannon, Western Pub. Co. (Racine, WI), 1994.

(As Constance Allen) *Peek-a-boo!,* illustrated by David Prebenna, Western Pub. Co. (Racine, WI), 1994.

(As Constance Allen) *What's the Monster Making?,* illustrated by Joel Schick, Western Pub. Co. (Racine, WI), 1994.

Big Bird at Bat, illustrated by Tom Brannon, Random House/Children's Television Workshop (New York, NY), 1995.

Christmas for Polar Bear, illustrated by Ann Hubbard Thornburg, Troll Associates (Mahwah, NJ), 1995.

(As Constance Allen) *Grouches on Parade,* illustrated by Tom Brannon, Western Pub. Co. (Racine, WI), 1995.

Elmo's Twelve Days of Christmas, illustrated by Maggie Swanson, Western Pub. Co. (Racine, WI), 1996.

(As Constance Allen) *I Am a Baby,* illustrated by Tom Brannon, Western Pub. Co. (Racine, WI), 1996.

(As Constance Allen) *Rise and Shine!,* illustrated by David Prebenna, Western Pub. Co. (Racine, WI), 1996.

The Curious Little Duckling, illustrated by Barbara Lanza, Troll Associates (Mahwah, NJ), 1996.

There's a Ghost in My House, illustrated by Kathy Mitchell, Troll Associates (Mahwah, NJ), 1996.

(As Sarah Willson) *A Baby's Got to Grow!,* illustrated by Peter Panas, Simon & Schuster (New York, NY), 1997.

Big Bird's Ticklish Christmas, illustrated by Joe Ewers, Golden Books (New York, NY), 1997.

Chelli Tells the Truth, illustrated by Carol O'Malia, Golden Books (Racine, WI), 1997.

Chelli and the Great Sandbox Adventure, illustrated by Andrew Shiff, Golden Books (New York, NY), 1997.

(As Constance Allen) *Chelli, Be Mine!,* illustrated by Laurent Linn, Golden Books (New York, NY), 1997.

Elmo Loves You: A Poem by Elmo, illustrated by Maggie Swanson, Golden Books (New York, NY), 1997.

(As Constance Allen) *Elmo Says, "Don't Wake the Baby!",* illustrated by David Prebenna, Golden Books (New York, NY), 1997.

(As Constance Allen) *Elmo's Christmas Colors,* illustrated by David Prebenna, Golden Books (New York, NY), 1997.

Elmo's Counting Game, illustrated by Joe Ewers, Golden Books (Racine, WI), 1997.

(As Sarah Willson) *Follow the Leader,* illustrated by Bryan Mon and Adam Devaney, Mouse Works (New York, NY), 1997.

I Can Do It!: Featuring Jim Henson's Sesame Street Muppets, illustrated by Larry DiFiori, Random House (New York, NY), 1997.

(As Sarah Willson) *It's a Circus!,* illustrated by Peter Panas, Simon Spotlight (New York, NY), 1997.

James's Treasure Hunt, illustrated by Kathryn Mitter, Little Simon (New York, NY), 1997.

Ron's Animal Friends, illustrated by Kathryn Mitter, Little Simon (New York, NY), 1997.

Talent Show, illustrated by Joe Ewers, Random House (New York, NY), 1997.

The Bunny Hop, illustrated by Maggie Swanson, Golden Books (Racine, WI), 1997.

The Hurry-up Halloween Costume, illustrated by Laurent Linn, Golden Books (Racine, WI), 1997.

(As Sarah Willson) *The Rugrats' Book of Chanukah,* illustrated by Barry Goldberg, Simon Spotlight (New York, NY), 1997.

(As Sarah Willson) *Tommy and Chuckie on the Go!*, illustrated by Peter Panas, Simon Spotlight (New York, NY), 1997.

Are We There Yet?, illustrated by Tom Brannon, Golden Books (New York, NY), 1998.

Double Trouble: A Story about Twins, illustrated by David Prebenna, Golden Books (New York, NY), 1998.

Elmo Loves You, Golden Books (New York, NY), 1998.

Elmo Says . . ., Golden Books (New York, NY), 1998.

(As Catherine Samuel) *Elmo's Good Manners Game*, illustrated by Maggie Swanson, Golden Books (New York, NY), 1998.

(As Catherine Samuel) *Elmo's New Puppy*, illustrated by Maggie Swanson, Golden Books (New York, NY), 1998.

Elmo's Tricky Tongue Twisters, illustrated by Maggie Swanson, Golden Books (New York, NY), 1998.

(As Sarah Willson) *Happy Days*, illustrated by Jim Valeri, Mouse Works (Los Angeles, CA), 1998.

(As Constance Allen) *Let's Eat!*, illustrated by David Prebenna, Golden Books (New York, NY), 1998.

My Best Friend Is out of This World, illustrated by Nate Evans, Golden Books (New York, NY), 1998.

(As Sarah Willson) *One Colorful Picnic*, illustrated by DiCicco Digital Arts, Mouse Works (New York, NY), 1998.

Shall We Dance?: A Book of Opposites, illustrated by Carol Nicklaus, Golden Books (New York, NY), 1998.

Space Invaders!, illustrated by Ron Zalme, Simon Spotlight (New York, NY), 1998.

(As Sarah Willson) *Sweet Victory*, illustrated by Peter Panas, Simon Spotlight (New York, NY), 1998.

The Dragon's Scales, illustrated by John Manders, Random House (New York, NY), 1998.

(As Sarah Willson) *The House That Chuckie Built*, illustrated by Peter Panas, Simon & Schuster (New York, NY), 1998.

(As Sarah Willson) *The Rugrats Movie Storybook*, illustrated by John Kurtz and Sandrina Kurtz, Simon Spotlight/Nickelodeon (New York, NY), 1998.

(As Sarah Willson) *The Rugrats and the Zombies*, illustrated by Barry Goldberg, Simon Spotlight/Nickelodeon (New York, NY), 1998.

Brought to You by the Number 1, illustrated by Tom Brannon, Random House (New York, NY), 1999.

Brought to You by the Number 2, illustrated by Tom Brannon, Random House (New York, NY), 1999.

Brought to You by the Number 3, illustrated by Tom Brannon, Random House (New York, NY), 1999.

My New Pet Is the Greatest, illustrated by Nate Evans, Golden Books (New York, NY), 1999.

(As Sarah Willson) *The Perfect Formula*, illustrated by Mel Grant, Simon Spotlight/Nickelodeon (New York, NY), 1999.

(As Sarah Willson) *Tricked for Treats!: A Rugrats Halloween*, illustrated by Don Cassity, Simon Spotlight/Nickelodeon (New York, NY), 1999.

(As Constance Allen) *Unwelcome to Grouchland*, illustrated by Joe Ewers, Random House (New York, NY), 1999.

(As Sarah Willson) *Up and Away, Reptar!*, illustrated by Cary Rillo, Simon Spotlight/Nickelodeon (New York, NY), 1999.

Very First Things to Know about Monkeys, illustrated by John Dawson, Workman Pub. (New York, NY), 1999.

Are We There Yet?, illustrated by Tom Brannon, Random House (New York, NY), 2000.

Blue's Lunchbox, illustrated by Karen Craig, Simon Spotlight/Nick Jr. (New York, NY), 2000.

Blue's Travel Game, illustrated by Steve Celmer, Simon Spotlight/Nick Jr. (New York, NY), 2000.

(As Sarah Willson) *Chuckie Meets the Beastie Bunny*, illustrated by Philip Felix, Vince Giarrano, and Byron Talman, Simon Spotlight/Nickelodeon (New York, NY), 2000.

Double Trouble: A Story about Twins, illustrated by David Prebenna, Random House (New York, NY), 2000.

Elmo Loves You, illustrated by Maggie Swanson, Random House (New York, NY), 2000.

Elmo Says, Achoo!, illustrated by Tom Brannon, Random House (New York, NY), 2000.

Elmo's Ducky Day, illustrated by Normand Chartier, Random House (New York, NY), 2000.

(As Constance Allen) *I Am a Baby*, illustrated by Tom Brannon, Random House (New York, NY), 2000.

(As Sarah Willson) *Just Wanna Have Fun*, illustrated by Gary Fields, Simon Spotlight/Nickelodeon (New York, NY), 2000.

(As Catherine Lukas) *Rosie the Riveter*, illustrated by Richard Torrey, Little Simon (New York, NY), 2000.

(As Sarah Willson) *Santa's Workshop*, illustrated by Anne Thornburgh, Little Simon (New York, NY), 2000.

The Oreo Cookie Counting Book, illustrated by Victoria Raymond, Little Simon (New York, NY), 2000.

(As Sarah Willson) *The Quest for the Holey Pail*, Simon Spotlight/Nickelodeon (New York, NY), 2000.

(As Catherine Lukas) *Time Traveling*, illustrated by Richard Torrey, Little Simon (New York, NY), 2000.

Time for Bed, Elmo!, illustrated by Maggie Swanson, Random House (New York, NY), 2000.

Watch out for Banana Peels and Other Important Sesame Street Safety Tips, illustrated by Tom Brannon, Random House (New York, NY), 2000.

Ahoy, Uncle Roy!, illustrated by Ilja Bereznickas, Golden Books (New York, NY), 2001.

Elmo Goes to the Doctor, illustrated by Tom Brannon, Random House (New York, NY), 2001.

Elmo's First Babysitter, illustrated by Tom Brannon, Random House (New York, NY), 2001.

Ernie's Joke Book, illustrated by Joe Mathieu, Random House (New York, NY), 2001.

(As Sarah Willson) *Have No Fear, Chuckie's Here!*, illustrated by Robert Roper, Simon Spotlight/Nickelodeon (New York, NY), 2001.

I Don't Want to Go to School, illustrated by Tom Brannon, Random House (New York, NY), 2001.

If You're Happy and You Know It—Clap Your Paws!, illustrated by Joe Mathieu, Random House (New York, NY), 2001.

Monsters Are Red, Monsters Are Blue, illustrated by Tom Brannon, Random House (New York, NY), 2001.

My Baby Brother Is a Little Monster, illustrated by Tom Brannon, Random House (New York, NY), 2001.

No Cookies?, illustrated by Carol Nicklaus, Random House (New York, NY), 2001.

(As Sarah Willson) *Picture-perfect Tommy,* illustrated by Robert Roper, Simon Spotlight/Nickleodeon (New York, NY), 2001.

(As Sarah Willson) *Prince Chuckie,* illustrated by Ed Resto, Simon Spotlight/Nickelodeon (New York, NY), 2001.

(As Constance Allen) *Shake a Leg!,* illustrated by Maggie Swanson, Random House (New York, NY), 2001.

Spring Fever, illustrated by Carol Nicklaus, Random House (New York, NY), 2001.

(As Catherine Lukas) *The Honeywood Street Fair,* illustrated by Barry Goldberg, Simon Spotlight/Nick Jr. (New York, NY), 2001.

The Monsters on the Bus, illustrated by Joe Ewers, Random House (New York, NY), 2001.

(As Catherine Lukas) *Who's Hiding, Little Bill?,* illustrated by Barry Goldberg, Simon Spotlight/Nick Jr. (New York, NY), 2001.

A Perfect Picnic, Random House (New York, NY), 2002.

Bath Time Brain Quest: 175 Stories, Poems, Questions and Answers—Even Jokes and Riddles—To Read Together with a Little Duck Named Gus, illustrated by Kimble Mead, Workman Pub. (New York, NY), 2002.

(As Catherine Lukas) *Blue's Twelve Days of Christmas,* illustrated by Karen Craig, Simon Spotlight/Nick Jr. (New York, NY), 2002.

Elmo Loves You, illustrated by Maggie Swanson, Random House (New York, NY), 2002.

Give It a Try, Zoe!, Random House (New York, NY), 2002.

Hooray for Our Heroes!, Random House (New York, NY), 2002.

Just like You, Random House (New York, NY), 2002.

(As Catherine Lukas) *Little Bill's Big Book of Words,* illustrated by Robert Powers, Simon Spotlight/Nick Jr. (New York, NY), 2002.

(As Sarah Willson) *Rugrats in the Ring,* illustrated by BKN Studios, Simon Spotlight/Nickelodeon (New York, NY), 2002.

(As Sarah Willson) *Secret-agent Dad,* illustrated by Idea + Design Works, Simon Spotlight/Nickelodeon (New York, NY), 2002.

(As Catherine Lukas) *Super Detective Little Bill: Spin the Wheel, Find the Answer!,* illustrated by Andy Mastrocinque, Simon Spotlight/Nick Jr. (New York, NY), 2002.

Too Many Heroes to Count, Random House (New York, NY), 2002.

Blue's First 100 Days of School, illustrated by Victoria Miller, Simon Spotlight/Nick Jr. (New York, NY), 2003.

Clever Trevor, illustrated by Paige Billin-Frye, Kane Press (New York, NY), 2003.

(As Sarah Willson) *Dora's Halloween Adventure,* illustrated by Steven Savitsky, Simon Spotlight/Nick Jr. (New York, NY), 2003.

(As Sarah Willson) *Dora's Thanksgiving,* illustrated by Robert Roper, Simon Spotlight/Nick Jr. (New York, NY), 2003.

Dragon Tales: Nutcracker Sweet, Random House (New York, NY), 2003.

Dragon Tales: Something Wonderful, Random House (New York, NY), 2003.

Elmo Says Achoo!, illustrated by Tom Brannon, Random House (New York, NY), 2003.

(As Catherine Lukas) *Hello, Santa!,* illustrated by Bernie Cavender and Etsu Kahata, Simon Spotlight/Nick Jr. (New York, NY), 2003.

(As Catherine Lukas) *Hooray for Mother's Day!,* illustrated by Bernie Cavender, Simon Spotlight/Nick Jr. (New York, NY), 2003.

Listen to Your Fish: Terrific Tips for Pet Care, illustrated by Tom Brannon, Random House (New York, NY), 2003.

(As Catherine Lukas) *Little Bill's Birthday Party,* illustrated by Robert Powers, Simon Spotlight/Nick Jr. (New York, NY), 2003.

My Best Friend Is Out of This World, illustrated by Nate Evans, Random House (New York, NY), 2003.

(As Sarah Willson) *My Dress-up Party,* illustrated by Jennifer Oxley, Simon Spotlight (New York, NY), 2003.

My New Pet Is the Greatest, illustrated by Nate Evans, Random House (New York, NY), 2003.

Take Us out to the Ball Game, Random House (New York, NY), 2003.

The Dragon's Scales: A Math Reader, illustrated by John Manders, Random House (New York, NY), 2003.

(As Sarah Willson) *Travis and Scoop's Big Race: A Lift-the-flap Story,* illustrated by Giuseppe Castellano, Simon Spotlight (New York, NY), 2003.

(As Sarah Willson) *A Super Silly Fiesta,* llustrated by Robert Roper, Simon Spotlight/Nick Jr. (New York, NY), 2004.

(As Sarah Willson) *Baby-sitter Blues,* illustrated by Sharon Ross with Kevin Gallegly, Scholastic, Inc. (New York, NY), 2004.

A Visit from the Tooth Fairy, illustrated by Karen Craig, Simon Spotlight (New York, NY), 2004.

(As Sarah Willson) *Hocus Focus,* illustrated by Amy Wummer, Kane Press (New York, NY), 2004.

(As Catherine Lukas) *Is It My Turn Now?,* illustrated by Bernie Cavender, Simon Spotlight/Nick Jr. (New York, NY), 2004.

(As Sarah Willson) *Pirates of the Kiddy Pool,* illustrated by Bob Roper, Scholastic, Inc. (New York, NY), 2004.

(As Sarah Willson) *Blue's Pop-up Surprise!,* illustrated by Zina Saunders, Simon Spotlight/Nick, Jr. (New York, NY), 2005.

(As Sarah Willson) *Bob's Spring Parade,* illustrated by Mike Giles, Simon Spotlight (New York, NY), 2005.

Celebrate with Blue!: A Book of Winter Holidays, illustrated by Victoria Miller, Simon Spotlight/Nick Jr. (New York, NY), 2005.

(As Sarah Willson) *Cookie Crisis!,* illustrated by Sharon Ross and Shannon Bergman, Simon Spotlight/Nickelodeon (New York, NY), 2005.

Costume Capers, illustrated by Artful Doodlers, Simon Spotlight/Nick Jr. (New York, NY), 2005.

Elmo's Ducky Day, illustrated by Normand Chartier, Random House (New York, NY), 2005.

(As Catherine Lukas) *Let's Help!,* photographs by Ken Karp, Simon Spotlight (New York, NY), 2005.

(As Sarah Willson) *Pet Peeves,* illustrated by John Nez, Kane Press (New York, NY), 2005.

(As Catherine Lukas) *Shake, Rattle, and Roll!,* photographs by Ken Karp, Simon Spotlight/Nick Jr. (New York, NY), 2005.

(As Catherine Samuel) *Timmy's Eggs-ray Vision,* illustrated by Zina Saunders, Simon Spotlight/Nickelodeon (New York, NY), 2005.

Blue's Opposites Game, Simon Spotlight/Nick Jr. (New York, NY), 2006.

(With Kate Delaney) *Cheetahs,* Reader's Digest Young Families (Pleasantville, NY), 2006.

(Reteller) *Chicken Little: A Tale about Common Sense,* illustrated by Atelier Philippe Harchy, Reader's Digest Young Families (Pleasantville, NY), 2006.

Chimpanzees, Reader's Digest Young Families (Pleasantville, NY), 2006.

(As Sarah Willson) *Class Confusion,* illustrated by Robert Dress, Simon Spotlight/Nickelodeon (New York, NY), 2006.

Elephants, Reader's Digest Young Families (Pleasantville, NY), 2006.

(Reteller) *Grandpa Mouse and Little Mouse: A Tale about Respecting Elders,* illustrated by AKY-AKA Créations and Olga Lonaytis, Readers Digest Young Families (Pleasantville, NY), 2006.

Hello, Cat, Hello, Dog, illustrated by Tom Leigh, Reader's Digest Young Families (Pleasantville, NY), 2006.

It's Quite True!: A Story about Telling Tales, illustrated by Artful Doodlers, Reader's Digest Young Families (Pleasantville, NY), 2006.

Max Can Fix That, illustrated by Joel Schick, Reader's Digest Young Families (Pleasantville, NY), 2006.

(As Sarah Willson) *Mother Knows Best,* Simon Spotlight/Nickelodeon (New York, NY), 2006.

Off to Bed, illustrated by Len Ebert, Reader's Digest Young Families (Pleasantville, NY), 2006.

One for Me, One for You: A Book about Sharing, illustrated by Karen Craig, Simon Spotlight/Nick Jr. (New York, NY), 2006.

(As Catherine Lukas) *Rescue Patrol,* illustrated by The Artifact Group, Simon Spotlight/Nick Jr. (New York, NY), 2006.

(As Sarah Willson) *See My Valentine,* illustrated by Artful Doodlers, Simon Spotlight/Nickelodeon (New York, NY), 2006.

The Fastest Drawer in the West, illustrated by Dave Aikins, Scholastic, Inc. (Danbury, CT), 2006.

(Reteller) *The Grasshopper and the Ant: A Tale about Planning,* illustrated by Dennis Hockerman, Reader's Digest Young Families (Pleasantville, NY), 2006.

(Reteller) *The Nightingale: A Tale of Compassion,* illustrated by Beverly Branch, Reader's Digest Young Families (Pleasantville, NY), 2006.

(Reteller) *The Queen and the Mouse: A Story about Friendship,* illustrated by Renate Lohmann, Reader's Digest Young Families (Pleasantville, NY), 2006.

The Rooster and the Fox: A Tale about Being Clever, illustrated by Artful Doodlers, Reader's Digest Young Families (Pleasantville, NY), 2006.

(Reteller) *The Tale of Two Bad Mice: A Story about Respecting the Property of Others,* illustrated by Maggie Swanson, Reader's Digest Young Families (Pleasantville, NY), 2006.

(As Sarah Willson) *Valentine Villains,* illustrated by Artful Doodlers, Simon Spotlight (New York, NY), 2006.

(As Sarah Willson) *What's with Dad?,* illustrated by Larissa Marantz and Katharine DiPaolo, Simon Spotlight/Nickelodeon (New York, NY), 2006.

Where Is Pig?, illustrated by Walter Velez, Reader's Digest Young Families (Pleasantville, NY), 2006.

(As Sarah Willson) *Behold, No Cavities!: A Visit to the Dentist,* illustrated by Harry Moore, Simon Spotlight/Nickelodeon (New York, NY), 2007.

(As Catherine Lukas) *Jingle Bell Christmas,* illustrated by The Artifact Group, Simon Spotlight/Nick Jr. (New York, NY), 2007.

(As Sarah Willson) *Just Say Please!,* illustrated by Harry Moore, Simon Spotlight/Nickelodeon (New York, NY), 2007.

(As Sarah Willson) *SpongeBob Rippedpants,* illustrated by Heather Martinez, Simon Spotlight/Nickelodeon (New York, NY), 2007.

(As Catherine Lukas) *Three Wishes,* illustrated by Susan Hall, Simon Spotlight/Nick Jr. (New York, NY), 2007.

(As Catherine Lukas) *Trouble on the Train,* illustrated by the Artifact Group, Simon Spotlight/Nick Jr. (New York, NY), 2007.

(As Catherine Lukas) *Backyardigans and the Beanstalk,* illustrated by Susan Hall, Simon Spotlight/Nick Jr. (New York, NY), 2008.

(As Constance Allen) *Happy and Sad, Grouchy and Glad,* illustrated by Tom Brannon, Candlewick Press (Somerville, MA), 2008.

(As Catherine Lukas) *Bears,* Gareth Stevens (Pleasantville, NY), 2009.

(As Sarah Willson) *Man Sponge Saves the Day,* illustrated by the Artifact Group, Simon Spotlight/Nickelodeon (New York, NY), 2009.

(As Constance Allen) *Shake a Leg!,* Random House (New York, NY), 2010.

(As Sarah Willson) *The Best Mom,* illustrated by Dave Aikins, Simon Spotlight/Nickelodeon (New York, NY), 2010.

Poop Happened!: A History of the World from the Bottom Up, ilustrated by Robert Leighton, Walker Books (New York, NY), 2010.

Author of script for animated film *Elmo and the Orchestra.* Adaptor of teleplays, under names Catherine Lukas and Sarah Willson.

Sidelights

Writing under her own name as well as several pseudonyms, Sarah Albee entertained and educated a generation of fans of the *Sesame Street* and *Blue's Clues* television programs in her stories featuring beloved series characters. Born in Ohio, Albee opted for a career in writing after working as a cartoonist and a semiprofessional basketball player shortly after earning her degree at Harvard University. She began producing stories featuring Bert and Ernie, Grover, Big Bird, and others in the early 1990s, sometimes publishing them as Constance Allen, Catherine Lukas, or Sarah Willson. Over the years she has expanded her focus, creating engaging texts for board books and toddler concept books as well as interactive lift-the-flap stories, several of which have even made it to *New York Times* bestseller status. *Clever Trevor,* one of Albee's contributions to the "Science Solves It!" series, focuses on a boy who discovers a novel use for the fulcrum and lever first popularized by ancient Greek scientist Archimedes, while *Hocus Focus* finds nearsighted Jack and farsighted Gina teaming up to make it through the school day without eyeglasses. Praising *Clever Trevor* in *School Library Journal,* Anne Knickerbocker noted that it features the series' characteristic mix of "interesting stories with child-pleasing themes," while Erlene Bishop Killeen wrote in the same publication that *Hocus Focus* features a "solid combination . . . of story and science."

Albee's best-known book combines a giggle-inducing title with what *School Library Journal* critic Brian Odom cited as a "fluid writing style that ensnares and holds readers' attention." In *Poop Happened!: A History of the World from the Bottom Up!* she focuses on the human quandary of what to do with excrement, especially when many people live together in permanent settlements. Beginning with the ancient world, she travels through time and space to reveal the role urine and feces played in determining the course of human civilization. She also shows how the lack of proper sewage systems led to tragic outbreaks of bubonic plague and cholera. Unspoken but tantalizing question—such as how astronauts "go to the bathroom"—combine with memorable trivia—for example, the ancients' use of urine to clean their clothing—to produce a pun-filled text that "will elicit groans from adults but will resonate with kids," according to a *Kirkus Reviews* writer. In *Publishers Weekly* a contributor cited Albee's "candid humor" and mix of "delightfully uncouth anecdotes" and social and scientific history, while in *Booklist* John Peters praised Robert Leighton's cartoon art with appropriate "sludgy green highlights."

Biographical and Critical Sources

PERIODICALS

Booklist, July, 1998, Carolyn Phelan, review of *The Dragon's Scales,* p. 1890; March 15, 2004, Carolyn Phelan, review of *Hocus Focus,* p. 1312; February 15, 2010, John Peters, review of *Poop Happened!: A History of the World from the Bottom Up,* p. 75.
Children's Bookwatch, August, 2010, review of *Poop Happened!*
Kirkus Reviews, April 15, 2010, review of *Poop Happened!*

Publishers Weekly, July 10, 2000, review of *The Oreo Cookie Counting Book,* p. 65; May 3, 2010, review of *Poop Happened!,* p. 50.
School Library Journal, June, 2003, Anne Knickerbocker, review of *Clever Trevor,* p. 96, June, 2004, Erlene Bishop Killeen, review of *Hocus Focus,* p. 110; September, 2005, Christine E. Carr, review of *Pet Peeves,* p. 164; May, 2010, Brian Odom, review of *Poop Happened!,* p. 126.

ONLINE

Sarah Albee Home Page, http://sarahalbeebooks.com (April 20, 2011).
TeacherBuzz Web site, http://www.authorbuzz.com/teacherbuzz/ (June 15, 2011), "Sarah Albee."*

*   *   *

ALLEN, Constance
See ALBEE, Sarah

*   *   *

AVASTHI, Swati 1971-

Personal

Name pronounced "SWA-thee Of-US-thee"; born May 26, 1971; married; husband's name John; children: two. *Education:* University of Chicago, B.A. (literature and theatre); University of Minnesota, M.F.A.

Addresses

Home—Minneapolis, MN. *E-mail*—swatiavasthi@gmail.com.

Career

Author and educator. Presenter at conferences and workshops; guest lecturer. Member of awards committee, Minnesota Book Awards.

Member

Association of Writers and Writing Programs, Society of Children's Book Writers and Illustrators, Children's Literature Network.

Awards, Honors

Minnesota State Arts Board grant; Loft's Mentor Series Award; Pushcart Prize nomination; Parents' Choice Silver Award, CYBILS award, and Minnesota Book Award nomination, all 2010, and Best Books for Young Adults designation, American Library Association/YALSA, 2011, all for *Split.*

Writings

Split, Alfred A. Knopf (New York, NY), 2010.

Contributor to periodicals, including *Portland Review* and *Water-Stone Review*

Adaptations

Split was adapted for audiobook by Listening Library, 2010.

Sidelights

Minnesota-based writer Swati Avasthi became a reader at a young age and she quickly discovered the magical "Little House" books of Laura Ingalls Wilder as well as works by Emily Brontë and other classic novelists. In her own first novel, *Split,* Avasthi draws on the narrative talents of the writers who inspired her, creating a compelling story featuring a first-person narration that *School Library Journal* contributor Erin Carrillo characterized as "raw and intimate, dramatic and poetic."

As a student at the University of Chicago, Avasthi earned her B.A. in literature and theater. Viewing her future in a practical manner, she decided to earn a degree in law while also maintaining her passion for literature through teaching and lecturing. "I was signing up for the LSAT (Law School Admission Test) when the computer quit, just shut down," she recalled to an

Cover of Swati Avasthi's young-adult novel Split, *which finds a teen hoping to make a clean break with his abusive family.* (Copyright © 2010 by Knopf Children. Used by permission of Alfred A. Knopf, an imprint of Random House Children's Books, a division of Random House, Inc.)

interviewer on the Friends of Saint Paul Public Library Web site. Viewing this as an omen, she refocused on writing and began teaching at Minneapolis's Loft Literary Center. As marriage and beginning a family followed, Avasthi has continued to write. Her move from fantasy to contemporary teen fiction coupled with memories of her first-hand experience coordinating a domestic violence legal clinic to produce *Split.*

In *Split* readers meet sixteen-year-old Jace Witherspoon just as he is pummeled and thrown out on the street by his abusive dad. With no where else to go, Jace travels from Chicago to New Mexico where he is taken in by older brother Christian, who he has not seen in six years. Although the teen attempts to make a fresh start, worries over his mother's safety in an abusive relationship as well as a haunting secret force him to confront a past that will otherwise become his own destiny. Calling *Split* a "taut, complex family drama," a *Kirkus Reviews* writer added that Avasthi's story focuses on "healing, growth and learning to take responsibility for one's own anger." Jace's efforts to rekindle a relationship with Christian, and the brothers' efforts to "turn to each other to escape from their father's shadow, is touching," observed Carrillo, and a *Publishers Weekly* critic noted the "array of unexpected emotions" that surface once the teen is separated from his tormentor. Avasthi does not resolve her story with a happy ending; instead she crafts a tale in which "suspense . . . is perfectly counterbalanced by the nuanced growth and development" of her troubled characters, according to *Horn Book* critic Jonathan Hunt. In *Booklist* Daniel Kraus deemed *Split* "a nuanced and mournful work" and recommended Avasthi as "a writer to watch."

Biographical and Critical Sources

PERIODICALS

Booklist, January 1, 2010, Daniel Kraus, review of *Split,* p. 70.
Bulletin of the Center for Children's Books, April, 2010, Deborah Stevenson, review of *Split,* p. 323.
Horn Book, May-June, 2010, Jonathan Hunt, review of *Split,* p. 74.
Kirkus Reviews, March 1, 2010, review of *Split.*
Publishers Weekly, January 25, 2010, review of *Split,* p. 121.
School Library Journal, March, 2010, Erin Carrillo, review of *Split,* p. 151.

ONLINE

Friends of Saint Paul Public Library Web site, http://www.thefriends.org/ (June 20, 2011), "Swati Avasthi."
Swati Avasthi Home Page, http://www.swatiavasthi.com (June 20, 2011).
Swati Avasthi Web log, http://swatiavasthi.blogspot.com (June 20, 2011).*

B

BACHEM, Paul

Personal
Born in NY; married; wife's name Janice (a painter and sculptor). *Education:* Studied with Harold and Alma Stevenson, 1975-77. *Hobbies and other interests:* Playing classical guitar.

Addresses
Home—Locust Valley, NY. *E-mail*—pbachem@optonline.net.

Career
Illustrator and fine artist. *Exhibitions:* Work included in exhibits at galleries, including Gallery North, Setauket, NY, LaMantia Gallery, Northport, NY, and Robert Paul Galleries, Stowe, VT. Work included in permanent collection of Forbes Gallery, New York, NY.

Member
New York Plein Air Painters (associate member), Long Island Plein Air Painters Society (founding member).

Awards, Honors
Society of Illustrators Certificate of Merit; awards in juried shows.

Illustrator
Pony Pals: How to Draw Ponies, Scholastic, Inc. (New York, NY), 1994.

Sir Arthur Conan Doyle, *The Mysteries of Sherlock Holmes,* Grosset & Dunlap (New York, NY), 1996.

Jennifer Johnson Garrity, *The Bushwhacker: A Civil War Adventure,* Peachtree (Atlanta, GA), 1999.

Hilary Hyland, *The Wreck of the Ethie,* Peachtree (Atlanta, GA), 1999.

Sylvia M. James, *Salmon,* Mondo (New York, NY), 2000.

(With Laszlo Kubinyi) Megan McDonald, *Shadows in the Glasshouse* ("History Mysteries" series), Pleasant Company (Middleton, WI), 2000.

Alison Hart, *Anna's Blizzard,* Peachtree (Atlanta, GA), 2005.

Alison Hart, *Emma's River,* Peachtree (Atlanta, GA), 2010.

Contributor to books, including *Ancient Rome* and *Ancient Greece,* by Judith Simpson, Time-Life Books (Alexandria, VA), 1997.

"PONY PALS" SERIES

Jeanne Betancourt, *A Pony in Trouble,* Scholastic Inc. (New York, NY), 1995.

Jeanne Betancourt, *Give Me Back My Pony,* Scholastic Inc. (New York, NY), 1995.

Jeanne Betancourt, *Pony to the Rescue,* Scholastic Inc. (New York, NY), 1995.

Jeanne Betancourt, *The Baby Pony* ("Super Specials"), Scholastic, Inc. (New York, NY), 1996.

Jeanne Betancourt, *Circus Pony,* Scholastic Inc. (New York, NY), 1996.

Jeanne Betancourt, *Too Many Ponies,* Scholastic Inc. (New York, NY), 1996.

Jeanne Betancourt, *Don't Hurt My Pony,* Scholastic, Inc. (New York, NY), 1996.

Jeanne Betancourt, *Good-bye Pony,* Scholastic Inc. (New York, NY), 1996.

Jeanne Betancourt, *Keep Out, Pony!,* Scholastic, Inc. (New York, NY), 1996.

Jeanne Betancourt, *The Blind Pony,* Scholastic, Inc. (New York, NY), 1997.

Jeanne Betancourt, *The Girl Who Hated Ponies,* Scholastic, Inc. (New York, NY), 1997.

Jeanne Betancourt, *The Ghost Pony* ("Super Special"), Scholastic, Inc. (New York, NY), 1997.

Jeanne Betancourt, *The Story of Our Ponies* ("Super Special"), Scholastic, Inc. (New York, NY), 1997.

Jeanne Betancourt, *The Missing Pony,* Scholastic, Inc. (New York, NY), 1997.

Jeanne Betancourt, *Detective Pony,* Scholastic, Inc. (New York, NY), 1998.

Randi Hacker, *Pony Pals Cookbook,* Scholastic Inc. (New York, NY), 1999.

Jeanne Betancourt, *The Wild Pony,* Scholastic, Inc. (New York, NY), 1999.

Jeanne Betancourt, *The Newborn Pony,* Scholastic Inc. (New York, NY), 2000.

Jeanne Betancourt, *The Pony and the Missing Dog,* Scholastic, Inc. (New York, NY), 2000.

Jeanne Betancourt, *Pony Sitters,* Scholastic, Inc. (New York, NY), 2000.

Jeanne Betancourt, *He's My Pony!,* Scholastic, Inc. (New York, NY), 2001.

Jeanne Betancourt, *Lost and Found Pony,* Scholastic, Inc. (New York, NY), 2001.

Jeanne Betancourt, *Ponies from the Past,* Scholastic, Inc. (New York, NY), 2001.

Jeanne Betancourt, *Pony-4-sale,* Scholastic, Inc. (New York, NY), 2001.

Jeanne Betancourt, *The Fourth Pony Pal* ("Super Special"), Scholastic, Inc. (New York, NY), 2001.

Jeanne Betancourt, *What's Wrong with My Pony?,* Scholastic, Inc. (New York, NY), 2001.

Jeanne Betancourt, *Magic Pony,* Scholastic, Inc. (New York, NY), 2002.

Jeanne Betancourt, *The Pony and the Lost Swan,* Scholastic, Inc. (New York, NY), 2002.

Biographical and Critical Sources

PERIODICALS

Booklist, June 1, 2010, Abby Nolan, review of *Emma's River,* p. 66.

Children's Bookwatch, April, 2010, review of *Emma's River.*

Kirkus Reviews, September 15, 2005, review of *Anna's Blizzard,* p. 1027; March 1, 2010, review of *Emma's River.*

School Library Journal, April, 2000, Patricia B. McGee, review of *The Bushwacker: A Civil War Adventure,* p. 134, and William C. Schadt, review of *The Wreck of the Ethie,* p. 136; February, 2001, Kristen Oravec, review of *Shadows in the Glasshouse,* p. 118; October, 2005, Kathleen E. Gruver, review of *Anna's Blizzard,* p. 115; January, 2007, Lucinda Snyder Whitehurst, review of *Shadows in the Glasshouse,* p. 53; July, 2010, Necia Blundy, review of *Emma's River,* p. 90.

ONLINE

Paul Bachem Home Page, http://paulbachem.com (June 20, 2011).*

* * *

BANCKS, Tristan 1974-

Personal

Born 1974, in Australia. *Education:* University of New England, B.A. (English and film). *Hobbies and other interests:* Sports, travel, reading, spending time with family.

Addresses

Home—New South Wales, Australia. *E-mail*—contact@tristanbancks.com.

Career

Actor and author. Actor at Q Theatre, Sydney, New South Wales, Australia. Television roles include: (debut; as Tug O'Neale) *Home and Away,* 1992-94; (as Dean) *Dust,* 2002; (as Grub) *Beneath Clouds,* 2006; (as Grub) *Remote Area Nurse,* 2006; and presenter of television programming on U.K. television, including ITV, Channel Four, and British Broadcasting Corporation, until 1999. Director of short films, including *The Long Wet, The New Boots, Soar,* 2004, and *Every Day at Schools.* Speaker at schools, libraries, and festivals.

Awards, Honors

Numerous film festival awards for *Soar.*

Writings

Hanging out Together, Scholastic Education (Linfield, New South Wales, Australia), 2005.

Space Stations: Cities of the Future?, Scholastic Education (Linfield, New South Wales, Australia), 2005.

It's a Wild Ride!, Scholastic Education (Linfield, New South Wales, Australia), 2005.

Make 'em Laugh, Scholastic Education (Linfield, New South Wales, Australia), 2005.

(With Tempany Deckert) *It's Yr Life* (young-adult novel), Random House Australia (North Sydney, New South Wales, Australia), 2009.

Galactic Adventures: First Kids in Space, University of Queensland Press (St. Lucia, Queensland, Australia), 2011.

My Life and Other Stuff I Made Up, illustrated by Gus Gordon, Random House (North Sydney, New South Wales, Australia), 2011.

Contributor to anthologies, including *Picture This 2,* Pearson Australia (Port Melbourne, Victoria, Australia), 2009. Also author of short films.

"KIDS INC." SERIES

Behind the Scenes, illustrated by David Clarke, Macmillan Education Australia (South Yarra, Victoria, Australia), 2007.

Kart Games, illustrated by Heath McKenzie, Macmillan Education Australia (South Yarra, Victoria, Australia), 2007.

The Amazing Race, illustrated by Heath McKenzie, Macmillan Education Australia (South Yarra, Victoria, Australia), 2007.

Dream Racers Are Go!, illustrated by Heath McKenzie, Macmillan Education Australia (South Yarra, Victoria, Australia), 2007.

"MAC SLATER, COOLHUNTER" MIDDLE-GRADE NOVEL SERIES

The Rules of Cool, Random House (North Sydney, New South Wales, Australia), 2008, published as *Mac Slater Hunts the Cool,* Simon & Schuster Books for Young Readers (New York, NY), 2010.

I Heart NY, Random House (North Sydney, New South Wales, Australia), 2009, published as *Mac Slater vs. the City,* Simon & Schuster Books for Young Readers (New York, NY), 2011.

"NITBOY" SERIES

Lift Off!, illustrated by Heath McKenzie, Laguna Bay Publishing (Mosman, New South Wales, Australia), 2009.

Bug Out!, illustrated by Heath McKenzie, Laguna Bay Publishing (Mosman, New South Wales, Australia), 2009.

Adaptations

The "Nit Boy" series was adapted for Australian television.

Sidelights

Although Tristan Bancks has acted in television since his teen years and has also produced several short films, his largest fan following in his native Australia has come through his writing, which includes the middle-grade "Mac Slater" novels as well as chapters books and young-adult fiction. As Bancks explained on his home page in reviewing his multifaceted creative career, "Making two and a half hours of TV a week is a fantastic baptism of fire for a young actor and instills a professional work ethic that's come in handy."

As a teenager, Bancks trained as an actor at Sydney's Q Theatre, and then spent two years performing the role of Tug O'Neale on the television program *Home and Away.* After helping to develop a behind-the-scenes series for U.K.-based ITV in the mid-1990s, he relocated to England where he wrote and presented the program. Bancks remained in England for four years, working as a television presenter and journalist while also learning more about the craft of writing and filming for television. He returned to Australia in 1999 and completed his bachelor's degree at the University of New England. After appearing in several television programs, he shifted to the other side of the camera, directing the short films *The Long Wet, The New Boots, Soar,* and *Every Day at School.* Bancks also tapped his natural storytelling ability to produce not only his "Mac Slater" books but also the two volumes in his "Kids, Inc." and "Nitboys" stories for younger readers and the collaborative young-adult novel *It's Yr Life,* coauthored by former *Home and Away* costar Tempany Deckert.

Bancks' "Mac Slater" books include *The Rules of Cool* and *I Heart NY,* which were released to U.S. readers as *Mac Slater Hunts the Cool* and *Mac Slater vs. the City*

respectively. In the series opener, readers meet Australian eighth grader Mac, who lives in Kings Bay, a bohemian seaside town that may be one of the region's coolest places to live. Mac is an inventor, and when he is tapped by Web company Coolhunters to track down and report on new trends he recognizes that his status as middle-grade geek and iconoclast means that he has no knowledge of what is or has been in. While Mac is helped in his task by equally geeky best buddy Paul, calculating classmate Cat DeVrees believes that Mac's job for Coolhunters is destined to be hers . . . or else. *Mac Slater Hunts the Cool* "affirms a truth adolescents need to be reminded of: that true cool comes from within and can't be obtained with a credit card," noted *School Library Journal* contributor Jeffrey Hastings. In a *Kirkus Reviews* appraisal of Bancks' novel, a critic deemed the work "diverting," adding that *Mac Slater Hunts the Cool* presents preteen readers with "a timely tome for today," and *Booklist* critic Shauna Yusko dubbed Bancks' young hero "a likeable character who will appeal to a wide range of readers."

Mac takes his search for the latest and greatest to the streets of Manhattan in *Mac Slater vs. the City,* a

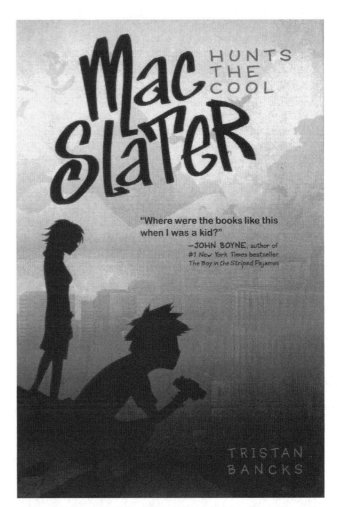

Cover of Tristan Bancks' middle-grade novel **Mac Slater Hunts the Cool,** *part of an entertaining series that features cover art by Gianluca Fallone.* (Copyright © 2008 by Tristan Bancks. Reproduced with permission of Simon & Schuster Books for Young Readers, an imprint of Simon & Schuster Children's Publishing Division.)

"breezy sequel" to *Mac Slater Hunts the Cool* that "provides some fast food for thought," according to a *Kirkus Reviews* writer. Reviewing Bancks' story, which finds Mac and Paul competing with three other trend-savvy preteens, Patty Saidenberg wrote in *School Library Journal* that *Mac Slater vs. the City* "takes twists and turns that are both surprising and rewarding," making the book a popular choice among middle-grade readers.

On his home page, Bancks noted that his career is gradually refocusing itself. "Some of my recent work melds my interest in social action and filmmaking," he noted, referencing his film *Every Day at School,* which was produced by Film Australia as part of a campaign promoting positive activism among primary school students. However, Bancks also views writing as a way of making a difference to young people, and he spends much of his time promoting reading and writing to students in Australian schools. "Writing fiction is pure storytelling," he added on his home page, "and I think it's the best job in the world."

Biographical and Critical Sources

PERIODICALS

Booklist, April 1, 2010, Shauna Yusko, review of *Mac Slater Hunts the Cool,* p. 39.
Kirkus Reviews, March 1, 2010, review of *Mac Slater Hunts the Cool;* February 1, 2011, review of *Mac Slater vs. the City.*
School Library Journal, March, 2010, Jeffrey Hastings, review of *Mac Slater Hunts the Cool,* p. 151; April, 2011, Patty Saidenberg, review of *Mac Slater vs. the City,* p. 166.

ONLINE

Lateral Learning Web site, http://www.laterallearning.com/ (June 20, 2011), "Tristan Bancks."
Tristan Bancks Home Page, http://www.tristanbancks.com (June 20, 2011).

*   *   *

BENNETT, Kelly 1958-
(Kelly Goldman Bennett, Jill Max, a joint pseudonym)

Personal

Born 1958, in Santa Cruz, CA; married Curtis Bennett; children: Max, Alexis. *Education:* Fullerton College, A.A. (liberal arts); attended California State University, Fullerton; San Jose State University, degree (communications); attended Tulsa Community College; Vermont College, M.F.A. (writing for children and young adults).

Addresses

Home—Houston, TX; Jakarta, Indonesia.

Career

Author and journalist. Presenter at schools.

Member

International Reading Association, Author's Guild, Society of Children's Book Writers and Illustrators, American Library Association, Texas Library Association.

Awards, Honors

Children's Choice selection, and Oppenheim Toy Portfolio Gold Medal, both 2005, both for *Not Norman;* National Parenting Publications Award Honor designation, 2010, for *Dad and Pop.*

Writings

FOR CHILDREN

(Adapter, with Ronnie Davidson under joint pseudonym Jill Max) Dorothèe Böhlke, *Cokolina and the Wild Island* (translation of *Cokolina und die wilde Insel*), Garrett Educational (Ada, OK), 1991.
(Editor, with Ronnie Davidson under joint pseudonym Jill Max) *Spider Spins a Story: Fourteen Legends from Native America,* illustrated by Robert Annesley and others, Rising Moon (Flagstaff, AZ), 1997.
Arbor Day, Children's Press (New York, NY), 2003.
Flag Day, Children's Press (New York, NY), 2003.
Delaware, Children's Press (New York, NY), 2004.
Not Norman: A Goldfish Story, illustrated by Noah Z. Jones, Candlewick Press (Cambridge, MA), 2005.
(With Ronnie Davidson under joint pseudonym Jill Max) *Strangers in Black: A Young Boy's Struggle to Survive in Khmer Rouge Cambodia,* Royal Fireworks Press (Unionville, NY), 2006.
Chesapeake Bay, Childrens Press (New York, NY), 2006.
Dance, Y'all, Dance, illustrated by Terri Murphy, Bright Sky Press (Houston, TX), 2009.
Dad and Pop: An Ode to Fathers and Stepfathers, illustrated by Paul Meisel, Candlewick Press (Somerville, MA), 2010.
Your Daddy Was Just like You, illustrated by David Walker, G.P. Putnam's Sons (New York, NY), 2010.
Your Mommy Was Just like You, illustrated by David Walker, G.P. Putnam's Sons (New York, NY), 2011.

Contributor to periodicals, including *Ranger Rick* and *Now! Jakarta.*

"MAGIC MOUNTAIN FABLES" SERIES

(Adaptor, with Ronnie Davidson under joint pseudonym Jill Max) *Annie's City Adventures* (based on *Besuche in der Stadt* by Marek Mann), Garrett Educational (Ada, OK), 1991.

(Adaptor, with Ronnie Davidson under joint pseudonym Jill Max) *Annie's High Sea Adventure* (based on *Urlaub am Meer* by Marek Mann), Garrett Educational (Ada, OK), 1991.

(Adaptor, with Ronnie Davidson under joint pseudonym Jill Max) *Dino, the Star Keeper* (based on *Dino, der Saurier* by Marek Mann), Garrett Educational (Ada, OK), 1991.

Sidelights

Kelly Bennett was born in California, and although her family moved out of the state during her elementary-grade years, she returned to complete high school and earn a degree in communications at San Jose State University. An M.F.A. in writing for children and young adults from Vermont College has added to Bennett's credentials as a children's author, as have her curiosity, her experiences traveling, and her time raising her own children. In addition to her own stories, which include *Dad and Pop: An Ode to Fathers and Stepfathers* and *Not Norman: A Goldfish Story*, Bennett has also col-laborated with fellow writer Ronnie Davidson, publishing under the joint pseudonym Jill Max. "Picture books are like icebergs, so much of what goes on goes unseen," Bennett explained in discussing the craft of writing on her home page. "I start with a big, messy jumble of words, pages of words, blocks of words, and just start chipping away," she added. "When I'm finished, I hope what's left is as pure and simply stated as I can write it."

A child's desire for a pet is at the heart of *Not Norman*, a picture book illustrated by Noah Z. Jones. For the young narrator of Bennett's tale, a goldfish named Norman is not exactly the pet of his dreams. When the opportunity comes to introduce Norman to his classmates during show-and-tell, he views it as a chance to find the fish a new owner. As the boy begins to extoll Norman's virtues to his classmates, however, he realizes that a goldfish has talents that cats and dogs do not. The story ends with what *Booklist* critic Carolyn Phelan described as a "verbally clever turnaround" to an "amusing" tale.

Kellyy Bennett teams up with artist Paul Meisel to present a multigenerational ode to fathers of all sorts in **Dad and Pop.** (Illustration copyright © 2010 by Paul Meisel. Reproduced by permission of Candlewick Press, Somerville, MA.)

Praising Bennett's use of "simple, straightforward language," Grace Oliff added in *School Library Journal* that *Not Norman* "is a sweet story" that effectively illustrates "the pitfalls of making snap judgments about pets—or people." A *Publishers Weekly* critic observed of Bennett's tale that her "off-the-cuff yet kidlike prose ideally suits [Jones'] . . . bright, crisp digital drawings."

Bennett focuses on family relationships in both *Dad and Pop* and *Your Daddy Was Just like You,* the latter featuring colorful paintings by David Walker. In the first, a little girl describes the many ways in which the two men in her life—her biological father and her stepfather—are alike despite their differences. While they do not share hobbies, physical looks, or preferences, the two men are united in their ability to make her feel loved and secure. With a multigenerational approach, *Your Daddy Was Just like You* finds an elderly grandmother recalling the antics of her own son to her grandson, using both the family photograph album and many well-remembered stories to show the child that his own father was a carefree boy before he grew up to become a daddy. With artwork by Paul Meisel, *Dad and Pop* presents "a positive and playful portrayal of a blended family," according to *School Library Journal* contributor Heidi Estrin, and Randall Enos noted in his *Booklist* review that Bennett's story takes a unique perspective on step-parenting. Appraising *Your Daddy Was Just like You* in *School Library Journal,* Anne Beier wrote that Bennett's "humorous text is in perfect sync with the simple illustrations," while Abby Nolan predicted in *Booklist* that Walker's "appealing pictures . . . will prompt loving memories from children's own grandparents."

Biographical and Critical Sources

PERIODICALS

Booklist, December 15, 1997, Karen Hutt, review of *Spider Spins a Story: Fourteen Legends from Native America,* p. 694; February 15, 2005, Carolyn Phelan, review of *Not Norman: A Goldfish Story,* p. 1082; February 1, 2010, Abby Nolan, review of *Your Daddy Was Just like You,* p. 52; February 15, 2010, Randall Enos, review of *Dad and Pop: An Ode to Fathers and Stepfathers,* p. 80.

Bulletin of the Center for Children's Books, April, 2005, Deborah Stevenson, review of *Not Norman,* p. 328.

Kirkus Reviews, February 1, 2005, review of *Not Norman,* p. 173.

Publishers Weekly, March 21, 2005, review of *Not Norman,* p. 50; April 19, 2010, reviews of *Your Dad Was Just like You* and *Dad and Pop,* both p. 52.

School Library Journal, January, 1998, Darcy Schild, review of *Spider Spins a Story,* p. 103; March, 2005, Grace Oliff, review of *Not Norman,* p. 166; March, 2010, Heidi Estrin, review of *Your Dad Was Just like You,* p. 114.

ONLINE

Kelly Bennett Home Page, http://kellybennett.com (June 20, 2011).

Jill Max Web site, http://www.jillmax.com (June 20, 2011).*

* * *

BENNETT, Kelly Goldman
See BENNETT, Kelly

* * *

BIRDSALL, Jeanne 1951-

Personal

Born 1951; married William Diehl, 1994; children: two stepchildren. *Education:* Attended Boston University, 1969; attended California College of Arts and Crafts, 1972.

Addresses

Home—Northampton, MA. *Agent*—Barbara S. Kouts Literary Agency, P.O. Box 560, Bellport, NY 11713.

Career

Children's book author. Formerly worked as a photographer. *Exhibitions:* Photographs included in exhibitions and permanent collections.

Awards, Honors

Booklist Top Ten First Novels for Youth inclusion, *School Library Journal* Best Books designation, and National Book Award for Young People's Literature, all 2005, all for *The Penderwicks;* Title for Reading and Sharing, New York Public Library, Children's Book Sense Top-Ten selection, and Cuffie Award for Best Sequel, all 2008, and Heidelberger Leander Award, 2009, all for *The Penderwicks on Gardam Street.*

Writings

The Penderwicks: A Summer Tale of Four Sisters, Two Rabbits, and a Very Interesting Boy, Knopf (New York, NY), 2005.

The Penderwicks on Gardam Street, illustrated by David Frankland, Alfred A. Knopf (New York, NY), 2008.

Flora's Very Windy Day, illustrated by Matt Phelan, Clarion Books (New York, NY), 2010.

The Penderwicks at Point Mouette, illustrated by David Frankland, Alfred A. Knopf (New York, NY), 2011.

Lucky and Squash Run Away, illustrated by Jane Dyer, Harper (New York, NY), 2012.

Author's work has been translated into several languages, including Chinese, Czech, Dutch, German, Greek, Hebrew, Hungarian, Indonesian, Italian, Korean, and Spanish.

Adaptations

The Penderwicks was adapted for audiobook, read by Susan Denaker, Listening Library, 2006. *The Penderwicks on Gardam Street* was adapted for audiobook, read by Denaker, Listening Library, 2008.

Sidelights

No one was more surprised than Jeanne Birdsall herself when she was awarded the 2005 National Book Award for Young People's Literature for her first-ever published book, *The Penderwicks: A Summer Tale of Four Sisters, Two Rabbits, and a Very Interesting Boy*. The four sisters whose imaginative adventures play out Birdsall's award-winning debut return in the sequels *The Penderwicks on Gardam Street* and *The Penderwicks at Point Mouette*, and the author also turns to younger readers in creating her picture books *Flora's Very Windy Day* and *Lucky and Squash Run Away*.

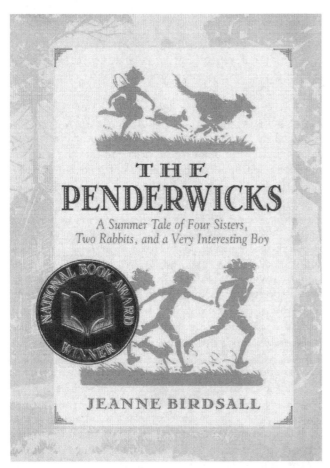

Cover of Jeanne Birdsall's award-winning middle-grade fantasy novel **The Penderwicks,** *featuring cover art b David Frankland.* (Illustration copyright © 2005 by David Frankland. Used by permission of Alfred A. Knopf, an imprint of Random House Children's Books, a division of Random House, Inc.)

Growing up in Strafford, Pennsylvania, Birdsall's childhood was scarred by alcoholism. Reading became a way for her to escape into another world, and her love of children's literature continued into adulthood. Although she eventually established her primary career in the visual arts and has become well known for her art photography, at age forty-two she decided to fulfill a childhood goal: write a book that carries on the legacy of children's fantasy writers E. Nesbit and Edward Eager. *The Penderwicks* was the result.

Described as "so retro, it's almost radical" by *School Library Journal* interviewer Rick Margolis, *The Penderwicks* introduces twelve-year-old Rosalind, eleven-year-old Skye, ten-year-old Jane, and four-year-old Batty Penderwick. Together with their widowed father, a loving but rather absentminded botany professor, the four sisters and the family dog vacation in a cozy cottage on a country estate called Arundel Hall. With few other children living nearby, the girls soon befriend Jeffrey, the lonely son of the hall's upper-crusty owner, Mrs. Tifton. As the summer passes, the children encounter a series of adventures in which the magic comes from their imaginative view of their novel surroundings. Jeffrey's doomed fate—to be sent to a dreaded military school—is something to be liberated from, while the usually dependable Rosalind suddenly finds herself doe-eyed over the hall's handsome young gardener. Feisty Skye battles the restrictions placed on the children by the snooty Mrs. Tifton, while Jane narrates the children's activities with a wry yet humorously melodramatic eye.

Praise for *The Penderwicks* was wide-ranging, many critics acknowledging Birdsall's nod to a pantheon of writers that range from Louisa May Alcott and Frances Hodgson Burnett to Elizabeth Enright and Lemony Snicket. "Nostalgic but never stale, this fresh, satisfying novel is like a cool breeze on a summer's day," concluded *Horn Book* contributor Carolyn Shute, describing *The Penderwicks* as "suffused with affectionate humor." In her "timeless tale," Birdsall captures "spirited family dynamics and repartee," wrote a contributor to *Publishers Weekly*, the critic adding that the Penderwick sisters exhibit "delightfully diverse personalities" that "propel the plot." Praising the author's "superb writing style," B. Allison Gray wrote in *School Library Journal* that Birdsall's "wonderful, humorous book . . . features characters whom readers will immediately love," characters who engage in what a *Kirkus Reviews* writer described as "the sorts of lively plots and pastoral pastimes we don't read much about these days."

The Penderwicks return to their western Massachusetts home town in *The Penderwicks on Gardam Street*, which a *New York Times Book Review* critic described as a "comforting comedy in an Austen-and Alcott-like vein." In the story, Aunt Claire arrives to visit her brother, Mr. Penderwick, and decides to become matchmaker to the widower. Now Rosalind, Skye, Jane, and

Batty are forced to sabotage the woman's efforts in order to avoid getting saddled with a stepmother. While the sisters band together to implement their "Save Daddy Plan," each is also battling a problem of her own. For Rosalind, attentive but annoying neighbor boy Tommy Geiger is becoming a pest; competitive Skye loses her temper during a game on the school soccer field; Jane's love of creative writing leads her into unexpected trouble; and Batty fixates on the mother and daughter who have just moved in next door. "Birdsall again delivers genuinely funny scenes and tender moments between father and daughters," wrote Carolyn L. Shute in her *Horn Book* review of *The Penderwicks on Gardam Street,* while *School Library Journal* critic Tim Wadams wrote that "laugh-out-loud moments abound and the humor comes naturally from the characters and situations." Praising the novel for possessing "even more charm than the original," a *Publishers Weekly* critic added that "it's sheer pleasure to spend time with these exquisitely drawn characters."

Their newly married father's honeymoon trip to England provides the impetus for the birls' adventures in *The Penderwicks at Point Mouette,* Birdsall's third book featuring the engaging Penderwick family. This time out the sisters are separated: while Rosalind spends the summer with friends, Skye, Jane, and Batty head for the rocky Maine coastline, where Aunt Claire and friend Jeffrey await. The pressure is now on for Skye to take the role of oldest sister, but Batty's constant surprises and Jane's romantic flightiness may be more than the teen can handle. "The girls are, as usual, kind, endearing, self-possessed, self-aware and comforting," observed a *Kirkus Reviews* writer in appraising the third "Penderwick" story, and Ilene Cooper asserted in *Booklist* that Birdsall "enlivens everyday happenings with excitement" and the small-town Maine setting "is so lovingly portrayed that readers will be longing to vacation there themselves."

Birdsall treats younger children to an example of her fanciful storytelling in Flora's Very Windy Day, *featuring artwork by Matt Phelan.* (Illustration copyright © 2010 by Matt Phelan. Reproduced with permission of Clarion Books, an imprint of Houghton Mifflin Harcourt Publishing Company.)

Birdsall turns from middle-grade readers to younger children in creating the stories for the picture books *Flora's Very Windy Day* and *Lucky and Squash Run Away,* the latter illustrated by Jane Dyer. In *Flora's Very Windy Day* Flora's number-one challenge is coping with pesky little brother Crispin. When the siblings are ordered to play outside by their mother on a particularly blustery fall day, Crispin is caught by the wind and pulled into the sky. Flora realizes how much she cares about her little brother when she sails up into the sky to retrieve him, declining the requests of an eagle, a cloud, and even a rainbow to keep the little boy. "This gem of a book will resonate with older siblings everywhere," predicted *School Library Journal* contributor Mary Jean Smith, and in *Booklist* Carolyn Phelan wrote that Birdsall "blends homely and fantastic elements as naturally as a child at play." Matt Phelan's soft-toned illustrations for the book "can be melt-your-heart beguiling," the critic added, while in *Publishers Weekly* a reviewer noted the similarities between *Flora's Very Windy Day* and the "Penderwick" novels: "believable characters, a tightly constructed story line, and a nod to past children's literature."

In her writing Birdsall openly pays homage to the books she loved as a child: escapist fiction featuring a band of curious children, a daunting challenge, and an everyday world that is transformed by the imagination into a place rife with the possibility of adventure. Each novel in her "Penderwick" series is also an investment in time, taking three years to complete. When Birdsall approached publishers with her first manuscript, she was advised to add a strong dose of adolescent strife, and make her story reflect what publishers maintained is demanded by modern readers weaned on so-called "problem novels." Fortunately, the story fell into the hands of a more open-minded editor at Knopf, and *The Penderwicks* was ultimately published with relatively minor changes. As Birdsall explained to Rick Margolis in *School Library Journal,* "People are saying children who lead traumatic lives need books that validate the trauma, and I'm not saying they're wrong. But I also think because it worked so well for me, that there are children who lead difficult lives who need to understand that it doesn't have to be so bad. I also think that there are a lot of children out there who are still leading wonderful lives, and . . . they need to have something to read too."

While continuing work on her "Penderwick" stories—a total of five novels featuring the entertaining siblings are planned—Birdsall makes her home in Western Massachusetts, together with her husband and assorted cats, rabbits, and a troublemaking but loveable dog. As she remarked of writing in an interview on her home page: "Most authors do work very hard. I know that I do, partly because I write slowly, so I have to write almost every day to make any progress at all. But mostly I work hard because I'm happiest when I'm writing."

Biographical and Critical Sources

PERIODICALS

Booklist, April 1, 2005, Ilene Cooper, review of *The Penderwicks: A Summer Tale of Four Sisters, Two Rabbits, and a Very Interesting Boy,* p. 1358; May 1, 2008, Ilene Cooper, review of *The Penderwicks on Gardam Street,* p. 89; July 1, 2010, Carolyn Phelan, review of *Flora's Very Windy Day,* p. 62.

Bulletin of the Center for Children's Books, September, 2005, Timnah Card, review of *The Penderwicks,* p. 9; July-August, 2008, Karen Coats, review of *The Penderwicks on Gardam Street,* p. 460; October, 2010, Deborah Stevenson, review of *Flora's Very Windy Day,* p. 63.

Christian Science Monitor, June 20, 2008, Jenny Sawyer, review of *The Penderwicks on Gardam Street,* p. 25.

Horn Book, July-August, 2005, Carolyn Shute, review of *The Penderwicks,* p. 465; July-August, 2008, Carolyn L. Shute, review of *The Penderwicks on Gardam Street,* p. 439.

Kirkus Reviews, June 1, 2005, review of *The Penderwicks,* p. 633; March 15, 2008, review of *The Penderwicks on Gardam Street;* July 1, 2010, review of *Flora's Very Windy Day;* May 1, 2011, review of *The Penderwicks at Point Mouette.*

Kliatt, September, 2006, Melody Moxley, review of *The Penderwicks,* p. 46.

New York Times Book Review, July 13, 2008, review of *The Penderwicks on Gardam Street,* p. 15.

Publishers Weekly, July 25, 2005, review of *The Penderwicks,* p. 77; April 28, 2008, review of *The Penderwicks on Gardam Street,* p. 138; July 12, 2010, review of *Flora's Very Windy Day,* p. 46.

School Library Journal, July, 2005, B. Allison Gray, review of *The Penderwicks,* p. 95; January, 2006, Rick Margolis, "Seems like Old Times" (interview), p. 60; March, 2008, Tim Wadham, review of *The Penderwicks on Gardam Street,* p. 194; July, 2010, Mary Jean Smith, review of *Flora's Very Windy Day,* p. 55.

ONLINE

Boston Globe Online, http://www.boston.com/ (December 12, 2005), David Mehegan, "A Storybook Beginning."

Jeanne Birdsall Home Page, http://www.jeannebirdsall. com (July 15, 2011).

R. Michelson Galleries Web site, http://www.rmichelson. com/ (April 26, 2006), "Jeanne Birdsall."

*   *   *

BLACKALL, Sophie

Personal

Born in Australia; daughter of Simon Blackall (a journalist and publisher); immigrated to United States, 2000; married; children: two. *Education:* Attended college.

Addresses

Home and office—Brooklyn, NY. *E-mail*—sophie@ sophieblackall.com.

Career

Illustrator and author of books for children.

Awards, Honors

Ezra Jack Keats New Illustrator Award, 2003, for *Ruby's Wish,* by Shirin Yim Bridges; Society of Illustrators Founders Award, 2005; Ten Best Illustrated Children's Books inclusion, *New York Times,* 2010, for *Big Red Lollipop* by Rukhsana Kahn.

Writings

SELF-ILLUSTRATED

Twenty Party Tricks to Amuse and Amaze Your Friends, Chronicle Books (New York, NY), 1997.
Are You Awake?, Henry Holt (New York, NY), 2011.

Creator and illustrator of Web logs *Mixed Connections* and *Drawn from My Father's Adventures.*

ILLUSTRATOR

Leith Hillard, *A Giraffe for France,* Watermark Press (Sydney, New South Wales, Australia), 1998.
Shirin Yim Bridges, *Ruby's Wish,* Chronicle Books (San Francisco, CA), 2002.
(With Meg Rosoff) *Meet Wild Boars,* Henry Holt (New York, NY), 2005.
Phillis and David Gershator, *Summer Is Summer,* Henry Holt (New York, NY), 2006.
Cari Best, *What's So Bad about Being an Only Child?,* Farrar, Straus & Giroux (New York, NY), 2007.
Deborah Noyes, *Red Butterfly: How a Princess Smuggled the Secrets of Silk out of China,* Candlewick Press (Cambridge, MA), 2007.
(With Meg Rosoff) *Jumpy Jack and Googily,* Henry Holt (New York, NY), 2008.
(With Meg Rosoff) *Wild Boars Cook,* Henry Holt (New York, NY), 2008.
Carol Diggory Shields, *Wombat Walkabout,* Dutton Children's Books (New York, NY), 2009.
Rukhsana Khan, *Big Red Lollipop,* Viking (New York, NY), 2010.
April Stevens, *Edwin Speaks Up,* Schwartz & Wade (New York, NY), 2010.
Jacqueline Woodson, *Pecan Pie Baby,* G.P. Putnam's Sons (New York, NY), 2010.
Lisa Wheeler, *Spinster Goose,* Atheneum Books for Young Readers (New York, NY), 2011.
Aldous Huxley, *The Crows of Pearblossom,* Abrams Books for Young Readers (New York, NY), 2011.

Matthew Olshan, *The Boxer Lalouche,* Schwartz & Wade (New York, NY), 2012.

Contributor of illustrations to periodicals, including *Gourmet, New York Times, Real Simple,* and *Wall Street Journal.* Illustrator of Web log *Drawn from My Father's Adventures,* authored by father, Simon Blackall.

ILLUSTRATOR; "IVY AND BEAN" SERIES BY ANNIE BARROWS

Ivy and Bean, Chronicle Books (New York, NY), 2006.
Ivy and Bean and the Ghost That Had to Go, Chronicle Books (New York, NY), 2006.
Ivy and Bean Break the Fossil Record, Chronicle Books (New York, NY), 2007.
Ivy and Bean: Bound to Be Bad, Chronicle Books (San Francisco, CA), 2008.
Ivy and Bean Take Care of the Babysitter, Chronicle Books (San Francisco, CA), 2008.
Ivy and Bean: Doomed to Dance, Chronicle Books (San Francisco, CA), 2009.
Ivy and Bean: What's the Big Idea?, Chronicle Books (San Francisco, CA), 2010.
Ivy and Bean: No News Is Good News, Chronicle Books (San Francisco, CA), 2011.

Sidelights

Born and raised in Australia, illustrator Sophie Blackall completed her first illustration project for children, Leith Hillard's *A Giraffe for France,* in her native country before relocating to the United States in 2000. Blackall has been honored with the Ezra Jack Keats Award for New Illustrator in recognition of the artwork she created for Shirin Yim Bridges' semi-autobiographical picture book *Ruby's Wish,* and she has also brought to life stories by several other authors, among them Cari Best, Meg Rosoff, Phillis and David Gershator, Carol Diggory Shields, and Rukhsana Khan. Reviewing her artwork for Shields' humorous *Wombat Walkabout,* "Blackall uses a 'less is more' approach to the art that successfully allows readers to focus on the animals, their expressions, and the flora around them," noted *School Library Journal* critic Catherine Callegari, and a *Kirkus Reviews* writer hailed the "uncluttered, downright adorable watercolors" as a main strength of the "satisfying" picture book.

Blackall grew up in Australia, where stories by Beatrix Potter and E.H. Shepard captured her young imagination. As she later recalled to a *Mom Culture* online interviewer, "I grew up by the sea, drawing in the sand with sticks, which was very bad for my sense of perspective, but my canvas was huge. From there I graduated to butcher's paper, and would give the butcher 15 cents for a wad of sheets, which makes it sound as though I was a child in the Great Depression." Deciding on a career path as an artist by age twelve, she studied design and developed her artistic techniques independently, painting signs and photo backdrops, as well as creating spot art for magazines. Inspired by

Japanese woodcuts and Chinese poster and graphic designs, Blackall works primarily in Chinese ink and watercolor, although her early illustrations also feature collage and opaque gouache.

Prior to tackling *A Giraffe for France,* Blackall created *Twenty Party Tricks to Amuse and Amaze Your Friends,* in which her art and text combine to instruct readers in tricks such as floating a needle, seemingly transforming water into wine, and fitting a hard-boiled egg into a narrow-necked glass bottle. The move to the United States, which Blackall made accompanied by her husband and young children, coincided with her decision to expand her work in picture books. After making the rounds of New York City publishers, she was approached by Chronicle Books as one of three illustrators they were considering for *Ruby's Wish.* As Blackall recalled to *Communication Arts* contributor Maria Piscopo, the publisher "had each of us illustrate the same passage. . . . It was a Chinese story and there were so many possible ways to approach it visually. In the end I decided to make the picture I would want to see."

Set in China during the first part of the twentieth century, *Ruby's Wish* finds young Ruby encouraged to pursue her love of learning and dreams of attending college by her wise grandfather. In a review of the book, Jody McCoy wrote in *School Library Journal* that "the beauty of Asian art and motifs is captured page after page" in Blackall's "exquisite" opaque watercolor art. Another Asian-themed story, Deborah Noyes' *Red Butterfly: How a Princess Smuggled the Secret of Silk out of China,* features the artist's delicate images in a story about a young girl who is sent from her father's verdant lands to marry the king of a desert region. Blackall's "splendid ink-and-watercolor illustrations" for Noyes' story "poignantly capture the princess's leave-taking as well as details of palace life in images evocative of Chinese screen paintings," according to a *Kirkus Reviews* writer.

Paired with the upbeat rhyming text of the Gershators' *Summer Is Summer,* Blackall's "whimsical watercolor illustrations feature a dreamy world of fantasy and reality," noted *School Library Journal* contributor Marge Loch-Wouters. She turns from fantasy to the classic ups and downs of childhood in *What's So Bad about Being an Only Child?,* a story by Best that finds young Rosemary alternately wishing she had a sibling to enjoying the fact that she is the center of her parents' world. Praising the work as "jovial," Blair Christolon added in *School Library Journal* that Blackall's "animated" and "dramatic" images contribute humor through her use of "mismatches stockings" and other wardrobe *faux pas* to highlight Rosemary's "personality and individuality." "Blackall . . . elevates everything she illustrates," asserted *Booklist* critic Ilene Cooper, and in *What's So Bad about Being an Only Child?* she demonstrates her "knack for using clever details to get the humor across . . . in the costumes, the decoration, and especially in the expressions."

***Sophie Blackall teams up with author Jacqueline Woodson to create an reassuring story about a soon-to-be larger family in* Pecan Pie Baby.**

A larger family is the focus of *Big Red Lollipop,* Kahn's story about a little sister who overshadows her sibling after inviting herself to a party. The author's "honest, even moving, commentary" on sibling relationships in an immigrant family is captured "in Blackall's spot-on illustrations," according to *Booklist* critic Cooper, while a *Publishers Weekly* critic cited the artist's "subtly textured" images as aomng the story's strengths. In *School Library Journal* Sara Lissa Paulson also bestowed special praise on the book's art, writing that "the beauty of the muted tones and spareness of the illustrations" in

Big Red Lollipop include "stylistic scattering of East Indian motifs" and a use of varied perspectives that make Blackall's images "priceless."

The humorous picture book *Meet Wild Boars* also benefits from Blackall's artwork: here the artist's depiction of four "hulking, hairy boars . . . make a wonderful visual articulation of and counterpoint to Rosoff's arch, mock-cautionary prose," according to a *Publishers Weekly* contributor. "Blackall's roll-on-the-ground-in-laughter illustrations" bring to life Rosoff's ill-mannered but "disgustingly delightful group," concluded Cooper in an appraisal of the same work, while *School Library Journal* contributor Mary Elam accorded special praise to "the artist's attention to detail." The ill-behaved characters return in *Wild Boars Cook,* as the wild and smelly creatures attempt to cook up a giant pudding big enough to satisfy their hunger . . . for a minute or so. Here the story's "tongue-in-cheek text and the full-throttle hilarity of Blackall's illustrations are a perfect match," according to Cooper. Another collaboration between Rosoff and Blackall, the standalone picture book *Jumpy Jack and Googily,* prompted a *Publishers Weekly* critic to comment that author and artist "make a waggish team . . . with Rossoff comically understating the obvious and Blackall providing visual punch lines."

Through her art, Blackall also brings to life Annie Barrows' easy-reading "Ivy and Bean" chapter books, which focus on a pair of second-grade best friends and include *Ivy and Bean, Ivy and Bean Break the Fossil Record, Ivy and Bean and the Ghost That Had to Go, Ivy and Bean: Doomed to Dance,* and *Ivy and Bean: No News Is Good News.* Writing that the art in *Ivy and Bean* "captures the girls' spirit," Cooper added that the illustrations "take . . . the book to a higher level." Appraising *Ivy and Bean and the Ghost That Had to Go* in *School Library Journal,* Adrienne Furness cited Blackall's "expressive illustrations," and Sharon R. Pearce wrote in the same publication that artist's "humorous drawings add to the fun" that plays out in *Ivy and Bean Break the Fossil Record.* Another story in the series, *Ivy and Bean Take Care of the Babysitter,* find young Bean getting into trouble when her older sister is charged to baby sit her for the day. Here Blackall's gently tinted ink-drawn images "capture the mood and carefree attitude" of Barrows' story, according to *School Library Journal* critic Krista Tokarz.

In addition to her book illustration, Blackall has also created artwork for magazines and animation, and her Web logs such as *Missed Connections* have been treasured by those who have discovered them. "I was looking for an idea to stretch out and one where I could do exactly as I pleased," the artist explained in her *Mom Culture* online interview in discussing the inspiration behind *Missed Connections.* "I had been collecting various forms of what I think of as accidental poetry for a while; everything from other people's shopping lists, to lost pet posters, to a stranger's diaries found at flea markets. When I stumbled on the Missed Connections posts on Craigslist I felt as though I'd struck gold."

Biographical and Critical Sources

PERIODICALS

Booklist, November 15, 2002, Linda Perkins, review of *Ruby's Wish,* p. 608; March 15, 2005, Ilene Cooper, review of *Meet Wild Boars,* p. 1287; April 1, 2006, Il-

ene Cooper, review of *Ivy and Bean,* p. 42; April 15, 2006, Hazel Rochman, review of *Summer Is Summer,* p. 51; October 15, 2006, Ilene Cooper, review of *Ivy and Bean and the Ghost That Had to Go,* p. 44; July 1, 2007, Kay Weisman, review of *Ivy and Bean Break the Fossil Record,* p. 58; September 1, 2007, Ilene Cooper, review of *What's So Bad about Being an Only Child?,* p. 130; February 1, 2010, Ilene Cooper, review of *Big Red Lollipop,* p. 44; August 1, 2010, Hazel Rochman, review of *Pecan Pie Baby,* p. 61.

Bulletin of the Center for Children's Books, October, 2002, review of *Ruby's Wish,* p. 49; June, 2006, Deborah Stevenson, review of *Ivy and Bean,* p. 440.

Communication Arts (illustration annual), July, 2007, Maria Piscopo, "Getting Published—Myth or Reality?"

Horn Book, July-August, 2008, Jennifer M. Brabander, review of *Ivy and Bean Take Care of the Babysitter,* p. 438; March-April, 2009, Robin L. Smith, review of *Wombat Walkabout,* p. 187; January-February, 2010, Jennifer M. Brabander, review of *Ivy and Bean: Doomed to Dance,* p. 80.

Kirkus Reviews, August 15, 2002, review of *Ruby's Wish,* p. 1217; April 15, 2005, review of *Meet Wild Boars,* p. 481; May 1, 2006, review of *Ivy and Bean,* p. 454; May 15, 2006, review of *Summer Is Summer,* p. 518; September 15, 2006, review of *Ivy and Bean and the Ghost That Had to Go,* p. 946; June 1, 2007, review of *Ivy and Bean Break the Fossil Record*; October 1, 2007, review of *Red Butterfly: How a Princess Smuggled the Secrets of Silk out of China*; April 15, 2008, review of *Jumpy Jack and Googily*; February 15, 2009, review of *Wombat Walkabout.*

Publishers Weekly, August 19, 2002, review of *Ruby's Wish,* p. 88; March 28, 2005, review of *Meet Wild Boars,* p. 78; May 15, 2006, review of *Ivy and Bean,* p. 72; October 1, 2007, review of *What's So Bad about Being an Only Child?,* p. 56; November 19, 2007, review of *Red Butterfly,* p. 56; May 26, 2008, review of *Jumpy Jack and Googily,* p. 65; July 14, 2008, review of *Wild Boars Cook,* p. 65; January 5, 2009, review of *Wombat Walkabout,* p. 48; March 1, 2010, review of *Big Red Lollipop,* p. 49; September 27, 2010, review of *Pecan Pie Baby,* p. 59; December 6, 2010, review of *Manners Mash-Up: A Goofy Guide to Good Behavior,* p. 48.

School Library Journal, February, 2003, Jody McCoy, review of *Ruby's Wish,* p. 102; July, 2005, Mary Elam, review of *Meet Wild Boars,* p. 82; June, 2006, Marge Loch-Wouters, review of *Summer Is Summer,* p. 122; July, 2006, Eve Ottenberg Stone, review of *Ivy and Bean,* p. 68; February, 2007, Adrienne Furness, review of *Ivy and Bean and the Ghost That Had to Go,* p. 84; July, 2007, Sharon R. Pearce, review of *Ivy and Bean Break the Fossil Record,* p. 67; May, 2008, Rachael Vilmar, review of *Jumpy Jack and Googily,* p. 107; August, 2008, Judith Constantinides, review of *Wild Boars Cook,* p. 101; January, 2010, Sarah Polace, review of *Ivy and Bean: Doomed to Dance,* p. 68; March, 2010, Sara Lissa Paulson, review of *Big Red Lollipop,* p. 120; October, 2010, Mary N. Oluonye, review of *Pecan Pie Baby,* p. 97.

ONLINE

Mom Culture Web site, http://momcultureonline.com/ (November 13, 2009), interview with Blackall.

Rumpus Online, http://therumpus.net/ (May 5, 2010), Sona Avakian, interview with Blackall.

Sophie Blackall Home Page, http://www.sophieblackall.com (June 25, 2011).*

*   *   *

BRIGHT, Paul 1949-

Personal

Born 1949, in Welwyn, Hertfordshire, England; married; has children. *Education:* Studied engineering and materials science.

Addresses

Home and office—Kent, England.

Career

Author of stories and poems for children. Former plastics engineer at a chemical company based in the United Kingdom.

Awards, Honors

Practical Pre-School Silver Award, 2003, for *Under the Bed;* Blue Peter Book Award shortlist, 2004, for *Quiet!;* Stockport School's Book Award shortlist, Stockport Metropolitan Borough Council, 2007, for *I'm Not Going out There!*

Writings

Under the Bed, illustrated by Ben Cort, Little Tiger Press (London, England), 2003, Good Books (Intercourse, PA), 2004.

Quiet!, illustrated by Guy Parker-Rees, Orchard Books (New York, NY), 2003.

Nobody Laughs at a Lion!, illustrated by Matt Buckingham, Good Books (Intercourse, PA), 2005.

I Am Not Going out There!, illustrated by Ben Cort, Good Books (Intercourse, PA), 2006.

The Bears in the Bed and the Great Big Storm, illustrated by Jane Chapman, Good Books (Intercourse, PA), 2008.

Fidgety Flash and Friends, illustrated by Ruth Galloway, Little Tiger Press (London, England), 2008.

Grumpy Badger's Christmas, illustrated by Jane Chapman, Good Books (Intercourse, PA), 2009.

Charlie's Superhero Underpants, illustrations by Lee Wildish, Little Tiger Press (London, England), 2009, Good Books (Intercourse, PA), 2010.

Crunch Munch Dinosaur Lunch!, illustrated by Mike Terry, Little Tiger Press (London, England), 2009, Good Books (Intercourse, PA), 2010.

What's More Scary than a Shark?, illustrated by Michael Terry, Little Tiger Press (London, England), 2009.

Fuzzy Wuzzy Bugs, illustrated by Jack Tickle, Little Tiger Press (London, England), 2010.

The Not-So Scary Snorklum, illustrated by Jane Chapman, Little Tiger Press (London, England), 2011.

Boris's Big Boogey, illustrated by Hannah George, Little Tiger Press (London, England), 2011.

Contributor of poetry to anthologies.

Author's work has been translated into Welsh.

Sidelights

Paul Bright began his writing career creating stories for his own children while working by day as a plastics engineer, but he now devotes himself to writing full time. The majority of Bright's picture-book texts are geared for preschool-aged audiences and focus on universal childhood themes such as fear and individuality. In *Nobody Laughs at a Lion!,* for example, a clumsy lion is discouraged when it realizes that other jungle animals have talents it does not possess: it cannot climb trees as quickly as the monkeys and cannot run as fast as a cheetah. When Lion tries to outdo the jungle animals at contests that draw on the unique talents of others, it fails miserably, but discovers its own special skill when roaring loudly is the test. A *Kirkus Reviews* critic praised Bright's story in *Nobody Laughs at a Lion!* as "a simple but fun read."

In his career as a plastics engineer in the chemical industry, Bright and his family moved from their native England, living for a time in Switzerland and the Netherlands as well as in Spain. "I used to make notes for stories when I was sitting in boring meetings, or travelling on trains and planes . . . ," he recalled on his home page. "I started writing stories for my children, when they were small, but it was a long time before I had anything accepted for publication. My children have now grown up and left home, so I've been working on my writing for a long, long time."

After several of his poems made it to print, Bright's first picture book, *Under the Bed,* was released, and his second, *Quiet!,* was shortlisted for England's Blue Peter Book Award. His rhyming text also takes center stage in *I'm Not Going out There!,* one of several picture books that feature artwork by Ben Cort. In *I'm Not Going out There!* a young boy hides under his bed and vehemently declares that he will not come out. As a host of scary characters are described—everything from witches to monsters to ghosts—each creature appears, but becomes so frightened of the thing that has terrified the boy that it joins him in his under-the-box-spring refuge. Ultimately, the terror reveals itself: it is the boy's little sister, busy having a temper tantrum. Praising

Paul Bright's whimsical story in* Charlie's Superhero Underpants *is brought to life in art by Lee Wildish. (Illustration copyright © 2009 by Lee Wildish. Reproduced with permission of Little Tiger Books.)

Cort's "bold and colorful" illustrations, Maren Ostergard wrote in *School Library Journal* that *I'm Not Going out There!* is "a rhyming tale with a twist," and a *Kirkus Reviews* writer cited the book's "bouncy rhymes, bright colors and . . . entertaining punch line." A second *Kirkus Reviews* writer deemed *Under the Bed* another successful collaboration between author and illustrator, writing that the "soothing" bedtime tale is enlivened by "Bright's vivid imagery and Cort's grand detonations of color."

Bright has also teamed up with artist Jane Chapman on the picture books *The Bears in the Bed and the Great Big Storm* and *Grumpy Badger's Christmas,* In the first story three little bearcubs awaken their parents during the night, leaving their father awake and vigilant when a nighttime visitor comes a-knocking. As the holiday season approaches, the title character in *Grumpy Badger's Christmas* is determined to play Scrooge, until the succession of good-wishes givers knocking on his door

change his negative outlook. "Young children . . . will be comforted by the fact that adults can be frightened too," noted Donna Atmur in her *School Library Journal* review of *The Bears in the Bed and the Great Big Storm*, while a *Kirkus Reviews* critic cited Bright's use of repetition in a "mildly amusing . . . story about a classic issue." "Chapman's cheery acrylic paintings are perfectly suited to" Bright's story in *Grumpy Badger's Christmas,* wrote *School Library Journal* critic Linda Israelson, and a *Kirkus Reviews* writer observed that the animal characters achieves a "certain appeal due to their restrained British mannerisms."

A little boy's efforts to corral his bright-red underpants after they blow away on wash day provide the humor in *Charlie's Superhero Underpants,* featuring illustrations by Lee Wildish. Another story by Bright, *Crunch Munch Dinosaur Lunch!,* pairs Mike Terry's colorful cartoon art with a rhyming story about a big-boy T-rex and his loving but pesky little sister. "The silliness of the story line and spirited portrayals of the various animals will induce giggles," predicted a *Publishers Weekly* critic in reviewing *Charlie's Superhero Underpants.*

"A picture book has to have a 'shape'—made up of rhyme or repetition of a phrase, or a pattern of words," Bright noted in discussing the craft of writing on his home page. "Once I have worked out the 'shape' I can start filling in the text and the story. Maybe other writers have different processes, but that is what works for me."

Biographical and Critical Sources

PERIODICALS

Kirkus Reviews, May 15, 2004, review of *Under the Bed,* p. 488; May 15, 2005, review of *Nobody Laughs at a Lion,* p. 585; September 15, 2006, review of *I'm Not Going out There!,* p. 947; September 15, 2008, review of *The Bears in the Bed and the Great Big Storm;* September 15, 2009, review of *Grumpy Badger's Christmas;* May 1, 2010, review of *Crunch Munch Dinosaur Lunch!*

Library Media Connection, January, 2004, review of *Quiet!,* p. 56.
Publishers Weekly, April 26, 2010, review of *Charlie's Superhero Underpants,* p. 105.
School Library Journal, December, 2003, Andrea Tarr, review of *Quiet!,* p. 104; August, 2004, Sheilah Kosco, review of *Under the Bed,* p. 84; November, 2006, Maren Ostergard, review of *I'm Not Going out There!,* p. 84; December, 2008, Donna Atmur, review of *The Bears in the Bed and the Great Big Storm,* p. 85; October, 2009, Linda Israelson, review of *Grumpy Badger's Christmas,* p. 78; June, 2010, Gloria Koster, review of *Charlie's Superhero Underpants,* p. 65.
School Librarian, winter, 2003, review of *Quiet!,* p. 185; winter, 2003, review of *Under the Bed,* p. 185; spring, 2006, Derek Lomas, review of *Nobody Laughs at a Lion,* p. 17; winter, 2006, Joyce Banks, review of *I'm Not Going out There!,* p. 181.

ONLINE

Paul Bright Home Page, http://www.paulbright.co.uk (June 25, 2011).
World Book Day Web site, http://www.worldbookday.com/ (August 6, 2007).*

C

CALLEN, Liz 1951-

Personal

Born 1951. *Education:* Attended University of California, Santa Barbara; Art Center College of Design, B.F.A. (illustration), 1975.

Addresses

Home—WA. *E-mail*—liz@callendoodles.com.

Career

Illustrator. Commercial artist, beginning 1975.

Member

Society of Children's Book Writers and Illustrators.

Awards, Honors

Cooperative Children's Book Center Choice designation, 2011, for *Wolf Pie* by Brenda Seabrooke.

Illustrator

Katy Hall and Lisa Eisenberg, *Oddball Baseball,* Random House (New York, NY), 1990.
Pamela R. Bishop, *Exploring Your Skeleton: Funny Bones and Not-so-funny Bones,* F. Watts (New York, NY), 1991.
Deborah Eaton, *Bo Peep's Sheep,* Scholastic (New York, NY), 1998.
Anne Miranda, *Neat Pete: A Pig's Tale,* Scholastic (New York, NY), 2002.
Jan Jones, *The Thingamajig,* Scholastic (New York, NY), 2002.
Dave Crawley, *Reading, Rhyming, and 'Rithmetic,* Wordsong (Honesdale, PA), 2010.
Brenda Seabrooke, *Wolf Pie,* Clarion Books (Boston, MA), 2010.

Sidelights

Liz Callen has worked as a commercial illustrator since the mid-1970s, after graduating from California's Art Center College of Design. In addition to advertising and product designs, her brightly colored, humorously drawn ink cartoon images have appeared on greeting cards, wrapping paper, other paper products as well as on coffee mugs, T-shirts, and the like. Callen moved into book illustration in 1989, when editors at Random House chose her to create the artwork for Katy Hall and Lisa Eisenberg's humorous picture book *Oddball Baseball.* Although her commercial work continues to consume most of her time, she has continued to entertain young readers with her engaging art for stories by Deborah Eaton, Jan Jones, Dave Crawley, and Brenda Seabrooke, among others. Reviewing Crawley's poetry collection *Reading, Rhyming, and 'Rithmetic* for *School Library Journal,* Julie Roach took note of Callen's contribution, writing that her "colorful cartoon illustrations . . . suit the poetry's bright humor," while a *Kirkus Reviews* writer observed that the book's "rather droll pen-and-ink-and-watercolor illustrations" fuel the humor in Crawley's "school-themed" anthology.

With an easy-reading text by Seabrooke, the chapter book *Wolf Pie* presents a novel take on the traditional story of the three little pigs. The three Pygg brothers—Marvin, James, and Lester—are having a pleasant day at home when they are visited by the persistent but dapperly dressed Wilfong the wolf. Although Wilfong's plans initially involved huffing and puffing, after observing the antics of the happy-go-lucky Pyggs, he begins to view the rotund brothers as potential friends, especially when several long-toothed wolves arrive with thoughts of a tasty pork dinner on their mind. Characterizing *Wolf Pie* as a "sophisticated" take on the age-old story, Lucinda Snyder Whitehurst added in her *School Library Journal* review that Callen's illustrations "are surprisingly abstract," and her use of unusual viewpoints and "a flattened 2-D perspective" help to reinforce "the characters' personalities." A *Publishers Weekly* critic also enjoyed the picture book, writing that the illustrator's "watercolors add to the slapstick humor" and "that will have children laughing and wanting more."

Liz Callen combines fun and learning in her artwork for Reading, Rhyming, and 'Rithmetic, *a verse collection by Dave Crawley.* (Illustration copyright © 2010 by Liz Callen. Reproduced with permission of Wordsong, an imprint of Boyds Mills Press, Inc.)

Biographical and Critical Sources

PERIODICALS

Kirkus Reviews, February 15, 2010, review of *Reading, Rhyming, and 'Rithmetic.*

Publishers Weekly, June 14, 2010, review of *Wolf Pie,* p. 52.

School Library Journal, November, 1991, Dorcas Hand, review of *Exploring Your Skeleton: Funny Bones and Not-so-funny Bones,* p. 126; April, 2010, Julie Roach, review of *Reading, Rhyming, and 'Rithmetic,* p. 144; August, 2010, Lucinda Snyder Whitehurst, review of *Wolf Pie,* p. 86.

ONLINE

Liz Callen Home Page, http://www.callendoodles.com (June 20, 2011).*

*   *   *

CARDINALE, Christopher

Personal

Son of teachers. *Education:* University of New Mexico, B.F.A. (studio arts; summa cum laude), 1996.

Addresses

Home—Brooklyn, NY. *E-mail*—info@christophercardinale.com.

Career

Illustrator, sequential artist, and muralist. Resident artist at Blue Mountain Center, 2002, 2005; community activist. *Exhibitions:* Work included in solo and group exhibitions in New York, NY, and at Lump Gallery, Raleigh, NC; Philley Center Gallery, Seattle, WA; ARC Gallery, Albuquerque, NM; Eidelon Gallery, Santa Fe,

***Christopher Cardinale captures the magic of Mexican poet Luis Alberto Urrea's text in his illustrations for the graphic-novel adaptation of* Mr. Mendoza's Paintbrush.** (Illustration copyright © 2010 by Christopher Cardinale. Reproduced with permission of Cinco Puntos Press.)

NM; and La Panaderia Galeria, Mexico City, Mexico. Creator of mural installations throughout Brooklyn and New York, NY, including at Sprungs High School, on Riker's Island; and in Italy, Greece, and Mexico.

Illustrator

Luis Alberto Urrea, *Mr. Mendoza's Paintbrush* (graphic novel), Cinco Puntos Press (El Paso, TX), 2010.

George Ella Lyon, *Which Side Are You On?: The Story of a Song,* Cinco Puntos Press (El Paso, TX), 2011.

Contributor to periodicals, including *New York Press, New York Times, Punk Planet, Time,* and *World War 3 Illustrated.*

Sidelights

On his home page, Christopher Cardinale describes himself as "a socially conscious artist who creates monumental figurative and narrative images in the form of murals, paintings, prints and illustrations." In his body of work, Cardinale does indeed combine a concern for social issues with visual images that distill such issues into a narrative that make them resonate with viewers. As a muralist, he has worked with communities to make visible shared viewpoints regarding warfare and economic global dominance, and the universality of such viewpoints has earned him appreciative audiences in the United States as well as in Greece and Mexico. As an illustrator, Cardinale's work has appeared in counterculture periodicals such as *Punk Planet* and *World War 3,* the latter a venue for uncensored commentary regarding contemporary culture that includes political comics, stories, and illustrations.

Cardinale's greatest exposure as an artist has come from his work on *Mr. Mendoza's Paintbrush,* a graphic novel that is based on a short story by Mexican poet Alberto Luis Urrea. In the story, Urrea recalls his youth in Rosario, a village where older women take charge of day-to-day affairs and the narrator and his cousin Jaime attempt to avoid and outwit them. Although the townspeople view their community highly, their placid lives are constantly marred by Mr. Mendoza, a strange elderly man who wanders the town with paintbrush in hand, intent on inscribing meaningfully moralizing, often witty, but sometimes obscure phrases on every available surface. His efforts cut short the mischief-making of the two boys on more than once occasion; in one instance, Mr. Mendoza brushes admonitions about improper behavior onto the cousins' buttocks after catching them spying on a group of girls bathing in a lake.

Calling Urrea's text "absolutely sparkling, wry, warm, and funny with a satirical edge that counterbalances the [building] magical realism," Deborah Stevenson added in the *Bulletin of the Center for Children's Books* that Cardinale's wood-cut-style art evokes the comix of R. Crumb while his "line evinces a delicacy in the designerly, regular barring that provides shading and depth." The earthen tones featured in the story also enhance its

setting, and the "mixture of crosshatching and scratch-board style . . . makes each panel resemble a static woodcut—but one that interacts dynamically" to fuel the story's "building action," according to a *Publishers Weekly* critic. "Not only does the art perfectly capture the mood of the piece . . . but it also reinforces the lucid dreamlike quality of its magical realism," asserted *Horn Book* contributor Jonathan Hunt, while the *Publishers Weekly* critic maintained that Cardinale's art is, perhaps, "the ideal way to present magical realism graphically." In *School Library Journal* Sadie Mattox wrote that "Urrea's delightful tale of morality and meaning is rendered masterfully by Cardinale's boisterous illustrations," becoming "a cheeky tour through elements of Latin pop culture" as well as "an enchanting exploration of life's myriad mysteries." Praising *Mr. Mendoza's Paintbrush* as an example of "sequential-art storytelling at its finest," *Booklist* contributor Francisca Goldsmith predicted that the sophisticated story will appeal to teen readers "who appreciate Mexican lore and art."

Biographical and Critical Sources

PERIODICALS

Booklist, May 1, 2010, Francisca Goldsmith, review of *Mr. Mendoza's Paintbrush,* p. 75.

Bulletin of the Center for Children's Books, September, 2010, Deborah Stevenson, review of *Mr. Mendoza's Paintbrush,* p. 48.

Horn Book, July-August, 2010, Jonathan Hunt, review of *Mr. Mendoza's Paintbrush,* p. 124.

Kirkus Reviews, April 15, 2010, review of *Mr. Mendoza's Paintbrush.*

Library Journal, May 15, 2010, Martha Cornog, review of *Mr. Mendoza's Paintbrush.*

Publishers Weekly, May 3, 2010, review of *Mr. Mendoza's Paintbrush,* p. 36.

San Francisco Chronicle, June 20, 2010, John McMurtrie, review of *Mr. Mendoza's Paintbrush.*

School Library Journal, July, 2010, Sadie Mattox, review of *Mr. Mendoza's Paintbrush,* p. 111.

ONLINE

Christopher Cardinale Home Page, http://christophercardinale.com (June 20, 2011).*

*   *   *

CARTER, Scott William (Jack Nolte)

Personal

Born in MN; married; children: two. *Education:* University of Oregon, B.A. (English), 1994.

Addresses

Home—OR.

Career

Author. Worked variously as a bookstore owner, ski instructor, and computer trainer.

Awards, Honors

Best Children's Book citation, Bank Street College of Education, and Oregon Book Award for Young Adult Literature, both 2011, both for *The Last Great Getaway of the Water Balloon Boys.*

Writings

The Liberators (ebook), Flying Raven Press, 2009.
The Dinosaur Diaries, and Other Tales across Space and Time, Fantastic Books, 2010.
A Web of Black Widows, and Other Stories of Love and Loss, PS Publishing, 2010.

Cover of Scott William Carter's high-energy teen novel The Last Great Getaway of the Water Balloon Boys, *which takes readers on a cross-country adventure.* (Simon & Schuster Books for Young Readers. Jacket photograph © DiMaggio/Kalish/Corbis.)

The Last Great Getaway of the Water Balloon Boys, Simon & Schuster Books for Young Readers (New York, NY), 2010.
(Under pseudonym Jack Nolte) *The Gray and Guilty Sea,* Flying Raven Press, 2010.
Drawing a Dark Way (ebook), Flying Raven Press, 2011.
President Jock, Vice President Geek, Flying Raven Press, 2011.
(Under pseudonym Jack Nolte) *Everybody Loves a Hero,* Flying Raven Press, 2011.

Contributor of short stories to periodicals, including *Analog, Asimov's, Ellery Queen Mystery Magazine, Realms of Fantasy,* and *Weird Tales.* Work published in anthologies, including *Mystery Date,* edited by Denise Little, DAW (New York, NY), 2008.

Sidelights

Oregon author Scott William Carter began writing adventure fiction at age seven, impressing his second-grade teacher and developing the talent for story telling that would come to characterize his fantasy fiction. Carter's first novel-length book, *The Last Great Getaway of the Water Balloon Boys,* comes on the heels of numerous short stories that have been anthologized and published in the pages of genre magazines such as *Analog, Ellery Queen Mystery Magazine,* and *Weird Tales.* In addition, Carter has been active in e-publishing, producing adventure novels under the pen name Jack Nolte.

Carter sets *The Last Great Getaway of the Water Balloon Boys* in his home state, where shy, artistic sixteen-year-old Charlie Hill and former best friend Jake Tucker are at a life-changing crossroads although they do not know it. As narrated by Charlie, events begin to spin out of control the day Jake rescues his friend from a school bully. Street-wise due to his time in foster care, Jake has cavalierly stolen the school principal's prized 1967 Mustang to come to Charlie's aid. One misstep now leads to another as the teens eventually find themselves hurdling down the interstate toward Colorado, with the state police in hot pursuit.

Praising Carter's debut as "touching and impressive," a *Publishers Weekly* critic added that *The Last Great Getaway of the Water Balloon Boys* features "on target" storytelling containing "believable characters with interesting stories to tell." "Well-developed characters and twists and turns along the way reveal the complexity of friendship, the redemptive power of second chances, . . . and the lasting effects of choices," asserted *School Library Journal* contributor Danielle Serra, the critic praising Carter's novel as "well-paced" and "compelling" and recommending it as "a good choice for reluctant readers."

Biographical and Critical Sources

PERIODICALS

Publishers Weekly, March 29, 2010, review of *The Last Great Getaway of the Water Balloon Boys,* p. 61.

School Library Journal, April, 2010, Danielle Serra, review of *The Last Great Getaway of the Water Balloon Boys,* p. 152.

ONLINE

Jack Nolte Web site, http://www.jacknolte.com (June 15, 2011).
Scott William Carter Home Page, http://scottwilliamcarter. com (June 15, 2011).*

*   *   *

COLE, Joanna 1944-
(Ann Cooke)

Personal

Born August 11, 1944, in Newark, NJ; daughter of Mario and Elizabeth (Reid) Basilea; married Philip A. Cole (an artist and psychotherapist), October 8, 1965; children: Rachel Elizabeth. *Education:* Attended University of Massachusetts at Amherst and Indiana University—Bloomington; City College of New York (now of the City University of New York), B.A., 1967.

Addresses

Home—CT.

Career

New York City Board of Education, New York, NY, elementary school librarian and instructor, 1967-68; *Newsweek,* New York, NY, letters correspondent, 1968-71; Scholastic, Inc., New York, NY, associate editor of See-Saw Book Club, 1971-73; Doubleday & Co., Garden City, NY, senior editor of books for young readers, 1973-80; full-time writer, 1980—.

Member

Authors Guild, Authors League of America, Society of Children's Book Writers and Illustrators, American Association for the Advancement of Science.

Awards, Honors

Child Study Association of America's Children's Books of the Year selection, 1971, for *Cockroaches,* 1972, for *Giraffes at Home* and *Twins: The Story of Multiple Births,* 1973, for *My Puppy Is Born* and *Plants in Winter,* 1974, for *Dinosaur Story,* 1975, for *A Calf Is Born,* and 1985, for *Large as Life: Daytime Animals, Large as Life: Nighttime Animals,* and *The New Baby at Your House;* Children's Book Showcase selection, Children's Book Council, 1977, for *A Chick Hatches;* New York Academy of Sciences Children's Science Honor book selection, 1981, and Children's Choice selection, International Reading Association/Children's Book Council (IRA/CBC), 1982, both for *A Snake's Body;* Golden Kite Honor Book designation, Society of Children's Book Writers and Illustrators, and Notable Children's Book selection, Association for Library Service to Children, both 1984, both for *How You Were Born;* Irma Simonton Black Award for Excellence in Children's Literature, 1986, for *Doctor Change; Boston Globe/Horn Book* Honor Book for Nonfiction selection, 1987, for *The Magic School Bus at the Waterworks;* IRA/CBC Children's Choice award, 1990, for *The Magic School Bus inside the Earth;* Eva L. Gordon Award, American Nature Study Society, 1990, for science and nature writing; *Washington Post*/Children's Book Guild Award for Nonfiction, 1991, for body of work; David McCord Children's Literature Citation, Framingham (MA) State College/Nobscot Council of the IRA, 1994, for significant contribution to excellence in children's literature. Recipient of state children's book awards, including Garden State Award for nonfiction, 1992, for *The Magic School Bus inside the Human Body,* and 1993, for *The Magic School Bus Lost in the Solar System.* Many of Cole's books have received best book or notable book citations from the American Library Association, *Horn Book,* and *School Library Journal;* numorous Outstanding Science Trade Books for Children designations, National Science Teachers Association/CBC designations.

Writings

NONFICTION; FOR CHILDREN

Cockroaches, illustrated by Jean Zallinger, Morrow (New York, NY), 1971.
(Under pseudonym Ann Cooke) *Giraffes at Home,* illustrated by Robert Quackenbush, Crowell (New York, NY), 1972.
(With Madeleine Edmondson) *Twins: The Story of Multiple Births,* illustrated by Salvatore Raciti, Morrow (New York, NY), 1972.
Plants in Winter, illustrated by Kazue Mizumura, Crowell (New York, NY), 1973.
My Puppy Is Born, photographs by Jerome Wexler, Morrow (New York, NY), 1973, revised edition, photographs by Margaret Miller, 1991.
Fleas, illustrated by Elsie Wrigley, Morrow (New York, NY), 1973.
Dinosaur Story, illustrated by Mort Kunstler, Morrow (New York, NY), 1974.
A Calf Is Born, photographs by Jerome Wexler, Morrow (New York, NY), 1975.
A Chick Hatches, photographs by Jerome Wexler, Morrow (New York, NY), 1976.
Saber-toothed Tiger and Other Ice-Age Mammals, illustrated by Lydia Rosier, Morrow (New York, NY), 1977.
A Fish Hatches, photographs by Jerome Wexler, Morrow (New York, NY), 1978.
(With Jerome Wexler) *Find the Hidden Insect,* photographs by Jerome Wexler, Morrow (New York, NY), 1979.

A Frog's Body, photographs by Jerome Wexler, Morrow (New York, NY), 1980.

A Horse's Body, photographs by Jerome Wexler, Morrow (New York, NY), 1981.

A Snake's Body, photographs by Jerome Wexler, Morrow (New York, NY), 1981.

A Cat's Body, photographs by Jerome Wexler, Morrow (New York, NY), 1982.

A Bird's Body, photographs by Jerome Wexler, Morrow (New York, NY), 1982.

Cars and How They Go, illustrated by Gail Gibbons, Crowell (New York, NY), 1983.

An Insect's Body, photographs by Jerome Wexler and Raymond A. Mendez, Morrow (New York, NY), 1984.

How You Were Born, Morrow (New York, NY), 1984, revised edition, with photographs by Margaret Miller, 1994.

The New Baby at Your House, photographs by Hella Hammid, Morrow (New York, NY), 1985, revised edition, with photographs by Margaret Miller, 1998.

Cuts, Breaks, Bruises, and Burns: How Your Body Heals, illustrated by True Kelly, Crowell (New York, NY), 1985.

Large as Life: Daytime Animals, illustrated by Kenneth Lilly, Knopf (New York, NY), 1985.

Large as Life: Nighttime Animals, illustrated by Kenneth Lilly, Knopf (New York, NY), 1985, published as *Large as Life Animals in Beautiful Life-Size Paintings,* 1990.

A Dog's Body, photographs by Jim and Ann Monteith, Morrow (New York, NY), 1985.

Hungry, Hungry Sharks, illustrated by Patricia Wynne, Random House (New York, NY), 1986.

The Human Body: How We Evolved, illustrated by Walter Gaffney-Kessell and Juan Carlos Barberis, Morrow (New York, NY), 1987.

Evolution, illustrated by Aliki, Crowell (New York, NY), 1987.

Asking about Sex and Growing Up: A Question-and-Answer Book for Boys and Girls, illustrated by Alan Tiegreen, Morrow (New York, NY), 1988, new edition published as *Asking about Sex and Growing Up: A Question-and-Answer Book for Kids,* HarperCollins (New York, NY), 2009.

A Gift from Saint Francis: The First Crèche, illustrated by Michele Lemieux, Morrow (New York, NY), 1989.

Your New Potty, illustrated by Margaret Miller, Morrow (New York, NY), 1989.

Your Insides, illustrated by Paul Meisel, Putnam (New York, NY), 1992.

You Can't Smell a Flower with Your Ear!: All about Your Five Senses, illustrated by Mavis Smith, Putnam (New York, NY), 1994.

(With Stephanie Calmenson) *Crazy Eights and Other Card Games,* illustrated by Alan Tiegreen, Morrow (New York, NY), 1994.

My New Kitten, photographs by Margaret Miller, Morrow (New York, NY), 1995.

Spider's Lunch: All about Garden Spiders, illustrated by Ron Broda, Grosset & Dunlap (New York, NY), 1995.

Riding Silver Star, photographs by Margaret Miller, Morrow (New York, NY), 1996.

(With Stephanie Calmenson) *The Rain or Shine Activity Book: Fun Things to Make or Do,* illustrated by Alan Tiegreen, Morrow (New York, NY), 1997.

(With Stephanie Calmenson) *The Any Day Book,* Morrow (New York, NY), 1997.

(With Stephanie Calmenson and Michael Street) *Marbles: 101 Ways to Play,* illustrated by Alan Tiegreen, Morrow (New York, NY), 1998.

(With Stephanie Calmenson and Michael Street) *Fun on the Run: Travel Games and Songs,* illustrated by Alan Tiegreen, Morrow (New York, NY), 1999.

My Big Girl Potty, illustrated by Maxie Chambliss, Morrow (New York, NY), 2000.

My Big Boy Potty, illustrated by Maxie Chambliss, Morrow (New York, NY), 2000.

Card Games, Morrow (New York, NY), 2000.

Hopscotch and Sidewalk Game, Morrow (New York, NY), 2000.

When You Were inside Mommy, illustrated by Maxie Chambliss, HarperCollins (New York, NY), 2001.

When Mommy and Daddy Go to Work, illustrated by Maxie Chambliss, HarperCollins (New York, NY), 2001.

Sharing Is Fun, illustrated by Maxie Chambliss, HarperCollins (New York, NY), 2004.

"MAGIC SCHOOL BUS" SERIES; NONFICTION

The Magic School Bus at the Waterworks, illustrated by Bruce Degen, Scholastic (New York, NY), 1986, special edition, Scholastic/New York City Department of Environmental Protection, 1990.

The Magic School Bus inside the Earth, illustrated by Bruce Degen, Scholastic (New York, NY), 1987.

The Magic School Bus inside the Human Body, illustrated by Bruce Degen, Scholastic (New York, NY), 1989.

The Magic School Bus Lost in the Solar System, illustrated by Bruce Degen, Scholastic (New York, NY), 1990.

The Magic School Bus on the Ocean Floor, illustrated by Bruce Degen, Scholastic (New York, NY), 1992.

The Magic School Bus in the Time of the Dinosaurs, illustrated by Bruce Degen, Scholastic (New York, NY), 1994.

The Magic School Bus inside a Hurricane, illustrated by Bruce Degen, Scholastic (New York, NY), 1995.

The Magic School Bus Gets Baked in a Cake, illustrated by Bruce Degen, Scholastic (New York, NY), 1995.

The Magic School Bus Plants Seeds, illustrated by Bruce Degen, Scholastic (New York, NY), 1995.

The Magic School Bus Briefcase, illustrated by Bruce Degen, Scholastic (New York, NY), 1995.

The Magic School Bus Meets the Rot Squad, illustrated by Bruce Degen, Scholastic (New York, NY), 1995.

The Magic School Bus Hello out There, illustrated by Bruce Degen, Scholastic (New York, NY), 1995.

The Magic School Bus in the Haunted Museum, illustrated by Bruce Degen, Scholastic (New York, NY), 1995.

The Magic School Bus Hops Home, illustrated by Bruce Degen, Scholastic (New York, NY), 1995.

The Magic School Bus Gets All Dried Up, illustrated by Bruce Degen, Scholastic (New York, NY), 1996.

The Magic School Bus Wet All Over, illustrated by Bruce Degen, Scholastic (New York, NY), 1996.

The Magic School Bus inside a Beehive, illustrated by Bruce Degen, Scholastic (New York, NY), 1996.

The Magic School Bus out of This World, illustrated by Bruce Degen, Scholastic (New York, NY), 1996.

The Magic School Bus Gets Eaten, illustrated by Bruce Degen, Scholastic (New York, NY), 1996.

The Magic School Bus Blows Its Top, illustrated by Bruce Degen, Scholastic (New York, NY), 1996.

The Magic School Bus Ups and Downs, illustrated by Bruce Degen, Scholastic (New York, NY), 1997.

The Magic School Bus and the Electric Field Trip, illustrated by Bruce Degen, Scholastic (New York, NY), 1997.

The Magic School Bus Goes Upstream, illustrated by Bruce Degen, Scholastic (New York, NY), 1997.

The Magic School Bus Gets Planted, illustrated by Bruce Degen, Scholastic (New York, NY), 1997.

The Magic School Bus Shows and Tells: A Book about Archaeology, illustrated by Bruce Degen, Scholastic (New York, NY), 1997.

The Magic School Bus in a Pickle, illustrated by Bruce Degen, Scholastic (New York, NY), 1997.

The Magic School Bus Plays Ball, illustrated by Bruce Degen, Scholastic (New York, NY), 1998.

The Magic School Bus in the Arctic, illustrated by Bruce Degen, Scholastic (New York, NY), 1998.

The Magic School Bus in the Rain Forest, illustrated by Bruce Degen, Scholastic (New York, NY), 1998.

The Magic School Bus Explores the Senses, illustrated by Bruce Degen, Scholastic (New York, NY), 1999.

The Magic School Bus Sees Stars, illustrated by Bruce Degen, Scholastic (New York, NY), 1999.

The Magic School Bus Answers Questions, illustrated by Bruce Degen, Scholastic (New York, NY), 1999.

The Magic School Bus Taking Flight, illustrated by Bruce Degen, Scholastic (New York, NY), 1999.

The Magic School Bus Going Batty, illustrated by Bruce Degen, Scholastic (New York, NY), 1999.

The Magic School Bus Gets Ants in Its Pants, illustrated by Bruce Degen, Scholastic (New York, NY), 1999.

Ms. Frizzle's Adventures in Egypt, illustrated by Bruce Degen, Scholastic (New York, NY), 2000.

Ms. Frizzle's Adventures: Medieval Castle, illustrated by Bruce Degen, Scholastic (New York, NY), 2002.

The Magic School Bus Flies from the Nest, illustrated by Carolyn Bracken, Scholastic (New York, NY), 2004.

The Magic School Bus: Lost in the Snow, illustrated by Carolyn Bracken, Scholastic (New York, NY), 2004.

Ms. Frizzle's Adventures: Imperial China, Scholastic (New York, NY), 2005.

The Magic School Bus at the First Thanksgiving, illustrated by Carolyn Bracken, Scholastic (New York, NY), 2006.

The Magic School Bus and the Science Fair Expedition, illustrated by Bruce Degen, Scholastic Press (New York, NY), 2006.

FICTION FOR CHILDREN

Cousin Matilda and the Foolish Wolf, Albert Whitman (Morton Grove, IL), 1970.

The Secret Box, Morrow (New York, NY), 1971.

Fun on Wheels, illustrated by Whitney Darrow, Morrow (New York, NY), 1976.

The Clown-Arounds, illustrated by Jerry Smath, Parents Magazine Press, 1981.

The Clown-Arounds Have a Party, illustrated by Jerry Smath, Parents Magazine Press, 1982.

Golly Gump Swallowed a Fly, illustrated by Bari Weissman, Parents Magazine Press, 1982.

Get Well, Clown-Arounds!, illustrated by Jerry Smath, Parents Magazine Press, 1982.

The Clown-Arounds Go on Vacation, illustrated by Jerry Smath, Parents Magazine Press, 1983.

Aren't You Forgetting Something, Fiona?, illustrated by Ned Delaney, Parents Magazine Press, 1983.

Bony-Legs, illustrated by Dirk Zimmer, Four Winds Press (New York, NY), 1983.

Sweet Dreams, Clown-Arounds, illustrated by Jerry Smath, Parents Magazine Press, 1985.

Monster Manners, illustrated by Jared Lee, Scholastic (New York, NY), 1986.

This Is the Place for Me, illustrated by William Van Horn, Scholastic (New York, NY), 1986.

Doctor Change, illustrated by Donald Carrick, Morrow (New York, NY), 1986.

Monster Movie, illustrated by Jared Lee, Scholastic (New York, NY), 1987.

Norma Jean, Jumping Bean, illustrated by Lynn Munsinger, Random House (New York, NY), 1987, reprinted, 2003.

Mixed-up Magic, illustrated by True Kelly, Scholastic (New York, NY), 1987.

(With husband, Philip Cole) *Hank and Frank Fix up the House,* illustrated by William Van Horn, Scholastic (New York, NY), 1988.

Animal Sleepyheads: One to Ten, illustrated by Jeni Bassett, Scholastic (New York, NY), 1988.

The Missing Tooth, illustrated by Marilyn Hafner, Random House (New York, NY), 1988, reprinted, 2004.

(With Philip Cole) *Big Goof and Little Goof,* illustrated by M.K. Brown, Scholastic (New York, NY), 1989.

Who Put the Pepper in the Pot?, illustrated by R.W. Alley, Parents Magazine Press, 1989.

It's Too Noisy!, illustrated by Kate Duke, Crowell (New York, NY), 1989.

Buster Cat Goes Out, illustrated by Rose Mary Berlin, Western Publishing, 1989.

Bully Trouble: A Step Two Book, illustrated by Marilyn Hafner, Random House (New York, NY), 1989, reprinted, 2003.

Monster Valentines, illustrated by Jared Lee, Scholastic (New York, NY), 1990.

Don't Call Me Names!, illustrated by Lynn Munsinger, Random House (New York, NY), 1990.

Don't Tell the Whole World!, illustrated by Kate Duke, Crowell (New York, NY), 1990.

How I Was Adopted: Samantha's Story, illustrated by Maxie Chambliss, Morrow (New York, NY), 1995.

(With Stephanie Calmenson) *The Gator Girls,* illustrated by Lynn Munsinger, Morrow (New York, NY), 1995.

Monster and Muffin, illustrated by Karen Lee Schmidt, Grosset & Dunlap (New York, NY), 1996.

(With Stephanie Calmenson) *Bug in a Rug: Reading Fun for Just Beginners,* illustrated by Alan Tiegreen, Morrow (New York, NY), 1996.

(With Stephanie Calmenson) *Rockin' Reptiles,* illustrated by Lynn Munsinger, Morrow (New York, NY), 1997.

I'm a Big Brother, illustrated by Maxie Chambliss, Morrow (New York, NY), 1997, revised edition, 2004, illustrated by Bridget Strevens-Marzo, HarperCollins Children's Books (New York, NY), 2008, illustrated by Rosalinda Kightly, HarperFestival (New York, NY), 2010.

I'm a Big Sister, illustrated by Maxie Chambliss, Morrow (New York, NY), 1997, revised edition, 2004, illustrated by Bridget Strevens-Marzo, HarperCollins Children's Books (New York, NY), 2008, illustrated by Rosalinda Kightly, HarperFestival (New York, NY), 2010.

(With Stephanie Calmenson) *Get Well, Gators!,* illustrated by Lynn Munsinger, Morrow (New York, NY), 1998.

Liz Sorts It Out, Scholastic (New York, NY), 1998.

Liz Looks for a New Home, Scholastic (New York, NY), 1998.

(With Stephanie Calmenson) *Gator Halloween,* Morrow (New York, NY), 1999.

Jump Rope Rhymes, Morrow (New York, NY), 2000.

Street Rhymes, Morrow (New York, NY), 2000.

My Friend the Doctor, illustrated by Maxie Chambliss, HarperCollins (New York, NY), 2005.

(With Rachel Cole) *Remember Your Manners,* illustrated by Rosalinda Kightley, HarperFestival (New York, NY), 2011.

EDITOR; FOR CHILDREN

(And author of introduction) *Best-Loved Folktales of the World,* illustrated by Jill K. Schwarz, Doubleday (New York, NY), 1982.

A New Treasury of Children's Poetry: Old Favorites and New Discoveries, illustrated by Judith Gwyn Brown, Doubleday (New York, NY), 1983.

(With Stephanie Calmenson) *The Laugh Book,* illustrated by Marilyn Hafner, Doubleday (New York, NY), 1986.

(With Stephanie Calmenson) *The Read-aloud Treasury: Favorite Nursery Rhymes, Poems, Stories & More for the Very Young,* illustrated by Ann Schweninger, Doubleday (New York, NY), 1988.

Anna Banana: 101 Jump Rope Rhymes, illustrated by Alan Tiegreen, Morrow (New York, NY), 1989.

(With Stephanie Calmenson) *Miss Mary Mack, and Other Children's Street Rhymes,* illustrated by Alan Tiegreen, Morrow (New York, NY), 1990.

(With Stephanie Calmenson) *Ready . . . Set . . . Read! The Beginning Reader Treasury,* illustrated by Anne Burgess, Doubleday (New York, NY), 1990.

(With Stephanie Calmenson) *The Scary Book,* illustrated by Chris Demarest, Morrow (New York, NY), 1991.

(With Stephanie Calmenson) *The Eentsy, Weentsy Spider: Fingerplays and Action Rhymes,* illustrated by Alan Tiegreen, Morrow (New York, NY), 1991.

(With Stephanie Calmenson) *Pat-a-Cake, and Other Play Rhymes,* illustrated by Alan Tiegreen, Morrow (New York, NY), 1992.

(With Stephanie Calmenson) *Pin the Tail on the Donkey, and Other Party Games,* illustrated by Alan Tiegreen, Morrow (New York, NY), 1993.

(With Stephanie Calmenson) *Six Sick Sheep: One Hundred Tongue Twisters,* illustrated by Alan Tiegreen, Morrow (New York, NY), 1993.

(With Stephanie Calmenson) *Give a Dog a Bone: Stories, Poems, Jokes, and Riddles about Dogs,* illustrated by John Speirs, Scholastic (New York, NY), 1994.

(With Stephanie Calmenson) *Why Did the Chicken Cross the Road?, and Other Riddles Old and New,* illustrated by Alan Tiegreen, Morrow (New York, NY), 1994.

(With Stephanie Calmenson) *A Pocketful of Laughs: Stories, Poems, Jokes, and Riddles,* illustrated by Marilyn Hafner, Doubleday (New York, NY), 1995.

(With Stephanie Calmenson) *Ready, Set, Read—and Laugh!: A Funny Treasury for Beginning Readers,* Doubleday (New York, NY), 1995.

(With Stephanie Calmenson) *Yours till Banana Splits: 201 Autograph Rhymes,* illustrated by Alan Tiegreen, Morrow (New York, NY), 1995.

OTHER

The Parents' Book of Toilet Teaching, Ballantine, Morrow (New York, NY), 1983.

(With Stephanie Calmenson) *Safe from the Start: Your Child's Safety from Birth to Age Five,* Facts on File (New York, NY), 1990.

(With Wendy Saul) *On the Bus with Joanna Cole: A Creative Autobiography,* Heinemann (London, England), 1996.

Also contributor of articles to *Parents.*

Adaptations

An animated series for PBS-TV based on the "Magic School Bus" books began in 1994 and features the voices of Lily Tomlin as Ms. Frizzle, Robby Benson, Carol Channing, and Malcolm-Jamal Warner; the series is also available in a CD-ROM version by Microsoft Home and Scholastic, Inc. The "Magic School Bus" series was the basis of the American Library Association's 1994 reading program, "Reading Is a Magic Trip," and were adapted as Scholastic's "Adventures of the Magic Schoolbus" science chapter-book series. Cassette recordings have been made of *Bony-Legs,* Random House, 1985, and *Monster Movie* and *Dinosaur Story,* both Scholastic, 1989.

Sidelights

Joanna Cole is the author of a wealth of children's books and her subjects are as varied as any young reader's interests. Cole's fertile imagination has produced beginning readers with jokes and puzzles, humorous tales of the Clown-Around family, retellings of folk tales and myths, and books about science that dazzle, inspire, and inform. The winner of numerous awards from the American Library Association, the National Science Teachers Association/Children's Book Council, and various state reading associations, Cole follows her own widespread interests to write about the life cycle of an insect, field questions on human sexuality, talk about potty training, and even take readers on a trip to the stars in her popular Magic School Bus. She is credited with introducing the fascinating world of science to legions of young readers through her stand-alone titles as well as through book series such as the hugely popular "Magic School Bus" books, which ultimately inspired its own television program. A thorough researcher, Cole is praised for her scientific accuracy, but her books gain most of their effectiveness from her humor and her frank, easily understood explanations of sometimes complicated technical subjects.

Born in New Jersey, Cole began taking her writing seriously when she was in grade school. "I discovered in the fifth grade what I liked to do; write reports and stories, make them interesting and/or funny and draw pictures to go along with the words," she once commented. "Except for the pictures, I still do that. I remember grade school very clearly when I sat at my desk, happily interested in whatever subject I was writing about. Science was my favorite. Our teacher, Miss Bair, would assign us to read a science trade book every week. And each week, she would choose one student to do an experiment and report on it to the class. I would have done an experiment every week if she had let me. Grade school was very important to me, much more influential than my later education. Maybe that's why as an adult I ended up writing books for children."

After receiving a bachelor's degree from the City College of New York, Cole pursued her interest in books by working variously as a librarian, teacher, and editor. It was during her first job at an elementary school that she was inspired by an article about cockroaches in the *Wall Street Journal*. Realizing that this was a subject she had never read about in school, Cole decided to write about it herself. The first publisher she submitted her manuscript to rejected the idea, but the author had more luck when she sent her book to the publishing house of William Morrow, where editor Connie C. Epstein helped Cole hone her skills in science writing. Beginning with that debut book, Cole has gone on to pen both nonfiction and fiction for younger readers. In 1980, after a decade of editing children's books, she became a full-time writer.

Many of Cole's nonfiction works focus on the life sciences. In her "Animal Bodies" series she introduces young readers to the anatomy of animals such as horses, frogs, dogs, birds, cats, and snakes. Reviewing *An Insect's Body* in *Horn Book*, Sarah S. Gagne commented that "if it is possible for Joanna Cole to improve on the unparalleled series of books about animal bodies that she has written over the years, she has now done so." Using the cricket as a representative insect, Cole examined its body structure and how this corresponds to the insect's environment. *Booklist* reviewer Ilene Cooper,

reviewing the same title, remarked that "anyone whose curiosity is intact cannot help but be captivated by this fascinating work." The series concludes with *The Human Body: How We Evolved,* which explains how archaeologists piece together the evolutionary history of mankind and how human anatomy compares to that of apes, chimpanzees, gorillas, and man's other primate cousins. Cooper called this volume a "fine introduction to evolution that will go a long way toward answering children's questions about their origins," while Jason R. Taylor, writing in *Science Books and Films,* deemed *The Human Body* "an excellent, extremely well-researched book."

Cole is very aware that young children's feelings affect their reactions to factual material. In her series on animals' births, which includes *A Calf Is Born, My Puppy Is Born, How You Were Born,* and *My New Kitten,* she explains the physiology of birth with candor and accuracy and is careful to include the gentle care baby mammals need to grow, care that mirrors children's own experience. Reviewing a revised edition of *How You Were Born,* Denise L. Moll noted in *School Library Journal* that "Cole relates the process of conception and birth in a personalized manner," and added that while other books on the same subject are available, "Cole's book continues to set the standard." A related title, *My New Kitten,* "promotes warm, fuzzy feelings and at the same time gives youngsters just a peek at the creatures' developmental stages," according to Margaret Chatham writing in *School Library Journal.*

A number of Cole's books focus on child development, among them *The New Baby at Your House, My Big Boy Potty, When You Were inside Mommy,* the companion books *I'm a Big Brother* and *I'm a Big Sister,* and *How I Was Adopted: Samantha's Story.* The first-named title deals with the arrival of a new infant, including sibling rivalry, while *When You Were inside Mommy* describes the development of a baby with "simplicity and sensitivity" according to *Booklist* contributor Carolyn Phelan. Martha Topol, writing in *School Library Journal,* felt that *The New Baby at Your House* "gives honest, practical advice on helping youngsters prepare for and cope with a new arrival." Similar advice is passed on in the companion volumes *I'm a Big Brother* and *I'm a Big Sister.* Dina Sherman, reviewing both books in *School Library Journal,* felt that "familiar situations, as well as positive reinforcement of individuality and importance as part of the family, are good reasons to put th[em] . . . into the hands of children who will soon be older siblings."

Adoption gets the Cole treatment in *How I Was Adopted,* in which a young girl tells her own story. A contributor to *Publishers Weekly* wrote that the book presents a "cheerful, informative approach" to the subject. Stephanie Zvirin, writing in *Booklist,* noted that "Cole expertly negotiates a middle course that provides children with some excellent, age-appropriate background on adoption." Other books featuring health and developmental issues include *My Friend the Doctor* and *Ask-*

ing about Sex and Growing Up: A Question-and-Answer Book for Kids, the latter a revised version of a children's reference Cole first published in 1988. "Cole and [illustrator Maxie] Chambliss hit just the right note in this picture-book version of a visit to the pediatrician's office," concluded Phelan in her *Booklist* review of *My Friend the Doctor.*

An age-appropriate approach to another important subject—toilet training—is provided in Cole's gender-specific duo *My Big Boy Potty* and *My Big Girl Potty.* In each volume she collaborates with Chambliss to provide encouragement to toddlers ready to take a major step toward independence. In a *Publishers Weekly* review a writer praised Cole's "gradual approach"—a favorite stuffed animal goes through the appropriate motions in advance of the potty-using novice—and Kathy Broderick noted in *Booklist* that the "reassuring" companion volumes benefit from "Cole's matter-of-fact text."

Of all her science books, Cole's "Magic School Bus" series has proved enduringly popular since first appearing in 1986. The "Magic School Bus" books combine science and imaginative fun in stories that have been warmly received by critics and readers alike. As a writer for *Children's Books and Their Creators* explained, Cole "has given the term nonfiction new meaning" with the long-running series in which, through "a masterly combination of scientific facts, humor, and fantasy, . . . turn[s] science class into story hour." In each book a class of school children is led by eccentric teacher Ms. Frizzle and sometimes accompanied by Assistant Principal Mr. Wilde on a new adventure of discovery. Illustrator Bruce Degen shows the unlimited possibilities for travel in the amazing bus, which can dig through the earth, travel through time, shrink to microscopic size, and even blast off into space. Each page combines a fact-and fun-filled text that blends with and sometimes competing for room with Degen's artwork. "Just as 'Sesame Street' revolutionized the teaching of letters

Cover of Joanna Cole's entertaining series installment **The Magic School Bus on the Ocean Floor,** *featuring artwork by Bruce Degen* (Illustration copyright © 1992 by Bruce Degen. Reproduced by permission of Scholastic, Inc.)

Cole addresses a topic of contemporary interest as Ms. Frizzle stars in The Magic School Bus and the Climate Challenge. (Illustration copyright © 2010 by Bruce Degen. Reproduced with permission of Scholastic Press, an imprint of Scholastic, Inc.)

and numbers by making it so entertaining that children had no idea they were actually learning something, so the 'Magic School Bus' books make science so much fun that the information is almost incidental," wrote Katherine Bouton in the *New York Times Book Review*. Bouton declared that Cole's books offer "the freshest, most amusing approach to science for children that I've seen," while Andrea Cleghorn, writing in *Publishers Weekly*, commented that the "Magic School Bus" books "serve science with a sizzle," noting that specialists in the field check all books in the series for accuracy.

Cole based the character of Ms. Frizzle, on her own favorite science teacher, Miss Bair, although, as she once commented, "Miss Bair did not dress at all like Ms. Frizzle!" The kids in the "Magic School Bus" books may grumble a bit about the adventures they experience, but in their hearts they love their teacher and are proud to be in her class. "In 'The Magic School Bus' books I use the same criteria as I do in all my science

books," Cole explained. "I write about ideas, rather than just facts. I try to ask an implicit question—such as, How do our bodies get energy from the food we eat? or How do scientists guess what dinosaurs were like? Then I try to answer the question in writing the book." The success of Cole's "Magic School Bus" books, which have sold in the millions worldwide, has carried over to television, where the Public Broadcasting Service adapted them as an animated series; Cole and illustrator Degen served as consultants.

Adventures on the school bus take the students, Ms. Frizzle, and Mr. Wilde inside the human body, down to the waterworks, inside a dog's nose or beehive or hurricane, back in time to the world of the dinosaurs, or through space to the stars. "Climb aboard," John Peters encouraged readers in a *School Library Journal* review of *The Magic School Bus in the Time of the Dinosaurs*, "there's never a dull moment with 'the Friz' at the wheel!" Reviewing *The Magic School Bus Explores the*

Senses, Christine A. Moesch remarked in *School Library Journal* that it is "another fun, fact-filled adventure," while *The Magic School Bus and the Electric Field Trip,* according to Blair Christolon in *School Library Journal,* "makes a complex subject fun to read about and simple to understand." More recent installments in the series include the "Miss Frizzle's Adventures" books, which allow readers to follow Cole's charismatic tour guide back in time to ancient Egypt, the medieval age, and imperial China.

Ms. Frizzle and company continue their adventures in *The Magic School Bus and the Science Fair Expedition,* a book that marked the twenty-year anniversary of Cole's "Magic School Bus" series. In this installment, students are trying to figure out what to construct for the upcoming school science fair, and during a field trip they are transported back in time and meet the men and women who made some of science's most pivotal discoveries. Contemporary questions about the earth's climate and ecology are addressed by Cole in *The Magic School Bus and the Climate Challenge,* which finds the Magic School Bus "going Green" as a hybrid vehicle before a trip into the clouds allows its young passengers to witness the chemical changes occurring in the atmosphere. *The Magic School Bus and the Science Fair Expedition* "cements the series' long-standing reputation as one of the most exciting, approachable elementary-

Cole's popular teacher branches out into new territory in a series of books that include **Ms. Frizzle's Adventures: Medieval Castle** *and feature Degen's cartoon art.* (Illustration copyright © 2003 by Bruce Degen. Reproduced by permission of Scholastic, Inc.)

school science resources," asserted Gillian Engberg in her *Booklist* review, and Betty Carter wrote in *Horn Book* that Cole's illustration of the scientific method in action shows readers that "science is not static but constantly being revised." *The Magic School Bus and the Climate Challenge* will "inspire kids to become citizen scientists and advocates," concluded *School Library Journal* contributor Sara Lissa Pauson, while a *Kirkus Reviews* writer maintained that Cole's "tested formula" in the "Magic School Bus" series is "as effective as ever for cluing in younger readers with a mix of instruction and droll side remarks."

Although Cole is more often recognized for her science books, she is also the author of a number of stories for children, has compiled anthologies of children's literature, and has written books for adults on parenting and child development. Early in her career Cole also wrote a series of amusing easy-readers featuring the Clown-Arounds, a silly family whose members sleep in shoes and generally approach life from a goofy angle. Popular retellings of folk tales from Cole include *Bony-Legs,* "a bang-up read," according to Nancy Palmer writing in *School Library Journal,* and *Don't Tell the Whole World!,* an example of "fine storytelling," as a *Publishers Weekly* contributor noted.

Working with frequent collaborator Stephanie Calmenson, Cole has produced nonfiction anthologies as well as stories in the "Gator Girls" series. In *Ready, Set, Read—and Laugh: A Funny Treasury for Beginning Readers* Cole and Calmenson compile a collection of stories, poems, jokes, and games that, according to *Booklist* contributor Hazel Rochman, "will turn readers on to the fun of books." "Kids will delight in the word play and the nonsense," Rochman continued, "and they'll want to read more." Other popular titles include *Give a Dog a Bone, The Rain or Shine Activity Book, Marbles: One Hundred One Ways to Play,* and *Bug in a Rug.*

In the "Gator Girls" series the coauthors present reptilian bff's Allie and Amy Gator in adventures that range from attending summer camp to getting over an illness. In the debut volume, *The Gator Girls,* the two girls want to cram all their summertime activities into the few days they have before going off to camp. *Booklist* reviewer Mary Harris Veeder wrote that in this beginning chapter book "the joys of true-blue friendship are humorously realized." *Get Well, Gators!* sees the duo fighting swamp fever in time to take part in a local street fair. "Give this one to chapter-book readers looking for a funny book," advised Kay Weisman in a *Booklist* review. In *Gator Halloween* the girls "are up to their old tricks," according to Stephanie Zvirin in *Booklist,* referencing the girls' efforts to win the best costume prize in the local Halloween parade. Zvirin called the book "fun, with a dash of over-the-top comedy and wonderful illustrations."

Whether sharing the antics of Ms. Frizzle and her dauntless crew in search of scientific knowledge, having fun

Enlivened with Degen's art, Cole's "Magic School Bus" series has inspired a television series as well as spin-off books by others, such as **The Adventures of the Magic School Bus: Inside Ralphie.** (Illustration copyright © by Bruce Degen. Reprinted by permission of Scholastic, Inc.)

with rhymes and jokes, or making everyday developmental activities into a meaningful experience, Cole knows what it takes to hook a young reader and bring him or her back for more. "Always keeping mind the emotional level of her audience, Joanna Cole presents her information in a reassuring, caring tone, with great respect for children," concluded the critic for *Children's Books and Their Creators.* For Cole, being able to write for children is the fulfillment of a childhood dream; for her legions of contented readers it is a windfall.

Biographical and Critical Sources

BOOKS

Authors of Books for Young People, 3rd edition, Scarecrow Press (Metuchen, NJ), 1990.
Children's Books and Their Creators, edited by Anita Silvey, Houghton Mifflin (Boston, MA), 1995.
Children's Literature Review, Gale (Detroit, MI), Volume 5, 1983, Volume 40, 1996.

PERIODICALS

Booklist, June 15, 1984, Ilene Cooper, review of *An Insect's Body,* p. 1482; September 1, 1987, Ilene Cooper, review of *The Human Body: How We Evolved,* p.

61; June 15, 1988, Denise M. Wilms, review of *Asking about Sex and Growing Up: A Question-and-Answer Book for Boys and Girls,* pp. 1733-1734; April 15, 1995, Mary Harris Veeder, review of *The Gator Girls,* p. 1497; August, 1995, Stephanie Zvirin, review of *How I Was Adopted: Samantha's Story,* p. 1955; October 1, 1995, Hazel Rochman, review of *Ready, Set, Read—and Laugh!: A Funny Treasury for Beginning Readers,* p. 329; November 15, 1998, Kay Weisman, review of *Get Well, Gators!,* p. 590; September 1, 1999, S. Zvirin, review of *Gator Halloween,* p. 145; February 1, 2001, Kathy Broderick, reviews of *My Big Boy Potty* and *My Big Girl Potty,* both p. 1055; August, 2001, Carolyn Phelan, reviews of *When Mommy and Daddy Go to Work* and *When You Were inside Mommy,* both p. 2124; July, 2003, Carolyn Phelan, review of *Mrs. Frizzle's Adventures: Medieval Castle,* p. 1881; June 1, 2005, Jennifer Mattson, review of *Mrs. Frizzle's Adventures: Imperial China,* p. 1815; July, 2005, Carolyn Phelan, review of *My Friend the Doctor,* p. 1929; September 15, 2006, Gillian Engberg, review of *The Magic School Bus and the Science Fair Expedition,* p. 63; February 15, 2010, Carolyn Phelan, review of *The Magic School Bus and the Climate Challenge,* p. 87.
Horn Book, October, 1984, Sarah S. Gagne, review of *An Insect's Body,* p. 627; September-October, 2005, Margaret A. Chang, review of *Mrs. Frizzle's Adventures: Imperial China,* p. 600; November-December, 2006,

Betty Carter, review of *The Magic School Bus and the Science Fair Expedition,* p. 732; March-April, 2010, Martha V. Parravano, review of *The Magic School Bus and the Climate Challenge,* p. 80.

Kirkus Reviews, March 1, 1988, review of *Asking about Sex and Growing Up,* p. 361; July 1, 2003, review of *Ms. Frizzle's Adventures: Medieval Castle,* p. 907; June 15, 2005, review of *Ms. Frizzle's Adventures: Imperial China,* p. 679; January 1, 2010, review of *The Magic School Bus and the Climate Challenge.*

Nature, March 4, 2010, Nicola Jones, interview with Cole, p. 36.

Publishers Weekly, October 12, 1990, review of *Don't Tell the Whole World!,* p. 63; January 25, 1991, Andrea Cleghorn, "Aboard the Magic School Bus," pp. 27-28; October 2, 1995, review of *How I Was Adopted,* p. 74.

School Library Journal, December, 1983, Nancy Palmer, review of *Bony-Legs,* p. 79; April, 1993, Denise L. Moll, review of *How You Were Born,* p. 110; September, 1994, John Peters, review of *The Magic School Bus in the Time of the Dinosaurs,* pp. 206, 226; April, 1995, Margaret Chatham, review of *My New Kitten,* p. 123; April, 1997, Dina Sherman, reviews of *I'm a Big Brother* and *I'm a Big Sister,* both pp. 96-97; November, 1997, Blair Christolon, review of *The Magic School Bus and the Electric Field Trip,* p. 106; April, 1998, Martha Topol, review of *The New Baby at Your House,* p. 114; February, 1999, Christine A. Moesch, review of *The Magic School Bus Explores the Senses,* p. 96; November, 2000, Jane Marino, review of *My Big Boy Potty,* p. 112; November, 2001, Marilyn Ackerman, review of *When Mommy and Daddy Go to Work,* p. 113; December, 2001, Kathleen Kelly MacMillan, review of *When You Were inside Mommy,* p. 97; July, 2003, Joyce Adams Burner, review of *How You Were Born,* p. 77, and Anne Chapman Callaghan, review of *Ms. Frizzle's Adventures: Medieval Castle,* p. 112; August, 2004, Rachel G. Payne, review of *Sharing Is Fun,* p. 85; August, 2005, Suzanne Myers Harold, review of *Mrs. Frizzle's Adventures: Imperial China,* p. 112; September, 2005, Laurel L. Iakovakis, review of *My Friend the Doctor,* p. 167; February, 2010, Sara Lissa Paulson, review of *The Magic School Bus and the Climate Challenge,* p. 99, and Kathy Piehl, review of *Asking about Sex and Growing Up: A Question-and-Answer Book for Kids,* p. 128.

Science Books and Films, January-February, 1988, Jason R. Taylor, review of *The Human Body,* pp. 174-175.

ONLINE

Scholastic Home Page, http://www2.scholastic.com/ (July 13, 2011), "Joanna Cole."

OTHER

Riding the Magic School Bus with Joanna Cole and Bruce Degen (videotape), Scholastic (New York, NY), 1993.*

*   *   *

COOKE, Ann
See COLE, Joanna

CORRIVEAU, Art

Personal

Born in Barre, VT; father a fire chief, mother a teacher. *Education:* Boston University, B.A. (French)/B.S. (mass communications); University of Michigan, M.F.A. (fiction writing); Centre Universitaire d'Études Françaises, University of Grenoble), diploma in French language; College of Santa Fe, certificate in screenwriting.

Addresses

Home—Williamstown, VT; Zürich, Switzerland. *E-mail*—artcorriveau@me.com.

Career

Novelist and travel writer. Brand consultant, copywriter, and marketing consultant to businesses and institutions. Fellow at art colonies, including Yaddo, MacDowell, and Djerrasi. Fiction writing instructor; visiting writer at high schools; writing mentor.

Member

Author's Guild.

Awards, Honors

New Mexico Book Award finalist in Junior Book category, 2010, for *How I, Nicky Flynn, Finally Get a Life (and a Dog).*

Writings

Housewrights (adult novel), Penguin Books (New York, NY), 2002.

Blood Pudding (collected stories), Esplanade Books (Montreal, Quebec, Canada), 2007.

How I, Nicky Flynn, Finally Get a Life (and a Dog) (middle-grade novel; also see below), Amulet Books (New York, NY), 2010.

Author of screenplay *Nicky Flynn Finally Gets a Life* (adaptation of his novel). Contributor to literary journals, including *American Short Fiction, First Fictions, Metropolitan, New York Native, Queen's Quarterly, Southwest Review,* and *Story,* and to anthologies *Neonlit: Time Out Book of New Writing,* edited by Nicholas Royle, Quartet (London, England), 1998.

Author's work has been translated into German.

Sidelights

As a travel writer, Vermont resident Art Corriveau has sampled life in locations as varied as France, the Netherlands, and Thailand. Corriveau's 2002 adult novel, *Housewrights,* was praised by *Booklist* contributor

Art Corriveau (Photograph by Timothy Horn. Reproduced by permission.)

Joanne Wilkinson as "sparely constructed and elegantly told," and his short stories have appeared in periodicals and been collected in the anthology *Blood Pudding.* The author turns to a younger readership in *How I, Nicky Flynn, Finally Get a Life (and a Dog),* which follows the adventures of a boy who comes to terms with his life while trying to run away from it.

Born into a northern New England family with roots stretching back several generations, Corriveau studied French literature and communications at Boston University and then traveled west to earn his M.F.A. in fiction writing at the University of Michigan, Ann Arbor. While his short fiction appeared in literary journals both in the United States and United Kingdom, Corriveau developed a career in marketing, both as a brand consultant and a copywriter specializing in travel, language, and cross-cultural exchange.

In his first adult novel, *Housewrights,* Corriveau plays out an early twentieth-century drama that involves the emotional lives of three childhood friends—Lily and the twin Pritchard brothers Oren and Ian—as they grow up and deal with a tangle of complex emotions. Set in small-town Vermont, where Corriveau was raised, *Housewrights* was praised for both its "compelling" story and "convincing finale" by *Library Journal* reviewer David A. Berona, while Wilkinson deemed the author's fiction debut "a surprisingly rich novel that offers many pleasures." "Corriveau is a smooth, evocative writer who creates engaging if somewhat odd charac-

ters," noted a *Publishers Weekly* critic, and in *Housewrights* he crafts what the critics described as an "accomplished, thought-provoking debut."

For eleven-year-old Nicky Flynn, the hero of *How I, Nicky Flynn, Finally Get a Life (and a Dog),* the arrival of Reggie the dog is not the exciting event it would have been if Nicky's parents had still been together. Since their divorce, the boy has moved with his working mom into an apartment in a run-down section of Boston and now has to battle bullies and friendlessness as the new kid at school. Reggie arrives with baggage of his own, however; a full-grown German shepherd, he was dropped at the city pound after working as a seeing-eye dog. On their walks through the city, boy and dog become friends, and soon Nicky decides that Reggie may be the only thing in life he can count on in trying to reconnect with his dad and the way things used to be. Corriveau's story follows Nicky and Reggie as they run away from home. Its "characters are vividly drawn without sentimentality," noted *Booklist* critic Hazel Rochman, and the "elemental bond" between dog and boy "will hold readers." For Nancy P. Reeder, reviewing the novel in *School Library Journal, How I, Nicky Flynn, Finally Get a Life (and a Dog)* "is told in the

Cover of Corriveau's engaging middle-grade novel **How I, Nicky Flynn, Finally Get a Life (and a Dog).** (Jacket photograph copyright © 2010 Getty Images; jacket design by Maria T. Middleton. Reproduced with permission of Amulet Books, an imprint of Abrams.)

authentic voice of a boy who is dealing with too much upheaval in his life," and a *Publishers Weekly* critic recommended Corriveau's "touching and engrossing story" to "readers who have had troubles at home or have struggled to fit in."

Biographical and Critical Sources

PERIODICALS

Booklist, June 1, 2002, Joanne Wilkinson, review of *Housewrights,* p. 1680; March 1, 2010, Hazel Rochman, review of *How I, Nicky Flynn, Finally Get a Life (and a Dog),* p. 70.

Bulletin of the Center for Children's Books, July-August, 2010, Karen Coats, review of *How I, Nicky Flynn, Finally Get a Life (and a Dog),* p. 477.

Kirkus Reviews, May 1, 2002, review of *Housewrights,* p. 593.

Library Journal, June 1, 2002, David A. Berona, review of *Housewrights,* p. 194.

Publishers Weekly, June 24, 2002, review of *Housewrights,* p. 36; May 3, 2010, review of *How I, Nicky Flynn, Finally Get a Life (and a Dog),* p. 51.

School Library Journal, May, 2010, Nancy P. Reeder, review of *How I, Nicky Flynn, Finally Get a Life (and a Dog),* p. 108.

ONLINE

Art Corriveau Home Page, http://www.artcorriveau.com (April 20, 2011).

* * *

CUSICK, Richie Tankersley 1952-

Personal

Born April 1, 1952, in New Orleans, LA; daughter of Dick (a petroleum engineer) and Louise (a homemaker) Tankersley; married Rick Cusick (a book designer, calligrapher, and graphic artist), October 4, 1980. *Education:* University of Southwestern Louisiana, B.A. (English), 1975. *Hobbies and other interests:* Animals, reading, watching movies, listening to music (country, ethnic, pop, soundtracks), collecting, traveling.

Addresses

Home—MO.

Career

Novelist. Ochsner Foundation Hospital, New Orleans, LA, ward clerk, summers, 1970-72; Hallmark Cards, Inc., Kansas City, MO, writer, 1975-84; freelance writer.

Member

Humane Society of the United States, National Wildlife Federation, Doris Day Animal League.

Awards, Honors

Children's Choice Award, International Reading Association, 1989, for *The Lifeguard;* Book for the Teen Age selection, New York Public Library, 1990, for *Trick or Treat;* Edgar Award nomination, Mystery Writers of America, 1993, for *Help Wanted.*

Writings

YOUNG-ADULT NOVELS

The Ink and the Paper, 1984.
Evil on the Bayou, Dell (New York, NY), 1984.
The Lifeguard, Scholastic (New York, NY), 1988.
Trick or Treat, Scholastic (New York, NY), 1989.
April Fools, Scholastic (New York, NY), 1990.
Teacher's Pet, Scholastic (New York, NY), 1990.
Vampire, Pocket Books (New York, NY), 1991.
Fatal Secrets, Pocket Books (New York, NY), 1992.
The Mall, Pocket Books (New York, NY), 1992.
Silent Stalker, Pocket Books (New York, NY), 1993.
Help Wanted, Pocket Books (New York, NY), 1993.
The Drifter, Pocket Books (New York, NY), 1994.
The Locker, Pocket Books (New York, NY), 1994.
Someone at the Door, Pocket Books (New York, NY), 1994.
Overdue, Pocket Books (New York, NY), 1995.
Summer of Secrets, Pocket Books (New York, NY), 1996.
Starstruck, Pocket Books (New York, NY), 1996.
The House Next Door, Simon Pulse (New York, NY), 2002.
Walk of the Spirits, Speak (New York, NY), 2008.
Shadow Mirror (sequel to *Walk of the Spirits*), Speak (New York, NY), 2010.

"BUFFY" NOVEL SERIES; BASED ON THE FILM AND TELEVISION SERIES BY JOSH WHEEDON

Buffy, the Vampire Slayer, Pocket Books (New York, NY), 1992.
The Harvest, Pocket Books (New York, NY), 1997.
The Angel Chronicles 2, Pocket Books (New York, NY), 1999.

"UNSEEN" NOVEL SERIES

The Unseen, Scholastic Children's Books (London, England), 2003, published as *It Begins,* Speak (New York, NY), 2005.
The Unseen II, Scholastic Children's Books (London, England), 2004, published as *Rest in Peace,* Speak (New York, NY), 2005.
The Unseen III, Scholastic Children's Books (London, England), 2005, published as *Blood Brothers,* Speak (New York, NY), 2006.
The Unseen. IV, Scholastic Children's Books (London, England), 2005, published as *Sin and Salvation,* Speak (New York, NY), 2006.

FOR ADULTS

Scarecrow, Pocket Books, (New York, NY), 1990.
Blood Roots, Pocket Books (New York, NY), 1992.

Adaptations

Several of Cusick's books have been adapted for audiobook, including *Walk of the Spirits,* 2010.

Sidelights

While she enjoys exploring the dark side of human nature in her horror novels for teens and adults, Richie Tankersely Cusick also focuses on the challenges of growing up in novels such as *Fatal Secrets, The Locker, Shadow Mirror,* and her "Unseen" novel series. In addition, Cusick was chosen to adapt the popular 1992 screenplay for *Buffy the Vampire Slayer* into novel form as well as producing *The Harvest* and *The Angel Chronicles,* which were based on the first seasons of the popular *Buffy* television series. "Teen readers can . . . identify with her central characters, who often come

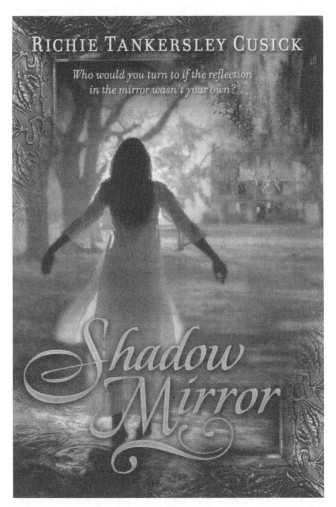

Focusing on a young woman who is capable of communicating with spirits, Richie Tankersley Cusick's Shadow Mirror *features artwork by Kamil Vojnar.* (Illustration copyright © 2010 by Kamil Vojnar. Used by permission of Speak, a division of Penguin Young Readers Group, a member of Penguin Group (USA) Inc., 345 Hudson St., New York, NY 10014. All rights reserved.)

from broken homes and must deal with difficult relationships, some familial and some romantic," Cosette Kies explained in the *St. James Guide to Young-Adult Writers*. "They often learn self-reliance in their struggles with the unknown evil and begin to understand the complexities of human behavior."

Cusick grew up in Louisiana, where mysteries and ghosts from the South's past were everywhere. She remained in the region after high-school graduation, eventually earning an English degree at the University of Southwestern Louisiana. A move to Kansas City, Missouri, followed, where she spent nine years working as a staff writer at Hallmark Cards. Composing greeting-card verses by day, Cusick wrote fiction by night, focusing on the teen horror genre that made R.L. Stine and Christopher Pike such popular novelists in the mid-1980s. After she sold the manuscript for *Evil on the Bayou*—a novel about a volunteer nurse who caretake an elderly woman in a house full of secrets—she was able to quit her job and make writing her full-time occupation.

In *Fatal Secrets* high-school senior Ryan McCauley is grieving over her sister's death in a tragic accident. The college girl had fallen through the ice, and Ryan feels guilty because they had recently fought. Ryan's single mother is consoled by one of Marissa's young college friends, whom she begins to date. Ryan soon discovers that Marissa knew about a drug stash near their house, and strange things begin to happen to Ryan who begins to believe that her sister's death might not have been an accident after all. Stacey M. Conrad, reviewing *Fatal Secrets* for *Kliatt,* wrote that Cusick's "story has a nice mix of suspense and romance."

In *The Locker* Cusick crafts a thriller about a young girl named Marlee whose parents were killed in an accident. She and her brother now live with a free-spirited aunt who is constantly moving, and when the story opens, Marlee is again the new girl in school. She soon finds out that the hall locker assigned to her once belonged to a female student who mysteriously disappeared. Now, when Marlee opens the locker, she sees a horrifying vision. Apparently Marlee is able to see events that have happened to people when she comes into contact with their possessions. She resigns herself to solving the mystery of the girl who disappeared and herself becomes involved in unbelievable events.

Elaine Baran Black, writing in *School Library Journal,* called *The House Next Door* a "hauntingly good read." In this story by Cusick, Emma Donavan accepts a dare from her twin brother to spend the night in the creepy house next door, which is said to be haunted. While there, she meets a ghost that turns out to be her true love from another lifetime and who was killed trying to rescue her from her abusive father. His spirit is trapped and Emma risks her life to set him free, while her brother and friend Val try to stop her before history is repeated. Reviewing *The House Next Door* in *Booklist,* Roger Leslie praised Cusick for her ability to craft

Cusick's four-part "The Unseen" series includes the mesmerizing installment **Blood Brothers.** (Cover art copyright © 2005 by Tony Sahara. Reproduced with permission of Speak, a division of Penguin Young Readers Group, a member of Penguin Group (USA) Inc., 345 Hudson St., New York, NY 10014. All rights reserved.)

"brisk dialogue, ingenious plot twists, and nerve-wracking suspense," and *Kliatt* critic Rebecca Rabinowitz dubbed the novel an "intense and riveting ghost story."

In *Walk of the Spirits* readers meet Miranda Barnes, a young woman who moves with her mom from hurricane-ravaged Florida to St. Yvette, Louisiana, where her grandfather lives in the family's ancestral home. While getting used to her new surroundings, Miranda soon finds that she has a greater problem: she hears whispers and voices and sees strange shadows and reflections that turn out to be caused by spirits of the dead. Etienne, a boy she is crushing on in school, is the only one who does not think she is losing her mind. The knowledge that she has a special gift inherited from her grandfather comes as little consolation when Miranda realizes that this gift brings with it the responsibility to help these earthbound spirits find peace. Cusick's sequel, *Shadow Mirror*, finds Miranda commun-

ing with the dead while also building a relationship with the understanding—and adorable—Etienne, even as a secret from his past threatens to derail their budding romance. "Romance, danger and supernatural thrills abound," noted a *Kirkus Reviews* writer in reviewing *Walk of the Spirits.*

In Cusick's "The Unseen" novels, which include *It Begins, Rest in Peace, Blood Brothers,* and *Sin and Salvation,* a tumble into a girl's open and occupied grave at the local cemetery signals the start of a series of supernatural events involving Lucy Dennison. Locating the murdered girl's still-living brother, Byron, gives Lucy some peace of mind as well as a confidante in Byron when frightening nightmares begin combining with the sense that someone—or some thing—will not let her out of its sight. Continued feelings of foreboding are supplemented by sadness at the loss of Byron during a tragic accident in *Rest in Peace,* and when Lucy meets her dead friend's long-lost brother in *Blood Brothers* she worries that he may have a sinister side. *Sin and Salvation* concludes the "Unseen" series and resolves Lucy's many questions even as it presents her with a crucial challenge. "The atmosphere of foreboding" in *It Begins* "is wonderfully done, and there's plenty of mystery to make the reader hungry for more," asserted Deirdre Root in her *Kliatt* review of the "Unseen" series opener, and *Rest in Peace* "is even better . . . , as the plot thickens and the red herrings fly."

"I've always believed in the supernatural," Cusick once told *SATA,* "and I grew up with a ghost in my house. I've always loved scary books and movies—even though my parents didn't want me to watch horror films. I'd sometimes manage to sneak in and turn on the television when my folks weren't in the room. In Girl Scouts, I was the troop storyteller and would make up tales of haunted houses and murderers. Next to Christmas, Halloween is my favorite holiday, and I really decorate, including a hanged woman in our front hallway, a dead body laid out in our parlor, and tombstones around our front porch.

"I've always loved to write; being an only child, I found it a great way to entertain myself and invent friends and adventures. My best buddies and mentors were my dog and my grandmother Dereatha Tankersley. She has always been my biggest inspiration.

"I also love working at home. . . . My studio is upstairs at the back of our house, and my favorite tree . . . stands guard outside my window. I love storms, rain, fog, and dark winter weather; my favorite part of the day is twilight, that dream state between dark and light. I love to watch the seasons change . . . as I sit and write at my haunted roll-top desk, which belonged to a funeral director in the 1800s.

"Writing is very important to me: being able to create people, adventures, worlds where readers can lose themselves for a little while. It's very hard work, but very rewarding. I hate it when a book ends and I have to tell my characters goodbye. I get so close to them that they linger in my own personality for days . . . and I guess when it comes right down to it, I never really lose them. They just become another part of me . . . or perhaps they were all along!"

Biographical and Critical Sources

BOOKS

Drew, Bernard, *The 100 Most Popular Young-Adult Authors,* Libraries Unlimited (Englewood, CO), 1996.
St. James Guide to Young-Adult Writers, St. James Press (Detroit, MI), 1999.
Science Fiction and Fantasy Literature, 1975-1991, Gale (Detroit, MI), 1992.

PERIODICALS

Booklist, January 1, 2002, Roger Leslie, review of *The House Next Door,* p. 841.

Kirkus Reviews, March 15, 2008, review of *Walk of the Spirits*; January 15, 2010, review of *Shadow Mirror.*
Kliatt, April, 1992, Stacey M. Conrad, review of *Fatal Secrets,* pp. 4, 6; March, 2002, Rebecca Rabinowitz, review of *The House Next Door,* p. 20; September, 2005, Deirdre Root, reviews of *It Begins* and *Rest in Peace,* both p. 26.
School Library Journal, February, 2002, Elaine Baran Black, review of *The House Next Door,* p. 130; October, 2005, Emily Rodriguez, review of *It Begins,* p. 158; June, 2008, Christi Voth Esterle, review of *Walk of the Spirits,* p. 136.
Voice of Youth Advocates, April, 2010, review of *Shadow Mirror,* p. 67.

ONLINE

Richie Tankersely Cusick Home Page, http://richietankerselycusick.com (July 1, 2011).
SlayerLit Web site, http://slayerlit.us/ (July 1, 2011), "Richie Tankersley Cusick."*

D-E

DAY, Susie 1975-

Personal
Born 1975, in Penarth, Wales.

Addresses
Home—Oxford, England. *E-mail*—susie@susieday.com.

Career
Author of young-adult fiction. Worked as a tour guide; resident warden at an international boarding school in Oxford, England.

Awards, Honors
British Broadcasting Corporation Talent Children's Fiction Prize, 2003, for *Whump! In Which Bill Falls 632 Miles down a Manhole.*

Writings

Whump! In Which Bill Falls 632 Miles down a Manhole, BBC Children's Books (London, England), 2004.

Big Woo!: Serafina67 Urgently Requires Life, Marion Lloyd (London, England), 2008, published as *Serafina67 *Urgently Requires Life*,*Scholastic Press (New York, NY), 2008.

Girl Meets Cake, Marion Lloyd (London, England), 2009, published as *My Invisible Boyfriend,* Scholastic Press (New York, NY), 2010.

Sidelights
Welsh-born writer Susie Day got her big career break when she won the 2003 British Broadcasting Corporation's Talent Children's Fiction Prize for the manuscript that became her first published novel, *Whump! In Which Bill Falls 632 Miles down a Manhole.* Day's whimsical view of life has continued to inspire her writing, pro-

ducing the young-adult novels *Serafina67 *Urgently Requires Life** and *My Invisible Boyfriend.* Adolescence is "such a fascinatingly horrible period of your life," Day noted on her home page in discussing her decision to write for teens. "You're enduring this continuous

Cover of Susie Day's young-adult novel **My Invisible Boyfriend,** *in which a teen's fictitious love interest creates several real-life problem.*
(Jacket photography © 2010 by Michael Frost. Reproduced with permission of Scholastic Press, an imprint of Scholastic, Inc.)

identity crisis, you're supposed to make all these important life-changing decisions even though you don't even control what kind of milk you pour on your cereal, and adults want to tell you how very lucky you are all the time. You're doing lots of things for the first time, which makes things much more likely to go horribly wrong—and Things Going Horribly Wrong is integral to a lot of storytelling."

The heroine of *Serafina67 *Urgently Requires Life** is Serafina Duffy, a teen whose new screen name is a way to project her very mature new self in her new Web log on her very new laptop computer. Disguised in Serafina's animated blog entries are worries about her father's upcoming marriage, her friend's eating disorder, and her mom's moodiness, not to mention the typical adolescent drama involving boys, dating, and friendships. Sarafina's goal is to get everything sorted out by the blog's first anniversary. She keeps her optimistic even when things seem to be spiraling out of control in a novel that Shari Fesko praised in *School Library Journal* for its "sympathetic" heroine and intriguing blog format.

Originally published as *Girl Meets Cake*, *My Invisible Boyfriend* finds another teen attempting to solve her problems in a creative way. For Heidi, a sophomore at a private boarding school where both her parents work, a small lie and a secret-agent raincoat have been the key to achieving social success. The problem is now that the lie—a made-up boyfriend named Ed with an online profile that makes him sound like the perfect guy—has inspired way too much interest in the fictitious beau: her friends are even e-mailing Ed for advice! Further complications to Heidi's school life include a production of Shakespeare's *Twelfth Night* and a string of anonymous messages sent by someone who claims know the truth about the mysterious Ed. Reviewing *My Invisible Boyfriend* for *School Library Journal*, Kelley Siegrist dubbed Day's novel "a fun read sprinkled with a bit of teen angst."

Biographical and Critical Sources

PERIODICALS

Bulletin of the Center for Children's Books, July-August, 2010, Deborah Stevenson, review of *My Invisible Boyfriend*, p. 478.

Kirkus Reviews, March 1, 2010, review of *My Invisible Boyfriend*.

Publishers Weekly, March 22, 2010, review of *My Invisible Boyfriend*, p. 71.

School Library Journal, March, 2009, Shari Fesko, review of *Serafina 67 *Urgently Requires Life**, p. 143; March, 2010, Kelley Siegrist, review of *My Invisible Boyfriend*, p. 154.

ONLINE

Susie Day Home Page, http://www.susieday.com (July 12, 2011).

Wondrous Reads Web site, http://www.wondrousreads.com/ (May 19, 2005), interview with Day.*

*   *   *

DERTING, Kimberly 1968-

Personal

Born 1968, in WA; married; children: three.

Addresses

Home—WA. *E-mail*—kim@kimberlyderting.com.

Career

Novelist.

Writings

The Body Finder, Harper (New York, NY), 2010.
Desires of the Dead, HarperCollins (New York, NY), 2011.

Sidelights

A native of the Pacific Northwest, Kimberly Derting writes novels for young adults that feature supernatural elements. A writer since the seventh grade, when she took her first journalism class, Derting quipped on her home page that the weather near her home in Seattle, Washington has helped to inspire her novels *The Body*

Kimberly Derting (Photograph by Celeste Morrision. Reproduced by permission.)

Finder and *Desires of the Dead.* The region's overcast days make it "the ideal place to be writing anything dark or creepy . . . ," she asserted; "A gloomy day can set the perfect mood."

In *The Body Finder* Derting introduces Violet Ambrose, a high-school junior living in a small town in Washington that is currently being terrorized by a serial killer. While Violet spends much of her time mooning over increasingly handsome friend and classmate Jay Heaton, she also recognizes that her long-held ability to sense the presence of the corporeal dead also extends to those among the living who have murdered others. As more and more girls fall victim to violent deaths at the killer's hand, Violet realizes that she may be able to end the terror with Jay's help. Teens will enjoy the novel's secondary plot, which focuses on the budding romance between Violet and Jay, predicted a *Kirkus Reviews* writer, and in *Booklist* Frances Bradburn deemed *The Body Finder* "a real page-turner" that "will have readers checking behind themselves and refusing to go anywhere alone." In her fiction debut Derting "demonstrates unusual skill in weaving together contemporary

teenage preoccupations with its paranormal plot twist," wrote a *Publishers Weekly* critic, the contributor going on to hail Derting as "a promising author."

Violet returns in *Desires of the Dead,* and her ability to sense the presence of murderers and their victims once again threatens to draw the sixteen year old into danger. Although her relationship with Jay seems stable, he spends so much time with his new friend Mike Russo that Violet begins to worry. Then the body of a missing boy surfaces and she quickly becomes part of the FBI's investigation into the crime. Ultimately, a link is found between Mike and the young victim, forcing Violet to confront a mystery that may threaten her love life and her own life as well. Reviewing *Desires of the Dead* in *Booklist,* Shelle Rosenfeld praised Derting for melding "suspense, steamy romance, [and] supernatural elements" into a "fast-paced, compelling read," while Rayna Patton predicted in *Voice of Youth Advocates* that "a perfect boyfriend and a suspenseful plot will keep teens turning pages." Also appraising the "absorbing" novel, a *Kirkus Reviews* writer maintained that the author's characters and story show marked improvement over *The Body Finder.* "Imaginative, convincing, and successful suspense" characterize *Desires of the Dead,* according to the critic, and "Derting convinces readers to believe in Violet's supernatural abilities."

Biographical and Critical Sources

PERIODICALS

Booklist, October 15, 2009, Frances Bradburn, review of *The Body Finder,* p. 58; March 15, 2011, Shelle Rosenfeld, review of *Desires of the Dead,* p. 56.
Bulletin of the Center for Children's Books, April, 2010, Kate Quealy-Gainer, review of *The Body Finder,* p. 331.
Kirkus Reviews, January 1, 2010, review of *The Body Finder;* February 1, 2011, review of *Desires of the Dead.*
Library Media Connection, March-April, 2010, Lu Ann Staheli, review of *The Body Finder,* p. 70.
Publishers Weekly, March 1, 2010, review of *The Body Finder,* p. 54.
School Library Journal, May, 2010, Anthony C. Doyle, review of *The Body Finder,* p. 110.
Voice of Youth Advocates, December, 2009, Etiene Vallee, review of *The Body Finder,* p. 419; April, 2011, Rayna Patton, review of *Desires of the Dead,* p. 79.

ONLINE

Kimberly Derting Home Page, http://www.kimberlyderting.com (June 20, 2011).

Cover of Derting's YA thriller **The Body Finder,** *in which a teen realizes that she may hold the key to discovering the identity of a local serial killer.* (Jacket art copyright © 2010 by Gustavo Marx/MergeLeftReps. Reproduced with permission of MergeLeftReps, artist's agent.)

*   *   *

EMOND, Stephen 1979(?)-

Personal

Born c. 1979, in CT. *Education:* Middlesex Community Technical College (Middletown, CT), earned degree.

Stephen Emond (Photograph by Cori Payne. Reproduced by permission.)

Addresses

Home—Middletown, CT. *E-mail*—emoboyrocks@
yahoo.com.

Career

Comic creator and screenwriter.

Awards, Honors

Andrew McMeel/Follett College Store Tomorrow's Top
Cartoonist talent search winner, 1999.

Writings

Happyface, Little, Brown & Co. (New York, NY), 2010.
Winter Town, Little, Brown & Co. (New York, NY), 2011.

Author of comic strips, including "Steverino," "Emo
Boy," and "Full House." Author of screenplay based on
"Emo Boy." Contributor to anthology *Strip Search: Re-
vealing Today's Best College Cartoonist,* Andrews Mc-
Meel (Kansas City, MO), 1999.

Author's work has been translated into German.

Sidelights

Connecticut native Stephen Emond first made a name
for himself as a college student when he beat out artists
in more high-profile art-education programs as the winner of publisher Andrew McMeel's nationwide Strip
Search talent contest for emerging cartoonists. Emond's
passion for cartooning began in his teens, and his innovative adult work includes the "Emo Boy" comic and
the teen novels *Happyface* and *Winter Town,* both which
feature a mix of visual and verbal storytelling.

Emond's first comic strip was "Steverino," an autobiographical sequential-art story that he released in monthly
twenty-five-page segment and distributed to friends,
family, and other interested parties. "'Steverino' was me
pouring my lonely heart out, a sad comic about a naïve
lovelorn boy," he explained in a guest post for *Teen-
reads.com.* "I barely hid myself in the work; it was my
way of saying all the things I was too shy to say aloud."
Since surviving adolescence, Emond has become less-
grounded in realism. "I [still] used a lot of life experience and how I felt as a teen in writing 'Emo Boy,'" he
explained of his more-recent comic. "But here I ob-
scured myself a bit more, concentrating more on outlandish concepts and story arcs." First published as a
Xeroxed mini-comic that tells the story of an angst-
ridden teen who hopes to harness his out-of-control super powers for constructive uses, "Emo Boy" was eventually picked up by SLG Publishing and published in
comic-book form.

Through a fan of "Emo Boy" who also worked in New
York City publishing, Emond had the opportunity to
create the unique illustrated Y-A novel *Happy Face,* a
story that *School Library Journal* contributor Joyce Adams Burner described as "by turns funny, wrenching,

**Emond moves from comic books to illustrated prose in his uniquely il-
lustrated teen novel Happyface.** (Copyright © 2010 by Stephen Emond. Hachette
Book Group, Inc. Reproduced with permission of Little, Brown & Company, a division of
Hachette Book Group, Inc.)

quirky, and redemptive." Formatted as the illustrated journal of a shy high-school sophomore who expresses himself through his art, *Happyface* follows the ups and downs of the school year as he suffers the pangs of unrequited love, worries over his parents' disintegrating marriage, and feels the pressures of following in the path of a high-achieving older brother. Midway through the year something pivotal (but unnamed) happens and he winds up in a new school. The teen decides to deal with the upheaval by joking around and pretending that everything is wonderful. Describing *Happy Face* as "a sketchbook of sorts" that also contains instant-message threads and e-mail interchanges, Emond discussed his concept for the book on his home page. "It's a journal, but it's illustrated. A little of the story is told in comic form, there's realistic beautiful drawings and silly cartoony ones. I thought it showed what you really can't write. It was very personal and intimate, and it does look different from anything else." In tracking his narrator's gradual realization that his upbeat mask is neither sincere or honest, Emond produces in *Happy Face*, what a *Kirkus Reviews* writer praised as an "engaging and absolutely heartfelt tale," and Matthew Weaver asserted in a *Voice of Youth Advocates* review that the author/illustrator "has mastered the voice of the awkward adolescent male" in "a character readers will come to love." Commenting on the illustrations in *Happyface*, a *Publishers Weekly* reviewer was equally laudatory, noting that "they can be whimsical, thoughtful, boyishly sarcastic, off-the-cuff, or achingly beautiful."

Biographical and Critical Sources

PERIODICALS

Kirkus Reviews, March 1, 2010, review of *Happyface.*
Publishers Weekly, January 25, 2010, review of *Happyface,* p 120.
School Library Journal, March, 2010, Joyce Adams Burner, review of *Happyface,* p. 156.
Voice of Youth Advocates, June, 2010, Matthew Weaver, review of *Happyface,* p. 152.

ONLINE

Stephen Emond Home Page, http://www.stephenemond.com (April 20, 2011).
Teenreads Web log, http://www.teenreads.com/blog/ (March 3, 2010), Stephen Emond, "Journals and Self-Expression."

*   *   *

ENGEL, Christiane

Personal

Born in Bremen, Germany; immigrated to United Kingdom, 2001. *Education:* School of Art (Kassal, Ger-

many), degree (animation and illustration); Leeds Metropolitan University, M.A. (graphic art and design).

Addresses

Home—London, England. *Agent*—Good Illustration, Ltd., 11-15 Betterton St., Covent Garden WC2H 9BP, England. *E-mail*—me@desertfriends.com.

Career

Illustrator, author, textile designer, and handlettering artist. Formerly worked as a translator. *Exhibitions:* Work exhibited at Portland Prints Society, Portland, OR; Drawgasmic Gallery, St. Louis, MO; and Inkygoodness, London, England.

Writings

SELF-ILLUSTRATED

Louis and Bobo: We Are Moving, Chrysalis Books (London, England), 2005.
Knick Knack Paddy Whack (with musical CD), vocals by SteveSongs, Barefoot Books (Cambridge, MA), 2008.
Twinkle Twinkle Little Star (pop-up book), Silver Dolphin Books, 2009.
Little Green Helpers Grow! (interactive board book), Campbell Books, 2010.
Little Green Helpers Recycle! (interactive board book), Campbell Books, 2010.

Also creator of books for Froebel Publishing.

SELF-ILLUSTRATED; "BUSY, BUSY BABIES" BOARD-BOOK SERIES

Very Hungry, Chrysalis Books (London, England), 2006.
Art Class, Chrysalis Books (London, England), 2006.
All Dressed Up!, Chrysalis Books (London, England), 2006.
A Busy Day, Chrysalis Books (London, England), 2006.

ILLUSTRATOR

Emma Dodd, *Grande o pequeña, es mi pelota,* Combel (Barcelona, Spain), 2004.
Crystal Bowman and Cindy Kenney, *My Read and Rhyme Bible Storybook,* Tyndale House Publishers (Carol Stream, IL), 2009.
Ellen Olson-Brown, *Ooh La La Polka-Dot Boots,* Tricycle Press (Berkeley, CA), 2010.

Contributor of illustrations to periodicals.

Sidelights

Christiane Engel is an illustrator whose work in acrylics, pen-and-ink, and digital collage is enlivened by its humor, retro appeal, and use of typographical elements.

Christiane Engel created the art for Ellen Olson-Brown's amusing and upbeat story in **Ooh La La Polka-Dot Boots.** (Illustration copyright © 2010 by Christiane Engel. Used by permission of Tricycle Press, an imprint of the Crown Publishing Group, a division of Random House, Inc.)

Born in Germany, Engel now works in London, England, where her artwork has been commissioned for use in advertising as well as in magazines, textile designs, and as part of promotional campaigns. Although her images have been popular in fashion and editorial illustration, they have also found a natural fit within children's literature. Engel has quickly established a reputation for creating engaging self-illustrated books for very young children, and has also been sought out by publishers to create illustrations for stories by other writers.

Engel received training in animation and illustration in Germany before moving to England to earn her master's degree in graphic art and design. Her master's project, a series of stories featuring a boy named Louis and his dog Bobo, eventually resulted in her first published book, *Louis and Bobo: We Are Moving*, released in 2005. At this point Engel was supporting herself with various day jobs and pursuing her illustration career in her free time. Picture books soon began to take up more

of her time as she created the "Busy, Busy Babies" board-book series as well as starting work on *Knick Knack Paddy Whack,* a combination counting book and songbook featuring a CD with vocals by SteveSongs. Reviewing *Knick Knack Paddy Whack* in *Booklist*, Hazel Rochman praised Engel's "bright . . . digital collage" art depicting children of many cultures and concluded that her colorful and animated images combine with the "music [to] make for joyful sharing many times over." "With colorful acrylic and collage illustrations and varying fonts, each spread is alive with activity," asserted Jane Marino in reviewing the same book for *School Library Journal.*

Another illustration project that captures Engel's unique illustration style, Ellen Olson-Brown's *Ooh La La Polka-Dot Boots* focuses on busy children who are engaged in a variety of outdoor activities that becomes more fun when one is wearing colorful, flamboyant footwear. Joining what *School Library Journal* critic Lynn K. Vanca praised as a "bouncy text," Engel's "multicultural cast . . . showcases an array of fashion styles" in art that "offers many little details for [young readers] . . . to find." The "bright primary colors" featured in the book's "acrylic-and-digital collage illustrations are ideally suited for the preschool audience," concluded a *Kirkus Reviews* writer, and in *Booklist* Hazel Rochman predicted that *Ooh La La Polka-Dot Boots* will inspire children to "move on to their own dress-up games with the duds they love."

Engel described her work process to *Pikaland* online interviewer Amy Ng. "I always decide on a setting first, . . . so I get to do some virtual traveling," she explained. "I also write and scribble a lot about the characters that I'm illustrating even if the story was written by someone else; it helps me to visualize them." In her work, she begins with a pencil sketch, then adds color digitally. Asked to list her inspirations, Engel casts a broad net: "Films, nature, folk tales, lino cuts, old signs, old maps, wildlife documentaries, German Expressionists, factual books for kids, geography, lettering, the outdoors, autumn, holiday snap shots or traveling itself and the things that happen, stories in general, social interaction, music with lyrics that put images in my head."

Biographical and Critical Sources

PERIODICALS

Booklist, April 1, 2008, Hazel Rochman, review of *Knick Knack Paddy Whack,* p. 53; January 1, 2010, Hazel Rochman, review of *Ooh La La Polka-Dot Boots,* p. 98.

Kirkus Reviews, March 1, 2010, review of *Ooh La La Polka-Dot Boots.*

School Library Journal, May, 2008, Jane Marino, review of *Knick Knack Paddy Whack,* p. 115; April, 2010, Lynn K. Vanca, review of *Ooh La La Polka-Dot Boots,* p. 136.

ONLINE

Christiane Engel Home Page, http://www.desertfriends. com (April 28, 2011).

Pikaland Web log, http://pikaland.com/ (March 12, 2010), Amy Ng, interview with Engel.*

*   *   *

ENGLE, Margarita 1951-

Personal

Born September 2, 1951, in Pasadena, CA; daughter of Martin (an artist) and Eloisa (a quilter) Mondrus; married Curtis E. Engle (a research entomologist), 1978; children: Victor, Nicole. *Ethnicity:* "Cuban-American."

Education: California State Polytechnic University, B.S., 1974; Iowa State University, M.S., 1977; doctoral study at University of California, Riverside, 1983. *Politics:* "Human rights advocate." *Religion:* Christian. *Hobbies and other interests:* Horsemanship, western equitation, trail riding.

Addresses

Agent—Julie Castiglia, 1155 Camino Del Mar, Ste. 510, Del Mar, CA 92014. *E-mail*—margarita@margarita engle.com.

Career

Botanist, poet, novelist, and journalist. California State Polytechnic University, Pomona, associate professor of agronomy, 1978-82.

Member

Pen USA West, Amnesty International, Freedom House of Human Rights, Freedom to Write Committee.

Awards, Honors

CINTAS fellowship, Arts International, 1994-95; San Diego Book Award, 1996, for *Skywriting;* Willow Review Poetry Award, 2005; Américas Award for Children's and Young-Adult Literature, Consortium of Latin-American Studies Programs, Pura Belpré Award, American Library Association (ALA), International Reading Association Children's Book Award and Teachers' Choice award, ALA Best Book for Young Adults selection, Notable Children's Books in the Language Arts selection, National Council of Teachers of English, Best Books designation, Bank Street College of Education, Best Books for the Teen Age selection, New York Public Library, and Cooperative Children's Book Center Choice selection, all c. 2008, all for *The Poet Slave of Cuba;* Américas Award, 2008, and Pura Belpré Award, Newbery Medal Honor Book designation, Jane Addams Award, Claudia Lewis Poetry Award, Lee Bennett Hopkins Honor designation, ALA Notable Book selection, and Notable Social Studies Book selection, National Council of Social Studies (NCSS)/ Children's Book Council (CBC), all c. 2009, all for *The Surrender Tree;* Sydney Taylor Book Award, Association of Jewish Libraries, Paterson Prize, Américas Award Commended Title, and 100 Titles for Reading and Sharing selection, New York Public Library, all c. 2009, all for *Tropical Secrets;* Pura Belpré Honor Book designation, Jane Addams Award finalist, NCSS/CBC Notable Social Studies Book selection, IRA Notable Book for a Global Society selection, and California Book Award finalist, all 2010, all for *The Firefly Letters;* NCSS/CBC Notable Social Studies Book selection, 2010, for *Summer Birds;* ALA Best Books for Young Adults listee nomination, 2011, for *Hurricane Dancers.*

Writings

Singing to Cuba (adult novel), Arte Público Press (Houston, TX), 1993.

Skywriting: A Novel of Cuba (adult novel), Bantam (New York, NY), 1995.

The Poet Slave of Cuba: A Biography of Juan Francisco Manzano (nonfiction for children), illustrated by Sean Qualls, Henry Holt (New York, NY), 2006.

The Surrender Tree: Poems of Cuba's Struggle for Freedom (for young adults), Henry Holt (New York, NY), 2008.

Tropical Secrets: Holocaust Refugees in Cuba, Henry Holt (New York, NY), 2009.

Summer Birds: The Butterflies of Maria Merian, illustrated by Julie Paschkis, Holt (New York, NY), 2010.

The Firefly Letters: A Suffragette's Journey to Cuba, Henry Holt (New York, NY), 2010.

Hurricane Dancers: The First Caribbean Pirate Shipwreck, Henry Holt (New York, NY), 2011.

The Wild Book (verse novel), illustrated by Yuyi Morales, Harcourt (New York, NY), 2012.

Contributor to periodicals, including *Atlanta Review, Bilingual Review, California Quarterly, Caribbean Writer, Hawai'i Pacific Review,* and *Nimrod.*

Adaptations

The Surrender Tree and *Tropical Secrets* were adapted for audiobook by Listening Library, 2008 and 2009 respectively.

Sidelights

The author of adult novels as well as books for young readers, Cuban-American writer Margarita Engle has been honored with some of the top awards in her field, including the Pura Belpré award, the Américas award, and the prestigious Newbery Medal. In addition to her award-winning free-verse novels *The Surrender Tree: Poems of Cuba's Struggle for Freedom* and *The Wild Book,* Engle has also authored the picture books *The Poet Slave of Cuba: A Biography of Juan Francisco Manzano* and *Summer Birds: The Butterflies of Maria Merian,* the latter illustrated by Julie Paschkis. Her stories for older children include *Tropical Secrets: Holocaust Refugees in Cuba* and *Hurricane Dancers: The First Caribbean Pirate Shipwreck. The Firefly Letters: A Suffragette's Journey to Cuba,* Engle's fictionalized narrative of a middle-aged Swedish traveler who befriended two other women during her visit to the island in 1851, received the sort of critical reception that has been characteristic when discussing her work. "Using elegant free verse and alternating among each character's point of view, Engle offers powerful glimpses into Cuban life," noted *School Library Journal* contributor Leah J. Sparks, while a *Kirkus Reviews* critic wrote of the author that her "poetry is a gossamer thread of subtle beauty weaving together three memorable characters who together find hope and courage."

Engle fell in love with reading and writing as a young child. While growing up, her mother instilled her with a love for Cuba, recounting to the young Engle many stories of her homeland. Despite Engle's love of stories and poetry, she decided to go to school to study agronomy and botany, a form of rebellion as well as a way to connect with the wilderness she had missed while growing up in Los Angeles. She eventually became a professor of agronomy and married Curtis Engle, an agricultural entomologist. While raising her two children, she revisited her love of writing, submitting her haiku and having it published, as well as writing editorial columns for news organizations. After a trip to Cuba in 1991, thirty years after visiting the island as a child, Engle was inspired to write two adult novels about Cuba: *Singing to Cuba* and *Skywriting: A Novel of Cuba.*

While traveling in Cuba, Engle learned the story of Juan Franciso Manzano, a slave who became a well-known poet. She struggled for years to write an historical novel about Manzano, but the words never came. Eventually, she changed directions and crafted a picture-book biography of Manzano in verse. A *Kirkus Reviews* contributor called *The Poet Slave of Cuba*—which won the Américas Award and the Pura Belpré Award—a "powerful and accessible biography." Engle "achieves an impressive synergy between poetry and biography," wrote a critic for *Publishers Weekly.* Commenting on Engle's depiction of Manzano telling himself stories while being beaten by his owners, Hazel Rochman wrote in *Booklist* that "today's readers will hear the stories . . . and never forget them," while in *School Library Journal* Carol Jones Collins concluded that *The Poet Slave of Cuba* "should be read by young and old, black and white, Anglo and Latino."

Like *The Poet Slave of Cuba, The Surrender Tree* is a story told in poetry that focuses on the life of a Cuban slave. Rosa la Bayamesa was born into slavery, but after she was freed by her owner she became a rebel, fighting for Cuban independence from Spain. She worked as a nurse, healing the wounded on both sides of the conflict. "*The Surrender Tree* is hauntingly beautiful, revealing pieces of Cuba's troubled past through the poetry of hidden moments," wrote Jill Heritage Maza, the *School Library Journal* critic adding that the small details in Engle's poetry illuminate the larger story. Jane Lopez-Santillana, writing in *Horn Book,* called Engle's poetry "haunting," and a *Kirkus Reviews* contributor concluded of *The Surrender Tree* that "young readers will come away inspired by these portraits of courageous ordinary people."

Engle once again returns readers to Cuba in *Tropical Secrets,* but here the events occurring throughout Europe due to World War II overshadow the beauty of the island for at least one young boy. For Daniel, Cuba is far from his native Germany, and it is also the last port of call for the thirteen year old since his ship was repelled from both Ellis Island and a hoped-for safe harbor in Canada. Like many of his shipmates, Daniel is a Jewish refugee escaping Nazi persecution; without his parents, he eventually finds others—such as the elderly Russian Jew David—who share his faith and his European cultural heritage and learns to make Cuba his home. Praising Engle's free-verse text, Geri Diorio added in *School Library Journal* that *Tropical Secrets* will captivate even reluctant readers due to its "eloquent poems and compelling characters." Engle's "tireless drive to give voice to the silenced in Cuban history provides fresh options for young readers," asserted a *Kirkus Reviews* writer, noting the author's characteristic use of "alternating first-person narrative poems." Also praising the evocative novel, a *Publishers Weekly* critic concluded of *Tropical Secrets* that "Engle gracefully packs a lot of information into a spare and elegant narrative that will make this historical moment accessible to a wide range of readers."

Described by *School Library Journal* contributor Jeffrey Hastings as a "welcome antidote" to the many "one-sided accounts of [the] brave European explorers" whose exploits established the historical record of the so-called Age of Conquest, *Hurricane Dancers* focuses on the half-Taino slave Quebrado, who has spent most of his life on the Caribbean, working aboard a succession of Spanish pirate ships. Because of the boy's knowledge of the native language, his current captain employs Quebrado as translator, hoping to deceive the locals when they harbor their vessel. When a severe storm destroys the pirate ship, Quebrado swims to shore where he now has the chance to create a new future for himself. He also has the chance to reconcile his past by

meting out justice to those of his former masters who also survived and are now prisoners of the Taino. While Quebrado is a fictional character, the other central actors in the story are real people, and Engle documents their stories in the source material contained in a concluding author's note. Employing "potent rhythms, sounds, and original, unforgettable imagery," in the words of *Booklist* contributor Gillian Engberg, *Hurricane Dancers* successfully "capture[s] elemental identity questions and the infinite sorrows of slavery and dislocation." Hastings deemed the novel both "unique and inventive," predicting that the author's "highly readable" verse will "provide . . . plenty of fodder for discussion" among thoughtful readers. Also praising the novel, a *Kirkus Reviews* writer asserted that the five intertwining verse narratives in *Hurricane Dancer* "work together elegantly" to further Engle's study of "issues of captivity and freedom in the historical setting of her ancestors."

Engle turns to younger readers in *Summer Birds,* which is set in Germany during the seventeenth century and focuses on thirteen-year-old Maria Sibylla Merian. Maria is fascinated by butterflies (then called "summer birds") and spends a great deal of time observing them. As she watches caterpillars spin cocoons and emerge as winged creatures, she questions the prevailing scientific wisdom that accepts spontaneous generation: the belief that insects can be created from decomposing earth or

Margarita Engle's biographical picture book Summer Birds *features colorful stylized illustrations by Julia Paschkis.* (Illustration copyright © 2010 by Julie Paschkis. Reproduced with permission of Henry Holt & Company, LLC.)

plant material. Although her view is considered somewhat heretical, Maria has the artistic and observational skills to document her theory, and her paintings and writings eventually influenced Swedish botanist and taxonomist Carl Linnaeus. In addition to providing readers with a "fascinating glimpse of a woman far head of her time," *Summer Birds* "offers a fresh perspective on the study of insects," according to *School Library Journal* critic Carol S. Surges, and a *Kirkus Reviews* writer noted that Paschkis's "rich, gouache folk-style paintings" capture Merian's "joy in the natural world."

Engle once noted: "I write to express my hopes, passions, fears, and beliefs. I write to communicate, explore, and understand. Usually I am haunted by a theme, or by characters, a setting, or events. Until I have experimented with them, I do not understand them clearly. I go through a slow process of trial and error, false starts, wrong turns, and humbling misjudgments. For every one hundred publishable pages, I have discarded perhaps 1,000 pages of 'error.' The process is emotionally exhausting, but I know I am always striving to be honest about the general themes of freedom and faith, and about specific tales of the search for freedoms, both personal and political. I have been deeply influenced by the suffering of my relatives in Cuba and by my love for the island, despite its desperation."

Biographical and Critical Sources

PERIODICALS

Booklist, February 15, 2006, Hazel Rochman, review of *The Poet Slave of Cuba: A Biography of Juan Francisco Manzano,* p. 95; March 15, 2008, Hazel Rochman, review of *The Surrender Tree: Poems of Cuba's Struggle for Freedom,* p. 53; January 1, 2009, Hazel Rochman, review of *Tropical Secrets: Holocaust Refugees in Cuba,* p. 74; December 15, 2009, Hazel Rochman, review of *Firefly Letters: A Suffragette's Journey to Cuba,* p. 32; January 1, 2010, Jeannine Atkins, interview with Engle, p. S38; March 15, 2010, Gillian Engberg, review of *Summer Birds: The Butterflies of Maria Merian,* p. 43; January 1, 2011, Gillian Engberg, review of *Hurricane Dancers: The First Caribbean Pirate Shipwreck,* p. 88.

Bulletin of the Center for Children's Books, April, 2010, Maggie Hommel, review of *The Firefly Letters,* p. 334.

Fresno Bee, February 18, 2008, Felicia Cousart Matlosz, "Paying Homage to a Poet."

Horn Book, July-August, 2006, Lelac Almagor, review of *The Poet Slave of Cuba,* p. 459; July-August, 2008, Jane Lopez-Santillana, review of *The Surrender Tree,* p. 465; March-April, 2010, Sarah Ellis, review of *The Firefly Letters,* p. 54.

Kirkus Reviews, March 15, 2006, review of *The Poet Slave of Cuba,* p. 289; March 15, 2008, review of *The Surrender Tree*; February 1, 2009, review of *Tropical Secrets*; January 1, 2010, review of *The Firefly Letters*; March 1, 2010, review of *Summer Birds;* January 15, 2011, review of *Hurricane Dancers.*

MELUS, spring, 1998, Gisele M. Requeña, "The Sounds of Silence: Remembering and Creating in Margarita Engle's *Singing to Cuba,* p. 147.

Publishers Weekly, June 5, 1995, review of *Skywriting,* p. 52; April 17, 2006, review of *The Poet Slave of Cuba,* p. 190; April 6, 2009, review of *Tropical Secrets,* p. 48; March 15, 2010, review of *The Firefly Letters,* p. 55.

School Library Journal, April, 2006, Carol Jones Collins, review of *The Poet Slave of Cuba,* p. 154; June, 2008, Jill Heritage Maza, review of *The Surrender Tree,* p. 158; June, 2009, Geri Diorio, review of *Tropical Secrets,* p. 122; February, 2010, review of *The Firefly Letters,* p. 129; July, 2010, review of *Summer Birds,* p. 74; March, 2011, Jeffrey Hastings, review of *Hurricane Dancers,* p. 160.

Voice of Youth Advocates, June, 2011, Nancy Wallace, review of *Hurricane Dancers,* p. 162.

ONLINE

Macmillan Web site, http://us.macmillan.com/ (July 15, 2011), "Margarita Engle."

Poet Seers Web site, http://www.poetseers.org/ (October 2, 2008), Margarita Engle, "Layers of Time."

School Library Journal Online, http://www.schoollibrary journal.com/ (March 4, 2009), Debra Lau Whelan, "Margarita Engle's Historic Newbery Honor."*

F

FALCONE, L.M. 1951-
(Lucy M. Falcone)

Personal

Born January 10, 1951, in Toronto, Ontario, Canada; daughter of Antonio Falcone (a public works department employee) and Maria Donata Zita (a homemaker). *Education:* University of Toronto, B.A., 1973, Teacher's College, Primary Specialist certification, 1974. *Politics:* "Liberal." *Hobbies and other interests:* Tai Chi, reading, traveling.

Addresses

Home—Toronto, Ontario, Canada. *E-mail*—contact@ lmfalcone.com.

Career

Screenwriter, children's book author, and producer. Formerly worked as a kindergarten teacher, artist, and private investigator; Northwind Productions, founder and film producer. Presenter at schools.

Member

Writers Guild of Canada, Canadian Society of Children's Authors, Illustrators, and Performers, Writers Union of Canada.

Awards, Honors

Hart House Award for best short story, 1981, for "Solitaire"; Bronze Award for Best Television Pilot, Houston International Film & Television Festival, 1992, for *Choir Practice;* Red Cedar Award nomination, 2006, for *The Mysterious Mummer;* Silver Birch Award, Diamond Willow Award, and Manitoba Young Readers Choice designation, all 2007, all for *Walking with the Dead;* Arthur Ellis Award nomination, 2007, Manitoba Young Readers Choice designation, 2008, and Red Cedar Award, 2009, all for *The Devil, the Banshee, and Me;* Diamond Willow Award nomination, 2011, for *The Midnight Curse.*

L.M. Falcone (Photograph by Victoria Jackson. Reproduced by permission.)

Writings

The Mysterious Mummer, Kids Can Press (Toronto, Ontario, Canada), 2003.
Walking with the Dead, Kids Can Press (Toronto, Ontario, Canada), 2005.
The Devil, the Banshee, and Me, Kids Can Press (Toronto, Ontario, Canada), 2006.
The Midnight Curse, Kids Can Press (Toronto, Ontario, Canada), 2010.

Contributor to screenplay *The Decision,* Tiempo Productions, 1984. Script writer for television series, including *The Littlest Hobo,* CTV, 1983; (and producer)

Choir Practice (pilot), 1991; *The New Monkees!,* Columbia Broadcast System, Inc., 1991; and *Are You Afraid of the Dark?,* Nickelodeon, 1994-95.

Author's work has been translated into French and Turkish.

Sidelights

Toronto-based author L.M. Falcone is a former television writer for such series as *The Littlest Hobo, The New Monkees!,* and the hugely popular pre-teen series *Are You Afraid of the Dark?* Focusing her talents on high-interest, suspenseful stories that will encourage reading among middle-grade students, Falcone's works include *The Mysterious Mummer, Walking with the Dead, The Devil, the Banshee, and Me,* and *The Midnight Curse.*

Falcone worked as an elementary-school teacher before transitioning her career to pursue writing. "My soul would have shriveled up and died, if I hadn't," she once admitted to *SATA.* After a decade spent writing for television and film in Los Angeles, California, as well as starting her own production company, she returned to her native Canada. After a four-year stint writing picture-book texts proved unsuccessful, Falcone decided to switch genres and focus on middle-grade suspense. Ultimately, she made a good choice; her first novel, *The Mysterious Mummer,* was published in 2003.

In *The Mysterious Mummer* Joey reluctantly spends the holiday season with his widowed aunt at her home on the coast of Newfoundland. Here spectral sightings and the woman's strange behavior combine in what *School Library Journal* critic Susan Patron described as "some genuinely creepy plot twists" and Joan Marshall recommended in *Resource Links* as "a fast-moving, compelling ghost story that will have middle school students glued to the action."

A mummy named Costas, who once lived in ancient Greece and was unjustly accused of a crime, sparks the action in Falcone's *Walking with the Dead,* as twelve-year-old Alex and friend Freddie find themselves battling a hoard of mythological monsters while aiding the ancient spirit on its journey to rest in the underworld. In addition to praising *Walking with the Dead* as "an amusing adventure," *Booklist* critic Todd Morning recommended Falcone's second novel as "an inventive and lighthearted introduction" to Greek mythology, while Elaine E. Knight noted the "quiet message about personal responsibility and courage" that weaves within the high-action story.

Falcone continues to entertain readers in *The Devil, the Banshee, and Me,* in which a preteen named Will stumbles into an adventure while going on an innocent errand to borrow eggs from a neighbor who lives in a cemetery. Mrs. MacGregor and her daughter Megan seem nice enough, but a wailing banshee, the Devil's nephew, and the evil demons that have tagged along with them are more than Will can take. Trying to make

sense of it all, the boy becomes embroiled in a mystery of supernatural proportions as he tries to save Megan from the Banshee's clutches on her thirteenth birthday. "With a blend of chills, humour and suspense, short chapters and clever word play, this fast paced thriller will keep readers turning pages until the end," according to *Canadian Review of Materials* contributor Jane Bridle in her review of *The Devil, the Banshee, and Me.*

A trio of ghosts and a creaky old mansion animate Falcone's novel *The Midnight Curse.* When their widowed mother inherits the family estate in England, twins Charlie and Lacey know that something exciting is bound to happen. While exploring sprawling Blaxton Manor they learn about the presence of three resident spectres, one of which is a poltergeist. When Charlie is jinxed with the family curse, the children turn to a local psychic as their only hope of freeing him in a story that "contains a good deal of threats, ghosts, and spookiness," according to *School Library Journal* critic Walter Minkel. In *Booklist,* Ilene Cooper recommended *The Midnight Curse* as a good choice for reluctant readers, noting that there "is dialogue propelled with plenty of eerie action on every page."

Cover of Canadian writer Falcone's middle-grade mystery novel **Walking with the Dead.** (Illustration © Images.com. Reproduced with permission of Kids Can Press Ltd.)

Falcone continues to scare young readers with her novel **The Midnight Curse,** *which features a haunted mansion, psychic powers, and a family mystery.* (Reproduced with permission of KCP Fiction, an imprint of Kids Can Press, Ltd.)

No stranger to variety, Falcone has worked as a private investigator for the Acadia Investigation Bureau, catered for the cast and crew of the television series *The Golden Girls,* and once applied for a job as a fish plucker. She enjoys traveling when researching new writing projects and has lived in an Amish community in Pennsylvania; in an 1860s-era cottage in New Brunswick (with no phone, no car, no TV); and on a sheep farm in England, in the very village where Robin Hood lived! Falcone's advice to aspiring authors is rather surprising coming from a former television scriptwriter: "Turn off that darn TV and start living! Stories are everywhere but you'll find them only if you're open to receiving them."

Biographical and Critical Sources

PERIODICALS

Booklist, March 15, 2005, Todd Morning, review of *Walking with the Dead,* p. 1292; May 1, 2010, Ilene Cooper, review of *The Midnight Curse,* p. 53.

Canadian Review of Materials, May 12, 2006, review of *The Devil, the Banshee, and Me.*
Kirkus Reviews, February 15, 2005, review of *Walking with the Dead;* January 1, 2010, review of *The Midnight Curse.*
Kliatt, November, 2003, Claire Rosser, review of *The Mysterious Mummer,* p. 5.
Resource Links, February, 2004, Joan Marshall, review of *The Mysterious Mummer,* p. 12; June, 2005, K.V. Johansen, review of *Walking with the Dead,* p. 13.
School Library Journal, October, 2003, Susan Patron, review of *The Mysterious Mummer,* p. 62; June, 2005, Elaine E. Knight, review of *Walking with the Dead,* p. 156; July, 2006, Michele Capozzella, review of *The Devil, the Banshee, and Me,* p. 101; April, 2010, Walter Minkel, review of *The Midnight Curse,* p. 156.

ONLINE

Canadian Association of Children's Authors, Illustrators, and Performers Web site, http://www.canscaip.org/ (June 20, 2011), "L.M. Falcone."
L.M. Falcone Web site, http://www.lmfalcone.com (June 20, 2011).

*   *   *

FALCONE, Lucy M.
See FALCONE, L.M.

*   *   *

FORD, A.G.

Personal

Born in TX. *Education:* Columbus College of Art and Design, B.F.A. (illustration), 2007. *Hobbies and other interests:* Fitness.

Addresses

Home—Dallas, TX. *Agent*—Steven Malk, Writers' House, smalk@writershouse.com. *E-mail*—agford@agfordillustration.com.

Career

Illustrator. Presenter at schools.

Awards, Honors

(With others) Image Award for Outstanding Literary Work for Children, National Association for the Advancement of Colored People (NAACP), 2010, for *Our Children Can Soar* by Michelle Cook.

Illustrator

Jonah Winter, *Barack,* Katherine Tegen Books (New York, NY), 2008.

A.G. Ford's illustration projects include Mina Javaherbin's sports-centered picture book **Goal!** (Illustration copyright © 2010 by A.G. Ford. Reproduced by permission of Candlewick Press, Somerville, MA.)

(With others) Michelle Cook, *Our Children Can Soar: A Celebration of Rosa, Barack, and the Pioneers of Change,* Bloomsbury (New York, NY), 2009.

Deborah Hopkinson, *Michelle,* Katherine Tegen Books (New York, NY), 2009.

Deborah Hopkinson, *First Family,* Katherine Tegen Books (New York, NY), 2010.

Mina Javaherbin, *Goal!,* Candlewick Press (Somerville, MA), 2010.

Teresa E. Harris, *Summer Jackson: Grown Up,* Katherine Tegen Books (New York, NY), 2011.

Contributor to periodicals, including *Black Enterprise, Boy's Life, Dallas Observer, Highlights for Children, Ohio Magazine,* and *Santa Barbara Independent.* Work featured in annuals, including *Spectrum.*

Sidelights

A Texas native, A.G. Ford established his illustration career shortly after graduating from the Columbus College of Art and Design, where he studied under illustrator C.F. Payne and was acknowledged by his inclusion in the Society of Illustrators' student competition. In addition to his illustrations for the high-profile picturebooks *First Family, Michelle,* and *Barack,* all which were published to commemorate the historic 2008 U.S. presidential election, Ford has contributed his detailed illustrations to stories by Mina Javaherbin and Teresa E. Harris. His work is also represented in the NAACP Image Award-winning *Our Children Can Soar: A Celebration of Rosa, Barack, and the Pioneers of Change,* featuring a text by Michelle Cook. Interestingly, Ford showed his professionalism from the very start; in his first illustration project, Jonathan Winter's text for *Barack,* he was allotted only months to complete over twenty realistic paintings for the book. Praising Deborah Hopkinson's profile of the new First Lady in *Michelle,* a *Publishers Weekly* critic added that Ford's paintings for the "warm, respectful" picture-book biography "captur[e] . . . facial expressions and nuances of posture and gesture with uncanny realism."

Another illustration project, Javaherbin's *Goal!,* takes readers to South Africa, where a group of six boys learns to deal effectively with some bullies in order to keep possession of their new regulation-sized soccer ball. Ford found illustrating *Goal!* to be a unique challenge because establishing the harsh reality of the story's setting is so crucial to Javaherbin's tale. "The drawings of the shanty homes had to be accurate in height, and the textures had to appear rough and worn due to weather, wind, and the everyday wear and tear that is created by the hot sun, years of rain, and rust," he explained on a *Brown Bookshelf* online interview. "Dirt and dust needed to appear smoky and brutal, clothes needed to look worn out, and soccer balls needed to fly!" Writing in *School Library Journal,* Blair Christolon praised the artist's ability to create "expressive facial features" and added that the "large and colorful action shots . . . keep the story moving at a quick pace."

In *Booklist* Gillian Engberg also had praise for *Goal!,* writing that the artist "uses unusual angles to intensify the . . . exciting action, the tense confrontation, and the reality of shantytown life."

Although Ford works primarily in acrylics and oils, he experiments with a looser, cartoon style in his watercolor-and-ink work for Harris's picture book *Summer Jackson: Grown Up.* In the story, a spunky seven year old is certain that it is time to take on adult life, a life that includes fancy high-heeled shoes, staying up late, and acting just like her mom and dad. Enriching his artwork with shades of girl-friendly pink and pale purple, Ford captures "every emotion" of Harris's young heroine, according to a *Kirkus Reviews* contributor. In addition to its mix of story and art, *Summer Jackson* as a good story-time choice for yet another reason, the critic added: "African-American girls are rarely depicted in picture books," especially one like summer, "with a little bit of sparkle and a whole lot of sass."

Ford views the work of an artist as one of constant growth and constant refinement, and the success of his first illustrated children's books have not prompted him to rest on his laurels. His advice to aspiring illustrators? Recognize that illustration is a profession as well as an art, and that trends change over time. "Don't give up, research what you are doing, and really lose yourself in the art world," he recommended in his *Brown Bookshelf* interview. "Be a student of the arts, stay focused, work ten times harder than everyone around you, and be emersed in it and maximize your potential."

Biographical and Critical Sources

PERIODICALS

Booklist, November 15, 2008, Daniel Kraus, review of *Barack,* p. 47; November 1, 2009, Hazel Rochman, review of *Michelle,* p. 50; March 1, 2010, Gillian Engberg, review of *Goal!,* p. 77.

Kirkus Reviews, October 1, 2008, review of *Barack;* May 1, 2011, review of *Summer Jackson: Grown Up.*

Publishers Weekly, September 15, 2008, review of *Barack,* p. 65; October 12, 2009, review of *Michelle,* p. 48; January 4, 2010, review of *First Family,* p. 44.

School Library Journal, December, 2008, Kathy Piehl, review of *Barack,* p. 117; February, 2010, Blair Christolon, review of *Goal!,* p. 88.

ONLINE

A.G. Ford Home Page, http://www.agfordillustration.com (May 28, 2011).

A.G. Ford Web Log, http://agford.blogspot.com (May 28, 2011).

Brown Bookshelf Web site, http://thebrownbookshelf.com/ (February 2, 2010), interview with Ford.

Seven Impossible Things before Breakfast Web log, http://
blaine.org/sevenimpossiblethings/ (June 1, 2010), Julie
Danielson, interview with Ford.*

*   *   *

FROMENTAL, Jean-Luc 1950-

Personal

Born 1950, in Tunis, Tunisia; immigrated to France.

Addresses

Home—France.

Career

Author and journalist. Script writer for television, beginning 1983; novelist and author of children's books.

Appeared in films, including *Sac de nuds,* 1985, and
T'es où mère-grand?!, 2003.

Awards, Honors

Boston Globe/Horn Book Honor Book designation,
2006, for *365 Penguins.*

Writings

Paris-noir, Dernier Terrain Vague (France), 1980.
(With François Landon) *Le Système de l'homme-mort*
(novel), Albin Michel (Paris, France), 1981.
(With José-Louis Bocquet and others) *L'Année de la bande
Dessinée, 81-82,* Temps Futurs (Paris, France), 1981.
En pleine guerre froide, illustrated by Jean-Louis Floch,
Les Humanoïdes Associés, 1984.
Ma vie, Les Humanoïdes Associés, 1985.

Cover of the English translation of Jean-Luc Fromental's popular French-language picture book Little Penguins, *featuring artwork by Joëlle Jolivet.*
(Reproduced with permission of Abrams Books for Young Readers, an imprint of Abrams.)

Les contes de la soif, illustrated by Didier Eberoni and others, Albin Michel (Paris, France), 1990.

(With Miles Hyman) *Le carnet noir,* Editions Nathan (Paris, France), 1991.

Jamais deux sans trois, illustrated by Miles Hyman, Albin Michel (Paris, France), 1991.

Figures de la BD, photographs by Hervé Bruhat, Editions Hoëbeke (Paris, France), 1993.

Le poulet de Broadway, illustrated by Miles Hyman, Seuil Jeunesse (Paris, France), 1993, translated as *Broadway Chicken,* Hyperion Books for Children (New York, NY), 1995.

Air Utopia, Payot (Paris, France), 1994.

Le cochon à l'oreille coupée, illustrated by Miles Hyman, Seuil Jeunesse (Paris, France), 1994.

Le pygmée géant, illustrated by Jano, Seuil Jeunesse (Paris, France), 1996.

Monsieur Troublevenue et son brochet: Un conte des cinq sens, illustrated by Joëlle Jolivet, Seuil Jeunesse (Paris, France), 2002.

365 pingouins, illustrated by Joëlle Jolivet, Naïve (Paris, France), 2006, translated as *365 Penguins,* Abrams Books for Young Readers (New York, NY), 2006.

Oups!, illustrated by Joëlle Jolivet, Hélium (Paris, France), 2009, translated by Thomas Connors as *Oops!,* Abrams Books for Young Readers (New York, NY), 2010.

P'tits pingouins: un livre animé pour jouer à compter (pop-up book), illustrated by Joëlle Jolivet, Hélium (Paris, France), 2010, translated by Amanda Katz as *Ten Little Penguins,* Abrams Books for Young Readers (New York, NY), 2010.

Le coup de Prague, illustrated by Miles Hyman, Dupuis (France), 2011.

Author of French-language television scripts, including for series *Médecins de nuit, Hôtel de police, Navarro,* and *Mandarine et Cow* and for movie *Opération Bugs Bunny.* Translator into French of works by Eric Ambler, Peter Benchley, Charles Bukowski, Edgar Rice Burroughs, William S. Burroughs, Troy Conway, Matt Groening, Chester Himes, Herbert Kastle, Rudyard Kipling, Sara Midda, Michael Moorcock, Ralph Nader, Bob Ottum, David Reuben, Jon Scieszka, Posy Simmonds, Ralph Steadman, Robert Louis Stevenson, Mike Storey, and Alan Williams.

Sidelights

Jean-Luc Fromental is a journalist and author who has also written for television in his native France since the early 1980s. A novelist and translator of the works of a pantheon of well-known English-language writers, Fromental has also gained many young fans through his stories for young children. Fortunately for English-language readers, several of Fromental's works have become available in translation, among them the math concept books *365 Penguins* and *Ten Little Penguins* as well as *Oops!* and *Broadway Chicken.*

Featuring artwork by French illustrator Joëlle Jolivet, *365 Penguins* focuses on a family whose life changes radically when their doorbell rings on New Years' Day

and a penguin is delivered. As Fromental's young narrator breathlessly explains in this oversized picture book, the same thing continues to happen for the rest of the week, and then the rest of the month. By the end of March there are almost a hundred penguins living in the house, and the deliveries show no sign of stopping. Calculations are required every day to determine whether the house can hold the bulk and weight of so many birds, and also to figure out how much fish to purchase for the chubby, orange-footed house guests. Finally the mystery is solved when an environmentally conscious relative arrives and takes responsibility for the birds. A handful of the Arctic birds return in *Ten Little Penguins,* a pop-up book that counts down from ten to one as the playful birds leave their penguin games one at a time, disappearing and reappearing with the reader's help. Praising the book's "striking mod design" and bright, high-contrast illustrations, a *Publishers Weekly* critic added that "comical math problems and an ecological message form a memorable counterpoint" in *365 Penguins.* As Randall Enos asserted in his *Booklist* review of *Ten Little Penguins,* while "the premise is goofy, . . . the math is fun" in Fromental's "lively romp."

Originally published as *Le poulet de Broadway, Broadway Chicken* features another humorous story alongside illustrations by Miles Hyman. In classic rags-to-riches fashion, a dancing chicken named Charlie earns his living performing for the nickels tossed by audiences at an arcade in New York's Chinatown. The bird's life changes when talent-spotting Sam Z. Fowler swoops him up and sets up a series of performances that take Charlie all the way to Broadway, where he headlines as the Broadway Bantam. After migrating to Hollywood, Charlie stars in films such as *Elmer Poultry.* Ultimately, however, fame eclipses the bird's early passion for self-expression and while furthering his cinematic career he winds up destroying the unique flaw that was the source of his dancing talent. With his dancing days now over, Charlie returns to his roost in Chinatown, a well-traveled but wiser bird. "Chicken humor abounds in this well-drafted, expressive, oversize picture book," asserted *Booklist* contributor April Judge, the critic adding of *Broadway Chicken* that Hyman's pastel-toned "impressionistic paintings . . . help set the nostalgic mood and carry out . . . [Fromental's] sophisticated spoof." "The endless poultry-inspired wordplay alone is worth the price of admission," wrote a *Publishers Weekly* critic, dubbing Fromental's poultry-centered nostalgic fantasy "dazzling."

Like *Broadway Chicken, Oops!* showcases Fromental's whimsical storytelling style. Again collaborating with illustrator Jolivet, he presents a humorous example of the spillover of unintended consequences that descend on a family (the same people who shared their home in *365 Penguins*) attempting to reach the Paris airport in time to board the plane that will take them on their summer holiday. From escaping zoo animals and swarms of angry bees to a road-blocking parade and a display of colorful fireworks, events conspire to delay the family's trip and force the vacationers to employ curious and sometimes desperate modes of transportation. Judging *Oops!* to be "fun for anyone willing to surrender to the looniness," a *Kirkus Reviews* writer added that children "will pore over the pages, laugh out loud and just enjoy." In her *School Library Journal* review of Fromental's book, Marzena Currie praised Jolivet's "quirky and fairly abstract illustrations" and suggested that *Oops!* "can be used for all sorts of memory and observation games" due to its brightly colored and busy mod-styled art.

Biographical and Critical Sources

PERIODICALS

Booklist, December 15, 1995, April Judge, review of *Broadway Chicken,* p. 704; January 1, 2007, Randall Enos, review of *365 Penguins,* p. 114.

Horn Book, January-February, 2008, Anita Silvey, review of *365 Penguins,* p. 20.

Kirkus Reviews, November 15, 2006, review of *365 Penguins*; April 15, 2010, review of *Oops!*

Publishers Weekly, October 16, 1995, review of *Broadway Chicken,* p. 61; November 27, 2006, review of *365 Penguins,* p. 49.

Quill & Quire, September, 1995, review of *Broadway Chicken,* p. 76.

New York Times Book Review, November 12, 1995, Frank Rich, review of *Broadway Chicken;* November 12, 2006, Polly Shulman, review of *365 Penguins,* p. 24.

School Librarian, autumn, 2010, Marzena Currie, review of *Oops!,* p. 154.

School Library Journal, February, 1996, Cynthia K. Richey, review of *Broadway Chicken,* p. 84; December, 2006, Barbara Auerbach, review of *365 Penguins,* p. 100; April, 2010, Marge Loch-Wouters, review of *Oops!,* p. 124.

Washington Post Book World, December 10, 2006, Jabari Asim, review of *365 Penguins,* p. 8.*

G

GILANI, Fawzia
See GILANI-WILLIAMS, Fawzia

* * *

GILANI-WILLIAMS, Fawzia 1967-
(Fawzia Gilani)

Personal

Born October 2, 1967, in Walsall, England; immigrated to United States; married Robert Williams; children: Muslimah. *Education:* University of Wolverhampton, degree (primary education); University of Birmingham, degree (Islamic studies); University of Worcester, doctoral studies (children's Islamic literature).

Addresses

Home—Oberlin, OH.

Career

Educator, librarian, and author. Teacher at Islamic schools in England and the United States, 1993-2001, and administrator, 2001-04; educational consultant; currently works as reference librarian in OH.

Writings

The Adventures of Musab, illustrated by Rin Warrilow, Ta-Ha Publishers (London, England), 2002.

The Emir and the Verse of the Throne, illustrated by Ramendranath Sarkar, Goodword Publishing (New Delhi, India), 2004.

A Khimar for Nadia, illustrated by Rin Warrilow, Ta-Ha (London, England), 2004.

The Troublesome Eid Jinn, illustrated by Rin Warrilow, Ta-Ha (London, England), 2004.

Eid Kareem Ameer Sahab!, illustrated by Jagdish Joshi, Goodword Publishing (New Delhi, India), 2004.

Aminah and Aisha's Eid Gifts, illustrated by Neeta Gangopadhyay, Goodword Publishing (New Delhi, India), 2004.

Eid and Ramadan Songs, illustrated by Chaitali Chatterjee, Goodword Publishing (New Delhi, India), 2004.

Celebrating Eid-ul Fitr with Ama Fatima, illustrated by Sujata Bansal, Goodword Publishing (New Delhi, India), 2004.

Eid Songs, illustrated by Sudha Chowdhry, Goodword Publishing (New Delhi, India), 2004.

Salaam Li and the Dacoits, [New Delhi, India], 2006.

Ihtisham and the Eid Shoes, [New Delhi, India], 2006.

A Poor Widow's Eid, [New Delhi, India], 2006.

A Beggar Boy, [New Delhi, India], 2006.

A Samosah Maker, [New Delhi, India], 2006.

An Old Man Who Trusts in Allah, [New Delhi, India], 2006.

Father Ant and the Pious Groom, [New Delhi, India], 2006.

The Lost Ring, illustrated by Kulthum Burgess, Islamic Foundation (Markfield, England), 2007.

Husna and the Eid Party, illustrated by Kulthum Burgess, Islamic Foundation (Markfield, England), 2007.

(Reteller) *Ismat's Eid,* illustrated by Proiti Roy, Tulika Publishers (Chennai, India), 2007.

(Reteller) *Nabeel's New Pants: An Eid Tale,* illustrated by Proiti Roy, Marshall Cavendish Children (Tarrytown, NY), 2010.

Cinderella: An Islamic Tale, illustrated by Shireen Adams, Kube Publishing (Markfield, Leicestershire, England), 2011.

Work included in anthology *Between Love, Hope, and Fear,* An-Najm (London, England), 2007. Contributor of book reviews to *School Library Journal.*

Sidelights

Born in England but now making her home in the United States, Fawzia Gilani-Williams trained as a primary-school teacher, then pursued graduate degrees in both Islamic studies and Islamic children's literature. Gilani-Williams began writing as an outgrowth of her work as a teacher and librarian, and she was inspired in her work by her own experiences as a Muslim living in a predominately Christian society. Designed to reinforce cultural pride among Islamic children, her books focus mainly on the Muslim holiday Eid ul-Fitr, which occurs in December and marks the end of the month of fasting known as Ramadan. Colorfully illustrated, her stories include *Eid Kareem Ameer Sahab!*, *Aminah and Aisha's Eid Gifts*, *The Adventures of Musab*, and *Nabeel's New Pants: An Eid Tale*, as well as an Islamic retelling of the "Cinderella" story.

Eid ul-Fitr marks both the end of the Ramadan fast and, like the secular New Year's celebration, an opportunity for a fresh start. Extending over three days, it begins with a large gathering for a pre-sunrise prayer. Then families visit friends and relatives to exchange good wishes, share special foods, and perform other rituals, including sermons and blessings. Illustrated by Proiti Roy, *Nabeel's New Pants* focuses on a shoemaker whose work has continued right up to the beginning of Eid. At the last minute he goes shopping for a new pair of trousers to wear to the early-morning prayers, as well as for gifts for his family. In his haste, Nabeel has purchased trousers that are far too long, but the women in his extended family are busy with Eid preparations and have not time to hem them. Although Nabeel quietly handles the sewing task himself and then goes to sleep, his appreciative wife, mother, and daughter find a moment to handle the alteration, each without knowing that the pants have already been shortened. "A fine choice for read-aloud fun," according to Margaret Bush in *School Library Journal*, *Nabeel's New Pants* "is a simple introduction to Muslim culture that will evoke empathetic chuckles when . . . Nabeel dons his knee-length pants on the morning of Eid." "The [illustrations'] warm colors and [Gilani-Williams'] language work well, depicting the family working cooperatively to prepare for the sacred moment," asserted a *Kirkus Reviews* writer, and *Booklist* contributor Hazel Rochman predicted that "kids will laugh right along with the loving characters, who sew the missing pants pieces back together to give Nabeel perfectly fitting trousers in the end."

"Children need a sense of belonging and a sense of place," Gilani-Williams noted in an interview for *Ummah Reads* online. While acknowledging that publishers of children's books have started to embrace multiculturalism, she maintains that Islamic traditions and history are still under-represented in many schools and libraries. One winter she visited her local library on a regular basis, and as the December holidays approached "the children's area was filled with displays of Christ-

mas and Hanukkah books and even Kwanzaa. But there was nothing on Eid. Not one book. It was very sad and embarrassing that my child's religious celebration—the second largest in the world—was not acknowledged in any shape, way or form. It was at that moment that I made a silent prayer to address the gap. When I was hired at the library I contacted all English-speaking national libraries (USA, Canada, England, Ireland, Australia, New Zealand, Scotland, Wales, Jamaica, etc.) and provided them with a bibliography of Eid stories so that they could improve their collection. . . . I believe that as educators and parents we need to follow the example of the Jews and make Eid as visible as Hanukkah is today."

Biographical and Critical Sources

PERIODICALS

Booklist, March 15, 2010, Hazel Rochman, review of *Nabeel's New Pants: An Eid Tale*, p. 50.

Kirkus Reviews, March 1, 2010, review of *Nabeel's New Pants*.

Publishers Weekly, April 5, 2010, review of *Nabeel's New Pants*, p. 59.

School Library Journal, April, 2010, Margaret Bush, review of *Nabeel's New Pants*, p. 126.

ONLINE

Goodword Islamic Books Web site, http://www.good wordbooks.com/ (July 13, 2011), "Fawzia Gilani-Williams."

Ummah Reads Web log, http://muslimkidsbooks.word press.com/ (March 29, 2011), interview with Gilani-Williams.*

*   *   *

GONZÁLEZ, Christina Díaz 1969-

Personal

Born 1969; daughter of Delfin and Esperanza Diaz; married; children: two sons. *Education:* University of Miami, B.B.A. (accounting; with honors), 1991; Colegio Universitario (Madrid, Spain), International Law Certificate, 1992; Florida State University, J.D. (magna cum laude), 1994. *Hobbies and other interests:* Writing.

Addresses

Home—Miami, FL.

Career

Attorney and author. Practicing attorney specializing in immigration and social security disability, beginning 1994; González & Rembold, Miami, FL, principal; currently of counsel for Sanchez-Medina, González, Quesada, Lage, Crespo, Gomez & Machado, Coral Gables, FL. Member, Latino Identity Leadership Consortium.

Member

Society of Children's Book Writers and Illustrators, Cuban American Bar Association, Florida Bar Association.

Awards, Honors

Children's Cooperative Book Center Choice selection, Best Fiction for Young Adults selection, American Library Association, Teacher's Choice selection, International Reading Association, Florida Book Award Gold Medal, and International Latino Book Award Silver Medal, all c. 2010, all for *The Red Umbrella.*

Writings

The Red Umbrella, Alfred A. Knopf (New York, NY), 2010.
A Thunderous Whisper, 2012.

Sidelights

While growing up in the American South, Christina Díaz González was raised in two worlds: the Cuban culture of her parents and the typical middle-class suburban world where free time was spent riding bicycles, playing with friends, and reading. As a teen, González moved with her family to Miami, and eventually earned an accounting degree at the University of Miami. Law school followed, and she has gone on to build a successful career in immigration law. When her own two sons were old enough to begin reading, González discovered her own talent for writing. Based on her short story, "Flight from Neverland," her first book, *The Red Umbrella,* was the result.

The Red Umbrella was inspired by the story of González' grandparents, who were airlifted from Cuba to the United States when their own parents grew concerned over the policies of communist dictator Fidel Castro. A joint operation of the U.S. Department of State, the Catholic Church in Miami, Florida, and numerous Cubans who opposed Castro's government, Operation Pedro Pan transported over 14,000 children to Miami between 1960 and 1962. In the novel, fourteen-year-old Lucía Álvarez and younger brother Frankie lead a comfortable life in their small town of Puerto Mijares, Cuba. However, even the children realize that something is wrong in their country when they see soldiers on the street, are prohibited from visiting certain areas, and overhear rumors regarding the townspeople who have mysteriously vanish. While several of her friends are overjoyed by the new government—including her boyfriend Manuel—Lucía's own feelings are sobered by her parents' growing apprehension and her father's job loss. Her carefree childhood ends abruptly when she is told that she and her brother are to be sent to the United States on their own. After she finds herself in rural Nebraska, the young Cuban exile must become a parent to Frankie while also learning English and adapting to a new culture. Lucía must also juggle her growing affection for her kindly foster family with her loyalty to her parents as well as dealing with her worries regarding the safety of the relatives and friends left behind under Castro's oppressive and isolationist regime.

González' "well-written novel has a thoroughly believable protagonist and well-chosen period details," wrote *School Library Journal* contributor Rhona Campbell, the critic adding that *The Red Umbrella* "could generate some excellent classroom discussions" about the history of U.S.-Cuban relations. A *Kirkus Reviews* writer cited "Lucía's captivating voice" for effectively describing Cuba's "drastic transformation . . . into a communist system," while a *Publishers Weekly* contributor noted that González' "compelling, atmospheric" story presents readers with "a moving portrait of resilience and reinvention." "Through the eyes of this likable young narrator, readers will understand a compelling part of history," concluded Augusta Scattergood in her review of *The Red Umbrella* for the *Christian Science Monitor.* "Kudos to Christina Díaz González for sharing her family's story, and for telling it so well."

Biographical and Critical Sources

PERIODICALS

Christian Science Monitor, August 5, 2010, Augusta Scattergood, review of *The Red Umbrella.*
Kirkus Reviews, April 15, 2010, review of *The Red Umbrella.*
Miami Herald, May 22, 2010, Sue Corbett, "A Novel Experience from Real Life."
Publishers Weekly, May 3, 2010, review of *The Red Umbrella,* p. 53.
School Library Journal, May, 2010, Rhona Campbell, review of *The Red Umbrella,* p. 114.

ONLINE

Christina Díaz González Home Page, http://christinagonzalez.com (July 15, 2011).
Christina Díaz González Web log, http://christina-dg.livejournal.com (July 15, 2011).
SMGQ Law Web site, http://www.smgqlaw.com/ (July 15, 2011), "Christina Díaz González."

GRAY, Steve 1950-

Personal

Born 1950, in Hornell, NY.

Addresses

Home—Redondo Beach, CA. *E-mail*—stevegray1@ yahoo.com.

Career

Cartoonist, illustrator, and animator.

Illustrator

Bob Fellows, *Easily Fooled,* Mind Matters (Minneapolis, MN), 1989.

Kathleen W. Kranking, *Earth: Where Would We Be without It?,* Golden Books (New York, NY), 1999.

(With others) Richie Chevat and Jackie Ball, *Electricity,* Gareth Stevens (Milwaukee, WI), 2003.

Katy Duffield, *Farmer McPeepers and His Missing Milk Cows,* Rising Moon (Flagstaff, AZ), 2003.

Lisa Trumbauer, *A Tooth Is Loose,* Children's Press (New York, NY), 2004.

Jackie Franza, *It's Raining Cats and Dogs: Making Sense of Animal Phrases,* BowTie Press (Irvine, CA), 2005.

Gray's quirky illustration style can be seen in his humorous cartoon titled "Pirate with a Bounty on His Head." (Courtesy of the illustrator.)

Jennifer Ward, *There Was a Coyote Who Swallowed a Flea,* Rising Moon (Flagstaff, AZ), 2007.

Jennifer Ward, *There Was an Old Monkey Who Swallowed a Frog,* Marshall Cavendish Children (New York, NY), 2010.

Jennifer Ward, *There Was an Old Pirate Who Swallowed a Fish,* Marshall Cavendish Children (New York, NY), 2013.

Creator of short film *Santa's Camels.*

Sidelights

"For the first twenty years of my career I work as a humorous illustrator in advertising," Steve Gray told *SATA.* "I worked for a number of clients including McDonalds, Carls Jr., Pizza Hut, Sizzler, Baskin Robbins, Disney, Warner Brothers, Knott's Berry Farm, Sea World and American Express. My first children's book was published in 1999." In the years since, Gray's many illustration projects have included collaborating with writer Jennifer Ward on the humorous stories *There Was an Old Monkey Who Swallowed a Frog, There Was a Coyote Who Swallowed a Flea,* and *There Was an Old Pirate Who Swallowed a Fish.*

Steve Gray (Photograph by Tom Beavers. Reproduced by permission.)

Gray's google-eyed character add extra laughts to Jennifer Ward's humorous story in **There Was an Old Monkey Who Swallowed a Frog.** (Illustration copyright © 2010 by Steve Gray. Reproduced with permission of Marshall Cavendish Books.)

Biographical and Critical Sources

PERIODICALS

Booklist, March 15, 2010, Hazel Rochman, review of *There Was an Old Monkey Who Swallowed a Frog,* p. 45.

Kirkus Reviews, March 1, 2010, review of *There Was an Old Monkey Who Swallowed a Frog.*

ONLINE

Steve Gray Home Page, http://www.stevegrayillustration. com (May 28, 2011).

H

HARRIS, Maria Guadalupe
See HARRIS, M.G.

* * *

HARRIS, M.G.
(Maria Guadalupe Harris)

Personal

Born in Mexico City, Mexico; immigrated to England; married; children: two daughters. *Education:* St. Catherine's College Oxford, B.S. (biochemistry), M.A., Ph.D. (molecular biology). *Hobbies and other interests:* Salsa dancing, mixology.

Addresses

Home—Oxford, England. *Agent*—Peter Cox, Redhammer Management.

Career

Writer. Formerly worked as a research scientist; founder of an internet business.

Writings

"JOSHUA FILES" MIDDLE-GRADE NOVEL SERIES

Invisible City, Scholastic (London, England), 2008, Walker & Co. (New York, NY), 2010.
Ice Shock, Scholastic (London, England), 2009, Walker Books for Young Readers (New York, NY), 2011.
Zero Moment, Scholastic (London, England), 2010.
Dark Parallel, Scholastic (London, England), 2011.

Sidelights

M.G. Harris has an unusual resumé for a writer. Born in Mexico and raised in both Germany and England, she earned her Ph.D. in molecular biology and worked as a scientist before making the switch to novelist. A skiing accident was the catalyst: bedridden following surgery, Harris finally had the time to ponder an idea for a thriller that had been germinating in her imagination for years. Although her first novel was rejected by publishers, it allowed her to develop the writing habit. For her next book Harris again looked back, this time to her teen years in Mexico and her fascination with the Yucatan and its Mayan ruins. Research into Mayan writing led to *Invisible City,* the first novel in Harris's "Joshua Files" novel series.

In the mix of narrative and blog entries in *Invisible City* readers meet thirteen-year-old Joshua Garcia just as his world is rocked by news of his father's death in a plane crash. The cause of the accident is sketchy and does not seem to jibe with his father's work: as an archeologist, he was searching for an ancient codex (a bound book) containing information regarding the purported end of the Mayan calendar—and maybe the world—on December 22, 2012. Josh decides to investigate for himself and is joined by two friends on his trip from England to the Mexican jungle. As he retraces his father's path, the teen uncovers the existence of Ixchel, a sister he never knew, as well as a secret society whose members have knowledge of aviation so advanced that it may have alien origins. While Josh searches for the truth, a nest of international secret agents hunts him down, resulting in what *School Library Journal* contributor Steven Engelfried described as "an action-packed adventure involving conspiracy theories, end-of-the-world prophecies, government agents, futuristic technology, and a bit of the supernatural." While Ilene Cooper wrote in her *Booklist* review that Harris's story ratchets the level of action fairly high, "the end-of-the-world scenario" in *Invisible City* "is hard to resist, and appealing Josh makes a solid hero."

Harris's "Joshua Files" stories continue in *Ice Shock, Zero Moment,* and *Dark Parallel* as Josh continues his race to save the world from an ancient Mayan prophecy. In *Ice Shock* the search for a hidden grave in the lost city of Ek Naab leads to the knowledge that Mr.

Garcia also sought another ancient artifact: the Bracelet of Itzamna. *Zero Moment* finds the teen mastering time travel, but should he use this knowledge to save his father? Ixchel knows what he intends to do. Should she stop him? Before this question is answered, Ixchel, is abducted by those who hope to doom mankind. Josh and Ixchel travel back to the time of the Mayan in *Dark Parallel,* but while they hoped to learn the truth of the doomsday predictions they make a discovery that prompts them to question their entire quest. *Ice Shock* "is one of the rare sequels that improve upon the original," asserted a *Kirkus Reviews* writer, the critic noting that "touches of science fiction and fantasy add flavor to the adventure and action, as do Borgesian allusions and a charming tale of two long-dead lovers."

Biographical and Critical Sources

PERIODICALS

Booklist, May 1, 2010, Ilene Cooper, review of *Invisible City,* p. 49.
Bulletin of the Center for Children's Books, July-August, 2010, April Spisak, review of *Invisible City,* p. 483.
Financial Times (London, England), February 2, 2008, James Lovegrove, review of *Invisible City,* p. 41.
Kirkus Reviews, April 1, 2010, review of *Invisible City;* June 15, 2011, review of *Ice Shock.*
Publishers Weekly, July 12, 2010, review of *Invisible City,* p. 48.
School Library Journal, July, 2010, Steven Engelfried, review of *Invisible City,* p. 89.

ONLINE

Joshua Files Web site, http://www.joshuafiles.co.uk/ (July 15, 2011).
M.G. Harris Home Page, http://www.mgharris.net (July 15, 2011).
Scholastic Web site, http://www5.scholastic.co.uk/ (July 15, 2011), "M.G. Harris."*

* * *

HEWITT, Sally 1949-

Personal

Born August 8, 1949, in Worthing, Sussex, England; daughter of Norman Sidney (a businessman) and Cynthia Elizabeth Lacey; married Gavin James Hewitt (a news correspondent), September 2, 1972; children: Rebecca Jane, Daniel James. *Education:* Stockwell College of Education, B.Ed., 1971. *Hobbies and other interests:* Singing, bicycling, spending time with family.

Addresses

Home—Richmond, Surrey, England. *E-mail*—sally hewitt@blueyonder.co.uk.

Career

Teacher in primary schools in Worthing, Sussex, England, 1971-73; music teacher in primary schools in Brighton, Sussex, 1973-77; science teacher in primary schools in Richmond, Sussex, 1974-78; worked previously as a project editor; freelance writer. Presenter at schools and libraries.

Writings

NONFICTION; FOR CHILDREN

Busy Little Artist (craft book), illustrated by Penny Dann, Octopus (London, England), 1990.
Activity Atlas, Apple (London, England), 1997.
Me and My Body (home-learning activity book), Levinson, 1997.
Happy Holidays (home-learning activity book), Levinson, 1997.
Around the World (home-learning activity book), Levinson, 1997.
Maths (boxed activity book; includes math supplies), illustrated by Helen Holroyd, Apple (London, England), 1997.
The Human Body (boxed activity book), Quarto (London, England), 1997.
I Can Print ("Look and Make" series), illustrated by Michael Evans, F. Watts (London, England), 1997.
Miss George and the Dragon (home-learning activity book), Levinson, 1998.
Wolves ("Look Out" series), Two-Can (London, England), 1999.
Animal Homes, World Book (Chicago, IL), 1999.
Nature for Fun Projects, Copper Beech (Brookfield, CT), 2000.
Plants, Copper Beech Books (Brookfield, CT), 2001.
Animal Life, Copper Beech Books (Brookfield, CT), 2002.
Jungle Beasts Pop-up: A Face-to-Face Safari (pop-up book), illustrated by Chris Gilvan-Cartwright, Poppy Red (High Wycombe, England), 2002, Harry N. Abrams (New York, NY), 2003.
Cars, Chrysalis Education (North Mankato, MN), 2003.
Earth and Space, Chrysalis Education (North Mankato, MN), 2003.
Energy, Chrysalis Education (North Mankato, MN), 2003.
Planes, Chrysalis Education (North Mankato, MN), 2003.
Plants, Chrysalis Education (North Mankato, MN), 2003.
Pop-up Bugs: Creepy Crawlers Face to Face (pop-up book), illustrated by Chris Gilvan-Cartwright, Poppy Red (High Wycombe, England), 2003, Harry Abrams (New York, NY), 2011.
Minibeasts ("Adventures in Science" series), Chrysalis Education (North Mankato, MN), 2003.
Forces and Motion ("Adventures in Science" series), Chrysalis Education (North Mankato, MN), 2003.
Going to the Dentist ("First Experiences" reader series), QEB Publications (North Mankato, MN), 2004.
Life Cycles: from Caterpillar to Butterfly ("Start Thinking" series), QEB Publications (North Mankato, MN), 2004.

Going to School ("First Experiences" reader series), QEB Publications (North Mankato, MN), 2005.

Where's My Shirt? ("Reading and Thinking" series), QEB Publications (North Mankato, MN), 2005.

The Tidy Fairy ("Reading and Thinking" series), QED (London, England), 2005, published as *The Spick-and-Span Fairy*, QEB Publications (North Mankato, MN), 2005.

Keeping Healthy, QEB Publications (North Mankato, MN), 2005.

Life Cycles: from Tadpole to Frog ("Start Thinking" series), F. Watts (London, England), 2005.

Color: I Like Red!, Stargazer Books (North Mankato, MN), 2008.

Pop-up Sea Creatures: Squirmy, Scary Fish Face to Face (pop-up book), illustrated by Chris Gilvan-Cartwright, Poppy Red (High Wycombe, England), Harry Abrams (New York, NY), 2011,

Also author of "Bear Sticker Book" series, illustrated by Andy Cooke, Quarto (London, England), 1996; and "First Crosswords" series, illustrated by Sasha Lipscomb, Hodder (London, England), 1996. Author of story board books *Sheep, Pig, Cat, Cow,* and *Horse,* illustrated by Paul Cemmick, Zigzag, 1999.

Author's works have been translated into Irish and Welsh.

"BASIC SKILLS" SERIES

Mr. Goon Flies to the Moon, illustrated by Paul Davies, Tesco (St. Albans, Hertfordshire, England), 1992.

Winnie's Workshop, illustrated by Peter Wingham, Tesco (St. Albans, Hertfordshire, England), 1992.

The Crazy Cooks (math skills), illustrated by Ainslie MacLeod, Tesco (St. Albans, Hertfordshire, England), 1992.

A Day with the Monsters (language skills), illustrated by Michael Brownlow, Tesco (St. Albans, Hertfordshire, England), 1992.

"FLYERS TRANSPORT" SERIES

(With Nicola Wright) *Diggers and Cranes,* illustrated by Rachael O'Neill, F. Watts (London, England), 1993.

(With Nicola Wright) *Ships and Boats,* illustrated by Rachael O'Neill, F. Watts (London, England), 1993.

(With Nicola Wright) *Planes and Helicopters,* illustrated by Rachael O'Neill, F. Watts (London, England), 1993.

(With Nicola Wright) *Cars and Trucks,* illustrated by Rachael O'Neill, F. Watts (London, England), 1993, packaged with toy cars, Zigzag (Hurstpierpoint, England), 1994.

(With Nicola Wright) *Things That Go,* illustrated by Rachael O'Neill, Zigzag (Hurstpierpoint, England), 1995.

"GET SET . . . GO!" SERIES

Pluck and Scrape, illustrated by Peter Millard, F. Watts (London, England), 1993, Children's Press (Chicago, IL), 1994.

Puff and Blow, illustrated by Peter Millard, F. Watts (London, England), 1993, Children's Press (Chicago, IL), 1994.

Bang and Rattle, illustrated by Peter Millard, F. Watts (London, England), 1993, Children's Press (Chicago, IL), 1994.

Squeak and Roar, illustrated by Peter Millard, F. Watts (London, England), 1993, Children's Press (Chicago, IL), 1994.

"NOW I KNOW" SERIES

All around Me, illustrated by Amelia Rosato, Thompson (New York, NY), 1995.

Animals, illustrated by Steve Holmes, Thompson (New York, NY), 1995.

"TAKE OFF" SERIES

Take Off with Maths Puzzles, Evans Bros. (London, England), 1995, Raintree Steck-Vaughn (Austin, TX), 1996.

Take Off with Measuring, Evans Bros. (London, England), 1995, Raintree Steck-Vaughn (Austin, TX), 1996.

Take Off with Numbers, Evans Bros. (London, England), 1995, Raintree Steck-Vaughn (Austin, TX), 1996.

Take Off with Shapes, Evans Bros. (London, England), 1995, Raintree Steck-Vaughn (Austin, TX), 1996.

Take Off with Sorting and Sets, Evans Bros. (London, England), 1995, Raintee Steck-Vaughn, 1996.

Take Off with Time, Evans Bros. (London, England), 1995, Raintree Steck-Vaughn, 1996.

"FOOTSTEPS IN TIME" SERIES

The Greeks, F. Watts (London, England), 1995.

The Romans, F. Watts (London, England), 1995.

The Aztecs, Children's Press (New York, NY), 1996.

The Plains People, Children's Press (New York, NY), 1996.

"FEELINGS" SERIES

Feeling Angry, illustrated by Rhian Nest-James, F. Watts (London, England), 1996.

Feeling Jealous, illustrated by Rhian Nest-James, F. Watts (London, England), 1997.

Feeling Shy, illustrated by Rhian Nest-James, F. Watts (London, England), 1997.

Feeling Worried, illustrated by Rhian Nest-James, F. Watts (London, England), 1997.

"LOOK AROUND YOU" SERIES

(With Jane Rowe) *The Things We Use,* Raintree Steck-Vaughn (Austin, TX), 1997.

(With Jane Rowe) *The Clothes We Wear,* Raintree Steck-Vaughn (Austin, TX), 1997.

(With Jane Rowe) *The Homes We Live In,* Raintree Steck-Vaughn (Austin, TX), 1997.

(With Jane Rowe) *The Toys We Play With,* Raintree Steck-Vaughn (Austin, TX), 1997.

"IT'S SCIENCE!" SERIES

Forces around Us, F. Watts (London, England), 1997, Children's Press (New York, NY), 1998.

Full of Energy, F. Watts (London, England), 1997, Children's Press (New York, NY), 1998.

Machines We Use, F. Watts (London, England), 1997, Children's Press (New York, NY), 1998.

Solid, Liquid, or Gas?, F. Watts (London, England), 1997, Children's Press (New York, NY), 1998.

Growing Up, F. Watts (London, England), 1998, Children's Press (New York, NY), 1999.

Hearing Sounds, Children's Press (New York, NY), 1998.

Light and Dark, Children's Press (New York, NY), 1998.

All Kinds of Animals, Children's Press (New York, NY), 1998.

All Kinds of Habitats, F. Watts (London, England), 1998, Children's Press (New York, NY), 1999.

Plants and Flowers, Children's Press (New York, NY), 1998.

You and Your Body, F. Watts (London, England), 1998, Children's Press (New York, NY), 1999.

The Five Senses, F. Watts (London, England), 1998, Children's Press (New York, NY), 1999.

Air and Flight, Children's Press (New York, NY), 1999.

Time, Children's Press (New York, NY), 1999.

Water, Children's Press (New York, NY), 1999.

Weather, F. Watts (London, England), 1999, Children's Press (New York, NY), 2000.

Hot and Cold, F. Watts (London, England), 1999, Children's Press (New York, NY), 2000.

Food, F. Watts (London, England), 1999, Children's Press (New York, NY), 2000.

"DISCOVERING NATURE" SERIES

Seashores, Ponds, and Rivers, F. Watts (London, England), 1999, published as *Rivers, Ponds, and Seashore,* Copper Beech Books (Brookfield, CT), 1999.

Weather, Copper Beech Books (Brookfield, CT), 1999.

Nature Garden, F. Watts (London, England), 2000.

Life Cycles, Copper Beech Books (Brookfield, CT), 2000.

Woods and Meadows, Copper Beech Books (Brookfield, CT), 2000.

All Year 'Round, Copper Beech Books (Brookfield, CT), 2000.

Your Backyard, illustrated by Tony Kenyon, Stuart Squires, and Mike Atkinson, Copper Beech Books (Brookfield, CT), 2000.

"START MATHS" SERIES

Pirates at Sea, illustrated by Serena Feneziani, Belitha Press (London, England), 2000, Thameside Press (North Mankato, MN), 2001.

Knights in Armour, illustrated by Serena Feneziani, Belitha Press (London, England), 2000.

Aliens and Astronauts, illustrated by Serena Feneziani, Belitha Press (London, England), 2000, Thameside Press (North Mankato, MN), 2001.

Explorers on Safari, illustrated by Serena Feneziani, Belitha Press (London, England), 2000, Thameside Press (North Mankato, MN), 2001.

"IN YOUR NEIGHBOURHOOD" SERIES

Where We Live, photographs by Chris Fairclough, F. Watts (London, England), 2000.

Places We Share, photographs by Chris Fairclough, F. Watts (London, England), 2000.

In the Street, photographs by Chris Fairclough, F. Watts (London, England), 2000.

Schools, photographs by Chris Fairclough, F. Watts (London, England), 2000.

Shopping, photographs by Chris Fairclough, F. Watts (London, England), 2000.

Travelling About, photographs by Chris Fairclough, F. Watts (London, England), 2000.

"NUMBER TEAM" SERIES

In the Jungle, illustrated by Ruth Rivers, Thameside Press (North Mankato, MN), 2001.

Party Time, illustrated by Ruth Rivers, Belitha Press (London, England), 2001, published as *The Numbers Team Have a Party,* Thameside Press (North Mankato, MN), 2001.

To the Rescue, illustrated by Ruth Rivers, Thameside Press (North Mankato, MN), 2001.

The Great Race, illustrated by Ruth Rivers, Thameside Press (North Mankato, MN), 2001.

"WHY CAN'T I . . ." SERIES

Why Can't I . . . Live Underwater with the Fish?, illustrated by Ruth Thomson, Thameside Press (North Mankato, MN), 2001.

Why Can't I . . . Just Eat Sweets?, illustrated by Ruth Thompson, Belitha Press (London, England), 2001.

Why Can't I . . . Fly like a Superhero?, Thameside Press (North Mankato, MN), 2001.

Why Can't I . . . Jump up to the Moon?, and Other Questions about Energy, Thameside Press (Mankato, MN), 2002.

Why Can't I . . . Sleep on a Bed of Bubbles?, and Other Questions about Materials, Smart Apple Media (North Mankato, MN), 2002.

Why Can't I . . . Slide down a Rainbow?, and Other Questions about Light, Smart Apple Media (North Mankato, MN), 2002.

Why Can't I . . . Roar like a Lion?, and Other Questions about Sound, Smart Apple Media (North Mankato, MN), 2002.

"TAKING PART" SERIES

Pupil Parliament, photographs by Chris Fairclough, F. Watts (London, England), 2002.
An Eco-School, photographs by Chris Fairclough, F. Watts (London, England), 2002.
A Caring School, photographs by Chris Fairclough, F. Watts (London, England), 2002.
Community Helpers, photographs by Chris Fairclough, F. Watts (London, England), 2002.
Twinned Schools, photographs by Chris Fairclough, F. Watts (London, England), 2002.

"FASCINATING SCIENCE PROJECTS" SERIES

Light, Copper Beech Books (Brookfield, CT), 2002.
Animal Kingdom, F. Watts (London, England), 2002.
Air, F. Watts (London, England), 2003.

"SCIENCE AROUND US" SERIES

Pull and Push, Chrysalis Education (North Mankato, MN), 2003.
Dark and Light, Chrysalis Education (North Mankato, MN), 2003.
Using Machines, Chrysalis Education (North Mankato, MN), 2003.
Sound, Chrysalis Education (North Mankato, MN), 2003.
Energy, Chrysalis Education (North Mankato, MN), 2003.

"I CAN REMEMBER" SERIES

World War II, F. Watts (London, England), 2003.
The 1950s, F. Watts (London, England), 2003.
The 1960s, F. Watts (London, England), 2003.
The 1970s, F. Watts (London, England), 2003.
The 1980s, F. Watts (London, England), 2005.
The 1930s, F. Watts (London, England), 2005.

"SEASONS" SERIES

A Year at the Seaside, photographs by Chris Fairclough, F. Watts (London, England), 2004.
A Year in the City, photographs by Chris Fairclough, F. Watts (London, England), 2004.
A Year in the Village, photographs by Chris Fairclough, F. Watts (London, England), 2004.
A Year on the Farm, photographs by Chris Fairclough, F. Watts (London, England), 2004.

"WAYS INTO HISTORY" SERIES

Seaside Holiday, F. Watts (London, England), 2004.
Toys and Games, F. Watts (London, England), 2004.
Houses and Homes, F. Watts (London, England), 2004.
The Great Fire of London, F. Watts (London, England), 2004.

Brunel: The Great Engineer, F. Watts (London, England), 2004.
Florence Nightingale, F. Watts (London, England), 2004.

"STARTERS" READER SERIES

Human Body, Aladdin (London, England), 2004, Stargazer Books (North Mankato, MN), 2006.
Sorting Plants: What Is a Flower?, Aladdin (London, England), 2004, Stargazer Books (North Mankato, MN), 2006.
Sorting Materials: Tough Toys, Soft Toys, Aladdin (London, England), 2004, Stargazer Books (Mankato, MN), 2006.
Forces: Tractors, F. Watts (London, England), 2005, Stargazer Books (North Mankato, MN), 2006.
Heat: Too Hot or Too Cold?, F. Watts (London, England), 2005, Stargazer Books (North Mankato, MN), 2007.
Life Processes: What's Inside Me?, F. Watts (London, England), 2005, Stargazer Books (North Mankato, MN), 2006.
Animal Kingdom: Ants to Whales, F. Watts (London, England), 2005, Stargazer Books (North Mankato, MN), 2006.
Springs: How Far Does It Stretch?, F. Watts (London, England), 2005, Stargazer Books (Mankato, MN), 2006.
Looking after Myself, F. Watts (London, England), 2005, Stargazer Books (North Mankato, MN), 2006.
Local Wildlife: What's in My Garden?, F. Watts (London, England), 2005, Stargazer Books (North Mankato, MN), 2006.
Time: What Time Is It?, F. Watts (London, England), 2005, Stargazer Books (North Mankato, MN), 2008.
Measuring: How Big Is It?, F. Watts (London, England), 2006, Stargazer Books (North Mankato, MN), 2008.
Living Things: Is It Alive?, F. Watts (London, England), 2006, Stargazer Books (Norht Mankato, MN), 2007.
Routes and Journeys: I Know the Way, F. Watts (London, England), 2006, Stargazer Books (North Mankato, MN), 2007.
Friction: Wheels and Brakes, F. Watts (London, England), 2007, Stargazer Books (North Mankato, MN), 2008.
Rocks and Soil: Gems, Metals, and Minerals, F. Watts (London, England), 2007, Stargazer Books (North Mankato, MN), 2008.
Space: Sun, Moon, and Stars, F. Watts (London, England), 2007, Stargazer Books (North Mankato, MN), 2008.

"LET'S START! SCIENCE" SERIES

Hear This!, QED (London, England), 2005, Crabtree Pub. (New York, NY), 2008, published as *Listen Up!,* QEB Publications (North Mankato, MN), 2005.
Look Here!, QED (London, England), 2005, Crabtree (New York, NY), 2008, published as *Look Out!,* QEB Publications (North Mankato, MN), 2005.
Smell It!, QED (London, England), 2005, Crabtree (New York, NY), 2008, published as *Smell That!,* QEB Publications (North Mankato, MN), 2005.

Tastes Good!, QEB Publications (North Mankato, MN), 2005.

Touch That!, QEB Publications (North Mankato, MN), 2005.

"A WALK" SERIES

A Walk in the Town, photographs by Chris Fairclough, F. Watts (London, England), 2005.

A Walk in the Park, photographs by Chris Fairclough, F. Watts (London, England), 2005.

A Walk by the Seaside, photographs by Chris Fairclough, F. Watts (London, England), 2005.

A Walk by the River, photographs by Chris Fairclough, F. Watts (London, England), 2005.

A Walk around a School, photographs by Chris Fairclough, F. Watts (London, England), 2005.

"HOW CAN I DEAL WITH. . ." SERIES

Bullying, F. Watts (London, England), 2007, Black Rabbit Books (Mankato, MN), 2009.

My Parents' Divorce, F. Watts (London, England), 2007, Smart Apple Media (Mankato, MN), 2009.

My Stepfamily, F. Watts (London, England), 2007, Smart Apple Media (Mankato, MN), 2009.

Our New Baby, F. Watts (London, England), 2007, Smart Apple Media (Mankato, MN), 2009.

Racism, F. Watts (London, England), 2007, Smart Apple Media (Mankato, MN), 2009.

When People Die, F. Watts (London, England), 2007, Smart Apple Media (Mankato, MN), 2009.

"AMAZING SCIENCE" SERIES

Amazing Electricity, Wayland (London, England), 2006, Crabtree Pub. (New York, NY), 2008.

Amazing Forces and Movement, Wayland (London, England!), 2006, Crabtree Pub. (New York, NY), 2008.

Amazing Light, Wayland (London, England), 2006, Crabtree Pub. (New York, NY), 2008.

Amazing Materials, Wayland (London, England), 2006, Crabtree Pub. (New York, NY), 2008.

Amazing Plants, Wayland (London, England), 2006, Crabtree Pub. (New York, NY), 2008.

Amazing Sound, Wayland (London, England), 2006, Crabtree Pub. (New York, NY), 2008.

"STARTING HISTORY" SERIES

World War II, F. Watts (London, England), 2006.

The Vikings, F. Watts (London, England), 2006, Smart Apple Media (North Mankato, MN), 2008.

The Anglo-Saxons, F. Watts (London, England), 2006.

The Tudors, F. Watts (London, England), 2006.

The Victorians, F. Watts (London, England), 2006.

The Romans, F. Watts (London, England), 2006, Smart Apple Media (North Mankato, MN), 2008.

The Egyptians, F. Watts (London, England), 2006, Smart Apple Media (North Mankato, MN), 2008.

The Greeks, F. Watts (London, England), 2006, Smart Apple Media (North Mankato, MN), 2008.

"GOOD FOR ME" SERIES

Fruit, Wayland (London, England), 2007, PowerKids Press (New York, NY), 2008.

Grains and Cereals, Wayland (London, England), 2007, PowerKids Press (New York, NY), 2008.

Meat and Fish, Wayland (London, England), 2007, PowerKids Press (New York, NY), 2008.

Milk and Cheese, Wayland (London, England), 2007, PowerKids Press (New York, NY), 2008.

Vegetables, Wayland (London, England), 2007, PowerKids Press (New York, NY), 2008.

Water, Wayland (London, England), 2007, PowerKids Press (New York, NY), 2008.

"MY BODY" SERIES

My Bones, QEB Publications (Mankato, MN), 2008.

My Brain, QEB Publications (Laguna Hills, CA), 2008.

My Digestive System, QEB Publications (Laguna Hills, CA), 2008.

My Heart and Lungs, QEB Publications (Laguna Hills, CA), 2008.

"GREEN TEAM" SERIES

Reduce and Reuse, F. Watts (London, England), 2008, Crabtree (New York, NY), 2009.

Using Energy, F. Watts (London, England), 2008, Crabtree (New York, NY), 2009.

Using Water, F. Watts (London, England), 2008, Crabtree (New York, NY), 2009.

Waste and Recycling, F. Watts (London, England), 2008, Crabtree (New York, NY), 2009.

Your Food, F. Watts (London, England), 2008, Crabtree (New York, NY), 2009.

Your Local Environment, F. Watts (London, England), 2008, Crabtree (New York, NY), 2009.

"STARTING SCIENCE" SERIES

Sound, F. Watts (London, England), 2009.

Forces, F. Watts (London, England), 2009.

Materials, F. Watts (London, England), 2009.

Light, F. Watts (London, England), 2009.

"STARTING GEOGRAPHY" SERIES

By the Sea, F. Watts (London, England), 2009, Amicus (Mankato, MN), 2010.

Caring for Our Earth, F. Watts (London, England), 2009, Amicus (Mankato, MN), 2010.

Homes, F. Watts (London, England), 2009, Amicus (Mankato, MN), 2010.

Maps, F. Watts (London, England), 2009, Amicus (Mankato, MN), 2010.

Mountains, F. Watts (London, England), 2009, Amicus (Mankato, MN), 2011.

Rivers, F. Watts (London, England), 2009, Amicus (Mankato, MN), 2011.

Transportation, F. Watts (London, England), 2009, Amicus (Mankato, MN), 2011.

Weather, F. Watts (London, England), 2009, Amicus (Mankato, MN), 2011.

OTHER

Including Pupils with Autism at Break and Lunchtimes, National Association for Special Educational Needs (Tamworth, England), 2003.

Specialist Support Approaches to Autism Spectrum Disorder Students in Mainstream Settings, Jessica Kingsley (London, England), 2005.

Sidelights

A former teacher who now specializes in writing nonfiction books for young children, Sally Hewitt is a pro-

Cover of Sally Hewitt's **Forces around Us,** *a book for budding scientists that features cover photography by Ray Moller.* (Franklin Watts, 1998. Reproduced by permission of Hachette Publishing Group.)

lific author whose published books include *Mr. Goon Flies to the Moon, All Kinds of Habitats,* and numerous titles in the "It's Science!," "Now I Know," "Amazing Science," "I Can Remember," "Starters," and "Green Team" reader series. Commenting on her contributions to the "Now I Know" books, *Children's Book Review Service* reviewer Ursula Adams praised Hewitt's *Now I Know about Animals* and *Now I Know All around Me* as "a wonderful introduction to the world of learning." Another series, "My Body," encompasses the books *My Bones, My Brain, My Digestive System,* and *My Heart and Lungs* and was praised by *School Library Journal* contributor Karen Hoth for its ability to "present facts in a colorful, easy-to-understand manner."

Born in Sussex, England, in 1949, Hewitt earned a bachelor's degree in education at the Stockwell College of Education before going on to specialize in the teaching of music and science in British primary schools. In 1990 she began her career as a freelance writer by teaming up with the publishing firm of Conran to create *Busy Little Artist,* a craft book featuring photographs of children's art. From there she has gone on to produce a wide range of nonfiction books for children ranging in age from toddlers to pre-teens, many of which provide young people with basic introductions to nature and scientific concepts. "For me, the challenge of being an author is to write clear, attractive information books for children," Hewitt once explained to *SATA.* "I started my career as a teacher, so I know the difference that bright, creative books can make. I want to write books that inspire children to pore over detail, ask questions, learn something new, and find out more for themselves. Visiting schools and libraries as a writer helps me to find out what really works with children, parents, and teachers." Hewitt's books can be found in schools and libraries in both Great Britain and the United States.

The "It's Science!" series presents a wide range of science-related subjects, and Hewitt's contributions include *Forces around Us, Weather, Light and Dark,* and *Hearing Sounds.* The series is presented in a basic format that *Times Educational Supplement* contributor Wilson Flood described as "ideal for children from about six to eight." Connections between scientific terms and everyday objects are clearly drawn, and each book in the series contains color photographs and hands-on activities that increase knowledge of the physical properties of planet Earth. While some critics faulted Hewitt's presentation as overly basic, *School Librarian* critic Wilfred Ashworth wrote that books in the "It's Science!" series "succeed . . . in making [science] seem easy."

Other science-based series by Hewitt include the "Amazing Science," "Starting Science," and "Let's Start! Science" series. Praising the five volumes in "Let's Start! Science"—*Smell It!, Touch That!, Taste's Good!, Look Here!,* and *Hear This!*—Rachel Gooden characterized the project as "a great introduction to

learning about the five senses" that combines "clear, simple language" and "bright, clear" photographs. The "Amazing Science" series is geared for older readers and focuses on physics in books such as *Amazing Electricity, Amazing Forces and Movement,* and *Amazing Sound.* Here Hewitt "does a great job of introducing science concepts in a very simple manner," according to Kelley McGuire, another *Resource Links* writer. According to *Science and Children* contributor Marilyn Cook, the series features "a clear introduction to basic concepts" and works well "as a springboard for further study and investigation."

Hewitt has also contributed a number of titles to the "Take Off" series, an introduction to mathematics that presents basic concepts in books such as *Take Off with Time, Take Off with Puzzles,* and *Take Off with Sorting and Sets.* Praising the books' format as "accessible to young children," *Booklist* contributor Carolyn Phelan added that Hewitt's *Take Off with Puzzles* includes not only counting activities, but also advanced concepts such as predicting and sorting by pattern and shape. Ending with a quiz, *Take Off with Time* encourages young readers to learn about the concept of time through photographs of a variety of timepieces, as well as a project that results in a paper clock. Praising the series as a whole for containing "a playfulness and open-

Hewitt presents readers with a wealth of ways to keep busy and also learn about the complex world of nature in **Nature for Fun Projects,** *featuring artwork by Tony Kenyon, Stuart Squires, and Mike Atkinson.*
(Copper Beech, 2000. Reproduced in the U.S. by permission of Millbrook Press, in the rest of the world by permission of Aladdin Books.)

endedness that could give learning mathematics a good name," *Appraisal* contributor Linda F. Wiener noted that the "Take Off" books will serve both parents and teachers as an effective means by which to teach basic math skills because their "simple and clear" texts are helpful in encouraging "learning by doing."

Hewitt focuses on environmental issues in her "Green Team" books, which include *Using Water, Waste and Recycling, Your Food, Using Energy,* and *Reduce and Reuse.* In *School Library Journal* Kathy Piehl wrote that Hewitt balances a discussion about the topic at hand with "action suggestions" that include projects allowing readers to make constructive changes within their own family and community. Reviewing *Waste and Recycling,* Ilene Cooper noted in *Booklist* that Hewitt's "attractive offering is an upbeat answer to a serious problem." *Science and Children* contributor Teri Cosentino wrote that in *Using Water* Hewitt structures her text to "increase awareness through action" and also "connect children from one culture to another" as fellow occupants of Mother Earth.

In *Jungle Beasts Pop-up: A Face to Face Safari, Pop-up Bugs: Creepy Crawlers Face to Face,* and *Pop-up Sea Creatures: Squirmy, Scary Fish Face to Face* Hewitt teams up with artist Chris Gilvan-Cartwright to entertain young children and also introduce a variety of exotic creatures. In *Jungle Beasts Pop-up* six brightly colored animals rise from sturdy paper pages, and are brought to life in Hewitt's rhyming text. "Younger children especially will be startled, then delighted, by each in-your-face encounter," predicted John Peters in his *School Library Journal* review of the book.

In describing her job as a children's writer Hewitt expressed great appreciation for the guidance she has received from the editors, designers, and illustrators she has had the pleasure to work with since the beginning of her writing career. Despite her busy writing schedule, Hewitt still finds time for her favorite pastimes. "I sing in a choir," she once explained to *SATA,* "cycle along the Thames and in Richmond Park, and love sitting down to a meal I have cooked with my family." Regarding her career as a children's book author? "Seeing children fully engaged and excited by books is magic," Hewitt told a *Word Pool* Web site interviewer. "Writing books for children is a dream come true."

Biographical and Critical Sources

PERIODICALS

Appraisal, fall, 1996, Linda F. Wiener, review of "Take Off" series, pp. 67-68.
Booklist, May 15, 1996, Carolyn Phelan, review of "Take Off" series, p. 1589; February 15, 2009, Ilene Cooper, review of *Waste and Recycling,* p. 90.

Hewitt addresses a science-related topic of contemporary concern in her book Using Energy, *which examines the past and future of global power sources.* (Crabtree Publishing Company, 2009. Photo reproduced by permission of Shutterstock.)

Children's Book Review Service, December, 1995, Ursula Adams, review of "Now I Know" series, p. 39.
Resource Links, February, 2008, Kelley McGuire, review of "Amazing Science" series, p. 22; June, 2008, Rachelle Gooden, review of "Let's Start Science!" series, p. 13.
School Librarian, May, 1996, Marie Imeson, review of "Now I Know" series, p. 67; August, 1996, Joan Nellist, reviews of *The Plains People* and *The Aztecs,* both p. 112; summer, 1998, Wilfred Ashworth, reviews of *Forces around Us, Full of Energy,* and *Machines We Use,* all p. 92.
School Library Journal, June, 1996, JoAnn Rees, review of "Take Off" series, p. 116; May, 1999, Christine A. Moesch, reviews of *The Five Senses* and *All Kinds of Habitats,* both pp. 107-108; January, 2001, Jody McCoy, review of *Animal Homes,* p. 117; July, 2003, John Peters, review of *Face to Face Safari,* p. 98; April, 2006, Sandra Welzenbach, review of *Animal Kingdom: Ants to Whales,* p. 126; November, 2008, Kathy Piehl, review of "Green Team" series; August, 2009, Karen Hoth, review of "My Body" series, p. 90; November, 2010, Lisa Crandall, reviews of *By the Sea, Homes,* and *Maps,* all p. 92.

Science and Children, October, 2008, Marilyn Cook, review of *Amazing Plants,* p. 70; December, 2008, Marilyn Cook, review of *Amazing Materials,* p. 61; February, 2009, Teri Cosentino, review of *Reduce and Reuse,* p. 66; April-May, 2009, Marilyn Cook, review of *Amazing Sound,* p. 71; December, 2009, Marilyn Cook, review of *Amazing Electricity,* p. 64; February, 2010, Teri Cosentino, review of *Using Water,* p. 75.

Times Educational Supplement, February 27, 1998, Wilson Flood, reviews of *Full of Energy, Forces around Us,* and *Solid, Liquid, or Gas?,* all p. 56.

ONLINE

Word Pool Web site, http://www.wordpool.co.uk/ (June 28, 2011), interview with Hewitt.*

* * *

HOUSTON, Dick 1943-

Personal

Born December 18, 1943, in Ashtabula, OH. *Education:* Kent State University, B.A. (English); Edinboro University of Pennsylvania, M.A. (English).

Addresses

Home—Ashtabula, OH. *E-mail*—dhoustonelefence@ yahoo.com.

Career

Conservationist, safari leader, educator, and writer. Leader of overland safari expeditions across Sahara Desert, beginning c. 1960s; teacher of English in Africa for American Embassy schools; freelance writer. Elefence International (conservation group), Zambia, cofounder and president. Film-speaker for African Adventure programs at schools.

Awards, Honors

Distinguished Alumni Award, Edinboro University of Pennsylvania, 1994; Roger T. Beitler Award for Arts and Humanities, Kent State University; named honorary trustee, Martin and Osa Johnson Safari Museum (KS); Best Book citation, Bank Street College of Education, 2011, for *Bulu.*

Writings

(And photographer) *Safari Adventure* (memoir), Cobblehill Books (New York, NY), 1991.

Bulu: African Wonder Dog, Random House (New York, NY), 2010.

Contributor of articles to periodicals, including *Los Angeles Times, New York Times, Readers Digest,* and *Smithsonian.*

Sidelights

Dick Houston took his first adventure trek as a seven year old growing up in the Midwest, and he fulfilled his dream of living in the wild years later, while working in Africa as a safari leader and conservationist. As a safari leader, Houston has led journeys across the Sahara Desert, through rain forests, and into the African bush, and his growing concern over the continent's threatened wildlife prompted him to join a friend in founding the conservation nonprofit Elefence International to educate the world about elephant conservation. Houston was inspired to write his first young-adult book, *Bulu: African Wonder Dog,* while visiting Zambia's South Luangwa National Park on behalf of Elefence and hearing the story of a remarkable Jack Russell terrier.

Born in Ohio, Houston attended Kent State University and Edinboro University of Pennsylvania, ultimately graduating with a master's degree in English. He went to work as a teacher and continued to teach English when his travels took him to Venezuela and thence to Kenya, Zambia, and South Africa. In *Safari Adventure* Houston recounts the first month-long trek he made in

A spunky Jack Russell terrier is the star of Dick Houston's Bulu: African Wonder Dog, *featuring photography by Steve and Anna Tolan.* (Photograph courtesy of Steve and Anna Tolan. Reproduced with permission of Dick Houston.)

Africa: a 1972 journey from Nairobi to Lake Paradise that also included a climb up Kilimanjaro. Reviewing *Safari Adventure* in *School Library Journal*, Doris A. Fong praised the work as "everything a well-written travelogue should be," weaving Houston's "vivid prose" with you-are-there-style photographs that allow young readers to travel the lands of the heroic Maasai warrior.

In *Bulu* readers meet a Jack Russell pup who was born on a Zambian crocodile farm. Bulu was an unwanted runt until he was adopted by Anna and Steve Tolan, a British couple who were fulfilling their dream of living in the African bush. With a name that means "wild dog" in the language of the local Nyanja tribe, Bulu had a gentle nature that made him an affective foster parent for the many animals that the Tolans rescued and cared for in their new African home. The pup's charges included everything from baboons and monkeys to warthogs, buffalo, and even a young elephant, and he bravely defended his young, defenseless charges when predators such as crocodiles and even hungry lions became a threat. 'Houston's account is an animal-lovers delight," asserted *Booklist* contributor Anne O'Malley, while in *School Library Journal* Denise Moore predicted that *Bulu* "will hold the interest of even the most reluctant readers," whether they are in search of a thrilling adventure or a story that channels their love of man's best friend.

Biographical and Critical Sources

PERIODICALS

Houston, Dick, *Safari Adventure,* Cobblehill Books (New York, NY), 1991.

PERIODICALS

Booklist, March 15, 2010, Anne O'Malley, review of *Bulu: African Wonder Dog,* p. 40.
Bulletin of the Center for Children's Books, October, 1991, review of *Safari Adventure,* p. 39.
Cleveland, December, 2010, Jennifer Keirn, "Wild Life."
School Library Journal, November, 1991, Doris A. Fong, review of *Safari Adventure,* p. 139; May, 2010, Denise Moore, review of *Bulu,* p. 132.
Voice of Youth Advocates, December, 1991, review of *Safari Adventure,* p. 336; April, 2010, Barbara Johnston, review of *Bulu,* p. 80.

ONLINE

Bulu: African Wonder Dog Web site, http://www.buluafricanwonderdog.com/ (June 15, 2011).
Elefence International Web site, http://www.elefence.org/ (June 15, 2011).

HOUTMAN, Jacqueline 1960-
(Jacqueline Jaeger Houtman)

Personal

Born 1960; married Carl Houtman (a chemical engineer); children: one son. *Education:* University of Delaware, B.A. (biological science; with distinction; cum laude), 1981, M.S. (animal science), 1989; University of Wisconsin—Madison, Ph.D. (medical microbiology and immunology), 1996.

Addresses

Home—P.O. Box 259815, Madison, WI 53725.

Career

Science writer, editor, and novelist, beginning 1997. Presenter at schools.

Member

National Association of Science Writers, American Medical Writers Association, Society of Children's Book Writers and Editors.

Awards, Honors

Tofte/Wright Children's Literature Award, Council for Wisconsin Writers, and Cooperative Children's Book Center Choice selection, both 2011, both for *The Reinvention of Edison Thomas.*

Writings

The Reinvention of Edison Thomas, Front Street (Honesdale, PA), 2010.

Contributor to periodicals, including *Advances in Experimental Medicine and Biology, AMWA Journal, Avian Diseases, Cleveland Clinic Magazine, Clinical and Experimental Allergy, Journal of Lipid Research, Journal of NeroVirology,* and *Wisconsin State Journal.*

Sidelights

Science writer and editor Jacqueline Houtman had something special to celebrate the year she turned fifty: she was now a published novelist. In her novel *The Reinvention of Edison Thomas,* Houtman introduces middle graders to a new way of looking at the world: through the eyes of a preteen whose ability to deal with typical adolescent worries are made more challenging because he also has Asperger's syndrome.

When readers first meet Eddy Thomas in *The Reinvention of Edison Thomas,* the middle grader is beginning his first year at Drayton Middle School. Although Eddy's spectrum disorder is high functioning—he cannot tolerate loud noises or illogical, inefficient actions, and cannot "read" people's facial language—orienting himself to his new environment is very distressing. The way the boy deals with the unpredictable human element—teachers, classmates, and potential new friends—is to shut it out in favor of channeling his analytical and mnemonic abilities into learning Morse code, memorizing the entire periodic table, and jumping up and down on the school's trampoline. Fortunately, Eddy makes some special friends among Drayton's geeky contingent; Justin and Terry understand the way Edison's mind works enough to join the school counselor in helping him interact better with his other classmates. When a school crossing guard is laid off due to town budget cuts, Eddy begins to mull over the problems that result, problems that could actually endanger Drayton Middle School students. Mining his supply of broken appliances and scraps of machinery, the preteen creates a device to caution auto traffic at the crossing guard's old post, showing others that a smile is not the only way of showing affection.

"It's curious to walk with a mind that works differently, where channels are isolated, fraught, and amplified, but readers will get a chance to do just that" by getting to know Eddy, wrote Alison Follos in her review of *The Reinvention of Edison Thomas* for *School Library Journal*. Citing the story's "quirky humor and authentic characters," a *Publishers Weekly* critic praised Houtman's novel as "a perceptive look at a complicated mind," and Cindy Dobrez observed in *Booklist* that the author's inclusion of "scientific facts . . . will intrigue budding scientists." A *Kirkus Reviews* writer observed that Houtman "has a particularly engaging way of tracking Eddie's thought processes as he struggles to wrest order from a seemingly chaotic world," and dubbed the hero of *The Reinvention of Edison Thomas* a preteen "worth knowing."

Biographical and Critical Sources

PERIODICALS

Booklist, April 1, 2010, Cindy Dobrez, review of *The Reinvention of Edison Thomas,* p. 41.
Bulletin of the Center for Children's Books, April, 2010, Deborah Stevenson, review of *The Reinvention of Edison Thomas,* p. 338.
Kirkus Reviews, March 1, 2010, review of *The Reinvention of Edison Thomas.*
Publishers Weekly, March 15, 2010, review of *The Reinvention of Edison Thomas,* p. 53.
School Library Journal, June, 2010, Alison Follos, review of *The Reinvention of Edison Thomas,* p. 104.
Wisconsin State Journal, March 23, 2010, Doug Moe, "Science Writer Becomes Children's Novelist," p. A2.

ONLINE

Jacqueline Houtman Home Page, http://jjhoutman.com (July 15, 2011).
Jacqueline Houtman Web log, http://jjhoutman/livejournal.com (July 15, 2011).*

* * *

HOUTMAN, Jacqueline Jaeger
See HOUTMAN, Jacqueline

* * *

HOXTER, Holly Nicole 1983-

Personal

Born 1983, in Baltimore, MD; married. *Education:* University of Maryland, College Park, B.A. (English). *Hobbies and other interests:* Reading, running.

Addresses

Home—Baltimore, MD. *E-mail*—holly.nicole.hoxter@gmail.com.

Cover of Jacqueline Houtman's middle-grade novel The Reinvention of Edison Thomas. *(Jacket photographs © 2010 by JupiterImages Corporation. Reproduced with permission of Front St., an imprint of Boyds Mills Press, Inc.)*

Career

Author and medical transcriptionist. Worked variously as a cashier, relay operator for the deaf, legal word processor, and pet sitter. Presenter at literary festivals.

Writings

Holly Nicole Hoxter, *The Snowball Effect,* HarperTeen (New York, NY), 2010.

Sidelights

Holly Nicole Hoxter began to take her writing seriously when she realized how many would-be authors were working mundane jobs instead of pursuing their passion. While working by day as a medical transcriptionist, Hoxter set to work to produce a novel-length work, and her diligence resulted in her first published novel, *The Snowball Effect.* "Expertly weaving together quirky family stories, realistic characters and tough decisions," *The Snowball Effect* illustrates that "teens need not just go with the flow but can and should control their own destinies," according to a *Kirkus Reviews* writer.

When readers meet Lainey Pike, the central character in *The Snowball Effect,* she is marveling at the number of deaths budding out along the newest branches of her family tree. Her grandmother's stroke, her stepfather's dramatic motorcycle accident, and her own mother's recent suicide in the basement of the family home have left Lainey and her five-year-old brother Colin orphaned. When Vallery, Lainey's older half-sister, returns to take care of the emotionally traumatized Colin, the recent high-school graduate feels like life has taken control of her. The fact that her boyfriend, Riley, is beginning to talk about settling down also makes the young woman feel confined, and her long-time friends provide only pat advice even though everything in her world is now different. Afraid of settling for the easy solution, the eighteen year old hopes to escape the confines of her fatalistic family when she meets a young man with no ties to her past. Through this new relationship, Lainey is able to disconnect from her current worries and clearly reflect on her need for independence and her desire to reconcile this with her love of family and the things that are truly most important.

Praising *The Snowball Effect* in *Booklist,* Francisca Goldsmith noted that in Lainey Hoxter "creates a compelling character who develops . . . emotional maturity" while responding to "conflicting demands." While the plot of the novel might verge on melodrama, the debut author "gives a masterful portrayal of the effects of grief" and Lainey's coming-of-age "feels authentic and earned," according to a *Publishers Weekly* critic.

Cover of Holly Nicole Hoxter's coming-of-age novel The Snowball Effect, *in which a new friendship allows a young teen to break from her emotionally confining family.* (HarperCollins, 2010. Photograph copyright © by OJO Images Photography/Veer.)

Biographical and Critical Sources

PERIODICALS

Booklist, February 15, 2010, Francisca Goldsmith, review of *The Snowball Effect,* p. 72.
Bulletin of the Center for Children's Books, May, 2010, Deborah Stevenson, review of *The Snowball Effect,* p. 38.
Kirkus Reviews, March 1, 2010, review of *The Snowball Effect.*
Publishers Weekly, March 22, 2010, review of *The Snowball Effect,* p. 70.
School Library Journal, April, 2010, Rhona Campbell, review of *The Snowball Effect,* p. 160.

ONLINE

Cynsations Web log, http://cynthialeitichsmith.blogspot.com/ (July 6, 2010), Cynthia Leitich Smith, interview with Hoxter.
Holly Nicole Hoxter Home Page, http://www.hollynicolehoxter.com (June 20, 2011).*

J

JAY, Stacey 1978(?)-

Personal

Born c. 1978, in AR; married; children: four. *Education:* B.F.A. (acting). *Hobbies and other interests:* Cooking, photography, reading.

Addresses

Home—Maumelle, AR.

Career

Author. Worked variously as an actor dancer, waiter, math tutor, and yoga instructor; freelance writer, beginning 2005.

Writings

YOUNG-ADULT NOVELS

You Are So Undead to Me, Razorbill (New York, NY), 2009.
Undead Much? (sequel to *You Are So Undead to Me*), Razorbill (New York, NY), 2010.
My So-called Death, Flux (Woodbury, MN), 2010.
Juliet Immortal, Delacorte Press (New York, NY), 2011.
The Locket, Razorbill (New York, NY), 2011.

OTHER

Dead on the Delta (adult urban fantasy novel), 2011.

Author of adult romance novels under a pseudonym.

Adaptations

You Are So Undead to Me and *Undead Much?* were adapted for audiobook.

Sidelights

Stacey Jay channels her unusual fascination for zombies in a constructive fashion: she writes horror fiction for teen readers that mixes in a healthy dose of humor and a dash of romance. Her YA novels include the companion stories *You Are So Undead to Me* and *Undead Much?* as well as *My So-called Death, The Locket,* and *Juliet Immortal,* the last a thriller based on the ill-fated love affair in Shakespeare's *Romeo and Juliet.* "I'm a young adult at heart," Jay explained on her home page, discussing why she writes for teen readers. "I have a lot of energy and enthusiasm and hope, but I also spend a lot of time wondering what the heck is going on," she added. "Life is big and confusing and never more so than when you're trying to grow up. I haven't stopped growing up yet, so young adult novels still feel very authentic for me to write."

During her own confusing teen years, Jay was a cheerleader and dancer, and her fictional characters exhibit a cheerleader's characteristic high-energy optimism and competitive spirit. In *You Are So Undead to Me,* for example, fifteen-year-old Megan Berry is a cheerleader. She is also a Zombie Settler: a human whose task it is to help the undead resolve personal issues in order to move to their ultimate resting place. While zombies are, by nature, well . . . zombies, Megan worries that a sudden rash of zombie attacks means that someone has harnessed them as vicious puppets to further some nefarious purpose. Megan returns in *Undead Much?,* as she finds herself on the radar of the recently reanimated. While the perky high-school sophomore teams up with friend and fellow pom squader Monica to save the world from a wave of zombie aggression, she also finds time for truly important things, like pom-pom squad practice and hanging out with boyfriend Ethan. Citing the "brisk clip" of the action in *Undead Much?,* a *Publishers Weekly* critic wrote that Jay's "light and engaging" prose features "lively and likeable" teen characters. In *Booklist* Francisca Goldsmith deemed the same novel a "delicious sequel" to *You Are So Undead to Me.*

Cover of Stacey Jay's quirky and humorously horrific middle-grade novel **My So-called Death.** (Cover image © 2010 Rob Melnychuk/Digital Vision/PunchStock. Reproduced with permission from Flux, an imprint of Llewellyn Publications.)

Another cheerleader, high-school freshman Karen Vera, pits her wits against a zombie menace in *My So-called Death.* Karen had been blissfully unaware of zombies until a fall during cheerleading practice left her with a cracked skull and a messy brain leakage. Now technically dead, Karen nonetheless is still standing due to the genetic mutation that creates zombies. Fortunately, an enterprising educator has set up a school for these young undead, and Karen is soon shipped off to Dead High. Now she shares a dorm room with a Goth girl who despises her, lines up for the most disgusting dining-hall food imaginable, and finds herself crushing on a cute un-dead who she suspects of stealing the damaged brains of Dead High students. "Peppered with gross-out humor, the camp flows freely" in Jay's amusing horror story, wrote a *Kirkus Reviews* writer, and a *Publishers Weekly* reviewer predicted that "the premise and gruesome details" in *My So-called Death* "should appeal to those with a dark sense of humor." Jay's "plot is swiftly paced and appropriately wacky," asserted *Booklist* critic Debbie Carton, "but the real draws" of *My So-called Death* "are the satirical portrayal of the popular set and the black humor of zombie life."

Jay sidesteps zombies in *The Locket* and instead focuses on more subtle manifestations of the paranormal. On her seventeenth birthday, Katie discovers a locket and decides that to wear it will give her good luck. When she is dumped (for just cause) by boyfriend Isaac, the locket lets Katie travel two weeks into the past and avoid the relational misstep that led to Isaac's rejection. While her love life now stabilizes, other things in Katie's world seem oddly "off," and now she wonders whether monkeying around with the past has allowed her to avoid unpleasant consequences after all. Although *The Locket* "could stand as an example of the perils of underage drinking," Suanne Rousch added in her *School Library Journal* review of the novel that "the paranormal aspects will keep even the most reluctant reader devouring" Jay's story.

In an online interview with Brittany Geragotelis for *American Cheerleader* online, Jay offered advice to budding writers. "Read and write," she advised. "Read everything you can get your hands on—each book will teach you something about storytelling. Write every day—because you can't get better if you don't practice. (Something every cheerleader knows, of course.)"

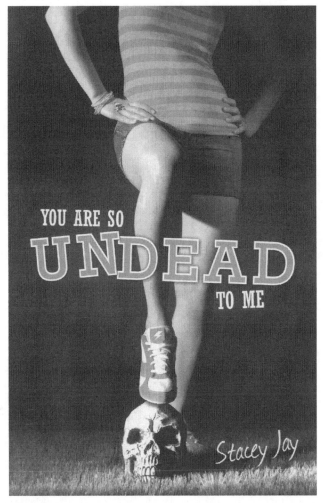

Life after death continues to be the theme in Jay's teen novel **You Are So Undead to Me.** (Cover photograph © Michael Frost. Used by permission of Razorbill, a division of Penguin Young Readers Group, a member of Penguin Group (USA) Inc., 345 Hudson St., New York, NY 10014. All rights reserved.)

Biographical and Critical Sources

PERIODICALS

Booklist, December 1, 2009, Francisca Goldsmith, review of *Undead Much?,* p. 41; February 15, 2010, Debbie Carton, review of *My So-called Death,* p. 71.

Bulletin of the Center for Children's Books, May, 2009, Karen Coats, review of *You Are So Undead to Me,* p. 365; January, 2011, Claire Gross, review of *The Locket,* p. 240.

Kirkus Reviews, February 15, 2009, review of *You Are So Undead to Me;* March 1, 2010, review of *My So-called Death.*

Publishers Weekly, January 18, 2010, review of *Undead Much?,* p. 50; March 8, 2010, review of *My So-called Death,* p. 58.

School Library Journal, March, 2011, Suanne Roush, review of *The Locket,* p. 164.

Voice of Youth Advocates, June, 2009, Kristin Anderson, review of *You Are So Undead to Me,* p. 152; February, 2010, Teri Lesesne, review of *Undead Much?,* p. 508; February, 2011, Marla K. Unruh and Nicole Jacques, review of *The Locket,* p. 570.

ONLINE

Stacey Jay Home Page, http://www.staceyjay.com (April 28, 2011).

Stacey Jay Web log, http://staceyjayya.blogspot.com (July 15, 2011).

American Cheerleader Online, http://www.americancheerleader.com/ (January 1, 2010), Brittany Geragotelis, interview with Jay.

*   *   *

JENNINGS, Sharon 1954-

Personal

Born January 21, 1954, in Toronto, Ontario, Canada; daughter of Alfred Joseph (a mechanic) and Eileen Estella (a homemaker) Jennings; married Anthony DiLena (a lawyer), October 20, 1979; children: Adrian, Guy, Mia. *Education:* University of York, M.A. (English), 1978; Royal Conservatory of Music (University of Toronto), diplomas in speech arts (drama), 1978, 1979. *Hobbies and other interests:* Swimming, running, theatre, ballet, reading, tobogganing.

Addresses

Home—Toronto, Ontario, Canada. *E-mail*—sharonjennings@sympatico.ca.

Career

Editor and author. Harcourt Brace Jovanovich, Toronto, Ontario, Canada, senior editor of textbooks, 1982-86; Nelson Canada, Toronto, senior editor, 1986-87; writer. Presenter at schools.

Sharon Jennings (Reproduced by permission.)

Member

International Board of Books for Young People (IBBY-Canada), Canadian Society of Composers, Authors, Illustrators and Publishers, Writers' Union of Canada, Canadian Children's Book Centre.

Awards, Honors

Best Kids' Books of the Year citation, *Parents* magazine, 1990, for *Jeremiah and Mrs. Ming;* Blue Spruce Award, Ontario Library Association, 1999, for *The Byebye Pie;* Mr. Christie's Award Silver Seal, 2001, for *Priscilla and Rosy;* Governor General's Award for Children's Fiction shortlist, 2009, and TD Canadian Children's Award finalist, 2010, both for *Home Free.*

Writings

FOR CHILDREN

Jeremiah and Mrs. Ming, illustrated by Mireille Levert, Annick Press (Toronto, Ontario, Canada), 1990.

When Jeremiah Found Mrs. Ming, illustrated by Mireille Levert, Annick Press (Toronto, Ontario, Canada), 1992.

Sleep Tight, Mrs. Ming, illustrated by Mireille Levert, Annick Press (Toronto, Ontario, Canada), 1993.

The Bye-bye Pie, illustrated by Ruth Ohi, Fitzhenry & Whiteside (Markham, Ontario, Canada), 1999.

Into My Mother's Arms, illustrated by Ruth Ohi, Fitzhenry & Whiteside (Markham, Ontario, Canada), 2000.

Priscilla and Rosy, illustrated by Linda Hendry, Fitzhenry & Whiteside (Markham, Ontario, Canada), 2001.

Priscilla's Paw de Deux, illustrated by Linda Hendry, Fitzhenry & Whiteside (Markham, Ontario, Canada), 2002.

When You Get a Baby, illustrated by Joanne Fitzgerald, Fitzhenry & Whiteside (Markham, Ontario, Canada), 2002.

No Monsters Here, illustrated by Ruth Ohi, Fitzhenry & Whiteside (Markham, Ontario, Canada), 2004.

Bearcub and Mama, illustrated by Melanie Watt, Kids Can Press (Toronto, Ontario, Canada), 2005.

The Happily Ever Afternoon, illustrated by Ron Lightburn, Annick Press (Toronto, Ontario, Canada), 2006.

(With Nora Hilb) *Wiggle Giggle Tickle Train,* photographs by Marcela Cabezas Hilb, illustrated by Nora Hilb, Annick Press (Toronto, Ontario, Canada), 2009.

A Chanukah Noel: A True Story, illustrated by Gillian Newland, Second Story Press (Toronto, Ontario, Canada), 2010.

C'mere, Boy!, illustrated by Ashley Spires, Kids Can Press (Toronto, Ontario, Canada), 2010.

Author's work has been translated into French.

JUVENILE NOVELS

Pump!, High Interest Publications (Toronto, Ontario, Canada), 2006.

Dancing on the Edge, illustrated by Catherine Doherty, High Interest Publications (Toronto, Ontario, Canada), 2008.

Home Free, Second Story Press (Toronto, Ontario, Canada), 2009.

"BATS" CHAPTER-BOOK SERIES

Bats and Burglars, illustrated by John Mardon, Fitzhenry & Whiteside (Markham, Ontario, Canada), 2000.

Bats out the Window, illustrated by John Mardon, Fitzhenry & Whiteside (Markham, Ontario, Canada), 2001.

Bats in the Garbage, illustrated by John Mardon, Fitzhenry & Whiteside (Markham, Ontario, Canada), 2003.

Bats past Midnight, illustrated by John Mardon, Fitzhenry & Whiteside (Markham, Ontario, Canada), 2005.

Bats in the Graveyard, illustrated by John Mardon, Fitzhenry & Whiteside (Markham, Ontario, Canada), 2006.

Jingle Bats, High Interest Publications (Toronto, Ontario, Canada), 2006.

Batnapped, High Interest Publications (Toronto, Ontario, Canada), 2008.

Baseball Bats, High Interest Publications (Toronto, Ontario, Canada), 2010.

Bats on Break, High Interest Publications (Toronto, Ontario, Canada), 2010.

"FRANKLIN" READER SERIES; BASED ON THE TELEVISION SERIES

(With Paulette Bourgeois) *Franklin's Valentines,* illustrated by Brenda Clark, Kids Can Press (Toronto, Ontario, Canada), 1998.

(With Paulette Bourgeois) *Franklin's Class Trip,* illustrated by Brenda Clark, Scholastic (New York, NY), 1999.

Franklin's Neighbourhood, illustrated by Brenda Clark, Kids Can Press (Toronto, Ontario, Canada), 1999.

Franklin Says Sorry, illustrated by Brenda Clark, Kids Can Press (Toronto, Ontario, Canada), 1999.

Franklin and the Hero, illustrated by Sean Jeffrey and others, Kids Can Press (Toronto, Ontario, Canada), 2000.

Franklin Forgets, illustrated by Sean Jeffrey and others, Scholastic (New York, NY), 2000.

Franklin Goes to the Hospital, illustrated by Brenda Clark, Kids Can Press (Toronto, Ontario, Canada), 2000.

Franklin Plants a Tree, illustrated by Sean Jeffrey, Mark Koren, and Jelena Sisic, Scholastic (New York, NY), 2001.

Franklin Runs Away, illustrated by Sean Jeffrey and others, Scholastic (New York, NY), 2001.

Franklin's Birthday Party, illustrated by Sean Jeffrey and others, Kids Can Press (Toronto, Ontario, Canada), 2001.

Franklin and the Babysitter, illustrated by Mark Koren and others, Scholastic (New York, NY), 2001.

Franklin's Thanksgiving, illustrated by Brenda Clark, Scholastic (New York, NY), 2001.

Franklin and Otter's Visit, illustrated by Mark Koran and others, Kids Can Press (Toronto, Ontario, Canada), 2002.

Franklin and the Magic Show, illustrated by Sean Jeffrey and others, Kids Can Press (Toronto, Ontario, Canada), 2002.

Franklin Plays Hockey, illustrated by Mark Koren, John Lei, and Jelena Sisic, Scholastic (New York, NY), 2002.

Franklin and His Friend, illustrated by Mark Koren, Alice Sinkner, and Jelena Sisic, Scholastic (New York, NY), 2002.

Franklin and the Big Kid, illustrated by Sean Jeffrey, Jelena Sisic, and Shelley Southern, Scholastic (New York, NY), 2002.

Franklin's Canoe Trip, illustrated by Sean Jeffrey, Mark Koren, and Jelena Sisic, Scholastic (New York, NY), 2002.

Franklin's Music Lessons, illustrated by Sean Jeffrey, Alice Sinkner, and Shelley Southern, Scholastic (New York, NY), 2002.

Franklin Makes a Deal, illustrated by Sean Jeffrey and others, Scholastic (New York, NY), 2003.

Franklin Snoops, illustrated by Sean Jeffrey and others, Scholastic (New York, NY), 2003.

Franklin Stays Up, illustrated by Sean Jeffrey, Shelley Southern, and Jelena Sisic, Scholastic (New York, NY), 2003.

Franklin's Trading Cards, illustrated by Sean Jeffrey and others, Kids Can Press (Toronto, Ontario, Canada), 2003.

Franklin's Surprise, illustrated by Sean Jeffrey and others, Kids Can Press (Toronto, Ontario, Canada), 2003.

Franklin Wants a Badge, illustrated by Shelley Southern, Jelena Sisic, and Alice Sinkner, Scholastic (New York, NY), 2003.

Franklin and the Computer, illustrated by John Lei and others, Scholastic (New York, NY), 2003.

Franklin's Reading Club, illustrated by Sean Jeffrey, Mark Koren, and Alice Sinkner, Scholastic (New York, NY), 2003.

Franklin Forgives, illustrated by Céleste Gagnon, Alice Sinkner, and Shelley Southern, Scholastic (New York, NY), 2004.

Franklin the Detective, illustrated by Céleste Gagnon and others, Scholastic (New York, NY), 2004.

Franklin's Pumpkin, illustrated by Sasha McIntyre, Kids Can Press (Toronto, Ontario, Canada), 2004.

Franklin and the Scooter, illustrated by Céleste Gagnon, Kids Can Press (Toronto, Ontario, Canada), 2004.

Franklin and the New Teacher, illustrated by Céleste Gagnon, Kids Can Press (Toronto, Ontario, Canada), 2004.

Franklin and the Contest, illustrated by Sean Jeffrey and others, Kids Can Press (Toronto, Ontario, Canada), 2004.

Franklin's Nickname, illustrated by John Lei, Sasha McIntyre, and Jelena Sisic, Scholastic (New York, NY), 2004.

Franklin's Library Book, illustrated by Céleste Gagnon and others, Scholastic (New York, NY), 2005.

Franklin and the Tin Flute, illustrated by Céleste Gagnon, Kids Can Press (Toronto, Ontario, Canada), 2005.

Franklin Celebrates, illustrated by Sean Jeffrey and others, Kids Can Press (Toronto, Ontario, Canada), 2005.

Franklin's Pond Phantom, illustrated by Sasha McIntyre and others, Kids Can Press (Toronto, Ontario, Canada), 2005.

Ashley Spires contributes humorous cartoon art to Jennings' engaging story in **C'Mere Boy!** (Illustration copyright © 2010 by Ashley Spires. Reproduced with permission of Kids Can Press Ltd.)

Franklin and the Cookies, illustrated by Céleste Gagnon and others, Kids Can Press (Toronto, Ontario, Canada), 2005.

Franklin Has the Hiccups, illustrated by Céleste Gagnon and others, Kids Can Press (Toronto, Ontario, Canada), 2006.

Franklin's Picnic, illustrated by Sasha McIntyre, Kids Can Press (Toronto, Ontario, Canada), 2006.

Franklin and the Bubble Gum, illustrated by Sasha McIntyre, Kids Can Press (Toronto, Ontario, Canada), 2006.

Franklin and the Stopwatch, illustrated by Sasha McIntyre, Kids Can Press (Toronto, Ontario, Canada), 2007.

Franklin and the Duckling, illustrated by Sasha McIntyre, Kids Can Press (Toronto, Ontario, Canada), 2007.

Franklin's Soapbox Derby, illustrated by Sean Jeffrey, Sasha McIntyre, and Jalena Sisic, Kid's Can Press (Toronto, Ontario, Canada), 2007.

Books in the "Franklin" series have been translated into Spanish.

Sidelights

With a passion for the theatre and a talent for writing, Canadian author Sharon Jennings has transitioned her career as a textbook editor into work crafting entertaining stories for children of many ages. Her picture books for younger readers include *Jeremiah and Mrs. Ming, Priscilla and Rosy, C'mere, Boy!, The Happily Ever Afternoon,* and *Wiggle Giggle Tickle Train.* Also the author of chapter books and middle-grade novels such as *Pumped!* and *Dancing on the Edge,* Jennings mixes vocabulary-building skills and likeable characters into her easy-reading "Bats" mystery series, which stars best friends Sam and Simon and includes *Bats and Burglers, Bats in the Garbage,* and *Baseball Bats.* A frequent visitor to schools, Jennings includes theatrics in her engaging language-arts program. "I try to draw kids into my books by having them identify with the characters and situations," she explained on the Annick Press Web site. "I want children to realize that books are about themselves. Books come alive when children bring their own experience to the story."

Jennings grew up in Toronto, Ontario, where she joined her friends in writing, acting, and directing short plays. She sought out drama groups throughout high school and college, and also mentored children with a similar love of the theatre. She earned a master's degree in English at York University, as well as two dramatic arts diplomas, and then found a job editing textbooks for Toronto-based publishers Harcourt Brace Jovanovich and Nelson Canada.

Jennings came up with the idea for her first book, *Jeremiah and Mrs. Ming,* one night when her first child had difficulty falling asleep. In the story, Jeremiah tells Mrs. Ming that he cannot sleep, switching from one imaginative excuse to another to defend his continued shuffling down the hall from his bedroom. Meanwhile, Mrs. Ming keeps busy baking cookies, practicing her ballet, and reading the newspaper, and she performs the same good-night ritual each time she is interrupted by the wide-awake boy. A "simple, cumulative, and repetitive" story, *Jeremiah and Mrs. Ming* has a "mysterious" effect in showing young children that "the world is crazy but safe," commented *Horn Book* reviewer Sarah Ellis, while *Canadian Children's Literature* critic Jetske Sybesma wrote that Jennings' "text and pictures succeed in presenting a positive attitude" toward Canada's ethnic diversity.

Jennings followed her first picture book with two sequels: *When Jeremiah Found Mrs. Ming* and *Sleep Tight, Mrs. Ming.* The first grew out of the time her children, standing in the midst of a pile of toys, announced that they could find fun nothing to do. When Jeremiah presents the marvelous Mrs. Ming with the same problem in *When Jeremiah Found Mrs. Ming,* he is rewarded with a series of wacky adventures. In *Sleep Tight, Mrs. Ming* Jeremiah calls on Mrs. Ming to deal with his nighttime problems and fears, but a turn-around occurs later when a sleeping Mrs. Ming is awakened by a thunderstorm and turns to the boy for comfort. "Jennings has clearly captured a small child's idea of a good time," noted Ellis in her *Quill & Quire* review of *When Jeremiah Found Mrs. Ming,* while *Canadian Review of Materials* critic Ila D. Scott asserted that the story "reinforces the strong message that whenever there is nothing to do, reading is a way to bring many exciting things to pass." Artist Mireille Levert earned a Governor General's award for her illustrations in *When Jeremiah Found Mrs. Ming,* which *Canadian Book Review Annual* critic Steve Pitt hailed as "the third terrific book about the enigmatic relationship between Mrs. Ming and Jeremiah."

Other interlinking picture books by Jennings include *Priscilla and Rosy* and *Pricilla's Paw de Deux,* both which feature a rodent that usually does not appear in picture books. Rather that white-tummied field mice, Priscilla and Rosy are alley rats, and their extreme rattiness is captured in amusing line-and-opaque watercolor art by Linda Hendry. In *Priscilla and Rosy* Priscilla is tempted to back out on a promised visit with Rosy when she gets a better offer from another friend planning a boat ride. *Pricilla's Paw de Deux* captures Priscilla's frustration when her rat hole proves to be too crowded with treasures to allow her to frolic and dance. With Rosy's help, she discovers Mme. Genevieve's Dance Studio, which seems perfect for dancing practice until a watch-cat makes its presence known. In *Kirkus Reviews* a contributor dubbed *Priscilla and Rosy* "charming" and likened Hendry's artwork to Beth and Joe Krush's illustrations for Mary Norton's *The Borrowers.* Jennings' "warm, satisfying story of friendship and persistence will especially appeal to dance lovers," predicted *Booklist* critic Susan Dove Lempke in a review of *Priscilla's Paw de Deux,* while in *School Library Journal* Beth Tegart noted that "Hendry's attention to minuscule details adds a delightful touch."

Standalone picture books by Jennings include *C'mere, Boy!, The Happily Ever Afternoon, A Chanukah Noel: A True Story,* and *The Bye-bye Pie,* the last which captures the mix of emotions that comes from being an older sibling. Illustrated by Ashley Spires in earth-toned cartoon art, *C'mere Boy!* presents a quirky twist on the boy-wants-dog formula that will appeal to "those who enjoy the wry and somewhat skewed," according to a *Kirkus Reviews* writer. *The Happily Ever Afternoon* serves up what *Resource Links* critic Wendy Hogan unabashedly described as "a banquet of joy, truly delightful" in its illustrated tale of a small boy's humorous attempts to sample the food for a family party in advance, and in *Booklist* Carolyn Phelan recommended the same book as "an imaginative experience for young children enchanted by fairy tales." *Wiggle Giggle Tickle Train,* a collaboration between Jennings and artist Nora Hilb, combines thirteen poems with collages of humorous art and photos. In *School Library Journal* Linda Staskus recommended this story for "parents [hoping] to interact with their children in imaginative-play activities."

A Chanukah Noel transports readers to rural France, where Charlotte has moved with her family. In addition to being Canadian, she is also Jewish and she feels left out when her school engages in holiday traditions that she is unfamiliar with. When she befriends Colette, a classmate who is too poor to participate in the class gift exchange, Charlotte finds a way to participate in the Christmas tradition of giving while also honoring her Jewish faith and the celebration of Chanukah. Captured in dramatic artwork by Gillian Newland, *A Chanukah Noel* is imbued with "both the holiday spirit and the feeling of a French village," according to *Booklist* critic Ilene Cooper. Eva Mitnick recommended Jennings' story in *School Library Journal* as "a fine crosscultural choice."

In *Dancing on the Edge* Jennings turns to older readers, crafting a story that *School Library Journal* contributor H.H. Henderson characterized as "*Flashdance* meets *Fame.*" In the novel, Bonnie Lee has been admitted to the prestigious City Arts High School, which means that they have left the friends in their working-class neighborhood behind and now attend classes with teens from far more affluent families. Although Lee has talent and loves to dance, she finds that success as a dancer in her new school requires more than just talent when she realizes that even her teacher questions whether she is a City Arts student to fill a quota. Part of the "Edge" series published by High Interest Publishing, *Dancing on the Edge* was designed to attract even reluctant readers through its tension-building storyline featuring a likeable teen who is dealing with realistic problems that high schoolers can relate to.

Jennings' long-running "Franklin" beginning-reader stories are based on a television series created by Canadian author Paulette Bourgeois and illustrator Brenda Clark that focuses on the adventures of an engaging toddler stand-in: a green turtle. In *Franklin's Reading Club* a new book by a favorite author sends the turtle and his friends on a bookstore search, while *Franklin Plants a Tree* finds Franklin learning about patience and the fun of watching things grow when he plants a tree seedling for Earth Day. *Franklin's Soapbox Derby* and *Franklin's Thanksgiving* continue the turtle's adventures while also challenging beginning readers with "sentences that are a bit longer" and animation-style "illustrations that . . . children should be able to read along with just a minimal amount of assistance," according to a *Resource Links* critic.

Biographical and Critical Sources

PERIODICALS

Booklist, March 1, 1999, Shelley Townsend-Hudson, review of *Franklin's Class Trip,* p. 1218; November 15, 1999, John Peters, review of *The Bye-bye Pie,* p. 636; May 15, 2000, Helen Rosenberg, review of *Into My Mother's Arms,* p. 1748; September 15, 2001, Carolyn Phelan, review of *Franklin's Thanksgiving,* p. 235; December 15, 2002, Susan Dove Lempke, review of *Pricilla's Paw de Deux,* p. 768; September 1, 2004, Carolyn Phelan, review of *No Monsters Here,* p. 133; February 15, 2005, Ilene Cooper, review of *Bearcub and Mama,* p. 1084; August 1, 2006, Carolyn Phelan, review of *The Happily Ever Afternoon,* p. 88; November 1, 2010, Ilene Cooper, review of *A Chanukah Noel: A True Story,* p. 74.

Canadian Book Review (annual), 1990, Ila D. Scott, review of *When Jeremiah Found Mrs. Ming,* p. 6046.

Canadian Children's Literature, number 62, 1991, Jetske Sybesma, "Overt and Covert Content in Current Illustrated Children's Books," pp. 99-100.

Canadian Review of Materials, October, 1992, Steve Pitt, review of *When Jeremiah Found Mrs. Ming,* p. 263.

Horn Book, January-February, 1991, Sarah Ellis, "News from the North," p. 110.

Kirkus Reviews, October 1, 2001, review of *Priscilla and Rosy;* February 15, 2005, review of *Bearcub and Mama;* January 15, 2010, review of *C'mere, Boy!*

Publishers Weekly, October 29, 2001, review of *Priscilla and Rosy,* p. 63; October 11, 2010, review of *A Chanukah Noel,* p. 41.

Quill & Quire, September, 1992, Sarah Ellis, review of *When Jeremiah Found Mrs. Ming.*

Resource Links, December, 1999, review of *The Bye-bye Pie;* June, 2000, review of *Into My Mother's Arms,* p. 3; June, 2001, Joanne de Groot, review of *Franklin Plants a Tree,* p. 3; February, 2002, Linda Irvine, review of *Bats out the Window,* p. 12; April, 2002, Ann Abel, review of *Franklin's Canoe Trip,* p. 5; February, 2007, review of *Franklin's Soapbox Derby,* p. 4.

School Library Journal, July, 2000, Susan Garland, review of *Into My Mother's Arms,* p. 80; September, 2001, Wendy S. Carroll, review of *Franklin's Thanksgiving,* p. 191; January, 2002, Kathleen Kelly MacMillan, review of *Priscilla and Rosy,* p. 102; February, 2003,

Beth Tegart, review of *Priscilla's Paw de Deux,* p. 114; May, 2004, Marilyn Taniguchi, review of *Franklin's Reading Club,* p. 116; October, 2004, Maryann H. Owen, review of *No Monsters Here,* p. 119; July, 2008, H.H. Henderson, review of *Dancing on the Edge,* p. 100; December, 2009, Linda Staskus, review of *Wiggle Giggle Tickle Train,* p. 84; April, 2010, Catherine Callegari, review of *C'mere Boy!,* p. 130; October, 2010, Eva Mitnick, review of *A Chanukah Noel,* p. 72.

ONLINE

Annick Press Web site, http://www.annickpress.com/ (June 15, 2011).
Sharon Jennings Home Page, http://www.sharonjennings.ca (June 15, 2011).

*   *   *

JOHNSON, Dianne
See JOHNSON, Dinah

*   *   *

JOHNSON, Dinah 1960-
(Dianne Johnson)

Personal

Born August 6, 1960, in Charleston, SC; daughter of Douglas L., Sr. (an army colonel in the Medical Service Corps) and Beatrice (a teacher) Johnson; children: Niani Sekai Feelings. *Education:* Princeton University, A.B. (English/creative writing), 1982; Yale University, M.A. (African-American studies), 1984, Ph.D. (American studies), 1988. *Hobbies and other interests:* Photography.

Addresses

Home and office—P.O. Box 782, Santee, SC 29142. *E-mail*—dinahsdesk@gmail.com.

Career

Author and educator. University of South Carolina, Columbia, SC, professor of English, beginning 1990, interim director of African-American studies program, 1998-2000. Member of advisory board, Children's Defense Fund's Langston Hughes Library, Clinton, TN.

Member

Society of Children's Book Writers and Illustrators, Modern Language Association, Children's Literature Association, American Library Association.

Awards, Honors

Notable Children's Trade Book in the Field of Social Studies selection, Children's Book Council/National Council for the Social Studies, 1997, for *The Best of*

The Brownies' Book; National Endowment for the Humanities Summer Institute on Black Film fellowship, University of Central Florida, 1999.

Writings

FOR CHILDREN

All around Town: The Photographs of Richard Samuel Roberts, Henry Holt (New York, NY), 1998.
Sunday Week, illustrated by Tyrone Geter, Henry Holt (New York, NY), 1999.
Quinnie Blue, illustrated by James Ransome, Henry Holt (New York, NY), 2000.
Sitting Pretty: A Celebration of Black Dolls (poetry), photographs by Myles Pinkney, Henry Holt (New York, NY), 2000.
Hair Dance!, photographs by Kelly Johnson, Henry Holt (New York, NY), 2007.
Black Magic, illustrated by R. Gregory Christie, Henry Holt (New York, NY), 2010.

OTHER; UNDER NAME DIANNE JOHNSON

Telling Tales: The Pedagogy and Promise of African-American Literature for Youth, Greenwood Press (Westport, CT), 1990.
Presenting Laurence Yep, Twayne (New York, NY), 1995.
(Editor) *The Best of The Brownies' Book,* Oxford University Press (New York, NY), 1996.

Editor, with Catherine Lewis, of *African American Review,* spring, 1998 (special issue on African-American children's literature). Contributor of essays to *BookBird* and *African American Review;* contributor to anthology *African American Writers,* second edition, edited by Valerie Smith, Scribner's (New York, NY), 2001. Some work published under name Dianne Johnson-Feelings.

Sidelights

Dinah Johnson is an author and educator who has been an active force in promoting the representation of many cultures in children's literature. In addition to her academic work, which includes *Telling Tales: The Pedagogy and Promise of African-American Literature for Youth* and is published under the name Dianne Johnson, Johnson has produced entertaining stories for children of a variety of ages. In addition to her picture books *Sunday Week, Black Magic,* and *Hair Day!,* Johnson has also produces the award-winning *Quinnie Blue,* a story written to honor the elderly women in her own family.

Johnson was born in Charleston, South Carolina, the daughter of a school teacher. Because of her father's career in the U.S. Army, she and her family moved frequently. "Along with my older sister, Debbi, and my younger brother and sister, Dougie and Loretta, we lived in ten different states in the United States, and also in Iran and Germany," the author explained on her home page. "Growing up around the world has given me an appreciation for the richness and uniqueness of various places: the sounds, the smells, the color palettes are all unique," Johnson also commented in an online interview with *The Brown Bookshelf.* "The people in different places, collectively, have their own ways of expressing themselves, their own relationships with the concept of time. . . . They have their own orientation to the world. Seeing different places gives me an informed appreciation for the richness of human cultures and reminds me, as a writer, to make my writing 'truthful' to the extent that is possible. And if I tell the truth of a particular character, the specifics make the story rich, while also depicting a character whose humanity is evident to all readers."

Inspired by a sixth-grade teacher who combined classroom work with field trips, films, and numerous opportunities for creative writing, Johnson began composing poetry as a young teen, developing the writing habit that continues to be part of her life. After high school she attended Princeton University and then moved to Yale University to complete a master's degree in African-American studies and a Ph.D. in American studies. In 1990 she began her teaching career in the English department at the University of South Carolina.

Johnson's first book for children, *All around Town: The Photographs of Richard Samuel Roberts,* introduces a little-known African-American photographer who worked during the 1920s and 1930s. After describing the self-taught photographer's life, the author relates what is little known of the individuals captured in Roberts' photographs, filling in the gaps with educated guesses based on clues hidden in the images themselves. "Johnson's text invites young readers to think about the lives behind the pictures," remarked Deborah Taylor in her *Horn Book* review of *All around Town,* and a *Publishers Weekly* critic predicted that "readers will likely be left with a feeling that they've visited a long-ago time that has much in common with their own."

In *Sunday Week* Johnson focuses on the importance of the spirit in an African-American community. Her story opens with the Monday-morning blues, but the week gradually brightens as it winds its way toward Sunday, when everyone dresses up in their best, goes to church, and then enjoys a feast during Sunday dinner. "Although Johnson's expression of these tender feelings borders on the cliché, her lyric verse evokes warm and honest images of home and love and God," wrote Susan P. Bloom in her *Horn Book* review of *Sunday Week.*

Nostalgia for the past is also at the heart of *Quinnie Blue,* a reverential inquiry into the life of Johnson's African-American grandmother. The story's young narrator, Quinnie Blue, was named for her grandmother and she imagines her grandmother's life running parallel to her own in the book's lyrical text and James Ransome's light-filled paintings. As they have with her other books for children, critics singled out Johnson's poetic prose for special praise. The author's "lilting text is practically music," remarked Ilene Cooper in her *Booklist* appraisal of the book.

In *Sitting Pretty: A Celebration of Black Dolls* Johnson's verses are inspired by the black dolls she has collected from all over the world. In her focus on dolls and doll-making, the author also celebrates African and African-American crafts and culture and "lovingly captures the unique spirit of the African diaspora," according to Veronica Stevenson-Moudamane in the *Black Issues Book Review.* "This is a book that speaks to children but will be well loved by adults, and should find many uses beyond its classification as poetry," concluded Nina Lindsay in her *School Library Journal* review. *Sitting Pretty* "explores my feelings about being part of the larger family of people of the African diaspora," Johnson once told *SATA.* "I've written poems to go along with my dolls from the United States and various parts of Africa and the Caribbean. They are poems about black girls, boys, women, and men who are sitting pretty in the sense that they know who they are and where they are going. I hope that it is a book that, like all of my books, will be enjoyed by readers of all ages."

Johnson continues her upbeat celebration of black culture in the picture books *Black Magic* and *Hair Dance!* Featuring inspiring artwork by R. Gregory Christie, *Black Magic* shows the magical, inspiring, delicious, and even whimsical things that are black in hue, from zebra stripes and an inky dusky sky to extra-dark chocolate and stylish braided hair. Praising Johnson's text as "crisp and definitive," Cooper added praise for Christie's "stylized, riotously colored" gouache images, depicted strikingly on a velvety black backdrop. Johnson's "free-flowing verse" is "buoyant yet reflective," according to a *Publishers Weekly* critic. Also praising the book, Mary Landrum noted in *School Library Journal* that Johnson's "vivid descriptions of black will enrich children's vocabulary by introducing them to similes for this color." *Black Magic* is a "winning celebration of blackness," asserted a *Kirkus Reviews* writer, the critic predicting that grown ups "will find this book a great conversation starter with little ones."

Hair Day! features photographs by Kelly Johnson that depict African-American women and capture the many tones, styles, and textures of African-American hair, whether long or short, smooth or curly, braided or twisted or left to go its own way. Noting Johnson's upbeat, energetic rhyming text, Cooper also cited the many "appealing photographs" of black girls "looking strong and beautiful." In *School Library Journal* Teresa Pfeifer wrote that *Hair Day!* "read[s] aloud like a jump-rope rhyme," and its "lighthearted" design "matches the text's effervescent tone."

"People who know me as an English professor and literary critic call me Dianne Johnson," Johnson once told

SATA: "In that part of my life, I teach courses on African-American literature, children's and young adult literature, black film, and multiethnic autobiography. One of the scholarly projects I'm proud of is my book *Presenting Laurence Yep* on the life and work of one of my favorite writers. The other scholarly project that really was a labor of love is *The Best of The Brownies' Book,* selections of poetry, fiction, folklore, photographs, letters, current events, and art from a black children's magazine produced in 1920 and 1921. Edited by W.E.B. Du Bois and Jessie Fauset, the twenty-four issues of this magazine represent for me the beginning of African-American children's literature. As 'Dinah'—the name my parents have always called me—I am thrilled to now be a part of this tradition."

Discussing her books for children, Johnson noted that they are "all . . . connected in some way to my strong feelings about my family and about my home state of South Carolina, where I live with my daughter Niani Feelings. But I've had the privilege of traveling all around the world." "I love writing books," she added. "It is fascinating to see one's idea become a book that can be held in people's hands or be read out loud—there must be music in my words. And I hope that there is magic as well. . . . I think that in some ways, literature is a luxury. But in other ways, it is a necessity. I always remind myself that reading was once against the law for black Americans. And so I'll never take this gift for granted, I've hung in my office a poster of Frederick Douglass with his philosophy that 'Once you learn to read you will be forever free.' So here's to the pleasures and power of books and my small contribution to the world of words."

Biographical and Critical Sources

PERIODICALS

Black Issues Book Review, January, 2001, Veronica Stevenson-Moudamane, review of *Sitting Pretty: A Celebration of Black Dolls,* p. 80.

Booklist, February 15, 1998, Hazel Rochman, review of *All around Town: The Photographs of Richard Samuel Roberts,* p. 1014; February 15, 1999, Ilene Cooper, review of *Sunday Week,* p. 1075; April 15, 2000, Ilene Cooper, review of *Quinnie Blue,* p. 1552; October 1, 2000, Carolyn Phelan, review of *Sitting Pretty: A Celebration of Black Dolls,* p. 333; December 15, 2007, Ilene Cooper, review of *Hair Dance!,* p. 49; February 1, 2010, Ilene Cooper, review of *Black Magic,* p. 61.

Bulletin of the Center for Children's Books, December, 2007, Karen Coats, review of *Hair Dance!,* p. 175.

Horn Book, March-April, 1998, Deborah Taylor, review of *All around Town,* p. 235; March, 1999, Susan P. Bloom, review of *Sunday Week,* p. 191.

Publishers Weekly, January 12, 1998, review of *All around Town,* p. 60; February 22, 1999, review of *Sunday Week,* p. 94; May 29, 2000, review of *Quinnie Blue,* p. 82; January 11, 2010, review of *Black Magic,* p. 48.

School Library Journal, March, 1998, Starr E. Smith, review of *All around Town,* p. 196; June, 1999, Alicia Eames, review of *Sunday Week,* p. 98; June, 2000, Louise L. Sherman, review of *Quinnie Blue,* p. 116; October, 2000, Nina Lindsay, review of *Sitting Pretty,* p. 148; November, 2007, Teresa Pfeifer, review of *Hair Dance!,* p. 108; February, 2010, Mary Landrum, review of *Black Magic,* p. 88.

ONLINE

Brown Bookshelf Web log, http://thebrownbookshelf.com/ (February 17, 2010), interview with Johnson.

Dinah Johnson Home Page, http://www.dinahjohnson.com (June 20, 2011).

*   *   *

JUTTE, Jan 1953-

Personal

Born October 1, 1953, in Arnhem, Netherlands; married Nanouk Masselink (an author); children: Melle (son). *Education:* Academie voor Beeldende Kunsten, degree (drawing and painting), 1980; teaching certification.

Addresses

Home—Netherlands. *Agent*—Scott Treimel NY, 434 Lafayette St., New York, NY 10003. *E-mail*—info@ janjutte.nl.

Career

Illustrator. Freelance illustrator, beginning 1983; Hendrik Pierson College, Zetten, Netherlands, instructor in drawing and art history, 1984-2000; Academie voor Beeldende Kunsten, Arnhem, Netherlands, instructor in illustration, 1988-92;

Awards, Honors

Gouden Penseel award, 1994, for *Lui, Lei, Enzo* by Rindert Kromhout, 2001, for *Tien stoute katjes* by Mensje van Keulen, 2004, for *Een muts voor de maan* by Sjoerd Kuyper; Gouden Plaque award (with Nanouk Masselink), 1999, for *Opstaan!;* Gouden Uil award, 2003, for *Schaap met laarsjes* by Marritgen Matter, and nomination, 2008, for *Van mij en van jou* by Hans and Monique Hagen.

Writings

(With wife Nanouk Masselink) *Opstaan!,* Leopold (Amsterdam, Netherlands), 1998.

Hoempapa!, Leopold (Amsterdam, Netherlands), 2001.

Op de step, Leopold (Amsterdam, Netherlands), 2001.

Tip en Olle, Leopold (Amsterdam, Netherlands), 2001.

(With Nanouk Masselink) *Ruimtereis,* Leopold (Amsterdam, Netherlands), 2001.

Pak me dan!, Leopold (Amsterdam, Netherlands), 2002.

Nat!, Leopold (Amsterdam, Netherlands), 2002.

ILLUSTRATOR

Annie M.G. Schmidt, *Het beertje Pippeloentje,* Querido (Amsterdam, Netherlands), 1983.

Toon Tellegen, *Er ging geen dag voorbij: Negenenveertig verhalen over de eekhoorn en de andere dieren,* Querido (Amsterdam, Netherlands), 1984.

Rindert Kromhout, *Vannacht als iedereen slaapt,* Querido (Amsterdam, Netherlands), 1985.

Paul van Loon, *Wat zit er in het bos?,* Zwijsen (Tilburg, Netherlands), 1985.

Rindert Kromhout, *Olaf de rover,* Querido (Amsterdam, Netherlands), 1986.

Uri Orlev, *Moedertje Brei,* Querido (Amsterdam, Netherlands), 1986.

Corrie Hafkamp, *Het huis in het bos,* Zwijsen (Tilburg, Netherlands), 1986.

Doeschka Meijsing, *Beer en jager,* Querido (Amsterdam, Netherlands), 1987.

Rita Törnqvist, *Achter de bergen light de zee,* Querido (Amsterdam, Netherlands), 1987.

Jetty Krever, *De hond aan de boom,* Wolters-Noordhoff (Groningen, Germany), 1987.

Jetty Krever, *In dat huis woont een sppok,* Wolters-Noordhoff (Groningen, Germany), 1987.

Rindert Kromhout, *Jip op de wip,* Zwijsen (Tilburg, Netherlands), 1987.

Guus Kuijer, *Tin Toeval,* Querido (Amsterdam, Netherlands), 1987.

Guus Kuijer, *Tin Toeval en het geheim van Tweebeenseiland,* Querido (Amsterdam, Netherlands), 1987.

Guus Kuijer, *Tin Toeval en de kunst van het verdwalen,* Querido (Amsterdam, Netherlands), 1987.

Jos de Valk, *Vuurvogel Daan,* Van Goor (Amsterdam, Netherlands), 1988.

Robert Francissen, *Een raar verhaal,* Zwijsen (Tilburg, Germany), 1988.

Gertie Evenhuis, *Papegaaitje leef je nog?,* Van Goor (Amsterdam, Netherlands), 1989.

(With Mance Post) Guus Kuijer, *Tin Toeval en de kunst van Madelief,* Querido (Amsterdam, Netherlands), 1989.

Rindert Kromhout, *Wedden dat het lukt,* Zwijsen (Tilburg, Netherlands), 1989.

Nina Bawden, *Freddie,* Querido (Amsterdam, Netherlands), 1989.

Sjoerd Kuyper, *Josje,* Leopold (Amsterdam, Netherlands), 1989, translated by Patricia Crampton as *The Swan's Child,* Holiday House (New York, NY), 2006.

Paul van Loon, *Schilpad ontvoerd,* Zwijsen (Tilburg, Netherlands), 1989.

Paul van Loon, *Sam Schoffel meester-speurder,* Zwijsen (Tilburg, Netherlands), 1989.

Rindert Kromhout, *Het witte meisje,* Zwijsen (Tilburg, Netherlands), 1990.

Bart Moeyaert, *Een kuil om in te wonen,* Zwijsen (Tilburg, Netherlands), 1990.

Margaret Mahy, *Olifantekaas en nijlpaardemelk,* Querido (Amsterdam, Netherlands), 1990.

Paul van Loon, *Baby geroofd,* Zwijsen (Tilburg, Netherlands), 1990.

Mensje van Keulen, *Van Aap tot Zet,* Querido (Amsterdam, Netherlands), 1990.

Burny Bos, *Eén April kikker in je bil,* 2nd edition, Leopold (The Hague, Netherlands), 1990.

Burny Bos, *Zand op je boterham,* 2nd edition, Leopold (The Hague, Netherlands), 1990.

Rindert Kromhout, *Peppino,* Querido (Amsterdam, Netherlands), 1990.

Ben Kuipers, *Jandoedel: Mijn opa en ik,* Sjaloom (Amsterdam, Netherlands), 1991.

Vivian den Hollander, *De oma van Niels,* Van Kolkema & Warendorf (Houten, Netherlands), 1991.

Gertie Evenhuis, *Papegaaitje, praat je nog?,* Van Goor (Amsterdam, Netherlands), 1991.

Rindert Kromhout, *Olaf de geweldige,* Querido (Amsterdam, Netherlands), 1991.

Peter Noland, *Wie krabt mijn rug?,* Van Goor (Amsterdam, Netherlands), 1992.

Mensje van Keulen, *Meneer Ratti,* Querido (Amsterdam, Netherlands), 1992.

Mieke Vanpol, *Ich nenn dich einfach Ib,* Dressler (Hamburg, Germany), 1992.

Sjoerd Kuyper, *Josje's droom,* Leopold (Amsterdam, Netherlands), 1992.

Rindert Kromhout, *Hup naar huis,* Zwijsen (Tilburg, Netherlands), 1992.

Els Pelgrom, *Ongeboren Roulf,* Querido (Amsterdam, Netherlands), 1992.

Toon Tellegen, *Er ging geen dag voorbij: negenenveertig verhalen over de eekhoorn en de andere dieren,* Querido (Amsterdam, Netherlands), 1993.

Els Pelgrom, *Vielspeuk,* Zwijsen (Tilburg, Netherlands), 1993.

Paul van Loon, *De allesdief,* Zwijsen (Tilburg, Netherlands), 1993.

Rindert Kromhout, *De Paljas en de vuurvreter,* Querido (Amsterdam, Netherlands), 1993.

Guus Kuijer, *Tin Toeval in de onderwereld,* Querido (Amsterdam, Netherlands), 1993.

Rindert Kromhout, *Lui Lei Enzo,* Zwijsen (Tilburg, Netherlands), 1993.

Marianne Busser and Ron Schröder, *Liselotje gaat logeren,* Holkema & Warendorf (Houten, Netherlands), 1993.

Marianne Busser and Ron Schröder, *Liselotje op het potje,* Holkema & Warendorf (Houten, Netherlands), 1993.

Burny Bos, *Snap je dan niet dat dat pijn doet,* 2nd edition, Leopold (The Hague, Netherlands), 1994.

Burny Bos, *Wie praat daar met de poes?,* 2nd edition, Leopold (The Hague, Netherlands), 1994.

Mensje van Keulen, *Snottebel Lies en andere portretten,* Querido (Amsterdam, Netherlands), 1994.

Marianne Busser and Ron Schröder, *Liselotje naar de speelzaal,* Holkema & Warendorf (Houten, Netherlands), 1994.

Marianne Busser and Ron Schröder, *Liselotje krijgt een zusje,* Holkema & Warendorf (Houten, Netherlands), 1994.

Rindert Kromhout, *In de weg uit de weg,* Zwijsen (Tilburg, Netherlands), 1994.

Rindert Kromhout, *Katten vangen,* Zwisjen (Tilburg, Netherlands), 1994.

Sjoerd Kuyper, *Het eiland Klassje,* Leopold (Amsterdam, Netherlands), 1994.

Rindert Kromhout, *De troep van Joep,* Zwijsen (Tilburg, Netherlands), 1994.

Elly Bennink, *Klap eens in je handjes: liedjes en versjes voor peuters en kleuters,* Kosmos (Utrecht, Netherlands), 1994.

Rindert Kromhout, *Rare vogels,* Leopold (Amsterdam, Netherlands), 1995.

Rindert Kromhout, *De twee vrienden,* Zwijsen (Tilburg Netherlands), 1995.

Rindert Kromhout, *Vieze beesten,* Zwijsen (Tilburg, Netherlands), 1995.

Marianne Busser and Ron Schröder, *Liselotje krijgt een fiets,* Holkema & Warendorf (Houten, Netherlands), 1995.

Marianne Busser and Ron Schröder, *Liselotje zet haar schoen,* Holkema & Warendorf (Houten, Netherlands), 1995.

Sjoerd Kuyper, *Majesteit, Uw ontbijt,* Leopold (Amsterdam, Netherlands), 1995.

Bies van Ede, *Ik wil geen ridder worden,* Zwijsen (Tilburg, Netherlands), 1995.

Erik van Os, *Er loopt een liedje door de lucht,* Zwijsen (Tilburg, Netherlands), 1995.

Paul van Loon, *Een spook in de school,* Zwijsen (Tilburg, Netherlands), 1996.

Guus Kuijer, *De grote Tin Toeval* (omnibus), Querido (Amsterdam, Netherland), 1996.

Marianne Busser and Ron Schröder, *Liselotje krijgt een vriendje,* Holkema & Warendorf (Houten, Netherlands), 1996.

Mensje van Keulen, *Pas op voor Bez,* Leopold (Amsterdam, Netherlands), 1996.

Marianne Busser and Ron Schröder, *Liselotje en het kerstfeest,* Holkema & Warendorf (Houten, Netherlands), 1996.

Toon Tellegen, *Teunis,* Querido (Amsterdam, Netherlands), 1996.

Rindert Kromhout, *Rita Ramp,* Zwijsen (Tilburg, Netherlands), 1996.

Rindert Kromhout, *Wedden dat ik lees!,* Leopold (Amsterdam, Netherlands), 1996.

Burny Bos, *Ot Jan Dikke!,* Leopold (Amsterdam, Netherlands), 1997.

Marianne Busser and Ron Schröder, *Liselotje gaat naar zwemles,* Holkema & Warendorf (Houten, Netherlands), 1997.

Marianne Busser and Ron Schröder, *Liselotje is jarig,* Holkema & Warendorf (Houten, Netherlands), 1997.

Annie M.G. Schmidt, *Broodjes,* Silvester (Leiden, Netherlands), 1997.

Rindert Kromhout, *Allez hop!,* Leopold (Amsterdam, Netherlands), 1997.

Sjoerd Kuyper, *Een spook voor het raam,* Zwijsen (Tilburg, Netherlands), 1997.

Marianne Busser and Ron Schröder, *Liselotje en het paasfeest,* Holkema & Warendorf (Houten, Netherlands), 1998.

Marianne Busser and Ron Schröder, *Liselotje gaat kamperen,* Holkema & Warendorf (Houten, Netherlands), 1998.

Maria van Eeden, *Het land van de vrije prinses,* Leopold (Amsterdam, Netherland), 1998.

Leendert Witvliet, *Apen kijken,* Querido (Amsterdam, Netherlands), 1998.

Rindert Kromhout, *Een dief in huis,* Zwijsen (Tilburg, Netherlands), 1998.

Rindert Kromhout, *Vreemde vrienden,* Leopold (Amsterdam, Netherlands), 1999.

Het huis is vol, Zwijsen (Tilburg, Netherlands), 1999.

Rindert Kromhout, *Pas op de oppas,* Zwijsen (Tilburg, Netherlands), 1999.

Rindert Kromhout, *Feest!,* Zwijsen (Tilburg, Netherlands), 1999.

Marianne Busser and Ron Schröder, *Het grote avontureboek van Liselotje* (omnibus), Holkema & Warendorf (Houten, Netherlands), 1999.

Edward van de Vendel, *Jaap deelt klapen uit,* Querido (Amsterdam, Netherlands), 1999.

Wat een verhaal!, Zwijsen (Tilburg, Netherlands), 1999.

Sjoerd Kuyper, *Het boek van Josje* (omnibus), Leopold (Amsterdam, Netherlands), 1999.

Sjoerd Kuyper, *Die meid is een heks, Vos,* Zwijsen (Tilburg, Netherlands), 2000.

Rindert Kromhout, *Weer en wind,* Zwijsen (Tilburg, Netherlands), 2000.

Rindert Kromhout, *De grote wedstrijd vrouwen sjouwen,* Zwijsen (Tilburg, Netherlands), 2000.

Mensje van Keulen, *Tien stoute katjes,* Leopold (Amsterdam, Netherlands), 2000, multilingual edition published as *Ten stoute katjes=Ten Naughty Kittens,* Atlas (Amsterdam, Netherlands), 2009.

Rindert Kromhout, *De dichte doos,* Zwijsen (Tilburg, Netherlands), 2000.

Rindert Kromhout, *Een fijne verjaardag,* Zwijsen (Tilburg, Netherlands), 2001.

Sjoerd Kuyper, *Vos koopt een hoed,* Zwijsen (Tilburg, Netherlands), 2001.

Jules Welling, *Mat!: Het eerste schaakboek,* Van Reemst (Houten, Netherlands), 2001.

Ivo de Wijs, *Het opperhoofd,* Zwijsen (Tilburg, Netherlands), 2001.

Gerard Tonen, *O, was ik maar een aap,* Zwijsen (Tilburg, Netherlands), 2001.

Annie M.G. Schmidt, *De prins van Hoedeli Doedli Douw,* De Uitvreter (Zoeterwoude, Netherlands), 2001.

Mensje van Keulen, *Eerst de muziek,* Contact (Amsterdam, Netherlands), 2001.

Dirk Nielandt, *Mees op nieuwe sokken,* Zwijsen (Tilburg, Netherlands), 2002.

Sjoerd Kuyper, *Uil en de valse katten,* Zwijsen (Tilburg, Netherlands), 2002.

Maritgen Matter, *Schaap met laarsjes,* Querido (Amsterdam, Netherlands), 2002.

Sylvia Vanden Heede, *Ik kan huilen!*, Zwijsen (Tilburg, Netherlands), 2002.

Bibi Dumon Tak, *Wat een circus!*, Querido (Amsterdam, Netherlands), 2002.

Haye van der Heyden, *Max: de gelukkigste hond van de wereld*, Leopold (Amsterdam, Netherlands), 2002.

Jules Welling, *Van pion tot konig: wunderkinderen aan zet*, Van Olkema & Warendorf (Houten, Netherlands), 2002.

Rindert Kromhout, *Bil en Wil: wijf kleine avonturen van twee grote vrienden*, Leopold (Amsterdam, Netherlands), 2003.

Anke Kranendonk, *Ties en tos verliefd*, Zwijsen (Tilburg, Netherlands), 2003.

Rindert Kromhout, *Rita Ramp*, Zwijsen (Tilburg, Netherlands), 2003.

Sjoerd Kuyper, *Een muts voor de maan*, Leopold (Amsterdam, Netherlands), 2003.

Ik en mijn broertje, Zwijsen (Tilburg, Netherlands), 2003.

Sjoerd Kuyper, *Een bos vol tover*, Leopold (Amsterdam, Netherlands), 2003.

Karel Verleyen, *Geld telt!*, Biblion (Leidschendam, Netherlands), 2003.

Anke Kranendonk, *De bruiloft van Ties en Tos*, Zwijsen (Tilburg, Netherlands), 2004.

Maria van Eeden, *Ik pas op het huis*, Zwijsen (Tilburg, Netherlands), 2004.

Maria van Eeden, *Op zoek naar oom Koos*, Zwijsen (Tilburg, Netherlands), 2004.

Maria van Eeden, *Sim!*, Zwijsen (Tilburg, Netherlands), 2004.

Maria van Eeden, *Sip?*, Zwijsen (Tilburg, Netherlands), 2004.

Maria van Eeden, *Ris, ris!*, Zwijsen (Tilburg, Netherlands), 2004.

Maria van Eeden, *Kaat en de boot*, Zwijsen (Tilburg, Netherlands), 2004.

Mensje van Keulen, *Titus raakt zoek*, Leopold (Amsterdam, Netherlands), 2004.

Rindert Kromhout, *Italië*, Querido (Amsterdam, Netherlands), 2004.

Lydia Rood, *Bezoek in de nacht*, Zwijsen (Tilburg, Netherlands), 2004.

Toon Tellegen, *Er ging geen dag voorbij*, Querido (Amsterdam, Netherlands), 2004.

Rindert Kromhout, *Toen de weg weg was*, Zwijsen (Tilburg, Netherlands), 2004.

Rindert Kromhout, *De dag dat Zil kwam*, Zwijsen (Tilburg, Netherlands), 2004.

Lydia Rood, *Zoenen is vies, zei Darma Appelgat*, Kinderboekenmarkt ('s-Gravenhage, Netherlands), 2004.

Anke Kranendonk, *Ties en Tos op reis*, Zwijsen (Tilburg, Netherlands), 2004.

Rindert Kromhout, *Ik ben niet boos!*, Zwijsen (Tilburg, Netherlands), 2005.

Rindert Kromhout, *Krijg nou wat!*, Zwijsen (Tilburg, Netherlands), 2005.

Rindert Kromhout, *Bie en Wil: vrienden voor altijd*, Leopold (Amsterdam, Netherlands), 2005.

Dirk Weber, *Kies mij!*, Querido (Amsterdam, Netherlands), 2005.

Toon Tellegen, *m n o p q*, Querido (Amsterdam, Netherlands), 2005.

Rindert Kromhout, *Een fiets voor twee*, Zwijsen (Tilburg, Netherlands), 2005.

Rindert Kromhout, *Wat een Billen!*, Zwijsen (Tilburg, Netherlands), 2005.

Rindert Kromhout, *Bil en Wil: wat een wagen!*, Leopold (Amsterdam, Netherlands), 2005.

Anke Kranendonk, *Ties en Tos naar het strand*, Zwijsen (Tilburg, Netherlands), 2006.

Margje Kuyper and Sjoerd Kuyper, *Welkom thuis, leeuw!*, Zwijsen (Tilburg, Netherlands), 2006.

Nanouk, *Met vis naar zee*, Zwijsen (Tilburg, Netherlands), 2006.

Ienne Biermans, *Paperasje*, Neiuw Amsterdam (Amsterdam, Netherlands), 2006.

Hans Hagen and Monique Hagen, *Van mij en van jou*, Querido (Amsterdam, Netherlands), 2007.

Tamara Bos, *Brammetje Baas*, Zwijsen (Tilburg, Netherlands), 2007.

Selma Noort, *Ik vertel het niet!*, Zwijsen (Tilburg, Netherlands), 2007.

Burny Bos, *Ot Jan Dikkie is cool*, Leopold (Amsterdam, Netherlands), 2007.

Jacques Vriens and others, *Het januarimeisje en andere verhalen*, Stichting Lezen (Amsterdam, Netherlands), 2008.

Paul van Loon, *Echte boeven?*, Zwijsen (Tilburg, Netherlands), 2008.

Driek van Wissen, *Wat een land!*, Van Goor (Houten, Netherlands), 2008.

Ienne Biemans, *Paperasje ging op reis*, Neiuw Amsteram (Amsterdam, Netherlands), 2008.

Eric-Jan Lens, *Fiets foetsie*, Zwijsen (Tilburg, Netherlands), 2008.

Selma Noort, *De den van Tijs en Pip*, Leesleeuw (Tilburg, Netherlands), 2008.

(And puppet designer) Rindert Kromhout, *De avonturen van Leentje en Beentje: verhalen met handpoppen*, Zwijsen (Tilburg, Netherlands), 2009.

Annie M.G. Schmidt, *Sebastiaan*, Raadgeep (Delft, Netherlands), 2009.

Maria van Eeden, *Het boek van Teun*, Zwijsen (Tilburg, Netherlands), 2009.

Barbara Joosse, *Roawr!*, Philomel Books (New York, NY), 2009.

Barbara Joosse, *Sleepover at Gramma's House*, Philomel Books (New York, NY), 2010.

Simon van der Geest, *Dissus*, Querido (Amsterdam, Netherlands), 2010.

Toon Tellegen, *Waar is Mo?*, Rubinstein (Amsterdam, Netherlands), 2010.

Bil en Wil: Wat een verhalen!, Zwijsen (Tilburg, Netherlands), 2010.

(With Georgien Overwater) Rindert Kromhout, *Hens up!*, Leopold (Amsterdam, Netherlands), 2010.

Rindert Kromhout, *Weet jij het al?*, SP (Rotterdam, Netherlands), 2010.

Contributor to anthologies, including *Ik ben jarig: verhalen en versjes*, Leopold (Amsterdam, Netherlands), 1996; *Schatkist instap*, Zwijsen (Tilberg, Netherlands),

1998; *Zoek de dieren van het paleis,* Stichting Konin-klijk Paleis (Amsterdam, Netherlands), 1998; *Heb je wel gehoord,* Stichting Averoes (Amsterdam, Netherlands), 2000; and *Help, ik krimp! en anderen verhalen,* Zwijsen, 2001.

Books featuring Jutte's illustrations have been translated into Chinese, Czech, French, German, Italian, Japanese, Korean, Portuguese, Russian, Slovenian, Spanish, and Swedish.

Biographical and Critical Sources

PERIODICALS

Booklist, December 1, 2008, Daniel Kraus, review of *Roawr!,* p. 58; May 1, 2010, Ilene Cooper, review of *Sleepover at Gramma's House,* p. 85.

Children's Bookwatch, September, 2006, review of *The Swan's Child.*

Kirkus Reviews, February 15, 2006, review of *The Swan's Child,* p. 185; April 15, 2010, review of *Sleepover at Gramma's House.*

Publishers Weekly, March 23, 2009, review of *Roawr!,* p. 58; April 26, 2010, review of *Sleepover at Gramma's House,* p. 105.

School Library Journal, March, 2006, Elizabeth Bird, review of *The Swan's Child,* p. 195; March, 2009, Susan Weitz, review of *Roawr!,* p. 118; June, 2010, Marge Loch-Wouters, review of *Sleepover at Gramma's House,* p. 76.

ONLINE

Jan Jutte Home Page, http://www.janjutte.nl (June 28, 2011).*

K

KATZ, Alan
(I.B. Wrongo)

Personal

Married; wife's name Rose (a journalist); children: Simone, Andrew, Nathan, David.

Addresses

Home—CT. *E-mail*—alankatzbooks@aol.com.

Career

Children's writer and television writer. XM Radio, host of *Dr. I.B. Wrongo* radio show. Presenter at schools and libraries.

Awards, Honors

Emmy Award nominations for work on *Rosie O'Donnell Show* and *Raw Toonage*; Cuffie Award, *Publishers Weekly,* for *Take Me out of the Bathtub, and Other Silly Dilly Songs.*

Writings

FOR CHILDREN

Take Me out of the Bathtub, and Other Silly Dilly Songs, illustrated by David Catrow, Margaret K. McElderry Books (New York, NY), 2001.

I'm Still Here in the Bathtub: Brand New Silly Dilly Songs, illustrated by David Catrow, Margaret K. McElderry Books (New York, NY), 2003.

Where Did They Hide My Presents?: Silly Dilly Christmas Songs, illustrated by David Catrow, Margaret K. McElderry Books (New York, NY), 2005.

Stinky Thinking: The Big Book of Gross Games and Brain Teasers, illustrated by Laurie Keller, Aladdin (New York, NY), 2005.

(With Caissie St. Onge) *United Jokes of America,* illustrated by Mike Lester, Scholastic (New York, NY), 2005.

Stinky Thinking Number Two: Another Big Book of Gross Games and Brain Teasers, illustrated by Jennifer Kalis, Aladdin (New York, NY), 2005.

(With Pete Fornatale) *Elfis: A Christmas Tale,* illustrated by Dani Jones, Price Stern Sloan (New York, NY), 2006.

Are You Quite Polite?: Silly Dilly Manners Songs, illustrated by David Catrow, Margaret K. McElderry Books (New York, NY), 2006.

The Flim-Flam Fairies, Running Press (Philadelphia, PA), 2007.

Oops!, illustrated by Edward Koren, Margaret K. McElderry Books (New York, NY), 2007.

Don't Say That Word!, illustrated by David Catrow, Margaret K. McElderry Books (New York, NY), 2007.

On Top of the Potty, and Other Get-up-and-Go Songs, illustrated by David Catrow, Margaret K. McElderry Books (New York, NY), 2008.

Smelly Locker: Silly Dilly School Songs, illustrated by David Catrow, Margaret K. McElderry Books (New York, NY), 2008.

Oops!, illustrated by Edward Koren, Margaret K. McElderry Books (New York, NY), 2008.

Going, Going, Gone!, and Other Silly Dilly Sports Songs, illustrated by David Catrow, Margaret K. McElderry Books (New York, NY), 2009.

Karate Pig, illustrated by Daniel Moreton, Little Simon (New York, NY), 2009.

Too Much Kissing!, and Other Silly Dilly Songs about Parents, illustrated by David Catrow, Margaret K. McElderry Books (New York, NY), 2009.

Let's Get a Checkup!, illustrated by Pascal Lemaître, Little Simon (New York, NY), 2010.

Stalling, illustrated by Elwood H. Smith, Margaret K. McElderry Books (New York, NY), 2010.

Mosquitoes Are Ruining My Summer!, and Other Silly Dilly Camp Songs, illustrated by David Catrow, Margaret K. McElderry Books (New York, NY), 2011.

Poems I Wrote When No One Was Looking, illustrated by Edward Koren, Margaret K. McElderry Books (New York, NY), 2011.

Ricky Vargas #1: The Funniest Kid in the World, illustrated by Stacy Curtis, Little Apple (New York, NY), 2011.

FOR ADULTS

(As told to Katz by Dr. Juice) *The Cat Not in the Hat!,* illustrated by Chris Wrinn, Dove (Beverly Hills, CA), 1996.

Wackronyms, Avon (New York, NY), 1996.

C'Mere, Kitty: A Cat Lover's Guide to Pestering Your Pet, Avon (New York, NY), 1998.

Maternity the Musical!: Funny Songs about Cravings, Sonograms, and Everything Else an Expectant Mom's Got or Gonna Get, Andrews McMeel (Kansas City, MO), 2004.

OTHER

Writer for television programs including *Rosie O'Donnell Show,* Warner Brothers Animation's *Taz-Mania,* and Disney's *Raw Toonage,* as well as programs on Nickelodeon and ABC Television. Contributor of humor essays to *New York Times.*

Sidelights

Comedy writer Alan Katz has been successful in a career that draws on his ability to stay young at heart. "When a six-year old boy thinks like a grown man, they call him a child prodigy," Katz observed on his home page. "But what's the best way to describe a grown man who thinks like a six-year old boy? That's the problem my wife faces every time she has to introduce me." Whether writing his "Silly Dilly" song books or working on television cartoons for Disney or Nickelodeon, Katz uses his ability to think like a child to make sure the silliness and jokes with which he fills his books appeal to young readers. Along with his books, Katz is also the creator of the trivia program "That's Right, That's Wrong!" which is hosted by his fictional alter ego Dr. I.B. Wrongo and airs regularly on XM Radio. He also visits schools and libraries to do readings, sing songs, and tell jokes.

Take Me out of the Bathtub, and Other Silly Dilly Songs was Katz's first book for young readers. Featuring a collection of original lyrics paired with traditional tunes and brought to life in artwork by David Catrow, *Take Me out of the Bathtub, and Other Silly Dilly Songs* containst tunes lyrics "so clever that kids will want to burst into song immediately," according to Jane Marino in her review for *School Library Journal.* Ginny Gustin, writing in the same periodical, felt that in the collection, old songs "are given new life," while a *Publishers Weekly* contributor predicted that these new versions "will have kids giggling as they sing." The fun continues in *I'm Still Here in the Bathtub: Brand New Silly Dilly Songs.*

In *Where Did They Hide My Presents?: Silly Dilly Christmas Songs* Katz sets his humorous lyrics to familiar holiday music, focusing on seasonal events ranging from shopping to decorating rooftops with colorful lights. "The child's-perspective lyrics are often about the seemingly ridiculous lengths adults go to" during the holidays, noted Bridget T. McCaffrey in *Horn Book.* Although a *Kirkus Reviews* contributor deemed some of the rewrites "gross," the critic added that "most provide the sort of irreverent humor beloved by children." Other "Silly Dilly" titles include *Going, Going, Gone!, and Other Silly-Dilly Sports Songs, Too Much Kissing!, and Other Silly Dilly Songs about Parents,* and *Mosquitoes Are Ruining My Summer!, and Other Silly Dilly Camp Songs,* the last described by Shelle Rosenfeld in *Booklist* as a collection of "witty takes on summer camp" life in which Catrow's "lively cartoon-style illustrations extend the hyperbolic humor." "Children old enough to enjoy a good parody will have a field day with this sports-themed book," wrote Carolyn Phelan in reviewing *Going, Going, Gone!* in the same periodical.

Consistently silly, Katz's books frequently have an educational purpose as well. For example, the cunningly titled *On Top of the Potty, and Other Get-up-and-Go Songs* is designed to help young listeners with potty training. Both *Stinky Thinking: The Big Book of Gross*

Alan Katz teams up with artist David Catrow in the humorous picture book **Don't Say That Word!** (Illustration copyright © 2007 by David Catrow. Reproduced by permission of Margaret K. McElderry Books, an imprint of Simon & Schuster Children's Publishing Division.)

Katz's story in the aptly titled **Stalling** *comes to life in Elwood H. Smith's characteristically quirky art.* (Illustration copyright © 2010 by Elwood H. Smith. Reproduced with permission of Margaret K. McElderry Books, an imprint of Simon & Schuster Children's Publishing Division.)

Games and Brain Teasers and *Stinky Thinking Number Two: Another Big Book of Gross Games and Brain Teasers* use bathroom humor to ask real quiz questions, such as the number of Supreme Court justices in the United States. *Are You Quite Polite?: Silly Dilly Manners Songs* and *Don't Say That Word!*, both of which feature quirky illustrations by Catrow, also double as off-beat guides to good manners. Noting the contrasting pairing of model behavior and bad habits in *Are You Quite Polite?* a *Kirkus Reviews* contributor wrote that Katz's examples "will induce hilarity." Hazel Rochman, writing in *Booklist,* concluded that "the gross humor" in *Don't Say That Word!* "is right-on for slapstick."

Teaming up with *New Yorker* cartoonist Edward Koren, Katz's *Oops!* and *Uh-oh!* were characterized by a *Kirkus Reviews* writer as "rhymed . . . knee-slappers paired to scribbly ink drawings." In *Oops!* Katz collects over a hundred short poems that children can easily memorize for opportune recitation when commentary on annoying parents, pesky siblings, and school situations is required. "Puns and other groaners abound and are sure to delight young readers, especially boys," predicted *School Library Journal* critic Donna Cardon, and a *Kirkus Reviews* critic asserted that *Oops!* makes "a strong bid for the year's most uproarious set of new verse." *Uh-oh!* continues the silliness, as another grand batch of Katz's short poems are illuminated by clever black-and-white images by Koren that a *New York Times Book Review* critic characterized as full of "scruffy charm." "Filled with puns and rhymes, the verse blends the silly and the gross," according to a *Publishers Weekly* critic.

Biographical and Critical Sources

PERIODICALS

Booklist, August, 2003, Shelle Rosenfeld, review of *I'm Still Here in the Bathtub: Brand New Silly Dilly Songs,* p. 1985; November 15, 2006, Julie Cummins, review of *Are You Quite Polite?: Silly Dilly Manners Songs,* p. 50; July 1, 2007, Hazel Rochman, review of *Don't Say That Word!,* p. 64; March 1, 2008, Hazel Rochman, review of *Oops!,* p. 64; June 1, 2008, Hazel Rochman, review of *On Top of the Potty, and Other Get-Up-and-Go Songs,* p. 84; January 1, 2009, Carolyn Phelan, review of *Going, Going, Gone!, and Other Silly Dilly Sports Songs,* p. 78; January 1, 2010, Hazel Rochman, review of *Uh-Oh!,* p. 76; April 15, 2011, Shelle Rosenfeld, review of *Mosquitoes Are Ruining My Summer!, and Other Silly Dilly Camp Songs,* p. 48.

Bulletin of the Center for Children's Books, December, 2006, review of *Where Did They Hide My Presents?: Silly Dilly Christmas Songs,* p. 188.

Horn Book, November-December, 2005, Bridget T. McCafferty, review of *Where Did They Hide My Presents?,* p. 695; September-October, 2008, Roger Sutton, review of *Smelly Locker: Silly Dilly School Songs,* p. 604.

Kirkus Reviews, March 1, 2003, review of *I'm Still Here in the Bathtub,* p. 389; November 1, 2005, review of *Where Did They Hide My Presents?,* p. 1194; September 15, 2006, review of *Are You Quite Polite?,* p. 957; February 15, 2008, reviews of *On Top of the Potty, and Other Get-Up-and-Go Songs* and *Oops!;* June 15, 2008, review of *Smelly Locker;* July 1, 2008, review of *The Flim-Flam Fairies;* May 15, 2009, review of *Karate Pig;* January 1, 2010, review of *Uh-Oh.*

New York Times Book Review, July 13, 2008, review of *Oops!,* p. 15.

Publishers Weekly, April 16, 2001, review of *Take Me out of the Bathtub, and Other Silly Dilly Songs,* p. 63; March 24, 2003, review of *I'm Still Here in the Bathtub,* p. 78; June 25, 2007, review of *Don't Say That Word!,* p. 59; March 17, 2008, review of *Oops!,* p. 70; September 6, 2010, review of *Stalling,* p. 37.

School Library Journal, April, 2001, Jane Marino, review of *Take Me out of the Bathtub, and Other Silly Dilly Songs,* p. 132; July, 2003, Nina Lindsay, review of *I'm Still Here in the Bathtub,* p. 114; December, 2004, Ginny Gustin, review of *Take Me out of the Bathtub, and Other Silly Dilly Songs,* p. 59; June, 2005, Steven Engelfried, review of *Take Me out of the Bathtub, and Other Silly Dilly Songs,* p. 56; October, 2006, Grace Oliff, review of *Are You Quite Polite?,* p. 136; July, 2007, Mary Hazelton, review of *Don't Say That Word!,* p. 78; March, 2008, Martha Simpson, review of *On Top of the Potty, and Other Get-Up-and-Go Songs,* p. 185; April, 2008, Donna Cardon, review of *Oops!,* p. 164; October, 2008, Mary Elam, review of *Smelly Locker,* p. 132; February, 2009, Martha Simpson, review of *Going, Going, Gone!, and Other Silly Dilly Sports Songs,* p. 92; April, 2010, Erlene Bishop Killeen, review of *Too Much Kissing!, and Other Silly Dilly Songs about Parents,* p. 146.

ONLINE

Alan Katz Home Page, http://www.alankatzbooks.com (July 15, 2011).

Authors on the Web, http://www.authorsontheweb.com/ (December 2, 2007), "Alan Katz."

Book Report Web site, http://www.thebookreport.net/ (November 1, 2006), podcast interview with Katz.

Simon & Schuster Web site, http://www.simonsays.com/ (July 15, 2011), "Alan Katz."*

*   *   *

KELLEY, J.A.
See KELLEY, Jane

*   *   *

KELLEY, Jane 1954-
(J.A. Kelley)

Personal

Born 1954, in WI; father an electrical engineer, mother a librarian; married; children: one daughter. *Education:* Northwestern University, B.S., 1976.

Addresses

Home—Brooklyn, NY. *E-mail*—janekelley@janekelley books.com.

Career

Writer. Presenter at schools.

Writings

(As J.A. Kelley) *Meteor Showers* (nonfiction), Children's Press (New York, NY), 2010.

Nature Girl, illustrated by Heather Palisi, Random House (New York, NY), 2010.

The Girl behind the Glass, Random House Children's Books (New York, NY), 2011.

Author of science and social-studies books.

Sidelights

Jane Kelley grew up in Wisconsin where her mother's love of books made reading an important part of everyday life. Kelley's grandmother, Katharine Carson, had

Cover of Jane Kelley's teen novel **Nature Girl,** *featuring artwork by Heather Palisi.* (Illustration copyright © 2010 by Heather Palisi. Used by permission of Random House Children's Books, a division of Random House, Inc.)

been a novelist in the 1940s. Reading inspired Kelley with possibilities, and she decided to become an actress when she grew up: "My own [life] seemed kind of plain to me compared to the girls I read about," she recalled on her home page. Years later, after writing several nonfiction books on science and social-studies topics, Kelley decided to tackle her first work of novel-length fiction. Inspired by a love of the outdoors and experiences hiking parts of the Appalachian trail that runs up the east-coast mountain range from Georgia to Maine, *Nature Girl* became Kelley's first published novel.

Illustrated by Heather Palisi, *Nature Girl* introduces eleven-year-old Megan, a New York City native who is devastated to discover that her artist parents are forcing the family to spend the entire summer in a corner of Vermont with limited modern technology. While grudgingly accompanying her older sister and boyfriend on a short hike, Megan gets pouty and stomps off onto a side path that links up with the Appalachian trail. Lost, but accompanied by the family dog, the seventh grader decides to follow the historic trail south to Massachusetts, where she can be reunited with her best friend Lucy. Megan's naive understanding of life in the wild results in some tense moments as brown bears, hunger, a downpour, bugs, and insufficient food, water, and shelter make her view the word "necessity" in a new light. Calling *Nature Girl* a wilderness tale that "gets to the heart of real survival," Delia Carruthers added in *School Library Journal* that Megan comes across as "believable and honest, and her journey is both a physical and emotional success." In *Booklist* Debbie Carton recommended Kelley's novel as "right on target" for preteen nature lovers, and Deborah Stevenson predicted in the *Bulletin of the Center for Children's Books* that *Nature Girl* depicts "the kind of survival" most middle graders are "realistically . . . able to manage, and they'll relish seeing one of their unpromising own reach her surprising goal."

Kelley turns to mystery in *The Girl behind the Glass,* as eleven-year-old twins Anna and Hannah move with their parents to an old, musty-smelling house on rural Hemlock Road. Although the siblings are initially unified by their dislike of the new house, they soon find themselves disagreeing with one another over trivial things. Anna becomes content with new friends, while Hannah begins picking up strange, angry feelings from something who can neverforgive or forget what happened at the house eighty years ago. Hannah's sympathy for it soon places her at risk. In *Kirkus Reviews* a critic noted that Kelley mixes "mounting creepiness with well-placed spine-tingling moments" in *The Girl behind the Glass,* and her use of "a seemingly third-person narration that subtly morphs into a first-person" narrative adds a sinister element to the tale.

"Some of you might be writers too," Kelley commented, addressing *SATA* readers. "Maybe you'd like to be, but aren't sure how to begin?

"One thing is true for everybody, no matter who you are or whether you want to be a musician, a physicist, a screenwriter or an artist. No matter how successful you are, how many awards you have won, or if it's your first attempt, each time you begin a project, you must face the same thing: the exhilarating, terrifying BLANK PAGE.

"Everything anybody creates starts with an empty space that someone begins to fill. But unfortunately not everybody keeps at it. I didn't know if I would finish writing my novel *Nature Girl.* And I certainly didn't know it would get published.

"In many ways, Megan's journey parallels my own as a writer. Megan completely underestimates how long it will take her to hike from Vermont to Massachusetts. When I began *Nature Girl.* in the summer of 2006, I had no idea that the novel wouldn't be on the shelves until April 2010. I didn't know I would rewrite it nine times. I didn't know if it would ever be read by anybody who wasn't my relative. I knew one thing for certain. If I kept writing, I might succeed. But if I didn't, I never would. One of my characters actually says, 'You can do it! The only way to fail is to quit. So keep going!' I know I certainly needed to be reminded of that, too.

"Megan faces all kinds of challenges as she hikes the Appalachian Trail. A 'yucky voice' in her head constantly tells her, 'You'll never make it anyway, so why even bother to try?' But Megan tries to ignore that voice. Step by step, she gets closer to her goal. Then, one day, the 'yucky voice' is gone. Hiking on the trail has boosted Megan's confidence. Being in Nature has given her a new perspective on what's really important in her life. She has outwitted bears, found food in the wilderness and accomplished many other things she didn't think she could do.

"And so can you. If you refuse to listen to your 'yucky voice' that tells you not to even try.

"Many people wait for someone to give them permission to create. But you don't need anyone's approval. All you need is determination—and that terrifying, exhilarating BLANK PAGE."

Biographical and Critical Sources

PERIODICALS

Booklist, April 1, 2010, Debbie Carton, review of *Nature Girl,* p. 41.
Bulletin of the Center for Children's Books, April, 2010, Deborah Stevenson, review of *Nature Girl,* p. 340.
Kirkus Reviews, March 1, 2010, review of *Nature Girl;* July 1, 2011, review of *The Girl behind the Glass.*
Publishers Weekly, April 12, 2010, review of *Nature Girl,* p. 49.

School Library Journal, March, 2010, Delia Carruthers, review of *Nature Girl,* p. 160.

ONLINE

Jane Kelley Home Page, http://www.janekelleybooks.com (July 15, 2011).
Jane Kelley Web log, http://www.janekelley.blogspot.com (July 15, 2011).*

*   *   *

KHAN, Rukhsana 1962-

Personal

First name is pronounced "ruk-SA-na"; born March 13, 1962, in Lahore, Pakistan; immigrated to Canada, 1965; daughter of Muhammad Anwar (a tool-and-die maker) and Iftikhar Shahzadi (a homemaker) Khan; married Irfan Haseeb Alli (a condominium manager), March 31, 1979; children: three daughters, one son. *Education:* Seneca College of Applied Arts and Technology, degree (biological-chemical technician); attended University of Toronto. *Religion:* Islam.

Addresses

Home—Toronto, Ontario, Canada. *Agent*—Charlotte Sheedy, 928 Broadway, Ste. 901, New York, NY 10010. *E-mail*—rukhsana@rukhsanakhan.com.

Career

Writer and storyteller. Presenter at schools throughout United States and Canada.

Member

Society of Children's Book Writers and Illustrators, Writer's Union of Canada, Canadian Society of Children's Authors, Illustrators, and Performers, Storytellers of Canada, Storytelling School of Toronto.

Awards, Honors

Honorary Januscz Korczak International Literature Award, Polish section of International Board on Books for Young People, 1998, for *The Roses in My Carpets;* Writers' Reserve grant, Ontario Arts Council, 1998, 2003, 2009; Artists in Education grant, 1998-99; Ruth Schwartz Award shortlist, Canadian Booksellers Association/Ontario Arts Council, and Red Maple Award shortlist, Ontario Library Association, both 2000, and Manitoba Young Reader's Choice Honour Award, Manitoba Library Association, 2001, all for *Dahling If You Luv Me Would You Please, Please Smile;* Hackmatack Award shortlist, and Canadian Children's Book Centre Choice designation, both 2001, both for *Muslim Child;* Toastmaster District 60 Communication and Leadership Award, 2004; Arts and Literature Award,

Rukhsana Khan (Reproduced by permission.)

Canadian Islamic Congress, 2004; Council for the Advancement of Muslim Professionals (Toronto, Ontario chapter) Award of Excellence, 2008; Middle East Book Award in Youth Fiction category, Society of School Librarians International Honor Book selection, and U.S. Board on Books for Youth Outstanding International Books selection, all 2009, and IODE Violet Downey Award shortlist, Hackmatack Award shortlist, Rocky Mountain Book Award shortlist, International Reading Association Notable Books for a Global Society selection, Capital Choices Noteworthy Titles for Children and Teens inclusion, and Canadian Children's Book Centre Best Books designation, all 2010, all for *Wanting Mor;* Society of School Librarians International Honor selection, Notable Books for a Global Society selection, International Reading Association, and *New York Times* Top-ten Illustrated Books selection, all 2010, and Best Book of the Year selection, Bank Street College of Education, Golden Kite Award for Best Picturebook Text, and Charlotte Zolotow Award, all 2011, all for *Big Red Lollipop.*

Writings

PICTURE BOOKS

Bedtime Ba-a-a-lk, illustrated by Kristi Frost, Stoddart Kids (Toronto, Ontario, Canada), 1998.
The Roses in My Carpets, illustrated by Ronald Himler, Holiday House (New York, NY), 1998.

King of the Skies, illustrated by Laura Fernandez and Rick Jacobson, North Winds Press (Markham, Ontario, Canada), 2001.

Ruler of the Courtyard, illustrated by R. Gregory Christie, Viking (New York, NY), 2003.

Silly Chicken, illustrated by Yunmee Kyong, Viking (New York, NY), 2005.

Big Red Lollipop, illustrated by Sophie Blackall, Viking (New York, NY), 2010.

OTHER

Dahling If You Luv Me, Would You Please, Please Smile (young-adult novel), Stoddart Kids (Toronto, Ontario, Canada), 1999.

Muslim Child: A Collection of Short Stories and Poems, illustrated by Patty Gallinger, Napoleon (Toronto, Ontario, Canada), 1999, published as *Muslim Child: Understanding Islam through Stories and Poems,* Albert Whitman (Morton Grove, IL), 2002.

Many Windows: Six Kids, Five Faiths, One Community (short-story collection), Dundurn Press, 2002.

Coming to Canada (novella), Citizenship and Immigration Canada, 2008, published as *A New Life,* Groundwood (Toronto, Ontario, Canada), 2009.

Wanting Mor (middle-grade novel), Groundwood Books (Toronto, Ontario, Canada), 2009, published as *Jameela,* Allen & Unwin (East Melbourne, Victoria, Australia), 2010.

Contributor of short stories to anthology *Hoping for Home: Stories of Arrival,* Scholastic Canada (Toronto, Ontario, Canada), 2011, and to magazines, including *Message International* and *Kahani;* and of articles to *Horn Book* and *School Library Journal.* Contributor of songs to *Adam's World* (children's videos), produced by Sound Vision, and to story for *Driver Dan's Story Train* television series.

Sidelights

Pakistan-born Canadian writer and storyteller Rukhsana Khan draws on her experiences living within two very different cultures in her award-winning books for young readers. In picture books as well as novels for preteens and young adults, Khan's characters cope with the universal challenges faced while growing up within a Muslim culture.

In her first picture book, *Bedtime Ba-a-a-lk,* Khan provides a twist on the usual scenario of a child counting sheep in order to be reluctantly lulled to sleep. Here, a little girl conjures up a flock of imaginary sheep to aid in her efforts to fall asleep, but she meets resistance from the wooly creatures on every front. First they require her to imagine more light on the far side of the fence so they can see what they are jumping into, then they get bored by the activity they have performed so many times before and demand entertainment instead. When the girl conjures up an imaginary carnival, the sheep become so entranced that they forget to jump at

all. *Quill & Quire* reviewer Patty Lawlor praised Khan's soothing text, writing that *Bedtime Ba-a-a-lk* "opens almost poetically with lyrical language, phrasing and pacing, immediately creating an effective sleepytime mood." A reviewer for *Kirkus Reviews* praised the book's illustrations and text for their "light touch": "A little bit of dream manipulation goes a long way in this lullaby tale," the reviewer stated.

Striking a decidedly different tone, *The Roses in My Carpets* was inspired by Khan's visit with her Afghan refugee foster child in a refugee camp in Peshawar in 1992. The book introduces a young Afghan refugee who lives with his mother and younger sister. At the beginning of his day, the boy rises early after a recurrent nightmare, prays at the mosque, eats, goes to school, prays again, then practices the craft of weaving. Learning to weave is the highlight of his day; his work is the only beautiful thing he sees in the grim world of the camp and becoming proficient at this skill offers him hope that he will one day be able to support his family through his earnings from work. While at his weaving lesson, the boy learns that his sister has been hit by a truck, though she will recover. That night his worries and hopes for the future transform his earlier nightmare. In *The Roses in My Carpets* "Khan hints at the boy's powerful emotions in spare prose, and handles her difficult subject matter sensitively," commented a reviewer in *Publishers Weekly. Booklist* critic Linda

***Ronald Himler captures the dreams of a young Afghani weaver in his illustrations for Khan's* The Roses in My Carpets.** (Illustration copyright © 1998 by Ronald Himler. Reproduced by permission of Holiday House, Inc.)

Perkins noted that, while youngsters will likely need supplemental information on the Islamic religion and the war in Afghanistan, Khan's story presents "a rare and welcome glimpse into a culture [American] children usually don't see." Khan used the earnings from *The Roses in My Carpets* to sponsor other refugees and help found a library in an orphanage in Kabul.

The disabled young boy who serves as the protagonist in Khan's *King of the Skies* is a native of Pakistan, and he shares his excitement about the upcoming kite festival celebrated in the city of Lahore each spring. Showing the results of much practice, skill, and concentration, he navigates his own kite, the yellow Guddi Chore, among others in the festival as his siblings help clear fallen kites from the path of his wheelchair. In *Canadian Review of Materials* a reviewer praised *King of the Skies* as "beautiful and satisfying," adding that Khan's "eloquence is matched by . . . luminous oil paintings" created by Rick Jacobson and Laura Fernandez. *King of the Skies* "is an excellent example of a story which carries the reader to another place," maintained *Resource Links* writer Kathryn McNaughton, the critic predicting that Khan's "fascinating" story, in addition to its multicultural elements, "may also spark conversations about children with diverse abilities."

Also set in Pakistan, *Ruler of the Courtyard* and *Silly Chicken* focus on chickens, although these birds of a feather do not share similar temperaments. In *Ruler of the Courtyard* a young girl named Saba lives in fear of the flock of sharp-beaked chickens which run unchecked through the courtyard of her rural home. The hold the dumb birds have over her is broken, however, when Sabba gains self-confidence after bravely confronting a far more deadly threat. Praising *Ruler of the Courtyard* as "perfectly paced," a *Kirkus Reviews* contributor added that the tale's exciting storyline and "positive message" combine to make Khan's book "a winner for reading aloud." A *Publishers Weekly* critic cited Khan's "message about self-reliance and courage," while in *Horn Book* Susan P. Bloom commented favorably on the tale's "wonderful energy and use of language," from "short, staccato sentences" to "smooth soaring language" as the girl overcomes her fears.

Sibling rivalry is the focus of the poignant *Silly Chicken,* which is based on a true story told about Khan's grandmother by Khan's mother. Main character Rani—short for "maharani" or queen—is named after Khan's mother; the chicken's name, Bibi, means "miss." In the story Rani feels competition from pet chicken Bibi, which seems to take most of Rani's mother's attention. When Bibi meets an unfortunate end at the hand of a cruel neighbor, however, Raini realizes her mistake and determines to be a loving guardian of the creature that will hatch from the egg the pet chicken has left behind. Noting the happy ending that concludes *Silly Chicken,* a *Kirkus Reviews* writer wrote that Khan's "language is conversational and spare and the [story's] pacing just

A young girl braves a predator while caring for her family's flock of chickens in Khan's novel **Ruler of the Courtyard,** *featuring artwork by* **R. Gregory Christie.**

right," while in *Booklist* reviewer Carolyn Phelan explained that the tale "clearly depicts a child's jealousy" while sidestepping "the usual schmaltz."

Another picture book, *Big Red Lollipop*, finds Khan teaming up with artist Sophie Blackall to describe the jealousies that can spring up between sisters. Rubina and Sana are young Pakistani immigrants, and Rubina, the oldest, is excited to attend a friend's birthday party. When middle sister Sana insists that she go too, she ends up ruining the party for her sister. Sana eventually receives a party invitation as well, and now she balks when her littlest sister demands that she attend as well. Despite her anger at Sana, Rubina recognizes that she can influence her mother into making a decision that will allow her younger sister to enjoy her special time with friends in a story that *Booklist* critic Ilene Cooper described as "an honest, even moving, commentary on sisterly relationships." For a *Publishers Weekly* contributor, *Big Red Lollipop* takes on more than sibling rivalry: it deals with "hard-won lessons emerging from clashes of identity and assimilation," according to the critic. For *School Library Journal* critic Sara Lissa Paulson, Blackall's illustrations add to the story's resonance. Her use of shifting perspectives as well as "muted tones and [the] spareness of the illustrations allow readers to feel the small conflicts in the text," Paulson maintained.

"*Big Red Lollipop* began as an incidental paragraph in my teen novel *Dahling If You Luv Me Would You Please Please Smile,* then turned into an oral story I told for more than ten years to audiences of all ages. It wasn't until my editor suggested that I write the story from the older sister's point of view, did it become the current award-winning version. When writing the story, I used an abbreviated version of my own name for the character that represents me, thinking that everyone would figure out that Rukh-SANA is writing the story. *Big Red Lollipop* was dedicated to the memory of my older sister Bushra, who passed away of breast cancer in 2003, and her two children. Bushra only ever got to hear the story in oral form. On the day that occurred, she was laughing louder than anyone else in the audience and then came up to me and took me to task for the one thing I'd changed in the story. Bushra said, 'Wait a minute! You never gave me the green lollipop!' I replied, 'I know, but I should have.' I consider having written the story as my atonement."

While her picture books introduce cultural differences through gentle stories, Khan's anthology *Muslim Child: Understanding Islam through Stories and Poems* takes a more direct route, collecting eight stories featuring young Muslims living in North America as well as Nigeria, and Pakistan. A *Kirkus Reviews* contributor praised the "earnest tone" Khan brings to her stories and poems, adding that readers' understanding of Islam will increase through the author's inclusion of passages from the Qu'ran, quotations by Muhammad, and sidebars that contains information about many aspects of the Muslim faith. While noting that Khan's motive is to educate Western readers, *School Library Journal* contributor Coop Renner wrote of *Muslim Child* that the book's "most avid audience . . . may be American Muslim children excited finally to find stories with characters to whom they can relate."

Khan describes an almost-universal battle between children and their parents in her picture book Bedtime Ba-a-a-lk, *featuring artwork by Kristi Frost.* (Illustration copyright © 1998 by Kristi Frost. Reproduced by permission of Fitzhenry & Whiteside Limited.)

Geared for middle-grade readers, Khan's novel *Wanting Mor* is based on a true story set in war-torn Afghanistan during 2001. Jameela lives in the countryside with her parents when U.S. troops enter the country to battle the Taliban, and after her mother is killed she moves with her father to the city of Kabul. The woman who then marries her father does not want Jameela as a daughter because of the girl's devotion to Islam and her appearance (she has a cleft lip), and she convinces her new husband to abandon the girl. Fortunately, Jameela's hardships are now over: she is discovered and taken to an orphanage where her lip is treated and she is given the opportunity to gain an education in preparation for a better life. Through Jameela's first-person narrative Western readers can visualize "the far-off world of rural and urban Afghanistan," according to Kathleen Isaacs in *Horn Book,* and *School Library Journal* contributor Lynn Rutan praised Khan's "compelling" tale for including examples of Afghan's Pushto language along with a glossary. *Wanting Mor* "fills a niche" in middle-grade fiction, asserted a *Kirkus Reviews* writer, "and [it] does so with respect for the people and places described—and with sometimes downright lovely language."

Khan turns to teen readers in *Dahling if You Luv Me, Would You Please, Please Smile*, a contemporary novel addressing mature themes of conformity, bullying, racism, and suicide. In the story, Zainab is a young Muslim teen who is trying to fit in to her new Canadian surroundings. Through Zainab's story, Khan explores the way people are manipulated: from the obvious sexual manipulation faced by Zainab's best friend Jenny to the more subtle religious manipulation being perpetrated on the young woman herself. Reviewing the novel in the *Toronto Star,* Deirdre Baker wrote that *Dahling if You Luv Me, Would You Please, Please Smile* contains "wonderful warmth, humour and complexity."

"Growing up Muslim in North America was very difficult," Khan once recalled to *SATA,* explaining that "the release of each mega-blockbuster depicting Muslims as merciless bumbling terrorists or ignorant taxi drivers" made them "look . . . like a bunch of barbaric idiots." Moving with her family to Ontario in the mid-1960s, she also experienced racial prejudice first hand. "My father worked at a tool and die company, and his coworkers used to call him 'black bastard' right to his face," she recalled to *Canadian Review of Materials* interviewer Dave Jenkinson. "They hardly ever called him by his name, and he put up with it because he had four kids to feed. My father had chosen to live in Canada because he wanted to get away from those cultural influences which said girls are expendable. He also wanted to raise us as Muslims, and he wanted a good neighborhood."

Because Khan's family was one of only two Indian families living in their Ontario town, their differences were apparent to everyone. "Because we stuck out so much, we were persecuted from day one," the author continued to Jenkinson. "If it hadn't been for that negative treatment, I don't think I would have become a

Sophie Blackall created the award-winning artwork that pairs with Khan's picture-book text in **Big Red Lollipop.** (Illustration copyright © 2010 by Sophie Blackall. Used by permission of Viking Children's Books, a division of Penguin Young Readers Group, a member of Penguin Group (USA) Inc., 345 Hudson St., New York, NY 10014. All rights reserved.)

writer because my growing up was so horrible that I went to books to escape. Having no friends, I spent my recesses among the trees. I used to think a lot, and that's when I really came to terms with what my beliefs are, who I am, and what my place is in the universe."

While developing her skills as an author, Khan wrote stories, began attending writing conferences and seminars, and did extensive reading. From the start, her primary aim has been to tell good stories, set within her Muslim culture in the hope that these stories will help 'humanize' Muslims to unfamiliar readers.

At one conference Khan attended, a Western woman spoke about a novel she had written that was set in Muslim culture. It was about a Muslim child, and "this white lady had gotten the culture all wrong," Khan explained to *SATA*. "It was clear, almost from the beginning of the book, that a 'white feminist' had imposed her sensibilities on a girl who wouldn't have been exposed to them within the scope of the novel. There was some merit in the book, but unfortunately the book did perpetuate a lot of the prevalent Muslim stereotypes that so upset me."

"At that moment, what I really was up against fully hit me," Khan remembered. "Here I was, a Pakistani immigrant with quaint old-fashioned principles, trying to show this big amorphous blob of Western society that they'd pegged us 'Moslems' all wrong. How could I even aspire to such a lofty goal? Who did I think I was?

"What I eventually realized is that people . . . will write all kinds of garbage about Islam. In order to fight them, I'll have to be better.

"I'm working on it."

Biographical and Critical Sources

PERIODICALS

Booklist, November 15, 1998, Linda Perkins, review of *The Roses in My Carpets,* p. 596; February 15, 2002, John Green, review of *Muslim Child: A Collection of Short Stories and Poems,* p. 1011; January 1, 2005, Carolyn Phelan, review of *Silly Chicken,* p. 879; April 1, 2009, Lynn Rutan, review of *Wanting Mor,* p. 40; February 1, 2010, Ilene Cooper, review of *Big Red Lollipop,* p. 44.

Childhood Education, summer, 2010, Connie Green, review of *Wanting Mor,* p. 277.

Horn Book, March-April, 2003, Susan P. Bloom, review of *Ruler of the Courtyard,* p. 204; March-April, 2005, Kitty Flynn, review of *Silly Chicken,* p. 190; July-August, 2009, Kathleen Isaacs, review of *Wanting Mor,* p. 426; September-October, 2009, Rukhsana Khan, "It's How You Say It," p. 499.

Kirkus Reviews, June 15, 1998, review of *Bedtime Ba-a-a-lk,* p. 896; February 1, 2002, review of *Muslim Child,* p. 182; December 15, 2002, review of *Ruler of the Courtyard,* p. 1851; February 15, 2005, review of *Silly Chicken,* p. 230; April 15, 2009, review of *Wanting Mor;* January 15, 2010, review of *Big Red Lollipop.*

New York Times Book Review, November 7, 2010, Lawrence Downes, review of *Big Red Lollipop,* p. 18.

Publishers Weekly, October 5, 1998, review of *The Roses in My Carpets,* p. 90; February 11, 2002, review of *Muslim Child,* p. 189; January 6, 2003, review of *Ruler of the Courtyard,* p. 59; April 4, 2005, review of *Silly Chicken,* p. 59; March 1, 2010, review of *Big Red Lollipop,* p. 49.

Quill & Quire, March, 1998, Patty Lawlor, review of *Bedtime Ba-a-a-lk,* pp. 71-72.

Resource Links, December, 2001, Kathryn McNaughton, review of *King of the Skies,* p. 6.

School Library Journal, November, 1998, pp. 87-88; February, 2002, Coop Renner, review of *Muslim Child,* p. 122; February, 2003, Dona Ratterree, review of *Ruler of the Courtyard,* p. 114; January, 2005, Ann W. Moore, review of *Muslim Child,* p. 55; April, 2005, Joy Fleishhacker, review of *Silly Chicken,* p. 105; September, 2006, Rukhsana Khan, "Muslims in Children's Books: An Author Looks Back and at the Ongoing Publishing Challenges," p. 36; March, 2010, Sara Lissa Paulson, review of *Big Red Lollipop,* p. 120.

Toronto Star, April 18, 1999, Deirdre Baker, review of *Dahling if You Luv, Me Would You Please, Please Smile,* p. D31.

ONLINE

Canadian Review of Materials Online, http://www.umanitoba.ca/outreach/cm/ (September 24, 1999), David Jenkinson, interview with Khan; (February 4, 2000) David Jenkinson, review of *Muslim Child;* (November 2, 2001) review of *King of the Skies;* (April 29, 2005) Valerie Nielsen, review of *Silly Chicken.*

Canadian Society of Children's Authors, Illustrators, and Performers Web site, http://www.canscaip.org/ (May 28, 2005), "Rukhsana Khan."

Rukhsana Khan Home Page, http://www.rukhsanakhan.com (July 10, 2011).

Rukhsana Khan Web log, http://blog.rukhsanakhan.com (July 15, 2011).

*   *   *

KURILLA, Renée 1981-

Personal

Born May 14, 1981, in Scranton, PA. *Education:* Art Institute of Boston, B.F.A. (illustration), diploma (graphic design). *Hobbies and other interests:* Playing guitar, sewing, painting in oils.

Addresses

Home—Boston, MA. *E-mail*—renee@kurillastration. com.

Career

Animator and illustrator. FableVision Studios (educational media company), Boston, MA, animation artist, beginning 2005. Presenter at workshops.

Illustrator

Sharon Emerson, *Zebrafish* (based on the animated character created by Peter H. Reynolds and FableVision), Atheneum Books for Young Readers (New York, NY), 2010.

Creator of *Goodbye, My 20's* Web log.

Sidelights

Renée Kurilla became a children's book illustrator through her connection with FableVision, an animation studio located in her adopted home town of Boston, Massachusetts. A native of Scranton, Pennsylvania, Kurilla moved to Boston to study illustration and graphic design at the city's Art Institute, and she went to work at educational media company FableVision after several years of freelancing. In addition to her duties designing animation for the Cartoon Network, Discovery Kids, and other television channels, she is also the illustrator of *Zebrafish,* a graphic novel based on an animated character created by illustrator and animator Peter H. Reynolds.

Geared for middle-grade readers, *Zebrafish* focuses on Vita, an aspiring, purple-haired rock musician who is also the new girl at school. Fortunately, Vita's desire to start a band she calls Zebrafish combines with her willingness to help classmates with a similar dream but less than stellar musical skills. Soon the band's new members are working together on a music video . . . except for Tayna, who constantly misses rehearsals. At first Vita is frustrated by this seeming lack of commitment, but when she discovers the reason for Tanya's absences she also gains a lesson in compassion in a "bouncy cartoon story" that "mines equally serious territory," according to *Booklist* critic Francisca Goldsmith. Reviewing *Zebrafish* in *School Library Journal,* Janet Weber praised Kurilla's "clear and sharply inked" four-color sequential panel art, adding that her use of contrast "creates balance and tone throughout" the work. Based on an online animated cartoon series, *Zebrafish* also marked a collaboration between FableVision and the Boston Children's Hospital; a portion of all proceeds from book sales benefit the hospital's work.

Renee Kurilla's illustration projects include creating the cartoon artwork for Sharon Emerson's **Zebrafish.** (Illustration copyright © 2010 by Children's Hospital Boston. Reproduced with permission of Atheneum Books for Young Readers, an imprint of Simon & Schuster Children's Publishing Division.)

Biographical and Critical Sources

PERIODICALS

Booklist, March 15, 2010, Francisca Goldsmith, review of *Zebrafish,* p. 62.
Bulletin of the Center for Children's Books, September, 2010, review of *Zebrafish,* p. 15.
School Library Journal, May, 2010, Janet Weber, review of *Zebrafish,* p. 139.

ONLINE

FableVision Web site, http://www.fablevisionstudios.com/ (June 15, 2011), "Renée Kurilla."
Goodbye, My 20's Web Log, http://goodbymy20s.blogspot. com (June 15, 2011).
Renée Kurilla Home Page, http://www.kurillastration.com (June 15, 2011).
Renée Kurilla Web Log, http://kurillastration.blogspot.com (June 15, 2011).

L

LACY, Rick

Personal
Male. *Education:* School of Visual Arts, B.A. (animation), 2002.

Addresses
Home—New York, NY. *E-mail*—ricklacy@gmail.com.

Career
Animator, character designer, and concept artist. Venture Bros., Inc., character designer and story artist, 2001-09; Gameloft, NY, animator and second artist for computer games, 2009—. Teacher of sequential art at Bergen Street Comics, Brooklyn, NY.

Illustrator
(With Ben Caldwell) Tim Mucci, adaptor, *The Odyssey* ("All-Actions Classics" series), three volumes, Sterling (New York, NY), 2010.

Illustrator of "Labor Days" comic-book series, text by Philip Gelatt, Oni Press, c. 2008-09. Contributor to comic-book series, including "Star Wars: Clone Wars Adventures," "Rex Steele," "Indiana Jones Adventures," and "Hellboy Animated."

Biographical and Critical Sources

PERIODICALS

School Library Journal, July, 2010, Andrea Lipinski, review of *The Odyssey,* volume 3, p. 107.

ONLINE

Rick Lacy Web log, http://www.ricklacy.blogspot.com (June 26, 2011).*

LAGOS, Joseph

Personal
Born in Montevideo, Uruguay; immigrated to United States at age two; married; has children.

Addresses
Home—Houston, TX. *Agent*—Jill Grinberg, Anderson Grinberg Literary Management, 244 5th Ave., 11th Fl., New York, NY 10001; jill@grinbergliterary.com.

Career
Author and businessman.

Writings

"SONS OF LIBERTY" GRAPHIC-NOVEL SERIES

(With brother Alexander Lagos) *The Sons of Liberty,* illustrated by Steve Walker and Oren Kramek, Random House Children's Books (New York, NY), 2010.
(With Alexander Lagos) *Death and Taxes,* illustrated by Steve Walker and Oren Kramek, Random House Children's Books (New York, NY), 2011.

Sidelights
Joseph Lagos teams up with brother Alexander Lagos to create the "Sons of Liberty" graphic novel series, which weaves together the superhero elements of classic adventure comics with actual people and events from U.S. history. Featuring dramatic artwork by Steve Walker and Oren Kramek, the "Sons of Liberty" books are designed to capture the interest of comic-book fans, history buffs, and particularly reluctant readers and their stories may inspire thoughtful reflection about the actions and choices underlying the course of the nation's founding. In a review of the first installment in the La-

gos brothers' graphic-novel series, a *Kirkus Reviews* writer cited the "Sons of Liberty" books for their "distinctly different take on the American Revolution."

Lagos was born in Uruguay and immigrated to the United States when he was two years old. Growing up in Elizabeth, New Jersey, a town steeped in history, he became fascinated with the colonial era. Although he now makes his home in Texas, where he has joined his family's woodcarving business, Lagos's continued interest in the American Revolution prompted him to look for a way to work this historical era into a story that would inspire the same interest in other readers. He found a ready collaborator in brother Alexander Lagos,

who was born in Elizabeth and shares his interest and enthusiasm. Because Alexander lives in Brooklyn, New York, the two brothers often rely on communication technology to engage in their creative collaboration.

In *The Sons of Liberty* the setting is rural Pennsylvania, near Philadelphia, where tobacco is grown. Brothers Graham and Brody are slaves who have been brought from Africa, and they decide to escape from their master after an act of particular cruelty. Advised to search for a man named Benjamin, they locate inventor and statesman Benjamin Franklin. Franklin's son William shares his father's inventive genius, but he channels it toward destructive ends. After he uses the two escaped

Joseph Lagos joins brother Alexander Lagos to write the text for **The Sons of Liberty,** *a graphic novel featuring artwork by Steve Walker and Oren Kramek.* (Art by Steve Walker. Used by permission of Random House Children's Books, a division of Random House, Inc.)

slaves in an experiment, William leaves them with unusual powers that they must learn to harness. Still in hiding, they locate another Benjamin, Quaker abolitionist Benjamin Lay, who channels their new abilities through his knowledge of the African fighting technique called Dambe. Now able to defend themselves, Graham and Brody are also able to stop the work of vicious slave hunters as well as avenge the tragic murder of their friend and mentor. The brothers' adventures continue in *Death and Taxes,* as tensions over British policies within the colonies begin to flame into violence.

Predicting that the colorful digitized artwork in *The Sons of Liberty* will attract younger readers, Jesse Karp added in his *Booklist* review that the Lagos brothers' incorporation of "well-researched (but embellished) history" with well-realized characters and a cliffhanger ending "makes for an uncommonly complex, literate, and satisfying adventure." Reviewing the same installment in *Voice of Youth Advocates,* Kat Kan suggested that the Lagos's decision to mix "historical fiction with super hero elements . . . could attract reluctant readers," and a *Publishers Weekly* critic predicted that all but true sticklers for historical veracity "should appreciate the fast pace and creativity" on exhibit in the pages of the illustrated saga. While "not a source of accurate history," the *Kirkus Reviews* contributor admitted, *The Sons of Liberty* is nonetheless "hard to put down."

The "Sons of Liberty" series "deals with controversial subject matters during a very hard time in American history," Lagos noted in an online interview with Melissa Buron, and he explained that he and his brother strive to keep their text for the work "respectful." "We have a responsibility to research historical events, compile supporting data and images, check for accuracy, and identify key players that are consistent with history," he added; "but then, of course, we throw in masked super heroes and make the whole thing entertaining as well as educational."

Biographical and Critical Sources

PERIODICALS

Booklist, June 1, 2010, Jesse Karp, review of *The Sons of Liberty,* p. 70.

Kirkus Reviews, April 15, 2010, review of *The Sons of Liberty.*

Library Journal, March 15, 2011, Martha Cornog, review of *Death and Taxes,* p. 104.

Publishers Weekly, May 3, 2010, review of *The Sons of Liberty,* p. 55.

School Library Journal, July, 2010, Douglas P. Davey, review of *The Sons of Liberty,* p. 106.

Voice of Youth Advocates, August, 2010, Kat Kan, review of *The Sons of Liberty,* p. 238.

ONLINE

Joseph Lagos Home Page, http://thesonsoflibertybook.com (July 15, 2011).

Melissa Buron Web log, http://melissaburon.livejournal.com/ (March 20, 2010), Melissa Buron, interview with Lagos.*

*　　*　　*

LARBALESTIER, Justine

Personal

Surname pronounced "Lar-bal-est-ee-air"; born in Sydney, New South Wales, Australia; daughter of anthropologists; married Scott Westerfeld (a writer). *Education:* Ph.D. *Hobbies and other interests:* Cricket.

Addresses

Home—Sydney, New South Wales, Australia; New York, NY. *Agent*—Jill Grinberg, Anderson Grinberg Literary Management, 244 5th Ave., 11th Fl., New York, NY 10001; jill@grinbergliterary.com.

Career

Novelist. Formerly worked as an academic.

Awards, Honors

Susan Koppleman Award, William Atheling, Jr., Award, and British Science Fiction Award shortlist, all c. 2006, all for *Daughters of Earth;* Best Teen Books selection, Bank Street College of Education, Best Books for Young Adults selection, American Library Association, and Ethel Turner Award shortlist, New South Wales Premier's Literary Awards, all 2006, and Andre Norton Award, 2007, all for *Magic or Madness;* Aurealis Award for Best Australian Young-Adult Novel, Cooperative Center for Children's Books Choice designation, and Locus Award shortlist, all c. 2006, all for *Magic Lessons.*

Writings

FICTION

How to Ditch Your Fairy, Bloomsbury U.S.A. (New York, NY), 2008.

Liar, Bloomsbury U.S.A. Children's Books (New York, NY), 2009.

"MAGIC OR MADNESS" YOUNG-ADULT NOVEL TRILOGY

Magic or Madness, Razorbill (New York, NY), 2005.

Magic Lessons, Razorbill (New York, NY), 2006.

Magic's Child, Razorbill (New York, NY), 2007.

OTHER

Opulent Darkness: The Werewolves of Tanith Lee, Nimrod Publications (New Lambton, New South Wales, Australia), 1999.

The Battle of the Sexes in Science Fiction, Wesleyan University Press (Middletown, CT), 2002.

(Editor) *Daughters of Earth: Feminist Science Fiction in the Twentieth Century,* Wesleyan University Press (Middletown, CT), 2006.

(Compiler with Holly Black) *Zombies vs. Unicorns,* Margaret K. McElderry Books (New York, NY), 2010.

Author of screenplay *A Legend of King Midas,* Australian Film, Television, and Radio School, 1999; coauthor of radio program. Work represented in anthologies, including *Four Scenarios, . . . Is This a Cat?,* edited by Christopher Rowe, Fortress of Words (Lexington, KY), 2002; *Say . . . Was That a Kiss?,* edited by Rowe, Fortress of Words, 2002; *The Best of Strange Horizons, Year Two,* edited by Kelli Carlson, Lethe Press (Maple Shade, NJ), 2004; *Agog! Smashing Stories,* edited by Cat Sparks, Agog Press (Wollongong, New South Wales, Australia), 2004; and *Love Is Hell,* HarperTeen (New York, NY), 2008. Contributor of essays and short stories to periodicals, including *Strange Horizons* and *Foundation: The International Review of Science Fiction.*

Adaptations

Liar was adapted for audiobook by Brilliance Audio, narrated by Channie Waites, 2009.

Sidelights

Australian educator Justine Larbalestier made her literary debut with *The Battle of the Sexes in Science Fiction,* an academic work that was an outgrowth of her Ph.D. thesis. Continuing her study of science fiction as a literary genre, Larbalestier has edited the award-winning *Daughters of Earth: Feminist Science Fiction in the Twentieth Century* and joined fellow author Holly Black to produce the anthology *Zombies vs. Unicorns,* in which a dozen writers—including Libba Bray, Meg Cabot, Margo Lanagan, and Larbalestier's husband, writer Scott Westerfeld—defend their position in the ongoing debate about which fantasy creature is more popular. *Zombies vs. Unicorns* "is a must-have for fantasy collections," asserted *School Library Journal* contributor Jessica Miller, the critic adding that the "highly entertaining anthology" benefits from "the snarky dialogue between the coeditors."

Larbalestier also contributes to the genre that has been her main topic of study in her young-adult science-fiction trilogy "Magic or Madness," which includes the novels *Magic or Madness, Magic Lessons,* and *Magic's Child.* As *Magic or Madness* opens, fifteen-year-old mathematical prodigy Reason Cansino learns that she must now live with her grandmother, a woman rumored

to be an evil, deranged witch. Attempting to escape, Reason opens a door that proves to be a portal to New York City, where she learns that things are not always what they seem and flees the evil creatures that now pursue her. A *Kirkus Review* contributor called *Magic or Madness* "a cleverly creepy fantasy with likable, complex characters and a sinister conclusion," while Melissa Moore wrote in *School Library Journal* that the novel treats readers to "a fantasy adventure and a thoughtful examination of relationships." In *Booklist* contributor Jennifer Mattson also recommended *Magic or Madness,* citing "Larbalestier's fine writing."

In *Magic Lessons* Reason's powers force her and her mother to move constantly after she causes a boy's death by radiating her uncontrollable anger. In New York City the teen is attracted to a young man who has no magical powers, and now she must decide whether this relationship is worth relinquishing her own powers. Reason returns in *Magic's Child* as the now-pregnant teen joins friends Jay-Tee and Tom to map an uncertain future and also ponder a life without their magical pow-

Cover of Justine Larbalestier's novel Magic or Madness, ***featuring artwork by Silva Otto and Kamil Vojnar.*** (Cover photographs © by Silvia Otte/ Photonica & Kamil Vojnar/Photonica. Used by permission of Razorbill, a division of Penguin Young Readers Group, a member of Penguin Group (USA) Inc., 345 Hudson St., New York, NY 10014. All rights reserved.)

Cover of Larbalestier's series installment **Magic Lessons,** *featuring artwork by Kamil Vojnar.* (Cover photographs © by Kamil Vojnar/Photonica & Scott Westerfield. Used by permission of Razorbill, a division of Penguin Young Readers Group, a member of Penguin Group (USA) Inc., 345 Hudson St., New York, NY 10014. All rights reserved.)

ers. In a review of *Magic Lessons* for *School Library Journal,* Beth L. Meister wrote that Larbalestier "creates complex relationships among her characters." In *Booklist* Jennifer Mattson cited the "inventive premise and amiable teen characters" in *Magic's Child,* while Meister praised the same work as "a strong conclusion to a compelling trilogy" featuring "a sympathetic and conflicted protagonist." Writing in *Kirkus Reviews,* a critic recommended the "crackling blend of fantastic adventure and soap-opera angst" in Larbalestier's "Magic or Madness" books and predicted that the saga will leave teens "pondering their own hard choices."

Larbalestier mixes fantasy and futuristic fiction in *How to Ditch Your Fairy,* which takes readers to a country— New Avalon—where every resident has a fairy as a constant companion. While this may sound like a good deal, Charlie and Fiorenze would disagree. Their fairy companions are specialized, and Charlie's fairy spends her time providing the fourteen year old non-driver with available parking spaces. Meanwhile, Fiorenze's fairy concentrates on making every boy crush on her human companion. When the two teens team up to stop

fairy interference they wind up switching fairies, and a *Publishers Weekly* critic noted that this plot twist propels Larbalestier's "vividly imagined story" "to some serious (and seriously funny) extremes." "Charlie is totally likable, smart, and sarcastic, a perfectly self-involved, insecure teen," asserted Connie Tyrrell Burns in her *School Library Journal* appraisal of *How to Ditch Your Fairy,* and *Horn Book* critic Claire E. Gross stated that "Larbalestier's half-fantasy, half-sci-fi setting is fully realized and strikingly original."

In the thriller *Liar* Larbalestier turns to an older readership and introduces Micah Wilkins, a seventeen-year-old high-school senior who lives in New York City. As Micah recounts the chain of events that led her to become a suspect in the murder of another student at her private high school, readers must temper her narrative with Micah's up-front admission that she is a compulsive prevaricator. While the teen's "suspenseful, supernatural tale is engrossing," cautioned *School Library Journal* critic Patricia N. McClune, "the wise [reader] will be wary of her spin and read carefully for subtle slipups and foreshadowing." In fact, Micah slowly peels layers of lies from her tale, recounting three successive versions of events and asserting before each one that it is more truthful than her previous explanation. In the end, however, it is left to the reader to evaluate what is true and what is a creation of Micah's inner psyche. As a narrator, "Micah is wonderfully complex, both irritating and immensely likeable," according to *Booklist* contributor Debbie Carton, Praising *Liar* as a "dark, gripping page-turner," a *Kirkus Reviews* writer added that Larbalestier's "engrossing story of teenage life on the margins" resolves into an ending that most will not anticipate. "Micah's story makes compulsive reading," concluded *Horn Book* critic Lauren Adams, "and the ambiguous ending will leave readers haunted long after closing the book."

On her home page, Larbalestier encouraged aspiring writers to read with an eye to what they like best. "Don't be in too much of a hurry to get published," she added. "Learning to write well is the main thing. If you try to publish before you're ready you can wind up very discouraged. While you're learning to write you should have fun with it. Try different styles, different genres, mess about, get your hands dirty!"

Biographical and Critical Sources

PERIODICALS

Booklist, March 15, 2005, Jennifer Mattson, review of *Magic or Madness,* p. 1286; April 15, 2007, Jennifer Mattson, review of *Magic's Child,* p. 38; September 1, 2009, Debbie Carton, review of *Liar,* p. 84; September 1, 2010, Daniel Kraus, review of *Zombies vs. Unicorns,* p. 103.

Extrapolation, fall, 2002, Javier A. Martinez review of *The Battle of the Sexes in Science Fiction,* p. 354; summer, 2008, Erin McQuiston, review of *Daughters of Earth: Feminist Science Fiction in the Twentieth Century,* p. 334.

Horn Book, January-February, 2009, Claire E. Gross, review of *How to Ditch Your Fairy,* p. 95; November-December, 2009, Lauren Adams, review of *Liar,* p. 676.

Kirkus Reviews, February 1, 2005, review of *Magic or Madness,* p. 178; March 1, 2006, review of *Magic Lessons,* p. 233; March 1, 2007, review of *Magic's Child*; August 15, 2008, review of *How to Ditch Your Fairy*; September 15, 2009, review of *Liar.*

Kliatt, March, 2006, review of *Magic Lessons,* p. 14.

Publishers Weekly, May 20, 2002, review of *The Battle of the Sexes in Science Fiction,* p. 52; October 6, 2008, review of *How to Ditch Your Fairy,* p. 55; August 24, 2009, review of *Liar,* p. 63; August 23, 2010, review of *Zombies vs. Unicorns,* p. 51.

School Library Journal, March, 2005, Melissa Moore, review of *Magic or Madness,* p. 213; June, 2006, Beth L. Meister, review of *Magic Lessons,* p. 161; May, 2007, Beth L. Meister, review of *Magic's Child,* p. 136; October, 2008, Connie Tyrell Burns, review of *How to Ditch Your Fairy,* p. 152; October, 2009, Patricia N. McClune, review of *Liar,* p. 129; October, 2010, Jessica Miller, review of *Zombies vs. Unicorns,* p. 108.

Wilson Quarterly, winter, 2003, Robert Masello, review of *The Battle of the Sexes in Science Fiction,* p. 114.

Women's Review of Books, January, 2003, Cecilia Tan, review of *The Battle of the Sexes in Science Fiction,* pp. 22-23.

ONLINE

Insideadog, http://www.insideadog.com.au/ (August 12, 2006), "Justine Larbalestier."

Justine Larbalestier Home Page, http://www.justinelarbalestier.com (July 15, 2011).

Writertopia, http://www.writertopia.com/ (August, 12, 2006), "Justine Larbalestier."*

*   *   *

LLOYD, Alison 1966-

Personal

Born 1966, in Australia; married; children: two. *Education:* College degree. *Hobbies and other interests:* Reading, walking, cycling.

Addresses

Home—Melbourne, Victoria, Australia.

Career

Writer. Australian Department of Foreign Affairs and Trade, former member of staff.

Awards, Honors

Children's Book Council of Australia Award shortlist, 2011, for *Wicked Warriors and Evil Emperors.*

Writings

Year of the Tiger, Puffin Books Australia (Camberwell, Victoria, Australia), 2008, Holiday House (New York, NY), 2010.

China, illustrated by Terry Denton, Penguin Books Australia (Camberwell, Victoria, Australia), 2010.

Wicked Warriors and Evil Emperors, illustrated by Terry Denton, Penguin Books Australia (Camberwell, Victoria, Australia), 2010.

"LETTY" CHAPTER-BOOK SERIES

Meet Letty, illustrated by Lucia Masciullo, Penguin Books Australia (Camberwell, Victoria, Australia), 2011.

Letty's Christmas, illustrated by Lucia Masciullo, Penguin Books Australia (Camberwell, Victoria, Australia), 2011.

Letty on the Land, illustrated by Lucia Masciullo, Penguin Books Australia (Camberwell, Victoria, Australia), 2011.

Letty and the Stranger's Lace, illustrated by Lucia Masciullo, Penguin Books Australia (Camberwell, Victoria, Australia), 2011.

Biographical and Critical Sources

PERIODICALS

Booklist, April 15, 2010, Ian Chipman, review of *Year of the Tiger,* p. 60.

Publishers Weekly, April 5, 2010, review of *Year of the Tiger,* p. 61.

School Library Journal, June, 2010, Jennifer Rothschild, review of *Year of the Tiger,* p. 110.

ONLINE

Alison Lloyd Home Page, http://www.alisonlloyd.com.au (June 22, 2011).*

*   *   *

LUKAS, Catherine
See ALBEE, Sarah

M

MACKLER, Carolyn 1973-

Personal

Born July 13, 1973, in Brockport, NY; married Jonas Rideout, June, 2003; children: two sons. *Education:* Vassar College, B.A. (art history), 1995. *Hobbies and other interests:* Reading, bicycling, walking in Central Park, swimming, spending time with family.

Addresses

Home—New York, NY. *E-mail*—carolyn@carolynmackler.com.

Career

Writer and editor.

Member

Authors League.

Awards, Honors

American Library Association Quick Pick for Reluctant Readers selection, and International Reading Association Young Adults Choice designation, both 2000, both for *Love and Other Four-Letter Words;* Michael J. Printz Honor Book selection, for *The Earth, My Butt, and Other Big Round Things.*

Writings

Love and Other Four-Letter Words, Delacorte (New York, NY), 2000.
The Earth, My Butt, and Other Big Round Things, Candlewick Press (Cambridge, MA), 2003.
Vegan Virgin Valentine, Candlewick Press (Cambridge, MA), 2004.
Guyaholic: A Story of Finding, Flirting, Forgetting . . . and the Boy Who Changes Everything, Candlewick Press (Cambridge, MA), 2007.

Tangled, HarperTeen (New York, NY), 2010.

Also author of e-book *The Class of 2000.* Contributor to anthologies *250 Ways to Make America Better,* 1999, and *Body Outlaws.* Contributor of short stories and articles to periodicals, including *American Girl, CosmoGIRL!, Girl's Life, Glamour, Jump, Los Angeles Times, Self, Seventeen, Shape, Storyworks,* and *Teen People.* Contributing editor, *Ms.*

Author's works have been translated into several languages, including Czech, Danish, Dutch, French, German, Hebrew, Indonesian, Italian, and Korean.

Sidelights

In a series of teen novels that features such eye-catching, quirky titles as *Love and Other Four-Letter Words, The Earth, My Butt, and Other Big Round Things, Vegan Virgin Valentine,* and *Guyaholic: A Story of Finding, Flirting, Forgetting . . . and the Boy Who Changes Everything,* Carolyn Mackler introduces ordinary young women who feel awkward about themselves and are trying to find their place in the world. Often setting her novels in her native New York City, Mackler also shares her insights in short stories and articles she has published in *Seventeen, Girl's Life,* and *American Girl.* "I'm a professional snoop," she admitted in an interview posted on her home page. "As I ride in the subway or walk in Central Park, I eavesdrop on any teenager who comes within earshot." "None of the events in my novels have happened to me," she added. "But at the same time, when I'm writing a story, I often draw on my feelings (about my parents' divorce or my first relationship or a challenging friendship) and that helps me create more realistic characters."

Mackler grew up in western New York State in a house of storytellers. Her mother read to her constantly, while her father told stories about his life. At age four or five, Mackler used a tape recorder to record herself reciting her own stories; in high school, she moved to writing in daily journals, mostly about the boys she had crushes on. While attending Vassar College, she began to formally write stories and poems, and an internship at *Ms.* magazine gave her the experience needed to start a freelance career writing for several high-profile magazines. Graduated from Vassar in 1995 with a degree in art history, Mackler continued freelancing and two years later she attended a writing class at New York University. It was here that she started the manuscript that became her first novel, *Love and Other Four-Letter Words.* In 1999, after four years' work writing and rewriting, she found a publisher.

Love and Other Four-Letter Words is a coming-of-age story about sixteen-year-old Sammie Davis, whose parents are going through a trial separation. While her college-professor father decides to go to California, her overwhelmed mother becomes withdrawn and refuses to get out of bed, leaving Sammie to take care of things in their newly downsized New York City apartment.

Cover of Carol Mackler's teen novel Love, and Other Four-letter Words, *which humorously explores the ups and down of adolescent relationships.* (Jacket cover copyright © 2002 by Delacorte, an imprint of Random House Children' Books. Used with permission of Delacorte Press, an imprint of Random House Children's Books, a division of Random House Inc.)

Meanwhile, Sammie's self-absorbed best friend Kitty has become sexually active and too involved with a new boyfriend to be much use as a confidante. Sammie also struggles with her self-image, concerned over her heavy-set figure and her inexperience with boys. Vicki Reutter, reviewing *Love and Other Four-Letter Words* for *School Library Journal,* wrote that, "despite the stressful situation, there is a lighthearted element to the novel that keeps the mood balanced." "Many teens will read this for the facts about sex and growing up as well as the story," Hazel Rochman added in *Booklist,* calling Mackler's debut a "funny first novel."

In *The Earth, My Butt, and Other Big Round Things* Mackler again features a character with a self-image problem. Virginia Shreves belongs to the "perfect family." Her older sister Anaïs is in Africa with the Peace Corps; her brother Byron is a rugby star attending college; and her mother is a psychologist. Still at home, overweight Virginia is being pressured by her mother to go on a diet, and with best friend Shanna out of state for the semester, she feels lonely and alone. Besides, the big question looms as to whether boyfriend Froggy really cares about her. When Byron is accused of date rape and kicked out of school, Virginia begins to realize that maybe her "perfect family" is not so perfect after all. Michele Winship, reviewing the novel in *Kliatt,* called *The Earth, My Butt, and Other Big Round Things* "funny, touching, and very real," while a critic for *Kirkus Reviews* wrote that "Virginia's emotions progress from despondence to anger, joy, and strong independence, all portrayed with clarity." A critic for *Publishers Weekly* maintained that "the heroine's transformation into someone who finds her own style and speaks her own mind is believable—and worthy of applause."

A type-A teen is the focus of *Vegan Virgin Valentine,* which finds high-school senior Mara Valentine vying with an ex-boyfriend for the valedictorian spot. She hopes that this success might make up for the disappointment her parents feel over the foibles of an older sister who is now in her mid-thirties. Then her sister's daughter Vivienne, or V—who is slightly younger than Mara—comes to live with the family. Mara's life and assumptions are suddenly thrown into a tailspin: V smokes marijuana, cuts class, wears skimpy clothes, and breaks all the rules. With V's help, when a new romance blooms with a less-than-"perfect" guy, Mara assesses the situation with a new perspective and is open to new possibilities in a "fast, often humorous" book that touches on "the universal theme of growing up and figuring out what's important," according to *School Library Journal* reviewer Karyn N. Silverman. Although V also makes a turn-around and discovers her talent for acting, her character serves primarily as a "catalyst" for Mara, noted *Booklist* contributor Ilene Cooper. Citing Mara's decision to let go of her feelings of responsibility for her parents and become less strident in her opin-

Cover of Mackler's popular young-adult novel The Earth, My Butt, and Other Big Round Things. (Jacket photograph © 2003 by Richard Pontes. Reproduced by permission of Candlewick Press, Inc., Somerville, MA.)

ions, Cooper added that Mackler's protagonist undergoes a "transformation . . . [that is] entirely credible and, for readers, . . . thoroughly enjoyable."

The free-spirited V returns in *Guyaholic,* and this time it is her turn to make life changes. During a school sporting event, V is beaned by a hockey puck and schoolmate Sam Almond catches her before she hits the ground. Sam is the kind of guy who V would normally discount: he is focused, plays by the rules, and is also a virgin. Although the two feel an attraction to each other, the push toward commitment and the lack of drama in their relationship feel uncomfortable to V. When she dates someone else and a brokenhearted Sam leaves for the West Coast to start college, she decides that a visit with her mother in Texas will help her understand what NOT to do in a relationship. V's trip from New York to the Lone Star State "ends up being a journey of self-discovery," according to *School Library Journal* contributor Kathleen E. Gruver. Mackler's heroine "comes across as an engaging character whose struggles seem very real," noted Cooper in *Booklist,* and a *Kirkus Reviews* writer asserted that "V's narration is simple and accessible as she learns to be brave." Calling Mackler

"an accomplished writer for older YA readers," Claire Rosser added in *Kliatt* that *Guyaholic* "is heartfelt, gritty . . . , and psychologically illuminating."

A summer vacation at a Caribbean resort aptly called Paradise becomes a life-changing experience for the four teens readers meet in Mackler's novel *Tangled.* Even though Jena and Skye are the daughters of two best friends, their moms' scheme of sending the girls on a joint "getting to know you" holiday may prove to be a flawed idea. Popular and beautiful, teen actress Skye cannot be bothered helping to build the self-esteem of overweight and self-deprecating Jena, at least until Jena starts paling around with geeky Owen and Owen's über-cute wild-boy brother Dakota. During their holiday as well as after, the four teens are forced by their interactions to confront their own foibles and limitations and are also challenged to break old habits. In what a *Publishers Weekly* critic described as "distinct, engaging voices," each teen takes a turn recording the thoughts behind his or her actions, and through these narratives the emotion-driven plot of *Tangled* "builds in poignant layers," according to *Booklist* contributor Gillian Engberg. "Themes of understanding, respecting others, and the power of good communication are carefully and ef-

Cover of Mackler's teen novel Tangled, *a coming-of-age story featuring cover art by Howard Huang.* (Cover art by Howard Huang. Reproduced with permission of Howard Huang Photography.)

fectively woven throughout a story that begs for discussion," concluded Diane P. Tuccillo in her *School Library Journal* review of the novel and a *Kirkus Reviews* writer asserted that Mackler's "emotionally generous, character-driven" story is "brimming with girl appeal."

Biographical and Critical Sources

PERIODICALS

American Libraries, December, 2001, Beverly Goldberg, "Principal Bans Love," p. 25.

Booklist, August, 2000, Hazel Rochman, review of *Love and Other Four-Letter Words,* p. 2131; June 1, 2004, Ilene Cooper, review of *Vegan Virgin Valentine,* p. 1720; September 15, 2007, Ilene Cooper, review of *Guyaholic: A Story of Finding, Flirting, Forgetting . . . and the Boy Who Changes Everything,* p. 74; January 1, 2010, Gillian Engberg, review of *Tangled,* p. 71.

Bookseller, November 9, 2001, review of *Love and Other Four-Letter Words,* p. 36.

Journal of Adolescent and Adult Literacy, November, 2002, review of *Love and Other Four-Letter Words,* p. 216.

Kirkus Reviews, June 15, 2003, review of *The Earth, My Butt, and Other Big Round Things,* p. 861; July 1, 2004, review of *Vegan Virgin Valentine,* p. 632; August 15, 2007, review of *Guyaholic;* December 15, 2009, review of *Tangled.*

Kliatt, July, 2003, Michele Winship, review of *The Earth, My Butt, and Other Big Round Things,* p. 14; July, 2004, Claire Rosser, review of *Vegan Virgin Valentine,* p. 10; September, 2007, Claire Rosser, review of *Guyaholic,* p. 15.

New York Times Book Review, September 15, 2007, Julie Just, review of *Guyaholic,* p. 19.

Observer (London, England), February 17, 2002, review of *Love and Other Four-Letter Words.*

Publishers Weekly, September 25, 2000, review of *Love and Other Four-Letter Words,* p. 118; July 21, 2003, review of *The Earth, My Butt, and Other Big Round Things,* p. 197; June 21, 2004, review of *Vegan Virgin Valentine,* p. 64; November 23, 2009, review of *Tangled,* p. 59.

School Library Journal, December, 1999, Becky Ferrall, review of *250 Ways to Make America Better,* p. 166; September, 2000, Vicki Reutter, review of *Love and Other Four-Letter Words,* p. 233; August, 2004, Karyn N. Silverman, review of *Vegan Virgin Valentine,* p. 126; January, 2008, Kathleen E. Gruver, review of *Guyaholic,* p. 122; January, 2010, Diane P. Tuccillo, review of *Tangled,* p. 108.

ONLINE

Carolyn Mackler Home Page, http://www.carolynmackler. com (July 15, 2011).

Carolyn Mackler Web log, http://dearwriter.tumblr.com (July 15, 2011).*

MARINO, Gianna

Personal

Born in San Francisco, CA. *Hobbies and other interests:* Travel.

Addresses

Home—CA.

Career

Fine-art painter and author/illustrator of children's books. Formerly worked as a toy designer. Presenter at schools.

Awards, Honors

Northern California Book Award in Children's Literature nomination, 2006, for *Zoopa.*

Writings

Zoopa: An Animal Alphabet, Chronicle Books (San Francisco, CA), 2005.

One Too Many: A Seek and Find Counting Book, Chronicle Books (San Francisco, CA), 2010.

Sidelights

California native Gianna Marino gains much of the inspiration for her fine-art paintings from her travels. Although she lived for a time in Europe, where many of the great works of Western art are houses, Marino was influenced far more by the plants and animals she encountered in exotic locales, such as Burma, Nepal, Thailand, China, New Zealand, Tahiti, and western Africa. She began working as a painter after designing toys for several years, and her medium of choice has evolved from gouache to a mix of artistic media. As an illustrator, her work has appeared in travel magazines as well as in the pages of the wordless children's books *Zoopa: An Animal Alphabet* and *One Too Many: A Seek and Find Counting Book.*

An A-to-Z guide to colorful critters, *Zoopa* uses a brimming bowl of soup on a blue-and-white check tablecloth as a way to teach young children about the alphabet as well as various animals. As Marino's story begins, readers are introduced to the first letters via alphabet noodles that bring with them an ant and a butterfly. With each turn of the page two or three more noodles and animals make readers' acquaintance, all in alphabetical order and some hidden to encourage interactive storytimes. By the time the V for vulture and Y for yak appear, the book's pages are crowded to overflowing, with animals appearing in both the pattern decorating the soup bowl and spoon as well as in and around the bowl itself. Marino's "playful gouache illustrations depict the colorful crew having as much fun as readers will surely have identifying them," asserted Barbara Auerbach in her *School Library Journal* review of *Zoopa*. A *Kirkus Reviews* writer also had praise for the picture-book debut, noting that its animal characters are "drawn naturalistically but with big, expressive eyes and mobile features." Marino also includes a visual key to help children with animal identification, providing "a big help to children a little hazy on their hedgehogs," according to the *Kirkus Reviews* writer. "Marino's concept is well orchestrated," wrote a *Publishers Weekly* contributor, "and her decision to eschew any text should encourage youngsters to spend extra time" on animal observation. After *Zoopa*, "alphabet soup will never look the same," the critic concluded.

Marino moves from the lunch table to the barnyard in *One Too Many*, and here her menagerie full of engaging animals is used to help reinforce counting skills. At first readers meet a single flea as it jumps to the watering trough; then two thirsty cows appear. As the species count increases, so does the numeral that appears at the upper right-hand corner of each two-page spread. During the course of a day, horses, bunnies, sheep and pigs, geese, and more stop and stay by the water, until dusk brings a nocturnal critter that causes the other animals to scatter. Praising *One Too Many* as a "remarkable counting book," Mary Jean Smith added in *School Library Journal* that "Marino's naturalistic [gouache] illustrations" will encourage repeat readings. The artist's "marvelously striking" images feature "animals that are largely black and white, with a bit of sepia, against blue sky . . . and sandy barnyard," wrote a *Kirkus Reviews* writer, and her artwork holds "additional challenges for eagle-eyed readers," according to a *Publishers Weekly* critic.

Biographical and Critical Sources

PERIODICALS

Booklist, April 15, 2010, Randall Enos, review of *One Too Many: A Seek and Find Counting Book*, p. 52.
Kirkus Reviews, August 1, 2005, review of *Zoopa: An Animal Alphabet*, p. 854; April 15, 2010, review of *One Too Many*.
New York Times Book Review, January 15, 2006, Emily Jenkins, review of *Zoopa*, p. 18.
Publishers Weekly, August 15, 2005, review of *Zoopa*, p. 57; April 26, 2010, review of *One Two Many*, p. 106.
School Library Journal, October, 2005, Barbara Auerbach, review of *Zoopa*, p. 120; May, 2010, Mary Jean Smith, review of *One Too Many*, p. 88.

ONLINE

Gianna Marino Home Page, http://www.giannamarino.com (July 15, 2011).*

MAX, Jill
See BENNETT, Kelly

*   *   *

McGHEE, Alison 1960-

Personal

Born 1960, in NY; children: three children.

Addresses

Home—Minneapolis, MN. *Office*—Metropolitan State University, 700 E. 7th St., St. Paul, MN 55106-5000. *Agent*—(children's books) Pippin Properties, 155 E. 38th St., Ste. 2H, New York, NY 10016; (adult books) Doug Stewart, Sterling Lord Literistic, 65 Bleecker St., New York, NY 10012. *E-mail*—alison_mcghee@hotmail.com; alison.mcghee@metrostate.edu.

Career

Author and educator. Metropolitan State University, St. Paul, MN, professor of creative writing and department coordinator; previously taught writing at Carleton College, Hamline University, Macalester College, the Loft, Vermont College, and University of Minnesota. Presenter at schools and conferences.

Awards, Honors

Minnesota Book Award, 1999, and Great Lakes College Association National Fiction Award, both for *Rainlight*; Minnesota Book Award, 2001, and Pulitzer Prize nomination, Columbia University, both for *Shadow Baby;* Minnesota Book Award, 2003, and Oppenheim Gold Toy Portfolio Award, both for *Countdown to Kindergarten;* Minnesota Book Award finalist, 2003, for *Was It Beautiful?*, 2004, for *Snap*, 2007, for *Falling Boy*, 2008, for *Julia Gillian (and the Art of Knowing);* Ezra Jack Keats Award, 2009, for *Only a Witch Can Fly;* (with Kate DiCamillo) Theodor Seuss Geisel Award, 2011, for *Bink and Gollie*.

Writings

NOVELS

Rainlight, Papier-Maché Press (Watsonville, CA), 1998.
Shadow Baby, Harmony Books (New York, NY), 2000.
Was It Beautiful?, Shaye Areheart Books (New York, NY), 2003.
Snap (young-adult novel), Candlewick Press (Cambridge, MA), 2004.
All Rivers Flow to the Sea (young-adult novel), Candlewick Press (Cambridge, MA), 2005.
Falling Boy (young-adult novel), Picador (New York, NY), 2007.

Contributor of articles and short fiction to various literary periodicals.

Author's work has been published in Braile editions.

"JULIA GILLIAN" CHAPTER-BOOK SERIES

Julia Gillian (and the Art of Knowing), illustrated by Drazen Kozjan, Scholastic (New York, NY), 2008.
Julia Gillian (and the Quest for Joy), illustrated by Drazen Kozjan, Scholastic (New York, NY), 2009.
Julia Gillian (and the Dream of the Dog), illustrated by Drazen Kozjan, Scholastic Press (New York, NY), 2010.

FOR CHILDREN

Countdown to Kindergarten, illustrated by Harry Bliss, Harcourt (San Diego, CA), 2002.
Mrs. Watson Wants Your Teeth, illustrated by Harry Bliss, Harcourt (Orlando, FL), 2004.
A Very Brave Witch, illustrated by Harry Bliss, Simon & Schuster Books for Young Readers (New York, NY), 2006.
Someday, illustrated by Peter H. Reynolds, Atheneum Books for Young Readers (New York, NY), 2007.
Little Boy, illustrated by Peter H. Reynolds, Atheneum Books for Young Readers (New York, NY), 2008.
Bye-bye, Crib, illustrated by Ross MacDonald, Simon & Schuster Books for Young Readers (New York, NY), 2008.
Only a Witch Can Fly, illustrated by Taeeun Yoo, Feiwel and Friends (New York, NY), 2009.
Always, illustrated by Pascal Lemaître, Simon & Schuster Books for Young Readers (New York, NY), 2009.
Song of Middle C, illustrated by Scott Menchin, Candlewick Press (Somerville, MA), 2009.
(With Kate DiCamillo) *Bink and Gollie,* illustrated by Tony Fucile, Candlewick Press (Somerville, MA), 2010.
So Many Days, illustrated by Taeeun Yoo, Atheneum Books for Young Readers (New York, NY), 2010.
Making a Friend, illustrated by Marc Rosenthal, Atheneum Books for Young Readers (New York, NY), 2011.

Contributor of articles and short fiction to various literary periodicals.

Adaptations

A Very Brave Witch was adapted as an animated film by Weston Woods. *Shadow Baby, Snap,* and *Julia Gillian (and the Art of Knowing)* were adapted as audiobooks. *Someday* was adapted as an anime short film by Pierrot Plus (Japanese studio), 2011.

Sidelights

Minnesota-based author Alison McGhee writes adult and young-adult novels in addition to creating the "Julia Gillian" chapter-book series and picture books featuring artwork by a range of talented illustrators. With a passion for writing that fueled her through six years of relentless effort until her first short story was published, McGhee's debut novel, *Rainlight,* won both a Great Lakes College Association National Fiction award and a Minnesota Book award, while her follow-up effort, *Shadow Baby,* was nominated for a Pulitzer prize in literature. When she is not writing, McGhee shares her skills as a teacher in the creative-writing program at Metropolitan State University and has also taught in the M.F.A. program at Vermont College. Reviewing her young-adult novel *Falling Boy,* which focuses on a recently handicapped sixteen year old and the complex relationships he develops after a move to a new town, a *Publishers Weekly* predicted that teens "will be charmed by McGhee's tender and affecting coming-of-age tale."

In *Rainlight* McGhee tells the story of the sudden, accidental death of husband and father Starr Williams, and how the family and friends William has left behind handle their grief. Not only does McGhee address the impact of the man's death, but she also illustrates how his life continues to affect the people around him even after he is gone. Margaret Flanagan, contributing to *Booklist,* wrote that "this heartrending yet ultimately affirmative eulogy is laden with both despair and hope," comprising "a stunning debut." A reviewer for *Publishers Weekly* called *Rainlight* a "vivid, poetically charged (and occasionally overwritten) first novel."

Shadow Baby, McGhee's second novel, revisits themes of loss and grief as it examines the world through the eyes of young Clara Winter. Clara befriends the elderly Georg Kominsky as part of a school history project, and Georg soon becomes a major adult influence in her life. They trade stories of the hardships they have experienced; Clara's twin sister died at birth and her mother refuses to speak of the past, while Georg was forced to abandon his injured brother during a snowstorm on their way to America and never saw the boy again. Following a tragic climax, Clara is able to open herself to the other adults in her life as a result of what Georg has taught her. Becky Ferrall, in a review for *School Library Journal,* commented of *Shadow Baby* that "Clara's insights bring both introspection and humor to this skillfully told story about seeing and finding the possibilities in life," while Michelle Kaske remarked in *Booklist* that "McGhee's work, full of contrasts and transformations, is a strong, solid novel with quiet feminist undertones." A *Publishers Weekly* contributor wrote that, "with a mix of deadpan humor and pathos, McGhee perfectly captures the voice of a sensitive, wise child on the cusp of adulthood, at once knowing and naive."

In the novel *Was It Beautiful?* William T. Jones, a dairy trucker from the Adirondack Mountains, allows his grief to get the better of him when his grown son, William J., is hit by a train and dies. Haunted by the young man's death, which he witnessed, William T. draws into himself, rebuffing the concerned overtures of both his wife and his best friend. A *Publishers Weekly* critic described *Was It Beautiful?* as "gracefully wrought," while *Library Journal* critic Beth E. Andersen called McGhee's story "hypnotic, wrenching, and powerful in its promise of hope in the face of impossible grief."

With *Snap* McGhee turns her attention to a young-adult audience. The novel follows Edwina "Eddie" Beckly, who wears colored rubber bands around her arm and snaps them to be reminded of various things. One reminder regards her best friend's grandmother, Willie, who is dying of a blood disease. Ilene Cooper, in *Booklist,* remarked that *Snap* "is pregnant with tragedy, but it's not so much what happens as the way McGhee . . . writes it. Her writing is precise, evocative, and sure." *School Library Journal* reviewer Susan Hepler wrote that the novel "features memorable characters and a tolerance for eccentricity, emotional subtlety, and complexity, themes of acceptance, of death and love, and a spare and poetic text that begs to be reread and savored."

Also for young adults, *All Rivers Flow to the Sea* finds teenager Rose traumatized by the accident that put her sister in a coma. Ultimately, Rose struggles with coming to terms with this new reality and recover from the pain she has caused herself by seeking solace in the wrong places. A contributor to *Publishers Weekly* commented of *All Rivers Flow to the Sea* that "McGhee writes confidently as one who remembers the ordinariness of adolescence as well as its angst," and Holly Koelling concluded in *Booklist* that, "despite its literary imperfections, this remains an insightful work that will touch readers." *Kliatt* contributor Myrna Marler agreed that *All Rivers Flow to the Sea* offers readers "a window into the process of grieving" and went on to call the novel "one of those rare books that somehow manages to express the inexpressible."

Featuring illustrations by Drazen Kozjan, McGhee's "Julia Gillian" chapter books are geared for older elementary graders and include *Julia Gillian (and the Art of Knowing), Julia Gillian (and the Quest for Joy),* and *Julia Gillian (and the Dream of the Dog).* The star of these easy-reading stories is nine-year-old Julia Gillian, a creative yet thoughtful girl who lives with her mom and dad and Bigfoot the dog in a third-floor apartment, where she enjoys crafting colorful masks from papier mache. In the first novel, the summer before fifth grade seems to hold a series of small setbacks and disappointments for Julia as her parents opt for college courses over family excursions to the local water park, newspaper headlines warn of doom and gloom, and the novel she started with such enthusiasm seems to be leading her toward a sad ending. With lots of time on her own to wander her neighborhood with Bigfoot in tow, Julia develops the titular "art of knowing" as she observes the daily ebb and flow of life in her neighborhood.

In *Julia Gillian (and the Quest for Joy)* fifth grade has started but life seems just as challenging as Julia's best friend acts unusually standoffish and evasive, her mastery of the trumpet seems to have reached a snag, and her favorite lunch lady has departed, leaving the grouchy Dumpling Man in her stead. Worries over the ever-aging Bigfoot overshadow any enjoyment Julia is having in sixth grade in *Julia Gillian (and the Dream of the Dog),* and her dislike for reading should have but does not make her exempt from the school's Reading Extravaganza program. Fortunately, the advice of an elderly neighbor is there to help the preteen deal with an inevitable heartbreak.

Calling Julia "utterly likeable," a *Publishers Weekly* critic noted of *Julia Gillian (and the Art of Knowing)* that McGhee's "well paced" story effectively captures the girl's "slightly whimsical personality," while *Horn Book* critic Christine M. Heppermann wrote that the author's "affectionate" depiction of her heroine's struggles in the follow-up volume "reveals a keen perception of elementary-school worries." Rather than an upbeat Pollyanna, Julia is a serious-minded girl who is "acutely conscious of achieving a new maturity" as she approaches adolescence, according to *School Library Journal* critic Lillian Heckler, and Marie Orlando noted in

Alison McGhee introduces a likeable preteen in her novel series that includes Julia Gillian (and the Dream of the Dog) *and features illustrations by Drazen Kozjan.* (Illustration copyright © 2010 by Drazen Kozjan. Reproduced with permission of the illustrator's agent, Pippin Properties and Scholastic Press, an imprint of Scholastic, Inc.)

the same periodical that *Julia Gillian (and the Quest for Joy)* benefits from "wonderfully quirky characters; rich, playful language; funny dialogue; and lots of heart."

McGhee's works for younger children include *Countdown to Kindergarten, Mrs. Watson Wants Your Teeth,* and *A Very Brave Witch,* all which feature artwork by Harry Bliss. In *Countdown to Kindergarten* the young narrator's fears of starting kindergarten increase when an older child tells her that everyone is expected to know how to tie his or her own shoes. As the fateful first day of school approaches, nothing can take her mind off of her fear, not even shoe-tying lessons from her father or a favorite spaghetti dinner. Once school begins, however, the child is relieved to learn she is not the only one who cannot knot their laces. A reviewer for *Publishers Weekly* stated that in *Countdown to Kindergarten* "McGhee combines a puckishly structured counting book . . . with an amiable exploration of new-school anxiety."

McGhee's nervous little heroine returns in *Mrs. Watson Wants Your Teeth,* but here she has graduated to the first grade. Unfortunately, unfounded rumors still circulate, and she starts the year believing that her teacher has a purple tongue and likes to steal students' baby teeth. A contributor to *Kirkus Reviews* remarked of *Mrs. Watson Wants Your Teeth* that McGhee "keeps the dialogue crisp, bringing out the sweet gullibility of the first-grader and the second-grader's mischief-making."

For the young musician in *Song of Middle C,* stage fright is the big concern as the first piano recital looms in her near future. Practice makes perfect, even when it is practicing in front of a stuffed-toy audience, and wearing her special good-luck underwear will not hurt, either, the girl decides. Although she looks forward to the recital feeling confident in her talent, the girl still experiences momentary jitters when it is her turn to step out on stage, and the "feelings and concerns" McGhee captures in her first-person story "will be familiar to any child who had been in a performance situation, noted Joy Fleischacker in *School Library Journal.*

In *Always,* another picture-book story by McGhee, a young girl is again the focus, but this time the worries are not hers. Instead, her young puppy is the narrator and, as brought to life in Pascal Lemaître's art, it imagines all the dangers that it might face while protecting her in their shared future. Youngsters "will recognize the physicality, the loyalty, and the powerful connection between animal and child" in *Always,* according to *Booklist* critic Hazel Rochman, and a *Publishers Weekly* critic predicted of the same book that "only the stony-hearted could withstand its charms."

More spiritual in approach, *So Many Days* presents what *School Library Journal* contributor Marianne Saccardi described as "a philosophical offering that encourages youngsters to face life head on" in its story about a young child pondering the possibilities that life holds in store, while McGhee's use of the French sestina form in *Only a Witch Can Fly* results in a rhyming description of a young girl's Halloween fantasy that is "both languorous and incantatory," according to *New York Times Book Review* contributor Lawrence Downes.

Winner of the 2011 Theodor Seuss Geisel Award, *Bink and Gollie* is a collaboration among McGhee, fellow author Kate DiCamillo, and illustrator Tony Fucile. In the story, short and carefree Bink lives in a tumbledown cottage while Gollie is tall and sophisticated and lives in an upscale and impeccably decorated home. Although they are opposite in almost every way, they are also the best of friends, as the book's three interconnected stories show. Bink's love of flamboyant and colorful socks raises the eyebrow of her stylish friend in one tale, while a new pet causes temporary jealousy in another. In a third, the coauthors broach the importance of alone-time, even among best friends, the feelings of the engaging main characters captured in what Gillian Engberg described in *Booklist* as "expressive, cartoon-style drawings" which "extend the sense of character, story, and madcap adventure." In *School Library Journal* Nancy Menaldi-Scanlan noted that McGhee and DiCamillo's use of "short sentences, abundant dialogue, and . . . contemporary expressions" combine to create "delightful portrayals of two headstrong characters." Calling Bink and Gollie "welcome human newcomers in a world of easy readers largely populated by animals," Sarah Ellis added in her *New York Times Book Review* appraisal that these engaging young characters "join the ranks of George and Martha, Frog and Toad, Zelda and Ivy and all the other resilient pairs that celebrate the challenges and strengths of a great friendship."

"I'm the luckiest person in the world," McGhee told *SATA.* "I get to spend my days doing what I most love to do, which is write books. I began writing novels for adults and have now branched into writing in all forms for all ages. I have three children of my own and have taught high school, college and adult students. Writing for children is a great joy and something I'm honored to do. Happy reading!"

Biographical and Critical Sources

PERIODICALS

Booklist, March 15, 1998, Margaret Flanagan, review of *Rainlight,* p. 1202; April 1, 2000, Michelle Kaske, review of *Shadow Baby,* p. 1436; August, 2002, Carolyn Phelan, review of *Countdown to Kindergarten,* p. 1974; May 15, 2004, Ilene Cooper, review of *Snap,* p. 1621; October 15, 2005, Holly Koelling, review of *All Rivers Flow to the Sea,* p. 42; February 15, 2007, Gillian Engberg, review of *Falling Boy,* p. 36; August 1, 2009, Hazel Rochman, review of *Always,* p. 75; February 1, 2010, Gillian Engberg, review of *So Many Days*, p. 51; September 15, 2010, Gillian Engberg, review of *Bink and Gollie*, p. 68.

Children's Bookwatch, December 1, 2005, review of *All Rivers Flow to the Sea.*

Daughters, January-February, 2003, Alison McGhee, "Refusing to Keep Quiet," p. 15.

Denver Post, March 16, 2003, review of *Was It Beautiful?*

Instructor, August, 2003, Judy Freeman, review of *Countdown to Kindergarten,* p. 61.

Kirkus Reviews, July 1, 2002, review of *Countdown to Kindergarten,* p. 959; December 1, 2002, review of *Was It Beautiful?,* p. 1723; March 1, 2004, review of *Snap,* p. 227; July 1, 2004, review of *Mrs. Watson Wants Your Teeth,* p. 633; October 15, 2005, review of *All Rivers Flow to the Sea,* p. 1143; July 1, 2006, review of *A Very Brave Witch,* p. 679; October 1, 2006, review of *Falling Boy,* p. 981; March 1, 2007, review of *Someday,* p. 228; February 15, 2008, review of *Bye-Bye, Crib*; April 1, 2009, review of *Song of Middle C*; July 15, 2009, review of *Only a Witch Can Fly.*

Kliatt, November 1, 2005, Myrna Marler, review of *All Rivers Flow to the Sea,* p. 8; September, 2007, Nola Theiss, review of *Falling Boy,* p. 24.

Library Journal, April 1, 2000, Lisa S. Nussbaum, review of *Shadow Baby,* p. 130; December, 2002, Beth E. Andersen, review of *Was It Beautiful?,* p. 179.

Minneapolis Observer Quarterly, February 19, 2006, Anne Geske, author interview.

Publishers Weekly, January 5, 1998, review of *Rainlight,* p. 57; February 14, 2000, review of *Shadow Baby,* p. 170; July 8, 2002, review of *Countdown to Kindergarten,* pp. 48-49; February 17, 2003, review of *Was It Beautiful?,* p. 59; April 12, 2004, review of *Snap,* p. 66; July 5, 2004, review of *Mrs. Watson Wants Your Teeth,* p. 54; November 14, 2005, review of *All Rivers Flow to the Sea,* p. 71; August 14, 2006, review of *A Very Brave Witch,* p. 204; October 16, 2006, review of *Falling Boy,* p. 27; February 12, 2007, review of *Someday,* p. 84; March 24, 2008, review of *Little Boy,* p. 69; June 8, 2009, review of *Always,* p. 43; December 14, 2009, review of *So Many Days,* p. 57; November 8, 2010, review of *Bink and Gollie,* p. 34.

School Library Journal, June, 2001, Becky Ferrall, review of *Shadow Baby,* p. 184; September, 2002, Mary Elam, review of *Countdown to Kindergarten,* p. 201; April, 2004, Susan Hepler, review of *Snap,* p. 157; July, 2004, Lisa G. Kropp, review of *Countdown to Kindergarten,* p. 43; September, 2004, Mary Elam, review of *Mrs. Watson Wants Your Teeth,* p. 173; November, 2005, Emily Garrett, review of *All Rivers Flow to the Sea,* p. 141; August, 2006, Wanda Meyers-Hines, review of *A Very Brave Witch,* p. 93; March, 2007, Carolyn Janssen, review of *Someday,* p. 176; April, 2007, Jamie Watson, review of *Falling Boy,* p. 168; February, 2008, Kathy Krasniewicz, review of *Bye-bye, Crib,* p. 92; June, 2008, Linda M. Kenton, review of *Little Boy,* p. 110; May, 2009, Judith Constantinides, review of *Always,* p. 83; August, 2009, Joy Fleischhacker, review of *Song of Middle C,* p. 80; September, 2009, Kathleen Finn, review of *Only a Witch Can*

Fly, p. 129; March, 2010, Marianne Saccardi, review of *So Many Days,* p. 124; August, 2010, Lauralyn Persson, review of *Julia Gillian (and the Dream of the Dog),* p. 106.

ONLINE

Alison McGhee Home Page, http://www.alisonmcghee. com (June 15, 2011).

Pippin Properties Web site, http://www.pippinproperties. com/ (June 15, 2011), "Alison McGhee."

Small Spiral Notebook Web site, http://www.smallspiral notebook.com/ (June 25, 2007), Mary Phillips, interview with McGhee.

*   *   *

MESSER, Stephen 1972-

Personal

Born 1972, in ME; married.

Addresses

Home—Durham, NC. *Agent*—Josh Adams, Adams Literary, info@adamsliterary.com.

Career

Author. Presenter at schools.

Writings

Windblowne, Random House (New York, NY), 2010.

The Death of Yorik Mortwell, illustrated by Gris Grimly, Random House Children's Books (New York, NY), 2011.

Colossus, Random House (New York, NY), 2013.

Sidelights

While growing up, Stephen Messer developed two loves that have continues into adulthood: a love of kite flying and a love of reading. Messer's decision to write books for younger readers was inspired by these childhood passions, and kite flying fuels the fantasy in his first middle-grade novel, *Windblowne.*

In *Windblowne* readers meet Oliver as he looks forward to the town of Windblowne's annual kite-flying festival, despite the fact that he is not able to keep a kite aloft. Determined that this year he will be a contender, Oliver visits his great-uncle Gilbert for some kite-flying advice, only to watch the man attacked by a hoard of sharp-edged kites. The boy now sets out and travels through several parallel worlds in search of his recently vanished relative, but in an alternative Windblowne Gilbert's evil twin has mastered time travel and plans to take over the world. While noting the novel's complexity, Connie Tyrell Burns added in *School Library Journal* that "Messer's allegorical fantasy is imaginative and contains a strong ecological message as well as the worthy theme of the importance of finding one's own unique talent." The "easy, unforced writing" in *Windblowne* adds to the story, asserted Andrew Medlar in his *Booklist* review of Messer's debut, and a *Publishers Weekly* critic deemed the novel "an inventive . . . fantasy" that "moves along at a powerful, steady pace to a climactic faceoff."

Messer turns to dark fantasy in *The Death of Yorik Mortwell,* a Dickensian story about an orphaned boy who, along with his little sister, becomes a servant to the spoiled young lord at Ravenby Manor. When a rock-throwing incident results in Yorik's death, he finds that he is a servant in the afterlife as well. At first he is thrilled to be ordered by the Princess of the Aviary Glade to haunt the home of his former master. Unfortunately, he soon finds himself trying to save his little sister from something that has entered Ravensby from the wrong side of evil, and Yorick's tale is captured in macabre illustrations by Gris Grimley.

Biographical and Critical Sources

PERIODICALS

Booklist, May 15, 2010, Andrew Medlar, review of *Windblowne,* p. 53.
Bulletin of the Center for Children's Books, May, 2010, Kate Quealy-Gainer, review of *Windblowne,* p. 390.
Kirkus Reviews, April 1, 2010, review of *Windblowne;* May 15, 2011, review of *The Death of Yorik Mortwell.*
School Library Journal, June, 2010, Connie Tyrrell Burns, review of *Windblowne,* p. 112.

ONLINE

Stephen Messer Home Page, http://stephenmesser.com (July 15, 2011).*

*   *   *

MONTALBANO, Andrea

Personal

Born in Key Biscayne, FL; daughter of William Montalbano (a foreign correspondent); married Diron Jebejian; children: Lily, William. *Education:* Harvard University, degree, 1990; Columbia University, M.A. (journalism).

Addresses

Home—Bronxville, NY. *Office*—Esther Newberg, ICM, 825 8th Ave., New York, NY 10019.

Career

Author and journalist. ABC News Radio, New York, NY, member of staff, beginning early 1990; NBC News, New York, NY, researcher, then supervising producer of *Today* television program until 2005.

Awards, Honors

Inducted into Varsity Club Hall of Fame.

Writings

Breakaway, Philomel (New York, NY), 2010.

Sidelights

Andrea Montalbano grew up playing soccer, and the heroine of her first middle-grade novel, *Breakaway,* share her talent and passion for the sport. Although Montalbano exhibited good sportsmanship throughout her athletic career, Lily James—known as LJ—her protagonist in *Breakaway,* still has a few lessons to learn about being part of a competitive team.

Cover of Andrea Montalbano's teen novel Breakaway, *featuring artwork by Michael Frost.* (Cover art copyright © 2010 by Michael Frost. Used by permission of Philomel Books, a division of Penguin Young Readers Group, a member of Penguin Group (USA) Inc., 345 Hudson St., New York, NY 10014. All rights reserved.)

Montalbano haunted the soccer fields of Key Biscayne, Florida, while growing up, and in school she participated in a competitive girls' soccer program that was advanced for its time. Twice named Miami-Dade County Player of the Year, she went on to excel as captain of the women's team at Harvard University. Montalbano pursued a career in journalism at Columbia University after completing her bachelor's degree, following in the footsteps of her father, a foreign correspondent and writer. She worked for ABC News Radio but turned to television as a supervising producer of the popular *Today* shop after jumping networks to NBC. In 2007, while working on a manuscript for an adult thriller, Montalbano was asked to craft an essay reflecting on her athletic career, and this essay eventually morphed into *Breakaway.*

When readers meet twelve-year-old LJ in *Breakaway* they quickly realize that soccer is the girl's life. Because she is good at the sport, LJ has earned a measure of respect from her fellow students, but she confuses the team's overall success with her own personal accomplishment. Soon LJ begins to openly show her frustration for her fellow players, but her pride precedes a big fall. Determined to win a crucial game, she keeps control of the ball and refuses to pass it off to her teammates. This ball-hogging results in LJ's suspension from the team for two games, and she also receives a comeuppance at home when a temper tantrum earns her a stint working in the family restaurant. In *School Library Journal* Blair Christolon noted the "excellent play-by-play action scenes" that energize Montalbano's upbeat "tale of friendship through teamwork," while a *Kirkus Reviews* writer asserted that the "compelling" story "provides a valuable life lesson." Praising *Breakaway* as a good choice for sports-minded girls, a *Publishers Weekly* critic added that the author's "crackerjack, play-by-play account . . . brings the story to a winning end."

Biographical and Critical Sources

PERIODICALS

Kirkus Reviews, April 15, 2010, review of *Breakaway.*

Publishers Weekly, May 17, 2010, review of *Breakaway,* p. 50.

School Library Journal, July, 2010, Blair Christolon, review of *Breakaway,* p. 94.

ONLINE

Andrea Montalbano Home Page, http://www.andreamon talbano.com (July 15, 2011).*

N-O

NA, Il Sung

Personal

Born in Seoul, South Korea. *Education:* Attended Chelsea College of Arts, 2002-03; Kingston University, B.A. (illustration and animation; with honors), 2006.

Addresses

Home—South Korea. *E-mail*—ilsungna@hotmailcom.

Career

Author and illustrator of children's books. Illustrator for advertising; art appeared on greeting cards. *Exhibitions:* Work exhibited in Best of British Contemporary Illustration touring show, 2007-08, and at Fidra Gallery, Edinburgh, Scotland, 2009; ChungmooArt Hall, Seoul, South Korea, 2009; and SeoJeongWook Gallery, Seoul, 2009.

Awards, Honors

Image 31 New Talent selection, Association of Illustrators, 2007; Big Picture Best New Illustrators Award nomination, 2008; White Ravens Award selection, and British Book Design and Production Award nomination, both 2008, both for *ZZzzz.*

Writings

SELF-ILLUSTRATED

ZZzzz: A Book of Sleep, Meadowside Children's (London, England), 2007, published as *A Book of Sleep,* Alfred A. Knopf (New York, NY), 2009.
The Thingamabob, Meadowside Children's (London, England), 2008, Alfred A. Knopf (New York, NY), 2010.
Brrrr: A Book of Winter, Meadowside Children's (London, England), 2010.

Snow Rabbit, Spring Rabbit: A Book of Changing Seasons, Alfred A. Knopf (New York, NY), 2011.
Hide and Seek, Meadowside Children's (London, England), 2011.

Also author/illustrator of books published in Korea, including *The King of the Golden River,* 2009.

Author's work has been translated into several languages, including Dutch, German, Japanese, Korean, and Spanish.

ILLUSTRATOR

Lucy M. George, *Teacup in a Storm,* Meadowside Children's (London, England), 2009.

Sidelights

Born in South Korea, Il Sung Na studied illustration at England's Kingston University, where he developed the sketchy and loosely tinted illustration style that has delighted fans of what Pamela Paul referred to in the *New York Times Book Review* as his "deceptively simple storybooks." Na's mixture of colorful multimedia art—he uses oils, pen and ink, and digital manipulation—and simple, spare storytelling can be found in *A Book of Sleep, The Thingamabob,* and *Snow Rabbit, Spring Rabbit: A Book of Changing Seasons.* According to Paul, the "straightforward tale of nature" the author/illustrator shares with readers in *Snow Rabbit, Spring Rabbit* "is elevated by distinctive illustration into a somewhat more enchanted realm than that of mere snowfall and frozen dirt."

"It is difficult to praise *A Book of Sleep* . . . without sounding as if I'm knocking it," quipped Daniel Handler in his laudatory review of Na's illustrated tale for the *New York Times Book Review:* "'The literary equivalent of Tylenol PM' is an unlikely blurb for the paperback, but it is apt, so thoroughly does the book inhabit its sleepy world." In *A Book of Sleep* Na's story follows

Il Sung Na pairs his unique illustrations with an engaging story in the picture book **A Book of Sleep.** (Copyright © 2007 by Il Sung Na. Used by permission of Alfred A. Knopf, an imprint of Random House Children's Books, a division of Random House, Inc.)

Owl as he tours his territory and observes a variety of woodland animal families preparing for sleep. Reviewing the tale, which was release in the United Kingdom as *ZZzzz: A Book of Sleep,* Abby Nolan wrote in *Booklist* that the artist's "wonderfully illustrated debut" features a "text [that] is spare but informative, and soothing in its rhythms." Meg Smith wrote in *School Library Journal* that the "starry wonderland" revealed in *A Book of Sleep* "soothes young listeners through succinct phrasing and powerful spacing," while a *Publishers Weekly* critic noted the "captivating aura that emanates from every [two-page] spread," likening Na's illustration style to the "limpid charm of [twentieth-century painter] Paul Klee." *A Book of Sleep* "deserves a cozy place on the shelf for reading to children at 7 p.m.," recommended Handler, "or, in the case of other people's children, 4:30."

Another story by Na, *The Thingamabob,* follows its very large hero, a pale elephant, as he discovers a long, red, collapsible object (a red umbrella) and embarks on a quest of discovery. Because he has never seen such an amazing thing before, the elephant is flummoxed and queries his animal friends regarding the unnamed object. After attempting to use the umbrella as a sail as well as a shield, a sprinkle of rain prompts the pachyderm to use the "thingamabob" for the purpose it was intended, resulting in a picture-book "celebration of curiosity and perception," according to a *Publishers Weekly* critic. "Sumptuous colors and swirling textures turn this slight, silly story into a visual feast," asserted *Booklist* critic Ian Chipman, and Maryann H. Owen wrote in *School Library Journal* that Na's "intriguing artwork" is "worthy of close study."

Biographical and Critical Sources

PERIODICALS

Booklist, November 1, 2009. Abby Nolan, review of *A Book of Sleep,* p. 34; February 1, 2010, Ian Chipman, review of *The Thingamabob,* p. 51; January 1, 2011, Andrew Medlar, review of *Snow Rabbit, Spring Rabbit: A Book of Changing Seasons,* p. 114.
Kirkus Reviews, March 1, 2010, review of *The Thingamabob*; December 1, 2010, review of *Snow Rabbit, Spring Rabbit.*
New York Times Book Review, December 6, 2009, Daniel Handler, review of *A Book of Sleep,* p. 52; February 22, 2011, Pamela Paul, review of *Snow Rabbit, Spring Rabbit.*
Publishers Weekly, September 14, 2009, review of *A Book of Sleep,* p. 46; February 8, 2010, review of *The Thingamabob,* p. 47.
School Library Journal, November, 2009, Meg Smith, review of *A Book of Sleep,* p. 84; March, 2010, Maryann H. Owen, review of *The Thingamabob,* p. 128; February, 2011, Roxanne Burg, review of *Snow Rabbit, Spring Rabbit,* p. 88.

ONLINE

Il Sung Na Home Page, http://www.ilsungna.com (July 15, 2011).*

*   *   *

NOLTE, Jack
See CARTER, Scott William

*   *   *

OFFERMANN, Andrea

Personal

Born in Cologne, Germany. *Education:* Attended medical school (Lubeck, Germany); Art Center College of Design, B.A. (illustration).

Addresses

Home—Hamburg, Germany.

Career

Illustrator and painter. *Exhibitions:* Work exhibited in galleries, including at David B. Smith Gallery, Denver, CO, 2009; Gallery Nucleus, Alhambra, CA, 2009, 2010; Chicago Art Source, Chicago, IL, 2010; and Thinkspace Gallery, Culver City, CA, 2010.

Illustrator

Will Gmehling, *Kleine Angst vor schafen,* Carlsen Verlag (Hamburg, Germany), 2008.
Kate Milford, *The Boneshaker,* Clarion (New York, NY), 2010.
Sonya Hartnett, *The Midnight Zoo,* Candlewick Press (New York, NY), 2011.

Contributor to anthologies, including *Flight, Volume 4,* 2007.

Biographical and Critical Sources

PERIODICALS

Booklist, May 15, 2010, Ian Chipman, review of *The Boneshaker,* p. 52.
Kirkus Reviews, April 15, 2010, review of *The Boneshaker.*
School Library Journal, June, 2010, Heather M. Campbell, review of *The Boneshaker,* p. 113.

ONLINE

Andrea Offermann Home Page, http://www.andreaoffermann.com (June 22, 2011).

Andrea Offermann Web log, http://andreaoffermann. blogspot.com (June 22, 2011).

Flight Comics Web log, http://www.flightcomics/blog/ (September 17, 2007), interview with Offermann.*

*   *   *

OLANDER, Johan 1967-

Personal

Born 1967, in Sweden; married: children: a daughter. *Education:* School of Visual Arts, B.F.A. (painting), 1994.

Addresses

Home—Brooklyn, NY. *E-mail*—olander.j@gmail.com.

Career

Author, illustrator, and photographer.

Writings

SELF-ILLUSTRATED

A Field Guide to Monsters: Googly-eyed Wart Floppers, Shadow-casters, Toe-eaters, and Other Creatures, Marshall Cavendish (New York, NY), 2007.

A Field Guide to Aliens: Intergalactic Worrywarts, Bubblonauts, Sliver-slurpers, and Other Extraterrestrials, Marshall Cavendish Children (New York, NY), 2010.

ILLUSTRATOR

Jennifer Cole Judd and Laura Wynkoop, editors, *An Eyeball in My Garden, and Other Spine-tingling Poems,* Marshall Cavendish Children's (New York, NY), 2010.

Sidelights

Touting himself as a "world famous monstrologist," Swedish-born author and artist Johan Olander mixes humor, whimsy, and a dash of the grotesque in his unique self-illustrated field guides for children. As their titles make plain, both *A Field Guide to Monsters: Googly-eyed Wart Floppers, Shadow-casters, Toe-eaters, and Other Creatures* and *A Field Guide to Aliens: Intergalactic Worrywarts, Bubblonauts, Sliver-slurpers, and Other Extraterrestrials* are not for the squeamish. Olander also hosts a tongue-in-cheek Web log, *Monster Watch,* which features sketches and received letters from "young, but extremely brave and gifted" novice monster hunters. His line drawings also appear in the edited anthology *An Eyeball in My Gar-*

den, and Other Spine-tingling Poems, which "straddles the line between scary and innocently goofy," according to *School Library Journal* critic Julie Roach.

In *A Field Guide to Monsters* Olander devotes a double-page spread to each of the twenty-seven monsters he introduces to young adventurers. In addition to the Latin name, the creature's diet (which sometimes includes children), life cycle, preferred habitat, and general de-

Johan Olander presents a useful guidebook for young adventurers in his self-illustrated **A Field Guide to Aliens, Intergalactic Worrywarts, Bubblonauts, Sliver-slurpers, and Other Extraterrestrials.** (Illustration copyright © 2010 by Johan Olander. Reproduced with permission of Marshall Cavendish Books.)

scription are included. Of major importance is the advice the author gives regarding how to behave if one encounters the monster in question, and chuckle-inducing accounts of actual monster sightings are also included. Composed digitally from a collage of ink drawings, pencil sketches, and oil paintings, the book mimics a well-traveled journal stuffed with handwritten field notes and sketches, coffee-stained scribblings, and scraps of monster-related ephemera. Writing that "Olander's sketches are the real stars in this book," Jeff Mann added in his *Voice of Youth Advocates* review that *A Field Guide to Monsters* "is handsomely put together" and a good choice for reluctant readers due to its inclusion of "imaginative creatures, creative drawings, and humorous tidbits of information." While posting a warning to "squeamish readers," Kirsten Cutler asserted in *School Library Journal* that *A Field Guide to Monsters* is a "superb, playfully farcical presentation" that will "capture children's imagination."

Olander's discovery that, according to a *Voice of Youth Advocates* contributor, "45 percent of all monster sightings reported are actually alien sightings," inspired his second book, *A Field Guide to Aliens.* Like *A Field Guide to Monsters,* this useful work includes factual data on creatures as diverse as Space Worms, Cloudians, and Dolfini, and it also mimics what *School Library Journal* critic Walter Minkel described as "a stained, doodle-filled scrapbook, full of sketches, text, and clippings." While characterizing Olander's mix of text and art as "silly and gross," the *Voice of Youth Advocated* critic predicted that these very same characteristics should guarantee *A Field Guide to Aliens* a loyal readership among preteen boys.

Biographical and Critical Sources

PERIODICALS

Publishers Weekly, May 31, 2010, review of *A Field Guide to Aliens: Intergalactic Worrywarts, Bubblonauts, Sliver-slurpers, and Other Extraterrestrials,* p. 49; August 9, 2010, review of *An Eyeball in My Garden, and Other Spine-tingling Poems,* p. 50.

School Library Journal, November, 2007, Kirsten Cutler, review of *A Field Guide to Monsters: Googly-eyed Wart Floppers, Shadow-casters, Toe-eaters, and Other Creatures,* p. 97; June, 2010, Walter Minkel, review of *A Field Guide to Aliens,* p. 116; November, 2010, Julie Roach, review of *An Eyeball in My Garden, and Other Spine-tingling Poems,* p. 140.

Voice of Youth Advocates, December, 2007, Jeff Mann, review of *A Field Guide to Monsters,* p. 451; April, 2010, review of *A Field Guide to Aliens.*

ONLINE

Johan Olander Home Page, http://www.johanolander.com (May 2, 2011).

Johan Olander Web log, http://monstrologist.blogspot.com (June 15, 2011).*

P

PALMER, Gary

Personal
Married; wife's name Rebecca; children: Joel, Evan. *Education:* Ringling School of Art and Design, B.F.A., 1978. *Hobbies and other interests:* Camping, fishing.

Addresses
Home—Charlotte, NC. *E-mail*—gary@garypalmerillus tration.com.

Career
Artist and illustrator. *Exhibitions:* Work exhibited at North Carolina Museum of Natural Science.

Illustrator
Carol Crane, *T Is for Tar Heel: A North Carolina Alphabet,* Sleeping Bear Press (Chelsea, MI), 2003.
Carol Crane, *Wright Numbers: A North Carolina Number Book,* Sleeping Bear Press (Chelsea, MI), 2005.
Carol Crane, *Net Numbers: A South Carolina Number Book,* Sleeping Bear Press (Chelsea, MI), 2006.
Judy Young, *H Is for Hook: A Fishing Alphabet,* Sleeping Bear Press (Chelsea, MI), 2008.
Carol Crane, *The Handkerchief Quilt,* Sleeping Bear Press (Ann Arbor, MI), 2010.

Biographical and Critical Sources

PERIODICALS

School Library Journal, September, 2010, Sarah Polace, review of *The Handkerchief Quilt,* p. 120.

ONLINE

Gary Palmer Home Page, http://www.garypalmerillustra tion.com (May 2, 2011).*

Gary Palmer (Reproduced by permission.)

*   *   *

PATT, Beverly

Personal
Born in IL; daughter of Gale and Joan Lyle; married Jerry Patt; children: four. *Education:* University of Illi-

nois, B.A. (psychology); Northeast Illinois University, M.A. (special education). *Hobbies and other interests:* Tennis, knitting, reading.

Addresses

Home—Chicago, IL. *E-mail*—beverlypatt@gmail.com.

Career

Educator and author. Special-education teacher for seven years. Presenter at schools.

Writings

(With Gary Burge) *Time for Learning: Bible,* Publications International (Lincolnwood, IL), 2003.
Haven (middle-grade novel), Blooming Tree Press, 2009.
Best Friends Forever: A World War II Scrapbook, illustrated by Shula Klinger, Marshall Cavendish Children (New York, NY), 2010.

Contributor to periodicals, including *Highlights for Children.*

Sidelights

Beverly Patt taught special education for seven years in her home state of Illinois before leaving to raise her children and explore her potential as a writer. After co-authoring a work of children's nonfiction, she turned to middle-grade fiction. *Haven* is the story of Rudy Morris, a preteen who must rethink his decision to befriend adventurous orphaned friend Latonya and aid in her plan to escape from foster care. In *Best Friends Forever: A World War II Scrapbook* Patt mixes fiction and nonfiction, weaving history about the internment of Japanese Americans during World War II with a fictional story inspired by her mother's childhood memories.

First produced as a magazine article and then enriched with additional insights from Dave and Margaret Masuoka, friends who shared their own memories of living in internment camps, *Best Friends Forever* introduces two young Americans whose race puts them at the effect of wartime hysteria. Louise Kessler, a fourteen-year-old German immigrant, and Japanese American Dottie Masuoka are best friends. When the Masuoka family is relocated to a government internment camp in south-central Washington State, Louise begins a scrapbook that includes her diary entries and Dottie's letters and drawings along with newspaper clippings and wartime posters, photographs, and other ephemera commemorating the girls' friendship. Illustrated by Shula Klinger, *Best Friends Forever* features an "authentic" format and an approach to its subject that will draw "readers . . . into the continuing debate about what makes a 'real' American," according to *Booklist* critic

Hazel Rochman. In *Publishers Weekly* a critic predicted that Patt's story "should inspire readers to learn more about the history of internment" and *School Library Journal* critic Emma Burkhart praised *Best Friends Forever* as "appealing and accessible" as well as a "heartwarming tale of steadfast friendship."

Biographical and Critical Sources

PERIODICALS

Booklist, April 15, 2010, Hazel Rochman, review of *Best Friends Forever: A World War II Scrapbook,* p. 55.
Bulletin of the Center for Children's Books, July-August, 2010, Elizabeth Bush, review of *Best Friends Forever,* p. 497.
Kirkus Reviews March 15, 2010, review of *Best Friends Forever.*
Publishers Weekly, May 3, 2010, review of *Best Friends Forever,* p. 50.
School Library Journal, April, 2010, Emma Burkhart, review of *Best Friends Forever,* p. 166.
Voice of Youth Advocates, April, 2010, Kelly Czarnecki, review of *Best Friends Forever,* p. 61.

ONLINE

Beverly Patt Home Page, http://www.beverlypatt.com (July 15, 2011).
Beverly Patt Web log, http://beberly.livejournal.com (July 15, 2011).
Class of 2K9 Web site, http://www.classof2k9.com/ (July 15, 2011), "Beverly Patt."
Discovering Nikkei Web site, http://www.discoveringnikkei.org/ (September 16, 2010), Leslie Yamaguchi, interview with Patt.

*   *   *

PAULSEN, Gary 1939-

Personal

Born May 17, 1939, in Minneapolis, MN; son of Oscar (an army officer) and Eunice Paulsen; married third wife, Ruth Ellen Wright (an artist), May 5, 1971; children: (first marriage) two; (third marriage) James Wright. *Education:* Attended Bemidji College, 1957-58, and University of Colorado, 1976. *Politics:* "As Russian author Alexander Solzhenitsyn has said, 'If we limit ourselves to political structures we are not artists.'" *Religion:* "Spiritual progress."

Addresses

Home—La Luz, NM; Willow, AK. *Agent*—Jennifer Flannery, 34-34 28th St., No. 5, Long Island City, NY 11106.

Gary Paulsen (Reproduced by permission.)

Career

Novelist and author of nonfiction. Freelance writer beginning 1966; worked variously as a teacher, field engineer, editor, actor, director, farmer, rancher, truck driver, trapper, professional archer, migrant farm worker, singer, and sailor. Participant in iditarods, 1983, 1985. *Military service:* U.S. Army, 1959-62; attained rank of sergeant.

Awards, Honors

Society of Midland Authors Book Award, 1985, for *Tracker;* Parents' Choice Award, Parents' Choice Foundation, 1985, and Newbery Honor Book citation, and Children's Book of the Year Award, Child Study Association of America, both 1986, all for *Dogsong;* Newbery Honor Book citation, 1988, and Dorothy Canfield Fisher Children's Book Award, 1989, both for *Hatchet; Parenting* magazine Reading Magic Award, and Teachers' Choice Award, International Reading Association (IRA), both 1990, both for *The Voyage of the Frog;* Newbery Honor Book citation, Judy Lopez Memorial Award, and *Parenting* Best Book of the Year citation, all 1990, all for *The Winter Room;* Parents' Choice Award, 1991, for *The Boy Who Owned the School;* ALAN Award, 1991; Society of Midland Authors Book

Award, and Spur Award, Western Writers of America, both 1991, both for *Woodsong;* Spur Award, 1993, for *The Haymeadow;* Children's Choice citation, IRA/ Children's Book Council (CBC), 1994, for both *Nightjohn* and *Dogteam;* Children's Literature Award finalist, PEN Center USA West, 1994, for *Sisters/Hermanas;* Margaret A. Edwards Award, 1997, for lifetime achievement in writing for young adults; Parents' Choice Award, and *Chicago Tribune* Young-Adult Book Prize, both 2007, National Council for Social Studies/CBC Notable Children's Trade Books in the Field of Social Studies designation, New Mexico Land of Enchantment Book Award, Texas Bluebonnet Award nomination, and ALA Quick Pick for Reluctant Readers designation, all 2008, and Sequoyah Book Award for Children's Literature, 2010, all for *Lawn Boy.* Paulsen's books have been selected as American Library Association (ALA) Best Books for Young Adults and Notable Children's Books, National Council of Teachers of English (NCTE) Notable Books in the Language Arts, Notable Children's Books in the Social Studies, and New York Public Library Books for the Teen Age, and have won numerous state awards.

Writings

JUVENILE FICTION

Mr. Tucket, illustrated by Noel Sickles, Funk & Wagnalls (New York, NY), 1968.

The C.B. Radio Caper, illustrated by John Asquith, Raintree Press (Milwaukee, WI), 1977.

The Curse of the Cobra, illustrated by John Asquith, Raintree Press (Milwaukee, WI), 1977.

Winterkill, Thomas Nelson (Nashville, TN), 1977.

The Foxman, Thomas Nelson (Nashville, TN), 1977.

Tiltawhirl John, Thomas Nelson (Nashville, TN), 1977.

The Golden Stick, illustrated by Jerry Scott, Raintree Press (Milwaukee, WI), 1977.

The Night the White Deer Died, Thomas Nelson (Nashville, TN), 1978.

(With Ray Peekner) *The Green Recruit,* Independence Press (Independence, MO), 1978.

The Spitball Gang, Elsevier (New York, NY), 1980.

Popcorn Days and Buttermilk Nights, Lodestar Books (New York, NY), 1983.

Dancing Carl, Bradbury (Scarsdale, NY), 1983, reprinted, Aladdin (New York, NY), 2007.

Tracker, Bradbury (Scarsdale, NY), 1984, reprinted, Aladdin (New York, NY), 2007.

Dogsong, Bradbury (Scarsdale, NY), 1985, reprinted, Simon Pulse (New York, NY), 2007.

Sentries, Bradbury (Scarsdale, NY), 1986, reprinted, Simon Pulse (New York, NY), 2007.

The Crossing, Orchard Books (New York, NY), 1987.

Hatchet, Bradbury (Scarsdale, NY), 1987.

The Island, Orchard Books (New York, NY), 1988.

The Voyage of the Frog, Orchard Books (New York, NY), 1989.

The Winter Room, Orchard Books (New York, NY), 1989.

The Boy Who Owned the School, Orchard Books (New York, NY), 1990.

Canyons, Delacorte (New York, NY), 1990.

Woodsong, illustrated by wife, R.W. Paulsen, Bradbury (Scarsdale, NY), 1990.

The Cookcamp, Orchard Books (New York, NY), 1991.

The River, Delacorte (New York, NY), 1991.

The Monument, Delacorte (New York, NY), 1991.

The Haymeadow, Delacorte (New York, NY), 1992.

Christmas Sonata, illustrated by Leslie Bowman, Delacorte (New York, NY), 1992.

Nightjohn, Delacorte (New York, NY), 1993.

Sisters/Hermanas, Harcourt (New York, NY), 1993.

Dogteam, illustrated by R.W. Paulsen, Delacorte (New York, NY), 1993.

Harris and Me: A Summer Remembered, Harcourt (New York, NY), 1993, reprinted, Harcourt (Orlando, FL), 2007.

The Car, Harcourt (New York, NY), 1994.

The Tortilla Factory, paintings by R.W. Paulsen, Harcourt (New York, NY), 1995.

Call Me Francis Tucket, Delacorte (New York, NY), 1995.

The Tent: A Parable in One Sitting, Harcourt (New York, NY), 1995.

The Rifle, Harcourt (New York, NY), 1995.

Brian's Winter, Delacorte (New York, NY), 1996.

Worksong, illustrated by R.W. Paulsen, Harcourt (New York, NY), 1997.

Tucket's Ride, Delacorte (New York, NY), 1997.

The Schernoff Discoveries, Delacorte (New York, NY), 1997.

Sarny: A Life Remembered, Delacorte (New York, NY), 1997.

The Transall Saga, Delacorte (New York, NY), 1998.

Soldier's Heart: A Novel of the Civil War, Delacorte (New York, NY), 1998.

Canoe Days, illustrated by R.W. Paulsen, Doubleday (New York, NY), 1999.

The White Fox Chronicles, Delacorte (New York, NY), 1999.

Brian's Return, Delacorte (New York, NY), 1999.

Alida's Song, Delacorte (New York, NY), 1999.

Tucket's Gold, Delacorte (New York, NY), 1999.

Escape, Delacorte (New York, NY), 2000.

Tucket's Home, Delacorte (New York, NY), 2000.

Brian's Hunt, Wendy Lamb Books (New York, NY), 2003.

Shelf Life: Stories by the Book, Simon & Schuster (New York, NY), 2003.

The Glass Café; or, The Stripper and the State: How My Mother Started a War with the System That Made Us Kind of Rich and a Little Bit Famous, Wendy Lamb Books (New York, NY), 2003.

The Quilt, Wendy Lamb Books (New York, NY), 2004.

Molly McGinty Has a Really Good Day, Wendy Lamb Books (New York, NY), 2004.

The Time Hackers, Wendy Lamb Books (New York, NY), 2005.

The Legend of Bass Reeves: Being the True and Fictional Account of the Most Valiant Marshal in the West, Wendy Lamb Books (New York, NY), 2006.

The Amazing Life of Birds: The Twenty-Day Puberty Journal of Duane Homer Leech, Wendy Lamb Books (New York, NY), 2006.

Lawn Boy, Wendy Lamb Books (New York, NY), 2007.

Mudshark, Wendy Lamb Books (New York, NY), 2009.

Notes from the Dog, Wendy Lamb Books (New York, NY), 2009.

Lawn Boy Returns (sequel to *Lawn Boy*), Wendy Lamb Books (New York, NY), 2010.

Masters of Disaster, Wendy Lamb Books (New York, NY), 2010.

Woods Runner, Wendy Lamb Books (New York, NY), 2010.

Liar, Liar: The Theory, Practice, and Destructive Properties of Deception, Wendy Lamb Books (New York, NY), 2011.

"CULPEPPER ADVENTURES" SERIES

The Case of the Dirty Bird, Dell (New York, NY), 1992.

Dunc's Doll, Dell (New York, NY), 1992.

Culpepper's Cannon, Dell (New York, NY), 1992.

Dunc Gets Tweaked, Dell (New York, NY), 1992.

Dunc's Halloween, Dell (New York, NY), 1992.

Dunc Breaks the Record, Dell (New York, NY), 1992.

Dunc and the Flaming Ghost, Dell (New York, NY), 1992.

Amos Gets Famous, Dell (New York, NY), 1993.

Dunc and Amos Hit the Big Top, Dell (New York, NY), 1993.

Dunc's Dump, Dell (New York, NY), 1993.

Dunc and the Scam Artist, Dell (New York, NY), 1993.

Dunc and Amos and the Red Tattoos, Dell (New York, NY), 1993.

The Wild Culpepper Cruise, Dell (New York, NY), 1993.

Dunc's Undercover Christmas, Dell (New York, NY), 1993.

Dunc and the Haunted House, Dell (New York, NY), 1993.

Cowpokes and Desperadoes, Dell (New York, NY), 1994.

Dunc and the Greased Sticks of Doom, Dell (New York, NY), 1994.

Amos's Killer Concert Caper, Dell (New York, NY), 1994.

Amos Gets Married, Dell (New York, NY), 1995.

Amos Goes Bananas, Dell (New York, NY), 1995.

Dunc and Amos Go to the Dogs, Dell (New York, NY), 1996.

Amos and the Vampire, Dell (New York, NY), 1996.

Amos and the Chameleon Caper, Dell (New York, NY), 1996.

Super Amos, Dell (New York, NY), 1997.

Dunc and Amos on Thin Ice, Dell (New York, NY), 1997.

Amos Binder, Secret Agent, Dell (New York, NY), 1997.

"GARY PAULSEN WORLD OF ADVENTURE" SERIES

The Legend of Red Horse Cavern, Dell (New York, NY), 1994.

Escape from Fire Mountain (also see below), Dell (New York, NY), 1995.

The Rock Jockeys, Dell (New York, NY), 1995.

The Gorgon Slayer, Dell (New York, NY), 1995.

Danger on Midnight River (also see below), Dell (New York, NY), 1995.

Hook 'Em Snotty! (also see below), Dell (New York, NY), 1995.

Rodomonte's Revenge, Dell (New York, NY), 1995.

Captive!, Dell (New York, NY), 1996.

Project: A Perfect New World, Dell (New York, NY), 1996.

Skydive!, Dell (New York, NY), 1996.

The Treasure of El Patron, Dell (New York, NY), 1996.

The Seventh Crystal, Dell (New York, NY), 1996.

The Creature of Black Water Lake, Dell (New York, NY), 1997.

The Grizzly, Dell (New York, NY), 1997.

Thunder Valley, Dell (New York, NY), 1998.

Curse of the Ruins, Dell (New York, NY), 1998.

Time Benders, Dell (New York, NY), 1998.

Flight of the Hawk, Dell (New York, NY), 1998.

World of Adventure Trio (includes *Escape from Fire Mountain, Hook 'Em, Snotty!,* and *Danger on Midnight River*), Yearling (New York, NY), 2006.

JUVENILE NONFICTION

(With Dan Theis) *Martin Luther King: The Man Who Climbed the Mountain,* Raintree Press (Milwaukee, WI), 1976.

The Small Ones, illustrated by K. Goff, photographs by Wilford Miller, Raintree Press (Milwaukee, WI), 1976.

The Grass-Eaters: Real Animals, illustrated by K. Goff, photographs by Wilford Miller, Raintree Press (Milwaukee, WI), 1976.

Dribbling, Shooting, and Scoring Sometimes, photographs by Heinz Kluetmeier, Raintree Press (Milwaukee, WI), 1976.

Hitting, Pitching, and Running Maybe, photographs by Heinz Kluetmeier, Raintree Press (Milwaukee, WI), 1976.

Tackling, Running, and Kicking—Now and Again, photographs by Heinz Kluetmeier, Raintree Press (Milwaukee, WI), 1977.

Riding, Roping, and Bulldogging—Almost, photographs by Heinz Kluetmeier, Raintree Press (Milwaukee, WI), 1977.

Careers in an Airport, photographs by R. Nye, Raintree Press (Milwaukee, WI), 1977.

Running, Jumping, and Throwing—If You Can, photographs by Heinz Kluetmeier, Raintree Press (Milwaukee, WI), 1978, revised with Roger Barrett as *Athletics,* Macdonald (Milwaukee, WI), 1980.

Forehanding and Backhanding—If You're Lucky, photographs by Heinz Kluetmeier, Raintree Press (Milwaukee, WI), 1978, revised with Roger Barrett as *Tennis,* Macdonald (Milwaukee, WI), 1980.

(With John Morris) *Hiking and Backpacking,* illustrated by R.W. Paulsen, Simon & Schuster (New York, NY), 1978.

(With John Morris) *Canoeing, Kayaking, and Rafting,* illustrated by John Peterson and Jack Storholm, Simon & Schuster (New York, NY), 1979.

Downhill, Hotdogging, and Cross-Country—If the Snow Isn't Sticky, photographs by Heinz Kluetmeier and Willis Wood, Raintree Press (Milwaukee, WI), 1979,

revised with Roger Barrett as *Skiing,* Macdonald (Milwaukee, WI), 1980.

Facing Off, Checking, and Goaltending—Perhaps, photographs by Heinz Kluetmeier and Melchior DiGiacomo, Raintree Press (Milwaukee, WI), 1979, revised with Roger Barrett as *Ice Hockey,* Macdonald (Milwaukee, WI), 1980.

Going Very Fast in a Circle—If You Don't Run out of Gas, photographs by Heinz Kluetmeier and Bob D'Olivo, Raintree Press (Milwaukee, WI), 1979, revised with Roger Barrett as *Motor Racing,* Macdonald (Milwaukee, WI), 1980.

Pummeling, Falling, and Getting Up—Sometimes, photographs by Heinz Kluetmeier and Joe DiMaggio, Raintree Press (Milwaukee, WI), 1979.

Track, Enduro, and Motocross—Unless You Fall Over, photographs by Heinz Kluetmeier, Raintree Press (Milwaukee, WI), 1979, revised with Roger Barrett as *Motor-cycling,* Macdonald (Milwaukee, WI), 1980.

Launching, Floating High, and Landing—If Your Pilot Light Doesn't Go Out, photographs by Heinz Kluetmeier, Raintree Press (Milwaukee, WI), 1979, published as *Full of Hot Air: Launching, Floating High, and Landing,* photographs by Mary A. Heltshe, Delacorte (New York, NY), 1993.

(With Art Browne, Jr.) *TV and Movie Animals,* Messner (Englewood Cliffs, NJ), 1980.

Sailing: From Jibs to Jibing, illustrated by R.W. Paulsen, Messner (Englewood Cliffs, NJ), 1981.

Father Water, Mother Woods: Essays on Fishing and Hunting in the North Woods, illustrated by R.W. Paulsen, Delacorte (New York, NY), 1994.

My Life in Dog's Years, drawings by R.W. Paulsen, Delacorte (New York, NY), 1998.

The Beet Fields: Memories of a Sixteenth Summer, Delacorte (New York, NY), 2000.

Guts: The True Story behind Hatchet and the Brian Books, Delacorte (New York, NY), 2001.

Caught by the Sea: My Life on Boats, Delacorte (New York, NY), 2001.

How Angel Peterson Got His Name, and Other Outrageous Tales about Extreme Sports, Wendy Lamb Books (New York, NY), 2003.

FICTION; FOR ADULTS

The Implosion Effect, Major Books (Canoga Park, CA), 1976.

The Death Specialists, Major Books (Canoga Park, CA), 1976.

C.B. Jockey, Major Books (Canoga Park, CA), 1977.

The Sweeper, Harlequin (Tarrytown, NY), 1981.

Campkill, Pinnacle Books (New York, NY), 1981.

Clutterkill, Harlequin (Tarrytown, NY), 1982.

Murphy, Walker & Co. (New York, NY), 1987.

Murphy's Gold, Walker & Co. (New York, NY), 1988.

The Madonna Stories, Van Vliet (Minneapolis, MN), 1988.

Murphy's Herd, Walker & Co. (New York, NY), 1989.

(With Brian Burks) *Murphy's Stand,* Walker & Co. (New York, NY), 1993.

(With Brian Burks) *Murphy's Ambush,* Walker & Co. (New York, NY), 1995.

(With Brian Burks) *Murphy's Trail,* Walker & Co. (New York, NY), 1996.

PLAYS

Communications (one-act), produced in New Mexico, 1974.
Together-Apart (one-act), produced in Denver, CO, 1976.

OTHER

(With Raymond Friday Locke) *The Special War,* Sirkay (Los Angeles, CA), 1966.
Some Birds Don't Fly, Rand McNally (Chicago, IL), 1969.
The Building a New, Buying an Old, Remodeling a Used, Comprehensive Home and Shelter Book, Prentice-Hall (New York, NY), 1976.
Farm: A History and Celebration of the American Farmer, Prentice-Hall (New York, NY), 1977.
Successful Home Repair, Structures (Farmington, MI), 1978.
Money-saving Home Repair Guide, Ideals (State College, PA), 1981.
Beat the System: A Survival Guide, Pinnacle Books (New York, NY), 1983.
Kill Fee, Donald I. Fine (New York, NY), 1990.
Night Rituals, Bantam (New York, NY), 1991.
Clabbered Dirt, Sweet Grass (adult nonfiction), illustrated by R.W. Paulsen, Harcourt (New York, NY), 1992.
Eastern Sun, Winter Moon (adult nonfiction), Harcourt (New York, NY), 1993.
Winterdance: The Fine Madness of Running the Iditarod (adult nonfiction), Harcourt (New York, NY), 1994.
(Author of introduction) Jack London, *The Call of the Wild,* illustrated by Barry Moser, Macmillan (New York, NY), 1994.
Puppies, Dogs, and Blue Northers: Reflections on Being Raised by a Pack of Sled Dogs (adult nonfiction), Harcourt (New York, NY), 1996.
Pilgrimage on a Steel Ride: A Memoir about Men and Motorcycles (adult nonfiction), Harcourt (New York, NY), 1997.

Contributor of short stories and articles to periodicals, including *Child Life.*

Paulsen's works have been published in German, Japanese, Danish, Dutch, Russian, Norwegian, Italian, Spanish, French, Swedish, and Chinese.

Adaptations

Dogsong was released as a filmstrip with cassette, Random House/Miller-Brody, 1986. *Hatchet* was released as a filmstrip with cassette, Random House, 1988. *Woodsong* was released as an audiocassette, Bantam Audio, 1991. *Canyons, Hatchet,* and *The River* were released as audiocassettes, all read by Peter Coyote, Bantam Audio, 1992. *The Haymeadow* and *The Monument* were released as audiocassettes, both Bantam Audio, 1992. *Woods Runner* was adapted for audiobook, read by Danny Campbell, Listening Library, 2010.

Sidelights

A writer of popular and finely wrought young-adult novels and nonfiction, Gary Paulsen joined a select group of YA writers when he received the 1997 Margaret A. Edwards Award honoring an author's lifetime achievement in writing books for teens. His work is widely praised by critics, and he has been awarded Newbery Medal Honor Book citations for three of his books: *Dogsong, Hatchet,* and *The Winter Room.* Although Paulsen has also written for adult readers, since the mid-1990s his focus has been primarily on teens. "Adults are locked into car payments and divorces and work," he told *New York Times Book Review* interviewer Anne Goodwin Sides. "They haven't got time to think fresh. Name the book that made the biggest impression on you. I bet you read it before you hit puberty. In the time I've got left, I intend to write artistic books—for kids—because they're still open to new ideas."

In lean prose that critics have cited for containing echoes of novelist Ernest Hemingway, Paulsen creates powerful young-adult fiction, often setting his stories in wilderness or rural areas and featuring teenagers who arrive at self-awareness by way of experiences in nature—through challenging tests of their own survival instincts—or through the ministrations of understanding adults. He displays an "extraordinary ability to picture for the reader how man's comprehension of life can be transformed with the lessons of nature," according to Evie Wilson writing in *Voice of Youth Advocates.* "With humor and psychological genius, Paulsen develops strong adolescent characters who lend new power to youth's plea to be allowed to apply individual skills in their risk-taking." In addition to writing young-adult fiction, Paulsen has also authored numerous picture books with his illustrator wife R.W. Paulsen, penned children's nonfiction, and authored two plays and many works of adult fiction and nonfiction.

Paulsen was born in Minnesota in 1939, the son of first-generation Danish and Swedish parents. During his childhood, he saw little of his father, who served in the military in Europe during World War II. He also saw little of his mother, who worked in a Chicago ammunitions factory. "I was reared by my grandmother and several aunts," he once told *SATA.* "I first saw my father when I was seven in the Philippines where my parents and I lived from 1946 to 1949." Writing of that experience a half century later in *Riverbank Review,* Paulsen noted that he "lived essentially as a street child in Manila, because my parents were alcoholics and I was not supervised. The effect was profound and lasting."

When Paulsen's family returned to the United States, they continued to move frequently. 'The longest time I spent in one school was for about five months," Paulsen once told *SATA.* "I was an 'Army brat,' and it was a miserable life. School was a nightmare because I was unbelievably shy, and terrible at sports. . . . I wound up skipping most of the ninth grade." In addition to problems at school, he faced ordeals at home, where "my father drank a lot, and there would be terrible arguments." Eventually Paulsen was sent to live with relatives and he worked to support himself with jobs as a newspaper boy and as a pin-setter in a bowling alley.

After just barely graduating from high school in Thief River Falls, Minnesota, in 1959, Paulsen attended Bemidji College in Minnesota for two years, paying for his tuition with money he had earned as a trapper for the state of Minnesota. When he flunked out of college, he joined the U.S. Army, serving from 1959 to 1962, and working with missiles. After his tour of duty was completed, he took extension courses to become a certified field engineer, finding work in the aerospace industry. While working for the Bendix and Lockheed corporations, it occurred to him that he might try and become a writer. "I'd finished reading a magazine article on flight-testing . . . and thought, gad, what a way to make a living—writing about something you like and getting paid for it!," he told F. Serdahely in *Writer's Digest.* "I remembered writing some of my past reports, some fictionalized versions I'd included. And I thought: 'What the hell, I am an engineering writer.' But, conversely, I also realized I didn't know a thing about writing professionally. After several hours of hard thinking, a way to learn came to me. All I had to do was go to work editing a magazine."

Creating a fictitious resumé, Paulsen obtained an associate editor position on a men's magazine in Southern California. Although it soon became apparent to his employers that he had no editorial experience, "they could see I was serious about wanting to learn, and they were willing to teach me." He spent nearly a year with the magazine, finding it "the best of all possible ways to learn about writing. It probably did more to improve my craft and ability than any other single event in my life." Living near Hollywood at the time, he also found work as a film extra and took up sculpting as a hobby, even winning first prize in a local exhibition.

Paulsen's first book, *The Special War,* was published in 1966, and he soon proved himself to be one of the most prolific authors in the United States. During his first decade, while working mainly out of northern Minnesota—where he returned after becoming disillusioned with Hollywood—he published several dozen books and close to 200 articles and stories for magazines. Among Paulsen's diverse titles were a number of children's nonfiction books about animals, a biography of Martin Luther King, Jr., several humorous titles in the "Sports on the Light Side" series published by Raintree Press, two plays, adult fiction and nonfiction, and several ventures into juvenile fiction. On a bet with a friend, he once wrote eleven articles and short stories inside four days and sold all of them.

Paulsen's prolific output was interrupted by a libel lawsuit brought against his 1977 young-adult novel *Winterkill,* the powerful story of a semi-delinquent boy who

is befriended by a hard-bitten cop named Duda in a small Minnesota town. Paulsen eventually won the case, but, as he noted, "the whole situation was so nasty and ugly that I stopped writing. I wanted nothing more to do with publishing and burned my bridges, so to speak." Unable to earn any other type of living, he went back to trapping for the state of Minnesota, working his sixty-mile trap line on foot or skis, and he soon returned to writing as well.

Paulsen's acclaimed young-adult fiction—all written since the early 1980s—often centers around teenage characters who arrive at an understanding of themselves and their world through pivotal experiences with nature. His writing has been praised for its almost poetic effect, and he is also credited with creating vivid descriptions of his characters' emotional states. One of his first coming-of-age stories, *Tracker,* tells about a thirteen-year-old boy who faces his first season of deer hunting alone while his grandfather is bedridden and dying of

Cover of Paulsen's coming-of-age novel Brian's Winter, *featuring artwork by Neal McPheeters.* (Copyright © 1996 by Delacorte Kids. Used by permission of Delacorte Press, an imprint of Random House Children's Books, a division of Random House, Inc.)

cancer. Ronald A. Jobe praised the novel in *Language Arts* as "powerfully written," adding that Paulsen "explores with the reader the innermost frustrations, hurts, and fears of the young boy. "*Tracker* was the first book by Paulsen to receive wide critical and popular recognition.

To help Paulsen in his hunting and trapping, a friend offered him a team of sled dogs, and this gift had profound consequences. "One day, about midnight, we were crossing Clear Water Lake, which is about three miles long," Paulsen recounted. "There was a full moon shining so brightly on the snow you could read by it. There was no one around, and all I could hear was the rhythm of the dogs' breathing as they pulled the sled." The intensity of the moment prompted an impulsive seven-day trip by Paulsen through northern Minnesota. "I didn't go home—my wife was frantic—I didn't check lines, I just ran the dogs. . . . For food, we had a few beaver carcasses. . . . I was initiated into this incredibly ancient and very beautiful bond, and it was as if everything that had happened to me before ceased to exist." Paulsen afterwards made a resolution to give up hunting and trapping and pursue dogsled racing as a hobby. He entered the grueling 1,200-mile Iditarod in Alaska in both 1983 and 1985, and this experience provided the basis for his award-winning novel *Dogsong.*

Dogsong, a Newbery Medal Honor Book selection, is a rite-of-passage novel about a young Inuit boy named Russel who wishes to abandon the increasingly modern ways of his people. Through the guidance of a tribal elder, Russel learns to bow-hunt and dogsled and eventually leads his own pack of dogs on a trip across Alaska and back. "While the language of . . . [*Dogsong*] is lyrical, Paulsen recognizes the reality of Russel's world—the dirty smoke and the stinking yellow fur of the bear," wrote Nel Ward in the *Voice of Youth Advocates.* "He also recognizes the reality of killing to save lives, and of dreaming to save sanity, in the communion between present and past, life and death, reality and imagination, in this majestic exploration into the Alaskan wilderness by a master author who knows his subject well."

Also the recipient of a Newbery Honor designation, *Hatchet* tells the story of Brian, a thirteen-year-old thoroughly modern boy who is forced to survive alone in the Canadian woods after a plane crash. Like Russel in *Dogsong, Hatchet*'s hero is also transformed by the wilderness. "By the time he is rescued, Brian is permanently changed," noted Suzanne Rahn in *Twentieth-Century Children's Writers;* "he is far more observant and thoughtful, and knows what is really important in his life." As noted in *Children's Books and Their Creators, Hatchet* became "one of the most popular adventure stories of all time," combining "elementary language with a riveting plot to produce a book both comprehensible and enjoyable for those children who frequently equate reading with frustration."

Hatchet proved so popular with readers that they demanded, and won, a number of sequels: *The River, Brian's Winter, Brian's Return,* and *Brian's Hunt.* In *Brian's Hunt* Paulsen "delivers a gripping, gory tale about survival in the north woods, based on a real bear attack," noted Paula Rohrlick in *Kliatt.*

The experiences of growing up in rural America are chronicled by Paulsen in both *Harris and Me: A Summer Remembered* and *The Amazing Life of Birds: The Twenty-Day Puberty Journal of Duane Homer Leech.* Raised by abusive and alcoholic parents, the preteen narrator in *Harris and Me* is sent to live with his uncle's family. In this new environment, the boy finds a degree of normalcy, although his new friend Harris leads him in escapades involving playing Tarzan in the barn's hayloft and using pig pens as the stage for G.I. Joe games. "Through it all," explained a reviewer for the *Bulletin of the Center for Children's Books,* "the lonely hero imperceptibly learns about belonging." In her review of *Harris and Me* for *Voice of Youth Advocates,* Penny Blubaugh pointed out that, "for the first time in his life [the narrator] finds himself surrounded by love."

The twelve-year-old narrator of *The Amazing Life of Birds* shares his uncomfortable experience of adolescence in a humorous journal that "manages to both entertain and reassure," according to *Kliatt* contributor Paula Rohrlick. Contemplative by nature, Duane finds that his ongoing observations of a bird preparing to leave the nest outside his bedroom window parallel his own growing need for independence. Describing *The Amazing Life of Birds* as "a quick and enjoyable take on school and family," *Booklist* contributor Todd Morning maintained that Paulsen captures the interest of reluctant readers by sustaining a "tone [that is] light and amusing."

The narrator of Paulsen's award-winning middle-grade novel *Lawn Boy* is the same age as Duane, although he has a very different set of problems. In fact, the book's twelve-year-old narrator is overwhelmed by success. When he receives an old riding lawn mower as a birthday gift from his grandmother, Paulsen's preteen protagonist decides to capitalize on the fact that he lives in a large suburban neighborhood. When he begins a lawn-mowing service, he quickly finds his service in great demand. When a cash-strapped client barters his expertise as an investment consultant for regular lawn maintanence, Lawn Boy gets a crash course in capitalism but finds that a growing portfolio can quickly translate into a growing headache. In a sequel, *Lawn Boy Returns,* the twelve year old is propelled to the status of a newsworthy celebrity after several savvy investment decisions pan out and he gains public recognition as the result of a television appearance. "With all the energy of a bull market and a farce that grows as steadily as crabgrass," *Lawn Boy* "has summer escapism written all over it," Betty Carter noted in *Horn Book,* and in *School*

Library Journal Terry Ann Lawler dubbed *Lawn Boy Returns* "an extremely fast and funny story" that is "good for struggling and reluctant readers."

Fourteen-year-old loner Finn is the focus of *Notes from the Dog,* and for Finn the prospect of entrepreneurism is a fearsome one. Although he knows that his dad expects him to get a summer job, Finn would rather spend time with Dylan, the family dog, and his best friend Matthew. When he meets new next-door-neighbor Johanna, a twenty-something graduate student who is battling breast cancer, she immediately steals Finn's heart. As the teen empathizes with Joanna's troubles and her ability to remain positive, he begins to move beyond his self-absorbed shyness, and when she provides him a summer job that allows him to gradually enlarge his circle of friends, the teen discovers a surprising new talent. The author's technique of combining "sorrow and humor . . . demonstrates to the middle-school audience that taking action to help is much better than turning away," wrote Susan Dove Lempke in her *Horn Book* review of *Notes from the Dog.* Paulsen's "quiet, steady story" becomes "an effective homage to cancer survivors everywhere," Daniel Kraus wrote in his *Booklist* review, and a *Publishers Weekly* critic praised the novel as a "touching story about human kindness and humanity" that "will note disappoint."

Paulsen continues his focus on spunky preteens in novels such as *Masters of Disaster, Mudshark,* and *Liar, Liar: The Theory, Practice, and Destructive Properties of Deception.* In *Masters of Disaster* twelve-year-old Henry convinces buddies Reed and Riley to undertake a sequence of ill-conceived but exciting challenges in order to test their mettle, among them flipping a portable toilet, dabbling with wilderness survival, and riding a bicycle off the roof of a house. The young sleuth in *Mudshark* has what it takes in the mystery-solving department, and when all the erasers vanish from the school he is called on the case by the school principal. For Kevin, the young hero of Paulsen's easy-reading novel *Liar, Liar,* a natural talent for obfuscation does not endear him to his school principal, or impress any one among his friends or family. Noting the "over-the-top exploits" of the young heroes who star in *Masters of Disaster,* Carolyn Phelan predicted in *Booklist* that even reluctant readers "will enjoy plenty of laughs along the way," while Ian Chipman noted in the same periodical that "Paulsen's deft hand with detailing and sometimes-light, sometimes-heavy touches of humor draw the story along" in *Mudshark.*

In books like *Nightjohn, Mr. Tucket, The Legend of Bass Reeves: Being the True and Fictional Account of the Most Valiant Marshal in the West,* and *Woods Runner* Paulsen draws on history for literary inspiration. *Nightjohn* is set in the nineteenth-century American South and revolves around Sarny, a young slave girl who risks severe punishment when she is taught to read by Nightjohn, a runaway slave who has just been recap-

Cover of Paulsen's middle-grade adventure novel **Call Me Francis Tucket,** *featuring artwork by Jos. A Smith.* (Jacket cover copyright © 1996 Yearling, an imprint of Random House Children's Books. Used by permission of Yearling, an imprint of Random House Children's Books, a division of Random House, Inc.)

tured. A commentator for *Kirkus Reviews* called *Nightjohn* "a searing picture of slavery" and an "unbearably vivid book."

Sarny returns in *Sarny: A Life Remembered,* in which the former slave looks back on her life in 1930, at the ripe old age of ninety-four. A focal point of the woman's story is the fact that she learned to read: this skill saved her on more than one occasion. Sarny's "story makes absorbing reading," concluded Bruce Anne Shook in a *School Library Journal* review of the book.

In *Mr. Tucket* fourteen-year-old Francis Tucket has a number of hair-raising adventures after he is captured by the Pawnee while wandering away from his family's Oregon-bound wagon train. After Francis escapes from the tribe, a one-armed fur trader named Jason Grimes continues the young teen's frontier education. Tucket's adventures are continued in several more works by Paulsen, including *Call Me Francis Tucket, Tucket's Ride,* and *Tucket's Home.*

In a mix of fact and fiction, Paulsen brings to life a fascinating character from America's mythic Wild West in

The Legend of Bass Reeves. Born a slave, the African-American Reeves learned cowboy skills such as riding and shooting while helping to defend the property of his master, a Texas rancher, from Indian attacks. Although much of Reeves' childhood remains unknown, Paulsen creates an entertaining backstory for the man, showing Reeves escaping from an unjust master, fleeing to the Oklahoma Territory in the 1840s, and becoming an officer of the law. In fact, Reeve became a legendary federal marshal, and was known for never drawing his gun first. *The Legend of Bass Reeves* was praised by *Kliatt* critic Janice Flint-Ferguson as "a fascinating story of what it took to survive in the American West" that is enriched by Paulsen's introductory comments regarding the crafting of the novel from original newspaper accounts. Reeves becomes "a fully fleshed-out character whose story is made all the more satisfying by the truth behind it," concluded Laurie Slagenwhite in her *School Library Journal* review of the book.

Paulsen takes readers even further into the past in *Woods Runner,* which finds a thirteen-year-old boy drawn into the growing conflict between Pennsylvania colonists and British forces that will become known as the American Revolution. Samuel and his parents live in a frontier community where news of the colonial uprising is slow to be known. While the boy is away from home on a hunting trip, his community is attacked by Iroquois scouts under orders of the King's army. Samuel returns to find his parents kidnaped and many others left for dead. The teen is determined to free them, and his wilderness skills come to the fore as he starts his journey north to New York, where he hopes to find help from those in the patriot underground. A "fast-paced" adventure, *Woods Runner* "will leave readers with a new sense of admiration for those who lost their lives in the creation of the nation," according to *School Library Journal* critic Denise Moore. Woven within Paulsen's story are "brief segments on spy networks, weaponry, war orphans, Hessians and floating prisons," noted a *Kirkus Reviews* writer, and Roger Sutton asserted in *Horn Book* that such "details . . . are helpful and interesting, and [serve to] accent . . . rather than slow . . . the momentum." In *Booklist* Ian Chipman recommended the realism in Paulsen's story, writing that *Woods Runner* "provides a stark glimpse of just how awful the war really was for those who suffered through it."

The White Fox Chronicles is a departure for Paulsen in its futuristic setting and a plot that a *Publishers Weekly* reviewer likened to that of a "shoot-'em-up computer game." The novel's hero is fourteen-year-old Cody, who has been captured by the nefarious Confederation of Consolidated Republics. This group has overrun the United States and is hatching Nazi-like purges of its enemies. A *Publishers Weekly* reviewer noted that the work will cause readers to "cheer on the good guys without ever fearing that they might not triumph in the end." Paulsen's *The Time Hackers* also employs elements of science fiction, as a seventh-grader discovers that he is able to travel through time using his laptop

computer. "Paulsen writes with his usual skill, creating believable characters and moving the action along at a fairly fast pace," noted *Booklist* contributor Cindy Welch.

In *My Life in Dog's Years, The Beet Fields: Memories of a Sixteenth Summer, Eastern Sun, Winter Moon, Caught by the Sea: My Life on Boats,* and *Guts: The True Stories behind Hatchet and the Brian Books* Paulsen recounts stories from his own life, many of which he has fictionalized in his young-adult novels. While most of the remembrances are intended for an adult audience, one of his most powerful memoirs for young readers is *Woodsong,* an autobiographical account of Paulsen's life in Minnesota and Alaska while preparing his sled dogs to run the Iditarod. A reviewer noted in *Horn Book* that the "lure of the wilderness is always a potent draw, and Paulsen evokes its mysteries as well as anyone since Jack London." In another memoir intended for a teen readership, *How Angel Peterson Got His Name, and Other Outrageous Tales about Extreme Sports,* Paulsen recalls a number of daredevil stunts he and his friends performed during their early

Cover of Paulsen's high-adventure historical novel **Woods Runner,** *featuring artwork by Richard Tuschman.* (Cover art copyright © 2010 by Richard Tuschman. Reproduced with permission of Wendy Lamb Books, an imprint of Random House Children's Books, a division of Random House, Inc.)

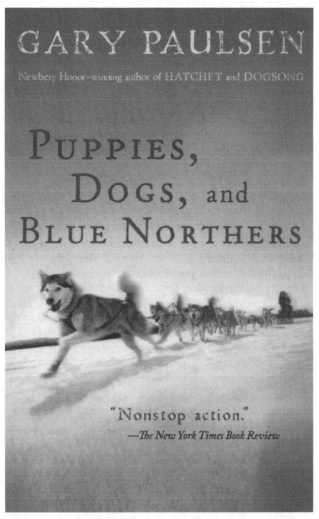

GARY PAULSEN

Newbery Honor-winning author of HATCHET and DOGSONG

PUPPIES, DOGS, and BLUE NORTHERS

"Nonstop action."
—*The New York Times Book Review*

Cover of Paulsen's Puppies, Dogs, and Blue Northers, *which draws from its author's Iditerod adventures.* (Illustration copyright © 1996 by Ruth Wright Paulsen. Reproduced by permission of Houghton Mifflin Harcourt Publishing Company.)

teen years. "Paulsen laces his tales with appealing '50s details and broad asides about the boys' personalities, ingenuity, and idiocy," noted a reviewer in *Publishers Weekly.*

A prolific author whose career has spanned over five decades, Paulsen follows a rigorous writing schedule. As he related to Sharon Miller Cindrich in *Writer,* he has been known to work eighteen-hour days and seven-day weeks. "People don't do that anymore," he added. "They don't study. The dedication, obsession, the compulsion-driven need to be like me is just not done anymore." "There is no motivation; it's just what I do," he added. "The stories are like a river that's going by all the time, and I just 'bucket in' and up comes a story. It's a cliché, but it's like that."

Paulsen's concern with literacy is personal; as he told David Gale in a *School Library Journal* interview celebrating his Margaret A. Edwards Award, "there's nothing that has happened to me that would have happened if a librarian hadn't got me to read. . . . All of our knowledge, everything we are—is locked up in books,

and if you can't read, it's lost." Waging a one-writer campaign against illiteracy, Paulsen consciously crafts his books with clean, spare language in order to attract reluctant readers, and it has been this empathic power that has made him such a popular and respected author. As Gary M. Salvner commented in *Writers for Young Adults:* "Whether angry or happy, whether writing about survival or growing up, Gary Paulsen is always a hopeful writer, for he believes that young people must be respected as they are guided into adulthood. And he continues to write enthusiastically, commenting that he has 'fallen in love with writing, with the dance of it.' Taken together, Gary Paulsen's sense of purpose and love of writing ensure that he will continue to write enjoyable and effective books for young adults for years to come."

Biographical and Critical Sources

BOOKS

Beacham's Guide to Literature for Young Adults, Beacham (Osprey, FL), Volume 6, 1994, Volume 7, 1994, Volume 8, 1994, Volume 10, Gale (Detroit, MI), 2000, Volume 11, 2001.
Children's Books and Their Creators, edited by Anita Silvey, Houghton Mifflin (Boston, MA), 1995.
Children's Literature Review, Gale (Detroit, MI), Volume 19, 1990, Volume 54, 1999.
Drew, Bernard A., *The 100 Most Popular Young Adult Authors: Biographical Sketches and Bibliographies,* Libraries Unlimited, Inc., 1996.
Peters, Stephanie True, *Gary Paulsen,* Learning Works, 1999.
St. James Guide to Young-Adult Writers, St. James Press (Detroit, MI), 1999.
Salvner, Gary M., *Presenting Gary Paulsen,* Twayne (New York, NY), 1996.
Twentieth-Century Children's Writers, 4th edition, St. James Press (Detroit, MI), 1995.
Writers for Young Adults, Scribner (New York, NY), 1997.

PERIODICALS

Booklist, December 15, 1992, Hazel Rochman, review of *Nightjohn,* pp. 727-728; January 15, 1993, Ilene Cooper, review of *Eastern Sun, Winter Moon: An Autobiographical Odyssey,* p. 850; February 15, 1994, Hazel Rochman, review of *Winterdance: The Fine Madness of Running the Iditarod,* p. 1051; March 15, 1995, review of *Harris and Me: A Summer Remembered,* p. 1323; December 15, 1995, Hazel Rochman, review of *Brian's Winter,* p. 700; January 1, 1998, Stephanie Zvirin, review of *My Life in Dog Years,* p. 799; May 15, 1998, Roger Leslie, review of *The Transall Saga,* p. 1623; June 1, 1998, Carolyn Phelan, review of *Soldier's Heart: A Novel of the Civil War,* p. 1750; January 1, 1999, reviews of *My Life in Dog Years* and *Soldier's Heart,* p. 782, and Stephanie Zvirin, interview with Paulsen, p. 864; February 1, 1999, review of *Brian's Return,* p. 975, and Kay Weisman, review of *Canoe Days*, p. 982; February 15, 1999, Karen Harris, review of *Sarny: A Life Remembered*, p. 1084; June 1, 1999, Roger Leslie, review of *Alida's Song*, p. 1816; December 1, 1999, Kay Weisman, review of *Tucket's Gold*, p. 707; July, 2000, review of *The Beet Fields: Memories of a Sixteenth Summer*, p. 2033; August, 2000, Gillian Engberg, review of *The White Fox Chronicles*, p. 2131; September 1, 2000, Kay Weisman, review of *Tucket's Home*, p. 119; December 1, 2000, Stephanie Zvirin, review of *The Beet Fields*, p. 693; February 15, 2001, Kelly Milner Halls, review of *Guts: The True Story behind Hatchet and the Brian Books*, p. 1128; August, 2001, Elaine Hanson, review of *Tucket's Home*, p. 2142; September 15, 2001, review of *Caught by the Sea: My Life on Boats*, p. 222; December 15, 2002, GraceAnne A. DeCandido, review of *How Angel Peterson Got His Name, and Other Outrageous Tales about Extreme Sports*, p. 754; August, 2003, Kathleen Odean, review of *Shelf Life: Stories by the Book*, p. 1983; September 1, 2003, Ilene Cooper, review of *The Glass Café; or, The Stripper and the State: How My Mother Started a War with the System That Made Us Kind of Rich and a Little Bit Famous*, p. 115; January 1, 2004, Michael Cart, review of *Brian's Hunt*, p. 848; May 15, 2004, Hazel Rochman, review of *The Quilt*, p. 1632; January 1, 2005, Cindy Welch, review of *The Time Hackers*, p. 860; July 1, 2006, Todd Morning, review of *The Amazing Life of Birds: The Twenty-Day Puberty Journal of Duane Homer Leech*, p. 52; February 15, 2009, Ian Chipman, review of *Mudshark*, p. 83; August 1, 2009, Daniel Kraus, review of *Notes from the Dog*, p. 70; January 1, 2010, Ian Chipman, review of *Woods Runner*, p. 72; October 1, 2010, Carolyn Phelan, review of *Masters of Disaster*, p. 91.

Bulletin of the Center for Children's Books, February, 1993, review of *Nightjohn*, pp. 187-188; January, 1994, review of *Harris and Me*, pp. 164-165; June, 1995, review of *The Tent: A Parable in One Sitting*, pp. 356-357; October, 1995, review of *The Rifle*, pp. 64-65; March, 1998, review of *My Life in Dog Years*, pp. 254-255; September, 1998, review of *Soldier's Heart*, p. 26; September, 1999, review of *Alida's Song*, pp. 26-27; October, 2000, review of *The Beet Fields*, p. 79; February, 2003, review of *How Angel Peterson Got His Name, and Other Outrageous Tales about Extreme Sports*, p. 247.

Horn Book, July-August, 1983, Dorcas Hand, review of *Dancing Carl*, pp. 446-447; November-December, 1990, review of *Woodsong*, p. 762; November, 1998, Nancy Vasilakis, review of *Soldier's Heart*, p. 737, and Kristi Beavin, review of *Sarny*, p. 768; January, 1999, review of *Brian's Return*, p. 69; September, 2001, review of *Three Days*, p. 590; July-August, 2007, Abby Carter, review of *Lawn Boy*, p. 402; September-October, 2009, Susan Dove Lempke, review of *Notes from the Dog*, p. 572; July-August, 2010, Betty Carter, review of *Lawn Boy Returns*, p. 118; March-April, 2010, Roger Sutton, review of *Woods Runner*, p. 66.

Journal of Adolescent and Adult Literacy, April, 2010, Lisa Arter, review of *Notes from the Dog*, p. 615.

Journal of Adolescent & Adult Literacy, October, 2004, Jo Ann Yazzie, review of *The Glass Café*, p. 175.

Kirkus Reviews, July 15, 1987, review of *The Crossing*, p. 1074; June 15, 1991, review of *The River*, p. 792; January 1, 1993, review of *Eastern Sun, Winter Moon*, p. 48; January 1, 1993, review of *Nightjohn*, p. 67; June 1, 2003, review of *The Glass Café*, p. 809; November 15, 2003, review of *Brian's Hunt*, p. 1362; April 1, 2004, review of *The Quilt*, p. 335; September 1, 2004, review of *Molly McGinty Has a Really Good Day*, p. 872; May 15, 2007, review of *Lawn Boy*; April 1, 2009, review of *Mudshark*; January 1, 2010, review of *Woods Runner*.

Kliatt, March, 2003, Jennifer Banas, review of *Guts*, p. 44; July, 2003, Paula Rohrlick, review of *The Glass Café*, p. 16; January, 2004, Paula Rohrlick, review of *Brian's Hunt*, pp. 10-11; May, 2004, Tom Adamich, review of *Caught by the Sea*, p. 34; May, 2006, Paula Rohrlick, review of *The Amazing Life of Birds*, p. 13; July, 2006, Janis Flint-Ferguson, review of *The Legend of Bass Reeves: Being the True and Fictional Account of the Most Valiant Marshal in the West*, p. 12.

Language Arts, September, 1984, Ronald A. Jobe, review of *Tracker*, p. 527.

Los Angeles Times Book Review, March 21, 1993, Tim Winton, "His Own World War," pp. 1, 11.

New York Times Book Review, August 26, 2006, Anne Goodwin Sides, "On the Road and between the Pages, an Author Is Restless for Adventure"

Publishers Weekly, September 29, 1989, review of *The Winter Room*, p. 69; December 14, 1992, review of *Nightjohn*, p. 58; July 3, 1995, review of *Call Me Francis Tucket*, p. 62; August 11, 1997, review of *Sarny*, p. 403; May 25, 1998, review of *The Transall Saga*, p. 91; July 20, 1998, review of *Soldier's Heart*, p. 221; January 11, 1999, review of *Brian's Return*, p. 26; May 31, 1999, review of *Alida's Song*, pp. 94-95; September 6, 1999, review of *Sarny*, p. 106; February 14, 2000, Leonard S. Marcus, interview with Paulsen, p. 98; June 26, 2000, review of *The White Fox Chronicles*, p. 75; September 4, 2000, review of *The Beet Fields*, p. 109; June 25, 2001, review of *Canoe Days*, p. 75; November 18, 2002, review of *Guts*, p. 63; January 20, 2003, review of *How Angel Peterson Got His Name*, p. 83; June 30, 2003, reviews of *Shelf Life*, p. 79, and *The Glass Café*, p. 81; August 30, 2004, review of *Molly McGinty Has a Really Good Day*, p. 56; January 24, 2005, review of *The Time Hackers*, p. 245; June 11, 2007, review of *Lawn Boy*, p. 61; April 20, 2009, review of *Mudshark*, p. 50; July 20, 2009, review of *Notes from the Dog*, p. 141.

Riverbank Review, spring, 1999, Gary Paulsen, "The True Face of War," pp. 25-26.

School Library Journal, August, 1993, Carol Clark, review of *Eastern Sun, Winter Moon*, pp. 208-209; January, 1994, Lee Bock, review of *Harris and Me*, p. 132; May, 1995, Tom S. Hurlburt, review of *The Tent*, p. 122; August, 1995, review of *Winterdance*, p. 38; November, 1996, Mollie Bynum, review of *Puppies, Dogs, and Blue Northers: Reflections on Being Raised by a Pack of Sled Dogs*, p. 130; June, 1997, David Gale, "The Maximum Expression of Being Human," pp. 24-29; September, 1997, Bruce Anne Shook, review of *Sarny*, p. 224; March, 1998, review of *Woodsong*, p. 238; May, 1998, John Peters, review of *The Transall Saga*, p. 147; September, 1998, Steve Engelfried, review of *Soldier's Heart*, p. 206; August, 1999, Suzette Kragenbrink, review of *The Transall Saga*, p. 70; October, 1999, Coop Renner, review of *Tucket's Gold*, p. 156; January, 2000, Barbara S. Wysocki, review of *Soldier's Heart*, p. 74; August, 2000, Trish Anderson, review of *The White Fox Chronicles*, p. 188; September, 2000, Vicki Reutter, review of *The Beet Fields*, and Victoria Kidd, review of *Tucket's Home*, p. 235; October, 2001, Vicki Reutter, review of *Caught by the Sea*, p. 190; February, 2003, Vicki Reutter, review of *How Angel Peterson Got His Name*, p. 168; August, 2003, Edward Sullivan, review of *Shelf Life*, p. 164; November, 2003, Carol Fazioli, review of *The Beet Fields*, p. 84; December, 2003, Sean George, review of *Brian's Hunt*, p. 158; May, 2004, Vicki Reutter, review of *Guts*, p. 65, and review of *Winterdance*, p. 66, and Edith Ching, review of *The Quilt*, p. 156; September, 2004, Jean Gaffney, review of *Molly McGinty Has a Really Good Day*, p. 215; January, 2005, Diana Pierce, review of *The Time Hackers*, pp. 134-135; August, 2006, Laurie Slagenwhite, review of *The Legend of Bass Reeves*, p. 128; June, 2007, Kathryn Kosiorek, review of *Lawn Boy*, p. 157; May, 2009, Caitlin Augusta, review of *Mudshark*, p. 116; September, 2009, Alison Follos, review of *Notes from the Dog*, p. 170; February, 2010, Denise Moore, review of *Woods Runner*, p. 122; June, 2010, Terry Ann Lawler, review of *Lawn Boy Returns*, p. 116; November, 2010, Elaine E. Knight, review of *Masters of Disaster*, p. 124.

Voice of Youth Advocates, December, 1985, Nel Ward, review of *Dogsong*, pp. 321-322; June, 1988, Evie Wilson, review of *The Island*, pp. 89-90; February, 1994, Penny Blubaugh, review of *Harris and Me*, p. 371; April, 1994, review of *Mr. Tucket*, p. 29; October, 1994, review of *Winterdance*, p. 234; February, 1996, review of *The Rifle*, p. 375; February, 1997, Helen Turner, review of *Brian's Winter*, p. 332, and review of *Puppies, Dogs, and Blue Northers*, p. 352; April, 1998, reviews of *Hatchet*, p. 42, and *My Life in Dog Years*, p. 71.

Wilson Library Bulletin, January, 1993, Frances Bradburn, review of *Nightjohn*, pp. 87-88.

Writer, June, 2004, Sharon Miller Cindrich, "Gary Paulsen's Love Affair with Writing," p. 22.

Writer's Digest, January, 1980, F. Serdahely, "Prolific Paulsen."

ONLINE

Random House Web site, http://www.randomhouse.com/ (July 15, 2011), "Gary Paulsen."*

*   *   *

POGUE, David 1963-

Personal

Born March 9, 1963, in Shaker Heights, OH; son of Richard (an attorney) and Patricia Pogue; married; children: three. *Education:* Yale University, B.A. (music; summa cum laude), 1985. *Hobbies and other interests:* Playing piano, performing magic.

Addresses

Home—CT. *E-mail*—david@pogueman.com; pogue@nytimes.com.

Career

Technology journalist, commentator, composer, and author. Music Theatre International, New York, NY, conductor or arranger for musical stage productions; composer of musical scores. Freelance journalist, beginning 1988; correspondent and commentator for *New York Times*, beginning 2000, and other media outlets, including Columbia Broadcasting Service and CNBC. Host of television series *It's All Geek to Me*, 2007, and *Making Stuff*, 2011. Teacher of beginning magic at New School for Social Research and Learning Annex, New York, NY, c. 1990s. Keynote speaker at conferences and other gatherings focusing on business, education, and technology.

Awards, Honors

Honorary D.Mus., Shenandoah University, 2007; Gerald Loeb Award for Distinguished Business Journalism, 2010, for *Pogue's Posts* Web log.

Writings

FICTION

Hard Drive (adult novel), 1993.
Abby Carnelia's One and Only Magical Power, Roaring Brook Press (New York, NY), 2010.

NONFICTION

Macs for Dummies, IDG Books Worldwide (San Mateo, CA), 1992, foreword by John Kander, 1996, new edition, John Wiley & Co. (Hoboken, NJ), 2004.
(With Joseph Schorr) *Macworld Macintosh Secrets*, IDG Books (San Mateo, CA), 1993, new edition, 1999.
(With Joseph Schorr) *Macworld Mac and Power Mac Secrets*, IDG Books (San Mateo, CA), 1994.
More Macs for Dummies, foreword by Carly Simon, IDG Books (San Mateo, CA), 1994.
Macworld Mac FAQs, IDG Books (Foster City, CA), 1995.
(With Scott Speck) *Classical Music for Dummies*, preface by Zarin Mehta, foreword by Glenn Dicterow, IDG Books (Foster City, CA), 1997.
(With Scott Speck) *Opera for Dummies*, foreword by Roger Pines, IDG Books (Foster City, CA), 1997.
(Editor) *The Microsloth Joke Book: A Satire*, Berkley Books (New York, NY), 1997.

(With Enfert Fenton) *The Weird Wide Web,* IDG Books (Foster City, CA), 1997.

Magic for Dummies, IDG Books (Foster City, CA), 1998.

(Editor) *Tales from the Tech Line: Hilarious Strange-but-True Stories from the Computer Industry's Technical-Support Hotlines,* Berkley Books (New York, NY), 1998.

The Great Macintosh Easter Egg Hunt, Berkley Books (New York, NY), 1998.

The iMac for Dummies, IDG Books (Foster City, CA), 1998.

(With Adam C. Engst) *Crossing Platforms: A Macintosh/Windows Phrasebook,* O'Reilly (Sebastopol, CA), 1999.

PalmPilot: The Ultimate Guide, O'Reilly (Sebastopol, CA), 1999.

The iBook for Dummies, IDG Books (Foster City, CA), 2000.

The Flat Screen iMac for Dummies, John Wiley & Sons (New York, NY), 2002.

(With Andrea Butter) *Piloting Palm: The Inside Story of Palm, Handspring, and the Birth of the Billion-dollar Handheld Industry,* John Wiley & Sons (New York, NY), 2002.

The World according to Twitter, Workman Publishing (New York, NY), 2009.

Author's work has been translated into numerous languages.

"MISSING MANUAL" SERIES

Mac OS 9, Pogue Press/O'Reilly (Sebastopol, CA), 2000.

Windows Me, Pogue Press/O'Reilly (Sebastopol, CA), 2000.

iMovie, Pogue Press/O'Reilly (Sebastopol, CA), 2000.

iMovie 2, Pogue Press/O'Reilly (Sebastopol, CA), 2001.

Mac OS X, Pogue Press/O'Reilly (Sebastopol, CA), 2002.

(With Joseph Schorr and Derrick Story) *iPhoto,* Pogue Press/O'Reilly (Sebastopol, CA), 2002.

iMovie 3 and iDVD, Pogue Press/O'Reilly (Sebastopol, CA), 2003.

Mac OS X Panther Edition, Pogue Press/O'Reilly (Sebastopol, CA), 2003.

Switching to the Mac, Pogue Press/O'Reilly (Sebastapol, CA), 2003.

(With Craig Zacker and LJ. Zacker) *Windows XP Pro,* Pogue Press/O'Reilly (Sebastopol, CA), 2003.

(With Joseph Schorr and Derrick Story) *iPhoto 2,* Pogue Press/O'Reilly (Sebastapol, CA), 2003.

GarageBand, Pogue Press/O'Reilly (Sebastopol, CA), 2004.

iLife '04, Pogue Press/O'Reilly (Sebastopol, CA), 2004.

iMovie 4 and iDVD, Pogue Press/O'Reilly (Sebastopol, CA), 2004.

Windows XP Home Edition, Pogue Press/O'Reilly (Sebastopol, CA), 2004.

(With Craig Zacker and L.J. Zacker) *Windows XP Pro,* Pogue Press/O'Reilly (Sebastopol, CA), 2004.

(With Derrick Story) *iPhoto 4,* Pogue Press/O'Reilly (Sebastopol, CA), 2004.

(Editor) J.D. Biersdorfer, *iPod and iTunes,* Pogue Press/O'Reilly (Sebastopol, CA), 2004, new edition, 2006.

GarageBand 2, Pogue Press/O'Reilly (Sebastopol, CA), 2005.

iMovie HD and iDVD 5: The Missing Manual, Pogue Press/O'Reilly (Sebastopol, CA), 2005.

Mac OS X, Tiger Edition, Pogue Press/O'Reilly (Sebastopol, CA), 2005.

iLife '05, Pogue Press/O'Reilly (Sebastopol, CA), 2005.

(With David Storey) *iPhoto 5,* Pogue Press/O'Reilly (Sebastopol, CA), 2005.

(Editor) David Sawyer McFarland, *Dreamweaver 8,* Pogue Press/O'Reilly (Sebastopol, CA), 2006.

(With J.D. Biersdorfer) *The Internet,* Pogue Press/O'Reilly (Sebastopol, CA), 2006.

iMovie 6 and iDVD, Pogue Press/O'Reilly (Sebastopol, CA), 2006.

Windows Vista, Pogue Press/O'Reilly (Sebastopol, CA), 2006.

(With Derrick Story) *iPhoto 6,* Pogue Press/O'Reilly (Sebastopol, CA), 2006.

Mac OS X Leopard Edition, Pogue Press/O'Reilly (Sebastopol, CA), 2007.

Windows Vista for Starters, O'Reilly (Sebastopol, CA), 2007.

iMovie '08 and iDVD, Pogue Press/O'Reilly (Sebastopol, CA), 2007.

iPhone, Pogue Press/O'Reilly (Sebastopol, CA), 2007.

Switching to the Mac: Leopard Edition, Pogue Press/O'Reilly (Sebastopol, CA), 2008.

(With Derrick Story) *iPhoto '08,* Pogue Press/O'Reilly (Sebastopol, CA), 2008.

(With J.D. Biersdorfer) *iPod,* Pogue Press/O'Reilly (Sebastapol, CA), 2008.

David Pogue's Digital Photography, Pogue Press/O'Reilly (Sebastopol, CA), 2009.

MAC OS X: Snow Leopard, Pogue Press/O'Reilly (Sebastopol, CA), 2009.

Switching to the Mac: Snow Leopard Edition, Pogue Press/O'Reilly (Sebastopol, CA), 2009.

(With Aaron Miller) *iMovie '09 and iDVD,* Pogue Press/O'Reilly (Sebastopol, CA), 2009.

(With J.D. Biersdorfer) *iPhoto '09,* Pogue Press/O'Reilly (Sebastopol, CA), 2009.

Windows 7, Pogue Press/O'Reilly (Sebastopol, CA), 2010.

(With Aaron Miller) *iMovie '11 and iDVD,* Pogue Press/O'Reilly (Sebastopol, CA), 2011.

(With Lesa Snider) *iPhoto '11,* Pogue Press/O'Reilly (Sebastopol, CA), 2011.

Author of "State of the Art" column in *New York Times,* beginning 2000; contributor to periodicals, including *Macworld,* beginning 1988, and *Scientific American.*

Adaptations

Abby Carnelia's One and Only Magical Power was adapted for audiobook, Brilliance Audio, 2010.

Sidelights

Technology writer David Pogue has made a name for himself by helping people keep track of the constantly upgraded electronic gadgetry and programs that are wo-

Cover of David Pogue's middle-grade novel Abby Carnelia's One and Only Magical Power, *featuring artwork by Antonio Cáparo.* (Jacket illustration copyright © 2010 by Antonio Caparo. Reproduced with permission of Roaring Brook Press, a division of Holtzbrinck Publishing Holdings Limited.)

ven into our daily life: from smart phones and iPhones to new-generation operating systems to digital cameras and flat-screen television. In addition to his helpful "Missing Manual" books, which allow purchasers to opt for a paper guidebook rather than run the gauntlet of online "Help" menus when learning to operate new electronic devices, Pogue has also contributed to the long-running "Dummies" series, writes a technology column for the *New York Times,* and has hosted television specials and appeared as an on-air technological expert. While his 2009 book *The World according to Twitter* was novel in its use of "tweets" from 500,000 of his Twitter followers, Pogue entered an even more

unusual arena with *Abby Carnelia's One and Only Magical Power,* a novel for upper-elementary and middle-grade readers.

In *Abby Carnelia's One and Only Magical Power* Pogue draws on his love of magic, an interest he has had since childhood. The novel's eleven-year-old heroine discovers, while making a salad, that she has a magical ability when she tugs on her earlobes and the hardboiled egg on the counter in front of her starts to spin. Excited by her new talent but unsure what purpose it might serve, Abby attends Camp Cadabra, where she meets other children with interesting but often just-as-useless skills. More than eggs start spinning out of control when she learns, too late, that Camp Cadabra is actually a cover for something quite sinister in a novel that *Booklist* critic Kara Dean commended for its "leisurely pace" and "snappy dialogue." In *School Library Journal* Amanda Raklovits also noted the accessibility of Pogue's story, writing that his "original" idea and mix of "short chapters and plenty of dialogue" will keep children turning the pages. "Abby is bright and fully sympathetic," asserted a *Kirkus Reviews* writer, the critic adding that *Abby Carnelia's One and Only Magical Power* "makes the nice point that all kids are special, magical power or no."

Biographical and Critical Sources

PERIODICALS

Booklist, May 15, 2010, Kara Dean, review of *Abby Carnelia's One and Only Magical Power,* p. 52.
Kirkus Reviews, April 15, 2010, review of *Abby Carnelia's One and Only Magical Power.*
New York Times Book Review, July 18, 2010, Susannah Meadows, review of *Abby Carnelia's One and Only Magical Power,* p. 15.
School Library Journal, May, 2010, Amanda Raklovits, review of *Abby Carnelia's One and Only Magical Power,* p. 121.

ONLINE

David Pogue Home Page, http://www.davidpogue.com (May 2, 2011).
Pogue's Posts Web log, http://pogue.blogs.nytimes.com/ (June 27, 2011).*

R

RAVE, Friederike 1970-

Personal

Born 1970, in Flensburg, Germany. *Education:* University of Wuppertal, degree (communication design and illustration), 2002.

Addresses

Home—Wuppertal, Germany. *E-mail*—friederike.rave@rave-illustrationen.de.

Career

Illustrator, graphic artist, and author.

Writings

SELF-ILLUSTRATED

Der Fuchs, die Hüner und das Wurstbrot, NordSüd (Zürich, Switzerland), 2010, translated as *Outfoxing the Fox,* NorthSouth (New York, NY), 2010.
Es begab sich aber zu der Zeit die Weihnachtsgeschichte nach dem Lukasevangelium, Präsenz Kunst & Buch (Hünfelden-Gnadenthal, Germany), 2010.

ILLUSTRATOR

Dieter Vieweger and Claudia Voigt, *Das Geheimnis des Tells—Eine archäologische Reise in den Orient,* Philipp Von Zabern Verlag (Mainz am Rhein, Germany), 2005.
Henning Mankell, *Der Hund de unterwegs zu einem Stern war,* Cornelson Verlag (Berlin, Germany), 2006.
Barbara Wohlrab, *Helden der City. Ein Leseprojekt zu dem gleichnamigen Jugendbuch von Kristina Dunker,* Cornelsen (Berlin, Germany), 2007.
Ursula Poznanski, *Pauline Pechfee,* Residenz Verlag (St. Pölten, Austria), 2007.

Benno Pludra, *Jacob Heimatlos. Ein Leseprojekt zu dem gleichnamigen* (novel), Cornelsen Verlag (Berlin, Germany), 2007.
Monika Wittmann, *Meine großes Wimmel-und-Wörterbuch,* Carlsen (Hamburg, Germany), book 5: *Ritter und Burgen,* 2008, book 6: *Die Jahreszeiten,* 2009.
Bruno Hachler, *Annas Wunsch,* NordSüd (Zürich, Switzerland), 2008, translated as *Anna's Wish,* NorthSouth (New York, NY), 2008.
Claudia Haas and others, *Ich fahr Rad! Sicher unterwegs im Straßenverkehr,* Sauerländer (Düsseldorf, Germany), 2008.
Cornelia Witzmann, *Behalt das Leben leib. Ein Leseprojekt zu dem gleichnamingen Roman von Jaap ter Haar,* Cornelsen (Berlin, Germany), 2008.
Corinna Gieseler, *Die Elfe mit den Gummistiefeln,* Ellermann (Hamburg, Germany), 2009.
Isabelle Erler, *Mein Körper,* Carlsen (Hamburg, Germany), 2009.
Ursula Poznanski, *Theo Piratenkönig,* Rezidenz Verlag (St. Pölten, Austria), 2010.
Brigitte Hoffman, *Strand und Watt,* Carlsen (Hamburg, Germany), 2010.
Gabriele Klassmann, *Die Schatten wachsen in der dämmerung. Ein Leseprojekt zu dem gleichnamigen Jugendbuch von Henning Mankell,* Cornelsen (Berlin, Germany), 2010.
Thilo Guschas, *Weltreligionen,* Carlsen (Hamburg, Germany), 2011.
Bruno Hächler, *Die lustige Osterwerkstatt,* NordSüd (Zürich, Switzerland), 2011.
Andrea Erne, *Pixi Wissen, Band 63: Steinzeit,* Carlsen (Hamburg, Germany), 2011.
Donatella Capriz, *Paola, Fabio und das Familienfest,* Carlsen (Hamburg, Germany), 2011.

Works featuring Rave's art have been translated into Chinese and French.

Biographical and Critical Sources

PERIODICALS

Booklist, October 15, 2008, Carolyn Phelan, review of *Anna's Wish,* p. 44.

Kirkus Reviews, September 15, 2008, review of *Anna's Wish.*

School Library Journal, October, 2008, Donna Cardon, review of *Anna's Wish,* p. 110; May, 2010, Samantha Larsen Hastings, review of *Outfoxing the Fox,* p. 90.

ONLINE

Friederike Rave Home Page, http://www.rave-illustra tionen.de (May 2, 2011).*

*   *   *

ROCKWELL, Thomas 1933-

Personal

Born March 13, 1933, in New Rochelle, NY; son of Norman (an artist) and Mary Rockwell; married Gail Sudler (an artist), July 16, 1955; children: Barnaby, Abigail. *Education:* Bard College, B.A., 1956.

Addresses

Home—Poughkeepsie, NY. *Agent*—Joan Raines, Raines & Raines Agency, 71 Park Ave., Ste. 4A, New York, NY 10016.

Career

Writer. Worked variously in book sales, as a teacher, and in television and advertising.

Awards, Honors

Mark Twain Award, California Young Readers' Medal, and Golden Archer Award, all 1975, South Carolina Children's Book Award, Massachusetts Children's Book Award, Sequoyah Award, and Nene Award, all 1976, Young Hoosier Book Award, 1977, Arizona Young Readers' Award, and Tennessee Children's Choice selection, both 1979, and Iowa Children's Choice selection, 1980, all for *How to Eat Fried Worms.*

Writings

FOR CHILDREN

Rackety-Bang and Other Verses, illustrated by wife, Gail Rockwell, Pantheon (New York, NY), 1969.

Humpf!, illustrated by Muriel Batherman, Pantheon (New York, NY), 1971.

Squawwwk!, illustrated by Gail Rockwell, Little, Brown (Boston, MA), 1972.

The Neon Motorcycle, illustrated by Michael Horen, F. Watts (New York, NY), 1973.

How to Eat Fried Worms (also see below), illustrated by Emily McCully, F. Watts (New York, NY), 1973.

Hiding Out, illustrated by Charles Molina, Bradbury (Scarsdale, NY), 1974.

The Portmanteau Book, illustrated by Gail Rockwell, Little, Brown (Boston, MA), 1974.

Tin Cans, illustrated by Saul Lambert, Bradbury (Scarsdale, NY), 1975.

The Thief, illustrated by Gail Rockwell, Delacorte (New York, NY), 1977.

How to Eat Fried Worms, and Other Plays, illustrated by Joel Schick, Delacorte (New York, NY), 1980.

Hey, Lover Boy, Delacorte (New York, NY), 1981.

Oatmeal Is Not for Mustaches, illustrated by Eileen Christelow, Holt (New York, NY), 1984.

How to Fight a Girl (sequel to *How to Eat Fried Worms*), illustrated by Gioia Fiammenghi, Franklin Watts (New York, NY), 1987.

How to Get Fabulously Rich, illustrated by Anne Canevari Green, Franklin Watts (New York, NY), 1990.

Emily Stew: With Some Side Dishes, illustrated by David McPhail, Roaring Brook Press (New York, NY), 2010.

OTHER

Norman Rockwell's Hometown, illustrated by father, Norman Rockwell, Windmill Books (New York, NY), 1970.

(Coauthor) Norman Rockwell, *Norman Rockwell: My Adventures as an Illustrator,* Curtis Publishing (Indianapolis, IN), 1979.

(Editor) *The Best of Norman Rockwell,* Courage Books (Philadelphia, PA), 1988.

Adaptations

How to Eat Fried Worms was adapted as a television film, 1985, and as a feature film by Bob Dolman, New Line Cinema, 2006.

Sidelights

In his writing for children, Thomas Rockwell fashions stories from a unique mix of outlandish elements and universal, sometimes serious issues. Rockwell's books are also distinguished by their irreverent tone and sometimes crude humor, a humor that appeals to young readers while raising adult eyebrows. Despite the penchant for fun exhibited in books such as *Squawwwk!, How to Eat Fried Worms, The Portmanteau Book, Oatmeal Is Not for Mustaches,* and *How to Get Fabulously Rich,* he takes his young audience seriously; as he mused in his Sequoyah Award acceptance speech (as transcribed in *Oklahoma Librarian*), "I suppose one of the reasons I write books for children is because I feel I can be more outrageous than if I were writing for adults." In a review of *The Portmanteau Book,* a *Kirkus Reviews* contributor concluded of Rockwell that he "doesn't intend to please grownups." In fact, the critic added, "his readiness to offend them is the basis of his appeal."

Rockwell grew up in rural Vermont, the second son of renowned painter and *Saturday Evening Post* cover illustrator Norman Rockwell. While his siblings were

Thomas Rockwell entices young readers with his intriguingly titled **How to Eat Fried Worms,** *a story featuring illustrations by Emily Mc-Cully.* (Illustration copyright © 2006 by Yearling, an imprint of Random House Children's Books. Used by permission of Yearling, an imprint of Random House Children's Books, a division of Random House, Inc.)

drawn to art, young Rockwell was more intrigued by the written word. Although his interest in children's literature waned as he grew older, it was rekindled once he became a father and read to his own young son. Rockwell's first literary venture, *Rackety-Bang and Other Verses,* was published in 1969 and prompted *Library Journal* contributor Barbara Gibson to credit the author with a "fertile imagination."

Rockwell produced several other children's stories, including *Humpf!, Squawwwk!,* and *The Neon Motorcycle,* before securely establishing his position as a children's author with 1973's *How to Eat Fried Worms.* Eventually adapted as a play and also filmed, *How to Eat Fried Worms* details Billy Forrester's fifty-dollar bet with a group of skeptical friends that he can eat fifteen worms in fifteen days. A budding culinary genius, Billy dreams up various worm-based menus, such as fried worm with ketchup, mustard, and horseradish and baked worm with onions and sour cream. As Billy methodically executes his side of the bargain, his friends realize that they had better scramble in order to produce the expected cash. In *Childhood Education* Patricia Tonkin dubbed *How to Eat Fried Worms* "fun" while warning "nervous parents" of the possibility that copycat readers will take the same dare as Billy. A *Booklist* reviewer branded the work "a hilarious story that will revolt and delight" and singled out Rockwell's "colorful, original writing" for special praise.

Billy Forrester returns in several other stories. In *How to Fight a Girl* he uses his winnings from the bet to purchase a new bicycle. By constantly showing off,

however, Billy tries the patience of his friends, however, and soon they are plotting to find a way to motivate his mom to confiscate the bike. *How to Get Fabulously Rich* finds the preteen casting about for a moneymaking venture and deciding to purchase a lottery ticket. With the help of one friend old enough to purchase the ticket and with numbers selected by his baby sister, Billy wins. Unfortunately, the boy and his parents have totally different ideas about what to buy with the money. Rockwell has "a knack for capturing the feelings of kids," according to a *Bulletin of the Center for Children's Books* reviewer, and Cynthia Samuels noted in the *Washington Post Book World* that *How to Fight a Girl* is a "sweet and decent tale." Appraising *How to Get Fabulously Rich,* a reviewer for the *Bulletin of the Center for Children's Books* praised its "unsentimental, uncondescending vision" of a boy's life, and a *Publishers Weekly* critic cited Rockwell's "highly dramatic" prose style and "lighthearted and fanciful storytelling."

Since the success of *How to Eat Fried Worms,* Rockwell has continued to intermittently produce distinctive books for young readers, teaming up with a variety of illustrators that include David McPhail, Gail Rockwell, and Gioia Fiammenghi. He offers a mixed bag of activities in *The Portmanteau Book,* as his use of the word *portmanteau*—something combining more than one use—conveys the nature of the book which offers a hodgepodge of stories, poems, and quizzes. Even the index doles out zany bits of information. A reviewer for *Booklist* explained that the book's "diversity of content and levels of meaning defy pigeonholing."

Tin Cans functions as both a fantasy and a moralizing story about the methods used to obtain wanted goods. The tale concerns David who, while visiting his aunt, meets Jane, a foster child who survives by scrounging at garbage dumps. The duo finds a magic Campbell's soup can that, when pointed at an object, will retrieve it. A conflict ensues, however, when the pair debates—from starkly different socio-economic vantage points—the ethics of keeping the device. Carolyn Johnson, writing in *School Library Journal,* assessed *Tin Cans* as a "smooth fantasy [that] moves to a credible conclusion."

Rockwell returns to a light-hearted subject in *Hey, Lover Boy,* as seventh grader Paul demonstrates his skill at playing pranks on his classmates. The situation is reversed, however, when one of Paul's victims, Margaret, decides to seek revenge. The story's plot, coupled with Paul's education on the finer points of sex, produces what several reviewers contended is an accurate portrayal of middle-school life. A *Kirkus Reviews* contributor noted of *Hey, Lover Boy* that Rockwell's "funny story" is "told with . . . a real awareness of the intensities and overwhelming uncertainties of adolescence."

Praised by a *Kirkus Reviews* writer as a "wildly inventive poetic portrait of a riveting character, *Emily Stew: With Some Side Dishes* comes to life in engaging ink

Rockwell teams up with artist David McPhail to tell an imaginative story in **Emily Stew: With Some Side Dishes.** (Illustration copyright © 2010 by David McPhail. Reproduced with permission of Roaring Brook Press, a division of Holtzbrinck Publishing Holdings Limited.)

drawings by artist David McPhail. As readers learn from Rockwell's series of descriptive scenes, young Emily is a girl of many contradictions who exhibits extreme reactions to both real and imaginary things around her. Noting the book's appeal to both children and adults, the *Kirkus Reviews* writer added that the "sophisticated silliness" of Rockwell's rhyming text mixes humorous comments with "the occasional wry philosophical observation."

Biographical and Critical Sources

BOOKS

Children's Books and Their Creators, edited by Anita Silvey, Houghton (Boston, MA), 1995.

Children's Literature Review, Volume 6, Gale (Detroit, MI), 1984, pp. 234-240.

PERIODICALS

Booklist, November 15, 1973, review of *How to Eat Fried Worms,* p. 342; November 1, 1974, review of *The Portmanteau Book,* p. 294.

Bulletin of the Center for Children's Books, December, 1987, review of *How to Fight a Girl,* p. 74; December, 1990, review of *How to Get Fabulously Rich,* p. 99.

Childhood Education, March, 1974, Patricia Tonkin, review of *How to Eat Fried Worms,* p. 294.

Kirkus Reviews, November 15, 1974, review of *The Portmanteau Book,* p. 1205; September 1, 1981, review of *Hey, Lover Boy,* p. 108; January 1, 2010, review of *Emily Stew: With Some Side Dishes.*

Library Journal, October, 1969, Barbara Gibson, review of *Rackety-Bang and Other Verses,* p. 143.

New York Times, August 6, 2006, Kristopher Tapley, "Ick! Ugh! Luring Boys with Worms," p. AR14.

Oklahoma Librarian, July, 1976, Thomas Rockwell, transcript of Sequoyah Award Acceptance Speech, pp. 4-6, 15.

Publishers Weekly, May 26, 1969, review of *Rackety-Bang and Other Verses,* p. 55; September 28, 1990, review of *How to Get Fabulously Rich,* p. 103.

School Library Journal, October, 1975, Carolyn Johnson, review of *Tin Cans,* p. 101.

Washington Post Book World, November 8, 1987, Cynthia Samuels, "Doing the Real Right Thing," p. 18.

ROSS, Sylvia 1937-

Personal

Born 1937, in Los Angeles, CA; married Bob Ross (a teacher); children: four sons. *Ethnicity:* "Native American/Chukchansi." *Education:* Fresno State University, B.A. (writing; cum laude), 1969. *Hobbies and other interests:* Cooking, drawing, restoring old photographs.

Addresses

Home—CA.

Career

Educator, poet, and author/illustrator. Walt Disney Productions, Burbank, CA, worked in ink and paint department, 1954-58; teacher at Belleview Elementary School, Porterville, CA, c. 1970s; teacher at Vandalia Elementary School, Tule River Indian Reservation, Tulare County, CA.

Writings

(And illustrator) *Lion Singer,* Heyday Books (Berkeley, CA), 2005.

(And illustrator) *Blue Jay Girl,* Heyday Books (Berkeley, CA), 2010.

Contributor to periodicals, including *Dry Crik Review* and *News from Native California.* Work included in anthologies, including *The Dirt Is Red Here: Art and Poetr from Native California,* Heyday Books (Berkeley, CA), 2002; *Spring Salmon, Hurry to Me,* 2008; and *The Illuminated Landscape: A Sierra Nevada Anthology;* and to cookbook *Seaweed, Salmon, and Manzanita Cider: A California Indian Feast,* by Margaret Dubin and Sara-Larus Tolley, Heyday Books, 2008.

Biographical and Critical Sources

PERIODICALS

Children's Bookwatch, November, 2005, review of *Lion Singer.*

School Library Journal, October, 2005, DeAnn Tabuchi, review of *Lion Singer,* p. 127.

ONLINE

Heyday Books Web site, http://www.heydaybooks.com/ (June 15, 2011), "Sylvia Ross."*

S

SALERNI, Dianne K.

Personal

Married; husband's name Bob; children: Gabrielle, Gina. *Education:* University of Delaware, B.S. (elementary education); University of Pennsylvania, M.Ed. (language-arts education).

Addresses

Home—West Grove, PA. *Agent*—Sara Crowe, Harvey Klinger, Inc., sara@harveyklinger.com. *E-mail*—dksalerni@gmail.com.

Career

Educator and author. Avon Grove School District, PA, teacher of fourth-and fifth-grade students, beginning c. 1990. Presenter at schools.

Writings

High Spirits, iUniverse (e-book), 2007, published as *We Hear the Dead,* Sourcebooks (Naperville, IL), 2010.

Short fiction anthologized in *Visions,* three volumes, edited by C. Edward Sellner and Michael S. Katz, Strider Nolan Media, beginning 2009.

Adaptations

We Hear the Dead was optioned for film by Open Eye Studio.

Sidelights

In *We Hear the Dead,* her first novel for teen readers, teacher and writer Dianne K. Salerni draws on an actual story of the paranormal that took place in Hydesville, New York, in 1848. Interestingly, Salerni intended to write a humorous novel about a nineteenth-century spiritualist until her research led her to the story of two sisters, Maggie and Kate Fox. The fact that these two teens were able to captivate the nation and inspire an interest in contacting the spiritual realm fascinated Salerni and she knew that it would fascinate historical-fiction fans as well.

Living with their parents in Hydesville, New York, fourteen-year-old Maggie and eleven-year-old Kate become local celebrities when they claimed to have communicated, through rapping, with the spirit of a murder victim who was secretly buried in the basement of their home. Although the rapping was actually a ruse designed by the girls to frighten away a visiting cousin, Mrs. Fox took her daughters seriously and soon word of the sisters' strange ability has attracted even wider attention. Leah Fox Fish, their married older sister, convinces Maggie and Kate to continue the prank, realizing the potential money to be made from gullible people looking for reassurance from their dearly departed. As the sisters' spirit circles are reported in newspapers, they become nationally known as mediums and are alternately loved or reviled by the press and populace. Although she wanted to end the deception, Kate and Leah insisted that the ruse must continue, but Maggie's worries over her unusual career become increasingly complicated after she meets and falls in love with a well-known world explorer, Elisha Kent Kane. Although Maggie publicly exposed the deception four decades later, belief in the power of séances remained undiminished and has continued to this day.

In *We Hear the Dead* Salerni weaves Kane's actual correspondence with Maggie into her story, as well as including the verses he penned for his beloved. The book weaves these letters into a narrative that alternates Maggie's pragmatic perspective with that of Kate, who believed wholeheartedly that human spirits could be contacted in the afterlife. In addition to following the sisters' intertwined stories, the novel also "details . . . their troubled family dynamics," drawing on facts that "are inherently fascinating," according to *Booklist* critic

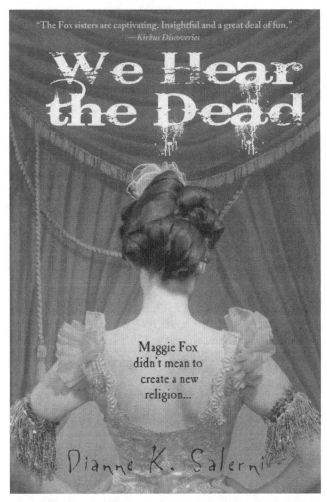

Cover of Dianne K. Salerni's We Hear the Dead, *an intriguingly told tale that is based on actual characters from the late 1800s.* (Cover image © Big Cheese Photo/Jupiter Images. Reproduced with permission of Sourcebooks Fire, an imprint of Sourcebooks, Inc.)

Gillian Engberg. Deeming *We Hear the Dead* to be an example of "historical fiction at its best," Maggie Knapp added in *School Library Journal* that Salerni "paints vivid scenes of life" as it was actually lived during the mid-nineteenth century.

Biographical and Critical Sources

PERIODICALS

Booklist, April 15, 2010, Gillian Engberg, review of *We Hear the Dead,* p. 58.

School Library Journal, June, 2010, Maggie Knapp, review of *We Hear the Dead,* p. 119.

Voice of Youth Advocates, June, 2010, Sarah Flowers, review of *We Hear the Dead,* p. 159.

ONLINE

Dianne Salerni Home Page, http://www.highspiritsbook.com (May 28, 2011).

Dianne Salerni Web log, http://diannesalerni.blogspot.com (May 28, 2011).

*   *   *

SCHERTLE, Alice 1941-

Personal

Surname rhymes with "turtle"; born April 7, 1941, in Los Angeles, CA; daughter of Floyd C. (a real estate investor) and Marguerite (a teacher) Sanger; married Richard Schertle (a general contractor), December 21, 1963; children: Jennifer, Katherine, John. *Education:* University of Southern California, B.S. (cum laude), 1963.

Addresses

Home—Plainfield, MA.

Career

Highland School, Inglewood, CA, elementary school teacher, 1963-65; writer, 1965—.

Member

National Council of Teachers of English, Authors Guild, Authors League, Society of Children's Book Writers and Illustrators.

Awards, Honors

Parents' Choice Picture Book Award, 1989, and Christopher Award, 1990, both for *William and Grandpa;* Parents' Choice Picture Book Award, 1991, for *Witch Hazel;* Best Books citation, *School Library Journal,* 1995, for *Advice for a Frog, and Other Poems;* National Parenting Publications Award, 1995, for *How Now, Brown Cow?,* and 1996, for *Down the Road;* Notable Children's Books citations, American Library Association, 1996, for both *Advice for a Frog, and Other Poems* and *Down the Road;* Oppenheim Toy Portfolio Gold Award, 2002, for *All You Need for a Snowman;* Children's Books of the Year selection, Bank Street College School of Education, and Myers Outstanding Book Award honorable mention, Gustavus Myers Center for the Study of Bigotry and Human Rights in North America, both 2007, both for *We.*

Writings

FOR CHILDREN

The Gorilla in the Hall, illustrated by Paul Galdone, Lothrop (New York, NY), 1977.

The April Fool, illustrated by Emily Arnold McCully, Lothrop (New York, NY), 1981.

Hob Goblin and the Skeleton, illustrated by Katherine Coville, Lothrop (New York, NY), 1982.

In My Treehouse, illustrated by Meredith Dunham, Lothrop (New York, NY), 1983.

Bim Dooley Makes His Move, illustrated by Victoria Chess, Lothrop (New York, NY), 1984.

Goodnight, Hattie, My Dearie, My Dove, illustrated by Linda Strauss, Lothrop (New York, NY), 1985, illustrated by Ted Rand, Harcourt (San Diego, CA), 2002.

My Two Feet, illustrated by Meredith Dunham, Lothrop (New York, NY), 1985.

That Olive!, illustrated by Cindy Wheeler, Lothrop (New York, NY), 1986.

Jeremy Bean's St. Patrick's Day, illustrated by Linda Shute, Lothrop (New York, NY), 1987.

Bill and the Google-eyed Goblins, illustrated by Patricia Coombs, Lothrop (New York, NY), 1987.

Gus Wanders Off, illustrated by Cheryl Harness, Lothrop (New York, NY), 1988.

William and Grandpa, illustrated by Lydia Dabcovich, Lothrop (New York, NY), 1989.

That's What I Thought, illustrated by John Wallner, Harper (New York, NY), 1990.

Witch Hazel, illustrated by Margot Tomes, Harper (New York, NY), 1991.

Little Frog's Song, illustrated by Leonard Everett Fisher, HarperCollins (New York, NY), 1992.

How Now, Brown Cow?, illustrated by Amanda Schaffer, Browndeer Press (San Diego, CA), 1994.

Down the Road, illustrated by Margot Tomes, HarperCollins (New York, NY), 1994, illustrated by E.B. Lewis, Browndeer Press (San Diego, CA), 1995.

Maisie, illustrated by Lydia Dabcovich, Lothrop (New York, NY), 1995.

Advice for a Frog, and Other Poems, illustrated by Norman Green, Lothrop (New York, NY), 1995.

Keepers, illustrated by Ted Rand, Lothrop (New York, NY), 1996.

I Am the Cat, illustrated by Mark Buehner, Harcourt (San Diego, CA), 1999.

A Lucky Thing, illustrated Wendell Minor, Harcourt (San Diego, CA), 1999.

All You Need for a Snowman, illustrated by Barbara Lavallee, Harcourt (San Diego, CA), 2002.

Teddy Bear, Teddy Bear, illustrated by Linda Hill Griffith, HarperCollins (New York, NY), 2003.

When the Moon Is High, illustrated by Julia Noonan, HarperCollins (New York, NY), 2003.

(Adapter into English) Alma Flor Ada and F. Isabel Campoy, *¡Pío Peep!: Traditional Spanish Nursery Rhymes,* illustrated by Viví Escrivá, HarperCollins (New York, NY), 2003.

The Skeleton in the Closet, HarperCollins (New York, NY), 2003.

All You Need for a Beach, Harcourt (San Diego, CA), 2004.

A Very Hairy Bear, Harcourt (San Diego, CA), 2004.

One, Two, I Love You, illustrated by Emily Arnold McCully, Chronicle Books (San Francisco, CA), 2004.

The Adventures of Old Bo Bear, illustrated by David Parkins, Chronicle Books (San Francisco, CA), 2006.

Very Hairy Bear, illustrated by Matt Phelan, Harcourt (Orlando, FL), 2007.

We, illustrated by Kenneth Addison, Lee & Low Books (New York, NY), 2007.

Button Up!: Wrinkled Rhymes, illustrated by Petra Mathers, Harcourt (Orlando, FL), 2008.

Little Blue Truck, illustrated by Jill McElmurry, Harcourt (Orlando, FL), 2008.

Jeremy Bean, illustrated by David Slonim, Chronicle Books (San Francisco, CA), 2008.

An Anaconda Ate My Homework!, illustrated by Aaron Renier, Disney/Hyperion Books (New York, NY), 2009.

Little Blue Truck Leads the Way, illustrated by Jill McElmurry, Harcourt Children's Books (Boston, MA), 2009.

Look out, Jeremy Bean!, illustrated by David Slonim, Chronicle Books (San Francisco, CA), 2009.

Work included in anthologies, including *Hamsters, Shells, and Spelling Bees: School Poems,* edited by Lee Bennett Hopkins, HarperCollins (New York, NY), 2008; and *Sky Matic,* edited by Hopkins, Dutton (New York, NY), 2009. Contributor to periodicals, including *Instructor* and *Storyworks.*

"CATHY AND COMPANY" SERIES

Cathy and Company and Mean Mr. Meeker, illustrated by Cathy Pavia, Children's Press (New York, NY), 1980.

Cathy and Company and Bumper the Bully, illustrated by Cathy Pavia, Children's Press (New York, NY), 1980.

Cathy and Company and the Green Ghost, illustrated by Cathy Pavia, Children's Press (New York, NY), 1980.

Cathy and Company and the Nosy Neighbor, illustrated by Cathy Pavia, Children's Press (New York, NY), 1980.

Cathy and Company and the Double Dare, illustrated by Cathy Pavia, Children's Press (New York, NY), 1980.

Cathy and Company and Hank the Horse, illustrated by Cathy Pavia, Children's Press (New York, NY), 1980.

Sidelights

A former elementary-grade teacher, Alice Schertle is the author of dozens of engaging books for children, among them *William and Grandpa, Down the Road, We,* and *Little Blue Truck Leads the Way.* "I write children's books because I love them—always have," Schertle once stated. "The various seasons of my childhood are identified in my memory with the books that were important to me then. There was the year Mary Poppins floated into the lives of Jane and Michael Banks and me. And my sixth-grade year I think I spent with *Black Stallion* [by Walter Farley] and [Marguerite Henry's] *King of the Wind.*" As an author who now provides such moments for new generations of young people, Schertle takes her work seriously; as she once asserted, "We who write for young children share the considerable responsibility and the wonderful opportunity of showing them that words can paint pictures too."

Schertle was born and raised in Los Angeles, California. "As a child, I could usually be found folded into some unlikely position (as often as not I was in a tree) either reading a story or trying to write one," she once told *SATA*. "My writing was always very much influenced by the book I was reading at the moment. *The Wizard of Oz* and *Mary Poppins* inspired me to try my hand at fantasy. *The Black Stallion* led to a rash of horse stories. And after a summer of reading Nancy Drew books, I churned out mysteries peppered with words like 'sleuth' and 'chum.'"

After graduating from the University of Southern California in 1963, Schertle married and began teaching elementary school students in Inglewood, California. Following the birth of her first child two years later, she left teaching to devote herself full time to raising what would soon be three children. It was not until 1975, when her kids were old enough to allow her some free time, that she began writing again. Her first book for children, *The Gorilla in the Hall*, tells the story of a young boy's vivid imagination and was published in 1977.

Although *The Gorilla in the Hall* received little notice from critics, Schertle's next book, *The April Fool*, was proclaimed a winner. An amusing story about a curmudgeonly king's search for a pair of shoes that will not hurt his feet, *The April Fool* was described by *School Library Journal* reviewer Patt Hays as "a satisfying story." For Schertle, the story "almost seem[ed] to write itself, from beginning to end. . . . I started with 'Once there was a king whose feet hurt,' and wrote through to 'the end' with scarcely a hitch along the way."

In her early work, Schertle often found story ideas in the activities of her three children. "*In My Treehouse* was inspired by my son's adventures in his own tree house," she once told *SATA*. "As a child, I spent a good deal of time in trees, so I took John up on his invitation to join him in his house in a big fruitless mulberry. In fact, I did a lot of writing up there, though I find they're not making tree houses as big as they used to." With *In My Treehouse* Schertle translates the experience of being in her son's tree fort into a book about a young boy's love of being apart from the hustle and bustle of the world at large, and about gaining independence.

Living with cats as well as with children provided Schertle the inspiration for *That Olive!*, a picture book about a mischievous kitty that Lucy Young Clem described in *School Library Journal* as "a hall-of-fame cat story." Andy spends a lot of time looking for his cat, Olive, and Olive spends a lot of time playing hide-and-seek with Andy. Only the lure of tunafish sandwiches brings the elusive Olive out into the open and into Andy's arms. Animals of another sort star in *Goodnight, Hattie, My Dearie, My Dove*, as Schertle deals with the familiar theme of the bedtime routine. First published in 1985 and reissued with new illustrations in 2002, this picture book describes how Hattie assembles a parade of stuffed animals to take to bed with her, creating a "reassuring and recognizable bedtime (and counting) story," as a *Kirkus Reviews* contributor noted.

Schertle focuses on multigenerational relationships in several of her books, among them the award-winning *William and Grandpa*. When Willie comes to stay with his lonely grandfather, the two share a host of simple activities—singing songs, catching shadows, making shaving cream moustaches, and telling old stories about Willie's father—that bond them into a close and loving relationship. "The continuity of generations and the warm relationship between children and the elderly are communicated equally through story and pictures," noted Carolyn Caywood in *School Library Journal*.

Another story about making friends, *Jeremy Bean's St. Patrick's Day* features a first grader whose excitement about his school's St. Patrick's Day party withers when he arrives at school and realizes that he has neglected to wear his green sweater. Noting Schertle's "clear prose and sympathetic observation of small children and their concerns," a *Kirkus Reviews* critic praised *Jeremy Bean's St. Patrick's Day* as a good book about making friends, even with school principals. The story is included in the chapter book *Look out, Jeremy Bean!*, which pairs illustrations by David Slonim with two additional stories that find the boy endeavoring to assemble a collection of something to show to his classmates as well as finding an unusual new pet hiding in a clump of dust under the couch. "Youngsters will empathize with the everyday occurrences in these funny, totally childlike tales," predicted Carrie Rogers-Whitehead in her review of *Look out Jeremy Bean!* for *School Library Journal*.

In *Witch Hazel*, which a *Publishers Weekly* writer called a "touching story of the triumph of imagination,"

Julia Noonan creates the evocative artwork in Alice Schertle's bedtime picture book **When the Moon Is High.** (Illustration © 2003 by Julia Noonan. Reproduced by permission of HarperCollins Children's Division, a division of HarperCollins Publishers.)

Schertle tells the story of Johnny, a young boy who is raised by his two grown brothers, Bill and Bart, after the death of their parents. Bill and Bart are farmers who can do without the young boy's help as they work their small farm. When they give their young brother some pumpkin seed and a branch of witch hazel, Johnny plants the seeds and makes a scarecrow lady out of the tree branch, dressing "her" in one of his mother's old dresses. When Bill and Bart leave Johnny and take their crop to market after the fall harvest, Johnny dreams that the scarecrow, "Witch Hazel," has tossed his huge orange pumpkin up into the sky, where it has remained, transformed into a full, round harvest moon.

Little Frog's Song tells of the adventures and fears of a young frog that is washed from his lily pad during a fierce rain shower and must now find his way home. "The text . . . is a song, rich with images and the rhythm of repetition reminiscent of the writing of Margaret Wise Brown," commented Katie Cerra in *Five Owls.* Equally lyrical is Schertle's *How Now, Brown Cow?*, in which everything from milking time to a cow's longing to jump the moon is covered in verse. A *Publishers Weekly* reviewer described *How Now, Brown Cow?* as "by turns funny and tender, cheeky and thoughtful" while *Booklist* critic Ilene Cooper dubbed it "beauteously bovine."

A number of Schertle's prose titles deal with family situations, such as *Maisie,* which gives an overview of Grandmother Maisie's life, and *Down the Road,* which recounts young Hetty's first experience going to the store alone. When Hetty is asked to go and buy eggs for the family's breakfast, she takes the responsibility seriously. Everything goes fine until she is homeward bound. Reaching up to pick an apple at the side of the road, she accidentally drops the fragile eggs on the ground. Hetty is afraid to return home empty-handed so she climbs the apple tree, where her worried parents eventually find and soothe her. As Martha V. Parravano commented in *Horn Book, Down the Road* unites themes of temptation and redemption with "a modern lesson in supportive parenting techniques," thereby creating a "unique story," and *Booklist* reviewer Shelley Townsend-Hudson dubbed it "a fine book that speaks straight to the heart."

A poetry collection about memories and mementos, *Keepers* elicits a variety of memories in different moods, ranging from comical to pensive. In fact, *Booklist* critic Susan Dove Lempke found many of Schertle's poems here to be "thought provoking" and suggested that they would be best understood by an audience more sophisticated than the intended one. On the other hand, *I Am the Cat,* a mix of narrative verses and haikus, takes a fresh look at a common subject, demonstrating in "this somewhat surprising book . . . that cats aren't always soft, cuddly felines," to quote Stephanie Zvirin in *Booklist.* A *Publishers Weekly* reviewer remarked that the feline-focused collection "distills the essence of cat with humor and wry eloquence."

A *Horn Book* reviewer cited as noteworthy the poems' "sinuous" rhythms, "irony, surprise, and humor," concluding that *I Am the Cat* "holds its own in the cat-poetry category."

Looking at the world with a fresh perspective is often the role of poetry. In *A Lucky Thing,* written for somewhat older readers, Schertle creates a thematically unified and "thoughtful book of poems [that] celebrates the creative process," a *Publishers Weekly* reviewer noted. The work garnered favorable reviews. By reflecting the girl narrator's point of view of life on the farm, Schertle allows children to "see the ordinary with new eyes," commented Lempke, the critic adding that readers might be inspired to write verse of their own. Among the work's other enthusiasts numbered a *Horn Book* reviewer, who appreciated the "humor," "rhythmic assurance," and "robust language" of these fourteen lyric poems. Comparing the verses favorably to those of Nancy Larrick, *Bulletin of the Center for Children's Books* reviewer Deborah Stevenson praised *A Lucky Thing* for its "delicate and imaginative precision" and the "unmannered lyricism [that] brings a freshness to oft-elegized subjects." Stevenson even suggested that Schertle's book might transform some children into poetry lovers.

The companion titles *All You Need for a Snowman* and *All You Need for a Beach* are geared to the preschool crowd. With its "bouncy and light" text instructions, *All You Need for a Snowman* "rolls along like hand-packed snow," wrote Martha Topol in *School Library Journal.* Even with such rhythmic drive, Phelan asserted that the text goes on "without ever falling into lockstep predictability." The word "except" ends each page, encouraging readers and listeners to turn the pages of this "wintertime treat," as a *Publishers Weekly* reviewer dubbed the picture book. Joanna Rudge predicted in *Horn Book* that *All You Need for a Snowman* would make "a wonderfully childlike and ebullient addition to the winter repertoire," while a *Kirkus Reviews* contributor suggested that the work would be "read again and again."

Schertle opts for fun in *The Skeleton in the Closet,* as a clackety creature ransacks a little boy's bedroom looking for something to cover its bare bones. A critic in *Kirkus Reviews* praised the author's "humorous upbeat rhyme," and Lempke pointed out in *Horn Book* that the story's non-Halloween focus makes *The Skeleton in the Closet* useful "to chill and thrill story-hour audiences year-round." *An Anaconda Ate My Homework!* pairs another lighthearted story by Schertle with artwork by Aaron Renier, this time for slightly older children. When Digby is assigned a way-too-long homework assignment, he trudges home despondently. Then the adventures begin, as the boy is carried off by a raptor and menaced by a hungry anaconda, a frisky gorilla, and a charging elephant. Each time, Digby manages to save himself, and he is ultimately rewarded when the president of the United States vetoes the dreaded homework assignment. "Schertle's over-the-top text and zany situ-

Schertle's wintertime tale in **All You Need for a Snowman** ***is brought to life in Barbara Lavallee's colorful art.*** (Illustration © 2002 by Barbara Lavallee. Reproduced by permission of Houghton Mifflin Harcourt Publishing Company. This material may not be reproduced in any form or by any means without the prior written permission of the publisher.)

ations will appeal to children who enjoy . . . frenetically paced adventures," predicted *School Library Journal* contributor Grace Oliff in review of the story.

For *¡Pío Peep!: Traditional Spanish Nursery Rhymes,* Schertle provides adaptations of the rhymes into English. It was a project she found absorbing and satisfying: "Since these are not literal translations," she noted, "but poetic recreations, my challenge was to work out English lines that would fall easily on the ear while retaining the humor and charm and delight of the originals." Ilene Cooper, in *Booklist,* wrote that both the Spanish and English versions "have a sweet, rhythmic simplicity," and Ann Welton called *¡Pío Peep!* "a wonderful reassuring lap book" in her review for *School Library Journal.*

In *One, Two, I Love You,* Schertle's take on the popular "Buckle My Shoe" rhyme, a mother elephant and her young son spend an adventurous day riding a train, playing hide-and-seek, and catching falling stars. The author's "verse is lyrical and charming," noted *School Library Journal* contributor Jane Barrer, and Phelan wrote in *Booklist* that the work "offers a counting rhyme with an affectionate tone." *The Adventures of Old Bo Bear* centers on a little boy and his well-worn teddy bear. After Bo emerges from the washing machine missing an ear, his owner conjures a number of fanciful scenarios that contributed to his toy's condition, including a battle with pirates, a thrilling ride on a bucking bronco, and a showdown with some outlaws in the Old West. "The tale slyly segues between the real and imagined worlds," a *Publishers Weekly* critic observed in a review of *The Adventures of Old Bo Bear.*

The yearly life cycle of a large brown bear is the focus of *Very Hairy Bear,* "a terrific way to introduce little ones to the seasons," according to Cooper. Schertle follows the lumbering creature as it fishes for salmon, forages for berries, and prepares for hibernation. The author's "patterned language sets up a playful cadence," wrote a *Kirkus Reviews* contributor. "Schertle makes frequent use of interior rhymes and alliteration to move the action along," Wendy Lukehart noted in a *School Library Journal* review.

Little Blue Truck, a "pointed tribute to good hearts and amiable natures everywhere," according to *Booklist* reviewer John Peters, examines themes of kindness and courtesy. As it passes through the countryside each day, Little Blue, a pickup truck, cheerfully greets the rural residents, in stark contrast to rude, noisy, and obnoxious Dump Truck. When Dump gets stuck in the mud, its calls for help go unanswered until Little Blue comes to the rescue. "This old-fashioned picture book has a timeless, if well-trod, message," remarked *Horn Book* critic Kitty Flynn, while also citing the humorous gouache illustrations by Jill McElmurry. A contributor in *Publishers Weekly* remarked that Schertle's "rhyming stanzas are succinct," and a *Kirkus Reviews* critic noted that the author's "rhythmic text . . . fairly chants itself." A se-

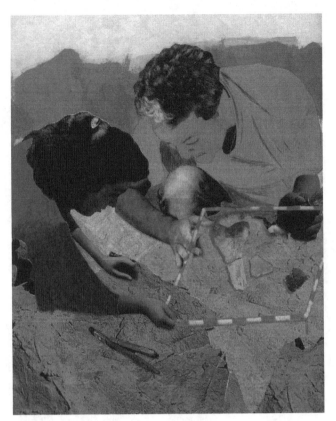

Schertle's simply titled picture book We *follows the story of humans and the evolution of civilized societies throughout the world.* (Illustration copyright © 2005 by Kenneth Addison. Reproduced by permission of Lee & Low Books, Inc.)

quel, *Little Blue Truck Leads the Way,* follows Blue into the big city, where the pickup truck is crowded by noisy cars, busses, taxis, and even a street sweeper. In *Booklist* Hazel Rochman dubbed Schertle's story "welcome fuel for many preschoolers' imaginative play."

In the award-winning *We* Schertle offers a "panoramic, free-verse view of the human story," remarked a contributor in *Kirkus Reviews.* Illustrated by Kenneth Addison, the book traces human evolution from its origins in Africa to the contemporary, and her spare text explores humankind's many achievements in the arts and sciences. According to *Booklist* critic Rochman, Schertle's tale "is about the diffusion of cultures and the rich connections." Writing in *Publishers Weekly,* a critic described *We* as "a compelling work that celebrates humankind's shared beginnings as much as its diversity and achievements."

"When I talk to classes of children and tell them about the unfinished stories I used to write, they usually laugh and say they do the same thing," Schertle once explained to *SATA.* "Sometimes I suggest they try writing the last half of a story first, and then go back and write the beginning. That's something I occasionally do now with my books. Sometimes a funny, or exciting, or ridiculous situation will pop into my head, an idea that would make a good middle of a story. So I'll sit down and write about some characters who find themselves in that situation, though I haven't yet any idea how they got there or what will finally happen to them. Then comes the hard part—writing the beginning and the ending, and making the parts fit together smoothly and logically.

"One of the nicest things about being an author is that it gives me the opportunity to talk to classes of children about books and writing. I always tell them that the best way to learn to write is to read and read and read. It's advice I take myself. There's a tall stack of books precariously balanced on my bedside table, and a good many of them are children's books. One lifetime will never be long enough for me to read all the books I want to read, but it'll be fun to try."

Biographical and Critical Sources

PERIODICALS

Booklist, September 15, 1994, Ilene Cooper, review of *How Now, Brown Cow?,* p. 133; April 15, 1995, Stephanie Zvirin, review of *Maisie,* p. 1508; September 15, 1995, Shelley Townsend-Hudson, review of *Down the Road,* p. 161; October 15, 1996, Susan Dove Lempke, review of *Keepers,* p. 428; March 15, 1999, Susan Dove Lempke, review of *A Lucky Thing,* p. 1340; April 1, 1999, Stephanie Zvirin, review of *I Am the Cat,* p. 1417; April 1, 2002, Shelley Townsend-Hudson, review of *Good Night, Hattie, My Dearie, My Dove,* p. 1335; November 15, 2002, Carolyn Phelan, review of *All You Need for a Snowman,* p. 612; October 1, 2004, Carolyn Phelan, review of *One, Two, I Love You,* p. 338; February 1, 2006, Julie Cummins, review of *The Adventures of Old Bo Bear,* p. 57; May 1, 2007, Hazel Rochman, review of *We,* p. 94; October 1, 2007, Ilene Cooper, review of *Very Hairy Bear,* p. 67; April 1, 2008, John Peters, review of *Little Blue Truck,* p. 55; May 15, 2009, Kathleen Isaacs, review of *Button Up!: Wrinkled Rhymes,* p. 41; July 1, 2009, Hazel Rochman, review of *Little Blue Truck Leads the Way,* p. 70.

Bulletin of the Center for Children's Books, June, 1999, Deborah Stevenson, review of *A Lucky Thing,* pp. 364-365; January, 2003, review of *All You Need for a Snowman,* p. 210; September, 2003, Janice Del Negro, review of *The Skeleton in the Closet,* p. 33; June, 2004, Hope Morrison, review of *All You Need for a Beach,* p. 436; December, 2007, Jeannette Hulick, review of *Very Hairy Bear,* p. 187; June, 2008, Deborah Stevenson, review of *Little Blue Truck,* p. 442; June, 2009, Deborah Stevenson, review of *Button Up!,* p. 419.

Five Owls, April, 1992, Katie Cerra, review of *Little Frog's Song,* pp. 76-77.

Horn Book, September-October, 1991, Ann A. Flowers, review of *Witch Hazel,* p. 589; March-April, 1996, Martha V. Parravano, review of *Down the Road,* pp. 191-192; May, 1999, review of *A Lucky Thing,* p. 347; September, 1999, review of *I Am the Cat,* p. 621;

November-December, 2002, Joanna Rudge, review of *All You Need for a Snowman,* p. 739; May-June, 2008, Kitty Flynn, review of *Little Blue Truck,* p. 299; May-June, 2009, Joanna Rudge Long, review of *Button Up!,* p. 316; July-August, 2009, Robin L. Smith, review of *Look Out, Jeremy Bean!,* p. 431.

Kirkus Reviews, January 15, 1987, review of *Jeremy Bean's St. Patrick's Day,* p. 132; March 1, 1999, review of *I Am the Cat,* pp. 381-382; March 1, 2002, review of *Good Night, Hattie, My Dearie, My Dove,* p. 345; September 15, 2002, review of *All You Need for a Snowman,* pp. 1399-1400; March 1, 2003, review of *When the Moon Is High,* p. 397; April 1, 2003, review of *Teddy Bear, Teddy Bear,* p. 539; April 15, 2003, review of *¡Pío Peep!: Traditional Spanish Nursery Rhymes,* p. 603; July 15, 2003, review of *The Skeleton in the Closet,* p. 968; January 15, 2006, review of *The Adventures of Old Bo Bear,* p. 89; April 15, 2007, review of *We;* October 1, 2007, review of *Very Hairy Bear;* April 1, 2008, review of *Little Blue Truck;* April 15, 2009, review of *Look Out, Jeremy Bean!;* September 15, 2009, review of *Little Blue Truck Leads the Way.*

New York Times Book Review, February 2, 1997, review of *Keepers,* p. 18.

Publishers Weekly, January 16, 1981, review of *The April Fool,* p. 80; June 27, 1986, review of *That Olive!,* p. 85; January 16, 1987, review of *Jeremy Bean's St. Patrick's Day,* p. 73; July 10, 1987, review of *Bill and the Google-eyed Goblins,* p. 68; May 19, 1989, review of *William and Grandpa,* p. 82; June 28, 1991, review of *Witch Hazel,* p. 101; September 5, 1994, review of *How Now, Brown Cow?,* pp. 110-111; March 15, 1999, review of *I Am the Cat,* p. 59; May 10, 1999, review of *A Lucky Thing,* p. 68; September 18, 2000, review of *Down the Road,* p. 113; October 21, 2002, review of *All You Need for a Snowman,* p. 73; April 21, 2003, review of *Teddy Bear, Teddy Bear,* pp. 64-65; August 4, 2003, review of *The Skeleton in the Closet,* p. 80; October 4, 2004, review of *One, Two, I Love You,* p. 86; February 27, 2006, review of *The Adventures of Old Bo Bear,* p. 60; April 30, 2007, review of *We,* p. 160; September 17, 2007, review of *A Very Hairy Bear,* p. 52; April 28, 2008, review of *Little Blue Truck,* p. 137; February 9, 2009, review of *Button Up!,* p. 48.

Reading Teacher, December, 1997, review of *Keepers,* p. 330.

School Library Journal, August, 1980, Diane Meyer, review of *Cathy and Company and the Nosy Neighbor,* p. 70; October, 1981, Patt Hays, review of *The April Fool,* p. 135; October, 1982, review of *Hob Goblin and the Skeleton,* p. 145; May, 1983, review of *In My Treehouse,* p. 66; May, 1984, Diane S. Rogoff, review of *Bim Dooley Makes His Move,* pp. 71-72; October, 1985, Ginny Caine Cooper, review of *Goodnight, Hattie, My Dearie, My Dove,* p. 162; November, 1985, Joan McGrath, review of *My Two Feet,* p. 77; August, 1986, Lucy Young Clem, review of *That Olive!,* p. 87; October, 1987, David Gale, review of *Jeremy Bean's St. Patrick's Day,* p. 118; January, 1988, Pamela Miller Ness, review of *Bill and the Google-eyed Goblins,* p.

70; March, 1989, Sally R. Dow, review of *Gus Wanders Off,* p. 170; August, 1989, Carolyn Caywood, review of *William and Grandpa,* p. 132; January, 1991, Carolyn Vang Schuler, review of *That's What I Thought,* p. 80; September, 1991, Ruth K. MacDonald, review of *Witch Hazel,* p. 240; July, 1992, Joy Fleishhacker, review of *Little Frog's Song,* p. 64; April, 1995, Jane Gardner Connor, review of *Maisie,* p. 116, and Sue Norris, review of *How Now, Brown Cow?,* p. 129; September, 1995, Ellen Donohue Warwick, review of *Advice for a Frog,* p. 197; April, 1996, Vanessa Elder, review of *Down the Road,* pp. 117-118; December, 1996, Kathleen Whalin, review of *Keepers,* p. 117; June, 1999, Joan Zaleski, review of *A Lucky Thing,* and Margaret Bush, review of *I Am the Cat,* both p. 120; June, 2002, Heather E. Miller, review of *Goodnight, Hattie, My Dearie, My Dove,* p. 110; December, 2002, Martha Topol, review of *All You Need for a Snowman,* p. 108; July, 2003, Lee Bock, review of *Teddy Bear, Teddy Bear,* p. 19, Maryann H. Owen, review of *When the Moon Is High,* p. 106, and Ann Welton, review of *¡Pío Peep!,* p. 121; September, 2003, Gay Lynn Van Vleck, review of *The Skeleton in the Closet,* p. 190; January, 2005, Jane Barrer, review of *One, Two, I Love You,* p. 97; February, 2006, Marge Loch-Wouters, review of *The Adventures of Old Bo Bear,* p. 109; May, 2007, Marianne Saccardi, review of *We,* p. 124; December, 2007, Wendy Lukehart, review of *Very Hairy Bear,* p. 99; July, 2008, Rachael Vilmar, review of *Little Blue Truck,* p. 81; May, 2009, Julie Roach, review of *Button Up!,* p. 98; August, 2009, Carrie Rogers-Whitehead, review of *Look out, Jeremy Bean!,* p. 84; October, 2009, Grace Oliff, reviews of *Little Blue Truck Leads the Way* and *An Anaconda Ate My Homework!,* both p. 104.

ONLINE

Children's Literature Network, http://www.childrenslitera turenetwork.org/ (July 15, 2011), "Alice Schertle."
Lee & Low Web site, http://www.leeandlow.com/ (July 15, 2011), "Alice Schertle."
Teaching PreK-8 Web site, http://www.teachingk-8.com/ (August 15, 2008), Lee Bennett Hopkins, "Alice Schertle."*

*   *   *

SCHMID, Paul

Personal

Married Linda Wallace (a photo artistic director); children: Anna. *Education:* American Academy of Art, degree (graphic art), 1982. *Hobbies and other interests:* Kayaking, backpacking.

Addresses

Home—Seattle, WA. *Agent*—Steven Malk, Writer's House, smalk@writersHouse.com. *E-mail*—paul@ paulschmidstudio.com.

Career

Fine-art painter and author/illustrator of children's books. Art director at Grey Advertising, 1982-83, and Carmichael Lynch, 1983-86; *Seattle Times,* Seattle, WA, graphic artist and designer, 1989-2006; freelance author and illustrator of children's books.

Member

Society of Children's Book Writers and Illustrators (Western Washington chapter), Puget Sound Group of Northwest Painters.

Awards, Honors

Union League Club Exhibition Purchase Prize, 1981; awards from Society of Illustrators and Society of Children's Book Writers and Illustrators (Western Washington), AIGA, Society of News Design, Society of American Travel Writers, and Sunday Magazine Editors Association.

Writings

SELF-ILLUSTRATED

A Pet for Petunia, Harper (New York, NY), 2011.
Hugs from Pearl, Harper (New York, NY), 2011.
Petunia Goes Wild, Harper (New York, NY), 2012.
Percy's Big Idea, Harper (New York, NY), 2012.

ILLUSTRATOR

Amy Krouse Rosenthal, *The Wonder Book,* Harper (New York, NY), 2010.

Contributor to periodicals, including *Seattle Times.* Work has appeared in illustration annuals, including *Communication Arts* and *Print.*

Sidelights

Based in Seattle, Washington, Paul Schmid hails from a long line of artists, but he has expanded his family's creative pedigree to include writing and illustrating books for children. An award-winning watercolor painter while still in college, Schmid eventually moved to the Pacific Northwest, where he contributed to the *Seattle Times* in addition to working in advertising. More recently returned to his roots in landscape painting, he also established himself in children's publishing through his illustration work for Amy Krouse Rosenthal's *The Wonder Book.* Original books that pair his entertaining art with engaging, child-centered stories included *A Pet for Petunia, Hugs from Pearl,* and *Petunia Goes Wild.* Writing in *Kirkus Reviews,* a critic noted of *The Wonder Book* that Schmid's "dynamic and expressive" line art is "integral to the . . . meaning" of

Paul Schmid's illustration projects include creating the whimsical cartoon art for Amy Krouse Rosenthal's **The Wonder Book.** (Harper, 2010. Reproduced by permission of Harper, an imprint of HarperCollins Children's Books, a division of HarperCollins Publishers.)

Rosenthal's verses, while *Booklist* contributor Julie Cummins likened Schmid's illustrations for the book as "reminiscent" of the work of beloved children's author/illustrator Shel Silverstein.

A skunk is the star of *A Pet for Petunia,* Schmid's story about a little girl who longs for a pet. For some reason that Petunia cannot fathom, Mom and Dad do not exhibit enthusiasm at the prospect of sharing their home with a cute, black-and-white-striped, button-nosed, fluffy-tailed skunk. The determined child tries every tack ever encountered by a resolute parent, begging, pleading, promising, and wheeling and dealing . . . until a serendipitous encounter causes her to rethink her choice of a favorite pet. A *Publishers Weekly* critic enjoyed Schmid's "enthusiastic and single-minded" young narrator, adding that in *A Pet for Petunia* the author/illustrator's "line drawings are simple, fluid, and convey lots of valuable information."

Biographical and Critical Sources

PERIODICALS

Booklist, January 1, 2010, Julie Cummins, review of *The Wonder Book,* p. 84.

Bulletin of the Center for Children's Books, March, 2010, Deborah Stevenson, review of *The Wonder Book,* p. 303.
Kirkus Reviews, March 1, 2010, review of *The Wonder Book.*
Publishers Weekly, February 8, 2010, review of *The Wonder Book,* p. 48; January 3, 2011, review of *A Pet for Petunia,* p.47.
School Library Journal, March, 2010, Kathleen Finn, review of *The Wonder Book,* p. 143.

ONLINE

Paul Schmid Home Page, http://www.paulschmidbooks. com (May 20, 2011).
Paul Schmid Web log, http://paulschmidstudio.blogspot. com (May 20, 2011).

*   *   *

SHEA, Bob

Personal

Married; wife's name Colleen (a graphic designer); children: Ryan.

Addresses

Home—CT. *E-mail*—bob@bobshea.com.

Career

Author, illustrator, and graphic artist. Creator of animation and graphics airing on PBS Kids.

Awards, Honors

Best Book designation, *Horn Book,* 2008, and Blue Ribbon selection, *Bulletin of the Center for Children's Books,* both for *Dinosaur vs. Bedtime.*

Writings

SELF-ILLUSTRATED

New Socks, Little, Brown (New York, NY), 2007.
Dinosaur vs. Bedtime, Hyperion Books for Children (New York, NY), 2008.
Oh, Daddy!, Balzer + Bray (New York, NY), 2010.
Race You to Bed, Katherine Tegen Books (New York, NY), 2010.
I'm a Shark!, Balzer + Bray (New York, NY), 2011.
Dinosaur vs. the Potty, Hyperion Books for Children (New York, NY), 2011.
Dinosaur vs. the Library, Hyperion Books for Children (New York, NY), 2011.

Contributor to periodicals, including *Nick Jr.*

FOR CHILDREN

Big Plans, illustrated by Lane Smith, Hyperion Books for Children (New York, NY), 2008.

ILLUSTRATOR

Kelly DiPucchio, *Gilbert Goldfish Wants a Pet,* Dial Books for Young Readers (New York, NY), 2011.

Tammi Sauer, *Me Want Pet,* Simon & Schuster Books for Young Readers (New York, NY), 2012.

Adaptations

New Socks was adapted as an animated film with voiceover by Shea.

Sidelights

Beginning with his self-illustrated *New Socks,* Bob Shea has transferred his talent for creating engaging animated non-human characters into a career as a picture-book author and illustrator. A story that captures the excitement of a toddler who discovers that something new and colorful and interactive has entered his world, *New Socks* employs what has become Shea's characteristic formula: colorful black-lined cartoon art, a simple text, and an engaging creature that serves as a toddler stand-in. The formula also makes a success of *Dinosaur vs. Bedtime, Dinosaur vs. the Library,* and *Dinosaur vs. Bedtime,* a series of books in which a round-headed, smiling red dinosaur engages in typical childish antics. *Oh, Daddy!, Race You to Bed,* and *I'm a Shark!* also feature Shea's paired story and art, while fellow author/illustrator Lane Smith takes over the visual storytelling

***Bob Shea's original self-illustrated picture books include the humorous* Race You to Bed.** (Copyright © 2010 by Bob Shea. Reproduced with permission of Katherine Tegen Books, an imprint of HarperCollins Children's Books, a division of HarperCollins Publishers.)

in *Big Plans,* which imagines the future plans of an ambitious young lad for whom the sky is not the limit. Reviewing *Big Plans* in *Publishers Weekly,* a reviewer noted that "Shea . . . gives readers a bold and funny motto to proclaim against small setbacks," while a *Kirkus Reviews* critic predicted that the story will leave readers "undoubtedly hatching some BIG PLANS of their own."

For the young red reptilian in *Dinosaur vs. Bedtime,* everyday encounters provide exciting opportunities to gain the upper hand. While eating bowls of spaghetti, mastering the playground slide, and talking to grown-up dinosaurs are all challenging, Dinosaur tackles each with a "Roar!" and gains in confidence. However, there is one obstacle to independence that remains stubbornly fixed no matter how much roaring he does, in an illustrated tale featuring what a *Publishers Weekly* described as "freewheeling compositions [that] convey both a beguiling spontaneity and a preschooler's sense of invincibility." Another showdown is brewing in *Dinosaur vs. the Potty,* as the author/illustrator's "bright, busy, and not-so-ferocious red dinosaur is back" for another "high-energy offering," according to *School Library Journal* contributor Alison Donnelly. With their "strong lines and bright colors," Shea's images "keep the energy high without being cluttered," maintained *School Library Journal* critic Kristine M. Casper in her review of *Dinosaur vs. Bedtime,* while Donnelly wrote that the digitized cartoon illustrations "perfectly complement . . . the spare but spot-on text" in *Dinosaur vs. the Potty.*

Like he does in *Dinosaur vs. Bedtime,* Shea tackles the dreaded lights-out routine in *Race You to Bed.* Here a bright-eyed young bunny inspires young listeners to transform traditional bedtime footdragging into a fun-filled race to the finish. Commonly held but highly imaginative fears of childhood are diffused by Shea in yet another picture book, *I'm a Shark!,* while in *Oh, Daddy!* two blue-skinned hippo characters capture the playful nature of a father-child relationship through Shea's mix of simple story and colorful art. Comparing Shea's work with that of popular animator/author Mo Willems, *Booklist* critic Ilene Cooper wrote that the "frantic rabbit" in *Race You to Bed* leads readers on "a circuitous route" that includes hills, railway and bus travel, and traversing patches of poison ivy and "croc-infested waters." Shea's "lively romp of a bedtime book" is "full of non sequiturs" and resolves in a "clever, bedtime-friendly ending," according to a *Publishers Weekly,* critic, while in *School Library Journal* Ieva Bates praised Shea's story for containing "a clever twist" capable of "engaging children in an active way." In *Booklist* Karen Cruze dubbed *Oh, Daddy* "stylistically simple and undeniably hip" and "sure to captivate the under-five set," while *School Library Journal* contributor Amy Lilien-Harper heralded the same work as a "humorous paean to fatherhood" that serves as "an antidote to the cloyingly sweet parent-child books glutting the market."

Shea invests his dino characters with terrifyingly toddler characteristics in his self-illustrated picture book **Dinosaur vs. Bedtime.** (Illustration copyright © 2008 by Bob Shea. Reproduced with permission of Hyperion Books for Children, an imprint of Disney Book Group.)

Biographical and Critical Sources

PERIODICALS

Booklist, February 15, 2008, Julie Cummins, review of *Big Plans,* p. 84; February 15, 2010, Karen Cruze, review of *Oh, Daddy!,* p. 80; April 1, 2010, Ilene Cooper, review of *Race You to Bed,* p. 48.

Horn Book, September-October, 2008, Martha V. Parravano, review of *Dinosaur vs. Bedtime,* p. 574.

Kirkus Reviews, March 1, 2007, review of *New Socks,* p. 231; April 1, 2008, review of *Big Plans;* July 15, 2008, review of *Dinosaur vs. Bedtime;* January 1, 2010, review of *Race You to Bed.*

New York Times Book Review, December 21, 2008, Julie Just, review of *Dinosaur vs. Bedtime,* p. 13.

Publishers Weekly, March 5, 2007, review of *New Socks,* p. 59; March 31, 2008, review of *Big Plans,* p. 61; September 8, 2008, review of *Dinosaur vs. Bedtime,* p. 50; January 11, 2010, review of *Race You to Bed,* p. 47.

School Library Journal, April, 2007, Joy Fleischhacker, review of *New Socks,* p. 116; June, 2008, Ieva Bates, review of *Big Plans,* p. 114; November, 2008, Rick Margolis, interview with Shea, p. 28; February, 2010, Ieva Bates, review of *Race You to Bed,* p. 94; April, 2010, Amy Lilien-Harper, review of *Oh, Daddy!,* p. 140; October, 2010, Alison Donnelly, review of *Dinosaur vs. the Potty,* p. 94.

ONLINE

Bob Shea Home Page, http://www.bobshea.com (July 15, 2011).*

* * *

SMITH, Jim W.W.

Personal
Born in Canada.

Addresses
Home—Victoria, British Columbia, Canada. *E-mail*—juniorskeptic@skeptic.com.

Career
Graphic designer and cartoonist.

Member
Computer Graphics Society.

Awards, Honors
Silver Birch Nonfiction Award nomination, 2011, for *Evolution* by Daniel Loxton.

Writings

Daniel Loxton, *Evolution: How We and All Living Things Came to Be,* Kids Can Press (Toronto, Ontario, Canada), 2010.

Author of online comic "big noggins." Contributing illustrator to *Junior Skeptic* supplement, *Skeptic* magazine.

Biographical and Critical Sources

PERIODICALS

School Library Journal, May, 2010, Patricia Manning, review of *Evolution: How We and All Living Things Came to Be,* p. 133.

ONLINE

Jim Smith Home Page, http://monkeyboyblue.com (May 2, 2011).
Skeptic Online, http://www.skeptic.com/ (May 2, 2011), "Jim W.W. Smith."*

* * *

SMITH HERNÁNDEZ, Duncan Tonatiuh
See TONATIUH, Duncan

STONE, Mary Hanlon

Personal
Father an attorney; married Richard Stone (an attorney and judge); children: two. *Education:* University of Michigan, B.A. (English), 1982, J.D., 1985.

Addresses
Home—Beverly Hills, CA. *Agent*—Claire Gerus Literary Agency, gerus.claire@gmail.com. *E-mail*—mary@maryhanlonstone.com.

Career
Attorney and author. Civil attorney in Chicago, IL, for one year; State of California District Attorney's Office, Los Angeles, deputy district attorney. Presenter at schools.

Writings

Invisible Girl, Philomel (New York, NY), 2010.
The Comedown Life, Philomel (New York, NY), 2011.

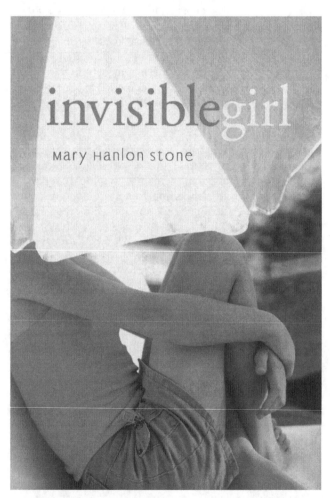

Cover of Mary Hanlon Stone's middle-grade novel **Invisible Girl,** *in which a young teen must decide whether upholding her principals is more important to her than popularity.* (Cover photographs © Veer Incorporated. Used by permission of Philomel Books, a division of Penguin Young Readers Group, a member of Penguin Group (USA), Inc., 345 Hudson St., New York, NY 10014. All rights reserved.)

Sidelights

Raised in a large, rambunctious family, Mary Hanlon Stone developed an early love of reading: stealing away into a quiet corner with a favorite book provided both an escape from household chores and a vehicle for her vivid childhood imagination. Now grown and with a family of her own, Stone works as a prosecuting attorney who advocates on behalf of abused and neglected children. In 2010 she also became a published novelist with the release of *Invisible Girl*. "As a deputy district attorney, I have specialized in prosecuting criminals who hurt kids and young adults," Stone explained on her home page. "I chose these cases because I love taking care of the victims. . . . *Invisible Girl* was inspired by the courage of many of the young girls I have met through work."

In *Invisible Girl* fourteen-year-old Stephanie lives in Boston with her parents until her alcoholic mom walks out on the family. Unable to cope, Stone's dad sends the teen to the West Coast to live with one of his friends, a wealthy man with a daughter, Annie, who is Stephanie's age. Life in an affluent Los Angeles suburb is a far cry from her own family's working-class Boston neighborhood, and finding herself without the blonde hair, high-fashion wardrobe, and sun-kissed good looks of her peers she uses her self-deprecating humor as a way to make friends. Although Annie welcomes her new roommate into her exclusive clique of friends, Stephanie's problematic past comes back to haunt her and she is eventually targeted by the clique for expulsion. When the group's disdain subsequently refocuses on a new Muslim student named Amal, Stephanie is happy to become socially invisible until her ability to empathize with the new girl forges a true friendship in a novel that a *Publishers Weekly* critic described as "a careful and challenging examination of clique politics." *Invisible Girl* features "smart insights into how Annie's circle operates and how hard Stephanie works to be part of it," the critic added. *School Library Journal* critic Geri Diorio wrote of *Invisible Girl* that Stephanie's "naivete is heartbreaking" and "Stone portrays her growth believably, in small increments, with many slip-ups along the way."

Biographical and Critical Sources

PERIODICALS

Bulletin of the Center for Children's Books, May, 2010, Deborah Stevenson, review of *Invisible Girl,* p. 401.

Kirkus Reviews, April 15, 2010, review of *Invisible Girl.*

Publishers Weekly, May 3, 2010, review of *Invisible Girl,* p. 53.

School Library Journal, July, 2010, Geri Diorio, review of *Invisible Girl,* p. 97.

ONLINE

Mary Hanlon Stone Home Page, http://www.maryhanlon stone.com (June 25, 2011).*

SWINBURNE, Stephen R. 1952-

Personal

Born November 8, 1952, in London, England; immigrated to United States, 1960; son of William Walter and Lillian Swinburne; married May 19, 1984; wife's name Heather; children: Hayley, Devon. *Education:* Castleton State College, B.A. (English and biology) *Hobbies and other interests:* Gardening, playing guitar, bird watching, travel, canoeing.

Addresses

Home and office—P.O. Box 2005, Main St., South Londonderry, VT 05155.

Career

Writer, photographer, and naturalist. U.S. National Park Service, former park ranger.

Member

Society of Children's Book Writers and Illustrators, Children's Book Insider.

Writings

FOR CHILDREN

Guide to Cumberland Island National Seashore, illustrated by Casey French Alexander, Eastern Acorn Press (New York, NY), 1984.

Swallows in the Birdhouse, illustrated by Robin Brickman, Millbrook Press (Brookfield, CT), 1996.

Water for One, Water for Everyone: A Counting Book of African Animals, illustrated by Melinda Levine, Millbrook Press (Brookfield, CT), 1998.

Moon in Bear's Eyes, illustrated by Crista Forest, Millbrook Press (Brookfield, CT), 1998.

Safe, Warm, and Snug (poems), illustrated by José Aruego and Ariane Dewey, Harcourt (San Diego, CA), 1999.

Once a Wolf: How Wildlife Biologists Fought to Bring Back the Gray Wolf ("Scientists in the Field" series), photographs by Jim Brandenburg, Houghton Mifflin (Boston, MA), 1999.

Unbeatable Beaks (poems), illustrated by Joan Paley, Henry Holt (New York, NY), 1999.

The Woods Scientist ("Scientists in the Field" series), photographs by Susan C. Moore, Houghton Mifflin (Boston, MA), 2003.

Turtle Tide: The Way of Sea Turtles, illustrated by Bruce Hiscock, Boyds Mills Press (Honesdale, PA), 2005.

Wings of Light: The Migration of the Yellow Butterfly, illustrated by Bruce Hiscock, Boyds Mills Press (Honesdale, PA), 2006.

Armadillo Trail: The Northward Journey of the Armadillo, illustrated by Bruce Hiscock, Boyds Mills Press (Honesdale, PA), 2009.

Ocean Soup: Tide Pool Poems, illustrated by Mary Peterson, Charlesbridge (Watertown, MA), 2010.

Wiff and Dirty George: The Z.E.B.R.A. Incident, Boyds Mills Press (Honesdale, PA), 2010.

FOR CHILDREN; AND PHOTOGRAPHER

Lots and Lots of Zebra Stripes: Patterns in Nature, Boyds Mills Press (Honesdale, PA), 1998.

In Good Hands: Behind the Scenes at a Center for Orphaned and Injured Birds, Sierra Club Books for Children (San Francisco, CA), 1998.

Coyote: North America's Dog, Boyds Mills Press (Honesdale, PA), 1999.

Guess Whose Shadow?, Boyds Mills Press (Honesdale, PA), 1999.

What's Opposite?, Boyds Mills Press (Honesdale, PA), 2000.

What's a Pair? What's a Dozen?, Boyds Mills Press (Honesdale, PA), 2001.

Bobcat: North America's Cat, Boyds Mills Press (Honesdale, PA), 2001.

Boxing Rabbits, Bellowing Alligators, and Other Animal Showoffs, Millbrook Press (Brookfield, CT), 2002.

Go, Go, Go!: Kids on the Move, Boyds Mills Press (Honesdale, PA), 2002.

What Color Is Nature?, Boyds Mills Press (Honesdale, PA), 2002.

Black Bear: North America's Bear, Boyds Mills Press (Honesdale, PA), 2003.

Saving Manatees, Boyds Mills Press (Honesdale, PA), 2006.

Whose Shoes?: A Shoe for Every Job, Boyds Mills Press (Honesdale, PA), 2010.

Contributor to periodicals, including *Country Journal, Family Fun, Highlights for Children,* and *Vermont Life.*

Sidelights

Writer, photographer, and naturalist Stephen R. Swinburne shares his love of nature in his many works for children. The adventures to be experienced within the pages of Swinburne's books include stalking elusive bobcats as they range through North America, learning about the innovative ways different animals protect their offspring, watching a field biologist studying animals in the wild, and witnessing a lumbering sea turtle's laborious journey to land and her efforts to battle predators in order to hatch at least one of her many eggs. Swin-

***Stephen R. Swinburne's photographs, taken during his many travels around the world, are featured in picture books such as* Guess Whose Shadow?**
(Photograph copyright © 1999 by Stephen R. Swinburne. Reproduced by permission.)

burne's books often feature original photographs that help very young children visualize concepts such as "a pair," "a dozen," "shadows," and "opposites." In a *Booklist* review of *The Woods Scientist,* Gillian Engberg described Swinburne's writing as "immediate, clear, and filled with moment-by-moment observations," and Margaret Bush wrote in *School Library Journal* that the author/photographer's books "offer many invitations for personal involvement in studying wildlife."

Swinburne was born in London, England, but just before he turned eight he immigrated with his parents and two siblings to the United States aboard the grand ocean liner the *Queen Mary.* The middle child, he loved reading and listening to the Beatles, and he began writing in journals during his teens, when his family life became unstable due to his parents' impending divorce. His dreams of travel and adventure came true, in a fashion, when Swinburne added biology classes to his English studies and found work as a ranger in several national parks following college graduation. His skill with a camera and his talent for writing combined with his passion for nature to inspire his eventual career as a children's author.

Swallows in the Birdhouse, one of Swinburne's early picture books, finds a brother and sister building a birdhouse. As time passes, readers can watch along with the siblings as a pair of tree swallows finds the birdhouse, builds a nest, and successfully hatches a brood of chicks. At the end of the book, the swallows amass in great numbers for a communal flight. In *Booklist,* Lauren Peterson commended *Swallows in the Birdhouse* as a work mixing "lovely descriptive language" with helpful facts on swallow biology and birdhouse building.

In his nonfiction works, Swinburne focuses primarily on creatures native to North America. In both *Moon in Bear's Eyes* and *Black Bear: North America's Bear* he introduces readers to the region's two bear species: the grizzly bear common to the American West and as the black bear common to the boreal forests that cover the northeastern United States. April Judge wrote in *Booklist* that *Moon in Bear's Eyes* "reads like an adventure story" in its focus on a family of grizzlies while also covering the essential biology and ecology of the species. *Black Bear* profiles the bear that is finding its way into suburban backyards as its numbers increase and the eastern forests reemerge. While presenting an overview of the species and teaching readers to spot bear signs, Swinburne also "counters some common misconceptions" and shares "his own brief encounters with black bears," wrote *Booklist* critic John Peters. In *School Library Journal,* Nancy Call praised the book's color photographs and "lively text," adding that *Black Bear* provides readers with an "intriguing introduction to these fascinating animals.

Bears join coyotes and bobcats as the most illusive large predators prowling the North America wilderness. In *Bobcat: North America's Cat* Swinburne documents

Swinburne works with nature photographer Jim Brandenburg in several of his nonfiction books, among them **Once a Wolf.** (Photograph copyright © 1999 by Jim Brandenburg. Reprinted by permission of Houghton Mifflin Harcourt Publishing Company. All rights reserved.)

his search for the beautiful feline predator, accompanied by professional trackers as well as by a class of curious sixth graders. Interspersing the account of this trek, he shares information with his readers information regarding the bobcat's survival skills and its passion for privacy. In *School Library Journal,* Margaret Bush wrote that Swinburne's personal anecdotes "lend an inviting immediacy" to the narrative, while *Booklist* contributor Ilene Cooper predicted that *Bobcat* will encourage readers to contemplate "the relationship between animals and their prey." Swinburne takes a similar approach in *Saving Manatees,* as he joins a class of fourth graders on a ranger-guided visit to a Florida wildlife refuge known for its giant manatee population. The author's "enthusiastic descriptions of his experiences with the animals are contagious and will draw children right into the subject," predicted Engberg of the large-format work.

Realizing the opportunities Nature provides for teaching useful concepts, Swinburne has created several well-received picture books that feature his original full-color photographs. *Lots and Lots of Zebra Stripes: Patterns in Nature* uses living examples to teach preschoolers about pattern, while the questions he poses in *What's Opposite?, What's a Pair? What's a Dozen?,* and *What Color Is Nature?* are answered in vivid images of objects that young children will recognize, even if they have never seen them so vividly presented. The jobs grown-ups perform are captured in the photographs Swinburne creates for *Whose Shoes?: A Shoe for Every Job,* which find children sampling future careers by donning the appropriate footwear. Lauren Peterson, writing in *Booklist,* called *Lots and Lots of Zebra Stripes* a "gorgeous photo-essay," and *Booklist* correspondent Carolyn Phelan dubbed *What's Opposite?* a "handsome book of photographs." In *School Library Journal* Kristina Aaronson described *What's a Pair? What's a Dozen?* as a good introduction to mathematical concepts, while a *Kirkus Reviews* writer recommended *Whose Shoes?* as a "lighthearted look at occupations" featuring a "rhythmic" text that "will read aloud well."

Employing a theme designed to appeal to younger children, Swinburne's *Safe, Warm, and Snug* uses rhyming verses to offer glimpses into the many ways that animals protect their young. From toads to penguins to marsupials, the book covers some of the most bizarre parental behavior on the planet. Featuring engaging pastel-toned artwork by Mary Peterson, *Ocean Soup: Tide Pool Poems* also addresses a younger audience. Here Swinburne adopts the voice of a range of small oceanic creatures as each describes its path to an ephemeral coastal pool and the main characteristics of its species. In her *School Library Journal* review, Marian Drabkin called *Safe, Warm, and Snug* "a celebration of the animal world" that offers the added attraction of giving children "reassurance that parents are protectors." In *Ocean Soup* the author "shows his lighter side . . . in pleasing and sometimes amusing verse," wrote *Booklist* contributor Phelan, and a *Publishers Weekly* critic asserted that while the book's "brief paragraphs provide factual tidbits, . . . the focus is definitely on fun."

In the course of his travels Swinburne frequently works alongside wildlife biologists, both professional and amateur. In *In Good Hands: Behind the Scenes at a Center for Orphaned and Injured Birds* he introduces sixteen-year-old Hannah, a volunteer nursing an injured baby owl in preparation for its release into the wild. Sally Margolis, reviewing the book for *School Library Journal,* cited the "immediacy" imparted by Hannah's personal interactions with both the owl and with human visitors to the shelter. In her *Booklist* review of *In Good Hands* Kathleen Squires wrote that Swinburne's "bittersweet" ending "will tug on the heartstrings."

Inspired by his work with scientists, Swinburne has contributed several books to Houghton Mifflin's respected "Scientists in the Field" series, which is geared for older readers. In *The Woods Scientist* he profiles the work of Susan C. Morse, a fourth-generation wildlife biologist and forester who lives and works in Vermont. Illustrated with Morse's own photographs, the book focuses on the many creatures that make their home in the boreal forests of the New England region: bears, deer, bobcats, raccoons, foxes, deer, among many others. In his narrative, Swinburne "brings young readers close to the excitement of scientific discovery," according to Engberg in *Booklist.*

Also part of the "Scientist in the Field" series, *Once a Wolf: How Wildlife Biologists Fought to Bring Back the Gray Wolf* pairs Swinburne's text with photographs by noted nature photographer Jim Brandenburg. Donna Beales, writing in *Booklist,* declared that the work "packs a lot of information" about a species that has been reviled by the farmers and ranchers invading its habitat while also demonstrating a keen intelligence. *Once a Wolf* focuses in particular on the efforts to reintroduce gray wolves to Yellowstone National Park and its environs, despite the objections of neighboring farmers and ranchers. Swinburne presents both sides of

Swinburne collaborates with noted illustrators José Aruego and Ariane Dewey in the nature-centered picture book Safe, Warm, and Snug.

the controversy: the wolves' crucial role in the region's ecology as well as the economic impact of this talented predator on area ranches. A *Horn Book* critic deemed *Once a Wolf* "bracingly journalistic," and Ruth S. Vose in *School Library Journal* praised "the excitement of science in action" to be found in its pages.

The natural world is not always a kind world, and Swinburne illustrates this fact in several of his books for slightly older children. *Turtle Tide: The Ways of Sea Turtles* is one of several collaborations between Swinburne and watercolor artist Bruce Hiscock. In this picture book, author and illustrator follow a large Loggerhead turtle as she clambers from the Atlantic Ocean onto a sandy beach and digs the nest in which she lays the many eggs that, after her departure, will be vulnerable to gulls, raccoons, crabs, and sand sharks as they mature. Noting that the sea turtle is one of the oldest creatures on Earth, Bush wrote in *Horn Book* that the "spare prose and fine paintings" in *Turtle Tide* reveal the drama of Nature, as "animal encounters . . . reduce the eggs and hatchlings to one lone survivor."

Praised by Phelan as "a well-written and beautifully illustrated picture book," *Wings of Light: The Migration of the Yellow Butterfly* again pairs the talents of Swinburne and Hiscock, this time as they follow a flock of cloudless sulfur butterflies on its daunting migration from Mexico's Yucatán rain forest north along the east coast of the United States to its destination in northern New England. Another collaboration, *Armadillo Trail: The Northward Journey of the Armadillo*, allows young naturalists to observe the efforts of a female nine-banded armadillo to protect her four pups during their first months exploring the wider world and journeying from Texas to rural Kansas. Noting the book's ability to inspire, a *Kirkus Reviews* writer commented of *Wings of Light* that "young readers will come away with a sense of wonder and admiration for the frail creature's remarkable flight." By positioning the struggles of his animal characters within the wider cycle of animal reproduction, *Armadillo Trail* brings to its subject a "refreshing lack of sensationalism and sentimentality about events in the animals' lives," according to Phelan. Swinburne's "clear text" combines with Hiscock's "detailed watercolors" to "brings readers into the journey without actual personification," wrote a *Kirkus Reviews* writer, and in *School Library Journal* Kirsten Cutler dubbed *Armadillo Trail* an "informative and appealing introduction" to an intriguing and uniquely North American animal.

In a change of pace for the nature writer, Swinburne draws on memories of his own teen years in his elementary-grade novel *Wiff and Dirty George: The Z.E.B.R.A. Incident*. Growing up in London, Swinburne's rather unkept best friend was dubbed "Dirty George" by his mother, while Swinburne went by the nickname Wiff. In their imagine-driven adventures, the two twelve year olds accidentally find themselves in the know regarding a secret plot by a crazy scientist who happens to be one of Wiff's distant relatives. When the man realizes that the boys intend to thwart his scheme to take over the world by kidnaping Queen Elizabeth II, he employs a series of fantastical means to stop them, at one point encasing them in glass bubbles. Set against a backdrop of Beatlemania and the Peter Maxx-patterned culture of the 1960s, *Wiff and Dirty George* "is light on character development but strong in fun plot elements," asserted *School Library Journal* critic Misti Tidman, the reviewer recommending the quirky preteen adventure to fans of the "Shredderman" stories by Wendelin van Draanen.

Biographical and Critical Sources

PERIODICALS

Booklist, June 1, 1996, Lauren Peterson, review of *Swallows in the Birdhouse*, p. 1729; May 1, 1998, April Judge, review of *Moon in Bear's Eyes*, p. 1520; July, 1998, Kathleen Squires, review of *In Good Hands: Behind the Scenes at a Center for Orphaned and Injured Birds*, p. 1880; September 15, 1998, Lauren Peterson, review of *Lots and Lots of Zebra Stripes: Patterns in Nature*, p. 233; March 1, 1999, Stephanie Zvirin, review of *Once a Wolf: How Wildlife Biologists Fought to Bring Back the Gray Wolf*, p. 1211; June 1, 1999, Kay Weisman, review of *Safe, Warm, and Snug*, p. 1835; October 15, 1999, Donna Beales, review of *Coyote: North America's Dog*, p. 440; March 15, 2000, Shelle Rosenfeld, review of *What's a Pair? What's a Dozen?*, p. 1384; September 1, 2000, Carolyn Phelan, review of *What's Opposite?*, p. 120; April 1, 2001, Ilene Cooper, review of *Bobcat: North America's Cat*, p. 1468; June 1, 2002, Carolyn Phelan, review of *What Color Is Nature?*, p. 1732; March 15, 2003, Gillian Engberg, review of *The Woods Scientist*, p. 1326; January 1, 2004, John Peters, review of *Black Bear: North America's Bear*, p. 851; April 1, 2005, John Peters, review of *Turtle Tide: The Ways of Sea Turtles*, p. 1362; April 1, 2006, Carolyn Phelan, review of *Wings of Light: The Migration of the Yellow Butterfly*, p. 46; September 1, 2006, Gillian Engberg, review of *Saving Manatees*, p. 123; February 1, 2009, Carolyn Phelan, review of *Armadillo Trail: The Northward Journey of the Armadillo*, p. 45; January 1, 2010, Carolyn Phelan, review of *Ocean Soup: Tide-Pool Poems*, p. 89; February 1, 2010, Carolyn Phelan, review of *Whose Shoes?: A Shoe for Every Job*, p. 46.

Horn Book, July, 1999, review of *Once a Wolf*, p. 487; May-June, 2005, Margaret A. Bush, review of *Turtle Tide*, p. 351; May-June, 2010, Betty Carter, review of *Whose Shoes?*, p. 73.

Kirkus Reviews, September 1, 2003, review of *North America's Bear*, p. 1131; March 15, 2005, review of *Turtle Tide*, p. 358; April 1, 2006, review of *Wings of Light*, p. 358; September 15, 2006, review of *Saving Manatees*, p. 969; January 1, 2009, review of *Armadillo Trail*; January 1, 2010, review of *Ocean Soup*; January 15, 2010, review of *Whose Shoes?*

Publishers Weekly, May 3, 1999, review of *Safe, Warm, and Snug*, p. 75; February 8, 2010, review of *Ocean Soup*, p. 48.

Swinburne's skill as a photographer is one of the attractions of his evocative children's book **Coyote: North America's Dog.** (Photograph copyright © 1999 by Stephen R. Swinburne. All rights reserved. Reproduced by permission.)

School Library Journal, June, 1996, Helen Rosenberg, review of *Swallows in the Birdhouse,* p. 118; August, 1998, Ruth S. Vose, review of *In Good Hands,* p. 184; January, 1999, Arwen Marshall, review of *Lots and Lots of Zebra Stripes,* p. 122; May, 1999, Ruth S. Vose, review of *Once a Wolf,* p. 140; June, 1999, Marian Drabkin, review of *Safe, Warm, and Snug,* p. 122; April, 2000, Kristina Aaronson, review of *What's a Pair? What's a Dozen?,* p. 126; October, 2000, Lucinda Snyder Whitehurst, review of *What's Opposite?,* p. 154; August, 2001, Margaret Bush, review of *Bobcat,* p. 205; April, 2003, Margaret Bush, review of *The Woods Scientist,* p. 193; August, 2003, Kathy Piehl, review of *Once a Wolf,* p. 117; November, 2003, Nancy Call, review of *Black Bear,* p. 132; September,

2004, Janet Dawson Hamilton, review of *What's a Pair? What's a Dozen?,* p. 59; March, 2005, Patricia Manning, review of *Turtle Tide,* p. 204; May, 2006, Margaret Bush, review of *Wings of Light,* p. 118; November, 2006, Christine Markley, review of *Saving Manatees,* p. 165; March, 2009, Kirsten Cutler, review of *Armadillo Trail,* p. 139; April, 2010, Susan Scheps, review of *Ocean Soup,* p. 149, and Misti Tidman, review of *Wiff and Dirty George: The Z.E.B.R.A. Incident,* p. 169.

ONLINE

Stephen R. Swinburne Home Page, http://www.steveswinburne.com (July 15, 2011).*

T

TEPLIN, Scott

Personal

Male. *Education:* University of Wisconsin—Madison, B.S. (fine art), 1995; University of Washington, M.F.A. (printmaking), 1998.

Addresses

Home—New York, NY.

Career

Illustrator and fine arts painter. *New York Times,* New York, NY, photo-graphics editor, 1998-2010; Sotheby's (auction house), New York, NY, photo editor, beginning 2010. Web master, Elizabeth Foundation for the Arts; cofounder and member of board of advisors, Brooklyn Artist Alliance. *Exhibitions:* Work exhibited in group shows throughout the United States and Europe and in solo shows at Howard House, Seattle, WA, 1999; Jessica Murray Projects, Brooklyn, NY, 2001, 2003; Adam Baumgold Gallery, New York, NY, 2002, 2004, 2008, 2010; DiverseWorks, Houston, TX, 2003; and g-module, Paris, France, 2007. Work included in numerous permanent collections, including at California College of Arts and Crafts, Progressive Insurance Corp., University of Washington, Seattle, Harvard University, San Francisco Museum of Modern Art, Stanford University, Yale University, Smithsonian Institution, Occidental College, Brooklyn Museum of Art, Altoids Collection, and Spencer Art Museum, Lawrence, KS.

Awards, Honors

Elizabeth Foundation for the Arts free studio fellowship, 2009.

Illustrator

(With Adam Rex) Mac Barnett and Eli Horowitz, *The Clock without a Face,* McSweeney's (San Francisco, CA), 2010.

Contributor to periodicals, including *Art Actuel, ART-Forum, ARTnews, Art Review, Creative Review, Houston Magazine, Lucky Peach, McSweeney's, New Yorker, New York Sun, New York Times* and *Rolling Stone.*

Sidelights

In addition to his work as a photo/graphics editor and Web developer, Scott Teplin is a fine artist and illustrator who is noted for created meticulously detailed drawings that echo the comix-style art of R. Crumb. Based in New York City, Teplin has exhibited his art in both the United States and Europe, and his illustrations have appeared in magazines such as *ARTnews,* the *New Yorker,* and *Rolling Stone. New York Times* art reviewer Grace Glueck characterized Teplin's exhibited work as "halfway between comic strips and children's book illustration" due to his use of minute detail to organically deconstruct everything from human teeth to machinery. In one collection of his works, for example, Teplin uses ink and airbrush to create twenty-six fantasy dwellings, each designed in the shape of a capital letter and all intricately designed and maze-like. Reinforcing Glueck's assessment, his detailed images have found their way into the pages of Mac Barnett and Eli Horowitz's *The Clock without a Face,* where Teplin shares illustration duties with fellow artist Adam Rex.

A trip to Florence, Italy, following his junior year at the University of Wisconsin—Madison inspired the then-twenty-one-year-old Teplin to pursue a career in art. After graduating, he relocated to New York City due to its vibrant arts community. Despite the competition for illustration jobs, he worked diligently for over a year to build up his portfolio and eventually earned assignments with high-profile magazines such as *Rolling Stone.* In addition to appearing in magazines and as part of exhibitions and art collections throughout the United States, Teplin's work found a place in book publishing with *The Clock without a Face.*

Pentagonal in shape, *The Clock without a Face* matched perfectly with Teplin's unique style: an interactive and highly visual puzzle book, it allows readers to follow

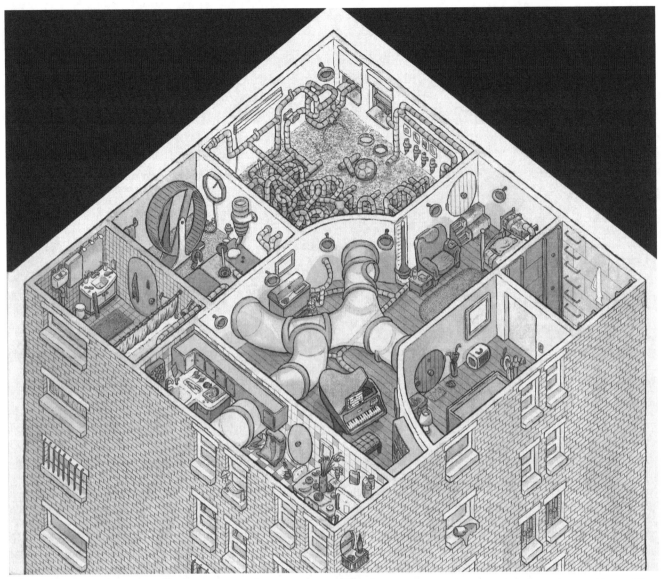

Artist Scott Teplin takes on illustrator duties, collaborating with coauthors Mac Barnett and Eli Horowitz on the offbeat The Clock without a Face.
(McSweeney's Books, 2010. Illustration copyright © 2010 by Scott Teplin. Reproduced by permission of Scott Teplin.)

the efforts of ace detective Roy Dodge and his sidekick to track down the twelve bejeweled numerals that have been stolen from an antique clock and are now hidden somewhere in a thirteen-storey apartment building. Cited for providing "hours of fun for sharp-eyed puzzle fans" by a *Kirkus Reviews* writer, *The Clock without a Face* also benefits from what a *Publishers Weekly* critic described as "pages of intricate details" that emerge as Dodge interviews "bizarre residents in equally eccentric apartments."

Biographical and Critical Sources

PERIODICALS

Kirkus Reviews, April 15, 2010, review of *The Clock without a Face.*

New York Times, July 12, 2002, Grace Glueck, "Scott Teplin" (exhibit review), p. E38.
Publishers Weekly, April 26, 2010, review of *The Clock without a Face,* p. 108.

ONLINE

Scott Teplin Home Page, http://www.teplin.com (July 15, 2011).*

*   *   *

TONATIUH, Duncan (Duncan Tonatiuh Smith Hernández)

Personal

Born in Mexico City, Mexico. *Education:* Parsons School of Design, B.F.A. (integrated design); Eugene Lange College, B.A.

Addresses

Home—San Miguel de Allende, Mexico. *E-mail*—duncansito@yahoo.com.

Career

Author and illustrator. Activist on behalf of worker's rights.

Awards, Honors

Tbilisi International Festival Grand Prize for Best Project, 2010, for *Journey of a Mixteco;* Chicago Public Library Best of the Best selection, Notable Children's Book selection, Association of Library Service to Children, and Pura Belpré Award honorable mention, all 2010, and Notable Book for a Global Society listee, and Américas Award Commended selection, both 2011, all for *Dear Primo.*

Writings

Dear Primo: A Letter to My Cousin, Abrams Books for Young Readers (New York, NY), 2010.
Diego Rivera: His World and Ours, Abrams Books for Young Readers (New York, NY), 2011.

Author and illustrator of "Journey of a Mixteco" (serialized story), posted on Topshelfcomix.com. Illustrator for books published by ST-Editorial, Mexico.

Sidelights

Duncan Tonatiuh grew up in San Miguel de Allende, Mexico, the son of a Mexican mother and an American father. After age sixteen, he received his education in the United States, where his studies at a Massachusetts boarding school inspired him to pursue a career in art. Tonatiuh earned his B.F.A. at Manhattan's prestigious Parsons School of Design while also earning a joint bachelor's degree at Eugene Lang College. His senior project, the five-part sequential-art story "Journey of a Mixteco," earned the talented student an award for best thesis and was eventually published online. The work also attracted the attention of an editor at Abrams Books for Young Readers, who saw the potential of Tonatiuh's unique illustration style and awarded him a contract for *Dear Primo: A Letter to My Cousin.*

Dear Primo showcases Tonatiuh's stylized images, which are inspired by the work of Mixtec and other ancient Mexican civilizations. The book tells the story of two cousins who live in different cultures. While Charlie lives in New York City, Carlitos makes his home in rural Mexico, where his family owns a farm. The letters between the two boys illustrate both the similarities and differences in their daily lives, from going to school and playing with friends to what they eat, how they celebrate holidays, and how each of their families spends

its time. Featuring a bilingual English-Spanish text, *Dear Primo* also showcases the author/illustrator's "clever use of colors" as he contrasts the "Mayan blue and Indian red" of Carlitos's world with "bright colors for the U.S. urban scenes" that are familiar to Charlie. Tonatiuh's "writing is simple yet peppered with imagery that enhances it significantly," wrote Grace Oliff in *School Library Journal,* while his artwork "accurately reflects [Mesoamerica's ancient] Mixtec tradition." Also praising Tonatiuh's debut picture book, a *Publishers Weekly* critic dubbed *Dear Primo* "a subtly reflective story about friendship and commonalities," while Andrew Medlar wrote in *Booklist* that it "reinforces the sense that kids around the world are more alike than different."

Tonatiuh's second book, *Diego Rivera: His World and Ours,* mixes a biography of the noted twentieth-century Mexican muralist with thought-provoking questions regarding the nature of artistic inspiration. If Rivera was alive today, what would his murals depict?, wonders the author, thereby "establishing a link [with] . . . modern readers" and defining "art" as "both aspiration and action," according to a *Kirkus Reviews* writer. Praising the biography for adopting an "inspired approach that combines child appeal, cultural anthropology, and art history," Wendy Lukehart added in her *School Library Journal* review of *Diego Rivera* that the book's illustrations feature "scenes both thoughtful and humorous."

Biographical and Critical Sources

PERIODICALS

Booklist, February 1, 2010, Andrew Medlar, review of *Dear Primo: A Letter to My Cousin,* p. 48.
Kirkus Reviews, March 1, 2010, review of *Dear Primo;* May 1, 2011, review of *Diego Rivera: His World and Ours.*
Publishers Weekly, March 15, 2010, review of *Dear Primo,* p. 52.
School Librarian, summer, 2010, Lucinda Jacob, review of *Dear Primo,* p. 94.
School Library Journal, March, 2010, Grace Oliff, review of *Dear Primo,* p. 134; April, 2011, Wendy Lukehart, review of *Diego Rivera,* p. 165.

ONLINE

Duncan Tonatiuh Home Page, http://www.duncantonatiuh. com (May 2, 2011).
Duncan Tonatiuh Web log, http://duncantonatiuh. wordpress.com/ (June 25, 2011).
Parsons School of Design Web site, http://www.newschool. edu/parsons/ (June 25, 2011), "Duncan Tonatiuh Smith."
Top Shelf Comix Web site, http://www.topshelfcomix.com/ (June 25, 2011), "Duncan Tonatiuh."

TOWNSEND, Michael 1981-

Personal

Born July 1, 1981. *Education:* School of Visual Arts, B.F.A.

Addresses

Home—Lansdale, PA. *Agent*—Paul Rodeen, Paul@rodeenliterary.com. *E-mail*—MTtheGREAT@aol.com.

Career

Children's book author and illustrator.

Awards, Honors

Gryphon Award, Center for Children's Books, 2008, for *Billy Tartle in Say Cheese!;* Gryphon Award Honor Book selection, 2010, for *Kit Feeny: On the Move.*

Writings

Billy Tartle in Say Cheese!, Alfred A. Knopf (New York, NY), 2007.

Kit Feeny: On the Move (graphic novel), Alfred A. Knopf (New York, NY), 2009.

Kit Feeny: The Ugly Necklace (graphic novel), Alfred A. Knopf (New York, NY), 2009.

Amazing Greek Myths of Wonder and Blunders, Dial Books for Young Readers (New York, NY), 2010.

Monkey and Elephant's Worst Fight Ever!, Alfred A. Knopf (New York, NY), 2011.

Sidelights

Michael Townsend's debut picture book *Billy Tartle in Say Cheese!* was published shortly after its author/illustrator's graduation from New York City's School of Visual Arts. With this start in children's publishing, Townsend has gone on to create several more stories in the same tradition, as well as two graphic novels for slightly older readers: *Kit Feeny: On the Move* and *Kit Feeny: The Ugly Necklace.* Townsend readily admits to an obsession with monkeys, and observant fans can spot the frisky simians in each of his books, sometimes as main characters and other times hiding in the story's animated cartoon art.

In *Billy Tartle in Say Cheese!* Townsend introduces an energetic and well-meaning young hero who is looking forward to picture day at his elementary school. For Billy, the key to a fantastic picture is a fantastic haircut, and this knowledge sparks a power struggle between Billy and his mother on a pre-picture trip to the barber shop. Barber Ken must play mediator in the battle between a bright pink, spiky Mohawk and a tidy, good-boy haircut. When Mom wins, it is left to the resourceful Billy to find another way to shake up picture day. In

Publishers Weekly a critic predicted that "readers with a rascally bent will likely get a kick out of Billy's overactive imagination and puckish behavior." Linda M. Kenton wrote in *School Library Journal* that Townsend's digitized comic-book art is "sharp and bright," and a *Kirkus Reviews* contributor enjoyed the author/illustrator's "definite predilection for tomfoolery."

Townsend's love of monkeys inspired *Monkey and Elephant's Worst Fight Ever,* which focuses on the ups and downs of two best friends. Monkey is excited to surprise friend Elephant with some home-baked cupcakes, but at Elephant's house a party seems to be underway to which Monkey has not been invited. Hurt, Monkey sneaks back later and hides all of Elephant's stuffed toys in the freezer, prompting Elephant to retaliate by filling Monkey's home with a multigenerational family of rabbits. Fortunately, the other animals band together to stop the feud from escalating much further in a picture book that relates its "instructive tale with pitch-perfect notes of humor and silliness that never approach the didactic," according to a *Kirkus Reviews* writer.

Silliness once again reigns in *Amazing Greek Myths of Wonder and Blunders,* as Townsend turns ancient history on its head. Here the classic myths about Pandora, Midas, Perseus, Demeter, Icarus, Midas, Arachne, Hercules, Persephone, and Pyramus and Thisbe are recast as humorous comic-book tales in which whimsical elements such as a roaming toaster, special slippers, rap lyrics, and silly sheep are all part of the mix. "Brash colors, quirky humor, and authentic retellings combine to make this compilation of stories . . . both bright and engaging," asserted *Booklist* critic Francisca Goldsmith, while a *Publishers Weekly* reviewer noted that Townsend's "entertaining, lively, and action-packed stories are spiced with slapstick" and retain their time-honored lessons. The author's use of "conversational, up-to-date language and broad jokes help to make the stories accessible," noted Paula Willey in a *School Library Journal* review, and *Kirkus Reviews* critic remarked on the author's inclusion of his emblematic monkey—in this case "an army of monkeys"—in the story of Icarus and his flight too close to the sun.

Kit Feeny, the star of both *Kit Feeny: On the Move* and *Kit Feeny: The Ugly Necklace*, is a big-eared, round-headed preteen stand-in who loves comic books and hatches all sorts of wacky and improbable schemes. In the first book in Townsend's series, Kit's family is moving out of town, and now he must hit upon a scheme for replacing his best friend, Arnold. When no one at his new school makes the grade, Kit is forced to rethink his pigeonhole approach to people, and his imaginative negotiation of interpersonal relationships is as insightful as it is entertaining. The challenge of finding the perfect birthday gift for his mom is tackled in *Kit Feeny: The Ugly Necklace,* although Kit's idea of perfect is limited by his childish perspective and hampered by his last-minute approach. "Townsend's bright-eyed bear-

***Michael Townsend's art and story pair up in the entertaining graphic story* Kit Feeny: On the Move.** (Copyright © 2009 by Michael Townsend. Used by permission of Alfred A. Knopf, an imprint of Random House Children's Books, a division of Random House, Inc.)

hamster-pooch people and enthusiastically bizarre sense of humor will make this two-color graphic novel a hot item," predicted a *Kirkus Reviews* writer in appraising *Kit Feeny: On the Move. School Library Journal* critic Benjamin Russell wrote of Townsend's sequel that, "long on charm, the childish spirit of Kit and [new best friend] Hoff is infectious, and their ramshackle inventions are recognizable as the products of real, home-spun imagination." "Mischievous, [and] silly," according to *Booklist* critic Courtney Jones, "Kit is an easy hero to cheer for."

"Long ago, when I was a young mud-throwing grubby little boy, reading comic books was one of my favorite activities," Townsend told *SATA*. "Now that I am a mature and sophisticated (mud-throwing) adult, reading comic books still remains one of my favorite activities. The only real difference is, now, I also make them. The art of combining pictures and words together, then sequencing them one after another to tell stories, is a beautiful thing to me and I love doing it. I also appreciate that more and more teachers and librarians are treat-

ing comics as a legitimate story-telling art form instead of insisting that ALL comics will rot your brains out. There are only a few comics that have ever been proven to rot brains out and, thankfully, they are no longer in print."

Biographical and Critical Sources

PERIODICALS

Booklist, September 1, 2009, Courtney Jones, review of *Kit Feeny: On the Move,* p. 90; October 15, 2009, Courtney Jones, review of *The Ugly Necklace,* p. 44; January 1, 2010, Francisca Goldsmith, review of *Amazing Greek Myths of Wonder and Blunders,* p. 73.

Bulletin of the Center for Children's Books, July-August, 2007, Deborah Stevenson, review of *Billy Tartle in Say Cheese!*

Kirkus Reviews, June 15, 2007, review of *Billy Tartle in Say Cheese!;* September 1, 2009, review of *Kit Feeny:*

On the Move; January 1, 2010, review of *Amazing Greek Myths of Wonder and Blunders;* February 15, 2011, review of *Monkey and Elephant's Worst Fight Ever!*

Publishers Weekly, July 9, 2007, review of *Billy Tartle in Say Cheese!,* p. 53; January 4, 2010, review of *Amazing Greek Myths of Wonder and Blunders,* p. 49.

School Library Journal, July, 2007, Linda M. Kenton, review of *Billy Tartle in Say Cheese!,* p. 86; November, 2009, Benjamin Russell, review of *Kit Feeny: The Ugly Necklace,* p. 142; January, 2010, Paula Willey, review of *Amazing Greek Myths of Wonders and Blunders,* p. 126; March, 2010, Carrie Rogers-Whitehead, review of *Kit Feeny: On the Move,* p. 187; March, 2011, Wendy Lukehart, review of *Monkey and Elephant's Worst Fight Ever!,* p. 137.

ONLINE

Curled up with a Good Kid's Book Web site, http://www.curledupkids.com/ (October 13, 2008), Zane Ewton, review of *Billy Tartle in Say Cheese!*

Michael Townsend Home Page, http://www.mikeisgreathelikeschocolatecake.com (July 15, 2011).

Random House Web site, http://www.randomhouse.ca/ (July 15, 2011), "Michael Townsend."

V-Z

VOGEL, Carole Garbuny 1951-

Personal

Born 1951, in Pittsburgh, PA; daughter of Max (a physicist) and Melitta (a math teacher) Garbuny; married Mark A. Vogel (an electrical engineer); children: Joshua, Kate. *Education:* Kenyon College, B.S. (biology), 1972; University of Pittsburgh, M.A.T., 1973. *Hobbies and other interests:* Hiking, kayaking, camping, traveling, geneaology.

Addresses

Office—P.O. Box 444, Branchville, NJ 07826. *E-mail*—cvogel@recognitionscience.com.

Career

Educator, author, science editor, and genealogist. Elementary-school teacher in Pittsburgh, PA, 1973-78; freelance editor and author, beginning 1978; developer of trade books, textbooks, activities, and science-related teacher's guides for grades 3-12. Presenter at schools; public speaker. Genealogist, beginning 1990.

Member

Society of Children's Book Writers and Illustrators, Authors Guild, Boston Authors Club.

Awards, Honors

(With Kathryn Allen Goldner) Outstanding Science Trade Book for Children designation, National Science Teachers Association (NSTA), 1990, and Children's Choice selection, International Reading Association/ Children's Book Council (CBC), 1991, both for *The Great Yellowstone Fire;* Anna Cross Giblin nonfiction work-in-progress grant, Society of Children's Book Writers and Illustrators, 1994, and *Storytelling World* honor designation, Society of School Librarians International Honor Book selection, and Notable Social Studies Trade Book for Young People designation, National Council for the Social Studies/CBC, all 2000, all for *Legends of Landforms;* Joan Fassler Memorial Book Award, Association for the Care of Children's Health, and Honor Book selection in science category, Society of School Librarians, both 1996, both for *Will I Get Breast Cancer?;* Will Solimene Award of Excellence in Medical Communication, American Medical Writers Association (New England Chapter), NSTA/CBC Outstanding Science Trade Book for Children designation, and Books for the Teen Age selection, New York Public Library, all 2002, all for *Breast Cancer;* Best Children's Books selection, Bank Street College of Education, 2002, for both *Breast Cancer* and *Weather Legends;* Boston Authors Club Book of the Year, 2001, for *Nature's Fury;* (with Yossi Leshem) *Smithsonian* magazine Notable Children's Book selection, 2009, and *Skipping Stones* Honor Book designation, and Sydney Taylor Notable Book designation, both 2010, all for *The Man Who Flies with Birds.*

Writings

(With Kathryn Allen Goldner) *Why Mount St. Helens Blew Its Top,* illustrated by Roberta Aggarwal, Dillon Press (Minneapolis, MN), 1981.

(With Kathryn Allen Goldner) *The Dangers of Strangers,* illustrated by Lynette Schmidt, Dillon Press (Minneapolis, MN), 1983.

(With Kathryn Allen Goldner) *HBJ Science: Activity Workbooks for Levels 3-6,* Harcourt (New York, NY), 1984.

(With Kathryn Allen Goldner) *Humphrey, the Wrong-Way Whale,* Dillon Press (Minneapolis, MN), 1987.

(With Kathryn Allen Goldner) *The Great Yellowstone Fire,* Sierra Club/Little, Brown (Boston, MA), 1990.

(Editor) *We Shall Not Forget! Memories of the Holocaust,* Temple Isaiah (Lexington, MA), 1994.

The Great Midwest Flood, Little, Brown (Boston, MA), 1995.

Will I Get Breast Cancer?: Questions and Answers for Teenage Girls, Silver Burdett, 1995, revised edition published as *Breast Cancer: Questions and Answers for Young Women,* Twenty-first Century Books (Brookfield, CT), 2001.

Shock Waves through Los Angeles: The 1994 Northridge Earthquake, Little, Brown (Boston, MA), 1996.

Inside Earth ("Science Explorer" textbook series), Prentice Hall, 1999.

Legends of Landforms: Native American Lore and the Geology of the Land, Millbrook Press (Brookfield, CT), 1999.

Nature's Fury: Eyewitness Reports of Natural Disasters, Scholastic Reference (New York, NY), 2000.

Weather Legends: Native American Lore and the Science of Weather, Millbrook Press (Brookfield, CT), 2001.

(With Yossi Leshem) *The Man Who Flies with Birds,* Kar-Ben Pub. (Minneapolis, MN), 2009.

Contributor to periodicals, including *Avotaynu: The International Review of Jewish Genelogy, Working Mother, 3-2-1 Contact, Good Housekeeping, Ladies' Home Journal,* and *Writer.* Contributor to books, including *Hidden Worlds,* National Geographic Society, 1981; *3-2-1 Contact Activity Book,* Silver Burdett, 1983; *Facts on File Scientific Yearbook 1985,* Facts on File (New York, NY), 1985; *The New Golden Book Encyclopedia,* Macmillan (New York, NY), 1988; *Invitations to Literacy: Level 4,* Houghton Mifflin (Boston, MA), 1996; *Earth Explorer,* Sonic Images, 1995; *Newfangled Fairy Tales,* Meadowbrook Press (Minnetonka, MN), 1997; and *A Second Chicken Soup for the Woman's Soul,* Health Communications, 1998.

"RESTLESS SEA" NONFICTION SERIES

Dangerous Crossings, Franklin Watts (New York, NY), 2003.

Human Impact, Franklin Watts (New York, NY), 2003.

Ocean Wildlife, Franklin Watts (New York, NY), 2003.

Savage Waters, Franklin Watts (New York, NY), 2003.

Shifting Shores, Franklin Watts (New York, NY), 2003.

Underwater Exploration, Franklin Watts (New York, NY), 2003.

Sidelights

Carole Garbuny Vogel is fascinated by nature, and she shares her enthusiasm with young readers in many works of nonfiction, among them *Shock Waves through Los Angeles: The 1994 Northridge Earthquake, Nature's Fury: Eyewitness Reports of Natural Disasters, The Man Who Flies with Birds,* and her six-volume "Restless Sea" series, the last which inspires middle graders with its detailed depiction of Earth's largest ecosystem. "My friends and colleagues have dubbed me the "Queen of Natural Disasters,'" Vogel once explained

to *SATA.* "I hardly look the part but it certainly describes my passion for writing about Mother Nature's wrath. Volcanoes, hurricanes, tornadoes, and other natural disasters have always fascinated me." Vogel's books have been praised by reviewers for describing events in terms that children can comprehend while also adding new vocabulary and explanations designed to increase their interest in the field of science.

Reflecting on the roots of her writing career, Vogel recalls one childhood occurrence in particular: an unusually violent thunderstorm that took place when she was about two years old. "My older sister and I watched the lightning display from my parents' bedroom window while my father tried to soothe us with scientific explanations," the author later recalled to *SATA.* "I didn't understand a word, but I knew I needn't be afraid." In school, a lesson about the volcanic eruption that buried the ancient city of Pompeii further fueled Vogel's interest in the power of nature: "I was fascinated by the images of people frozen in motion by Vesuvius's fury. From that point on I was hooked."

Vogel's books have included discussions of the eruption of Washington State's Mount St. Helens in 1980, the Yellowstone fire of 1988, the Midwest flood of 1993, and the Northridge, California, earthquake of 1994. "I don't experience first-hand the disasters I write about," Vogel once noted. "Instead, I pore over newspaper clippings, magazine articles, and videotapes. I surf the Web, and conduct extensive telephone interviews with eyewitnesses, scientists, and other experts. However, I do need to feel the impact of nature's wrath emotionally. My writing contains strong action verbs, and getting into the subject helps me get into the spirit."

In 1980, near the beginning of her writing career, Vogel teamed up with Kathryn Allen Goldner, a science editor, to create a number of books and magazine articles. Their partnership, which lasted nine years, enabled both women to establish viable writing careers and still have time to devote to their families. Among their most notable collaborative efforts are *The Great Yellowstone Fire, Why Mount St. Helens Blew Its Top, Humphrey the Wrong-Way Whale,* and *The Dangers of Strangers.*

In *The Great Yellowstone Fire* Vogel and Goldner explain the events surrounding the huge blaze that destroyed much of Yellowstone National Park in 1988. Not only the fire, but the forestry policies that contributed to its severity and its impact on area wildlife are discussed in descriptive text that "vividly conveys events and their significance as history," according to *Horn Book* reviewer Margaret A. Bush. A *Kirkus Reviews* critic proclaimed *The Great Yellowstone Fire* "well organized, gracefully written, and beautifully produced," and an *Appraisal* contributor declared the book to be a "model of good science writing."

In *The Great Midwest Flood* the deluge that laid waste to many Midwestern states in 1993 is described by Vogel in a text geared for younger readers. Beginning with the history of the Mississippi River up until the moment that it burst its banks, the author goes on to explain the mechanisms created to control river flow, as well as the costs of the flood cleanup in both human misery and money. Calling Vogel's analysis of the causes and effects of the 1993 disaster "insightful and well founded," *School Library Journal* contributor Charlyn Lyons dubbed *The Great Midwest Flood* "clear and concise," while *Booklist* critic Chris Sherman wrote that the book "captures the drama and tension" of the natural disaster. In *Appraisal,* Ellen Rappaport maintained that Vogel's text contains "scientific, historical, and human interest [elements that] involve the reader in the power of nature to transform the environment."

Shock Waves through Los Angeles describes the cause and impact of the 1994 Los Angeles quake that destroyed 112,000 buildings and caused the deaths of fifty-eight people. In reporting the earthquake and its aftermath, Vogel concentrates on "acts of heroism and the tragedies that followed the natural disaster," according to *School Library Journal* contributor Anne Connor, the critic praising Vogel for her "clear prose" and her avoidance of sensationalism. The inclusion of full-color photographs and maps in *Shock Waves through Los Angeles* provide young readers the opportunity to "see for themselves" what happened during the quake, "without the inclusion of any grisly images," in the opinion of *Booklist* reviewer Susan Dove Lempke. Lempke added that Vogel "adeptly walks the line between scientific information and the irresistible fascination with disasters . . . and she puts it all at child level."

In *The Legends of Landforms: Native American Lore and the Geology of the Land* Vogel describes the exploits of fearsome dragons, bloodthirsty serpents, mighty giants, and other spirit beings that ancient Native Americans attributed to the creation of such spectacular landforms as the Grand Canyon and Niagara Falls. Juxtaposed with these legends is a discussion of the physical forces that actually shaped earth's terrain, from colliding continents and simmering volcanoes to earth-rattling quakes and colossal floods. Vogel turns to weather in the related *Weather Legends: Native American Lore and the Science of Weather,* which uses recent weather anomalies to "link ancient myths to modern-day realities," according to *Booklist* critic Ellen Mandel.

Vogel's discovery of the work of Israeli ornithologist Yossi Leshem inspired her work on *The Man Who Flies with Birds.* As a Ph.D. student, Leshem learned about the hazards birds pose to military pilots; a bird-plane collision, or "bird strike," was usually fatal to the bird and sometimes to the pilot as well, in addition to causing destruction to the aircraft. In 1983 he began studying the migration of larger bird species, such as hawks, pelicans, storks, and buzzards, then used his understanding of migratory patterns to help the Israeli military reduce the incidence of bird strikes by over seventy-five percent. "I loved Yossi's passion for birds and his use of science to resolve the conflict between birds and planes," Vogel remarked in an interview on the Kar-Ben Publishing Web site. "Yossi's message about bringing peace to the Middle East one bird lover at a time resonated deeply with me, as did his pro-environmental activism." Vogel used her interviews with Leshem to create the text for *The Man Who Flies with Birds,* supplementing it with maps, diagrams, and full-page color photographs. Calling *The Man Who Flies with Birds* an "inspiring title on a most timely topic," Scheps added that Vogel and Leshem's work "will appeal to those who are fascinated with wildlife, Earth science, and technology," while in *Science Teacher* Elizabeth Hayward touched upon the international scope of the ornithologist's work by noting that it "may also serve as a starting point for peace among nations traditionally at war."

In contrast to much of her writing, which features natural disasters, Vogel's *Will I Get Breast Cancer? Questions and Answers for Teenage Girls* was inspired by a good friend who died of the disease while in her early thirties. "I wanted to show my friend's daughter that her mother's fate did not have to be her own," the author explained. Using a question-and-answer approach, Vogel's book imparts valuable information on a topic of concern for many young women and has been more-recently updated as *Breast Cancer: Questions and Answers for Young Women. Will I Get Breast Cancer?* drew praise from *Booklist* commentator Stephanie Zvirin, who called it "a fine book . . . that not only always keeps its teenage audience in mind, but also presents the facts without patronizing or pretending." In *School Library Journal* Mary R. Hofmann noted of Vogel's revised work that her "excellent reference" features "two pivotal chapters [that] address the myriad emotional and physical issues involved when one's mother has breast cancer."

When choosing a subject to write about, Vogel always keeps her readers in mind and she keeps atuned to their evolving interests by visiting schools and libraries. "Kids don't think of my books as science books even though my writing is laced with scientific explanations," she once explained. "I feel a great obligation to make my text as accurate as possible, so I always have a series of experts review my manuscripts."

Biographical and Critical Sources

PERIODICALS

Appraisal, winter, 1991, review of *The Great Yellowstone Fire,* p. 55; summer, 1996, Ellen Rappaport, review of *The Great Midwest Flood,* p. 38.

Booklist, August, 1995, Stephanie Zvirin, review of *Will I Get Breast Cancer? Questions and Answers for Teenage Girls,* p. 1940; October 1, 1996, Susan Dove Lempke, review of *Shock Waves through Los Angeles: The Northridge Earthquake,* p. 346; September 1, 2001, Ellen Mandel, review of *Weather Legends: Native American Lore and the Science of Weather,* p. 102.

Bulletin of the Center for Children's Books, December, 1995, review of *The Great Midwest Flood,* p. 143; December, 2009, Deborah Stevenson, review of *The Man Who Flies with Birds,* p. 170.

Horn Book, May-June, 1990, Margaret A. Bush, review of *The Great Yellowstone Fire,* p. 351.

Kirkus Reviews, May 15, 1990, review of *The Great Yellowstone Fire,* p. 735; August 1, 2009, review of *The Man Who Flies with Birds.*

Publishers Weekly, July 10, 1987, Genevieve Stuttaford, review of *Humphrey the Wrong-Way Whale,* p. 72; October 7, 1996, review of *Shock Waves through Los Angeles,* p. 78.

School Library Journal, January, 1984, review of *The Dangers of Strangers,* p. 69; July, 1995, Martha Gordon, review of *Will I Get Breast Cancer?,* p. 103; January, 1996, Charlyn Lyons, review of *The Great Midwest Flood,* pp. 126-127; October, 1996, Anne Connor, review of *Shock Waves through Los Angeles,* p. 119; May, 2001, Mary R. Hofmann, review of *Breast Cancer: Questions and Answers for Young Women,* p. 172; December, 2009, Susan Scheps, review of *The Man Who Flies with Birds,* p. 143.

Voice of Youth Advocates, October, 1995, review of *Will I Get Breast Cancer?,* p. 262; August, 2001, review of *Breast Cancer,* p. 227.

ONLINE

Carole Garbuny Vogel Home Page, http://www.recognitionscience.com/cgv (June 15, 2011).

Cynsations Web log, http://cynthialeitichsmith.blogspot.com (January 25, 2010, Cynthia Leitich Smith, interview with Vogel.

Kar-Ben Publishing Web log, http://karbenbooks.blogspot.com? (November, 2009), interview with Vogel.*

*   *   *

WABER, Paulis

Personal

Born in New York, NY; daughter of Bernard (a children's author) and Ethel Waber; married; children: three.

Addresses

Home—Washington, DC. *E-mail*—pauliswaber@gmail.com.

Career

Illustrator and artist. Presenter at schools.

Illustrator

Bernard Waber, *Lyle Walks the Dogs: A Counting Book,* Houghton Mifflin Books for Children (Boston, MA), 2010.

Bernard Waber, *Lyle, Lyle, Hello, Hello,* Houghton Mifflin Books for Children (Boston, MA), 2011.

Sidelights

Paulis Waber grew up not only around children's books but also around one of their most beloved creators. As the daughter of author/illustrator Bernard Waber, she is well aware of the time and effort that each colorful picture-book can entail. When her father's diminishing vision required that he have assistance in adapting his popular character Lyle the Crocodile for stories geared for very young children, Paulis Waber was only too happy to volunteer. Bernard Waber's nine original "Lyle the Crocodile" books focus on emotions and family situations that many children experience. The sprightly green, city-dwelling crocodile first made his appearance in 1962, in *The House on East 88th Street,* which featured a dedication to a then-very-young Paulis. When Lyle reappeared in 2010's *Lyle Walks the Dogs: A Counting Book,* his new story bore a dual dedication: from father to daughter and from daughter to dad.

In *Lyle Walks the Dogs* Lyle the Crocodile is embarking on a new career as a dog walker. While he begins with only one dog in his care, the crocodile does such a good job that the next day he finds himself with two, then three, and so forth up to ten dogs. As young listeners practice their counting skills with the encouragement of Bernard Waber's simple text, they also enjoy Lyle's upbeat personality and his ability to find a way to keep even the most rambunctious pup under control. Describing *Lyle Walks the Dogs* as a "peppy story," a *Publishers Weekly* critic added that Paulis Waber's "watercolor, ink, and pencil drawings flawlessly replicate that airiness and humor of her father's iconic art." Also praising the father-daughter collaboration, Kathleen Kelly MacMillan added in *School Library Journal* that the crocodile's "sunny disposition has lost none of its appeal."

"My father's talent, the fact that Lyle was his original creation, and the great popularity of these books did create apprehension for me," Waber admitted to *Publishers Weekly* interviewer Sally Lodge in discussing her work on the collaborative picture-book project. Lyle "remind[s] me of my father, and he's been a part of my life for so long that he seems very real. He is so sweet, self-effacing, and concerned with other people. Doing this book, it helped that I knew Lyle so well because I know my father so well."

Paulis Waber created the artwork that pairs with her father, Bernard Waber's text in the engaging concept book Lyle Walks the Dogs. (Illustration copyright © 2010 by Paulis Waber. Reproduced with permission of Houghton Mifflin Books for Children, an imprint of Houghton Mifflin Harcourt Publishing Company.)

Biographical and Critical Sources

PERIODICALS

Publishers Weekly, April 15, 2010, Sally Lodge, "Father-Daughter Team Brings Back Lyle the Crocodile"; April 19, 2010, review of *Lyle Walks the Dogs: A Counting Book,* p. 50.
School Library Journal, May, 2010, Kathleen Kelly Macmillan, review of *Lyle Walks the Dogs,* p. 94.

ONLINE

Houghton Mifflin Web site, http://www.houghtonmifflin books.com/ (June 25, 2011), "Paulis Waber."

Paulis and Bernard Waber Web log, http://waberchat.word press.com (June 25, 2011).*

*   *   *

WIEWANDT, Thomas 1945-

Personal

Born 1945. *Education:* University of Arizona, M.S. (zoology); Cornell University, Ph.D. (ecology), 1977.

Addresses

Home and office—P.O. Box 5118, Tucson, AZ 85703.

Career

Photographer and videographer, ecoguide, and author. Freelance photographer and wildlife tour leader, beginning 1985. Artist in residence at Petrified Forest National Park, 2006. Chief scientific advisor, International Reptile Conservation Foundation; member, International Union for Conservation of Nature Species Survival Commission. *Exhibitions:* Work exhibited at numerous juried shows and galleries.

Member

International Association of Panoramic Photographers, American Society of Media Photographers, American Society of Picture Professionals, North American Nature Photographers Association, Authors Guild, International Union for the Conservation of Nature (member, Iguana Specialist Group), International Reptile Conservation Foundation.

Awards, Honors

Four Cine Golden Eagles awards, 1982-87; Emmy Award nomination for cinematography, 1987; Eastman Kodak Outstanding Photographic Achievement Award, 1987; Gold Apple Award, National Education Film and Video Festival, 1987; John Burroughs Outstanding Nature Books for Young Readers listee, 1990, for *Hidden Life of the Desert;* iParenting Media Award, 2001, for *The Southwest Inside Out;* Gold Benjamin Franklin Award, 2002; Gold Independent Publishers Award, 2002; Best Book Award, Arizona Book Publishers Association, 2003; winner in wildlife category, Photography Masters Cup Awards, 2008.

Writings

AND PHOTOGRAPHER

Hidden Life of the Desert, Crown Publishers (New York, NY), 1990, new edition, Mountain Press Publishing (Missoula, MT), 2010.

(With Maureen Wilks) *The Southwest Inside Out: An Illustrated Guide to the Land and Its History,* Wild Horizons (Tucson, AZ), 2001.

Contributor of photographs to periodicals, including *Arizona Highways, Audubon, Geo, Smithsonian,* and publications of the National Geographic Society and National Wildlife Federation.

Sidelights

Photographer Thomas Wiewandt specializes in capturing the multifaceted beauty of the natural world in his photographs, which have been widely published and exhibited. A videographer as well as a still photographer, Wiewandt has created award-winning films for the British Broadcasting Corporation and the National Geo-

graphic Society. *Hidden Life of the Desert* he introduces the complex desert ecosystem that surrounds the Arizona-based photographer, and he continues to explore this region in *The Southwest Inside Out: An Illustrated Guide to the Land and Its History.*

In *Hidden Life of the Desert* Wiewandt leads readers on a tour of the Sonoran Desert, a fascinating region in which contrasts abound. While stretches of sands, sharply cut mountains, and the occasional cactus might register at first glance, Wiewandt shows that numerous plants and animals have found creative ways to make the harsh desert environment their home, and he moves through the region's five seasons—spring, dry summer, wet summer, fall, and winter—to capture myriad forms of life shifting across the desert's canvas. Originally published in 1990, *Hidden Life of the Desert* was updated in 2010 with a new chapter that addresses the region's future as a changing climate threatens water availability. In addition, Wiewandt adds maps and a glossary, a list of both English-and Spanish-language online and print resources for further study, and many new photographs. "Striking photographs of Sonoran desert scenery and wildlife illustrate this celebration of an ecosystem," wrote a *Kirkus Reviews* writer in appraising the new edition of *Hidden Life of the Desert,* the critic concluding that Wiewandt's book "deserves more than regional attention."

Thomas Wiewandt's artful nature photography pairs with his illuminating text to introduce an amazing ecosystem in **Hidden Life of the Desert.** (Copyright © 2010 by Thomas Wiewandt. Reproduced with permission of the photographer and author.)

Collaborating with noted geologist Maureen Wilks, Wiewandt continues his exploration of America's desert regions in *The Southwest Inside Out*. A natural-history tour of Arizona, New Mexico, California, Colorado, Nevada, and Utah that is accessible to the general reader, the book ranges in focus from volcanoes, caves, and canyons to rivers, lakes, and the region's ever-shifting sea of sand, mixing interesting geological facts with the region's social history. Complete with more than 300 full-color photographs by Wiewandt, *The Southwest Inside Out* combines "stunning color photographs and [an] engaging text," according to John McCormick in *Library Journal*.

"A deeper understanding of all living things has helped to fuel my creative passions," noted Wiewandt in an artist's statement posted on the Petrified Forest National Park Web site, "and the medium of photography has allowed me to comfortably bring the worlds of art and science together. . . . Much of my thinking and photography is aimed at telling stories. To a great extent this comes from my academic background and desire to communicate ideas and experiences with depth. My love of wildlife and animal behavior led me to motion picture work. Cinematography is a great story-telling medium and relieves the frustration of using stills to portray a world that never stands still."

Biographical and Critical Sources

PERIODICALS

Children's Bookwatch, May, 2010, review of *Hidden Life of the Desert.*
Kirkus Reviews, April 15, 2010, review of *Hidden Life of the Desert.*
Library Journal, September 1, 2001, John McCormick, review of *The Southwest Inside Out: An Illustrated Guide to the Land and Its History,* p. 214.

ONLINE

Petrified Forest National Park Web site, http://www.nps. gov/pefo/ (July 15, 2011), "Thomas Wiewandt."
Thomas Wiewandt Home Page, http://www.wildhorizons. com (July 15, 2011).*

*   *   *

WILDISH, Lee

Personal

Born in England. *Education:* B.A. (with honors).

Addresses

Home—Nottingham, England. *Agent*—Bright Agency, Studio 102, 250 York Rd., Battersea, London SW11 3SJ, England. *E-mail*—enquiries@wildishillustration. com.

Career

Illustrator. Worked as a graphic designer, Nottingham, England; former studio manager for printers and newspapers; manager of production development for greeting-card company for five years; freelance illustrator.

Illustrator

Leigh Attaway Wilcox, *All Better: A Touch-and-Heal Book,* Piggy Toes Press (Atlanta, GA), 2007.
Sue Graves, *Fizz Whiz,* Franklin Watts (London, England), 2007.
Jonny Zucker, *MP3 Mind Control,* Stone Arch Books (Minneapolis, MN), 2008.
Victoria Roberts, *I've Finished,* Caterpillar Books (England), 2008.
Jane West, *Self Defender,* Stone Arch Books (Minneapolis, MN), 2008.
The Boy Who Cried Wolf, Sterling (New York, NY), 2008.
Kes Gray, *Mom and Dad Glue,* Barron's (Hauppauge, NY), 2009, published as *Mum and Dad Glue,* Hodder Children's (London, England), 2009.
Sam Taplin and Stephanie Jones, *This Is My Dinosaur* (interactive book), Usborne (London, England), 2009.
Snuggly Bunny, Scholastic (New York, NY), 2009.
Paul Bright, *Charlie's Superhero Underpants,* Little Tiger Press (London, England), 2009, Good Books (Intercourse, PA), 2010.
Lynne Rickards, *Jacob O'Reilly Wants a Pet,* Barron's Educational, 2010.
Steve Smallman, *Dragon Stew,* Good Books (Intercourse, PA), 2010.
Marilyn Singer, *Nose to Nose, Tail to Tail: Love Poems from the Animal Kingdom,* Alfred A. Knopf (New York, NY), 2010.
Mairi Mackinnon, *Wild School,* Usborne (London, England), 2010.
Tamsyn Murray, *Showbiz Sensation* ("Stunt Bunny" series), Simon & Schuster (London, England), 2010.
Shutta Crum, *Thomas and the Dragon Queen,* Alfred A. Knopf (New York, NY), 2010.
Anna Claybourne, *Don't Wake the Lion,* Caterpillar Books (England), 2010.
Kes Gray, *Leave Me Alone,* Hodder Children's (London, England), 2011.
Tamsyn Murray, *Tour Troubles* ("Stunt Bunny" series), Simon & Schuster (London, England), 2011.
Tamsyn Murray, *Rabbit Racer* ("Stunt Bunny" series), Simon & Schuster (London, England), 2011.
Andrew Weale, *The Spooky Spooky House,* Picture Corgi (London, England), 2011.
Tamsyn Murray, *Medal Mayhem* ("Stunt Bunny" series), Simon & Schuster (London, England), 2012.

Also illustrator of educational readers.

Books featuring Wildish's art have been translated into several languages, including French, German, Italian, Spanish, and Welsh.

"NOISY BOOKS" INTERACTIVE BOARD-BOOK SERIES

Sam Taplin, *Noisy Jungle*, Usborne (London, England), 2009.

Sam Taplin, *Noisy Football Match*, Usborne (London, England), 2009.

Sam Taplin, *Noisy Zoo*, Usborne (London, England), 2009.

Sam Taplin, *Noisy Spooky Book*, Usborne (London, England), 2010.

Jessica Greenwell, *Noisy Monsters*, Usborne (London, England), 2010.

Jessica Greenwell, *Noisy Body Book*, Usborne (London, England), 2011.

"GRUNT AND THE GROUCH" READER SERIES

Tracey Corderoy, *The Grunt and the Grouch*, Little Tiger Press (London, England), 2010.

Tracey Corderoy, *Beastly Feast*, Little Tiger Press (London, England), 2010.

Tracey Corderoy, *Pick 'n' Mix*, Little Tiger Press (London, England), 2010.

Sidelights

Lee Wildish began his creative career as a graphic designer and worked in several different areas before turning to book illustration. A job as a studio manager for a printer and newspaper allowed Wildish to experience the commercial side of being an artist, and during his five-year stint creating art and designs for a greeting-card company he was able to follow his concepts from start to finish. As a freelance illustrator, Wildish's work has proved to be a natural fit for children's books, and it has been paired with texts by authors ranging from

Shutta Crum and Kes Gray to Steve Smallman and Marilyn Singer. "I find Nature and people the biggest influence in my work," Wildish noted on his home page, and he tries "to get as much character and expression into each piece of work as possible." Of course, he added, the best part is being able to add a dash of humor. "There is nothing more warming than seeing people enjoying and laughing at a published book that you have illustrated."

Early in his book-illustration career Wildish created artwork for *All Better: A Touch-and-Heal Book,* which pairs a simple text by Leigh Attaway Wilcox with Velcro bandages that enable pre-readers to administer to young animals with boo boos. Other books for very young children include *Noisy Zoo, Noisy Jungle,* and *Noisy Monsters,* all part of a series of board books that feature Wildish's round-headed characters along with interactive elements such as push buttons and pull tabs.

Moving to a slightly older audience, Wildish has collaborated with Gray on several books for children in the early elementary grades. *Mom and Dad Glue* addresses the issue of divorce and how it affects the family, while *Leave Me Alone* finds a group of friends helping a youngster stand up to a school bully. Reviewing the first book in *School Library Journal,* Julie Roach cited the mix of "warm cartoon illustrations and bouncy rhymes" in *Mom and Dad Glue* while a *Publishers Weekly* critic wrote that Wildish's depiction of Gray's "little but large-headed hero is instantly sympathetic in both his determination and vulnerability."

A more fantastical story plays out in his art for Paul Bright's *Charlie's Superhero Underpants,* as an adventurous young lad is determined to follow his bright red

Lee Wildish injects added humor into Paul Bright's story of a boy's missing unmentionables in his imaginative artwork for **Charlie's Superhero Underpants.** (Illustration copyright © 2009 by Lee Wildish. Reproduced with permission of Little Tiger Books.)

underpants after they are carried off the clothesline by a gust of wind. "Wildish's humorous illustrations capture the streets of Paris, the Serengeti plain, a Peruvian plateau, the waters of the Mississippi, and the mountains of Nepal," observed *School Library Journal* critic Gloria Koster in reviewing Bright's far-flung story, and a *Publishers Weekly* critic praised the artist's work for "providing the bulk of the book's zip and humor."

A determined young boy reflects the yearnings of many children in *Jacob O'Reilly Wants a Pet*, a story that combines Wildish's line-and-watercolor art with a rhyming text by Lynne Rickards that *Booklist* critic Connie Fletcher characterized as "boisterous." Fletcher also recommended the book's "riotous illustrations," while *School Library Journal* critic contributor Linda L. Walkins noted that the illustrator "deftly captures the unique personalities of the individual animals" which young Jacob encounters on his search for the perfect pet. For Thomas, the young hero of Crum's chapter book *Thomas and the Dragon Queen*, animals are part of the problem when the safety of a kidnapped princess is at stake. Taking stock of Wildish's black-and-white illustrations for Crum's story, *School Library Journal* critic Robyn Gioia deemed them "expressive," while a *Publishers Weekly* critic concluded that the "high-spirited" cartoon art in *Thomas and the Dragon Queen* "enhance[s] the ample action and humor" in Crum's "taut fantasy."

Biographical and Critical Sources

PERIODICALS

Booklist, April 15, 2010, Connie Fletcher, review of *Jacob O'Reilly Wants a Pet,* p. 51; July 1, 2010, Carolyn Phelan, review of *Thomas and the Dragon Queen,* p. 61.

Bookseller, December 18, 2009, Marilyn Brocklehurst, review of *Jacob O'Reilly Wants a Pet,* p. 25.

Horn Book, July-August, 2010, Robin C. Smith, review of *Thomas and the Dragon Queen,* p. 104.

Publishers Weekly, November 23, 2009, review of *Mom and Dad Glue,* p. 55; April 26, 2010, review of *Charlie's Superhero Underpants,* p. 105; June 21, 2010, review of *Thomas and the Dragon Queen,* p. 46.

School Librarian, summer, 2010, Jane Doonan, review of *Mum and Dad Glue,* p. 88; autumn, 2010, Angela Redfern, review of *Jacob O'Reilly Wants a Pet,* p. 160.

School Library Journal, February, 2010, Julie Roach, review of *Mom and Dad Glue,* p. 84; May, 2010, Linda L. Walkins, review of *Jacob O'Reilly Wants a Pet,* p. 90; June, 2010, Gloria Koster, review of *Charlie's Superhero Underpants,* p. 65; August, 2010, Robyn Gioia, review of *Thomas and the Dragon Queen,* p. 72; December, 2010, Tanya Boudreau, review of *Dragon Stew,* p. 88.

ONLINE

Lee Wildish Home Page, http://www.wildishillustration. com (June 25, 2011).

*   *   *

WILLSON, Sarah
See ALBEE, Sarah

*   *   *

WRONGO, I.B.
See KATZ, Alan

*   *   *

YUE, Stephanie 1984-

Personal

Born 1984. *Education:* Pratt Institute, B.F.A. (communication design and illustration), 2006.

Addresses

Home—Providence, RI. *E-mail*—quezzie@gmail.com.

Career

Illustrator, designer, animator, and sequential artist. Creator of concept art and character design for Gamelab, 2006, and Curious Pictures, 2006-07; Lifemeter Comics, editor, co-creator, and artist, 2006-08.

Illustrator

Prudence Breitrose, *Thumb-top,* Disney/Hyperion (New York, NY), 2011.

Contributor to periodicals, including *Nickelodeon* and *Purple Sky.* Creator, with Zack Giallongo, of "Novasett Island" mini comics.

"GUINEA PIG, PET SHOP PRIVATE EYE" SERIES

Colleen A.F. Venable, *And Then There Were Gnomes,* Graphic Universe (Minneapolis, MN), 2010.

Colleen A.F. Venable, *Hamster and Cheese,* Graphic Universe (Minneapolis, MN), 2010.

Colleen A.F. Venable, *The Ferret's a Foot,* Graphic Universe (Minneapolis, MN), 2011.

Sidelights

On her path to becoming an illustrator, Stephanie Yue was inspired by her father's collection of "Calvin and Hobbes" comic strips, as well as by "Tintin," the comic-book series created by Belgian artist Hergé that is noted for its uniformly clean-lined, two-dimensional sequential art. Yue began creating sequential art while studying illustration at Brooklyn's Pratt Institute, and she started her illustration career after graduating in 2006. In addition to creating the "Novasett Island" mini-comic with Zack Giallongo, she has also contributed the artwork to the books in Colleen A.F. Venable's "Guinea Pig, Pet Shop Private Eye" series.

With titles such as *And Then There Were Gnomes, Hamster and Cheese,* and *The Ferret's a Foot,* Venable's stories promise humor, and Yue's art helps to fulfil that promise. In the first "Pet Shop Private Eye" book, *Hamster and Cheese,* readers meet Sasspants, a guinea pig whose voracious reading habit has given her the knowledge to solve mysteries. It is no surprise, then that Hamisher, one of the pet shop hamsters, asks for Sasspants' advice when the befuddled shop owner's lunchtime sandwiches start to disappear. Described by a *Publishers Weekly* critic as "a lively and entertaining book," *Hamster and Cheese* features "colorful art [that] uses a straightforward panel design that's easy to follow," in the opinion of *Booklist* critic Kat Kan. Appraising the sequel, *And Then There Were Gnomes,* which raises the possibility that the pet shop may be haunted, another *Publishers Weekly* contributor concluded of Venable and Yue's illustrated series that "everything about it could be described as cute, from the art to the characters' personalities."

Biographical and Critical Sources

PERIODICALS

Booklist, March 15, 2010, Kat Kan, review of *Hamster and Cheese,* p. 62.
Publishers Weekly, September 6, 2010, review of *And Then There Were Gnomes,* p. 43.
School Library Journal, May, 2010, Marilyn Ackerman, review of *Hamster and Cheese,* p. 143.

ONLINE

Stephanie Yue Web log, http://jellycity.com (June 25, 2011).*

*   *   *

ZAKANITCH, Robert Rahway 1935-
(Robert S. Zakanitch)

Personal

Born 1935, in Elizabeth, NJ. *Education:* Newark School of Fine and Industrial Art, B.A., 1958.

Addresses

Home—New York, NY. *E-mail*—robert@zakanitch.com.

Career

Illustrator and fine-art painter. Worked for advertising agencies and studios in New York, NY, 1958-60s. Teacher at schools, including University of California, San Diego, 1972-73, Oklahoma Summer Arts Institute, 1988, 1999, and Boston Museum School, 1996; visiting artist at Art Institute of Chicago, 1977; lecturer and panelist. *Exhibitions:* Work included in numerous exhibitions, including at Institute of Contemporary Art, Philadelphia, PA, 1981; Sidney Janis Gallery, New York, NY, 1982; Norton Gallery of Art, West Palm Beach, Fl, 1983; Locks Gallery, Philadelphia, 1986, 1999, 2008; Jason McCoy Gallery, New York, NY, 1994; Scrips College, Claremont, CA, 1997; and Spike Gallery, New York, NY, 2003-06. Work included in collections at art institutions, including Albright-Knox Museum, Buffalo, NY; Brooklyn Museum, Brooklyn, NY; Whitney Museum of American Art, New York, NY; High Museum of Art, Atlanta, GA; Phoenix Art Museum, Phoenix, AZ; Milwaukee Art Museum, Milwaukee, WI; Hirshhorn Museum and Sculpture Garden, Washington, DC; Denver Art Museum, Denver, CO; in museums in France, Portugal, Switzerland, and Germany; and in numerous private collections. *Military service:* U.S. Army, c. 1958-59.

Awards, Honors

New York CAPS grant, 1970; John Simon Guggenheim Foundation grant, 1995.

Illustrator

Maya Gottfried, *Last Night I Dreamed a Circus,* Alfred A. Knopf (New York, NY), 2003.
Maya Gottfried, *Good Dog,* Alfred A. Knopf (New York, NY), 2005.
Maya Gottfried, *Our Farm: By the Animals of Farm Sanctuary,* Alfred A. Knopf (New York, NY), 2010.

Sidelights

The son of Czech immigrants, painter Robert Rahway Zakanitch helped establish the Pattern and Decoration movement which drew on the decorative elements of domestic arts and crafts and inspired several New York City artists during the mid-1970s. Although art aficionados may know his work through his many gallery exhibits, Zakanitch's paintings have also been paired with poems by Maya Gottfried in the books *Last Night I Dreamed a Circus, Good Dog,* and *Our Farm: By the Animals of Farm Sanctuary.*

Last Night I Dreamed a Circus allows readers to experience the life of a circus performer, as Gottfried's young narrator imagines being a clown, a horseback rider, a trapeze artist, and even a four-legged performer such as a dancing circus dog or a caged African lion. Zakanitch enhances the drama of the colorful setting by positioning each of these performers against an inky black background, incorporating rich colors and intri-

Fine-art painter Robert Rahway Zakanitch teams up with poet Maya Gottfried to introduce readers to the residents of a farm sanctuary in Our Farm.
(Illustration copyright © 2010 by Robert Rahway Zakanitch. Used by permission of Alfred A. Knopf, an imprint of Random House Children's Books, a division of Random House, Inc.)

cate patterns in a way that evokes what *Booklist* critic GraceAnne A. DeCandido referenced as "the Cirque du Soleil as well as . . . Eastern European folk art." While noting the "static" quality of Zakanitch's work, Kathie Meizner added in her *School Library Journal* review that *Last Night I Dreamed a Circus* is "visually intriguing," and a *Kirkus Reviews* writer wrote that Gottfried's poems seem "sprinkled delicately through the pages" of a field of "enchanting" art.

Good Dog started as a series of sixteen oil paintings, each depicting a unique breed of dog, from a stoic bulldog to a well-pedigreed Maltese to a harried, excitable Chihuahua. With their gessoed black backgrounds, Zakanitch's colorful paintings focus attention on the colors and textures that differentiate the various breeds, and the name of the breed, written in white chalk, adds a static, graphic quality. These paintings are linked by loose pencil drawings, and Gottfried's free-verse poems thread through the art to transform the whole into a cohesive picture book. Praising the poems in *Good Dog* for their "warm humor," a *Publishers Weekly* critic added that the verses pair with Zakanitch's "inviting artwork" to "do these dogs proud." For Linda Ludke, writing in *School Library Journal*, the "beautifully designed" picture book with its "stunning oil paintings" treats "animal lovers . . . [to a] captivating dog show," while a *Kirkus Reviews* writer described *Good Dog* as a "simple but memorable artistic composition."

Continuing his creative collaboration with Gottfried, Zakanitch also brings to life the poems in *Our Farm,* a "homage to the shelter for neglected and abused farm animals where Gottfried served as a volunteer," according to *School Library Journal* critic Susan Weitz. Here his highly textured colored paintings stand out against bright white pages and are supplemented by penciled drawings that serve as spot art and sometimes become the illustrated background for an animal-authored poem. Narrators include Maya the cow, a sheep named Hilda, a rooster named Mayfly, and even a free-running black-and-white piglet named J.D., and their free-verse or haiku musings capture the bucolic pace of life in their adopted farm home. Gottfried closes *Our Farm* with a brief discussion of the animal farm movement, which provides a quiet environment for creatures that have been rescued or discarded from commercial farms.

Praising Zakanitch's "handsome" watercolor paintings and drawings, Hazel Rochman added in *Booklist* that his "images about the joy of home will move young animal lovers." Each of the artist's "superb" paintings "exhibit[s] . . . a masterful technique, tenderness, subtlety, and humor," asserted Susan Weitz in her *School Library Journal* review of *Our Farm,* and a *Publishers Weekly* contributor dubbed the book "aesthetically intriguing and fun."

Biographical and Critical Sources

PERIODICALS

Booklist, February 1, 2003, GraceAnne A. DeCandido, review of *Last Night I Dreamed a Circus,* p. 1000; March 1, 2010, Hazel Rochman, review of *Our Farm: By the Animals of Farm Sanctuary,* p. 75.
Children's Bookwatch, April, 2010, review of *Our Farm.*
Kirkus Reviews, November 15, 2002, review of *Last Night I Dreamed a Circus,* p. 1692; January 1, 2005, review of *Good Dog,* p. 51; February 15, 2010, review of *Our Farm.*
Publishers Weekly, December 2, 2002, review of *Last Night I Dreamed a Circus,* p. 51; January 24, 2005, review of *Good Dog,* p. 242; January 11, 2010, review of *Our Farm,* p. 47.
School Library Journal, May, 2003, Kathie Meizner, review of *Last Night I Dreamed a Circus,* p. 119; April, 2005, Linda Ludke, review of *Good Dog,* p. 122; January, 2010, Susan Weitz, review of *Our Farm,* p. 86.

ONLINE

Archives of American Art Web site, http://www.aaa.si.edu/ (June 25, 2011), Paul Cummings, "Oral History Interview with Robert Zakanitch, 1972 Aub. 23-30" (transcript).
Robert Rahway Zakanitch Home Page, http://www.zakanitch.com (June 25, 2011).*

* * *

ZAKANITCH, Robert S.
See ZAKANITCH, Robert Rahway

Illustrations Index

(In the following index, the number of the *volume* in which an illustrator's work appears is given *before* the colon, and the *page number* on which it appears is given *after* the colon. For example, a drawing by Adams, Adrienne appears in Volume 2 on page 6, another drawing by her appears in Volume 3 on page 80, another drawing in Volume 8 on page 1, and so on and so on. . . .)

YABC

Index references to *YABC* refer to listings appearing in the two-volume *Yesterday's Authors of Books for Children,* also published by Gale, Cengage Learning. *YABC* covers prominent authors and illustrators who died prior to 1960.

A

Aas, Ulf *5:* 174
Abbe, S. van
  See van Abbe, S.
Abel, Raymond *6:* 122; *7:* 195; *12:* 3; *21:* 86; *25:* 119
Abelliera, Aldo *71:* 120
Abolafia, Yossi *60:* 2; *93:* 163; *152:* 202
Abrahams, Hilary *26:* 205; *29:* 24, 25; *53:* 61
Abrams, Kathie *36:* 170
Abrams, Lester *49:* 26
Abulafia, Yossi *154:* 67; *177:* 3
Accardo, Anthony *191:* 3, 8
Accornero, Franco *184:* 8
Accorsi, William *11:* 198
Acs, Laszlo *14:* 156; *42:* 22
Acuna, Ed *198:* 79
Adams, Adrienne *2:* 6; *3:* 80; *8:* 1; *15:* 107; *16:* 180; *20:* 65; *22:* 134, 135; *33:* 75; *36:* 103, 112; *39:* 74; *86:* 54; *90:* 2, 3
Adams, Connie J. *129:* 68
Adams, John Wolcott *17:* 162
Adams, Kathryn *224:* 1
Adams, Lynn *96:* 44
Adams, Norman *55:* 82
Adams, Pam *112:* 1, 2
Adams, Sarah *98:* 126; *164:* 180
Adams, Steve *209:* 64
Adamson, George *30:* 23, 24; *69:* 64
Addams, Charles *55:* 5
Addison, Kenneth *192:* 173; *231:* 166
Addy, Sean *180:* 8; *222:* 31
Ade, Rene *76:* 198; *195:* 162
Adinolfi, JoAnn *115:* 42; *176:* 2; *217:* 79
Adkins, Alta *22:* 250
Adkins, Jan *8:* 3; *69:* 4; *144:* 2, 3, 4; *210:* 11, 17, 18, 19
Adl, Shirin *225:* 2
Adler, Kelynn *195:* 47
Adler, Peggy *22:* 6; *29:* 31
Adler, Ruth *29:* 29
Adlerman, Daniel *163:* 2
Adragna, Robert *47:* 145
Agard, Nadema *18:* 1
Agee, Jon *116:* 8, 9, 10; *157:* 4; *196:* 3, 4, 5, 6, 7, 8
Agre, Patricia *47:* 195
Aguirre, Alfredo *152:* 218
Ahl, Anna Maria *32:* 24

Ahlberg, Allan *68:* 6, 7, 9; *165:* 5; *214:* 9
Ahlberg, Janet *68:* 6, 7, 9; *214:* 9
Ahlberg, Jessica *229:* 2, 191
Aicher-Scholl, Inge *63:* 127
Aichinger, Helga *4:* 5, 45
Aitken, Amy *31:* 34
Ajhar, Brian *207:* 126; *220:* 2
Akaba, Suekichi *46:* 23; *53:* 127
Akasaka, Miyoshi *YABC 2:* 261
Akib, Jamel *181:* 13; *182:* 99; *220:* 74
Akino, Fuku *6:* 144
Alain *40:* 41
Alajalov *2:* 226
Albert, Chris *200:* 64
Alborough, Jez *86:* 1, 2, 3; *149:* 3
Albrecht, Jan *37:* 176
Albright, Donn *1:* 91
Alcala, Alfredo *91:* 128
Alcantará, Felipe Ugalde *171:* 186
Alcorn, John *3:* 159; *7:* 165; *31:* 22; *44:* 127; *46:* 23, 170
Alcorn, Stephen *110:* 4; *125:* 106; *128:* 172; *150:* 97; *160:* 188; *165:* 48; *201:* 113; *203:* 39; *207:* 3; *226:* 25
Alcott, May *100:* 3
Alda, Arlene *44:* 24; *158:* 2
Alden, Albert *11:* 103
Aldridge, Andy *27:* 131
Aldridge, George *105:* 125
Aldridge, Sheila *192:* 4
Alejandro, Cliff *176:* 75
Alex, Ben *45:* 25, 26
Alexander, Claire *228:* 2
Alexander, Ellen *7:* 3
Alexander, Lloyd *49:* 34
Alexander, Martha *3:* 206; *11:* 103; *13:* 109; *25:* 100; *36:* 131; *70:* 6, 7; *136:* 3, 4, 5; *169:* 120; *230:* 78
Alexander, Paul *85:* 57; *90:* 9
Alexeieff, Alexander *14:* 6; *26:* 199
Alfano, Wayne *80:* 69
Aliki
  See Brandenberg, Aliki
Alko, Selina *218:* 2
Allamand, Pascale *12:* 9
Allan, Judith *38:* 166
Alland, Alexandra *16:* 255
Allen, Gertrude *9:* 6
Allen, Graham *31:* 145
Allen, Jonathan *131:* 3, 4; *177:* 8, 9, 10
Allen, Joy *168:* 185; *217:* 6, 7

Allen, Pamela *50:* 25, 26, 27, 28; *81:* 9, 10; *123:* 4, 5
Allen, Raul *207:* 94
Allen, Rowena *47:* 75
Allen, Thomas B. *81:* 101; *82:* 248; *89:* 37; *104:* 9
Allen, Tom *85:* 176
Allender, David *73:* 223
Alley, R.W. *80:* 183; *95:* 187; *156:* 100, 153; *169:* 4, 5; *179:* 17
Allison, Linda *43:* 27
Allon, Jeffrey *119:* 174
Allport, Mike *71:* 55
Almquist, Don *11:* 8; *12:* 128; *17:* 46; *22:* 110
Aloise, Frank *5:* 38; *10:* 133; *30:* 92
Alsenas, Linas *186:* 2
Alter, Ann *206:* 4, 5
Althea
  See Braithwaite, Althea
Altschuler, Franz *11:* 185; *23:* 141; *40:* 48; *45:* 29; *57:* 181
Alvin, John *117:* 5
Ambrus, Victor G. *1:* 6, 7, 194; *3:* 69; *5:* 15; *6:* 44; *7:* 36; *8:* 210; *12:* 227; *14:* 213; *15:* 213; *22:* 209; *24:* 36; *28:* 179; *30:* 178; *32:* 44, 46; *38:* 143; *41:* 25, 26, 27, 28, 29, 30, 31, 32; *42:* 87; *44:* 190; *55:* 172; *62:* 30, 144, 145, 148; *86:* 99, 100, 101; *87:* 66, 137; *89:* 162; *134:* 160
Ames, Lee J. *3:* 12; *9:* 130; *10:* 69; *17:* 214; *22:* 124; *151:* 13; *223:* 69
Amini, Mehrdokht *211:* 119
Amon, Aline *9:* 9
Amoss, Berthe *5:* 5
Amstutz, André *152:* 102; *214:* 11, 16; *223:* 99
Amundsen, Dick *7:* 77
Amundsen, Richard E. *5:* 10; *24:* 122
Ancona, George *12:* 11; *55:* 144; *145:* 7; *208:* 13
Anderson, Alasdair *18:* 122
Andersen, Bethanne *116:* 167; *162:* 189; *175:* 17; *191:* 4, 5; *218:* 20
Anderson, Bob *139:* 16
Anderson, Brad *33:* 28
Anderson, Brian *211:* 8
Anderson, C.W. *11:* 10
Anderson, Carl *7:* 4
Anderson, Catherine Corley *72:* 2
Anderson, Cecil *127:* 152
Anderson, David Lee *118:* 176

Anderson, Derek *169:* 9; *174:* 180
Anderson, Doug *40:* 111
Anderson, Erica *23:* 65
Anderson, G.E. *223:* 181
Anderson, Laurie *12:* 153, 155
Anderson, Lena *99:* 26
Anderson, Peggy Perry *179:* 2
Anderson, Sara *173:* 3
Anderson, Scoular *138:* 13; *201:* 6
Anderson, Stephanie *225:* 3
Anderson, Susan *90:* 12
Anderson, Tara *188:* 132; *211:* 115
Anderson, Wayne *23:* 119; *41:* 239; *56:* 7; *62:* 26; *147:* 6; *202:* 4, 5
Andreasen, Daniel *86:* 157; *87:* 104; *103:* 201, 202; *159:* 75; *167:* 106, 107; *168:* 184; *180:* 247; *186:* 9; *212:* 101; *220:* 110, 111; *221:* 56; *227:* 3, 4, 5, 6
Andrew, Ian *111:* 37; *116:* 12; *166:* 2
Andrew, John *22:* 4
Andrews, Benny *14:* 251; *31:* 24; *57:* 6, 7; *183:* 8
Andrews, Vaughn *166:* 28
Anelay, Henry *57:* 173
Angel, Marie *47:* 22
Angelo, Valenti *14:* 8; *18:* 100; *20:* 232; *32:* 70
Anglund, Joan Walsh *2:* 7, 250, 251; *37:* 198, 199, 200
Anholt, Catherine *74:* 8; *131:* 7; *141:* 5
Anholt, Laurence *141:* 4
Anno, Mitsumasa *5:* 7; *38:* 25, 26, 27, 28, 29, 30, 31, 32; *77:* 3, 4; *157:* 10, 11
Antal, Andrew *1:* 124; *30:* 145
Antram, David *152:* 133
Apostolou, Christy Hale
See Hale, Christy
Apple, Margot *33:* 25; *35:* 206; *46:* 81; *53:* 8; *61:* 109; *64:* 21, 22, 24, 25, 27; *71:* 176; *77:* 53; *82:* 245; *92:* 39; *94:* 180; *96:* 107; *152:* 4, 5; *162:* 192, 194; *173:* 44; *214:* 21, 22, 23, 24
Appleyard, Dev *2:* 192
Aragones, Sergio *48:* 23, 24, 25, 26, 27
Araneus *40:* 29
Arbo, Cris *103:* 4; *220:* 4, 5
Archambault, Matt *85:* 173; *138:* 19, 20; *143:* 33; *145:* 144; *179:* 103; *187:* 7; *219:* 2
Archer, Janet *16:* 69; *178:* 156
Ardizzone, Edward *1:* 11, 12; *2:* 105; *3:* 258; *4:* 78; *7:* 79; *10:* 100; *15:* 232; *20:* 69,178; *23:* 223; *24:* 125; *28:* 25, 26, 27, 28, 29, 30, 31,33, 34, 35, 36, 37; *31:* 192, 193; *34:* 215, 217; *60:* 173; *64:* 145; *87:* 176; *YABC 2:* 25
Arena, Jill *176:* 49
Arenella, Roy *14:* 9
Argemi, David *197:* 2
Argent, Kerry *103:* 56; *138:* 17; *158:* 134
Arihara, Shino *201:* 98
Arisman, Marshall *162:* 50
Armer, Austin *13:* 3
Armer, Laura Adams *13:* 3
Armer, Sidney *13:* 3
Armitage, David *47:* 23; *99:* 5; *155:* 4
Armitage, Eileen *4:* 16
Armstrong, George *10:* 6; *21:* 72
Armstrong, Shelagh *102:* 114; *224:* 4
Armstrong-Ellis, Carey *185:* 196
Arno, Enrico *1:* 217; *2:* 22, 210; *4:* 9; *5:* 43; *6:* 52; *29:* 217, 219; *33:* 152; *35:* 99; *43:* 31, 32, 33; *45:* 212, 213, 214; *72:* 72; *74:* 166; *100:* 169
Arnold, Alli *187:* 40, 41
Arnold, Andrew *219:* 155; *221:* 155
Arnold, Caroline *174:* 5
Arnold, Emily *76:* 7, 9, 10
Arnold, Katya *115:* 11; *168:* 2, 3
Arnold, Tedd *116:* 14; *133:* 152; *160:* 5; *208:* 24, 25, 26, 176

Arnosky, Jim *22:* 20; *70:* 9, 10, 11; *118:* 3, 5; *160:* 8, 10; *189:* 5, 7, 8, 9, 10; *217:* 11, 12, 13, 14
Arnsteen, Katy Keck *105:* 97; *116:* 145
Arsenault, Isabelle *207:* 7; *226:* 109
Arrowood, Clinton *12:* 193; *19:* 11; *65:* 210
Artell, Mike *89:* 8
Arting, Fred J. *41:* 63
Artzybasheff, Boris *13:* 143; *14:* 15; *40:* 152, 155
Aruego, Ariane *6:* 4
Aruego, José *4:* 140; *6:* 4; *7:* 64; *33:* 195; *35:* 208; *68:* 16, 17; *75:* 46; *93:* 91, 92; *94:* 197; *109:* 65, 67; *125:* 2, 3, 4, 5; *127:* 188; *143:* 25; *178:* 17, 19, 74; *188:* 166; *202:* 164; *231:* 176
Arzoumanian, Alik *177:* 12; *194:* 115
Asare, Meshack *86:* 9; *139:* 19
Ascensios, Natalie *105:* 139
Asch, Frank *5:* 9; *66:* 2, 4, 6, 7, 9, 10; *102:* 18, 19,21; *154:* 12
Ashby, Gail *11:* 135
Ashby, Gil *146:* 4
Ashby, Gwynneth *44:* 26
Ashley, C.W. *19:* 197
Ashmead, Hal *8:* 70
Ashton, Tim *211:* 204
Aska, Warabe *56:* 10
Assel, Steven *44:* 153; *77:* 22, 97
Astrop, John *32:* 56
Atene, Ann *12:* 18
Atherton, Lisa *38:* 198
Atkinson, Allen *60:* 5
Atkinson, J. Priestman *17:* 275
Atkinson, Janet *86:* 147; *103:* 138
Atkinson, Mike *127:* 74
Atkinson, Wayne *40:* 46
Attard, Karl *196:* 22, 23
Attebery, Charles *38:* 170
Atwell, Debby *150:* 6
Atwood, Ann *7:* 9
Aubrey, Meg Kelleher *77:* 159
Auch, Herm *173:* 7, 8
Auch, Mary Jane *173:* 7
Augarde, Steve *25:* 22; *159:* 7; *210:* 43, 44
Austerman, Miriam *23:* 107
Austin, Margot *11:* 16
Austin, Robert *3:* 44
Austin, Virginia *81:* 205; *127:* 221
Auth, Tony *51:* 5; *192:* 18
Avendano, Dolores *158:* 74
Avedon, Richard *57:* 140
Averill, Esther *1:* 17; *28:* 39, 40, 41
Avilés, Martha *218:* 6
Axeman, Lois *2:* 32; *11:* 84; *13:* 165; *22:* 8; *23:* 49; *61:* 116; *101:* 124
Axtel, David *155:* 110
Ayer, Jacqueline *13:* 7
Ayer, Margaret *15:* 12; *50:* 120
Ayers, Alan *91:* 58; *107:* 169
Ayliffe, Alex *95:* 164
Ayto, Russell *111:* 5; *112:* 54; *206:* 7, 8; *213:* 56
Azarian, Mary *112:* 9, 10; *114:* 129; *117:* 171; *137:* 163; *171:* 4, 5; *181:* 161; *188:* 128

B

B.T.B.
See Blackwell, Basil T.
Baasansuren, Bolormaa *216:* 40
Babbitt, Bradford *33:* 158
Babbitt, Natalie *6:* 6; *8:* 220; *68:* 20; *70:* 242, 243; *194:* 8, 9
Baca, Maria *104:* 5
Bacchus, Andy *94:* 87
Bacha, Andy *109:* 169
Bachelet, Gilles *196:* 18
Bachem, Paul *48:* 180; *67:* 65; *144:* 206

Back, Adam *63:* 125
Back, George *31:* 161
Backes, Nick *190:* 72
Backhouse, Colin *78:* 142
Bacon, Bruce *4:* 74
Bacon, Paul *7:* 155; *8:* 121; *31:* 55; *50:* 42; *56:* 175; *62:* 82, 84
Bacon, Peggy *2:* 11, 228; *46:* 44
Baek, Matthew J. *169:* 95; *202:* 8
Baer, Julie *161:* 2
Baicker-McKee, Carol *177:* 15; *180:* 215
Bailey, Peter *58:* 174; *87:* 221; *194:* 12
Bailey, Sheila *155:* 11
Baker, Alan *22:* 22; *61:* 134; *93:* 11, 12; *146:* 6, 7, 10
Baker, Charlotte *2:* 12
Baker, Garin *89:* 65
Baker, Jeannie *23:* 4; *88:* 18, 19, 20
Baker, Jim *22:* 24
Baker, Joe *82:* 188; *111:* 55; *124:* 70; *197:* 73
Baker, Keith *179:* 6, 7; *222:* 36
Baker, Leslie *112:* 214; *132:* 103, 246; *180:* 74, 246
Baker-Smith, Grahame *223:* 10; *225:* 132
Baldacci, Rudy *184:* 9
Baldridge, Cyrus LeRoy *19:* 69; *44:* 50
Baldus, Jackie *216:* 81
Baldus, Zachary *152:* 231; *187:* 60
Balet, Jan *11:* 22
Balian, Lorna *9:* 16; *91:* 16
Balit, Christina *102:* 24; *159:* 9; *162:* 118, 119; *212:* 2, 3
Ballantyne, R.M. *24:* 34
Ballis, George *14:* 199
Balouch, Kristen *176:* 11
Baltzer, Hans *40:* 30
Banbery, Fred *58:* 15
Bancroft, Bronwyn *216:* 42
Banfill, A. Scott *98:* 7; *112:* 59
Bang, Molly *24:* 37, 38; *69:* 8, 9, 10; *111:* 7,9, 10, 11; *140:* 11; *158:* 37, 38, 39; *195:* 3; *215:* 11, 12, 13, 14
Banik, Yvette Santiago *21:* 136
Banks, Erin Bennett *211:* 12
Banner, Angela
See Maddison, Angela Mary
Bannerman, Helen *19:* 13, 14
Banning, Greg *202:* 98
Bannon, Laura *6:* 10; *23:* 8
Bantock, Nick *74:* 229; *95:* 6
Banyai, Istvan *185:* 209; *193:* 14, 16; *209:* 155; *223:* 166, 167
Baptist, Michael *37:* 208
Baracca, Sal *135:* 206
Baranaski, Marcin *182:* 113
Barasch, Lynne *126:* 16; *186:* 15
Barbarin, Lucien C., Jr. *89:* 88
Barbour, Karen *96:* 5; *74:* 209; *170:* 16
Bare, Arnold Edwin *16:* 31
Bare, Colleen Stanley *32:* 33
Barger, Jan *147:* 11
Bargery, Geoffrey *14:* 258
Barkat, Jonathan *149:* 177; *164:* 254; *181:* 106; *184:* 186; *196:* 11; *198:* 148
Barker, Carol *31:* 27
Barker, Cicely Mary *49:* 50, 51
Barkley, James *4:* 13; *6:* 11; *13:* 112
Barks, Carl *37:* 27, 28, 29, 30, 31, 32, 33, 34
Barling, Joy *62:* 148
Barling, Tom *9:* 23
Barlow, Gillian *62:* 20
Barlow, Perry *35:* 28
Barlowe, Dot *30:* 223
Barlowe, Wayne *37:* 72; *84:* 43; *105:* 5
Barnard, Bryn *88:* 53; *13:* 55; *169:* 13; *193:* 194
Barneda, David *206:* 11
Barner, Bob *29:* 37; *128:* 33; *136:* 19, 20; *177:* 27
Barnes, Hiram P. *20:* 28
Barnes, Tim *137:* 28

Barnes-Murphy, Rowan *88:* 22
Barnett, Charles II *175:* 150
Barnett, Ivan *70:* 14
Barnett, Moneta *16:* 89; *19:* 142; *31:* 102; *33:* 30, 31, 32; *41:* 153; *61:* 94, 97
Barney, Maginel Wright *39:* 32, 33, 34; *YABC 2:* 306
Barnum, Jay Hyde *11:* 224; *20:* 5; *37:* 189, 190
Baron, Alan *80:* 3; *89:* 123
Barr, George *60:* 74; *69:* 64
Barragán, Paula S. *134:* 116; *186:* 158; *216:* 43, 44, 197
Barrall, Tim *115:* 152
Barraud, Martin *189:* 38
Barrauds *33:* 114
Barrer-Russell, Gertrude *9:* 65; *27:* 31
Barret, Robert *85:* 134
Barrett, Angela *40:* 136, 137; *62:* 74; *75:* 10; *76:* 142; *144:* 137; *145:* 14; *223:* 14
Barrett, Jennifer *58:* 149
Barrett, John E. *43:* 119
Barrett, Moneta *74:* 10
Barrett, Peter *55:* 169; *86:* 111
Barrett, Robert *62:* 145; *77:* 146; *82:* 35
Barrett, Ron *14:* 24; *26:* 35
Barron, John N. *3:* 261; *5:* 101; *14:* 220
Barrow, Ann *136:* 27
Barrows, Walter *14:* 268
Barry, Ethelred B. *37:* 79; *YABC 1:* 229
Barry, James *14:* 25
Barry, Katharina *2:* 159; *4:* 22
Barry, Robert E. *6:* 12
Barry, Scott *32:* 35
Barshaw, Ruth McNally *203:* 9
Bartenbach, Jean *40:* 31
Barth, Ernest Kurt *2:* 172; *3:* 160; *8:* 26; *10:* 31
Bartholomew, Caty *208:* 153
Bartholomew, Marie *200:* 66
Bartlett, Alison *101:* 88; *165:* 93; *209:* 51
Barton, Byron *8:* 207; *9:* 18; *23:* 66; *80:* 181; *90:* 18, 19, 20, 21; *126:* 29, 30
Barton, Harriett *30:* 71
Barton, Jill *129:* 108; *135:* 120; *145:* 185, 189; *184:* 177; *224:* 142, 143
Barton, Patrice *226:* 14
Bartram, Robert *10:* 42
Bartram, Simon *218:* 8
Bartsch, Jochen *8:* 105; *39:* 38
Bascove, Barbara *45:* 73
Base, Graeme *101:* 15, 16, 17, 18; *162:* 8, 10, 12
Baseman, Gary *174:* 12
Bash, Barbara *132:* 9
Baskin, Leonard *30:* 42, 43, 46, 47; *49:* 125, 126, 128, 129,133; *173:* 120
Bass, Saul *49:* 192
Bassett, Jeni *40:* 99; *64:* 30
Basso, Bill *99:* 139; *189:* 134
Batchelor, Joy *29:* 41, 47, 48
Bate, Norman *5:* 16
Bates, Amy June *188:* 170; *189:* 27, 28
Bates, Leo *24:* 35
Batet, Carmen *39:* 134
Batherman, Muriel *31:* 79; *45:* 185
Battaglia, Aurelius *50:* 44
Batten, John D. *25:* 161, 162
Batten, Mary *162:* 14, 15
Battles, Asa *32:* 94, 95
Bauer, Carla *193:* 6
Bauer, Jutta *150:* 32
Bauernschmidt, Marjorie *15:* 15
Baum, Allyn *20:* 10
Baum, Willi *4:* 24, 25; *7:* 173
Bauman, Leslie *61:* 121
Baumann, Jill *34:* 170
Baumhauer, Hans *11:* 218; *15:* 163, 165, 167
Baxter, Glen *57:* 100
Baxter, Leon *59:* 102
Baxter, Robert *87:* 129

Bayer, Herbert *181:* 16
Bayley, Dorothy *37:* 195
Bayley, Nicola *40:* 104; *41:* 34, 35; *69:* 15; *129:* 33, 34, 35
Baylin, Mark *158:* 233
Baynes, Pauline *2:* 244; *3:* 149; *13:* 133, 135,137, 141; *19:* 18, 19, 20; *32:* 208, 213, 214; *36:* 105, 108; *59:* 12, 13, 14, 16, 17, 18, 20; *100:* 158, 159, 243; *133:* 3, 4
Beach, Lou *150:* 150; *207:* 117, 118
Beame, Rona *12:* 40
Bean, Jonathan *196:* 102
Bear's Heart *73:* 215
Beard, Alex *222:* 40
Beard, Dan *22:* 31, 32
Beard, J.H. *YABC 1:* 158
Bearden, Romare *9:* 7; *22:* 35
Beardshaw, Rosalind *169:* 22; *190:* 22; *224:* 12; *225:* 6, 7, 8; *226:* 71
Beardsley, Aubrey *17:* 14; *23:* 181; *59:* 130, 131
Bearman, Jane *29:* 38
Beaton, Cecil *24:* 208
Beaton, Clare *125:* 28; *208:* 67; *220:* 10, 11, 12
Beauce, J.A. *18:* 103
Beaujard, Sophie *81:* 54
Beavers, Ethen *225:* 9
Beccia, Carlyn *189:* 29
Bechtold, Lisze *208:* 29
Beck, Andrea *226:* 16
Beck, Charles *11:* 169; *51:* 173
Beck, Ian *138:* 27; *182:* 150; *190:* 25; *225:* 130
Beck, Melinda *203:* 112
Beck, Ruth *13:* 11
Becker, Harriet *12:* 211
Beckerman, Jonathan *208:* 194
Beckett, Sheilah *25:* 5; *33:* 37, 38
Beckhoff, Harry *1:* 78; *5:* 163
Beckhorn, Susan Williams *189:* 32
Beckman, Kaj *45:* 38, 39, 40, 41
Beckman, Per *45:* 42, 43
Beddows, Eric *72:* 70
Bedford, F.D. *20:* 118, 122; *33:* 170; *41:* 220, 221,230, 233
Bee, Joyce *19:* 62
Bee, William *188:* 6
Beeby, Betty *25:* 36
Beech, Carol *9:* 149
Beech, Mark *192:* 122
Beek *25:* 51, 55, 59
Beeke, Tiphanie *177:* 127; *204:* 140; *212:* 178; *218:* 102
Beekman, Doug *125:* 146, 148
Beerbohm, Max *24:* 208
Beeson, Bob *108:* 57
Begin, Mary Jane *82:* 13; *206:* 13
Beha, Philippe *172:* 85
Behr, Joyce *15:* 15; *21:* 132; *23:* 161
Behrens, Hans *5:* 97
Beier, Ellen *135:* 170; *139:* 47; *183:* 164; *221:* 177; *222:* 151
Beingessner, Laura *220:* 14
Beinicke, Steve *69:* 18
Beisner, Monika *46:* 128, 131; *112:* 127
Belden, Charles J. *12:* 182
Belina, Renate *39:* 132
Bell, Corydon *3:* 20
Bell, Graham *54:* 48
Bell, Julia *151:* 214
Bell, Julie *159:* 172; *165:* 18
Bell, Thomas P. *76:* 182
Bellamy, Glen *127:* 15
Beltran, Alberto *43:* 37
Bemelmans, Ludwig *15:* 19, 21; *100:* 27
Ben-Ami, Doron *75:* 96; *84:* 107; *108:* 132; *110:* 63; *159:* 157; *197:* 142
Bendall-Brunello, John *150:* 4; *157:* 163; *185:* 3, 4; *203:* 5

Benda, Wladyslaw T. *15:* 256; *30:* 76, 77; *44:* 182
Bender, Robert *77:* 162; *79:* 13; *160:* 23
Bendick, Jeanne *2:* 24; *68:* 27, 28
Benioff, Carol *121:* 42; *175:* 23
Benner, Cheryl *80:* 11
Bennett, Charles H. *64:* 6
Bennett, Erin Susanne *165:* 216
Bennett, F.I. *YABC 1:* 134
Bennett, James *146:* 240
Bennett, Jill *26:* 61; *41:* 38, 39; *45:* 54
Bennett, Rainey *15:* 26; *23:* 53
Bennett, Richard *15:* 45; *21:* 11, 12, 13; *25:* 175
Bennett, Susan *5:* 55
Benny, Mike *142:* 78; *203:* 13, 14; *207:* 85
Benoit, Elise *77:* 74
Benson, Linda *60:* 130; *62:* 91; *75:* 101; *79:* 156; *134:* 129
Benson, Patrick *68:* 162; *147:* 17, 18, 19, 20
Bentley, Carolyn *46:* 153
Bentley, James *149:* 30
Bentley, Roy *30:* 162
Benton, Jim *172:* 22
Benton, Thomas Hart *2:* 99
Bereal, JaeMe *228:* 16
Berelson, Howard *5:* 20; *16:* 58; *31:* 50
Berenstain, Jan *12:* 47; *64:* 33, 34, 36, 37, 38, 40, 42, 44; *135:* 25, 28, 31, 35
Berenstain, Stan *12:* 47; *64:* 33, 34, 36, 37, 38, 40, 42, 44; *135:* 25, 28, 31, 35
Berenzy, Alix *65:* 13; *73:* 6; *78:* 115
Berg, Joan *1:* 115; *3:* 156; *6:* 26, 58
Berg, Ron *36:* 48, 49; *48:* 37, 38; *67:* 72
Bergen, David *115:* 44; *207:* 34
Berger, Barbara *77:* 14
Berger, Carin *185:* 6
Berger, Joe *221:* 9
Berger, William M. *14:* 143; *YABC 1:* 204
Bergherr, Mary *74:* 170; *151:* 123
Bergin, Mark *114:* 8, 9; *143:* 95; *160:* 26, 27
Bergstreser, Douglas *69:* 76
Bergum, Constance R. *121:* 14, 15; *208:* 31, 32, 33; *209:* 176
Bering, Claus *13:* 14
Berkeley, Jon *139:* 218
Berkowitz, Jeanette *3:* 249
Berman, Paul *66:* 14
Berman, Rachel *217:* 26
Bernal, Richard *154:* 176
Bernadette
  See Watts, Bernadette
Bernard, Gary *216:* 71
Bernardin, James *112:* 24; *167:* 94; *227:* 14, 15
Bernasconi, Pablo *183:* 10, 11
Bernath, Stefen *32:* 76
Berner, Rotraut Susanne *214:* 32
Bernhard, Durga *80:* 13
Bernstein, Michel J. *51:* 71
Bernstein, Ted *38:* 183; *50:* 131
Bernstein, Zena *23:* 46
Berridge, Celia *86:* 63
Berrill, Jacquelyn *12:* 50
Berry, Erick
  See Best, Allena
Berry, Holly *205:* 116; *210:* 49, 50
Berry, William D. *14:* 29; *19:* 48
Berry, William A. *6:* 219
Berson, Harold *2:* 17, 18; *4:* 28, 29, 220; *9:* 10; *12:* 19; *17:* 45; *18:* 193; *22:* 85; *34:* 172; *44:* 120; *46:* 42; *80:* 240
Bertholf, Bret *187:* 9; *189:* 32, 33
Berton, Patsy *99:* 16
Bertschmann, Harry *16:* 1
Besco, Don *70:* 99
Beskow, Elsa *20:* 13, 14, 15
Bess, Clayton *63:* 94
Best, Allena *2:* 26; *34:* 76
Betera, Carol *74:* 68
Bethell, Thomas N. *61:* 169

Bethers, Ray *6:* 22
Betteridge, Deirdre *214:* 34
Bettina
    See Ehrlich, Bettina
Betts, Ethel Franklin *17:* 161, 164, 165; *YABC 2:* 47
Betz, Rudolf *59:* 161
Bewick, Thomas *16:* 40, 41, 43, 44, 45, 47; *54:* 150; *YABC 1:* 107
Beyer, Paul J. III *74:* 24
Bezencon, Jacqueline *48:* 40
Biamonte, Daniel *40:* 90
Bianchi, John *91:* 19
Bianco, Pamela *15:* 31; *28:* 44, 45, 46
Bible, Charles *13:* 15
Bice, Clare *22:* 40
Biedrzycki, David *186:* 170; *219:* 7
Bierman, Don *57:* 184
Biggers, John *2:* 123
Biggs, Brian *192:* 38; *196:* 15; *207:* 170
Bikadoroff, Roxanna *201:* 74
Bileck, Marvin *3:* 102; *40:* 36, 37
Bilibin, Ivan *61:* 8, 9, 12, 13, 14, 15, 151, 152, 154, 162
Billington, Patrick *98:* 71
Billout, Guy *144:* 38, 39
Bimen, Levent *5:* 179
Binch, Caroline *81:* 18; *140:* 15, 16; *144:* 115; *211:* 82
Binder, Hannes *169:* 163
Bing, Christopher *126:* 34
Binger, Bill *121:* 46
Binks, Robert *25:* 150
Binzen, Bill *24:* 47
Birch, Reginald *15:* 150; *19:* 33, 34, 35, 36; *37:* 196,197; *44:* 182; *46:* 176; *YABC 1:* 84; *2:* 34, 39
Birch, Wendy *223:* 70
Birchall, Mark *123:* 188
Bird, Esther Brock *1:* 36; *25:* 66
Birdsong, Keith *167:* 85; *219:* 105
Birkett, Georgie *204:* 121
Birkett, Rachel *78:* 206
Birling, Paul *109:* 30
Birmingham, Christian *132:* 243; *143:* 114; *209:* 58; *220:* 20
Birmingham, Lloyd P. *12:* 51; *83:* 13
Biro, Val *1:* 26; *41:* 42; *60:* 178; *67:* 23, 24; *84:* 242, 243
Bischoff, Ilse *44:* 51
Bishop, Don *199:* 133
Bishop, Gavin *97:* 17, 18; *144:* 42, 44; *216:* 52, 55, 56, 57
Bishop, Kathleen Wong *115:* 67
Bishop, Rich *56:* 43
Bite, I. *60:* 14
Bittinger, Ned *93:* 117; *205:* 115
Bjorklund, Lorence *3:* 188, 252; *7:* 100; *9:* 113; *10:* 66; *19:* 178; *33:* 122, 123; *35:* 36, 37, 38, 39,41, 42, 43; *36:* 185; *38:* 93; *47:* 106; *66:* 194; *YABC 1:* 242
Björkman, Steve *91:* 199; *160:* 110; *198:* 18; *218:* 188; *223:* 20, 21
Blabey, Aaron *214:* 35
Black Sheep *164:* 100
Blackburn, Loren H. *63:* 10
Blackall, Sophie *194:* 140; *209:* 157; *231:* 31, 115
Blackford, John *137:* 105; *180:* 36
Blackwell, Basil T. *YABC 1:* 68, 69
Blackwood, Freya *199:* 9
Blackwood, Gary L. *118:* 17
Blades, Ann *16:* 52; *37:* 213; *50:* 41; *69:* 21; *99:* 215
Blair, Jay *45:* 46; *46:* 155
Blaisdell, Elinore *1:* 121; *3:* 134; *35:* 63
Blake, Anne Catharine *189:* 71
Blake, Francis *198:* 4
Blake, Quentin *3:* 170; *10:* 48; *13:* 38; *21:* 180; *26:* 60; *28:* 228; *30:* 29, 31; *40:* 108; *45:* 219; *46:* 165, 168; *48:* 196; *52:* 10, 11, 12,13, 14, 15, 16, 17; *73:* 41, 43; *78:* 84, 86; *80:* 250, 251; *84:* 210, 211, 212; *87:* 177; *96:* 24, 26, 28; *124:* 79; *125:* 32, 34; *181:* 139; *211:* 26, 27; *227:* 176; *229:* 167
Blake, Robert J. *37:* 90; *53:* 67; *54:* 23; *160:* 28, 29
Blake, William *30:* 54, 56, 57, 58, 59, 60
Blakeslee, Lys *218:* 11, 105
Blanchard, N. Taylor *82:* 140
Blass, Jacqueline *8:* 215
Blazek, Scott R. *91:* 71
Bleck, Cathie *118:* 116
Bleck, Linda *204:* 124
Blegvad, Erik *2:* 59; *3:* 98; *5:* 117; *7:* 131; *11:* 149; *14:* 34, 35; *18:* 237; *32:* 219; *60:* 106; *66:* 16, 17, 18, 19; *70:* 233; *76:* 18; *82:* 106; *87:* 45; *100:* 188; *129:* 125; *132:* 17, 18, 19, 20; *176:* 14; *200:* 100; *YABC 1:* 201
Blessen, Karen *93:* 126
Bliss, Corinne Demas *37:* 38
Bliss, Harry *196:* 27, 28, 29
Blitt, Barry *179:* 199; *187:* 13; *225:* 198
Bloch, Lucienne *10:* 12
Blondon, Herve *129:* 48; *183:* 22
Bloom, Lloyd *35:* 180; *36:* 149; *47:* 99; *62:* 117; *68:* 231; *72:* 136; *75:* 185; *83:* 99; *108:* 19; *229:* 114
Bloom, Suzanne *172:* 23, 24
Blossom, Dave *34:* 29
Blumenschein, E.L. *YABC 1:* 113, 115
Blumer, Patt *29:* 214
Blundell, Kim *29:* 36
Bluthenthal, Diana Cain *93:* 32; *104:* 106; *177:* 26
Blythe, Benjamin *128:* 7
Blythe, Gary *112:* 52; *181:* 166; *182:* 64; *185:* 7; *186:* 116, 117
Boake, Kathy *176:* 185
Board, Perry *171:* 99
Boardman, Gwenn *12:* 60
Boase, Susan *224:* 53
Boatwright, Phil *211:* 195
Bober, Richard *125:* 145; *132:* 40
Bobri *30:* 138; *47:* 27
Bock, Vera *1:* 187; *21:* 41
Bock, William Sauts *8:* 7; *14:* 37; *16:* 120; *21:* 141; *36:* 177; *62:* 203
Bodecker, N(iels) M(ogens) *8:* 13; *14:* 2; *17:* 55, 56, 57; *73:* 22, 23, 24
Boehm, Linda *40:* 31
Bogacki, Tomek *138:* 31, 32; *144:* 123; *202:* 13
Bogan, Paulette *197:* 152; *201:* 17
Bogdan, Florentina *107:* 43
Bohdal, Susi *22:* 44; *101:* 20
Bohlen, Nina *58:* 13
Boies, Alex *96:* 53
Bok, Chip *205:* 16
Bolam, Emily *101:* 216; *159:* 12; *205:* 59
Bolian, Polly *3:* 270; *4:* 30; *13:* 77; *29:* 197
Bolle, Frank *87:* 100; *208:* 101
Bollen, Roger *79:* 186; *83:* 16
Bolling, Vickey *114:* 44
Bollinger, Peter *101:* 7; *128:* 198; *172:* 26
Bolognese, Don *2:* 147, 231; *4:* 176; *7:* 146; *17:* 43; *23:* 192; *24:* 50; *34:* 108; *36:* 133; *71:* 24, 25; *103:* 131; *129:* 39, 40
Bolster, Rob *186:* 169
Bolton, A.T. *57:* 158
Bond, Arnold *18:* 116
Bond, Barbara Higgins *21:* 102
Bond, Bruce *52:* 97
Bond, Felicia *38:* 197; *49:* 55, 56; *89:* 170; *90:* 171; *126:* 37
Bond, Higgins *177:* 22, 23; *209:* 175; *220:* 22, 23, 24
Bone, J. *230:* 11, 181
Bonn, Pat *43:* 40
Bonner, Hannah *197:* 13, 14
Bonners, Susan *41:* 40; *85:* 36; *94:* 99, 100; *151:* 105, 106
Bonnet, Rosalinde *230:* 79
Bono, Mary *184:* 73
Bonsall, Crosby *23:* 6
Booker, Philip *225:* 16
Boon, Debbie *103:* 6; *144:* 188
Boon, Emilie *86:* 23, 24
Boone, Debbie *165:* 77
Boore, Sara *60:* 73
Bootman, Colin *155:* 13; *159:* 35; *174:* 192; *222:* 128
Booth, Franklin *YABC 2:* 76
Booth, George *191:* 13
Booth, Graham *32:* 193; *37:* 41, 42
Borda, Juliette *102:* 188
Bordier, Georgette *16:* 54
Boren, Tinka *27:* 128
Borges, Jose Francisco *119:* 62
Borja, Robert *22:* 48
Born, Adolf *49:* 63
Bornstein, Ruth *14:* 44; *88:* 45, 46; *107:* 30
Borten, Helen *3:* 54; *5:* 24
Bosin, Blackbear *69:* 104
Bossom, Naomi *35:* 48
Bostock, Mike *83:* 221; *114:* 14; *188:* 205
Boston, Peter *19:* 42
Bosustow, Stephen *34:* 202
Boszko, Ron *75:* 47
Bottner, Barbara *14:* 46
Boucher, Joelle *41:* 138
Boulat, Pierre *44:* 40
Boulet, Susan Seddon *50:* 47
Bouma, Paddy *118:* 25; *128:* 16
Bour, Daniele *66:* 145
Bourke-White, Margaret *15:* 286, 287; *57:* 102
Boutavant, Marc *200:* 136
Boutet de Monvel, M. *30:* 61, 62, 63, 65
Bowen, Betsy *105:* 222
Bowen, Richard *42:* 134
Bowen, Ruth *31:* 188
Bower, Ron *29:* 33
Bowers, David *95:* 38; *115:* 20; *127:* 169, 170; *165:* 57; *207:* 11
Bowers, Tim *185:* 35; *201:* 41; *218:* 13
Bowman, Claire *174:* 177
Bowman, Eric *151:* 23
Bowman, Leslie *85:* 203; *105:* 108; *116:* 76; *128:* 234; *182:* 24, 25
Bowman, Peter *146:* 214, 215; *150:* 115
Bowser, Carolyn Ewing *22:* 253
Boxall, Ed *178:* 28
Boyd, Aaron *158:* 242
Boyd, Patti *45:* 31
Boyle, Eleanor Vere *28:* 50, 51
Boynton, Sandra *57:* 13, 14, 15; *107:* 36, 37; *152:* 12, 13, 14
Bozzo, Frank *4:* 154
Brabbs, Derry *55:* 170
Brace, Eric *132:* 193, 194; *152:* 71; *184:* 195; *197:* 6; *201:* 54
Brackers de Hugo, Pierre *115:* 21
Bradford, June *158:* 138
Bradford, Ron *7:* 157
Bradley, David P. *69:* 105
Bradley, Richard D. *26:* 182
Bradley, William *5:* 164
Brady, Irene *4:* 31; *42:* 37; *68:* 191
Bragg, Michael *32:* 78; *46:* 31
Bragg, Ruth Gembicki *77:* 18
Brainerd, John W. *65:* 19
Braithwaite, Althea *23:* 12, 13; *119:* 16
Brak, Syd *146:* 187
Bralds, Braldt *90:* 28; *91:* 151
Bram, Elizabeth *30:* 67
Bramley, Peter *4:* 3
Brandenberg, Aliki *2:* 36, 37; *24:* 222; *35:* 49, 50, 51,52, 53, 54, 56, 57; *75:* 15, 17; *92:* 205; *113:* 18, 19, 20; *157:* 28; *156:* 111
Brandenburg, Alexa *75:* 19
Brandenburg, Jim *47:* 58; *150:* 212
Brandi, Lillian *31:* 158
Brandon, Brumsic, Jr. *9:* 25

Brannen, Sarah S. *202:* 15; *216:* 199
Bransom, Paul *17:* 121; *43:* 44
Braren, Loretta Trezzo *87:* 193
Brassard, France *186:* 22
Braun, Wendy *80:* 17, 18; *213:* 14
Brautigam, Don *115:* 175, 176; *225:* 109
Brazell, Derek *75:* 105; *79:* 9
Breathed, Berkeley *86:* 27, 28, 29; *161:* 13, 14; *229:* 10, 11, 12
Breckenreid, Julia *192:* 209
Breen, Steve *186:* 23
Brennan, Steve *83:* 230; *101:* 184
Brenner, Fred *22:* 85; *36:* 34; *42:* 34
Brett, Bernard *22:* 54
Brett, Harold M. *26:* 98, 99, 100
Brett, Jan *30:* 135; *42:* 39; *71:* 31, 32; *130:* 23, 24, 25, 26, 27; *171:* 15, 16
Brewer, Paul *106:* 115; *145:* 202; *230:* 13
Brewer, Sally King *33:* 44
Brewster, Patience *40:* 68; *45:* 22, 183; *51:* 20; *66:* 144; *89:* 4; *97:* 30, 31; *212:* 99
Brick, John *10:* 15
Brickman, Robin D. *131:* 88; *142:* 150; *155:* 18; *178:* 109; *184:* 32
Bridge, David R. *45:* 28
Bridgman, L.J. *37:* 77
Bridwell, Norman *4:* 37; *138:* 36, 37, 40
Brierley, Louise *91:* 22; *96:* 165; *183:* 51
Briggs, Harry *172:* 187
Briggs, Raymond *10:* 168; *23:* 20, 21; *66:* 29, 31, 32; *131:* 28, 29; *184:* 15, 16
Brigham, Grace A. *37:* 148
Bright, Robert *24:* 55
Brighton, Catherine *107:* 39; *206:* 23
Brinckloe, Julie *13:* 18; *24:* 79, 115; *29:* 35; *63:* 140; *81:* 131
Brion *47:* 116
Brisley, Joyce L. *22:* 57
Brisson, James F. *110:* 60
Brittingham, Geoffrey *88:* 37
Brix-Henker, Silke *81:* 194
Broadway, Hannah *208:* 104
Brock, Charles E. *15:* 97; *19:* 247, 249; *23:* 224, 225; *36:* 88; *42:* 41, 42, 43, 44, 45; *100:* 189; *YABC 1:* 194, 196, 203
Brock, Emma *7:* 21
Brock, Henry Matthew *15:* 81; *16:* 141; *19:* 71; *34:* 115; *40:* 164; *42:* 47, 48, 49; *49:* 66
Brocksopp, Arthur *57:* 157
Broda, Ron *136:* 180; *174:* 123
Brodkin, Gwen *34:* 135
Brodovitch, Alexi *52:* 22
Bromhall, Winifred *5:* 11; *26:* 38
Bromley, Lizzy *159:* 179
Bronson, Linda *150:* 210; *174:* 133; *203:* 16, 17; *225:* 178
Brooke, L. Leslie *16:* 181, 182, 183, 186; *17:* 15, 16, 17; *18:* 194
Brooker, Christopher *15:* 251
Brooker, Kyrsten *111:* 94; *140:* 28; *162:* 111; *175:* 108; *186:* 42, 225; *199:* 12; *201:* 30; *219:* 98
Brooks, Erik *166:* 52; *182:* 30
Brooks, Karen Stormer *186:* 110; *220:* 65
Brooks, Maya Itzna *92:* 153
Brooks, Ron *94:* 15; *197:* 188; *212:* 6, 7, 8, 9
Brooks, S.G. *178:* 127
Broomfield, Maurice *40:* 141
Brotman, Adolph E. *5:* 21
Brown, Buck *45:* 48
Brown, Calef *179:* 18; *210:* 206; *217:* 30, 31; *225:* 201
Brown, Christopher *62:* 124, 125, 127, 128
Brown, Craig *73:* 28; *84:* 65; *224:* 18
Brown, Dan *61:* 167; *115:* 183, 184; *116:* 28, 29; *193:* 190; *200:* 21, 23
Brown, David *7:* 47; *48:* 52
Brown, Denise *11:* 213
Brown, Don *172:* 59
Brown, Elbrite *195:* 39; *198:* 5
Brown, Ford Madox *48:* 74

Brown, Gayle *224:* 184
Brown, Hunter *191:* 111, 112
Brown, Judith Gwyn *1:* 45; *7:* 5; *8:* 167; *9:* 182, 190; *20:* 16, 17, 18; *23:* 142; *29:* 117; *33:* 97; *36:* 23, 26; *43:* 184; *48:* 201, 223; *49:* 69; *86:* 227; *110:* 188; *153:* 7
Brown, Kathryn *98:* 26
Brown, Lisa *187:* 175
Brown, Laurie Krasny *99:* 30
Brown, Leo *225:* 18
Brown, Marc (Tolon) *10:* 17, 197; *14:* 263; *51:* 18; *53:* 11, 12, 13, 15, 16, 17; *75:* 58; *80:* 24, 25, 26; *82:* 261; *99:* 29; *145:* 22, 23, 25, 27; *162:* 198; *224:* 136
Brown, Marcia *7:* 30; *25:* 203; *47:* 31, 32, 33, 34, 35,36, 37, 38, 39, 40, 42, 43, 44; *YABC 1:* 27
Brown, Margery W. *5:* 32, 33; *10:* 3
Brown, Martin *101:* 43
Brown, Mary Barrett *97:* 74
Brown, Palmer *36:* 40
Brown, Paul *25:* 26; *26:* 107
Brown, Richard *61:* 18; *67:* 30
Brown, Rick *78:* 71; *150:* 154; *224:* 16
Brown, Robert S. *85:* 33
Brown, Rod *157:* 142
Brown, Ruth *55:* 165; *86:* 112, 113; *105:* 16, 17, 18; *171:* 178
Brown, Trevor *99:* 160; *139:* 247; *189:* 206
Browne, Anthony *45:* 50, 51, 52; *61:* 21, 22, 23, 24, 25; *105:* 21, 22, 23, 25
Browne, Dik *8:* 212; *67:* 32, 33, 35, 37, 39
Browne, Gordon *16:* 97; *64:* 114, 116, 117, 119, 121
Browne, Hablot K. *15:* 65, 80; *21:* 14, 15, 16, 17, 18, 19,20; *24:* 25
Browne, Jane *165:* 222
Browning, Coleen *4:* 132
Browning, Mary Eleanor *24:* 84
Bruce, Robert *23:* 23
Brude, Dick *48:* 215
Bruel, Nick *166:* 41; *205:* 17, 18
Brule, Al *3:* 135
Brumbeau, Jeff *157:* 29
Bruna, Dick *43:* 48, 49, 50; *76:* 27, 28
Brundage, Frances *19:* 244
Brunhoff, Jean de *24:* 57, 58
Brunhoff, Laurent de *24:* 60; *71:* 35, 36, 37
Brunkus, Denise *84:* 50; *123:* 117; *178:* 209; *193:* 99; *204:* 10, 11, 12; *209:* 202
Brunson, Bob *43:* 135
Bryan, Ashley *31:* 44; *72:* 27, 28, 29; *107:* 92; *116:* 192; *132:* 24; *178:* 33, 34, 35; *208:* 83
Bryant, Laura J. *176:* 36; *183:* 168; *214:* 141; *222:* 49, 152
Bryant, Michael *93:* 74
Brychta, Alex *21:* 21
Bryer, Diana *107:* 121
Bryson, Bernarda *3:* 88, 146; *39:* 26; *44:* 185; *131:* 40
Buba, Joy *12:* 83; *30:* 226; *44:* 56
Buchanan, George *166:* 198
Buchanan, Lilian *13:* 16
Buchanan, Rachel *171:* 71
Bucholtz-Ross, Linda *44:* 137
Buchs, Thomas *40:* 38
Buck, Margaret Waring *3:* 30
Buckhardt, Marc *172:* 59
Buckley, Mike *166:* 180
Budwine, Greg *175:* 172
Buehner, Mark *104:* 12, 15; *105:* 160; *119:* 98; *157:* 188; *159:* 39, 40, 43; *192:* 111; *219:* 13, 14, 15, 16; *221:* 17, 18, 19
Buehr, Walter *3:* 31
Buell, Carl *222:* 68
Buff, Conrad *19:* 52, 53, 54
Buff, Mary *19:* 52, 53
Bull, Charles Livingston *18:* 207; *88:* 175, 176
Bullen, Anne *3:* 166, 167
Buller, Jon *205:* 21
Bullock, Kathleen *77:* 24

Bumgarner-Kirby, Claudia *77:* 194
Burbank, Addison *37:* 43
Burchard, Peter Duncan *3:* 197; *5:* 35; *6:* 158, 218; *143:* 17
Burckhardt, Marc *94:* 48; *110:* 89; *196:* 41; *199:* 116
Burden, Andrea *227:* 26
Burger, Carl *3:* 33; *45:* 160, 162
Burgeson, Marjorie *19:* 31
Burgess, Anne *76:* 252
Burgess, Gelett *32:* 39, 42
Burgess, Mark *157:* 31
Burke, Jim *179:* 19; *185:* 63
Burke, Phillip *95:* 117
Burkert, Nancy Ekholm *18:* 186; *22:* 140; *24:* 62, 63,64, 65; *26:* 53; *29:* 60, 61; *46:* 171; *YABC 1:* 46
Burkhardt, Bruce *142:* 86
Burkhardt, Melissa A. *142:* 86
Burleson, Joe *104:* 35; *172:* 139; *227:* 124
Burn, Doris *6:* 172
Burn, Jeffrey *89:* 125; *152:* 132
Burn, Ted
    See Burn, Thomas E.
Burn, Thomas E. *151:* 41
Burnard, Damon *115:* 23
Burnett, Lindy *210:* 59
Burnett, Virgil *44:* 42
Burningham, John *9:* 68; *16:* 60, 61; *59:* 28, 29, 30,31, 32, 33, 35; *111:* 18, 19, 21; *160:* 37; *225:* 21, 24
Burns, Howard M. *12:* 173
Burns, Jim *47:* 70; *86:* 32; *91:* 197; *123:* 16
Burns, M.F. *26:* 69
Burns, Raymond *9:* 29
Burns, Robert *24:* 106
Burr, Dan *65:* 28; *108:* 134; *164:* 203; *182:* 68
Burr, Dane *12:* 2
Burra, Edward *YABC 2:* 68
Burrell, Galen *56:* 76
Burri, Rene *41:* 143; *54:* 166
Burridge, Marge Opitz *14:* 42
Burris, Burmah *4:* 81
Burroughs, John Coleman *41:* 64
Burroughs, Studley O. *41:* 65
Burton, Marilee Robin *46:* 33
Burton, Virginia Lee *2:* 43; *44:* 49, 51; *100:* 46, 47; *YABC 1:* 24; *147:* 56
Bush, Timothy *228:* 138
Busoni, Rafaello *1:* 186; *3:* 224; *6:* 126; *14:* 5; *16:* 62, 63
Butchkes, Sidney *50:* 58
Butler, Geoff *94:* 20
Butler, Ralph *116:* 212
Butterfield, Ned *1:* 153; *27:* 128; *79:* 63
Butterworth, Ian *184:* 48, 49
Butterworth, Nick *106:* 43, 44; *149:* 34
Buxton, John *123:* 12
Buzelli, Christopher *105:* 149
Buzonas, Gail *29:* 88
Buzzell, Russ W. *12:* 177
Byard, Carole *39:* 44; *57:* 18, 19, 20; *60:* 60; *61:* 93, 96; *69:* 210; *78:* 246; *79:* 227
Byars, Betsy *46:* 35
Byfield, Barbara Ninde *8:* 18
Byfield, Graham *32:* 29
Bynum, Janie *176:* 50
Byrd, Robert *13:* 218; *33:* 46; *158:* 70; *212:* 100; *226:* 39, 40; *229:* 102
Byrd, Samuel *123:* 104

C

Cabat, Erni *74:* 38
Cabban, Vanessa *138:* 73; *176:* 39; *185:* 65; *227:* 70
Cabrera, Jane *103:* 24; *152:* 27; *182:* 33, 34
Caceres, Ana Palmero *198:* 106
Caddy, Alice *6:* 41

Cady, Harrison *17:* 21, 23; *19:* 57, 58
Caffrey, Aileen *72:* 223; *141:* 154
Cairns, Julia *177:* 37
Caldecott, Randolph *16:* 98, 103; *17:* 32, 33, 36, 38, 39; *26:* 90; *100:* 49, 50; *YABC 2:* 172
Calder, Alexander *18:* 168
Calderón, Gloria *179:* 5
Calderon, W. Frank *25:* 160
Caldwell, Ben *105:* 75; *149:* 60; *195:* 61
Caldwell, Clyde *98:* 100; *116:* 39; *208:* 145
Caldwell, Doreen *23:* 77; *71:* 41
Caldwell, John *46:* 225
Call, Greg *126:* 135; *165:* 49; *182:* 105, 163; *197:* 18, 19; *200:* 159; *209:* 166; *212:* 161; *229:* 122
Callahan, Kevin *22:* 42
Callahan, Philip S. *25:* 77
Callan, Jamie *59:* 37
Callen, Liz *231:* 37
Calvert, Rosemary *218:* 96
Calvin, James *61:* 92
Camburn-Bracalente, Carol A. *118:* 22
Cameron, Chad *190:* 144
Cameron, Julia Margaret *19:* 203
Cameron, Scott *99:* 18
Camm, Martin *140:* 208, 209, 210
Campbell, Ann *11:* 43; *123:* 182; *183:* 68
Campbell, Bill *89:* 39
Campbell, Ken *126:* 143; *205:* 162
Campbell, Robert *55:* 120
Campbell, Rod *51:* 27; *98:* 34
Campbell, Walter M. *YABC 2:* 158
Camps, Luis *28:* 120, 121; *66:* 35
Canga, C.B. *187:* 165
Caniglia, Jeremy *201:* 89
Cann, Helen *124:* 50; *141:* 78; *170:* 138; *179:* 22, 23
Cannell, Jon *196:* 43
Cannon, Janell *78:* 25; *128:* 40
Canright, David *36:* 162
Cantone, AnnaLaura *182:* 146; *196:* 80
Canty, Thomas *85:* 161; *92:* 47; *113:* 192; *134:* 60; *185:* 117
Canyon, Christopher *150:* 44; *151:* 112
Cáparo, Antonio Javier *204:* 128; *218:* 88; *220:* 114; *221:* 167; *227:* 125; *231:* 154
Caple, Laurie *228:* 9
Caporale, Wende *70:* 42
Capp, Al *61:* 28, 30, 31, 40, 41, 43, 44
Cappon, Manuela *154:* 64; *218:* 149
Caras, Peter *36:* 64
Caraway, Caren *57:* 22
Caraway, James *3:* 200, 201
Carbe, Nino *29:* 183
Cardinale, Christopher *231:* 38
Cares, Linda *67:* 176
Carigiet, Alois *24:* 67
Carle, Eric *4:* 42; *11:* 121; *12:* 29; *65:* 32,33, 34, 36; *73:* 63, 65; *163:* 55, 56
Carling, Amelia Lau *164:* 46
Carlino, Angela *168:* 43; *188:* 20
Carlson, Nancy L. *41:* 116; *56:* 25; *90:* 45; *144:* 48, 50; *213:* 24, 25, 26
Carluccio, Maria *175:* 129; *221:* 119
Carmi, Giora *79:* 35; *149:* 40; *208:* 126
Carpenter, Nancy *76:* 128; *86:* 173; *89:* 171; *131:* 186; *134:* 8; *138:* 215; *153:* 204; *159:* 93; *165:* 232; *211:* 134; *216:* 113
Carr, Archie *37:* 225
Carrick, Donald *5:* 194; *39:* 97; *49:* 70; *53:* 156; *63:* 15, 16, 17, 18, 19, 21; *80:* 131; *86:* 151; *118:* 24
Carrick, Malcolm *28:* 59, 60
Carrick, Paul *118:* 26; *194:* 28
Carrick, Valery *21:* 47
Carrier, Lark *71:* 43
Carroll, Jim *88:* 211; *140:* 177; *153:* 99; *195:* 75
Carroll, Lewis
    See Dodgson, Charles L.

Carroll, Michael *72:* 5
Carroll, Pamela *84:* 68; *128:* 214; *199:* 130
Carroll, Ruth *7:* 41; *10:* 68
Carter, Abby *81:* 32; *97:* 121; *102:* 61; *163:* 139; *164:* 125; *184:* 22, 23; *191:* 85; *222:* 51
Carter, Barbara *47:* 167, 169
Carter, David A. *114:* 24, 25; *170:* 42, 43; *228:* 29
Carter, Don *124:* 54; *184:* 100; *192:* 43, 44, 45
Carter, Harry *22:* 179
Carter, Helene *15:* 38; *22:* 202, 203; *YABC 2:* 220, 221
Carter, Penny *173:* 91
Cartlidge, Michelle *49:* 65; *96:* 50, 51
Cartwright, Reg *63:* 61, 62; *78:* 26; *143:* 4
Cartwright, Shannon *176:* 81
Carty, Leo *4:* 196; *7:* 163; *58:* 131
Cary, Page *12:* 41
Cary *4:* 133; *9:* 32; *20:* 2; *21:* 143
Casale, Paul *71:* 63; *109:* 122; *136:* 28
Case, Chris *209:* 23
Case, Sandra E. *16:* 2
Caseley, Judith *87:* 36; *159:* 47, 48, 49
Casilla, Robert *78:* 7; *167:* 124; *211:* 41; *212:* 165
Casino, Steve *85:* 193
Cassel, Lili
    See Wronker, Lili Cassel
Cassel-Wronker, Lili
    See Wronker, Lili Cassel
Cassels, Jean *8:* 50; *150:* 119; *173:* 37; *186:* 182
Cassen, Melody *140:* 51
Cassity, Don *104:* 24
Cassler, Carl *75:* 137, 138; *82:* 162
Casson, Hugh *65:* 38, 40, 42, 43
Castellon, Federico *48:* 45, 46, 47, 48
Castle, Jane *4:* 80
Castro L., Antonio *84:* 71; *226:* 43
Casu, Danny "casroc" *201:* 10
Catalano, Dominic *94:* 79; *163:* 60, 61; *162:* 54
Catalanotto, Peter *63:* 170; *70:* 23; *71:* 182; *72:* 96; *74:* 114; *76:* 194, 195; *77:* 7; *79:* 157; *80:* 28, 67; *83:* 157; *85:* 27; *108:* 11; *113:* 30, 31, 33, 34, 36; *114:* 27, 28, 29; *117:* 53; *124:* 168; *159:* 54, 55; *195:* 19, 20, 21, 22, 24, 174; *200:* 156; *207:* 103; *209:* 184; *226:* 4
Catania, Tom *68:* 82
Cather, Carolyn *3:* 83; *15:* 203; *34:* 216
Catlin, George *214:* 172
Catrow, David *117:* 179; *152:* 31, 33; *173:* 24; *206:* 29; *231:* 107
Catusanu, Mircea *222:* 53
Cauley, Lorinda Bryan *44:* 135; *46:* 49
Cayard, Bruce *38:* 67
Cazet, Denys *52:* 27; *99:* 39, 40; *163:* 65, 66; *191:* 25, 27, 28
Ceccoli, Nicoletta *181:* 39; *188:* 99; *199:* 118; *209:* 6
Cecil, Randy *127:* 132, 133; *187:* 16, 17; *191:* 168; *209:* 5; *223:* 37, 38; *224:* 83
Cellini, Joseph *2:* 73; *3:* 35; *16:* 116; *47:* 103
Cepeda, Joe *90:* 62; *109:* 91; *134:* 172; *159:* 57, 58, 164; *197:* 157; *203:* 69, 95; *215:* 38, 39, 40
Chabrian, Debbi *45:* 55
Chabrian, Deborah *51:* 182; *53:* 124; *63:* 107; *75:* 84; *79:* 85; *82:* 247; *89:* 93; *101:* 197; *212:* 13
Chagnon, Mary *37:* 158
Chalmers, Mary *3:* 145; *13:* 148; *33:* 125; *66:* 214
Chamberlain, Christopher *45:* 57
Chamberlain, Margaret *46:* 51; *106:* 89; *188:* 193; *212:* 16, 17; *224:* 181
Chamberlain, Nigel *78:* 140
Chambers, C.E. *17:* 230
Chambers, Dave *12:* 151
Chambers, Jill *134:* 110

Chambers, Mary *4:* 188
Chambliss, Maxie *42:* 186; *56:* 159; *93:* 163, 164; *103:* 178; *186:* 33, 34; *196:* 39; *223:* 182
Champlin, Dale *136:* 124
Chan, Harvey *96:* 236; *99:* 153; *143:* 218; *179:* 144; *211:* 219
Chan, Peter *207:* 21; *221:* 39
Chandler, David P. *28:* 62
Chaney, Howard *139:* 27
Chang, Warren *101:* 209
Chapel, Jody *68:* 20
Chapman, C.H. *13:* 83, 85, 87
Chapman, Frederick T. *6:* 27; *44:* 28
Chapman, Gaye *203:* 133
Chapman, Gaynor *32:* 52, 53
Chapman, Jane *145:* 186; *150:* 56; *166:* 220; *174:* 202; *176:* 43, 44; *179:* 131; *202:* 189; *212:* 20, 21, 22; *216:* 123, 225; *221:* 181, 182
Chapman, Lynne *175:* 31; *197:* 25; *208:* 44
Chapman-Crane, Jeff *220:* 101
Chappell, Warren *3:* 172; *21:* 56; *27:* 125
Charles, Donald *30:* 154, 155
Charlip, Remy *4:* 48; *34:* 138; *68:* 53, 54; *119:* 29, 30; *210:* 63, 64
Charlot, Jean *1:* 137, 138; *8:* 23; *14:* 31; *48:* 151; *56:* 21
Charlot, Martin *64:* 72
Charlton, Michael *34:* 50; *37:* 39
Charmatz, Bill *7:* 45
Chartier, Normand *9:* 36; *52:* 49; *66:* 40; *74:* 220; *145:* 169; *168:* 91; *177:* 108
Chase, Lynwood M. *14:* 4
Chast, Roz *97:* 39, 40; *212:* 25
Chastain, Madye Lee *4:* 50
Chateron, Ann *152:* 19
Chatterton, Martin *68:* 102; *152:* 19; *225:* 42
Chau, Tungwai *140:* 35
Chauncy, Francis *24:* 158
Chayka, Doug *145:* 97; *177:* 150; *196:* 46; *212:* 58
Chee, Cheng-Khee *79:* 42; *81:* 224; *180:* 245
Chen, Chih-sien *90:* 226
Chen, Tony *6:* 45; *19:* 131; *29:* 126; *34:* 160
Chen, Wendy *221:* 76
Chen, Yong *183:* 34
Cheney, T.A. *11:* 47
Cheng, Andrea *205:* 28
Cheng, Judith *36:* 45; *51:* 16
Chermayeff, Ivan *47:* 53
Cherry, David *93:* 40
Cherry, Lynne *34:* 52; *65:* 184; *87:* 111; *99:* 46, 47
Chesak, Lina *135:* 118
Chess, Victoria *12:* 6; *33:* 42, 48, 49; *40:* 194; *41:* 145; *69:* 80; *72:* 100; *92:* 33, 34; *104:* 167
Chessare, Michele *41:* 50; *56:* 48; *69:* 145
Chesterton, G.K. *27:* 43, 44, 45, 47
Chestnutt, David *47:* 217
Chesworth, Michael *75:* 24, 152; *88:* 136; *94:* 25; *98:* 155; *160:* 42; *207:* 23, 24, 25; *214:* 145
Chetham, Celia *134:* 34
Chetwin, Grace *86:* 40
Cheung, Irving *158:* 96
Chevalier, Christa *35:* 66
Chew, Ruth *7:* 46; *132:* 147
Chewning, Randy *92:* 206
Chichester Clark, Emma *72:* 121; *77:* 212; *78:* 209; *87:* 143; *117:* 37, 39, 40; *144:* 138; *156:* 24, 25; *209:* 26
Chifflart *47:* 113, 127
Child, Lauren *119:* 32; *183:* 30, 31
Chin, Alex *28:* 54
Chitwood, Susan Tanner *163:* 16
Cho, Shinta *8:* 126
Chodos-Irvine, Margaret *52:* 102, 103, 107; *152:* 44

Choi, Yangsook *171:* 134; *173:* 135; *178:* 38, 39, 40
Choksi, Nishant *222:* 54
Chollat, Emilie *170:* 203
Chollick, Jay *25:* 175
Choma, Christina *99:* 169
Chomey, Steve *188:* 53
Chorao, Kay *7:* 200, 201; *8:* 25; *11:* 234; *33:* 187; *35:* 239; *69:* 35; *70:* 235; *123:* 174; *193:* 179; *215:* 43, 44, 45, 46; *229:* 174
Chorney, Steve *221:* 63
Chow, Frances J. Soo Ping *206:* 36
Chowdhury, Subrata *62:* 130; *162:* 22, 23
Christelow, Eileen *38:* 44; *83:* 198, 199; *90:* 57, 58; *184:* 26
Christensen, Bonnie *93:* 100; *153:* 67; *213:* 29, 30
Christensen, Gardell Dano *1:* 57
Christensen, James C. *140:* 226
Christiana, David *90:* 64; *135:* 13; *171:* 7; *195:* 26, 27
Christiansen, Per *40:* 24
Christie, R. Gregory *116:* 107; *127:* 20, 21; *162:* 179; *164:* 114; *165:* 137; *174:* 157; *179:* 172; *185:* 17, 18, 19; *200:* 2; *204:* 85; *215:* 207; *218:* 57; *220:* 80, 130; *225:* 45, 46, 47; *226:* 211; *231:* 113
Christy, Howard Chandler *17:* 163, 164, 165, 168, 169; *19:* 186, 187; *21:* 22, 23, 24, 25
Christy, Jana *194:* 21
Chronister, Robert *23:* 138; *63:* 27; *69:* 167
Church, Caroline Jayne *179:* 27; *219:* 28, 29
Church, Frederick *YABC 1:* 155
Chute, Marchette *1:* 59
Chwast, Jacqueline *1:* 63; *2:* 275; *6:* 46, 47; *11:* 125; *12:* 202; *14:* 235
Chwast, Seymour *3:* 128, 129; *18:* 43; *27:* 152; *92:* 79; *96:* 56, 57, 58; *146:* 32, 33; *197:* 99
Cieslawski, Steve *101:* 142; *127:* 116; *158:* 169, 171; *190:* 174; *212:* 85; *228:* 123
Cinelli, Lisa *146:* 253
Cirlin, Edgard *2:* 168
Clairin, Georges *53:* 109
Clapp, John *105:* 66; *109:* 58; *126:* 7; *129:* 148; *130:* 165; *195:* 48; *220:* 102
Clark, Brenda *119:* 85; *153:* 55
Clark, David *77:* 164; *134:* 144, 145; *216:* 66, 67
Clark, Emma Chichester
    See Chichester Clark, Emma
Clark, Robert *227:* 170
Clark, Victoria *35:* 159
Clarke, Greg *169:* 134; *215:* 47, 115
Clarke, Gus *72:* 226; *134:* 31
Clarke, Harry *23:* 172, 173
Clarke, Peter *75:* 102
Claverie, Jean *38:* 46; *88:* 29
Clavis, Philippe Goossens *182:* 167
Clay, Wil *203:* 29
Clayton, Elaine *159:* 60; *209:* 32
Clayton, Robert *9:* 181
Cleary, Brian P. *186:* 37
Cleaver, Elizabeth *8:* 204; *23:* 36
Cleland, Janet *225:* 111; *226:* 48
Cleland, T.M. *26:* 92
Clemens, Peter *61:* 125
Clement, Charles *20:* 38
Clement, Gary *186:* 79; *191:* 32
Clement, Janet *182:* 50
Clement, Nathan *200:* 30
Clement, Rod *97:* 42
Clement, Stephen *88:* 3
Clementson, John *84:* 213
Clemesha, David *192:* 49, 50
Cleminson, Kate *221:* 26
Clevin, Jorgen *7:* 50
Clifford, Judy *34:* 163; *45:* 198
Clokey, Art *59:* 44
Clouse, Dennis *187:* 158
Clouse, James *84:* 15

Clouse, Nancy L. *78:* 31; *114:* 90; *225:* 117
Clover, Peter *152:* 45
Cneut, Carll *156:* 166; *165:* 67; *197:* 26
Coalson, Glo *9:* 72, 85; *25:* 155; *26:* 42; *35:* 212; *53:* 31; *56:* 154; *94:* 37, 38, 193
Cober, Alan E. *17:* 158; *32:* 77; *49:* 127
Cober-Gentry, Leslie *92:* 111
Cocca-Leffler, Maryann *80:* 46; *136:* 60; *139:* 193; *194:* 31, 33, 34
Cochran, Bobbye *11:* 52
Cochran, Josh *221:* 27
CoConis, Ted *4:* 41; *46:* 41; *51:* 104
Cocozza, Chris *87:* 18; *110:* 173; *111:* 149
Cockroft, Jason *152:* 20
Coerr, Eleanor *1:* 64; *67:* 52
Coes, Peter *35:* 172
Cogancherry, Helen *52:* 143; *69:* 131; *77:* 93; *78:* 220; *109:* 204; *110:* 129; *203:* 92
Coggins, Jack *2:* 69
Cohen, Alix *7:* 53
Cohen, Lisa *225:* 49
Cohen, Miriam *155:* 23, 24
Cohen, Nancy R. *165:* 35
Cohen, Santiago *164:* 26; *215:* 52, 199
Cohen, Sheldon *105:* 33, 34; *166:* 46, 47
Cohen, Vincent O. *19:* 243
Cohen, Vivien *11:* 112
Coker, Paul *51:* 172
Colbert, Anthony *15:* 41; *20:* 193
Colby, C.B. *3:* 47
Cole, Babette *58:* 172; *96:* 63, 64; *155:* 29
Cole, Brock *68:* 223; *72:* 36, 37, 38, 192; *127:* 23; *136:* 64, 65; *197:*
Cole, Gwen *87:* 185
Cole, Henry *178:* 120; *181:* 42, 43; *189:* 60; *213:* 35, 36; *222:* 139
Cole, Herbert *28:* 104
Cole, Michael *59:* 46
Cole, Olivia H.H. *1:* 134; *3:* 223; *9:* 111; *38:* 104
Cole, Rachael *209:* 39
Colin, Paul *102:* 59; *123:* 118; *126:* 152; *192:* 129
Colley, Jacqui *202:* 20
Collicott, Sharleen *98:* 39; *143:* 29, 30
Collier, Bryan *126:* 54; *151:* 166; *174:* 16, 17, 18; *204:* 18, 19; *208:* 84; *211:* 143; *228:* 128
Collier, David *13:* 127
Collier, John *27:* 179; *208:* 154
Collier, Steven *50:* 52
Collier-Morales, Roberta *168:* 61
Collins, Heather *66:* 84; *67:* 68; *81:* 40; *98:* 192, 193; *129:* 95, 96, 98
Collins, Matt *167:* 90; *231:* 9
Collins, Ross *140:* 23, 24; *200:* 36, 37; *209:* 54
Colman, Audrey *146:* 161
Colón, Raul *108:* 112; *113:* 5; *117:* 167; *134:* 112; *146:* 23; *159:* 92; *166:* 73; *180:* 107; *186:* 156; *190:* 6; *193:* 24, 205; *202:* 21, 22, 23; *217:* 68; *220:* 126, 157; *226:* 118; *227:* 165
Colonna, Bernard *21:* 50; *28:* 103; *34:* 140; *43:* 180; *78:* 150
Comport, Sally Wern *117:* 169; *169:* 104; *190:* 42; *207:* 50
Conahan, Carolyn *215:* 17
Conde, J.M. *100:* 120
Condon, Grattan *54:* 85 Condon, Ken *161:* 44; *195:* 28, 29
Cone, Ferne Geller *39:* 49
Cone, J. Morton *39:* 49
Conklin, Paul *43:* 62
Connelly, Gwen *212:* 30
Connelly, James *198:* 12
Connolly, Howard *67:* 88
Connolly, Jerome P. *4:* 128; *28:* 52
Connolly, Peter *47:* 60
Conoly, Walle *110:* 224
Conover, Chris *31:* 52; *40:* 184; *41:* 51; *44:* 79; *213:* 39

Conroy, Melissa *226:* 54
Constantin, Pascale *207:* 159
Contreras, Gerry *72:* 9
Converse, James *38:* 70
Conway *62:* 62
Conway, Michael *69:* 12; *81:* 3; *92:* 108
Cook, Ande *188:* 135
Cook, G.R. *29:* 165
Cook, Joel *108:* 160
Cook, Lynette *228:* 211
Cookburn, W.V. *29:* 204
Cooke, Donald E. *2:* 77
Cooke, Tom *52:* 118
Coomaraswamy, A.K. *50:* 100
Coombs, Charles *43:* 65
Coombs, Deborah *139:* 175
Coombs, Patricia *2:* 82; *3:* 52; *22:* 119; *51:* 32, 33, 34, 35, 36, 37, 38, 39, 40, 42, 43
Cooney, Barbara *6:* 16, 17, 50; *12:* 42; *13:* 92; *15:* 145; *16:* 74, 111; *18:* 189; *23:* 38, 89, 93; *32:* 138; *38:* 105; *59:* 48, 49, 51, 52, 53; *74:* 222; *81:* 100; *91:* 25; *96:* 71, 72, 74; *100:* 149; *YABC2:* 10
Cooper, Elisha *157:* 38, 39
Cooper, Floyd *79:* 95; *81:* 45; *84:* 82; *85:* 74; *91:* 118; *96:* 77, 78; *103:* 149; *144:* 54; *145:* 151; *159:* 198; *176:* 133, 134; *187:* 26, 27, 28, 29; *188:* 22; *199:* 175; *219:* 66; *227:* 38, 39, 40, 42
Cooper, Heather *50:* 39
Cooper, Helen *102:* 42, 43, 44
Cooper, Mario *24:* 107
Cooper, Marjorie *7:* 112
Cope, Jane *61:* 201; *108* 52
Copeland, Mark *180:* 12
Copelman, Evelyn *8:* 61; *18:* 25
Copley, Heather *30:* 86; *45:* 57
Corace, Jen *208:* 48
Corbett, Grahame *30:* 114; *43:* 67
Corbino, John *19:* 248
Corcos, Lucille *2:* 223; *10:* 27; *34:* 66
Cordell, Matthew *197:* 93; *199:* 20, 21
Córdova, Amy *220:* 194
Corey, Robert *9:* 34
Corlass, Heather *10:* 7
Cornell, James *27:* 60
Cornell, Jeff *11:* 58
Cornell, Laura *94:* 179; *95:* 25
Corr, Christopher *204:* 98
Corral, Ridrigs *212:* 87
Corrigan, Barbara *8:* 37
Corrigan, Patrick *145:* 149
Corwin, Judith Hoffman *10:* 28
Corwin, Oliver *191:* 119
Cory, Fanny Y. *20:* 113; *48:* 29
Cosentino, Ralph *169:* 32
Cosgrove, Margaret *3:* 100; *47:* 63; *82:* 133
Costabel, Eva Deutsch *45:* 66, 67
Costanza, John *58:* 7, 8, 9
Costello, Chris *86:* 78
Costello, David F. *23:* 55
Côté, Geneviéve *184:* 37, 39; *210:* 256; *211:* 151
Cote, Nancy *126:* 139; *156:* 101; *174:* 101; *182:* 53, 54, 55; *222:* 49
Cottenden, Jeff *190:* 45
Couch, Greg *94:* 124; *110:* 13; *162:* 31; *168:* 149; *199:* 22; *216:* 144; *229:* 103
Councell, Ruth Tietjen *79:* 29
Courtney, Cathy *58:* 69, 144; *59:* 15; *61:* 20, 87
Courtney, R. *35:* 110
Counihan, Claire *133:* 106
Cousineau, Normand *89:* 180; *112:* 76; *227:* 75
Cousins, Lucy *172:* 53, 54; *205:* 34, 35
Couture, Christin *41:* 209
Covarrubias, Miguel *35:* 118, 119, 123, 124, 125
Coville, Katherine *32:* 57; *36:* 167; *92:* 38
Covington, Neverne *113:* 87

Cowdrey, Richard *169:* 170; *178:* 205; *204:* 22, 23; *215:* 31
Cowell, Cressida *140:* 39
Cowell, Lucinda *77:* 54
Cowles, Rose *203:* 164, 167
Cox *43:* 93
Cox, Charles *8:* 20
Cox, David *56:* 37; *90:* 63; *119:* 38
Cox, Palmer *24:* 76, 77
Cox, Paul *226:* 57, 58
Cox, Steve *140:* 96
Coxe, Molly *69:* 44
Coxon, Michele *158:* 80
Crabb, Gordon *70:* 39
Crabtree, Judith *98:* 42
Craft, Kinuko *22:* 182; *36:* 220; *53:* 122, 123, 148,149; *74:* 12; *81:* 129; *86:* 31; *89:* 139; *127:* 27, 28, 29; *132:* 142; *139:* 38
Craig, Daniel *177:* 67; *180:* 11; *185:* 203; *211:* 212; *224:* 27; *229:* 59
Craig, David *136:* 198; *205:* 37
Craig, Helen *49:* 76; *62:* 70, 71, 72; *69:* 141; *94:* 42, 43, 44; *112:* 53; *135:* 101, 102; *213:* 45, 46, 47, 55, 81, 82
Crane, Alan H. *1:* 217
Crane, H.M. *13:* 111
Crane, Jack *43:* 183
Crane, Jordan *174:* 21
Crane, Walter *18:* 46, 47, 48, 49, 53, 54, 56, 57, 59, 60, 61; *22:* 128; *24:* 210, 217; *100:* 70, 71
Cravath, Lynne Avril *98:* 45; *182:* 58, 59; *216:* 48; *219:* 61; *220:* 124; *224:* 183; *228:* 74; *229:* 89
Crawford, Allen *212:* 181
Crawford, Denise *137:* 213
Crawford, Will *43:* 77
Credle, Ellis *1:* 69
Czekaj, Jef *217:* 44; *218:* 77
Czernecki, Stefan *154:* 104; *178:* 68, 69
Crespi, Francesca *87:* 90
Cressy, Michael *124:* 55; *203:* 132
Crews, Donald *32:* 59, 60; *76:* 42, 43, 44
Crews, Nina *97:* 49
Crichlow, Ernest *74:* 88; *83:* 203
Crilley, Mark *210:* 71
Croft, James *150:* 57
Crofut, Bob *80:* 87; *81:* 47
Crofut, Susan *23:* 61
Croll, Carolyn *80:* 137; *102:* 52
Cross, Peter *56:* 78; *63:* 60, 65
Crossman, David A. *219:* 38
Crowe, Elizabeth *88:* 144
Crowell, Pers *3:* 125
Cruikshank, George *15:* 76, 83; *22:* 74, 75, 76, 77, 78, 79,80, 81, 82, 84, 137; *24:* 22, 23
Crump, Fred H. *11:* 62
Cruz, Ray *6:* 55; *70:* 234; *123:* 173; *172:* 192
Csatari, Joe *44:* 82; *55:* 152; *63:* 25, 28; *102:* 58
Cuetara, Mittie *158:* 85
Cuffari, Richard *4:* 75; *5:* 98; *6:* 56; *7:* 13,84, 153; *8:* 148, 155; *9:* 89; *11:* 19; *12:* 55, 96,114; *15:* 51, 202; *18:* 5; *20:* 139; *21:* 197; *22:* 14, 192; *23:* 15, 106; *25:* 97; *27:* 133; *28:* 196; *29:* 54; *30:* 85; *31:* 35; *36:* 101; *38:* 171; *42:* 97; *44:* 92, 192; *45:* 212, 213; *46:* 36, 198; *50:* 164; *54:* 80, 136, 137, 145; *56:* 17; *60:* 63; *66:* 49, 50; *70:* 41; *71:* 132; *77:* 157; *78:* 58, 149; *79:* 120; *85:* 2, 152
Cugat, Xavier *19:* 120
Cumings, Art *35:* 160
Cummings, Chris *29:* 167
Cummings, Michael *159:* 142
Cummings, Pat *42:* 61; *61:* 99; *69:* 205; *71:* 57,58; *78:* 24, 25; *93:* 75; *107:* 49, 50; *164:* 259; *203:* 45, 46
Cummings, Richard *24:* 119
Cummings, Terrance *227:* 49, 172
Cunette, Lou *20:* 93; *22:* 125
Cunningham, Aline *25:* 180

Cunningham, David *11:* 13
Cunningham, Imogene *16:* 122, 127
Cunningham, Kelley *176:* 159
Cupples, Pat *107:* 12; *126:* 109; *182:* 13; *198:* 68; *217:* 21, 22
Curlee, Lynn *98:* 48; *141:* 39; *190:* 48
Currey, Anna *190:* 145; *202:* 130, 132
Curry, John Steuart *2:* 5; *19:* 84; *34:* 36; *144:* 126
Curry, Tom *127:* 131; *185:* 25, 26
Curtis, Bruce *23:* 96; *30:* 88; *36:* 22
Curtis, Neil *167:* 30
Curtis, Stacy *205:* 38
Cusack, Margaret *58:* 49, 50, 51
Cushman, Doug *65:* 57; *101:* 39, 40; *133:* 179; *157:* 45; *186:* 157; *210:* 76, 77
Cutting, Ann *196:* 194
Cyrus, Kurt *132:* 39; *179:* 36, 37
Czechowski, Alicia *95:* 21; *171:* 37
Czernecki, Stefan *117:* 173

D

Dabcovich, Lydia *25:* 105; *40:* 114; *99:* 75, 76
Dacey, Bob *82:* 175; *152:* 65
d'Achille, Gino *127:* 175, 176
Daily, Don *78:* 197; *220:* 154
Dain, Martin J. *35:* 75
Dale, Penny *127:* 224; *151:* 57; *160:* 89; *197:* 75
Dale, Rae *72:* 197
Daley, Joann *50:* 22
Dalton, Anne *40:* 62; *63:* 119
Daly, Deborah M. *74:* 213
Daly, Jim *103:* 60; *150:* 48
Daly, Jude *138:* 118, 119; *213:* 41; *222:* 56, 57
Daly, Nicholas *37:* 53; *76:* 48, 49
Daly, Niki *107:* 15; *114:* 38, 39, 40; *164:* 86; *192:* 53; *198:* 26, 27
Daly, Paul *97:* 205
Dalziel, Brothers *33:* 113
D'Amato, Alex *9:* 48; *20:* 25
D'Amato, Janet *9:* 48; *20:* 25; *26:* 118
D'Amico, Steve *170:* 52
Danalis, Johnny *167:* 27
D'Andrea, Domenick *183:* 108
Daniel, Alan *23:* 59; *29:* 110; *76:* 50, 53, 55, 56; *153:* 76 *115:* 74; *134:* 70
Daniel, Lea *76:* 53, 55; *153:* 76
Daniel, Lewis C. *20:* 216
Daniels, Beau *73:* 4
Daniels, Steve *22:* 16
Daniels, Stewart *56:* 12
Dann, Bonnie *31:* 83
Dann, Penny *82:* 128
Danska, Herbert *24:* 219
Danyell, Alice *20:* 27
Darbyshire, Kristen *218:* 41
Dardik, Helen *208:* 200
Darley, F.O.C. *16:* 145; *19:* 79, 86, 88, 185; *21:* 28,36; *35:* 76, 77, 78, 79, 80, 81; *YABC 2:* 175
Darling, Lois *3:* 59; *23:* 30, 31
Darling, Louis *1:* 40, 41; *2:* 63; *3:* 59; *23:* 30,31; *43:* 54, 57, 59; *121:* 53
Darnell, K.L. *210:* 247
Darrow, David R. *84:* 101
Darrow, Whitney, Jr. *13:* 25; *38:* 220, 221
Darwin, Beatrice *43:* 54
Darwin, Len *24:* 82
Dastolfo, Frank *33:* 179
Dauber, Liz *1:* 22; *3:* 266; *30:* 49
Daugherty, James *3:* 66; *8:* 178; *13:* 27, 28, 161; *18:* 101; *19:* 72; *29:* 108; *32:* 156; *42:* 84; *YABC 1:* 256; *2:* 174
d'Aulaire, Edgar Parin *5:* 51; *66:* 53
d'Aulaire, Ingri Parin *5:* 51; *66:* 53
Davalos, Felipe *99:* 197; *159:* 66; *174:* 163

Davenier, Christine *125:* 88; *127:* 32; *128:* 152; *179:* 39, 40; *216:* 84, 85, 86, 87; *218:* 62, 63; *224:* 73
Davick, Linda *151:* 124; *208:* 187
David, Jacques-Louis *193:* 22
David, Jonathan *19:* 37
Davidson, Kevin *28:* 154
Davidson, Raymond *32:* 61
Davie, Helen K. *77:* 48, 49
Davies, Andy Robert *205:* 169
Davies, Lottie *214:* 69
Davis, Allen *20:* 11; *22:* 45; *27:* 222; *29:* 157; *41:* 99; *47:* 99; *50:* 84; *52:* 105
Davis, Bette J. *15:* 53; *23:* 95
Davis, Dimitris *45:* 95
Davis, Eleanor *209:* 33
Davis, Hendon *151:* 122
Davis, Jack E. *145:* 139; *175:* 84, 85; *208:* 102; *210:* 81, 82; *213:* 151
Davis, Jim *32:* 63, 64
Davis, Katie *152:* 52, 53, 54; *208:* 52
Davis, Lambert *110:* 23, 24; *176:* 58
Davis, Marguerite *31:* 38; *34:* 69, 70; *100:* 34; *YABC 1:* 126, 230
Davis, Nelle *69:* 191
Davis, Paul *78:* 214
Davis, Rich *206:* 38
Davis, Stuart *211:* 69
Davis, Yvonne LeBrun *94:* 144
Davisson, Virginia H. *44:* 178
DaVolls, Andy *85:* 53
Dawson, Diane *24:* 127; *42:* 126; *52:* 130; *68:* 104
Dawson, Janine *215:* 198
Dawson, Willow *208:* 54; *216:* 119
Day, Alexandra *67:* 59; *97:* 54; *166:* 65; *169:* 40; *197:* 50, 51, 52, 54
Day, Larry *169:* 88; *185:* 59; *227:* 55
Day, Rob *94:* 110; *127:* 24; *197:* 32
Dean, Bob *19:* 211
Dean, David *192:* 55
de Angeli, Marguerite *1:* 77; *27:* 62, 65, 66, 67, 69, 70, 72; *100:* 75, 76; *YABC 1:* 166
DeArmond, Dale *70:* 47
Deas, Michael *27:* 219, 221; *30:* 156; *67:* 134; *72:* 24; *75:* 155; *84:* 206; *88:* 124
Deas, Rich *191:* 87; *193:* 10; *212:* 79
deBarros, Jim *196:* 60
Debon, Nicolas *151:* 60; *177:* 46
de Bosschere, Jean *19:* 252; *21:* 4; *186:* 44, 45
De Bruyn, M(onica) G. *13:* 30, 31
Decker, C.B. *172:* 120; *215:* 94
De Cuir, John F. *1:* 28, 29
Deeter, Catherine *74:* 110; *103:* 150; *137:* 50
Degen, Bruce *40:* 227, 229; *57:* 28, 29; *56:* 156; *75:* 229; *76:* 19; *81:* 36, 37; *92:* 26; *93:* 199; *97:* 56, 58, 59; *124:* 40; *147:* 39, 40, 41; *168:* 23; *205:* 45, 46; *231:* 46, 47, 48, 49
De Grazia *14:* 59; *39:* 56, 57
DeGrazio, George *88:* 40
deGroat, Diane *9:* 39; *18:* 7; *23:* 123; *28:* 200, 201; *31:* 58, 59; *34:* 151; *41:* 152; *43:* 88; *46:* 40, 200; *49:* 163; *50:* 89; *52:* 30, 34; *54:* 43; *63:* 5; *70:* 136; *71:* 99; *73:* 117,156; *77:* 34; *85:* 48; *86:* 201; *87:* 142; *90:* 72, 73, 143; *95:* 182; *111:* 123; *118:* 160; *126:* 8; *130:* 130; *138:* 93, 94; *169:* 46, 47
de Groot, Lee *6:* 21
Deines, Brian *110:* 139; *220:* 36, 37
DeJohn, Marie *89:* 78
Dekhteryov, B. *61:* 158
de Kiefte, Kees *94:* 107
Delacre, Lulu *36:* 66; *156:* 35; *202:* 10, 53; *209:* 36
Delaney, A. *21:* 78
Delaney, Michael *180:* 16
Delaney, Molly *80:* 43
Delaney, Ned *28:* 68; *56:* 80; *102:* 11
DeLapine, Jim *79:* 21
De La Roche Saint Andre, Anne *75:* 37

de Larrea, Victoria *6:* 119, 204; *29:* 103; *72:* 203; *87:* 199
Delehanty, Joan W. *223:* 165
DeLeon, Melanie *210:* 43
Delessert, Étienne *7:* 140; *46:* 61, 62, 63, 65, 67, 68; *130:* 38, 39, 40, 41, 42; *179:* 46, 47, 48, 49; *YABC 2:* 209
Delezenne, Christine *186:* 126
Delinois, Alix *228:* 40
Del Negro, Janice *196:* 161
Delon, Melanie *216:* 30
DeLorenzo, Christopher *154:* 149
Delulio, John *15:* 54
DeLuna, Tony *88:* 95
Demarest, Chris L. *45:* 68, 69, 70; *73:* 172, 173, 176; *78:* 106; *82:* 48, 49; *89:* 212; *92:* 86; *128:* 57, 58; *175:* 46, 48
De Mejo, Oscar *40:* 67
De Muth, Roger *205:* 184; *221:* 35
Demi *11:* 135; *15:* 245; *66:* 129, 130; *89:* 216; *102:* 66, 67, 68; *210:* 86, 87, 89
Denetsosie, Hoke *13:* 126; *82:* 34
Denise, Christopher *147:* 43, 44; *176:* 101; *193:* 35, 36, 37; *201:* 37
Dennis, Morgan *18:* 68, 69; *64:* 89
Dennis, Wesley *2:* 87; *3:* 111; *11:* 132; *18:* 71, 72, 73, 74; *22:* 9; *24:* 196, 200; *46:* 178; *69:* 94, 96; *129:* 62
Denos, Julia *202:* 26
Denslow, W.W. *16:* 84, 85, 86, 87; *18:* 19, 20, 24; *29:* 211; *100:* 21
Denton, Kady MacDonald *110:* 82; *130:* 70; *181:* 54, 55, 56; *192:* 75
Denton, Phil *220:* 6
Denton, Terry *72:* 163; *174:* 26; *186:* 52; *196:* 83, 84
DePalma, Mary Newell *132:* 114; *139:* 75; *185:* 30, 31; *186:* 121; *213:* 62
dePaola, Tomie *8:* 95; *9:* 93; *11:* 69; *25:* 103; *28:* 157; *29:* 80; *39:* 52, 53; *40:* 226; *46:* 187; *59:* 61, 62, 63, 64, 65, 66, 67, 68, 69, 71, 72, 74; *62:* 19; *108:* 63, 67, 68, 70; *155:* 62, 64, 66; *180:* 105; *200:* 47, 48, 49, 50; *226:* 116
Deraney, Michael J. *77:* 35; *78:* 148
deRosa, Dee *70:* 48; *71:* 210; *91:* 78
Dervaux, Isabelle *111:* 117
DeSaix, Deborah Durland *180:* 15; *188:* 24
De Saulles, Tony *119:* 39
de Sève, Peter *146:* 261; *207:* 78; *219:* 42
Deshaprabhu, Meera Dayal *86:* 192
Desimini, Lisa *86:* 68; *94:* 47; *96:* 7; *104:* 107; *125:* 194; *131:* 180; *172:* 56; *216:* 89, 90
de St. Menin, Charles *70:* 17
Detmold, Edward J. *22:* 104, 105, 106, 107; *35:* 120; *64:* 5; *YABC 2:* 203
Detrich, Susan *20:* 133
Deutermann, Diana *77:* 175
DeVelasco, Joseph E. *21:* 51
de Veyrac, Robert *YABC 2:* 19
DeVille, Edward A. *4:* 235
de Visser, John *55:* 119
Devito, Bert *12:* 164
Devlin, Harry *11:* 74; *74:* 63, 65; *136:* 77, 78
Dewan, Ted *108:* 73; *157:* 55; *165:* 129; *226:* 67, 68, 69
Dewar, Nick *133:* 122
Dewdney, Anna *184:* 43, 44
Dewey, Ariane *7:* 64; *33:* 195; *35:* 208; *68:* 16,17; *75:* 46; *93:* 91; *94:* 197; *109:* 65, 66, 67; *125:* 2, 3, 4, 5; *127:* 188; *143:* 25; *178:* 17, 19, 74; *188:* 166; *202:* 164; *231:* 176
Dewey, Jennifer (Owings) *58:* 54; *64:* 214; *65:* 207; *88:* 169; *103:* 45
Dewey, Kenneth *39:* 62; *51:* 23; *56:* 163
de Zanger, Arie *30:* 40
Diakité, Baba Wagué *174:* 28

Diamond, Donna *21:* 200; *23:* 63; *26:* 142; *35:* 83, 84, 85, 86, 87, 88, 89; *38:* 78; *40:* 147; *44:* 152; *50:* 144; *53:* 126; *69:* 46, 47, 48, 201; *71:* 133; *123:* 19
Dias, Ron *71:* 67
Diaz, David *80:* 213; *96:* 83, 84; *108:* 228; *110:* 29; *149:* 106; *150:* 63; *179:* 160; *184:* 95, 97; *189:* 51, 52, 53; *221:* 86; *229:* 37, 38, 39, 40
di Bartolo, Jim *225:* 53
Dibley, Glin *138:* 83; *141:* 128; *211:* 162; *221:* 61
DiCesare, Joe *70:* 38; *71:* 63, 106; *79:* 214; *93:* 147; *116:* 217; *143:* 111; *166:* 57
Dick, John Henry *8:* 181
Dickens, Frank *34:* 131
Dickey, Robert L. *15:* 279
Dickson, Mora *84:* 21
Didier, Sam *166:* 114
Dietz, James *128:* 223; *193:* 136
di Fate, Vincent *37:* 70; *90:* 11; *93:* 60; *109:* 219, 220
Di Fiori, Lawrence *10:* 51; *12:* 190; *27:* 97; *40:* 219; *93:* 57; *130:* 45
Digby, Desmond *97:* 180
Dignan, James *196:* 143
Di Grazia, Thomas *32:* 66; *35:* 241
Dillard, Annie *10:* 32
Dillard, Sarah *136:* 186; *217:* 53
Dillon, Corinne B. *1:* 139
Dillon, Diane *4:* 104, 167; *6:* 23; *13:* 29; *15:* 99; *26:* 148; *27:* 136, 201; *51:* 29, 48, 51, 52, 53, 54,55, 56, 57, 58, 59, 60, 61, 62; *54:* 155; *56:* 69; *58:* 127,128; *61:* 95; *62:* 27; *64:* 46; *68:* 3; *69:* 209; *74:* 89; *79:* 92; *86:* 89; *92:* 28, 177; *93:* 7, 210; *94:* 239, 240; *97:* 167; *106:* 58, 59,61, 64; *107:* 3; *139:* 246; *167:* 77; *189:* 202; *191:* 191; *194:* 45, 46, 48, 49
Dillon, Leo *4:* 104, 167; *6:* 23; *13:* 29; *15:* 99; *26:* 148; *27:* 136, 201; *51:* 29, 48, 51, 52, 53, 54,55, 56, 57, 58, 59, 60, 61, 62; *54:* 155; *56:* 69; *58:* 127,128; *61:* 95; *62:* 27; *64:* 46; *68:* 3; *69:* 209; *74:* 89; *79:* 92; *86:* 89; *92:* 28, 177; *93:* 7, 210; *94:* 239, 240; *97:* 167; *106:* 58, 59,61, 64; *107:* 3; *139:* 246; *167:* 77; *189:* 202; *191:* 191; *194:* 45, 46, 48, 49
Dillon, Sharon Saseen *59:* 179, 188
DiMaccio, Gerald *121:* 80
DiMaggio, Joe *36:* 22
DiMassi, Gina *169:* 17
Dinan, Carol *25:* 169; *59:* 75
Dines, Glen *7:* 66, 67
Dinesen, Thomas *44:* 37
Dinh, Pham Viet *167:* 184
Dinnerstein, Harvey *42:* 63, 64, 65, 66, 67, 68; *50:* 146
Dinsdale, Mary *10:* 65; *11:* 171
Dinyer, Eric *86:* 148; *109:* 163; *110:* 239; *124:* 11; *150:* 69; *170:* 4; *171:* 30
Dion, Nathalie *170:* 124; *213:* 52
DiPucchio, Kelly *230:* 3
DiRocco, Carl *181:* 23
DiSalvo-Ryan, DyAnne *59:* 77; *62:* 185; *117:* 46; *144:* 64; *150:* 153; *186:* 162
Disney, Walt *28:* 71, 72, 73, 76, 77, 78, 79, 80, 81, 87, 88, 89,90, 91, 94
DiTerlizzi, Tony *105:* 7; *147:* 22; *154:* 31, 32, 33; *214:* 74
Divito, Anna *83:* 159
Dixon, Don *74:* 17; *109:* 196
Dixon, Larry *127:* 125
Dixon, Maynard *20:* 165
Dizin, Pascal *230:* 25, 26
Doares, Robert G. *20:* 39
Dob, Bob *205:* 14
Dobias, Frank *22:* 162
Dobrin, Arnold *4:* 68
Dobson, Steven Gaston *102:* 103
Docherty, Thomas *218:* 45, 46

Dockray, Tracy *139:* 77
Docktor, Irv *43:* 70
Dodd, Ed *4:* 69
Dodd, Emma *203:* 57
Dodd, Julie *74:* 73
Dodd, Lynley *35:* 92; *86:* 71; *132:* 45, 46, 47
Dodge, Bill *96:* 36; *118:* 7, 8, 9; *133:* 135
Dodgson, Charles L. *20:* 148; *33:* 146; *YABC 2:* 98
Dodson, Bert *9:* 138; *14:* 195; *42:* 55; *54:* 8; *60:* 49; *101:* 125
Dodson, Liz Brenner *105:* 117; *111:* 15
Dohanos, Stevan *16:* 10
Dolce, J. Ellen *74:* 147; *75:* 41
Dolch, Marguerite P. *50:* 64
Dolesch, Susanne *34:* 49
Dollar, Diane *57:* 32
Dolobowsky, Mena *81:* 54
Dolson, Hildegarde *5:* 57
Domanska, Janina *6:* 66, 67; *YABC 1:* 166
Domi *134:* 113
Dominguez, El *53:* 94
Domjan, Joseph *25:* 93
Domm, Jeffrey C. *84:* 69; *135:* 70
Donahey, William *68:* 209
Donahue, Dorothy *76:* 170
Donahue, Vic *2:* 93; *3:* 190; *9:* 44
Donald, Elizabeth *4:* 18
Donalty, Alison *149:* 195, 196, 197
Donato *85:* 59; *149:* 204; *191:* 19
Donato, Michael A. *200:* 143
Doner, Kim *208:* 57
Doney, Todd L.W. *87:* 12; *93:* 112; *98:* 135; *101:* 57; *104:* 40; *118:* 163; *135:* 162, 163; *151:* 18; *227:* 79
Donna, Natalie *9:* 52
Donohue, Dorothy *95:* 2; *132:* 30; *176:* 54, 55; *178:* 77, 78, 79
Dooling, Michael *82:* 19; *105:* 55; *106:* 224; *125:* 135; *171:* 46; *172:* 12; *176:* 120; *197:* 89; *220:* 39, 40
Doran, Ben-Ami *128:* 189
Doran, Colleen *211:* 48
Dore, Gustave *18:* 169, 172, 175; *19:* 93, 94, 95, 96, 97, 98,99, 100, 101, 102, 103, 104, 105; *23:* 188; *25:* 197, 199
Doremus, Robert *6:* 62; *13:* 90; *30:* 95, 96, 97; *38:* 97
Dorfman, Ronald *11:* 128
Doriau *86:* 59; *91:* 152
Dorman, Brandon *197:* 35; *204:* 6; *210:* 104; *212:* 95; *216:* 156; *222:* 133
Dormer, Frank W. *200:* 55; *222:* 48
Dorros, Arthur *78:* 42, 43; *91:* 28
Doruyter, Karel *165:* 105
dos Santos, Joyce Audy *57:* 187, 189
Doty, Roy *28:* 98; *31:* 32; *32:* 224; *46:* 157; *82:* 71; *142:* 7
Doucet, Bob *132:* 238; *169:* 159
Dougherty, Charles *16:* 204; *18:* 74
Doughty, Rebecca *177:* 174; *222:* 159
Doughty, Thomas *118:* 31; *140:* 60
Douglas, Aaron *31:* 103
Douglas, Allen *223:* 53; *230:* 148
Douglas, Carole Nelson *73:* 48
Douglas, Goray *13:* 151
Dow, Brian *150:* 92
Dowd, Jason *132:* 51, 52; *164:* 244
Dowd, Vic *3:* 244; *10:* 92
Dowden, Anne Ophelia *7:* 70, 71; *13:* 120
Dowdy, Mrs. Regera *29:* 100
Downard, Barry *202:* 32
Downes, Belinda *180:* 29
Downing, Julie *60:* 140; *81:* 50; *86:* 200; *99:* 129
Doyle, Janet *56:* 31
Doyle, Richard *21:* 31, 32, 33; *23:* 231; *24:* 177; *31:* 87
Draper, Angie *43:* 84
Drath, Bill *26:* 34
Drawson, Blair *17:* 53; *126:* 65

Dray, Matt *177:* 47
Drescher, Henrik *105:* 60, 62, 63; *172:* 72
Drescher, Joan *30:* 100, 101; *35:* 245; *52:* 168; *137:* 52
Dressell, Peggy *186:* 41
Drew, Janet *201:* 177
Drew, Patricia *15:* 100
Dronzek, Laura *199:* 28, 29; *207:* 69
Drummond, Allan *209:* 41
Drummond, V.H. *6:* 70
Drury, Christian Potter *105:* 97; *186:* 224
Dubanevich, Arlene *56:* 44
Dubin, Jill *205:* 56; *217:* 25
Dubois, Claude K. *196:* 2
Dubois, Gerard *182:* 9
DuBurke, Randy *187:* 89; *222:* 136; *224:* 35
Ducak, Danilo *99:* 130; *108:* 214
Duchesne, Janet *6:* 162; *79:* 8
Duda, Jana *102:* 155; *209:* 134
Dudash, C. Michael *32:* 122; *77:* 134; *82:* 149; *212:* 93, 94
Duer, Douglas *34:* 177
Duewell, Kristina *195:* 76
Duffy, Daniel Mark *76:* 37; *101:* 196; *108:* 147, 148
Duffy, Joseph *38:* 203
Duffy, Pat *28:* 153
Dugan, Karen *181:* 26; *202:* 35
Dugin, Andrej *77:* 60
Dugina, Olga *77:* 60
Duke, Chris *8:* 195; *139:* 164
Duke, Kate *87:* 186; *90:* 78, 79, 80, 81; *192:* 21, 59, 60, 61, 63
Duke, Marion *165:* 87
Dulac, Edmund *19:* 108, 109, 110, 111, 112, 113, 114, 115, 117; *23:* 187; *25:* 152; *YABC 1:* 37; *2:* 147
Dulac, Jean *13:* 64
Dumas, Philippe *52:* 36, 37, 38, 39, 40, 41, 42, 43, 45; *119:* 40, 41, 42
Dunaway, Nancy *108:* 161
Dunbar, James *76:* 63
Dunbar, Polly *181:* 60, 61; *211:* 51, 52, 53; *212:* 42
Duncan, Beverly *72:* 92
Duncan, John *116:* 94
Dunn, H.T. *62:* 196
Dunn, Harvey *34:* 78, 79, 80, 81
Dunn, Iris *5:* 175
Dunn, Phoebe *5:* 175
Dunne, Jeanette *72:* 57, 173, 222
Dunnick, Regan *176:* 51; *178:* 83, 84; *219:* 36; *224:* 144; *229:* 83
Dunnington, Tom *3:* 36; *18:* 281; *25:* 61; *31:* 159; *35:* 168; *48:* 195; *79:* 144; *82:* 230
Dunn-Ramsey, Marcy *117:* 131
Dunrea, Olivier *59:* 81; *118:* 53, 54; *124:* 43
Duntze, Dorothee *88:* 28; *160:* 76
Dupasquier, Philippe *86:* 75; *104:* 76; *151:* 63
duPont, Lindsay Harper *207:* 39
DuQuette, Keith *90:* 83; *155:* 73, 74
Durand, Delphine *200:* 56
Durham, Sarah *192:* 248
Durney, Ryan *208:* 122
Duroussy, Nathalie *146:* 150
Durrell, Julie *82:* 62; *94:* 62
Dusíková, Maja *223:* 49
Dutz *6:* 59
Duvoisin, Roger *2:* 95; *6:* 76, 77; *7:* 197; *28:* 125; *30:* 101, 102, 103, 104, 105, 107; *47:* 205; *84:* 254
Dyer, Dale *141:* 71
Dyer, Jane *75:* 219; *129:* 28; *147:* 49, 50, 51; *168:* 121; *190:* 4; *191:* 57, 59, 60; *203:* 4
Dyer, Sarah *212:* 40
Dypold, Pat *15:* 37

E

E.V.B.
  See Boyle, Eleanor Vere (Gordon)
Eachus, Jennifer *29:* 74; *82:* 201; *164:* 153
Eadie, Bob *63:* 36
Eagle, Bruce *95:* 119
Eagle, Ellen *82:* 121; *89:* 3
Eagle, Jeremy *141:* 71
Eagle, Michael *11:* 86; *20:* 9; *23:* 18; *27:* 122; *28:* 57; *34:* 201; *44:* 189; *73:* 9; *78:* 235; *85:* 43
Earl-Bridges, Michele *159:* 128
Earle, Edwin *56:* 27
Earle, Olive L. *7:* 75
Earle, Vana *27:* 99
Earley, Lori *132:* 2; *186:* 4; *195:* 8
Early, Margaret *72:* 59
East, Jacqueline *218:* 198; *224:* 38
East, Stella *131:* 223
Eastman, P.D. *33:* 57
Easton, Reginald *29:* 181
Eaton, Tom *4:* 62; *6:* 64; *22:* 99; *24:* 124
Eaves, Edward *224:* 13
Ebbeler, Jeffrey *193:* 62; *206:* 45
Ebel, Alex *11:* 89
Eberbach, Andrea *192:* 115
Ebert, Len *9:* 191; *44:* 47
Echevarria, Abe *37:* 69
Echo Hawk, Bunky *187:* 192
Eckersley, Maureen *48:* 62
Eckert, Horst *72:* 62
Ede, Janina *33:* 59
Edens, Cooper *49:* 81, 82, 83, 84, 85; *112:* 58
Edens, John *109:* 115
Edgar, Sarah E. *41:* 97
Edgerton, Perky *195:* 144
Edliq, Emily S. *131:* 107
Edrien *11:* 53
Edwards, Freya *45:* 102
Edwards, George Wharton *31:* 155
Edwards, Gunvor *2:* 71; *25:* 47; *32:* 71; *54:* 106
Edwards, Jeanne *29:* 257
Edwards, Linda Strauss *21:* 134; *39:* 123; *49:* 88, 89
Edwards, Michelle *152:* 62, 63
Edwards, Wallace *170:* 55
Egan, Tim *155:* 76, 77, 78
Egge, David *102:* 71
Eggenhofer, Nicholas *2:* 81
Eggleton, Bob *74:* 40; *81:* 190, 191; *105:* 6; *121:* 183; *149:* 203; *166:* 215
Egielski, Richard *11:* 90; *16:* 208; *33:* 236; *38:* 35; *49:* 91, 92, 93, 95, 212, 213, 214, 216; *79:* 122; *106:* 67, 68, 69; *134:* 135; *144:* 244; *163:* 82, 84; *207:* 125; *225:* 200
Ehlert, Lois *35:* 97; *69:* 51; *112:* 7; *113:* 208; *128:* 63, 64, 65; *172:* 77, 79, 80; *220:* 43, 44, 45, 46, 47, 48
Ehrlich, Bettina *1:* 83
Eitan, Ora *160:* 165
Eichenberg, Fritz *1:* 79; *9:* 54; *19:* 248; *23:* 170; *24:* 200; *26:* 208; *50:* 67, 68, 69, 70, 71, 72, 73,74, 75, 77, 79, 80, 81; *60:* 165; *100:* 137; *YABC 1:* 104, 105; *2:* 213
Einsel, Naiad *10:* 35; *29:* 136
Einsel, Walter *10:* 37
Einzig, Susan *3:* 77; *43:* 78; *67:* 155; *129:* 154
Eisner, Will *165:* 82, 83
Eitzen, Allan *9:* 56; *12:* 212; *14:* 226; *21:* 194; *38:* 162; *76:* 218
Eldridge, H. *54:* 109
Eldridge, Harold *43:* 83
Elgaard, Greta *19:* 241
Elgin, Kathleen *9:* 188; *39:* 69
Ellacott, S.E. *19:* 118
Elliot, David *192:* 26; *208:* 62, 63

Elliott, Mark *93:* 69; *105:* 108; *107:* 123; *140:* 53; *165:* 189; *173:* 67; *195:* 95; *203:* 67; *210:* 99; *221:* 57, 70; *230:* 147
Elliott, Sarah M. *14:* 58
Ellis, Carson *216:* 210
Ellis, Dianne *130:* 208
Ellis, Jan Davey *88:* 50; *115:* 80
Ellis, Richard *130:* 47, 48
Ellison, Chris *196:* 66; *199:* 131; *207:* 193
Ellison, Pauline *55:* 21
Ellwand, David *213:* 60
Elmer, Richard *78:* 5
Elmore, Larry *90:* 8
Elschner, Géraldine *183:* 38
Elwell, Peter *195:* 150
Elwell, Tristan *110:* 39; *121:* 182; *127:* 46; *137:* 144; *141:* 173; *151:* 236; *158:* 264; *167:* 119, 120, 121; *169:* 20; *190:* 12; *202:* 16; *226:* 6
Elzbieta *88:* 80, 81
Ember, Kathi *214:* 147
Emberley, Ed *8:* 53; *70:* 53, 54; *146:* 65, 69, 70; *218:* 50
Emberley, Rebecca *218:* 50
Emberley, Michael *34:* 83; *80:* 72; *119:* 47, 48; *147:* 100; *158:* 115; *189:* 62, 64; *203:* 87, 89
Emerling, Dorothy *104:* 27
Emery, Leslie *49:* 187
Emmett, Bruce *49:* 147; *80:* 175; *101:* 206; *220:* 200
Emond, Stephen *231:* 59
Emry-Perrott, Jennifer *61:* 57
Emshwiller, Ed *174:* 45
Endle, Kate *191:* 167; *207:* 41
Engel, Christiane *231:* 61
Engel, Diana *70:* 57
Engle, Mort *38:* 64
Englebert, Victor *8:* 54
English, Mark *101:* 207; *220:* 201
Enik, Ted *142:* 39
Enos, Randall *20:* 183
Enright, Maginel Wright *19:* 240, 243; *39:* 31, 35, 36
Enrique, Romeo *34:* 135
Ensor, Barbara *180:* 30
Epstein, Stephen *50:* 142, 148
Erdogan, Buket *174:* 179
Erdrich, Louise *141:* 62
Erhard, Walter *1:* 152
Erickson, Jim *196:* 190
Erickson, Phoebe *11:* 83; *59:* 85
Erikson, Mel *31:* 69
Eriksson, Eva *63:* 88, 90, 92, 93; *203:* 99; *207:* 44
Ering, Timothy Basil *131:* 100; *176:* 63, 64; *202:* 29; *204:* 8
Erlbruch, Wolf *181:* 66
Ernst, Lisa Campbell *47:* 147; *95:* 47; *154:* 46, 47, 48; *164:* 88; *212:* 45
Esco, Jo *61:* 103
Escourido, Joseph *4:* 81
Escrivá, Viví *119:* 51; *181:* 36
Essakalli, Julie Klear *200:* 58
Este, Kirk *33:* 111
Estep, David *73:* 57
Estes, Eleanor *91:* 66
Estoril, Jean *32:* 27
Estrada, Pau *74:* 76
Estrada, Ric *5:* 52, 146; *13:* 174
Etchemendy, Teje *38:* 68
Etheredges, the *73:* 12
Etienne, Kirk-Albert *145:* 184
Ets, Marie Hall *2:* 102
Ettlinger, Doris *171:* 98; *186:* 106; *197:* 126; *214:* 125
Eulalie *YABC 2:* 315
Eustace, David *224:* 24
Evangelista, Theresa M. *213:* 67
Evans, Greg *73:* 54, 55, 56; *143:* 40, 41
Evans, Katherine *5:* 64

Evans, Leslie *144:* 227; *207:* 57; *214:* 88; *221:* 28

Evans, Shane W. *159:* 142; *160:* 190; *168:* 39; *188:* 88; *189:* 66, 67, 68; *229:* 150

Everitt, Betsy *151:* 110

Ewart, Claire *76:* 69; *145:* 59, 60

Ewing, Carolyn *66:* 143; *79:* 52

Ewing, Juliana Horatia *16:* 92

Eyolfson, Norman *98:* 154

F

Fabian, Limbert *136:* 114

Facklam, Paul *132:* 62

Falconer, Ian *125:* 66; *179:* 59

Falconer, Pearl *34:* 23

Falkenstern, Lisa *70:* 34; *76:* 133; *78:* 171; *127:* 16; *191:* 151

Fallone, Gianluca *231:* 23

Falls, C.B. *1:* 19; *38:* 71, 72, 73, 74

Falter, John *40:* 169, 170

Falwell, Cathryn *118:* 77; *137:* 185; *196:* 71, 72

Fancher, Lou *138:* 219; *141:* 64; *144:* 199; *177:* 51; *214:* 95; *221:* 63; *228:* 42, 43, 44; *230:* 44, 45, 46

Fanelli, Sara *89:* 63; *126:* 69

Faria, Rosana *150:* 143

Faricy, Patrick *185:* 182; *212:* 61

Farooqi, Musharraf Ali *207:* 46

Farmer, Andrew *49:* 102

Farmer, Peter *24:* 108; *38:* 75

Farnsworth, Bill *93:* 189; *116:* 147; *124:* 8; *135:* 52; *146:* 242, 243, 244; *182:* 176; *186:* 31, 83, 84, 85; *191:* 197; *222:* 2

Farquharson, Alexander *46:* 75

Farrell, Darren *228:* 45

Farrell, David *40:* 135

Farrell, Russell *196:* 38

Farris, David *74:* 42

Fasolino, Teresa *118:* 145

Fatigati, Evelyn *24:* 112

Fatus, Sophie *182:* 74; *190:* 218; *225:* 131

Faul-Jansen, Regina *22:* 117

Faulkner, Jack *6:* 169

Faulkner, Matt *161:* 174; *167:* 75

Faust, Anke *230:* 166

Fava, Rita *2:* 29

Fax, Elton C. *1:* 101; *4:* 2; *12:* 77; *25:* 107

Fay *43:* 93

Fearing, Mark *223:* 142; *224:* 39, 40

Fearnley, Jan *153:* 82, 83; *205:* 63, 64, 65

Fearrington, Ann *146:* 80

Federspiel, Marian *33:* 51

Fedorov, Nickolai Ivanovich *110:* 102

Feelings, Tom *5:* 22; *8:* 56; *12:* 153; *16:* 105; *30:* 196; *49:* 37; *61:* 101; *69:* 56, 57; *93:* 74; *105:* 88

Fehr, Terrence *21:* 87

Feiffer, Jules *3:* 91; *8:* 58; *61:* 66, 67, 70, 74, 76,77, 78; *111:* 47, 48, 49, 50; *132:* 122; *157:* 62; *201:* 48, 49, 50; *230:* 66

Feigeles, Neil *41:* 242

Feldman, Elyse *86:* 7

Feller, Gene *33:* 130

Fellows, Muriel H. *10:* 42

Felstead, Cathie *116:* 85

Felts, Shirley *33:* 71; *48:* 59

Fennell, Tracy *171:* 69

Fennelli, Maureen *38:* 181

Fenton, Carroll Lane *5:* 66; *21:* 39

Fenton, Mildred Adams *5:* 66; *21:* 39

Ferguson, Peter *177:* 30, 31; *181:* 154; *197:* 4; *199:* 40; *215:* 104; *221:* 66; *229:* 15, 16

Ferguson, Walter W. *34:* 86

Fernandes, Eugenie *77:* 67; *205:* 68

Fernandes, Stanislaw *70:* 28

Fernandez, Fernando *77:* 57

Fernandez, Laura *77:* 153; *101:* 117; *131:* 222; *170:* 119; *175:* 182

Ferrari, Alex *188:* 121

Ferrington, Susan *172:* 22

Fetz, Ingrid *11:* 67; *12:* 52; *16:* 205; *17:* 59; *29:* 105; *30:* 108, 109; *32:* 149; *43:* 142; *56:* 29; *60:* 34; *85:* 48; *87:* 146

Fiammenghi, Gioia *9:* 66; *11:* 44; *12:* 206; *13:* 57, 59; *52:* 126, 129; *66:* 64; *85:* 83; *91:* 161; *166:* 169

Fiedler, Joseph Daniel *96:* 42; *113:* 173; *129:* 164; *146:* 17; *159:* 68; *162:* 104

Field, Rachel *15:* 113

Fielding, David *70:* 124

Fieser, Stephen *152:* 36

Fine, Howard *159:* 159; *159:* 64; *165:* 134; *174:* 129; *181:* 68

Fine, Peter K. *43:* 210

Finger, Helen *42:* 81

Fink, Sam *18:* 119

Finlay, Winifred *23:* 72

Finney, Pat *79:* 215

Fiore, Peter *99:* 196; *125:* 139; *144:* 225; *160:* 169; *180:* 72; *212:* 103

Fiorentino, Al *3:* 240

Firehammer, Karla *174:* 202; *221:* 183; *228:* 84

Firmin, Charlotte *29:* 75; *48:* 70

Firmin, Peter *58:* 63, 64, 65, 67, 68, 70, 71

Firth, Barbara *81:* 208; *127:* 218; *179:* 62

Fischel, Lillian *40:* 204

Fischer, Hans *25:* 202

Fischer, Scott M. *207:* 37; *217:* 29

Fischer-Nagel, Andreas *56:* 50

Fischer-Nagel, Heiderose *56:* 50

Fisher, Carolyn *154:* 50

Fisher, Chris *79:* 62; *158:* 248; *188:* 195

Fisher, Cynthia *117:* 45; *137:* 118; *195:* 40

Fisher, Jeffrey *142:* 80

Fisher, Leonard Everett *3:* 6; *4:* 72, 86; *6:* 197; *9:* 59; *16:* 151, 153; *23:* 44; *27:* 134; *29:* 26; *34:* 87, 89, 90, 91, 93, 94, 95, 96; *40:* 206; *50:* 150; *60:* 158; *73:* 68, 70, 71, 72, 73; *176:* 71, 72, 73; *208:* 131; *YABC 2:* 169

Fisher, Lois *20:* 62; *21:* 7

Fisher, Valorie *177:* 55; *214:* 92

Fisk, Nicholas *25:* 112

Fitschen, Marilyn *2:* 20, 21; *20:* 48

Fitz-Maurice, Jeff *175:* 2

Fitzgerald, F.A. *15:* 116; *25:* 86, 87

Fitzgerald, Joanne *157:* 153, 154; *198:* 34, 35

Fitzgerald, Royce *205:* 5

Fitzhugh, Louise *1:* 94; *9:* 163; *45:* 75, 78

Fitzhugh, Susie *11:* 117

Fitzpatrick, Jim *109:* 130

Fitzpatrick, Marie-Louise *125:* 69, 70; *189:* 72, 73

Fitzsimmons, Arthur *14:* 128

Fix, Philippe *26:* 102

Flack, Marjorie *21:* 67; *100:* 93; *YABC 2:* 122

Flagg, James Montgomery *17:* 227

Flavin, Teresa *132:* 115; *186:* 119

Flax, Zeona *2:* 245

Fleetwood, Tony *171:* 51

Fleishman, Seymour *14:* 232; *24:* 87

Fleming, Denise *71:* 179; *81:* 58; *126:* 71, 72, 73; *173:* 52, 53

Fleming, Guy *18:* 41

Flesher, Vivienne *85:* 55

Fletcher, Claire *80:* 106; *157:* 159

Flint, Russ *74:* 80

Floate, Helen *111:* 163

Floca, Brian *155:* 88, 89; *190:* 10, 66, 67

Floethe, Richard *3:* 131; *4:* 90

Floherty, John J., Jr. *5:* 68

Flook, Helen *160:* 81

Flora, James *1:* 96; *30:* 111, 112

Florczak, Robert *166:* 51

Florian, Douglas *19:* 122; *83:* 64, 65; *125:* 71, 72, 74, 76; *128:* 130; *177:* 58, 60; *226:* 119

Flory, Jane *22:* 111

Flower, Renee *125:* 109

Floyd, Gareth *1:* 74; *17:* 245; *48:* 63; *62:* 35,36, 37, 39, 40, 41; *74:* 245; *79:* 56

Fluchere, Henri A. *40:* 79

Flynn, Alice *183:* 2

Flynn, Barbara *7:* 31; *9:* 70

Fogarty, Thomas *15:* 89

Foley, Greg *190:* 69

Folger, Joseph *9:* 100

Folkard, Charles *22:* 132; *29:* 128, 257, 258

Foott, Jeff *42:* 202

Forberg, Ati *12:* 71, 205; *14:* 1; *22:* 113; *26:* 22; *48:* 64, 65

Ford, A.G. *230:* 40; *231:* 69

Ford, George *24:* 120; *31:* 70, 177; *58:* 126; *81:* 103; *107:* 91; *136:* 100; *194:* 47; *208:* 81; *218:* 56

Ford, Gilbert *199:* 10

Ford, H.J. *16:* 185, 186

Ford, Jason *174:* 119

Ford, Pamela Baldwin *27:* 104

Fordham, John *168:* 160, 161

Foreman, Michael *2:* 110, 111; *67:* 99; *73:* 78, 79, 80,81, 82; *93:* 146; *135:* 55, 56, 57; *184:* 58, 59; *216:* 100, 101, 102, 103; *225:* 144

Forrester, Victoria *40:* 83

Forsey, Chris *140:* 210

Fortnum, Peggy *6:* 29; *20:* 179; *24:* 211; *26:* 76, 77, 78; *39:* 78; *58:* 19, 21, 23, 27; *YABC 1:* 148

Fortune, Eric *191:* 52

Foster, Brad W. *34:* 99

Foster, Genevieve *2:* 112

Foster, Gerald L. *7:* 78; *198:* 40

Foster, Jon *146:* 18; *198:* 7

Foster, Laura Louise *6:* 79

Foster, Marian Curtis *23:* 74; *40:* 42

Foster, Sally *58:* 73, 74

Fotheringham, Edwin *219:* 32

Foucher, Adele *47:* 118

Foust, Mitch *168:* 50

Fowler, Jim *184:* 190

Fowler, Mel *36:* 127

Fowler, Richard *87:* 219

Fowles, Shelley *165:* 127; *205:* 72

Fox, Charles Phillip *12:* 84

Fox, Christyan *188:* 36

Fox, Jim *6:* 187

Fox, Nathan *208:* 64

Fox-Davies, Sarah *76:* 150; *182:* 63; *199:* 42, 43

Frace, Charles *15:* 118

Frailey, Joy *72:* 108

Frame, Paul *2:* 45, 145; *9:* 153; *10:* 124; *21:* 71; *23:* 62; *24:* 123; *27:* 106; *31:* 48; *32:* 159; *34:* 195; *38:* 136; *42:* 55; *44:* 139; *60:* 39, 40, 41, 42, 43, 44, 46; *73:* 183

Frampton, David *85:* 72; *102:* 33; *139:* 182; *152:* 37; *189:* 171

Francis, Guy *198:* 164; *224:* 91; *225:* 65

Francois, Andre *25:* 117

Francoise

See Seignobosc, Francoise

Frank, Lola Edick *2:* 199

Frank, Mary *4:* 54; *34:* 100

Franke, Phil *45:* 91

Frankel, Alona *66:* 70

Frankel, Julie *40:* 84, 85, 202

Frankenberg, Robert *22:* 116; *30:* 50; *38:* 92, 94, 95; *68:* 111

Frankfeldt, Gwen *84:* 223; *110:* 92

Frankland, David *169:* 137; *182:* 164; *201:* 159; *224:* 7; *231:* 27

Franklin, Ashton *165:* 144; *225:* 107

Franklin, John *24:* 22

Franson, Leanne R. *111:* 57, 58; *151:* 7; *223:* 63, 64, 158

Frascino, Edward *9:* 133; *29:* 229; *33:* 190; *48:* 80, 81, 82, 83, 84, 85, 86

Frasconi, Antonio *6:* 80; *27:* 208; *53:* 41, 43, 45, 47,48; *68:* 145; *73:* 226; *131:* 68
Fraser, Betty *2:* 212; *6:* 185; *8:* 103; *31:* 72,73; *43:* 136; *111:* 76
Fraser, Eric *38:* 78; *41:* 149, 151
Fraser, F.A. *22:* 234
Fraser, James *171:* 68
Fraser, Mary Ann *137:* 63; *214:* 98
Frasier, Debra *69:* 60; *112:* 67; *182:* 81, 82, 83
Fraustino, Lisa Rowe *146:* 87
Frazee, Marla *72:* 98; *105:* 79, 80; *151:* 67, 68; *164:* 165; *171:* 190, 191; *187:* 53, 54, 55, 56, 143; *222:* 173; *225:* 68, 69, 70; *226:* 180
Frazetta, Frank *41:* 72; *58:* 77, 78, 79, 80, 81, 82, 83
Frazier, Craig *177:* 63; *221:* 47
Freas, John *25:* 207
Fredrickson, Mark *103:* 33
Freeland, Michael J. *118:* 115
Freeman, Don *2:* 15; *13:* 249; *17:* 62, 63, 65, 67, 68; *18:* 243; *20:* 195; *23:* 213, 217; *32:* 155; *55:* 129
Freeman, Irving *67:* 150
Freeman, Laura *144:* 111; *200:* 62, 63
Freeman, Pietri *140:* 223
Freeman, Tom *167:* 118
Freeman, Tor *164:* 93
Fregosi, Claudia *24:* 117
Fremaux, Charlotte Murray *138:* 29; *141:* 95
French, Fiona *6:* 82, 83; *75:* 61; *109:* 170; *132:* 79, 80, 81, 82
French, Martin *163:* 4
French, S. Terrell *216:* 106
Frendak, Rodney *126:* 97, 98
Freschet, Gina *175:* 73
Freynet, Gilbert *72:* 221
Fried, Janice *202:* 121
Frieden, Sarajo *213:* 119
Friedman, Judith *43:* 197; *131:* 221
Friedman, Marvin *19:* 59; *42:* 86
Frinta, Dagmar *36:* 42
Frith, Michael K. *15:* 138; *18:* 120
Fritz, Ronald *46:* 73; *82:* 124
Fromm, Lilo *29:* 85; *40:* 197
Frost, A.B. *17:* 6, 7; *19:* 123, 124, 125, 126, 127, 128, 129,130; *100:* 119; *YABC 1:* 156, 157, 160; *2:* 107
Frost, Helen *183:* 51
Frost, Kristi *118:* 113; *231:* 114
Frost, Michael *151:* 209; *209:* 44; *212:* 70
Froud, Brian *150:* 82, 83
Froud, Wendy *151:* 237
Fry, Guy *2:* 224
Fry, Rosalie *3:* 72; *YABC 2:* 180, 181
Fry, Rosalind *21:* 153, 168
Fryer, Elmer *34:* 115
Fuchs, Bernie *110:* 10; *162:* 46
Fuchs, Erich *6:* 84
Fuchshuber, Annegert *43:* 96
Fucile, Tony *221:* 48
Fufuka, Mahiri *32:* 146
Fuge, Charles *144:* 91, 93
Fujikawa, Gyo *39:* 75, 76; *76:* 72, 73, 74
Fulford, Deborah *23:* 159
Fuller, Margaret *25:* 189
Fulweiler, John *93:* 99
Funai, Mamoru *38:* 105
Funfhausen, Christian *196:* 30
Funk, Tom *7:* 17, 99
Furchgott, Terry *29:* 86
Furness, William Henry, Jr. *94:* 18
Furukawa, Mel *25:* 42
Fusari, Erika *164:* 227

G

Gaadt, David *78:* 212; *121:* 166; *201:* 171
Gaadt, George *71:* 9

Gaber, Susan *99:* 33; *115:* 57, 58; *164:* 195; *169:* 61, 62, 63; *185:* 50, 51; *188:* 124
Gaberell, J. *19:* 236
Gable, Brian *195:* 68, 69
Gabler, Mirko *99:* 71; *195:* 32
Gabor, Tim *216:* 61
Gackenbach, Dick *19:* 168; *41:* 81; *48:* 89, 90, 91, 92,93, 94; *54:* 105; *79:* 75, 76, 77
Gad, Victor *87:* 161
Gaetano, Nicholas *23:* 209
Gaffney-Kessell, Walter *94:* 219; *174:* 188
Gag, Flavia *17:* 49, 52
Gag, Wanda *100:* 101, 102; *YABC 1:* 135, 137, 138, 141, 143
Gagnon, Cecile *11:* 77; *58:* 87
Gaillard, Jason *200:* 69; *204:* 74
Gal, Laszlo *14:* 127; *52:* 54, 55, 56; *65:* 142; *68:* 150; *81:* 185; *96:* 104, 105
Gal, Susan *228:* 58
Galazinski, Tom *55:* 13
Galbraith, Ben *200:* 70
Galdone, Paul *1:* 156, 181, 206; *2:* 40, 241; *3:* 42,144; *4:* 141; *10:* 109, 158; *11:* 21; *12:* 118, 210; *14:* 12; *16:* 36, 37; *17:* 70, 71, 72, 73, 74; *18:* 111, 230; *19:* 183; *21:* 154; *22:* 150, 245; *33:* 126; *39:* 136, 137; *42:* 57; *51:* 169; *55:* 110; *66:* 80, 82, 139; *72:* 73; *100:* 84
Gale, Cathy *140:* 22; *143:* 52; *213:* 166
Gall, Chris *176:* 79, 80
Gallagher, Jack *187:* 100
Gallagher, S. Saelig *105:* 154; *198:* 91
Gallagher, Sears *20:* 112Gallagher-Cole, Mernie *206:* 56
Galloway, Ewing *51:* 154
Galouchka, Annouchka Gravel *95:* 55; *182:* 40
Galster, Robert *1:* 66
Galsworthy, Gay John *35:* 232
Galvez, Daniel *125:* 182
Gamble, Kim *112:* 64, 65; *124:* 77; *183:* 40, 42, 43, 56, 57; *187:* 170
Gammell, Stephen *7:* 48; *13:* 149; *29:* 82; *33:* 209; *41:* 88; *50:* 185, 186, 187; *53:* 51, 52, 53, 54, 55, 56,57, 58; *54:* 24, 25; *56:* 147, 148, 150; *57:* 27, 66; *81:* 62, 63; *87:* 88; *89:* 10; *106:* 223; *126:* 2; *128:* 71, 73, 74, 77; *154:* 34; *211:* 210; *226:* 80, 81, 82
Gamper, Ruth *84:* 198
Gampert, John *58:* 94
Ganly, Helen *56:* 56
Gannett, Ruth Chrisman *3:* 74; *18:* 254; *33:* 77, 78
Gannon, Ned *205:* 6
Gantschev, Ivan *45:* 32
Garafano, Marie *73:* 33
Garbot, Dave *131:* 106
Garbutt, Bernard *23:* 68
Garcia *37:* 71
Garcia, Geronimo *222:* 73
Garcia, Manuel *74:* 145
Garcia-Franco, Rebecca *173:* 46
Gardiner, Lindsey *178:* 128; *186:* 137
Gardner, Earle *45:* 167
Gardner, Joan *40:* 87
Gardner, Joel *40:* 87, 92
Gardner, John *40:* 87
Gardner, Lucy *40:* 87
Gardner, Richard
See Cummings, Richard
Gardner, Sally *171:* 177; *177:* 66, 68; *229:* 58
Gargiulo, Frank *84:* 158
Garland, Michael *36:* 29; *38:* 83; *44:* 168; *48:* 78, 221, 222; *49:* 161; *60:* 139; *71:* 6, 11; *72:* 229; *74:* 142; *89:* 187; *93:* 183; *104:* 110; *131:* 55; *139:* 209; *168:* 56; *208:* 72, 73, 75
Garland, Peggy *60:* 139
Garland, Sarah *62:* 45; *135:* 67, 68; *171:* 118
Garn, Aimee *75:* 47
Garner, Joan *128:* 170
Garneray, Ambroise Louis *59:* 140

Garnett, Eve *3:* 75
Garnett, Gary *39:* 184
Garns, Allen *80:* 125; *84:* 39; *165:* 231; *209:* 44
Garófoli, Viviana *186:* 123
Garraty, Gail *4:* 142; *52:* 106
Garrett, Agnes *46:* 110; *47:* 157
Garrett, Edmund H. *20:* 29
Garrett, Tom *107:* 194; *215:* 179
Garrick, Jacqueline *67:* 42, 43; *77:* 94
Garrison, Barbara *19:* 133; *104:* 146; *109:* 87
Garro, Mark *108:* 131; *128:* 210
Garvey, Robert *98:* 222
Garza, Carmen Lomas *80:* 211; *182:* 86
Garza, Xavier *184:* 64
Gates, Frieda *26:* 80
Gaughan, Jack *26:* 79; *43:* 185
Gaver, Becky *20:* 61
Gavril, David *211:* 196
Gawing, Toby *72:* 52
Gay, Marie-Louise *68:* 76, 77, 78; *102:* 136; *126:* 76, 78, 81, 83; *127:* 55, 56; *179:* 70, 72, 73, 74; *224:* 81
Gay, Zhenya *19:* 135, 136
Gaydos, Tim *62:* 201
Gazsi, Ed *80:* 48
Gazso, Gabriel *73:* 85
Geary, Clifford N. *1:* 122; *9:* 104; *51:* 74
Geary, Rick *142:* 44, 46
Gee, Frank *33:* 26
Geehan, Wayne *157:* 181
Geer, Charles *1:* 91; *3:* 179; *4:* 201; *6:* 168; *7:* 96; *9:* 58; *10:* 72; *12:* 127; *39:* 156,157, 158, 159, 160; *42:* 88, 89, 90, 91; *55:* 111, 116
Geerinck, Manuel *173:* 128
Gehm, Charlie *36:* 65; *57:* 117; *62:* 60, 138
Geis, Alissa Imre *189:* 77
Geisel, Theodor Seuss *1:* 104, 105, 106; *28:* 108, 109, 110,111, 112, 113; *75:* 67, 68, 69, 70, 71; *89:* 127, 128; *100:* 106, 107, 108
Geisert, Arthur *92:* 67, 68; *133:* 72, 73, 74; *165:* 97, 98; *171:* 64, 65
Geldart, William *15:* 121; *21:* 202
Genia *4:* 84
Gentry, Cyrille R. *12:* 66
Genzo, John Paul *136:* 74
George, Jean *2:* 113
George, Lindsay Barrett *95:* 57; *155:* 97, 98
Geraghty, Paul *130:* 60, 61
Gerard, Jean Ignace *45:* 80
Gerard, Rolf *27:* 147, 150
Gerber, Mark *61:* 105
Gerber, Mary Jane *112:* 124; *171:* 56
Gerber, Stephanie *71:* 195
Gerdstein, Mordecai *169:* 105
Gergely, Tibor *54:* 15, 16
Geritz, Franz *17:* 135
Gerlach, Geff *42:* 58
Gerrard, Roy *47:* 78; *90:* 96, 97, 98, 99
Gerritsen, Paula *177:* 69; *217:* 166
Gershinowitz, George *36:* 27
Gerstein, Mordicai *31:* 117; *47:* 80, 81, 82, 83, 84, 85, 86; *51:* 173; *69:* 134; *107:* 122; *142:* 49, 52; *165:* 209; *176:* 119; *178:* 95, 97, 99; *215:* 173; *222:* 76
Gervase *12:* 27
Geter, Tyrone *146:* 249; *150:* 86
Getz, Arthur *32:* 148
Gévry, Claudine *188:* 47
Gewirtz, Bina *61:* 81
Giancola, Donato *95:* 146; *164:* 226; *229:* 181
Gibala-Broxholm, Scott *205:* 76; *219:* 186
Gibbons, Gail *23:* 78; *72:* 77, 78, 79; *82:* 182; *104:* 65; *160:* 99, 100; *201:* 59, 60, 62
Gibbs, Tony *40:* 95
Gibran, Kahlil *32:* 116
Gibson, Barbara Leonard *205:* 77; *212:* 151
Gider, Iskender *81:* 193
Giebfried, Rosemary *170:* 135
Giesen, Rosemary *34:* 192, 193
Giffard, Hannah *83:* 70

Giguere, George *20:* 111
Gilbert, John *19:* 184; *54:* 115; *YABC 2:* 287
Gilbert, W.S. *36:* 83, 85, 96
Gilbert, Yvonne *116:* 70; *128:* 84; *149:* 119; *185:* 69; *192:* 25; *195:* 81
Gilchrist, Jan Spivey *72:* 82, 83, 84, 85, 87; *77:* 90; *105:* 89, 91; *130:* 63, 64; *155:* 105, 107; *182:* 67
Giles, Will *41:* 218
Gili, Phillida *70:* 73
Gill, Margery *4:* 57; *7:* 7; *22:* 122; *25:* 166; *26:* 146, 147
Gillen, Denver *28:* 216
Gillette, Henry J. *23:* 237
Gilliam, Stan *39:* 64, 81
Gillies, Chuck *62:* 31
Gilliland, Jillian *87:* 58
Gillman, Alec *98:* 105
Gilman, Esther *15:* 124
Gilman, Phoebe *104:* 70, 71
Gilpin, Stephen *213:* 68
Ginsberg, Sari *111:* 184
Ginsburg, Max *62:* 59; *68:* 194 *Girard, Roge 161:* 30
Girouard, Patrick *155:* 100; *218:* 165
Giovanopoulos, Paul *7:* 104; *60:* 36
Giovine, Sergio *79:* 12; *93:* 118; *139:* 118; *205:* 114
Gist, E.M. *206:* 60
Githens, Elizabeth M. *5:* 47
Gladden, Scott *99:* 108; *103:* 160; *193:* 46, 47
Gladstone, Gary *12:* 89; *13:* 190
Gladstone, Lise *15:* 273
Glanzman, Louis S. *2:* 177; *3:* 182; *36:* 97, 98; *38:* 120, 122; *52:* 141, 144; *71:* 191; *91:* 54, 56
Glaser, Byron *154:* 59, 60
Glaser, Milton *3:* 5; *5:* 156; *11:* 107; *30:* 26; *36:* 112; *54:* 141; *151:* 70
Glass, Andrew *36:* 38; *44:* 133; *48:* 205; *65:* 3; *68:* 43, 45; *90:* 104, 105; *150:* 89; *223:* 73, 74
Glass, Marvin *9:* 174
Glasser, Judy *41:* 156; *56:* 140; *69:* 79; *72:* 101
Glattauer, Ned *5:* 84; *13:* 224; *14:* 26
Glauber, Uta *17:* 76
Gleeson, J.M. *YABC 2:* 207
Glegg, Creina *36:* 100
Glienke, Amelie *63:* 150
Gliewe, Unada *3:* 78, 79; *21:* 73; *30:* 220
Gliori, Debi *72:* 91; *138:* 82; *162:* 37; *189:* 79, 81, 82
Glovach, Linda *7:* 105
Gobbato, Imero *3:* 180, 181; *6:* 213; *7:* 58; *9:* 150; *18:* 39; *21:* 167; *39:* 82, 83; *41:* 137, 251; *59:* 177
Goble, Paul *25:* 121; *26:* 86; *33:* 65; *69:* 68, 69; *131:* 79, 80
Goble, Warwick *46:* 78, 79; *194:* 143
Godal, Eric *36:* 93
Godbey, Cory *221:* 154
Godkin, Celia *145:* 84, 86
Godfrey, Michael *17:* 279
Godon, Ingrid *166:* 163; *186:* 99
Goede, Irene *208:* 87
Goembel, Ponder *42:* 124
Goffe, Toni *61:* 83, 84, 85; *89:* 11; *90:* 124; *178:* 118
Goffstein, M.B. *8:* 71; *70:* 75, 76, 77
Golbin, Andre *15:* 125
Gold, Robert *166:* 151, 152
Goldfeder, Cheryl *11:* 191
Goldfinger, Jennifer P. *185:* 71
Goldman, Todd H. *221:* 50, 51
Goldsborough, June *5:* 154, 155; *8:* 92, *14:* 226; *19:* 139; *54:* 165
Goldsmith, Robert *110:* 77
Goldstein, Barry *198:* 147
Goldstein, Leslie *5:* 8; *6:* 60; *10:* 106

Goldstein, Nathan *1:* 175; *2:* 79; *11:* 41, 232; *16:* 55
Goldstrom, Robert *98:* 36; *145:* 51, 52
Golembe, Carla *79:* 80, 81; *136:* 91; *144:* 113; *193:* 53
Golin, Carlo *74:* 112
Gomez, Elena *188:* 122; *191:* 72
Gomez, Elizabeth *127:* 70; *133:* 76
Gomi, Taro *64:* 102; *103:* 74, 76
Gon, Adriano *101:* 112
Gonsalves, Ron *178:* 213; *212:* 196
Gonzalez, Maya Christina *104:* 3; *136:* 92; *215:* 4, 5
Gonzalez, Thomas *226:* 157
Gonzalez, Yolanda *212:* 65
Good, Karen Hillard *212:* 143; *214:* 103
Goodall, John S. *4:* 92, 93; *10:* 132; *66:* 92, 93; *YABC 1:* 198
Goode, Diane *15:* 126; *50:* 183; *52:* 114, 115; *76:* 195; *84:* 94; *99:* 141; *114:* 76, 77, 78; *170:* 99, 101; *225:* 80, 81, 82, 83, 84
Goodelman, Aaron *40:* 203
Goodenow, Earle *40:* 97
Goodfellow, Peter *62:* 95; *94:* 202
Goodman, Joan Elizabeth *50:* 86
Goodman, Vivienne *82:* 251; *146:* 181, 182
Goodnow, Patti *117:* 33
Goodrich, Carter *221:* 52, 53
Goodwin, Harold *13:* 74
Goodwin, Philip R. *18:* 206
Goor, Nancy *39:* 85, 86
Goor, Ron *39:* 85, 86
Goossens, Philippe *195:* 71
Gorbachev, Valeri *89:* 96; *112:* 97; *143:* 63, 64; *184:* 66, 67, 68, 101; *222:* 84, 85, 86, 87
Gordon, David *216:* 159
Gordon, Gwen *12:* 151
Gordon, Margaret *4:* 147; *5:* 48, 49; *9:* 79
Gordon, Mike *101:* 62, 63, 64
Gordon, Russell *136:* 204; *137:* 214; *228:* 34
Gordon, Walter *138:* 9
Gore, Leonid *89:* 51; *94:* 74; *136:* 8; *158:* 117; *166:* 136; *168:* 36; *170:* 107; *181:* 94; *185:* 73; *222:* 89, 90, 91, 92
Gorecka-Egan, Erica *18:* 35
Gorey, Edward *1:* 60, 61; *13:* 169; *18:* 192; *20:* 201; *29:* 90, 91, 92, 93, 94, 95, 96, 97, 98, 99, 100; *30:* 129; *32:* 90; *34:* 200, *65:* 48; *68:* 24, 25; *69:* 79; *70:* 80, 82, 83, 84; *85:* 136; *127:* 62
Gorman, Mike *222:* 167
Gorsline, Douglas *1:* 98; *6:* 13; *11:* 113; *13:* 104; *15:* 14; *28:* 117, 118; *YABC 1:* 15
Gorton, Julia *108:* 94; *178:* 81, 82
Gosfield, Josh *118:* 165, 166; *149:* 67
Gosner, Kenneth *5:* 135
Gosney, Joy *167:* 142
Gotlieb, Jules *6:* 127
Goto, Scott *115:* 86; *136:* 69; *203:* 77, 78
Gott, Barry *197:* 95; *212:* 102
Gottlieb, Dale *67:* 162; *107:* 16; *149:* 6
Goudey, Ray *97:* 86
Gough, Alan *91:* 57
Gough, Philip *23:* 47; *45:* 90
Gould, Chester *49:* 112, 113, 114, 116, 117, 118
Gould, Jason *151:* 232
Gourbault, Martine *177:* 159
Govern, Elaine R. *26:* 94
Gower, Teri *102:* 184
Gowing, Toby *60:* 25; *63:* 33; *78:* 70, 252; *83:* 228; *86:* 187; *93:* 145; *108:* 133; *110:* 217; *184:* 125; *225:* 142
Grabianski *20:* 144
Grabianski, Janusz *39:* 92, 93, 94, 95
Graboff, Abner *35:* 103, 104
Graef, Renée *61:* 188; *72:* 207; *204:* 45; *210:* 249
Grafe, Max *156:* 173; *178:* 237; *192:* 240; *198:* 51
Graham, A.B. *11:* 61

Graham, Bob *101:* 66, 67, 68; *151:* 74, 75; *187:* 65, 67, 68, 70
Graham, Georgia *188:* 3; *190:* 75
Graham, L. *7:* 108
Graham, Margaret Bloy *11:* 120; *18:* 305, 307
Graham, Mark *88:* 208; *159:* 153; *182:* 3
Grahame-Johnstone, Janet *13:* 61
Grahame-Johnstone, Anne *13:* 61
Grainger, Sam *42:* 95
Gralley, Jean *166:* 86
Gramatky, Hardie *1:* 107; *30:* 116, 119, 120, 122, 123
Gran, Julie *168:* 118
Granahan, Julie *84:* 84
GrandPré, Mary *84:* 131; *109:* 199; *118:* 76; *180:* 65; *184:* 70, 71, 180; *192:* 87; *215:* 24; *229:* 68, 69, 70
Grandström, Brita *176:* 139
Grandville, J.J. *45:* 81, 82, 83, 84, 85, 86, 87, 88; *47:* 125; *64:* 10
Granger, Paul *39:* 153
Granström, Brita *162:* 35; *167:* 46; *224:* 56, 57
Grant, (Alice) Leigh *10:* 52; *15:* 131; *20:* 20; *26:* 119; *48:* 202
Grant, Gordon *17:* 230, 234; *25:* 123, 124, 125, 126; *52:* 69; *YABC 1:* 164
Grant, Melvyn *159:* 186, 187; *170:* 48, 49; *213:* 168, 169; *226:* 163
Grant, Michelle *210:* 95
Grant, Renee *77:* 40
Grant, Shirley *109:* 45
Graves, Elizabeth *45:* 101
Graves, Keith *167:* 89; *191:* 74; *216:* 34; *223:* 103
Gray, Harold *33:* 87, 88
Gray, Les *82:* 76; *83:* 232
Gray, Reginald *6:* 69
Gray, Steve *226:* 206; *231:* 77, 78
Greco, Tony *184:* 6
Greder, Armin *76:* 235
Green, Ann Canevari *62:* 48
Green, Eileen *6:* 97
Green, Elizabeth Shippen *139:* 109
Green, Jonathan *86:* 135; *105:* 109; *221:* 73
Green, Ken *111:* 68
Green, Michael *32:* 216
Green, Robina *87:* 138
Green, Jonathan *157:* 105
Greene, Jeffrey *117:* 93
Greenaway, Kate *17:* 275; *24:* 180; *26:* 107; *41:* 222, 232; *100:* 115, 116; *YABC 1:* 88, 89; *2:* 131, 133, 136,138, 139, 141
Greenberg, Melanie Hope *72:* 93; *80:* 125; *101:* 174; *133:* 180; *186:* 189; *214:* 105
Greenseid, Diane *178:* 106, 107
Greenstein, Elaine *150:* 100
Greenwald, Sheila *1:* 34; *3:* 99; *8:* 72
Greger, Carol *76:* 86
Gregorian, Joyce Ballou *30:* 125
Gregory, Emilian *177:* 146; *187:* 10
Gregory, Fran *130:* 4; *140:* 93
Gregory, Frank M. *29:* 107
Greiffenhagen, Maurice *16:* 137; *27:* 57; *YABC 2:* 288
Greiner, Robert *6:* 86
Gretter, J. Clemens *31:* 134
Gretz, Susanna *7:* 114
Gretzer, John *1:* 54; *3:* 26; *4:* 162; *7:* 125; *16:* 247; *18:* 117; *28:* 66; *30:* 85, 211; *33:* 235; *56:* 16
Grey, Mini *166:* 90; *192:* 71
Grey Owl *24:* 41
Gri *25:* 90
Grieder, Walter *9:* 84
Griesbach/Martucci *59:* 3
Grifalconi, Ann *2:* 126; *3:* 248; *11:* 18; *13:* 182; *46:* 38; *50:* 145; *66:* 99, 100, 101, 104, 106; *69:* 38; *70:* 64; *87:* 128; *90:* 53; *93:* 49; *128:* 48; *133:* 79, 81, 210:* 111
Griffin, Gillett Good *26:* 96
Griffin, James *30:* 166

Griffin, John Howard *59:* 186
Griffin, Rachel *131:* 23
Griffith, Gershom *94:* 214
Griffiths, Dave *29:* 76
Griffiths, Dean *168:* 180; *169:* 182
Grimly, Gris *186:* 102; *192:* 112; *197:* 86; *219:* 34
Grimsdell, Jeremy *83:* 75
Grimwood, Brian *82:* 89
Gringhuis, Dirk *6:* 98; *9:* 196
Gripe, Harald *2:* 127; *74:* 98
Grisha *3:* 71
Grobler, Piet *201:* 100
Grohmann, Susan *84:* 97
Gropper, William *27:* 93; *37:* 193
Gros *60:* 199
Grose, Helen Mason *YABC 1:* 260; *2:* 150
Grossman, Nancy *24:* 130; *29:* 101
Grossman, Robert *11:* 124; *46:* 39
Groth, John *15:* 79; *21:* 53, 54; *83:* 230
Grover, Lorie Ann *168:* 59
Grubb, Lisa *160:* 116
Grue, Lisa *187:* 193
Gruelle, Johnny *35:* 107
Gschwind, William *11:* 72
Guarnaccia, Steven *201:* 170, 173
Guay-Mitchell, Rebecca *110:* 95, 96; *135:* 240; *180:* 76; *181:* 71, 73; *216:* 77
Guback, Georgia *88:* 102
Gudeon, Karla *212:* 67
Guerguerion, Claudine *105:* 73
Guevara, Susan *97:* 87; *167:* 49; *194:* 54
Guggenheim, Hans *2:* 10; *3:* 37; *8:* 136
Guhathaakurta, Ajanta *183:* 199
Guida, Lisa Chauncy *172:* 188
Guilbeau, Honore *22:* 69
Guillette, Joseph *137:* 37
Guisewite, Cathy *57:* 52, 53, 54, 56, 57
Gukova, Julia *95:* 104; *154:* 103; *168:* 195
Gundersheimer, Karen *35:* 240; *82:* 100
Gunderson, Nick *57:* 120
Gunnella *192:* 144
Gurney, James *76:* 97; *86:* 32
Gurney, John Steven *75:* 39, 82; *110:* 175; *143:* 67, 68; *169:* 172; *217:* 50, 88; *227:* 86, 87, 88; *228:* 139, 140, 141
Gusman, Annie *38:* 62
Gustafson, Scott *34:* 111; *43:* 40
Gustavson, Adam *104:* 10; *171:* 183; *176:* 87; *197:* 94; *204:* 35; *219:* 187
Guthridge, Bettina *108:* 79; *186:* 92
Guthrie, R. Dale *64:* 143
Guthrie, Robin *20:* 122
Gutierrez, Akemi *172:* 87; *205:* 135
Gutierrez, Alan *136:* 31, 32
Gutierrez, Rudy *97:* 162; *203:* 79; *216:* 158
Gutmann, Bessie Pease *73:* 93, 94
Gwynne, Fred *41:* 94, 95
Gyberg, Bo-Erik *38:* 131

H

Haas, Irene *17:* 77; *87:* 46; *96:* 117
Hack, Konrad *51:* 127
Hader, Berta H. *16:* 126
Hader, Elmer S. *16:* 126
Haeffele, Deborah *76:* 99
Haemer, Alan *62:* 109
Hafner, Marylin *22:* 196, 216; *24:* 44; *30:* 51; *35:* 95; *51:* 25, 160, 164; *86:* 16; *105:* 196; *121:* 93, 94; *149:* 208, 209; *179:* 82, 83, 84, 115; *190:* 200; *201:* 29; *217:* 91
Hagerty, Sean *62:* 181
Hague, Michael *32:* 128; *48:* 98, 99, 100, 101, 103, 105,106, 107, 108, 109, 110; *49:* 121; *51:* 105; *64:* 14, 15; *79:* 134; *80:* 91, 92; *83:* 135; *100:* 241; *102:* 29; *129:* 101, 103, 104; *185:* 80, 81, 82; *215:* 89
Hair, Jonathan *115:* 135

Halas, John *29:* 41, 47, 48
Haldane, Roger *13:* 76; *14:* 202
Hale, Bruce *203:* 83
Hale, Christy *79:* 124; *84:* 200; *114:* 201; *128:* 2, 3; *146:* 203; *158:* 243; *167:* 99; *179:* 87
Hale, Irina *26:* 97
Hale, James Graham *88:* 207
Hale, Kathleen *17:* 79; *66:* 114, 116, 118
Hale, Nathan *210:* 115, 116; *214:* 179
Haley, Amanda *205:* 82, 83
Haley, Gail E. *43:* 102, 103, 104, 105; *78:* 65, 67; *136:* 106, 107
Hall, Amanda *96:* 110
Hall, Angus *224:* 192
Hall, August N. *217:* 74
Hall, Chuck *30:* 189
Hall, Douglas *15:* 184; *43:* 106, 107; *86:* 100; *87:* 82; *129:* 72
Hall, H. Tom *1:* 227; *30:* 210
Hall, Melanie *116:* 48, 49; *169:* 77, 78; *219:* 170; *228:* 65, 66, 67
Hall, Michael *228:* 69
Hall, Sydney P. *31:* 89
Hall, Tim *164:* 196; *202:* 41
Hall, Vicki *20:* 24
Hallinan, P.K. *39:* 98
Hallman, Tom *98:* 166
Hally, Greg *101:* 200; *151:* 224
Halperin, Wendy Anderson *96:* 151; *125:* 96, 97, 98, 99; *139:* 22; *140:* 84; *200:* 77, 78; *210:* 157; *215:* 65; *228:* 24, 76
Halpern, Joan *97:* 25
Halpern, Shari *174:* 172
Halsey, Megan *96:* 172; *114:* 185; *180:* 8; *185:* 85
Halstead, Virginia *125:* 105
Halverson, Janet *49:* 38, 42, 44
Hallensleben, Georg *134:* 5, 6; *172:* 17
Hallett, Mark *220:* 63
Hamanaka, Sheila *71:* 100
Hamann, Brad *78:* 151
Hamann, Sigune *104:* 115
Hamberger, John *6:* 8; *8:* 32; *14:* 79; *34:* 136; *88:* 78
Hamil, Tom *14:* 80; *43:* 163
Hamilton, Bill and Associates *26:* 215
Hamilton, Helen S. *2:* 238
Hamilton, J. *19:* 83, 85, 87
Hamilton, Laurie *116:* 210
Hamilton, Todd Cameron *84:* 15
Hamlin, Janet *97:* 136; *124:* 90; *137:* 157; *182:* 117
Hamlin, Louise *71:* 135
Hammill, Matt *206:* 65
Hammond, Chris *21:* 37
Hammond, Elizabeth *5:* 36, 203
Hampshire, Michael *5:* 187; *7:* 110, 111; *48:* 150; *51:* 129
Hampson, Denman *10:* 155; *15:* 130
Hampton, Blake *41:* 244
Handford, Martin *64:* 105, 106, 107, 109
Handforth, Thomas *42:* 100, 101, 102, 103, 104, 105, 107
Handville, Robert *1:* 89; *38:* 76; *45:* 108, 109
Hane, Roger *17:* 239; *44:* 54
Haney, Elizabeth Mathieu *34:* 84
Hanke, Ted *71:* 10
Hankinson, Phil *181:* 164
Hanley, Catherine *8:* 161
Hann, Jacquie *19:* 144
Hanna, Cheryl *91:* 133
Hanna, Wayne A. *67:* 145
Hannon, Mark *38:* 37
Hanrahan, Kelly-Anne *203:* 142
Hansen, Gaby *159:* 11; *186:* 25; *224:* 11
Hansen, Mia *149:* 76
Hanson, Glen *229:* 84
Hanson, Joan *8:* 76; *11:* 139
Hanson, Peter E. *52:* 47; *54:* 99, 100; *73:* 21; *84:* 79; *116:* 144
Hansson, Gunilla *64:* 111, 112

Harbour, Elizabeth *221:* 68
Hardcastle, Nick *121:* 82; *175:* 185; *222:* 135
Hardy, David A. *9:* 96; *119:* 74
Hardy, Paul *YABC 2:* 245
Hargis, Wes *219:* 70 Haring, Keith *145:* 65
Harlan, Jerry *3:* 96
Harlin, Greg *89:* 194; *103:* 82; *118:* 161; *121:* 167; *182:* 76; *201:* 172; *215:* 76
Harman, Dominic *206:* 48
Harness, Cheryl *106:* 80; *131:* 87; *178:* 111; *200:* 39
Harnischfeger *18:* 121
Harper, Arthur *YABC 2:* 121
Harper, Betty *126:* 90
Harper, Jamie *174:* 71; *214:* 212
Harper, Piers *79:* 27; *105:* 102; *161:* 67
Harrington, Glenn *82:* 18; *94:* 66, 68; *185:* 118
Harrington, Jack *83:* 162
Harrington, Richard *5:* 81
Harris, Andrew N. *191:* 78
Harris, Jim *127:* 130; *183:* 4
Harris, John *83:* 25
Harris, Nick *86:* 177
Harris, Susan Yard *42:* 121
Harrison, Florence *20:* 150, 152
Harrison, Harry *4:* 103
Harrison, Jack *28:* 149
Harrison, Mark *105:* 157; *165:* 190
Harrison, Ted *56:* 73
Harsh, Fred *72:* 107
Harston, Jerry *105:* 143
Hart, Lewis *98:* 115
Hart, Thomas *181:* 165
Hart, William *13:* 72
Hartland, Jessie *171:* 80, 81; *186:* 165; *223:* 58
Hartung, Susan Kathleen *150:* 107, 108; *173:* 106; *175:* 106; *192:* 78; *211:* 19
Hartelius, Margaret *10:* 24
Hartshorn, Ruth *5:* 115; *11:* 129
Harvey, Amanda *145:* 44
Harvey, Bob *48:* 219
Harvey, Gerry *7:* 180
Harvey, Lisa *97:* 21
Harvey, Paul *88:* 74
Harvey, Roland *71:* 88; *123:* 63; *179:* 94; *218:* 94; *219:* 74
Haskamp, Steve *195:* 36; *229:* 29
Hassall, Joan *43:* 108, 109
Hassell, Hilton *YABC 1:* 187
Hassett, John *162:* 59
Hasselriis, Else *18:* 87; *YABC 1:* 96
Hastings, Glenn *89:* 183
Hastings, Ian *62:* 67
Hauman, Doris *2:* 184; *29:* 58, 59; *32:* 85, 86, 87
Hauman, George *2:* 184; *29:* 58, 59; *32:* 85, 86, 87
Hausherr, Rosmarie *15:* 29
Haverfield, Mary *225:* 87
Hawkes, Kevin *78:* 72; *104:* 198; *105:* 197; *112:* 109; *126:* 87; *144:* 88; *149:* 210; *150:* 110, 135; *156:* 94; *164:* 35; *186:* 18; *190:* 197; *198:* 152; *201:* 70, 71, 72; *220:* 99; *221:* 90, 92, 93
Hawkins, Jacqui *112:* 86; *162:* 64
Hawkinson, John *4:* 109; *7:* 83; *21:* 64
Hawkinson, Lucy *21:* 64
Hawthorne, Mike *140:* 228
Haxton, Elaine *28:* 131
Haydock, Robert *4:* 95
Hayes, Geoffrey *26:* 111; *44:* 133; *91:* 85; *207:* 63
Hayes, Karel *207:* 65
Haynes, Max *72:* 107
Hays, Michael *73:* 207; *83:* 93; *139:* 197; *146:* 202, 250; *202:* 47
Haywood, Carolyn *1:* 112; *29:* 104
Heale, Jonathan *104:* 117
Healy, Daty *12:* 143

Healy, Deborah *58:* 181, 182; *101:* 111
Heap, Sue *102:* 207; *150:* 113, 114; *187:* 84, 85, 87
Hearn, Diane Dawson *79:* 99; *113:* 13; *209:* 71, 72; *211:* 106
Hearon, Dorothy *34:* 69
Heaslip, William *57:* 24, 25
Hechtkopf, H. *11:* 110
Heck, Ed *173:* 81
Hector, Julian *205:* 85
Hedderwick, Mairi *30:* 127; *32:* 47; *36:* 104; *77:* 86; *145:* 91, 93, 95
Heffernan, Phil *146:* 197; *195:* 172; *218:* 123
Hefter, Richard *28:* 170; *31:* 81, 82; *33:* 183
Hehenberger, Shelly *126:* 91
Heigh, James *22:* 98
Heighway, Richard *25:* 160; *64:* 4
Heighway-Bury, Robin *159:* 89
Heine, Helme *67:* 86; *135:* 91, 92
Heinly, John *45:* 113
Hellard, Susan *81:* 21; *204:* 82; *209:* 92
Hellebrand, Nancy *26:* 57
Heller, Linda *46:* 86
Heller, Ruth M. *66:* 125; *77:* 30, 32
Hellmuth, Jim *38:* 164
Helms, Georgeann *33:* 62
Helquist, Brett *142:* 203; *146:* 133, 134; *156:* 10; *173:* 25; *180:* 106; *187:* 90, 91; *193:* 12; *224:* 186; *226:* 117; *229:* 76, 77, 78
Helweg, Hans *41:* 118; *50:* 93; *58:* 22, 26
Hemingway, Edward *212:* 71
Hemphill, Helen *179:* 95
Henba, Bobbie *90:* 195
Henderling, Lisa *214:* 65
Henderson, Dave *73:* 76; *75:* 191, 192, 193, 194; *82:* 4
Henderson, D.F. *216:* 77
Henderson, Douglas *103:* 68
Henderson, Kathy *55:* 32; *155:* 118
Henderson, Keith *35:* 122
Henderson, Meryl *127:* 58, 60; *169:* 81; *228:*
Hendrix, John *187:* 133; *208:* 106, 107, 108; *216:* 115
Hendry, Linda *80:* 104; *83:* 83; *164:* 216
Hengeveld, Dennis *142:* 86
Henkes, Kevin *43:* 111; *108:* 106, 107, 108
Henneberger, Robert *1:* 42; *2:* 237; *25:* 83
Henriksen, Harold *35:* 26; *48:* 68
Henriquez, Celeste *103:* 137
Henriquez, Elsa *82:* 260
Henriquez, Emile F. *89:* 88; *211:* 56
Henry, Everett *29:* 191
Henry, Matthew *117:* 58
Henry, Paul *93:* 121; *194:* 125
Henry, Rohan *217:* 77
Henry, Thomas *5:* 102
Hensel *27:* 119
Henshaw, Jacqui *141:* 127
Henstra, Friso *8:* 80; *36:* 70; *40:* 222; *41:* 250; *73:* 100, 101
Henterly, Jamichael *93:* 4
Heo, Yumi *89:* 85, 86; *94:* 89, 90; *146:* 40, 137, 138; *163:* 227; *201:* 192
Hepple, Norman *28:* 198
Herbert, Helen *57:* 70
Herbert, Jennifer *189:* 47
Herbert, Wally *23:* 101
Herbster, Mary Lee *9:* 33
Herder, Edwin *182:* 104
Herge
    See Remi, Georges
Hermansen, Pal *133:* 113
Hermanson, Dennis *10:* 55
Hermes, Gertrude *54:* 161
Herr, Margo *57:* 191
Herr, Susan *83:* 163
Herriman, George *140:* 74, 75, 76, 77, 78
Herriman, Lisa *87:* 190
Herring, Michael *121:* 76; *182:* 103
Herrington, Roger *3:* 161
Herscovici, C. *165:* 240

Hescox, Richard *85:* 86; *90:* 30; *139:* 35
Heslop, Mike *38:* 60; *40:* 130
Hess, Lydia J. *85:* 17
Hess, Mark *111:* 146; *113:* 207
Hess, Paul *134:* 47; *166:* 133; *193:* 13
Hess, Richard *42:* 31
Hester, Ronnie *37:* 85
Heuser, Olga J. *121:* 116
Heusser, Sibylle *168:* 195
Heustis, Louise L. *20:* 28
Hewgill, Jody *201:* 90
Hewitson, Jennifer *74:* 119; *124:* 167
Hewitt, Kathryn *80:* 126; *149:* 105; *184:* 93; *196:* 36; *229:* 99
Hewitt, Margaret *84:* 112
Heyduck-Huth, Hilde *8:* 82
Heyer, Carol *74:* 122; *130:* 72, 73; *192:* 35; *203:* 78
Heyer, Hermann *20:* 114, 115
Heyer, Marilee *102:* 108
Heyman, Ken *8:* 33; *34:* 113
Heyne, Ulrike *146:* 151
Heywood, Karen *48:* 114
Hickling, P.B. *40:* 165
Hickman, Stephen *85:* 58; *136:* 33; *171:* 128
Hierstein, Judith *56:* 40; *162:* 168; *212:* 72; *227:* 46
Higashi, Sandra *154:* 59, 60
Higginbottom, J. Winslow *8:* 170; *29:* 105, 106
Higgins, Chester *101:* 79
Higham, David *50:* 104
Hilb, Nora *176:* 8
Hild, Anja *215:* 194
Hildebrandt, Greg *8:* 191; *55:* 35, 36, 38, 39, 40, 42, 46; *172:* 110
Hildebrandt, Tim *8:* 191; *55:* 44, 45, 46
Hilder, Rowland *19:* 207
Hill, Eric *66:* 127, 128; *133:* 91
Hill, Gregory *35:* 190
Hill, Pat *49:* 120
Hillenbrand, Will *84:* 115; *92:* 76, 80; *93:* 131; *104:* 168; *128:* 137; *145:* 187; *146:* 184; *147:* 105, 106, 107; *152:* 59; *184:* 179; *195:* 34, 180; *196:* 125; *210:* 122, 123, 124; *217:* 62; *224:* 145
Hilliard, Richard *183:* 74
Hillier, Matthew *45:* 205
Hillman, Priscilla *48:* 115
Hills, Tad *113:* 4; *137:* 147; *173:* 83; *208:* 199
Himler, Ronald *6:* 114; *7:* 162; *8:* 17, 84, 125; *14:* 76; *19:* 145; *26:* 160; *31:* 43; *38:* 116; *41:* 44, 79; *43:* 52; *45:* 120; *46:* 43; *54:* 44, 83; *58:* 180; *59:* 38; *68:* 146; *69:* 231; *70:* 98; *71:* 177, 178; *77:* 219; *79:* 212; *83:* 62; *89:* 5; *91:* 160; *92:* 91, 92, 93; *94:* 93; *95:* 69, 174, 194; *99:* 99, 112; *113:* 92; *118:* 114; *137:* 73, 74, 77, 167; *163:* 99; *165:* 138; *178:* 9, 220; *183:* 77, 79, 80, 81; *184:* 80, 83; *215:* 151; *231:* 11, 112
Himmelman, John *47:* 109; *65:* 87; *94:* 96, 97; *159:* 85; *221:* 79, 80, 81, 82
Hinds, Bill *37:* 127, 130
Hines, Anna Grossnickle *51:* 90; *74:* 124; *95:* 78, 79,80, 81
Hines, Bob *135:* 149, 150
Hirao, Amiko *203:* 98
Hiroko *99:* 61
Hiroshige *25:* 71
Hirsh, Marilyn *7:* 126
Hiscock, Bruce *137:* 80, 81; *204:* 51, 53
Hissey, Jane *103:* 90; *130:* 81
Hitch, Jeff *99:* 206; *128:* 86
Hitz, Demi *11:* 135; *15:* 245; *66:* 129, 130; *152:* 94, 95
Hnizdovsky, Jacques *32:* 96; *76:* 187
Ho, David *227:* 32
Ho, Kwoncjan *15:* 132
Hoban, Lillian *1:* 114; *22:* 157; *26:* 72; *29:* 53; *40:* 105, 107, 195; *41:* 80; *69:* 107, 108; *71:* 98; *77:* 168; *106:* 50; *113:* 86; *136:* 118

Hoban, Tana *22:* 159; *104:* 82, 83, 85
Hobbie, Holly *225:* 90, 91
Hobbie, Jocelyn *190:* 78; *196:* 92
Hobbie, Nathaniel *196:* 92
Hobbs, Leigh *166:* 95
Hoberman, Norman *5:* 82
Hobson, Sally *77:* 185
Hockerman, Dennis *39:* 22; *56:* 23
Hodgell, P.C. *42:* 114
Hodges, C. Walter *2:* 139; *11:* 15; *12:* 25; *23:* 34; *25:* 96; *38:* 165; *44:* 197; *45:* 95; *100:* 57; *YABC 2:* 62, 63
Hodges, David *9:* 98
Hodgetts, Victoria *43:* 132
Hofbauer, Imre *2:* 162
Hoff, Syd *9:* 107; *10:* 128; *33:* 94; *72:* 115,116, 117, 118; *138:* 114, 115
Hoffman, Rosekrans *15:* 133; *50:* 219; *63:* 97
Hoffman, Sanford *38:* 208; *76:* 174; *88:* 160, 161; *151:* 156
Hoffmann, Felix *9:* 109
Hoffnung, Gerard *66:* 76, 77
Hofsinde, Robert *21:* 70
Hogan, Inez *2:* 141
Hogan, Jamie *192:* 94; *198:* 177
Hogarth, Burne *41:* 58; *63:* 46, 48, 49, 50, 52, 53, 54, 55,56
Hogarth, Paul *41:* 102, 103, 104; *YABC 1:* 16
Hogarth, William *42:* 33
Hogenbyl, Jan *1:* 35
Hogner, Nils *4:* 122; *25:* 144
Hogrogian, Nonny *3:* 221; *4:* 106, 107; *5:* 166; *7:* 129; *15:* 2; *16:* 176; *20:* 154; *22:* 146; *25:* 217; *27:* 206; *74:* 127, 128, 129, 149, 152; *127:* 99; *YABC 2:* 84, 94
Hokanson, Lars *93:* 111; *172:* 137; *212:* 88
Hokusai *25:* 71
Hol, Colby *126:* 96
Holberg, Richard *2:* 51
Holbrook, Kathy *107:* 114
Holdcroft, Tina *38:* 109; *227:* 99, 100, 160
Holden, Caroline *55:* 159
Holder, Heidi *36:* 99; *64:* 9
Holder, Jim *204:* 163
Holder, Jimmy *151:* 224
Holderness, Grizelda *215:* 107
Hole, Stian *204:* 55
Holiday, Henry *YABC 2:* 107
Holl, F. *36:* 91
Holland, Brad *45:* 59, 159
Holland, Gay W. *128:* 105; *225:* 76
Holland, Janice *18:* 118
Holland, Marion *6:* 116
Holland, Richard *216:* 109, 124
Holldobler, Turid *26:* 120
Holliday, Keaf *144:* 236
Holling, Holling C. *15:* 136, 137
Hollinger, Deanne *12:* 116
Holm, Sharon Lane *114:* 84; *115:* 52
Holmes, B. *3:* 82
Holmes, Bea *7:* 74; *24:* 156; *31:* 93
Holmes, Dave *54:* 22
Holmes, Lesley *135:* 96
Holmgren, George Ellen *45:* 112
Holmlund, Heather D. *150:* 140
Holt, Norma *44:* 106
Holt, Pater *151:* 188
Holtan, Gene *32:* 192
Holub, Joan *149:* 72; *229:* 82
Holyfield, John *149:* 231; *227:* 101; *230:* 9
Holz, Loretta *17:* 81
Hom, Nancy *79:* 195
Homar, Lorenzo *6:* 2
Homer, Winslow *128:* 8; *YABC 2:* 87
Honey, Elizabeth *112:* 95, 96; *137:* 93, 94
Honeywood, Varnette P. *110:* 68, 70
Hong, Lily Toy *76:* 104
Honigman, Marian *3:* 2
Honore, Paul *42:* 77, 79, 81, 82
Hood, Alun *69:* 145, 218; *72:* 41; *80:* 226; *87:* 4; *95:* 139

Hood, Susan *12:* 43
Hook, Christian *104:* 103
Hook, Frances *26:* 188; *27:* 127
Hook, Jeff *14:* 137; *103:* 105
Hook, Richard *26:* 188
Hooks *63:* 30
Hooper, Hadley *177:* 145
Hoover, Carol A. *21:* 77
Hoover, Russell *12:* 95; *17:* 2; *34:* 156
Hope, James *141:* 116
Hopkins, Chris *99:* 127
Hopkinson, Leigh *202:* 70
Hopman, Philip *178:* 184
Hoppe, Paul *209:* 85
Hoppin, Augustus *34:* 66
Horacek, Judy *211:* 86
Horacek, Petr *163:* 117; *214:* 113
Horder, Margaret *2:* 108; *73:* 75
Horen, Michael *45:* 121
Horne, Daniel *73:* 106; *91:* 153; *109:* 127;
   110: 232; *164:* 176
Horne, Richard *111:* 80
Horowitz, Dave *204:* 58
Horse, Harry *128:* 195; *169:* 86
Horstman, Lisa *219:* 79
Horton, Anthony *211:* 98
Horvat, Laurel *12:* 201
Horvath, David *192:* 95
Horvath, Ferdinand Kusati *24:* 176
Horvath, Maria *57:* 171
Horwitz, Richard *57:* 174
Hotchkiss, De Wolfe *20:* 49
Hough, Charlotte *9:* 112; *13:* 98; *17:* 83; *24:*
   195
Houlihan, Ray *11:* 214
House, Caroline *183:* 121
Housman, Laurence *25:* 146, 147
Houston, James *13:* 107; *74:* 132, 134, 135
Hovland, Gary *88:* 172; *171:* 148
Hoyt, Eleanor *158:* 231
How, W.E. *20:* 47
Howard, Alan *16:* 80; *34:* 58; *45:* 114
Howard, Arthur *165:* 111, 112; *190:* 5; *229:* 30
Howard, J.N. *15:* 234
Howard, John *33:* 179
Howard, Kim *116:* 71
Howard, Paul *142:* 126, 129; *144:* 187
Howard, Rob *40:* 161
Howarth, Daniel *170:* 34; *222:* 97, 98; *224:*
   20; *225:* 77
Howe, John *79:* 101; *80:* 150; *115:* 47; *176:*
   106; *207:* 32, 35
Howe, Phillip *79:* 117; *175:* 115
Howe, Stephen *1:* 232
Howell, Karen *119:* 123
Howell, Pat *15:* 139
Howell, Troy *23:* 24; *31:* 61; *36:* 158; *37:*
   184; *41:* 76, 235; *48:* 112; *56:* 13; *57:* 3; *59:*
   174; *63:* 5; *74:* 46; *89:* 188; *90:* 231; *95:* 97,
   98; *99:* 189; *153:* 156, 157, 158; *176:*
   104; *199:* 96, 98; *222:* 65
Howells, Tania *229:* 87
Howes, Charles *22:* 17
Hoyt, Ard *145:* 141; *190:* 82; *207:* 148
Hranilovich, Barbara *127:* 51
Hu, Ying-Hwa *116:* 107; *152:* 236; *173:* 171
Huang, Benrei *137:* 55
Huang, Zhong-Yang *117:* 30, 32; *213:* 18
Hubbard, Woodleigh Marx *98:* 67; *115:* 79;
   160: 138; *214:* 120
Hubbell, Patricia *222:* 31
Hubley, Faith *48:* 120, 121, 125, 130, 131,
   132, 134
Hubley, John *48:* 125, 130, 131, 132, 134
Hudak, Michal *143:* 74
Hudnut, Robin *14:* 62
Huerta, Catherine *76:* 178; *77:* 44, 45; *90:*
   182; *210:* 202
Huffaker, Sandy *10:* 56
Huffman, Joan *13:* 33

Huffman, Tom *13:* 180; *17:* 212; *21:* 116; *24:*
   132; *33:* 154; *38:* 59; *42:* 147
Hughes, Arthur *20:* 148, 149, 150; *33:* 114,
   148, 149
Hughes, Darren *95:* 44
Hughes, David *36:* 197
Hughes, Shirley *1:* 20, 21; *7:* 3; *12:* 217; *16:*
   163; *29:* 154; *63:* 118; *70:* 102, 103, 104;
   73: 169; *88:* 70; *110:* 118, 119; *159:* 103
Hugo, Victor *47:* 112
Huliska-Beith, Laura *204:* 108; *220:* 137
Hull, Cathy *78:* 29
Hull, Richard *95:* 120; *123:* 175; *172:* 195
Hulsmann, Eva *16:* 166
Hume, Lachie *189:* 93
Hummel, Berta *43:* 137, 138, 139
Hummel, Lisl *29:* 109; *YABC 2:* 333, 334
Humphrey, Henry *16:* 167
Humphreys, Graham *25:* 168
Humphries, Tudor *76:* 66; *80:* 4; *124:* 4, 5;
   226: 112
Huneck, Stephen *183:* 88, 89
Hunt, James *2:* 143
Hunt, Jonathan *84:* 120
Hunt, Paul *119:* 104; *129:* 135; *139:* 160; *173:*
   112
Hunt, Robert *110:* 206, 235; *147:* 136, 137;
   170: 3; *211:* 76; *226:* 189
Hunt, Scott *190:* 143
Hunter, Anne *133:* 190; *178:* 150
Huntington, Amy *180:* 99
Hurd, Clement *2:* 148, 149; *64:* 127, 128, 129,
   131, 133, 134,135, 136; *100:* 37, 38
Hurd, Peter *24:* 30, 31,; *YABC 2:* 56
Hurd, Thacher *46:* 88, 89; *94:* 114, 115, 116;
   123: 81, 82, 84; *219:* 82
Hurlimann, Ruth *32:* 99
Hurst, Carol Otis *185:* 92
Hurst, Elise *221:* 98
Hurst, Philip *196:* 79
Hurst, Tracey *192:* 238
Hussar, Michael *114:* 113; *117:* 159
Hustler, Tom *6:* 105
Hutchins, Laurence *55:* 22
Hutchins, Pat *15:* 142; *70:* 106, 107, 108; *178:*
   131, 132
Hutchinson, Sascha *95:* 211
Hutchinson, William M. *6:* 3, 138; *46:* 70
Hutchison, Paula *23:* 10
Hutton, Clarke *YABC 2:* 335
Hutton, Kathryn *35:* 155; *89:* 91
Hutton, Warwick *20:* 91
Huyette, Marcia *29:* 188
Hyatt, John *54:* 7
Hyatt, Mitch *178:* 162
Hyde, Maureen *82:* 17; *121:* 145, 146
Hyman, David *117:* 64
Hyman, Miles *210:* 132
Hyman, Trina Schart *1:* 204; *2:* 194; *5:* 153;
   6: 106; *7:* 138, 145; *8:* 22; *10:* 196; *13:* 96;
   14: 114; *15:* 204; *16:* 234; *20:* 82; *22:* 133;
   24: 151; *25:* 79, 82; *26:* 82; *29:* 83; *31:* 37,
   39; *34:* 104; *38:* 84, 100, 128; *41:* 49; *43:*
   146; *46:* 91, 92, 93, 95, 96, 97, 98, 99, 100,
   101, 102, 103, 104, 105,108, 109, 111, 197;
   48: 60, 61; *52:* 32; *60:* 168; *66:* 38; *67:* 214;
   72: 74; *75:* 92; *79:* 57; *82:* 95, 238; *89:* 46;
   95: 91, 92, 93; *100:* 33, 199; *132:* 12; *147:*
   33, 35, 36; *167:* 58, 60; *177:* 189, 190; *211:*
   188

Ibarra, Rosa *147:* 91
Ibatoulline, Bagram *156:* 48; *174:* 33, 82; *202:*
   30; *211:* 213; *224:* 84; *225:* 98, 99
Ichikawa, Satomi *29:* 152; *41:* 52; *47:* 133,
   134,135, 136; *78:* 93, 94; *80:* 81; *146:* 143,
   145, 146; *208:* 117, 118, 119

Ide, Jacqueline *YABC 1:* 39
Idle, Molly Schaar *223:* 95
Ilsley, Velma *3:* 1; *7:* 55; *12:* 109; *37:* 62; *38:*
   184
Imai, Ayano *190:* 85, 86
in den Bosch, Nicole *150:* 204
Inga *1:* 142
Ingman, Bruce *134:* 50; *182:* 91, 92; *214:* 10
Ingpen, Robert *109:* 103, 104; *132:* 138; *137:*
   177; *166:* 103; *181:* 140; *229:* 169
Ingraham, Erick *21:* 177; *84:* 256; *103:* 66
Inkpen, Mick *99:* 104, 105; *106:* 44
Innerst, Stacy *149:* 104
Innocenti, Roberto *21:* 123; *96:* 122; *159:* 111,
   197; *199:* 176
Inoue, Yosuke *24:* 118
Iofin, Michael *97:* 157
Iosa, Ann *63:* 189
Ipcar, Dahlov *1:* 124, 125; *49:* 137, 138, 139,
   140, 141, 142,143, 144, 145; *147:* 122, 124,
   126
Irvin, Fred *13:* 166; *15:* 143, 144; *27:* 175
Irving, Jay *45:* 72
Irving, Laurence *27:* 50
Isaac, Joanne *21:* 76
Isaacs, Gary *170:* 188
Isadora, Rachel *43:* 159, 160; *54:* 31; *79:* 106,
   107,108; *121:* 100, 102; *165:* 116, 117; *204:*
   61, 63, 64
Ishmael, Woodi *24:* 111; *31:* 99
Isol *220:* 73
Ives, Ruth *15:* 257
Iwai, Melissa *149:* 233; *183:* 92; *199:* 115
Iwamura, Kazuo *213:* 87

J

Jabar, Cynthia *101:* 201; *210:* 134, 135
Jackness, Andrew *94:* 237
Jackson, Julian *91:* 104, 106
Jackson, Michael *43:* 42
Jackson, Shelley *79:* 71; *99:* 109; *187:* 82
Jacob, Murv *89:* 30
Jacobi, Kathy *62:* 118
Jacobs, Barbara *9:* 136
Jacobs, Lou, Jr. *9:* 136; *15:* 128
Jacobsen, Laura *176:* 98; *177:* 85, 86
Jacobson, Rick *131:* 222; *170:* 119; *222:* 52
Jacobus, Tim *79:* 140; *109:* 126; *129:* 180
Jacques, Robin *1:* 70; *2:* 1; *8:* 46; *9:* 20; *15:*
   187; *19:* 253; *32:* 102, 103, 104; *43:* 184;
   73: 135; *YABC 1:* 42
Jaeggi, Yoshiko *186:* 184
Jaffee, Al *66:* 131, 132
Jago *216:* 122
Jagr, Miloslav *13:* 197
Jahn-Clough, Lisa *88:* 114; *152:* 104; *193:* 70,
   71
Jahnke, Robert *84:* 24
Jainschigg, Nicholas *80:* 64; *91:* 138; *95:* 63;
   99: 25; *108:* 50; *171:* 41
Jakesevic, Nenad *85:* 102; *226:* 215
Jakobsen, Kathy *116:* 83
Jakubowski, Charles *14:* 192
Jambor, Louis *YABC 1:* 11
James, Ann *73:* 50; *82:* 113; *158:* 61; *183:* 44
James, Brian *140:* 91
James, Curtis E. *182:* 93
James, Derek *35:* 187; *44:* 91; *61:* 133; *74:* 2;
   80: 57; *86:* 88; *130:* 30; *179:* 29; *218:* 31
James, Gilbert *YABC 1:* 43
James, Gordon C. *195:* 89
James, Harold *2:* 151; *3:* 62; *8:* 79; *29:* 113;
   51: 195; *74:* 90
James, Kennon *126:* 211
James, Robin *50:* 106; *53:* 32, 34, 35
James, Simon *202:* 73, 74
James, Will *19:* 150, 152, 153, 155, 163

Janosch
See Eckert, Horst
Janovitch, Marilyn 68: 168
Janovitz, Marilyn 87: 187; 130: 198; 194: 91
Jansons, Inese 48: 117
Jansson, Alexander 216: 59
Jansson, Tove 3: 90; 41: 106, 108, 109, 110, 111, 113, 114
Jaques, Faith 7: 11, 132, 133; 21: 83, 84; 69: 114,116; 73: 170
Jaques, Frances Lee 29: 224
Jarka, Jeff 221: 94
Jarrett, Clare 201: 77
Jarrie, Martin 219: 86
Jauss, Anne Marie 1: 139; 3: 34; 10: 57, 119; 11: 205; 23: 194
Jay, Alison 158: 97, 98; 183: 126, 127; 196: 95, 96, 97, 98; 200: 72, 73, 74; 212: 39
Jeffers, Oliver 175: 111; 213: 89
Jeffers, Susan 17: 86, 87; 25: 164, 165; 26: 112; 50: 132, 134, 135; 70: 111, 112, 113; 137: 107, 108, 109, 110, 111; 202: 77, 78
Jefferson, Louise E. 4: 160
Jenkin-Pearce, Susie 78: 16
Jenkins, Debra Reid 85: 202; 114: 89; 173: 134; 225: 116
Jenkins, Jean 98: 79, 102
Jenkins, Leonard 157: 169; 167: 128; 189: 96, 97; 190: 89
Jenkins, Patrick 72: 126
Jenkins, Steve 124: 177; 154: 90, 91, 92, 93; 185: 194; 188: 81, 82, 83, 84, 85, 86; 218: 67, 69, 70, 71, 72
Jenks, Aleta 73: 117; 124: 225
Jenkyns, Chris 51: 97
Jensen, Bruce 95: 39
Jensinius, Kirsten 56: 58
Jeram, Anita 89: 135; 102: 122, 123; 129: 112; 154: 96, 97, 98; 164: 154; 203: 123, 124; 219: 88, 89, 90, 91
Jernigan, E. Wesley 85: 92
Jerome, Elaine 227: 45
Jerome, Karen A. 72: 194
Jeruchim, Simon 6: 173; 15: 250
Jeschke, Susan 20: 89; 39: 161; 41: 84; 42: 120
Jessel, Camilla 29: 115
Jessell, Tim 159: 3; 177: 87; 181: 95; 205: 4; 213: 74; 223: 187; 225: 102; 226: 190
Jeyaveeran, Ruth 182: 100
Jiang, Cheng An 109: 108
Jiang, Wei 109: 108
Jimenez, Maria 77: 158; 93: 127
Jobling, Curtis 138: 74
Jocelyn, Marthe 118: 83; 137: 219; 163: 119, 120; 198: 62
Joerns, Consuelo 38: 36; 44: 94
John, Diana 12: 209
John, Helen 1: 215; 28: 204
Johns, Elizabeth 127: 33
Johns, Jasper 61: 172
Johns, Jeanne 24: 114
Johnson, Adrian 143: 50
Johnson, Bruce 9: 47
Johnson, Cathy 92: 136; 218: 112
Johnson, Crockett
See Leisk, David
Johnson, D. William 23: 104
Johnson, D.B. 183: 98, 139
Johnson, David A. 175: 18; 191: 91; 218: 19
Johnson, Gillian 119: 175; 164: 217; 215: 99
Johnson, Harper 1: 27; 2: 33; 18: 302; 19: 61; 31: 181; 44: 46, 50, 95
Johnson, Ingrid 37: 118
Johnson, James Ralph 1: 23, 127
Johnson, James David 12: 195
Johnson, Jane 48: 136
Johnson, Joel Peter 98: 18; 128: 111; 201: 13; 213: 189
Johnson, John E. 34: 133
Johnson, Kevin 72: 44

Johnson, Kevin Eugene 109: 215
Johnson, Larry 47: 56; 123: 107; 159: 203
Johnson, Layne 187: 94; 209: 63; 222: 100, 101
Johnson, Margaret S. 35: 131
Johnson, Meredith Merrell 71: 181; 83: 158; 89: 103; 104: 88
Johnson, Milton 1: 67; 2: 71; 26: 45; 31: 107; 60: 112; 68: 96
Johnson, Pamela 16: 174; 52: 145; 62: 140; 73: 116; 85: 52
Johnson, Paul Brett 83: 95; 132: 119
Johnson, Stephen T. 80: 15; 131: 35; 141: 96; 145: 40; 164: 187; 175: 32; 189: 99, 100; 208: 43
Johnson, Steve 138: 219; 141: 64; 144: 199; 177: 51; 214: 95; 221: 63; 228: 42, 43, 44; 230: 44, 45, 46
Johnson, William R. 38: 91
Johnson-Petrov, Arden 115: 206
Johnston, David McCall 50: 131, 133
Johnston, Lynne 118: 85, 87, 89; 216: 127, 128, 131
Johnstone, Anne 8: 120; 36: 89
Johnstone, Janet Grahame 8: 120; 36: 89
Jolivet, Joëlle 231: 71
Jonas, Ann 50: 107, 108, 109; 135: 113
Jones, Bob 71: 5; 77: 199
Jones, Carol 5: 131; 72: 185, 186; 153: 111, 112
Jones, Chuck 53: 70, 71
Jones, Curtis 211: 144
Jones, Davy 89: 176
Jones, Douglas B. 185: 192; 202: 82
Jones, Elizabeth Orton 18: 124, 126, 128, 129
Jones, Harold 14: 88; 52: 50
Jones, Holly 127: 3
Jones, Laurian 25: 24, 27
Jones, Margaret 74: 57
Jones, Noah Z. 182: 37; 203: 159
Jones, Randy 131: 104
Jones, Richard 127: 222
Jones, Robert 25: 67
Jones, Wilfred 35: 115; YABC 1: 163
Jordan, Charles 89: 58
Jordan, Jess 158: 136; 203: 111
Jordan, Martin George 84: 127
Jordan, Richard 84: 36
Jorgenson, Andrea 91: 111
Jorisch, Stéphane 153: 56, 193; 177: 29; 178: 138, 139; 187: 23; 211: 182
Joseph, James 53: 88
Joudrey, Ken 64: 145; 78: 6
Joyce, William 72: 131, 132, 133, 134; 73: 227; 145: 37
Joyner, Jerry 34: 138
Joyner, Loraine M. 209: 17
Joysmith, Brenda 210: 237
Juan, Ana 175: 38; 179: 111, 112; 213: 9
Jucker, Sita 5: 93
Judge, Lita 192: 99
Judkis, Jim 37: 38
Juhasz, Victor 31: 67
Jullian, Philippe 24: 206; 25: 203
Jung, Tom 91: 217
Junge, Alexandra 183: 37
Junge, Walter 67: 150
Jupo, Frank 7: 148, 149
Jurisch, Stephane 154: 105
Justice, Martin 34: 72

K

Kabatova-Taborska, Zdenka 107: 153
Kachik, John 165: 230
Kaczman, James 156: 98
Kadair, Deborah Ousley 184: 45, 89

Kahl, David 74: 95; 97: 35; 109: 174; 110: 213; 198: 15
Kahl, M.P. 37: 83
Kahl, Virginia 48: 138
Kahn, Katherine Janus 90: 135; 211: 155; 218: 75, 76; 220: 89,90
Kakimoo, Kozo 11: 148
Kalett, Jim 48: 159, 160, 161
Kalin, Victor 39: 186
Kalis, Jennifer 207: 82; 219: 62
Kalman, Maira 96: 131, 132; 137: 115
Kalmenoff, Matthew 22: 191
Kalow, Gisela 32: 105
Kamen, Gloria 1: 41; 9: 119; 10: 178; 35: 157; 78: 236; 98: 82
Kaminsky, Jef 102: 153
Kandell, Alice 35: 133
Kane, Henry B. 14: 90; 18: 219, 220
Kane, Robert 18: 131
Kanfer, Larry 66: 141
Kangas, Juli 200: 88
Kappes, Alfred 28: 104
Karalus, Bob 41: 157
Karas, G. Brian 80: 60; 99: 179; 115: 41; 118: 50; 136: 168; 145: 166; 149: 245; 159: 65; 171: 192; 178: 142, 143; 202: 38; 209: 142; 222: 106, 107, 108, 109; 225: 62
Karasz, Ilonka 128: 163
Karlin, Eugene 10: 63; 20: 131
Karlin, Nurit 63: 78; 103: 110
Karpinski, Tony 134: 160
Kasamatsu, Shiro 139: 155
Kasparavicius, Kestutis 139: 210
Kassian, Olena 64: 94
Kastner, Jill 79: 135; 117: 84, 85
Kasuya, Masahiro 41: 206, 207; 51: 100
Kasza, Keiko 191: 99, 100, 101, 102, 103
Katona, Robert 21: 85; 24: 126
Katz, Avi 199: 55
Katz, Karen 158: 123
Kauffer, E. McKnight 33: 103; 35: 127; 63: 67
Kaufman, Angelika 15: 156
Kaufman, Joe 33: 119
Kaufman, John 13: 158
Kaufman, Stuart 62: 64; 68: 226; 137: 44
Kaufmann, John 1: 174; 4: 159; 8: 43, 1; 10: 102; 18: 133, 134; 22: 251
Kaye, Graham 1: 9; 67: 7, 8
Kaye, M.M. 62: 95
Kazalovski, Nata 40: 205
Keane, Bil 4: 135
Kearney, David 72: 47; 121: 83
Keating, Pamel T. 77: 37
Keats, Ezra Jack 3: 18, 105, 257; 14: 101, 102; 33: 129; 57: 79, 80, 82, 83, 84, 87
Keegan, Charles 166: 211
Keegan, Marcia 9: 122; 32: 93
Keeler, Patricia A. 81: 56; 183: 102, 103
Keely, Jack 119: 95
Keely, John 26: 104; 48: 214
Keen, Eliot 25: 213
Keep, Richard C. 170: 122
Keeping, Charles 9: 124, 185; 15: 28, 134; 18: 115; 44: 194, 196; 47: 25; 52: 3; 54: 156; 69: 123, 124; 74: 56; 155: 9
Keeter, Susan 168: 46; 183: 192
Keith, Eros 4: 98; 5: 138; 31: 29; 43: 220; 52: 91, 92, 93, 94; 56: 64, 66; 60: 37; 79: 93
Keleinikov, Andrei 65: 101, 102
Kelen, Emery 13: 115
Keller, A.J. 62: 198
Keller, Arthur I. 26: 106
Keller, Dick 36: 123, 125
Keller, Holly 45: 79; 76: 118, 119, 120, 121; 108: 137, 138, 140; 157: 117, 118, 119; 216: 136
Keller, Katie 79: 222; 93: 108
Keller, Laurie 196: 105, 106
Keller, Ronald 45: 208
Kelley, Gary 183: 105; 216: 78; 217: 95, 96, 97

Kelley, Marty *211:* 91
Kelley, True *41:* 114, 115; *42:* 137; *75:* 35; *92:* 104, 105; *124:* 62; *130:* 100, 101; *179:* 120, 121, 122; *192:* 251
Kellogg, Steven *8:* 96; *11:* 207; *14:* 130; *20:* ; *201:* 38 58; *29:* 140, 141; *30:* 35; *41:* 141; *57:* 89, 90, 92,93, 94, 96; *59:* 182; *73:* 141; *77:* 129; *130:* 105, 106; *177:* 94, 95, 96, 97; *199:* 57; *217:* 61; *YABC 1:* 65, 73
Kelly, Billy *158:* 143
Kelly, Geoff *97:* 196; *112:* 25
Kelly, Irene *147:* 134; *210:* 144, 145
Kelly, Jennifer *230:* 137
Kelly, John *194:* 186
Kelly, Joseph *174:* 94
Kelly, Kathleen M. *71:* 109
Kelly, Laura *89:* 217
Kelly, True *163:* 87
Kelly, Walt *18:* 136, 137, 138, 139, 140, 141, 144, 145, 146, 148, 149
Kemble, E.W. *34:* 75; *44:* 178; *YABC 2:* 54, 59
Kemly, Kathleen *209:* 165
Kemp-Welsh, Lucy *24:* 197; *100:* 214
Kendall, Jane *150:* 105; *186:* 109
Kendall, Peter *152:* 85
Kendrick, Dennis *79:* 213
Kennaway, Adrienne *60:* 55, 56; *171:* 88, 89
Kennedy, Anne *212:* 34
Kennedy, Doug *189:* 104
Kennedy, Paul Edward *6:* 190; *8:* 132; *33:* 120
Kennedy, Richard *3:* 93; *12:* 179; *44:* 193; *100:* 15; *YABC 1:* 57
Kent, Jack *24:* 136; *37:* 37; *40:* 81; *84:* 89; *86:* 150; *88:* 77
Kent, Rockwell *5:* 166; *6:* 129; *20:* 225, 226, 227,229; *59:* 144
Kenyon, Tony *81:* 201; *127:* 74; *231:* 86
Kepes, Juliet *13:* 119
Kerins, Anthony *76:* 84
Kerr, Judity *24:* 137
Kerr, Phyllis Forbes *72:* 141
Kessler, Leonard *1:* 108; *7:* 139; *14:* 107, 227; *22:* 101; *44:* 96; *67:* 79; *82:* 123
Kest, Kristin *168:* 99; *173:* 23
Kesteven, Peter *35:* 189
Ketcham, Hank *28:* 140, 141, 142
Kettelkamp, Larry *2:* 164
Key, Alexander *8:* 99
Khalsa, Dayal Kaur *62:* 99
Kiakshuk *8:* 59
Kid, Tom *207:* 54
Kidd, Chip *94:* 23
Kidd, Richard *152:* 110
Kidd, Tom *64:* 199; *81:* 189; *185:* 173
Kiddell-Monroe, Joan *19:* 201; *55:* 59, 60; *87:* 174; *121:* 112
Kidder, Harvey *9:* 105; *80:* 41
Kidwell, Carl *43:* 145
Kieffer, Christa *41:* 89
Kiesler, Kate *110:* 105; *136:* 142
Kiff, Ken *40:* 45
Kilaka, John *223:* 107
Kilbride, Robert *37:* 100
Kilby, Don *141:* 144
Kim, David *201:* 79; *202:* 97
Kim, Glenn *99:* 82
Kimball, Anton *78:* 114; *119:* 105
Kimball, Yeffe *23:* 116; *37:* 88
Kimber, Murray *171:* 91
Kimmel, Warren *176:* 112
Kincade, Orin *34:* 116
Kindersley, Barnabas *96:* 110
Kindred, Wendy *7:* 151
King, Colin *53:* 3
King, Robin *10:* 164, 165
King, Stephen Michael *141:* 31; *197:* 191; *218:* 81, 82
King, Tara Calahan *139:* 172
King, Tony *39:* 121
Kingman, Dong *16:* 287; *44:* 100, 102, 104

Kingsley, Charles *YABC 2:* 182
Kingston, Julie *147:* 14
Kingston, Maxine Hong *53:* 92
Kinney, Jeff *187:* 97
Kipling, John Lockwood *YABC 2:* 198
Kipling, Rudyard *YABC 2:* 196
Kipniss, Robert *29:* 59
Kirchherr, Astrid *55:* 23
Kirchhoff, Art *28:* 136
Kirk, Daniel *153:* 115, 116, 117; *173:* 101; *196:* 113, 114, 115, 116
Kirk, David *117:* 88, 89; *161:* 97, 98
Kirk, Ruth *5:* 96
Kirk, Steve *170:* 37
Kirk, Tim *32:* 209, 211; *72:* 89; *83:* 49
Kirmse, Marguerite *15:* 283; *18:* 153
Kirsch, Vincent X. *124:* 207
Kirschner, Ruth *22:* 154
Kirwan, Wednesday *198:* 73
Kish, Ely *73:* 119; *79:* 2
Kitamura, Satoshi *62:* 102; *98:* 91; *101:* 147; *138:* 2; *143:* 83, 85, 86; *201:* 83; *223:* 3, 4
Kiss, Andrew *168:* 115
Kitchel, JoAnn E. *133:* 32
Kitchen, Bert *70:* 126; *193:* 49
Kittelsen, Theodor *62:* 14
Kiuchi, Tatsuro *114:* 71
Kiwak, Barbara *172:* 135
Klahr, Susan *176:* 196
Klapholz, Mel *13:* 35
Klee, Jutte *209:* 136
Klein, Bill *89:* 105
Klein, Robert *55:* 77
Klein, Suzanna *63:* 104
Kleinman, Zalman *28:* 143
Kleven, Elisa *173:* 96, 97; *217:* 100, 102
Kliban, B. *35:* 137, 138
Kline, Michael *127:* 66
Klinger, Shula *230:* 55
Klise, M. Sarah *180:* 117, 118; *181:* 97; *221:* 100, 102
Knabel, Lonnie *73:* 103; *75:* 187, 228; *194:* 216
Kneen, Maggie *140:* 139; *221:* 104, 105
Knight, Ann *34:* 143
Knight, Christopher *13:* 125
Knight, Hilary *1:* 233; *3:* 21; *15:* 92, 158, 159; *16:* 258, 259, 260; *18:* 235; *19:* 169; *35:* 242; *46:* 167; *52:* 116; *69:* 126, 127; *132:* 129; *YABC 1:* 168, 169, 172
Knorr, Laura *200:* 91
Knorr, Peter *126:* 92, 93
Knotts, Howard *20:* 4; *25:* 170; *36:* 163
Knutson, Barbara *112:* 134; *202:* 108
Knutson, Kimberley *115:* 90
Kobayashi, Ann *39:* 58
Kochalka, James *196:* 120, 121, 122
Kocsis, J.C.
See Paul, James
Kodman, Stanislawa *201:* 85; *224:* 72
Koehler, Hanne Lore *176:* 203
Koehn, Ilse *34:* 198; *79:* 123
Koelsch, Michael *99:* 182; *107:* 164; *109:* 239; *138:* 142; *150:* 94; *176:* 105; *187:* 63; *198:* 63; *230:* 204
Koering, Ursula *3:* 28; *4:* 14; *44:* 5; *64:* 140,141; *85:* 46
Koerner, Henry
See Koerner, W.H.D.
Koerner, W.H.D. *14:* 216; *21:* 88, 89, 90, 91; *23:* 211
Koetsch, Mike *166:* 68
Koffler, Camilla *36:* 113
Kogan, Deborah Ray *161:* 101, 102
Koide, Yasuko *50:* 114
Kolado, Karen *102:* 228
Kolesova, Juliana *217:* 81; *222:* 185; *229:* 183
Komarck, Michael *227:* 48
Komoda, Kiyo *9:* 128; *13:* 214
Kompaneyets, Marc *169:* 92
Konashevich, Vladimir *61:* 160

Konashevicha, V. *YABC 1:* 26
Konigsburg, E.L. *4:* 138; *48:* 141, 142, 144, 145; *94:* 129, 130; *126:* 129, 130, 131; *194:* 95, 98
Kono, Erin Eitter *177:* 99
Kooiker, Leonie *48:* 148
Koonook, Simon *65:* 157
Koontz, Robin Michal *136:* 155
Koopmans, Loek *101:* 121
Kopelke, Lisa *154:* 107
Kopper, Lisa *72:* 152, 153; *105:* 135, 136
Korach, Mimi *1:* 128, 129; *2:* 52; *4:* 39; *5:* 159; *9:* 129; *10:* 21; *24:* 69
Koren, Edward *5:* 100; *65:* 65, 67
Kosaka, Fumi *164:* 130
Koscielniak, Bruce *99:* 122; *153:* 120, 121, 122
Koshkin, Alexander *92:* 180
Kossin, Sandy *10:* 71; *23:* 105
Kostin, Andrej *26:* 204
Kosturko, Bob *164:* 56
Kotzky, Brian *68:* 184
Kovacevic, Zivojin *13:* 247
Kovalski, Maryann *58:* 120; *84:* 88; *97:* 124, 125, 126; *158:* 3; *186:* 80
Kozjan, Drazen *209:* 99; *231:* 130
Krahn, Fernando *2:* 257; *34:* 206; *49:* 152
Krall, Dan *218:* 84, 85
Kramek, Oren *231:* 119
Kramer, Anthony *33:* 81
Kramer, David *96:* 162; *109:* 132; *150:* 220
Kramer, Frank *6:* 121
Krantz, Kathy *35:* 83
Kratter, Paul *139:* 65
Kraus, Robert *13:* 217; *65:* 113; *93:* 93, 94
Krause, Jon *176:* 62
Krauss, Trisha *174:* 10
Kredel, Fritz *6:* 35; *17:* 93, 94, 95, 96; *22:* 147; *24:* 175; *29:* 130; *35:* 77; *YABC 2:* 166, 300
Kreloff, Eliot *189:* 107, 108; *205:* 182
Krementz, Jill *17:* 98; *49:* 41
Krenina, Katya *117:* 106; *125:* 133; *176:* 117; *221:* 107
Kresin, Robert *23:* 19
Kretschmar, Sonia *226:* 97
Krieger, Salem *54:* 164
Kriegler, Lyn *73:* 29
Krinitz, Esther Nisenthal *193:* 196
Krommes, Beth *128:* 141; *149:* 136; *181:* 100, 101; *184:* 105; *188:* 125; *208:* 135; *209:* 185
Krone, Mike *101:* 71
Kronheimer, Ann *135:* 119
Krosoczka, Jarrett J. *155:* 142; *200:* 93, 94
Kruck, Gerald *88:* 181
Krudop, Walter Lyon *199:* 19
Krupinski, Loretta *67:* 104; *102:* 131; *161:* 105, 106
Krupp, Robin Rector *53:* 96, 98
Krush, Beth *1:* 51, 85; *2:* 233; *4:* 115; *9:* 61; *10:* 191; *11:* 196; *18:* 164, 165; *32:* 72; *37:* 203; *43:* 57; *60:* 102, 103, 107, 108, 109
Krush, Joe *2:* 233; *4:* 115; *9:* 61; *10:* 191; *11:* 196; *18:* 164, 165; *32:* 72, 91; *37:* 203; *43:* 57; *60:* 102, 103, 107, 108, 109
Krych, Duane *91:* 43
Krykorka, Vladyana *96:* 147; *143:* 90, 91; *168:* 14
Kubick, Dana *165:* 91; *212:* 104, 105, 212
Kubinyi, Laszlo *4:* 116; *6:* 113; *16:* 118; *17:* 100; *28:* 227; *30:* 172; *49:* 24, 28; *54:* 23; *167:* 149
Kubricht, Mary *73:* 118
Kucharik, Elena *139:* 31
Kuchera, Kathleen *84:* 5
Kuhn, Bob *17:* 91; *35:* 235
Kulikov, Boris *163:* 185; *185:* 23; *205:* 99, 100; *217:* 160
Kulka, Joe *188:* 110
Kukalis, Romas *90:* 27; *139:* 37
Kuklin, Susan *63:* 82, 83, 84

Kunhardt, Dorothy *53:* 101
Kunhardt, Edith *67:* 105, 106
Kunstler, Mort *10:* 73; *32:* 143
Kurchevsky, V. *34:* 61
Kurczok, Belinda *121:* 118
Kurelek, William *8:* 107
Kuriloff, Ron *13:* 19
Kurisu, Jane *160:* 120
Kurilla, Renée *231:* 117
Kuskin, Karla *2:* 170; *68:* 115, 116; *111:* 116
Kutzer, Ernst *19:* 249
Kuzma, Steve *57:* 8; *62:* 93
Kuznetsova, Berta *74:* 45
Kvasnosky, Laura McGee *93:* 103; *142:* 83; *182:* 108
Kwas, Susan Estelle *179:* 116; *217:* 90
Kyong, Yunmee *165:* 139

L

LaBlanc, Andre *24:* 146
Laboccetta, Mario *27:* 120
LaBrose, Darcie *157:* 134
Labrosse, Darcia *58:* 88; *108:* 77; *178:* 89
LaCava, Vince *95:* 118
Laceky, Adam *32:* 121
Lacis, Astra *85:* 117
Lacome, Julie *174:* 96, 97
La Croix *YABC 2:* 4
Ladd, London *206:* 50
Ladwig, Tim *98:* 212; *117:* 76; *215:* 32; *223:* 111, 112
La Farge, Margaret *47:* 141
LaFave, Kim *64:* 177; *72:* 39; *97:* 146; *99:* 172; *106:* 123; *149:* 126; *196:* 128, 129
Lafontaine, Roger *167:* 158
Lafrance, Marie *197:* 109
Lagarrigue, Jerome *136:* 102; *187:* 81
Laimgruber, Monika *11:* 153
Laínez, René Colato *226:* 50
Laio, Jimmy *213:* 57
Laite, Gordon *1:* 130, 131; *8:* 209; *31:* 113; *40:* 63; *46:* 117
Laliberté, Louise-Andrée *169:* 98
LaMarche, Jim *46:* 204; *61:* 56; *94:* 69; *114:* 22; *129:* 163; *162:* 78, 80
Lamb, Jim *10:* 117
Lambase, Barbara *101:* 185; *150:* 221; *166:* 234
Lambert, J.K. *38:* 129; *39:* 24
Lambert, Sally Anne *133:* 191
Lambert, Saul *23:* 112; *33:* 107; *54:* 136
Lambert, Stephen *109:* 33; *174:* 99
Lambo, Don *6:* 156; *35:* 115; *36:* 146
Lamontagne, Jacques *166:* 227
Lamut, Sonja *57:* 193
Lamut, Sonya *85:* 102
Landa, Peter *11:* 95; *13:* 177; *53:* 119
Landau, Jacob *38:* 111
Landon, Lucinda *79:* 31
Landshoff, Ursula *13:* 124
Landström, Lena *146:* 165, 166
Landström, Olof *146:* 166, 168; *170:* 22
Lane, Daniel *112:* 60
Lane, John R. *8:* 145
Lane, John *15:* 176, 177; *30:* 146
Lane, Nancy *166:* 74
Lang, G.D. *48:* 56
Lang, Gary *73:* 75
Lang, Glenna *221:* 113
Lang, Jerry *18:* 295
Langdon, Bryan *186:* 187; *191:* 113, 114, 115
Lange, Dorothea *50:* 141
Langley, Jonathan *162:* 128
Langner, Nola *8:* 110; *42:* 36
Lanino, Deborah *105:* 148
Lantz, Paul *1:* 82, 102; *27:* 88; *34:* 102; *45:* 123

Larkin, Bob *84:* 225
Laroche, Giles *126:* 140; *146:* 81; *221:* 116, 117
LaRochelle, David *171:* 97
Larrañaga, Ana Martín *229:* 106
Larrecq, John *44:* 108; *68:* 56
Larsen, Suzanne *1:* 13
Larson, Gary *57:* 121, 122, 123, 124, 125, 126, 127
Larsson, Carl *35:* 144, 145, 146, 147, 148, 149, 150, 152, 153, 154
Larsson, Karl *19:* 177
Lartitegui, Ana G. *105:* 167
LaRue, Jenna *167:* 20
La Rue, Michael D. *13:* 215
Lasker, Joe *7:* 186, 187; *14:* 55; *38:* 115; *39:* 47; *83:* 113, 114, 115
Latham, Barbara *16:* 188, 189; *43:* 71
Lathrop, Dorothy *14:* 117, 118, 119; *15:* 109; *16:* 78, 79, 81; *32:* 201, 203; *33:* 112; *YABC 2:* 301
Lattimore, Eleanor Frances *7:* 156
Lauden, Claire *16:* 173
Lauden, George, Jr. *16:* 173
Laune, Paul *2:* 235; *34:* 31
Laure, Jason *49:* 53; *50:* 122
Lauter, Richard *63:* 29; *67:* 111; *77:* 198
Lavallee, Barbara *74:* 157; *92:* 154; *96:* 126; *145:* 193; *166:* 125, 126; *186:* 155; *192:* 172; *231:* 165
Lave, Fitz Hugh *59:* 139
Lavis, Steve *43:* 143; *87:* 137, 164, 165; *222:* 161; *225:* 121
Layton, Neal *152:* 120, 121; *182:* 65; *187:* 103, 105, 106
Law, Jenny *201:* 31
Lawrason, June *168:* 30
Lawrence, John *25:* 131; *30:* 141; *44:* 198, 200; *214:* 7
Lawrence, Stephen *20:* 195
Lawson, Carol *6:* 38; *42:* 93, 131; *174:* 56; *189:* 89; *209:* 59
Lawson, George *17:* 280
Lawson, Robert *5:* 26; *6:* 94; *13:* 39; *16:* 11; *20:* 100, 102, 103; *54:* 3; *66:* 12; *100:* 144, 145; *YABC 2:* 222, 224, 225, 227, 228, 229, 230, 231, 232, 233, 234, 235, 237, 238, 239, 240, 241
Layfield, Kathie *60:* 194
Lazare, Jerry *44:* 109; *74:* 28
Lazarevich, Mila *17:* 118
Lazarus, Claire *103:* 30
Lazarus, Keo Felker *21:* 94
Lazzaro, Victor *11:* 126
Lea, Bob *166:* 208; *203:* 108
Lea, Tom *43:* 72, 74
Leacroft, Richard *6:* 140
Leaf, Munro *20:* 99
Leake, Donald *70:* 41
Leander, Patricia *23:* 27
Lear, Edward *18:* 183, 184, 185
Lear, Rebecca *149:* 46
Lebenson, Richard *6:* 209; *7:* 76; *23:* 145; *44:* 191; *87:* 153
Le Cain, Errol *6:* 141; *9:* 3; *22:* 142; *25:* 198; *28:* 173; *68:* 128, 129; *86:* 49
Lechon, Daniel *113:* 211
Leder, Dora *129:* 172
Ledger, Bill *181:* 58
Leduc, Bernard *102:* 36
Lee, Alan *62:* 25, 28
Lee, Bryce *99:* 60; *101:* 195; *196:* 53
Lee, Chinlun *181:* 138; *182:* 112
Lee, Declan *191:* 20
Lee, Dom *83:* 118, 120; *93:* 123; *121:* 121, 126; *146:* 174, 175, 206, 207; *174:* 204
Lee, Doris *13:* 246; *32:* 183; *44:* 111
Lee, Hector Viveros *115:* 96
Lee, Ho Baek *200:* 160
Lee, Huy Voun *217:* 106
Lee, Jeanne M. *158:* 56

Lee, Jared *93:* 200; *157:* 229; *215:* 113, 191, 192, 193; *228:* 177
Lee, Jody *81:* 121; *82:* 225; *91:* 155; *100:* 182
Lee, Jody A. *127:* 124, 126, 127
See also Lee, Jody
Lee, Manning de V. *2:* 200; *17:* 12; *27:* 87; *37:* 102, 103, 104; *YABC 2:* 304
Lee, Margaret *213:* 179
Lee, Marie G. *138:* 157
Lee, Paul *97:* 100; *105:* 72, 209; *109:* 177; *128:* 113; *202:* 45
Lee, Robert J. *3:* 97; *67:* 124
Lee, Victor *96:* 228; *105:* 182; *140:* 196; *208:* 191
Lee, Virginia *208:* 139, 140; *218:* 28
Leech, Dorothy *98:* 76
Leech, John *15:* 59
Leedy, Loreen *84:* 142; *128:* 144, 145, 146; *175:* 125, 126, 127
Leeman, Michael *44:* 157
Leeming, Catherine *87:* 39
Lees, Harry *6:* 112
LeFever, Bill *88:* 220, 221
Legenisel *47:* 111
Legrand, Edy *18:* 89, 93
Lehman, Barbara *73:* 123; *170:* 130
Lehrman, Rosalie *2:* 180
Leichman, Seymour *5:* 107
Leick, Bonnie *205:* 104
Leighton, Clare *25:* 130; *33:* 168; *37:* 105, 106, 108,109
Leisk, David *1:* 140, 141; *11:* 54; *30:* 137, 142, 143,144
Leister, Bryan *89:* 45; *106:* 37; *114:* 67; *149:* 236; *222:* 181
Leloir, Maurice *18:* 77, 80, 83, 99
Lemaître, Pascal *144:* 175; *176:* 130; *189:* 135; *225:* 124, 125
Lemieux, Michele *100:* 148; *139:* 153
Lemke, Horst *14:* 98; *38:* 117, 118, 119
Lemke, R.W. *42:* 162
Lemon, David Gwynne *9:* 1
LeMoult, Adolph *82:* 116
Lenn, Michael *136:* 89
Lennon, John *114:* 100
Lennox, Elsie *95:* 163; *143:* 160
Lenski, Lois *1:* 144; *26:* 135, 137, 139, 141; *100:* 153, 154
Lent, Blair *1:* 116, 117; *2:* 174; *3:* 206, 207; *7:* 168, 169; *34:* 62; *68:* 217; *133:* 101; *183:* 60
Leon, Jana *226:* 214
Leonard, David *212:* 149
Leonard, Richard *91:* 128
Leonard, Tom *207:* 95; *219:* 55
Leone, Leonard *49:* 190
Lerner, Carol *86:* 140, 141, 142
Lerner, Judith *116:* 138
Lerner, Sharon *11:* 157; *22:* 56
Leroux-Hugon, Helene *132:* 139
Leslie, Cecil *19:* 244
Lessac, Frané *80:* 182, 207; *96:* 182; *202:* 58; *209:* 104
Lessing, Erich *167:* 52; *173:* 60
Lester, Alison *50:* 124; *90:* 147, 148; *129:* 130; *218:* 91, 93
Lester, Mike *208:* 50
Lethcoe, Jason *191:* 116, 117
Le Tord, Bijou *49:* 156; *95:* 112
Leutz, Emanuel *165:* 27
Levai, Blaise *39:* 130
Levert, Mireille *211:* 101
Levin, Ted *12:* 148
Levine, David *43:* 147, 149, 150, 151, 152; *64:* 11
Levine, Joe *71:* 88; *219:* 74
Levine, Marge *81:* 127
Levinson, David *178:* 232
Levit, Herschel *24:* 223
Levstek, Ljuba *131:* 192; *134:* 216; *149:* 65; *168:* 180

Levy, Jessica Ann *19:* 225; *39:* 191
Levy, Lina *117:* 126
Lewin, Betsy *32:* 114; *48:* 177; *90:* 151; *91:*
    125; *92:* 85; *115:* 105; *169:* 110, 111; *178:*
    47; *186:* 188; *194:* 201; *222:* 120; *226:* 139
Lewin, Ted *4:* 77; *8:* 168; *20:* 110; *21:* 99,100;
    27: 110; 28; 96, 97; *31:* 49; *45:* 55; *48:* 223;
    60: 20, 119, 120; *62:* 139; *66:* 108; *71:* 12;
    72: 21; *74:* 226; *76:* 139, 140; *77:* 82; *79:*
    87; *85:* 49, 177; *86:* 55; *88:* 182; *93:* 28, 29;
    94: 34, 182, 194; *99:* 156; *104:* 8; *115:* 123;
    118: 74; *119:* 114, 116; *131:* 54; *145:* 99;
    165: 151; *177:* 75; *178:* 42; *190:* 30; *192:*
    86; *195:* 101, 102; *203:* 52; *222:* 119; *226:*
    136, 137, 138, 139
Lewis, Allen *15:* 112
Lewis, Anthony *227:* 114
Lewis, E.B. *88:* 143; *93:* 109; *119:* 79; *124:*
    113; *128:* 49; *151:* 167; *168:* 110; *173:* 121;
    174: 66; *176:* 7; *184:* 150; *185:* 191; *211:*
    108, 109, 110, 111; *223:* 17
Lewis, H.B. *170:* 124
Lewis, J. Patrick *162:* 83
Lewis, Jan *81:* 22
Lewis, Kim *136:* 165; *217:* 109, 111
Lewis, Richard W. *52:* 25
Lewis, Robin Baird *98:* 193
Lew-Vriethoff, Joanne *225:* 181
Leydon, Rita Floden *21:* 101
Li, Xiojun *187:* 172
Liao, Jimmy *202:* 100
Lichtenheld, Tom *152:* 125, 126; *222:* 160;
    224: 9
Lieblich, Irene *22:* 173; *27:* 209, 214
Lieder, Rick *108:* 197; *199:* 58, 59, 60
Lies, Brian *92:* 40; *141:* 101; *150:* 138; *190:*
    97, 98, 99
Liese, Charles *4:* 222
Liew, Sonny *219:* 108
Life, Kay *79:* 49
Lifton, Robert Jay *66:* 154
Lightburn, Ron *86:* 153; *91:* 122
Lightfoot, Norman R. *45:* 47
Lignell, Lois *37:* 114
Lill, Debra *121:* 70
Lilly, Charles *8:* 73; *20:* 127; *48:* 53; *72:* 9,16;
    77: 98; *102:* 94
Lilly, Ken *37:* 224
Lim, John *43:* 153
Limona, Mercedes *51:* 183
Lin, Grace *143:* 217; *162:* 86, 87; *174:* 185
Lincoln, Patricia Henderson *27:* 27; *78:* 127
Lindahn, Ron *84:* 17
Lindahn, Val *84:* 17
Lindberg, Howard *10:* 123; *16:* 190
Lindberg, Jeffrey *64:* 77; *77:* 71; *79:* 54; *80:*
    149; *174:* 109; *179:* 52
Linden, Seymour *18:* 200, 201; *43:* 140
Lindenbaum, Pija *144:* 143; *183:* 113
Linder, Richard *27:* 119
Lindman, Maj *43:* 154
Lindsay, Norman *67:* 114
Lindsay, Vachel *40:* 118
Lindstrom, Jack *145:* 118
Line, Les *27:* 143
Linell
    See Smith, Linell
Lintern, Tom *228:* 101
Lionni, Leo *8:* 115; *72:* 159, 160, 161
Lipinsky, Lino *2:* 156; *22:* 175
Lippincott, Gary A. *70:* 35; *119:* 118; *220:*
    105, 106, 107
Lippman, Peter *8:* 31; *31:* 119, 120, 160
Lisi, Victoria *89:* 145
Lisker, Emily *169:* 114
Lisker, Sonia O. *16:* 274; *31:* 31; *44:* 113, 114
Lisowski, Gabriel *47:* 144; *49:* 157
Lissim, Simon *17:* 138
Little, Ed *89:* 145; *151:* 53
Little, Harold *16:* 72
Little, Mary E. *28:* 146

Littlewood, Karen *165:* 126; *211:* 112
Litty, Julie *111:* 63
Litzinger, Rosanne *151:* 101; *176:* 118; *196:*
    133, 134, 135; *208:* 129; *209:* 147
Liu, Lesley *143:* 72
Lively, Lorna *19:* 216
Livingston, Susan *95:* 22
Liwska, Renata *164:* 113; *199:* 25, 69; *220:* 79
Ljungkvist, Laura *180:* 120
Llerena, Carlos Antonio *19:* 181
Lloyd, Errol *11:* 39; *22:* 178
Lloyd, Megan *77:* 118; *80:* 113; *97:* 75; *117:*
    94, 95; *189:* 121, 122; *208:* 128; *211:* 72
Lloyd, Sam *183:* 116, 117
Lo, Beth *165:* 154
Lo, Koon-chiu *7:* 134
Loates, Glen *63:* 76
Lobel, Anita *6:* 87; *9:* 141; *18:* 248; *55:* 85,86,
    87, 88, 93, 104; *60:* 67; *78:* 263; *82:* 110;
    96: 157, 159; *101:* 84; *132:* 35; *162:* 93, 94
Lobel, Arnold *1:* 188, 189; *5:* 12; *6:* 147; *7:*
    167, 209; *18:* 190, 191; *25:* 39, 43; *27:* 40;
    29: 174; *52:* 127; *55:* 89, 91, 94, 95, 97, 98,
    99, 100, 101, 102,103, 105, 106; *60:* 18, 31;
    66: 181, 183; *75:* 57; *82:* 246; *136:* 146
Lobel, Gillian *190:* 21
Lobo, Jen *229:* 53
Locker, Thomas *109:* 134
Lodge, Bernard *107:* 125, 126; *153:* 93
Loeb, Jeph *153:* 177
Lodge, Jo *112:* 119
Loefgren, Ulf *3:* 108
Loescher, Ann *20:* 108
Loescher, Gil *20:* 108
Loew, David *93:* 184; *171:* 120; *211:* 187
Lofting, Hugh *15:* 182, 183; *100:* 161, 162
Lofts, Pamela *60:* 188
Loh, George *38:* 88
Lomberg, Jon *58:* 160
Lonette, Reisie *11:* 211; *12:* 168; *13:* 56; *36:*
    122; *43:* 155
Long, Ethan *168:* 146; *178:* 12; *182:* 120, 121;
    196: 124; *223:* 116, 117
Long, Laurel *162:* 135; *190:* 11; *203:* 113,
    114; *228:* 212
Long, Loren *99:* 176; *172:* 65; *182:* 78; *188:*
    114, 115
Long, Melinda *152:* 128
Long, Miles *115:* 174
Long, Sally *42:* 184
Long, Sylvia *74:* 168; *132:* 63; *179:* 134
Longoni, Eduardo *73:* 85
Longtemps, Ken *17:* 123; *29:* 221; *69:* 82
Looser, Heinz *YABC 2:* 208
Lopez, Loretta *190:* 100
López, Rafael *197:* 160; *198:* 85
Lopshire, Robert *6:* 149; *21:* 117; *34:* 166; *73:*
    13
Lord, John Vernon *21:* 104; *23:* 25; *51:* 22
Lorenz, Albert *40:* 146; *115:* 127
Lorenzen, Geoffrey *229:* 24
Loretta, Sister Mary *33:* 73
Lorraine, Walter H. *3:* 110; *4:* 123; *16:* 192;
    103: 119
Los, Marek *146:* 22; *193:* 23
Loss, Joan *11:* 163
Louderback, Walt *YABC 1:* 164
Loughridge, Stuart *214:* 131
Louis, Catherine *212:* 186
Lousada, Sandra *40:* 138
Louth, Jack *149:* 252; *151:* 191, 192
Love, Judy *173:* 43; *196:* 40
Lovelock, Brian *214:* 132, 197
Low, Joseph *14:* 124, 125; *18:* 68; *19:* 194;
    31: 166; *80:* 239
Low, William *62:* 175; *80:* 147; *112:* 194; *150:*
    202; *169:* 175; *177:* 110; *192:* 27
Lowe, Vicky *177:* 130
Lowenheim, Alfred *13:* 65, 66
Lowenstein, Sallie *116:* 90, 91
Lowery, Mike *227:* 115

Lowitz, Anson *17:* 124; *18:* 215
Lowrey, Jo *8:* 133
Loxton, Daniel *229:* 109
Lubach, Vanessa *142:* 152
Lubell, Winifred *1:* 207; *3:* 15; *6:* 151
Lubin, Leonard B. *19:* 224; *36:* 79, 80; *45:*
    128, 129,131, 132, 133, 134, 135, 136, 137,
    139, 140, 141; *70:* 95; *YABC2:* 96
Lucas, David *208:* 148
Lucht, Irmgard *82:* 145
Ludwig, Helen *33:* 144, 145
Luebs, Robin *212:* 109
Lufkin, Raymond *38:* 138; *44:* 48
Luhrs, Henry *7:* 123; *11:* 120
Lujan, Tonita *82:* 33
Lum, Bernice *230:* 70
Lupo, Dom *4:* 204
Lustig, Loretta *30:* 186; *46:* 134, 135, 136,
    137
Lutes, Jason *210:* 163
Luthardt, Kevin *172:* 125, 126; *217:* 2
Luxbacher, Irene *153:* 145; *219:* 112, 113
Luzak, Dennis *52:* 121; *99:* 142
Lydbury, Jane *82:* 98
Lydecker, Laura *21:* 113; *42:* 53
Lynch, Charles *16:* 33
Lynch, Marietta *29:* 137; *30:* 171
Lynch, P.J. *126:* 228; *129:* 110; *132:* 247; *183:*
    64; *207:* 184; *213:* 100, 101, 102
Lyne, Alison Davis *188:* 118, 198
Lyon, Carol *102:* 26
Lyon, Elinor *6:* 154
Lyon, Fred *14:* 16
Lyon, Lea *212:* 110
Lyon, Tammie *175:* 170
Lyons, Oren *8:* 193
Lyster, Michael *26:* 41

M

Maas, Dorothy *6:* 175
Maas, Julie *47:* 61
Macaulay, David *46:* 139, 140, 141, 142, 143,
    144, 145, 147, 149, 150; *72:* 167, 168, 169;
    137: 129, 130, 131, 132
MacCarthy, Patricia *69:* 141
Macdonald, Alister *21:* 55
Macdonald, Roberta *19:* 237; *52:* 164
MacDonald, Norman *13:* 99
MacDonald, Ross *201:* 103
MacDonald, Suse *54:* 41; *109* 138; *130:* 156;
    193: 106, 107, 109, 110
Mace, Varian *49:* 159
MacEachern, Stephen *206:* 2
Macguire, Robert Reid *18:* 67
Machetanz, Fredrick *34:* 147, 148
MacInnes, Ian *35:* 59
MacIntyre, Elisabeth *17:* 127, 128
Mack, Jeff *161:* 128; *194:* 119, 120; *219:* 67;
    225: 135
Mack, Stan *17:* 129; *96:* 33
Mackay, Donald *17:* 60
MacKaye, Arvia *32:* 119
Mackenzie, Robert *204:* 78
Mackenzie, Stuart *73:* 213
MacKenzie, Garry *33:* 159
Mackie, Clare *87:* 134
Mackinlay, Miguel *27:* 22
MacKinstry, Elizabeth *15:* 110; *42:* 139, 140,
    141, 142, 143,144, 145
MacLeod, Lee *91:* 167
Maclise, Daniel *YABC 2:* 257
Macnaughton, Tina *182:* 145; *218:* 106, 107
MacRae, Tom *181:* 112
Madden, Don *3:* 112, 113; *4:* 33, 108, 155; *7:*
    193; *78:* 12; *YABC 2:* 211
Maddison, Angela Mary *10:* 83
Madrid, Erwin *229:* 117

Madsen, Jim *146:* 259; *152:* 237; *184:* 106; *197:* 21; *202:* 103, 104

Maestro, Giulio *8:* 124; *12:* 17; *13:* 108; *25:* 182; *54:* 147; *59:* 114, 115, 116, 117, 118, 121, 123, 124, 125,126, 127; *68:* 37, 38; *106:* 129, 130, 131, 136, 137, 138

Maffia, Daniel *60:* 200

Maggio, Viqui *58:* 136, 181; *74:* 150; *75:* 90; *85:* 159; *90:* 158; *109:* 184; *193:* 113

Magnus, Erica *77:* 123

Magnuson, Diana *28:* 102; *34:* 190; *41:* 175

Magoon, Scott *181:* 104; *217:* 165; *222:* 126

Magovern, Peg *103:* 123; *218:* 164

Maguire, Sheila *41:* 100

Magurn, Susan *91:* 30

Mahony, Will *37:* 120

Mahony, Will *85:* 116

Mahood, Kenneth *24:* 141

Mahurin, Matt *164:* 225; *175:* 95; *189:* 37; *196:* 14; *209:* 163; *229:* 179

Maik, Henri *9:* 102

Maione, Heather *106:* 5; *178:* 8; *189:* 126, 127; *193:* 58

Maisto, Carol *29:* 87

Maitland, Antony *1:* 100, 176; *8:* 41; *17:* 246; *24:* 46; *25:* 177, 178; *32:* 74; *60:* 65, 195; *67:* 156; *87:* 131; *101:* 110

Majewski, Dawn W. *169:* 95

Mak, Kam *72:* 25; *75:* 43; *87:* 186; *97:* 24; *102:* 154; *149:* 195; *186:* 28; *209:* 132

Makie, Pam *37:* 117

Maktima, Joe *116:* 191

Maland, Nick *99:* 77

Male, Alan *132:* 64

Malone, James Hiram *84:* 161

Malone, Nola Langner *82:* 239

Malone, Peter *191:* 121, 122, 123

Malsberg, Edward *51:* 175

Malvern, Corinne *2:* 13; *34:* 148, 149

Manchess, Gregory *165:* 241; *203:* 119

Mancusi, Stephen *63:* 198, 199

Mandelbaum, Ira *31:* 115

Manders, John *138:* 152, 155; *188:* 171; *190:* 92; *199:* 5; *217:* 52; *219:* 35; *219:* 115, 116, 117

Mandine, Selma *228:* 103

Manet, Edouard *23:* 170

Mangiat, Jeff *173:* 127

Mangurian, David *14:* 133

Manham, Allan *42:* 109; *77:* 180; *80:* 227

Manley, Matt *103:* 167; *117:* 98; *172:* 49; *212:* 207

Manna, Giovanni *178:* 44

Manniche, Lise *31:* 121

Manning, Jane *96:* 203

Manning, Jo *63:* 154

Manning, Lawrence *191:* 153

Manning, Maurie J. *211:* 116

Manning, Mick *176:* 139; *224:* 57

Manning, Samuel F. *5:* 75

Mantel, Richard *57:* 73; *63:* 106; *82:* 255

Mantha, John *205:* 164; *217:* 117

Maraja *15:* 86; *YABC 1:* 28; *2:* 115

Marcellino, Fred *20:* 125; *34:* 222; *53:* 125; *58:* 205; *61:* 64, 121, 122; *68:* 154, 156, 157, 158, 159; *72:* 25; *86:* 184; *98:* 181; *118:* 129, 130, 131; *149:* 218; *194:* 7

Marchesi, Stephen *34:* 140; *46:* 72; *50:* 147; *66:* 239; *70:* 33; *73:* 18, 114, 163; *77:* 47, 76,147; *78:* 79; *80:* 30; *81:* 6; *89:* 66; *93:* 21,130; *94:* 94; *97:* 66; *98:* 96; *114:* 115, 116

Marchiori, Carlos *14:* 60

Marciano, John Bemelmans *118:* 133; *167:* 110, 111, 112

Marconi, Guilherme *220:* 143

Marcus, Barry David *139:* 248; *145:* 18

Maren, Julie *199:* 73

Margules, Gabriele *21:* 120

Mariana
    See Foster, Marian Curtis

Mariano, Michael *52:* 108

Marino, Dorothy *6:* 37; *14:* 135

Mario, Heide Stetson *101:* 202

Maris, Ron *71:* 123

Maritz, Nicolaas *85:* 123

Mark, Mona *65:* 105; *68:* 205; *116:* 213

Markham, R.L. *17:* 240

Marklew, Gilly *211:* 118

Marks, Alan *104:* 104; *109:* 182; *164:* 92; *185:* 134; *187:* 120, 121, 122; *218:* 114, 115; *230:* 165

Marks, Cara *54:* 9

Marks, Colin *203:* 129

Marokvia, Artur *31:* 122

Marquez, Susan *108:* 121; *219:* 95

Marrella, Maria Pia *62:* 116

Marriott, Pat *30:* 30; *34:* 39; *35:* 164, 165, 166; *44:* 170; *48:* 186, 187, 188, 189, 191, 192, 193; *91:* 92

Mars, W.T. *1:* 161; *3:* 115; *4:* 208, 225; *5:* 92, 105, 186; *8:* 214; *9:* 12; *13:* 121; *27:* 151; *31:* 180; *38:* 102; *48:* 66; *62:* 164, 165; *64:* 62; *68:* 229; *79:* 55

Marschall, Ken *85:* 29

Marsh, Christine *3:* 164

Marsh, James *73:* 137

Marsh, Reginald *17:* 5; *19:* 89; *22:* 90, 96

Marshall, Anthony D. *18:* 216

Marshall, Felicia *170:* 190

Marshall, James *6:* 160; *40:* 221; *42:* 24, 25, 29; *51:* 111, 112, 113, 114, 115, 116, 117, 118, 119, 120, 121; *64:* 13; *75:* 126, 127, 128, 129; *102:* 10, 12; *216:* 26, 28

Marshall, Janet *97:* 154

Marstall, Bob *55:* 145; *84:* 153, 170; *104:* 145; *154:* 166, 167, 168

Martchenko, Michael *50:* 129, 153, 155, 156, 157; *83:* 144,145; *154:* 137, 138, 139

Marten, Ruth *129:* 52

Martin, Brad *199:* 186

Martin, Charles E. *70:* 144

Martin, Courtney A. *214:* 28

Martin, David Stone *24:* 232; *62:* 4

Martin, Fletcher *18:* 213; *23:* 151

Martin, Rene *7:* 144; *42:* 148, 149, 150

Martin, Richard E. *51:* 157; *131:* 203

Martin, Ron *32:* 81

Martin, Stefan *8:* 68; *32:* 124, 126; *56:* 33

Martin, Whitney *166:* 137

Martinez, Ed *58:* 192; *72:* 231; *77:* 33; *80:* 214; *167:* 123

Martinez, John *6:* 113; *118:* 13; *139:* 143

Martinez, Sergio *158:* 190; *220:* 156

Martini, Angela *183:* 161; *226:* 195

Martiniere, Stephan *171:* 130

Marton, Jirina *95:* 127, 128; *144:* 145; *230:* 73, 74, 75

Martorell, Antonio *84:* 6; *97:* 161

Martucci, Griesbach *52:* 106

Marvin, Frederic *83:* 86

Marx, Robert F. *24:* 143

Marzollo, Jean *190:* 127

Masefield, Judith *19:* 208, 209

Masheris, Robert *78:* 51

Masiello, Ralph *186:* 171; *214:* 134

Mason, George F. *14:* 139

Mason, Robert *84:* 96

Masse, Josée *208:* 45; *217:* 19; *221:* 134

Massey, Barbara *68:* 142

Massie, Diane Redfield *16:* 194

Massie, Kim *31:* 43

Massini, Sarah *213:* 79

Mataya, David *121:* 66

Mathers, Petra *119:* 135; *163:* 104; *176:* 143, 144; *187:* 142; *196:* 101

Mathewuse, James *51:* 143

Mathieu, Joseph *14:* 33; *39:* 206; *43:* 167; *56:* 180; *79:* 126; *94:* 147; *185:* 140

Matje, Martin *169:* 177, 178; *172:* 180

Matsubara, Naoko *12:* 121

Matsuda, Shizu *13:* 167

Matsuoka, Mei *192:* 135; *214:* 84

Matte, L'Enc *22:* 183

Mattelson, Marvin *36:* 50, 51

Mattheson, Jenny *180:* 132; *222:* 153

Matthews, Elizabeth *194:* 128; *223:* 35

Matthews, F. Leslie *4:* 216

Matthews, Tina *190:* 130

Mattingly, David *71:* 76, 77; *82:* 64; *91:* 216, 217; *109:* 25

Matulay, Laszlo *5:* 18; *43:* 168

Matus, Greta *12:* 142

Maughan, Bill *181:* 31; *211:* 211

Mauldin, Bill *27:* 23

Mauterer, Erin Marie *119:* 5

Mawicke, Tran *9:* 137; *15:* 191; *47:* 100

Mawson, Matt *74:* 115

Max, Peter *45:* 146, 147, 148, 149, 150

Maxie, Betty *40:* 135

Maxwell, John Alan *1:* 148

May, Katie *225:* 128

May, Steve *204:* 30

Mayan, Earl *7:* 193

Maydak, Michael S. *220:* 117

Mayer, Bill *200:* 138

Mayer, Danuta *117:* 103

Mayer, Marianna *32:* 132

Mayer, Mercer *11:* 192; *16:* 195, 196; *20:* 55, 57; *32:* 129, 130, 132, 133, 134; *41:* 144, 248, 252; *58:* 186; *73:* 140, 142, 143; *137:* 137, 138

Mayforth, Hal *166:* 77

Mayhew, James *85:* 121; *138:* 187; *149:* 140; *204:* 81

Mayhew, Richard *3:* 106

Mayo, Gretchen Will *38:* 81; *84:* 166

Mays, Victor *5:* 127; *8:* 45, 153; *14:* 245; *23:* 50; *34:* 155; *40:* 79; *45:* 158; *54:* 91; *66:* 240

Mazal, Chanan *49:* 104

Maze, Deborah *71:* 83

Mazellan, Ron *75:* 97, 98; *210:* 169

Mazetti, Alan *112:* 72

Mazille, Capucine *96:* 168

Mazza, Adriana Saviozzi *19:* 215

Mazzella, Mary Jo *82:* 165

Mazzetti, Alan *45:* 210

McAfee, Steve *135:* 146; *167:* 176; *191:* 84; *210:* 117; *218:* 34

McAlinden, Paul *112:* 128

McBride, Angus *28:* 49; *103:* 40

McBride, Will *30:* 110

McCaffery, Janet *38:* 145

McCall, Bruce *209:* 119

McCallum, Graham *78:* 78

McCallum, Stephen *141:* 143; *156:* 5; *166:* 228

McCann, Gerald *3:* 50; *4:* 94; *7:* 54; *41:* 121

McCarthy, Dan *174:* 74

McCarthy, Linda *177:* 128; *218:* 104

McCarthy, Meghan *168:* 134; *199:* 74

McCauley, Adam *157:* 36; *184:* 199; *193:* 100; *209:* 122

McCay, Winsor *41:* 124, 126, 128, 129, 130, 131; *134:* 77, 79

McClary, Nelson *1:* 111

McClements, George *196:* 146

McClennan, Connie *210:* 181

McClintock, Barbara *57:* 135; *95:* 130; *146:* 190; *213:* 3, 5, 107, 108

McClintock, Theodore *14:* 141

McCloskey, Robert *1:* 184, 185; *2:* 186, 187; *17:* 209; *39:* 139, 140, 141, 142, 143, 146, 147, 148; *85:* 150, 151; *100:* 172, 173, 174

McClung, Robert *2:* 189; *68:* 166, 167

McClure, Gillian *31:* 132; *150:* 53

McClure, Nikki *218:* 120

McConnel, Jerry *31:* 75, 187

McConnell, Mary *102:* 49

McCord, Kathleen Garry *78:* 236

McCormack, John *66:* 193

McCormick, A.D. *35:* 119

McCormick, Dell J. *19:* 216
McCoy, Glenn *212:* 132
McCrady, Lady *16:* 198; *39:* 127
McCrea, James *3:* 122; *33:* 216
McCrea, Ruth *3:* 122; *27:* 102; *33:* 216
McCue, Lisa *65:* 148, 149; *77:* 54; *80:* 132;
    175: 33; *177:* 133, 135; *212:* 136, 137, 138
McCully, Emily Arnold *2:* 89; *4:* 120, 121,
    146, 197; *5:* 2, 129; *7:* 191; *11:* 122; *15:*
    210; *33:* 23; *35:* 244; *37:* 122; *39:* 88; *40:*
    103; *50:* 30,31, 32, 33, 34, 35, 36, 37; *52:*
    89, 90; *57:* 6; *62:* 3; *70:* 195; *86:* 82; *96:*
    192; *97:* 93; *110:* 143,144; *117:* 47; *167:* 96;
    210: 175, 176; *225:* 179; *231:* 157
McCurdy, Michael *13:* 153; *24:* 85; *81:* 160;
    82: 157, 158; *86:* 125; *97:* 92; *117:* 178;
    132: 6; *147:* 159, 160
McCusker, Paul *99:* 19
McDaniel, Jerry *132:* 135
McDaniel, Preston *160:* 206; *170:* 139
McDermott, Beverly Brodsky *11:* 180
McDermott, Gerald *16:* 201; *74:* 174, 175;
    163: 150, 151
McDermott, Mike *96:* 187
McDonald, Jill *13:* 155; *26:* 128
McDonald, Mercedes *169:* 118
McDonald, Ralph J. *5:* 123, 195
McDonnell, Flora *146:* 199, 200
McDonnell, Patrick *179:* 153, 154; *221:* 136,
    137, 138
McDonough, Don *10:* 163
McElligott, Matt *196:* 147
McElmurry, Jill *137:* 148; *163:* 141; *202:* 186
McElrath-Eslick, Lori *129:* 145; *142:* 21; *173:*
    123; *202:* 194; *204:* 88, 89
McEntee, Dorothy *37:* 124
McEwan, Keith *88:* 116; *165:* 122, 123
McEwen, Katharine *169:* 34
McFall, Christie *12:* 144
McFeely, Daniel *160:* 213
McGaw, Laurie *109:* 243; *143:* 216; *211:* 218
McGee, Barbara *6:* 165
McGee, Marni *163:* 153
McGillvray, Kim *158:* 171; *165:* 213; *186:*
    183; *190:* 175
McGinley-Nally, Sharon *131:* 19
McGinnis, Robert *110:* 113; *177:* 80
McGovern, Tara *98:* 171
McGraw, Sheila *83:* 146
McGregor, Barbara *200:* 155
McGregor, Malcolm *23:* 27
McGrory, Anik *193:* 120
McGuire, Robert *204:* 57; *209:* 86
McGuirk, Leslie *152:* 159
McHale, John *138:* 190
McHenry, E.B. *193:* 122
McHugh, Tom *23:* 64
McIntosh, Jon *42:* 56
McKay, Donald *2:* 118; *32:* 157; *45:* 151, 152
McKean, Dave *150:* 71; *174:* 156; *197:* 83,
    118; *229:* 45, 46
McKeating, Eileen *44:* 58
McKee, David *10:* 48; *21:* 9; *70:* 154, 155;
    107: 139, 140, 141; *134:* 218; *158:* 148, 149,
    150, 151; *228:* 171
McKee, Diana *109:* 185
McKelvey, Patrick *164:* 141
McKendry, Joe *170:* 136
McKeveny, Tom *164:* 60; *173:* 79
McKie, Roy *7:* 44
McKie, Todd *205:* 181
McKillip, Kathy *30:* 153
McKinney, Ena *26:* 39
McKinnon, James *136:* 75
McKowen, Scott *172:* 63; *202:* 49
McLachlan, Edward *5:* 89
McLaren, Chesley *133:* 53; *213:* 112; *219:* 31
McLaren, Kirsty *123:* 99; *124:* 226
Mclean, Andrew *113:* 117, 118, 120, 121; *172:*
    130, 131
Mclean, Janet *172:* 130

McLean, Meg *94:* 196
McLean, Sammis *32:* 197
McLean, Wilson *90:* 29; *113:* 195
McLoughlin, John C. *47:* 149
McLoughlin, Wayne *102:* 230; *134:* 178; *216:*
    196
McMahon, Robert *36:* 155; *69:* 169
McManus, Shawn *85:* 71
McMenemy, Sarah *156:* 139; *211:* 93; *224:*
    139; *226:* 152
McMillan, Bruce *22:* 184
McMullan, James *40:* 33; *67:* 172; *87:* 142;
    99: 63, 64; *189:* 133; *196:* 51
McMullen, Nigel *146:* 177
McNeely, Tom *162:* 55
McNaught, Harry *12:* 80; *32:* 136
McNaughton, Colin *39:* 149; *40:* 108; *92:* 144,
    145, 146; *134:* 104, 106; *211:* 122, 123, 124
McNicholas, Maureen *38:* 148
McNicholas, Shelagh *173:* 61; *191:* 125, 126
McPhail, David *14:* 105; *23:* 135; *37:* 217,
    218, 220,221; *47:* 151, 152, 153, 154, 155,
    156, 158, 159, 160, 162, 163, 164; *71:* 211;
    81: 139, 140, 142; *86:* 123; *132:* 150; *140:*
    129, 131, 132; *183:* 134, 135, 137; *189:* 132;
    219: 121, 122, 123, 124, 125; *231:* 158
McPhee, Richard B. *41:* 133
McPheeters, Neal *78:* 132; *86:* 90; *99:* 162;
    111: 141; *142:* 162; *231:* 146
McQuade, Jacqueline *124:* 223
McQueen, Lucinda *28:* 149; *41:* 249; *46:* 206;
    53: 103
McQuillan, Mary *153:* 97; *200:* 140
McVay, Tracy *11:* 68
McVicker, Charles *39:* 150
McWilliam, Howard *219:* 135
Mead, Ben Carlton *43:* 75
Meade, Holly *90:* 102; *94:* 101; *149:* 8; *151:*
    107
Mecray, John *33:* 62
Meddaugh, Susan *20:* 42; *29:* 143; *41:* 241;
    77: 50; *84:* 173, 174, 175, 176, 177, 178;
    125: 160, 161, 162; *176:* 148, 149, 150, 151
Meehan, Dennis B. *56:* 144
Meents, Len W. *73:* 147, 150
Meers, Tony *99:* 113
Meisel, Paul *98:* 137; *124:* 18; *162:* 180; *179:*
    16; *181:* 62; *194:* 154; *221:* 5; *224:* 100,
    101, 102, 133; *231:* 25
Melanson, Luc *149:* 229; *198:* 97, 98; *221:*
    166
Melendez, Francisco *72:* 180
Melling, David *202:* 199
Melnychuk, Monika *153:* 65
Melo, Esperança *196:* 90
Melo, John *16:* 285; *58:* 203
Meloni, Maria Teresa *98:* 62
Meltzer, Ericka
    See O'Rourke, Ericka
Menasco, Milton *43:* 85
Menchin, Scott *188:* 129
Mendelson, Steven T. *86:* 154
Mendelssohn, Felix *19:* 170
Mendola, Christopher *88:* 223
Meng, Heinz *13:* 158
Merian, Maria Sibylla *140:* 88
Mero, Lee *34:* 68
Merrell, David *205:* 3
Merrill, Frank T. *16:* 147; *19:* 71; *YABC 1:*
    226, 229,273
Merriman, Rachel *98:* 108; *114:* 122; *149:* 142
Merveille, David *200:* 142
Meryman, Hope *27:* 41
Meryweather, Jack *10:* 179
Meseldzija, Petar *168:* 97
Meserve, Jessica *184:* 137; *211:* 127
Messick, Dale *64:* 150, 151, 152
Meth, Harold *24:* 203
Meyer, Alex Eben *226:* 60
Meyer, Herbert *19:* 189
Meyer, Renate *6:* 170

Meyers, Bob *11:* 136
Meyers, Nancy *172:* 124
Meynell, Louis *37:* 76
Micale, Albert *2:* 65; *22:* 185
Miccuci, Charles *82:* 163; *144:* 150
Micich, Paul *164:* 163
Middleton, Charlotte *230:* 81
Middleton, Jeffrey *177:* 173; *222:* 157
Middleton, Joshua *208:* 146; *219:* 24
Middleton-Sandford, Betty *2:* 125
Mieke, Anne *45:* 74
Mighell, Patricia *43:* 134
Miglio, Paige *101:* 203; *151:* 223; *201:* 118,
    119; *204:* 162
Mikec, Larry *204:* 125
Mikolaycak, Charles *9:* 144; *12:* 101; *13:* 212;
    21: 121; *22:* 168; *30:* 187; *34:* 103, 150; *37:*
    183; *43:* 179; *44:* 90; *46:* 115, 118, 119; *49:*
    25; *78:* 121, 122, 205, 207; *81:* 4
Milelli, Pascal *129:* 66; *135:* 153; *187:* 45
Miles, Elizabeth *117:* 77
Miles, Jennifer *17:* 278
Milgrim, David *158:* 157; *187:* 125, 126, 128;
    223: 124, 125, 126, 127
Milhous, Katherine *15:* 193; *17:* 51
Millais, John E. *22:* 230, 231
Millar, H.R. *YABC 1:* 194, 195, 203
Millard, C.E. *28:* 186
Millard, Kerry *105:* 124; *204:* 93, 94
Miller, Don *15:* 195; *16:* 71; *20:* 106; *31:* 178
Miller, Edna *29:* 148
Miller, Edward *115:* 64; *183:* 140, 141; *218:*
    129, 130, 131
Miller, Frank J. *25:* 94
Miller, Grambs *18:* 38; *23:* 16
Miller, Ian *99:* 128
Miller, Jane *15:* 196
Miller, Marcia *13:* 233
Miller, Marilyn *1:* 87; *31:* 69; *33:* 157
Miller, Mitchell *28:* 183; *34:* 207
Miller, Phil *175:* 150
Miller, Shane *5:* 140
Miller, Virginia *81:* 206
Millman, Isaac *172:* 18
Mills, Elaine *72:* 181
Mills, Judith Christine *130:* 168, 169
Mills, Lauren *92:* 170
Mills, Yaroslava Surmach *35:* 169, 170; *46:*
    114
Millsap, Darrel *51:* 102
Milone, Karen *89:* 169; *222:* 149
Milord, Susan *147:* 163, 164; *200:* 144
Milot, René *226:* 127
Milton, Debbie *162:* 161
Mims, Ashley *170:* 51
Min, Willemien *222:* 62
Miner, Julia *98:* 69
Minor, Wendell *39:* 188; *52:* 87; *56:* 171; *58:*
    116; *62:* 56; *66:* 109; *74:* 93; *78:* 129; *94:*
    67; *117:* 12, 13; *124:* 84, 86; *136:* 121; *164:*
    168, 169; *170:* 71; *199:* 79, 80, 81, 82; *217:*
    63; *223:* 149; *226:* 90, 91, 92
Minter, Daniel *176:* 154; *179:* 177
Mirocha, Paul *81:* 133; *192:* 148; *194:* 36
Misako Rocks! *192:* 149, 150
Mitchell, Judith *109:* 117
Mitchell, Mark *91:* 208
Mitchell, Tracy *190:* 15
Mitgutsch, Ali *76:* 161
Mitsuhashi, Yoko *45:* 153
Miyake, Yoshi *38:* 141
Mizumura, Kazue *10:* 143; *18:* 223; *36:* 159
Mochi, Ugo *8:* 122; *38:* 150
Mock, Paul *55:* 83; *123:* 32
Modarressi, Mitra *90:* 236; *126:* 168; *173:*
    165, 166; *200:* 147, 148
Modell, Frank *39:* 152
Mogenson, Jan *74:* 183
Mohn, Susan *89:* 224
Mohr, Mark *133:* 201
Mohr, Nicholasa *8:* 139; *113:* 127

Molan, Christine *60:* 177; *84:* 183
Moldon, Peter L. *49:* 168
Molk, Laurel *92:* 150; *230:* 217, 219
Mollica, Gene *197:* 11
Momaday, N. Scott *48:* 159
Mombourquette, Paul *112:* 91; *126:* 142
Monk, Julie *165:* 231; *191:* 96
Monks, Lydia *189:* 136, 137
Monroe, Chris *219:* 133
Monroy, Manuel *199:* 192
Montgomery, Lucy *150:* 126
Montgomery, Michael G. *208:* 159
Montgomery-Higham, Amanda *169:* 131
Monteiel, David *201:* 95
Montiel, David *69:* 106; *84:* 145
Montijo, Rhode *193:* 164
Montresor, Beni *2:* 91; *3:* 138; *38:* 152, 153,
    154,155, 156, 157, 158, 159, 160; *68:* 63
Montserrat, Pep *128:* 135; *181:* 119; *184:* 53
Moon, Carl *25:* 183, 184, 185
Moon, Eliza *14:* 40
Moon, Ivan *22:* 39; *38:* 140
Moore, Adrienne *67:* 147
Moore, Agnes Kay Randall *43:* 187
Moore, Cyd *117:* 107, 108; *159:* 137, 138;
    186: 148, 149, 151; *203:* 15; *214:* 138, 139
Moore, Gustav *127:* 181, 182; *170:* 162, 163
Moore, Jackie *128:* 79
Moore, Janet *63:* 153
Moore, Margie *176:* 156; *221:* 125; *224:* 106,
    107
Moore, Mary *29:* 160
Moore, Patrick *184:* 121
Moore, Yvette *101:* 11, 12; *154:* 141
Mora, Giovanni *179:* 127; *184:* 11
Mora, Raul Mina *20:* 41
Moraes, Odilon *102:* 144
Morales, Magaly *225:* 137
Morales, Yuyi *154:* 144; *226:* 120
Moran, Rosslyn *111:* 26
Moran, Tom *60:* 100
Mordan, C.B. *193:* 115
Mordvinoff, Nicolas *15:* 179
Moreno, René King *169:* 59; *190:* 133, 209;
    212: 52
Morgan, Barbara *169:* 116
Morgan, Jacqui *58:* 57
Morgan, Mary *114:* 133, 134, 135; *123:* 11;
    213: 115, 116, 117
Morgan, Tom *42:* 157
Morgan, Pierr *173:* 148
Morgenstern, Michael *158:* 7, 57; *171:* 103;
    174: 60; *226:* 12
Morice, Dave *93:* 142
Morin, Paul *73:* 132; *79:* 130; *88:* 140; *137:*
    143
Moriuchi, Mique *177:* 203
Morozumi, Atsuko *110:* 155; *217:* 126, 127
Morrill, Leslie *18:* 218; *29:* 177; *33:* 84; *38:*
    147; *42:* 127; *44:* 93; *48:* 164, 165, 167,
    168, 169, 170,171; *49:* 162; *63:* 136, 180;
    70: 72; *71:* 70, 91,92; *72:* 228; *80:* 163, 164,
    165; *90:* 121; *121:* 88; *178:* 117
Morrill, Rowena A. *84:* 16; *98:* 163
Morris *47:* 91
Morris, Frank *55:* 133; *60:* 28; *76:* 2
Morris, Harry O. *119:* 138
Morris, Jackie *128:* 194; *144:* 119; *151:* 146;
    202: 126, 127; *204:* 83; *211:* 80; *214:* 163
Morris, Jennifer E. *179:* 157
Morris, Oradel Nolen *128:* 180
Morris, Tony *62:* 146; *70:* 97
Morrison, Bill *42:* 116; *66:* 170; *69:* 40
Morrison, Gordon *87:* 150; *113:* 93; *128:* 181,
    182; *183:* 144, 145, 146
Morrison, Frank *169:* 162; *205:* 156; *224:* 121;
    226: 154
Morrison, Taylor *159:* 144, 145; *187:* 131
Morrow, Gray *2:* 64; *5:* 200; *10:* 103, 114; *14:*
    175
Morse, Scott *200:* 149, 150

Morton, Lee Jack *32:* 140
Morton, Marian *3:* 185
Mosberg, Hilary *117:* 195; *118:* 164; *149:* 55
Moser, Barry *56:* 68, 117, 118, 119, 120, 121,
    122, 123, 124; *59:* 141; *60:* 160; *79:* 91,
    147, 149, 151, 152; *82:* 81; *90:* 118; *91:* 35;
    95: 210; *97:* 91, 93; *102:* 152; *126:* 4; *128:*
    175; *133:* 141; *138:* 167, 171, 174; *153:*
    205; *174:* 130; *185:* 152, 154; *195:* 163;
    204: 115; *209:* 201
Moser, Cara *90:* 118; *138:* 167
Moses, Grandma *18:* 228
Moses, Will *178:* 170, 171
Moskof, Martin Stephen *27:* 152
Mosley, Francis *57:* 144
Moss, Donald *11:* 184
Moss, Geoffrey *32:* 198
Moss, Marissa *71:* 130; *104:* 127; *163:* 156;
    216: 164, 165, 166
Most, Bernard *48:* 173; *91:* 142, 143; *134:* 120
Mourning, Tuesday *205:* 25; *220:* 68; *221:* 42
Mowll, Joshua *188:* 133
Mowry, Carmen *50:* 62
Moxley, Sheila *96:* 174; *169:* 26; *206:* 16
Moyers, William *21:* 65
Moyler, Alan *36:* 142
Mozley, Charles *9:* 87; *20:* 176, 192, 193; *22:*
    228; *25:* 205; *33:* 150; *43:* 170, 171, 172,
    173, 174; *YABC2:* 89
Mueller, Hans Alexander *26:* 64; *27:* 52, 53
Mugnaini, Joseph *11:* 35; *27:* 52, 53; *35:* 62
Mujica, Rick *72:* 67; *88:* 95; *111:* 53; *180:*
    185; *197:* 70
Mullen, Douglas *180:* 178
Muller, Robin *86:* 161
Muller, Steven *32:* 167
Muller, Jorg *35:* 215; *67:* 138, 139
Mulock, Julie *163:* 112
Mullins, Edward S. *10:* 101
Mullins, Patricia *51:* 68
Multer, Scott *80:* 108
Munari, Bruno *15:* 200
Munch, Edvard *140:* 143
Munowitz, Ken *14:* 148; *72:* 178, 179
Muñoz, Claudio *208:* 161
Munoz, William *42:* 160
Munro, Roxie *58:* 134; *136:* 177; *137:* 218;
    184: 133, 134; *223:* 130, 132, 133
Munsinger, Lynn *33:* 161; *46:* 126; *71:* 92; *82:*
    80; *89:* 218; *92:* 125; *94:* 157, 158, 159,
    160; *98:* 196; *103:* 198; *142:* 143; *145:* 133,
    134, 136; *153:* 203; *176:* 162; *177:* 140, 141,
    142; *189:* 113, 114, 116, 117; *201:* 42; *221:*
    148, 149,150
Munson, Russell *13:* 9
Munster, Sebastian *166:* 107
Munzar, Barbara *149:* 75
Murdocca, Salvatore *73:* 212; *98:* 132; *111:*
    168; *157:* 228; *164:* 257
Murphy, Bill *5:* 138; *130:* 170
Murphy, Jill *37:* 142; *70:* 166; *142:* 132, 134
Murphy, Kelly *130:* 212; *143:* 119; *176:* 158;
    190: 135
Murphy, Liz *210:* 183; *212:* 157
Murphy, Mary *196:* 158
Murphy, Tom *192:* 40
Murr, Karl *20:* 62
Murray, Joe *175:* 37
Murray, Ossie *43:* 176
Mussino, Attilio *29:* 131; *100:* 164
Mutchler, Dwight *1:* 25
Myers, Bernice *9:* 147; *36:* 75; *81:* 146, 147,
    148
Muth, Jon J. *165:* 169; *167:* 109; *190:* 227;
    193: 59; *228:* 206
Myers, Christopher *183:* 150; *193:* 139
Myers, Duane O. *99:* 145
Myers, Tim *147:* 168
Myers, V.G. *142:* 41
Myers, Lou *11:* 2

N

Na, Il Sung *231:* 136
Nachreiner, Tom *29:* 182
Nacht, Merle *65:* 49
Nadler, Ellis *88:* 91
Nagle, Shane *180:* 223
Nagy, Ian *195:* 64
Najaka, Marlies *62:* 101
Nakai, Michael *30:* 217; *54:* 29
Nakata, Hiroe *157:* 156; *162:* 30; *205:* 124,
    125
Nakatani, Chiyoko *12:* 124
Narahashi, Keiko *77:* 188; *82:* 213; *115:* 142,
    143, 144
Nascimbene, Yan *133:* 128; *173:* 132, 133
Nash, Lesa *87:* 135
Nash, Linell *46:* 175
Nash, Scott *130:* 36; *188:* 196; *224:* 180
Naso, John *33:* 183
Nason, Thomas W. *14:* 68
Nasser, Muriel *48:* 74
Nast, Thomas *21:* 29; *28:* 23; *51:* 132, 133,
    134, 135,136, 137, 138, 139, 141
Nasta, Vincent *78:* 185
Natale, Vincent *76:* 3; *78:* 125; *112:* 47; *166:*
    81; *174:* 189; *185:* 212; *197:* 59; *218:* 35
Natchev, Alexi *96:* 177
Nathan, Charlott *125:* 151
Nathan, Cheryl *150:* 104; *186:* 112
Natti, Susanna *20:* 146; *32:* 141, 142; *35:* 178;
    37: 143; *71:* 49; *93:* 98; *125:* 166, 168; *126:*
    228; *151:* 6; *178:* 8; *188:* 106; *231:* 10
Navarra, Celeste Scala *8:* 142
Naylor, Penelope *10:* 104
Nazz, James *72:* 8
Nebel, M. *45:* 154
Neebe, William *7:* 93
Needham, Dave *196:* 85
Needler, Jerry *12:* 93
Neel, Alice *31:* 23
Neely, Beth *119:* 184
Neely, Keith R. *46:* 124
Neff, Leland *78:* 74
Negri, Rocco *3:* 213; *5:* 67; *6:* 91, 108; *12:*
    159
Negrin, Fabian *174:* 125; *175:* 15; *223:* 91
Neidigh, Sherry *128:* 53; *204:* 101, 102, 103;
    222: 95
Neilan, Eujin Kim *180:* 241; *200:* 151, 152
Neill, John R. *18:* 8, 10, 11, 21, 30; *100:* 22
Neilsen, Cliff *158:* 131; *177:* 112, 121; *209:* 8;
    215: 150; *230:* 62
Neilsen, Terese *116:* 74
Nelson, Craig *62:* 151; 153; *183:* 86
Nelson, Gail White *68:* 140
Nelson, Jennifer *129:* 152; *199:* 132
Nelson, Kadir *151:* 185; *154:* 146, 147; *157:*
    189, 222; *181:* 122, 124; *197:* 155; *213:* 122,
    123, 124
Nelson, Melissa *224:* 87
Nelson, S.D. *131:* 34; *181:* 126, 127; *228:* 23
Ness, Evaline *1:* 164, 165; *2:* 39; *3:* 8; *10:*
    147; *12:* 53; *26:* 150, 151, 152, 153; *49:* 30,
    31, 32; *56:* 30; *60:* 113
Neubecker, Robert *170:* 143; *214:* 157
Neville, Vera *2:* 182
Nevins, Daniel *191:* 173
Nevwirth, Allan *79:* 168
Newberry, Clare Turlay *1:* 170
Newbold, Greg *108:* 125; *145:* 199; *151:* 23;
    193: 178; *197:* 10; *199:* 92, 93
Newfeld, Frank *14:* 121; *26:* 154
Newland, Gillian *220:* 132
Newman, Andy *149:* 61; *195:* 63
Newman, Ann *43:* 90
Newman, Barbara Johansen *191:* 137, 138;
    231: 13
Newsham, Ian *143:* 162

Newsom, Carol *40:* 159; *44:* 60; *47:* 189; *65:* 29; *70:* 192; *80:* 36; *85:* 137, 138; *92:* 167; *191:* 82
Newsom, Tom *49:* 149; *71:* 13, 62; *75:* 156; *91:* 113
Newton, Jill *83:* 105; *200:* 154
Nez, John *218:* 136
Ng, Michael *29:* 171
Ng, Simon *167:* 7
Ngui, Marc *229:* 50
Nguyen, Vincent *189:* 49; *226:* 160; *229:* 172
Nichols, Sandy *219:* 103
Nicholson, William *15:* 33, 34; *16:* 48
Nickens, Bessie *104:* 153
Nicklaus, Carol *45:* 194; *62:* 132, 133
Nickle, John *181:* 128
Nickless, Will *16:* 139
Nicholas, Corasue *154:* 20
Nicolas *17:* 130, 132, 133; *YABC 2:* 215
Niebrugge, Jane *6:* 118
Nielsen, Cliff *95:* 207, 208; *105:* 58; *114:* 112; *124:* 12; *125:* 91, 92; *132:* 224; *135:* 187; *136:* 40; *137:* 168; *145:* 54; *149:* 28; *158:* 129; *165:* 64, 158; *168:* 169; *170:* 6; *175:* 114, 116; *187:* 75, 76; *194:* 107; *197:* 172; *201:* 14; *208:* 192; *211:* 186; *216:* 215; *217:* 67; *224:* 61, 62; *230:* 21
Nielsen, Jon *6:* 100; *24:* 202
Nielsen, Kay *15:* 7; *16:* 211, 212, 213, 215, 217; *22:* 143; *YABC 1:* 32, 33
Niemann, Christoph *191:* 141
Nikola-Lisa, W. *180:* 180
Niland, Deborah *25:* 191; *27:* 156; *135:* 50; *172:* 143
Niland, Kilmeny *25:* 191; *75:* 143
Nino, Alex *59:* 145
Ninon *1:* 5; *38:* 101, 103, 108
Nissen, Rie *44:* 35
Nithael, Mark *158:* 237
Nivola, Claire A. *78:* 126; *140:* 147; *208:* 164
Nixon, K. *14:* 152
Nobati, Eugenia *194:* 118
Noble, Louise *61:* 170
Noble, Marty *97:* 168; *125:* 171
Noble, Trinka Hakes *39:* 162; *84:* 157
Nobles, Scott *226:* 159
Noda, Takayo *168:* 143
Noguchi, Yoshie *30:* 99
Nolan, Dennis *42:* 163; *67:* 163; *78:* 189; *82:* 225; *83:* 26; *92:* 169, 170; *103:* 166; *111:* 35; *112:* 213; *127:* 171; *166:* 161; *194:* 218
Noll, Sally *82:* 171
Nolte, Larry *121:* 63, 65
Nones, Eric Jon *61:* 111; *76:* 38; *77:* 177
Noonan, Daniel *100:* 224
Noonan, Julia *4:* 163; *7:* 207; *25:* 151; *91:* 29; *95:* 149; *231:* 163
Norcia, Ernie *108:* 155; *140:* 47
Nordenskjold, Birgitta *2:* 208
Noreika, Robert *173:* 20; *217:* 24
Norling, Beth *149:* 153, 154; *209:* 77
Norman, Elaine *77:* 72, 176; *94:* 35; *136:* 63; *178:* 42
Norman, Mary *36:* 138, 147
Norman, Michael *12:* 117; *27:* 168
Normandin, Luc *227:* 180
Northway, Jennifer *85:* 96
Nostlinger, Christiana *162:* 131
Novak, Linda *166:* 205
Novak, Matt *104:* 132, 133; *165:* 173, 174; *204:* 104, 106
Novelli, Luca *61:* 137
Novgorodoff, Danica *215:* 133
Nugent, Cynthia *106:* 189; *205:* 126, 127; *209:* 180
Numberman, Neil *220:* 133
Numeroff, Laura Joffe *28:* 161; *30:* 177
Nurse, Chris *164:* 91
Nussbaumer, Paul *16:* 219; *39:* 117
Nutt, Ken *72:* 69; *97:* 170

Nyce, Helene *19:* 219
Nygren, Tord *30:* 148; *127:* 164

O

Oakley, Graham *8:* 112; *30:* 164, 165; *84:* 188,189, 190, 191, 192
Oakley, Thornton *YABC 2:* 189
Oberheide, Heide *118:* 37
Obligado, Lilian *2:* 28, 66, 67; *6:* 30; *14:* 179; *15:* 103; *25:* 84; *61:* 138, 139, 140, 141, 143
Oblinski, Rafael *190:* 139
Obrant, Susan *11:* 186
O'Brien, Anne Sibley *53:* 116, 117; *155:* 115; *213:* 127; *224:* 71; *227:* 9
O'Brien, John *41:* 253; *72:* 12; *89:* 59, 60; *98:* 16; *161:* 185; *169:* 16; *180:* 196; *228:* 38
O'Brien, Patrick *193:* 142, 143, 144
O'Brien, Teresa *87:* 89
O'Brien, Tim *93:* 25; *136:* 94; *164:* 57; *169:* 57; *173:* 55; *175:* 86; *184:* 192; *191:* 134; *193:* 137; *210:* 159; *224:* 28, 29; *229:* 140
O'Clair, Dennis *127:* 25
O'Connor, George *183:* 153; *228:* 113, 114
Odell, Carole *35:* 47
Odem, Mel *99:* 164; *167:* 84, 87
O'Donohue, Thomas *40:* 89
Oechsli, Kelly *5:* 144, 145; *7:* 115; *8:* 83, 183; *13:* 117; *20:* 94; *81:* 199
Ofer, Avi *208:* 143
Offen, Hilda *42:* 207
Ogden, Bill *42:* 59; *47:* 55
Ogg, Oscar *33:* 34
Ogle, Nancy Gray *163:* 144
Ohi, Ruth *90:* 175, 177; *131:* 63; *135:* 106; *175:* 107; *179:* 55
Ohlsson, Ib *4:* 152; *7:* 57; *10:* 20; *11:* 90; *19:* 217; *41:* 246; *82:* 106; *92:* 213
Ohtomo, Yasuo *37:* 146; *39:* 212, 213
O'Keefe, Jennifer *136:* 184
O'Kelley, Mattie Lou *36:* 150
Olbinski, Rafal *149:* 27; *158:* 77; *203:* 36
Oldland, Nicholas *223:* 136
O'Leary, Chris *208:* 166
Olander, Johan *231:* 138
Oleynikov, Igor *202:* 134
Oliver, Isaac *171:* 182
Oliver, Jenni *23:* 121; *35:* 112
Oliver, Narelle *152:* 192; *197:* 129, 130
Oller, Erika *128:* 186; *134:* 126
Olschewski, Alfred *7:* 172
Olsen, Ib Spang *6:* 178, 179; *81:* 164
Olson, Alan *77:* 229
Olson-Brown, Ellen *183:* 154
Olugebefola, Ademola *15:* 205
O'Malley, Kevin *94:* 180; *106:* 8; *113:* 108; *136:* 70; *157:* 193; *191:* 146; *203:* 78; *217:* 84; *230:* 115, 117, 118
O'Neil, Dan IV *7:* 176
O'Neill, Catharine *72:* 113; *84:* 78; *134:* 153
O'Neill, Jean *22:* 146
O'Neill, Martin *187:* 39; *203:* 118
O'Neill, Michael J. *54:* 172
O'Neill, Rose *48:* 30, 31
O'Neill, Steve *21:* 118
Ono, Chiyo *7:* 97
Orbaan, Albert *2:* 31; *5:* 65, 171; *9:* 8; *14:* 241; *20:* 109
Orbach, Ruth *21:* 112
Orback, Craig *197:* 132
Orfe, Joan *20:* 81
Org, Ed *119:* 93
Ormai, Stella *72:* 129
Ormerod, Jan *55:* 124; *70:* 170, 171; *90:* 39; *132:* 172, 173, 174; *147:* 98
Ormsby, Virginia H. *11:* 187

O'Rourke, Ericka *108:* 216; *117:* 194; *111:* 142; *119:* 194; *137:* 152; *150:* 134; *167:* 64; *172:* 164; *188:* 163; *191:* 172; *201:* 15; *203:* 75; *209:* 130; *219:* 99
O'Rourke, Ericka Meltzer
    See O'Rourke, Ericka
Orozco, Jose Clemente *9:* 177
Orr, Forrest W. *23:* 9
Orr, N. *19:* 70
Ortiz, Vilma *88:* 158
Osborn, Kathy *152:* 232; *199:* 101, 102; *206:* 67
Osborn, Robert *65:* 49
Osborne, Billie Jean *35:* 209
Osmond, Edward *10:* 111
Ostow, David *223:* 138
O'Sullivan, Tom *3:* 176; *4:* 55; *78:* 195
Otani, June *124:* 42; *156:* 53
Otis, Rebecca *185:* 92
Ottley, Matt *147:* 221; *171:* 133
Otto, Svend *22:* 130, 141; *67:* 188, 189
Oudry, J.B. *18:* 167
Oughton, Taylor *5:* 23; *104:* 136
Overeng, Johannes *44:* 36
Overlie, George *11:* 156
Owens, Carl *2:* 35; *23:* 521
Owens, Gail *10:* 170; *12:* 157; *19:* 16; *22:* 70; *25:* 81; *28:* 203, 205; *32:* 221, 222; *36:* 132; *46:* 40; *47:* 57; *54:* 66, 67, 68, 69, 70, 71, 72, 73; *71:* 100; *73:* 64; *77:* 157; *80:* 32; *82:* 3; *99:* 226; *224:* 198
Owens, Mary Beth *113:* 202, 203; *191:* 148, 149
Owens, Nubia *84:* 74
Oxenbury, Helen *3:* 150, 151; *24:* 81; *68:* 174, 175,176; *81:* 209; *84:* 213, 245; *129:* 56; *149:* 159; *184:* 181; *224:* 147
Oz, Robin *88:* 167; *185:* 181

P

Padgett, Jim *12:* 165
Page, Gail *205:* 128
Page, Homer *14:* 145
Page, Mark *162:* 70
Paget, Sidney *24:* 90, 91, 93, 95, 97
Paget, Walter *64:* 122
Paillot, Jim *173:* 89
Pajouhesh, Noushin *160:* 121
Pak *12:* 76
Pak, Yu Cha *86:* 174
Paladino, Lance *134:* 30
Palazzo, Tony *3:* 152, 153
Palecek, Josef *56:* 136; *89:* 158
Palen, Debbie *135:* 88; *195:* 148, 149
Palencar, John Jude *84:* 12, 45; *85:* 87; *92:* 187; *99:* 128; *110:* 204; *150:* 122; *171:* 86; *207:* 36
Palin, Nicki *81:* 201; *89:* 161
Palisi, Heather *231:* 109
Palladini, David *4:* 113; *40:* 176, 177, 178, 179, 181,224, 225; *50:* 138; *78:* 186
Pallarito, Don *43:* 36
Palmer, Carol *158:* 230; *195:* 187
Palmer, Heidi *15:* 207; *29:* 102
Palmer, Jan *42:* 153; *82:* 161
Palmer, Judd *153:* 160, 161
Palmer, Juliette *6:* 89; *15:* 208
Palmer, Kate Salley *104:* 143; *154:* 169
Palmer, Lemuel *17:* 25, 29
Palmisciano, Diane *110:* 62; *162:* 26; *202:* 138, 139
Palmquist, Eric *38:* 133
Pamintuan, Macky *214:* 160
Panesis, Nicholas *3:* 127
Panter, Gary *182:* 191
Panton, Doug *52:* 99
Paparone, Pamela *129:* 174
Papas, William *11:* 223; *50:* 160

Papin, Joseph 26: 113
Papish, Robin Lloyd 10: 80
Papp, Robert 198: 41; 205: 130; 219: 53
Paradis, Susan 40: 216
Paraquin, Charles H. 18: 166
Pardo DeLange, Alex 179: 128; 211: 135, 136
Paris, Peter 31: 127
Parisi, Elizabeth B. 141: 82; 164: 57
Park, Nick 113: 143
Park, Seho 39: 110
Park, W.B. 22: 189
Parker, Ant 82: 87, 88; 104: 121
Parker, Buzz 227: 154
Parker, Jake 227: 134
Parker, Lewis 2: 179
Parker, Nancy Winslow 10: 113; 22: 164; 28: 47, 144; 52: 7; 69: 153; 91: 171, 174; 132: 175
Parker, Robert 4: 161; 5: 74; 9: 136; 29: 39
Parker, Robert Andrew 11: 81; 29: 186; 39: 165; 40: 25; 41: 78; 42: 123; 43: 144; 48: 182; 54: 140; 74: 141; 91: 24; 111: 115; 151: 201; 154: 156; 200: 163, 164; 211: 67
Parker-Rees, Guy 149: 145; 193: 149, 150
Parkin, Trevor 140: 151
Parkins, David 114: 123; 146: 176; 176: 168; 192: 107; 218: 139, 140, 141, 148; 224: 92
Parkinson, Kathy 71: 143; 144: 234
Parkinson, Keith 70: 66
Parks, Gordon, Jr. 33: 228
Parlato, Stephen 222: 137
Parnall, Peter 5: 137; 16: 221; 24: 70; 40: 78; 51: 130; 69: 17, 155; 136: 22, 23, 24
Parnall, Virginia 40: 78
Paros, Jennifer 210: 197
Parow, Lorraine 158: 127
Parr, Todd 134: 139, 140; 179: 163, 164, 165
Parra, John 225: 150
Parrish, Anne 27: 159, 160
Parrish, Dillwyn 27: 159
Parrish, Maxfield 14: 160, 161, 164, 165; 16: 109; 18: 12, 13; YABC 1: 149, 152, 267; 2: 146, 149
Parry, David 26: 156
Parry, Marian 13: 176; 19: 179
Parsons, Garry 197: 135
Partch, Virgil 45: 163, 165
Pascal, David 14: 174
Paschkis, Julie 177: 153, 154; 220: 140, 141; 231: 64
Pasquier, J.A. 16: 91
Pastel, Elyse 201: 123
Pasternak, Robert 119: 53
Paterson, Diane 13: 116; 39: 163; 59: 164, 165, 166,167; 72: 51, 53; 129: 175; 177: 156, 157
Paterson, Helen 16: 93
Patkau, Karen 112: 123
Paton, Jane 15: 271; 35: 176
Patricelli, Leslie 207: 129
Patrick, John 139: 190
Patrick, Pamela 90: 160; 93: 211; 105: 12
Patrick, Tom 190: 103
Patterson, Geoffrey 54: 75
Patterson, Robert 25: 118
Patti, Joyce 187: 145, 146
Patz, Nancy 111: 40; 154: 161; 214: 80
Paul, James 4: 130; 23: 161
Paul, Korky 102: 85
Paull, Grace 24: 157; 87: 127
Paulsen, Ruth Wright 79: 160, 164; 189: 146; 231: 150
Pavlov, Elena 80: 49
Payne, Adam S. 135: 166
Payne, C.F. 145: 138, 140; 179: 168
Payne, Joan Balfour 1: 118
Payne, Tom 170: 27
Payson, Dale 7: 34; 9: 151; 20: 140; 37: 22
Payzant, Charles 21: 147
Peacock, Phyllis Hornung 230: 124
Peacock, Ralph 64: 118

Peake, Mervyn 22: 136, 149; 23: 162, 163, 164; YABC2: 307
Pearce, Carl 228: 107; 229: 148
Pearson, Larry 38: 225
Pearson, Tracey Campbell 64: 163, 164, 167, 168, 169; 118: 51; 156: 169, 171, 172; 163: 140; 219: 140, 141, 142, 143
Peat, Fern B. 16: 115
Peck, Anne Merriman 18: 241; 24: 155
Peck, Beth 66: 242; 79: 166; 80: 136; 91: 34; 95: 9; 101: 77; 164: 197; 190: 170
Peddicord, Jane Ann 199: 106
Pedersen, Janet 193: 152; 217: 57; 218: 15; 228: 85
Pedersen, Judy 66: 217; 121: 36; 172: 67
Pedersen, Vilhelm YABC 1: 40
Pederson, Sharleen 12: 92
Pedlar, Elaine 161: 45
Peek, Merle 39: 168
Peet, Bill 2: 203; 41: 159, 160, 161, 162, 163; 78: 158, 159, 160, 161
Peguero, Adrian 116: 133
Peguero, Gerard 116: 133
Pels, Winslow Pinney 55: 126
Peltier, Leslie C. 13: 178
Peltzer, Marc 202: 92
Penberthy, Mark 171: 78
Pendle, Alexy 7: 159; 13: 34; 29: 161; 33: 215; 86: 62
Pendola, Joanne 76: 203; 81: 125; 105: 181; 178: 152, 153
Pene du Bois, William 4: 70; 10: 122; 26: 61; 27: 145, 211; 35: 243; 41: 216; 68: 180, 181; 73: 45
Penfound, David 102: 185
Pennington, Eunice 27: 162
Peppe, Mark 28: 142
Peppe, Rodney 4: 164, 165; 74: 187, 188, 189
Pepper, Hubert 64: 143
Percy, Graham 63: 2
Pericoli, Matteo 178: 177
Perini, Ben 173: 77
Perkins, David 60: 68
Perkins, Lucy Fitch 72: 199
Perkins, Lynne Rae 172: 146; 212: 153
Perl, Susan 2: 98; 4: 231; 5: 44, 45, 118; 6: 199; 8: 137; 12: 88; 22: 193; 34: 54, 55; 52: 128; YABC 1: 176
Perlman, Janet 222: 141
Perrone, Donna 78: 166
Perry, Marie Fritz 165: 180
Perry, Patricia 29: 137; 30: 171
Perry, Roger 27: 163
Perske, Martha 46: 83; 51: 108, 147
Persson, Stina 175: 166
Pesek, Ludek 15: 237
Petach, Heidi 149: 166; 200: 207
Peters, David 72: 205; 182: 116
Petersen, Jeff 181: 95
Petersham, Maud 17: 108, 147, 148, 149, 150, 151, 152, 153
Petersham, Miska 17: 108, 147, 148, 149, 150, 151, 152, 153
Peterson, Eric 109: 125
Peterson, Nisse 99: 27
Peterson, R.F. 7: 101
Peterson, Russell 7: 130
Petie, Haris 2: 3; 10: 41, 118; 11: 227; 12: 70
Petit-Roulet, Philippe 227: 12
Petricic, Dusan 153: 75, 76, 77; 170: 12; 172: 13; 176: 170; 179: 56
Petrides, Heidrun 19: 223
Petrone, Valeria 159: 160; 171: 92; 186: 173; 204: 49; 216: 208; 220: 98
Petrosino, Tamara 177: 40; 193: 154, 155
Petruccio, Steven James 67: 159; 127: 5
Pettingill, Ondre 64: 181; 70: 64; 222: 167, 168
Peyo 40: 56, 57
Peyton, K.M. 15: 212
Pfeifer, Herman 15: 262

Pfister, Marcus 83: 165, 166, 167; 146: 152; 150: 160; 207: 132, 134, 135, 136
Pfloog, Jan 124: 60
Pham, LeUyen 160: 48; 175: 154, 156; 179: 149; 201: 124, 125, 126, 127; 204: 28; 208: 206; 217: 92
Phelan, Matt 182: 160; 184: 222; 215: 140, 141; 221: 157; 231: 28
Phillipps, J.C. 218: 142
Phillips, Craig 70: 151; 207: 74; 221: 159; 229: 22
Phillips, Douglas 1: 19
Phillips, F.D. 6: 202
Phillips, Gary R. 223: 23
Phillips, Louise 133: 67
Phillips, Matt 184: 173
Phillips, Thomas 30: 55
Philpot, Glyn 54: 46
Phiz
    See Browne, Hablot K.
Piatti, Celestino 16: 223
Pica, Steve 115: 181
Picarella, Joseph 13: 147
Picart, Gabriel 121: 165; 201: 169
Picasso, Pablo 228: 131
Pichon, Liz 174: 139
Pickard, Charles 12: 38; 18: 203; 36: 152
Picken, George A. 23: 150
Pickens, David 22: 156
Pickering, Jimmy 195: 152; 197: 163
Pien, Lark 222: 143, 144
Pienkowski, Jan 6: 183; 30: 32; 58: 140, 141, 142,143, 146, 147; 73: 3; 87: 156, 157; 131: 189
Pieper, Christiane 200: 168
Pignataro, Anna 163: 220; 223: 143 Pile, Emma 218: 156 Pileggi, Steve 145: 122
Pilkey, Dav 68: 186; 115: 164, 166; 166: 173, 174, 175
Pimlott, John 10: 205
Pincus, Harriet 4: 186; 8: 179; 22: 148; 27: 164, 165; 66: 202
Pini, Wendy 89: 166
Pinkett, Neil 60: 8
Pinkney, Brian 81: 184, 185; 94: 107; 113: 146, 147; 117: 121, 166; 132: 145; 158: 108, 191; 160: 189; 200: 8
Pinkney, Jerry 8: 218; 10: 40; 15: 276; 20: 66; 24: 121; 33: 109; 36: 222; 38: 200; 41: 165, 166, 167, 168, 169, 170, 171, 173, 174; 44: 198; 48: 51; 53: 20; 56: 61, 68; 58: 184; 60: 59; 61: 91; 71: 146, 148, 149; 72: 17; 73: 149; 74: 159,192; 75: 45; 80: 206; 81: 44; 85: 144; 95: 50; 107: 158, 159, 160; 108: 164; 112: 114, 115; 133: 58; 195: 140; 227: 131
Pinkwater, Daniel Manus 8: 156; 46: 180, 181, 182, 185, 188, 189, 190; 151: 161 76: 178, 179, 180; 210: 203
Pinkwater, Manus
    See Pinkwater, Daniel Manus
Pinkwater, Jill 114: 160, 161; 158: 179; 188: 143, 145, 146
Pinto, Ralph 10: 131; 45: 93
Pinto, Sara 200: 165
Pinon, Mark 74: 22
Piven, Hanoch 173: 142
Pistolesi 73: 211
Pitcairn, Ansel 188: 10; 227: 20
Pittman, Helena Clare 71: 151
Pitz, Henry C. 4: 168; 19: 165; 35: 128; 42: 80; YABC 2: 95, 176
Pitzenberger, Lawrence J. 26: 94
Pitzer, Susanna 181: 131
Place, François 218: 42
Plant, Andrew 214: 166
Player, Stephen 82: 190
Plecas, Jennifer 84: 201; 106: 124; 149: 168; 205: 180; 220: 81; 229: 152, 153, 154
Ploog, Mike 180: 19
Plowden, David 52: 135, 136

Plume, Ilse *170:* 149
Plummer, William *32:* 31
Podevin, Jean François *184:* 185
Podwal, Mark *56:* 170, 173; *101:* 154, 155, 157; *149:* 176; *160:* 194; *224:* 127, 128, 129
Pohrt, Tom *67:* 116; *104:* 80; *152:* 199; *195:* 154; *199:* 85
Poirson, V.A. *26:* 89
Polacco, Patricia *74:* 195, 196, 197, 198; *123:* 121, 122, 123; *180:* 189, 190, 191, 193, 194; *212:* 168, 170, 171
Polgreen, John *21:* 44
Polhemus, Coleman *210:* 209
Politi, Leo *1:* 178; *4:* 53; *21:* 48; *47:* 173,174, 176, 178, 179, 180, 181
Pollack, Barbara *219:* 60
Pollema-Cahill, Phyllis *123:* 126
Pollen, Samson *64:* 80
Polonsky, Arthur *34:* 168
Polseno, Jo *1:* 53; *3:* 117; *5:* 114; *17:* 154; *20:* 87; *32:* 49; *41:* 245
Pomaska, Anna *117:* 148
Pons, Bernadette *184:* 100
Ponter, James *5:* 204
Poole, Colin *111:* 27
Poortvliet, Rien *6:* 212; *65:* 165, 166, 167
Pope, Kevin *183:* 158
Popp, Wendy *72:* 122; *158:* 68
Poppel, Hans *71:* 154, 155
Porfirio, Guy *76:* 134
Portal, Colette *6:* 186; *11:* 203
Porter, George *7:* 181
Porter, Janice Lee *136:* 175; *164:* 37
Porter, John *113:* 47
Porter, Pat Grant *84:* 112; *125:* 101
Porter, Sue *146:* 246, 247; *213:* 139, 140, 141; *221:* 91
Porter, Walter *124:* 175
Porto, James *221:* 14
Posada, Mia *187:* 151
Posen, Michael *175:* 82
Posthuma, Sieb *150:* 163
Postier, Jim *202:* 140; *204:* 25
Postma, Lidia *79:* 17
Potter, Beatrix *100:* 194, 195; *132:* 179, 180, 181, 182; *YABC 1:* 208, 209, 210, 212, 213
Potter, Giselle *117:* 123; *143:* 44; *144:* 170, 197; *149:* 7; *150:* 165; *187:* 152, 153; *190:* 198; *196:* 152; *200:* 12; *225:* 60; *227:* 105
Potter, Katherine *104:* 147; *171:* 135; *173:* 136; *217:* 130, 131
Potter, Miriam Clark *3:* 162
Poulin, Stephane *98:* 140, 141
Poullis, Nick *146:* 210
Powell, Constance Buffington *174:* 141
Powell, Gary *151:* 208
Powell, Ivan *67:* 219
Power, Margaret *105:* 122
Powers, Daniel *161:* 173
Powers, Richard M. *1:* 230; *3:* 218; *7:* 194; *26:* 186
Powledge, Fred *37:* 154
Powzyk, Joyce *74:* 214
Poydar, Nancy *96:* 149; *190:* 180, 181, 182
Pracher, Richard *91:* 166
Prachaticka, Marketa *126:* 126
Prange, Beckie *181:* 169
Prap, Lila *177:* 165
Prater, John *103:* 142, 143, 144; *149:* 172
Pratt, Charles *23:* 29
Pratt, Christine Joy *214:* 167
Pratt, George *116:* 208; *212:* 37
Pratt, Pierre *150:* 73; *166:* 183; *168:* 172; *201:* 27; *208:* 171, 172, 173
Prebenna, David *73:* 174
Preiss-Glasser, Robin *123:* 176; *152* 40; *172:* 194
Press, Jenny *116:* 95
Preston, Mark *152:* 162

Pretro, Korinna *91:* 126
Prevost, Mikela *209:* 111
Price, Christine *2:* 247; *3:* 163, 253; *8:* 166
Price, Cynthia *118:* 156
Price, Edward *33:* 34
Price, Garrett *1:* 76; *2:* 42
Price, Hattie Longstreet *17:* 13
Price, Nick *216:* 173; *220:* 7
Price, Norman *YABC 1:* 129
Price, Willard *48:* 184
Priceman, Marjorie *81:* 171; *136:* 169; *156:* 200; *168:* 153, 154; *188:* 45; *226:* 7
Priestley, Alice *168:* 33; *227:* 142
Priestley, Chris *198:* 144
Primavera, Elise *26:* 95; *58:* 151; *73:* 37; *80:* 79; *86:* 156; *105:* 161; *213:* 157; *230:* 132, 133, 134
Primrose, Jean *36:* 109
Prince, Alison *86:* 188, 189
Prince, Leonora E. *7:* 170
Pritchett, Shelley *116:* 148
Prittie, Edwin J. *YABC 1:* 120
Proimos, James *176:* 4; *217:* 132, 133, 134
Proimos, John *173:* 144
Prosmitsky, Jenya *132:* 33
Provensen, Alice *37:* 204, 215, 222; *70:* 176, 177, 178, 180, *71:* 213; *147:* 184; *191:* 190
Provensen, Martin *37:* 204, 215, 222; *70:* 176, 177, 178, 180; *71:* 213; *191:* 190
Pucci, Albert John *44:* 154
Pudlo *8:* 59
Puggaard, Ulla *196:* 25
Pullen, Zachary *211:* 161
Pulver, Harry, Jr. *129:* 159
Pulver, Robin *160:* 4
Punchatz, Don *99:* 57
Purdy, Susan *8:* 162
Pursell, Weimer *55:* 18
Purston, Oliver *229:* 156
Purtscher, Alfons *97:* 6
Puskas, James *5:* 141
Pyk, Jan *7:* 26; *38:* 123
Pyle, Chuck *99:* 149; *191:* 83
Pyle, Howard *16:* 225, 226, 227, 228, 230, 231, 232, 235; *24:* 27; *34:* 124, 125, 127, 128; *59:* 132; *100:* 198

Q

Quackenbush, Robert *4:* 190; *6:* 166; *7:* 175, 178; *9:* 86; *11:* 65, 221; *41:* 154; *43:* 157; *70:* 185, 186; *71:* 137; *85:* 47; *92:* 148; *133:* 154, 164, 169
Qualls, Sean *177:* 167, 168; *193:* 43; *228:* 108
Quennell, Marjorie (Courtney) *29:* 163, 164
Quidor, John *19:* 82
Quirk, John *62:* 170
Quirk, Thomas *12:* 81

R

Rackham, Arthur *15:* 32, 78, 214-227; *17:* 105, 115; *18:* 233; *19:* 254; *20:* 151; *22:* 129, 131, 132, 133; *23:* 175; *24:* 161, 181; *26:* 91; *32:* 118; *64:* 18; *100:* 9, 16, 203, 204; *YABC 1:* 25, 45, 55, 147; *2:* 103, 142, 173, 210
Racz, Michael *56:* 134
Raczka, Bob *191:* 155, 156
Radcliffe, Andrew *82:* 215
Rader, Laura *101:* 219; *197:* 147; *203:* 53
Radunsky, Vladimir *177:* 170; *192:* 30
Radzinski, Kandy *212:* 174
Rafilson, Sidney *11:* 172
Raglin, Tim *125:* 24

Raible, Alton *1:* 202, 203; *28:* 193; *35:* 181; *110:* 207
Raine, Patricia *82:* 74; *88:* 154
Ramá, Sue *173:* 45; *185:* 186; *190:* 184
Ramhorst, John *117:* 11
Ramirez, Gladys *177:* 19
Ramirez, Jose *207:* 27
Ramsey, James *16:* 41
Ramsey, Marcy Dunn *82:* 11; *180:* 186
Ramus, Michael *51:* 171
Rand, Paul *6:* 188
Rand, Ted *67:* 9, 10, 121, 123; *74:* 190; *84:* 170; *103:* 170; *112:* 6; *114:* 73; *139:* 168; *143:* 194; *156:* 154; *161:* 9, 10; *200:* 38; *204:* 7
Randazzo, Tony *81:* 98
Randell, William *55:* 54
Rane, Walter *93:* 144; *143:* 109; *184:* 126
Rankin, Joan *163:* 40; *212:* 176
Rankin, Laura *176:* 173, 174; *179:* 150
Ransome, Arthur *22:* 201
Ransome, James E. *74:* 137; *75:* 80; *84:* 181; *94:* 108; *117:* 115; *123:* 128, 129, 130; *158:* 101, 102; *159:* 205; *178:* 188, 189, 190; *216:* 114; *227:* 146, 148, 149, 150
Rantz, Don *119:* 184
Rao, Anthony *28:* 126
Raphael, Elaine *23:* 192; *71:* 24, 25
Rappaport, Eva *6:* 190
Raschka, Chris *80:* 187, 189, 190; *97:* 211; *115:* 210; *117:* 151, 152, 153, 154; *143:* 195; *145:* 153; *166:* 190, 191; *170:* 114; *207:* 140, 143, 144, 145; *208:* 82; *220:* 85
Rash, Andy *158:* 178; *162:* 172; *210:* 204; *219:* 145; *226:* 194
Raskin, Ellen *2:* 208, 209; *4:* 142; *13:* 183; *22:* 68; *29:* 139; *36:* 134; *38:* 173, 174, 175, 176, 177, 178,179, 180, 181; *60:* 163; *86:* 81
Rathmann, Peggy *93:* 32; *94:* 168; *157:* 212, 214
Ratkus, Tony *77:* 133
Rattray, Gail *227:* 96
Ratzkin, Lawrence *40:* 143
Rau, Margaret *9:* 157
Raverat, Gwen *YABC 1:* 152
Ravid, Joyce *61:* 73
Ravielli, Anthony *1:* 198; *3:* 168; *11:* 143
Ravilious, Robin *77:* 169
Rawlins, Donna *72:* 198; *73:* 15, 129
Rawlins, Janet *76:* 79
Rawlings, Steve *143:* 139; *151:* 54; *208:* 150
Rawlinson, Debbie *75:* 132
Ray, Deborah Kogan *8:* 164; *29:* 238; *50:* 112, 113; *62:* 119; *78:* 191; *203:* 149, 150, 151
Ray, Jane *96:* 166; *97:* 104; *152:* 208; *190:* 221; *196:* 165
Ray, Ralph *2:* 239; *5:* 73
Rayann, Omar *162:* 205; *186:* 29, 30
Rayevsky, Robert *64:* 17; *70:* 173; *80:* 204; *117:* 79; *190:* 187, 188
Raymond, Larry *31:* 108; *97:* 109
Rayner, Hugh *151:* 170
Rayner, Mary *22:* 207; *47:* 140; *72:* 191; *87:* 171, 172; *192:* 104
Rayner, Shoo
  See Rayner, Hugh
Raynes, John *71:* 19
Raynor, Dorka *28:* 168
Raynor, Paul *24:* 73
Rayyan, Omar *110:* 222; *112:* 17; *125:* 131
Razzi, James *10:* 127
Read, Alexander D. *20:* 45
Reader, Dennis *71:* 157
Reasoner, Charles *53:* 33, 36, 37
Rebenschied, Shane *203:* 76; *215:* 124
Reczuch, Karen *115:* 132; *145:* 131
Redlich, Ben *163:* 221; *198:* 193
Reddy, Mike *203:* 67
Reed, Joseph *116:* 139
Reed, Lynn Rowe *115:* 173; *171:* 146; *208:* 177; *215:* 144, 145

Reed, Mike *211:* 147; *215:* 131
Reed, Tom *34:* 171
Reeder, Colin *74:* 202; *77:* 113
Rees, Mary *134:* 219
Reese, Bob *60:* 135
Reeve, Philip *171:* 50
Reeves, Eira B. *130:* 173, 174; *141:* 151
Reeves, Rick *181:* 179
Reeves, Rosie *202:* 200
Regan, Dana *117:* 116
Regan, Laura *103:* 198; *153:* 206
Reichert, Renée *169:* 127
Reid, Barbara *82:* 178; *92:* 17; *93:* 169, 170; *222:* 45
Reid, Stephen *19:* 213; *22:* 89
Reim, Melanie *104:* 151; *150:* 98
Reinert, Kirk *89:* 138; *195:* 129
Reinertson, Barbara *44:* 150; *62:* 103
Reiniger, Lotte *40:* 185
Reisberg, Mira *119:* 2
Reisch, Jesse *158:* 130
Reiser, Lynn *81:* 175; *138:* 184; *180:* 200
Reiss, John J. *23:* 193
Relf, Douglas *3:* 63
Relyea, C.M. *16:* 29; *31:* 153
Remi, Georges *13:* 184
Remington, Frederic *19:* 188; *41:* 178, 179, 180, 181, 183,184, 185, 186, 187, 188; *62:* 197
Remkiewicz, Frank *67:* 102; *77:* 171; *80:* 130; *113:* 107; *152:* 116; *152:* 211, 212; *157:* 148; *217:* 120, 138, 139, 140, 141
Rendon, Maria *116:* 141; *192:* 134; *134:* 152
Renfro, Ed *79:* 176
Renier, Aaron *202:* 141; *207:* 119
Renlie, Frank *11:* 200
Reschofsky, Jean *7:* 118
Rethi *60:* 181
Rethi, Lili *2:* 153; *36:* 156
Reusswig, William *3:* 267
Revell, Cindy *195:* 93
Rex, Adam *156:* 172; *169:* 91; *186:* 178, 179; *215:* 103; *223:* 11; *225:* 154
Rex, Michael *157:* 147; *191:* 159, 160; *221:* 124
Rey, H.A. *1:* 182; *26:* 163, 164, 166, 167, 169; *69:* 172, 173, 174, 175; *86:* 195, 196, 197; *100:* 211; *YABC 2:* 17
Rey, Luis V. *201:* 162
Reynish, Jenny *222:* 155
Reynolds, Adrian *192:* 159, 160
Reynolds, Doris *5:* 71; *31:* 77
Reynolds, Peter H. *142:* 12; *179:* 175, 176; *202:* 113, 114; *226:* 30, 166, 167; *228:* 132
Rhead, Louis *31:* 91; *100:* 228
Rhodes, Andrew *38:* 204; *50:* 163; *54:* 76; *61:* 123, 124; *87:* 200
Ribbons, Ian *3:* 10; *37:* 161; *40:* 76
Ricci, Regolo *93:* 22; *164:* 148
Rice, Elizabeth *2:* 53, 214
Rice, Eve *34:* 174, 175; *91:* 172
Rice, James *22:* 210; *93:* 173
Rich, Anna *212:* 180
Rich, Martha *195:* 16
Richards, Chuck *170:* 154
Richards, George *40:* 116, 119, 121; *44:* 179
Richards, Henry *YABC 1:* 228, 231
Richardson, Ernest *2:* 144
Richardson, Frederick *18:* 27, 31
Richardson, John *110:* 88
Richman, Hilda *26:* 132
Richmond, George *24:* 179
Riddell, Chris *114:* 170, 195; *166:* 179; *199:* 164, 166, 167; *218:* 146, 148; *219:* 149, 150, 152, 153; *228:* 125
Riddle, Tohby *74:* 204; *151:* 179; *223:* 154, 156
Riding, Peter *63:* 195
Rieniets, Judy King *14:* 28
Riger, Bob *2:* 166

Riggio, Anita *73:* 191; *85:* 63; *137:* 184; *172:* 165
Rigano, Giovanni *219:* 45
Riley, Jon *74:* 70
Riley, Kenneth *22:* 230
Riley, Terry *203:* 100
Riley-Webb, Charlotte *153:* 143
Rim, Sujean *225:* 157
Rinaldi, Angelo *165:* 60, 69; *227:* 53
Ringgold, Faith *71:* 162; *114:* 173, 174, 176; *187:* 160, 161, 163
Ringi, Kjell *12:* 171
Rios, Tere
　　See Versace, Marie
Rioux, Jo *215:* 110; *226:* 170
Ripper, Charles L. *3:* 175
Ripplinger, Henry *117:* 31
Ritchie, Scot *217:* 145
Ritchie, William *74:* 183
Ritter, John *175:* 14
Ritz, Karen *41:* 117; *72:* 239; *87:* 125; *102:* 7; *106:* 6
Rivas, Victor *209:* 193; *226:* 144
Rivers, Ruth *178:* 193
Rivkin, Jay *15:* 230
Rivoche, Paul *45:* 125
Roach, Marilynne *9:* 158
Robbin, Jodi *44:* 156, 159
Robbins, Frank *42:* 167
Robbins, Ken *147:* 191, 192
Robbins, Ruth *52:* 102
Roberton, Fiona *230:* 142
Roberts, Cliff *4:* 126
Roberts, David *154:* 4, 6; *191:* 162; *196:* 184; *197:* 105; *210:* 257
Roberts, Doreen *4:* 230; *28:* 105
Roberts, Jim *22:* 166; *23:* 69; *31:* 110
Roberts, Tony *109:* 195, 214
Roberts, W. *22:* 2, 3
Robertson, M.P. *197:* 153
Robins, Arthur *137:* 172; *151:* 225; *204:* 161
Robinson, Aminah Brenda Lynn *86:* 205; *103:* 55; *159:* 175
Robinson, Charles [1870-1937] *17:* 157, 171, 172, 173, 175, 176; *24:* 207; *25:* 204; *YABC 2:* 308, 309, 310, 331
Robinson, Charles *3:* 53; *5:* 14; *6:* 193; *7:* 150; *7:* 183; *8:* 38; *9:* 81; *13:* 188; *14:* 248, 249; *23:* 149; *26:* 115; *27:* 48; *28:* 191; *32:* 28; *35:* 210; *36:* 37; *48:* 96; *52:* 33; *53:* 157; *56:* 15; *62:* 142; *77:* 41; *111:* 148
Robinson, Fiona *225:* 158
Robinson, Jerry *3:* 262
Robinson, Joan G. *7:* 184
Robinson, Lolly *90:* 227
Robinson, T.H. *17:* 179, 181, 182, 183; *29:* 254
Robinson, W. Heath *17:* 185, 187, 189, 191, 193, 195, 197, 199, 202; *23:* 167; *25:* 194; *29:* 150; *YABC 1:* 44; *2:* 183
Rocco, John *187:* 4; *188:* 151; *208:* 180, 181, 182; *213:* 94; *222:* 34
Roche, Christine *41:* 98
Roche, Denis *99:* 184; *180:* 32; *196:* 168
Roche, P.K. *57:* 151, 152
Rocker, Fermin *7:* 34; *13:* 21; *31:* 40; *40:* 190,191
Rocklen, Margot *101:* 181
Rockwell, Anne *5:* 147; *33:* 171, 173; *71:* 166, 167,168; *114:* 183, 184; *194:* 152, 155
Rockwell, Gail *7:* 186
Rockwell, Harlow *33:* 171, 173, 175
Rockwell, Lizzy *114:* 182; *162:* 182; *185:* 189
Rockwell, Norman *23:* 39, 196, 197, 199, 200, 203, 204, 207; *41:* 140, 143; *123:* 47; *YABC 2:* 60
Rockwood, Richard *119:* 75
Rodanas, Kristina *156:* 183, 184; *221:* 127
Rodegast, Roland *43:* 100
Rodgers, Frank *69:* 177
Rodriguez, Albert G. *182:* 50

Rodriguez, Christina *184:* 12; *225:* 94
Rodriguez, Edel *204:* 86
Rodriguez, Joel *16:* 65
Rodriguez, Robert *145:* 145; *212:* 33
Rodriguez-Howard, Pauline *177:* 18
Roe, Monika *210:* 94
Roeckelein, Katrina *134:* 223
Roennfeldt, Robert *66:* 243
Roever, J.M. *4:* 119; *26:* 170
Roffey, Maureen *33:* 142, 176, 177
Rogasky, Barbara *46:* 90
Rogé *173:* 160
Rogers, Carol *2:* 262; *6:* 164; *26:* 129
Rogers, Chris M. *150:* 59; *196:* 61
Rogers, Forest *87:* 160; *101:* 76
Rogers, Frances *10:* 130
Rogers, Gregory *104:* 76; *126:* 57; *171:* 26
Rogers, Jacqueline *78:* 249; *80:* 34; *86:* 54 *103:* 70; *115:* 72; *129:* 173; *131:* 57, 225; *143:* 211; *153:* 100; *193:* 186; *203:* 51; *213:* 144, 145, 146; *214:* 142
Rogers, Sherry *191:* 66
Rogers, Walter S. *31:* 135, 138; *67:* 65, 168; *100:* 81
Rogers, William A. *15:* 151, 153, 154; *33:* 35
Rogoff, Barbara *95:* 20
Rohmann, Eric *103:* 152; *198:* 151
Rojankovsky, Feodor *6:* 134, 136; *10:* 183; *21:* 128,129, 130; *25:* 110; *28:* 42; *68:* 120
Rolfsen, Alf *62:* 15
Rolston, Steve *209:* 154; *223:* 113
Romain, Trevor *134:* 157
Roman, Barbara J. *103:* 171
Romas *114:* 111; *165:* 63
Romano, Robert *64:* 68
Romero, Alejandro *187:* 185
Roos, Maryn *168:* 198; *225:* 160; *226:* 143
Root, Barry *80:* 212; *90:* 196; *146:* 78; *156:* 165; *159:* 161; *182:* 18, 172
Root, Kimberly Bulcken *86:* 72; *98:* 21; *108:* 111; *127:* 114; *159:* 162; *176:* 134; *192:* 163
Roper, Bob *65:* 153
Roraback, Robin *111:* 156
Rorer, Abigail *43:* 222; *85:* 155
Rosales, Melodye *80:* 35
Rosamilia, Patricia *36:* 120
Rose, Carl *5:* 62
Rose, David S. *29:* 109; *70:* 120
Rose, Gerald *68:* 200, 201; *86:* 48
Rose, Naomi C. *228:* 136
Rose, Ted *93:* 178
Rosen, Elizabeth *205:* 137
Rosenbaum, Jonathan *50:* 46
Rosenberg, Amye *74:* 207, 208
Rosenberry, Vera *87:* 22, 26; *144:* 212, 213; *158:* 120; *219:* 163, 164
Rosenblum, Richard *11:* 202; *18:* 18
Rosenstiehl, Agnès *203:* 153
Rosier, Lydia *16:* 236; *20:* 104; *21:* 109; *22:* 125; *30:* 151, 158; *42:* 128; *45:* 214; *77:* 227, 228
Rosing, Jens *85:* 142
Ross
　　See Thomson, Ross
Ross, Christine *83:* 172, 173
Ross, Clare Romano *3:* 123; *21:* 45; *48:* 199
Ross, Dave *32:* 152; *57:* 108
Ross, Graham *199:* 4
Ross, Herbert *37:* 78
Ross, John *3:* 123; *21:* 45
Ross, Johnny *32:* 190
Ross, Larry *47:* 168; *60:* 62
Ross, Ruth *109:* 233
Ross, Tony *17:* 204; *56:* 132; *65:* 176, 177, 179; *90:* 123; *123:* 186, 187, 190; *130:* 188, 190, 191, 192; *132:* 242; *174:* 159; *176:* 181, 182, 183; *202:* 198; *225:* 168, 170
Rossetti, Dante Gabriel *20:* 151, 153
Rostant, Larry *180:* 221; *194:* 108; *195:* 96; *197:* 12; *207:* 53; *210:* 189; *226:* 22
Roth, Arnold *4:* 238; *21:* 133

Roth, Julie Jersild *180:* 206
Roth, Marci *135:* 223
Roth, R.G. *184:* 50
Roth, Rob *105:* 98; *146:* 41
Roth, Robert *176:* 159
Roth, Roger *61:* 128; *190:* 192
Roth, Ruby *216:* 185
Roth, Stephanie *136:* 171, 172
Roth, Susan L. *80:* 38; *93:* 78; *134:* 165, 166;
    181: 145, 146
Rothenberg, Joani Keller *162:* 190, 191
Rothman, Michael *139:* 62; *184:* 34 *Rotman,*
    Jeffrey L. 145: 30
Rotondo, Pat *32:* 158
Roughsey, Dick *35:* 186
Rouille, M. *11:* 96
Rounds, Glen *8:* 173; *9:* 171; *12:* 56; *32:* 194;
    40: 230; *51:* 161, 162, 166; *56:* 149; *70:*
    198, 199; *YABC 1:* 1, 2, 3; *112:* 163
Roundtree, Katherine *114:* 88; *168:* 102
Rovetch, Lissa *201:* 164
Rowan, Evadne *52:* 51
Rowe, Eric *111:* 161
Rowe, Gavin *27:* 144; *72:* 47; *88:* 201
Rowe, John *132:* 70, 71; *180:* 126
Rowell, Kenneth *40:* 72
Rowen, Amy *52:* 143
Rowena *116:* 101
Rowland, Andrew *164:* 136
Rowland, Jada *83:* 73
Rowles, Daphne *58:* 24
Roy, Jeroo *27:* 229; *36:* 110
Royo *118:* 32; *144:* 105, 106, 108; *165:* 19;
    166: 166
Rubbino, Salvatore *220:* 147
Rubel, Nicole *18:* 255; *20:* 59; *81:* 66, 67; *95:*
    169, 170; *119:* 60; *135:* 177, 179, 180; *169:*
    68; *181:* 150
Rubel, Reina *33:* 217
Rud, Borghild *6:* 15
Ruddell, Gary *110:* 238; *116:* 207
Rudolph, Norman Guthrie *17:* 13
Rue, Leonard Lee III *37:* 164
Rueda, Claudia *183:* 170, 171
Ruelle, Karen Gray *126:* 193
Ruff, Donna *50:* 173; *72:* 203; *78:* 49; *80:*
    120,121; *93:* 162; *164:* 121
Ruffins, Reynold *10:* 134, 135; *41:* 191, 192,
    193, 194, 195, 196; *125:* 187, 188, 189; *162:*
    197
Ruhlin, Roger *34:* 44
Rui, Paolo *217:* 115
Ruiz, Art *95:* 154; *110:* 91
Rumford, James *193:* 167
Runnerstroem, Bengt Arne *75:* 161
Ruse, Margaret *24:* 155
Rush, Ken *98:* 74
Rush, Peter *42:* 75
Russell, Charles M. *167:* 171
Russell, E.B. *18:* 177, 182
Russell, Jim *53:* 134
Russell, Natalie *218:* 170, 171
Russell, P. Craig *80:* 196; *146:* 102; *162:* 186
Russo, Marisabina *84:* 51; *106:* 164; *151:* 183;
    188: 153, 154, 155, 156
Russo, Susan *30:* 182; *36:* 144
Russon, Mary *87:* 145
Ruth, Greg *183:* 125
Ruth, Rod *9:* 161
Rutherford, Alexa *110:* 108
Rutherford, Jenny *78:* 5
Rutherford, Meg *25:* 174; *34:* 178, 179; *69:*
    73; *72:* 31
Rutland, Jonathan *31:* 126
Ruurs, Margriet *147:* 195
Ruzzier, Sergio *159:* 176, 177; *163:* 184; *210:*
    214, 216
Ryan, Amy *188:* 50
Ryan, Will *86:* 134
Rycroft, Nina *228:* 143
Ryden, Hope *8:* 176

Rylant, Cynthia *112:* 170, 172
Rymer, Alta M. *34:* 181
Ryniak, Christopher *178:* 11
Rystedt, Rex *49:* 80

S

Saaf, Chuck *49:* 179
Saaf, Donald *101:* 220; *124:* 180
Sabaka, Donna R. *21:* 172
Sabin, Robert *45:* 35; *60:* 30; *99:* 161; *223:* 29
Sabuda, Robert *170:* 166, 167, 168
Sacker, Amy *16:* 100
Sadler, Sonia Lynn *230:* 42, 163
Saelig, S.M. *129:* 73; *173:* 59
Saffioti, Lino *36:* 176; *48:* 60; *223:* 26
Saflund, Birgitta *94:* 2
Sagsoorian, Paul *12:* 183; *22:* 154; *33:* 106;
    87: 152
Sahara, Tony *168:* 106; *177:* 181; *178:* 228;
    186: 132; *207:* 89; *231:* 54
Sahlberg, Myron *57:* 165
Saidens, Amy *145:* 162; *191:* 131; *210:* 129
Saint Exupery, Antoine de *20:* 157
Saint James, Synthia *152:* 220; *188:* 90; *200:*
    7
Sakai, Komako *213:* 148
Saldutti, Denise *39:* 186; *57:* 178
Sale, Morton *YABC 2:* 31
Sale, Tim *153:* 177
Salerno, Steven *150:* 79; *176:* 188; *202:* 39;
    216: 190
Salter, George *72:* 128, 130
Saltzberg, Barney *135:* 184, 185; *194:* 160
Saltzman, David *86:* 209
Salwowski, Mark *71:* 54
Salzman, Yuri *86:* 12
Sambourne, Linley *YABC 2:* 181
Sampson, Katherine *9:* 197
Samson, Anne S. *2:* 216
San Souci, Daniel *40:* 200; *96:* 199, 200; *113:*
    171; *157:* 149; *170:* 69; *192:* 167, 168; *220:*
    152; *221:* 126
Sancha, Sheila *38:* 185
Sanchez, Enrique O. *155:* 84
Sand, George X. *45:* 182
Sandberg, Lasse *15:* 239, 241
Sanders, Beryl *39:* 173
Sanderson, Ruth *21:* 126; *24:* 53; *28:* 63; *33:*
    67; *41:* 48, 198, 199, 200, 201, 202, 203; *43:*
    79; *46:* 36,44; *47:* 102; *49:* 58; *62:* 121, 122;
    85: 3; *109:* 207, 208, 209, 210; *172:* 157,
    158; *223:* 85; *224:* 152, 153, 154
Sandia *119:* 74
Sandin, Joan *4:* 36; *6:* 194; *7:* 177; *12:*
    145,185; *20:* 43; *21:* 74; *26:* 144; *27:* 142;
    28: 224, 225; *38:* 86; *41:* 46; *42:* 35; *59:* 6;
    80: 136; *94:* 188; *140:* 116; *153:* 179, 180;
    197: 168
Sandland, Reg *39:* 215
Sandoz, Edouard *26:* 45, 47
Sanford, John *66:* 96, 97
Sanger, Amy Wilson *205:* 140
Sankey, Tom *72:* 103
Sano, Kazuhiko *153:* 208; *195:* 171; *203:* 21;
    221: 71
Santat, Dan *188:* 160; *221:* 62; *223:* 163; *224:*
    157, 158, 159
Santiago, Wilfred *210:* 48
Santore, Charles *54:* 139; *200:* 171, 172
Santoro, Christopher *74:* 215
Santos, Jesse J. *99:* 24
Sapieha, Christine *1:* 180
Saport, Linda *123:* 137, 138; *215:* 29
Sara
    See De La Roche Saint Andre, Anne
Sarcone-Roach, Julia *215:* 158
Sardinha, Rick *175:* 151
Sarg, Tony *YABC 2:* 236

Sargent, Claudia *64:* 181
Sargent, Robert *2:* 217
Saris *1:* 33
Sarony *YABC 2:* 170
Saroff, Phyllis V. *202:* 160
Sasaki, Goro *170:* 46
Sasaki, Ellen Joy *216:* 49
Sasek, Miroslav *16:* 239, 240, 241, 242
Sassman, David *9:* 79
Sattler, Jennifer Gordon *218:* 175
Satty *29:* 203, 205
Sauber, Robert *40:* 183; *76:* 256; *78:* 154; *87:*
    92
Saunders, Dave *85:* 163, 164, 165
Savadier, Elivia *84:* 50; *145:* 45; *164:* 206;
    228: 146
Savage, Naomi *56:* 172
Savage, Steele *10:* 203; *20:* 77; *35:* 28
Savage, Stephen *174:* 182
Savio *76:* 4
Savitt, Sam *8:* 66, 182; *15:* 278; *20:* 96; *24:*
    192; *28:* 98
Sawyer, Kem Knapp *84:* 228, 229
Say, Allen *28:* 178; *69:* 182, 183, 232; *110:*
    194, 195,196; *161:* 154, 155
Sayles, Elizabeth *82:* 93; *105:* 155; *109:* 116;
    180: 64; *220:* 160, 161
Scabrini, Janet *13:* 191; *44:* 128
Scalora, Suza *224:* 160
Scanlan, Peter *83:* 27; *153:* 165; *187:* 149
Scanlon, Paul *83:* 87
Scannell, Reece *105:* 105
Scarry, Huck *35:* 204, 205
Scarry, Richard *2:* 220, 221; *18:* 20; *35:* 193,
    194, 195,196, 197, 198, 199, 200, 201, 202;
    75: 165, 167, 168
Schachner, Judith Byron *88:* 180; *92:* 163; *93:*
    102; *142:* 82; *178:* 199, 200; *190:* 140; *228:*
    83
Schade, Susan *205:* 21
Schaeffer, Mead *18:* 81, 94; *21:* 137, 138, 139;
    47: 128
Schaffer, Amanda *90:* 206
Schallau, Daniel *222:* 164
Schanzer, Rosalyn *138:* 192, 193
Scharl, Josef *20:* 132; *22:* 128
Scheel, Lita *11:* 230
Scheffler, Axel *180:* 23, 24; *230:* 169, 170
Scheib, Ida *29:* 28
Schermer, Judith *30:* 184
Schick, Eleanor *82:* 210, 211; *144:* 222
Schick, Joel *16:* 160; *17:* 167; *22:* 12; *27:*
    176; *31:* 147, 148; *36:* 23; *38:* 64; *45:* 116,
    117; *52:* 5, 85; *104:* 159
Schields, Gretchen *75:* 171, 203
Schindelman, Joseph *1:* 74; *4:* 101; *12:* 49;
    26: 51; *40:* 146; *56:* 158; *73:* 40
Schindler, Edith *7:* 22
Schindler, S.D. *38:* 107; *46:* 196; *74:* 162; *75:*
    172, 173; *99:* 133; *112:* 177; *118:* 185, 186;
    121: 71; *136:* 159; *143:* 45; *149:* 120; *156:*
    30; *169:* 135; *171:* 161, 162, 163; *172:* 9;
    186: 163; *194:* 109; *195:* 35; *198:* 170, 171,
    172
Schlesinger, Bret *7:* 77
Schlossberg, Elisabeth *221:* 161
Schmid, Eleanore *12:* 188; *126:* 196, 197
Schmid, Paul *231:* 169
Schmiderer, Dorothy *19:* 224
Schmidt, Bill *73:* 34; *76:* 220, 222, 224
Schmidt, Elizabeth *15:* 242
Schmidt, George Paul *132:* 122
Schmidt, Karen Lee *54:* 12; *71:* 174; *92:* 56;
    94: 190, 191; *127:* 103
Schmidt, Lynette *76:* 205
Schmitz, Tamara *207:* 147
Schneider, Christine M. *171:* 165
Schneider, Howie *181:* 159
Schneider, Rex *29:* 64; *44:* 171
Schnurr, Edward *170:* 62
Schoberle, Cecile *80:* 200; *92:* 134; *218:* 113

Schoenherr, Ian *32:* 83; *173:* 41
Schoenherr, John *1:* 146, 147, 173; *3:* 39, 139; *17:* 75; *29:* 72; *32:* 83; *37:* 168, 169, 170; *43:* 164, 165; *45:* 160, 162; *51:* 127; *66:* 196, 197, 198; *68:* 83; *72:* 240; *75:* 225; *88:* 176
Scholder, Fritz *69:* 103
Schomburg, Alex *13:* 23
Schongut, Emanuel *4:* 102; *15:* 186; *47:* 218, 219; *52:* 147, 148, 149, 150; *185:* 27
Schoonover, Frank *17:* 107; *19:* 81, 190, 233; *22:* 88,129; *24:* 189; *31:* 88; *41:* 69; *YABC 2:* 282, 316
Schories, Pat *164:* 210
Schottland, Miriam *22:* 172
Schramm, Ulrik *2:* 16; *14:* 112
Schreiber, Elizabeth Anne *13:* 193
Schreiber, Ralph W. *13:* 193
Schreiter, Rick *14:* 97; *23:* 171; *41:* 247; *49:* 131
Schroades, John *214:* 129
Schroeder, Binette *56:* 128, 129
Schroeder, E. Peter *12:* 112
Schroeder, Ted *11:* 160; *15:* 189; *30:* 91; *34:* 43
Schrotter, Gustav *22:* 212; *30:* 225
Schubert, Dieter *101:* 167, 168; *217:* 151, 152, 153, 155
Schubert, Ingrid *217:* 151, 152, 153, 155
Schubert-Gabrys, Ingrid *101:* 167, 168
Schucker, James *31:* 163
Schuett, Stacey *72:* 137; *208:* 204
Schulder, Lili *146:* 29
Schulke, Debra *57:* 167
Schulke, Flip *57:* 167
Schulz, Barbara *167:* 24
Schulz, Charles M. *10:* 137, 138, 139, 140, 141, 142; *118:* 192, 193, 194, 196, 199
Schutzer, Dena *109:* 32
Schwark, Mary Beth *51:* 155; *72:* 175
Schwartz, Amy *47:* 191; *82:* 100; *83:* 178, 179, 180,181; *129:* 107; *131:* 197, 198; *189:* 166, 168; *226:* 174
Schwartz, Carol *124:* 41; *130:* 199
Schwartz, Charles *8:* 184
Schwartz, Daniel *46:* 37
Schwartz, Joanie *124:* 170
Schwartzberg, Joan *3:* 208
Schwarz, Viviane *204:* 132
Schweitzer, Iris *2:* 137; *6:* 207
Schweninger, Ann *29:* 172; *82:* 246; *159:* 202; *168:* 166; *211:* 193
Schwinger, Laurence *84:* 44; *91:* 61
Scofield, Penrod *61:* 107; *62:* 160
Scott, Anita Walker *7:* 38
Scott, Art *39:* 41
Scott, Frances Gruse *38:* 43
Scott, Jane Wooster *226:* 181
Scott, Julian *34:* 126
Scott, Roszel *33:* 238
Scott, Sally *87:* 27
Scott, Steve *166:* 230, 231; *171:* 93
Scott, Trudy *27:* 172
Scotton, Rob *214:* 183
Scrace, Carolyn *143:* 95, 96
Scrambly, Crab *198:* 196
Scribner, Joanne *14:* 236; *29:* 78; *33:* 185; *34:* 208; *78:* 75; *164:* 237; *203:* 73
Scrofani, Joseph *31:* 65; *74:* 225
Scroggs, Kirk *187:* 169
Seaman, Mary Lott *34:* 64
Searle, Ronald *24:* 98; *42:* 172, 173, 174, 176, 177, 179; *66:* 73, 74; *70:* 205, 206, 207
Searle, Townley *36:* 85
Sebree, Charles *18:* 65
Sedacca, Joseph M. *11:* 25; *22:* 36
Seder, Jason *108:* 102
Seeger, Laura Vaccaro *172:* 162
Seegmiller, Don *174:* 57
Seely, David *164:* 173
Seeley, Laura L. *97:* 105

Segal, John *178:* 202
Segar, E.C. *61:* 179, 181
Segur, Adrienne *27:* 121
Seibold, J. Otto *83:* 188, 190, 191; *149:* 212, 214, 215, 216; *196:* 177, 179; *215:* 204
Seignobosc, Francoise *21:* 145, 146
Sejima, Yoshimasa *8:* 187
Selig, Sylvie *13:* 199
Seltzer, Isadore *6:* 18; *133:* 59
Seltzer, Meyer *17:* 214
Selven, Maniam *144:* 133
Selway, Martina *169:* 157
Selznick, Brian *79:* 192; *104:* 25; *117:* 175; *126:* 156; *134:* 171; *158:* 76, 78; *169:* 70; *171:* 172, 173; *191:* 106; *192:* 130; *197:* 158; *203:* 35; *205:* 92; *210:* 219, 220, 221, 222
Sempe, Jean-Jacques *47:* 92; *YABC 2:* 109
Sendak, Maurice *1:* 135, 190; *3:* 204; *7:* 142; *15:* 199; *17:* 210; *27:* 181, 182, 183, 185, 186, 187, 189,190, 191, 192, 193, 194, 195, 197, 198, 199, 203; *28:* 181, 182; *32:* 108; *33:* 148, 149; *35:* 238; *44:* 180, 181; *45:* 97, 99; *46:* 174; *73:* 225; *91:* 10, 11 *YABC1:* 167; *113:* 163, 165, 167, 168; *118:* 153; *127:* 161
Senders, Marci *180:* 79
Sengler, Johanna *18:* 256
Senn, Steve *60:* 145
Seredy, Kate *1:* 192; *14:* 20, 21; *17:* 210
Sergeant, John *6:* 74
Serra, Sebastía *212:* 215
Servello, Joe *10:* 144; *24:* 139; *40:* 91; *70:* 130, 131; *146:* 159
Seton, Ernest Thompson *18:* 260-269, 271
Seuss, Dr.
  See Geisel, Theodor
Severin, John Powers *7:* 62
Sewall, Marcia *15:* 8; *22:* 170; *37:* 171, 172, 173; *39:* 73; *45:* 209; *62:* 117; *69:* 185, 186; *71:* 212; *90:* 232; *96:* 127; *102:* 101; *107:* 129; *119:* 176, 177, 178, 180
Seward, James *70:* 35
Seward, Prudence *16:* 243
Sewell, Helen *3:* 186; *15:* 308; *33:* 102; *38:* 189, 190, 191, 192
Seymour, Stephen *54:* 21
Sfar, Joann *182:* 183
Shachat, Andrew *82:* 179
Shadbolt, Robert *203:* 68
Shahn, Ben *39:* 178; *46:* 193
Shalansky, Len *38:* 167
Shanks, Anne Zane *10:* 149
Shannon, David *57:* 137; *107:* 184; *112:* 216; *135:* 12; *152:* 223, 224, 225; *158:* 192; *212:* 159, 160, 163; *228:* 162, 163, 164, 165
Sharkey, Niamh *213:* 152
Sharp, Paul *52:* 60
Sharp, William *6:* 131; *19:* 241; *20:* 112; *25:* 141
Sharratt, Nick *102:* 207, 208; *104:* 163; *153:* 198; *175:* 176; *192:* 208; *199:* 141, 142, 143, 184, 187, 188
Shaw, Barclay *74:* 14, 16; *118:* 138
Shaw, Charles *21:* 135; *38:* 187; *47:* 124; *126:* 219
Shaw, Charles G. *13:* 200
Shaw, Hannah *227:* 163, 164
Shaw-Smith, Emma *144:* 117
Shea, Bob *231:* 170, 171
Shea, Edmund *56:* 19
Shearer, Ted *43:* 193, 194, 195, 196
Sheban, Chris *182:* 185; *190:* 102, 104; *202:* 28; *204:* 112, 114; *209:* 150; *210:* 107; *220:* 103; *224:* 185
Shecter, Ben *16:* 244; *25:* 109; *33:* 188, 191; *41:* 77
Shed, Greg *74:* 94; *84:* 204; *129:* 149, 167; *91:* 192; *223:* 104
Sheeban, Chris *144:* 190; *158:* 163
Shefcik, James *48:* 221, 222; *60:* 141

Shefelman, Karl *58:* 168
Shefelman, Tom *204:* 137
Shefts, Joelle *48:* 210
Shein, Bob *139:* 189
Sheinkin, Stephen *204:* 139
Shekerjian, Haig *16:* 245
Shekerjian, Regina *16:* 245; *25:* 73
Sheldon, David *184:* 174; *185:* 204; *211:* 189
Shelley, John *186:* 223
Shemie, Bonnie *96:* 207
Shenton, Edward *45:* 187, 188, 189; *YABC 1:* 218, 219, 221
Shepard, Ernest H. *3:* 193; *4:* 74; *16:* 101; *17:* 109; *25:* 148; *33:* 152, 199, 200, 201, 202, 203, 204, 205, 206,207; *46:* 194; *98:* 114; *100:* 111, 178, 179, 217, 219, 220,221; *YABC 1:* 148, 153, 174, 176, 180, 181
Shepard, Mary *4:* 210; *22:* 205; *30:* 132, 133; *54:* 150, 152, 153, 157, 158; *59:* 108, 109, 111; *100:* 246
Shepherd, Amanda *198:* 14
Shepherd, Irana *171:* 112
Sheppard, Kate *195:* 176
Shepperson, Rob *96:* 153; *177:* 163; *178:* 204; *197:* 34; *205:* 108
Sheridan, Brian *196:* 193
Sherman, Theresa *27:* 167
Sherwan, Earl *3:* 196
Shields, Charles *10:* 150; *36:* 63
Shields, Leonard *13:* 83, 85, 87
Shiffman, Lena *139:* 167; *168:* 136
Shiga, Jason *228:* 168
Shigley, Neil K. *66:* 219
Shillabeer, Mary *35:* 74
Shilston, Arthur *49:* 61; *62:* 58
Shimin, Symeon *1:* 93; *2:* 128, 129; *3:* 202; *7:* 85; *11:* 177; *12:* 139; *13:* 202, 203; *27:* 138; *28:* 65; *35:* 129; *36:* 130; *48:* 151; *49:* 59; *56:* 63, 65, 153
Shimizu, Yuko *215:* 197
Shine, Andrea *104:* 165; *128:* 34
Shinn, Everett *16:* 148; *18:* 229; *21:* 149, 150, 151; *24:* 218
Shinn, Florence Scovel *63:* 133, 135
Shore, Robert *27:* 54; *39:* 192, 193; *YABC 2:* 200
Shortall, Leonard *4:* 144; *8:* 196; *10:* 166; *19:* 227, 228, 229, 230; *25:* 78; *28:* 66, 167; *33:* 127; *52:* 125; *73:* 12, 212
Shortt, T.M. *27:* 36
Shpitalnik, Vladimir *83:* 194
Shroades, John *230:* 24
Shropshire, Sandy *170:* 191
Shtainments, Leon *32:* 161
Shulevitz, Uri *3:* 198, 199; *17:* 85; *22:* 204; *27:* 212; *28:* 184; *50:* 190, 191, 192, 193, 194, 195, 196,197, 198, 199, 201; *106:* 181, 182, 183; *165:* 203, 205; *166:* 138
Shulman, Dee *180:* 140
Shupe, Bobbi *139:* 80, 81
Shute, A.B. *67:* 196
Shute, Linda *46:* 59; *74:* 118
Siberell, Anne *29:* 193
Sibley, Don *1:* 39; *12:* 196; *31:* 47
Sibthorp, Fletcher *94:* 111, 112
Sidjakov, Nicolas *18:* 274
Siebel, Fritz *3:* 120; *17:* 145
Siebold, J. Otto *158:* 227
Siegel, Hal *74:* 246
Sieger, Ted *189:* 172
Siegl, Helen *12:* 166; *23:* 216; *34:* 185, 186
Silin-Palmer, Pamela *184:* 102
Sill, John *140:* 194; *141:* 157; *221:* 163; *222:* 171
Sills, Joyce *5:* 199
Silva, Simon *108:* 122
Silver, Maggie *85:* 210
Silveria, Gordon *96:* 44
Silverstein, Alvin *8:* 189
Silverstein, Shel *33:* 211; *92:* 209, 210
Silverstein, Virginia *8:* 189

Silvey, Joe *135:* 203
Simard, Rémy *95:* 156; *221:* 144
Siminovich, Laura *219:* 172
Simmons, Elly *110:* 2; *127:* 69; *134:* 181
Simon, Eric M. *7:* 82
Simon, Hilda *28:* 189
Simon, Howard *2:* 175; *5:* 132; *19:* 199; *32:* 163, 164, 165
Simont, Marc *2:* 119; *4:* 213; *9:* 168; *13:* 238,240; *14:* 262; *16:* 179; *18:* 221; *26:* 210; *33:* 189, 194; *44:* 132; *58:* 122; *68:* 117; *73:* 204, 205, 206; *74:* 221; *126:* 199, 200; *133:* 195; *163:* 40; *164:* 128; *223:* 28
Sims, Agnes *54:* 152
Sims, Blanche *44:* 116; *57:* 129; *75:* 179, 180; *77:* 92; *104:* 192; *152:* 117; *156:* 160; *160:* 70; *168:* 174, 175; *198:* 17
Singer, Edith G. *2:* 30
Singer, Gloria *34:* 56; *36:* 43
Singer, Julia *28:* 190
Singh, Jen *178:* 146
Sinquette, Jaclyn *215:* 83
Siomades, Lorianne *134:* 45; *204:* 48; *217:* 157
Siracusa, Catherine *68:* 135; *82:* 218
Sís, Peter *67:* 179, 181, 183, 184, 185; *96:* 96, 98; *106:* 193, 194, 195; *149:* 224, 226; *180:* 177; *192:* 180, 182; *222:* 64
Sivard, Robert *26:* 124
Sivertson, Liz *116:* 84
Skardinski, Stanley *23:* 144; *32:* 84; *66:* 122; *84:* 108
Slack, Michael *185:* 108; *189:* 173, 174
Slackman, Charles B. *12:* 201
Slade, Christian *193:* 187; *204:* 134
Slade, Paul *61:* 170
Slark, Albert *99:* 212; *205:* 161
Slater, Rod *25:* 167
Slavin, Bill *182:* 14, 15; *196:* 90; *199:* 148, 149, 150; *217:* 20
Sloan, Joseph *16:* 68
Sloane, Eric *21:* 3; *52:* 153, 154, 155, 156, 157, 158, 160
Sloat, Teri *164:* 231
Slobodkin, Louis *1:* 200; *3:* 232; *5:* 168; *13:* 251; *15:* 13, 88; *26:* 173, 174, 175, 176, 178, 179; *60:* 180
Slobodkina, Esphyr *1:* 201
Slonim, David *166:* 167, 168
Small, David *50:* 204, 205; *79:* 44; *95:* 189, 190, 191; *126:* 203, 204; *136:* 119; *143:* 201, 202, 203; *144:* 246; *150:* 5; *161:* 176; *183:* 181, 182, 183, 184; *200:* 211; *212:* 86; *216:* 202, 203, 204; *230:* 222
Small, W. *33:* 113
Smalley, Janet *1:* 154
Smath, Jerry *198:* 179, 180
Smedley, William T. *34:* 129
Smee, David *14:* 78; *62:* 30
Smee, Nicola *167:* 156
Smith, A.G., Jr. *35:* 182
Smith, Ali *204:* 68
Smith, Alvin *1:* 31, 229; *13:* 187; *27:* 216; *28:* 226; *48:* 149; *49:* 60
Smith, Andy *188:* 20; *207:* 151
Smith, Anne *194:* 147
Smith, Anne Warren *41:* 212
Smith, Barry *75:* 183
Smith, Brian *200:* 183
Smith, Carl *36:* 41
Smith, Cat Bowman *146:* 39; *164:* 219; *201:* 55, 184
Smith, Craig *97:* 197; *172:* 175; *206:* 40; *215:* 19; *217:* 129; *220:* 145
Smith, Donald A. *178:* 7
Smith, Doris Susan *41:* 139
Smith, Douglas *189:* 159; *213:* 170
Smith, Duane *171:* 152; *208:* 97
Smith, E. Boyd *19:* 70; *22:* 89; *26:* 63; *YABC 1:* 4, 5, 240, 248, 249
Smith, Edward J. *4:* 224

Smith, Elwood H. *157:* 231; *181:* 79; *203:* 160, 161, 162; *231:* 108
Smith, Eunice Young *5:* 170
Smith, Gary *113:* 216
Smith, George *102:* 169
Smith, Howard *19:* 196
Smith, J. Gerard *95:* 42
Smith, Jacqueline Bardner *27:* 108; *39:* 197
Smith, Jay J. *61:* 119
Smith, Jeff *93:* 191
Smith, Jessie Willcox *15:* 91; *16:* 95; *18:* 231; *19:* 57, 242; *21:* 29, 156, 157, 158, 159, 160, 161; *34:* 65; *100:* 223; *YABC 1:* 6; *2:* 180, 185, 191, 311, 325
Smith, Jos. A. *52:* 131; *72:* 120; *74:* 151; *84:* 147, 148; *85:* 146; *87:* 96; *94:* 219; *96:* 97; *104:* 33; *108:* 126, 127, 128; *111:* 140; *136:* 145; *181:* 173; *200:* 213; *201:* 94; *231:* 148
Smith, Kenneth R. *47:* 182
Smith, Keri *216:* 60
Smith, Kevin Warren *89:* 112
Smith, Kristin *209:* 197
Smith, L.H. *35:* 174
Smith, Lane *76:* 211, 213; *88:* 115; *105:* 202, 203,204, 205; *131:* 207; *160:* 217, 221; *179:* 183, 184, 185, 186; *199:* 122, 123, 124, 126; *224:* 164
Smith, Lee *29:* 32
Smith, Linell Nash *2:* 195
Smith, Maggie Kaufman *13:* 205; *35:* 191; *110:* 158; *178:* 226; *190:* 204; *209:* 145
Smith, Mavis *101:* 219
Smith, Moishe *33:* 155
Smith, Philip *44:* 134; *46:* 203
Smith, Ralph Crosby *2:* 267; *49:* 203
Smith, Robert D. *5:* 63
Smith, Sally J. *84:* 55
Smith, Susan Carlton *12:* 208
Smith, Terry *12:* 106; *33:* 158
Smith, Virginia *3:* 157; *33:* 72
Smith, William A. *1:* 36; *10:* 154; *25:* 65
Smith-Moore, J.J. *98:* 147
Smolinski, Dick *84:* 217
Smoljan, Joe *112:* 201
Smollin, Mike *39:* 203
Smyth, Iain *105:* 207
Smyth, M. Jane *12:* 15
Smythe, Fiona *151:* 213
Smythe, Theresa *141:* 37
Snair, Andy *176:* 4
Sneed, Brad *125:* 25; *191:* 175, 176; *211:* 194
Snow, Sarah *228:* 47
Snyder, Andrew A. *30:* 212
Snyder, Betsy *230:* 173
Snyder, Jerome *13:* 207; *30:* 173
Snyder, Joel *28:* 163
So, Meilo *162:* 201; *208:* 188
Soentpiet, Chris K. *97:* 208; *110:* 33; *159:* 184; *161:* 10; *163:* 130
Sofia *1:* 62; *5:* 90; *32:* 166; *86:* 43
Sofilas, Mark *93:* 157
Sogabe, Aki *207:* 153; *221:* 110
Sohn, Jiho *182:* 78
Sokol, Bill *37:* 178; *49:* 23
Sokolov, Kirill *34:* 188
Solbert, Ronni *1:* 159; *2:* 232; *5:* 121; *6:* 34; *17:* 249
Solomon, Michael *174:* 115
Solonevich, George *15:* 246; *17:* 47
Soloviov, Michael *223:* 122
Soma, Liana *81:* 118
Soman, David *90:* 122; *102:* 126; *140:* 120; *93:* 188; *43:* 89; *200:* 180, 181
Sommer, Robert *12:* 211
Song, Jae *203:* 27
Soo, Kean *201:* 185
Sorel, Edward *4:* 61; *36:* 82; *65:* 191, 193; *126:* 214
Sorensen, Henri *196:* 58
Sorensen, Henrik *62:* 16

Sorensen, Svend Otto *22:* 130, 141; *67:* 188, 189
Sorra, Kristin *155:* 80; *229:* 85
Sosa, Hernan *198:* 66
Sostre, Maria *187:* 36
Sotomayor, Antonio *11:* 215
Souhami, Jessica *112:* 128; *176:* 193
Sousa, Natalie C. *209:* 89
Souza, Diana *71:* 139
Sovak, Jan *115:* 190
Sowards, Ben *215:* 62
Soyer, Moses *20:* 177
Spaenkuch, August *16:* 28
Spafford, Suzy *160:* 228
Spain, Valerie *105:* 76
Spain, Sunday Sahara *133:* 204
Spalenka, Greg *149:* 69; *151:* 228; *184:* 195; *191:* 21; *196:* 12; *198:* 181, 182, 201; *208:* 92
Spanfeller, James *1:* 72, 149; *2:* 183; *19:* 230, 231,232; *22:* 66; *36:* 160, 161; *40:* 75; *52:* 166; *76:* 37
Spangler, Brie *212:* 188
Sparks, Mary Walker *15:* 247
Spearing, Craig J. *228:* 172
Spears, Rick *182:* 187; *220:* 67
Speidel, Sandra *78:* 233; *94:* 178; *134:* 180; *210:* 67
Speirs, John *67:* 178
Spence, Geraldine *21:* 163; *47:* 196
Spence, Jim *38:* 89; *50:* 102
Spencer, Laurie *113:* 12
Spencer, Mark *57:* 170
Spengler, Kenneth J. *146:* 256
Sperling, Andrea *133:* 182
Spiegel, Beth *184:* 203
Spiegel, Doris *29:* 111
Spiegelman, Art *109:* 227
Spier, Jo *10:* 30
Spier, Peter *3:* 155; *4:* 200; *7:* 61; *11:* 78; *38:* 106; *54:* 120, 121, 122, 123, 124, 125, 126, 127, 128, 129, 130,131, 132, 133, 134
Spilka, Arnold *5:* 120; *6:* 204; *8:* 131
Spires, Ashley *231:* 96
Spirin, Gennady *95:* 196, 197; *113:* 172; *128:* 9; *129:* 49; *134:* 210; *153:* 9; *204:* 143, 144, 145; *220:* 153
Spiro, Ruth *208:* 197
Spivak, I. Howard *8:* 10; *13:* 172
Spohn, David *72:* 233
Spohn, Kate *87:* 195; *147:* 201, 202
Spollen, Christopher J. *12:* 214
Spooner, Malcolm *40:* 142
Spoor, Mike *220:* 92
Spowart, Robin *82:* 228; *92:* 149; *133:* 131; *176:* 163; *177:* 183, 184; *217:* 123, 124
Sprague, Kevin *150:* 60; *196:* 62
Spranger, Nina *201:* 199
Sprattler, Rob *12:* 176
Spring, Bob *5:* 60
Spring, Ira *5:* 60
Springer, Harriet *31:* 92
Spudvilas, Anne *110:* 74; *197:* 192; *199:* 154
Spurll, Barbara *78:* 199; *88:* 141, 142; *99:* 215
Spurrier, Steven *28:* 198
Spuvilas, Anne *85:* 114
Spy
    See Ward, Leslie
Squires, Stuart *127:* 74
St. Aubin, Bruno *179:* 54
St. John, J. Allen *41:* 62
Staake, Bob *209:* 168, 169; *229:* 132
Stabin, Victor *101:* 131; *164:* 158
Stadler, John *62:* 33; *204:* 149
Stadnyk, Greg *212:* 55
Staffan, Alvin E. *11:* 56; *12:* 187
Stahl, Ben *5:* 181; *12:* 91; *49:* 122; *71:* 128; *87:* 206; *112:* 107
Stair, Gobin *35:* 214
Stallwood, Karen *73:* 126
Stamaty, Mark Alan *12:* 215; *230:* 175

Stammen, JoEllen McAllister *113:* 14
Stamp, Jørgen *225:* 184
Stampnick, Ken *51:* 142
Stanbridge, Joanne *150:* 91
Stanley, Diane *3:* 45; *37:* 180; *80:* 217, 219
Stanley, Sanna *145:* 228
Star, Lindsay *219:* 39
Starcke, Helmut *86:* 217
Stark, Ken *197:* 102
Starr, Branka *73:* 25
Stasiak, Krystyna *49:* 181; *64:* 194
Staub, Leslie *103:* 54
Stauffer, Brian *220:* 123
Staunton, Ted *112:* 192
Stawicki, Matt *164:* 250
Stead, L. *55:* 51, 56
Steadman, Broeck *97:* 185, 186; *99:* 56; *121:* 48; *208:* 190
Steadman, Henry *211:* 130
Steadman, Ralph *32:* 180; *123:* 143, 145
Stearn, Nick *183:* 26
Stearn, Todd *218:* 179
Steckler, June *90:* 178
Steele, Robert Gantt *169:* 174
Steichen, Edward *30:* 79
Steig, William *18:* 275, 276; *70:* 215, 216, 217, 218; *111:* 173, 174, 175, 176, 177
Stein, David Ezra *211:* 168
Stein, Harve *1:* 109
Steinberg, Saul *47:* 193
Steinel, William *23:* 146
Steiner, Charlotte *45:* 196
Steiner, Joan *110:* 219; *199:* 160, 161
Steirnagel, Michael *80:* 56
Stemp, Eric *60:* 184
Stengel, Christopher *229:* 200
Stephens, Alice Barber *66:* 208, 209
Stephens, Charles H. *YABC 2:* 279
Stephens, Pam *198:* 69
Stephens, Pat *126:* 110; *128:* 101
Stephens, William M. *21:* 165
Stephenson, Kristina *224:* 169
Steptoe, Javaka *151:* 203, 204; *190:* 169; *213:* 163, 164
Steptoe, John *8:* 197; *57:* 9; *63:* 158, 159, 160, 161,163, 164, 165, 166, 167; *96:* 4; *105:* 87
Stern, Simon *15:* 249, 250; *17:* 58; *34:* 192, 193
Sterret, Jane *53:* 27
Stetsios, Debbie *165:* 108, 109
Steven, Kat *158:* 237
Stevens, David *62:* 44
Stevens, Helen *189:* 31; *207:* 83
Stevens, Janet *40:* 126; *57:* 10, 11; *80:* 112; *90:* 221, 222; *109:* 156; *130:* 34; *166:* 202; *176:* 53, 116; *193:* 199, 200, 202; *208:* 127; *212:* 182
Stevens, Mary *11:* 193; *13:* 129; *43:* 95
Stevenson, Harvey *66:* 143; *80:* 201, 221; *153:* 60; *191:* 166
Stevenson, James *42:* 182, 183; *51:* 163; *66:* 184; *71:* 185, 187, 188; *78:* 262; *87:* 97; *113:* 182, 183,184, 185; *161:* 182, 183
Stevenson, Sucie *92:* 27; *104:* 194, 195; *112:* 168; *160:* 202; *194:* 172, 173; *195:* 166
Stewart, April Blair *75:* 210
Stewart, Arvis *33:* 98; *36:* 69; *60:* 118; *75:* 91; *127:* 4
Stewart, Charles *2:* 205
Stewart, Joel *151:* 205; *211:* 170, 171; *229:* 168
Stieg, William *172:* 58
Stiles, Fran *26:* 85; *78:* 56; *82:* 150
Stillman, Susan *44:* 130; *76:* 83
Stimpson, Tom *49:* 171
Stimson, James *208:* 46
Stinemetz, Morgan *40:* 151
Stinson, Paul *110:* 86
Stirnweis, Shannon *10:* 164
Stites, Joe *86:* 96

Stobbs, William *1:* 48, 49; *3:* 68; *6:* 20; *17:* 117, 217; *24:* 150; *29:* 250; *60:* 179; *87:* 204, 205,206
Stock, Catherine *37:* 55; *65:* 198; *72:* 7; *99:* 225; *114:* 197, 198, 199; *126:* 3; *145:* 161; *161:* 82; *173:* 149; *208:* 210; *214:* 192, 194; *224:* 196, 197
Stockman, Jack *113:* 24
Stoeke, Janet Morgan *90:* 225; *136:* 196; *202:* 182, 183
Stoerrle, Tom *55:* 147
Stolp, Jaap *49:* 98
Stolp, Todd *89:* 195
Stone, David L. *87:* 154
Stone, David *9:* 173
Stone, David K. *4:* 38; *6:* 124; *9:* 180; *43:* 182; *60:* 70
Stone, Helen V. *6:* 209
Stone, Helen *44:* 121, 122, 126
Stone, Kazuko G. *134:* 43
Stone, Kyle M. *202:* 185
Stone, Phoebe *86:* 212; *134:* 213; *162:* 188; *205:* 145
Stone, Steve *166:* 213; *208:* 185; *220:* 57,58; *224:* 124
Stone, Tony *150:* 34, 35
Storms, Patricia *217:* 163
Storrings, Michael *191:* 108; *216:* 217
Stoud, Virginia A. *89:* 31
Stover, Jill *82:* 234
Stower, Adam *217:* 89; *227:* 53
Strachan, Bruce *205:* 146
Stratton, Helen *33:* 151
Stratton-Porter, Gene *15:* 254, 259, 263, 264, 268, 269
Straub, Matt *192:* 176; *229:* 176
Straub, Phillip *197:* 22
Streano, Vince *20:* 173
Street, Janet Travell *84:* 235
Streeter, Clive *121:* 2
Strickland, Shadra *209:* 179
Stringer, Lauren *129:* 187; *154:* 172, 173; *161:* 127; *183:* 187, 188
Strodl, Daniel *47:* 95
Strogart, Alexander *63:* 139
Stromoski, Rick *111:* 179; *124:* 161, 190
Strong, Joseph D., Jr. *YABC 2:* 330
Stroyer, Poul *13:* 221
Strugnell, Ann *27:* 38
Struzan, Drew *117:* 6
Stubbs, William *73:* 196
Stubis, Talivaldis *5:* 182, 183; *10:* 45; *11:* 9; *18:* 304; *20:* 127
Stubley, Trevor *14:* 43; *22:* 219; *23:* 37; *28:* 61; *87:* 26
Stuck, Marion *104:* 44
Stuecklen, Karl W. *8:* 34, 65; *23:* 103
Stull, Betty *11:* 46
Stutzman, Mark *119:* 99
Stutzmann, Laura *73:* 185
Suarez, Maribel *162:* 208; *200:* 202
Suave, Gordon *209:* 66
Suba, Susanne *4:* 202, 203; *14:* 261; *23:* 134; *29:* 222; *32:* 30
Sue, Majella Lue *209:* 182; *212:* 146
Sueling, Barbara *98:* 185
Sueling, Gwenn *98:* 186
Sugarman, Tracy *3:* 76; *8:* 199; *37:* 181, 182
Sugimoto, Yugo *170:* 144; *223:* 137
Sugita, Yutaka *36:* 180, 181
Suh, John *80:* 157
Sullivan, Dorothy *89:* 113
Sullivan, Edmund J. *31:* 86
Sullivan, James F. *19:* 280; *20:* 192
Sully, Tom *104:* 199, 200; *182:* 77
Sumichrast, Jozef *14:* 253; *29:* 168, 213
Sumiko *46:* 57
Summers, Leo *1:* 177; *2:* 273; *13:* 22
Summers, Mark *118:* 144
Summers, Mike *190:* 176
Sutton, Judith *94:* 164

Svarez, Juan *56:* 113
Svendsen, Mark *181:* 176
Svolinsky, Karel *17:* 104
Swain, Carol *172:* 182
Swain, Su Zan Noguchi *21:* 170
Swan, Susan *22:* 220, 221; *37:* 66; *60:* 146; *145:* 205; *181:* 168
Swann, Susan *86:* 55
Swanson, Karl *79:* 65; *89:* 186
Swarner, Kristina *203:* 62; *215:* 184
Swayne, Sam *53:* 143, 145
Swayne, Zoa *53:* 143, 145
Swearingen, Greg *152:* 56; *165:* 135; *173:* 2; *224:* 32; *225:* 188
Sweat, Lynn *25:* 206; *57:* 176; *73:* 184; *168:* 178
Sweet, Darrell K. *60:* 9; *69:* 86; *74:* 15; *75:* 215; *76:* 130, 131; *81:* 96, 122; *82:* 253; *83:* 11; *84:* 14; *85:* 37; *89:* 140; *90:* 6; *91:* 137,139; *95:* 160, 161; *126:* 25; *185:* 175; *195:* 132
Sweet, Darrell K. *1:* 163; *4:* 136; *164:* 175
Sweet, Melissa *71:* 94; *72:* 172; *111:* 82; *139:* 53, 58; *141:* 88; *142:* 231; *155:* 121; *159:* 121, 122; *172:* 185; *188:* 127; *209:* 81; *211:* 174, 175; *218:* 21
Sweet, Ozzie *31:* 149, 151, 152
Sweetland, Robert *12:* 194
Swiatkowska, Gabi *132:* 43; *175:* 139; *180:* 218; *183:* 176
Swope, Martha *43:* 160; *56:* 86, 87, 89
Sylvada, Peter *154:* 174
Sylvester, Natalie G. *22:* 222
Szafran, Gene *24:* 144
Szasz, Susanne *13:* 55, 226; *14:* 48
Szekeres, Cyndy *2:* 218; *5:* 185; *8:* 85; *11:* 166; *14:* 19; *16:* 57, 159; *26:* 49, 214; *34:* 205; *60:* 150, 151, 152, 153, 154; *73:* 224; *74:* 218; *131:* 213, 215
Szpura, Beata *81:* 68; *119:* 65; *168:* 201
Szuc, Jeff *220:* 188

T

Taback, Simms *40:* 207; *52:* 120; *57:* 34; *80:* 241; *104:* 202, 203; *170:* 176, 177; *205:* 183
Taber, Patricia *75:* 124
Tabor, Nancy Maria Grande *89:* 210; *161:* 188
Taddei, Richard *112:* 13, 14
Tadgell, Nicole *150:* 77; *161:* 20; *177:* 186; *209:* 16; *220:* 190, 191
Tadiello, Ed *133:* 200
Tafuri, Nancy *39:* 210; *75:* 199, 200; *92:* 75; *130:* 215, 216, 217
Tailfeathers, Gerald *86:* 85
Tait, Douglas *12:* 220; *74:* 105, 106
Takabayashi, Mari *113:* 112; *130:* 22; *156:* 169
Takahashi, Hideko *136:* 160; *187:* 6; *209:* 152, 187
Takakjian, Portia *15:* 274
Takashima, Shizuye *13:* 228
Talarczyk, June *4:* 173
Talbott, Hudson *84:* 240; *163:* 100; *212:* 191, 192, 193
Tallarico, Tony *116:* 197
Tallec, Olivier *218:* 4
Tallon, Robert *2:* 228; *43:* 200, 201, 202, 203, 204, 205,206, 207, 209
Tamaki, Jillian *201:* 188
Tamas, Szecsko *29:* 135
Tamburine, Jean *12:* 222
Tanaka, Yoko *215:* 187
Tancredi, Sharon *215:* 127
Tandy, H.R. *13:* 69
Tandy, Russell H. *65:* 9; *100:* 30, 131
Tang, Charles *81:* 202; *90:* 192
Tang, Susan *80:* 174; *108:* 158
Tang, You-shan *63:* 100
Tankersley, Paul *69:* 206; *133:* 219

Tannenbaum, Robert *48:* 181
Tanner, Jane *87:* 13; *97:* 37
Tanner, Tim *72:* 192; *84:* 35
Tanobe, Miyuki *23:* 221
Tarabay, Sharif *110:* 149; *113:* 123; *169:* 83
Tarkington, Booth *17:* 224, 225
Tarlow, Phyllis *61:* 198
Tate, Don *159:* 141, 191; *183:* 69; *186:* 120
Tauss, Herbert *95:* 179
Tauss, Marc *117:* 160; *126:* 155; *178:* 221;
    197: 7; *223:* 168
Tavares, Matt *159:* 192, 193; *198:* 188, 189,
    190; *199:* 86
Taylor, Ann *41:* 226
Taylor, Dahl *129:* 157
Taylor, Geoff *93:* 156; *197:* 173, 175; *204:*
    151, 152
Taylor, Isaac *41:* 228
Taylor, Jennifer *226:* 128
Taylor, Mike *143:* 99, 100
Teague, Mark *83:* 6; *139:* 241; *170:* 180, 181;
    205: 150, 151
Teale, Edwin Way *7:* 196
Teason, James *1:* 14
Teckentrup, Britta *200:* 191, 192
Teeple, Lyn *33:* 147
Tee-Van, Helen Damrosch *10:* 176; *11:* 182
Teevee, Ningeokuluk *223:* 173
Teicher, Dick *50:* 211
Teichman, Mary *77:* 220; *124:* 208; *127:* 22;
    197: 33
Telgemeier, Raina *228:* 180, 181, 182
Temertey, Ludmilla *96:* 232; *104:* 43, 45; *109:*
    244
Tempest, Margaret *3:* 237, 238; *88:* 200
Temple, Frances *85:* 185, 186, 187
Temple, Herbert *45:* 201
Templeton, Owen *11:* 77
ten Cate, Marijke *183:* 193
Tenggren, Gustaf *18:* 277, 278, 279; *19:* 15;
    28: 86; *YABC2:* 145
Tennent, Julie *81:* 105
Tenneson, Joyce *153:* 166
Tenney, Gordon *24:* 204
Tenniel, John *74:* 234, 235; *100:* 89; *YABC 2:*
    99; *153:* 63
Teplin, Scott *231:* 180
Tepper, Matt *116:* 80
Terkel, Ari *103:* 162
Terry, Michael *180:* 209
Terry, Will *131:* 73; *205:* 155; *223:* 105
Teskey, Donald *71:* 51
Tessler, Manya *200:* 193
Thacher, Mary M. *30:* 72
Thackeray, William Makepeace *23:* 224, 228
Thamer, Katie *42:* 187
Tharlet, Eve *146:* 149
Thelwell, Norman *14:* 201
Theobalds, Prue *40:* 23
Theurer, Marilyn Churchill *39:* 195
Thiesing, Lisa *89:* 134; *95:* 202; *156:* 190;
    159: 195
Thiewes, Sam *133:* 114
Thisdale, François *223:* 55
Thistlethwaite, Miles *12:* 224
Thollander, Earl *11:* 47; *18:* 112; *22:* 224
Thomas, Allan *22:* 13
Thomas, Art *48:* 217
Thomas, Eric *28:* 49
Thomas, Harold *20:* 98
Thomas, Jacqui *125:* 95
Thomas, Jan *197:* 180; *226:* 198
Thomas, Mark *42:* 136
Thomas, Martin *14:* 255
Thomas, Middy *177:* 114; *230:* 63
Thompson, Arthur *34:* 107
Thompson, Carol *85:* 189; *95:* 75; *102:* 86;
    147: 166; *189:* 179, 180, 181; *190:* 84; *207:*
    18
Thompson, Colin *95:* 204

Thompson, Ellen *51:* 88, 151; *60:* 33; *67:* 42;
    77: 148; *78:* 75, 219; *79:* 122, 170; *84:* 219;
    85: 97; *87:* 37; *88:* 192, 194; *89:* 80; *93:* 37;
    98: 59; *132:* 14
Thompson, George W. *22:* 18; *28:* 150; *33:*
    135
Thompson, John *58:* 201; *102:* 226; *124:* 154;
    128: 228; *129:* 157; *150:* 49; *185:* 160; *191:*
    192; *224:* 110
Thompson, Julie *44:* 158
Thompson, Katherine *132:* 146
Thompson, K. Dyble *84:* 6
Thompson, Miles *152:* 77
Thompson, Sharon *74:* 113; *158:* 60; *165:* 87
Thomson, Arline K. *3:* 264
Thomson, Bill *186:* 160
Thomson, Hugh *26:* 88
Thomson, Ross *36:* 179
Thorkelson, Gregg *95:* 183, 184; *98:* 58; *165:*
    30, 31; *225:* 31, 32
Thorn, Lori *189:* 119
Thornberg, Dan *104:* 125
Thornburgh, Rebecca McKillip *143:* 37
Thorne, Diana *25:* 212
Thornhill, Jan *77:* 213
Thorpe, Peter *58:* 109
Thorvall, Kerstin *13:* 235
Threadgall, Colin *77:* 215
Thurber, James *13:* 239, 242, 243, 245, 248,
    249
Thurman, Mark *63:* 173; *168:* 116
Tibbles, Jean-Paul *115:* 200
Tibbles, Paul *45:* 23
Tibo, Gilles *67:* 207; *107:* 199, 201
Tichenor, Tom *14:* 207
Tichnor, Richard *90:* 218
Tiegreen, Alan *36:* 143; *43:* 55, 56, 58; *77:*
    200; *94:* 216, 217; *121:* 54, 59
Tierney, Tom *113:* 198, 200, 201
Tildes, Phyllis Limbacher *210:* 240
Tilley, Debbie *102:* 134; *133:* 226; *137:* 101;
    159: 96; *190:* 211, 212; *213:* 51
Tillman, Nancy *211:* 129, 178
Tillotson, Katherine *224:* 175
Tilney, F.C. *22:* 231
Timbs, Gloria *36:* 90
Timmins, Harry *2:* 171
Timmons, Bonnie *194:* 189
Tinkelman, Murray *12:* 225; *35:* 44
Titherington, Jeanne *39:* 90; *58:* 138; *75:* 79;
    135: 161
Tjader, Ella *209:* 14
Tobin, Nancy *145:* 197
Toddy, Irving *172:* 144
Tokunbo, Dimitrea *181:* 183; *187:* 182, 183;
    226: 209
Tolbert, Jeff *128:* 69
Toledo, Francisco *197:* 182; *198:* 199
Toledo, Natalia *197:* 182
Tolford, Joshua *1:* 221
Tolkien, J.R.R. *2:* 243; *32:* 215
Tolman, Marije *195:* 43
Tolmie, Ken *15:* 292
Tomei, Lorna *47:* 168, 171
Tomes, Jacqueline *2:* 117; *12:* 139
Tomes, Margot *1:* 224; *2:* 120, 121; *16:* 207;
    18: 250; *20:* 7; *25:* 62; *27:* 78, 79; *29:* 81,
    199; *33:* 82; *36:* 186, 187, 188, 189, 190;
    46: 129; *56:* 71; *58:* 183; *70:* 228; *75:* 73,
    75; *80:* 80; *83:* 97; *90:* 205
Tommaso, Rich *200:* 198
Tommorow, Tom *223:* 176
Toner, Raymond John *10:* 179
Tong, Gary *66:* 215
Tongier, Stephen *82:* 32
Tooke, Susan *173:* 162
Toothill, Harry *6:* 54; *7:* 49; *25:* 219; *42:* 192
Toothill, Ilse *6:* 54
Topaz, Ksenia *224:* 94
Topolski, Feliks *44:* 48
Torbert, Floyd James *22:* 226

Torgersen, Don *55:* 157
Torline, Kevin *169:* 171
Tormey, Bertram M. *75:* 3, 4
Torrecilla, Pablo *176:* 207
Torres, Leyla *156:* 199, 201
Torrey, Helen *87:* 41
Torrey, Marjorie *34:* 105
Torrey, Richard *189:* 182; *205:* 24
Toschik, Larry *6:* 102
Totten, Bob *13:* 93
Townsend, Michael *231:* 183
Toy, Julie *128:* 112
Trachok, Cathy *131:* 16; *228:* 10
Tracy, Libba *82:* 24
Trago, Keith *158:* 253
Trail, Lee *55:* 157
Trang, To Ngoc *167:* 180
Trang, Winson *89:* 151
Trapani, Iza *116:* 202; *214:* 203
Travers, Bob *49:* 100; *63:* 145
Treatner, Meryl *95:* 180
Tremain, Ruthven *17:* 238
Tresilian, Stuart *25:* 53; *40:* 212
Trez, Alain *17:* 236
Trezzo, Loretta *86:* 45
Trier, Walter *14:* 96
Trimby, Elisa *47:* 199
Trinkle, Sally *53:* 27
Triplett, Gina *182:* 193; *188:* 100; *198:* 38
Tripp, F.J. *24:* 167
Tripp, Wallace *2:* 48; *7:* 28; *8:* 94; *10:* 54,76;
    11: 92; *31:* 170, 171; *34:* 203; *42:* 57; *60:*
    157; *73:* 182
Trivas, Irene *53:* 4; *54:* 168; *82:* 46, 101
Trnka, Jiri *22:* 151; *43:* 212, 213, 214, 215;
    YABC 1: 30, 31
Trondheim, Lewis *182:* 183
Troughton, Joanna *37:* 186; *48:* 72
Troyer, Johannes *3:* 16; *7:* 18
Trudeau, G.B. *35:* 220, 221, 222; *48:* 119,
    123, 126, 127,128, 129, 133; *168:* 189
Trueman, Matthew *165:* 208; *183:* 191; *220:*
    61; *222:* 174
Truesdell, Sue *55:* 142; *108:* 219, 220; *212:*
    202; *220:* 78
Tryon, Leslie *84:* 7; *139:* 214; *143:* 10; *181:*
    10
Tseng, Jean *72:* 195; *94:* 102; *119:* 126; *151:*
    106; *173:* 138, 139; *200:* 158
Tseng, Mou-sien *72:* 195; *94:* 102; *119:* 126;
    151: 106; *173:* 138, 139; *200:* 158
Tsinajinie, Andy *2:* 62
Tsinganos, Jim *180:* 142
Tsugami, Kyuzo *18:* 198, 199
Tucker, Ezra *156:* 31
Tuckwell, Jennifer *17:* 205
Tudor, Bethany *7:* 103
Tudor, Tasha *18:* 227; *20:* 185, 186, 187; *36:*
    111; *69:* 196, 198; *100:* 44;
    YABC 2: 46, 314; *160:* 234
Tuerk, Hanne *71:* 201
Tugeau, Jeremy *199:* 170; *203:* 96
Tulloch, Maurice *24:* 79
Tunis, Edwin *1:* 218, 219; *28:* 209, 210, 211,
    212
Tunnicliffe, C.F. *62:* 176, 177, 178, 179; 181
Turkle, Brinton *1:* 211, 213; *2:* 249; *3:* 226;
    11: 3; *16:* 209; *20:* 22; *50:* 23; *67:* 50; *68:*
    65; *79:* 205, 206, 207; *128:* 47; *YABC 1:* 79
Turnbull, Christopher J. *143:* 99, 100
Turner, Gwenda *59:* 195
Turner, Helen *203:* 154
Turska, Krystyna *12:* 103; *31:* 173, 174, 175;
    56: 32,34; *100:* 66
Tusa, Tricia *72:* 242; *111:* 180, 181; *157:* 165;
    164: 186; *189:* 40; *201:* 9; *207:* 163, 164
Tusan, Stan *6:* 58; *22:* 236, 237
Tuschman, Richard *219:* 100; *224:* 188; *225:*
    175; *231:* 149
Tworkov, Jack *47:* 207
Tyers, Jenny *89:* 220

Tylden-Wright, Jenny *114:* 119
Tyrol, Adelaide Murphy *103:* 27
Tyrrell, Frances *107:* 204
Tzimoulis, Paul *12:* 104

U

Uchida, Yoshiko *1:* 220
Uderzo *47:* 88
Udovic, David *189:* 185; *195:* 201
Ueno, Noriko *59:* 155
Ugliano, Natascia *196:* 186
Ulm, Robert *17:* 238
Ulrich, George *73:* 15; *75:* 136, 139; *99:* 150
Ulriksen, Mark *101:* 58; *182:* 43; *210:* 243
Unada *84:* 67; *227:* 80
    See Gliewe, Unada
Underhill, Liz *53:* 159
Underwood, Beck *192:* 36
Underwood, Clarence *40:* 166
Unger, Jim *67:* 208
Ungerer, Tomi *5:* 188; *9:* 40; *18:* 188; *29:* 175; *33:* 221, 222, 223, 225; *71:* 48; *106:* 209, 210, 211, 212
Unwin, Nora S. *3:* 65, 234, 235; *4:* 237; *44:* 173, 174; *YABC 1:* 59; *2:* 301
Unzner, Christa *230:* 186
Upitis, Alvis *145:* 179
Urban, Helle *149:* 243
Urbanovic, Jackie *86:* 86; *189:* 186, 187
Urberuaga, Emilio *219:* 110, 175
U'ren, Andrea *213:* 177
Uris, Jill *49:* 188, 197
Ursell, Martin *50:* 51
Utpatel, Frank *18:* 114
Utz, Lois *5:* 190

V

Vagin, Vladimir *66:* 10; *142:* 215
Vaillancourt, Francois *107:* 199
Vainio, Pirkko *123:* 157, 158
Valério, Geraldo *180:* 225; *194:* 116
Vallejo, Boris *62:* 130; *72:* 212; *91:* 38; *93:* 61
Van Abbe, S. *16:* 142; *18:* 282; *31:* 90; *YABC 2:* 157, 161
Van Allsburg, Chris *37:* 205, 206; *53:* 161, 162, 163, 165,166, 167, 168, 169, 170, 171; *105:* 215, 216, 217, 218; *156:* 176, 177, 178
Vance, James *65:* 28
Van Der Linde, Henry *99:* 17
van der Meer, Ron *98:* 204, 205
van der Meer, Atie *98:* 204, 205
Vandivert, William *21:* 175
Van Dongen, H.R. *81:* 97
Van Dusen, Chris W. *173:* 169; *228:* 192
Vane, Mitch *210:* 160; *218:* 152
Van Everen, Jay *13:* 160; *YABC 1:* 121
Van Fleet, John *165:* 12, 13
Van Frankenhuyzen, Gijsbert *145:* 230; *149:* 164; *184:* 151; *210:* 248
van Genechten, Guido *165:* 226
van Haeringen, Annemarie *193:* 206
Van Horn, William *43:* 218
van Hout, Mies *195:* 191; *207:* 58
van Kampen, Vlasta *194:* 217
van Lawick, Hugo *62:* 76, 79
Van Lieshout, Maria *201:* 196; *223:* 119
Van Loon, Hendrik Willem *18:* 285, 289, 291
Van Munching, Paul *83:* 85
van Ommen, Sylvia *186:* 192
Van Patter, Bruce *183:* 195
Van Rynbach, Iris *102:* 192
Van Sciver, Ruth *37:* 162
VanSeveren, Joe *63:* 182
Van Stockum, Hilda *5:* 193

Van Vleet, John *213:* 180
Van Wassenhove, Sue *202:* 193
Van Wely, Babs *16:* 50; *79:* 16
Van Wright, Cornelius *72:* 18; *102:* 208; *116:* 107; *152:* 236; *173:* 170, 171; *199:* 185
Van Zyle, Jon *103:* 125; *160:* 181, 182; *176:* 199, 200; *221:* 128
Vardzigulyants, Ruben *90:* 54
Varga, Judy *29:* 196
Vargo, Kurt *79:* 224
Varley, Susan *61:* 199; *63:* 176, 177; *101:* 148; *134:* 220
Varon, Sara *195:* 208
Vasconcellos, Daniel *80:* 42
Vasiliu, Mircea *2:* 166, 253; *9:* 166; *13:* 58; *68:* 42
Vaughn, Frank *34:* 157
Vavra, Robert *8:* 206
Vawter, Will *17:* 163
Vayas, Diana *71:* 61
Vazquez, Carlos *125:* 184
Veeder, Larry *18:* 4
Velasquez, Eric *45:* 217; *61:* 45; *63:* 110, 111; *88:* 162; *90:* 34, 144; *94:* 213; *107:* 147; *132:* 192; *138:* 213; *159:* 126; *181:* 184; *184:* 96; *191:* 16; *192:* 234; *208:* 37; *214:* 81; *226:* 201, 203, 212
Velasquez, Jose A. *63:* 73
Velez, Walter *71:* 75; *91:* 154; *121:* 181; *168:* 49; *207:* 52
Velthuijs, Max *110:* 228, 229
Vendrell, Carme Sole *42:* 205
Venezia, Mike *54:* 17
Venti, Anthony Bacon *124:* 103; *126:* 26
Venturo, Piero *61:* 194, 195
Ver Beck, Frank *18:* 16, 17
Verkaaik, Ben *110:* 209
Verling, John *71:* 27
Verney, John *14:* 225; *75:* 8
Vernon, Ursula *204:* 157
Verrier, Suzanne *5:* 20; *23:* 212
Verroken, Sarah *223:* 178
Versace, Marie *2:* 255
Verstraete, Randy *108:* 193
Vess, Charles *215:* 201
Vestal, H.B. *9:* 134; *11:* 101; *27:* 25; *34:* 158
Vestergaard, Hope *190:* 203
Vicatan *59:* 146
Vickrey, Robert *45:* 59, 64
Victor, Joan Berg *30:* 193
Vieceli, Emma *210:* 245
Viereck, Ellen *3:* 242; *14:* 229
Vigna, Judith *15:* 293; *102:* 194, 195, 196, 197
Vila, Laura *207:* 172
Vilato, Gaspar E. *5:* 41
Villeneuve, Anne *230:* 189
Villiard, Paul *51:* 178
Vimnera, A. *23:* 154
Vincent, Eric *34:* 98
Vincent, Felix *41:* 237
Vincent, Gabrielle *121:* 175
Vip *45:* 164
Viskupic, Gary *83:* 48
Vitale, Stefano *109:* 71, 107; *114:* 219, 220; *123:* 106; *138:* 232; *180:* 228, 229; *212:* 38; *225:* 191, 192, 193
Vivas, Julie *51:* 67, 69; *96:* 225; *197:* 190; *199:* 71
Voake, Charlotte *114:* 221, 222; *180:* 232
Vo-Dinh, Mai *16:* 272; *60:* 191
Vogel, Ilse-Margret *14:* 230
Voigt, Erna *35:* 228
Vojnar, Kamil *95:* 31; *114:* 4; *115:* 62; *121:* 90; *124:* 72; *130:* 31; *141:* 81; *146:* 196; *150:* 123; *158:* 5, 6; *158:* 154; *171:* 119, 188; *179:* 15; *180:* 112; *203:* 74; *223:* 30; *229:* 43; *230:* 199; *231:* 53, 121, 122
Vojtech, Anna *42:* 190; *108:* 222, 223; *150:* 203; *174:* 173; *228:* 21
von Buhler, Cynthia *149:* 237; *162:* 177; *177:* 205; *180:* 77; *185:* 214, 215, 216

von Roehl, Angela *126:* 191
von Schmidt, Eric *8:* 62; *50:* 209, 210
von Schmidt, Harold *30:* 80
Vosburgh, Leonard *1:* 161; *7:* 32; *15:* 295, 296; *23:* 110; *30:* 214; *43:* 181
Voss, Tom *127:* 104
Voter, Thomas W. *19:* 3, 9
Vroman, Tom *10:* 29
Vulliamy, Clara *72:* 65
Vyner, Tim *228:* 198

W

Waber, Bernard *47:* 209, 210, 211, 212, 213, 214; *95:* 215, 216, 217; *156:* 203, 205, 206, 207
Waber, Paulis *231:* 189
Wachenje, Benjamin *194:* 170
Wack, Jeff *95:* 140; *110:* 90
Wagner, John *8:* 200; *52:* 104
Wagner, Ken *2:* 59
Wagner, Michael *211:* 159
Wahman, Wendy *218:* 186
Waide, Jan *29:* 225; *36:* 139
Wainwright, Jerry *14:* 85
Waites, Joan *171:* 2; *226:* 184
Wakeen, Sandra *47:* 97
Wakiyama, Hanako *171:* 96; *192:* 236; *200:* 16
Waldherr, Kris *81:* 186
Waldman, Bruce *15:* 297; *43:* 178
Waldman, Neil *35:* 141; *50:* 163; *51:* 180; *54:* 78; *77:* 112; *79:* 162; *82:* 174; *84:* 5, 56, 106; *94:* 232, 233, 234; *96:* 41; *111:* 139; *113:* 9; *118:* 30; *142:* 220, 223; *203:* 173, 174
Waldrep, Richard *111:* 147; *198:* 202
Waldron, Kevin *230:* 191
Walker, Brian *144:* 128
Walker, Charles *1:* 46; *4:* 59; *5:* 177; *11:* 115; *19:* 45; *34:* 74; *62:* 168; *72:* 218
Walker, Dugald Stewart *15:* 47; *32:* 202; *33:* 112
Walker, Gil *8:* 49; *23:* 132; *34:* 42
Walker, Jeff *55:* 154; *123:* 116
Walker, Jim *10:* 94
Walker, Mort *8:* 213
Walker, Norman *41:* 37; *45:* 58
Walker, Stephen *12:* 229; *21:* 174
Walker, Steve *231:* 119
Wallace, Beverly Dobrin *19:* 259
Wallace, Chad *229:* 198
Wallace, Cly *87:* 93
Wallace, Ian *53:* 176, 177; *56:* 165, 166; *58:* 4; *98:* 4; *101:* 191; *112:* 124; *141:* 197, 198, 199, 200; *151:* 212; *219:* 180, 182
Wallace, John *105:* 228
Wallace, Nancy Elizabeth *141:* 204; *186:* 195, 197, 199; *222:* 191, 192, 193, 194
Wallenta, Adam *123:* 180
Waller, S.E. *24:* 36
Wallner, Alexandra *15:* 120; *156:* 183
Wallner, John C. *9:* 77; *10:* 188; *11:* 28; *14:* 209; *31:* 56, 118; *37:* 64; *51:* 186, 187, 188, 189, 190, 191,192, 193, 194, 195; *52:* 96; *53:* 23, 26; *71:* 99; *73:* 158; *89:* 215; *141:* 9
Wallner, John *162:* 17
Wallower, Lucille *11:* 226
Walotsky, Ron *93:* 87
Walsh, Ellen Stoll *99:* 209; *147:* 219; *194:* 194, 195, 196
Walsh, Rebecca *158:* 193; *217:* 169, 170
Walsh, Vivian *149:* 215; *158:* 227
Walters, Anita *205:* 163
Walters, Audrey *18:* 294
Walther, Tom *31:* 179
Walton, Garry *69:* 149
Walton, Tony *11:* 164; *24:* 209; *153:* 8; *177:* 73
Waltrip, Lela *9:* 195

Waltrip, Mildred *3:* 209; *37:* 211
Waltrip, Rufus *9:* 195
Wan *12:* 76
Wan, Shelly *212:* 131
Wang, Lin *221:* 179
Wang, Shaoli *216:* 220
Wang, Suling *191:* 183; *213:* 194
Warburton, Sarah *154:* 187
Wappers, G. *121:* 40
Ward, Chad Michael *217:* 121
Ward, Fred *52:* 19
Ward, Helen *72:* 244; *144:* 240, 242
Ward, John *42:* 191; *96:* 54; *97:* 110; *123:* 105; *124:* 71; *173:* 66; *221:* 55
Ward, Keith *2:* 107; *132:* 69
Ward, Leslie *34:* 126; *36:* 87
Ward, Lynd *1:* 99, 132, 133, 150; *2:* 108, 158, 196, 259; *18:* 86; *27:* 56; *29:* 79, 187, 253, 255; *36:* 199,200, 201, 202, 203, 204, 205, 206, 207, 209; *43:* 34; *56:* 28; *60:* 116; *100:* 65
Ward, Peter *37:* 116
Waring, Geoff *172:* 84
Warhola, James *92:* 5; *115:* 85, 87; *118:* 174, 175, 177; *176:* 84; *187:* 189, 190; *223:* 102
Warner, Bob *230:* 5
Warner, Ben *159:* 171
Warner, Peter *14:* 87
Warner, Sally *214:* 210
Warnes, Tim *175:* 159; *202:* 188; *216:* 224
Warnick, Elsa *113:* 223
Warren, Betsy *2:* 101
Warren, Jim *85:* 81
Warren, Marion Cray *14:* 215
Warshaw, Jerry *30:* 197, 198; *42:* 165
Wasden, Kevin *102:* 162
Washington, Nevin *20:* 123
Washington, Phyllis *20:* 123
Wasserman, Amy L. *92:* 110; *209:* 95
Waterman, Stan *11:* 76
Watkins-Pitchford, D.J. *6:* 215, 217
Watling, James *67:* 210; *78:* 112; *101:* 81; *117:* 189, 190; *127:* 119, 120
Watson, Aldren A. *2:* 267; *5:* 94; *13:* 71; *19:* 253; *32:* 220; *42:* 193, 194, 195, 196, 197, 198, 199, 200, 201; *YABC 2:* 202
Watson, G. *83:* 162
Watson, Gary *19:* 147; *36:* 68; *41:* 122; *47:* 139
Watson, J.D. *22:* 86
Watson, Jesse Joshua *197:* 124; *199:* 181; *202:* 136
Watson, Karen *11:* 26
Watson, Mary *117:* 193
Watson, Richard Jesse *62:* 188, 189; *211:* 201
Watson, Wendy *5:* 197; *13:* 101; *33:* 116; *46:* 163; *64:* 12; *74:* 242, 243; *91:* 21; *142:* 228; *215:* 79
Watt, Mélanie *136:* 206; *193:* 211
Wattenberg, Jane *174:* 200; *185:* 46; *187:* 108
Watterson, Bill *66:* 223, 225, 226
Watts, Bernadette *4:* 227; *103:* 182, 183; *230:* 193, 194, 195
Watts, James *59:* 197; *74:* 145; *86:* 124
Watts, John *37:* 149
Watts, Leslie Elizabeth *150:* 207; *165:* 106; *209:* 67
Watts, Stan *116:* 205
Weatherby, Mark Alan *77:* 141
Web, Hannah *228:* 215
Webb, Jennifer *110:* 79
Webb, Lanny *142:* 175
Webb, Sophie *135:* 214
Webber, Helen *3:* 141
Webber, Irma E. *14:* 238
Weber, Erik *56:* 19, 20
Weber, Florence *40:* 153
Weber, Jill *127:* 227, 228; *189:* 163; *208:* 157; *209:* 190, 191; *216:* 46
Weber, Roland *61:* 204
Weber, Sam *190:* 227

Weber, William J. *14:* 239
Webster, Jean *17:* 241
Weeks, Sarah *162:* 39
Wegman, William *78:* 243
Wegner, Fritz *14:* 250; *20:* 189; *44:* 165; *86:* 62
Weidenear, Reynold H. *21:* 122
Weigel, Jeff *170:* 193
Weihs, Erika *4:* 21; *15:* 299; *72:* 201; *107:* 207, 208
Weil, Lisl *7:* 203; *10:* 58; *21:* 95; *22:* 188,217; *33:* 193
Weiman, Jon *50:* 162, 165; *52:* 103; *54:* 78, 79, 81; *78:* 80; *82:* 107; *93:* 82; *97:* 69; *105:* 179; *193:* 65
Weiner, Greg *215:* 21
Weiner, Sandra *14:* 240
Weiner, Scott *55:* 27
Weinhaus, Karen Ann *53:* 90; *71:* 50; *86:* 124
Weinman, Brad *197:* 20
Weinstock, Robert *204:* 165, 166
Weisgard, Leonard *1:* 65; *2:* 191, 197, 204, 264, 265; *5:* 108; *21:* 42; *30:* 200, 201, 203, 204; *41:* 47; *44:* 125; *53:* 25; *85:* 196, 198, 200, 201; *100:* 139,207; *YABC 2:* 13
Weisman, David *173:* 47
Weiss, Ellen *44:* 202
Weiss, Emil *1:* 168; *7:* 60
Weiss, Harvey *1:* 145, 223; *27:* 224, 227; *68:* 214; *76:* 245, 246, 247
Weiss, Nicki *33:* 229
Weissman, Bari *49:* 72; *90:* 125; *139:* 142
Weitzman, David L. *172:* 199
Welch, Sheila Kelly *130:* 221
Welkes, Allen *68:* 218
Wellington, Monica *99:* 223; *157:* 259, 260, 261; *222:* 197, 198, 199, 200
Welliver, Norma *76:* 94
Wellner, Fred *127:* 53
Wells, Frances *1:* 183
Wells, H.G. *20:* 194, 200
Wells, Haru *53:* 120, 121
Wells, Robert E. *184:* 208
Wells, Rosemary *6:* 49; *18:* 297; *60:* 32; *66:* 203; *69:* 215, 216; *114:* 227; *118:* 149, 150; *156:* 188, 189, 190, 191; *207:* 180, 181, 182, 183
Wells, Rufus III *56:* 111, 113
Wells, Susan *22:* 43
Wendelin, Rudolph *23:* 234
Wengenroth, Stow *37:* 47
Weninger, Brigitte *189:* 192, 194
Werenskiold, Erik *15:* 6; *62:* 17
Werner, Honi *24:* 110; *33:* 41; *88:* 122
Werth, Kurt *7:* 122; *14:* 157; *20:* 214; *39:* 128
Wesson,
West, Harry A. *124:* 38; *227:* 16
Westcott, Nadine Bernard *68:* 46; *84:* 49; *86:* 133; *106:* 199; *111:* 78; *113:* 111; *130:* 224; *139:* 54; *158:* 256; *194:* 199
Westerberg, Christine *29:* 226
Westerduin, Anne *105:* 229
Westerman, Johanna *162:* 206
Weston, Martha *29:* 116; *30:* 213; *33:* 85, 100; *53:* 181, 182, 183, 184; *77:* 95; *80:* 152; *119:* 196,197, 198, 199; *127:* 189; *133:* 196; *209:* 199
Wetherbee, Margaret *5:* 3
Wexler, Jerome *49:* 73; *150:* 129
Whalley, Peter *50:* 49
Whamond, Dave *222:* 203
Whatley, Bruce *186:* 93, 95; *207:* 127; *213:* 183, 184
Wheatley, Arabelle *11:* 231; *16:* 276
Wheeler, Cindy *49:* 205
Wheeler, Dora *44:* 179
Wheelright, Rowland *15:* 81; *YABC 2:* 286
Whelan, Michael *56:* 108; *70:* 27, 29, 67, 68, 148; *74:* 18; *84:* 14; *91:* 195, 196; *95:* 147; *98:* 150, 151; *106:* 157; *113:* 218, 220; *116:* 99, 100

Whelan, Patrick *135:* 145
Whistler, Rex *16:* 75; *30:* 207, 208
White, Beth *216:* 139
White, Craig *110:* 130; *119:* 193; *130:* 33; *179:* 31
White, David Omar *5:* 56; *18:* 6
White, Joan *83:* 225
White, Lee *221:* 176; *223:* 188, 189, 190
White, Martin *51:* 197; *85:* 127
Whitear *32:* 26
Whitehead, Beck *86:* 171
Whitehead, Jenny *221:* 16
Whitehead, S.B. *154:* 132
Whithorne, H.S. *7:* 49
Whitman, Candace *208:* 208
Whitney, George Gillett *3:* 24
Whitney, Jean *99:* 53
Whitson, Paul *102:* 161
Whittam, Geoffrey *30:* 191
Whyte, Mary *96:* 127
Wiberg, Harald *38:* 127; *93:* 215
Wick, Walter *77:* 128
Wickstrom, Sylvie *106:* 87; *169:* 180; *214:* 110
Wickstrom, Thor *200:* 205
Widener, Terry *105:* 230; *106:* 7; *163:* 23; *200:* 17; *209:* 195; *231:* 12
Wiese, Kurt *3:* 255; *4:* 206; *14:* 17; *17:* 18, 19; *19:* 47; *24:* 152; *25:* 212; *32:* 184; *36:* 211,213, 214, 215, 216, 217, 218; *45:* 161; *100:* 92
Wiesner, David *33:* 47; *51:* 106; *57:* 67; *58:* 55; *64:* 78, 79, 81; *69:* 233; *72:* 247, 248, 249, 251,252, 253, 254; *83:* 134; *104:* 31; *117:* 197, 199, 200, 202; *139:* 223, 224; *151:* 51; *181:* 189, 190
Wiesner, William *4:* 100; *5:* 200, 201; *14:* 262
Wight, Eric *218:* 190
Wiggins, George *6:* 133
Wijngaard, Juan *111:* 36; *114:* 124; *227:* 136; *230:* 202
Wikkelsoe, Otto *45:* 25, 26
Wikland, Ilon *5:* 113; *8:* 150; *38:* 124, 125, 130; *127:* 162
Wikler, Madeline *114:* 233
Wilbur, C. Keith, M.D. *27:* 228
Wilburn, Kathy *53:* 102; *68:* 234
Wilcox, Cathy *105:* 123
Wilcox, J.A.J. *34:* 122
Wilcox, Lydia *207:* 187
Wilcox, R. Turner *36:* 219
Wild, Jocelyn *46:* 220, 221, 222; *80:* 117
Wilde, George *7:* 139
Wildish, Lee *231:* 34, 193
Wildsmith, Brian *16:* 281, 282; *18:* 170, 171; *66:* 25; *69:* 224, 225, 227; *77:* 103; *83:* 218; *124:* 214,217, 219
Wildsmith, Mike *140:* 229
Wilhelm, Hans *58:* 189, 191; *73:* 157; *77:* 127; *135:* 229, 230, 233, 234; *196:* 209
Wilkin, Eloise *36:* 173; *49:* 208, 209, 210
Wilkinson, Barry *50:* 213
Wilkinson, Gerald *3:* 40
Wilkon, Jozef *31:* 183, 184; *71:* 206, 207, 209; *133:* 222
Wilks, Mike *34:* 24; *44:* 203; *224:* 193
Willems, Mo *154:* 245, 246, 247; *180:* 236, 237, 239; *228:* 204, 208
Willey, Bee *103:* 129; *139:* 159; *173:* 115
Willhoite, Michael A. *71:* 214
William, Maria *168:* 51
Williams, Berkeley, Jr. *64:* 75
Williams, Ferelith Eccles *22:* 238
Williams, Garth *1:* 197; *2:* 49, 270; *4:* 205; *15:* 198, 302, 304, 307; *16:* 34; *18:* 283, 298, 299, 300, 301; *29:* 177, 178, 179, 232, 233, 241, 242, 243, 244, 245, 248; *40:* 106; *66:* 229, 230, 231, 233, 234; *71:* 192; *73:* 218, 219, 220; *78:* 261; *100:* 251, 252, 255; *136:* 117; *YABC 2:* 15, 16, 19
Williams, J. Scott *48:* 28

Williams, Jennifer *102:* 201
Williams, Jenny *60:* 202; *81:* 21; *88:* 71
Williams, Kent *180:* 18
Williams, Kit *44:* 206, 207, 208, 209, 211, 212
Williams, Marcia *97:* 214; *159:* 208, 209
Williams, Maureen *12:* 238
Williams, Patrick *14:* 218
Williams, Richard *44:* 93; *72:* 229; *74:* 133; *78:* 155, 237; *91:* 178; *110:* 212; *136:* 201, 202, 203; *152:* 115
Williams, Sam *124:* 222; *153:* 11; *177:* 201, 202; *180:* 34; *212:* 49
Williams, Sophy *135:* 236
Williams, Vera B. *53:* 186, 187, 188, 189; *102:* 201, 202, 203; *210:* 65
Williamson, Alex *177:* 180; *205:* 50
Williamson, Mel *60:* 9
Willingham, Fred *104:* 206; *154:* 157
Willis, Adam *181:* 75; *209:* 11
Willmore, J.T. *54:* 113, 114
Wilsdorf, Anne *180:* 122; *189:* 124; *191:* 195
Wilson, Anne *160:* 114; *224:* 199, 200
Wilson, Charles Banks *17:* 92; *43:* 73
Wilson, Connie *113:* 179
Wilson, Dagmar *10:* 47
Wilson, Dawn *67:* 161; *81:* 120; *113:* 158
Wilson, Edward A. *6:* 24; *16:* 149; *20:* 220, 221; *22:* 87; *26:* 67; *38:* 212, 214, 215, 216, 217
Wilson, Forrest *27:* 231
Wilson, Gahan *35:* 234; *41:* 136
Wilson, George *76:* 87
Wilson, Helen Miranda *140:* 61
Wilson, Jack *17:* 139
Wilson, Janet *77:* 154; *96:* 114; *99:* 219, 220; *153:* 64 *106:* 122; *130:* 210; *145:* 178; *173:* 64
Wilson, John *22:* 240
Wilson, Maurice *46:* 224
Wilson, Patten *35:* 61
Wilson, Peggy *15:* 4; *84:* 20
Wilson, Phil *181:* 29
Wilson, Rowland B. *30:* 170
Wilson, Sarah *50:* 215
Wilson, Tom *33:* 232
Wilson, W.N. *22:* 26
Wilson-Max, Ken *170:* 196; *180:* 181
Wilton, Nicholas *103:* 52; *183:* 111
Wilwerding, Walter J. *9:* 202
Wimmer, Mike *63:* 6; *70:* 121; *75:* 186; *76:* 21,22, 23; *91:* 114; *97:* 45, 68; *98:* 28; *107:* 130; *146:* 21; *149:* 47; *173:* 126; *193:* 21, 25; *194:* 204, 205
Winborn, Marsha *78:* 34; *99:* 70; *192:* 20
Winch, John *165:* 233
Winchester, Linda *13:* 231
Wind, Betty *28:* 158
Windham, Kathryn Tucker *14:* 260
Windham, Sophie *184:* 212
Winfield, Alison *115:* 78; *214:* 121
Winfield, Wayne *72:* 23
Wing, Gary *64:* 147
Wing, Ron *50:* 85
Wingerter, Linda S. *132:* 199; *174:* 181; *200:* 196
Winick, Judd *124:* 227, 228, 229
Winn-Lederer, Ilene *202:* 91
Winnick, Karen B. *211:* 207
Winslow, Will *21:* 124
Winstead, Rosie *180:* 243
Winsten, Melanie Willa *41:* 41
Winter, Jeanette *151:* 240, 241, 242; *184:* 215, 217, 218, 219
Winter, Milo *15:* 97; *19:* 221; *21:* 181, 203, 204, 205; *64:* 19; *YABC 2:* 144
Winter, Paula *48:* 227
Winter, Susan *163:* 177; *182:* 201; *226:* 173
Winters, Greg *70:* 117
Winters, Nina *62:* 194
Wise, Louis *13:* 68
Wiseman, Ann *31:* 187

Wiseman, B. *4:* 233
Wishnefsky, Phillip *3:* 14
Wiskur, Darrell *5:* 72; *10:* 50; *18:* 246
Wisniewski, David *95:* 220, 221
Wisniewski, Robert *95:* 10; *119:* 192
Withee, Maureen *225:* 42
Witschonke, Alan *153:* 149, 150
Witt, Dick *80:* 244
Wittmann, Patrick *162:* 204
Wittman, Sally *30:* 219
Wittner, Dale *99:* 43
Wittwer, Hala *158:* 267; *195:* 80
Woehr, Lois *12:* 5
Wohlberg, Meg *12:* 100; *14:* 197; *41:* 255
Wohnoutka, Mike *137:* 68; *190:* 199; *195:* 218; *205:* 132; *221:* 6; *230:* 206, 207
Wojtowycz, David *167:* 168
Woldin, Beth Weiner *34:* 211
Wolf, Elizabeth *133:* 151; *208:* 175
Wolf, J. *16:* 91
Wolf, Janet *78:* 254
Wolf, Linda *33:* 163
Wolfe, Corey *72:* 213
Wolfe, Frances *216:* 227
Wolfe, Gillian *199:* 193
Wolff, Ashley *50:* 217; *81:* 216; *156:* 216, 217; *170:* 57; *174:* 174; *184:* 72; *203:* 181, 182, 183, 184
Wolff, Glenn *178:* 230
Wolff, Jason *213:* 186
Wolfsgruber, Linda *166:* 61
Wondriska, William *6:* 220
Wong, Janet S. *98:* 225; *152:* 43
Wong, Ken *224:* 23
Wong, Nicole *174:* 13; *214:* 216; *215:* 25
Wonsetler, John C. *5:* 168
Wood, Audrey *50:* 221, 222, 223; *81:* 219, 221; *198:* 206
Wood, Don *50:* 220, 225, 226, 228, 229; *81:* 218, 220; *139:* 239, 240
Wood, Grant *19:* 198
Wood, Heather *133:* 108
Wood, Ivor *58:* 17
Wood, Jakki *211:* 209
Wood, Muriel *36:* 119; *77:* 167; *171:* 55; *187:* 46
Wood, Myron *6:* 220
Wood, Owen *18:* 187; *64:* 202, 204, 205, 206, 208, 210
Wood, Rob *193:* 48
Wood, Ruth *8:* 11
Woodbridge, Curtis *133:* 138; *204:* 113
Wooding, Sharon L. *66:* 237
Woodruff, Liza *132:* 239; *182:* 46, 204
Woodruff, Thomas *171:* 73
Woods, John, Jr. *109:* 142
Woods, Maria *227:* 69
Woodson, Jack *10:* 201
Woodson, Jacqueline *94:* 242
Woodward, Alice *26:* 89; *36:* 81
Wool, David *26:* 27
Wooley, Janet *112:* 75; *227:* 74
Woolman, Steven *106:* 47; *163:* 73
Wooten, Vernon *23:* 70; *51:* 170
Worboys, Evelyn *1:* 166, 167
Word, Reagan *103:* 204
Wormell, Christopher *154:* 251; *202:* 206
Worth, Jo *34:* 143
Worth, Wendy *4:* 133
Wosmek, Frances *29:* 251
Wrenn, Charles L. *38:* 96; *YABC 1:* 20, 21
Wright, Barbara Mullarney *98:* 161
Wright, Cliff *168:* 203
Wright, Dare *21:* 206
Wright-Frierson, Virginia *58:* 194; *110:* 246
Wright, George *YABC 1:* 268
Wright, Joseph *30:* 160
Wronker, Lili Cassel *3:* 247; *10:* 204; *21:* 10
Wu, Donald *200:* 18
Wummer, Amy *154:* 181; *168:* 150; *176:* 85; *201:* 202, 203; *218:* 154

Wyant, Alexander Helwig *110:* 19
Wyatt, David *97:* 9; *101:* 44; *114:* 194; *140:* 20; *167:* 13; *188:* 48; *227:* 60
Wyatt, Stanley *46:* 210
Wyeth, Andrew *13:* 40; *YABC 1:* 133, 134
Wyeth, Jamie *41:* 257
Wyeth, N.C. *13:* 41; *17:* 252, 253, 254, 255, 256, 257, 258, 259, 264, 265, 266, 267, 268; *18:* 181; *19:* 80, 191, 200; *21:* 57, 183; *22:* 91; *23:* 152; *24:* 28, 99; *35:* 61; *41:* 65; *100:* 206; *YABC1:* 133, 223; *2:* 53, 75, 171, 187, 317
Wyman, Cherie R. *91:* 42
Wynne, Patricia J. *210:* 260; *223:* 184

X

Xuan, YongSheng *119:* 202, 207, 208; *140:* 36; *187:* 21; *226:* 221, 227, 230, 232, 233

Y

Yaccarino, Dan *141:* 208, 209; *147:* 171; *192:* 244, 245; *207:* 168
Yakovetic, Joe *59:* 202; *75:* 85
Yalowitz, Paul *93:* 33; *211:* 92
Yamaguchi, Marianne *85:* 118
Yamasaki, James *167:* 93
Yang, Belle *170:* 198
Yang, Jay *1:* 8; *12:* 239
Yap, Weda *6:* 176
Yaroslava
    See Mills, Yaroslava Surmach
Yashima, Taro *14:* 84
Yates, John *74:* 249, 250
Yates, Kelly *208:* 214
Yayo *178:* 88; *226:* 235
Yeatts, Tabatha *215:* 210
Yee, Cora *166:* 233
Yee, Wong Herbert *115:* 216, 217; *172:* 204, 205; *194:* 59
Yelchin, Eugene *204:* 4
Yeo, Brad *135:* 121; *192:* 106
Yerxa, Leo *181:* 195
Yezerski, Thomas F. *162:* 29
Ylla
    See Koffler, Camilla
Yohn, F.C. *23:* 128; *YABC 1:* 269
Yoo, Taeeun *191:* 198
Yorinks, Adrienne *144:* 248; *200:* 214
Yorke, David *80:* 178
Yoshida, Toshi *77:* 231
Yoshikawa, Sachiko *168:* 104; *177:* 28; *181:* 196, 197; *225:* 115
Youll, Paul *91:* 218
Youll, Stephen *92:* 227; *118:* 136, 137; *164:* 248; *202:* 92
Young, Amy L. *185:* 218; *190:* 46
Young, Cybéle *167:* 9
Young, Ed *7:* 205; *10:* 206; *40:* 124; *63:* 142; *74:* 250, 251, 252, 253; *75:* 227; *81:* 159; *83:* 98; *94:* 154; *115:* 160; *137:* 162; *YABC 2:* 242; *173:* 174, 175, 176; *205:* 29; *212:* 82; *221:* 72
Young, Mary O'Keefe *77:* 95; *80:* 247; *134:* 214; *140:* 213; *211:* 223, 225
Young, Noela *8:* 221; *89:* 231; *97:* 195; *230:* 145, 146
Young, Paul *190:* 222; *225:* 38
Young, Selina *153:* 12; *201:* 204, 205
Yuen, Sammy *223:* 46
Yum, Hyewon *211:* 228
Yun, Cheng Mung *60:* 143
Yung, Jennifer *220:* 136

Z

Zacharow, Christopher *88:* 98
Zacks, Lewis *10:* 161
Zadig *50:* 58
Zaffo, George *42:* 208
Zagwyn, Deborah Turney *138:* 227
Zahares, Wade *193:* 219
Zaid, Barry *50:* 127; *51:* 201
Zaidenberg, Arthur *34:* 218, 219, 220
Zalben, Jane Breskin *7:* 211; *79:* 230, 231, 233; *170:* 202
Zallinger, Jean *4:* 192; *8:* 8, 129; *14:* 273; *68:* 36; *80:* 254; *115:* 219, 220, 222
Zallinger, Rudolph F. *3:* 245
Zakanitch, Robert Rahway *231:* 195
Zakrajsek, Molly *177:* 146
Zappa, Ahmet *180:* 250
Zebot, George *83:* 214
Zecca, Katherine *207:* 195
Zeck, Gerry *40:* 232
Zeff, Joe *181:* 98; *221:* 101
Zeifert, Harriet *154:* 265, 267

Zeiring, Bob *42:* 130
Zeldich, Arieh *49:* 124; *62:* 120
Zeldis, Malcah *86:* 239; *94:* 198; *146:* 265, 266
Zelinsky, Paul O. *14:* 269; *43:* 56; *49:* 218-223; *53:* 111; *68:* 195; *102:* 219, 222, 221, 222; *154:* 255, 256, 257; *171:* 141; *185:* 96
Zelvin, Diana *72:* 190; *76:* 101; *93:* 207
Zemach, Kaethe *149:* 250
Zemach, Margot *3:* 270; *8:* 201; *21:* 210, 211; *27:* 204, 205, 210; *28:* 185; *49:* 22, 183, 224; *53:* 151; *56:* 146; *70:* 245, 246; *92:* 74
Zeman, Ludmila *153* 212
Zemsky, Jessica *10:* 62
Zepelinsky, Paul *35:* 93
Zerbetz, Evon *127:* 34; *158:* 109
Zezejl, Daniel *197:* 74
Zhang, Ange *101:* 190; *172:* 41
Zhang, Son Nang *163:* 113; *170:* 206
Ziegler, Jack *84:* 134
Zimdars, Berta *129:* 155
Zimet, Jay *147:* 94; *152:* 74; *196:* 75
Zimic, Tricia *72:* 95

Zimmer, Dirk *38:* 195; *49:* 71; *56:* 151; *65:* 214; *84:* 159; *89:* 26; *147:* 224
Zimmer, Tracie Vaughn *169:* 183
Zimmerman, Andrea *192:* 49, 50
Zimmermann, H. Werner *101:* 223; *112:* 197
Zimnik, Reiner *36:* 224
Zingone, Robin *180:* 134
Zinkeisen, Anna *13:* 106
Zinn, David *97:* 97
Zoellick, Scott *33:* 231
Zollars, Jaime *190:* 190
Zonia, Dhimitri *20:* 234, 235
Zorn, Peter A., Jr. *142:* 157
Zudeck, Darryl *58:* 129; *63:* 98; *80:* 52
Zug, Mark *88:* 131; *204:* 169
Zulewski, Tim *164:* 95
Zuma *99:* 36
Zvorykin, Boris *61:* 155
Zweifel, Francis *14:* 274; *28:* 187
Zwerger, Lisbeth *54:* 176, 178; *66:* 246, 247, 248; *130:* 230, 231, 232, 233; *181:* 92; *194:* 224, 225, 226
Zwinger, Herman H. *46:* 227
Zwolak, Paul *67:* 69, 71, 73, 74

Author Index

The following index gives the number of the volume in which an author's biographical sketch, Autobiography Feature, Brief Entry, or Obituary appears.

This index includes references to all entries in the following series, which are also published by The Gale Group.

YABC—*Yesterday's Authors of Books for Children: Facts and Pictures about Authors and Illustrators of Books for Young People from Early Times to 1960*
CLR—*Children's Literature Review: Excerpts from Reviews, Criticism, and Commentary on Books for Children*
SAAS—*Something about the Author Autobiography Series*

A

Aardema, Verna 1911-2000 107
  Obituary 119
  Earlier sketches in SATA :4, 68
  See also CLR 17
  See also SAAS 8
Aaron, Chester 1923- 216
  Autobiography Feature 216
  Earlier sketches in SATA 9, 74
  See also SAAS 12
Aaseng, Nate
  See Aaseng, Nathan
Aaseng, Nathan 1953- 172
  Brief entry 38
  Earlier sketches in SATA 51, 88
  See also CLR 54
  See also SAAS 12
Abadzis, Nick 1965- 193
Abalos, Rafael 1956-
  See Abalos, Rafael
Abalos, Rafael 1956- 197
Abbas, Jailan 1952- 91
Abbey, Lynn
  See Abbey, Marilyn Lorraine
Abbey, Marilyn Lorraine 1948- 156
Abbott, Alice
  See Borland, Kathryn Kilby
  and Speicher, Helen Ross S(mith)
Abbott, Jacob 1803-1879 22
Abbott, Manager Henry
  See Stratemeyer, Edward L.
Abbott, R(obert) Tucker 1919-1995 61
  Obituary 87
Abbott, Sarah
  See Zolotow, Charlotte
Abbott, Tony 1952- 205
  Earlier sketch in SATA 159
Abdelsayed, Cindy 1962- 123
Abdul, Raoul 1929- 12
Abeele, Veronique van den 196
Abel, Raymond 1911- 12
Abell, Kathleen 1938- 9
Abelove, Joan 110
Abels, Harriette S(heffer) 1926- 50
Abercrombie, Barbara 1939- 182
  Earlier sketch in SATA 16
Abercrombie, Barbara Mattes
  See Abercrombie, Barbara

Abercrombie, Lynn
  See Sorrells, Walter
Abernethy, Robert G(ordon) 1927- 5
Abisch, Roslyn Kroop 1927- 9
Abisch, Roz
  See Abisch, Roslyn Kroop
Ablow, Gail 1962- 198
Abodaher, David J. (Naiph) 1919- 17
Abolafia, Yossi 1944-
  See Abulafia, Yossi
Abolivier, Aurelie 219
Abouzeid, Chris 175
Abrahall, Clare Hoskyns
  See Hoskyns-Abrahall, Clare (Constance Drury)
Abrahams, Hilary (Ruth) 1938- 29
Abrahams, Peter 1947- 194
Abrahams, Robert David 1905-1998 4
Abramovitz, Anita (Zeltner Brooks) 1914- 5
Abrams, Joy 1941- 16
Abrams, Lawrence F. 58
  Brief entry 47
Abrashkin, Raymond 1911-1960 50
Abulafia, Yossi 1944- 177
  Brief entry 46
  Earlier sketch in SATA 60
Acampora, Paul 175
Accardo, Anthony 191
Acer, David 206
Achebe, Albert Chinualumogu
  See Achebe, Chinua
Achebe, Chinua 1930- 40
  Brief entry 38
  Earlier sketch in SATA 38
  See also CLR 156
Acheson, Alison 1964- 222
Ackerman, Diane 1948- 102
Ackerman, Eugene (Francis) 1888-1974 10
Ackerman, Karen 1951- 126
Ackerman, Susan Yoder 1945- 92
Ackison, Wendy Wassink 1956- 103
Ackley, Peggy Jo 1955- 58
Ackroyd, Peter 1949- 153
Acorn, John (Harrison) 1958- 79
Acredolo, Linda (Potter) 1947- 159
Acs, Laszlo (Bela) 1931- 42
  Brief entry 32
Acuff, Selma Boyd 1924- 45

Ada, Alma Flor 1938- 222
  Autobiography Feature 222
  Earlier sketches in SATA 43, 84, 143, 181
  See also CLR 62
Adair, Gilbert 1944- 98
Adair, Ian 1942- 53
Adair, Margaret Weeks (?)-1971 10
Adam, Cornel
  See Lengyel, Cornel Adam
Adam, Mark
  See Alexander, Marc
Adam, Paul 1958- 231
Adam, Robert 1948- 93
Adams, Adrienne 1906- 90
  Earlier sketch in SATA 8
  See also CLR 73
Adams, Andy 1859-1935
  See YABC 1
Adams, Barbara Johnston 1943- 60
Adams, Bruin
  See Ellis, Edward S.
Adams, Captain Bruin
  See Ellis, Edward S.
Adams, Captain J. F. C.
  See Ellis, Edward S.
Adams, Dale
  See Quinn, Elisabeth
Adams, Daniel
  See Nicole, Christopher
Adams, Debra
  See Speregen, Devra Newberger
Adams, Diane 1960- 217
Adams, Douglas 1952-2001 116
  Obituary 128
Adams, Douglas Noel
  See Adams, Douglas
Adams, Edith
  See Shine, Deborah
Adams, Florence 1932- 61
Adams, Georgie 1945- 216
Adams, Harriet S(tratemeyer) 1892(?)-1982 .. 1
  Obituary 29
Adams, Harrison
  See Rathborne, St. George (Henry)
  and Stratemeyer, Edward L.
Adams, Hazard 1926- 6
Adams, Hazard Simeon
  See Adams, Hazard
Adams, John Anthony 1944- 67

Adams, Kathryn *224*
Adams, Laurie 1941- *33*
Adams, Lowell
  See Joseph, James (Herz)
Adams, Nicholas
  See Pine, Nicholas
Adams, Nicholas
  See Smith, Sherwood
Adams, Nicholas
  See Doyle, Debra
  and Macdonald, James D.
Adams, Pam 1919- *112*
Adams, Pamela
  See Adams, Pam
Adams, Richard 1920- *69*
  Earlier sketch in SATA *7*
  See also CLR *121*
Adams, Richard George
  See Adams, Richard
Adams, Ruth Joyce *14*
Adams, S.J.
  See Selzer, Adam
Adams, Tricia
  See Kite, Pat
Adams, William Taylor 1822-1897 .... *28*
Adam Smith, Janet (Buchanan) 1905-1999 .. *63*
Adamson, Gareth 1925-1982(?) *46*
  Obituary *30*
Adamson, George 1906-1989
  Obituary *63*
Adamson, George (Worsley) 1913-2005 ...... *30*
Adamson, Graham
  See Groom, Arthur William
Adamson, Joy(-Friederike Victoria)
  1910-1980 .... *11*
  Obituary *22*
Adamson, Wendy Writson 1942- *22*
Addasi, Maha 1968- *205*
Addison, Kenneth 1949(?)-2005 .... *187*
Addison, Kenneth L.
  See Addison, Kenneth
Addona, Angelo F. 1925- *14*
Addy, Sean 1976- *222*
Addy, Sharon Hart 1943- *192*
  Earlier sketch in SATA *108*
Addy, Ted
  See Winterbotham, R(ussell) R(obert)
Adelberg, Doris
  See Orgel, Doris
Adelson, Leone 1908- *11*
Adinolfi, JoAnn *176*
Adkins, Jan 1944- *210*
  Autobiography Feature *210*
  Earlier sketches in SATA *8, 69, 144*
  See also CLR *77*
  See also SAAS *19*
Adl, Shirin 1975- *225*
Adler, C. S. 1932- *126*
  Earlier sketches in SATA *26, 63, 102*
  See also CLR *78*
  See also SAAS *15*
Adler, Carole Schwerdtfeger
  See Adler, C. S.
Adler, David A. 1947- *231*
  Earlier sketches in SATA *14, 70, 106, 151,
  178*
  See also CLR *108*
Adler, Emily *230*
Adler, Irene
  See Penzler, Otto
  and Storr, Catherine (Cole)
Adler, Irving 1913- *29*
  Autobiography Feature *164*
  Earlier sketch in SATA *1*
  See also CLR *27*
  See also SAAS *15*
Adler, Larry 1939- *36*
Adler, Peggy *22*
Adler, Ruth 1915-1968 .... *1*
Adlerman, Daniel (Ezra) 1963- *163*
  Earlier sketch in SATA *96*

Adlerman, Kim
  See Adlerman, Kimberly M(arie)
Adlerman, Kimberly M(arie) 1964- *163*
  Earlier sketch in SATA *96*
Adoff, Arnold 1935- *96*
  Earlier sketches in SATA *5, 57*
  See also CLR *7*
  See also SAAS *15*
Adoff, Jaime *163*
Adoff, Jaime Levi
  See Adoff, Jaime
Adorjan, Carol (Madden) 1934- *71*
  Earlier sketch in SATA *10*
Adrian, Frances
  See Polland, Madeleine A(ngela Cahill)
Adrian, Mary
  See Jorgensen, Mary Venn
Adshead, Gladys L(ucy) 1896-1985 .... *3*
Aesop 620(?)B.C.-560(?)B.C. *64*
  See also CLR *14*
Aesop, Abraham
  See Newbery, John
Affabee, Eric
  See Stine, R.L.
Agapida, Fray Antonio
  See Irving, Washington
Agard, John 1949- *223*
  Earlier sketch in SATA *138*
Agard, Nadema 1948- *18*
Agarwal, Deepa 1947- *141*
Agee, Jon 1960- *196*
  Earlier sketches in SATA *116, 157*
Agell, Charlotte 1959- *214*
  Earlier sketches in SATA *99, 150*
Agent Orange
  See Moseley, James W(illett)
Aghill, Gordon
  See Garrett, Randall
  and Silverberg, Robert
Agle, Nan Hayden 1905- *3*
  See also SAAS *10*
Agnew, Edith J(osephine) 1897-1988 .... *11*
Agnew, Lincoln *222*
Agonito, Joseph *177*
Agonito, Rosemary 1937- *177*
Aguilar, David *214*
Aguilar, David A.
  See Aguilar, David
Ahern, Margaret McCrohan 1921- *10*
Ahl, Anna Maria 1926- *32*
Ahlberg, Allan 1938- *214*
  Brief entry *35*
  Earlier sketches in SATA *68, 120, 165*
  See also CLR *18*
Ahlberg, Janet 1944-1994 .... *120*
  Brief entry *32*
  Obituary *83*
  Earlier sketch in SATA *68*
  See also CLR *18*
Ahlberg, Jessica 1980- *229*
Aho, Julia Kay
  See Kay, Julia
Aichinger, Helga 1937- *4*
Aiken, Clarissa (M.) Lorenz 1899-1992 .... *12*
  Obituary *109*
Aiken, Conrad 1889-1973 .... *30*
  Earlier sketch in SATA *3*
Aiken, Conrad Potter
  See Aiken, Conrad
Aiken, Joan (Delano) 1924-2004 .... *73*
  Autobiography Feature *109*
  Obituary *152*
  Earlier sketches in SATA *2, 30*
  See also CLR *90*
  See also SAAS *1*
Aillaud, Cindy Lou 1955- *184*
Ainsley, Alix
  See Steiner, Barbara A(nnette)
Ainsworth, Catherine Harris 1910- *56*
Ainsworth, Norma 1911-1987 .... *9*

Ainsworth, Ruth (Gallard) 1908- *73*
  Earlier sketch in SATA *7*
Ainsworth, William Harrison 1805-1882 ..... *24*
Aistrop, Jack 1916- *14*
Aitken, Amy 1952- *54*
  Brief entry *40*
Aitken, Dorothy 1916- *10*
Aitmatov, Chingiz 1928-2008 .... *56*
Aitmatov, Chingiz Torekulovich
  See Aitmatov, Chingiz
Ajhar, Brian 1957- *220*
Akaba, Suekichi 1910- *46*
Akers, Floyd
  See Baum, L. Frank
Akib, Jamel *181*
Aks, Patricia 1926-1994 .... *68*
al Abdullah, Rania 1970- *230*
Alagoa, Ebiegberi Joe 1933- *108*
Alain
  See Brustlein, Daniel
Alajalov, Constantin 1900-1987
  Obituary *53*
Alalou, Ali *203*
Alalou, Elizabeth *203*
Alan, David
  See Horsfield, Alan
Alan, Robert
  See Silverstein, Robert Alan
Alarcon, Francisco X. 1954- *215*
  Earlier sketch in SATA *104*
Alarcon, Francisco Xavier
  See Alarcon, Francisco X.
Alarcon, Karen Beaumont
  See Beaumont, Karen
Albee, Sarah 1962- *231*
Albert, Burton 1936- *22*
Albert, Louise 1928- *157*
Albert, Michael 1966- *202*
Albert, Richard E. 1909-1999 .... *82*
Albert, Susan Wittig 1940- *107*
Alberts, Frances Jacobs 1907-1989 .... *14*
Albertson, Susan
  See Wojciechowski, Susan
Albion, Lee Smith *29*
Alborough, Jez 1959- *149*
  Earlier sketch in SATA *86*
Albrecht, Lillie (Vanderveer H.)
  1894-1985 .... *12*
Albyn, Carole Lisa 1955- *83*
Alchemy, Jack
  See Gershator, David
Alcock, Gudrun 1908- *56*
  Brief entry *33*
Alcock, Vivien (Dolores) 1924-2003 .... *76*
  Brief entry *38*
  Obituary *148*
  Earlier sketch in SATA *45*
  See also CLR *26*
Alcorn, John 1935- *31*
  Brief entry *30*
Alcorn, Stephen 1958- *207*
  Earlier sketch in SATA *110*
Alcott, Louisa May 1832-1888 .... *100*
  See also YABC *1*
  See also CLR *109*
Alda, Arlene 1933- *205*
  Brief entry *36*
  Earlier sketches in SATA *44, 106, 158*
  See also CLR *93*
Alden, Isabella (Macdonald) 1841-1930 ..... *115*
  See also YABC *2*
Alden, Sue
  See Francis, Dorothy
Alderman, Clifford Lindsey 1902-1988 .... *3*
Alderson, Sue Ann 1940- *59*
  Brief entry *48*
Alding, Peter
  See Jeffries, Roderic
Aldis, Dorothy (Keeley) 1896-1966 .... *2*
Aldiss, Brian W. 1925- *34*

Aldiss, Brian Wilson
See Aldiss, Brian W.
Aldon, Adair
See Meigs, Cornelia Lynde
Aldous, Allan (Charles) 1911- *27*
Aldrich, Ann
See Meaker, Marijane
Aldrich, Bess Streeter 1881-1954
See CLR *70*
Aldrich, Thomas (Bailey) 1836-1907 .... *114*
Earlier sketch in SATA *17*
Aldridge, (Harold Edward) James 1918- *87*
Aldridge, Josephine Haskell *14*
Aldridge, Sheila 1974- *192*
Aleas, Richard
See Ardai, Charles
Alegria, Malin 1974(?)- *190*
Alegria, Ricardo E(nrique) 1921- *6*
Aleksin, Anatolii Georgievich 1924- *36*
Alenov, Lydia 1948- *61*
Alex, Ben (a pseudonym) 1946- *45*
Alex, Marlee (a pseudonym) 1948- *45*
Alexander, Alma 1963- *217*
Alexander, Anna B(arbara Cooke) 1913- *1*
Alexander, Anne
See Alexander, Anna B(arbara Cooke)
Alexander, Claire *228*
Alexander, Ellen 1938- *91*
Alexander, Frances (Laura) 1888-1979 .... *4*
Alexander, Janet 1907-1994 .... *97*
Earlier sketch in SATA *1*
Alexander, Jill S. 1964- *223*
Alexander, Jill Shurbet
See Alexander, Jill S.
Alexander, Jocelyn Anne Arundel 1930- *22*
Alexander, Linda 1935- *2*
Alexander, Lloyd 1924-2007 .... *135*
Obituary *182*
Earlier sketches in SATA *3, 49, 81, 129*
See also CLR *48*
See also SAAS *19*
Alexander, Lloyd Chudley
See Alexander, Lloyd
Alexander, Marc 1929- *117*
Alexander, Martha 1920- *136*
Earlier sketches in SATA *11, 70*
Alexander, Rae Pace
See Alexander, Raymond Pace
Alexander, Raymond Pace 1898-1974 .... *22*
Alexander, Robert *200*
Alexander, Rod
See Pellowski, Michael (Joseph)
Alexander, Sally Hobart 1943- *84*
Alexander, Sue 1933-2008 .... *136*
Obituary *195*
Earlier sketches in SATA *12, 89*
See also SAAS *15*
Alexander, Vincent Arthur 1925-1980
Obituary *23*
Alexeieff, Alexandre A. 1901-1979 .... *14*
Alger, Horatio, Jr.
See Stratemeyer, Edward L.
Alger, Horatio, Jr. 1832-1899 .... *16*
See also CLR *87*
Alger, Leclaire (Gowans) 1898-1969 .... *15*
Aliki
See Brandenberg, Aliki
Alkema, Chester Jay 1932- *12*
Al-Khalili, Jim 1962- *124*
Alkiviades, Alkis 1953- *105*
Alko, Selina 1968- *218*
Alkouatli, Claire *186*
Allaby, John Michael
See Allaby, Michael
Allaby, Michael 1933- *167*
Allamand, Pascale 1942- *12*
Allan, Mabel Esther 1915-1998 .... *75*
Earlier sketches in SATA *5, 32*
See also CLR *43*
See also SAAS *11*

Allan, Nicholas 1956- *123*
Earlier sketch in SATA *79*
Allan-Meyer, Kathleen 1918- *51*
Brief entry *46*
Allard, Harry, Jr. 1928- *216*
Earlier sketch in SATA *42, 102*
See also CLR *85*
Allard, Harry G.
See Allard, Harry, Jr.
Allee, Marjorie Hill 1890-1945 .... *17*
Allen, Adam
See Epstein, Beryl
and Epstein, Samuel
Allen, Alex B.
See Heide, Florence Parry
Allen, Allyn
See Eberle, Irmengarde
Allen, Betsy
See Harrison, Elizabeth (Allen) Cavanna
Allen, Bob 1961- *76*
Allen, Constance
See Albee, Sarah
Allen, Gertrude E(lizabeth) 1888-1984 .... *9*
Allen, Grace
See Hogarth, Grace (Weston Allen)
Allen, Jeffrey (Yale) 1948- *42*
Allen, John
See Perry, Ritchie (John Allen)
Allen, Jonathan 1957- *177*
Earlier sketch in SATA *131*
Allen, Jonathan Dean
See Allen, Jonathan
Allen, Joy 1948- *217*
Allen, Judy (Christina) 1941- *124*
Earlier sketch in SATA *80*
Allen, Kenneth S. 1913-1981 .... *56*
Allen, Leroy 1912- *11*
Allen, Linda 1925- *33*
Allen, Marjorie 1931- *22*
Allen, Maury 1932-2010 .... *26*
Allen, Merritt Parmelee 1892-1954 .... *22*
Allen, Nancy Kelly 1949- *171*
Earlier sketch in SATA *127*
Allen, Nina (Stroemgren) 1935- *22*
Allen, Pamela (Kay) 1934- *123*
Earlier sketches in SATA *50, 81*
See also CLR *44*
Allen, Raul *205*
Allen, Rodney F. 1938-1999 .... *27*
Allen, Roger MacBride 1957- *105*
Allen, Ruth
See Peterson, Esther (Allen)
Allen, Samuel W(ashington) 1917- *9*
Allen, T. D.
See Allen, Terril Diener
Allen, Terril Diener 1908- *35*
Allen, Terry D.
See Allen, Terril Diener
Allen, Thomas B. 1929- *193*
Earlier sketches in SATA *45, 140*
Allen, Thomas Benton
See Allen, Thomas B.
Allen, Tom
See Allen, Thomas B.
Allende, Isabel 1942- *163*
See also CLR *99*
Allerton, Mary
See Govan, (Mary) Christine Noble
Alley, Robert W.
See Alley, R.W.
Alley, R.W. *211*
Earlier sketch in SATA *169*
Alley, Zoe B. *214*
Alleyn, Ellen
See Rossetti, Christina
Allington, Richard L(loyd) 1947- *39*
Brief entry *35*
Allison, Amy 1956- *138*
Allison, Bob *14*
Allison, Diane Worfolk *78*
Allison, Jennifer *173*

Allison, Linda 1948- *43*
Allison, Margaret
See Klam, Cheryl
Allman, Barbara 1950- *137*
Allmendinger, David F(rederick), Jr. 1938- . *35*
Allred, Alexandra Powe 1965- *144*
Allred, Gordon T(hatcher) 1930- *10*
Allsop, Kenneth 1920-1973 .... *17*
Allsopp, Sophie *188*
Alma, Ann 1946- *201*
Almedingen, E. M.
See Almedingen, Martha Edith von
Almedingen, Martha Edith von 1898-1971 .... *3*
Almon, Russell
See Clevenger, William R.
and Downing, David A(lmon)
Almond, David 1951- *158*
Earlier sketch in SATA *114*
See also CLR *168*
Almond, Linda Stevens 1881(?)-1987
Obituary *50*
Almquist, Don 1929- *11*
Alonzo, Sandra *199*
Alphin, Elaine Marie 1955- *139*
Autobiography Feature *139*
Earlier sketches in SATA *80, 130*
Alsenas, Linas 1979- *186*
Alsop, Mary O'Hara 1885-1980 .... *34*
Obituary *24*
Earlier sketch in SATA *2*
Alter, Anna 1974- *206*
Earlier sketch in SATA *135*
Alter, Judith 1938- *101*
Earlier sketch in SATA *52*
Alter, Judith MacBain
See Alter, Judith
Alter, Judy
See Alter, Judith
Alter, Robert Edmond 1925-1965 .... *9*
Alter, Stephen 1956- *187*
Althea
See Braithwaite, Althea
Altman, Linda Jacobs 1943- *21*
Altman, Suzanne
See Orgel, Doris
and Schecter, Ellen
Alton, Steve *169*
Altscheler, Franz 1923- *45*
Altsheler, Joseph A(lexander) 1862-1919
See YABC *1*
Alvarez, John
See del Rey, Lester
Alvarez, Joseph A. 1930- *18*
Alvarez, Julia 1950- *129*
al-Windawi, Thura
See Windawi, Thura al-
Alyer, Philip A.
See Stratemeyer, Edward L.
Amado, Elisa *193*
Amann, Janet 1951- *79*
Amato, Carol A. 1942- *92*
Amato, Mary 1961- *178*
Earlier sketch in SATA *140*
Ambrose, Stephen E. 1936-2002 .... *138*
Earlier sketch in SATA *40*
Ambrose, Stephen Edward
See Ambrose, Stephen E.
Ambrus, Gyozo Laszlo 1935- *1*
See also SAAS *4*
Ambrus, Victor G.
See Ambrus, Gyozo Laszlo
Amend, Bill 1962- *147*
Amerman, Lockhart 1911-1969 .... *3*
Ames, Evelyn 1908-1990 .... *13*
Obituary *64*
Ames, Gerald 1906-1993 .... *11*
Obituary *74*
Ames, Lee J. 1921-2011 .... *151*
Earlier sketch in SATA *3*
Ames, Lee Judah
See Ames, Lee J.

Ames, Mildred 1919-1994 .... *85*
    Earlier sketches in SATA *22, 81*
Amico, Tom 1960(?)- *176*
Amit, Ofra 1966- *205*
Ammon, Richard 1942- *124*
Amon, Aline 1928- *9*
Amory, Jay
    See Lovegrove, James
Amoss, Berthe 1925- *112*
    Earlier sketch in SATA *5*
Amstutz, Andre 1925- *214*
Anastasio, Dina 1941- *94*
    Brief entry *30*
    Earlier sketch in SATA *37*
Anaya, Rudolfo 1937-
    See CLR *129*
Anaya, Rudolfo A.
    See Anaya, Rudolfo
Anaya, Rudolpho Alfonso
    See Anaya, Rudolfo
Anckarsvard, Karin Inez Maria 1915-1969 .... *6*
Ancona, George 1929- *208*
    Autobiography Feature *208*
    Earlier sketches in SATA *12, 85, 145, 192*
    See also SAAS *18*
Anders, C. J.
    See Bennett, Cherie
Anders, Isabel 1946- *101*
Anders, Lou *176*
Andersdatter, Karla M. 1938- *34*
Andersen, Bethanne 1954- *191*
Andersen, Hans Christian 1805-1875 .... *100*
    See also YABC *1*
    See also CLR *113*
Andersen, Ted
    See Boyd, Waldo T.
Andersen, Yvonne 1932- *27*
Anderson, Bernice G(oudy) 1894-1997 .... *33*
Anderson, Bob 1944- *139*
    Earlier sketch in SATA *136*
Anderson, Brad 1924- *33*
    Brief entry *31*
Anderson, Bradley Jay
    See Anderson, Brad
Anderson, Brian 1974- *211*
Anderson, C. C.
    See Anderson, Catherine Corley
Anderson, C(larence) W(illiam) 1891-1971 . *11*
Anderson, Carolyn Dunn
    See Dunn, Carolyn
Anderson, Catherine C.
    See Anderson, Catherine Corley
Anderson, Catherine Corley 1909-2001 .... *72*
    See Lee, Cora
Anderson, Clifford
    See Gardner, Richard (M.)
Anderson, Daryl Shon 1963- *93*
Anderson, Dave
    See Anderson, David
Anderson, David 1929- *60*
Anderson, Derek 1969- *169*
Anderson, Eloise Adell 1927- *9*
Anderson, George
    See Groom, Arthur William
Anderson, Grace Fox 1932- *43*
Anderson, J(ohn) R(ichard) L(ane)
    1911-1981 .... *15*
    Obituary *27*
Anderson, Jessica Lee 1980- *224*
Anderson, Jodi Lynn *182*
Anderson, John David *197*
Anderson, John L. 1905- *2*
Anderson, Joy 1928- *1*
Anderson, Kevin J. 1962- *117*
    Earlier sketch in SATA *74*
Anderson, Kevin James
    See Anderson, Kevin J.
Anderson, Kirsty 1978- *108*
Anderson, K.J.
    See Moesta, Rebecca

Anderson, Laurie Halse 1961- *186*
    Earlier sketches in SATA *95, 132*
    See also CLR *138*
Anderson, LaVere Francis Shoenfelt
    1907-1998 .... *27*
Anderson, Leone Castell 1923- *53*
    Brief entry *49*
Anderson, Lisa G. 1963- *108*
Anderson, Lonzo
    See Anderson, John L.
Anderson, Lucia (Lewis) 1922- *10*
Anderson, Madelyn Klein 1926-2005 .... *28*
Anderson, Margaret J(ean) 1931- *27*
    See also SAAS *8*
Anderson, Marilyn D. 1943- *144*
Anderson, Mary 1939- *82*
    Earlier sketch in SATA *7*
    See also SAAS *23*
Anderson, Matthew Tobin
    See Anderson, M.T.
Anderson, Mona 1910-2004 .... *40*
Anderson, Mrs. Melvin
    See Anderson, Catherine Corley
Anderson, M.T. 1968- *182*
    Earlier sketches in SATA *97, 146*
Anderson, Norman Dean 1928- *22*
Anderson, Peggy Perry 1953- *179*
    Earlier sketch in SATA *84*
Anderson, Poul 1926-2001 .... *90*
    Autobiography Feature *106*
    Brief entry *39*
    See also CLR *58*
Anderson, Poul William
    See Anderson, Poul
Anderson, Rachel 1943- *86*
    Earlier sketch in SATA *34*
    See also SAAS *18*
Anderson, Rebecca J.
    See Anderson, R.J.
Anderson, Rebecca M.
    See Moesta, Rebecca
Anderson, Rebecca Moesta
    See Moesta, Rebecca
Anderson, Richard
    See Anderson, J(ohn) R(ichard) L(ane)
Anderson, R.J. 1970(?)- *216*
Anderson, Sara *173*
Anderson, Scoular *201*
Anderson, (Tom) Scoular *138*
Anderson, Stephanie 1976- *225*
Anderson, Susan 1952- *90*
Anderson, Thomas Scoular
    See Anderson, Scoular
Anderson, W. B.
    See Schultz, James Willard
Anderson, Wayne 1946- *202*
    Earlier sketches in SATA *56, 147*
Andersson, Kenneth 1970- *200*
Andre, Evelyn M. 1924- *27*
Andre, Evelyn Marie
    See Andre, Evelyn M.
Andreasen, Dan *227*
    Earlier sketch in SATA *186*
Andreassen, Karl
    See Boyd, Waldo T.
Andreassi, K. Robert
    See DeCandido, Keith R.A.
Andree, Louise
    See Coury, Louise Andree
Andrew, Ian 1962- *166*
    Earlier sketch in SATA *116*
Andrew, Ian Peter
    See Andrew, Ian
Andrew, Prudence (Hastings) 1924- *87*
Andrews, Benny 1930-2006 .... *31*
    Obituary *178*
Andrews, Eleanor Lattimore
    See Lattimore, Eleanor Frances
Andrews, Elton V.
    See Pohl, Frederik
Andrews, F(rank) Emerson 1902-1978 .... *22*

Andrews, J(ames) S(ydney) 1934- *4*
Andrews, Jan 1942- *167*
    Brief entry *49*
    Earlier sketches in SATA *58, 98*
Andrews, Julie 1935- *153*
    Earlier sketch in SATA *7*
    See also CLR *85*
Andrews, Laura
    See Coury, Louise Andree
Andrews, Roy Chapman 1884-1960 .... *19*
Andrews, Tamra 1959- *129*
Andrews, V(irginia) C(leo) 1924(?)-1986
    Obituary *50*
Andrews, Wendy
    See Sharmat, Marjorie Weinman
Andrews, William G. 1930- *74*
Andrews, William George
    See Andrews, William G.
Andrezel, Pierre
    See Blixen, Karen
Andriani, Renee
    See Williams-Andriani, Renee
Andriola, Alfred J. 1912-1983
    Obituary *34*
Andrist, Ralph K. 1914-2004 .... *45*
Andronik, Catherine M. *189*
Andryszewski, Tricia 1956- *148*
    Earlier sketch in SATA *88*
Anelli, Melissa 1979- *215*
Angaramo, Roberta 1974- *229*
Angel, Ann 1952- *192*
Angel, Carl *178*
Angel, Marie 1923- *47*
Angeles, Peter A. 1931- *40*
Angeletti, Roberta 1964- *124*
Angeli, Marguerite (Lofft) de
    See de Angeli, Marguerite (Lofft)
Angell, Judie 1937- *78*
    Earlier sketch in SATA *22*
    See also CLR *33*
Angell, Madeline 1919- *18*
Angelo, Valenti 1897- *14*
Angelou, Maya 1928- *136*
    Earlier sketch in SATA *49*
    See also CLR *53*
Angier, Bradford -1997 .... *12*
Angle, Kimberly Greene *203*
Angle, Paul M(cClelland) 1900-1975
    Obituary *20*
Anglund, Joan Walsh 1926- *2*
    See also CLR *94*
Ango, Fan D.
    See Longyear, Barry B(rookes)
Angrist, Stanley W(olff) 1933- *4*
Anhalt, Ariela 1990(?)- *227*
Anholt, Catherine 1958- *131*
    Earlier sketch in SATA *74*
Anholt, Laurence 1959- *141*
    Earlier sketch in SATA *74*
Aninno, J.G.
    See Annino, Jan Godown
Anita
    See Daniel, Anita
Anmar, Frank
    See Nolan, William F.
Annett, Cora
    See Scott, Cora Annett (Pipitone)
Annie-Jo
    See Blanchard, Patricia
    and Suhr, Joanne
Annino, Jan Godown 1952- *228*
Annixter, Jane
    See Sturtzel, Jane Levington
Annixter, Paul
    See Sturtzel, Howard A(llison)
Anno, Mitsumasa 1926- *157*
    Earlier sketches in SATA *5, 38, 77*
    See also CLR *122*
Anrooy, Francine Van
    See Van Anrooy, Francine
Ansary, Mir Tamim 1948- *140*

Anstey, Caroline 1958- *81*
Antell, Will D. 1935- *31*
Anthony, Barbara
  See Barber, Antonia
Anthony, C. L.
  See Smith, Dorothy Gladys
Anthony, Edward 1895-1971 .... *21*
Anthony, John
  See Beckett, Ronald Brymer
  and Ciardi, John (Anthony)
  and Sabini, John Anthony
Anthony, Joseph Patrick 1964- *103*
Anthony, Patricia 1947- *109*
Anthony, Piers 1934- *129*
  Autobiography Feature *129*
  Earlier sketch in SATA *84*
  See also CLR *118*
  See also SAAS *22*
Anthony, Susan C(arol) 1953- *87*
Anticaglia, Elizabeth 1939- *12*
Antieau, Kim *214*
Antilles, Kem
  See Moesta, Rebecca
Antle, Nancy 1955- *102*
Antolini, Margaret Fishback 1904-1985
  Obituary *45*
Anton, Michael J(ames) 1940- *12*
Antonacci, Robert J(oseph) 1916- *45*
  Brief entry *37*
Anvil, Christopher 1925-2009 .... *102*
Anzaldua, Gloria (Evanjelina) 1942-2004
  Obituary *154*
Aoki, Hisako 1942- *45*
Aoyagi, Nora *229*
Apfel, Necia H(alpern) 1930- *51*
  Brief entry *41*
Aphrodite, J.
  See Livingston, Carole
Apikuni
  See Schultz, James Willard
Apostolina, M. *184*
Apostolina, Michael
  See Apostolina, M.
Apostolou, Christine Hale 1955- *179*
  Earlier sketches in SATA *82, 128*
Appel, Allen (R.) 1945- *115*
Appel, Benjamin 1907-1977 .... *39*
  Obituary *21*
Appel, Martin 1948- *45*
Appel, Martin Eliot
  See Appel, Martin
Appel, Marty
  See Appel, Martin
Appelbaum, Diana Muir Karter 1953- *132*
Appelt, Kathi 1954- *190*
  Earlier sketches in SATA *83, 129*
Apperley, Dawn 1969- *135*
Appiah, Peggy 1921-2006 .... *84*
  Earlier sketch in SATA *15*
  See also SAAS *19*
Apple, Margot *214*
  Brief entry *42*
  Earlier sketches in SATA *64, 152*
Applebaum, Stan 1922- *45*
Applegate, K.A.
  See Applegate, Katherine
Applegate, Katherine 1956- *196*
  Earlier sketches in SATA *109, 162*
  See also CLR *90*
Applegate, Katherine Alice
  See Applegate, Katherine
Appleton, Victor
  See Barrett, Neal, Jr.
  and Doyle, Debra
  and Stratemeyer, Edward L.
  and Vardeman, Robert E.
Appollo 1969- *214*
Appollodorus, Olivier
  See Appollo
Apsler, Alfred 1907-1982 .... *10*

Aragones, Sergio 1937- *48*
  Brief entry *39*
Araujo, Frank P. 1937- *86*
Arbo, Cris 1950- *220*
  Earlier sketch in SATA *103*
Arbuckle, Dorothy Fry 1910-1982
  Obituary *33*
Arbuthnot, May Hill 1884-1969 .... *2*
Archambault, John *163*
  Earlier sketches in SATA *67, 112*
Archambault, Matthew 1968- *219*
Archbold, Rick 1950- *97*
Archer, Colleen Rutherford 1949- *164*
Archer, Frank
  See O'Connor, Richard
Archer, Jules 1915- *85*
  Earlier sketch in SATA *4*
  See also SAAS *5*
Archer, Lily 1981- *193*
Archer, Marion Fuller 1917- *11*
Archer, Nathan
  See Watt-Evans, Lawrence
Archer, Peggy 1947- *199*
Archibald, Joe
  See Archibald, Joseph S(topford)
Archibald, Joseph S(topford) 1898-1986 .... *3*
  Obituary *47*
Ard, William
  See Jakes, John
Ardagh, Philip 1961- *154*
Ardai, Charles 1969- *85*
Arden, Barbi
  See Stoutenburg, Adrien (Pearl)
Arden, William
  See Lynds, Dennis
Ardizzone, Edward (Jeffrey Irving)
  1900-1979 .... *28*
  Obituary *21*
  Earlier sketch in SATA *1*
  See also CLR *3*
Ardley, Neil 1937- *121*
  Earlier sketch in SATA *43*
Ardley, Neil Richard
  See Ardley, Neil
Arehart-Treichel, Joan 1942- *22*
Arena, Felice 1968- *151*
Arenella, Roy 1939- *14*
Arevamirp, Esile
  See Primavera, Elise
Argent, Kerry 1960- *138*
Arguelles, Francisco Xavier
  See Stork, Francisco X.
Argueta, Jorge *179*
Arihara, Shino 1973- *201*
Arkin, Alan 1934- *59*
  Brief entry *32*
Arkin, Alan Wolf
  See Arkin, Alan
Arksey, Neil *158*
Arlen, Leslie
  See Nicole, Christopher
Arley, Robert
  See Jackson, Mike
Armer, Alberta (Roller) 1904-1986 .... *9*
Armer, Laura Adams 1874-1963 .... *13*
Armistead, John 1941- *130*
Armitage, David 1943- *155*
  Brief entry *38*
  Earlier sketch in SATA *99*
Armitage, Frank
  See Carpenter, John
Armitage, Ronda (Jacqueline) 1943- *155*
  Brief entry *38*
  Earlier sketches in SATA *47, 99*
Armour, Richard (Willard) 1906-1989 .... *14*
  Obituary *61*
Armstrong, Alan 1939- *172*
Armstrong, Alan W.
  See Armstrong, Alan
Armstrong, George D. 1927- *10*
Armstrong, Gerry (Breen) 1929- *10*

Armstrong, Jeannette (C.) 1948- *102*
Armstrong, Jennifer 1961- *165*
  Autobiography Feature *120*
  Earlier sketches in SATA *77, 111*
  See also CLR *66*
  See also SAAS *24*
Armstrong, Louise *43*
  Brief entry *33*
Armstrong, Martin Donisthorpe
  1882-1974 .... *115*
Armstrong, Matthew 1975- *188*
Armstrong, Matthew S.
  See Armstrong, Matthew
Armstrong, Ralph Richard
  See Armstrong, Richard
Armstrong, Richard 1903-1986 .... *11*
Armstrong, Shelagh 1961- *224*
Armstrong, William H(oward) 1914-1999 ..... *4*
  Obituary *111*
  See also CLR *117*
  See also SAAS *7*
Armstrong-Ellis, Carey (Fraser) 1956- *145*
Armstrong-Hodgson, Shelagh
  See Armstrong, Shelagh
Arndt, Ursula (Martha H.) *56*
  Brief entry *39*
Arneson, D(on) J(on) 1935- *37*
Arnett, Caroline
  See Cole, Lois Dwight
Arnett, Jack
  See Goulart, Ron
Arnette, Robert
  See Silverberg, Robert
Arno, Enrico 1913-1981 .... *43*
  Obituary *28*
Arnold, Ann 1953(?)- *207*
Arnold, Caroline 1944- *228*
  Brief entry *34*
  Earlier sketches in SATA *36, 85, 131, 174*
  See also CLR *61*
  See also SAAS *23*
Arnold, Elizabeth 1944- *164*
Arnold, Elliott 1912-1980 .... *5*
  Obituary *22*
Arnold, Emily 1939- *210*
  Autobiography Feature *134*
  Earlier sketches in SATA *5, 50, 76, 110, 134*
  See also CLR *46*
  See also SAAS *7*
Arnold, Gillian Clare
  See Cross, Gillian
Arnold, Katya 1947- *168*
  Earlier sketches in SATA *82, 115*
Arnold, Louise *175*
Arnold, Louise Claire
  See Arnold, Louise
Arnold, Marsha Diane 1948- *147*
  Earlier sketch in SATA *93*
Arnold, Nick 1961- *113*
Arnold, Oren 1900-1980 .... *4*
Arnold, Susan (Riser) 1951- *58*
Arnold, Tedd 1949- *208*
  Earlier sketches in SATA *69, 116, 160*
Arnoldy, Julie
  See Bischoff, Julia Bristol
Arnosky, James Edward 1946- *189*
  Earlier sketches in SATA *70, 118*
  See also CLR *93*
Arnosky, Jim
  See Arnosky, James Edward
Arnott, Kathleen 1914- *20*
Arnov, Boris, Jr. 1926- *12*
Arnow, Harriette (Louisa) Simpson
  1908-1986 .... *42*
  Obituary *47*
Arnsteen, Katy Keck 1934- *68*
Arnstein, Helene S(olomon) 1915- *12*
Arntson, Herbert E(dward) 1911-1982 .... *12*
Aroner, Miriam *82*
Aronin, Ben 1904-1980
  Obituary *25*

Aronson, Marc 1950- *189*
  Autobiography Feature *189*
  Earlier sketches in SATA *126, 175*
Aronson, Marc Henry
  See Aronson, Marc
Aronson, Sarah *196*
Aronson, Virginia 1954- *122*
Arora, Shirley (Lease) 1930- *2*
Arrasmith, Patrick *176*
Arrick, Fran
  See Angell, Judie
Arrigan, Mary 1943- *142*
Arrington, Aileen *183*
Arrington, Stephen L. 1948- *97*
Arrington, Stephen Lee
  See Arrington, Stephen L.
Arrley, Richmond
  See Delany, Samuel R., Jr.
Arrou-Vignod, Jean-Philippe 1958- *218*
Arrowood, (McKendrick Lee) Clinton
  1939- *19*
Arrowsmith, Pat 1930- *59*
Arsenault, Isabelle 1978- *207*
Artell, Mike 1948- *183*
  Earlier sketches in SATA *89, 134*
Arthur, Robert (Andrew) 1909-1969
  See Arthur, Robert, (Jr.)
Arthur, Robert, (Jr.) 1909-1969 .... *118*
Arthur, Ruth M(abel) 1905-1979 .... *26*
  Earlier sketch in SATA *7*
Artis, Vicki Kimmel 1945- *12*
Artzybasheff, Boris (Miklailovich)
  1899-1965 .... *14*
Aruego, Ariane
  See Dewey, Ariane
Aruego, Jose 1932- *178*
  Earlier sketches in SATA *6, 68, 125*
  See also CLR *5*
Aruego, Jose Espiritu
  See Aruego, Jose
Arundel, Honor (Morfydd) 1919-1973 .... *4*
  Obituary *24*
  See also CLR *35*
Arundel, Jocelyn
  See Alexander, Jocelyn Anne Arundel
Arvey, Michael 1948- *79*
Arzoumanian, Alik *177*
Asare, Meshack (Yaw) 1945- *139*
  Earlier sketch in SATA *86*
Asaro, Catherine 1955- *165*
  Earlier sketch in SATA *101*
Asaro, Catherine Ann 1955-
  See Asaro, Catherine
Asay, Donna Day 1945- *127*
Asbjornsen, Peter Christen 1812-1885 .... *15*
  See also CLR *104*
Asch, Frank 1946- *154*
  Earlier sketches in SATA *5, 66, 102*
Ash, Jutta 1942- *38*
Ashabranner, Brent 1921- *166*
  Earlier sketches in SATA *1, 67, 130*
  See also CLR *28*
  See also SAAS *14*
Ashabranner, Brent Kenneth
  See Ashabranner, Brent
Ashbless, William
  See Blaylock, James P.
  and Powers, Tim
Ashby, Gil 1958- *146*
Ashby, Gwynneth 1922- *44*
Ashby, Ruth *170*
Ashby, Yvonne 1955- *121*
Ashe, Arthur (Robert, Jr.) 1943-1993 .... *65*
  Obituary *87*
Ashe, Geoffrey (Thomas) 1923- *17*
  Autobiography Feature *125*
Ashe, Mary Ann
  See Lewis, Mary
Asher, Bridget
  See Baggott, Julianna

Asher, Sandra Fenichel
  See Asher, Sandy
Asher, Sandy 1942- *71*
  Autobiography Feature *158*
  Brief entry *34*
  Earlier sketch in SATA *36*
  See also SAAS *13*
Asheron, Sara
  See Moore, Lilian
Ashey, Bella
  See Breinburg, Petronella
Ashford, Daisy
  See Ashford, Margaret Mary
Ashford, Jeffrey
  See Jeffries, Roderic
Ashford, Margaret Mary 1881-1972 .... *10*
Ashland, Monk 1972- *207*
Ashley, Bernard (John) 1935- *155*
  Brief entry *39*
  Earlier sketches in SATA *47, 79*
  See also CLR *4*
Ashley, Elizabeth
  See Salmon, Annie Elizabeth
Ashley, Ray
  See Abrashkin, Raymond
Ashman, Linda 1960- *203*
  Earlier sketch in SATA *150*
Ashton, Lorayne
  See Gottfried, Theodore Mark
Ashton, Warren T.
  See Adams, William Taylor
Asimov, Isaac 1920-1992 .... *74*
  Earlier sketches in SATA *1, 26*
  See also CLR *79*
Asinof, Eliot 1919-2008 .... *6*
Asinof, Eliot Tager
  See Asinof, Eliot
Aska, Warabe
  See Masuda, Takeshi
Askani, Tanja 1962- *227*
Asprin, Robert 1946-2008 .... *92*
Asprin, Robert L.
  See Asprin, Robert
Asprin, Robert Lynn
  See Asprin, Robert
Asquith, Cynthia Mary Evelyn (Charteris)
  1887-1960 .... *107*
Asquith, Ros *153*
Astley, Juliet
  See Lofts, Norah (Robinson)
Aston, Dianna Hutts 1964- *176*
Aston, James
  See White, T(erence) H(anbury)
Ata, Te 1895-1976 .... *119*
Atene, Ann
  See Atene, (Rita) Anna
Atene, (Rita) Anna 1922- *12*
Atheling, William, Jr.
  See Blish, James
Atkins, Catherine *160*
Atkins, Jeannine 1953- *172*
  Earlier sketch in SATA *113*
Atkinson, Allen G. 1953(?)-1987 .... *60*
  Brief entry *46*
  Obituary *55*
Atkinson, Elizabeth *215*
Atkinson, Elizabeth Jane
  See Atkinson, Elizabeth
Atkinson, M. E.
  See Frankau, Mary Evelyn Atkinson
Atkinson, Margaret Fleming *14*
Atteberry, Kevan J. *186*
Attema, Martha 1949- *156*
  Earlier sketch in SATA *94*
Atticus
  See Davies, Hunter
  and Fleming, Ian
  and Pawle, Gerald Strachan
  and Wilson, (Thomas) Woodrow

Atwater, Florence 1896-1979 .... *66*
  Earlier sketch in SATA *16*
  See also CLR *19*
Atwater, Florence Hasseltine Carroll
  See Atwater, Florence
Atwater, Montgomery Meigs 1904-1976 ...... *15*
Atwater, Richard 1892-1948 .... *66*
  Brief entry *27*
  Earlier sketch in SATA *54*
  See also CLR *19*
Atwater, Richard Tupper
  See Atwater, Richard
Atwater-Rhodes, Amelia 1984- *170*
  Earlier sketch in SATA *124*
Atwell, Debby 1953- *150*
  Earlier sketch in SATA *87*
Atwood, Ann (Margaret) 1913-1992 .... *7*
Atwood, Margaret 1939- *170*
  Earlier sketch in SATA *50*
Atwood, Margaret Eleanor
  See Atwood, Margaret
Aubrey, Meg Kelleher 1963- *83*
Aubry, Claude B. 1914-1984 .... *29*
  Obituary *40*
Auch, Herm *173*
Auch, Mary Jane *173*
  Earlier sketch in SATA *138*
Auch, M.J.
  See Auch, Mary Jane
Auclair, Joan 1960- *68*
Auel, Jean 1936- *91*
Auel, Jean M.
  See Auel, Jean
Auel, Jean Marie
  See Auel, Jean
Auer, Martin 1951- *77*
Augarde, Steve 1950- *210*
  Earlier sketches in SATA *25, 159*
Augarde, Steven Andre
  See Augarde, Steve
Augelli, John P(at) 1921- *46*
Augustine, Mildred
  See Benson, Mildred
Ault, Phil
  See Ault, Phillip H(alliday)
Ault, Phillip H(alliday) 1914- *23*
Ault, Rosalie Sain 1942- *38*
Ault, Roz
  See Ault, Rosalie Sain
Aung, (Maung) Htin 1909- *21*
Auntie Deb
  See Coury, Louise Andree
Auntie Louise
  See Coury, Louise Andree
Aunt Weedy
  See Alcott, Louisa May
Auseon, Andrew 1976- *217*
  Earlier sketch in SATA *166*
Austen, Carrie
  See Bennett, Cherie
Austen, Catherine 1965- *223*
Austin, Carrie
  See Seuling, Barbara
Austin, Elizabeth S. 1907-1977 .... *5*
Austin, Harry
  See McInerny, Ralph
Austin, Margot 1909(?)-1990 .... *11*
  Obituary *66*
Austin, Michael *178*
Austin, Oliver L(uther), Jr. 1903-1988 .... *7*
  Obituary *59*
Austin, Patricia 1950- *137*
Austin, R. G.
  See Gelman, Rita Golden
  and Lamb, Nancy
Austin, Virginia 1951- *152*
  Earlier sketch in SATA *80*
Auteur, Hillary
  See Gottfried, Theodore Mark
Auth, Tony
  See Auth, William Anthony, Jr.

Auth, William Anthony, Jr. 1942- *192*
Autry, Gloria Diener
    See Allen, Terril Diener
Auvil, Peggy A 1954- *122*
Auvil, Peggy Appleby
    See Auvil, Peggy A
Avasthi, Swati 1971- *231*
Aveni, Anthony F. 1938- *181*
Aveni, Anthony Francis
    See Aveni, Anthony F.
Averbeck, Jim 1963- *201*
Averill, Esther (Holden) 1902-1992 .... *28*
    Obituary *72*
    Earlier sketch in SATA *1*
Avery, A. A.
    See Montgomery, Rutherford George
Avery, Al
    See Montgomery, Rutherford George
Avery, Gillian 1926- *137*
    Autobiography Feature *137*
    Earlier sketches in SATA *7, 75*
    See also SAAS *6*
Avery, Gillian Elise
    See Avery, Gillian
Avery, Kay 1908- *5*
Avery, Lorraine
    See Older, Effin
    and Older, Jules
Avery, Lynn
    See Cole, Lois Dwight
Avi 1937- *226*
    Earlier sketches in SATA *14, 71, 108, 156,
    190*
    See also CLR *68*
Aviles, Martha *218*
Avishai, Susan 1949- *82*
Avraham, Kate Aver *227*
Avril, Francois 1961- *191*
Avril, Lynne
    See Cravath, Lynne W.
Awdry, Christopher Vere 1940- *67*
Awdry, Wilbert Vere 1911-1997 .... *94*
    See also CLR *23*
Axelrod, Amy *131*
Axelsen, Stephen 1953- *165*
Axton, David
    See Koontz, Dean
Ayars, James S(terling) 1898-1986 .... *4*
Aye, A. K.
    See Edwards, Hazel (Eileen)
Ayer, Eleanor H. 1947-1998 .... *121*
    Earlier sketch in SATA *78*
Ayer, Jacqueline 1930- *13*
Ayer, Margaret (?)-1981 .... *15*
Aylesworth, Jim 1943- *213*
    Earlier sketches in SATA *38, 89, 139*
    See also CLR *89*
Aylesworth, Thomas G(ibbons) 1927-1995 .. *88*
    Earlier sketch in SATA *4*
    See also CLR *6*
    See also SAAS *17*
Ayliffe, Alex *190*
Aylward, Marcus
    See Alexander, Marc
Aymar, Brandt 1911- *22*
Ayme, Marcel (Andre) 1902-1967 .... *91*
    See also CLR *25*
Ayres, Becky
    See Hickox, Rebecca (Ayres)
Ayres, Katherine 1947- *187*
Ayres, Pam 1947- *90*
Ayres, Patricia Miller 1923-1985
    Obituary *46*
Aytmatov, Chingiz
    See Aitmatov, Chingiz
Ayto, Russell 1960- *206*
    Earlier sketches in SATA *111, 166*
Azaid
    See Zaidenberg, Arthur
Azar, Penny 1952- *121*

Azarian, Mary 1940- *171*
    Earlier sketch in SATA *112*
Azore, Barbara 1934- *188*

B

Baasansuren, Bolormaa 1982- *216*
Baastad, Babbis Friis
    See Friis-Baastad, Babbis Ellinor
Bab
    See Gilbert, W(illiam) S(chwenck)
Babbis, Eleanor
    See Friis-Baastad, Babbis Ellinor
Babbitt, Lucy Cullyford 1960- *85*
Babbitt, Natalie 1932- *194*
    Earlier sketches in SATA *6, 68, 106*
    See also CLR *141*
    See also SAAS *5*
Babbitt, Natalie Zane Moore
    See Babbitt, Natalie
Babcock, Chris 1963- *83*
Babcock, Dennis 1948- *22*
Babcock, Dennis Arthur
    See Babcock, Dennis
Baber, Carolyn Stonnell 1936- *96*
Baboni, Elena *198*
Baca, Ana 1967- *191*
Baca, Maria 1951- *104*
Baccalario, Pierdomenico 1974- *222*
Bach, Alice (Hendricks) 1942- *93*
    Brief entry *27*
    Earlier sketch in SATA *30*
Bach, Bellamy
    See Windling, Terri
Bach, Mary 1960- *125*
Bach, Richard 1936- *13*
Bach, Richard David
    See Bach, Richard
Bache, Ellyn 1942- *124*
Bachel, Beverly K. 1957- *142*
Bachelet, Gilles 1952- *196*
Bachem, Paul *231*
Bachman, Fred 1949- *12*
Bachman, Richard
    See King, Stephen
Bachorz, Pam 1973- *226*
Bachrach, Deborah 1943- *80*
Bacigalupi, Paolo 1973- *230*
Backus, James Gilmore 1913-1989
    Obituary *63*
Backus, Jim
    See Backus, James Gilmore
Bacmeister, Rhoda W(arner) 1893-1991 .... *11*
Bacon, Betty
    See Bacon, Elizabeth
Bacon, Elizabeth 1914-2001 .... *3*
    Obituary *131*
Bacon, Joan Chase
    See Bowden, Joan Chase
Bacon, Josephine Dodge (Daskam)
    1876-1961 .... *48*
Bacon, Margaret Frances
    See Bacon, Peggy
Bacon, Margaret Hope 1921- *6*
Bacon, Martha Sherman 1917-1981 .... *18*
    Obituary *27*
    See also CLR *3*
Bacon, Melvin 1950- *93*
Bacon, Melvin L.
    See Bacon, Melvin
Bacon, Peggy 1895-1987 .... *50*
Bacon, R(onald) L(eonard) 1924- *84*
    Earlier sketch in SATA *26*
Baddiel, Ivor 1963- *210*
Baden, Robert 1936- *70*
Baden-Powell, Robert (Stephenson Smyth)
    1857-1941 .... *16*
Badt, Karin L(uisa) 1963- *91*
Bae, Hyun-Joo *186*

Baehr, Kingsley M. 1937- *89*
Baehr, Patricia 1952- *65*
Baehr, Patricia Goehner
    See Baehr, Patricia
Baek, Matthew J. 1971- *202*
Baer, Jill
    See Gilbert, (Agnes) Joan (Sewell)
Baer, Judy 1951- *71*
Baer, Julie 1960- *161*
Baer-Block, Roxanna *172*
Baerg, Harry J(ohn) 1909-1996 .... *12*
Baeten, Lieve 1954- *83*
Bagert, Brod 1947- *191*
    Earlier sketch in SATA *80*
Baggette, Susan K. 1942- *126*
Baggott, Julianna 1969- *197*
Bagnold, Enid 1889-1981 .... *25*
    Earlier sketch in SATA *1*
Baguley, Elizabeth 1959- *199*
Bahlke, Valerie Worth -1994
    See Worth, Valerie
Bahous, Sally 1939- *86*
Bahr, Mary (Madelyn) 1946- *95*
Bahr, Robert 1940- *38*
Bahti, Tom 1926-1972 .... *57*
    Brief entry *31*
Bai, Durga *211*
Baicker-McKee, Carol 1958- *177*
Bailey, Alice Cooper 1890-1978 .... *12*
Bailey, Anne 1958- *71*
Bailey, Bernadine (Freeman) 1901-1995 ...... *14*
Bailey, Carolyn Sherwin 1875-1961 .... *14*
Bailey, Debbie 1954- *123*
Bailey, Donna (Veronica Anne) 1938- *68*
Bailey, Jane H(orton) 1916- *12*
Bailey, John (Robert) 1940- *52*
Bailey, Len *193*
Bailey, Linda 1948- *217*
    Earlier sketches in SATA *107, 182*
Bailey, Maralyn Collins (Harrison) 1941- *12*
Bailey, Matilda
    See Radford, Ruby L(orraine)
Bailey, Maurice Charles 1932- *12*
Bailey, Pearl (Mae) 1918-1990 .... *81*
Bailey, Peter 1946- *194*
Bailey, Ralph Edgar 1893-1982 .... *11*
Bailey, Sheila (Lucas) 1960- *155*
Baillie, Allan 1943- *151*
    Earlier sketch in SATA *87*
    See also CLR *49*
    See also SAAS *21*
Baillie, Allan Stuart
    See Baillie, Allan
Baines, John (David) 1943- *71*
Bains, Larry
    See Sabin, Louis
Baird, Alison 1963- *138*
Baird, Bil 1904-1987 .... *30*
    Obituary *52*
Baird, Thomas (P.) 1923-1990 .... *45*
    Brief entry *39*
    Obituary *64*
Baird, William Britton
    See Baird, Bil
Baity, Elizabeth Chesley 1907-1989 .... *1*
Baiul, Oksana 1977- *108*
Bajoria, Paul 1964- *187*
Bakeless, John (Edwin) 1894-1978 .... *9*
Bakeless, Katherine Little 1895-1992 .... *9*
Baker, Alan 1951- *146*
    Earlier sketches in SATA *22, 93*
Baker, Augusta 1911-1998 .... *3*
Baker, Barbara 1947- *192*
Baker, Betty Lou 1928-1987 .... *73*
    Obituary *54*
    Earlier sketch in SATA *5*
Baker, Carin Greenberg 1959- *79*
Baker, Charlotte 1910- *2*
Baker, Christina
    See Kline, Christina Baker
Baker, Christopher W. 1952- *144*

Baker, Deirdre 1955- 195
Baker, E.D. 190
Baker, (Mary) Elizabeth (Gillette) 1923- 7
Baker, Gayle Cunningham 1950- 39
Baker, James W. 1924- 65
 Earlier sketch in SATA 22
Baker, James W. 1926- 122
Baker, Janice E(dla) 1941- 22
Baker, Jeanette 178
Baker, Jeannie 1950- 156
 Earlier sketches in SATA 23, 88
 See also CLR 28
Baker, Jeffrey J(ohn) W(heeler) 1931- 5
Baker, Jim
 See Baker, James W.
Baker, Keith 1953- 222
 Earlier sketch in SATA 179
Baker, Ken 1962- 133
Baker, Laura Nelson 1911- 3
Baker, Margaret 1890-1965 4
Baker, Margaret J(oyce) 1918- 12
 See also SAAS 8
Baker, Mary Gladys Steel 1892-1974 12
Baker, (Robert) Michael (Graham) 1938- 4
Baker, Nina (Brown) 1888-1957 15
Baker, Pamela J. 1947- 66
Baker, Rachel 1904-1978 2
 Obituary 26
Baker, Roberta 206
Baker, Rosalie F. 1945- 166
Baker, Samm Sinclair 1909-1997 12
 Obituary 96
Baker, Sharon Reiss 1962- 207
Baker, Susan (Catherine) 1942-1991 29
Baker-Smith, Grahame 223
Balaam
 See Lamb, G(eoffrey) F(rederick)
Balan, Bruce 1959- 113
Balcavage, Dynise 1965- 137
Balch, Glenn 1902-1989 3
 Obituary 83
 See also SAAS 11
Baldacci, David 1960- 184
Baldacci, David G.
 See Baldacci, David
 and Baldacci, David
Balderose, Nancy Ward 1952- 93
Balderson, Margaret 1935- 151
Baldini, Michelle 205
Baldry, Cherith 1947- 167
 Earlier sketch in SATA 72
Balducci, Carolyn 1946- 5
Balducci, Carolyn Feleppa
 See Balducci, Carolyn
Baldwin, Alex
 See Griffin, W. E. B.
Baldwin, Anne Norris 1938- 5
Baldwin, Clara 11
Baldwin, Gordo
 See Baldwin, Gordon C(ortis)
Baldwin, Gordon C(ortis) 1908-1983 12
Baldwin, James 1841-1925 24
Baldwin, James 1924-1987 9
 Obituary 54
Baldwin, Louis 1919- 110
Baldwin, Margaret
 See Weis, Margaret
Baldwin, Stan(ley C.) 1929- 62
 Brief entry 28
Bales, Carol Ann 1940- 57
 Brief entry 29
Balet, Jan (Bernard) 1913- 11
Balgassi, Haemi 1971- 131
Balian, Lorna 1929- 91
 Earlier sketch in SATA 9
Balit, Christina 1961- 212
 Earlier sketches in SATA 102, 159
Ball, Duncan 1941- 73
Ball, Zachary
 See Janas, Frankie-Lee
 and Masters, Kelly R(ay)

Ballantine, Lesley Frost
 See Frost, Lesley
Ballantyne, R(obert) M(ichael) 1825-1894 ... 24
 See also CLR 137
Ballard, James G.
 See Ballard, J.G.
Ballard, James Graham
 See Ballard, J.G.
Ballard, Jane
 See Gorman, Carol
Ballard, J.G. 1930-2009 93
 Obituary 203
Ballard, Jim G.
 See Ballard, J.G.
Ballard, John 1945- 110
Ballard, Lowell C(lyne) 1904-1986 12
 Obituary 49
Ballard, (Charles) Martin 1929- 1
Ballard, Mignon F. 1934- 64
 Brief entry 49
Ballard, Mignon Franklin
 See Ballard, Mignon F.
Ballard, Robert D(uane) 1942- 85
 See also CLR 60
Ballard, Robin 1965- 126
Balliett, Blue 1955- 156
Ballinger, Bryan 1968- 161
Ballouhey, Pierre 1944- 90
Balog, Cyn 221
Balogh, Penelope 1916-1975 1
 Obituary 34
Balouch, Kristen 176
Balow, Tom 1931- 12
Baltazzi, Evan S(erge) 1921- 90
Balterman, Marcia Ridlon 1942- 22
Baltimore, J.
 See Catherall, Arthur
Baltzer, Hans (Adolf) 1900- 40
Balzano, Jeanne (Koppel) 1912- 7
Bambara, Toni Cade 1939-1995 112
Bamfylde, Walter
 See Bevan, Tom
Bamman, Henry A. 1918- 12
Banat, D. R.
 See Bradbury, Ray
Bancks, Tristan 1974- 231
Bancroft, Bronwyn 1958- 216
Bancroft, Griffing 1907-1999 6
Bancroft, Laura
 See Baum, L. Frank
Bandel, Betty 1912- 47
Baner, Skulda Vanadis 1897-1964 10
Banerjee, Anjali 174
Banfill, A. Scott 1956- 98
Bang, Betsy 1912- 48
 Brief entry 37
Bang, Garrett
 See Bang, Molly
Bang, Molly 1943- 215
 Earlier sketches in SATA 24, 69, 111, 158
 See also CLR 8
Bang, Molly Garrett
 See Bang, Molly
Bang-Campbell, Monika 1975(?)- 195
 Earlier sketch in SATA 140
Banjo, The
 See Paterson, A(ndrew) B(arton)
Banke, Cecile de
 See de Banke, Cecile
Banks, Erin Bennett 1978- 211
Banks, Kate 1960- 200
 Earlier sketches in SATA 134, 172
Banks, Laura Stockton Voorhees 1908(?)-1980
 Obituary 23
Banks, Lynne Reid
 See Reid Banks, Lynne
Banks, Merry 197
Banks, Michael A. 1951- 101
Banks, Paul 1952- 174
Banks, Sara
 See Harrell, Sara Gordon

Banks, Sara Jeanne Gordon Harrell
 See Harrell, Sara Gordon
Bannatyne-Cugnet, Elizabeth Jo-Anne
 See Bannatyne-Cugnet, Jo
Bannatyne-Cugnet, Jo 1951- 101
Banner, Angela
 See Maddison, Angela Mary
Bannerman, Helen (Brodie Cowan Watson)
 1862(?)-1946 19
 See also CLR 144
Banning, Evelyn I. 1903-1993 36
Bannon, Laura (?)-1963 6
Bannor, Brett 1959- 143
Bansch, Helga 1957- 224
Banta, Susan 181
Bantock, Nick 1950(?)- 95
Banyai, Istvan 193
Barakat, Ibtisam 1963- 186
Barasch, Lynne 1939- 186
 Earlier sketches in SATA 74, 126
Barbalet, Margaret 1949- 77
Barbary, James
 See Baumann, Amy Beeching
 and Beeching, Jack
Barbash, Shepard 1957- 84
Barbauld, Anna Laetitia 1743-1825
 See CLR 160
Barbe, Walter Burke 1926- 45
Barber, Alison 222
Barber, Antonia 1932- 163
 Earlier sketch in SATA 29
Barber, Atiim Kiambu
 See Barber, Tiki
Barber, Lynda
 See Graham-Barber, Lynda
Barber, Lynda Graham
 See Graham-Barber, Lynda
Barber, Richard (William) 1941- 35
Barber, Ronde 1975- 182
Barber, Tiki 1975- 182
Barbera, Joe 1911-2006 51
 Obituary 179
Barbera, Joseph
 See Barbera, Joe
Barbera, Joseph Roland
 See Barbera, Joe
Barberis, Juan C(arlos) 1920- 61
Barbour, Karen 1956- 170
 Earlier sketches in SATA 63, 121
Barbour, Ralph Henry 1870-1944 16
Barclay, Bill
 See Moorcock, Michael
Barclay, Isabel
 See Dobell, I(sabel) M(arian) B(arclay)
Barclay, William Ewert
 See Moorcock, Michael
Barclay, William Ewert
 See Moorcock, Michael
Bardhan-Quallen, Sudipta 1977- 214
 Earlier sketch in SATA 168
Bardoe, Cheryl 181
Bare, Arnold Edwin 1920- 16
Bare, Colleen Stanley 32
Bar-el, Dan 199
Barenholtz, Bernard 1914-1989
 Obituary 64
Bargar, Gary W. 1947-1985 63
Barger, Jan 1948- 147
Barish, Matthew 1907-2000 12
Barkan, Joanne 127
 Earlier sketch in SATA 77
Barker, Albert W. 1900- 8
Barker, Carol (Minturn) 1938- 31
Barker, Cicely Mary 1895-1973 49
 Brief entry 39
 See also CLR 88
Barker, Melvern 1907-1989 11
Barker, S. Omar 1894-1985 10
Barker, Squire Omar
 See Barker, S. Omar
Barker, Will 1913-1983 8

Barkin, Carol 1944- 52
    Earlier sketch in SATA 42
Barklem, Jill 1951- 96
    See also CLR 31
Barkley, Brad 178
Barkley, James Edward 1941- 6
Barks, Carl 1901-2000 37
Barley, Janet Crane 1934- 95
Barlow, Steve 1952- 211
Barnaby, Ralph S(tanton) 1893-1986 9
Barnard, A. M.
    See Alcott, Louisa May
Barnard, Bryn 1956- 169
    Earlier sketch in SATA 115
Barne, Kitty
    See Barne, Marion Catherine
Barne, Marion Catherine 1883-1957 97
Barneda, David 206
Barner, Bob 1947- 136
    Earlier sketch in SATA 29
Barnes, Dawn 1957- 175
Barnes, Derrick 191
Barnes, Derrick D.
    See Barnes, Derrick
Barnes, (Frank) Eric Wollencott 1907-1962 . 22
Barnes, Joyce Annette 1958- 85
Barnes, Laura T. 1958- 119
Barnes, Loutricia
    See Barnes-Svarney, Patricia L(ou)
Barnes, Malcolm 1909(?)-1984
    Obituary 41
Barnes, Michael 1934- 55
Barnes-Murphy, Frances 1951- 88
Barnes-Murphy, Rowan 1952- 88
Barnes-Svarney, Patricia L(ou) 1953- 67
Barnet, Nancy 1954- 84
Barnett, Ivan 1947- 70
Barnett, Lincoln (Kinnear) 1909-1979 36
Barnett, Mac 223
Barnett, Moneta 1922-1976 33
Barnett, Naomi 1927- 40
Barney, Maginel Wright 1881(?)-1966 39
    Brief entry 32
Barnhart, Clarence L(ewis) 1900-1993 48
    Obituary 78
Barnhouse, Rebecca 1961- 225
Barnouw, Adriaan Jacob 1877-1968
    Obituary 27
Barnouw, Victor 1915-1989 43
    Brief entry 28
Barnstone, Willis 1927- 20
Barnum, Jay Hyde 1888(?)-1962 20
Barnum, P. T., Jr.
    See Stratemeyer, Edward L.
Barnum, Richard 67
    Earlier sketch in SATA 1
Barnum, Theodore
    See Stratemeyer, Edward L.
Barnwell, Ysaye M. 1946- 200
Baron, Kathi 1956- 226
Baron, Kathy 1954- 90
Baron, Virginia Olsen 1931- 46
    Brief entry 28
Barr, Donald 1921-2004 20
    Obituary 152
Barr, George 1907-1992 2
Barr, Jene 1922-1985 16
    Obituary 42
Barr, Nevada 1952- 126
    Earlier sketch in SATA 115
Barragan, Paula 1963- 216
Barratt, Mark 1954- 224
Barrer, Gertrude
    See Barrer-Russell, Gertrude
Barrer-Russell, Gertrude 1921- 27
Barrett, Angela 1955- 223
Barrett, Angela (Jane) 1955- 145
    Earlier sketch in SATA 75
Barrett, Ethel 87
    Brief entry 44
Barrett, Joyce Durham 1943- 138

Barrett, Judi
    See Barrett, Judith
Barrett, Judith 1941- 204
    Earlier sketch in SATA 26
    See also CLR 98
Barrett, Robert T(heodore) 1949- 92
Barrett, Ron 1937- 14
Barrett, Susan (Mary) 1938- 113
Barrett, Tracy 1955- 207
    Earlier sketches in SATA 84, 115, 156
Barrett, William E(dmund) 1900-1986
    Obituary 49
Barretta, Gene 214
    Earlier sketch in SATA 176
Barretton, Grandall
    See Garrett, Randall
Barrie, Baronet
    See Barrie, J. M.
Barrie, J. M. 1860-1937 100
    See also YABC 1
    See also CLR 124
Barrie, James Matthew
    See Barrie, J. M.
Barringer, William 1940-1996 153
Barrington, Michael
    See Moorcock, Michael
Barris, George 1925- 47
Barrol, Grady
    See Bograd, Larry
Barron, Rex 1951- 84
Barron, T.A. 1952- 192
    Earlier sketches in SATA 83, 126
    See also CLR 86
Barron, Thomas Archibald
    See Barron, T.A.
Barron, Tom
    See Barron, T.A.
Barrow, Lloyd H. 1942- 73
Barrows, Annie 1962- 180
Barry, Dan 1958- 177
Barry, Dana (Marie Malloy) 1949- 139
Barry, James P(otvin) 1918- 14
Barry, Katharina Watjen 1936- 4
Barry, Robert 1931- 6
Barry, Robert Everett
    See Barry, Robert
Barry, Scott 1952- 32
Barry, Sheila Anne -2003 91
Barshaw, Ruth McNally 203
Bartell, Susan S. 175
Bartenbach, Jean 1918- 40
Barth, Edna 1914-1980 7
    Obituary 24
Barth, Kelly L. 1964- 152
Barthelme, Donald 1931-1989 7
    Obituary 62
Barth-Grozinger, Inge 1950- 185
Bartholomew, Barbara 1941- 86
    Brief entry 42
Bartholomew, Jean
    See Beatty, Patricia (Robbins)
Bartlett, Alison 153
Bartlett, Philip A. 1
Bartlett, Robert Merrill 1899-1995 12
Bartoletti, Susan Campbell 1958- 173
    Earlier sketches in SATA 88, 129, 135
Barton, Byron 1930- 126
    Earlier sketches in SATA 9, 90
Barton, Chris 224
Barton, Jill(ian) 1940- 75
Barton, May Hollis 67
    Earlier sketch in SATA 1
Barton, Pat
    See Arrowsmith, Pat
Barton, Patrice 1955- 226
Bartos-Hoeppner, Barbara 1923- 5
Bartram, Simon 218
    Earlier sketch in SATA 156
Bartsch, Jochen 1906- 39
Baruch, Dorothy W(alter) 1899-1962 21
Barunga, Albert 1912(?)-1977 120

Baryshnikov, Mikhail 1948- 192
Bas, Rutger
    See Rutgers van der Loeff-Basenau, An(na)
    Maria Margaretha
Base, Graeme 1958- 162
    Earlier sketches in SATA 67, 101
    See also CLR 22
Base, Graeme Rowland
    See Base, Graeme
Baseman, Gary 1960- 174
Bash, Barbara 1948- 132
Bashevis, Isaac
    See Singer, Isaac Bashevis
Bashevis, Yitskhok
    See Singer, Isaac Bashevis
Bashista, Adrienne Ehlert 203
Basile, Gloria Vitanza 1929- 180
Baskin, Leonard 1922-2000 120
    Brief entry 27
    Earlier sketch in SATA 30
Baskin, Nora Raleigh 1961- 189
    Earlier sketch in SATA 129
Bason, Lillian 1913- 20
Bass, Hester 1956- 223
Bass, L. G.
    See Geringer, Laura
Bassett, Jeni 1959- 64
    Brief entry 43
Bassett, John Keith
    See Keating, Lawrence A.
Bassett, Lisa 1958- 61
Bassil, Andrea
    See Nilsen, Anna
Bastyra, Judy 108
Basye, Dale E. 205
Bataille, Marion 1963- 209
Bat-Ami, Miriam 1950- 150
    Autobiography Feature 150
    Earlier sketches in SATA 82, 122
Bate, Lucy 1939-1993 18
Bate, Norman (Arthur) 1916- 5
Bateman, Colin 1962- 172
Bateman, Donna M. 190
Bateman, Teresa 1957- 216
    Earlier sketches in SATA 112, 168
Bates, Amy June 189
Bates, Barbara S(nedeker) 1919- 12
Bates, Betty
    See Bates, Elizabeth
Bates, Dianne 1948- 147
Bates, Elizabeth 1921- 19
Bates, Ivan 175
Bates, Katharine Lee 1859-1929 113
Bates, Martine
    See Leavitt, Martine
Bateson, Catherine 1960- 197
    Earlier sketch in SATA 157
Batey, Tom 1946- 52
    Brief entry 41
Bath, Kevin P.
    See Bath, K.P.
Bath, K.P. 1959- 171
Batherman, Muriel
    See Sheldon, Muriel
Batson, Larry 1930- 35
Batt, Tanya Robyn 1970- 131
Battaglia, Aurelius 1910- 50
    Brief entry 33
Batten, H(arry) Mortimer 1888-1958 25
Batten, Mary 1937- 162
    Earlier sketches in SATA 5, 102
Batterberry, Ariane Ruskin 1935- 13
Batterberry, Michael Carver 1932-2010 32
Battle-Lavert, Gwendolyn 1951- 155
    Earlier sketches in SATA 85, 131
Battles, (Roxy) Edith 1921- 7
Baudouy, Michel-Aime 1909- 7
Bauer, A.C.E. 201

Bauer, Caroline Feller 1935- 98
  Brief entry 46
  Earlier sketch in SATA 52
  See also SAAS 24
Bauer, Fred 1934- 36
Bauer, Helen 1900-1988 2
Bauer, Joan 1951- 160
  Earlier sketch in SATA 117
Bauer, Jutta 1955- 150
Bauer, Marion Dane 1938- 192
  Autobiography Feature 144
  Earlier sketches in SATA 20, 69, 113, 144
  See also SAAS 9
Bauer, Michael Gerard 1955(?)- 167
Bauer, Steven 1948- 125
Bauerschmidt, Marjorie 1926- 15
Baughman, Dorothy 1940- 61
Baum, Allyn Z(elton) 1924-1997 98
  Earlier sketch in SATA 20
Baum, L. Frank
  See Thompson, Ruth Plumly
Baum, L. Frank 1856-1919 100
  Earlier sketch in SATA 18
  See also CLR 107
Baum, Louis 1948- 182
  Brief entry 52
  Earlier sketch in SATA 64
Baum, Louis F.
  See Baum, L. Frank
Baum, Lyman Frank
  See Baum, L. Frank
Baum, Maxie 188
Baum, Willi 1931- 4
Bauman, Beth Ann 1964- 220
Baumann, Amy Beeching 1922- 10
Baumann, Amy Brown Beeching
  See Baumann, Amy Beeching
Baumann, Hans 1914- 2
  See also CLR 35
Baumann, Kurt 1935- 21
Baumgartner, Barbara 1939- 86
Baurys, Flo 1938- 122
Baurys, Florence
  See Baurys, Flo
Bausum, Ann 173
Bawden, Nina 1925- 132
  Earlier sketches in SATA 4, 72
  See also CLR 51
  See also SAAS 16
Bawden, Nina Mary Mabey
  See Bawden, Nina
Baxter, Andy
  See Dakin, Glenn
Baxter, Roberta 1952- 219
Baxter, Valerie
  See Meynell, Laurence Walter
Bay, Jeanette Graham 1928- 88
Bayer, Harold
  See Gregg, Andrew K.
Bayer, Jane E. (?)-1985
  Obituary 44
Bayley, Nicola 1949- 129
  Earlier sketches in SATA 41, 69
Baylor, Byrd 1924- 136
  Earlier sketches in SATA 16, 69
  See also CLR 3
Baynes, Pauline 1922-2008 133
  Obituary 196
  Earlier sketches in SATA 19, 59
Baynes, Pauline Diana
  See Baynes, Pauline
Bayoc, Cbabi 186
Bayrock, Fiona 215
BB
  See Watkins-Pitchford, Denys James
Beach, Charles
  See Reid, (Thomas) Mayne
Beach, Charles Amory 1
Beach, Edward L. 1918-2002 12
  Obituary 140

Beach, Edward Latimer
  See Beach, Edward L.
Beach, Lisa 1957- 111
Beach, Lynn
  See Lance, Kathryn
Beach, Stewart T(aft) 1899-1979 23
Beachcroft, Nina 1931- 18
Beagle, Peter S. 1939- 130
  Earlier sketch in SATA 60
Beagle, Peter Soyer
  See Beagle, Peter S.
Beaglehole, Helen 1946- 117
Beake, Lesley 1949- 209
Beaky, Suzanne 1971- 230
Beale, Fleur 107
Bealer, Alex W(inkler III) 1921-1980 8
  Obituary 22
Beales, Valerie 1915- 74
Beals, Carleton 1893-1979 12
Beals, Frank Lee 1881-1972
  Obituary 26
Beam, Matt 1970- 187
Beame, Rona 1934- 12
Beamer, Charles 1942- 43
Beamer, George Charles, Jr.
  See Beamer, Charles
Bean, Jonathan 1979- 194
Bean, Normal
  See Burroughs, Edgar Rice
Beaney, Jan
  See Udall, Jan Beaney
Beaney, Jane
  See Udall, Jan Beaney
Bear, Carolyn
  See Rayban, Chloe
Bear, Greg 1951- 105
  Earlier sketch in SATA 65
Bear, Gregory Dale
  See Bear, Greg
Bearanger, Marie
  See Messier, Claire
Beard, Alex 1970- 222
Beard, Charles A(ustin) 1874-1948 18
Beard, Dan(iel Carter) 1850-1941 22
Beard, Darleen Bailey 1961- 96
Bearden, Romare (Howard) 1914(?)-1988 ... 22
  Obituary 56
Beardmore, Cedric
  See Beardmore, George
Beardmore, George 1908-1979 20
Beardshaw, Rosalind 1969- 225
  Earlier sketch in SATA 190
Beardsley, Martyn R. 1957- 150
Bearman, Jane (Ruth) 1917- 29
Bearn, Emily 220
Beaton, Clare 1947- 220
  Earlier sketch in SATA 125
Beatty, Elizabeth
  See Holloway, Teresa (Bragunier)
Beatty, Hetty Burlingame 1907-1971 5
Beatty, Jerome, Jr. 1918- 5
Beatty, John (Louis) 1922-1975 6
  Obituary 25
Beatty, Patricia (Robbins) 1922-1991 73
  Obituary 68
  Earlier sketches in SATA 1, 30
  See also SAAS 4
Beaty, Andrea 186
Beaty, Mary (T.) 1947- 146
Beaudoin, Sean 210
Beauford, Jhenne Tyler
  See Beauford, Tyler
Beauford, Tyler 1990- 225
Beaumont, Karen 1954- 204
Beavers, Ethen 1971- 225
Beccia, Carlyn 189
Bechard, Margaret 1953- 164
  Earlier sketch in SATA 85
Bechtel, Louise Seaman 1894-1985 4
  Obituary 43
Bechtold, Lisze 208

Beck, Andrea 1956- 226
Beck, Barbara L. 1927- 12
Beck, Ian 1947- 190
  Earlier sketch in SATA 138
  See Beck, Ian Archibald
Beck, Peggy 1949- 171
Beck, Scott 197
Becker, Beril 1901-1999 11
Becker, Bonny 184
Becker, Deborah Zimmett 1955- 138
Becker, Helaine 1961- 142
Becker, John (Leonard) 1901- 12
Becker, John E(mil) 1942- 148
Becker, Joyce 1936- 39
Becker, May Lamberton 1873-1958 33
Becker, Neesa 1951- 123
Becker, Shari 174
Beckerman, Chad W. 198
Beckett, Sheilah 1913- 33
Beckhorn, Susan Williams 1953- 189
Beckles Willson, Robina 1930- 27
Beckman, Delores 1914-1994 51
Beckman, Gunnel 1910- 6
  See also CLR 25
  See also SAAS 9
Beckman, Kaj
  See Beckman, Karin
Beckman, Karin 1913- 45
Beckman, Per (Frithiof) 1913- 45
Bedard, Michael 1949- 154
  Earlier sketch in SATA 93
  See also CLR 35
Beddor, Frank 194
Beddows, Eric
  See Nutt, Ken
Bedford, A. N.
  See Watson, Jane Werner
Bedford, Annie North
  See Watson, Jane Werner
Bedford, David 224
  Earlier sketch in SATA 159
Bedford, David J.
  See Bedford, David
Bedoukian, Kerop 1907-1981 53
Bee, Jay
  See Brainerd, John W(hiting)
Bee, William 188
Beebe, B. F.
  See Johnson, B. F.
Beebe, (Charles) William 1877-1962 19
Beeby, Betty 1923- 25
Beech, Mark 1971- 191
Beech, Webb
  See Griffin, W. E. B.
Beecham, Jahnna 161
Beechcroft, William
  See Hallstead, William F(inn III)
Beeching, Jack 1922- 14
Beeke, Tiphanie 219
  Earlier sketch in SATA 163
Beeler, Janet
  See Shaw, Janet
Beeler, Nelson F(rederick) 1910-1978 13
Beere, Peter 1951- 97
Beers, Dorothy Sands 1917- 9
Beers, Lorna 1897-1989 14
Beers, V(ictor) Gilbert 1928- 130
  Earlier sketch in SATA 9
Beeton, Max
  See Redding, Robert Hull
Begay, Shonto 1954- 137
Begaye, Lisa Shook
  See Beach, Lisa
Begin, Mary Jane 1963- 82
Begin-Callanan, Mary Jane
  See Begin, Mary Jane
Begley, Kathleen A. 1948- 21
Begley, Kathleen Anne
  See Begley, Kathleen A.
Beguine, Anna
  See Saintcrow, Lilith

Beha, Eileen *221*
Beha, Philippe *211*
Behan, Leslie
  See Gottfried, Theodore Mark
Behler, Deborah A. 1947- *145*
Behler, John L. 1943-2006 .... *145*
  Obituary *173*
Behler, John Luther
  See Behler, John L.
Behn, Harry 1898-1973 .... *2*
  Obituary *34*
Behnke, Frances L. *8*
Behr, Joyce 1929- *15*
Behrens, Andy *228*
Behrens, June York 1925- *19*
Behrman, Carol H(elen) 1925- *144*
  Earlier sketch in SATA *14*
Beifuss, John, (Jr.) 1959- *92*
Beil, Karen Magnuson 1950- *221*
  Earlier sketch in SATA *124*
Beil, Michael D. *226*
Beiler, Edna 1923- *61*
Beingessner, Laura 1965- *220*
Beinicke, Steve 1956- *69*
Beirne, Barbara 1933- *71*
Beiser, Arthur 1931- *22*
Beiser, Germaine 1931- *11*
Belair, Richard L. 1934- *45*
Belaney, Archibald Stansfeld 1888-1938 ...... *24*
  See also CLR *32*
Belasen, Amy 1983- *213*
Belbin, David 1958- *164*
  Earlier sketch in SATA *106*
Belden, Wilanne Schneider 1925- *56*
Belfrage, Sally 1936-1994 .... *65*
  Obituary *79*
Belknap, B. H.
  See Ellis, Edward S.
Belknap, Boynton
  See Ellis, Edward S.
Belknap, Boynton M.D.
  See Ellis, Edward S.
Bell, Anthea 1936- *148*
  Earlier sketch in SATA *88*
Bell, Cathleen Davitt 1971- *203*
Bell, Cece *202*
Bell, Clare (Louise) 1952- *99*
Bell, Corydon Whitten 1894-1980 .... *3*
Bell, David Owen 1949- *99*
Bell, Emerson
  See Stratemeyer, Edward L.
Bell, Emily Mary
  See Cason, Mabel Earp
Bell, Frank
  See Benson, Mildred
Bell, Gertrude (Wood) 1911-1987 .... *12*
Bell, Gina
  See Balzano, Jeanne (Koppel)
Bell, Hilari 1958- *226*
  Earlier sketches in SATA *151, 197*
Bell, Jadrien
  See Golden, Christie
Bell, Janet
  See Clymer, Eleanor
Bell, Janet Cheatham 1937- *127*
Bell, Krista 1950- *215*
  Earlier sketch in SATA *126*
Bell, Krista Anne Blakeney
  See Bell, Krista
Bell, Margaret E(lizabeth) 1898-1990 .... *2*
Bell, Mary Reeves 1946- *88*
Bell, Norman (Edward) 1899- *11*
Bell, Raymond Martin 1907-1999 .... *13*
Bell, Siobhan *177*
Bell, Thelma Harrington 1896-1985 .... *3*
Bell, William 1945- *90*
  See also CLR *91*
Bellairs, John (Anthony) 1938-1991 .... *160*
  Obituary *66*
  Earlier sketches in SATA *2, 68*
  See also CLR *37*

Beller, Susan Provost 1949- *128*
  Earlier sketch in SATA *84*
  See also CLR *106*
Bellingham, Brenda 1931- *99*
  Brief entry *51*
Bello, Rosario de
  See De Bello, Rosario
Belloc, Hilaire 1870-1953 .... *112*
  See also YABC *1*
  See also CLR *102*
Belloc, Joseph Hilaire Pierre Sebastien Rene
  Swanton
  See Belloc, Hilaire
Belloc, Joseph Peter Rene Hilaire
  See Belloc, Hilaire
Belloc, Joseph Pierre Hilaire
  See Belloc, Hilaire
Belloli, Andrea P. A. 1947- *86*
Bell-Rehwoldt, Sheri 1962- *199*
Bellville, Cheryl Walsh 1944- *54*
  Brief entry *49*
Bell-Zano, Gina
  See Balzano, Jeanne (Koppel)
Belpre, Pura 1899-1982 .... *16*
  Obituary *30*
Belting, Natalia Maree 1915-1997 .... *6*
Belton, John Raynor 1931- *22*
Belton, Sandra 1939- *186*
  Earlier sketches in SATA *85, 134*
Belton, Sandra Yvonne
  See Belton, Sandra
Beltran, Alberto 1923- *43*
Beltran-Hernandez, Irene 1945- *74*
Belvedere, Lee
  See Grayland, Valerie (Merle Spanner)
Bemelmans, Ludwig 1898-1962 .... *100*
  Earlier sketch in SATA *15*
  See also CLR *93*
Benander, Carl D. 1941- *74*
Benary, Margot
  See Benary-Isbert, Margot
Benary-Isbert, Margot 1889-1979 .... *2*
  Obituary *21*
  See also CLR *12*
Benasutti, Marion 1908-1992 .... *6*
Benatar, Raquel 1955- *167*
Benchley, Nathaniel (Goddard) 1915-1981 .. *25*
  Obituary *28*
  Earlier sketch in SATA *3*
Benchley, Peter 1940-2006 .... *164*
  Earlier sketches in SATA *3, 89*
Benchley, Peter Bradford
  See Benchley, Peter
Bendall-Brunello, John *185*
Bender, Edna 1941- *92*
Bender, Esther 1942- *88*
Bender, Lucy Ellen 1942- *22*
Bender, Robert 1962- *160*
  Earlier sketch in SATA *79*
Bendick, Jeanne 1919- *135*
  Earlier sketches in SATA *2, 68*
  See also CLR *5*
  See also SAAS *4*
Bendick, Robert L(ouis) 1917- *11*
Benedetto, William R. 1928- *180*
Benedetto, William Ralph
  See Benedetto, William R.
Benedict, Andrew
  See Arthur, Robert, (Jr.)
Benedict, Dorothy Potter 1889-1979 .... *11*
  Obituary *23*
Benedict, Lois Trimble 1902-1967 .... *12*
Benedict, Rex 1920-1995 .... *8*
Benedict, Stewart H(urd) 1924- *26*
Beneduce, Ann Keay *128*
Benet, Laura 1884-1979 .... *3*
  Obituary *23*
Benet, Stephen Vincent 1898-1943
  See YABC *1*
Benet, Sula 1906-1982 .... *21*
  Obituary *33*

Ben-Ezer, Ehud 1936- *122*
Benezra, Barbara (Beardsley) 1921- *10*
Benham, Leslie 1922- *48*
Benham, Lois (Dakin) 1924- *48*
Benham, Mary Lile 1914-1991 .... *55*
Benjamin, E. M. J.
  See Bache, Ellyn
Benjamin, Floella 1949- *206*
Benjamin, Nora
  See Kubie, Nora Gottheil Benjamin
Benjamin, Saragail Katzman 1953- *86*
Benner, Cheryl 1962- *80*
Benner, Judith Ann 1942- *94*
Bennett, Alice
  See Ziner, Florence
Bennett, Artie *227*
Bennett, Cherie 1960- *158*
  Earlier sketch in SATA *97*
Bennett, Dorothea
  See Young, Dorothea Bennett
Bennett, Erin Susanne
  See Banks, Erin Bennett
Bennett, Holly 1957- *181*
Bennett, James (W.) 1942- *153*
  Autobiography Feature *153*
  Earlier sketches in SATA *93, 148*
Bennett, Jay 1912- *87*
  Brief entry *27*
  Earlier sketch in SATA *41*
  See also SAAS *4*
Bennett, Jill (Crawford) 1934- *41*
Bennett, John 1865-1956
  See YABC *1*
Bennett, Kelly 1958- *231*
Bennett, Kelly Goldman
  See Bennett, Kelly
Bennett, Penelope (Agnes) 1938- *94*
Bennett, Rachel
  See Hill, Margaret (Ohler)
Bennett, Rainey 1907-1998 .... *15*
  Obituary *111*
Bennett, Richard 1899- *21*
Bennett, Russell H(oradley) 1896- *25*
Bennett, Veronica 1953- *178*
Bennett, William (John) 1943- *102*
Benning, Elizabeth
  See Rice, Bebe Faas
Benny, Mike 1964- *203*
Benson, Elizabeth P(olk) 1924- *65*
Benson, Kathleen 1947- *183*
  Earlier sketches in SATA *62, 111*
Benson, Linda M(aria) 1959- *84*
Benson, Mildred 1905-2002 .... *100*
  Obituary *135*
  Earlier sketches in SATA *1, 65, 67*
Benson, Mildred Augustine Wirt
  See Benson, Mildred
Benson, Mildred Wirt
  See Benson, Mildred
Benson, Millie
  See Benson, Mildred
Benson, Patrick 1956- *147*
Benson, Sally 1900-1972 .... *35*
  Obituary *27*
  Earlier sketch in SATA *1*
Bentley, Judith (McBride) 1945- *89*
  Earlier sketch in SATA *40*
Bentley, Karen
  See Taschek, Karen
Bentley, Nancy (L.) 1946- *78*
Bentley, Nicolas Clerihew 1907-1978
  Obituary *24*
Bentley, Phyllis Eleanor 1894-1977 .... *6*
  Obituary *25*
Bentley, Roy 1947- *46*
Bentley, William (George) 1916- *84*
Bently, Peter 1960- *221*
Benton, Jim 1963- *172*
ben Uzair, Salem
  See Horne, Richard Henry Hengist

Ben-Zvi, Rebeccca Tova
  See O'Connell, Rebecca
Bercaw, Edna Coe 1961- 124
Berck, Judith 1960- 75
Bereal, JaeMe 1959(?)- 228
Berelson, Howard 1940- 5
Berends, Polly Berrien 1939- 50
  Brief entry 38
Berenstain, Jan 1923- 135
  Earlier sketches in SATA *12, 64, 129*
  See also CLR *150*
  See also SAAS *20*
Berenstain, Janice
  See Berenstain, Jan
Berenstain, Michael 1951- 220
  Earlier sketch in SATA *45*
Berenstain, Mike
  See Berenstain, Michael
Berenstain, Stan 1923-2005 135
  Obituary 169
  Earlier sketches in SATA *12, 64, 129*
  See also CLR *150*
  See also SAAS *20*
Berenstain, Stanley
  See Berenstain, Stan
Berenzy, Alix 1957- 168
  Earlier sketch in SATA *65*
Beresford, Elisabeth 1928-2010 141
  Earlier sketches in SATA *25, 86*
  See also SAAS *20*
Berg, Adriane G(ilda) 1948- 152
Berg, Dave
  See Berg, David
Berg, David 1920-2002 27
  Obituary 137
Berg, Elizabeth 1948- 104
Berg, Jean Horton 1913-1995 6
Berg, Joan
  See Victor, Joan Berg
Berg, Ron 1952- 48
Bergaust, Erik 1925-1978 20
Bergel, Colin J. 1963- 137
Bergen, Joyce 1949- 95
Berger, Barbara (Helen) 1945- 77
Berger, Carin 185
Berger, Gilda 1935- 88
  Brief entry 42
Berger, Joe 1970- 221
Berger, Josef 1903-1971 36
Berger, Lou 1950- 213
Berger, Melvin H. 1927- 158
  Autobiography Feature 124
  Earlier sketches in SATA *5, 88*
  See also CLR *32*
  See also SAAS *2*
Berger, Phil 1942-2001 62
Berger, Samantha 1969- 140
Berger, Samantha Allison
  See Berger, Samantha
Berger, Terry 1933- 8
Bergey, Alyce 1934- 45
Bergey, Alyce Mae
  See Bergey, Alyce
Bergin, Mark 1961- 160
  Earlier sketch in SATA *114*
Berglin, Ruth Marie 1970- 181
Bergman, Donna 1934- 73
Bergman, Mara 1956- 196
Bergman, Tamar 1939- 95
Bergren, Lisa T.
  See Bergren, Lisa Tawn
Bergren, Lisa Tawn 200
Bergsma, Jody Lynn 163
Bergstein, Rita M. 211
Bergum, Constance R. 1952- 208
  Earlier sketch in SATA *121*
Berk, Ari 208
Berk, Josh 1976- 227
Berkebile, Fred D(onovan) 1900-1978
  Obituary 26
Berkeley, Jon 1962- 204

Berkes, Marianne 217
  Earlier sketch in SATA *173*
Berkey, Barry Robert 1935- 24
Berkowitz, Freda Pastor 1908-1994 12
Berkus, Clara Widess 1909- 78
Berlan, Kathryn Hook 1946- 78
Berlfein, Judy Reiss 1958- 79
Berlin, Eric 1968- 195
Berliner, Don 1930- 33
Berliner, Franz 1930- 13
Berlitz, Charles (L. Frambach) 1914-2003 ... 32
  Obituary 151
Berman, Len 1947- 229
Berman, Linda 1948- 38
Berman, Paul (Lawrence) 1949- 66
Berman, Rachel 1946- 217
Berna, Paul 1910-1994 15
  Obituary 78
  See also CLR *19*
Bernadette
  See Watts, Bernadette
Bernard, Bruce 1928-2000 78
  Obituary 124
Bernard, George I. 1949- 39
Bernard, Jacqueline (de Sieyes) 1921-1983 ... 8
  Obituary 45
Bernard, Patricia 1942- 181
  Earlier sketch in SATA *106*
Bernard, Trish
  See Bernard, Patricia
Bernardin, James 1966- 227
  Earlier sketch in SATA *112*
Bernardo, Anilu 184
Bernards, Neal 1963- 71
Bernasconi, Pablo 1973- 183
Bernays, Anne 1930- 32
Berner, Rotraut Susanne 1948- 214
Bernhard, Durga T. 1961- 80
Bernhard, Emery 1950- 80
Bernheimer, Kate 201
Bernier-Grand, Carmen T. 1947- 202
Bernstein, Daryl (Evan) 1976- 81
Bernstein, Joanne E(ckstein) 1943- 15
Bernstein, Jonathan 217
Bernstein, Margery 1933- 114
Bernstein, Nina 1949- 180
Bernstein, Theodore M(enline) 1904-1979 ... 12
  Obituary 27
Berrien, Edith Heal
  See Heal, Edith
Berrill, Jacquelyn (Batsel) 1905- 12
Berrington, John
  See Brownjohn, Alan
Berry, B. J.
  See Berry, Barbara J.
Berry, Barbara J. 1937- 7
Berry, Erick
  See Best, (Evangel) Allena Champlin
Berry, Holly 1957- 210
Berry, James 1924- 110
  Earlier sketch in SATA *67*
  See also CLR *143*
Berry, Jane Cobb 1915(?)-1979
  Obituary 22
Berry, Joy 1944- 58
  Brief entry 46
Berry, Joy Wilt
  See Berry, Joy
Berry, Julie 1974- 218
Berry, Lynne 190
Berry, William D(avid) 1926- 14
Bersani, Shennen 1961- 164
Berson, Harold 1926- 4
Bertagna, Julie 1962- 151
Bertholf, Bret 189
Bertin, Charles-Francois
  See Berlitz, Charles (L. Frambach)
Bertolet, Paul
  See McLaughlin, Frank

Berton, Pierre (Francis de Marigny)
  1920-2004 99
  Obituary 158
Bertrand, Cecile 1953- 76
Bertrand, Diane Gonzales 1956- 177
  Earlier sketch in SATA *106*
Bertrand, Lynne 1963- 164
  Earlier sketch in SATA *81*
Beskow, Elsa (Maartman) 1874-1953 20
  See also CLR *17*
Bess, Clayton
  See Locke, Robert
Besson, Luc 1959- 199
Best, (Evangel) Allena Champlin 1892-1974 . 2
  Obituary 25
Best, Cari 1951- 200
  Earlier sketches in SATA *107, 149*
Best, (Oswald) Herbert 1894-1980 2
Bestall, A(lfred) E(dmeades) 1892-1986 97
  Obituary 48
Betancourt, Jeanne 1941- 148
  Brief entry 43
  Earlier sketches in SATA *55, 96*
Beth, Mary
  See Miller, Mary Beth
Bethancourt, T. Ernesto
  See Paisley, Tom
Bethel, Dell 1929- 52
Bethell, Jean (Frankenberry) 1922- 8
Bethers, Ray 1902-1973 6
Bethke, Bruce Raymond 1955- 114
Bethlen, T.D.
  See Silverberg, Robert
Bethune, J. G.
  See Ellis, Edward S.
Bethune, J. H.
  See Ellis, Edward S.
Betteridge, Anne
  See Potter, Margaret
Betteridge, Deirdre 214
Bettina
  See Ehrlich, Bettina Bauer
Bettmann, Otto Ludwig 1903-1998 46
Bettoli, Delana 187
Betts, James
  See Haynes, Betsy
Betz, Eva Kelly 1897-1968 10
Bevan, Tom 1868-1930(?)
  See YABC *2*
Bevis, Mary 1939- 202
Bewick, Thomas 1753-1828 16
Beyer, Audrey White 1916- 9
Beyer, Paul J. III 1950- 74
Beynon, John
  See Harris, John (Wyndham Parkes Lucas)
  Beynon
Bezencon, Jacqueline (Buxcel) 1924- 48
Bhatia, Jamunadevi 1919- 48
Bhatia, June
  See Bhatia, Jamunadevi
Bial, Morrison David 1917- 62
Bial, Raymond 1948- 225
  Earlier sketches in SATA *76, 116, 165*
Biala
  See Brustlein, Janice Tworkov
Biale, Rachel 1952- 99
Bialk, Elisa
  See Krautter, Elisa (Bialk)
Bianchi, John 1947- 91
Bianchi, Robert S(teven) 1943- 92
Bianco, Margery
  See Bianco, Margery Williams
Bianco, Margery Williams 1881-1944 15
  See also CLR *146*
Bianco, Pamela 1906- 28
Bibby, Violet 1908-1996 24
Bible, Charles 1937- 13
Bibo, Bobette
  See Gugliotta, Bobette
Bice, Clare 1909-1976 22

Bickerstaff, Isaac
  See Swift, Jonathan
Bidner, Jenni 1963- *193*
Biedrzycki, David 1955- *219*
Biegel, Paul 1925- *79*
  Earlier sketch in SATA *16*
  See also CLR *27*
  See also SAAS *18*
Biemiller, Carl L(udwig, Jr.) 1912-1979 ..... *40*
  Obituary *21*
Bienenfeld, Florence L(ucille) 1929- *39*
Bierhorst, John (William) 1936- *149*
  Autobiography Feature *149*
  Earlier sketches in SATA *6, 91*
  See also SAAS *10*
Biggar, Joan R. 1936- *120*
Biggar, Joan Rawlins
  See Biggar, Joan R.
Biggle, Lloyd, Jr. 1923-2002 .... *65*
Biggs, Brian 1968- *192*
Bilal, Abdel W(ahab) 1970- *92*
Bilbrough, Norman 1941- *111*
Bildner, Phil *230*
  Earlier sketch in SATA *173*
Bileck, Marvin 1920- *40*
Bilibin, Ivan (Iakolevich) 1876-1942 .... *61*
Bill, Alfred Hoyt 1879-1964 .... *44*
Bill, Tannis *228*
Billam, Rosemary 1952- *61*
Billings, Charlene W(interer) 1941- *41*
Billingsley, Franny 1954- *132*
Billington, Elizabeth T(hain) *50*
  Brief entry *43*
Billout, Guy (Rene) 1941- *144*
  Earlier sketch in SATA *10*
  See also CLR *33*
Bilson, Geoffrey 1938-1987 .... *99*
Binch, Caroline (Lesley) 1947- *140*
  Earlier sketch in SATA *81*
Bing, Christopher (H.) *126*
Bingham, Caroline 1962- *158*
Bingham, Jane M. 1941- *163*
Bingham, Jane Marie
  See Bingham, Jane M.
Bingham, Janet 1959- *200*
Bingham, Kelly 1967- *207*
Bingham, Sam 1944- *96*
Bingham, Samuel A.
  See Bingham, Sam
Bingley, Margaret (Jane Kirby) 1947- *72*
Binkley, Anne
  See Rand, Ann (Binkley)
Binzen, Bill
  See Binzen, William
Binzen, William *24*
Birch, David (W.) 1913-1996 .... *89*
Birch, Reginald B(athurst) 1856-1943 .... *19*
Birchman, David 1949- *72*
Birchmore, Daniel A. 1951- *92*
Bird, Carmel 1940- *124*
Bird, E(lzy) J(ay) 1911- *58*
Birdsall, Jeanne 1951- *231*
Birdsall, Jeanne 1952(?)- *170*
Birdseye, Tom 1951- *148*
  Earlier sketches in SATA *66, 98*
Birenbaum, Barbara 1941- *65*
Birmingham, Christian 1970- *220*
Birmingham, Lloyd P(aul) 1924- *83*
  Earlier sketch in SATA *12*
Birmingham, Ruth
  See Sorrells, Walter
Birney, Betty G. 1947- *169*
  Earlier sketch in SATA *98*
Biro, B.
  See Biro, B. S.
Biro, B. S. 1921- *1*
  See also CLR *28*
  See also SAAS *13*
Biro, Val
  See Biro, B. S.
Birtha, Becky 1948- *229*

Bischoff, Julia Bristol 1899-1970 .... *12*
Bishop, Bonnie 1943- *37*
Bishop, Claire Huchet 1899(?)-1993 .... *14*
  Obituary *74*
  See also CLR *80*
Bishop, Courtney
  See Ruemmler, John D(avid)
Bishop, Curtis (Kent) 1912-1967 .... *6*
Bishop, Elizabeth 1911-1979
  Obituary *24*
Bishop, Gavin 1946- *216*
  Earlier sketches in SATA *97, 144*
Bishop, Kathleen Wong 1954- *120*
Bishop, Kathy
  See Bishop, Kathleen Wong
Bishop, Nic 1955- *161*
  Earlier sketch in SATA *107*
Bishop, Rudine Sims *224*
Bisset, Donald 1910-1995 .... *86*
  Earlier sketch in SATA *7*
Bisson, Terry 1942- *99*
Bisson, Terry Ballantine
  See Bisson, Terry
Bitter, Gary G(len) 1940- *22*
Bixby, William (Courtney) 1920-1986 .... *6*
  Obituary *47*
Bjoerk, Christina 1938- *99*
  Earlier sketch in SATA *67*
  See also CLR *22*
Bjork, Christina
  See Bjoerk, Christina
Bjorklund, Lorence F. 1913-1978 .... *35*
  Brief entry *32*
Bjorkman, Lauren *222*
Bjorkman, Steve *223*
  Earlier sketch in SATA *163*
Blabey, Aaron 1975(?)- *214*
Black, Algernon David 1900-1993 .... *12*
  Obituary *76*
Black, Holly 1971- *210*
  Earlier sketch in SATA *147*
Black, Irma Simonton 1906-1972 .... *2*
  Obituary *25*
Black, Joe 1959- *224*
Black, Rabbi Joe
  See Black, Joe
Black, Kat *217*
Black, Katherine
  See Black, Kat
Black, Mansell
  See Trevor, Elleston
Black, MaryAnn
  See Easley, MaryAnn
Black, Susan Adams 1953- *40*
Blackall, Bernie 1956- *126*
Blackall, Sophie *231*
  Earlier sketch in SATA *182*
Blackburn, Claire
  See Altman, Linda Jacobs
Blackburn, John(ny) Brewton 1952- *15*
Blackburn, Joyce Knight 1920- *29*
Blacker, Terence 1948- *194*
Blacker, Tina
  See Louise, Tina
Blackett, Veronica Heath 1927- *12*
Blackie, Jean Cutler 1943- *79*
Blacklin, Malcolm
  See Chambers, Aidan
Blacklock, Dyan 1951- *112*
Blackman, Malorie 1962- *196*
  Earlier sketches in SATA *83, 128*
Blackton, Peter
  See Wilson, Lionel
Blackwood, Alan 1932- *70*
Blackwood, Freya *199*
Blackwood, Gary
  See Blackwood, Gary L.
Blackwood, Gary L. 1945- *226*
  Earlier sketches in SATA *72, 118, 169*

Blade, Alexander
  See Garrett, Randall
  and Hamilton, Edmond
  and Silverberg, Robert
Blades, Ann (Sager) 1947- *69*
  Earlier sketch in SATA *16*
  See also CLR *15*
Bladow, Suzanne Wilson 1937- *14*
Blaine, Chris
  See Gardner, Craig Shaw
Blaine, John
  See Goodwin, Harold L(eland)
Blaine, Marge
  See Blaine, Margery Kay
Blaine, Margery Kay 1937- *11*
Blair, Alison
  See Lerangis, Peter
Blair, Anne Denton 1914-1993 .... *46*
Blair, David Nelson 1954- *80*
Blair, Eric
  See Orwell, George
Blair, Jay 1953- *45*
Blair, Lucile
  See Yeakley, Marjory Hall
Blair, Margaret Whitman 1951- *227*
  Earlier sketch in SATA *124*
Blair, Mary 1911-1978 .... *195*
Blair, Pauline Hunter
  See Clarke, Pauline
Blair, Ruth Van Ness 1912-1999 .... *12*
Blair, Shannon
  See Kaye, Marilyn
Blair, Walter 1900-1992 .... *12*
  Obituary *72*
Blaisdell, Bob
  See Blaisdell, Robert
Blaisdell, Robert 1959- *105*
Blake, Bronwyn 1940- *149*
Blake, Francis *198*
Blake, Jon 1954- *171*
  Earlier sketch in SATA *78*
Blake, Olive
  See Supraner, Robyn
Blake, Quentin 1932- *211*
  Earlier sketches in SATA *9, 52, 96, 125*
  See also CLR *31*
Blake, Robert 1949- *42*
Blake, Robert J. *160*
Blake, Walker E.
  See Griffin, W. E. B.
Blake, William 1757-1827 .... *30*
  See also CLR *52*
Blakely, Gloria 1950- *139*
Blakely, Roger K. 1922- *82*
Blakeney, Jay D.
  See Chester, Deborah
Blakeslee, Lys 1985- *218*
Blakey, Nancy 1955- *94*
Blanc, Esther S. 1913-1997 .... *66*
Blanc, Mel 1908-1989
  Obituary *64*
Blanchard, Patricia *125*
Blanchet, M(uriel) Wylie 1891-1961 .... *106*
Blanco, Richard L(idio) 1926- *63*
Bland, E.
  See Nesbit, E.
Bland, Edith Nesbit
  See Nesbit, E.
Bland, Fabian
  See Nesbit, E.
Blane, Gertrude
  See Blumenthal, Gertrude
Blank, Clarissa Mabel 1915-1965 .... *62*
Blankenship, LeeAnn 1944- *181*
Blassingame, Wyatt Rainey 1909-1985 .... *34*
  Obituary *41*
  Earlier sketch in SATA *1*
Blatchford, Claire H. 1944- *94*
Blauer, Ettagale 1940- *49*
Bleck, Linda *207*
Bledsoe, Glen L. 1951- *108*

Bledsoe, Glen Leonard
See Bledsoe, Glen L.
Bledsoe, Karen E. 1962- 167
Earlier sketch in SATA 108
Bledsoe, Karen Elizabeth
See Bledsoe, Karen E.
Bledsoe, Lucy Jane 1957- 162
Earlier sketch in SATA 97
Bleeker, Sonia
See Zim, Sonia Bleeker
Blegen, Daniel M. 1950- 92
Blegvad, Erik 1923- 132
Earlier sketches in SATA 14, 66
Blegvad, Lenore 1926- 176
Earlier sketches in SATA 14, 66
Blessing, Charlotte 223
Bley, Anette 1967- 188
Blish, James 1921-1975 66
Blish, James Benjamin
See Blish, James
Blishen, Edward (William) 1920-1996 66
Obituary 93
Earlier sketch in SATA 8
Bliss, Corinne Demas 1947- 203
Earlier sketches in SATA 37, 131
Bliss, Frederick
See Card, Orson Scott
Bliss, Gillian
See Paton Walsh, Jill
Bliss, Harry 1964- 196
Earlier sketch in SATA 156
Bliss, Reginald
See Wells, H. G.
Bliss, Ronald G(ene) 1942- 12
Blitt, Barry 187
Bliven, Bruce, Jr. 1916-2002 2
Blixen, Karen 1885-1962 44
Blizzard, Gladys S. (?)-1992 79
Blobaum, Cindy 1966- 123
Bloch, Lucienne 1909-1999 10
Bloch, Marie Halun 1910-1998 6
See also SAAS 9
Bloch, Robert (Albert) 1917-1994 12
Obituary 82
Bloch, Serge 1956- 213
Blochman, Lawrence G(oldtree)
1900-1975 22
Block, Francesca Lia 1962- 213
Earlier sketches in SATA 80, 116, 158
See also CLR 116
See also SAAS 21
Block, Irvin 1917- 12
Blomgren, Jennifer (Alice) 1954- 136
Blonder, Terry Joyce
See Golson, Terry
Blood, Charles Lewis 1929- 28
Bloom, Barbara Lee 1943- 146
Bloom, Freddy 1914-2000 37
Obituary 121
Bloom, Lloyd 1947- 108
Brief entry 43
Bloom, Suzanne 1950- 172
Bloomfield, Michaela 1966- 70
Bloor, Edward 1950- 201
Earlier sketches in SATA 98, 155
Bloor, Edward William
See Bloor, Edward
Blos, Joan W. 1928- 153
Autobiography Feature 153
Brief entry 27
Earlier sketches in SATA 33, 69, 109
See also CLR 18
See also SAAS 11
Blos, Joan Winsor
See Blos, Joan W.
Blough, Glenn O(rlando) 1907-1995 1
Blue, Rose 1931- 166
Autobiography Feature 117
Earlier sketches in SATA 5, 91, 93
See also SAAS 24

Blue, Zachary
See Stine, R.L.
Bluemle, Elizabeth 209
Bluggage, Oranthy
See Alcott, Louisa May
Blumberg, Leda 1956- 59
Blumberg, Rhoda 1917- 123
Earlier sketches in SATA 35, 70
See also CLR 21
Blume, Judy 1938- 195
Earlier sketches in SATA 2, 31, 79, 142
See also CLR 69
Blume, Judy Sussman
See Blume, Judy
Blume, Lesley M.M. 1975- 180
Blumenthal, Deborah 204
Earlier sketch in SATA 161
Blumenthal, Gertrude 1907-1971
Obituary 27
Blumenthal, Shirley 1943- 46
Blutig, Eduard
See Gorey, Edward (St. John)
Bly, Janet 1945- 43
Bly, Janet Chester
See Bly, Janet
Bly, Stephen A(rthur) 1944- 116
Earlier sketch in SATA 43
Blyler, Allison Lee 1966- 74
Blythe, Gary 1959- 185
Blyton, Carey 1932-2002 9
Obituary 138
Blyton, Enid 1897-1968 25
See also CLR 31
Blyton, Enid Mary
See Blyton, Enid
Bo, Ben
See Richardson, V.A.
Boardman, Fon Wyman, Jr. 1911-2000 6
Boardman, Gwenn R.
See Petersen, Gwenn Boardman
Boase, Susan 226
Boase, Wendy 1944-1999 28
Obituary 110
Boatner, Mark Mayo III 1921- 29
Bobbe, Dorothie de Bear 1905-1975 1
Obituary 25
Bober, Natalie S. 1930- 134
Earlier sketch in SATA 87
See also SAAS 23
Bobette, Bibo
See Gugliotta, Bobette
Bobri, Vladimir V. 1898-1986 47
Brief entry 32
Bobritsky, Vladimir
See Bobri, Vladimir V.
Bochak, Grayce 1956- 76
Bock, Hal
See Bock, Harold I.
Bock, Harold I. 1939- 10
Bock, William Sauts Netamux'we 1939- 14
Bodanis, David 179
Bode, Janet 1943-1999 96
Obituary 118
Earlier sketch in SATA 60
Bode, N.E.
See Baggott, Julianna
Bodecker, N(iels) M(ogens) 1922-1988 73
Obituary 54
Earlier sketch in SATA 8
Bodeen, S. A. 1965- 158
Earlier sketch in SATA 114
Boden, Hilda
See Bodenham, Hilda Morris
Bodenham, Hilda Morris 1901- 13
Bodett, Thomas Edward 1955- 70
Bodett, Tom
See Bodett, Thomas Edward
Bodie, Idella F(allaw) 1925- 89
Earlier sketch in SATA 12
Bodker, Cecil
See Bodker, Cecil

Bodker, Cecil 1927- 133
Earlier sketch in SATA 14
See also CLR 23
Bodsworth, (Charles) Fred(erick) 1918- 27
Boeckman, Charles 1920- 12
Boegehold, Betty (Doyle) 1913-1985
Obituary 42
Boelts, Maribeth 1964- 200
Earlier sketches in SATA 78, 163
Boerst, William J. 1939- 170
Earlier sketch in SATA 121
Boesch, Mark J(oseph) 1917- 12
Boesen, Victor 1908- 16
Bogacki, Tomek 1950- 214
Earlier sketch in SATA 138
Bogaerts, Gert 1965- 80
Bogan, Paulette 1960- 201
Earlier sketch in SATA 129
Bogart, Jo Ellen 1945- 222
Earlier sketch in SATA 92
See also CLR 59
Boggs, Ralph Steele 1901-1994 7
Bograd, Larry 1953- 89
Earlier sketch in SATA 33
See also SAAS 21
Bogue, Gary 1938- 195
Bogue, Gary L.
See Bogue, Gary
Bohdal, Susi 1951- 101
Earlier sketch in SATA 22
Bohlen, Nina 1931- 58
Bohlmeijer, Arno 1956- 94
Bohner, Charles (Henry) 1927- 62
Bohnhoff, Maya Kaathryn 1954- 88
Boie, Kirsten 1950- 221
Boiger, Alexandra 178
Boissard, Janine 1932- 59
Bojunga, Lygia
See Nunes, Lygia Bojunga
Bojunga-Nunes, Lygia
See Nunes, Lygia Bojunga
Bok, Arthur
See Bok, Chip
Bok, Chip 1952- 205
Bolam, Emily 1969- 206
Boland, Janice 98
Bolden, Tonya 1959- 227
Earlier sketches in SATA 79, 138, 188
Bolden, Tonya Wilyce
See Bolden, Tonya
Boles, Paul Darcy 1916-1984 9
Obituary 38
Bolian, Polly 1925- 4
Bollen, Roger 1941(?)- 83
Brief entry 29
Bolliger, Max 1929- 7
Bollinger, Max 1929- 167
Bollinger, Peter 172
Bolognese, Don(ald Alan) 1934- 129
Earlier sketches in SATA 24, 71
Bolognese, Elaine 1933- 23
Bolotin, Norman (Phillip) 1951- 93
Bolton, Carole 1926- 6
Bolton, Elizabeth
See St. John, Nicole
Bolton, Evelyn
See Bunting, Eve
Bonar, Veronica
See Bailey, Donna (Veronica Anne)
Bond, B. J.
See Heneghan, James
Bond, Bruce 1939- 61
Bond, Felicia 1954- 219
Earlier sketches in SATA 49, 126
Bond, Gladys Baker 1912- 14
Bond, Higgins 1951- 220
Earlier sketches in SATA 83, 177
Bond, J. Harvey
See Winterbotham, R(ussell) R(obert)

Bond, (Thomas) Michael 1926- *157*
  Earlier sketches in SATA 6, 58
  See also CLR 95
  See also SAAS 3
Bond, Nancy 1945- *159*
  Autobiography Feature *159*
  Earlier sketches in SATA 22, 82
  See also CLR 11
  See also SAAS 13
Bond, Nancy Barbara
  See Bond, Nancy
Bond, Rebecca 1972- *214*
  Earlier sketch in SATA 130
Bond, Ruskin 1934- *87*
  Earlier sketch in SATA 14
Bondie, J. D.
  See Cunningham, Chet
Bondoux, Anne-Laure 1971- *175*
Bone, Ian 1956- *158*
  Earlier sketch in SATA 117
Bone, J. *230*
Bone, Jason
  See Bone, J.
Bonehill, Captain Ralph
  See Stratemeyer, Edward L.
Bonestell, Chesley 1888-1986
  Obituary *48*
Bonham, Barbara Thomas 1926- *7*
Bonham, Frank 1914-1989 .... *49*
  Obituary *62*
  Earlier sketch in SATA 1
  See also SAAS 3
Boniface, William 1963- *182*
  Earlier sketch in SATA 102
Bonino, Louise
  See Williams, Louise Bonino
Bonk, John J. *189*
Bonn, Pat
  See Bonn, Patricia Carolyn
Bonn, Patricia Carolyn 1948- *43*
Bonner, Hannah *197*
Bonner, Mary Graham 1890-1974 .... *19*
Bonner, Mike 1951- *121*
Bonners, Susan 1947- *85*
  Brief entry *48*
Bonnet, Rosalinde 1978- *226*
Bonnett-Rampersaud, Louise *173*
Bonning, Tony 1948- *169*
Bonsall, Crosby Barbara (Newell)
  1921-1995 .... *23*
  Obituary *84*
Bonsall, Joseph S. 1948- *119*
Bonsignore, Joan 1959- *140*
Bontemps, Arna 1902-1973 .... *44*
  Obituary *24*
  Earlier sketch in SATA 2
  See also CLR 6
Bontemps, Arnaud Wendell
  See Bontemps, Arna
Bonzon, Paul-Jacques 1908-1978 .... *22*
Boock, Paula 1964- *134*
Booher, Dianna Daniels 1948- *33*
Book, Rick 1949- *119*
Book, Rita
  See Holub, Joan
Bookman, Charlotte
  See Zolotow, Charlotte
Boon, Debbie 1960- *103*
Boon, Emilie (Laetitia) 1958- *86*
Boone, Charles Eugene
  See Boone, Pat
Boone, Pat 1934- *7*
Booraem, Ellen *211*
Boorman, Linda 1940- *46*
Boorman, Linda Kay
  See Boorman, Linda
Boorstin, Daniel J(oseph) 1914-2004 .... *52*
Boos, Ben 1971- *206*
Booth, Coe *187*
Booth, Ernest Sheldon 1915-1984 .... *43*
Booth, George 1926- *191*

Booth, Graham (Charles) 1935- *37*
Bootman, Colin *159*
Borden, Louise 1949- *190*
  Autobiography Feature *141*
  Earlier sketches in SATA 68, 104, 141
Bordier, Georgette 1924- *16*
Borgman, James
  See Borgman, Jim
Borgman, James Mark
  See Borgman, Jim
Borgman, Jim 1954- *122*
Borgo, Lacy Finn 1972- *194*
Boring, Mel 1939- *168*
  Earlier sketch in SATA 35
Borja, Corinne 1929- *22*
Borja, Robert 1923- *22*
Borland, Hal
  See Borland, Harold Glen
Borland, Harold Glen 1900-1978 .... *5*
  Obituary *24*
Borland, Kathryn Kilby 1916- *16*
Borlenghi, Patricia 1951- *79*
Born, Adolf 1930- *49*
Bornstein, Ruth Lercher
  See Bornstein-Lercher, Ruth
Bornstein-Lercher, Ruth 1927- *88*
  Autobiography Feature *107*
  Earlier sketch in SATA 14
Borris, Albert *221*
Borski, Lucia Merecka *18*
Borten, Helen Jacobson 1930- *5*
Bortolotti, Dan 1969- *157*
Borton, Elizabeth
  See Trevino, Elizabeth B(orton) de
Borton, Lady 1942- *98*
Borton de Trevino, Elizabeth
  See Trevino, Elizabeth B(orton) de
Bortstein, Larry 1942-2010 .... *16*
Bortz, Alfred B(enjamin) 1944- *139*
  Earlier sketch in SATA 74
Bortz, Fred
  See Bortz, Alfred B(enjamin)
Bosch, Pseudonymous *199*
Bosco, Jack
  See Holliday, Joseph
Bose, Mitali
  See Perkins, Mitali
Boshell, Gordon 1908-1991 .... *15*
Boshinski, Blanche 1922- *10*
Bosman, Paul 1929- *107*
Bosse, Malcolm (Joseph, Jr.) 1926-2002 .... *136*
  Earlier sketch in SATA 35
Bosserman, Charles Phillip
  See Bosserman, Phillip
Bosserman, Phillip 1931- *84*
Bossley, Michele Martin 1969- *219*
Bossom, Naomi 1933- *35*
Bostock, Mike 1962- *114*
Boston, L(ucy) M(aria Wood) 1892-1990 .... *19*
  Obituary *64*
  See also CLR 3
Bostrom, Kathleen (Susan) Long 1954- *139*
Bostrom, Kathy
  See Bostrom, Kathleen (Susan) Long
Boswell, Addie *208*
Boswell, Addie Kay
  See Boswell, Addie
Bosworth, J. Allan 1925- *19*
Bothwell, Jean (?)-1977 .... *2*
Botkin, B(enjamin) A(lbert) 1901-1975 .... *40*
Botsford, Ward 1927-2004 .... *66*
Botting, Douglas (Scott) 1934- *43*
Bottner, Barbara 1943- *170*
  Autobiography Feature *121*
  Earlier sketches in SATA 14, 93
  See also SAAS 26
Bottone, Frank G., Jr. 1969- *141*
Bouchard, David 1952- *213*
  Earlier sketch in SATA 117
Boucher, (Clarence) Carter 1954- *129*

Boudelang, Bob
  See Pell, Ed(ward)
Boughton, Richard 1954- *75*
Boulet, Susan Seddon 1941- *50*
Boulle, Pierre 1912-1994 .... *22*
  Obituary *78*
Boulle, Pierre Francois Marie-Louis
  See Boulle, Pierre
Boulton, Jane 1921- *91*
Bouma, Paddy 1947- *128*
Bour, Daniele 1939- *62*
Bourbonniere, Sylvie 1966- *182*
Bourdon, David 1934-1998 .... *46*
Bourgeois, Paulette 1951- *153*
Bourne, Lesley
  See Marshall, Evelyn
Bourne, Miriam Anne 1931-1989 .... *16*
  Obituary *63*
Boutavant, Marc 1970- *200*
Boutet de Monvel, (Louis) M(aurice)
  1850(?)-1913 .... *30*
  See also CLR 32
Bouwman, Heather M.
  See Bouwman, H.M.
Bouwman, H.M. *209*
Bova, Ben 1932- *133*
  Earlier sketches in SATA 6, 68
  See also CLR 96
Bova, Benjamin William
  See Bova, Ben
Bovaird, Anne E(lizabeth) 1960- *90*
Bow, Patricia 1946- *168*
Bowden, Joan Chase 1925- *51*
  Brief entry *38*
Bowe, Julie 1962- *194*
Bowen, Alexandria Russell *97*
Bowen, Andy Russell
  See Bowen, Alexandria Russell
Bowen, Anne 1952- *202*
  Earlier sketch in SATA 170
Bowen, Betty Morgan
  See West, Betty
Bowen, Catherine (Shober) Drinker
  1897-1973 .... *7*
Bowen, David
  See Bowen, Joshua David
Bowen, Fred 1953- *136*
Bowen, Joshua David 1930- *22*
Bowen, Rhys
  See Quin-Harkin, Janet
Bowen, Robert Sydney 1900-1977 .... *52*
  Obituary *21*
Bowermaster, Jon 1954- *135*
  Earlier sketch in SATA 77
Bowers, Richard J.
  See Bowers, Rick
Bowers, Rick 1952- *227*
Bowers, Terrell L. 1945- *101*
Bowers, Terry
  See Bowers, Terrell L.
Bowers, Tim *218*
  Earlier sketch in SATA 185
Bowie, C. W.
  See Old, Wendie C(orbin)
  and Wirths, Claudine (Turner) G(ibson)
Bowie, Jim
  See Norwood, Victor G(eorge) C(harles)
  and Stratemeyer, Edward L.
Bowkett, Stephen 1953- *67*
Bowler, Jan Brett
  See Brett, Jan
Bowler, Tim 1953- *209*
  Earlier sketch in SATA 149
Bowman, Catherine
  See Smith, Cat Bowman
Bowman, Crystal 1951- *105*
Bowman, James Cloyd 1880-1961 .... *23*
Bowman, John S(tewart) 1931- *16*
Bowman, Kathleen (Gill) 1942- *52*
  Brief entry *40*

Bowman, Leslie
See Bowman, Leslie W.
Bowman, Leslie W. *182*
Bowsher, Melodie *195*
Boxall, Ed *178*
Boyce, Frank Cottrell *182*
Boyce, George A(rthur) 1898- *19*
Boyd, Candy Dawson 1946- *72*
See also CLR *50*
Boyd, Pauline
See Schock, Pauline
Boyd, Selma
See Acuff, Selma Boyd
Boyd, Waldo T. 1918- *18*
Boyden, Linda 1948- *143*
Boyer, Allen B. 1963- *153*
Boyer, Robert E(rnst) 1929- *22*
Boyes, Vivien 1952- *106*
Boyes, Vivien Elizabeth
See Boyes, Vivien
Boyle, Ann (Peters) 1916- *10*
Boyle, Eleanor Vere (Gordon) 1825-1916 .... *28*
Boyle, Robert H. 1928- *65*
Boylston, Helen Dore 1895-1984 .... *23*
Obituary *39*
Boyne, John 1971- *181*
Boynton, Sandra (Keith) 1953- *152*
Brief entry *38*
Earlier sketches in SATA *57, 107*
See also CLR *105*
Boz
See Dickens, Charles
Bozarth, Jan *227*
Braasch, Gary *201*
Bracken, Charles
See Pellowski, Michael (Joseph)
Brackers de Hugo, Pierre 1960- *115*
Brackett, Dolli Tingle 1911-1993 .... *137*
Brackett, Virginia 1950- *166*
Earlier sketch in SATA *121*
Brackett, Virginia Roberts Meredith
See Brackett, Virginia
Bradbury, Bianca (Ryley) 1908-1982 .... *56*
Earlier sketch in SATA *3*
Bradbury, Edward P.
See Moorcock, Michael
Bradbury, Ray 1920- *123*
Earlier sketches in SATA *11, 64*
Bradbury, Ray Douglas
See Bradbury, Ray
Bradby, Marie *161*
Bradfield, Carl 1942- *91*
Bradford, Ann (Liddell) 1917- *56*
Brief entry *38*
Bradford, Barbara Taylor 1933- *66*
Bradford, Chris 1974- *215*
Bradford, Emma
See Perrin, Pat
Bradford, Karleen 1936- *96*
Earlier sketch in SATA *48*
Bradford, Lois J(ean) 1936- *36*
Bradford, Richard (Roark) 1932-2002 .... *59*
Obituary *135*
Bradford, Sally
See Bradford, Barbara Taylor
Bradley, Duane
See Sanborn, Duane
Bradley, Kimberly Brubaker 1967- *179*
Bradley, Marion Zimmer 1930-1999 .... *139*
Obituary *116*
Earlier sketch in SATA *90*
See also CLR *158*
Bradley, Timothy J. *193*
Bradley, Virginia 1912- *23*
Bradley, Will
See Strickland, Brad
Bradman, Tony 1954- *152*
Earlier sketch in SATA *81*
Bradshaw, Gillian (Joan) 1949- *118*
Bradshaw, Gillian 1956- *127*

Bradshaw, Gillian Marucha
See Bradshaw, Gillian
Bradstreet, T. J.
See Thesman, Jean
Brady, Esther Wood 1905-1987 .... *31*
Obituary *53*
Brady, Irene 1943- *4*
Brady, Kimberley S. 1953- *101*
Brady, Kimberley Smith
See Brady, Kimberley S.
Brady, Lillian 1902- *28*
Bragdon, Elspeth MacDuffie 1897-1980 .... *6*
Bragdon, Lillian Jacot *24*
Brager, Bruce L. 1949- *146*
Bragg, Georgia *225*
Bragg, Mabel Caroline 1870-1945 .... *24*
Bragg, Michael 1948- *46*
Bragg, Ruth Gembicki 1943- *77*
Brahm, Sumishta 1954- *58*
Brailsford, Frances
See Wosmek, Frances
Brainerd, John W(hiting) 1918- *65*
Braithwaite, Althea 1940- *23*
Autobiography Feature *119*
See also SAAS *24*
Brallier, Jess M. 1953- *226*
Bram, Elizabeth 1948- *30*
Bramsen, Carin *227*
Bramsen, Kirsten *228*
Brancato, Robin F. 1936- *97*
See also CLR *32*
See also SAAS *9*
Brancato, Robin Fidler
See Brancato, Robin F.
Branch, Muriel Miller 1943- *152*
Earlier sketch in SATA *94*
Brand, Christianna
See Lewis, Mary
Brand, Rebecca
See Charnas, Suzy McKee
Brande, Robin *194*
Brandel, Marc 1919- *71*
Brandenberg, Alexa (Demetria) 1966- *97*
Brandenberg, Aliki 1929- *157*
Earlier sketches in SATA *2, 35, 75, 113*
See also CLR *71*
Brandenberg, Franz 1932- *75*
Earlier sketches in SATA *8, 35*
Brandenburg, Jim 1945- *87*
Brandhorst, Carl T(heodore) 1898-1988 .... *23*
Brandis, Marianne 1938- *149*
Earlier sketches in SATA *59, 96*
Brandon, Brumsic, Jr. 1927- *9*
Brandon, Curt
See Bishop, Curtis (Kent)
Brandreth, Gyles 1948- *28*
Brandreth, Gyles Daubeney
See Brandreth, Gyles
Brandt, Catharine 1905-1997 .... *40*
Brandt, Keith
See Sabin, Louis
Brandt, Sue R(eading) 1916- *59*
Branfield, John (Charles) 1931- *11*
Branford, Henrietta 1946-1999 .... *106*
Branley, Franklyn M(ansfield) 1915-2002 .. *136*
Earlier sketches in SATA *4, 68*
See also CLR *13*
See also SAAS *16*
Brannen, Sarah S. *202*
Branscum, Robbie (Tilley) 1937-1997 .... *72*
Obituary *96*
Earlier sketch in SATA *23*
See also SAAS *17*
Bransom, (John) Paul 1885-1979 .... *43*
Brashares, Ann 1967- *188*
Earlier sketch in SATA *145*
See also CLR *113*
Brassard, France 1963- *186*
Braswell, E.J.
See Lynn, Tracy

Braswell, Elizabeth J.
See Lynn, Tracy
Braswell, Liz
See Lynn, Tracy
Bratton, Helen 1899-1986 .... *4*
Bratun, Katy 1950- *160*
Earlier sketch in SATA *83*
Braude, Michael 1936- *23*
Braun, Lilian Jackson 1916(?)-2011 .... *109*
Brautigan, Richard 1935-1984 .... *56*
Brautigan, Richard Gary
See Brautigan, Richard
Bray, Libba 1964- *203*
Earlier sketch in SATA *159*
Bray, Martha E.
See Bray, Libba
Braymer, Marjorie Elizabeth 1911-1988 .... *6*
Brazil, Angela 1869(?)-1947
See CLR *157*
Breathed, Berke 1957- *161*
Earlier sketch in SATA *86*
See Breathed, Berkeley
Breathed, Berkeley *229*
See Breathed, Berke
Breathed, Guy Berkeley
See Breathed, Berke
Brecht, Edith 1895-1975 .... *6*
Obituary *25*
Breck, Vivian
See Breckenfeld, Vivian Gurney
Breckenfeld, Vivian Gurney 1895-1992 .... *1*
Breda, Tjalmar
See DeJong, David C(ornel)
Bredeson, Carmen 1944- *163*
Earlier sketch in SATA *98*
Breen, M.E. *216*
Breen, Molly
See Breen, M.E.
Breen, Steve 1970- *186*
Breinburg, Petronella 1927- *11*
See also CLR *31*
Breisky, William J(ohn) 1928- *22*
Brenaman, Miriam *172*
Brenna, Beverley 1962- *226*
Brennan, Caitlin
See Tarr, Judith
Brennan, Gale (Patrick) 1927- *64*
Brief entry *53*
Brennan, Herbie 1940- *214*
Autobiography Feature *214*
Earlier sketches in SATA *140, 183*
Brennan, J. H.
See Brennan, Herbie
Brennan, James Herbert
See Brennan, Herbie
Brennan, Jan
See Brennan, Herbie
Brennan, Joseph Lomas 1903-2000 .... *6*
Brennan, Linda Crotta 1952- *130*
Brennan, Sarah Rees 1983- *221*
Brennan, Tim
See Conroy, John Wesley
Brennan-Nelson, Denise *203*
Brenner, Anita 1905-1974 .... *56*
Brenner, Barbara (Johnes) 1925- *124*
Earlier sketches in SATA *4, 42, 76*
See also SAAS *14*
Brenner, Fred 1920- *36*
Brief entry *34*
Brent, Hope 1935(?)-1984
Obituary *39*
Brent, Stuart 1912-2010 .... *14*
Breskin, Jane
See Zalben, Jane Breskin
Breslin, Theresa *128*
Autobiography Feature *128*
Earlier sketch in SATA *70*
Breslow, Maurice 1935- *72*
Breslow, Maurice A
See Breslow, Maurice
Breslow, Susan 1951- *69*

Brett, Bernard 1925- 22
Brett, Grace N(eff) 1900-1975 23
Brett, Jan 1949- 171
  Earlier sketches in SATA 42, 71, 130
  See also CLR 27
Brett, Jan Churchill
  See Brett, Jan
Brett Bowler, Jan
  See Brett, Jan
Brewer, Heather 1973- 196
Brewer, James D. 1951- 108
Brewer, Paul 1950- 230
Brewer, Sally King 1947- 33
Brewster, Benjamin
  See Folsom, Franklin (Brewster)
Brewster, Hugh 1950- 191
  Earlier sketch in SATA 95
Brewster, Patience 1952- 97
Brewton, John E(dmund) 1898-1982 5
Breznak, Irene 218
Brian, Dennis 1971- 229
Brian, Janeen (Paulette) 1948- 141
Briant, Ed 218
  Earlier sketch in SATA 180
Brick, John 1922-1973 10
Brickman, Robin D. 1954- 155
Bride, Nadja
  See Nobisso, Josephine
Bridgers, Sue Ellen 1942- 90
  Autobiography Feature 109
  Earlier sketch in SATA 22
  See also CLR 18
  See also SAAS 1
Bridges, Laurie
  See Bruck, Lorraine
Bridges, Ruby (Nell) 1954- 131
Bridges, William (Andrew) 1901-1984 5
Bridwell, Norman (Ray) 1928- 138
  Earlier sketches in SATA 4, 68
  See also CLR 96
Brier, Howard M(axwell) 1903-1969 8
Brierley, (Louise) 1958- 59
Briggs, Katharine Mary 1898-1980 101
  Obituary 25
Briggs, Peter 1921-1975 39
  Obituary 31
Briggs, Raymond 1934- 184
  Earlier sketches in SATA 23, 66, 131
  See also CLR 168
Briggs, Raymond Redvers
  See Briggs, Raymond
Bright, Paul 1949- 231
  Earlier sketch in SATA 182
Bright, Robert Sr.) 1902-1988 63
  Obituary 60
  Earlier sketch in SATA 24
Bright, Robert Douglas
  See Bright, Robert Sr.)
Bright, Sarah
  See Shine, Deborah
Brightfield, Richard 1927- 65
  Brief entry 53
Brightfield, Rick
  See Brightfield, Richard
Brighton, Catherine 1943- 206
  Earlier sketches in SATA 65, 107
Brill, Marlene Targ 1945- 124
  Earlier sketch in SATA 77
Brimberg, Stanlee 1947- 9
Brimner, Larry Dane 1949- 170
  Autobiography Feature 112
  Earlier sketch in SATA 79
Brin, David 1950- 65
Brin, Ruth Firestone 1921- 22
Brinckloe, Julie 1950- 13
Brinckloe, Julie Lorraine
  See Brinckloe, Julie
Brindel, June (Rachuy) 1919- 7
Brindle, Max
  See Fleischman, Sid
Brindze, Ruth 1903-1984 23

Brink, Carol Ryrie 1895-1981 100
  Obituary 27
  Earlier sketches in SATA 1, 31
  See also CLR 149
Brinsmead, H. F(ay)
  See Brinsmead, H(esba) F(ay)
Brinsmead, H. F.
  See Brinsmead, H(esba) F(ay)
Brinsmead, H(esba) F(ay) 1922- 78
  Earlier sketch in SATA 18
  See also CLR 47
  See also SAAS 5
Briquebec, John
  See Rowland-Entwistle, (Arthur) Theodore
  (Henry)
Brisbane, Henry R.
  See Ellis, Edward S.
Brisco, P. A.
  See Matthews, Patricia
Brisco, Patty
  See Matthews, Patricia
  and Matthews, Clayton (Hartley)
Briscoe, Jill (Pauline) 1935- 56
  Brief entry 47
Brisley, Joyce Lankester 1896-1978 22
  Obituary 84
Brissenden, Connie
  See Brissenden, Constance
Brissenden, Constance 1947- 150
Brisson, Pat 1951- 177
  Autobiography Feature 133
  Earlier sketches in SATA 67, 128, 133
Britt, Albert 1874-1969
  Obituary 28
Britt, Dell 1934- 1
Brittain, Bill
  See Brittain, William
Brittain, C. Dale 1948- 82
Brittain, William 1930- 76
  Earlier sketch in SATA 36
  See also SAAS 7
Brittingham, Geoffrey (Hugh) 1959- 76
Brittney, L. 209
Britton, Kate
  See Stegeman, Janet Allais
Britton, Louisa
  See McGuire, Leslie (Sarah)
Britton, Rick 1952- 82
Bro, Margueritte (Harmon) 1894-1977 19
  Obituary 27
Broach, Elise 1963- 173
Broadhead, Helen Cross 1913- 25
Broadway, Hannah 208
Brochmann, Elizabeth 1938- 41
Brock, Betty (Carter) 1923-2003 4
  Obituary 150
Brock, C(harles) E(dmund) 1870-1938 42
  Brief entry 32
Brock, Delia
  See Ephron, Delia
Brock, Emma L(illian) 1886-1974 8
Brock, H(enry) M(atthew) 1875-1960 42
Brockett, Eleanor Hall 1913-1967 10
Brockman, C(hristian) Frank 1902-1985 26
Brockmeier, Kevin 1972- 176
Broda, Ron 1954- 209
Broderick, Dorothy M. 1929- 5
Brodeur, Ruth Wallace
  See Wallace-Brodeur, Ruth
Brodie, Sally
  See Cavin, Ruth
Brodsky, Beverly
  See McDermott, Beverly Brodsky
Brody, Wendy
  See Staub, Wendy Corsi
Broekel, Rainer Lothar
  See Broekel, Ray
Broekel, Ray 1923- 38
Broekstra, Lorette 1964- 189
  Earlier sketch in SATA 124

Brogden, Sherryl
  See Jordan, Sherryl
Broger, Achim
  See Broger, Achim
Broger, Achim 1944- 31
Broida, Marian 154
Brokamp, Marilyn 1920- 10
Broman, Fred
  See Moseley, James W(illett)
Bromhall, Winifred 26
Brommer, Gerald F(rederick) 1927- 28
Brondfield, Jerome 1913-1998 22
Brondfield, Jerry
  See Brondfield, Jerome
Bronner, Stephen Eric 1949- 101
Bronowski, Jacob 1908-1974 55
Bronson, Alice
  See Watkins, Dawn L.
Bronson, Linda 203
Bronson, Lynn
  See Lampman, Evelyn Sibley
Bronson, Wilfrid Swancourt 1894-1985
  Obituary 43
Brook, Judith (Penelope) 1926- 59
  Brief entry 51
Brook, Judy
  See Brook, Judith (Penelope)
Brooke, L(eonard) Leslie 1862-1940 17
  See also CLR 20
Brooke, William J. 1946- 139
Brooke-Haven, P.
  See Wodehouse, P. G.
Brooker, Kyrsten 199
Brookins, Dana 1931- 28
Brooks, Anita
  See Abramovitz, Anita (Zeltner Brooks)
Brooks, Bill 1939- 59
Brooks, Bruce 1950- 112
  Brief entry 53
  Earlier sketch in SATA 72
  See also CLR 25
Brooks, Caryl 1924- 84
Brooks, Charlotte K(endrick) 1918-1998 24
  Obituary 112
Brooks, Erik 1972- 182
  Earlier sketch in SATA 152
Brooks, George
  See Baum, L. Frank
Brooks, Gwendolyn 1917-2000 6
  Obituary 123
  See also CLR 27
Brooks, Gwendolyn Elizabeth
  See Brooks, Gwendolyn
Brooks, Jerome 1931- 23
Brooks, Kevin 1959- 197
  Earlier sketch in SATA 150
Brooks, Kevin M.
  See Brooks, Kevin
Brooks, Laurie 209
Brooks, Lester 1924- 7
Brooks, Martha 1944- 134
  Autobiography Feature 134
  Earlier sketches in SATA 68, 121
Brooks, Maurice (Graham) 1900- 45
Brooks, Polly Schoyer 1912- 12
Brooks, Ron 1948- 212
  Brief entry 33
  Earlier sketch in SATA 94
Brooks, Ronald George
  See Brooks, Ron
Brooks, Terry 1944- 60
Brooks, Walter R(ollin) 1886-1958 17
Brooks-Hill, Helen (Mason) 1908-1994 59
Broome, Errol 1937- 158
  Earlier sketch in SATA 105
Brophy, Nannette 1963- 73
Brosnan, James Patrick 1929- 14
Brosnan, Jim
  See Brosnan, James Patrick
Brostoff, Anita 1931- 132

Brothers Grimm
  See Grimm, Jacob Ludwig Karl
  and Grimm, Wilhelm Karl
Brothers Hildebrandt, The
  See Hildebrandt, Greg
  and Hildebrandt, Tim
Broun, Emily
  See Sterne, Emma Gelders
Brouwer, S. W.
  See Brouwer, Sigmund (W.)
Brouwer, Sigmund (W.) 1959- 109
Brow, Thea 1934- 60
Brower, Millicent 8
Brower, Pauline 1929- 22
Browin, Frances Williams 1898-1986 5
Brown, Alexis
  See Baumann, Amy Beeching
Brown, Anne Ensign 1937- 61
Brown, Beverly Swerdlow 97
Brown, Bill
  See Brown, William L(ouis)
Brown, Billye Walker
  See Cutchen, Billye Walker
Brown, Bob
  See Brown, Robert Joseph
Brown, Buck 1936- 45
Brown, Calef 217
  Earlier sketch in SATA *179*
Brown, Cassie 1919-1986 55
Brown, Charlotte Lewis *181*
Brown, Conrad 1922- *31*
Brown, Craig 1947- *224*
Brown, Craig 1947- *224*
  Earlier sketch in SATA *73*
Brown, Craig McFarland
  See Brown, Craig
Brown, David
  See Brown, David A(lan)
  and Myller, Rolf
Brown, Dee 1908-2002 .... *110*
  Obituary *141*
  Earlier sketch in SATA *5*
Brown, Dee Alexander
  See Brown, Dee
Brown, Don 1949- 200
  Earlier sketch in SATA *172*
Brown, Drew T. III 1955- *83*
Brown, Drollene P. 1939- 53
Brown, Elbrite 198
Brown, Eleanor Frances 1908-1987 3
Brown, Elizabeth Ferguson 1937- 153
Brown, Elizabeth M(yers) 1915- 43
Brown, Fern G. 1918- 34
Brown, (Robert) Fletch 1923- 42
Brown, Fornan 1901-1996 71
  Obituary 88
Brown, George Earl 1883-1964 .... *11*
Brown, George Mackay 1921-1996 35
Brown, Irene Bennett 1932- 3
Brown, Irving
  See Adams, William Taylor
Brown, Ivor (John Carnegie) 1891-1974 5
  Obituary 26
Brown, Jane Clark 1930- *81*
Brown, Janet Mitsui 87
Brown, Jennifer 1972- 227
Brown, Jo 1964- *170*
Brown, Joanne 1933- *147*
Brown, Joe David 1915-1976 44
Brown, Joseph E(dward) 1929- 59
  Brief entry 51
Brown, Judith Gwyn 1933- 20
Brown, Kathryn 1955- *168*
  Earlier sketch in SATA *98*
Brown, Kathy
  See Brown, Kathryn
Brown, Ken (James) 129
Brown, Kevin 1960- 101
Brown, Laurene Krasny 1945- 99
  Earlier sketch in SATA *54*

Brown, Laurie Krasny
  See Brown, Laurene Krasny
Brown, Leo 225
Brown, Lloyd Arnold 1907-1966 36
Brown, Mahlon A.
  See Ellis, Edward S.
Brown, Marc (Tolon) 1946- 145
  Earlier sketches in SATA *10, 53, 80*
  See also CLR 29
Brown, Marcia (Joan) 1918- 47
  Earlier sketch in SATA *7*
  See also CLR 12
Brown, Margaret Wise 1910-1952 100
  See also YABC 2
  See also CLR *107*
Brown, Margery (Wheeler) 78
  Earlier sketch in SATA *5*
Brown, Marion Marsh 1908-2001 6
Brown, Myra Berry 1918- 6
Brown, Palmer 1919- 36
Brown, Pamela (Beatrice) 1924-1989 5
  Obituary 61
Brown, Paul 1942- 221
Brown, Peter 1979- *178*
Brown, Rachel W.N. 1947- 203
Brown, Reeve Lindbergh
  See Lindbergh, Reeve
Brown, Richard
  See Brown, Rick
Brown, Richard E.
  See Brown, Rick
Brown, Rick 1946- 226
  Earlier sketch in SATA *61*
Brown, Robert Joseph 1907-1989 14
Brown, Roderick (Langmere) Haig-
  See Haig-Brown, Roderick (Langmere)
Brown, Rosalie
  See Moore, Rosalie (Gertrude)
Brown, Roswell
  See Webb, Jean Francis (III)
Brown, Roy (Frederick) 1921-1982 51
  Obituary 39
Brown, Ruth 1941- 170
  Earlier sketch in SATA *105*
Brown, Scott 1971- *134*
Brown, Sue Ellen 1954- 81
Brown, Tricia 1954- *114*
Brown, Vinson 1912-1991 19
Brown, Walter R(eed) 1929- 19
Brown, Will
  See Ainsworth, William Harrison
Brown, William L(ouis) 1910-1964 5
Browne, Anthony 1946- 163
  Brief entry 44
  Earlier sketches in SATA *45, 61, 105*
  See also CLR *156*
Browne, Anthony Edward Tudor
  See Browne, Anthony
Browne, Dik
  See Browne, Richard Arthur Allen
Browne, Hablot Knight 1815-1882 21
Browne, Matthew
  See Rands, William Brighty
Browne, Nicki M.
  See Browne, N.M.
Browne, Nicky Matthews
  See Browne, N.M.
Browne, N.M. 1960- 167
Browne, Richard Arthur Allen 1917-1989 ... 67
  Brief entry 38
Browne, Vee F. 1956- 214
  Earlier sketch in SATA *90*
Browning, Robert 1812-1889
  See YABC *1*
  See also CLR 97
Browning, Tom 1949- 226
Brownjohn, Alan 1931- 6
Brownlee, Walter 1930- 62
Brownlie, Betty 1946- 159
Brownlow, Kevin 1938- 65
Brownlow, Mike *183*

Brownridge, William R(oy) 1932- 94
Broyles, Anne 1953- 201
Bruce, Dorita Fairlie 1885-1970
  Obituary 27
Bruce, Harry 1934- 77
Bruce, Mary 1927- *1*
Bruchac, Joseph III
  See Bruchac, Joseph
Bruchac, Joseph 1942- 228
  Autobiography Feature *176*
  Earlier sketches in SATA *42, 89, 131, 176*
  See also CLR 46
Bruchac, Margaret M.
  See Bruchac, Marge
Bruchac, Marge *181*
Bruck, Lorraine 1921- 55
  Brief entry 46
Bruel, Nick 205
  Earlier sketch in SATA *166*
Bruel, Robert O. 1929-2002 189
Bruemmer, Fred 1929- 47
Brugman, Alyssa (F.) 1974- 152
Brumbeau, Jeff 1955- 157
Bruna, Dick 1927- 76
  Brief entry 30
  Earlier sketch in SATA *43*
  See also CLR 7
Brunhoff, Jean de 1899-1937 24
  See also CLR *116*
Brunhoff, Laurent de 1925- 150
  Earlier sketches in SATA *24, 71*
  See also CLR *116*
Brunkus, Denise 204
Bruno, Elsa Knight 1935-2009 221
Brunskill, Elizabeth Ann Flatt
  See Flatt, Lizann
Brush, Karen A(lexandra) 1960- 85
Brussel-Smith, Bernard 1914- 58
Brust, Steven 1955- 121
  Earlier sketch in SATA *86*
Brust, Steven Karl Zoltan
  See Brust, Steven
Brustlein, Daniel 1904- 40
Brustlein, Janice Tworkov -2000 40
  Obituary 126
Brutschy, Jennifer 1960- 84
Bryan, Ashley 1923- *178*
  Earlier sketches in SATA *31, 72, 132*
  See also CLR 66
Bryan, Ashley F.
  See Bryan, Ashley
Bryan, Dorothy M. 1896(?)-1984
  Obituary 39
Bryan, Jennifer *190*
Bryan, Sean *192*
Bryant, Bernice (Morgan) 1908-1976 11
Bryant, Jen 1960- 218
  Earlier sketches in SATA *94, 175*
Bryant, Jennifer
  See Bryant, Jen
Bryant, Jennifer Fisher
  See Bryant, Jen
Bryant, Laura J. *176*
Brychta, Alex 1956- 21
Brynie, Faith H. 1946- *113*
Brynie, Faith Hickman
  See Brynie, Faith H.
Bryson, Bernarda 1903-2004 9
Buba, Joy Flinsch 1904- 44
Buchan, Bryan 1945- 36
Buchan, John 1875-1940
  See YABC 2
Buchan, Stuart 1942-1987
  Obituary 54
Buchanan, Debby 1952- 82
Buchanan, Deborah Leevonne
  See Buchanan, Debby
Buchanan, Jane 1956- *160*
Buchanan, Paul 1959- *116*
Buchanan, Sue 1939- *139*

Buchheimer, Naomi Barnett
 See Barnett, Naomi
Buchignani, Walter 1965- 84
Buchmann, Stephen L. 194
Buchwald, Art 1925-2007 10
Buchwald, Arthur
 See Buchwald, Art
Buchwald, Emilie 1935- 7
Buck, Gisela 1941- 101
Buck, Lewis 1925- 18
Buck, Margaret Waring 1905-1997 3
Buck, Nola
 See Godwin, Laura
Buck, Pearl S. 1892-1973 25
 Earlier sketch in SATA *1*
Buck, Pearl Sydenstricker
 See Buck, Pearl S.
Buck, Siegfried 1941- 101
Buckalew, Clare B.
 See Dunkle, Clare B.
Buckeridge, Anthony (Malcolm)
 1912-2004 85
 Earlier sketch in SATA *6*
Buckholtz, Eileen (Garber) 1949- 54
 Brief entry 47
Buckingham, Royce 1966- 210
Buckingham, Royce Scott
 See Buckingham, Royce
Buckler, Ernest 1908-1984 47
Buckless, Andrea K. 1968- 117
Buckley, Helen E(lizabeth) 1918- 90
 Earlier sketch in SATA *2*
Buckley, James, Jr. 1963- 166
 Earlier sketch in SATA *114*
Buckley, Michael 229
 Earlier sketch in SATA *177*
Buckley, Susan 184
Buckley, Susan Washburn
 See Buckley, Susan
Buckley-Archer, Linda 185
Buckmaster, Henrietta
 See Stephens, Henrietta Henkle
Bucks, Brad
 See Holub, Joan
Budd, E. S.
 See Sirimarco, Elizabeth
Budd, Lillian (Peterson) 1897-1989 7
Budhos, Marina 173
Buehler, Stephanie Jona 1956- 83
Buehner, Caralyn 1963- 219
 Earlier sketches in SATA *104, 159*
Buehner, Mark 1959- 221
 Earlier sketches in SATA *104, 159*
Buehr, Walter Franklin 1897-1971 3
Buell, Ellen Lewis
 See Cash, Ellen Lewis Buell
Buell, Janet 1952- 185
 Earlier sketch in SATA *106*
Buergel, Paul-Hermann H. 1949- 83
Buettner, Dan 1960- 95
Buff, Conrad 1886-1975 19
Buff, Mary (E. Marsh) 1890-1970 19
Buffett, Jimmy 1946- 110
 Earlier sketch in SATA *76*
Buffie, Margaret 1945- 161
 Earlier sketches in SATA *71, 107*
 See also CLR *39*
Bugbee, Emma 1888(?)-1981
 Obituary 29
Bugni, Alice 1951- 122
Buhhos, Marina Tamar
 See Budhos, Marina
Bujold, Lois McMaster 1949- 136
Bulfinch, Thomas 1796-1867 35
Bulion, Leslie 1958- 209
 Earlier sketch in SATA *161*
Bull, Angela (Mary) 1936- 45
Bull, Emma 1954- 190
 Autobiography Feature 103
 Earlier sketch in SATA *99*
Bull, Norman John 1916- 41

Bull, Peter (Cecil) 1912-1984
 Obituary 39
Bull, Schuyler M. 1974- 138
Bulla, Clyde R. 1914-2007 139
 Obituary 182
 Earlier sketches in SATA *2, 41, 91*
 See also SAAS *6*
Bullard, Lisa 1961- 142
Bullen, Alexandra 227
Buller, Jon 205
Bullock, Kathleen (Mary) 1946- 77
Bullock, Robert (D.) 1947- 92
Bulpin, (Barbara) Vicki 92
Bulwer-Lytton, Edward 1803-1873 23
Bulwer-Lytton, Edward George Earle Lytton
 See Bulwer-Lytton, Edward
Bumstead, Kathleen Mary 1918-1987 53
Bundles, A'Lelia Perry 1952- 76
Bunge, Daniela 1973- 207
Bunin, Catherine 1967- 30
Bunin, Sherry 1925- 30
Bunkers, Suzanne L. 1950- 136
Bunting, A.E.
 See Bunting, Eve
Bunting, Anne Evelyn
 See Bunting, Eve
Bunting, Eve 1928- 196
 Earlier sketches in SATA *18, 64, 110, 158*
 See also CLR *82*
Bunting, Glenn (Davison) 1957- 22
Bunyan, John 1628-1688
 See CLR *124*
Bupp, Walter
 See Garrett, Randall
Burack, Sylvia K. 1916-2003 35
 Obituary 143
Burbank, Addison (Buswell) 1895-1961 37
Burch, Joann J(ohansen) 75
Burch, Robert J(oseph) 1925- 74
 Earlier sketch in SATA *1*
 See also CLR *63*
Burchard, Peter Duncan 1921- 143
 Earlier sketches in SATA *5, 74*
 See also SAAS *13*
Burchard, S. H.
 See Burchard, Sue
Burchard, Sue 1937- 22
Burchardt, Nellie 1921- 7
Burckhardt, Marc 1962- 196
Burden, Andrea 1969-2009 227
Burdett, Lois 117
Burdick, Eugene (Leonard) 1918-1965 22
Burford, Eleanor
 See Hibbert, Eleanor Alice Burford
Burg, Ann E. 1954- 217
Burg, Shana 1968- 204
Burgan, Michael 1960- 167
 Earlier sketch in SATA *118*
Burger, Carl 1888-1967 9
Burgess, Ann Marie
 See Gerson, Noel Bertram
Burgess, Barbara Hood 1926- 69
Burgess, Em
 See Burgess, Mary Wyche
Burgess, (Frank) Gelett 1866-1951 32
 Brief entry 30
Burgess, Mark 157
Burgess, Mary Wyche 1916- 18
Burgess, Melvin 1954- 198
 Earlier sketches in SATA *96, 146*
Burgess, Michael
 See Gerson, Noel Bertram
Burgess, Robert F(orrest) 1927- 4
Burgess, Starling
 See Tudor, Tasha
Burgess, Thornton Waldo 1874-1965 17
Burgess, Trevor
 See Trevor, Elleston
Burgwyn, Mebane Holoman 1914-1992 7
Burke, David 1927- 46

Burke, Diana G.
 See Gallagher, Diana G.
Burke, Diana Gallagher
 See Gallagher, Diana G.
Burke, Dianne O'Quinn 1940- 89
Burke, Janine 1952- 139
Burke, Jim 1973- 179
Burke, John
 See O'Connor, Richard
Burke, Katie 1953- 168
Burke, Patrick 1958- 114
Burke, Ralph
 See Garrett, Randall
 and Silverberg, Robert
Burkert, Nancy Ekholm 1933- 24
 See also SAAS *14*
Burkett, D. Brent 194
Burke-Weiner, Kimberly 1962- 95
Burks, Brian 1955- 95
Burland, Brian (Berkeley) 1931- 34
Burland, C. A.
 See Burland, Cottie (Arthur)
Burland, Cottie (Arthur) 1905-1983 5
Burleigh, Robert 1936- 193
 Earlier sketches in SATA *55, 98, 146*
Burlingame, (William) Roger 1889-1967 2
Burman, Alice Caddy 1896(?)-1977
 Obituary 24
Burman, Ben Lucien 1896-1984 6
 Obituary 40
Burn, Doris 1923- 1
Burn, Ted
 See Burn, Thomas E.
Burn, Thomas E. 1940- 150
Burnard, Damon 1963- 115
Burnett, Constance Buel 1893-1975 36
Burnett, Frances Eliza Hodgson
 See Burnett, Frances Hodgson
Burnett, Frances Hodgson 1849-1924 100
 See also YABC *2*
 See also CLR *122*
Burnett, Lindy 210
Burnett Bossi, Lisa 193
Burney, Anton
 See Hopkins, (Hector) Kenneth
Burnford, Sheila (Philip Cochrane Every)
 1918-1984 3
 Obituary 38
 See also CLR *2*
Burnham, Gretchen
 See Sprague, Gretchen
Burnham, Nicole 1970- 161
Burnham, Niki
 See Burnham, Nicole
Burnham, Sophy 1936- 65
Burningham, John 1936- 225
 Earlier sketches in SATA *16, 59, 111, 160*
 See also CLR *9*
Burningham, Robin Yoko
 See Racoma, Robin Yoko
Burningham, Sarah O'Leary 216
Burns, Diane L. 1950- 81
 See also SAAS *24*
Burns, Eloise Wilkin
 See Wilkin, Eloise
Burns, Florence M. 1905-1988 61
Burns, Khephra 1950- 92
Burns, Loree Griffin 193
Burns, Marilyn 1941- 96
 Brief entry 33
Burns, Olive Ann 1924-1990 65
Burns, Patrick 1968- 227
Burns, Paul C. 5
Burns, Ray
 See Burns, Raymond (Howard)
Burns, Raymond (Howard) 1924- 9
Burns, Theresa 1961- 84
Burns, William A. 1909-1999 5
Burr, Dan 1951- 65
Burr, Dan 1960- 219
Burr, Lonnie 1943- 47

Burrell, Roy E(ric) C(harles) 1923- 72
Burroughs, Edgar Rice 1875-1950 41
  See also CLR *157*
Burroughs, Jean Mitchell 1908- 28
Burroughs, Polly 1925- 2
Burroway, Janet 1936- 23
Burroway, Janet Gay
  See Burroway, Janet
Burstein, Chaya M(alamud) 1923- 64
Burstein, Fred 1950- 83
Burstein, John 1949- 54
  Brief entry 40
Burstein, Stanley M.
  See Burstein, Stanley Mayer
Burstein, Stanley Mayer 1941- 175
Bursztynski, Sue 1953- 114
Burt, Jesse Clifton 1921-1976 46
  Obituary 20
Burt, Olive Woolley 1894-1981 4
Burtinshaw, Julie 185
Burton, Gennett 1945- 95
Burton, Hester (Wood-Hill) 1913-2000 74
  Earlier sketch in SATA *7*
  See also CLR *1*
  See also SAAS *8*
Burton, Leslie
  See McGuire, Leslie (Sarah)
Burton, Marilee Robin 1950- 82
  Earlier sketch in SATA *46*
Burton, Maurice 1898-1992 23
Burton, Rebecca 1970- 183
Burton, Robert (Wellesley) 1941- 22
Burton, Virginia Lee 1909-1968 100
  Earlier sketch in SATA *2*
  See also CLR *11*
Burton, William H(enry) 1890-1964 11
Busby, Ailie 192
Busby, Cylin 1970- 118
Busby, Edith (A. Lake) (?)-1964
  Obituary 29
Busby, John 1942- 209
Buscaglia, (Felice) Leo(nardo) 1924-1998 ... 65
Buscaglia, Leo F.
  See Buscaglia, (Felice) Leo(nardo)
Busch, Phyllis S. 1909- 30
Bush, Anne Kelleher
  See Kelleher, Anne
Bush, Catherine 1961- 128
Bush, Jenna 1981- 208
Bush, Laura 1946- 208
Bushmiller, Ernest Paul 1905-1982 31
Bushmiller, Ernie
  See Bushmiller, Ernest Paul
Bushnell, Jack 1952- 86
Busoni, Rafaello 1900-1962 16
Buss, Helen M.
  See Clarke, Margaret
Busse, Sarah Martin 194
Busselle, Rebecca 1941- 80
Bustard, Anne 1951- 173
Butcher, Kristin 1951- 140
Butenko, Bohdan 1931- 90
Butler, Beverly Kathleen 1932- 7
Butler, Bill
  See Butler, William Vivian
  and Butler, Ernest Alton
  and Butler, William Huxford
Butler, Charles 1963- 175
  Earlier sketch in SATA *121*
Butler, Charles Cadman
  See Butler, Charles
Butler, Dori Hillestad 1965- 207
  Earlier sketch in SATA *164*
Butler, Dorothy 1925- 73
Butler, Geoff 1945- 94
Butler, John 1952- 225
Butler, M. Christina 1934- 224
  Earlier sketches in SATA *72, 170*
Butler, Octavia 1947-2006 84
  See also CLR *65*

Butler, Octavia E.
  See Butler, Octavia
Butler, Octavia Estelle
  See Butler, Octavia
Butler, Vivian
  See Butler, William Vivian
Butler, William
  See Butler, William Vivian
Butler, William Vivian 1927-1987 79
Butterfield, Moira 1960- 219
Butters, Dorothy Gilman
  See Gilman, Dorothy
Butterworth, Emma Macalik 1928- 43
Butterworth, Nick 1946- 149
  Earlier sketch in SATA *106*
Butterworth, Oliver 1915-1990 1
  Obituary 66
Butterworth, W. E.
  See Griffin, W. E. B.
Butterworth, William E.
  See Griffin, W. E. B.
Butterworth, William Edmund III
  See Griffin, W. E. B.
Button, Lana 1968- 229
Butts, Ed 1951- 177
Butts, Edward P.
  See Butts, Ed
Butts, Ellen R. 1942- 93
Butts, Ellen Rubinstein
  See Butts, Ellen R.
Butzer, C. M. 1974- 212
Buxton, Ralph
  See Silverstein, Alvin
  and Silverstein, Virginia B.
Buzzeo, Toni 1951- 215
  Earlier sketch in SATA *135*
Byalick, Marcia 1947- 141
  Earlier sketch in SATA *97*
Byard, Carole (Marie) 1941- 57
Byars, Betsy 1928- 223
  Autobiography Feature 108
  Earlier sketches in SATA *4, 46, 80, 163*
  See also CLR *72*
  See also SAAS *1*
Byars, Betsy Cromer
  See Byars, Betsy
Byfield, Barbara Ninde 1930-1988 8
Byman, Jeremy 1944- 129
Bynum, Janie 133
Byrd, Elizabeth 1912-1989 34
Byrd, Nicole
  See Zach, Cheryl (Byrd)
Byrd, Robert 1942- 226
  Earlier sketches in SATA *33, 112, 158*
Byrd, Robert John
  See Byrd, Robert
Byrd, Tim 1964- 216
Byrne, Gayle 218
Byrne, Mary Gregg 1951- 162

C

C. 3. 3.
  See Wilde, Oscar
C. E. M.
  See Mastrangelo, Charles E(lmer)
Cabaniss, J(ames) Allen 1911-1997 5
Cabat, Erni 1914- 74
Cabban, Vanessa 1971- 176
Cable, Mary 1920- 9
Cabot, Meg 1967- 217
  Earlier sketches in SATA *127, 175*
  See also CLR *85*
Cabot, Meggin
  See Cabot, Meg
Cabot, Meggin Patricia
  See Cabot, Meg
Cabot, Patricia
  See Cabot, Meg

Cabral, O. M.
  See Cabral, Olga
Cabral, Olga 1909- 46
Cabrera, Cozbi A. 1963- 177
Cabrera, Jane 1968- 182
  Earlier sketches in SATA *103, 152*
Cabrera, Marcela 1966- 90
Caddy, Alice
  See Burman, Alice Caddy
Cade, Toni
  See Bambara, Toni Cade
Cadena, Beth 222
Cadmus and Harmonia
  See Buchan, John
Cadnum, Michael 1949- 225
  Earlier sketches in SATA *87, 121, 165*
  See also CLR *78*
Caduto, Michael J. 1955- 103
Cadwallader, Sharon 1936- 7
Cady, (Walter) Harrison 1877(?)-1970 19
Caffey, Donna (J.) 1954- 110
Cagle, Malcolm W(infield) 1918- 32
Cahn, Rhoda 1922- 37
Cahn, William 1912-1976 37
Cain, Arthur H(omer) 1913-1981 3
Cain, Christopher
  See Fleming, Thomas
Cain, Sheridan 1952- 186
Caine, Geoffrey
  See Walker, Robert W.
Caines, Jeannette (Franklin) 1938- 78
  Brief entry 43
  See also CLR *24*
Cairns, Trevor 1922- 14
Calabro, Marian 1954- 79
Caldecott, Moyra 1927- 22
Caldecott, Randolph (J.) 1846-1886 100
  Earlier sketch in SATA *17*
  See also CLR *110*
Calder, Charlotte 1952- 125
Calder, David 1932-1997 105
Calder, Lyn
  See Calmenson, Stephanie
Calder, Marie D(onais) 1948- 96
Calderone-Stewart, Lisa
  See Calderone-Stewart, Lisa-Marie
Calderone-Stewart, Lisa-Marie 1958- 123
Caldwell, Ben 1973- 230
Caldwell, Doreen (Mary) 1942- 71
Caldwell, John C(ope) 1913-1984 7
Caletti, Deb 1963- 221
  Earlier sketch in SATA *171*
Calhoun, B. B. 1961- 98
Calhoun, Chad
  See Barrett, Neal, Jr.
  and Cunningham, Chet
  and Goulart, Ron
Calhoun, Dia 1959- 183
  Earlier sketch in SATA *129*
Calhoun, Mary
  See Wilkins, Mary Huiskamp
Calhoun, T.B.
  See Bisson, Terry
Cali, Davide 1972- 190
Calif, Ruth 1922- 67
Calkhoven, Laurie 1959- 229
Calkins, Franklin
  See Stratemeyer, Edward L.
Call, Greg 197
Call, Hughie Florence 1890-1969 1
Callahan, Dorothy M. 1934- 39
  Brief entry 35
Callahan, Dorothy Monahan
  See Callahan, Dorothy M.
Callahan, Philip Serna 1923- 25
Callahan, Sean 1965- 222
Callan, Jamie 1954- 59
Callan, Jim 1951- 181
Callaway, Bernice (Anne) 1923- 48
Callaway, Kathy 1943- 36

Callen, Larry
  See Callen, Lawrence Willard, Jr.
Callen, Lawrence Willard, Jr. 1927- *19*
Callen, Liz 1951- *231*
Calley, Karin 1965- *92*
Calmenson, Stephanie 1952- *211*
  Brief entry *37*
  Earlier sketches in SATA *51, 84, 139*
Calonita, Jen *216*
Calvert, Elinor H.
  See Lasell, Elinor H.
Calvert, John
  See Leaf, (Wilbur) Munro
Calvert, Pam 1966- *205*
Calvert, Patricia 1931- *132*
  Earlier sketches in SATA *45, 69*
  See also SAAS *17*
Camburn, Carol A.
  See Camburn-Bracalente, Carol A.
Camburn-Bracalente, Carol A. 1962- *118*
Cameron, Ann 1943- *129*
  Earlier sketches in SATA *27, 89*
  See also SAAS *20*
Cameron, Edna M. 1905-1999 .... *3*
Cameron, Eleanor (Frances) 1912-1996 .... *25*
  Obituary *93*
  Earlier sketch in SATA *1*
  See also CLR *72*
  See also SAAS *10*
Cameron, Elizabeth
  See Nowell, Elizabeth Cameron
Cameron, Elizabeth Jane 1910-1976 .... *32*
  Obituary *30*
Cameron, Ian
  See Payne, Donald Gordon
Cameron, M(alcolm) G(ordon) Graham
  See Graham-Cameron, M(alcolm) G(ordon)
Cameron, M. Graham
  See Graham-Cameron, M(alcolm) G(ordon)
Cameron, Mike Graham
  See Graham-Cameron, M(alcolm) G(ordon)
Cameron, Natalie Russell
  See Russell, Natalie
Cameron, Polly 1928- *2*
Cameron, Scott 1962- *84*
Camp, Charles L. 1893-1975
  Obituary *31*
Camp, Lindsay 1957- *133*
Camp, Madeleine L'Engle
  See L'Engle, Madeleine
Camp, Walter (Chauncey) 1859-1925
  See YABC *1*
Campbell, (Elizabeth) Andrea 1963- *50*
Campbell, Ann R. 1925- *11*
Campbell, Bill 1960- *89*
Campbell, Bruce
  See Epstein, Samuel
Campbell, Camilla 1905-1992 .... *26*
Campbell, Carole R. 1939- *125*
Campbell, Hope 1925- *20*
Campbell, Hugh 1930- *90*
Campbell, Jane
  See Edwards, Jane Campbell
Campbell, Julie
  See Tatham, Julie Campbell
Campbell, Patricia J(ean) 1930- *45*
Campbell, Patty
  See Campbell, Patricia J(ean)
Campbell, Peter A. 1948- *99*
Campbell, R. W.
  See Campbell, Rosemae Wells
Campbell, Robin
  See Strachan, Ian
Campbell, Rod 1945- *98*
  Brief entry *44*
  Earlier sketch in SATA *51*
Campbell, Rosemae Wells 1909- *1*
Campbell, Sarah C. 1966- *207*
Camper, Cathy 1956- *170*
Campion, Nardi Reeder 1917-2007 .... *22*
Campling, Elizabeth 1948- *53*

Campos, Maria de Fatima *229*
Campoy, F. Isabel 1946- *181*
  Earlier sketch in SATA *143*
Camps, Luis 1928- *66*
Canales, Viola 1957- *141*
Candell, Victor 1903-1977
  Obituary *24*
Canfield, Dorothea F.
  See Fisher, Dorothy (Frances) Canfield
Canfield, Dorothea Frances
  See Fisher, Dorothy (Frances) Canfield
Canfield, Dorothy
  See Fisher, Dorothy (Frances) Canfield
Canfield, Jack 1944- *164*
Canfield, Jane White 1897-1984 .... *32*
  Obituary *38*
Canfield, Muriel 1935- *94*
Canga, C.B. 1976- *216*
Canga, Chris
  See Canga, C.B.
Caniff, Milton 1907-1988
  Obituary *58*
Caniff, Milton Arthur Paul
  See Caniff, Milton
Cann, Helen 1969- *179*
  Earlier sketch in SATA *124*
Cann, Kate 1954- *152*
  Earlier sketch in SATA *103*
Cannan, Joanna
  See Pullein-Thompson, Joanna Maxwell
Cannell, Jon *196*
Cannell, Jonathan C.
  See Cannell, Jon
Cannon, A.E. *202*
  Earlier sketches in SATA *93, 163*
Cannon, Ann Edwards
  See Cannon, A.E.
Cannon, Bettie (Waddell) 1922- *59*
Cannon, Curt
  See Hunter, Evan
Cannon, Eileen E(mily) 1948- *119*
Cannon, Frank
  See Mayhar, Ardath
Cannon, Janell 1957- *128*
  Earlier sketch in SATA *78*
  See also CLR *120*
Cannon, Marian G. 1923- *85*
Cannon, Taffy
  See Cannon, Eileen E(mily)
Cantone, AnnaLaura *182*
Cantrell, Julie 1973- *217*
Canusi, Jose
  See Barker, S. Omar
Canyon, Christopher 1966- *150*
  Earlier sketch in SATA *104*
Caparo, Antonio
  See Caparo, Antonio Javier
Caparo, Antonio Javier *205*
Capek, Michael 1947- *142*
  Earlier sketch in SATA *96*
Capes, Bernard (Edward Joseph)
  1854-1918 .... *116*
Caple, Kathy *193*
Caple, Laurie 1958- *201*
Caplin, Alfred Gerald 1909-1979 .... *61*
  Obituary *21*
Caponigro, John Paul 1965- *84*
Capote, Truman 1924-1984 .... *91*
Capp, Al
  See Caplin, Alfred Gerald
Cappel, Constance 1936- *22*
Cappetta, Cynthia 1949- *125*
Cappo, Nan Willard 1955- *143*
Capps, Benjamin (Franklin) 1922- *9*
Cappy Dick
  See Cleveland, George
Captain Kangaroo
  See Keeshan, Robert J.
Captain Wheeler
  See Ellis, Edward S.

Captain Young of Yale
  See Stratemeyer, Edward L.
Capucilli, Alyssa Satin 1957- *203*
  Earlier sketches in SATA *115, 163*
Capucine
  See Mazille, Capucine
Carafoli, Marci
  See Balterman, Marcia Ridlon
Caraher, Kim(berley Elizabeth) 1961- *105*
Caraker, Mary 1929- *74*
Caras, Roger A(ndrew) 1928-2001 .... *12*
  Obituary *127*
Caravantes, Peggy 1935- *140*
Caraway, Caren 1939- *57*
Carbone, Elisa 1954- *173*
  Earlier sketches in SATA *81, 137*
Carbone, Elisa Lynn
  See Carbone, Elisa
Carbonnier, Jeanne 1894-1974 .... *3*
  Obituary *34*
Card, Orson Scott 1951- *127*
  Earlier sketch in SATA *83*
  See also CLR *116*
Cardinale, Christopher *231*
Cardon, Laurent 1962- *230*
Care, Felicity
  See Coury, Louise Andree
Carew, Jan 1925- *51*
  Brief entry *40*
Carew, Jan Rynveld
  See Carew, Jan
Carey, Benedict 1960- *219*
Carey, Bonnie
  See Marshall, Bonnie C.
Carey, Charles W., Jr. 1951- *170*
Carey, Ernestine Gilbreth 1908-2006 .... *2*
  Obituary *177*
Carey, Janet Lee 1954(?)- *225*
  Earlier sketch in SATA *185*
Carey, Lisa *110*
Carey, M. V.
  See Carey, Mary V(irginia)
Carey, Mary V(irginia) 1925-1994 .... *44*
  Brief entry *39*
Carey, Peter 1943- *94*
Carey, Peter Philip
  See Carey, Peter
Carey, Valerie Scho 1949- *60*
Carheden, Gooel Kristina
  See Naaslund, Gooel Kristina
Carigiet, Alois 1902-1985 .... *24*
  Obituary *47*
  See also CLR *38*
Carini, Edward 1923- *9*
Carkeet, David 1946- *75*
Carle, Eric 1929- *163*
  Earlier sketches in SATA *4, 65, 120*
  See also CLR *72*
  See also SAAS *6*
Carleton, Captain L. C.
  See Ellis, Edward S.
Carleton, Captain Latham C.
  See Ellis, Edward S.
Carleton, Latham C.
  See Ellis, Edward S.
Carley, V(an Ness) Royal 1906-1976
  Obituary *20*
Carling, Amelia Lau 1949- *164*
  Earlier sketch in SATA *119*
Carlisle, Carolyn
  See Hawes, Louise
Carlisle, Clark
  See Holding, James (Clark Carlisle, Jr.)
Carlisle, Olga Andreyev 1930- *35*
Carlock, Miriam
  See Eyerly, Jeannette
Carls, Claudia 1978- *198*
Carlsen, G(eorge) Robert 1917- *30*
Carlsen, Ruth C(hristoffer) 1918- *2*
Carlson, Bernice Wells 1910- *8*
Carlson, Christopher C. *202*

Author Index

Carlson, Dale (Bick) 1935- *1*
Carlson, Daniel (Bick) 1960- 27
Carlson, Kirsten 1968- *192*
Carlson, Kirsten M.
    See Carlson, Kirsten
Carlson, Laurie 1952- *173*
    Earlier sketch in SATA *101*
Carlson, Laurie Winn
    See Carlson, Laurie
Carlson, Melody 1956- *171*
    Earlier sketch in SATA *113*
Carlson, Nancy 1953- *213*
    Brief entry 45
    Earlier sketches in SATA *56, 90, 144*
Carlson, Nancy L.
    See Carlson, Nancy
Carlson, Natalie Savage 1906-1997 68
    Earlier sketch in SATA *2*
    See also SAAS *4*
Carlson, Susan Johnston 1953- 88
Carlson, Vada F. 1897- 16
Carlstrom, Nancy White 1948- 215
    Brief entry 48
    Earlier sketches in SATA *53, 92, 156*
Carlton, Keith
    See Robertson, Keith (Carlton)
Carlton, Susan 1960- 195
Carlyon, Richard 55
Carman, Bill
    See Carman, William
Carman, Patrick 1966- 197
    Earlier sketch in SATA *161*
Carman, William 223
Carmer, Carl (Lamson) 1893-1976 37
    Obituary 30
Carmer, Elizabeth Black 1904- 24
Carmi, Giora 1944- 149
    Earlier sketch in SATA *79*
Carmichael, Carrie
    See Carmichael, Harriet
Carmichael, Clay 218
Carmichael, Harriet 40
Carmody, Isobelle 1958- 191
    Earlier sketch in SATA *161*
Carmody, Isobelle Jane
    See Carmody, Isobelle
Carney, Elizabeth 1981- 199
Carney, Jeff 1962- 196
Carney, Mary Lou 1949- 170
Carol, Bill J.
    See Knott, William C(ecil, Jr.)
Caron, Romi
    See Caron-Kyselkova', Romana
Caron-Kyselkova', Romana 1967- 94
Caroselli, Remus F(rancis) 1916- 36
Carpelan, Bo 1926- 8
Carpelan, Bo Gustaf Bertelsson
    See Carpelan, Bo
Carpenter, (John) Allan 1917- 81
    Earlier sketch in SATA *3*
Carpenter, Angelica Shirley 1945- 153
    Earlier sketch in SATA *71*
Carpenter, Frances 1890-1972 .... *3*
    Obituary 27
Carpenter, John 1948- 58
Carpenter, John Howard
    See Carpenter, John
Carpenter, Johnny
    See Carpenter, John
Carpenter, Nancy 215
Carpenter, Nancy Sippel
    See Carpenter, Nancy
Carpenter, Patricia (Healy Evans) 1920- 11
Carr, Glyn
    See Styles, (Frank) Showell
Carr, Harriett H(elen) 1899-1977 .... *3*
Carr, Jan 1953- 132
    Earlier sketch in SATA *89*
Carr, M. J.
    See Carr, Jan

Carr, Mary Jane 1899-1988 .... *2*
    Obituary 55
Carr, Philippa
    See Hibbert, Eleanor Alice Burford
Carr, Roger Vaughan 1937- 95
Carrel, Annette Felder 1929- 90
Carrick, Carol (Hatfield) 1935- *118*
    Earlier sketches in SATA *7, 63*
    See also SAAS *18*
Carrick, Donald (F.) 1929-1989 63
    Earlier sketch in SATA *7*
Carrick, Malcolm 1945- 28
Carrick, Paul 1972- *194*
Carrier, Lark 1947- *71*
    Brief entry 50
Carrier, Roch 1937- *166*
    Earlier sketch in SATA *105*
Carrighar, Sally 1898-1985 24
Carrillo, Patricia S.
    See Carrillo, P.S.
Carrillo, P.S. 209
Carrington, G. A.
    See Cunningham, Chet
Carrington, Marsha Gray 1954- *168*
    Earlier sketch in SATA *111*
Carris, Joan 1938- *182*
    Brief entry 42
    Earlier sketch in SATA *44*
Carris, Joan Davenport
    See Carris, Joan
Carroll, Curt
    See Bishop, Curtis (Kent)
Carroll, Elizabeth
    See Barkin, Carol
    and James, Elizabeth
Carroll, Jaye
    See Carroll, Michael
Carroll, Jenny
    See Cabot, Meg
Carroll, (Archer) Latrobe 1894-1996 7
Carroll, Laura
    See Parr, Lucy
Carroll, Lewis 1832-1898 .... *100*
    See also YABC *2*
    See also CLR *108*
Carroll, Michael 1966- 203
Carroll, Raymond 1924- 86
    Brief entry 47
Carruth, Hayden 1921-2008 47
    Obituary *197*
Carryl, Charles E. 1841-1920 .... *114*
Carryl, Charles Edward
    See Carryl, Charles E.
Carse, Robert 1902-1971 .... *5*
Carson, J(ohn) Franklin 1920-1981 .... *1*
    Obituary *107*
Carson, Mary Kay 1964- 200
    Earlier sketch in SATA *150*
Carson, Rachel 1907-1964 23
Carson, Rachel Louise
    See Carson, Rachel
Carson, Rosalind
    See Chittenden, Margaret
Carson, S. M.
    See Gorsline, (Sally) Marie
Carson, William C. 1928- *154*
Carter, Abby 222
    Earlier sketch in SATA *184*
Carter, Alden R 1947- *137*
    Earlier sketch in SATA *67*
    See also CLR *22*
    See also SAAS *18*
Carter, Alden Richardson
    See Carter, Alden R
Carter, Andy 1948- *134*
Carter, Angela 1940-1992 66
    Obituary 70
Carter, Angela Olive
    See Carter, Angela
Carter, Anne Laurel 1953- 209
    Earlier sketch in SATA *135*

Carter, Asa Earl
    See Carter, Forrest
Carter, Avis Murton
    See Allen, Kenneth S.
Carter, Bruce
    See Hough, Richard (Alexander)
Carter, Carol S(hadis) 1948- *124*
Carter, David A. 1957- 228
    Earlier sketches in SATA *114, 170*
Carter, Don 1958- *192*
    Earlier sketch in SATA *124*
Carter, Dorothy Sharp 1921- *8*
Carter, Forrest 1927(?)-1979 .... *32*
Carter, Helene 1887-1960 15
Carter, (William) Hodding, Jr. 1907-1972 ...... *2*
    Obituary 27
Carter, James Earl, Jr.
    See Carter, Jimmy
Carter, Jimmy 1924- 79
Carter, Katharine J(ones) 1905-1984 .... *2*
Carter, Lin(wood Vrooman) 1930-1988 91
Carter, Mike 1936- *138*
Carter, Nick
    See Avallone, Michael (Angelo, Jr.)
    and Ballard, (Willis) Todhunter
    and Crider, Bill
    and Cassiday, Bruce (Bingham)
    and Chastain, Thomas
    and Dey, Frederic (Merrill) Van Rensselaer
    and Garside, Jack
    and Hayes, Ralph E(ugene)
    and Henderson, M(arilyn) R(uth)
    and Lynds, Dennis
    and Lynds, Gayle (Hallenbeck)
    and Randisi, Robert J.
    and Rasof, Henry
    and Stratemeyer, Edward L.
    and Smith, Martin Cruz
    and Swain, Dwight V(reeland)
    and Vardeman, Robert E.
    and Wallmann, Jeffrey M(iner)
    and White, Lionel
Carter, Peter 1929- 57
Carter, Phyllis Ann
    See Eberle, Irmengarde
Carter, Samuel (Thomson) III 1904-1988 37
    Obituary 60
Carter, Scott William 231
Carter, Timothy 1972- 224
Carter, William E. 1926-1983 .... *1*
    Obituary 35
Cartlidge, Michelle 1950- 96
    Brief entry 37
    Earlier sketch in SATA *49*
Cartner, William Carruthers 1910- *11*
Cartwright, Ann 1940- 78
Cartwright, Reg(inald Ainsley) 1938- 64
Cartwright, Sally 1923- 9
Carusone, Al 1949- 89
Carvell, Marlene *172*
Carver, John
    See Gardner, Richard (M.)
Carwell, L'Ann
    See McKissack, Patricia C.
Cary
    See Cary, Louis F(avreau)
Cary, Barbara Knapp 1912(?)-1975
    Obituary *31*
Cary, Kate 1967(?)- *174*
Cary, Louis F(avreau) 1915- 9
Caryl, Jean
    See Kaplan, Jean Caryl Korn
Casanova, Mary 1957- *186*
    Earlier sketches in SATA *94, 136*
Cascone, A.G.
    See Cascone, Annette
    and Cascone, Gina
Cascone, Annette 1960- *103*
Cascone, Gina 1955- *103*
Case, Chris 1976- 209
Case, Marshal T(aylor) 1941- 9

Case, Michael
  See Howard, Robert West
Caseley, Judith 1951- 159
  Brief entry 53
  Earlier sketch in SATA 87
Casewit, Curtis W(erner) 1922-2002 4
Casey, Barbara (Louise) 1944- 147
  Earlier sketch in SATA 79
Casey, Brigid 1950- 9
Casey, Tina 1959- 141
Cash, Ellen Lewis Buell 1905-1989
  Obituary 64
Cash, John Carter 1970- 218
Cash, Megan Montague 160
Cashore, Kristin 1976(?)- 206
Casilla, Robert 1959- 211
  Earlier sketches in SATA 75, 146
Cason, Mabel Earp 1892-1965 10
Cass, Joan E(velyn) 1
Cass-Beggs, Barbara 1904- 62
Cassedy, Patrice (Rinaldo) 1953- 149
Cassedy, Sylvia 1930-1989 77
  Obituary 61
  Earlier sketch in SATA 27
  See also CLR 26
Cassel, Lili
  See Wronker, Lili Cassel
Cassels, Jean 173
Cassidy, Anne 1952- 166
Cassidy, Anne Josephine
  See Cassidy, Anne
Cassidy, Cathy 1962- 183
Cassino, Mark 228
Casson, Hugh Maxwell 1910-1999 65
  Obituary 115
Cassutt, Michael 1954- 78
Cassutt, Michael Joseph
  See Cassutt, Michael
Castaldi, Elicia 194
Castaldo, Nancy Fusco 1962- 151
  Earlier sketch in SATA 93
Castaneda, Omar S. 1954- 71
Castell, Megan
  See Williams, Jeanne
Castellanos, Jane Mollie Robinson
  1913-2001 9
Castellon, Federico 1914-1971 48
Castellucci, Cecil 1969- 176
Castillo, Edmund L. 1924-2005 1
  Obituary 167
Castillo, Lauren 195
Castle, Lee
  See Ogan, George F.
  and Ogan, Margaret E. (Nettles)
Castle, Paul
  See Howard, Vernon (Linwood)
Castle, Robert
  See Hamilton, Edmond
Castro L., Antonio 1941- 226
Castrovilla, Selene 1966- 186
Caswell, Brian 1954- 171
  Earlier sketch in SATA 97
Caswell, Deanna 223
Caswell, Helen (Rayburn) 1923- 12
Catalano, Dominic 1956- 163
  Earlier sketch in SATA 76
Catalano, Grace (A.) 1961- 99
Catalanotto, Peter 1959- 195
  Autobiography Feature 113
  Earlier sketches in SATA 70, 114, 159
  See also CLR 68
  See also SAAS 25
Catanese, P.W. 1961- 227
  Earlier sketch in SATA 179
Cate, Annette LeBlanc 196
Cate, Dick
  See Cate, Richard Edward Nelson
Cate, Richard Edward Nelson 1932- 28
Cather, Willa 1873-1947 30
  See also CLR 98

Catherall, Arthur 1906-1980 74
  Earlier sketches in SATA 3, 4
Cathon, Laura E(lizabeth) 1908-1991 27
Catlett, Elizabeth 1919(?)- 82
Catlin, Wynelle 1930- 13
Catlow, Nikalas
  See Catlow, Niki
Catlow, Niki 1975- 193
Cato, Heather 105
Cato, Sheila 114
Catran, Ken 1944- 190
Catrow, David
  See Catrow, David J. III
Catrow, David J. III 206
  Earlier sketch in SATA 152
Catt, Louis
  See French, Vivian
Cattell, James 1954- 123
Catton, (Charles) Bruce 1899-1978 2
  Obituary 24
Catusanu, Mircea 222
Catz, Max
  See Glaser, Milton
Caudell, Marian 1930- 52
Caudill, Rebecca 1899-1985 1
  Obituary 44
Cauley, Lorinda Bryan 1951- 46
  Brief entry 43
Caulfield, Peggy F. 1926-1987
  Obituary 53
Cauman, Samuel 1910-1971 48
Causley, Charles (Stanley) 1917-2003 66
  Obituary 149
  Earlier sketch in SATA 3
  See also CLR 30
Cavallaro, Ann (Abelson) 1918- 62
Cavallo, Diana 1931- 7
Cavanagh, Helen (Carol) 1939- 98
  Brief entry 37
  Earlier sketch in SATA 48
Cavanah, Frances 1899-1982 31
  Earlier sketch in SATA 1
Cavanna, Betty
  See Harrison, Elizabeth (Allen) Cavanna
Cavanna, Elizabeth
  See Harrison, Elizabeth (Allen) Cavanna
Cave, Kathryn 1948- 123
  Earlier sketch in SATA 76
Cavendish, Peter
  See Horler, Sydney
Caveney, Philip 1951- 219
Caveney, Philip Richard
  See Caveney, Philip
Cavin, Ruth 1918-2011 38
Cavin, Ruth Brodie
  See Cavin, Ruth
Cavoukian, Raffi 1948- 68
Cawley, Winifred 1915- 13
Cazeau, Charles J(ay) 1931- 65
Cazet, Denys 1938- 191
  Brief entry 41
  Earlier sketches in SATA 52, 99, 163
Cazzola, Gus 1934- 73
Cebulash, Mel 1937- 91
  Earlier sketch in SATA 10
Ceccoli, Nicoletta 181
Cecil, Randy 1968- 223
  Earlier sketch in SATA 187
Cecka, Melanie 199
Ceder, Georgiana Dorcas -1985 10
Celenza, Anna Harwell 133
Celestino, Martha Laing
  See Laing, Martha
Cepeda, Joe 215
  Earlier sketch in SATA 159
Cerf, Bennett (Alfred) 1898-1971 7
Cerf, Christopher (Bennett) 1941- 2
Cermak, Martin
  See Duchacek, Ivo D(uka)
Cerullo, Mary M. 1949- 145
  Earlier sketch in SATA 86

Cervon, Jacqueline
  See Moussard, Jacqueline
Cetin, Frank Stanley 1921- 2
Chabon, Michael 1963- 145
Chabrian, Deborah
  See Chabrian, Deborah L.
Chabrian, Deborah L. 212
Chaconas, D.J.
  See Chaconas, Dori
Chaconas, Dori 1938- 208
  Earlier sketches in SATA 145, 175
Chaconas, Doris J.
  See Chaconas, Dori
Chadda, Sarwat 224
Chadwick, Lester 67
  Earlier sketch in SATA 1
Chaffee, Allen 3
Chaffin, Lillie D(orton) 1925- 4
Chaikin, Miriam 1924- 152
  Earlier sketches in SATA 24, 102
Chall, Marsha Wilson 150
Challand, Helen J(ean) 1921- 64
Challans, Mary
  See Renault, Mary
Chalmers, Mary (Eileen) 1927- 6
  See also SAAS 14
Chamberlain, Barbara A.
  See Azore, Barbara
Chamberlain, Margaret 1954- 212
  Earlier sketch in SATA 46
Chamberlin, Kate 1945- 105
Chamberlin, Mary 1960- 177
Chamberlin, Rich 177
Chamberlin, Richard
  See Chamberlin, Rich
Chambers, Aidan 1934- 171
  Earlier sketches in SATA 1, 69, 108
  See also CLR 151
  See also SAAS 12
Chambers, Bradford 1922-1984
  Obituary 39
Chambers, Catherine E.
  See St. John, Nicole
Chambers, John W. 1933- 57
  Brief entry 46
Chambers, Kate
  See St. John, Nicole
Chambers, Margaret Ada Eastwood 1911- 2
Chambers, Peggy
  See Chambers, Margaret Ada Eastwood
Chambers, Robert W(illiam) 1865-1933 107
Chambliss, Maxie 186
Champlin, Susan 1961- 225
Chan, Gillian 1954- 147
  Earlier sketch in SATA 102
Chan, Peter 1980(?)- 207
Chance, James T.
  See Carpenter, John
Chance, John T.
  See Carpenter, John
Chance, Stephen
  See Turner, Philip (William)
Chandler, Caroline A(ugusta) 1906-1979 22
  Obituary 24
Chandler, David P. 1933- 28
Chandler, David Porter
  See Chandler, David P.
Chandler, Edna Walker 1908-1982 11
  Obituary 31
Chandler, Jennifer
  See Westwood, Jennifer
Chandler, Karen 1959- 122
Chandler, Kristen 230
Chandler, Linda S(mith) 1929- 39
Chandler, Pauline 175
Chandler, Robert 1953- 40
Chandler, Ruth Forbes 1894-1978 2
  Obituary 26
Chandonnet, Ann F. 1943- 92
Chaney, Jill 1932- 87
Chang, Chih-Wei 1966- 111

Chang, Cindy 1968- 90
Chang, Grace 1961- 226
Chang, Margaret 1941- 71
Chang, Margaret Scrogin
    See Chang, Margaret
Chang, Raymond 1939- 142
    Earlier sketches in SATA 71, 142 PEN
Chanin, Michael 1952- 84
Channel, A. R.
    See Catherall, Arthur
Chapian, Marie 1938- 29
Chapin, Alene Olsen Dalton 1915(?)-1986
    Obituary 47
Chapin, Tom 1945- 83
Chapman, Allen 67
    Earlier sketch in SATA 1
Chapman, Cheryl O(rth) 1948- 80
Chapman, (Constance) Elizabeth (Mann)
    1919- 10
Chapman, Gaye 1970- 200
Chapman, Gaye Coralie
    See Chapman, Gaye
Chapman, Gaynor 1935- 32
Chapman, Gillian 1955- 120
Chapman, Jane 1970- 212
    Earlier sketches in SATA 122, 176
Chapman, Jean 104
    Earlier sketch in SATA 34
    See also CLR 65
Chapman, John Stanton Higham 1891-1972
    Obituary 27
Chapman, Lee
    See Bradley, Marion Zimmer
Chapman, Linda 1969- 223
Chapman, Lynne 1960- 197
Chapman, Lynne F(erguson) 1963- 150
    Earlier sketch in SATA 94
Chapman, Maristan
    See Chapman, John Stanton Higham
Chapman, Vera (Ivy May) 1898-1996 33
Chapman, Walker
    See Silverberg, Robert
Chappell, Audrey 1954- 72
Chappell, Crissa-Jean 198
Chappell, Warren 1904-1991 68
    Obituary 67
    Earlier sketch in SATA 6
    See also SAAS 10
Chapra, Mimi 182
Charbonneau, Eileen 1951- 118
    Earlier sketch in SATA 84
Charbonnet, Gabrielle 1961- 227
    Earlier sketch in SATA 81
Chardiet, Bernice 1927(?)- 27
Chardiet, Bernice Kroll
    See Chardiet, Bernice
Charest, Emily MacLachlan 198
Charles, Donald
    See Meighan, Donald Charles
Charles, Louis
    See Stratemeyer, Edward L.
Charles, Nicholas
    See Kuskin, Karla
Charles, Nicholas J.
    See Kuskin, Karla
Charles, Norma 153
Charles, Veronika Martenova 182
Charlip, Remy 1929- 119
    Earlier sketches in SATA 4, 68
    See also CLR 8
Charlot, Jean 1898-1979 8
    Obituary 31
Charlot, Martin 1944- 64
Charlot, Martin Day
    See Charlot, Martin
Charlton, Michael (Alan) 1923- 34
Charlton-Trujillo, e.E. 189
Charmatz, Bill 1925-2005 7
Charnas, Suzy McKee 1939- 110
    Earlier sketch in SATA 61
Charosh, Mannis 1906- 5

Chartier, Normand L. 1945- 66
Chase, Alice
    See McHargue, Georgess
Chase, Alyssa 1965- 92
Chase, Andra 1942- 91
Chase, Emily
    See Aks, Patricia
    and Garwood, Julie
    and Sachs, Judith
    and White, Carol
Chase, Mary (Coyle) 1907-1981 17
    Obituary 29
Chase, Mary Ellen 1887-1973 10
Chase, Paula 214
Chase, Richard 1904-1988 64
    Obituary 56
Chase, Samantha
    See Glick, Ruth
Chast, Roz 1954- 212
    Earlier sketch in SATA 97
Chastain, Madye Lee 1908-1989 4
Chataway, Carol 1955- 140
Chatterjee, Debjani 1952- 83
Chatterton, Martin 1961- 225
Chauncy, Nan(cen Beryl Masterman)
    1900-1970 6
    See also CLR 6
Chaundler, Christine 1887-1972 1
    Obituary 25
Chayka, Doug 196
Chbosky, Stephen 1972- 164
Cheaney, Janie B.
    See Cheaney, J.B.
Cheaney, J.B. 1950- 188
Chee, Cheng-Khee 1934- 79
Cheese, Chloe 1952- 118
Chekhonte, Antosha
    See Chekhov, Anton
Chekhov, Anton 1860-1904 90
Chekhov, Anton Pavlovich
    See Chekhov, Anton
Chelushkin, Kirill 1968- 186
Chen, Anthony 1929- 6
Chen, Chih-Yuan 1975- 216
    Earlier sketch in SATA 155
Chen, Ju-Hong 1941- 78
Chen, Pauline 1966- 202
Chen, Sara
    See Odgers, Sally Farrell
Chen, Tony
    See Chen, Anthony
Chen, Yong 1963- 183
Chen, Yuan-tsung 1932- 65
Chen, Zhiyuan
    See Chen, Chih-Yuan
Chenault, Nell
    See Smith, Linell Nash
Chen Chih-Yuan
    See Chen, Chih-Yuan
Chenery, Janet (Dai) 1923- 25
Cheney, Cora 1916-1999 3
    Obituary 110
Cheney, Glenn (Alan) 1951- 99
Cheney, Lynne V. 1941- 152
Cheney, Lynne Vincent
    See Cheney, Lynne V.
Cheney, Ted
    See Cheney, Theodore Albert
Cheney, Theodore A. Rees
    See Cheney, Theodore Albert
Cheney, Theodore Albert 1928- 11
Cheng, Andrea 1957- 205
    Earlier sketches in SATA 128, 172
Cheng, Christopher 1959- 173
    Earlier sketch in SATA 106
Cheng, Judith 1955- 36
Cheng, Shan
    See Jiang, Cheng An
Cheripko, Jan 1951- 155
    Earlier sketch in SATA 83
Chermayeff, Ivan 1932- 47

Chernenko, Dan
    See Turtledove, Harry
Chernett, Dan 224
Chernoff, Dorothy A.
    See Ernst, (Lyman) John
Chernoff, Goldie Taub 1909- 10
Cherry, Carolyn Janice
    See Cherryh, C.J.
Cherry, Lynne 1952- 99
    Earlier sketch in SATA 34
Cherryh, C.J. 1942- 172
    Earlier sketch in SATA 93
Cherryholmes, Anne
    See Price, Olive
Cheshire, Simon 172
Chesler, Bernice 1932-2002 59
Chess, Victoria (Dickerson) 1939- 92
    Earlier sketch in SATA 33
Chessa, Francesca 191
Chester, Deborah 1957- 85
Chester, Kate
    See Guccione, Leslie Davis
Chesterton, G. K. 1874-1936 27
Chesterton, Gilbert Keith
    See Chesterton, G. K.
Chesworth, Michael 207
    Earlier sketch in SATA 160
Chetin, Helen 1922- 6
Chetwin, Grace 86
    Brief entry 50
Chevalier, Christa 1937- 35
Chevalier, Tracy 1962- 128
Chew, Ruth 1920-2010 7
Chichester Clark, Emma 1955- 209
    Earlier sketches in SATA 117, 156, 69
Chidsey, Donald Barr 1902-1981 3
    Obituary 27
Chiefari, Janet D. 1942- 58
Chien, Catia 193
Chien-min, Lin
    See Rumford, James
Child, L. Maria
    See Child, Lydia Maria
Child, Lauren 1965- 183
    Earlier sketches in SATA 119, 160
Child, Lincoln 1957- 113
Child, Lincoln B.
    See Child, Lincoln
Child, Lydia Maria 1802-1880 67
Child, Mrs.
    See Child, Lydia Maria
Child, Philip 1898-1978 47
Children's Shepherd, The
    See Westphal, Arnold Carl
Childress, Alice 1920-1994 81
    Earlier sketches in SATA 7, 48
    See also CLR 14
Childs, H(alla) Fay (Cochrane) 1890-1971 1
    Obituary 25
Chilton, Charles (Frederick William)
    1917- 102
Chima, Cinda Williams 226
    Earlier sketch in SATA 192
Chimaera
    See Farjeon, Eleanor
Chin, Jason 1978- 218
Chin, Richard (M.) 1946- 52
Chinery, Michael 1938- 26
Chin-Lee, Cynthia 1958- 102
Chin-Lee D., Cynthia
    See Chin-Lee, Cynthia
Chippendale, Lisa A. 158
Chipperfield, Joseph Eugene 1912-1980(?) .. 87
    Earlier sketch in SATA 2
Chisholm, P. F.
    See Finney, Patricia
Chislett, Gail (Elaine) 1948- 58
Chittenden, Elizabeth F. 1903-1999 9
Chittenden, Margaret 1935- 28
Chittum, Ida 1918- 7
Chitwood, Suzanne Tanner 1958- 160

Chmielarz, Sharon Lee 1940- 72
Choate, Judith (Newkirk) 1940- 30
Chocolate, Debbi 1954- 223
 Earlier sketch in SATA 96
Chocolate, Deborah H. Newton
 See Chocolate, Debbi
Chodos-Irvine, Margaret 211
 Earlier sketch in SATA 152
Choi, Sook Nyul 1937- 73
 Autobiography Feature 126
 See also CLR 53
Choi, Yangsook 178
Choksi, Nishant 1975- 222
Choldenko, Gennifer 1957- 182
 Earlier sketch in SATA 135
Chorao, Kay 1936- 215
Chorao, (Ann Mc)Kay (Sproat) 1936- 162
 Earlier sketches in SATA 8, 69
Choron, Sandra (Zena Samelson) 1950- 146
Choung, Eun-hee 199
Chown, Marcus 1959- 137
Choyce, Lesley 1951- 165
 Earlier sketch in SATA 94
Choyce, Lesley Willis
 See Choyce, Lesley
Chrisman, Arthur Bowie 1889-1953 124
 See also YABC 1
Christelow, Eileen 1943- 184
 Autobiography Feature 120
 Brief entry 35
 Earlier sketches in SATA 38, 90
Christensen, Bonnie 1951- 213
 Earlier sketches in SATA 110, 157
Christensen, Gardell Dano 1907-1991 1
Christensen, Laurie
 See Steding, Laurie
Christesen, Barbara 1940- 40
Christgau, Alice Erickson 1902-1977 13
Christian, Mary Blount 1933- 9
Christiana, David 195
Christie, Agatha 1890-1976 36
Christie, Agatha Mary Clarissa
 See Christie, Agatha
Christie, Ann Philippa
 See Pearce, Philippa
Christie, Gregory
 See Christie, R. Gregory
Christie, Philippa
 See Pearce, Philippa
Christie, R. Gregory 1971- 225
 Earlier sketches in SATA 127, 185
Christopher, John
 See Youd, Samuel
Christopher, Louise
 See Hale, Arlene
Christopher, Matt(hew Frederick)
 1917-1997 80
 Obituary 99
 Earlier sketches in SATA 2, 47
 See also CLR 119
 See also SAAS 9
Christopher, Milbourne 1914(?)-1984 46
Christy, Howard Chandler 1873-1952 21
Chrustowski, Rick 176
Chrystie, Frances N(icholson) 1904-1986 60
Chu, Daniel 1933- 11
Chukovsky, Kornei (Ivanovich) 1882-1969 . 34
 Earlier sketch in SATA 5
Church, Caroline Jayne 219
 Earlier sketch in SATA 179
Church, Richard 1893-1972 3
Churchill, E(lmer) Richard 1937- 11
Churchill, Elizabeth
 See Hough, Richard (Alexander)
Chute, B(eatrice) J(oy) 1913-1987 2
 Obituary 53
Chute, Marchette (Gaylord) 1909-1994 1
Chwast, Jacqueline 1932- 6
Chwast, Seymour 1931- 146
 Earlier sketches in SATA 18, 96

Ciardi, John (Anthony) 1916-1986 65
 Obituary 46
 Earlier sketch in SATA 1
 See also CLR 19
 See also SAAS 26
Ciccone, Madonna Louise Veronica
 See Madonna
Ciddor, Anna 1957- 213
Ciment, James D. 1958- 140
Cirrone, Dorian 182
Cisneros, Sandra 1954-
 See CLR 123
Citra, Becky 1954- 137
Citrin, Michael 1965(?)- 183
Claflin, Willy 1944- 208
Clair, Andree 19
Clampett, Bob 1914(?)-1985 44
 Obituary 38
Clampett, Robert
 See Clampett, Bob
Clapp, John 1968- 109
Clapp, Patricia 1912- 74
 Earlier sketch in SATA 4
 See also SAAS 4
Clare, Ellen
 See Sinclair, Olga
Clare, Helen
 See Clarke, Pauline
Claremont, Chris 1950- 87
Claremont, Christopher Simon
 See Claremont, Chris
Clark, Ann Nolan 1896-1995 82
 Obituary 87
 Earlier sketch in SATA 4
 See also CLR 16
 See also SAAS 16
Clark, Champ 1923-2002 47
Clark, Christopher (Anthony) Stuart
 See Stuart-Clark, Christopher (Anthony)
Clark, Clara Gillow 1951- 154
 Earlier sketch in SATA 84
Clark, David
 See Hardcastle, Michael
Clark, David Allen
 See Ernst, (Lyman) John
Clark, Emma Chichester
 See Chichester Clark, Emma
Clark, Frank J(ames) 1922- 18
Clark, Garel
 See Garelick, May
Clark, Halsey
 See Deming, Richard
Clark, Joan
 See Benson, Mildred
Clark, Joan 1934- 182
 Earlier sketches in SATA 59, 96
Clark, Leonard 1905-1981 30
 Obituary 29
Clark, M. R.
 See Clark, Mavis Thorpe
Clark, Margaret (D.) 1943- 126
Clark, Margaret Goff 1913- 82
 Earlier sketch in SATA 8
Clark, Mary Higgins 1929- 46
Clark, Mavis Thorpe 1909-1999 74
 Earlier sketch in SATA 8
 See also CLR 30
 See also SAAS 5
Clark, Merle
 See Gessner, Lynne
Clark, Patricia Denise
 See Robins, Patricia
Clark, Patricia Finrow 1929- 11
Clark, Ronald Harry 1904-1999 193
Clark, Ronald William 1916-1987 2
 Obituary 52
Clark, Sherryl 1956- 149
Clark, Van D(eusen) 1909-1974 2
Clark, Virginia
 See Gray, Patricia (Clark)
Clark, Walter Van Tilburg 1909-1971 8

Clarke, Arthur
 See Clarke, Arthur C.
Clarke, Arthur C. 1917-2008 115
 Obituary 191
 Earlier sketches in SATA 13, 70
 See also CLR 119
Clarke, Arthur Charles
 See Clarke, Arthur C.
Clarke, Clorinda 1917- 7
Clarke, Elizabeth L. 1934- 103
Clarke, Greg 1959- 215
Clarke, Gus 1948- 134
Clarke, J.
 See Clarke, Judith
Clarke, James Hall
 See Rowland-Entwistle, (Arthur) Theodore
 (Henry)
Clarke, Joan B. 1921- 42
 Brief entry 27
Clarke, John
 See Laklan, Carli
 and Sontup, Dan(iel)
Clarke, Judith 1943- 164
 Earlier sketches in SATA 75, 110
 See also CLR 61
Clarke, Julia 1950- 138
Clarke, Kenneth 1957- 107
Clarke, Lea
 See Rowland-Entwistle, (Arthur) Theodore
 (Henry)
Clarke, Margaret 1941-
 See CLR 99
Clarke, Mary Stetson 1911-1994 5
Clarke, Michael
 See Newlon, (Frank) Clarke
Clarke, Pauline 1921- 131
 Earlier sketch in SATA 3
 See also CLR 28
Clarkson, E(dith) Margaret 1915- 37
Clarkson, Ewan 1929- 9
Claudia, Susan
 See Goulart, Ron
 and Johnston, William
Claverie, Jean 1946- 38
Clay, Patrice 1947- 47
Clay, Wil 203
Clayman, Deborah Paula
 See Da Costa, Deborah
Claypool, Jane
 See Miner, Jane Claypool
Clayton, Elaine 1961- 209
 Earlier sketches in SATA 94, 159
Clayton, Lawrence (Otto, Jr.) 1945- 75
Clayton, Sally Pomme 218
Clayton, Sandra 1951- 110
Cle, Troy 202
Clea, Super
 See Hantman, Clea
Cleary, Beverly 1916- 121
 Earlier sketches in SATA 2, 43, 79
 See also CLR 72
 See also SAAS 20
Cleary, Beverly Atlee Bunn
 See Cleary, Beverly
Cleary, Brian P. 1959- 186
 Earlier sketches in SATA 93, 132
Cleaver, Bill
 See Cleaver, William J.
Cleaver, Carole 1934- 6
Cleaver, Elizabeth (Ann Mrazik)
 1939-1985 23
 Obituary 43
 See also CLR 13
Cleaver, Hylton Reginald 1891-1961 49
Cleaver, Vera 1919-1993 76
 Earlier sketch in SATA 22
 See also CLR 6
Cleaver, Vera Allen
 See Cleaver, Vera

Cleaver, William J. 1920-1981 22
  Obituary 27
  See also CLR 6
Cleishbotham, Jebediah
  See Scott, Sir Walter
Cleland, Janet 226
Cleland, Mabel
  See Widdemer, Mabel Cleland
Clem, Margaret H(ollingsworth) 1923- 90
Clemens, James
  See Rollins, James
Clemens, Samuel
  See Twain, Mark
Clemens, Samuel Langhorne
  See Twain, Mark
Clemens, Virginia Phelps 1941- 35
Clement, Gary 191
Clement, Janet 182
Clement, Nathan 1966- 200
Clement, Priscilla Ferguson 1942- 171
Clement, Rod 97
Clement-Moore, Rosemary 229
  Earlier sketch in SATA *188*
Clements, Andrew 1949- 203
  Earlier sketches in SATA *104, 158*
Clements, Bruce 1931- 178
  Earlier sketches in SATA *27, 94*
Clemesha, David 192
Cleminson, Katie 221
Clemons, Elizabeth
  See Nowell, Elizabeth Cameron
Clerk, N. W.
  See Lewis, C. S.
Cleveland, Bob
  See Cleveland, George
Cleveland, George 1903(?)-1985
  Obituary 43
Cleveland-Peck, Patricia 80
Cleven, Cathrine
  See Cleven, Kathryn Seward
Cleven, Kathryn Seward 2
Clevenger, William R. 1954- 84
Clevenger, William Russell
  See Clevenger, William R.
Clevin, Joergen 1920- 7
Clevin, Jorgen
  See Clevin, Joergen
Clewes, Dorothy (Mary) 1907-2003 86
  Obituary 138
  Earlier sketch in SATA *1*
Clifford, David
  See Rosenberg, Eth Clifford
Clifford, Eth
  See Rosenberg, Eth Clifford
Clifford, Harold B(urton) 1893-1988 10
Clifford, Margaret Cort 1929- 1
Clifford, Martin
  See Hamilton, Charles (Harold St. John)
Clifford, Mary Louise Beneway 1926- 23
Clifford, Peggy
  See Clifford, Margaret Cort
Clifford, Rachel Mark
  See Lewis, Brenda Ralph
Clifton, Lucille 1936-2010 128
  Earlier sketches in SATA *20, 69*
  See also CLR 5
Clifton, Thelma Lucille
  See Clifton, Lucille
Climo, Shirley 1928- 166
  Autobiography Feature 110
  Brief entry 35
  Earlier sketches in SATA *39, 77*
  See also CLR 69
Cline-Ransome, Lesa 201
Clinton, Catherine 1952- 203
Clinton, Cathryn 1957- 136
Clinton, Dirk
  See Silverberg, Robert
Clinton, Jon
  See Prince, J(ack) H(arvey)
Clippinger, Carol 193

Clish, (Lee) Marian 1946- 43
Clive, Clifford
  See Hamilton, Charles (Harold St. John)
Clokey, Art 1921- 59
Cloudsley-Thompson, J(ohn) L(eonard)
  1921- 19
Clouse, Nancy L. 1938- 78
Clover, Peter 1952- 215
  Earlier sketch in SATA *152*
Clutha, Janet
  See Frame, Janet
Clutha, Janet Paterson Frame
  See Frame, Janet
Clymer, Eleanor 1906-2001 85
  Obituary 126
  Earlier sketch in SATA *9*
  See also SAAS 17
Clyne, Patricia (Edwards) 31
Cneut, Carll 1969- 197
Coalson, Glo 1946- 94
  Earlier sketch in SATA *26*
Coates, Anna 1958- 73
Coates, Belle 1896-1986 2
Coates, Ruth Allison 1915- 11
Coats, Alice M(argaret) 1905-1976 11
Coatsworth, Elizabeth (Jane) 1893-1986 100
  Obituary 49
  Earlier sketches in SATA *2, 56*
  See also CLR 2
Cobalt, Martin
  See Mayne, William
Cobb, Jane
  See Berry, Jane Cobb
Cobb, Mary 1931- 88
Cobb, Vicki 1938- 136
  Autobiography Feature 136
  Earlier sketches in SATA *8, 69, 131*
  See also CLR 2
  See also SAAS 6
Cobbett, Richard
  See Pluckrose, Henry
Cober, Alan E(dwin) 1935-1998 7
  Obituary 101
Cobham, Sir Alan
  See Hamilton, Charles (Harold St. John)
Coburn, Jake 1978- 155
Cocagnac, Augustin Maurice(-Jean) 1924- 7
Cocca-Leffler, Maryann 1958- 194
  Earlier sketches in SATA *80, 136*
Cochran, Bill 187
Cochran, Bobbye A. 1949- 11
Cochran, Josh 221
Cochran, Thomas 1955- 198
Cochrane, Hamilton E.
  See Cochrane, Mick
Cochrane, Mick 1956- 215
Cockcroft, Jason 217
Cockett, Mary 3
Cocks, Peter 204
Cocovini, Abby 202
Coddell, Esme Raji
  See Codell, Esme Raji
Codell, Esme Raji 1968- 160
Cody, C. S.
  See Waller, Leslie
Cody, Jess
  See Cunningham, Chet
Cody, Matthew 229
Coe, Anne (E.) 1949- 95
Coe, Douglas
  See Epstein, Beryl
  and Epstein, Samuel
Coe, Lloyd 1899(?)-1976
  Obituary 30
Coen, Rena Neumann 1925- 20
Coerr, Eleanor (Beatrice) 1922- 67
  Earlier sketch in SATA *1*
Cofer, Judith Ortiz 1952- 164
  Earlier sketch in SATA *110*
Coffelt, Nancy 1961- 189

Coffey, Brian
  See Koontz, Dean
Coffin, Geoffrey
  See Mason, F(rancis) van Wyck
Coffin, M. T.
  See Stanley, George Edward
Coffin, M.T.
  See Stanley, George Edward
Coffman, Ramon Peyton 1896-1989 4
Cogan, Karen 1954- 125
Coggins, Jack (Banham) 1911-2006 2
Cohagan, Carolyn 1972- 228
Cohen, Barbara 1932-1992 77
  Obituary 74
  Earlier sketch in SATA *10*
  See also SAAS 7
Cohen, Daniel (E.) 1936- 70
  Earlier sketch in SATA *8*
  See also CLR 43
  See also SAAS 4
Cohen, Deborah Bodin 1968- 180
Cohen, Jan Barger
  See Barger, Jan
Cohen, Jene Barr
  See Barr, Jene
Cohen, Joan Lebold 1932- 4
Cohen, Judith Love 1933- 78
Cohen, Lisa 1963- 225
Cohen, Miriam 1926-1955 155
  Earlier sketches in SATA *29, 106*
  See also SAAS 11
Cohen, Nora 75
Cohen, Paul 1945- 58
Cohen, Paul S.
  See Cohen, Paul
Cohen, Peter Zachary 1931- 150
  Earlier sketch in SATA *4*
Cohen, Robert Carl 1930- 8
Cohen, Santiago 1954- 215
Cohen, Sholom 1951- 94
Cohn, Angelo 1914-1997 19
Cohn, Diana 194
Cohn, Rachel 1968- 228
  Earlier sketch in SATA *161*
Coit, Margaret Louise 1922-2003 2
  Obituary 142
Colasanti, Susane 1973- 214
Colato Lainez, Rene 1970- 226
  Earlier sketch in SATA *176*
Colbert, Anthony 1934-2007 15
Colbert, Nancy A. 1936- 139
Colby, C(arroll) B(urleigh) 1904-1977 35
  Earlier sketch in SATA *3*
Colby, Jean Poindexter 1909-1993 23
Cole, Annette
  See Steiner, Barbara A(nnette)
Cole, Babette 1949- 155
  Earlier sketches in SATA *61, 96*
Cole, Betsy 1940- 83
Cole, Brock 1938- 200
  Earlier sketches in SATA *72, 136*
  See also CLR 18
Cole, Davis
  See Elting, Mary
Cole, Hannah 1954- 74
Cole, Henry 1955- 213
  Earlier sketch in SATA *181*
Cole, Jack -1974
  See Stewart, John
Cole, Jackson
  See Curry, Thomas Albert
  and Germano, Peter B.
  and Heckelmann, Charles N(ewman)
  and Newton, D(wight) B(ennett)
  and Schisgall, Oscar
Cole, Jennifer
  See Zach, Cheryl (Byrd)
Cole, Joanna 1944- 231
  Brief entry 37
  Earlier sketches in SATA *49, 81, 120, 168*
  See also CLR 40

Cole, Lois Dwight 1903-1979 .... *10*
  Obituary *26*
Cole, Michael 1947- *59*
Cole, Samantha
  See Cole, Stephen
Cole, Sheila 1939- *171*
  Earlier sketches in SATA *24, 95*
Cole, Sheila R.
  See Cole, Sheila
Cole, Sheila Rotenberg
  See Cole, Sheila
Cole, Stephen 1971- *230*
  Earlier sketch in SATA *161*
Cole, Steve
  See Cole, Stephen
Cole, William (Rossa) 1919-2000 .... *71*
  Earlier sketch in SATA *9*
  See also SAAS *9*
Coleman, Andrew
  See Pine, Nicholas
Coleman, Clare
  See Bell, Clare (Louise)
  and Easton, M(alcolm) Coleman
Coleman, Janet Wyman *184*
Coleman, Loren 1947- *164*
Coleman, Loren Elwood, Jr.
  See Coleman, Loren
Coleman, Mary Ann 1928- *83*
Coleman, Michael
  See Jones, Allan Frewin
Coleman, Michael 1946- *199*
  Autobiography Feature *133*
  Earlier sketches in SATA *108, 133*
Coleman, Rowan *187*
Coleman, William L(eRoy) 1938- *49*
  Brief entry *34*
Coleman, Wim 1926- *212*
Coles, Robert (Martin) 1929- *23*
Colfer, Eoin 1965- *197*
  Earlier sketch in SATA *148*
  See also CLR *112*
Colin, Ann
  See Ure, Jean
Collard, Sneed B. III 1959- *184*
  Earlier sketches in SATA *84, 139*
Colledge, Anne 1939- *142*
Colley, Jacqui 1965- *202*
Collicott, Sharleen 1937- *143*
  Earlier sketch in SATA *98*
Collicutt, Paul *229*
Collier, Bryan *204*
  Earlier sketches in SATA *126, 174*
Collier, Christopher 1930- *70*
  Earlier sketch in SATA *16*
  See also CLR *126*
Collier, Ethel 1903-1999 .... *22*
Collier, James Lincoln 1928- *166*
  Earlier sketches in SATA *8, 70*
  See also CLR *126*
  See also SAAS *21*
Collier, Jane
  See Collier, Zena
Collier, Kristi *182*
Collier, Steven 1942- *61*
Collier, Zena 1926- *23*
Collings, Gillian 1939- *102*
Collington, Peter 1948- *99*
  Earlier sketch in SATA *59*
Collins, Ace 1953- *82*
Collins, Andrew J.
  See Collins, Ace
Collins, B. R. 1981- *214*
Collins, David R(aymond) 1940-2001 .... *121*
  Earlier sketch in SATA *7*
Collins, Heather 1946- *81*
Collins, Hunt
  See Hunter, Evan
Collins, Michael
  See Lynds, Dennis
Collins, Michael 1930- *58*

Collins, Pat Lowery 1932- *217*
  Earlier sketches in SATA *31, 151*
Collins, Paul 1954- *126*
Collins, Ross 1972- *200*
Collins, Ruth Philpott 1890-1975
  Obituary *30*
Collins, Suzanne 1963(?)- *224*
  Earlier sketch in SATA *180*
Collins, Yvonne *194*
Collinson, A. S.
  See Collinson, Alan S.
Collinson, Alan S. 1934- *80*
Collinson, Roger (Alfred) 1936- *133*
Collison, Linda 1953- *185*
Collodi, Carlo 1826-1890 .... *100*
  Earlier sketch in SATA *29*
  See also CLR *120*
Colloms, Brenda 1919- *40*
Colman, Hila 1909-2008 .... *53*
  Earlier sketch in SATA *1*
  See also SAAS *14*
Colman, Morris 1899(?)-1981
  Obituary *25*
Colman, Penny (Morgan) 1944- *160*
  Autobiography Feature *160*
  Earlier sketches in SATA *77, 114*
Colman, Warren (David) 1944- *67*
Coloma, Cindy
  See Martinusen-Coloma, Cindy
Colombo, John Robert 1936- *50*
Colon, Raul *156*
Colon, Raul 1952- *202*
Colonius, Lillian 1911-1992 .... *3*
Colorado, Antonio J.
  See Colorado (Capella), Antonio J(ulio)
Colorado (Capella), Antonio J(ulio)
  1903-1994 .... *23*
  Obituary *79*
Colquhoun, Glenn 1964- *165*
Colston, Fifi E. 1960- *150*
Colt, Martin
  See Epstein, Beryl
  and Epstein, Samuel
Colum, Padraic 1881-1972 .... *15*
  See also CLR *36*
Columbus, Chris 1959- *97*
Columbus, Christopher
  See Columbus, Chris
Columella
  See Moore, Clement Clarke
Colver, Anne 1908- *7*
Colvin, James
  See Moorcock, Michael
Colwell, Eileen (Hilda) 1904-2002 .... *2*
Colwyn, Stewart
  See Pepper, Frank S.
Coman, Carolyn 1951- *197*
  Earlier sketch in SATA *127*
Combres, Elisabeth 1967- *226*
Combs, Lisa M.
  See McCourt, Lisa
Combs, Robert
  See Murray, John
Comfort, Jane Levington
  See Sturtzel, Jane Levington
Comfort, Mildred Houghton 1886-1976 .... *3*
Comins, Ethel M(ae) *11*
Comins, Jeremy 1933- *28*
Commager, Henry Steele 1902-1998 .... *23*
  Obituary *102*
Comora, Madeleine *190*
Compere, Mickie
  See Davidson, Margaret
Compestine, Ying Chang 1963- *187*
  Earlier sketch in SATA *140*
Comport, Sally Wern *190*
Compton, Patricia A. 1936- *75*
Comte, The Great
  See Hawkesworth, Eric
Comus
  See Ballantyne, R(obert) M(ichael)

Comyns, Nance
  See Comyns-Toohey, Nantz
Comyns-Toohey, Nantz 1956- *86*
Conahan, Carolyn
  See Conahan, Carolyn Digby
Conahan, Carolyn Digby 1961- *216*
Conan Doyle, Arthur
  See Doyle, Sir Arthur Conan
Condie, Ally *204*
Condie, Allyson B.
  See Condie, Ally
Condit, Martha Olson 1913- *28*
Condon, Bill 1949- *142*
Condon, Judith *83*
Condon, Ken *195*
Condy, Roy 1942- *96*
Cone, Ferne Geller 1921- *39*
Cone, Molly (Lamken) 1918- *151*
  Autobiography Feature *151*
  Earlier sketches in SATA *1, 28, 115*
  See also SAAS *11*
Cone, Patrick 1954- *89*
Coney, Michael G. 1932-2005 .... *61*
  Obituary *170*
Coney, Michael Greatrex
  See Coney, Michael G.
Coney, Mike
  See Coney, Michael G.
Conford, Ellen 1942- *162*
  Earlier sketches in SATA *6, 68, 110*
  See also CLR *71*
Conger, Lesley
  See Suttles, Shirley (Smith)
Conklin, Gladys Plemon 1903- *2*
Conklin, Paul S. 1929(?)-2003 .... *43*
  Brief entry *33*
  Obituary *147*
Conkling, Hilda 1910-1986 .... *23*
Conlan, Kathleen Elizabeth 1950- *145*
Conlan, Kathy
  See Conlan, Kathleen Elizabeth
Conley, Robyn 1963- *125*
Conley-Weaver, Robyn
  See Conley, Robyn
Conlon-McKenna, Marita 1956- *71*
Conly, Jane Leslie 1948- *164*
  Earlier sketches in SATA *80, 112*
Conly, Robert Leslie 1918(?)-1973 .... *23*
  See also CLR *2*
Connell, Kirk
  See Chapman, John Stanton Higham
Connell, Tom *206*
Connelly, Gwen 1952- *212*
Connelly, Marc(us Cook) 1890-1980
  Obituary *25*
Connolly, Jerome P(atrick) 1931- *8*
Connolly, Pat 1943- *74*
Connolly, Peter 1935- *105*
  Earlier sketch in SATA *47*
Conover, Chris 1950- *213*
  Earlier sketch in SATA *31*
Conquest, Owen
  See Hamilton, Charles (Harold St. John)
Conrad, Joseph 1857-1924 .... *27*
Conrad, Pam 1947-1996 .... *133*
  Brief entry *49*
  Obituary *90*
  Earlier sketches in SATA *52, 80*
  See also CLR *18*
  See also SAAS *19*
Conroy, Jack
  See Conroy, John Wesley
Conroy, John Wesley 1899-1990 .... *19*
  Obituary *65*
Conroy, Melissa 1969- *226*
Conroy, Robert
  See Goldston, Robert (Conroy)
Constable, Kate 1966- *172*
Constant, Alberta Wilson 1908-1981 .... *22*
  Obituary *28*
Constantin, Pascale *185*

Conway, Celeste 210
Conway, David 1970- 213
Conway, Diana C. 1943- 91
Conway, Diana Cohen
    See Conway, Diana C.
Conway, Gordon
    See Hamilton, Charles (Harold St. John)
Cook, Ande 192
Cook, Bernadine 1924- 11
Cook, Fred J(ames) 1911-2003 2
    Obituary 145
Cook, Glen 1944- 171
    Earlier sketch in SATA 108
Cook, Glen Charles
    See Cook, Glen
Cook, Hugh 1956- 85
Cook, Hugh, Walter Gilbert
    See Cook, Hugh
Cook, Jean Thor 1930- 94
Cook, Joel 1934- 79
Cook, Joseph Jay 1924- 8
Cook, Lisa Broadie 157
Cook, Lyn
    See Waddell, Evelyn Margaret
Cook, Roy
    See Silverberg, Robert
Cook, Sally 207
Cook, Trish 175
Cooke, Ann
    See Cole, Joanna
Cooke, Arthur
    See Lowndes, Robert A(ugustine) W(ard)
Cooke, Barbara
    See Alexander, Anna B(arbara Cooke)
Cooke, David Coxe 1917- 2
Cooke, Donald Ewin 1916-1985 2
    Obituary 45
Cooke, Frank E. 1920- 87
Cooke, Jean (Isobel Esther) 1929- 74
Cooke, John Estes
    See Baum, L. Frank
Cooke, Trish 1962- 129
Cookson, Catherine (McMullen) 1906-1998 .. 9
    Obituary 116
Cooley, Beth 210
Cooley, Elizabeth
    See Cooley, Beth
Cooley, Regina Francoise 1940- 177
Coolidge, Olivia E(nsor) 1908- 26
    Earlier sketch in SATA 1
Cooling, Wendy 169
    Earlier sketch in SATA 111
Coombs, Charles I(ra) 1914-1994 43
    Earlier sketch in SATA 3
    See also SAAS 15
Coombs, Chick
    See Coombs, Charles I(ra)
Coombs, Jonathan 204
Coombs, Kate 190
Coombs, Patricia 1926- 51
    Earlier sketch in SATA 3
    See also SAAS 22
Cooney, Barbara 1917-2000 96
    Obituary 123
    Earlier sketches in SATA 6, 59
    See also CLR 23
Cooney, Caroline B. 1947- 218
    Brief entry 41
    Earlier sketches in SATA 48, 80, 113, 130,
    179
Cooney, Doug 181
Cooney, Nancy Evans 1932- 42
Coontz, Otto 1946- 33
Cooper, Ann (Catharine) 1939- 104
Cooper, Dutch
    See Kuyper, Sjoerd
Cooper, Elisha 1971- 157
    Earlier sketch in SATA 99
Cooper, Elizabeth Keyser -1992 47

Cooper, Floyd 227
    Earlier sketches in SATA 96, 144, 187
    See also CLR 60
Cooper, Gordon 1932- 23
Cooper, Helen 1963- 169
    Earlier sketch in SATA 102
Cooper, Henry S. F., Jr. 1933- 65
Cooper, Henry Spotswood Fenimore, Jr.
    See Cooper, Henry S. F., Jr.
Cooper, Ilene 1948- 145
    Earlier sketches in SATA 66, 97
Cooper, James Fenimore 1789-1851 19
    See also CLR 105
Cooper, John R. 1
Cooper, Kay 1941- 11
Cooper, Lee Pelham 1926- 5
Cooper, Lester (Irving) 1919-1985 32
    Obituary 43
Cooper, Lettice (Ulpha) 1897-1994 35
    Obituary 82
Cooper, Louise 1952-2009 152
Cooper, M.E.
    See Davis, Maggie S.
Cooper, M.E.
    See Lerangis, Peter
Cooper, Melrose
    See Kroll, Virginia L.
Cooper, Michael L. 1950- 181
    Earlier sketches in SATA 79, 117
Cooper, Michelle 1969- 226
Cooper, Patrick 1949- 134
Cooper, Susan 1935- 151
    Earlier sketches in SATA 4, 64, 104
    See also CLR 161
    See also SAAS 6
Cooper, Susan Mary
    See Cooper, Susan
Cope, Jane U(rsula) 1949- 108
Copeland, Helen 1920- 4
Copeland, Mark 1956- 180
Copeland, Paul W. 23
Coplans, Peta 1951- 84
Copley, (Diana) Heather Pickering 1918- 45
Coppard, A(lfred) E(dgar) 1878-1957
    See YABC 1
Copper, Melinda 1952- 172
Copper, Melinda McConnaughey
    See Copper, Melinda
Corace, Jen 208
Coralie
    See Anderson, Catherine Corley
Corbett, Grahame 43
    Brief entry 36
Corbett, Scott 1913- 42
    Earlier sketch in SATA 2
    See also CLR 1
    See also SAAS 2
Corbett, Sue 174
Corbett, W(illiam) J(esse) 1938- 102
    Brief entry 44
    Earlier sketch in SATA 50
    See also CLR 19
Corbin, Sabra Lee
    See Malvern, Gladys
Corbin, William
    See McGraw, William Corbin
Corbman, Marjorie 1987- 179
Corby, Dan
    See Catherall, Arthur
Corcoran, Barbara (Asenath) 1911-2003 77
    Autobiography Feature 125
    Earlier sketch in SATA 3
    See also CLR 50
    See also SAAS 20
Corcos, Lucille 1908-1973 10
Cordell, Alexander
    See Graber, Alexander
Cordell, Matthew 1975- 199
Corder, Zizou
    See Young, Louisa

Corella, Joseph
    See Odgers, Sally Farrell
Coren, Alan 1938-2007 32
    Obituary 187
Corey, Dorothy 23
Corey, Shana 1974- 219
    Earlier sketch in SATA 133
Corfe, Thomas Howell 1928- 27
Corfe, Tom
    See Corfe, Thomas Howell
Corfield, Robin Bell 1952- 74
Corke, Estelle 1969- 220
Corlett, William 1938-2005 46
    Brief entry 39
Cormack, M(argaret) Grant 1913- 11
Cormack, Maribelle B. 1902-1984 39
Cormier, Robert 1925-2000 83
    Obituary 122
    Earlier sketches in SATA 10, 45
    See also CLR 167
Cormier, Robert Edmund
    See Cormier, Robert
Cornelius, Carol 1942- 40
Cornelius, Kay 1933- 157
Cornell, J.
    See Cornell, Jeffrey
Cornell, James (Clayton, Jr.) 1938- 27
Cornell, Jean Gay 1920- 23
Cornell, Jeffrey 1945- 11
Cornell, Laura 189
Cornish, D.M. 1972- 185
Cornish, Sam(uel James) 1935- 23
Cornwall, Nellie
    See Sloggett, Nellie
Cornwell, Autumn 195
Corr, Christopher 1955- 189
Correy, Lee
    See Stine, G(eorge) Harry
Corrick, James A. 1945- 76
Corrigan, (Helen) Adeline 1909- 23
Corrigan, Barbara 1922- 8
Corrigan, Eireann 1977- 163
Corrin, Sara 1918- 86
    Brief entry 48
Corrin, Stephen 86
    Brief entry 48
Corriveau, Art 231
Corsi, Wendy
    See Staub, Wendy Corsi
Cort, M. C.
    See Clifford, Margaret Cort
Cort, Margaret
    See Clifford, Margaret Cort
Corwin, Judith H(offman) 1946- 10
Corwin, Oliver
    See Corwin, Oliver J.
Corwin, Oliver J. 206
Cory, Rowena
    See Lindquist, Rowena Cory
Cosby, Bill 1937- 110
    Earlier sketch in SATA 66
Cosby, William Henry, Jr.
    See Cosby, Bill
    and Cosby, Bill
Cosentino, Ralph 169
Cosgrave, John O'Hara II 1908-1968
    Obituary 21
Cosgrove, Margaret (Leota) 1926- 47
Cosgrove, Stephen E(dward) 1945- 53
    Brief entry 40
Coskey, Evelyn 1932- 7
Cosner, Shaaron 1940- 43
Cossi, Olga 1921- 216
    Earlier sketches in SATA 67, 102
Costabel, Eva Deutsch 1924- 45
Costabel-Deutsch, Eva
    See Costabel, Eva Deutsch
Costales, Amy 1974- 227
Coste, Marion 1938- 183
Costello, David 174
Costello, David F(rancis) 1904-1990 23

Cte, Genevieve 1964- *184*
Cote, Nancy 1952- *182*
Cott, Jonathan 1942- *23*
Cottam, Clarence 1899-1974 .... *25*
Cotten, Cynthia *188*
Cottin, Menena 1950- *213*
Cottle, Joan 1960- *135*
Cottler, Joseph 1899-1996 .... *22*
Cottonwood, Joe 1947- *92*
Cottrell, Leonard 1913-1974 .... *24*
Cottringer, Anne 1952- *150*
  Earlier sketch in SATA 97
Couch, Greg *199*
Coulman, Valerie 1969- *161*
Couloumbis, Akila 1932-2009 .... *225*
Couloumbis, Audrey *173*
Counsel, June 1926- *70*
Countryman, The
  See Whitlock, Ralph
Courlander, Harold 1908-1996 .... *6*
  Obituary *88*
Coursen, Valerie 1965(?)- *102*
Courtis, Stuart Appleton 1874-1969
  Obituary *29*
Courtland, Tyler
  See Stevens, Serita
Courtney, Dayle
  See Goldsmith, Howard
Coury, Louise Andree 1895(?)-1983
  Obituary *34*
Cousins, Linda 1946- *90*
Cousins, Lucy 1964- *205*
  Earlier sketch in SATA *172*
Cousins, Margaret 1905-1996 .... *2*
  Obituary *92*
Cousteau, Jacques 1910-1997 .... *98*
  Earlier sketch in SATA *38*
Cousteau, Jacques-Yves
  See Cousteau, Jacques
Couture, Christin 1951- *73*
Couvillon, Jacques *195*
Coverly, Dave 1964- *223*
Covert, Ralph 1968- *197*
Coville, Bruce 1950- *216*
  Autobiography Feature *155*
  Earlier sketches in SATA *32, 77, 118, 155*
Covington, Dennis *109*
Covington, Linda
  See Windsor, Linda
Cowan, Catherine *121*
Cowan, Rebecca M.
  See Moesta, Rebecca
Cowan, Rebecca Moesta
  See Moesta, Rebecca
Coward, Fiona 1963- *178*
Cowdrey, Richard 1959- *204*
Cowell, Cressida 1966- *140*
Cowen, Eve
  See Werner, Herma
Cowen, Ida 1898-1993 .... *64*
Cowie, Leonard W(allace) 1919- *4*
Cowles, Kathleen
  See Krull, Kathleen
Cowley, Cassia Joy
  See Cowley, Joy
Cowley, Joy 1936- *164*
  Autobiography Feature *118*
  Earlier sketches in SATA *4, 90*
  See also CLR 55
  See also SAAS 26
Cowley, Marjorie 1925- *111*
Cox, (Christopher) Barry 1931- *62*
Cox, Clinton 1934- *108*
  Earlier sketch in SATA *74*
Cox, David 1933- *56*
Cox, David Dundas
  See Cox, David
Cox, Donald William 1921- *23*
Cox, Jack
  See Cox, John Roberts
Cox, John Roberts 1915-1981 .... *9*

Cox, Judy 1954- *198*
  Earlier sketches in SATA *117, 160*
Cox, Marion Monroe 1898-1983
  Obituary *34*
Cox, Palmer 1840-1924 .... *24*
  See also CLR 24
Cox, Paul 1957- *226*
Cox, Vic 1942- *88*
Cox, Vicki 1945- *158*
Cox, Victoria 1945- *44*
Cox, Wallace 1924-1973 .... *25*
Cox, Wally
  See Cox, Wallace
Cox, William R(obert) 1901-1988 .... *46*
  Brief entry *31*
  Obituary *57*
Coxe, Molly 1959- *101*
  Earlier sketch in SATA *69*
Coxon, Michele 1950- *158*
  Earlier sketch in SATA *76*
Coy, Harold 1902-1986 .... *3*
Coy, John 1958- *171*
  Earlier sketch in SATA *120*
Craats, Rennay 1973- *131*
Crabtree, Judith 1928- *98*
  Earlier sketch in SATA *63*
Crabtree, Julie 1970- *214*
Cracker, Edward E.B.
  See Odgers, Sally Farrell
Craft, Elizabeth 1971(?)- *204*
Craft, K. Y.
  See Craft, Kinuko Y.
Craft, Kinuko Y. 1940- *127*
  Earlier sketch in SATA *65*
Craft, Kinuko Yamabe
  See Craft, Kinuko Y.
Craft, Ruth 1935- *87*
  Brief entry *31*
Craig, A. A.
  See Anderson, Poul
Craig, Alisa
  See MacLeod, Charlotte (Matilda)
Craig, David
  See James, Bill
Craig, Helen 1934- *213*
  Earlier sketches in SATA *46, 49, 94*
Craig, Joe 1979- *198*
Craig, Joe Alexander
  See Craig, Joe
Craig, John Eland
  See Chipperfield, Joseph Eugene
Craig, John Ernest 1921- *23*
Craig, Kit
  See Reed, Kit
Craig, M. F.
  See Craig, Mary (Francis) Shura
Craig, M. Jean *17*
Craig, M. S.
  See Craig, Mary (Francis) Shura
Craig, Margaret (Maze) 1911-1964 .... *9*
Craig, Mary
  See Craig, Mary (Francis) Shura
Craig, Mary Shura
  See Craig, Mary (Francis) Shura
Craig, Mary (Francis) Shura 1923-1991 .... *86*
  Obituary *65*
  Earlier sketch in SATA *6*
  See also SAAS 7
Craig, Ruth 1922- *95*
Craik, Mrs.
  See Craik, Dinah Maria (Mulock)
Craik, Dinah Maria (Mulock) 1826-1887 ..... *34*
Crandall, Court 1965- *175*
Crandell, Rachel 1943- *152*
Crane, Barbara (Joyce) 1934- *31*
Crane, Caroline 1930- *11*
Crane, Jordan 1973- *174*
Crane, M. A.
  See Wartski, Maureen (Ann Crane)
Crane, Royston Campbell 1901-1977
  Obituary *22*

Crane, Stephen 1871-1900
  See YABC 2
  See also CLR *132*
Crane, Stephen Townley
  See Crane, Stephen
Crane, Walter 1845-1915 .... *100*
  Earlier sketch in SATA *18*
  See also CLR 56
Crane, William D(wight) 1892-1976 .... *1*
Cranfield, Ingrid 1945- *74*
Cranshaw, Stanley
  See Fisher, Dorothy (Frances) Canfield
Crary, Elizabeth (Ann) 1942- *99*
  Brief entry *43*
Crary, Margaret (Coleman) 1906-1986 .... *9*
Craste, Marc *201*
Cravath, Lynne Avril
  See Cravath, Lynne W.
Cravath, Lynne W. 1951- *182*
  Earlier sketches in SATA *98, 148*
Craven, Thomas 1889-1969 .... *22*
Crawford, Brent 1975- *220*
Crawford, Charles P. 1945- *28*
Crawford, Deborah 1922- *6*
Crawford, John E(dmund) 1904-1971 .... *3*
Crawford, K(aren) Michael 1959- *155*
Crawford, Laura 1977(?)- *227*
Crawford, Mel 1925- *44*
  Brief entry *33*
Crawford, Phyllis 1899- *3*
Crawley, Dave *177*
Cray, Roberta
  See Emerson, Ru
Crayder, Dorothy *7*
Crayder, Teresa
  See Colman, Hila
Crayon, Geoffrey
  See Irving, Washington
Craz, Albert G. 1926- *24*
Crebbin, June 1938- *169*
  Earlier sketch in SATA *80*
Crecy, Jeanne
  See Williams, Jeanne
Credle, Ellis 1902-1998 .... *1*
Creech, Sharon 1945- *226*
  Earlier sketches in SATA *94, 139, 172*
  See also CLR *164*
Creeden, Sharon 1938- *91*
Creel, Ann Howard 1953- *187*
Creighton, (Mary) Helen 1899-1989
  Obituary *64*
Creighton, Jill 1949- *96*
Crelin, Bob 1959(?)- *221*
Crenson, Victoria 1952- *159*
  Earlier sketch in SATA *88*
Cresp, Gael 1954- *119*
Crespo, George 1962- *82*
Cresswell, Helen 1934-2005 .... *79*
  Obituary *168*
  Earlier sketches in SATA *1, 48*
  See also CLR 18
  See also SAAS 20
Cressy, Michael 1955- *124*
Cressy, Mike
  See Cressy, Michael
Cretan, Gladys (Yessayan) 1921- *2*
Cretzmeyer, Stacy (Megan) 1959- *124*
Crew, Gary 1947- *163*
  Earlier sketches in SATA *75, 110*
  See also CLR 42
Crew, Helen (Cecilia) Coale 1866-1941
  See YABC 2
Crew, Linda (Jean) 1951- *137*
  Earlier sketch in SATA *71*
Crewe, Megan 1980- *225*
Crews, Donald 1938- *76*
  Brief entry *30*
  Earlier sketch in SATA *32*
  See also CLR 7
Crews, Nina 1963- *158*
  Earlier sketch in SATA *97*

Crichton, John Michael
   See Crichton, Michael
Crichton, Michael 1942-2008 88
   Obituary 199
   Earlier sketch in SATA 9
Crider, Allen Billy
   See Crider, Bill
Crider, Bill 1941- 99
Crilley, Mark 1966- 210
   Autobiography Feature 148
   Earlier sketches in SATA 120, 148
Crilley, Paul 1975- 227
Crimi, Carolyn 1959- 219
   Earlier sketch in SATA 176
Cripps, Enid Margaret
   See Appiah, Peggy
Crisler, Curtis L. 188
Crisman, Ruth 1914- 73
Crisp, Marta Marie
   See Crisp, Marty
Crisp, Marty 1947- 128
Crispin, A(nn) C(arol) 1950- 86
Crist, James J. 1961- 168
Cristall, Barbara 79
Crist-Evans, Craig 1954- 153
Crocker, Carter 193
Crocker, Nancy 1956- 185
Crofford, Emily (Ardell) 1927- 61
Crofut, William E. III 1934- 23
Croggon, Alison 1962- 194
Croll, Carolyn 1945- 102
   Brief entry 52
   Earlier sketch in SATA 56
Croman, Dorothy Young
   See Rosenberg, Dorothy
Cromie, Alice Hamilton 1914-2000 24
Cromie, William J(oseph) 1930- 4
Crompton, Anne Eliot 1930- 73
   Earlier sketch in SATA 23
Crompton, Richmal
   See Lamburn, Richmal Crompton
Cronbach, Abraham 1882-1965 11
Crone, Ruth 1919-2003 4
Cronin, A(rchibald) J(oseph) 1896-1981 47
   Obituary 25
Cronin, Doreen (A.) 125
Cronin, Doreen 1966(?)- 178
   See also CLR 136
Cronin, Doreen A.
   See Cronin, Doreen
Cronn-Mills, Kirstin 1968- 224
Crook, Beverly Courtney 38
   Brief entry 35
Crook, Connie Brummel 1930- 168
   Earlier sketch in SATA 98
Crook, Constance
   See Crook, Connie Brummel
Crosby, Alexander L. 1906-1980 2
   Obituary 23
Crosby, Harry C.
   See Anvil, Christopher
Crosby, Margaret
   See Rathmann, Peggy
Crosher, G. R. 14
Cross, Gilbert B. 1939- 60
   Brief entry 51
Cross, Gillian 1945- 178
   Autobiography Feature 178
   Earlier sketches in SATA 38, 71, 110, 165
   See also CLR 28
Cross, Gillian Clare
   See Cross, Gillian
Cross, Helen Reeder
   See Broadhead, Helen Cross
Cross, Peter 1951- 95
Cross, Sarah 216
Cross, Shauna 1976(?)- 196
Cross, Tom 1954- 146
Cross, Verda 1914- 75
Cross, Wilbur Lucius III 1918- 2
Crossingham, John 1974- 226

Crossland, Caroline 1964- 83
Crossley-Holland, Kevin 1941- 165
   Earlier sketches in SATA 5, 74, 120
   See also CLR 84
   See also SAAS 20
Crossley-Holland, Kevin John William
   See Crossley-Holland, Kevin
Crossman, David A. 1951- 219
Crouch, Karen Hillard
   See Good, Karen Hillard
Crouch, Marcus 1913-1996 4
Crout, George C(lement) 1917- 11
Crow, Donna Fletcher 1941- 40
Crow, Francis Luther
   See Luther, Frank
Crow, Kristyn 208
Crowe, Andrew 111
Crowe, Carole 1943- 204
Crowe, Chris 206
Crowe, Ellie 203
Crowe, John
   See Lynds, Dennis
Crowe, (Bettina) Peter Lum 1911- 6
Crowell, Grace Noll 1877-1969 34
Crowell, Pers 1910-1990 2
Crowell, Robert Leland 1909-2001 63
Crowfield, Christopher
   See Stowe, Harriet Beecher
Crowley, Arthur 1945- 38
Crowley, Arthur McBlair
   See Crowley, Arthur
Crowley, John 1942- 140
   Earlier sketch in SATA 65
Crowley, Suzanne 1963- 196
Crowley, Suzanne Carlisle
   See Crowley, Suzanne
Crownfield, Gertrude 1867-1945
   See YABC 1
Crowther, James Gerald 1899-1983 14
Crowther, Kitty 1970- 220
Crowther, Robert 1948- 163
Cruikshank, George 1792-1878 22
   See also CLR 63
Cruise, Robin 1951- 179
Crum, Shutta 192
   Earlier sketch in SATA 134
Crummel, Susan Stevens 1949- 176
   Earlier sketch in SATA 130
Crump, Fred H., Jr. 1931- 76
   Earlier sketch in SATA 11
Crump, J(ames) Irving 1887-1979 57
   Obituary 21
Crump, William D(rake) 1949- 138
Crunden, Reginald
   See Cleaver, Hylton Reginald
Crunk, T.
   See Crunk, Tony
Crunk, Tony 1956- 130
Crutcher, Chris 1946- 196
   Earlier sketches in SATA 52, 99, 153
   See also CLR 159
Crutcher, Christopher C.
   See Crutcher, Chris
Cruz, Ray(mond) 1933- 6
Cruz Martinez, Alejandro (?)-1987 74
Crystal, Billy 1947- 154
Crystal, William
   See Crystal, Billy
Ctvrtek, Vaclav 1911-1976
   Obituary 27
Cuate, Melodie A. 219
Cuetara, Mittie 1957- 158
   Earlier sketch in SATA 106
Cuffari, Richard 1925-1978 66
   Obituary 25
   Earlier sketch in SATA 6
Cuffe-Perez, Mary 1946- 199
Cullen, Countee 1903-1946 18
Cullen, Lynn 190
Culliford, Pierre 1928-1992 40
   Obituary 74

Cullinan, Bernice E(llinger) 1926- 135
Culp, Louanna McNary 1901-1965 2
Culper, Felix
   See McCaughrean, Geraldine
Cumbaa, Stephen 1947- 72
Cumming, Peter 1951- 168
Cumming, Primrose Amy 1915- 24
Cumming, Robert 1945- 65
Cummings, Betty Sue 1918- 15
   See also SAAS 9
Cummings, John Michael 1963(?)- 216
Cummings, Mary 1951- 185
Cummings, Parke 1902-1987 2
   Obituary 53
Cummings, Pat 1950- 203
   Earlier sketches in SATA 42, 71, 107
   See also CLR 48
   See also SAAS 13
Cummings, Phil 1957- 123
   Earlier sketch in SATA 74
Cummings, Priscilla 1951- 170
   Earlier sketch in SATA 129
Cummings, Richard
   See Gardner, Richard (M.)
Cummings, Terrance 227
Cummins, Julie 200
Cummins, Maria Susanna 1827-1866
   See YABC 1
Cumpliano, Ina 207
Cuneo, Mary Louise -2001 85
Cunliffe, John Arthur 1933- 86
   Earlier sketch in SATA 11
Cunliffe, Marcus (Falkner) 1922-1990 37
   Obituary 66
Cunnane, Kelly 175
Cunningham, Bob
   See May, Julian
Cunningham, Captain Frank
   See Glick, Carl (Cannon)
Cunningham, Cathy
   See Cunningham, Chet
Cunningham, Chet 1928- 23
Cunningham, Dale S(peers) 1932- 11
Cunningham, Dru 91
Cunningham, E. V.
   See Fast, Howard
Cunningham, Julia (Woolfolk) 1916- 132
   Earlier sketches in SATA 1, 26
   See also SAAS 2
Cunningham, Lawrence J. 1943- 125
Cunningham, Virginia
   See Holmgren, Virginia C(unningham)
Cunxin, Li 1961- 220
Curiae, Amicus
   See Fuller, Edmund (Maybank)
Curie, Eve 1904-2007 1
   Obituary 188
Curlee, Lynn 1947- 190
   Earlier sketches in SATA 98, 141
Curley, Daniel 1918-1988 23
   Obituary 61
Curley, Marianne 1959- 175
   Earlier sketch in SATA 131
Currey, Anna 194
Currie, Robin 1948- 120
Currie, Stephen 1960- 132
   Earlier sketch in SATA 82
Curry, Ann (Gabrielle) 1934- 72
Curry, Jane L(ouise) 1932- 138
   Autobiography Feature 138
   Earlier sketches in SATA 1, 52, 90
   See also CLR 31
   See also SAAS 6
Curry, Peggy Simson 1911-1987 8
   Obituary 50
Curry, Tom 185
Curtis, Bruce (Richard) 1944- 30
Curtis, Chara M(ahar) 1950- 78
Curtis, Christopher Paul 1953- 187
   Earlier sketches in SATA 93, 140
   See also CLR 68

Curtis, Gavin 1965- *107*
Curtis, Jamie Lee 1958- *144*
   Earlier sketch in SATA 95
   See also CLR 88
Curtis, Jennifer Keats *185*
Curtis, Marci *160*
Curtis, Munzee
   See Caseley, Judith
Curtis, Neil 1950-2006 .... *202*
Curtis, Patricia 1921- *101*
   Earlier sketch in SATA 23
Curtis, Peter
   See Lofts, Norah (Robinson)
Curtis, Philip (Delacourt) 1920- *62*
Curtis, Richard 1937- *29*
Curtis, Richard Alan
   See Curtis, Richard
Curtis, Richard Hale
   See Deming, Richard
   and Levinson, Leonard
   and Rothweiler, Paul Roger
Curtis, Stacy *205*
Curtis, Wade
   See Pournelle, Jerry
Curtiss, A(rlene) B. 1934- *90*
Cusack, Margaret 1945- *58*
Cushman, Doug 1953- *210*
   Earlier sketches in SATA 65, 101, 157
Cushman, Jerome *2*
Cushman, Karen 1941- *147*
   Earlier sketch in SATA 89
   See also CLR 55
Cusick, Richie Tankersley 1952- *231*
   Earlier sketches in SATA 67, 140
Cusimano, Maryann K.
   See Love, Maryann Cusimano
Cutbill, Andy 1972- *201*
Cutchen, Billye Walker 1930- *15*
Cutchins, Judy 1947- *59*
Cutler, Daniel S. 1951- *78*
Cutler, Daniel Solomon
   See Cutler, Daniel S.
Cutler, Ebbitt 1923- *9*
Cutler, Ivor 1923-2006 .... *24*
   Obituary *174*
Cutler, Jane 1936- *162*
   Earlier sketches in SATA 75, 118
Cutler, May Ebbitt
   See Cutler, Ebbitt
Cutler, Samuel
   See Folsom, Franklin (Brewster)
Cutlip, Kimbra L(eigh-Ann) 1964- *128*
Cutrate, Joe
   See Spiegelman, Art
Cutt, W(illiam) Towrie 1898-1981 .... *16*
   Obituary *85*
Cuyler, Margery 1948- *229*
   Earlier sketches in SATA 39, 99, 156, 195
Cuyler, Margery Stuyvesant
   See Cuyler, Margery
Cuyler, Stephen
   See Bates, Barbara S(nedeker)
Cyrus, Kurt 1954- *179*
   Earlier sketch in SATA *132*
Czajkowski, James
   See Rollins, James
Czekaj, Jef 1969- *217*
Czernecki, Stefan 1946- *178*

D

Daagnese, Joseph *228*
Dabba Smith, Frank *174*
Dabcovich, Lydia *99*
   Brief entry *47*
   Earlier sketch in SATA 58
Dace, Dolores B(oelens) 1929- *89*
Da Costa, Deborah *193*
Daddo, Andrew 1967- *198*

Dadey, Debbie 1959- *217*
   Earlier sketches in SATA 73, 136
Dahl, Borghild (Margarethe) 1890-1984 .... *7*
   Obituary *37*
Dahl, Roald 1916-1990 .... *73*
   Obituary *65*
   Earlier sketches in SATA 1, 26
   See also CLR *111*
Dahlberg, Maurine F. 1951- *171*
Dahlstedt, Marden (Stewart) 1921-1983 .... *8*
   Obituary *110*
Dahme, Joanne *206*
Dain, Martin J. 1924-2000 .... *35*
Dakin, Glenn 1960- *224*
Dakos, Kalli 1950- *115*
   Earlier sketch in SATA 80
Dale, Anna 1971- *170*
Dale, Gary
   See Reece, Colleen L.
Dale, George E.
   See Asimov, Isaac
Dale, Jack
   See Holliday, Joseph
Dale, Kim 1957- *123*
Dale, Margaret J(essy) Miller 1911- *39*
Dale, Mitzi
   See Hemstock, Gillian
Dale, Norman
   See Denny, Norman (George)
Dale, Penny 1954- *151*
   Earlier sketch in SATA 70
Daley, Michael J. *170*
Dalgliesh, Alice 1893-1979 .... *17*
   Obituary *21*
   See also CLR 62
Dalkey, Kara 1953- *132*
Dalkey, Kara Mia
   See Dalkey, Kara
Dallas, Ruth 1919- *86*
Dalmas, John
   See Jones, John R(obert)
Dalton, Alene
   See Chapin, Alene Olsen Dalton
Dalton, Annie 1948- *140*
   Earlier sketch in SATA 40
Dalton, Kit
   See Cunningham, Chet
Dalton, Pamela
   See Johnson, Pamela
Dalton, Sean
   See Chester, Deborah
Dalton, Sheila 1949- *108*
D'Aluisio, Faith 1957- *205*
Daly, James *217*
Daly, Jim
   See Stratemeyer, Edward L.
Daly, Jude 1951- *222*
   Earlier sketch in SATA 177
Daly, Kathleen N(orah) *124*
   Brief entry *37*
Daly, Maureen 1921-2006 .... *129*
   Obituary *176*
   Earlier sketch in SATA 2
   See also CLR 96
   See also SAAS *1*
Daly, Nicholas
   See Daly, Niki
Daly, Niki 1946- *198*
   Earlier sketches in SATA 37, 76, 114, 164
   See also CLR 41
   See also SAAS 21
D'Amato, Alex 1919- *20*
D'Amato, Janet (Potter) 1925- *9*
Damerow, Gail 1944- *83*
Damerow, Gail Jane
   See Damerow, Gail
D'Amico, Carmela *170*
D'Amico, Steve *170*
Damrell, Liz 1956- *77*
Damrosch, Helen
   See Tee-Van, Helen Damrosch

Dana, Barbara 1940- *218*
   Earlier sketch in SATA 22
Dana, Richard Henry, Jr. 1815-1882 .... *26*
Danachair, Caoimhin O
   See Danaher, Kevin
Danaher, Kevin 1913-2002 .... *22*
Danakas, John 1963- *94*
Dandi
   See Mackall, Dandi Daley
D'Andrea, Kate
   See Steiner, Barbara A(nnette)
Dangerfield, Balfour
   See McCloskey, (John) Robert
Daniel, Alan 1939- *76*
   Brief entry *53*
Daniel, Anita 1893(?)-1978 .... *23*
   Obituary *24*
Daniel, Anne
   See Steiner, Barbara A(nnette)
Daniel, Becky 1947- *56*
Daniel, Claire 1949- *164*
Daniel, Colin
   See Windsor, Patricia
Daniel, Hawthorne 1890- *8*
Daniel, (Donna) Lee 1944- *76*
Daniel, Rebecca
   See Daniel, Becky
Daniels, Guy 1919-1989 .... *11*
   Obituary *62*
Daniels, Kit
   See Diver, Lucienne
Daniels, Lucy
   See Oldfield, Jenny
Daniels, Max
   See Gellis, Roberta
Daniels, Olga
   See Sinclair, Olga
Daniels, Patricia 1955- *93*
Daniels, Zoe
   See Laux, Constance
Dank, Gloria Rand 1955- *56*
   Brief entry *46*
Dank, Leonard D(ewey) 1929- *44*
Dank, Milton 1920- *31*
Dann, Max 1955- *62*
Danneberg, Julie 1958- *173*
Dantz, William R.
   See Philbrick, Rodman
Danzig, Dianne *213*
Danziger, Paula 1944-2004 .... *149*
   Brief entry *30*
   Obituary *155*
   Earlier sketches in SATA 36, 63, 102
   See also CLR 20
Darby, Gene Kegley
   See Darby, Jean (Kegley)
Darby, J. N.
   See Govan, (Mary) Christine Noble
Darby, Jean (Kegley) 1921- *68*
Darby, Patricia (Paulsen) *14*
Darby, Ray(mond) 1912-1982 .... *7*
Darbyshire, Kristen *218*
d'Arcy, Willard
   See Cox, William R(obert)
Dare, Geena
   See McNicoll, Sylvia (Marilyn)
D'arge, Mackie *218*
Darian, Shea 1959- *97*
Daringer, Helen Fern 1892-1986 .... *1*
Darke, Marjorie 1929- *87*
   Earlier sketch in SATA 16
Darley, F(elix) O(ctavius) C(arr)
   1822-1888 .... *35*
Darling, David J. 1953- *60*
   Brief entry *44*
Darling, Kathy
   See Darling, Mary Kathleen
Darling, Lois (MacIntyre) 1917-1989 .... *3*
   Obituary *64*
Darling, Louis, (Jr.) 1916-1970 .... *3*
   Obituary *23*

Darling, Mary Kathleen 1943- *124*
    Earlier sketches in SATA *9, 79*
Darling, Sandra Louise Woodward
    See Day, Alexandra
Darnell, K(athryn) L(ynne) 1955- *150*
Darroll, Sally
    See Odgers, Sally Farrell
Darrow, Sharon *181*
Darrow, Whitney, (Jr.) 1909-1999 .... *13*
    Obituary *115*
Darwin, Len
    See Darwin, Leonard
Darwin, Leonard 1916- *24*
Dasent, Sir George Webbe 1817-1896 .... *62*
    Brief entry *29*
Dash, Joan 1925- *142*
Daskam, Josephine Dodge
    See Bacon, Josephine Dodge (Daskam)
D'ath, Justin 1953- *174*
    Earlier sketch in SATA *106*
Dauer, Rosamond 1934- *23*
Daugherty, Charles Michael 1914- *16*
Daugherty, James (Henry) 1889-1974 .... *13*
    See also CLR *78*
Daugherty, Richard D(eo) 1922- *35*
Daugherty, Sonia Medwedeff (?)-1971
    Obituary *27*
d'Aulaire, Edgar Parin 1898-1986 .... *66*
    Obituary *47*
    Earlier sketch in SATA *5*
    See also CLR *21*
d'Aulaire, Ingri 1904-1980 .... *66*
    Obituary *24*
    Earlier sketch in SATA *5*
    See also CLR *21*
d'Aulaire, Ingri Mortenson Parin
    See d'Aulaire, Ingri
Dave, Dave
    See Berg, David
Daveluy, Paule Cloutier 1919- *11*
Davenier, Christine 1961- *216*
    Earlier sketches in SATA *127, 179*
Davenport, John 1960- *156*
Daves, Michael 1938- *40*
David, A. R.
    See David, A(nn) Rosalie
David, A(nn) Rosalie 1946- *103*
David, Jonathan
    See Ames, Lee J.
David, Lawrence 1963- *165*
    Earlier sketch in SATA *111*
David, Peter 1956- *72*
David, Peter Allen
    See David, Peter
David, Rosalie
    See David, A(nn) Rosalie
Davidson, Alice Joyce 1932- *54*
    Brief entry *45*
Davidson, Basil 1914-2010 .... *13*
Davidson, (Marie) Diane 1924- *91*
Davidson, Hugh
    See Hamilton, Edmond
Davidson, Jessica 1915-1986 .... *5*
Davidson, Judith 1953- *40*
Davidson, Lionel 1922-2009 .... *87*
Davidson, Margaret 1936- *5*
Davidson, Marion
    See Garis, Howard R.
Davidson, Mary R. 1885-1973 .... *9*
Davidson, Mary S. 1940- *61*
Davidson, Mickie
    See Davidson, Margaret
Davidson, Nicole
    See Jensen, Kathryn
Davidson, R.
    See Davidson, Raymond
Davidson, Raymond 1926- *32*
Davidson, Rosalie 1921- *23*
Davie, Helen K(ay) 1952- *148*
    Earlier sketch in SATA *77*
Davies, Andrew (Wynford) 1936- *27*

Davies, Andy Robert *200*
Davies, Bettilu D(onna) 1942- *33*
Davies, Hunter 1936- *55*
    Brief entry *45*
Davies, Jacqueline 1962- *186*
    Earlier sketch in SATA *155*
Davies, Joan 1934- *50*
    Brief entry *47*
Davies, Nicola 1958- *182*
    Earlier sketches in SATA *99, 150*
Davies, Peter J(oseph) 1937- *52*
Davies, Sumiko 1942- *46*
Davis, (A.) Aubrey 1949- *153*
Davis, Barbara Steincrohn
    See Davis, Maggie S.
Davis, Bette J. 1923- *15*
Davis, Burke 1913- *4*
Davis, Christopher 1928- *6*
Davis, D(elbert) Dwight 1908-1965 .... *33*
Davis, Daniel S(heldon) 1936- *12*
Davis, David R. 1948- *106*
Davis, Donald 1944- *169*
    Earlier sketch in SATA *93*
Davis, Donald D.
    See Davis, Donald
Davis, Eleanor 1983(?)- *209*
Davis, Emma
    See Davis, Maggie S.
Davis, Gibbs 1953- *102*
    Brief entry *41*
    Earlier sketch in SATA *46*
Davis, Grania 1943- *88*
    Brief entry *50*
Davis, H(arold) L(enoir) 1896-1960 .... *114*
Davis, Heather 1970- *221*
Davis, Hubert J(ackson) 1904-1997 .... *31*
Davis, Jack E. *210*
Davis, Jacky *204*
Davis, James Robert 1945- *32*
Davis, Jenny 1953- *74*
Davis, Jim
    See Davis, James Robert
Davis, Julia 1900(?)-1993 .... *6*
    Obituary *75*
Davis, Karen (Elizabeth) 1944- *109*
Davis, Katie 1959(?)- *208*
    Earlier sketch in SATA *152*
Davis, Lambert *176*
Davis, Leslie
    See Guccione, Leslie Davis
Davis, Louise Littleton 1921- *25*
Davis, Maggie S. 1943- *57*
Davis, Marguerite 1889- *34*
Davis, Mary L(ee) 1935- *9*
Davis, Mary Octavia 1901-1976 .... *6*
Davis, Nancy 1958(?)- *229*
Davis, Nelle 1958- *73*
Davis, Ossie 1917-2005 .... *81*
    See also CLR *56*
Davis, Paxton 1925-1994 .... *16*
Davis, Rich 1958- *206*
Davis, Robert 1881-1949
    See YABC *1*
Davis, Robin W(orks) 1962- *87*
Davis, Russell Gerard 1922- *3*
Davis, Tanita S. *212*
Davis, Tim(othy N.) 1957- *94*
Davis, Tony 1961- *222*
Davis, Verne Theodore 1889-1973 .... *6*
Davis, Yvonne 1927- *115*
Davol, Marguerite W. 1928- *146*
    Earlier sketch in SATA *82*
DaVolls, Andy (P.) 1967- *85*
DaVolls, Linda 1966- *85*
Davys, Sarah
    See Manning, Rosemary
Dawes, Claiborne 1935- *111*
Dawson, Arthur L. *207*
Dawson, Elmer A. *67*
    Earlier sketch in SATA *1*

Dawson, Imogen (Zoe) 1948- *126*
    Earlier sketch in SATA *90*
Dawson, Janine 1957- *196*
Dawson, Mary 1919- *11*
Dawson, Willow 1975- *208*
Day, A(rthur) Grove 1904-1994 .... *59*
Day, Alexandra 1941- *197*
    Autobiography Feature *197*
    Earlier sketches in SATA *67, 97, 169*
    See also CLR *22*
    See also SAAS *19*
Day, Beth (Feagles) 1924- *33*
Day, Donna
    See Asay, Donna Day
Day, Edward C. 1932- *72*
Day, Jon 1936(?)- *79*
Day, Karen *187*
Day, Larry 1956- *227*
    Earlier sketch in SATA *181*
Day, Nancy 1953- *140*
Day, Nancy Raines 1951- *148*
    Earlier sketch in SATA *93*
Day, Shirley 1962- *94*
Day, Susie 1975- *231*
Day, Thomas 1748-1789
    See YABC *1*
Day, Trevor 1955- *124*
Dazey, Agnes J(ohnston) *2*
Dazey, Frank M. *2*
Deacon, Alexis 1978- *139*
Deacon, Eileen
    See Geipel, Eileen
Deacon, Richard
    See McCormick, (George) Donald (King)
Deadman, Ronald 1919-1988(?)
    Obituary *56*
Deak, Erzsi 1959- *152*
Dean, Anabel 1915- *12*
Dean, Carolee 1962- *148*
Dean, Claire *215*
Dean, David 1976- *192*
Dean, Karen Strickler 1923- *49*
Dean, Ruth (Brigham) 1947- *145*
Dean, Zoey
    See Bennett, Cherie
de Angeli, Marguerite (Lofft) 1889-1987 ... *100*
    Obituary *51*
    Earlier sketches in SATA *1, 27*
    See also CLR *1*
Deans, Karen *195*
Deans, Sis Boulos 1955- *136*
    Earlier sketch in SATA *78*
DeArmand, Frances Ullmann 1904(?)-1984 . *10*
    Obituary *38*
DeArmond, Dale 1914- *70*
DeArmond, Dale Burlison
    See DeArmond, Dale
Deary, Terry 1946- *171*
    Brief entry *41*
    Earlier sketches in SATA *51, 101*
Deaver, Julie Reece 1953- *68*
de Banke, Cecile 1889-1965 .... *11*
De Bello, Rosario 1923- *89*
Debon, Nicolas *186*
    Earlier sketch in SATA *151*
de Bono, Edward 1933- *66*
de Brissac, Malcolm
    See Dickinson, Peter
de Brunhoff, Jean
    See Brunhoff, Jean de
De Brunhoff, Laurent
    See Brunhoff, Laurent de
De Bruyn, Monica G. 1952- *13*
De Bruyn, Monica Jean Grembowicz
    See De Bruyn, Monica G.
DeBry, Roger K. 1942- *91*
de Camp, Catherine Crook 1907-2000 .... *83*
    Earlier sketch in SATA *12*
de Camp, L. Sprague 1907-2000 .... *83*
    Earlier sketch in SATA *9*

de Camp, Lyon Sprague
  See de Camp, L. Sprague
DeCandido, Keith R.A. 112
Dechausay, Sonia E. 94
Decker, C.B. 172
Decker, Cynthia B.
  See Decker, C.B.
Decker, Duane 1910-1964 5
Decker, Timothy 1974- 197
DeClements, Barthe 1920- 131
  Earlier sketches in SATA 35, 71
  See also CLR 23
DeClements, Barthe Faith
  See DeClements, Barthe
de Clercq Zubli, Rita la Fontaine 1929- 199
de Conte, Sieur Louis
  See Twain, Mark
Dedman, Stephen 108
Dee, Barbara 1958- 220
Dee, Catherine 1964- 138
Dee, Ruby
  See Wallace, Ruby Ann
Deeble, Jason 1979- 221
Deedy, Carmen Agra 1960- 196
Deedy, John 1923- 24
Deegan, Paul Joseph 1937- 48
  Brief entry 38
Deem, James M. 1950- 191
  Autobiography Feature 191
  Earlier sketches in SATA 75, 134
Deem, James Morgan
  See Deem, James M.
Deeter, Catherine 1947- 137
DeFelice, Cynthia 1951- 165
  Earlier sketches in SATA 79, 121
DeFelice, Cynthia C.
  See DeFelice, Cynthia
Defoe, Daniel 1660(?)-1731 22
  See also CLR 164
de Fombelle, Timothee
  See Fombelle, Timothee de
DeFord, Deborah H. 123
deFrance, Anthony
  See DiFranco, Anthony (Mario)
Degen, Bruce 1945- 205
  Brief entry 47
  Earlier sketches in SATA 57, 97, 147
DeGering, Etta (Belle) Fowler 1898-1996 7
De Goldi, Kate 1959- 123
De Goldi, Kathleen Domenica
  See De Goldi, Kate
de Goursac, Olivier 1959- 184
De Grazia, Ettore 1909-1982 39
De Grazia, Ted
  See De Grazia, Ettore
deGroat, Diane 1947- 169
  Earlier sketches in SATA 31, 90
deGros, J. H.
  See Villiard, Paul
de Grummond, Lena Young 62
  Earlier sketch in SATA 6
de Hamel, Joan Littledale 1924- 86
De Haven, Tom 1949- 72
de Hugo, Pierre
  See Brackers de Hugo, Pierre
Deines, Brian 1955- 220
Deiss, Joseph Jay 1912-1999 12
de Jenkins, Lyll Becerra 1925-1997 102
DeJong, David C(ornel) 1905-1967 10
de Jong, Dola
  See de Jong, Dorothea Rosalie
de Jong, Dorothea Rosalie 1911-2003 7
  Obituary 149
DeJong, Meindert 1906-1991 2
  Obituary 68
  See also CLR 73
DeJonge, Joanne E. 1943- 56
Deka, Connie
  See Laux, Constance
de Kay, Ormonde (Jr.) 1923-1998 7
  Obituary 106

DeKeyser, Stacy 1959- 214
de Kiriline, Louise
  See Lawrence, Louise de Kiriline
Dekker, Carl
  See Laffin, John (Alfred Charles)
  and Lynds, Dennis
deKruif, Paul (Henry) 1890-1971 50
  Earlier sketch in SATA 5
Delacre, Lulu 1957- 209
  Earlier sketches in SATA 36, 156
DeLaCroix, Alice 1940- 195
  Earlier sketch in SATA 75
de la Cruz, Melissa 1971- 179
De la Garza, Phyllis 1942- 169
De Lage, Ida 1918- 11
de la Mare, Walter (John) 1873-1956 16
  See also CLR 148
Delaney, Harry 1932- 3
Delaney, Joseph 1945- 172
Delaney, M.C.
  See Delaney, Michael
Delaney, Michael 1955- 180
  Earlier sketch in SATA 96
Delaney, Michael Clark
  See Delaney, Michael
Delaney, Ned 1951- 28
Delaney, Thomas Nicholas III
  See Delaney, Ned
DeLange, Alex Pardo
  See Pardo DeLange, Alex
Delano, Hugh 1933- 20
Delano, Marfe Ferguson 215
Delany, Samuel R., Jr. 1942- 92
Delany, Samuel Ray
  See Delany, Samuel R., Jr.
de la Pena, Matt 205
De La Ramee, Marie Louise 1839-1908 20
de la Roche, Mazo 1879-1961 64
De La Roche Saint Andre, Anne 1950- 75
de Las Casas, Dianne 1970- 221
Delaune, (Jewel) Lynn (de Grummond) 7
DeLaurentis, Louise Budde 1920- 12
del Barco, Lucy Salamanca 1900(?)-1989
  Obituary 64
Delderfield, Eric R(aymond) 1909-1995 14
Delderfield, Ronald Frederick 1912-1972 20
DeLeeuw, Adele (Louise) 1899-1988 30
  Obituary 56
  Earlier sketch in SATA 1
De Leon, Nephtali 1945- 97
Delessert, Etienne 1941- 179
  Brief entry 27
  Earlier sketches in SATA 46, 130
  See also CLR 81
Delgado, James P. 1958- 122
Delinois, Alix 228
de Lint, Charles 1951- 207
  Earlier sketches in SATA 115, 157
de Lint, Charles Henri Diederick Hofsmit
  See de Lint, Charles
Delmar, Roy
  See Wexler, Jerome (LeRoy)
Del Negro, Janice M. 197
Deloria, Vine, Jr. 1933-2005 21
  Obituary 171
Deloria, Vine Victor, Jr.
  See Deloria, Vine, Jr.
del Rey, Lester 1915-1993 22
  Obituary 76
Delrio, Martin
  See Doyle, Debra
  and Macdonald, James D.
Delton, Judy 1931-2001 77
  Obituary 130
  Earlier sketch in SATA 14
  See also SAAS 9
Delulio, John 1938- 15
Delving, Michael
  See Williams, Jay
de Marcken, Gail 186

Demarest, Chris L. 1951- 175
  Brief entry 44
  Earlier sketches in SATA 45, 82, 128
Demarest, Christopher Lynn
  See Demarest, Chris L.
Demarest, Doug
  See Barker, Will
De Mari, Silvana 1953- 193
Demas, Corinne
  See Bliss, Corinne Demas
Demas, Vida 1927- 9
Dematons, Charlotte 1957- 203
DeMatteis, J.M. 1953- 180
DeMatteis, John Marc
  See DeMatteis, J.M.
De Mejo, Oscar 1911-1992 40
Demers, Dominique 1956- 177
de Messieres, Nicole 1930- 39
DeMeulemeester, Linda 1956- 230
Demi 1942- 210
  Earlier sketches in SATA 11, 66, 102, 152
  See also CLR 58
Demijohn, Thom
  See Disch, Thomas M.
  and Sladek, John
Deming, Richard 1915-1983 24
Deming, Sarah 191
de Monfreid, Dorothee 1973- 189
Demuth, Patricia Brennan 1948- 84
  Brief entry 51
De Muth, Roger 1948- 221
Dendinger, Roger E. 1952- 158
Denenberg, Barry 1940- 175
Dengler, Marianna (Herron) 1935- 103
Dengler, Sandy 1939- 54
  Brief entry 40
Denim, Sue
  See Pilkey, Dav
Denise, Anika 210
Denise, Christopher 1968- 193
  Earlier sketch in SATA 147
Denman, K.L. 1957- 186
Denmark, Harrison
  See Zelazny, Roger
Dennard, Deborah 1953- 136
  Earlier sketch in SATA 78
Denney, Diana 1910-2000 25
  Obituary 120
Dennis, Morgan 1891(?)-1960 18
Dennis, Wesley 1903-1966 18
Denniston, Elinore 1900-1978
  Obituary 24
Denny, Norman (George) 1901-1982 43
Denos, Julia 202
Denslow, Sharon Phillips 1947- 142
  Earlier sketch in SATA 68
Denslow, W(illiam) W(allace) 1856-1915 16
  See also CLR 15
Dent, Grace 1973- 187
Denton, Kady MacDonald 181
  Earlier sketches in SATA 66, 110
  See also CLR 71
Denton, Terry 1950- 186
Denver, Walt
  See Redding, Robert Hull
  and Sherman, Jory (Tecumseh)
Denzel, Justin F(rancis) 1917-1999 46
  Brief entry 38
Denzer, Ann Wiseman
  See Wiseman, Ann (Sayre)
DePalma, Mary Newell 1961- 185
  Earlier sketch in SATA 139
De Palma, Toni 199
dePaola, Thomas Anthony 1934- 200
  Earlier sketches in SATA 11, 59, 108, 155
  See also CLR 81
  See also SAAS 15
dePaola, Tomie
  See dePaola, Thomas Anthony
deParrie, Paul 1949- 74
DePauw, Linda Grant 1940- 24

De Pretto, Lorenzo 1966- *225*
DeRan, David 1946- *76*
Derby, Ken 1956- *181*
Derby, Kenneth R.
See Derby, Ken
Derby, Pat 1942- *172*
Derby, Sally 1934- *189*
Earlier sketches in SATA *89, 132*
de Regniers, Beatrice Schenk (Freedman)
1914-2000 .... *68*
Obituary *123*
Earlier sketch in SATA *2*
See also SAAS *6*
Dereske, Jo 1947- *72*
Deriso, Christine Hurley 1961- *210*
Derleth, August (William) 1909-1971 .... *5*
Derman, Martha (Winn) *74*
Derman, Sarah Audrey 1915- *11*
DeRoberts, Lyndon
See Silverstein, Robert Alan
Derom, Dirk 1980- *224*
de Roo, Anne Louise 1931-1997 .... *84*
Earlier sketch in SATA *25*
See also CLR *63*
deRosa, Dee *70*
Derrick, Lionel
See Cunningham, Chet
Derrickson, Jim 1959- *141*
Derry Down Derry
See Lear, Edward
Derting, Kimberly 1968- *231*
Dervaux, Isabelle 1961- *106*
Derwent, Lavinia *14*
Desai, Anita 1937- *126*
Earlier sketch in SATA *63*
DeSaix, Deborah Durland *188*
De Saulles, Tony 1958- *119*
Desbarats, Peter 1933- *39*
de Selincourt, Aubrey 1894-1962 .... *14*
de Seve, Peter 1958- *219*
de Seve, Randall *198*
Deshpande, Chris 1950- *69*
Desimini, Lisa 1964- *216*
Earlier sketches in SATA *86, 148*
Desjarlais, John 1953- *71*
Desjarlais, John J.
See Desjarlais, John
Desmoinaux, Christel 1967- *149*
Earlier sketch in SATA *103*
Desmond, Adrian 1947- *51*
Desmond, Adrian J.
See Desmond, Adrian
Desmond, Adrian John
See Desmond, Adrian
Desmond, Alice Curtis 1897-1990 .... *8*
Desnoettes, Caroline *183*
DeSpain, Pleasant 1943- *87*
Desputeaux, Helene 1959- *95*
Dessen, Sarah 1970- *172*
Earlier sketch in SATA *120*
Detine, Padre
See Olsen, Ib Spang
de Trevino, Elizabeth B.
See Trevino, Elizabeth B(orton) de
de Trevino, Elizabeth Borton
See Trevino, Elizabeth B(orton) de
Detwiler, Susan Dill 1956- *58*
Deuker, Carl 1950- *196*
Earlier sketches in SATA *82, 150*
Deutsch, Babette 1895-1982 .... *1*
Obituary *33*
Deutsch, Eva Costabel
See Costabel, Eva Deutsch
Deutsch, Helen 1906-1992 .... *76*
Deutsch, Kurt
See Singer, Kurt D.
De Valera, Sinead 1879(?)-1975
Obituary *30*
Devaney, John 1926-1994 .... *12*
de Varennes, Monique 1947- *168*
de Varona, Frank J. 1943- *83*

Devereux, Frederick L(eonard), Jr.
1914-1993 .... *9*
Devi, Nila
See Woody, Regina Jones
DeVillers, Julia 1967- *227*
deVinck, Christopher 1951- *85*
DeVita, James *195*
DeVito, Cara 1956- *80*
Devlin, Dorothy Wende
See Devlin, Wende
Devlin, Harry 1918-2001 .... *136*
Earlier sketches in SATA *11, 74*
Devlin, Wende 1918-2002 .... *74*
Earlier sketch in SATA *11*
Devon, Paddie 1953- *92*
Devons, Sonia 1974- *72*
Devorah-Leah *111*
de Vos, Gail 1949- *122*
de Vries, Anke 1936- *222*
DeVries, Douglas 1933- *122*
De Waard, E(lliott) John 1935- *7*
Dewan, Ted 1961- *226*
Earlier sketches in SATA *108, 157*
Dewdney, Anna *184*
Dewdney, Selwyn (Hanington) 1909-1979 ... *64*
DeWeese, Gene
See DeWeese, Thomas Eugene
DeWeese, Jean
See DeWeese, Thomas Eugene
DeWeese, Thomas Eugene 1934- *46*
Brief entry *45*
Dewey, Ariane 1937- *178*
Earlier sketches in SATA *7, 109*
Dewey, Jennifer (Owings) 1941- *103*
Brief entry *48*
Earlier sketch in SATA *58*
Dewey, Kenneth Francis 1940- *39*
Dewin, Howie
See Howie, Betsy
De Wire, Elinor 1953- *180*
deWit, Dorothy (May Knowles) 1916-1980 . *39*
Obituary *28*
Dexter, Alison 1966- *125*
Dexter, John
See Bradley, Marion Zimmer
Deyneka, Anita 1943- *24*
Deyrup, Astrith Johnson 1923- *24*
Dezern, Chad *201*
de Zubizarreta, Alma
See Ada, Alma Flor
Dhami, Narinder 1958- *152*
Dhondy, Farrukh 1944- *152*
Earlier sketch in SATA *65*
See also CLR *41*
Diakite, Baba Wague 1961- *174*
Diakite, Penda 1993(?)- *174*
Diamand, Emily 1971- *227*
Diamond, Arthur 1957- *76*
Diamond, Donna 1950- *69*
Brief entry *30*
Earlier sketch in SATA *35*
Diamond, Petra
See Sachs, Judith
Diamond, Rebecca
See Sachs, Judith
Dias, Earl Joseph 1916- *41*
Dias, Ron 1937- *71*
Diaz, David 1959(?)- *229*
Earlier sketches in SATA *96, 150, 189*
See also CLR *65*
di Bartolo, Jim *225*
Dibley, Glin *188*
DiCamillo, Kate 1964- *202*
Earlier sketches in SATA *121, 163*
See also CLR *117*
Di Certo, J(oseph) J(ohn) 1933- *60*
DiCianni, Ron 1952- *107*
Dick, Trella Lamson 1889-1974 .... *9*
Dickens, Charles 1812-1870 .... *15*
See also CLR *162*

Dickens, Charles John Huffam
See Dickens, Charles
Dickens, Frank
See Huline-Dickens, Frank William
Dickens, Monica (Enid) 1915-1992 .... *4*
Obituary *74*
Dickerson, Roy Ernest 1886-1965
Obituary *26*
Dickinson, Emily 1830-1886 .... *29*
Dickinson, Emily Elizabeth
See Dickinson, Emily
Dickinson, Mary 1949- *48*
Brief entry *41*
Dickinson, Mary-Anne
See Rodda, Emily
Dickinson, Peter 1927- *229*
Earlier sketches in SATA *5, 62, 95, 150*
See also CLR *125*
Dickinson, Peter Malcolm de Brissac
See Dickinson, Peter
Dickinson, Susan 1931- *8*
Dickinson, Terence 1943- *102*
Dickinson, W(illiam) Croft 1897-1963 .... *13*
Dickson, Gordon R. 1923-2001 .... *77*
Dickson, Gordon Rupert
See Dickson, Gordon R.
Dickson, Helen
See Reynolds, Helen Mary Greenwood Camp-
bell
Dickson, Naida 1916- *8*
Diehn, Gwen 1943- *80*
Dierssen, Andreas 1962- *190*
Diesen, Deborah 1967- *200*
Dieterich, Michele M. 1962- *78*
Dietz, David H(enry) 1897-1984 .... *10*
Obituary *41*
Dietz, Lew 1907-1997 .... *11*
Obituary *95*
Diffily, Deborah *159*
Di Fiori, Larry
See Di Fiori, Lawrence
Di Fiori, Lawrence 1934- *130*
DiFranco, Anthony (Mario) 1945- *42*
Digby, Anne 1935- *72*
Digges, Jeremiah
See Berger, Josef
Digman, Kristina 1959- *176*
D'Ignazio, Fred 1949- *39*
Brief entry *35*
D'Ignazio, Frederick
See D'Ignazio, Fred
Di Grazia, Thomas (?)-1983 .... *32*
Dijkstra, Lida 1961- *195*
Dikty, Julian May
See May, Julian
Dillard, Annie 1945- *140*
Earlier sketch in SATA *10*
Dillard, Kristine 1964- *113*
Dillard, Polly Hargis 1916- *24*
Dillard, Sarah 1961- *217*
Diller, Harriett 1953- *78*
Dillon, Anna
See Scott, Michael
Dillon, Barbara 1927- *44*
Brief entry *39*
Dillon, Diane 1933- *194*
Earlier sketches in SATA *15, 51, 106*
See also CLR *44*
Dillon, Diane Claire
See Dillon, Diane
Dillon, Eilis 1920-1994 .... *74*
Autobiography Feature *105*
Obituary *83*
Earlier sketch in SATA *2*
See also CLR *26*
Dillon, Jana (a pseudonym) 1952- *117*
Dillon, Leo 1933- *194*
Earlier sketches in SATA *15, 51, 106*
See also CLR *44*
Dillon, Sharon Saseen
See Saseen, Sharon (Dillon)

Dils, Tracey E. 1958- 83
Dilson, Jesse 1914-1988 24
Dinan, Carolyn 59
   Brief entry 47
Dines, Carol 1956- 175
Dines, (Harry) Glen 1925-1996 7
Dinesen, Isak
   See Blixen, Karen
Dinessi, Alex
   See Schembri, Jim
Dinneen, Betty 1929- 61
Dinnerstein, Harvey 1928- 42
Dinsdale, Tim(othy Kay) 1924-1987 11
Dion, Nathalie 1964- 213
Dionne, Erin 1975- 217
Diop, Birago (Ismael) 1906-1989
   Obituary 64
Diouf, Sylviane A. 168
Diouf, Sylviane Anna
   See Diouf, Sylviane A.
DiPucchio, Kelly 204
   Earlier sketch in SATA *159*
Dirk
   See Gringhuis, Richard H.
Dirks, Wilhelmina 1916- 59
Dirks, Willy
   See Dirks, Wilhelmina
Dirtmeister
   See Tomecek, Steve
DiSalvo, DyAnne 1960- 144
   Earlier sketch in SATA *59*
DiSalvo-Ryan, DyAnne
   See DiSalvo, DyAnne
Disch, Thomas M. 1940-2008 92
   Obituary 195
   See also CLR *18*
   See also SAAS *15*
Disch, Thomas Michael
   See Disch, Thomas M.
Disch, Tom
   See Disch, Thomas M.
Disher, Garry 1949- 125
   Earlier sketch in SATA *81*
Disney, Walt(er Elias) 1901-1966 28
   Brief entry 27
Ditchfield, Christin 1973- 226
   Earlier sketch in SATA *189*
DiTerlizzi, Tony 1969- 214
   Earlier sketch in SATA *154*
DiTerlooney, Tiny
   See DiTerlizzi, Tony
Divakaruni, Chitra Banerjee 1956- 222
   Earlier sketch in SATA *160*
Di Valentin, Maria (Amelia) Messuri
   1911-1985 7
Diver, Lucienne 1971- 218
Divine, Arthur Durham 1904-1987
   Obituary 52
Divine, David
   See Divine, Arthur Durham
Divine, L. 229
Dixon, Ann 1954- 212
   Earlier sketches in SATA *77, 127*
Dixon, Ann Renee
   See Dixon, Ann
Dixon, Dougal 1947- 190
   Earlier sketches in SATA *45, 127*
Dixon, Franklin W.
   See Barrett, Neal, Jr.
   and Goulart, Ron
   and Lantz, Francess L(in)
   and Lerangis, Peter
   and McFarlane, Leslie
   and Stanley, George Edward
   and Stratemeyer, Edward L.
Dixon, Jeanne 1936- 31
Dixon, Paige
   See Corcoran, Barbara (Asenath)
Dixon, Peter L(ee) 1931- 6
Dixon, Rachel 1952- 74
Dizin, Pascal 230

Djoleto, (Solomon Alexander) Amu 1929- ... 80
d'Lacey, Chris 1949- 227
   Earlier sketch in SATA *165*
Doak, Annie
   See Dillard, Annie
Doane, Pelagie 1906-1966 7
Dob, Bob 207
Dobell, I(sabel) M(arian) B(arclay)
   1909-1998 11
Dobie, J(ames) Frank 1888-1964 43
Dobkin, Alexander 1908-1975
   Obituary 30
Dobler, Lavinia G. 1910- 6
Dobrin, Arnold 1928- 4
Dobson, Jill 1969- 140
Dobson, Julia 1941- 48
Dobson, Mary 1954- 117
DoCampo, Valeria 1976- 217
Docherty, James
   See Docherty, Jimmy
Docherty, Jimmy 1976- 204
Docherty, Thomas 1955- 218
Dockery, Wallene T. 1941- 27
Dockray, Tracy 1962- 139
Dockrey, Karen 1955- 103
Doctor, Bernard
   See Doctor, Bernard Aquina
Doctor, Bernard Aquina 1950- 81
Doctor X
   See Nourse, Alan E(dward)
Dodd, Ed(ward Benton) 1902-1991 4
   Obituary 68
Dodd, Emma 1969- 203
Dodd, Lynley (Stuart) 1941- 132
   Earlier sketches in SATA *35, 86*
   See also CLR *62*
Dodd, Marty 1921- 142
Dodd, Quentin 1972- 137
Dodds, Bill 1952- 78
Dodds, Dayle Ann 1952- 201
   Earlier sketches in SATA *75, 150*
Doder, Josh 1968- 187
Dodge, Bertha S(anford) 1902-1995 8
Dodge, Fremont
   See Grimes, Lee
Dodge, Gil
   See Hano, Arnold
Dodge, Mary (Elizabeth) Mapes
   1831(?)-1905 100
   Earlier sketch in SATA *21*
   See also CLR *62*
Dodgson, Charles Lutwidge
   See Carroll, Lewis
Dodson, Kenneth MacKenzie 1907-1999 11
Dodson, Susan 1941- 50
   Brief entry 40
Doerrfeld, Cori 1964- 214
Dogar, Sharon 1962- 211
Dogyear, Drew
   See Gorey, Edward (St. John)
Doherty, Berlie 1943- 111
   Earlier sketch in SATA *72*
   See also CLR *21*
   See also SAAS *16*
Doherty, Charles Hugh 1913- 6
Doherty, Craig A. 1951- 169
   Earlier sketch in SATA *83*
Doherty, Katherine M(ann) 1951- 83
Doherty, Kieran 1945- 164
Dokas, Dara 1968- 216
Dokey, Cameron 1956- 97
Dolamore, Jaclyn 1982- 227
Dolan, Edward F(rancis), Jr. 1924- 94
   Brief entry 31
   Earlier sketch in SATA *45*
Dolan, Ellen M(eara) 1929-1998 88
Dolan, Sean J. 1958- 74
Dolce, J. Ellen 1948- 75
Dolch, Edward William 1889-1961 50
Dolch, Marguerite Pierce 1891-1978 50
Dollar, Diane (Hills) 1933- 57

Dolson, Hildegarde
   See Lockridge, Hildegarde (Dolson)
Domanska, Janina 1913(?)-1995 68
   Obituary 84
   Earlier sketch in SATA *6*
   See also CLR *40*
   See also SAAS *18*
Dominguez, Angel 1953- 76
Dominguez, Angela N. 1982- 219
Domino, John
   See Averill, Esther (Holden)
Domjan, Joseph (Spiri) 1907-1992 25
Domm, Jeffrey C. 1958- 84
Donahue, Dorothy 178
Donald, Rhonda Lucas 1962- 147
Donalds, Gordon
   See Shirreffs, Gordon D(onald)
Donaldson, Bryna
   See Stevens, Bryna
Donaldson, Gordon 1913-1993 64
   Obituary 76
Donaldson, Joan 1953- 227
   Earlier sketch in SATA *78*
Donaldson, Julia 1948- 226
   Earlier sketches in SATA *82, 132, 180*
Donaldson, Stephen R. 1947- 121
Donaldson, Stephen Reeder
   See Donaldson, Stephen R.
Doner, Kim 1955- 208
   Earlier sketch in SATA *91*
Doney, Todd L. W. 1959- 104
Dong-Sung, Kim 1970- 195
Dong-Sung Kim
   See Dong-Sung, Kim
Donkin, Andrew 219
Donkin, Nance (Clare) 1915- 95
Donna, Natalie 1934-1979 9
Donnelly, Elfie 1950-
   See CLR *104*
Donnelly, Jennifer 1963- 154
Donnelly, Matt 1972- 148
Donnio, Sylviane 188
Donofrio, Beverly 1950- 209
Donoghue, Emma 1969- 101
Donohue, Moira Rose 1954- 201
Donoughue, Carol 1935- 139
Donovan, Frank (Robert) 1906-1975
   Obituary 30
Donovan, Gail 1962- 217
Donovan, John 1928-1992 72
   Brief entry 29
   See also CLR *3*
Donovan, Mary Lee 1961- 86
Donovan, William
   See Berkebile, Fred D(onovan)
Donze, Mary Terese 1911- 89
Doob, Leonard W(illiam) 1909-2000 8
Doodler, Todd H.
   See Goldman, Todd Harris
Dooley, Norah 1953- 74
Dooling, Michael 1958- 220
   Earlier sketch in SATA *105*
Dor, Ana
   See Ceder, Georgiana Dorcas
Doran, Colleen 1963- 211
Dore, (Louis Christophe Paul) Gustave
   1832-1883 19
Doremus, Robert 1913-2010 30
Doren, Marion (Walker) 1928- 57
Dorenkamp, Michelle 1957- 89
Dorflinger, Carolyn 1953- 91
Dorfman, Joaquin 1979- 180
Dorfman, Joaquin Emiliano
   See Dorfman, Joaquin
Dorian, Edith M(cEwen) 1900-1983 5
Dorian, Harry
   See Hamilton, Charles (Harold St. John)
Dorian, Marguerite 7
Dorin, Patrick C(arberry) 1939- 59
   Brief entry 52
Dorman, Brandon 194

Dorman, Michael 1932- 7
Dorman, N. B. 1927- 39
Dormer, Frank W. 200
Dorris, Michael 1945-1997 75
    Obituary 94
    See also CLR 58
Dorris, Michael A.
    See Dorris, Michael
Dorris, Michael Anthony
    See Dorris, Michael
Dorritt, Susan
    See Schlein, Miriam
Dorros, Alex 1991- 194
Dorros, Arthur 1950- 168
    Earlier sketches in SATA *78, 122*
    See also CLR *42*
    See also SAAS *20*
Dorros, Arthur M.
    See Dorros, Arthur
Dorson, Richard M(ercer) 1916-1981 30
Doss, Helen (Grigsby) 1918- 20
Doss, Margot Patterson 6
dos Santos, Joyce Audy 1949- 57
    Brief entry 42
Dothers, Anne
    See Chess, Victoria (Dickerson)
Dotlich, Rebecca Kai 1951- 182
Dottig
    See Grider, Dorothy
Dotts, Maryann J. 1933- 35
Doty, Jean Slaughter 1929- 28
Doty, Roy 1922- 28
Doubtfire, Dianne (Abrams) 1918- 29
Doucet, Sharon Arms 1951- 144
    Autobiography Feature 144
    Earlier sketch in SATA *125*
Dougherty, Charles 1922- 18
Dougherty, Terri (L.) 1964- 146
Doughty, Rebecca 1955- 174
Douglas, Allen 223
Douglas, Blaise 1960- 101
Douglas, Carole Nelson 1944- 73
Douglas, Garry
    See Kilworth, Garry
Douglas, James McM.
    See Griffin, W. E. B.
Douglas, Kathryn
    See Ewing, Kathryn
Douglas, Leonard
    See Bradbury, Ray
Douglas, Lola
    See Zeises, Lara M.
Douglas, Marjory Stoneman 1890-1998 10
Douglas, Michael
    See Crichton, Michael
Douglas, Michael
    See Bright, Robert Sr.)
Douglas, Shirley Stewart
    See Tepper, Sheri S.
Douglass, Barbara 1930- 40
Douglass, Frederick 1817(?)-1895 29
Douglass, Keith
    See Cunningham, Chet
Douty, Esther M(orris) 1909-1978 8
    Obituary 23
Dow, Emily R. 1904-1987 10
Dow, Vicki
    See McVey, Vicki
Dowd, John David 1945- 78
Dowd, Siobhan 1960-2007 204
Dowdell, Dorothy (Florence) Karns 1910- ... 12
Dowden, Anne Ophelia Todd 1907-2007 7
    Obituary 180
    See also SAAS *10*
Dowdey, Landon Gerald 1923- 11
Dowdy, Mrs. Regera
    See Gorey, Edward (St. John)
Dowell, Frances O'Roark 1964- 205
    Earlier sketch in SATA *157*
Dower, Laura 1967- 185
Dowling, Terry 1947- 101

Downard, Barry 1956- 202
Downer, Ann 1960- 155
Downer, Marion 1892(?)-1971 25
Downes, Belinda 1962- 180
Downey, Fairfax D(avis) 1893-1990 3
    Obituary 66
Downey, Lisa 214
Downey, Lynn 1961- 185
Downham, Jenny 1964- 192
Downie, John 1931- 87
Downie, Mary Alice 1934- 171
    Earlier sketches in SATA *13, 87*
Downie, Mary Alice Dawe
    See Downie, Mary Alice
Downing, David A(lmon) 1958- 84
Downing, Johnette 184
Downing, Julie 1956- 148
    Earlier sketch in SATA *81*
Downing, Paula E. 1951- 80
Downing, Warwick
    See Downing, Wick
Downing, Wick 1931- 138
Dowswell, Paul 1957- 184
Doyle, A. Conan
    See Doyle, Sir Arthur Conan
Doyle, Sir Arthur Conan 1859-1930 24
    See also CLR *106*
Doyle, Brian 1935- 156
    Earlier sketches in SATA *67, 104*
    See also CLR *22*
    See also SAAS *16*
Doyle, Charlotte 1937- 178
    Earlier sketch in SATA *94*
Doyle, Charlotte Lackner
    See Doyle, Charlotte
Doyle, Conan
    See Doyle, Sir Arthur Conan
Doyle, Debra 1952- 165
    Earlier sketch in SATA *105*
Doyle, Donovan
    See Boegehold, Betty (Doyle)
Doyle, Eugenie 1952- 225
Doyle, John
    See Graves, Robert
Doyle, Malachy 1954- 165
    Earlier sketch in SATA *120*
    See also CLR *83*
Doyle, Richard 1824-1883 21
Doyle, Sir A. Conan
    See Doyle, Sir Arthur Conan
Dr. A
    See Asimov, Isaac
    and Silverstein, Alvin
    and Silverstein, Virginia B.
Dr. Alphabet
    See Morice, Dave
Dr. Fred
    See Bortz, Alfred B(enjamin)
Dr. Laura
    See Schlessinger, Laura (Catherine)
Dr. Seuss 1904-1991 100
    Obituary 67
    Earlier sketches in SATA *1, 28, 75*
    See also CLR *100*
Dr. Zed
    See Penrose, Gordon
Drabble, Margaret 1939- 48
Drackett, Phil(ip Arthur) 1922- 53
Draco, F.
    See Davis, Julia
Dracup, Angela 1943- 74
Dragisic, Patricia 116
Dragonwagon, Crescent 1952- 186
    Autobiography Feature 186
    Earlier sketches in SATA *11, 41, 75, 133*
    See also SAAS *14*
Drake, David 1945- 85
Drake, David Allen
    See Drake, David
Drake, Frank
    See Hamilton, Charles (Harold St. John)

Drake, Jane 1954- 82
Drake, Salamanda
    See Barlow, Steve
Drakeford, Dale B 1952- 113
Drakeford, Dale Benjamin
    See Drakeford, Dale B
Draper, Hastings
    See Jeffries, Roderic
Draper, Sharon
    See Draper, Sharon M.
Draper, Sharon M. 1948- 195
    Autobiography Feature 146
    Earlier sketches in SATA *98, 146*
    See also CLR *57*
Draper, Sharon Mills
    See Draper, Sharon M.
Drapier, M. B.
    See Swift, Jonathan
Drawson, Blair 1943- 126
    Earlier sketch in SATA *17*
Dray, Matt 1967- 177
Dray, Matthew Frederick
    See Dray, Matt
Dresang, Eliza (Carolyn Timberlake) 1941- . 19
Drescher, Henrik 1955- 172
    Earlier sketches in SATA *67, 105*
    See also CLR *20*
Drescher, Joan E(lizabeth) 1939- 137
    Earlier sketch in SATA *30*
Dressen-McQueen, Stacey 191
Dreves, Veronica R. 1927-1986
    Obituary 50
Drew, Patricia 1938- 15
Drew, Patricia Mary
    See Drew, Patricia
Drewery, Mary 1918- 6
Drewery, Melanie 1970- 165
Drewry, Henry N(athaniel) 1924- 138
Dreyer, Ellen 177
Drial, J. E.
    See Laird, Jean E(louise)
Drimmer, Frederick 1916-2000 60
    Obituary 124
Driskill, J. Lawrence 1920- 90
Driskill, Larry
    See Driskill, J. Lawrence
Driving Hawk, Virginia
    See Sneve, Virginia Driving Hawk
Dron, Laura
    See Matthews, L. S.
Dronzek, Laura 199
Drucker, Malka 1945- 214
    Brief entry 29
    Earlier sketches in SATA *39, 111*
Drucker, Olga Levy 1927- 79
Druitt, Tobias
    See Purkiss, Diane
Drummond, Allan 1957- 209
Drummond, Karona 1965- 220
Drummond, V(iolet) H(ilda) 1911-2000 6
Drummond, Walter
    See Silverberg, Robert
Drury, Clare Marie
    See Hoskyns-Abrahall, Clare (Constance Drury)
Drury, Roger W(olcott) 1914-1996 15
Druse, Eleanor
    See King, Stephen
Dryden, Pamela
    See St. John, Nicole
D.T., Hughes
    See Hughes, Dean
Duane, Diane (Elizabeth) 1952- 145
    Brief entry 46
    Earlier sketches in SATA *58, 95*
Dubanevich, Arlene 1950- 56
Dubelaar, Thea 1947- 60
Dubin, Jill 205
du Blane, Daphne
    See Groom, Arthur William
Duble, Kathleen Benner 1958- 164

Dubois, Claude K. 1960- *196*
DuBois, Rochelle Holt 1946- *41*
Du Bois, Shirley Graham 1907(?)-1977 .... *24*
  See Graham, Shirley
Du Bois, W. E. B. 1868-1963 .... *42*
Du Bois, William Edward Burghardt
  See Du Bois, W. E. B.
du Bois, William Pene
  See Pene du Bois, William (Sherman)
Duboise, Novella 1911-1999 .... *88*
Dubosarsky, Ursula 1961- *193*
  Earlier sketches in SATA *107, 147*
DuBose, LaRocque (Russ) 1926- *2*
Dubrovin, Vivian 1931- *139*
  Earlier sketch in SATA *65*
DuBurke, Randy *224*
  Earlier sketch in SATA *172*
Ducey, Jean Sparks 1915- *93*
Duchacek, Ivo D(uka) 1913-1988
  Obituary *55*
Du Chaillu, Paul (Belloni) 1835(?)-1903 ..... *26*
Ducharme, Dede Fox
  See Ducharme, Lilian Fox
Ducharme, Lilian Fox 1950- *122*
Ducornet, Erica 1943- *7*
Ducornet, Rikki
  See Ducornet, Erica
Duddle, Jonny 1971(?)- *219*
Duden, Jane 1947- *136*
Duder, Tessa 1940- *117*
  Earlier sketch in SATA *80*
  See also CLR *43*
  See also SAAS *23*
Dudley, Helen
  See Hope Simpson, Jacynth
Dudley, Martha Ward 1909(?)-1985
  Obituary *45*
Dudley, Nancy
  See Cole, Lois Dwight
Dudley, Robert
  See Baldwin, James
Dudley, Ruth H(ubbell) 1905-2001 .... *11*
Dudley-Smith, T.
  See Trevor, Elleston
Due, Linnea A. 1948- *64*
Dueck, Adele 1955- *97*
Dueland, Joy V(ivian) *27*
Duerr, Gisela 1968- *89*
Duey, Kathleen 1950- *199*
  Earlier sketch in SATA *132*
Dufault, Joseph Ernest Nephtali
  See James, Will(iam Roderick)
Duff, Annis (James) 1904(?)-1986
  Obituary *49*
Duff, Maggie
  See Duff, Margaret K(app)
Duff, Margaret K(app) 1916-2003 .... *37*
  Obituary *144*
Duffey, Betsy (Byars) 1953- *131*
  Earlier sketch in SATA *80*
Duffie, Charles 1960- *144*
Duffield, Katy S. 1961- *147*
Duffy, Carol Ann 1955- *165*
  Earlier sketch in SATA *95*
Duffy Stone, Heather *217*
Dugan, Jack
  See Griffin, W. E. B.
Dugan, John Kevin
  See Griffin, W. E. B.
Dugan, Karen *202*
Dugan, Karen M.
  See Dugan, Karen
Dugan, Michael (Gray) 1947- *15*
Duggan, Alfred Leo 1903-1964 .... *25*
Duggan, Maurice 1922-1974 .... *40*
  Obituary *30*
Duggan, Maurice Noel
  See Duggan, Maurice
Dugger, Elizabeth L.
  See Kanell, Beth
Duggleby, John 1952- *94*

Dugin, Andrej 1955- *77*
Dugina, Olga 1964- *77*
du Jardin, Rosamond Neal 1902-1963 .... *2*
Duka, Ivo
  See Duchacek, Ivo D(uka)
Duke, Kate 1956- *192*
  Earlier sketches in SATA *90, 148*
  See also CLR *51*
Duke, Will
  See Gault, William Campbell
Dulac, Edmund 1882-1953 .... *19*
Dumas, Alexandre (pere) 1802-1870 .... *18*
  See also CLR *134*
Dumas, Jacqueline 1946- *55*
Dumas, Philippe 1940- *119*
  Earlier sketch in SATA *52*
du Maurier, Daphne 1907-1989 .... *27*
  Obituary *60*
Dumbleton, Mike 1948- *206*
  Earlier sketches in SATA *73, 124*
Dunbar, Fiona 1961- *167*
Dunbar, Joyce 1944- *213*
  Earlier sketches in SATA *76, 112, 162*
Dunbar, Paul Laurence 1872-1906 .... *34*
Dunbar, Polly 1980(?)- *211*
  Earlier sketch in SATA *181*
Dunbar, Robert E(verett) 1926- *32*
Duncan, Alexandra
  See Moore, Ishbel (Lindsay)
Duncan, Alice Faye 1967- *168*
  Earlier sketch in SATA *95*
Duncan, Gregory
  See McClintock, Marshall
Duncan, Jane
  See Cameron, Elizabeth Jane
Duncan, Julia K.
  See Benson, Mildred
Duncan, Lois 1934- *219*
  Autobiography Feature *141*
  Earlier sketches in SATA *1, 36, 75, 133, 141*
  See also CLR *129*
  See also SAAS *2*
Duncan, Norman 1871-1916
  See YABC *1*
Duncan, Terence
  See Nolan, William F.
Duncombe, Frances (Riker) 1900-1994 .... *25*
  Obituary *82*
Dungy, Anthony
  See Dungy, Tony
Dungy, Tony 1955- *206*
Dunham, Montrew 1919- *162*
Dunham, Montrew Goetz
  See Dunham, Montrew
Dunkle, Clare B. 1964- *223*
  Earlier sketch in SATA *155*
Dunlap, Julie 1958- *84*
Dunleavy, Deborah 1951- *133*
Dunlop, Agnes M. R. (?)-1982 .... *87*
Dunlop, Eileen (Rhona) 1938- *76*
  Earlier sketch in SATA *24*
  See also SAAS *12*
Dunmore, Helen 1952- *201*
Dunn, Anne M. 1940- *107*
Dunn, Carolyn 1965- *208*
Dunn, Harvey T(homas) 1884-1952 .... *34*
Dunn, Herb
  See Gutman, Dan
Dunn, John M. (III) 1949- *93*
Dunn, Judy
  See Spangenberg, Judith Dunn
Dunn, Mary Lois 1930- *6*
Dunnahoo, Terry Janson 1927- *7*
Dunne, Jeanette 1952- *72*
Dunne, Kathleen 1933- *126*
Dunne, Marie
  See Clark, Ann Nolan
Dunne, Mary Collins 1914- *11*
Dunne, Mary Jo
  See Dunne, Mary Collins

Dunnett, Kaitlyn
  See Emerson, Kathy Lynn
Dunnett, Margaret (Rosalind) 1909-1977 ..... *42*
Dunnick, Regan *178*
Dunphy, Madeleine 1962- *219*
Dunrea, Olivier 1953- *160*
  Brief entry *46*
  Earlier sketches in SATA *59, 118*
Dunrea, Olivier Jean-Paul Dominique
  See Dunrea, Olivier
Dunstan Muller, Rachel *221*
Dunton, Dorothy 1912- *92*
Dupasquier, Philippe 1955- *151*
  Earlier sketch in SATA *86*
duPont, Lindsay *207*
duPont, Lindsay Harper
  See duPont, Lindsay
DuPrau, Jeanne 1944- *215*
  Earlier sketch in SATA *144*
Dupuy, T(revor) N(evitt) 1916-1995 .... *4*
  Obituary *86*
DuQuette, Keith 1960- *155*
  Earlier sketch in SATA *90*
Duran, Gloria 1924- *171*
Duran, Gloria Bradley
  See Duran, Gloria
Duranceau, Suzanne 1952- *162*
Durand, Delphine 1971- *200*
Durand, Hallie 1964(?)- *216*
Durango, Julia 1967- *215*
  Earlier sketch in SATA *173*
Durant, Alan 1958- *214*
  Earlier sketches in SATA *121, 165*
Durant, John 1902- *27*
Durbin, William 1951- *174*
  Earlier sketch in SATA *143*
Durell, Ann 1930- *66*
Durkee, Sarah *173*
Durney, Ryan *205*
Durrant, Lynda 1954- *212*
  Earlier sketches in SATA *96, 148*
Durrant, Sabine *210*
Durrell, Gerald (Malcolm) 1925-1995 .... *8*
  Obituary *84*
Durrell, Julie 1955- *94*
Durrett, Deanne 1940- *144*
  Earlier sketch in SATA *92*
Durst, Sarah Beth 1974- *203*
Dusikova, Maja 1946- *223*
Du Soe, Robert C. 1892-1958
  See YABC *2*
Dussling, Jennifer 1970- *143*
  Earlier sketch in SATA *96*
DuTemple, Lesley A. 1952- *113*
Dutton, Sandra *191*
Dutz
  See Davis, Mary Octavia
Duval, Katherine
  See James, Elizabeth
Duval, Kathy 1946- *181*
Duvall, Aimee
  See Thurlo, Aimee
  and Thurlo, David
Duvall, Evelyn Millis 1906- *9*
Duvall, Jill D. 1932- *102*
Duvall, Jill Donovan
  See Duvall, Jill D.
Duvoisin, Roger (Antoine) 1904-1980 .... *30*
  Obituary *23*
  Earlier sketch in SATA *2*
  See also CLR *23*
Dwiggins, Don(ald J.) 1913-1988 .... *4*
  Obituary *60*
Dwight, Allan
  See Cole, Lois Dwight
Dwyer, Deanna
  See Koontz, Dean
Dwyer, K.R.
  See Koontz, Dean
Dyck, Peter J. 1914- *75*
Dyer, Alan 1953- *218*

Dyer, Hadley 1973- 229
Dyer, James (Frederick) 1934- 37
Dyer, Jane 191
    Earlier sketch in SATA 147
Dyer, Sarah 1978- 212
Dyer, Sarah L.
    See Dyer, Sarah
Dyess, John (Foster) 1939- 76
Dygard, Thomas J. 1931-1996 97
    Obituary 92
    Earlier sketch in SATA 24
    See also SAAS 15
Dyke, John 1935- 35

E

E. V. L.
    See Lucas, E(dward) V(errall)
Eagar, Frances (Elisabeth Stuart)
    1940-1978 11
    Obituary 55
Eager, Edward (McMaken) 1911-1964 17
    See also CLR 43
Eager, George 1921- 56
Eager, George B.
    See Eager, George
Eagle, Ellen 1953- 61
Eagle, Kin
    See Adlerman, Daniel (Ezra)
    and Adlerman, Kimberly M(arie)
Eagle, Mike 1942- 11
Eamer, Claire 1947- 222
Earle, Olive L(ydia) 1888-1982 7
Earle, William
    See Johns, W(illiam) E(arle)
Earls, Nick 1963- 156
    Earlier sketch in SATA 95
Early, Jack
    See Scoppettone, Sandra
Early, Jon
    See Johns, W(illiam) E(arle)
Early, Margaret 1951- 72
Earnest, Peter 1934- 222
Earnshaw, Brian 1929- 17
Earnshaw, Micky 1939- 88
Earnshaw, Spencer Wright
    See Earnshaw, Micky
Easley, MaryAnn 94
Eason, Alethea 1957- 197
East, Jacqueline 224
Eastman, Charles A(lexander) 1858-1939
    See YABC 1
Eastman, P(hilip) D(ey) 1909-1986 33
    Obituary 46
Easton, Kelly 1960- 192
    Earlier sketch in SATA 141
Eastwick, Ivy (Ethel) O(live) 3
Eaton, Anne T(haxter) 1881-1971 32
Eaton, Anthony 1971- 167
Eaton, George L.
    See Verral, Charles Spain
Eaton, Janet
    See Givens, Janet E(aton)
Eaton, Jeanette 1886-1968 24
Eaton, Maxwell III 1981- 199
Eaton, Tom 1940- 22
Ebbeler, Jeff
    See Ebbeler, Jeffrey
Ebbeler, Jeffrey 1974- 206
Ebbitt, Carolyn Q. 1974(?)- 225
Ebel, Alex 1927- 11
Eber, Dorothy (Margaret) Harley 1930- 27
Eberhart, Sheri S.
    See Tepper, Sheri S.
Eberle, Irmengarde 1898-1979 2
    Obituary 23
Eble, Diane 1956- 74
Eboch, Chris 113
Eccles Williams, Ferelith 1920- 22

Echeverria-Bis, Olivia 217
Echeverria Gyorkos, Charmaine 216
Echlin, Kim 1955- 166
Eckblad, Edith Berven 1923- 23
Ecke, Wolfgang 1927-1983
    Obituary 37
Eckert, Allan W. 1931- 91
    Brief entry 27
    Earlier sketch in SATA 29
    See also SAAS 21
Eckert, Horst 1931- 72
    Earlier sketch in SATA 8
    See also CLR 26
Ecklar, Julia (Marie) 1964- 112
Eddings, David 1931-2009 91
Eddings, David Carroll
    See Eddings, David
Ede, Janina 1937- 33
Edell, Celeste 12
Edelman, Lily (Judith) 1915-1981 22
Edelson, Edward 1932- 51
Edens, Cooper 1945- 166
    Earlier sketches in SATA 49, 112
Edens, (Bishop) David 1926- 39
Edey, Maitland A(rmstrong) 1910-1992 25
    Obituary 71
Edgerton, Perky 196
Edgeworth, Maria 1768-1849 21
    See also CLR 153
Edgson, Alison 211
Edgy, Wardore
    See Gorey, Edward (St. John)
Edison, Theodore
    See Stratemeyer, Edward L.
Edler, Tim(othy) 1948- 56
Edmiston, Jim 1948- 80
Edmonds, I(vy) G(ordon) 1917- 8
Edmonds, Walter D(umaux) 1903-1998 27
    Obituary 99
    Earlier sketch in SATA 1
    See also SAAS 4
Edmund, Sean
    See Pringle, Laurence
Edsall, Marian (Stickney) 1920- 8
Edwards, Al
    See Nourse, Alan E(dward)
Edwards, Anne 1927- 35
Edwards, Audrey 1947- 52
    Brief entry 31
Edwards, Becky (Jane) 1966- 125
Edwards, Bertram
    See Edwards, Herbert Charles
Edwards, Bronwen Elizabeth
    See Rose, Wendy
Edwards, Cecile Pepin 1916- 25
Edwards, David 1962- 198
Edwards, Dorothy 1914-1982 88
    Obituary 31
    Earlier sketch in SATA 4
Edwards, F. E.
    See Nolan, William F.
Edwards, Frank B. 1952- 93
Edwards, Gunvor 32
Edwards, Harvey 1929- 5
Edwards, Hazel (Eileen) 1945- 135
Edwards, Herbert Charles 1912- 12
Edwards, Jane Campbell 1932- 10
Edwards, Julia
    See Stratemeyer, Edward L.
Edwards, Julie
    See Andrews, Julie
Edwards, Julie Andrews
    See Andrews, Julie
Edwards, June
    See Bhatia, Jamunadevi
Edwards, Linda Strauss 1948- 49
    Brief entry 42
Edwards, Margaret (Alexander) 1902-1988
    Obituary 56
Edwards, Michelle 1955- 152
    Earlier sketch in SATA 70

Edwards, Monica le Doux Newton
    1912-1998 12
Edwards, Olwen
    See Gater, Dilys
Edwards, Page (Lawrence, Jr.) 1941-1999 ... 59
Edwards, Pamela Duncan 189
Edwards, R. T.
    See Goulart, Ron
Edwards, Sally (Cary) 1929- 7
Edwards, Samuel
    See Gerson, Noel Bertram
Edwards, Wallace 1957(?)- 170
Edwardson, Debby Dahl 223
Eeckhout, Emmanuelle 1976- 208
Egan, E. W. 1922- 35
Egan, Edward Welstead
    See Egan, E. W.
Egan, Kerry 175
Egan, Lorraine Hopping 1960- 134
    Earlier sketch in SATA 91
Egan, Tim 1957- 191
    Earlier sketches in SATA 89, 155
Egermeier, Elsie E(milie) 1890-1986 65
Eggenberger, David 1918- 6
Eggleston, Edward 1837-1902 27
Egielski, Richard 1952- 220
    Earlier sketches in SATA 11, 49, 106, 163
Egypt, Ophelia Settle 1903-1984 16
    Obituary 38
Ehlert, Lois 1934- 172
    Earlier sketches in SATA 35, 69, 128
    See also CLR 28
Ehlert, Lois Jane
    See Ehlert, Lois
Ehling, Katalin Olah 1941- 93
Ehrenberg, Pamela 1972- 219
Ehrenfreund, Norbert 1921- 86
Ehrenhaft, Daniel 1970- 185
Ehrenhaft, Daniel Parker
    See Ehrenhaft, Daniel
Ehrhardt, Karen 1963- 184
Ehrlich, Amy 1942- 217
    Earlier sketches in SATA 25, 65, 96, 132
Ehrlich, Bettina Bauer 1903-1985 1
Ehrlich, Fred 205
Ehrlich, Fred M.D.
    See Ehrlich, Fred
Ehrlich, H. M.
    See Ziefert, Harriet
Eichenberg, Fritz 1901-1990 50
    Earlier sketch in SATA 9
Eichler, Margrit 1942- 35
Eichner, James A. 1927- 4
Eidson, Thomas 1944- 112
Eifert, Virginia (Louise) S(nider) 1911-1966 . 2
Eige, (Elizabeth) Lillian 1915- 65
Eiken, J. Melia 1967- 125
Einhorn, Edward 1970- 204
Einsel, Naiad 10
Einsel, Walter 1926- 10
Einzig, Susan 1922- 43
Eiseman, Alberta 1925- 15
Eisenberg, Azriel (Louis) 1903-1985 12
Eisenberg, Lisa 1949- 155
    Brief entry 50
    Earlier sketch in SATA 57
Eisenberg, Phyllis Rose 1924- 41
Eisner, Vivienne
    See Margolis, Vivienne
Eisner, Will 1917-2005 165
    Earlier sketch in SATA 31
Eisner, William Erwin
    See Eisner, Will
Eitzen, Allan 1928- 9
Eitzen, Ruth (Carper) 1924- 9
Ekwensi, C. O. D.
    See Ekwensi, Cyprian
Ekwensi, Cyprian 1921-2007 66
Ekwensi, Cyprian Odiatu Duaka
    See Ekwensi, Cyprian
Elam, Richard M(ace, Jr.) 1920- 9

Elborn, Andrew
  See Clements, Andrew
  and Clements, Andrew
Elboz, Stephen 1956- *152*
Eldin, Peter 1939- *154*
Eldon, Kathy 1946- *107*
Eldridge, Marion *199*
Eley, Robin *219*
Elfman, Blossom 1925- *8*
Elgin, Kathleen 1923- *39*
Elia
  See Lamb, Charles
Eliot, A. D.
  See Jewett, Sarah Orne
Eliot, Alice
  See Jewett, Sarah Orne
Eliot, Anne
  See Cole, Lois Dwight
Eliot, Dan
  See Silverberg, Robert
Elish, Dan 1960- *204*
  Earlier sketches in SATA *68, 129*
Elisha, Ron 1951- *104*
Elisofon, Eliot 1911-1973
  Obituary *21*
Elkeles, Simone 1970- *187*
Elkin, Benjamin 1911-1995 .... *3*
Elkins, Dov Peretz 1937- *5*
Ellacott, S(amuel) E(rnest) 1911- *19*
Elleman, Barbara 1934- *147*
Ellen, Jaye
  See Nixon, Joan Lowery
Eller, Scott
  See Holinger, William (Jacques)
  and Shepard, Jim
Ellery, Amanda *216*
Ellestad, Myrvin
  See Ellestad, Myrvin H.
Ellestad, Myrvin H. 1921- *120*
Elliot, Bruce
  See Field, Edward
Elliot, David 1952- *208*
  Earlier sketch in SATA *122*
Elliott, Bruce
  See Field, Edward
Elliott, David 1947- *201*
  Earlier sketch in SATA *163*
Elliott, Don
  See Silverberg, Robert
Elliott, Elizabeth Shippen Green
  See Green, Elizabeth Shippen
Elliott, Janice 1931-1995 .... *119*
Elliott, Joey
  See Houk, Randy
Elliott, Laura Malone 1957- *197*
Elliott, L.M.
  See Elliott, Laura Malone
Elliott, Louise *111*
Elliott, Mark 1949- *210*
Elliott, Odette 1939- *75*
Elliott, Patricia 1946- *176*
Elliott, Sarah M(cCarn) 1930- *14*
Elliott, (Robert) Scott 1970- *153*
Elliott, William
  See Bradbury, Ray
Elliott, Zetta *206*
Ellis, (Mary) Amabel (Nassau Strachey)
  Williams
  See Williams-Ellis, (Mary) Amabel (Nassau
  Strachey)
Ellis, Ann Dee *210*
Ellis, Anyon
  See Rowland-Entwistle, (Arthur) Theodore
  (Henry)
Ellis, Carson 1975- *190*
Ellis, Carson Friedman
  See Ellis, Carson
Ellis, Deborah 1960- *187*
  Earlier sketch in SATA *129*
Ellis, E. S.
  See Ellis, Edward S.

Ellis, Edward S. 1840-1916
  See YABC *1*
Ellis, Edward Sylvester
  See Ellis, Edward S.
Ellis, Ella Thorp 1928- *127*
  Earlier sketch in SATA *7*
  See also SAAS *9*
Ellis, Harry Bearse 1921-2004 .... *9*
Ellis, Herbert
  See Wilson, Lionel
Ellis, Julie 1961- *227*
Ellis, Mel(vin Richard) 1912-1984 .... *7*
  Obituary *39*
Ellis, Richard 1938- *130*
Ellis, Sarah 1952- *179*
  Earlier sketches in SATA *68, 131*
  See also CLR *42*
Ellison, Chris *196*
Ellison, Elizabeth Stow 1970- *209*
Ellison, Emily *114*
Ellison, Lucile Watkins 1907(?)-1979 .... *50*
  Obituary *22*
Ellison, Virginia H(owell) 1910- *4*
Ellsberg, Edward 1891-1983 .... *7*
Ellsworth, Loretta 1954- *199*
Ellsworth, Mary Ellen (Tressel) 1940- *146*
Ellwand, David 1965(?)- *213*
Elmer, Robert 1958- *154*
  Earlier sketch in SATA *99*
Elmore, (Carolyn) Patricia 1933- *38*
  Brief entry *35*
El-Moslimany, Ann P(axton) 1937- *90*
Elschner, Geraldine 1954- *183*
Elspeth
  See Bragdon, Elspeth MacDuffie
Elster, Jean Alicia 1953- *150*
Elting, Mary 1906- *88*
  Earlier sketch in SATA *2*
  See also SAAS *20*
Elvgren, Jennifer Riesmeyer *179*
Elwart, Joan Potter 1927- *2*
Elwell, Peter *220*
Elwood, Ann 1931- *55*
  Brief entry *52*
Elwood, Roger 1943-2007 .... *58*
Ely, Lesley *212*
Elya, Susan Middleton 1955- *202*
  Earlier sketches in SATA *106, 159*
Elzbieta *88*
Ember, Kathi *190*
Emberley, Barbara A. 1932- *146*
  Earlier sketches in SATA *8, 70*
  See also CLR *5*
Emberley, Barbara Anne
  See Emberley, Barbara A.
Emberley, Ed 1931- *146*
  Earlier sketches in SATA *8, 70*
  See also CLR *81*
Emberley, Edward Randolph
  See Emberley, Ed
Emberley, Michael 1960- *189*
  Earlier sketches in SATA *34, 80, 119*
Emberley, Rebecca 1958- *218*
Embry, Margaret Jacob 1919-1975 .... *5*
Emecheta, Buchi 1944- *66*
  See also CLR *158*
Emecheta, Florence Onye Buchi
  See Emecheta, Buchi
Emerson, Alice B.
  See Benson, Mildred
Emerson, Kate
  See Emerson, Kathy Lynn
Emerson, Kathy Lynn 1947- *63*
Emerson, Kevin *209*
Emerson, Ru 1944- *107*
  Earlier sketch in SATA *70*
Emerson, Sally 1952- *111*
Emerson, William K(eith) 1925- *25*
Emert, Phyllis R. 1947- *93*
Emert, Phyllis Raybin
  See Emert, Phyllis R.

Emery, Anne (McGuigan) 1907- *33*
  Earlier sketch in SATA *1*
Emmens, Carol Ann 1944- *39*
Emmett, Jonathan 1965- *188*
  Earlier sketch in SATA *138*
Emmons, Della (Florence) Gould 1890-1983
  Obituary *39*
Emond, Stephen 1979(?)- *231*
Emory, Jerry 1957- *96*
Emrich, Duncan (Black Macdonald)
  1908-1970(?) *11*
Emshwiller, Carol 1921- *174*
  Autobiography Feature *174*
Emshwiller, Carol Fries
  See Emshwiller, Carol
Emslie, M. L.
  See Simpson, Myrtle L(illias)
Ende, Michael (Andreas Helmuth)
  1929-1995 .... *130*
  Brief entry *42*
  Obituary *86*
  Earlier sketch in SATA *61*
  See also CLR *138*
Enderle, Dotti 1954- *203*
  Earlier sketch in SATA *145*
Enderle, Judith (Ann) Ross 1941- *89*
  Autobiography Feature *114*
  Earlier sketch in SATA *38*
  See also SAAS *26*
Endle, Kate *207*
Enell, Trinka (Gochenour) 1951- *79*
Enfield, Carrie
  See Smith, Susan Vernon
Engdahl, Sylvia Louise 1933- *4*
  Autobiography Feature *122*
  See also CLR *2*
  See also SAAS *5*
Engel, Christiane *231*
Engel, Diana 1947- *70*
Engelbreit, Mary 1952- *169*
Engelhart, Margaret S. 1924- *59*
Engelmann, Kim (V.) 1959- *87*
England, George Allan 1877-1936 .... *102*
Englart, Mindi Rose 1965- *146*
Engle, Eloise
  See Paananen, Eloise (Katherine)
Engle, Margarita 1951- *231*
  Earlier sketch in SATA *193*
Englebert, Victor 1933- *8*
English, James W(ilson) 1915- *37*
English, Karen *202*
Engstrom, Elizabeth 1951- *110*
Enright, D(ennis) J(oseph) 1920-2002 .... *25*
  Obituary *140*
Enright, Dominique *194*
Enright, Elizabeth (Wright) 1909-1968 .... *9*
  See also CLR *4*
Ensor, Barbara *180*
Ensor, Robert (T.) 1922- *93*
Enthoven, Sam 1974- *187*
Entwistle, (Arthur) Theodore (Henry) Rowland
  See Rowland-Entwistle, (Arthur) Theodore
  (Henry)
Enys, Sarah L.
  See Sloggett, Nellie
Epanya, Christian A(rthur Kingue) 1956- *91*
Ephraim, Shelly S(chonebaum) 1952- *97*
Ephron, Delia 1944- *197*
  Brief entry *50*
  Earlier sketch in SATA *65*
Epler, Doris M. 1928- *73*
Epp, Margaret A(gnes) 1913- *20*
Eppenstein, Louise (Kohn) 1892-1987
  Obituary *54*
Epple, Anne Orth 1927- *20*
Epstein, Anne Merrick 1931- *20*
Epstein, Beryl 1910- *31*
  Earlier sketch in SATA *1*
  See also CLR *26*
  See also SAAS *17*

Epstein, Beryl M. Williams
  See Epstein, Beryl
Epstein, Perle S(herry) 1938- 27
Epstein, Rachel S. 1941- 102
Epstein, Robin 1972- 230
Epstein, Samuel 1909-2000 31
  Earlier sketch in SATA *1*
  See also CLR *26*
  See also SAAS *17*
Erdman, Loula Grace 1905(?)-1976 .... *1*
Erdoes, Richard 1912- *33*
  Brief entry *28*
Erdogan, Buket *187*
Erdrich, Karen Louise
  See Erdrich, Louise
Erdrich, Louise 1954- *141*
  Earlier sketch in SATA *94*
Erickson, Betty J. 1923- *97*
Erickson, Betty Jean
  See Erickson, Betty J.
Erickson, John R. 1943- *136*
  Earlier sketch in SATA *70*
Erickson, Jon 1948- *141*
Erickson, Phoebe *59*
Erickson, Russell E(verett) 1932- *27*
Erickson, Sabra Rollins 1912-1995 .... *35*
Erickson, Walter
  See Fast, Howard
Ericson, Walter
  See Fast, Howard
Ericsson, Jennifer A. *170*
Erikson, Mel 1937- *31*
Eriksson, Eva 1949- *207*
Ering, Timothy Basil *176*
Erlanger, Baba
  See Trahey, Jane
Erlbach, Arlene 1948- *160*
  Earlier sketches in SATA *78, 115*
Erlbruch, Wolf 1948- *181*
Erlich, Lillian (Feldman) 1910-1983 .... *10*
Erlings, Fridrik 1962- *196*
Erlingsson, Friorik
  See Erlings, Fridrik
Ermatinger, James W. 1959- *170*
Ernest, William
  See Berkebile, Fred D(onovan)
Ernst, (Lyman) John 1940- *39*
Ernst, Kathleen
  See Ernst, Kathleen A.
Ernst, Kathleen A. 1959- *162*
Ernst, Kathryn (Fitzgerald) 1942- *25*
Ernst, Lisa Campbell 1957- *212*
  Brief entry *44*
  Earlier sketches in SATA *55, 95, 154*
Erskine, Kathryn *193*
Ervin, Janet Halliday 1923- *4*
Erwin, Will
  See Eisner, Will
Esbaum, Jill *213*
  Earlier sketch in SATA *174*
Esbensen, Barbara J(uster) 1925-1996 .... *97*
  Brief entry *53*
  Earlier sketch in SATA *62*
Eschbacher, Roger *160*
Eschmeyer, R. E. 1898-1989 .... *29*
Escriva, Vivi *182*
Eseki, Bruno
  See Mphahlele, Es'kia
Esekie, Bruno
  See Mphahlele, Es'kia
Eshmeyer, Reinhart Ernst
  See Eschmeyer, R. E.
Eskridge, Ann E. 1949- *84*
Espeland, Pamela (Lee) 1951- *128*
  Brief entry *38*
  Earlier sketch in SATA *52*
Espinosa, Laura *203*
Espinosa, Leo *203*
Espriella, Don Manuel Alvarez
  See Southey, Robert

Espy, Willard R(ichardson) 1910-1999 .... *38*
  Obituary *113*
Essakalli, Julie Klear *200*
Essrig, Harry 1912- *66*
Estep, Irene Compton *5*
Esterl, Arnica 1933- *77*
Estes, Eleanor (Ruth) 1906-1988 .... *91*
  Obituary *56*
  Earlier sketch in SATA *7*
  See also CLR *70*
Estoril, Jean
  See Allan, Mabel Esther
Estrada, Pau 1961- *200*
  Earlier sketch in SATA *74*
Etchemendy, Nancy 1952- *166*
  Earlier sketch in SATA *38*
Etchemendy, Nancy Elise Howell
  See Etchemendy, Nancy
Etchison, Birdie L(ee) 1937- *38*
Etchison, Craig 1945- *133*
Etherington, Frank 1945- *58*
Etnier, Jennifer L. *227*
Eton, Robert
  See Meynell, Laurence Walter
Ets, Marie Hall 1893-1984 .... *2*
  See also CLR *33*
Ettlinger, Doris 1950- *173*
Eugnia, Maria *222*
Eulberg, Elizabeth 1975- *227*
Eunson, (John) Dale 1904-2002 .... *5*
  Obituary *132*
Evan, Frances Y. 1951- *167*
Evanoff, Vlad 1916- *59*
Evans, Cambria 1981- *178*
Evans, Douglas 1953- *144*
  Earlier sketch in SATA *93*
Evans, Eva (Knox) 1905-1998 .... *27*
Evans, Freddi Williams 1957- *211*
  Earlier sketch in SATA *134*
Evans, Greg 1947- *143*
  Earlier sketch in SATA *73*
Evans, Hubert Reginald 1892-1986 .... *118*
  Obituary *48*
Evans, Katherine (Floyd) 1901-1964 .... *5*
Evans, Larry
  See Evans, Laurence Chubb
Evans, Laurence Chubb 1939- *88*
Evans, Lawrence Watt
  See Watt-Evans, Lawrence
Evans, Leslie 1953- *214*
Evans, Lezlie *180*
Evans, Mari 1923- *10*
Evans, Mark *19*
Evans, Nancy 1950- *65*
Evans, Nate *201*
Evans, Patricia Healy
  See Carpenter, Patricia (Healy Evans)
Evans, (Alice) Pearl 1927- *83*
Evans, Shane W. *189*
Evans, Shirlee 1931- *58*
Evans, Tabor
  See Cameron, Lou
  and Knott, William C(ecil, Jr.)
  and Wallmann, Jeffrey M(iner)
  and Whittington, Harry (Benjamin)
Evarts, Esther
  See Benson, Sally
Evarts, Hal G., (Jr.) 1915-1989 .... *6*
Everett, Gail
  See Hale, Arlene
Evernden, Margery 1916- *5*
Eversole, Robyn 1971- *74*
Eversole, Robyn H.
  See Eversole, Robyn
Eversole, Robyn Harbert
  See Eversole, Robyn
Evslin, Bernard 1922-1993 .... *83*
  Brief entry *28*
  Obituary *77*
  Earlier sketch in SATA *45*

Ewart, Claire 1958- *145*
  Earlier sketch in SATA *76*
Ewart, Franzeska G. 1950- *205*
Ewen, David 1907-1985 .... *4*
  Obituary *47*
Ewing, Juliana (Horatia Gatty) 1841-1885 ... *16*
  See also CLR *78*
Ewing, Kathryn 1921- *20*
Eyerly, Jeannette 1908-2008 .... *86*
  Obituary *196*
  Earlier sketch in SATA *4*
  See also SAAS *10*
Eyerly, Jeannette Hyde
  See Eyerly, Jeannette
Eyre, Dorothy
  See McGuire, Leslie (Sarah)
Eyre, Frank 1910-1988
  Obituary *62*
Eyre, Katherine Wigmore 1901-1970 .... *26*
Ezzell, Marilyn 1937- *42*
  Brief entry *38*

F

Fabe, Maxene 1943- *15*
Faber, Doris (Greenberg) 1924- *78*
  Earlier sketch in SATA *3*
Faber, Harold 1919-2010 .... *5*
Fabre, Jean Henri (Casimir) 1823-1915 .... *22*
Fabry, Glenn 1961- *205*
Facklam, Margaret
  See Thomas, Peggy
Facklam, Margery (Metz) 1927- *132*
  Earlier sketches in SATA *20, 85*
Fadden, David Kanietakeron *196*
Fadiman, Clifton (Paul) 1904-1999 .... *11*
  Obituary *115*
Fagan, Cary 1957- *186*
Fagan, Deva *220*
Fahs, Sophia Blanche Lyon 1876-1978 .... *102*
Failing, Barbara Larmon *182*
Fain, Sarah 1971- *204*
Fair, David 1952- *96*
Fair, Sylvia 1933- *13*
Fairfax-Lucy, Brian (Fulke Cameron-Ramsay)
  1898-1974 .... *6*
  Obituary *26*
Fairfield, Flora
  See Alcott, Louisa May
Fairlie, Gerard 1899-1983
  Obituary *34*
Fairman, Joan A(lexandra) 1935- *10*
Faithfull, Gail 1936- *8*
Falcone, L.M. 1951- *231*
  Earlier sketch in SATA *155*
Falcone, Lucy M.
  See Falcone, L.M.
Falconer, Ian 1959- *179*
  Earlier sketch in SATA *125*
  See also CLR *146*
Falconer, James
  See Kirkup, James
Falconer, Lee N.
  See May, Julian
Falkner, Brian 1962- *206*
Falkner, Leonard 1900-1977 .... *12*
Fall, Andrew
  See Arthur, Robert, (Jr.)
Fall, Thomas
  See Snow, Donald Clifford
Faller, Regis 1968- *187*
Falls, C(harles) B(uckles) 1874-1960 .... *38*
  Brief entry *27*
Falstein, Louis 1909-1995 .... *37*
Falvey, David 1982- *222*
Falwell, Cathryn 1952- *196*
Fancher, Lou 1960- *228*
  Earlier sketch in SATA *177*

Fanelli, Sara 1969- *126*
  Earlier sketch in SATA *89*
Fanning, Leonard M(ulliken) 1888-1967 .... *5*
Fantaskey, Beth 1965- *217*
Faralla, Dana 1909- *9*
Faralla, Dorothy W.
  See Faralla, Dana
Farb, Peter 1929-1980 .... *12*
  Obituary *22*
Farber, Norma 1909-1984 .... *75*
  Obituary *38*
  Earlier sketch in SATA *25*
Fardell, John 1967- *195*
Fardell, John William
  See Fardell, John
Faria, Rosana *213*
Farish, Terry 1947- *146*
  Earlier sketch in SATA *82*
Farjeon, (Eve) Annabel 1919-2004 .... *11*
  Obituary *153*
Farjeon, Eleanor 1881-1965 .... *2*
  See also CLR *34*
Farley, Carol (J.) 1936- *137*
  Earlier sketch in SATA *4*
Farley, Terri *165*
Farley, Walter (Lorimer) 1915-1989 .... *132*
  Earlier sketches in SATA *2, 43*
Farlow, James O(rville, Jr.) 1951- *75*
Farmer, Jacqueline *210*
Farmer, Nancy 1941- *161*
  Earlier sketches in SATA *79, 117*
Farmer, Patti 1948- *79*
Farmer, Penelope (Jane) 1939- *105*
  Brief entry *39*
  Earlier sketch in SATA *40*
  See also CLR *8*
  See also SAAS *22*
Farmer, Peter 1950- *38*
Farmer, Philip Jose
  See Farmer, Philip Jose
Farmer, Philip Jose 1918-2009 .... *93*
  Obituary *201*
Farmer, Philipe Jos
  See Farmer, Philip Jose
Farnham, Burt
  See Clifford, Harold B(urton)
Farnsworth, Bill 1958- *186*
  Earlier sketches in SATA *84, 135*
Farooqi, Musharraf Ali 1968- *207*
Farquhar, Margaret C(utting) 1905-1988 ...... *13*
Farquharson, Alexander 1944- *46*
Farquharson, Martha
  See Finley, Martha
Farr, Diana *82*
  Earlier sketch in SATA *3*
Farr, Finis (King) 1904-1982 .... *10*
Farr, Richard 1960- *209*
Farrar, Jill
  See Morris, Jill
Farrar, Susan Clement 1917- *33*
Farrell, Ben
  See Cebulash, Mel
Farrell, Darren *228*
Farrell, John 1951- *204*
Farrell, Patrick
  See Odgers, Sally Farrell
Farrell, Sally
  See Odgers, Sally Farrell
Farrer, Vashti *167*
Farrington, Benjamin 1891-1974
  Obituary *20*
Farrington, S(elwyn) Kip, Jr. 1904-1983 ...... *20*
Farris, Christine King 1927- *206*
Farshtey, Greg(ory T.) 1965- *148*
Farthing, Alison 1936- *45*
  Brief entry *36*
Farthing-Knight, Catherine 1933- *92*
Fassler, Joan (Grace) 1931- *11*
Fast, Howard 1914-2003 .... *7*
  Autobiography Feature *107*

Fast, Howard Melvin
  See Fast, Howard
Fasulo, Michael 1963- *83*
Fatchen, Max 1920- *84*
  Earlier sketch in SATA *20*
  See also SAAS *20*
Fate, Marilyn
  See Collins, Paul
Father Goose
  See Ghigna, Charles
Fatigati, Evelyn 1948- *24*
Fatigati, Frances Evelyn
  See Fatigati, Evelyn
Fatio, Louise 1904-1993 .... *6*
Fatus, Sophie 1957- *182*
Faulhaber, Martha 1926- *7*
Faulkner, Anne Irvin 1906- *23*
Faulkner, Frank
  See Ellis, Edward S.
Faulkner, Nancy
  See Faulkner, Anne Irvin
Faulknor, Cliff(ord Vernon) 1913- *86*
Faust, Anke 1971- *230*
Favole, Robert J(ames) 1950- *125*
Fawcett, Katie Pickard *229*
Fax, Elton Clay 1909-1993 .... *25*
Faxon, Lavinia
  See Russ, Lavinia (Faxon)
Feagles, Anita M.
  See Feagles, Anita MacRae
Feagles, Anita MacRae 1927- *9*
Feagles, Elizabeth
  See Day, Beth (Feagles)
Feague, Mildred H. 1915- *14*
Fearing, Mark 1968- *224*
Fearnley, Jan 1965- *205*
  Earlier sketch in SATA *153*
Fearrington, Ann (Peyton) 1945- *146*
Fecher, Constance
  See Heaven, Constance (Christina)
Feder, Chris Welles 1938- *81*
Feder, Harriet K. 1928- *73*
Feder, Paula (Kurzband) 1935- *26*
Federici, Debbie 1965- *175*
Federici, Debbie Tanner
  See Federici, Debbie
Feelings, Muriel 1938- *16*
  See also CLR *5*
  See also SAAS *8*
Feelings, Muriel Lavita Grey
  See Feelings, Muriel
Feelings, Thomas 1933-2003 .... *69*
  Obituary *148*
  Earlier sketch in SATA *8*
  See also CLR *58*
  See also SAAS *19*
Feelings, Tom
  See Feelings, Thomas
Fehler, Gene 1940- *201*
  Earlier sketch in SATA *74*
Fehrenbach, T(heodore) R(eed, Jr.) 1925- *33*
Feiffer, Jules 1929- *201*
  Earlier sketches in SATA *8, 61, 111, 157*
Feiffer, Jules Ralph
  See Feiffer, Jules
Feiffer, Kate 1964- *206*
  Earlier sketch in SATA *170*
Feig, Barbara Krane 1937- *34*
Feig, Paul *221*
Feikema, Feike
  See Manfred, Frederick (Feikema)
Feil, Hila 1942- *12*
Feilen, John
  See May, Julian
Feinberg, Barbara Jane 1938- *123*
  Earlier sketch in SATA *58*
Feinberg, Barbara Silberdick
  See Feinberg, Barbara Jane
Feinstein, John 1956- *195*
  Earlier sketch in SATA *163*
Feldman, Anne (Rodgers) 1939- *19*

Feldman, Elane *79*
Feldman, Eve B. *221*
Feldman, Jody *200*
Felin, M. Sindy *194*
Felix
  See Vincent, Felix
Fell, Derek 1939- *167*
Fell, Derek John
  See Fell, Derek
Fellowes, Julian 1950- *198*
Fellows, Muriel H. *10*
Fellows, Stan 1957- *177*
Fellows, Stanley
  See Fellows, Stan
Felsen, Henry Gregor 1916-1995 .... *1*
  See also SAAS *2*
Felstead, Cathie 1954- *192*
Feltenstein, Arlene 1934- *119*
Feltenstine, Arlene H.
  See Feltenstein, Arlene
Felton, Harold William 1902-1991 .... *1*
Felton, Ronald Oliver 1909- *3*
Felts, Shirley 1934- *33*
Felts, Susannah 1973- *214*
Fenderson, Lewis H., Jr. 1907-1983 .... *47*
  Obituary *37*
Fenner, Carol (Elizabeth) 1929-2002 .... *89*
  Obituary *132*
  Earlier sketch in SATA *7*
  See also SAAS *24*
Fenner, Phyllis R(eid) 1899-1982 .... *1*
  Obituary *29*
Fensham, Elizabeth *169*
Fenten, Barbara D(oris) 1935- *26*
Fenten, D(onald) X. 1932- *4*
Fenton, Carroll Lane 1900-1969 .... *5*
Fenton, Edward 1917-1995 .... *7*
  Obituary *89*
Fenton, Joe *213*
Fenton, Mildred Adams 1899-1995 .... *21*
Fenwick, Patti
  See Grider, Dorothy
Feravolo, Rocco Vincent 1922- *10*
Ferber, Brenda A. 1967- *184*
Ferber, Edna 1887-1968 .... *7*
Fergus, Charles *114*
Ferguson, Alane 1957- *182*
  Earlier sketch in SATA *85*
Ferguson, Bob
  See Ferguson, Robert Bruce
Ferguson, Cecil 1931- *45*
Ferguson, Peter 1968- *199*
Ferguson, Robert Bruce 1927-2001 .... *13*
Ferguson, Sarah 1959- *180*
  Earlier sketches in SATA *66, 110*
Ferguson, Sarah Margaret
  See Ferguson, Sarah
Ferguson, Walter (W.) 1930- *34*
Fergusson, Erna 1888-1964 .... *5*
Fermi, Laura 1907-1977 .... *6*
  Obituary *28*
Fern, Eugene A. 1919-1987 .... *10*
  Obituary *54*
Fern, Tracey E. *202*
Fernandes, Eugenie 1943- *205*
  Earlier sketches in SATA *77, 139*
Fernandez, Laura 1960- *171*
Ferraiolo, Jack D. *208*
Ferrari, Maria *123*
Ferrari, Michael *223*
Ferrari, Michael J.
  See Ferrari, Michael
Ferreiro, Carmen 1958- *158*
Ferrell, Nancy Warren 1932- *70*
Ferrer, Isabel
  See Riu, Isabel Ferrer
Ferri, Giuliano 1965- *197*
Ferrier, Lucy
  See Penzler, Otto
Ferris, Helen Josephine 1890-1969 .... *21*

Ferris, James Cody
See McFarlane, Leslie
Ferris, Jean 1939- 202
Brief entry 50
Earlier sketches in SATA *56, 105, 149*
Ferris, Jeri Chase 1937- 84
Ferry, Charles 1927- 92
Earlier sketch in SATA *43*
See also CLR 34
See also SAAS 20
Fetz, Ingrid 1915- 30
Feydy, Anne Lindbergh
See Sapieyevski, Anne Lindbergh
Fiammenghi, Gioia 1929- 66
Earlier sketch in SATA *9*
Fiarotta, Noel
See Ficarotta, Noel
Fiarotta, Phyllis
See Ficarotta, Phyllis
Ficarotta, Noel 1944- 15
Ficarotta, Phyllis 1942- 15
Fichter, George S. 1922-1993 7
Ficocelli, Elizabeth 189
Fidler, Kathleen (Annie) 1899-1980 87
Obituary 45
Earlier sketch in SATA *3*
Fiedler, Jean(nette Feldman) 4
Fiedler, Joseph Daniel 159
Fiedler, Lisa 185
Field, Dorothy 1944- 97
Field, Edward 1924- 109
Earlier sketch in SATA *8*
Field, Elinor Whitney 1889-1980
Obituary 28
Field, Eugene 1850-1895 16
Field, Gans T.
See Wellman, Manly Wade
Field, James 1959- 113
Field, Peter
See Drago, Harry Sinclair
and Dresser, Davis
and Mann, E(dward) B(everly)
Field, Rachel (Lyman) 1894-1942 15
See also CLR 21
Fielding, Kate
See Oldfield, Jenny
Fields, Bryan W. 1958(?)- 188
Fields, Lisa 1984(?)- 216
Fields, Terri 1948- 191
Fields, T.S.
See Fields, Terri
Fienberg, Anna 1956- 183
Earlier sketch in SATA *112*
Fiery, Ann
See Barrows, Annie
Fife, Dale (Odile Hollerbach) 1901- 18
Fighter Pilot, A
See Johnston, H(ugh) A(nthony) S(tephen)
Figler, Jeanie 1949- 123
Figley, Marty Rhodes 1948- 158
Earlier sketch in SATA *88*
Figueredo, D(anilo) H. 1951- 155
Figueroa, Pablo 1938- 9
Fijan, Carol 1918- 12
Filderman, Diane E(lizabeth) 1959- 87
Files, Meg 1946- 107
Fillmore, Parker H(oysted) 1878-1944
See YABC 1
Filstrup, Chris
See Filstrup, E(dward) Christian
Filstrup, E(dward) Christian 1942- 43
Filstrup, Janie
See Merrill, Jane
Finbarr, Desmond
See Zobel Nolan, Allia
Finchler, Judy 1943- 230
Earlier sketch in SATA *93*
Finder, Martin
See Salzmann, Siegmund
Findlay, Jamieson 1958- 169
Findon, Joanne 1957- 161

Fine, Anne 1947- 197
Earlier sketches in SATA *29, 72, 111, 160*
See also CLR 25
See also SAAS 15
Fine, Edith Hope 169
Fine, Howard 1961- 181
Fine, Jane
See Ziefert, Harriet
Finger, Charles J(oseph) 1869(?)-1941 42
Fink, William B(ertrand) 1916- 22
Finke, Blythe Foote 1922- 26
Finkel, George (Irvine) 1909-1975 8
Finkelstein, Norman H. 1941- 220
Earlier sketches in SATA *73, 137*
Finkelstein, Norman Henry
See Finkelstein, Norman H.
Finlay, Alice Sullivan 1946- 82
Finlay, Winifred Lindsay Crawford
(McKissack) 1910-1989 23
Finlayson, Ann 1925- 8
Finley, Martha 1828-1909 43
See also CLR 148
Finley, Mary Peace 1942- 83
Finn, Mary 208
Finney, Jack 1911-1995 109
Finney, Patricia 1958- 163
Finney, Shan 1944- 65
Finney, Walter Braden
See Finney, Jack
Firer, Ben Zion
See Firer, Benzion
Firer, Benzion 1914- 64
Fireside, Bryna J. 1932- 73
Firmin, Charlotte 1954- 29
Firmin, Peter 1928- 58
Earlier sketch in SATA *15*
Firth, Barbara 179
Fischbach, Julius 1894-1988 10
Fischer, John
See Fluke, Joanne
Fischer, R.J.
See Fluke, Joanne
Fischer, Scott M. 1971- 195
Fischer-Nagel, Andreas 1951- 56
Fischer-Nagel, Heiderose 1956- 56
Fischler, Shirley (Walton) 66
Fischler, Stan(ley I.) 66
Brief entry 36
Fischtrom, Harvey 1933-1974 3
Fishback, Margaret
See Antolini, Margaret Fishback
Fishbone, Greg R. 195
Fisher, Aileen (Lucia) 1906-2002 73
Obituary 143
Earlier sketches in SATA *1, 25*
See also CLR 49
Fisher, Barbara 1940- 44
Brief entry 34
Fisher, Carolyn 1968- 154
Fisher, Catherine 1957- 155
Fisher, Chris 1958- 80
Fisher, Clavin C(argill) 1912- 24
Fisher, Cynthia 195
Fisher, Dorothy (Frances) Canfield 1879-1958
See YABC 1
See also CLR 71
Fisher, Gary L. 1949- 86
Fisher, John 1909-1996 15
Fisher, John Oswald Hamilton
See Fisher, John
Fisher, Laura Harrison 1934- 5
Fisher, Leonard Everett 1924- 176
Autobiography Feature 122
Earlier sketches in SATA *4, 34, 73, 120*
See also CLR 18
See also SAAS 1
Fisher, Lois I. 1948- 38
Brief entry 35
Fisher, Margery (Turner) 1913-1992 20
Obituary 74
Fisher, Marshall Jon 1963- 113

Fisher, Nikki
See Strachan, Ian
Fisher, Robert (Tempest) 1943- 47
Fisher, Suzanne
See Staples, Suzanne Fisher
Fisher, Valorie 214
Earlier sketch in SATA *177*
Fishman, Cathy Goldberg 1951- 106
Fisk, Nicholas
See Higginbottom, David
Fisk, Pauline 1948- 160
Earlier sketch in SATA *66*
Fiske, Tarleton
See Bloch, Robert (Albert)
Fisscher, Catharina G. M. 1958- 142
Fisscher, Tiny
See Fisscher, Catharina G. M.
Fitch, Clarke
See Sinclair, Upton
Fitch, John IV
See Cormier, Robert
Fitch, Sheree 1956- 178
Earlier sketch in SATA *108*
Fitschen, Dale 1937- 20
Fitzalan, Roger
See Trevor, Elleston
FitzGerald, Captain Hugh
See Baum, L. Frank
FitzGerald, Cathleen 1932-1987
Obituary 50
Fitzgerald, Dawn 175
Fitzgerald, Edward Earl 1919-2001 20
Fitzgerald, F(rancis) A(nthony) 1940- 15
Fitzgerald, Joanne 1956- 198
Fitzgerald, John D(ennis) 1907(?)-1988 20
Obituary 56
See also CLR 1
Fitzgerald, Merni Ingrassia 1955- 53
Fitzgibbon, Terry 1948- 121
Fitzhardinge, Joan Margaret 1912- 73
Earlier sketch in SATA *2*
See also CLR 5
See also SAAS 3
Fitzhugh, Louise (Perkins) 1928-1974 45
Obituary 24
Earlier sketch in SATA *1*
See also CLR 72
Fitzhugh, Percy Keese 1876-1950 65
Fitzmaurice, Kathryn 217
Fitzpatrick, Becca 1979- 224
Fitzpatrick, Marie-Louise 1962- 189
Earlier sketch in SATA *125*
FitzRalph, Matthew
See McInerny, Ralph
Fitz-Randolph, Jane (Currens) 1915- 51
Fitzsimons, Cecilia 1952- 97
Fitzsimons, Cecilia A.L.
See Fitzsimons, Cecilia
Flack, Marjorie 1897-1958 100
See also YABC 2
See also CLR 28
Flack, Naomi John White -1999 40
Brief entry 35
Flake, Sharon G. 166
Flanagan, John 1944- 180
Flanagan, John Anthony
See Flanagan, John
Flannery, Kate
See De Goldi, Kate
Flatt, Lizann 1966- 88
Fleagle, Gail S(hatto) 1940- 117
Fleetwood, Jenni 1947- 80
Fleischer, Jane
See Oppenheim, Joanne
Fleischhauer-Hardt, Helga 1936- 30
Fleischman, Albert Sidney
See Fleischman, Sid
Fleischman, John 1948- 145

Fleischman, Paul 1952- *156*
  Brief entry *32*
  Earlier sketches in SATA *39, 72, 110*
  See also CLR *66*
  See also SAAS *20*
Fleischman, Sid 1920-2010 .... *185*
  Earlier sketches in SATA *8, 59, 96, 148*
  See also CLR *15*
Fleischner, Jennifer 1956- *188*
  Earlier sketch in SATA *93*
Fleisher, Paul 1948- *132*
  Earlier sketch in SATA *81*
Fleisher, Robbin 1951-1977 .... *52*
  Brief entry *49*
Fleishman, Seymour 1918- *66*
  Brief entry *32*
Fleming, A. A.
  See Arthur, Robert, (Jr.)
Fleming, Alice Mulcahey 1928- *9*
Fleming, Candace 1962- *225*
  Earlier sketches in SATA *94, 143, 190*
Fleming, Denise 1950- *173*
  Earlier sketches in SATA *81, 126*
Fleming, Elizabeth P. 1888-1985
  Obituary *48*
Fleming, Ian 1908-1964 .... *9*
Fleming, Ian Lancaster
  See Fleming, Ian
Fleming, Ronald Lee 1941- *56*
Fleming, Sally
  See Walker, Sally M.
Fleming, Stuart
  See Knight, Damon (Francis)
Fleming, Susan 1932- *32*
Fleming, Thomas 1927- *8*
Fleming, Thomas James
  See Fleming, Thomas
Fleming, Virginia (Edwards) 1923- *84*
Flesch, Y.
  See Flesch, Yolande
Flesch, Yolande 1950- *55*
Flesch, Yolande Catarina
  See Flesch, Yolande
Fletcher, Charlie *220*
Fletcher, Charlie May Hogue 1897-1977 .... *3*
Fletcher, Colin 1922-2007 .... *28*
Fletcher, Dirk
  See Cunningham, Chet
Fletcher, George U.
  See Pratt, (Murray) Fletcher
Fletcher, Helen Jill 1910- *13*
Fletcher, Ralph 1953- *195*
  Earlier sketches in SATA *105, 149*
  See also CLR *104*
Fletcher, Ralph J.
  See Fletcher, Ralph
Fletcher, Richard E. 1917(?)-1983
  Obituary *34*
Fletcher, Rick
  See Fletcher, Richard E.
Fletcher, Susan 1951- *181*
  Earlier sketches in SATA *70, 110*
Fletcher, Susan Clemens
  See Fletcher, Susan
Fleur, Paul
  See Pohl, Frederik
Flexner, James Thomas 1908-2003 .... *9*
Flinn, Alex 1966- *198*
  Earlier sketch in SATA *159*
Flint, Helen 1952- *102*
Flint, Russ 1944- *74*
Flitner, David, Jr. 1949- *7*
Flitner, David Perkins
  See Flitner, David, Jr.
Floca, Brian *190*
  Earlier sketch in SATA *155*
Floethe, Louise Lee 1913-1988 .... *4*
Floethe, Richard 1901-1998 .... *4*
Floherty, John Joseph 1882-1964 .... *25*
Flood, Bo
  See Flood, Nancy Bo

Flood, Nancy Bo 1945- *130*
Flood, Pansie Hart 1964- *140*
Flood, William 1942- *129*
Flooglebuckle, Al
  See Spiegelman, Art
Flora, James (Royer) 1914-1998 .... *30*
  Obituary *103*
  Earlier sketch in SATA *1*
  See also SAAS *6*
Flores-Galbis, Enrique 1952- *186*
Florian, Douglas 1950- *177*
  Earlier sketches in SATA *19, 83, 125*
Flory, Jane Trescott 1917- *22*
Flournoy, Valerie 1952- *95*
Flournoy, Valerie Rose
  See Flournoy, Valerie
Flowerdew, Phyllis -1994 .... *33*
Flowers, Pam 1946- *136*
Flowers, Sarah 1952- *98*
Floyd, Gareth 1940- *62*
  Brief entry *31*
Fluchere, Henri 1914-1991 .... *40*
Fluke, Joanne 1943- *88*
Flutsztejn-Gruda, Ilona 1930- *170*
Flynn, Barbara 1928- *9*
Flynn, Jackson
  See Bensen, Donald R.
  and Shirreffs, Gordon D(onald)
Flynn, Nicholas
  See Odgers, Sally Farrell
Flynn, Pat 1968- *214*
Flynn, Patrick
  See Flynn, Pat
Flynn, Rachel 1953- *171*
  Earlier sketch in SATA *109*
Flynn, Warren (G.) 1950- *154*
Fodor, R. V. 1944- *25*
Fodor, Ronald Victor
  See Fodor, R. V.
Fogelin, Adrian 1951- *175*
  Earlier sketch in SATA *129*
Foley, (Anna) Bernice Williams 1902-1987 . *28*
Foley, Greg E. 1969- *190*
Foley, June 1944- *44*
Foley, (Mary) Louise Munro 1933- *106*
  Brief entry *40*
  Earlier sketch in SATA *54*
Foley, Rae
  See Denniston, Elinore
Folke, Will
  See Bloch, Robert (Albert)
Follett, Helen Thomas 1884(?)-1970
  Obituary *27*
Folsom, Franklin (Brewster) 1907-1995 .... *5*
  Obituary *88*
Folsom, Michael (Brewster) 1938-1990 .... *40*
  Obituary *88*
Fombelle, Timothee de 1973- *218*
Fontenot, Mary Alice 1910-2003 .... *91*
  Obituary *209*
  Earlier sketch in SATA *34*
Fontes, Justine *172*
Fontes, Ron 1952- *183*
Foon, Dennis 1951- *119*
Fooner, Michael *22*
Foote, Timothy (Gilson) 1926- *52*
Forberg, Ati
  See Forberg, Beate Gropius
Forberg, Beate Gropius 1925- *22*
Forbes, Anna 1954- *101*
Forbes, Bryan 1926- *37*
Forbes, Cabot L.
  See Hoyt, Edwin P(almer), Jr.
Forbes, Esther 1891-1967 .... *100*
  Earlier sketch in SATA *2*
  See also CLR *147*
Forbes, Graham B. *1*
Forbes, Kathryn
  See McLean, Kathryn (Anderson)
Forbes, Robert
  See Arthur, Robert, (Jr.)

Ford, A.G. *231*
Ford, Albert Lee
  See Stratemeyer, Edward L.
Ford, Barbara *56*
  Brief entry *34*
Ford, Bernette *212*
Ford, Bernette G.
  See Ford, Bernette
Ford, B.G.
  See Ford, Bernette
Ford, Brian J(ohn) 1939- *49*
Ford, Carolyn 1938- *98*
Ford, Carolyn Mott
  See Ford, Carolyn
Ford, Christine 1953- *176*
Ford, David
  See Baldacci, David
  and Baldacci, David
Ford, David B.
  See Baldacci, David
Ford, David Baldacci
  See Baldacci, David
Ford, Elbur
  See Hibbert, Eleanor Alice Burford
Ford, Ellen 1949- *89*
Ford, George (Jr.) *31*
Ford, Hilary
  See Youd, Samuel
Ford, Hildegarde
  See Morrison, Velma Ford
Ford, Jerome W. 1949- *78*
Ford, Jerry
  See Ford, Jerome W.
Ford, John C. 1971- *221*
Ford, Juwanda G(ertrude) 1967- *102*
Ford, Marcia
  See Radford, Ruby L(orraine)
Ford, Nancy K(effer) 1906-1961
  Obituary *29*
Ford, Peter 1936- *59*
Ford, S. M.
  See Uhlig, Susan
Forde, Catherine 1961- *170*
Foreman, Mark *199*
Foreman, Michael 1938- *216*
  Earlier sketches in SATA *2, 73, 129, 135, 184*
  See also CLR *32*
  See also SAAS *21*
Foreman, Wilmoth 1939- *153*
Forest, Antonia 1915-2003 .... *29*
  Obituary *149*
Forest, Dial
  See Gault, William Campbell
Forest, Heather 1948- *185*
  Earlier sketch in SATA *120*
Forester, C. S. 1899-1966 .... *13*
Forester, Cecil Scott
  See Forester, C. S.
Forester, Victoria *214*
Forler, Nan *223*
Forman, Brenda 1936- *4*
Forman, James
  See Forman, James D.
Forman, James D. 1932-2009 .... *70*
  Earlier sketch in SATA *8*
Forman, James Douglas
  See Forman, James D.
Forman, Mark L.
  See Forman, M.L.
Forman, M.L. 1964- *215*
Forman, Ruth 1970- *186*
Formento, Alison *228*
Forrest, Elizabeth
  See Salsitz, Rhondi Vilott
Forrest, Mary
  See Pausacker, Jenny
Forrest, Sybil
  See Markun, Patricia Maloney
Forrestal, Elaine 1941- *165*
  Earlier sketch in SATA *117*

Forrester, Frank H. 1919(?)-1986
  Obituary 52
Forrester, Helen
  See Bhatia, Jamunadevi
Forrester, Jade
  See Pausacker, Jenny
Forrester, Marian
  See Schachtel, Roger
Forrester, Sandra 1949- 166
  Earlier sketch in SATA 90
Forrester, Victoria 1940- 40
  Brief entry 35
Forsee, (Frances) Aylesa -1986 1
Forsey, Chris 1950- 59
Forshay-Lunsford, Cin 1965- 60
Forster, E. M. 1879-1970 57
Forster, Edward Morgan
  See Forster, E. M.
Forsyth, Kate 1966- 154
Fort, Paul
  See Stockton, Francis Richard
Forte, Maurizio 1961- 110
Fortey, Richard 1946- 109
Fortey, Richard A.
  See Fortey, Richard
Fortey, Richard Alan
  See Fortey, Richard
Forth, Melissa D(eal) 96
Fortnum, Peggy
  See Nuttall-Smith, Margaret Emily Noel
Fortune, Eric 182
Forward, Robert L(ull) 1932-2002 82
Foster, Alan Dean 1946- 70
Foster, Brad W. 1955- 34
Foster, Doris Van Liew 1899-1993 10
Foster, E(lizabeth) C(onnell) 1902- 9
Foster, Elizabeth 1902- 12
Foster, Elizabeth 1905-1963 10
Foster, F. Blanche 1919- 11
Foster, G(eorge) Allen 1907-1969 26
Foster, Genevieve (Stump) 1893-1979 2
  Obituary 23
  See also CLR 7
Foster, Gerald L. 198
Foster, Hal
  See Foster, Harold
Foster, Harold 1892-1982 31
Foster, Jeanne
  See Williams, Jeanne
Foster, John
  See Foster, John L(ouis)
  and Furcolo, Foster
Foster, John (Thomas) 1925- 8
Foster, John L(ouis) 1941- 102
Foster, Juliana 196
Foster, Laura Louise (James) 1918- 6
Foster, Leila Merrell 1929- 73
Foster, Lynne 1937- 74
Foster, Margaret Lesser 1899(?)-1979
  Obituary 21
Foster, Marian Curtis 1909-1978 23
Foster, Mark 1961- 197
Foster, Sally 58
Fotheringham, Edwin 201
Foulds, E. V.
  See Foulds, Elfrida Vipont
Foulds, Elfrida Vipont 1902-1992 52
Fountas, Angela Jane 180
Fourie, Corlia 1944- 91
Fourth Brother, The
  See Aung, (Maung) Htin
Fowke, Edith (Margaret) 1913-1996 14
Fowles, John 1926-2005 22
  Obituary 171
Fowles, John Robert
  See Fowles, John
Fowles, Shelley 1956- 205
Fox, Aileen 1907-2005 58
  Obituary 170
Fox, Aileen Mary
  See Fox, Aileen

Fox, Annie 1950- 175
Fox, Charles Philip 1913-2003 12
  Obituary 150
Fox, Christyan 188
Fox, Diane 188
Fox, Eleanor
  See St. John, Wylly Folk
Fox, Fontaine Talbot, Jr. 1884-1964
  Obituary 23
Fox, Fred 1903(?)-1981
  Obituary 27
Fox, Freeman
  See Hamilton, Charles (Harold St. John)
Fox, Geoffrey 1941- 73
Fox, Grace
  See Anderson, Grace Fox
Fox, Helen 1962- 181
Fox, Karen C. 1969- 229
Fox, Larry 30
Fox, Lee 1958- 227
Fox, Lorraine 1922-1976 27
  Earlier sketch in SATA 11
Fox, Louisa
  See Kroll, Virginia L.
Fox, Mary Virginia 1919- 152
  Brief entry 39
  Earlier sketches in SATA 44, 88
Fox, Mem 1946- 211
  Earlier sketches in SATA 51, 103, 155
  See also CLR 80
Fox, Merrion Frances
  See Fox, Mem
Fox, Michael W(ilson) 1937- 15
Fox, Norma Diane
  See Mazer, Norma Fox
Fox, Paula 1923- 167
  Earlier sketches in SATA 17, 60, 120
  See also CLR 96
Fox, Robert J. 1927- 33
Fox, Robert Joseph
  See Fox, Robert J.
Fox-Davies, Sarah 1956- 199
Foyt, Victoria .... 187.
Fradin, Dennis
  See Fradin, Dennis Brindell
Fradin, Dennis Brindell 1945- 185
  Earlier sketches in SATA 29, 90, 135
Fradin, Judith Bloom 1945- 185
  Earlier sketches in SATA 90, 152
Frailey, Paige (Menefee) 1965- 82
Frame, Janet 1924-2004 119
Frame, Janet Paterson
  See Frame, Janet
Frame, Paul 1913-1994 60
  Brief entry 33
  Obituary 83
Frances, Miss
  See Horwich, Frances R(appaport)
Franchere, Ruth 18
Francis, Charles
  See Holme, Bryan
Francis, Dee
  See Haas, Dorothy F.
Francis, Dorothy 1926- 127
  Earlier sketch in SATA 10
Francis, Dorothy B.
  See Francis, Dorothy
Francis, Dorothy Brenner
  See Francis, Dorothy
Francis, Guy 225
Francis, Jaye
  See Pausacker, Jenny
Francis, Pamela (Mary) 1926- 11
Franck, Eddie
  See Cooke, Frank E.
Franco, Betsy 223
  Earlier sketches in SATA 150, 188
Franco, Eloise (Bauder) 1910- 62
Franco, Johan (Henri Gustave) 1908-1988 ... 62
Franco, Marjorie 38
Franco, Tom 224

Francois, Andre 1915-2005 25
Francoise
  See Seignobosc, Francoise
Frank, Anne 1929-1945 87
  Brief entry 42
  See also CLR 101
Frank, Annelies Marie
  See Frank, Anne
Frank, Daniel B. 1956- 55
Frank, Emily R.
  See Frank, E.R.
Frank, E.R. 1967- 157
Frank, Helene
  See Vautier, Ghislaine
Frank, Hillary 1976- 148
Frank, John 199
Frank, Josette 1893-1989 10
  Obituary 63
Frank, Lucy 1947- 166
  Earlier sketch in SATA 94
Frank, Mary 1933- 34
Frank, R., Jr.
  See Ross, Frank (Xavier), Jr.
Frankau, Mary Evelyn Atkinson 1899-1974 .. 4
Frankel, Alona 1937- 66
Frankel, Bernice 9
Frankel, Edward 1910- 44
Frankel, Ellen 1951- 78
Frankel, Julie 1947- 40
  Brief entry 34
Frankenberg, Robert 1911- 22
Frankland, David 207
Franklin, Cheryl J. 1955- 70
Franklin, Harold 1926- 13
Franklin, Kristine L. 1958- 124
  Earlier sketch in SATA 80
Franklin, Lance
  See Lantz, Francess L(in)
Franklin, Madeleine
  See L'Engle, Madeleine
Franklin, Madeleine L'Engle
  See L'Engle, Madeleine
Franklin, Madeleine L'Engle Camp
  See L'Engle, Madeleine
Franklin, Max
  See Deming, Richard
Franklin, Steve
  See Stevens, Franklin
Franson, Leanne 1963- 223
  Earlier sketch in SATA 111
Franson, Scott E. 1966- 192
Franzen, Nils-Olof 1916- 10
Frascino, Edward 48
  Brief entry 33
  See also SAAS 9
Frasconi, Antonio 1919- 131
  Earlier sketches in SATA 6, 53
  See also SAAS 11
Fraser, Betty
  See Fraser, Elizabeth Marr
Fraser, Elizabeth Marr 1928- 31
Fraser, Eric (George) 1902-1983 38
Fraser, Mary Ann 1959- 214
  Earlier sketches in SATA 76, 137
  See also SAAS 23
Fraser, Wynnette (McFaddin) 1925- 90
Frasier, Debra 1953- 182
  Earlier sketches in SATA 69, 112
Fraustino, Lisa Rowe 1961- 146
  Autobiography Feature 146
  Earlier sketch in SATA 84
Frazee, Marla 1958- 225
  Earlier sketches in SATA 105, 151, 187
Frazer, Megan 1977- 221
Frazetta, Frank 1928-2010 58
Frazier, Craig 1955- 221
  Earlier sketch in SATA 177
Frazier, Neta (Osborn) Lohnes 1890-1990 7
Frazier, Sundee T. 1968- 198
Frazier, Sundee Tucker
  See Frazier, Sundee T.

Frederic, Mike
    See Cox, William R(obert)
Frederick, Heather Vogel 207
Fredericks, Anthony D. 1947- 113
Freed, Alvyn M. 1913-1993 22
Freedman, Benedict 1919- 27
Freedman, Claire 227
    Earlier sketch in SATA 185
Freedman, Deborah 1960- 191
Freedman, Jeff 1953- 90
Freedman, Nancy 1920-2010 27
Freedman, Russell 1929- 175
    Earlier sketches in SATA 16, 71, 123
    See also CLR 71
Freedman, Russell Bruce
    See Freedman, Russell
Freeman, Barbara C. 1906-1999 28
Freeman, Barbara Constance
    See Freeman, Barbara C.
Freeman, Bill
    See Freeman, William Bradford
Freeman, Don 1908-1978 17
    See also CLR 90
Freeman, Ira Maximilian 1905-1987 21
Freeman, Kimberley
    See Wilkins, Kim
Freeman, Laura 200
Freeman, Lucy (Greenbaum) 1916-2004 24
Freeman, Mae 1907-1985 25
Freeman, Mae Blacker
    See Freeman, Mae
Freeman, Marcia S. 1937- 102
Freeman, Marcia Sheehan
    See Freeman, Marcia S.
Freeman, Martha 1956- 201
    Earlier sketches in SATA 101, 152
Freeman, Nancy 1932- 61
Freeman, Peter J.
    See Calvert, Patricia
Freeman, Sarah (Caroline) 1940- 66
Freeman, Tor 1977- 164
Freeman, VicToria
    See Freeman, Tor
Freeman, William Bradford 1938- 58
    Brief entry 48
Fregosi, Claudia (Anne Marie) 1946- 24
Freitas, Donna 1972- 205
French, Allen 1870-1946
    See YABC 1
French, Dorothy Kayser 1926- 5
French, Fiona 1944- 132
    Earlier sketches in SATA 6, 75
    See also CLR 37
    See also SAAS 21
French, Jackie 186
    Autobiography Feature 139
    Earlier sketches in SATA 108, 139
    See French, Jackie Anne
    and French, Jacqueline Anne
French, Kathryn
    See Mosesson, Gloria R(ubin)
French, Martin 176
French, Michael 1944- 49
    Brief entry 38
French, Paul
    See Asimov, Isaac
French, S. Terrell 216
French, Simon 1957- 147
    Earlier sketch in SATA 86
French, Vivian 209
    Earlier sketch in SATA 165
Frenette, Liza 126
Freschet, Gina 1960- 175
    Earlier sketch in SATA 139
Frewer, Glyn (M.) 1931- 11
Frey, Darcy 98
Freymann, Saxton 1958(?)- 178
Freymann-Weyr, Garret 1965- 145
Freymann-Weyr, Rhoda Garret Michaela
    See Freymann-Weyr, Garret

Frick, C. H.
    See Irwin, Constance (H.) Frick
Frick, Constance
    See Irwin, Constance (H.) Frick
Fricke, Aaron 1962- 89
Fridell, Ron 1943- 124
Fried, Janice 197
Friedlander, Joanne K(ohn) 1930- 9
Friedman, Aimee 1979- 189
Friedman, D. Dina 1957- 180
Friedman, Debra 1955- 150
Friedman, Estelle (Ehrenwald) 1920- 7
Friedman, Frieda 1905- 43
Friedman, Hal 230
    See Friedman, Harold
Friedman, Ina R(osen) 1926- 136
    Brief entry 41
    Earlier sketch in SATA 49
Friedman, Jerrold David
    See Gerrold, David
Friedman, Judi 1935- 59
Friedman, Laurie 1964- 219
    Earlier sketches in SATA 138, 179
Friedman, Marvin 1930- 42
    Brief entry 33
Friedman, Robin 1968- 219
    Earlier sketch in SATA 162
Friedmann, Stan 1953- 80
Friedrich, Otto (Alva) 1929-1995 33
Friedrich, Priscilla 1927- 39
Friend, Catherine 1957(?)- 194
Friend, David Michael 1975- 195
Friend, Natasha 1972- 184
Friendlich, Dick
    See Friendlich, Richard J.
Friendlich, Richard J. 1909- 11
Friermood, Elisabeth Hamilton 1903-1992 5
Friesen, Bernice (Sarah Anne) 1966- 105
Friesen, Gayle 1960- 200
    Earlier sketch in SATA 109
Friesen, Jonathan 1967(?)- 206
Friesner, Esther 1951- 207
    Earlier sketches in SATA 71, 168
Friesner, Esther M.
    See Friesner, Esther
Friis-Baastad, Babbis Ellinor 1921-1970 7
Frimmer, Steven 1928- 31
Frischmuth, Barbara 1941- 114
Friskey, Margaret (Richards) 1901-1995 5
Fritts, Mary Bahr
    See Bahr, Mary (Madelyn)
Fritz, Jean (Guttery) 1915- 163
    Autobiography Feature 122
    Earlier sketches in SATA 1, 29, 72, 119
    See also CLR 96
    See also SAAS 2
Froehlich, Margaret W(alden) 1930- 56
Frois, Jeanne 1953- 73
Froissart, Jean 1338(?)-1410(?) 28
Froman, Elizabeth Hull 1920-1975 10
Froman, Robert (Winslow) 1917- 8
Fromental, Jean-Luc 1950- 231
Fromm, Lilo 1928- 29
Frommer, Harvey 1937- 41
Frost, A(rthur) B(urdett) 1851-1928 19
Frost, Elizabeth
    See Frost-Knappman, Elizabeth
Frost, Erica
    See Supraner, Robyn
Frost, Helen 1949- 194
    Autobiography Feature 194
    Earlier sketches in SATA 157, 183
Frost, Helen Marie
    See Frost, Helen
Frost, Lesley 1899-1983 14
    Obituary 34
Frost, Robert 1874-1963 14
    See also CLR 67
Frost, Robert Lee
    See Frost, Robert
Frost, Shelley 1960- 138

Frost-Knappman, Elizabeth 1943- 179
Froud, Brian 1947- 150
Fry, Annette R(iley) 89
Fry, Christopher 1907-2005 66
Fry, Edward Bernard 1925- 35
Fry, Rosalie Kingsmill 1911-1992 3
    See also SAAS 11
Fry, Virginia Lynn 1952- 95
Frye, Sally
    See Moore, Elaine
Fuchs, Bernie 1932- 162
    Earlier sketch in SATA 95
Fuchs, Erich 1916- 6
Fuchshuber, Annegert 1940- 43
Fucile, Tony 221
Fuerst, Jeffrey B. 1956- 143
Fuertes, Gloria 1918-1998 115
Fuge, Charles 1966- 144
    Earlier sketch in SATA 74
Fujikawa, Gyo 1908-1998 76
    Brief entry 30
    Obituary 110
    Earlier sketch in SATA 39
    See also CLR 25
    See also SAAS 16
Fujita, Tamao 1905-1999 7
Fujiwara, Kim 1957- 81
Fujiwara, Michiko 1946- 15
Fuka, Vladimir 1926-1977
    Obituary 27
Fulcher, Jennifer
    See Westwood, Jennifer
Fuller, Catherine Leuthold 1916- 9
Fuller, Edmund (Maybank) 1914- 21
Fuller, Iola
    See McCoy, Iola Fuller
Fuller, John G(rant, Jr.) 1913-1990 65
Fuller, Kathleen
    See Gottfried, Theodore Mark
Fuller, Lois Hamilton 1915- 11
Fuller, Margaret 1810-1850 25
Fuller, Maud
    See Petersham, Maud
Fuller, Roy (Broadbent) 1912-1991 87
Fuller, Sarah Margaret
    See Fuller, Margaret
Fults, John Lee 1932- 33
Funk, Thompson 1911- 7
Funk, Tom
    See Funk, Thompson
Funke, Cornelia 1958- 209
    Earlier sketches in SATA 154, 174
    See also CLR 145
Funke, Cornelia Caroline
    See Funke, Cornelia
Funke, Lewis 1912-1992 11
Fuqua, Jonathon Scott 1966- 141
Furbee, Mary R.
    See Furbee, Mary Rodd
Furbee, Mary Rodd 1954- 138
Furchgott, Terry 1948- 29
Furlong, Monica (Mavis) 1930-2003 86
    Obituary 142
Furlonger, Patricia
    See Wrightson, Patricia
Furman, Gertrude Lerner Kerman 1909- 21
Furniss, Tim 1948- 49
Furrow, Robert 1985- 172
Furukawa, Toshi 1924- 24
Fusillo, Archimede 1962- 137
Futcher, Jane P. 1947- 76
Futehali, Zahida
    See Whitaker, Zai
Fyleman, Rose (Amy) 1877-1957 21
Fyson, Jenny Grace
    See Fyson, J.G.
Fyson, J.G. 1904-1998 42

G

Gaan, Margaret 1914- 65
Gaber, Susan 1956- 169
  Earlier sketch in SATA *115*
Gaberman, Judie Angell
  See Angell, Judie
Gabhart, Ann
  See Gabhart, Ann H.
Gabhart, Ann H. 1947- 75
Gable, Brian 1949- 195
Gabler, Mirko 1951- 77
Gabriel, Adriana
  See Rojany, Lisa
Gabrys, Ingrid Schubert
  See Schubert-Gabrys, Ingrid
Gackenbach, Dick 1927- 79
  Brief entry 30
  Earlier sketch in SATA *48*
Gadd, Jeremy 1949- 116
Gaddis, Vincent H. 1913-1997 35
Gadler, Steve J. 1905-1985 36
Gaeddert, Lou Ann (Bigge) 1931- 103
  Earlier sketch in SATA *20*
Gaeddert, Louann
  See Gaeddert, Lou Ann (Bigge)
Gaer, Joseph 1897-1969 118
Gaer, Yossef
  See Gaer, Joseph
Gaetz, Dayle Campbell 1947- 138
Gaffney, Timothy R. 1951- 170
  Earlier sketch in SATA *69*
Gaffron, Norma 1931- 97
Gaffron, Norma Bondeson
  See Gaffron, Norma
Gag, Flavia 1907-1979
  Obituary 24
Gag, Wanda (Hazel) 1893-1946 100
  See also YABC *1*
  See also CLR *150*
Gage, Brian 162
Gage, Wilson
  See Steele, Mary Q(uintard Govan)
Gagliano, Eugene M. 1946- 150
Gagliardo, Ruth Garver 1895(?)-1980
  Obituary 22
Gagnon, Cecile 1936- 58
Gaillard, Jason 1965- 200
Gaiman, Neil 1960- 228
  Earlier sketches in SATA *85, 146, 197*
  See also CLR *109*
Gaiman, Neil Richard
  See Gaiman, Neil
Gainer, Cindy 1962- 74
Gaines, Ernest J. 1933- 86
  See also CLR *62*
Gaines, Ernest James
  See Gaines, Ernest J.
Gaither, Gloria 1942- 127
Gal, Laszlo 1933- 96
  Brief entry 32
  Earlier sketch in SATA *52*
  See also CLR *61*
Gal, Susan 228
Galbraith, Ben 1980- 200
Galbraith, Kathryn O. 1945- 219
  Earlier sketch in SATA *85*
Galbraith, Kathryn Osebold
  See Galbraith, Kathryn O.
Galdone, Paul 1907(?)-1986 66
  Obituary 49
  Earlier sketch in SATA *17*
  See also CLR *16*
Galindo, Claudia 1979- 203
Galinsky, Ellen 1942- 23
Gall, Chris 1961- 176
Gallagher, Diana G. 1946- 153
Gallagher, Lurlene Nora
  See McDaniel, Lurlene
Gallagher-Cole, Mernie 1958- 206

Gallant, Roy A(rthur) 1924- 110
  Earlier sketches in SATA *4, 68*
  See also CLR *30*
Gallardo, Evelyn 1948- 78
Gallaz, Christophe 1948- 162
  See also CLR *126*
Gallego Garcia, Laura 1977- 173
Gallico, Paul 1897-1976 13
Gallico, Paul William
  See Gallico, Paul
Gallo, Donald R. 1938- 112
  Autobiography Feature 104
Gallo, Donald Robert
  See Gallo, Donald R.
Galloway, Owateka (S.) 1981- 121
Galloway, Priscilla 1930- 227
  Earlier sketches in SATA *66, 112*
Gallup, Joan 1957- 128
Galouchko, Annouchka Gravel 1960- 95
Galt, Thomas Franklin, Jr. 1908-1989 5
Galt, Tom
  See Galt, Thomas Franklin, Jr.
Galvin, Matthew R. 1950- 93
Galvin, Matthew Reppert
  See Galvin, Matthew R.
Gamble, Kim 1952- 183
  Earlier sketches in SATA *81, 124*
Gambrell, Jamey 82
Gamerman, Martha 1941- 15
Gammell, Stephen 1943- 226
  Earlier sketches in SATA *53, 81, 128*
  See also CLR *83*
Ganly, Helen (Mary) 1940- 56
Gannett, Ruth Chrisman (Arens)
  1896-1979 33
Gannett, Ruth Stiles 1923- 3
Gannij, Joan 208
Gannij, Joan Levine
  See Gannij, Joan
Gannon, Ned 1974- 205
Gannon, Robert Haines 1931- 8
Gano, Lila 1949- 76
Gans, Roma 1894-1996 45
  Obituary 93
Gant, Matthew
  See Hano, Arnold
Gantner, Susan (Verble) 1939- 63
Gantos, Jack 1951- 169
  Earlier sketches in SATA *20, 81, 119*
  See also CLR *85*
Gantos, John Bryan, Jr.
  See Gantos, Jack
Ganz, Yaffa 1938- 61
  Brief entry 52
Garafano, Marie 1942- 84
Garant, Andre J. 1968- 123
Garbe, Ruth Moore
  See Moore, Ruth (Ellen)
Garber, Esther
  See Lee, Tanith
Garcia, Cristina 1958- 208
Garcia, Emma 1969- 198
Garcia, Geronimo 1960- 222
Garcia, Kami 1972- 229
Garcia, Yolanda P. 1952- 113
Garcia, Yolanda Pacheco
  See Garcia, Yolanda P.
Gard, Janice
  See Latham, Jean Lee
Gard, Joyce
  See Reeves, Joyce
Gard, Robert Edward 1910-1992 18
  Obituary 74
Gard, (Sanford) Wayne 1899-1986
  Obituary 49
Gardam, Jane 1928- 130
  Brief entry 28
  Earlier sketches in SATA *39, 76*
  See also CLR *12*
  See also SAAS *9*

Gardam, Jane Mary
  See Gardam, Jane
Gardella, Tricia 1944- 96
Garden, Nancy 1938- 147
  Autobiography Feature 147
  Earlier sketches in SATA *12, 77, 114*
  See also CLR *51*
  See also SAAS *8*
Gardiner, John Reynolds 1944-2006 64
  Obituary 174
Gardiner, Lindsey 1971- 144
Gardner, Craig Shaw 1949- 99
Gardner, Dic
  See Gardner, Richard (M.)
Gardner, Graham 159
Gardner, Hugh 1910-1986
  Obituary 49
Gardner, Jane Mylum 1946- 83
Gardner, Jeanne LeMonnier 1925- 5
Gardner, John, Jr. 1933-1982 40
  Obituary 31
Gardner, John Champlin, Jr.
  See Gardner, John, Jr.
Gardner, John E(dward) 1917- 192
Gardner, Lyn 192
Gardner, Martin 1914-2010 142
  Earlier sketch in SATA *16*
Gardner, Miriam
  See Bradley, Marion Zimmer
Gardner, Richard (M.) 1931- 24
Gardner, Richard A(lan) 1931-2003 13
  Obituary 144
Gardner, Sally 229
  Earlier sketch in SATA *177*
Gardner, Sandra 1940- 70
Gardner, Scot 1968- 143
Gardner, Sheldon 1934- 33
Gardner, Ted
  See Gardner, Theodore Roosevelt II
Gardner, Theodore Roosevelt
  See Gardner, Theodore Roosevelt II
Gardner, Theodore Roosevelt II 1934- 84
Garelick, May 1910-1989 19
Garfield, James B. 1881-1984 6
  Obituary 38
Garfield, Leon 1921-1996 76
  Obituary 90
  Earlier sketches in SATA *1, 32*
  See also CLR *166*
Garfinkle, Debra L.
  See Garfinkle, D.L.
Garfinkle, D.L. 187
Garis, Howard R. 1873-1962 13
Garis, Howard Roger
  See Garis, Howard R.
Garland, Mark 1953- 79
Garland, Mark A.
  See Garland, Mark
Garland, Michael 1952- 208
  Earlier sketch in SATA *168*
Garland, Sarah 1944- 135
  Earlier sketch in SATA *62*
Garland, Sherry 1948- 145
  Autobiography Feature 145
  Earlier sketches in SATA *73, 114*
Garner, Alan 1934- 69
  Autobiography Feature 108
  Earlier sketch in SATA *18*
  See also CLR *130*
Garner, David 1958- 78
Garner, Eleanor Ramrath 1930- 122
Garner, James Finn 1960(?)- 92
Garnet, A. H.
  See Slote, Alfred
Garnett, Eve C. R. 1900-1991 3
  Obituary 70
Garofoli, Viviana 1970- 186
Garou, Louis P.
  See Bowkett, Stephen
Garraty, John A. 1920-2007 23
  Obituary 189

Garraty, John Arthur
　See Garraty, John A.
Garren, Devorah-Leah
　See Devorah-Leah
Garret, Maxwell R. 1917- 39
Garretson, Victoria Diane
　See Cox, Victoria
Garrett, Helen 1895- 21
Garrett, Randall 1927-1987 180
Garrett, Richard 1920- 82
Garrigue, Sheila 1931- 21
Garrison, Barbara 1931- 163
　Earlier sketch in SATA 19
Garrison, Frederick
　See Sinclair, Upton
Garrison, Mary 1952- 146
Garrison, Peter
　See Gardner, Craig Shaw
Garrison, Webb B(lack) 1919-2000 25
Garrity, Jennifer Johnson 1961- 124
Garrity, Linda K. 1947- 128
Garsee, Jeannine 199
Garst, Doris Shannon 1894-1981 1
Garst, Shannon
　See Garst, Doris Shannon
Garth, Will
　See Hamilton, Edmond
　and Kuttner, Henry
Garthwaite, Marion H(ook) 1893-1981 7
Garton, Malinda D(ean) (?)-1976
　Obituary 26
Garvie, Maureen 1944- 175
Garvie, Maureen McCallum
　See Garvie, Maureen
Garza, Carmen Lomas 1948- 182
Garza, Xavier 184
Gascoigne, Bamber 1935- 62
Gaskins, Pearl Fuyo 1957- 134
Gasperini, Jim 1952- 54
　Brief entry 49
Gater, Dilys 1944- 41
Gates, Doris 1901-1987 34
　Obituary 54
　Earlier sketch in SATA 1
　See also SAAS 1
Gates, Frieda 1933- 26
Gates, Susan 1950- 153
Gates, Viola R. 1931- 101
Gathorne-Hardy, Jonathan G. 1933- 124
　Earlier sketch in SATA 26
Gatti, Anne 1952- 103
Gatty, Juliana Horatia
　See Ewing, Juliana (Horatia Gatty)
Gauch, Patricia Lee 1934- 228
　Earlier sketches in SATA 26, 80
　See also CLR 56
　See also SAAS 21
Gauch, Sarah 223
Gaudasinska, Elzbieta 1943- 190
Gaul, Randy 1959- 63
Gault, Clare 1925- 36
Gault, Frank 1926-1982 36
　Brief entry 30
Gault, William Campbell 1910-1995 8
Gauthier, Gail 1953- 203
　Earlier sketches in SATA 118, 160
Gaver, Becky
　See Gaver, Rebecca
Gaver, Rebecca 1952- 20
Gavin, Jamila 1941- 223
　Earlier sketches in SATA 96, 125
Gay, Amelia
　See Hogarth, Grace (Weston Allen)
Gay, Francis
　See Gee, H(erbert) L(eslie)
Gay, Kathlyn 1930- 144
　Earlier sketch in SATA 9
Gay, Marie-Louise 1952- 179
　Earlier sketches in SATA 68, 126
　See also CLR 27
　See also SAAS 21

Gay, Michel 1947- 162
Gay, Zhenya 1906-1978 19
Gaze, Gillian
　See Barklem, Jill
Gear, Kathleen M. O'Neal
　See Gear, Kathleen O'Neal
Gear, Kathleen O'Neal 1954- 224
　Earlier sketches in SATA 71, 166
Gear, W. Michael 1955- 224
　Earlier sketches in SATA 71, 166
Geary, Rick 1946- 142
Geason, Susan 1946- 122
Gedalof, Robin
　See McGrath, Robin
Gedge, Pauline (Alice) 1945- 101
Gee, H(erbert) L(eslie) 1901-1977
　Obituary 26
Gee, Maurice 1931- 227
　Earlier sketches in SATA 46, 101
　See also CLR 56
Gee, Maurice Gough
　See Gee, Maurice
Geehan, Wayne (E.) 1947- 107
Geer, Charles 1922- 42
　Brief entry 32
Geeslin, Campbell 1925- 163
　Earlier sketch in SATA 107
Gehman, Mary W. 1923- 86
Gehr, Mary 1910(?)-1997 32
　Obituary 99
Geipel, Eileen 1932- 30
Geis, Alissa Imre 1976- 189
Geis, Darlene Stern 1918(?)-1999 7
　Obituary 111
Geisel, Helen 1898-1967 26
Geisel, Theodor Seuss
　See Dr. Seuss
Geisert, Arthur 1941- 171
　Brief entry 52
　Earlier sketches in SATA 56, 92, 133
　See also CLR 87
　See also SAAS 23
Geisert, Arthur Frederick
　See Geisert, Arthur
Geisert, Bonnie 1942- 165
　Earlier sketch in SATA 92
Geist, Ken 191
Gelber, Lisa 210
Geldart, William 1936- 15
Gelinas, Paul J. 1904-1996 10
Gellis, Roberta 1927- 128
Gellis, Roberta Leah Jacobs
　See Gellis, Roberta
Gellman, Marc 112
Gelman, Amy 1961- 72
Gelman, Jan 1963- 58
Gelman, Rita Golden 1937- 131
　Brief entry 51
　Earlier sketch in SATA 84
Gelman, Steve 1934- 3
Gemignani, Tony 1973- 220
Gemming, Elizabeth 1932- 11
Gendel, Evelyn W. 1916(?)-1977
　Obituary 27
Gennaro, Joseph F., Jr. 1924- 53
Gennaro, Joseph Francis, Jr.
　See Gennaro, Joseph F., Jr.
Gentieu, Penny 204
Gentile, Petrina 1969- 91
Gentle, Mary 1956- 48
Gentleman, David (William) 1930- 7
Gentry, Marita 215
Geoghegan, Adrienne 1962- 143
George, Barbara
　See Katz, Bobbi
George, Emily
　See Katz, Bobbi
George, Gail
　See Katz, Bobbi
George, Jean
　See George, Jean Craighead

George, Jean C.
　See George, Jean Craighead
George, Jean Craighead 1919- 226
　Earlier sketches in SATA 2, 68, 124, 170
　See also CLR 136
George, Jessica Day 1976- 210
George, John L(othar) 1916- 2
George, Kristine O'Connell 1954- 156
　Earlier sketch in SATA 110
George, Lindsay Barrett 1952- 206
　Earlier sketches in SATA 95, 155
George, S. C. 1898- 11
George, Sally
　See Orr, Wendy
George, Sidney Charles
　See George, S. C.
George, Twig C. 1950- 114
George, W(illiam) Lloyd 1900(?)-1975
　Obituary 30
Georgiou, Constantine 1927- 7
Georgiou, Theo
　See Odgers, Sally Farrell
Geraghty, Paul 1959- 130
Gerard, Jean Ignace Isidore 1803-1847 45
Geras, Adele 1944- 180
　Autobiography Feature 180
　Earlier sketches in SATA 23, 87, 129, 173
　See also SAAS 21
Geras, Adele Daphne Weston
　See Geras, Adele
Gerber, Carole 1947- 207
Gerber, Linda 213
Gerber, Merrill Joan 1938- 170
　Autobiography Feature 170
　Earlier sketches in SATA 64, 127
Gerber, Perren 1933- 104
Gerberg, Mort 1931- 64
Gergely, Tibor 1900-1978 54
　Obituary 20
Geringer, Laura 1948- 164
　Earlier sketches in SATA 29, 94
Gerler, William R(obert) 1917-1996 47
Gerrard, Jean 1933- 51
Gerrard, Roy 1935-1997 90
　Brief entry 45
　Obituary 99
　Earlier sketch in SATA 47
　See also CLR 23
Gerritsen, Paula 1956- 177
Gerrold, David 1944- 144
　Earlier sketch in SATA 66
Gershator, David 1937- 180
Gershator, Phillis 1942- 188
　Earlier sketches in SATA 90, 158
Gershon, Dann 1955- 187
Gershon, Gina 1962- 187
Gerson, Corinne 1927- 37
Gerson, Mary-Joan 136
　Earlier sketch in SATA 79
Gerson, Noel Bertram 1914-1988 22
　Obituary 60
Gerstein, Mordicai 1935- 222
　Brief entry 36
　Earlier sketches in SATA 47, 81, 142, 178
　See also CLR 102
Gertridge, Allison 1967- 132
Gervais, Bernadette 1959- 80
Gervay, Susanne 183
Gesner, Clark 1938-2002 40
　Obituary 143
Gessner, Lynne 1919- 16
Geter, Tyrone 150
Getz, David 1957- 91
Getzinger, Donna 1968- 128
Geus, Mireille 1964- 207
Gevirtz, Eliezer 1950- 49
Gevry, Claudine 188
Gewe, Raddory
　See Gorey, Edward (St. John)
Ghan, Linda (R.) 1947- 77
Ghent, Natale 1962- 148

Gherman, Beverly 1934- *123*
  Earlier sketch in SATA *68*
Ghigna, Charles 1946- *153*
  Earlier sketch in SATA *108*
Giacobbe, Beppe 1953- *174*
Giambastiani, Kurt R. A. 1958- *141*
Giannini, Enzo 1946- *68*
Gibala-Broxholm, Scott 1959(?)- *205*
Gibbons, Alan 1953- *198*
  Earlier sketch in SATA *124*
Gibbons, Faye 1938- *103*
  Earlier sketch in SATA *65*
Gibbons, Gail 1944- *201*
  Earlier sketches in SATA *23, 72, 104, 160*
  See also CLR *8*
  See also SAAS *12*
Gibbons, Gail Gretchen
  See Gibbons, Gail
Gibbons, Kaye 1960- *117*
Gibbs, Adrea 1960- *126*
Gibbs, Alonzo (Lawrence) 1915-1992 .... *5*
Gibbs, (Cecilia) May 1877-1969
  Obituary *27*
Gibbs, Stuart 1969- *230*
Gibbs, Tony
  See Gibbs, Wolcott, Jr.
Gibbs, Wolcott, Jr. 1935- *40*
Giblin, James Cross 1933- *197*
  Earlier sketches in SATA *33, 75, 122*
  See also CLR *29*
  See also SAAS *12*
Gibson, Andrew (William) 1949- *72*
Gibson, Barbara L. *205*
Gibson, Barbara Leonard
  See Gibson, Barbara L.
Gibson, Betty 1911- *75*
Gibson, Jo
  See Fluke, Joanne
Gibson, Josephine
  See Hine, Sesyle Joslin
  and Hine, Al(fred Blakelee)
Gibson, Marley 1966- *225*
Gibson, Sarah P. 1962- *211*
Gibson, William 1914-2008 .... *66*
  Obituary *199*
Gibson, William Ford
  See Gibson, William
Gidal, Nachum
  See Gidal, Tim Nachum
Gidal, Sonia (Epstein) 1922- *2*
Gidal, Tim Nachum 1909-1996 .... *2*
Gidalewitsch, Nachum
  See Gidal, Tim Nachum
Gideon, Melanie 1963- *175*
Giegling, John A(llan) 1935- *17*
Gifaldi, David 1950- *209*
  Earlier sketch in SATA *76*
Giff, Patricia Reilly 1935- *203*
  Earlier sketches in SATA *33, 70, 121, 160*
Giffard, Hannah 1962- *83*
Gifford, Carrie *224*
Gifford, Clive 1966- *198*
Gifford, Griselda 1931- *171*
  Earlier sketch in SATA *42*
Gifford, Kerri 1961- *91*
Gifford, Peggy 1952- *191*
Gilani, Fawzia
  See Gilani-Williams, Fawzia
Gilani-Williams, Fawzia 1967- *231*
Gilbert, Ann
  See Taylor, Ann
Gilbert, Anne Yvonne 1951- *185*
Gilbert, Barbara Snow 1954- *97*
Gilbert, Catherine
  See Murdock, Catherine Gilbert
Gilbert, Frances
  See Collings, Gillian
Gilbert, Harriett 1948- *30*
Gilbert, (Agnes) Joan (Sewell) 1931- *10*
Gilbert, John (Raphael) 1926- *36*

Gilbert, Nan
  See Gilbertson, Mildred Geiger
Gilbert, Roby Goodale 1966- *90*
Gilbert, Ruth Gallard Ainsworth
  See Ainsworth, Ruth (Gallard)
Gilbert, Sara (Dulaney) 1943- *82*
  Earlier sketch in SATA *11*
Gilbert, Sheri L. *157*
Gilbert, Suzie 1956- *97*
Gilbert, W(illiam) S(chwenck) 1836-1911 ... *36*
Gilbert, Yvonne
  See Gilbert, Anne Yvonne
Gilbertson, Mildred Geiger 1908-1988 .... *2*
Gilbreath, Alice 1921- *12*
Gilbreth, Frank B., Jr. 1911-2001 .... *2*
Gilbreth, Frank Bunker
  See Gilbreth, Frank B., Jr.
Gilchrist, Jan Spivey 1949- *130*
  Earlier sketch in SATA *72*
Gilden, Mel 1947- *97*
Giles, Gail *196*
  Earlier sketch in SATA *152*
Gilfond, Henry *2*
Gilge, Jeanette 1924- *22*
Gili, Phillida 1944- *70*
Gill, Derek (Lewis Theodore) 1919-1997 ...... *9*
Gill, Margery Jean 1925- *22*
Gill, Shelley *176*
Gill, Stephen 1932- *63*
Gillespie, Carol Ann 1951- *158*
Gillett, Mary (Bledsoe) *7*
Gillette, Henry Sampson 1915- *14*
Gillette, J. Lynett 1946- *103*
Gillette, Jan Lynett
  See Gillette, J. Lynett
Gilley, Jeremy 1969- *174*
Gillham, Bill
  See Gillham, W(illiam) E(dwin) C(harles)
Gillham, W(illiam) E(dwin) C(harles)
  1936- *42*
Gilliam, Stan 1946- *39*
  Brief entry *35*
Gilliland, Alexis A. 1931- *72*
Gilliland, Alexis Arnaldus
  See Gilliland, Alexis A.
Gilliland, (Cleburne) Hap 1918- *92*
Gilliland, Judith Heide *180*
Gillmor, Don 1954- *127*
Gilman, Dorothy 1923- *5*
Gilman, Esther 1925- *15*
Gilman, Laura Anne *178*
Gilman, Phoebe 1940-2002 .... *104*
  Obituary *141*
  Earlier sketch in SATA *58*
Gilmore, Iris 1900-1982 .... *22*
Gilmore, Kate 1931- *87*
Gilmore, Mary (Jean Cameron) 1865-1962 . *49*
Gilmore, Rachna 1953- *209*
Gilmore, Susan 1954- *59*
Gilpin, Stephen *213*
  Earlier sketch in SATA *177*
Gilroy, Beryl (Agatha) 1924- *80*
Gilson, Barbara
  See Gilson, Charles James Louis
Gilson, Charles James Louis 1878-1943
  See YABC *2*
Gilson, Jamie 1933- *176*
  Brief entry *34*
  Earlier sketches in SATA *37, 91*
Gimpel, Carolyn
  See Hart, Carolyn
Ginsberg, Blaze 1987- *222*
Ginsburg, Mirra 1909-2000 .... *92*
  Earlier sketch in SATA *6*
  See also CLR *45*
Giovanni, Nikki 1943- *208*
  Earlier sketches in SATA *24, 107*
  See also CLR *73*
Giovanni, Yolanda Cornelia
  See Giovanni, Nikki

Giovanni, Yolande Cornelia
  See Giovanni, Nikki
Giovanni, Yolande Cornelia, Jr.
  See Giovanni, Nikki
Giovanopoulos, Paul (Arthur) 1939- *7*
Gipson, Billie
  See Letts, Billie
Gipson, Fred(erick Benjamin) 1908-1973 ...... *2*
  Obituary *24*
Girard, Linda (Walvoord) 1942- *41*
Giraudon, David 1975- *215*
Girion, Barbara 1937- *78*
  Earlier sketch in SATA *26*
  See also SAAS *14*
Girl, Nerdy
  See Castellucci, Cecil
Girouard, Patrick 1957- *155*
Girzone, Joseph F. 1930- *76*
Girzone, Joseph Francis
  See Girzone, Joseph F.
Gise, Joanne
  See Mattern, Joanne
Gist, E.M. *206*
Gittings, Jo (Grenville) Manton 1919- *3*
Gittings, Robert (William Victor) 1911-1992 . *6*
  Obituary *70*
Givens, Janet E(aton) 1932- *60*
Givner, Joan 1936- *171*
Givner, Joan Mary
  See Givner, Joan
Gladstone, Eve
  See Werner, Herma
Gladstone, Gary 1935- *12*
Gladstone, M(yron) J. 1923- *37*
Glanville, Brian (Lester) 1931- *42*
Glanzman, Louis S. 1922- *36*
Glaser, Byron 1954- *154*
Glaser, Dianne E(lizabeth) 1937- *50*
  Brief entry *31*
Glaser, Isabel Joshlin 1929- *94*
Glaser, Linda *225*
Glaser, Milton 1929- *151*
  Earlier sketch in SATA *11*
Glaser, Shirley *151*
Glaspell, Susan 1882(?)-1948
  See YABC *2*
Glass, Andrew 1949- *223*
  Brief entry *46*
  Earlier sketches in SATA *90, 150*
Glass, Linzi *175*
Glass, Linzi Alex
  See Glass, Linzi
Glasscock, Amnesia
  See Steinbeck, John
Glassman, Bruce 1961- *76*
Glatt, Lisa 1963- *217*
Glauber, Uta (Heil) 1936- *17*
Glazer, Thomas (Zachariah) 1914-2003 .... *9*
Glazer, Tom
  See Glazer, Thomas (Zachariah)
Gleasner, Diana (Cottle) 1936- *29*
Gleason, Judith 1929- *24*
Gleason, Katherine (A.) 1960- *104*
Gleeson, Libby 1950- *142*
  Autobiography Feature *142*
  Earlier sketches in SATA *82, 118*
Gleiter, Jan 1947- *111*
Gleitzman, Morris 1953- *156*
  Earlier sketch in SATA *88*
  See also CLR *88*
Glen, Maggie 1944- *88*
Glendinning, Richard 1917-1988 .... *24*
Glendinning, Sally
  See Glendinning, Sara W(ilson)
Glendinning, Sara W(ilson) 1913-1993 .... *24*
Glenn, John W. *195*
Glenn, Mel 1943- *93*
  Brief entry *45*
  Earlier sketch in SATA *51*
  See also CLR *51*
Glenn, Patricia Brown 1953- *86*

Glenn, Sharlee *159*
Glenn, Sharlee Mullins
  See Glenn, Sharlee
Glennon, Karen M. 1946- *85*
Gles, Margaret Breitmaier 1940- *22*
Glick, Carl (Cannon) 1890-1971 .... *14*
Glick, Ruth 1942- *125*
Glick, Ruth Burtnick
  See Glick, Ruth
Glick, Virginia Kirkus 1893-1980
  Obituary *23*
Gliewe, Unada (Grace) 1927- *3*
Glimmerveen, Ulco 1958- *85*
Glines, Carroll V(ane), Jr. 1920- *19*
Gliori, Debi 1959- *189*
  Earlier sketches in SATA *72, 138*
Globe, Leah Ain 1900- *41*
Glori Ann
  See Blakely, Gloria
Glovach, Linda 1947- *105*
  Earlier sketch in SATA *7*
Glover, Denis (James Matthews) 1912-1980 . *7*
Glubok, Shirley (Astor) *146*
  Autobiography Feature *146*
  Earlier sketches in SATA *6, 68*
  See also CLR *1*
  See also SAAS *7*
Gluck, Felix 1923-1981
  Obituary *25*
Glyman, Caroline A. 1967- *103*
Glynne-Jones, William 1907-1977 .... *11*
Gobbato, Imero 1923- *39*
Gobbletree, Richard
  See Quackenbush, Robert M(ead)
Goble, Dorothy *26*
Goble, Paul 1933- *131*
  Earlier sketches in SATA *25, 69*
  See also CLR *21*
Goble, Warwick (?)-1943 .... *46*
Godden, (Margaret) Rumer 1907-1998 .... *36*
  Obituary *109*
  Earlier sketch in SATA *3*
  See also CLR *20*
  See also SAAS *12*
Gode, Alexander
  See Gode von Aesch, Alexander (Gottfried
  Friedrich)
Gode von Aesch, Alexander (Gottfried
  Friedrich) 1906-1970 .... *14*
Godfrey, Jane
  See Bowden, Joan Chase
Godfrey, Martyn
  See Godfrey, Martyn N.
  and Godfrey, Martyn N.
Godfrey, Martyn N. 1949-2000 .... *95*
  See also CLR *57*
Godfrey, William
  See Youd, Samuel
Godkin, Celia 1948- *145*
  Earlier sketch in SATA *66*
Godkin, Celia Marilyn
  See Godkin, Celia
Godon, Ingrid 1958- *186*
Godown, Jan
  See Annino, Jan Godown
Godwin, Laura 1956- *179*
Godwin, Sam
  See Pirotta, Saviour
Godwin, Sarah Massini
  See Massini, Sarah
Goede, Irene 1966- *208*
Goedecke, Christopher (John) 1951- *81*
Goekler, Susan
  See Wooley, Susan Frelick
Goembel, Ponder *204*
Goertzen, Glenda *172*
Goettel, Elinor 1930- *12*
Goetz, Delia 1898-1996 .... *22*
  Obituary *91*
Goffe, Toni 1936- *61*

Goffstein, Brooke
  See Goffstein, Marilyn Brooke
Goffstein, M. B.
  See Goffstein, Marilyn Brooke
Goffstein, Marilyn Brooke 1940- *70*
  Earlier sketch in SATA *8*
  See also CLR *3*
Goforth, Ellen
  See Francis, Dorothy
Gogol, Sara 1948-2004 .... *80*
Goh, Chan Hon 1969- *145*
Going, Kelly L.
  See Going, K.L.
Going, Kelly Louise
  See Going, K.L.
Going, K.L. *199*
  Earlier sketch in SATA *156*
Golann, Cecil Paige 1921-1995 .... *11*
Golbin, Andree 1923- *15*
Gold, Alison Leslie 1945- *104*
Gold, August 1955- *215*
Gold, Bernice *150*
Gold, Phyllis
  See Goldberg, Phyllis
Gold, Robert S(tanley) 1924- *63*
Gold, Sharlya *9*
Gold, Susan
  See Gold, Susan Dudley
Gold, Susan Dudley 1949- *147*
Goldbach, Veronica 1980- *220*
Goldberg, Grace 1956- *78*
Goldberg, Herbert S. 1926- *25*
Goldberg, Jacob 1943- *94*
Goldberg, Jake
  See Goldberg, Jacob
Goldberg, Myla 1972(?)- *210*
Goldberg, Phyllis 1941- *21*
Goldberg, Stan J. 1939- *63*
Goldberg, Susan 1948- *71*
Goldberg, Whoopi 1955- *119*
Goldberger, Judith M. 1948- *80*
Goldblatt, Stacey 1969(?)- *191*
Golden, Christie 1963- *167*
  Earlier sketch in SATA *116*
Goldentyer, Debra 1960- *84*
Goldfeder, Cheryl
  See Pahz, Cheryl Suzanne
Goldfeder, James
  See Pahz, James Alon
Goldfeder, Jim
  See Pahz, James Alon
Goldfinger, Jennifer P. 1963- *185*
Goldfrank, Helen Colodny 1912- *6*
Goldin, Augusta 1906-1999 .... *13*
Goldin, Barbara Diamond 1946- *129*
  Autobiography Feature *129*
  Earlier sketch in SATA *92*
  See also SAAS *26*
Goldin, David 1963- *101*
Golding, Julia 1969- *188*
Golding, Theresa Martin 1960- *150*
Golding, William 1911-1993
  See CLR *130*
Golding, William Gerald
  See Golding, William
Goldman, Alex J. 1917- *65*
Goldman, E. M. 1943- *103*
Goldman, Eleanor Maureen
  See Goldman, E. M.
Goldman, Elizabeth 1949- *90*
Goldman, Judy 1955- *212*
Goldman, Steven 1964- *207*
Goldman, Todd Harris *221*
Goldring, Ann 1937- *149*
Golds, Cassandra 1962- *226*
Goldsborough, June 1923- *19*
Goldschmidt, Judy *202*
Goldsmith, Connie 1945- *147*
Goldsmith, Howard 1943- *108*
  Earlier sketch in SATA *24*

Goldsmith, John Herman Thorburn 1903-1987
  Obituary *52*
Goldsmith, Oliver 1730(?)-1774 .... *26*
Goldsmith, Ruth M. 1919- *62*
Goldstein, Nathan 1927- *47*
Goldstein, Philip 1910-1997 .... *23*
Goldston, Robert (Conroy) 1927- *6*
Goldstone, Bruce *183*
Goldstone, Lawrence A.
  See Treat, Lawrence
Goldszmit, Henryk 1878-1942 .... *65*
  See also CLR *152*
Golembe, Carla 1951- *79*
Golenbock, Peter 1946- *99*
Goll, Reinhold W(eimar) 1897-1993 .... *26*
Gollub, Matthew 1960- *134*
  Earlier sketch in SATA *83*
Golson, Terry *213*
Golson, Terry Blonder
  See Golson, Terry
Gomes, Filomena 1965- *183*
Gomez, Elena *191*
Gomez, Elizabeth *133*
Gomez-Freer, Elizabeth
  See Gomez, Elizabeth
Gomi, Taro 1945- *103*
  Earlier sketch in SATA *64*
  See also CLR *57*
Gondosch, Linda 1944- *58*
Gonsalves, Rob 1959- *209*
Gonyea, Mark *194*
Gonzales, Chuck *230*
Gonzalez, Catherine Troxell 1917-2000 .... *87*
Gonzalez, Christina
  See Gonzalez, Maya Christina
Gonzalez, Christina Diaz 1969- *231*
Gonzalez, Gloria 1940- *23*
Gonzalez, Julie 1958- *174*
Gonzalez, Julie Sehers
  See Gonzalez, Julie
Gonzalez, Lucia M. 1957- *202*
Gonzalez, Maya
  See Gonzalez, Maya Christina
Gonzalez, Maya Christina 1964- *175*
  Earlier sketch in SATA *115*
Gonzalez, Rigoberto 1970- *147*
Goobie, Beth 1959- *128*
Good, Alice 1950- *73*
Good, Clare
  See Romano, Clare
Good, Karen Hillard *214*
Goodall, Daphne Machin
  See Machin Goodall, Daphne (Edith)
Goodall, Jane 1934- *111*
Goodall, John S(trickland) 1908-1996 .... *66*
  Obituary *91*
  Earlier sketch in SATA *4*
  See also CLR *25*
Goodbody, Slim
  See Burstein, John
Goode, Diane 1949- *225*
  Earlier sketches in SATA *15, 84, 114, 170*
Goode, Diane Capuozzo
  See Goode, Diane
Goode, Stephen Ray 1943- *55*
  Brief entry *40*
Goodenow, Earle 1913- *40*
Goodhart, Pippa 1958- *196*
  Earlier sketch in SATA *153*
Goodhue, Thomas W. 1949- *143*
Goodin, Sallie (Brown) 1953- *74*
Goodman, Alison 1966- *111*
Goodman, Deborah Lerme 1956- *50*
  Brief entry *49*
Goodman, Elaine 1930- *9*
Goodman, Emily *217*
Goodman, Joan Elizabeth 1950- *162*
  Earlier sketches in SATA *50, 94*
Goodman, Susan E. 1952- *181*
Goodman, Walter 1927-2002 .... *9*
Goodman Koz, Paula *211*

Goodrich, Carter 1959(?)- 221
Goodrich, Samuel Griswold 1793-1860 23
Goodsell, Jane Neuberger 1921(?)-1988
    Obituary 56
Goodweather, Hartley
    See King, Thomas
GoodWeather, Hartley
    See King, Thomas
Goodwin, Hal
    See Goodwin, Harold L(eland)
Goodwin, Harold L(eland) 1914-1990 51
    Obituary 65
    Earlier sketch in SATA *13*
Goodwin, William 1943- 117
Goor, Nancy (Ruth Miller) 1944- 39
    Brief entry 34
Goor, Ron(ald Stephen) 1940- 39
    Brief entry 34
Goossen, Agnes
    See Epp, Margaret A(gnes)
Goossens, Philippe 1963- 195
Gootman, Marilyn E. 1944- 179
Gopnik, Adam 1956- 171
Gorbachev, Valeri 1944- 222
    Autobiography Feature 143
    Earlier sketches in SATA *98, 143, 184*
Gordion, Mark
    See Turtledove, Harry
Gordon, Ad
    See Hano, Arnold
Gordon, Amy 1949- 197
    Earlier sketches in SATA *115, 156*
Gordon, Bernard Ludwig 1931-2010 27
Gordon, Colonel H. R.
    See Ellis, Edward S.
Gordon, David
    See Garrett, Randall
Gordon, Donald
    See Payne, Donald Gordon
Gordon, Dorothy 1893-1970 20
Gordon, Esther S(aranga) 1935- 10
Gordon, Frederick 1
Gordon, Gaelyn 1939-1997
    See CLR 75
Gordon, Garrett
    See Garrett, Randall
Gordon, Gary
    See Edmonds, I(vy) G(ordon)
Gordon, Hal
    See Goodwin, Harold L(eland)
Gordon, Jeffie Ross
    See Enderle, Judith (Ann) Ross
    and Gordon, Stephanie Jacob
Gordon, John
    See Gesner, Clark
Gordon, John (William) 1925- 84
Gordon, Lew
    See Baldwin, Gordon C(ortis)
Gordon, Margaret (Anna) 1939- 9
Gordon, Mike 1948- 101
Gordon, Mildred 1912-1979
    Obituary 24
Gordon, Selma
    See Lanes, Selma G.
Gordon, Sheila 1927- 88
    See also CLR 27
Gordon, Shirley 1921- 48
    Brief entry 41
Gordon, Sol 1923- 11
Gordon, Stephanie Jacob 1940- 89
    Autobiography Feature 114
    Earlier sketch in SATA *64*
    See also SAAS 26
Gordon, Stewart
    See Shirreffs, Gordon D(onald)
Gordons, The
    See Gordon, Mildred
    and Gordon, Gordon
Gore, Leonid 222
    Earlier sketch in SATA *185*

Gorelick, Molly C(hernow) 1920-2003 9
    Obituary 153
Gorey, Edward (St. John) 1925-2000 70
    Brief entry 27
    Obituary 118
    Earlier sketch in SATA *29*
    See also CLR 36
Gorham, Charles Orson 1868-1936 36
Gorham, Michael
    See Folsom, Franklin (Brewster)
Gorman, Carol 187
    Earlier sketch in SATA *150*
Gorman, Jacqueline Laks 1955- 148
Gorman, Mike 206
Gormley, Beatrice 1942- 202
    Brief entry 35
    Earlier sketches in SATA *39, 127*
Gorog, Judith (Katharine Allen) 1938- 75
    Earlier sketch in SATA *39*
Gorrell, Gena K. 1946- 170
Gorsline, Douglas (Warner) 1913-1985 11
    Obituary 43
Gorsline, (Sally) Marie 1928- 28
Gorsline, S. M.
    See Gorsline, (Sally) Marie
Gorton, Julia 218
Gorton, Kaitlyn
    See Emerson, Kathy Lynn
Gorton, Kathy Lynn
    See Emerson, Kathy Lynn
Goryan, Sirak
    See Saroyan, William
Goschke, Julia 1973- 208
Goscinny, Rene 1926-1977 47
    Brief entry 39
    See also CLR 37
Goss, Clay(ton E.) 1946- 82
Goss, Gary 1947- 124
Goss, Mini 1963- 186
Goto, Scott 203
Gott, Barry 197
Gottesman, S. D.
    See Kornbluth, C(yril) M.
    and Lowndes, Robert A(ugustine) W(ard)
    and Pohl, Frederik
Gottfried, Ted
    See Gottfried, Theodore Mark
Gottfried, Theodore Mark 1928- 150
    Earlier sketch in SATA *85*
Gottlieb, Gerald 1923- 7
Gottlieb, William P. 1917-2006 24
Gottlieb, William Paul
    See Gottlieb, William P.
Goudey, Alice E(dwards) 1898-1993 20
Goudge, Eileen 1950- 88
Goudge, Elizabeth (de Beauchamp)
    1900-1984 2
    Obituary 38
    See also CLR 94
Gough, Catherine
    See Mulgan, Catherine
Gough, Philip 1908-1986 45
Gough, Sue 1940- 106
Goulart, Ron 1933- 67
    Earlier sketch in SATA *1*
Goulart, Ronald Joseph
    See Goulart, Ron
Gould, Alberta 1945- 96
Gould, Chester 1900-1985 49
    Obituary 43
Gould, Jean R(osalind) 1909-1993 11
    Obituary 77
Gould, Lilian 6
Gould, Marilyn 1928- 76
    Earlier sketch in SATA *15*
Gould, Robert 154
Gould, Steven 1955- 95
Gould, Steven Charles
    See Gould, Steven
Gourley, Catherine 1950- 190
    Earlier sketch in SATA *95*

Gourse, Leslie 1939-2004 89
Govan, (Mary) Christine Noble 1898-1985 ... 9
Gove, Doris 1944- 72
Govenar, Alan 1952- 189
Govenar, Alan Bruce
    See Govenar, Alan
Govern, Elaine 1939- 26
Gowen, L. Kris 1968- 156
Graaf, Peter
    See Youd, Samuel
Graber, Alexander 1914-1997 98
    Earlier sketch in SATA *7*
Graber, George Alexander
    See Graber, Alexander
Graber, Janet 1942- 170
Graber, Richard (Fredrick) 1927- 26
Grabianski, Janusz 1928-1976 39
    Obituary 30
Graboff, Abner 1919-1986 35
Grace, Fran(ces Jane) 45
Grace, N.B.
    See Harper, Suzanne
Grace, Theresa
    See Mattern, Joanne
Gracza, Margaret Young 1928- 56
Graduate of Oxford, A
    See Ruskin, John
Grady, Denise 1952- 189
Graeber, Charlotte Towner 106
    Brief entry 44
    Earlier sketch in SATA *56*
Graef, Renee 1956- 204
Graeme, Roderic
    See Jeffries, Roderic
Graf, Michael
    See Graf, Mike
Graf, Mike 1960- 164
Grafe, Max 198
Graff, Lisa 1981- 188
Graff, Polly Anne Colver
    See Colver, Anne
Graff, (S.) Stewart 1908-2009 9
Graham, Ada 1931- 11
Graham, Alastair 1945- 74
Graham, Arthur Kennon
    See Harrison, David L.
Graham, Bob 1942- 187
    Earlier sketches in SATA *63, 101, 151*
    See also CLR 31
Graham, Brenda Knight 1942- 32
Graham, Charlotte
    See Bowden, Joan Chase
Graham, Christine 1952- 224
Graham, Eleanor 1896-1984 18
    Obituary 38
Graham, Ennis
    See Molesworth, Mary Louisa
Graham, Frank, Jr. 1925- 11
Graham, Georgia 1959- 190
Graham, Ian 1953- 229
    Earlier sketch in SATA *112*
Graham, John 1926-2007 11
Graham, Kennon
    See Harrison, David L.
Graham, Larry
    See Graham, Lawrence
Graham, Lawrence 1962- 63
Graham, Lawrence Otis
    See Graham, Lawrence
Graham, Linda
    See Graham-Barber, Lynda
Graham, Lorenz (Bell) 1902-1989 74
    Obituary 63
    Earlier sketch in SATA *2*
    See also CLR 10
    See also SAAS 5
Graham, Margaret Bloy 1920- 11
Graham, Robin Lee 1949- 7
Graham, Shirley 1896(?)-1977
    See Du Bois, Shirley Graham

Graham-Barber, Lynda 1944- *159*
Earlier sketch in SATA *42*
Graham-Cameron, M.
See Graham-Cameron, M(alcolm) G(ordon)
Graham-Cameron, M(alcolm) G(ordon)
1931- *53*
Brief entry *45*
Graham-Cameron, Mike
See Graham-Cameron, M(alcolm) G(ordon)
Grahame, Kenneth 1859-1932 .... *100*
See also YABC *1*
See also CLR *135*
Gralley, Jean *166*
Gramatky, Hardie 1907-1979 .... *30*
Obituary *23*
Earlier sketch in SATA *1*
See also CLR *22*
Grambling, Lois G. 1927- *206*
Earlier sketches in SATA *71, 148*
Grambo, Rebecca L(ynn) 1963- *109*
Grammer, June Amos 1927- *58*
Grand, Samuel 1912-1988 .... *42*
Grandits, John 1949- *192*
GrandPre, Mary 1954- *229*
Earlier sketch in SATA *184*
Grandville, J. J.
See Gerard, Jean Ignace Isidore
Grandville, Jean Ignace Isidore Gerard
See Gerard, Jean Ignace Isidore
Granfield, Linda 1950- *160*
Earlier sketch in SATA *96*
Grange, Peter
See Nicole, Christopher
Granger, Margaret Jane 1925(?)-1977
Obituary *27*
Granger, Michele 1949- *88*
Granger, Peggy
See Granger, Margaret Jane
Granowsky, Alvin 1936- *101*
Granstaff, Bill 1925- *10*
Granstrom, Brita 1969- *224*
Earlier sketches in SATA *111, 167*
Grant, Bruce 1893-1977 .... *5*
Obituary *25*
Grant, Cynthia D. 1950- *147*
Earlier sketches in SATA *33, 77*
Grant, Eva 1907-1996 .... *7*
Grant, Evva H. 1913-1977
Obituary *27*
Grant, Gordon 1875-1962 .... *25*
Grant, Gwen(doline Ellen) 1940- *47*
Grant, Judyann Ackerman *211*
Grant, Katie
See Grant, K.M.
Grant, Katie M.
See Grant, K.M.
Grant, K.M. *230*
Earlier sketch in SATA *175*
Grant, (Alice) Leigh 1947- *10*
Grant, Matthew G.
See May, Julian
Grant, Maxwell
See Gibson, Walter B(rown)
and Lynds, Dennis
Grant, Melvyn *183*
Grant, Myrna (Lois) 1934- *21*
Grant, Neil 1938- *154*
Earlier sketch in SATA *14*
Grant, Nicholas
See Nicole, Christopher
Grant, Richard 1948- *80*
Grant, Skeeter
See Spiegelman, Art
Grater, Michael 1923- *57*
Gratz, Alan 1972- *212*
Graullera, Fabiola
See Graullera Ramirez, Fabiola
Graullera Ramirez, Fabiola *225*
Gravel, Fern
See Hall, James Norman

Gravelle, Karen 1942- *166*
Earlier sketch in SATA *78*
Graves, Charles Parlin 1911-1972 .... *4*
Graves, Keith *191*
Earlier sketch in SATA *156*
Graves, Robert 1895-1985 .... *45*
Graves, Robert von Ranke
See Graves, Robert
Graves, Valerie
See Bradley, Marion Zimmer
Gravett, Emily 1972(?)- *189*
Gray, Betsy
See Poole, Gray Johnson
Gray, Caroline
See Nicole, Christopher
Gray, Claudia *213*
Gray, Dianne E. *183*
Gray, Elizabeth Janet
See Vining, Elizabeth Gray
Gray, Genevieve S(tuck) 1920-1995 .... *4*
Gray, Harold (Lincoln) 1894-1968 .... *33*
Brief entry *32*
Gray, Jenny
See Gray, Genevieve S(tuck)
Gray, John Lee
See Jakes, John
Gray, Judith A. 1949- *93*
Gray, Judith Anne
See Gray, Judith A.
Gray, Keith *151*
Gray, Kes 1960- *153*
Gray, Les 1929- *82*
Gray, Libba Moore 1937- *83*
Gray, Luli 1945- *149*
Earlier sketch in SATA *90*
Gray, Marian
See Pierce, Edith Gray
Gray, Nicholas Stuart 1922-1981 .... *4*
Obituary *27*
Gray, Nigel 1941- *104*
Earlier sketch in SATA *33*
Gray, (Lucy) Noel (Clervaux) 1898-1983 .... *47*
Gray, Patricia (Clark) *7*
Gray, Patsey
See Gray, Patricia (Clark)
Gray, Rita *184*
Gray, Steve 1950- *231*
Graydon, Shari 1958- *158*
Grayland, V. Merle
See Grayland, Valerie (Merle Spanner)
Grayland, Valerie (Merle Spanner) *7*
Grayson, Devin (Kalile) 1970- *119*
Grayson, Kristine
See Rusch, Kristine Kathryn
Grayson, Paul 1946- *79*
Graystone, Lynn
See Brennan, Joseph Lomas
Great Comte, The
See Hawkesworth, Eric
Greaves, Margaret 1914-1995 .... *87*
Earlier sketch in SATA *7*
Greaves, Nick 1955- *77*
Greban, Quentin 1977- *223*
Gree, Alain 1936- *28*
Green, Adam
See Weisgard, Leonard (Joseph)
Green, Anne Canevari 1943- *62*
Green, Brian
See Card, Orson Scott
Green, Cliff(ord) 1934- *126*
Green, Connie Jordan 1938- *80*
Green, D.
See Casewit, Curtis W(erner)
Green, Elizabeth Shippen 1871-1954 .... *139*
Green, Hannah
See Greenberg, Joanne (Goldenberg)
Green, Jane 1937- *9*
Green, Jessica *211*
Green, John 1977(?)- *170*
Green, Mary Moore 1906- *11*
Green, Morton 1937- *8*

Green, Norma B(erger) 1925- *11*
Green, Phyllis 1932- *20*
Green, Roger (Gilbert) Lancelyn 1918-1987 . *2*
Obituary *53*
Green, (James Le)Roy 1948- *89*
Green, Sheila Ellen 1934- *148*
Earlier sketches in SATA *8, 87*
Green, Timothy 1953- *91*
Greenaway, Kate 1846-1901 .... *100*
See also YABC *2*
See also CLR *111*
Greenbank, Anthony Hunt 1933- *39*
Greenberg, David 1954- *171*
Greenberg, David T.
See Greenberg, David
Greenberg, Harvey R. 1935- *5*
Greenberg, Jan 1942- *211*
Earlier sketches in SATA *61, 125*
Greenberg, Joanne (Goldenberg) 1932- *25*
Greenberg, Melanie Hope 1954- *214*
Earlier sketch in SATA *72*
Greenberg, Polly 1932- *52*
Brief entry *43*
Greenblat, Rodney Alan 1960- *106*
Greenburg, Dan 1936- *175*
Earlier sketch in SATA *102*
Greene, Bette 1934- *161*
Earlier sketches in SATA *8, 102*
See also CLR *140*
See also SAAS *16*
Greene, Carla 1916- *67*
Earlier sketch in SATA *1*
Greene, Carol *102*
Brief entry *44*
Earlier sketch in SATA *66*
Greene, Constance C(larke) 1924- *72*
Earlier sketch in SATA *11*
See also CLR *62*
See also SAAS *11*
Greene, Edgar
See Papademetriou, Lisa
Greene, Ellin 1927- *23*
Greene, Graham 1904-1991 .... *20*
Greene, Graham Henry
See Greene, Graham
Greene, Jacqueline Dembar 1946- *212*
Earlier sketches in SATA *76, 131*
Greene, Laura Offenhartz 1935- *38*
Greene, Meg
See Malvasi, Meg Greene
Greene, Michele 1962- *178*
Greene, Michele Dominguez
See Greene, Michele
Greene, Rhonda Gowler 1955- *160*
Earlier sketch in SATA *101*
Greene, Stephanie 1950- *221*
Earlier sketches in SATA *127, 173*
Greene, Wade 1933- *11*
Greene, Yvonne
See Flesch, Yolande
Greenfeld, Howard (Scheinman) 1928- *140*
Earlier sketch in SATA *19*
Greenfield, Josh(ua Joseph) 1928- *62*
Greenfield, Eloise 1929- *155*
Earlier sketches in SATA *19, 61, 105*
See also CLR *38*
See also SAAS *16*
Greenhaus, Thelma Nurenberg 1903-1984
Obituary *45*
Greenhut, Josh
See Mercer, Sienna
Greening, Hamilton
See Hamilton, Charles (Harold St. John)
Greenlaw, M. Jean 1941- *107*
Greenleaf, Barbara Kaye 1942- *6*
Greenleaf, Peter 1910-1997 .... *33*
Greenlee, Sharon 1935- *77*
Greeno, Gayle 1949- *81*
Greenseid, Diane 1948- *178*
Earlier sketch in SATA *93*

Greenspun, Adele Aron 1938- *142*
　Earlier sketch in SATA *76*
Greenstein, Elaine 1959- *150*
　Earlier sketch in SATA *82*
Greenwald, Sheila
　See Green, Sheila Ellen
Greenwood, Barbara 1940- *129*
　Earlier sketch in SATA *90*
Greenwood, Mark 1958- *202*
Greenwood, Pamela D. 1944- *115*
Greer, Richard
　See Garrett, Randall
　and Silverberg, Robert
Gregg, Andrew K. 1929- *81*
Gregg, Charles T(hornton) 1927- *65*
Gregg, Walter H(arold) 1919- *20*
Gregor, Arthur 1923- *36*
Gregor, Lee
　See Pohl, Frederik
Gregori, Leon 1919- *15*
Gregorian, Joyce Ballou 1946-1991 .... *30*
　Obituary *83*
Gregorich, Barbara 1943- *184*
　Earlier sketch in SATA *66*
Gregorowski, Christopher 1940- *30*
Gregory, Diana (Jean) 1933- *49*
　Brief entry *42*
Gregory, Harry
　See Gottfried, Theodore Mark
Gregory, Jean
　See Ure, Jean
Gregory, Kristiana 1951- *212*
　Earlier sketches in SATA *74, 136*
Gregory, Nan 1944- *192*
　Earlier sketch in SATA *148*
Gregory, Philippa 1954- *122*
Gregory, Stephen
　See Penzler, Otto
Gregory, Valiska 1940- *82*
Greif, Jean-Jacques 1944- *195*
Greisman, Joan Ruth 1937- *31*
Grendon, Stephen
　See Derleth, August (William)
Grenville, Pelham
　See Wodehouse, P. G.
Gretz, Susanna 1937- *7*
Gretzer, John *18*
Grewdead, Roy
　See Gorey, Edward (St. John)
Grey, Carol
　See Lowndes, Robert A(ugustine) W(ard)
Grey, Christopher *191*
Grey, Christopher Peter
　See Grey, Christopher
Grey, Jerry 1926- *11*
Grey, Mini *205*
　Earlier sketch in SATA *166*
Greybeard the Pirate
　See Macintosh, Brownie
Grey Owl
　See Belaney, Archibald Stansfeld
Gri
　See Denney, Diana
Gribbin, John 1946- *159*
Gribbin, John R.
　See Gribbin, John
Grice, Frederick 1910-1983 .... *6*
Grider, Dorothy 1915- *31*
Gridley, Marion E(leanor) 1906-1974 .... *35*
　Obituary *26*
Grieco-Tiso, Pina 1954- *108*
Grieder, Walter 1924- *9*
Griego, Tony A. 1955- *77*
Griese, Arnold A(lfred) 1921- *9*
Griessman, Annette 1962- *170*
　Earlier sketch in SATA *116*
Grieve, James 1934- *146*
Grifalconi, Ann 1929- *210*
　Earlier sketches in SATA *2, 66, 133*
　See also CLR *35*
　See also SAAS *16*

Griffin, Adele 1970- *195*
　Earlier sketches in SATA *105, 153*
Griffin, Elizabeth May 1985- *89*
Griffin, Gillett Good 1928- *26*
Griffin, Judith Berry *34*
Griffin, Kitty 1951- *137*
Griffin, Peni R. 1961- *193*
　Earlier sketches in SATA *67, 99*
Griffin, Steven A. 1953- *89*
Griffin, Steven Arthur
　See Griffin, Steven A.
Griffin, W. E. B. 1929- *5*
Griffith, Connie 1946- *89*
Griffith, Gershom 1960- *85*
Griffith, Helen V. 1934- *87*
　Autobiography Feature *107*
　Earlier sketch in SATA *39*
Griffith, Helen Virginia
　See Griffith, Helen V.
Griffith, Jeannette
　See Eyerly, Jeannette
Griffith, Saul 1974- *200*
Griffiths, Andy 1961- *196*
　Earlier sketch in SATA *152*
Griffiths, G(ordon) D(ouglas) 1910-1973
　Obituary *20*
Griffiths, Helen 1939- *86*
　Earlier sketch in SATA *5*
　See also CLR *75*
　See also SAAS *5*
Grigson, Jane (McIntire) 1928-1990 .... *63*
Grimes, Lee 1920- *68*
Grimes, Nikki 1950- *218*
　Earlier sketches in SATA *93, 136, 174*
　See also CLR *42*
Grimly, Gris *186*
Grimm, Jacob Ludwig Karl 1785-1863 .... *22*
　See also CLR *112*
Grimm, Wilhelm Karl 1786-1859 .... *22*
　See also CLR *112*
Grimm, William C(arey) 1907-1992 .... *14*
Grimm and Grim
　See Grimm, Jacob Ludwig Karl
　and Grimm, Wilhelm Karl
Grimm Brothers
　See Grimm, Jacob Ludwig Karl
　and Grimm, Wilhelm Karl
Grimsdell, Jeremy 1942- *83*
Grimshaw, Nigel (Gilroy) 1925- *23*
Grimsley, Gordon
　See Groom, Arthur William
Grindley, Jane Sally
　See Grindley, Sally
Grindley, Sally 1953- *148*
Gringhuis, Dirk
　See Gringhuis, Richard H.
Gringhuis, Richard H. 1918-1974 .... *6*
　Obituary *25*
Grinnell, David
　See Wollheim, Donald A(llen)
Grinnell, George Bird 1849-1938 .... *16*
Grinspoon, David
　See Grinspoon, David H.
Grinspoon, David H. 1959- *156*
Grinspoon, David Harry
　See Grinspoon, David H.
Gripe, Maria 1923- *74*
　Earlier sketch in SATA *2*
　See also CLR *5*
Gripe, Maria Kristina
　See Gripe, Maria
Gritton, Steve *223*
Grobler, Piet 1959- *201*
Groch, Judith (Goldstein) 1929- *25*
Grode, Redway
　See Gorey, Edward (St. John)
Groener, Carl
　See Lowndes, Robert A(ugustine) W(ard)
Groening, Matt 1954- *116*
　Earlier sketch in SATA *81*
Grohmann, Susan 1948- *84*

Grohskopf, Bernice *7*
Grol, Lini R(icharda) 1913- *9*
Grollman, Earl A. 1925- *22*
Groom, Arthur William 1898-1964 .... *10*
Grooms, Duffy 1964- *169*
Gross, Alan 1947- *54*
　Brief entry *43*
Gross, Ernie 1913- *67*
Gross, Philip 1952- *164*
　Earlier sketch in SATA *84*
Gross, Philip John
　See Gross, Philip
Gross, Ruth Belov 1929- *33*
Gross, Sarah Chokla 1906-1976 .... *9*
　Obituary *26*
Grosser, Morton 1931- *74*
Grosser, Vicky 1958- *83*
Grossman, Bill 1948- *126*
　Earlier sketch in SATA *72*
Grossman, Nancy 1940- *29*
Grossman, Patricia 1951- *73*
Grossman, Robert 1940- *11*
Grossmann-Hensel, Katharina 1973- *219*
Grote, JoAnn A. 1951- *113*
Groten, Dallas 1951- *64*
Groth, John (August) 1908-1988 .... *21*
　Obituary *56*
Groth-Fleming, Candace
　See Fleming, Candace
Grove, Vicki 1948- *151*
　Autobiography Feature *151*
　Earlier sketch in SATA *122*
Grover, Lorie Ann 1964- *168*
Grover, Wayne 1934- *69*
Groves, Georgina
　See Symons, (Dorothy) Geraldine
Groves, Maketa 1950- *107*
Groves, Seli *77*
Grubb, Lisa *160*
Gruber, Michael 1940- *173*
Gruber, Terry (deRoy) 1953- *66*
Gruelle, John 1880-1938 .... *35*
　Brief entry *32*
　See also CLR *34*
Gruelle, Johnny
　See Gruelle, John
Gruenberg, Sidonie Matsner 1881-1974 .... *2*
　Obituary *27*
Gruhzit-Hoyt, Olga (Margaret) 1922- *127*
　Earlier sketch in SATA *16*
Grummer, Arnold E(dward) 1923- *49*
Grunewalt, Pine
　See Kunhardt, Edith
Grunwell, Jeanne Marie 1971- *147*
Grupper, Jonathan *137*
Gryski, Camilla 1948- *72*
Guarino, Dagmar
　See Guarino, Deborah
Guarino, Deborah 1954- *68*
Guay, Georgette (Marie Jeanne) 1952- *54*
Guay, Rebecca *209*
Guay-Mitchell, Rebecca
　See Guay, Rebecca
Guback, Georgia *88*
Guccione, Leslie Davis 1946- *111*
　Earlier sketch in SATA *72*
Guck, Dorothy 1913-2002 .... *27*
Gudeon, Karla *212*
Guerny, Gene
　See Gurney, Gene
Guest, Elissa Haden 1953- *218*
　Earlier sketch in SATA *125*
Guest, Jacqueline 1952- *135*
Guevara, Susan *167*
　Earlier sketch in SATA *97*
Gugler, Laurel Dee *95*
Gugliotta, Bobette 1918-1994 .... *7*
Guianan, Eve 1965- *102*
Guiberson, Brenda Z. 1946- *211*
　Earlier sketches in SATA *71, 124*
Guibert, Emmanuel 1964- *181*

Guile, Melanie 1949- *152*
  Earlier sketch in SATA *104*
Guillaume, Jeanette G. Flierl 1899-1990 .... *8*
Guillot, Rene 1900-1969 .... *7*
  See also CLR 22
Guisewite, Cathy 1950- *57*
Guisewite, Cathy Lee
  See Guisewite, Cathy
Gulbis, Stephen 1959- *142*
Gulley, Judie 1942- *58*
Gump, P. Q.
  See Card, Orson Scott
Gundrey, Elizabeth 1924- *23*
Gunn, James E. 1923- *35*
Gunn, James Edwin
  See Gunn, James E.
Gunn, Robin Jones 1955- *84*
Gunnella 1956- *197*
Gunning, Monica Olwen 1930- *161*
Gunston, Bill
  See Gunston, William Tudor
Gunston, William Tudor 1927- *9*
Gunterman, Bertha Lisette 1886(?)-1975
  Obituary *27*
Gunther, John 1901-1970
Guravich, Dan 1918- *74*
Gurko, Leo 1914- *9*
Gurko, Miriam 1910(?)-1988 .... *9*
  Obituary *58*
Gurney, Gene 1924- *65*
Gurney, James 1958- *120*
  Earlier sketch in SATA *76*
Gurney, John Steven 1962- *227*
  Earlier sketches in SATA *75, 143*
Gustafson, Sarah R.
  See Riedman, Sarah R(egal)
Gustafson, Scott 1956- *34*
Gustavson, Adam 1974- *214*
  Earlier sketch in SATA *176*
Guthrie, A(lfred) B(ertram), Jr. 1901-1991 .. *62*
  Obituary *67*
Guthrie, Anne 1890-1979 .... *28*
Guthrie, Donna W. 1946- *105*
  Earlier sketch in SATA *63*
Gutierrez, Akemi *172*
Gutierrez, Rudy *203*
Gutman, Bill *128*
  Brief entry *43*
  Earlier sketch in SATA *67*
Gutman, Dan 1955- *221*
  Earlier sketches in SATA *77, 139, 188*
Gutman, Naham 1899(?)-1981
  Obituary *25*
Gutmann, Bessie Pease 1876-1960 .... *73*
Guy, Geoffrey 1942- *153*
Guy, Ginger Foglesong 1954- *171*
Guy, Rosa 1925- *122*
  Earlier sketches in SATA *14, 62*
  See also CLR *137*
Guy, Rosa Cuthbert
  See Guy, Rosa
Guy, Susan 1948- *149*
Guymer, (Wilhelmina) Mary 1909- *50*
Guzman, Lila 1952- *168*
Guzman, Rick 1957- *168*
Gwaltney, Doris 1932- *181*
Gwynne, Fred(erick Hubbard) 1926-1993 .... *41*
  Brief entry *27*
  Obituary *75*
Gwynne, Oscar A.
  See Ellis, Edward S.
Gwynne, Oswald A.
  See Ellis, Edward S.
Gyorkos, Charmaine Echeverria
  See Echeverria Gyorkos, Charmaine

H

Haab, Sherri 1964- *169*
  Earlier sketch in SATA *91*
Haar, Jaap ter
  See ter Haar, Jaap
Haarsma, P.J. *183*
Haas, Carolyn Buhai 1926- *43*
Haas, Dan 1957- *105*
Haas, Dorothy F. *46*
  Brief entry *43*
  See also SAAS *17*
Haas, Irene 1929- *96*
  Earlier sketch in SATA *17*
Haas, James E. 1943- *40*
Haas, James Edward
  See Haas, James E.
Haas, Jessie 1959- *215*
Haas, (Katherine) Jessie 1959- *135*
  Autobiography Feature *135*
  Earlier sketch in SATA *98*
Haas, Merle S. 1896(?)-1985
  Obituary *41*
Habenstreit, Barbara 1937- *5*
Haber, Karen 1955- *78*
Haber, Louis 1910-1988 .... *12*
Hacker, Randi 1951- *185*
Hacker, Randi Dawn
  See Hacker, Randi
Hackett, John Winthrop 1910-1997 .... *65*
Hacks, Peter 1928-2003
  Obituary *151*
Haddix, Margaret Peterson 1964- *224*
  Earlier sketches in SATA *94, 125, 187*
Haddon, Mark 1962- *223*
  Earlier sketch in SATA *155*
Hader, Berta (Hoerner) 1891(?)-1976 .... *16*
Hader, Elmer (Stanley) 1889-1973 .... *16*
Hadithi, Mwenye
  See Hobson, Bruce
Hadley, Franklin
  See Winterbotham, R(ussell) R(obert)
Hadley, Lee 1934-1995 .... *89*
  Brief entry *38*
  Obituary *86*
  Earlier sketch in SATA *47*
  See also CLR *40*
  See also SAAS *14*
Haeffele, Deborah 1954- *76*
Haenel, Wolfram 1956- *89*
  See also CLR *64*
Hafner, Marylin 1925- *179*
  Earlier sketches in SATA *7, 121*
Haft, Erin
  See Ehrenhaft, Daniel
Hager, Alan 1940- *176*
Hager, Alice Rogers 1894-1969
  Obituary *26*
Hager, Betty 1923- *89*
Hager, Jenna Bush
  See Bush, Jenna
Hager, Sarah *171*
Hager, Thomas 1953- *119*
Hager, Tom
  See Hager, Thomas
Hagerup, Klaus 1946- *186*
Haggard, H(enry) Rider 1856-1925 .... *16*
Haggerty, James J(oseph) 1920- *5*
Hagon, Priscilla
  See Allan, Mabel Esther
Hague, Kathleen 1949- *49*
  Brief entry *45*
Hague, Michael 1948- *185*
  Brief entry *32*
  Earlier sketches in SATA *48, 80, 129*
Hague, Michael R.
  See Hague, Michael
Hague, Susan Kathleen
  See Hague, Kathleen
Hahn, Emily 1905-1997 .... *3*
  Obituary *96*

Hahn, Hannelore *8*
Hahn, James (Sage) 1947- *9*
Hahn, Lynn 1949- *9*
Hahn, Mary Downing 1937- *208*
  Autobiography Feature *157*
  Brief entry *44*
  Earlier sketches in SATA *50, 81, 138, 157*
  See also SAAS *12*
Hahn, Michael T. 1953- *92*
Hahn, Mona Lynn
  See Hahn, Lynn
Haig, Matt 1975- *221*
Haig-Brown, Roderick (Langmere)
  1908-1976 .... *12*
  See also CLR *31*
Haight, Anne Lyon 1895-1977
  Obituary *30*
Haight, Rip
  See Carpenter, John
Haight, Sandy 1949- *79*
Haij, Vera
  See Jansson, Tove (Marika)
Hailstone, Ruth *219*
Haines, Gail Kay 1943- *11*
Haines, Margaret Ann Beck
  See Beck, Peggy
Haining, Peter 1940-2007 .... *14*
  Obituary *188*
Haining, Peter Alexander
  See Haining, Peter
Hains, Harriet
  See Watson, Carol
Hajdusiewicz, Babs Bell *163*
Hakim, Joy 1931- *173*
  Earlier sketch in SATA *83*
Halacy, D. S., Jr. 1919-2002 .... *36*
  See also SAAS *8*
Halacy, Dan
  See Halacy, D. S., Jr.
Halam, Ann
  See Jones, Gwyneth A.
Haldane, Roger John 1945- *13*
Hale, Arlene 1924-1982 .... *49*
Hale, Bruce 1957- *203*
  Earlier sketch in SATA *123*
Hale, Christy
  See Apostolou, Christine Hale
Hale, Dean 1972- *227*
Hale, Edward Everett 1822-1909 .... *16*
Hale, Glenn
  See Walker, Robert W.
Hale, Helen
  See Mulcahy, Lucille Burnett
Hale, Irina 1932- *26*
Hale, Kathleen 1898-2000 .... *66*
  Obituary *121*
  Earlier sketch in SATA *17*
Hale, Linda (Howe) 1929- *6*
Hale, Lucretia P.
  See Hale, Lucretia Peabody
Hale, Lucretia Peabody 1820-1900 .... *26*
  See also CLR *105*
Hale, Marian *194*
Hale, Nancy 1908-1988 .... *31*
  Obituary *57*
Hale, Nathan 1976- *210*
Hale, Shannon *200*
  Earlier sketch in SATA *158*
Haley, Amanda *205*
Haley, Gail E(inhart) 1939- *161*
  Autobiography Feature *161*
  Brief entry *28*
  Earlier sketches in SATA *43, 78, 136*
  See also CLR *21*
  See also SAAS *13*
Haley, Neale *52*
Halfmann, Janet 1944- *208*
Hall, Adam
  See Trevor, Elleston
Hall, Adele 1910- *7*
Hall, Anna Gertrude 1882-1967 .... *8*

Hall, August 207
Hall, Barbara 1961- 68
Hall, Becky 1950- 186
Hall, Beverly B. 1918- 95
Hall, Borden
    See Yates, Raymond F(rancis)
Hall, Brian P(atrick) 1935- 31
Hall, Cameron
    See del Rey, Lester
Hall, Caryl
    See Hansen, Caryl (Hall)
Hall, Donald 1928- 97
    Earlier sketch in SATA 23
Hall, Donald Andrew, Jr.
    See Hall, Donald
Hall, Douglas 1931- 43
Hall, Elizabeth 1929- 77
Hall, Elvajean 1910-1984 6
Hall, Francie 1940- 166
Hall, James Norman 1887-1951 21
Hall, Jesse
    See Boesen, Victor
Hall, Katy
    See McMullan, Kate
Hall, Kirsten Marie 1974- 67
Hall, Lynn 1937- 79
    Earlier sketches in SATA 2, 47
    See also SAAS 4
Hall, Malcolm 1945- 7
Hall, Marcellus 203
Hall, Marjory
    See Yeakley, Marjory Hall
Hall, Melanie 1949- 228
    Earlier sketches in SATA 78, 116, 169
Hall, Michael 1954- 228
Hall, Patricia 1940- 136
Hall, Rosalys Haskell 1914- 7
Hall, Teri 229
Hall, Willis 1929-2005 66
Hallard, Peter
    See Catherall, Arthur
Hallas, Richard
    See Knight, Eric
Hall-Clarke, James
    See Rowland-Entwistle, (Arthur) Theodore
    (Henry)
Hallensleben, Georg 1958- 173
Haller, Dorcas Woodbury 1946- 46
Hallett, Mark 1947- 220
    Earlier sketch in SATA 83
Halliburton, Richard 1900-1939(?) 81
Halliburton, Warren J. 1924- 19
Halliday, Brett
    See Dresser, Davis
    and Johnson, (Walter) Ryerson
    and Terrall, Robert
Halliday, William R(oss) 1926- 52
Hallin, Emily Watson 1916-1995 6
Hallinan, P. K. 1944- 39
    Brief entry 37
Hallinan, Patrick Kenneth
    See Hallinan, P. K.
Hallman, Ruth 1929- 43
    Brief entry 28
Hallowell, Tommy
    See Hill, Thomas
Hall-Quest, (Edna) Olga W(ilbourne)
    1899-1986 11
    Obituary 47
Halls, Kelly Milner 1957- 220
    Earlier sketch in SATA 131
Hallstead, William F(inn III) 1924- 11
Hallward, Michael 1889-1982 12
Halperin, Michael 156
Halperin, Wendy Anderson 1952- 200
    Earlier sketches in SATA 80, 125
Halpern, Julie 1975- 198
Halpin, Brendan 1968- 193
Halpin, Marlene 1927- 88
Halse, Laurie Beth
    See Anderson, Laurie Halse

Halsell, Grace (Eleanor) 1923-2000 13
Halsey, Megan 185
Halsted, Anna Roosevelt 1906-1975
    Obituary 30
Halter, Jon C(harles) 1941- 22
Halverson, Deborah 202
Halvorson, Adeline 218
Halvorson, Marilyn 1948- 123
Hamalian, Leo 1920- 41
Hamberger, John 1934- 14
Hamblin, Dora Jane 1920- 36
Hambly, Barbara 1951- 108
Hambly, Barbara Joan
    See Hambly, Barbara
Hamer, Martyn
    See Eldin, Peter
Hamerstrom, Frances 1907-1998 24
Hamil, Thomas Arthur 1928- 14
Hamill, Ethel
    See Webb, Jean Francis (III)
Hamilton, (John) Alan 1943- 66
Hamilton, Alice
    See Cromie, Alice Hamilton
Hamilton, Anita 1919- 92
Hamilton, Barbara
    See Hambly, Barbara
Hamilton, Buzz
    See Hemming, Roy G.
Hamilton, Carol (Jean Barber) 1935- 94
Hamilton, Charles (Harold St. John)
    1876-1961 13
Hamilton, Charles 1913-1996 65
    Obituary 93
Hamilton, Clive
    See Lewis, C. S.
Hamilton, Dorothy (Drumm) 1906-1983 12
    Obituary 35
Hamilton, Edith 1867-1963 20
Hamilton, Edmond 1904-1977 118
Hamilton, (Muriel) Elizabeth (Mollie)
    1906- 23
Hamilton, Emma Walton 1962- 177
Hamilton, Franklin
    See Silverberg, Robert
Hamilton, Gail
    See Corcoran, Barbara (Asenath)
    and Dodge, Mary Abigail
Hamilton, Kersten 1958- 204
    Earlier sketch in SATA 134
Hamilton, K.R.
    See Hamilton, Kersten
Hamilton, Martha 1953- 183
    Earlier sketch in SATA 123
Hamilton, Mary (E.) 1927- 55
Hamilton, Mollie
    See Kaye, M.M.
Hamilton, Morse 1943-1998 101
    Earlier sketch in SATA 35
Hamilton, Peter F. 1960- 109
Hamilton, Priscilla
    See Gellis, Roberta
Hamilton, Ralph
    See Stratemeyer, Edward L.
Hamilton, Virginia 1936-2002 123
    Obituary 132
    Earlier sketches in SATA 4, 56, 79
    See also CLR 127
Hamilton, Virginia Esther
    See Hamilton, Virginia
Hamilton-Paterson, James 1941- 82
Hamlet, Ova
    See Lupoff, Richard A(llen)
Hamley, D. C.
    See Hamley, Dennis
Hamley, Dennis 1935- 69
    Earlier sketch in SATA 39
    See also CLR 47
    See also SAAS 22
Hamley, Dennis C.
    See Hamley, Dennis
Hamlin, Peter J. 1970- 84

Hamm, Diane Johnston 1949- 78
Hammer, Charles 1934- 58
Hammer, Richard 1928- 6
Hammerman, Gay M(orenus) 1926- 9
Hammill, Matt 1982- 206
Hammond, Andrew 1970- 181
Hammond, Ralph
    See Hammond Innes, Ralph
Hammond, Winifred G(raham) 1899-1992 ... 29
    Obituary 107
Hammond Innes, Ralph 1913-1998 116
Hammontree, Marie (Gertrude) 1913- 13
Hample, Zack 1977- 161
Hampshire, Joyce Gregorian
    See Gregorian, Joyce Ballou
Hampshire, Susan 1942- 98
Hampson, (Richard) Denman 1929- 15
Hampson, Frank 1918(?)-1985
    Obituary 46
Hampton, Wilborn 1940- 196
    Earlier sketch in SATA 156
Hamre, Leif 1914- 5
Hamsa, Bobbie 1944- 52
    Brief entry 38
Han, Jenny 1981- 175
Han, Lu
    See Stickler, Soma Han
Han, Soma
    See Stickler, Soma Han
Han, Suzanne Crowder 1953- 89
Hancock, Mary A. 1923- 31
Hancock, Sibyl 1940- 9
Hand, Elizabeth 1957- 167
    Earlier sketch in SATA 118
Handford, Martin (John) 1956- 64
    See also CLR 22
Handforth, Thomas (Schofield) 1897-1948 .. 42
Handleman, Philip 1951- 222
Handler, Daniel
    See Snicket, Lemony
Handville, Robert (Tompkins) 1924- 45
Hane, Roger 1940-1974
    Obituary 20
Hanel, Wolfram
    See Haenel, Wolfram
Haney, Lynn 1941- 23
Hanff, Helene 1916-1997 97
    Earlier sketch in SATA 11
Hanft, Josh 1956- 197
Hanft, Joshua E.
    See Hanft, Josh
Hanley, Boniface Francis 1924- 65
Hanlon, Emily 1945- 15
Hann, Jacquie 1951- 19
Hann, Judith 1942- 77
Hanna, Bill
    See Hanna, William (Denby)
Hanna, Cheryl 1951- 84
Hanna, Dan 200
Hanna, Jack (Bushnell) 1947- 74
Hanna, Nell(ie L.) 1908- 55
Hanna, Paul R(obert) 1902-1988 9
Hanna, William (Denby) 1910-2001 51
    Obituary 126
Hannam, Charles 1925- 50
Hannan, Peter 1954- 187
Hannigan, Katherine 170
Hannon, Ezra
    See Hunter, Evan
Hann-Syme, Marguerite 127
Hano, Arnold 1922- 12
Hano, Renee Roth
    See Roth-Hano, Renee
Hanover, Terri
    See Huff, Tanya
Hansen, Amy S. 229
Hansen, Ann Larkin 1958- 96
Hansen, Brooks 1965- 104
Hansen, Caryl (Hall) 1929- 39
Hansen, Ian V. 1929- 113
Hansen, Jennifer 1972- 156

Hansen, Joyce 1942- *172*
  Autobiography Feature *172*
  Brief entry *39*
  Earlier sketches in SATA *46, 101*
  See also CLR *21*
  See also SAAS *15*
Hansen, Joyce Viola
  See Hansen, Joyce
Hansen, Mark Victor *112*
Hansen, Ron 1947- *56*
Hansen, Ronald Thomas
  See Hansen, Ron
Hansen, Thore 1942- *224*
Hanser, Richard (Frederick) 1909-1981 .... *13*
Hanson, Joan 1938- *8*
Hanson, Joseph E. 1894(?)-1971
  Obituary *27*
Hanson, Mary Elizabeth *188*
Hanson, Warren 1949- *155*
Hansson, Gunilla 1939- *64*
Hantman, Clea *200*
Hapka, C.A.
  See Hapka, Catherine
Hapka, Catherine *223*
Hapka, Cathy
  See Hapka, Catherine
Harald, Eric
  See Boesen, Victor
Harazin, S. A. *210*
Harbour, Elizabeth 1968- *221*
Harcourt, Ellen Knowles 1890(?)-1984
  Obituary *36*
Hard, Charlotte (Ann) 1969- *98*
Hardcastle, Michael 1933- *216*
  Brief entry *38*
  Earlier sketch in SATA *47*
Harding, Lee 1937- *32*
  Brief entry *31*
Hardinge, Frances 1973- *210*
Hardt, Helga Fleischhauer
  See Fleischhauer-Hardt, Helga
Hardwick, Richard Holmes, Jr. 1923- *12*
Hardy, Alice Dale *67*
  Earlier sketch in SATA *1*
Hardy, David A(ndrews) 1936- *9*
Hardy, Janice *222*
Hardy, Jon 1958- *53*
Hardy, LeAnne 1951- *154*
Hardy, Stuart
  See Schisgall, Oscar
Hare, Norma Q(uarles) 1924- *46*
  Brief entry *41*
Harel, Nira 1936- *154*
Harford, Henry
  See Hudson, W(illiam) H(enry)
Hargis, Wes *219*
Hargrave, Leonie
  See Disch, Thomas M.
Hargreaves, (Charles) Roger 1935-1988
  Obituary *56*
Hargrove, James 1947- *57*
  Brief entry *50*
Hargrove, Jim
  See Hargrove, James
Harik, Elsa
  See Marston, Elsa
Harik, Elsa M.
  See Marston, Elsa
Harik, Elsa Marston
  See Marston, Elsa
Hariton, Anca I. 1955- *79*
Hark, Mildred
  See McQueen, Mildred Hark
Harkaway, Hal
  See Stratemeyer, Edward L.
Harkins, Philip 1912-1997 .... *6*
  Obituary *129*
Harlan, Elizabeth 1945- *41*
  Brief entry *35*
Harlan, Glen
  See Cebulash, Mel

Harlan, Judith 1949- *135*
  Earlier sketch in SATA *74*
  See also CLR *81*
Harland, Richard 1947- *152*
Harlee, J. V.
  See Leese, Jennifer L.B.
Harler, Ann
  See Van Steenwyk, Elizabeth (Ann)
Harley, Avis *183*
Harley, Bill 1954- *208*
  Earlier sketch in SATA *87*
Harlow, Joan Hiatt 1932- *226*
  Earlier sketch in SATA *157*
Harman, Fred 1902(?)-1982
  Obituary *30*
Harman, Hugh 1903-1982
  Obituary *33*
Harmelink, Barbara (Mary) *9*
Harmer, Mabel 1894-1992 .... *45*
Harmon, Dan
  See Harmon, Daniel E(lton)
Harmon, Daniel E(lton) 1949- *157*
Harmon, Kate
  See Gibson, Marley
Harmon, Margaret 1906- *20*
Harmon, Michael 1969- *189*
Harmon, Michael B.
  See Harmon, Michael
Harmon, William (Ruth) 1938- *65*
Harnan, Terry 1920- *12*
Harness, Cheryl 1951- *178*
  Earlier sketch in SATA *131*
Harnett, Cynthia (Mary) 1893-1981 .... *5*
  Obituary *32*
Harper, Anita 1943- *41*
Harper, Betty 1946- *126*
Harper, Charise
  See Harper, Charise Mericle
Harper, Charise Mericle *226*
  Earlier sketch in SATA *179*
Harper, Elaine
  See Hallin, Emily Watson
Harper, Ellen
  See Noble, Marty
Harper, Jamie *174*
Harper, Jessica 1949- *148*
Harper, Jo 1932- *169*
  Earlier sketch in SATA *97*
Harper, Lee *201*
Harper, Mary Wood
  See Dixon, Jeanne
Harper, Piers 1966- *161*
  Earlier sketch in SATA *105*
Harper, Suzanne *194*
Harper, Wilhelmina 1884-1973 .... *4*
  Obituary *26*
Harrah, Madge 1931- *154*
Harrah, Michael 1940- *41*
Harrah, Monique
  See Harrah, Madge
Harrar, George E. 1949- *124*
Harrell, Beatrice Orcutt 1943- *93*
Harrell, Janice 1945- *70*
Harrell, Sara Gordon 1940- *26*
Harrell, Sara Jeanne Gordon
  See Harrell, Sara Gordon
Harries, Joan 1922- *39*
Harrill, Ronald 1950- *90*
Harrington, Denis J(ames) 1932- *88*
Harrington, Evelyn Davis 1911- *5*
Harrington, Janice N. 1956- *187*
Harrington, Lyn
  See Harrington, Evelyn Davis
Harris, Alan 1944- *71*
Harris, Aurand 1915-1996 .... *37*
  Obituary *91*
Harris, Bob
  See Harris, Robert J.
Harris, Carol Flynn 1933- *135*
Harris, Catherine
  See Ainsworth, Catherine Harris

Harris, Christie
  See Harris, Christie (Lucy) Irwin
Harris, Christie (Lucy) Irwin 1907-2002 ...... *74*
  Autobiography Feature *116*
  Earlier sketch in SATA *6*
  See also CLR *47*
  See also SAAS *10*
Harris, Christine 1955- *105*
Harris, Colver
  See Colver, Anne
Harris, David 1942- *118*
Harris, David William
  See Harris, David
Harris, Dorothy Joan 1931- *153*
  Earlier sketch in SATA *13*
Harris, Geraldine 1951- *54*
Harris, Geraldine Rachel
  See Harris, Geraldine
Harris, Jacqueline L. 1929- *62*
Harris, Janet 1932-1979 .... *4*
  Obituary *23*
Harris, Jesse
  See Standiford, Natalie
Harris, Joan 1946- *146*
Harris, Joe 1928- *201*
Harris, Joel Chandler 1848-1908 .... *100*
  See also YABC *1*
  See also CLR *128*
Harris, John (Wyndham Parkes Lucas) Beynon
  1903-1969 .... *118*
Harris, Johnson
  See Harris, John (Wyndham Parkes Lucas)
  Beynon
Harris, Jonathan 1921-1997 .... *52*
Harris, Larry Vincent 1939- *59*
Harris, Lavinia
  See St. John, Nicole
Harris, Leon A., Jr. 1926-2000 .... *4*
Harris, Lois V. *199*
Harris, Lorle K(empe) 1912-2001 .... *22*
Harris, Maria Guadalupe
  See Harris, M.G.
Harris, Marilyn
  See Springer, Marilyn Harris
Harris, Mark Jonathan 1941- *84*
  Earlier sketch in SATA *32*
Harris, Mary K(athleen) 1905-1966 .... *119*
Harris, M.G. *231*
Harris, Robert J. 1955- *195*
Harris, Robie H. 1940- *203*
  Brief entry *53*
  Earlier sketches in SATA *90, 147*
Harris, Robin
  See Shine, Deborah
Harris, Rosemary (Jeanne) *82*
  Earlier sketch in SATA *4*
  See also CLR *30*
  See also SAAS *7*
Harris, Ruth Elwin 1935- *164*
Harris, Sherwood 1932-2009 .... *25*
Harris, Stephen 1959- *230*
Harris, Steven Michael 1957- *55*
Harris, Trudy 1949- *191*
  Earlier sketch in SATA *128*
Harris-Filderman, Diane
  See Filderman, Diane E(lizabeth)
Harrison, C(hester) William 1913-1994 .... *35*
Harrison, Carol
  See Harrison, Carol Thompson
Harrison, Carol Thompson *113*
Harrison, David L. 1937- *186*
  Earlier sketches in SATA *26, 92, 150*
Harrison, Deloris 1938- *9*
Harrison, Edward Hardy 1926- *56*
Harrison, Elizabeth (Allen) Cavanna
  1909-2001 .... *30*
  Earlier sketch in SATA *1*
  See also SAAS *4*
Harrison, Harry 1925- *4*
Harrison, Harry Max
  See Harrison, Harry

Harrison, Mette Ivie 1970- 202
  Earlier sketch in SATA 149
Harrison, Michael 1939- 106
Harrison, Molly (Hodgett) 1909-2002 41
Harrison, Sarah 1946- 63
Harrison, Ted
  See Harrison, Edward Hardy
Harsh, Fred (T.) 1925- 72
Harshaw, Ruth H(etzel) 1890-1968 27
Harshman, Marc 1950- 109
  Earlier sketch in SATA 71
Hart, Alexandra 1939- 14
Hart, Alison
  See Leonhardt, Alice
Hart, Bruce 1938-2006 57
  Brief entry 39
Hart, Carole 1943- 57
  Brief entry 39
Hart, Carolyn 1936- 74
Hart, Carolyn G.
  See Hart, Carolyn
Hart, Carolyn Gimpel
  See Hart, Carolyn
Hart, Jan Siegel 1940- 79
Hart, Joyce 1954- 148
Hart, Karen 185
Hart, Lenore 171
Hart, Philip S. 1944- 180
Hart, Virginia 1949- 83
Harte, Bret 1836(?)-1902 26
Harte, Francis Brett
  See Harte, Bret
Harter, Debbie 1963- 107
Hartfield, Claire 1957- 147
Hartinger, Brent 1964- 217
  Earlier sketches in SATA 145, 174
Hartland, Jessie 171
Hartley, Ellen (Raphael) 1915-1980 23
Hartley, Fred Allan III 1953- 41
Hartley, William B(rown) 1913-1980 23
Hartling, Peter
  See Hartling, Peter
Hartling, Peter 1933- 66
  See also CLR 29
Hartman, Bob 1955- 224
Hartman, Carrie 226
Hartman, Cassie 202
Hartman, Dan 1955- 202
Hartman, Evert 1937- 38
  Brief entry 35
Hartman, Jane E. 1928- 47
Hartman, Jane Evangeline
  See Hartman, Jane E.
Hartman, Louis F(rancis) 1901-1970 22
Hartman, Rachel 174
Hartman, Victoria 1942- 91
Hartnett, Sonya 1968- 176
  Earlier sketches in SATA 93, 130
Hartry, Nancy 219
Hartshorn, Ruth M. 1928- 11
Hartung, Susan Kathleen 192
  Earlier sketch in SATA 150
Hartwig, Manfred 1950- 81
Harvey, Alyxandra 1974- 227
  Earlier sketch in SATA 189
Harvey, Brett 1936- 61
Harvey, Edith 1908(?)-1972
  Obituary 27
Harvey, Gill 189
Harvey, Karen D. 1935- 88
Harvey, Roland 1945- 219
  Earlier sketches in SATA 71, 123, 179
Harvey-Fitzhenry, Alyxandra
  See Harvey, Alyxandra
Harwick, B. L.
  See Keller, Beverly L(ou)
Harwin, Brian
  See Henderson, LeGrand
Harwood, Pearl Augusta (Bragdon)
  1903-1998 9

Haseley, Dennis 1950- 221
  Brief entry 44
  Earlier sketches in SATA 57, 105, 157
Hashmi, Kerri 1955- 108
Haskell, Arnold L(ionel) 1903-1981(?) 6
Haskins, James
  See Haskins, James S.
Haskins, James S. 1941-2005 132
  Autobiography Feature 132
  Earlier sketches in SATA 9, 69, 105
  See also CLR 39
  See also SAAS 4
Haskins, Jim
  See Haskins, James S.
Hasler, Eveline 1933- 181
Hasler, Joan 1931- 28
Hass, Robert 1941- 94
Hassall, Joan 1906-1988 43
  Obituary 56
Hassett, Ann 1958- 162
Hassett, John 162
Hassler, Jon 1933-2008 19
  Obituary 191
Hassler, Jon Francis
  See Hassler, Jon
Hastings, Beverly
  See Barkin, Carol
  and James, Elizabeth
Hastings, Graham
  See Jeffries, Roderic
Hastings, Ian 1912- 62
Hastings, Victor
  See Disch, Thomas M.
Haszard, Patricia Moyes 1923-2000 63
Hatch, Lynda S. 1950- 90
Hathaway, Barbara 164
Hathorn, Elizabeth
  See Hathorn, Libby
Hathorn, Elizabeth Helen
  See Hathorn, Libby
Hathorn, Libby 1943- 156
  Autobiography Feature 156
  Earlier sketches in SATA 74, 120
Hatkoff, Craig 1954- 192
Hatlo, Jimmy 1898-1963
  Obituary 23
Hatton, Caroline 1957- 205
Hauff, Wilhelm 1802-1827
  See CLR 155
Haugaard, Erik Christian 1923- 68
  Earlier sketch in SATA 4
  See also CLR 11
  See also SAAS 12
Haugaard, Kay 117
Haugen, Hayley Mitchell 1968- 172
Haugen, Tormod 1945- 66
Hauman, Doris 1898-1984 32
Hauman, George 1890-1961 32
Hauptly, Denis J. 1945- 57
Hauptly, Denis James
  See Hauptly, Denis J.
Hauser, Jill Frankel 1950- 127
Hauser, Margaret L(ouise) 1909- 10
Hausherr, Rosmarie 1943- 86
Hausman, Gerald 1945- 180
  Earlier sketches in SATA 13, 90, 132
  See also CLR 89
Hausman, Gerry
  See Hausman, Gerald
Hauth, Katherine B. 1940- 99
Hautman, Pete 1952- 173
  Earlier sketches in SATA 82, 128
Hautman, Peter Murray
  See Hautman, Pete
Hautzig, Deborah 1956- 106
  Earlier sketch in SATA 31
Hautzig, Esther Rudomin 1930-2009 148
  Earlier sketches in SATA 4, 68
  See also CLR 22
  See also SAAS 15
Havel, Geoff 1955- 152

Havel, Jennifer
  See Havill, Juanita
Havelin, Kate 1961- 143
Haven, Paul 1971(?)- 213
Haverfield, Mary 225
Havighurst, Walter (Edwin) 1901-1994 1
  Obituary 79
Haviland, Virginia 1911-1988 6
  Obituary 54
Havill, Juanita 1949- 224
  Earlier sketches in SATA 74, 155
Hawes, Judy 1913- 4
Hawes, Louise 1943- 180
  Earlier sketch in SATA 60
Hawk, Fran 222
Hawke, Rosanne 1953- 165
  Earlier sketch in SATA 124
Hawke, Rosanne Joy
  See Hawke, Rosanne
Hawkes, Kevin 1959- 201
  Earlier sketches in SATA 78, 150
Hawkes, Nigel 1943- 119
Hawkesworth, Eric 1921- 13
Hawking, Lucy 1969- 197
Hawkins, Arthur 1903-1985 19
Hawkins, Colin 1945- 162
  Earlier sketch in SATA 112
Hawkins, Jacqui 162
  Earlier sketch in SATA 112
Hawkins, Jimmy 1941- 188
Hawkins, Laura 1951- 74
Hawkins, (Helena Ann) Quail 1905-2002 6
  Obituary 141
Hawkins, Rachel 1979- 228
Hawkinson, John (Samuel) 1912-1994 4
Hawkinson, Lucy (Ozone) 1924-1971 21
Hawks, Robert 1961- 85
Hawley, Mabel C. 67
  Earlier sketch in SATA 1
Haworth, Danette 207
Haworth-Attard, Barbara 1953- 215
Hawthorne, Captain R. M.
  See Ellis, Edward S.
Hawthorne, Nathaniel 1804-1864
  See YABC 2
  See also CLR 163
Hay, Jeff T. 154
Hay, John 1915-2011 13
Hay, Samantha 213
Hay, Timothy
  See Brown, Margaret Wise
Hayashi, Leslie Ann 1954- 115
Hayashi, Nancy 1939- 186
  Earlier sketch in SATA 80
Haycak, Cara 1961- 180
Haycock, Kate 1962- 77
Haycraft, Howard 1905-1991 6
  Obituary 70
Haycraft, Molly Costain 1911- 6
Hayden, Gwendolen Lampshire 1904- 35
Hayden, Robert
  See Hayden, Robert Earl
Hayden, Robert C(arter), Jr. 1937- 47
  Brief entry 28
Hayden, Robert E.
  See Hayden, Robert Earl
Hayden, Robert Earl 1913-1980 19
  Obituary 26
Hayden, Torey L. 1951- 163
  Earlier sketch in SATA 65
Hayden, Torey Lynn
  See Hayden, Torey L.
Hayes, Carlton J(oseph) H(untley)
  1882-1964 11
Hayes, Daniel 1952- 109
  Earlier sketch in SATA 73
Hayes, Geoffrey 1947- 207
  Earlier sketches in SATA 26, 91
Hayes, Joe 1945- 131
  Earlier sketch in SATA 88
Hayes, John F. 1904-1980 11

Hayes, Karel 1949- 207
Hayes, Rosemary 227
   Earlier sketch in SATA 158
Hayes, Sarah 1945- 208
Hayes, Sheila 1937- 51
   Brief entry 50
Hayes, Will 7
Hayes, William D(imitt) 1913-1976 8
Haynes, Betsy 1937- 94
   Brief entry 37
   Earlier sketch in SATA 48
   See also CLR 90
Haynes, David 1955- 97
Haynes, Linda
   See Swinford, Betty (June Wells)
Haynes, Mary 1938- 65
Haynes, Max 1956- 72
Hays, Anna Jane 214
Hays, H(offmann) R(eynolds) 1904-1980 26
Hays, Thomas A.
   See Hays, Tony
Hays, Thomas Anthony
   See Hays, Tony
Hays, Tony 1957- 84
Hays, Wilma Pitchford 1909- 28
   Earlier sketch in SATA 1
   See also CLR 59
   See also SAAS 3
Hayward, Linda 1943- 185
   Brief entry 39
   Earlier sketch in SATA 101
Haywood, Carolyn 1898-1990 75
   Obituary 64
   Earlier sketches in SATA 1, 29
   See also CLR 22
Hazelaar, Cor 217
Hazell, Rebecca (Eileen) 1947- 141
Hazen, Barbara Shook 1930- 178
   Earlier sketches in SATA 27, 90
Hazen, Lynn E. 202
Head, Gay
   See Hauser, Margaret L(ouise)
Head, Tom 1978- 167
Headley, Elizabeth
   See Harrison, Elizabeth (Allen) Cavanna
Headley, Justina Chen 1968- 176
Headstrom, (Birger) Richard 1902-1985 8
Heady, Eleanor B(utler) 1917-1979 8
Heagy, William D. 1964- 76
Heal, Edith 1903-1995 7
Heal, Gillian 1934- 89
Heale, Jay (Jeremy Peter Wingfield) 1937- .. 84
Healey, Brooks
   See Albert, Burton
Healey, Karen 1981- 230
Healey, Larry 1927- 44
   Brief entry 42
Heap, Sue 1954- 187
   Earlier sketch in SATA 150
Heaps, Willard A(llison) 1908-1987 26
Hearn, Diane Dawson 1952- 209
   Earlier sketch in SATA 79
Hearn, Emily
   See Valleau, Emily
Hearn, Julie 1958- 212
   Earlier sketch in SATA 152
Hearn, Lian
   See Rubinstein, Gillian
Hearn, Sneed
   See Gregg, Andrew K.
Hearne, Betsy 1942- 146
   Earlier sketches in SATA 38, 95
Heath, Charles D(ickinson) 1941- 46
Heath, Veronica
   See Blackett, Veronica Heath
Heaven, Constance (Christina) 1911- 7
Hebert-Collins, Sheila 1948- 111
Hecht, George J(oseph) 1895-1980
   Obituary 22
Hecht, Henri Joseph 1922- 9
Hechtkopf, Henryk 1910- 17

Heck, Bessie (Mildred) Holland 1911-1995 . 26
Heck, Ed 1963- 173
Heckert, Connie K(aye Delp) 1948- 82
Hector, Julian 205
Hedderwick, Mairi 1939- 145
   Earlier sketches in SATA 30, 77
Hedges, Sid(ney) G(eorge) 1897-1974 28
Hedrick, Irene Hope 1920- 175
Heelan, Jamee Riggio 1965- 146
Heerboth, Sharon
   See Leon, Sharon
Heffernan, John 1949- 168
   Earlier sketch in SATA 121
Heffron, Dorris 1944- 68
Hefter, Richard 1942- 31
Hegamin, Tonya C. 1975- 209
Hegarty, Reginald Beaton 1906-1973 10
Hehenberger, Shelly 1968- 126
Heidbreder, Robert 1947- 196
   Earlier sketch in SATA 130
Heidbreder, Robert K.
   See Heidbreder, Robert
Heide, Florence Parry 1919- 192
   Earlier sketches in SATA 32, 69, 118
   See also CLR 60
   See also SAAS 6
Heiderstadt, Dorothy 1907-2001 6
Heidi Louise
   See Erdrich, Louise
Heidler, David S(tephen) 1955- 132
Heidler, Jeanne T. 1956- 132
Heilbroner, Joan Knapp 1922- 63
Heilbrun, Lois Hussey 1922(?)-1987
   Obituary 54
Heiligman, Deborah 1958- 193
   Earlier sketches in SATA 90, 144
Heilman, Joan Rattner 50
Heimann, Rolf 1940- 164
   Earlier sketch in SATA 120
Hein, Lucille Eleanor 1915-1994 20
Heine, Helme 1941- 135
   Earlier sketch in SATA 67
   See also CLR 18
Heinlein, Robert A. 1907-1988 69
   Obituary 56
   Earlier sketch in SATA 9
   See also CLR 75
Heinlein, Robert Anson
   See Heinlein, Robert A.
Heins, Ethel L(eah) 1918-1997 101
Heins, Paul 1909- 13
Heintze, Carl 1922- 26
Heinz, Bill
   See Heinz, W. C.
Heinz, Brian J. 1946- 181
   Earlier sketch in SATA 95
Heinz, Brian James
   See Heinz, Brian J.
Heinz, W. C. 1915-2008 26
Heinz, Wilfred Charles
   See Heinz, W. C.
Heinzen, Mildred
   See Masters, Mildred
Heisel, Sharon E(laine) 1941- 125
   Earlier sketch in SATA 84
Heitzmann, William Ray 1948- 73
Heitzmann, Wm. Ray
   See Heitzmann, William Ray
Helakoski, Leslie 178
Helberg, Shirley Adelaide Holden 1919- ... 138
Heldring, Thatcher 229
Helfer, Andrew 187
Helfer, Ralph 1937- 177
Helfman, Elizabeth S(eaver) 1911-2001 3
Helfman, Harry Carmozin 1910-1995 3
Helgerson, Joseph 1950- 181
Hellard, Susan 182
Hellberg, Hans-Eric 1927- 38
Heller, Linda 1944- 46
   Brief entry 40

Heller, Mike
   See Hano, Arnold
Heller, Ruth M. 1924- 112
   Earlier sketch in SATA 66
Hellman, Hal
   See Hellman, Harold
Hellman, Harold 1927- 4
Helman, Andrea (Jean) 1946- 160
   Earlier sketch in SATA 107
Helmer, Diana Star 1962- 86
Helmer, Marilyn 160
   Earlier sketch in SATA 112
Helps, Racey 1913-1971 2
   Obituary 25
Helquist, Brett 229
   Earlier sketches in SATA 146, 187
Helweg, Hans H. 1917- 50
   Brief entry 33
Helyar, Jane Penelope Josephine 1933- 5
   Autobiography Feature 138
   See also SAAS 2
Hemingway, Edith M. 1950- 223
Hemingway, Edith Morris
   See Hemingway, Edith M.
Hemingway, Edward 1969(?)- 212
Hemingway, Ernest 1899-1961
   See CLR 168
Hemingway, Ernest Miller
   See Hemingway, Ernest
Hemmant, Lynette 1938- 69
Hemming, Roy G. 1928-1995 11
   Obituary 86
Hemphill, Helen 1955- 179
Hemphill, Kris (Harrison) 1963- 118
Hemphill, Martha Locke 1904-1973 37
Hemphill, Michael 220
Hemphill, Stephanie 190
Hemstock, Gillian 1956- 173
Henba, Bobbie 1926- 87
Henbest, Nigel 1951- 55
   Brief entry 52
Henderley, Brooks 1
Henderson, Aileen Kilgore 1921- 178
Henderson, Aileen Mary
   See Fox, Aileen
Henderson, Gordon 1950- 53
Henderson, Kathy 1949- 155
   Brief entry 53
   Earlier sketches in SATA 55, 95
Henderson, Lauren 1966- 201
Henderson, LeGrand 1901-1965 9
Henderson, Nancy Wallace 1916- 22
Henderson, Zenna (Chlarson) 1917-1983 5
Hendrickson, Walter Brookfield, Jr. 1936- 9
Hendrix, John 1976- 208
Hendry, Diana 1941- 213
   Earlier sketches in SATA 68, 106
Hendry, Frances Mary 1941- 171
   Earlier sketch in SATA 110
Hendry, Linda (Gail) 1961- 83
Heneghan, James 1930- 160
   Earlier sketches in SATA 53, 97
Henkes, Kevin 1960- 207
   Earlier sketches in SATA 43, 76, 108, 154
   See also CLR 108
Henn, Astrid 214
Hennessy, Barbara G.
   See Hennessy, B.G.
Hennessy, Barbara Gulbrandsen
   See Hennessy, B.G.
Hennessy, B.G. 1951- 175
Hennessy, Carolyn 1962- 221
Henney, Carole Wells 1928- 102
Henriod, Lorraine 1925- 26
Henriquez, Emile F. 1937- 170
   Earlier sketch in SATA 89
Henry, April 1959- 174
Henry, Ernest 1948- 107
Henry, Joanne Landers 1927- 6
Henry, Maeve 1960- 75

Henry, Marguerite 1902-1997 .... *100*
  Obituary *99*
  See also CLR *4*
  See also SAAS *7*
Henry, Marie H. 1935- *65*
Henry, Marilyn 1939- *117*
Henry, Marion
  See del Rey, Lester
Henry, O. 1862-1910
  See YABC *2*
Henry, Oliver
  See Henry, O.
Henry, Rohan *217*
Henry, T. E.
  See Rowland-Entwistle, (Arthur) Theodore
  (Henry)
Henschel, Elizabeth Georgie *56*
Henson, Heather *206*
Henson, James Maury
  See Henson, Jim
Henson, Jim 1936-1990 .... *43*
  Obituary *65*
Henstra, Friso 1928- *73*
  Earlier sketch in SATA *8*
  See also SAAS *14*
Hentoff, Nat(han Irving) 1925- *133*
  Brief entry *27*
  Earlier sketches in SATA *42, 69*
  See also CLR *52*
Henty, G(eorge) A(lfred) 1832-1902 .... *64*
  See also CLR *76*
Heo, Yumi 1964- *206*
  Earlier sketches in SATA *94, 146*
Hepler, Heather *177*
Herald, Kathleen
  See Peyton, Kathleen Wendy
Herb, Angela M. 1970- *92*
Herbert, Cecil
  See Hamilton, Charles (Harold St. John)
Herbert, Don 1917-2007 .... *2*
  Obituary *184*
Herbert, Donald Jeffrey
  See Herbert, Don
Herbert, Frank 1920-1986 .... *37*
  Obituary *47*
  Earlier sketch in SATA *9*
Herbert, Frank Patrick
  See Herbert, Frank
Herbert, Helen (Jean) 1947- *57*
Herbert, Janis 1956- *139*
Herbert, Wally 1934-2007 .... *23*
Herbert, Walter William
  See Herbert, Wally
Herbst, Judith 1947- *74*
Herda, D.J. 1948- *80*
Herge
  See Remi, Georges
Heritage, Martin
  See Horler, Sydney
Herkimer, L(awrence) R(ussell) 1925(?)- *42*
Herlihy, Dirlie Anne 1935- *73*
Herlong, Madaline
  See Herlong, M.H.
Herlong, M.H. *211*
Herman, Charlotte 1937- *203*
  Earlier sketches in SATA *20, 99*
Hermanson, Dennis (Everett) 1947- *10*
Hermes, Jules 1962- *92*
Hermes, Patricia 1936- *191*
  Earlier sketches in SATA *31, 78, 141*
Hermes, Patricia Mary
  See Hermes, Patricia
Hernandez, Natalie Nelson 1929- *123*
Herndon, Ernest *91*
Herold, Ann Bixby 1937- *72*
Herrera, Diego
  See Yayo
Herrera, Juan Felipe 1948- *127*
Herrick, Steven 1958- *209*
  Earlier sketches in SATA *103, 156*
Herriman, George (Joseph) 1880-1944 .... *140*

Herriot, James 1916-1995 .... *135*
  Brief entry *44*
  Earlier sketch in SATA *86*
  See also CLR *80*
Herrmanns, Ralph 1933- *11*
Herrold, Tracey
  See Dils, Tracey E.
Herron, Carolivia 1947- *203*
Herron, Edward A(lbert) 1912- *4*
Herschler, Mildred Barger *130*
Hersey, John 1914-1993 .... *25*
  Obituary *76*
Hersey, John Richard
  See Hersey, John
Hershberger, Priscilla (Gorman) 1951- *81*
Hershenhorn, Esther 1945- *151*
Hershey, Kathleen M. 1934- *80*
Hershey, Mary *173*
Hershey, Mary L.
  See Hershey, Mary
Hersom, Kathleen 1911- *73*
Hertz, Grete Janus 1915- *23*
Herxheimer, Sophie 1963- *220*
Herzig, Alison Cragin 1935- *87*
Herzog, Brad 1968- *131*
Heslewood, Juliet 1951- *82*
Hess, Lilo 1916- *4*
Hess, Paul 1961- *134*
Hesse, Hermann 1877-1962 .... *50*
Hesse, Karen 1952- *215*
  Autobiography Feature *113*
  Earlier sketches in SATA *74, 103, 158*
  See also CLR *141*
  See also SAAS *25*
Hest, Amy 1950- *193*
  Earlier sketches in SATA *55, 82, 129*
Heuer, Karsten 1968(?)- *202*
Heuer, Kenneth John 1927- *44*
Heuman, William 1912-1971 .... *21*
Heuston, Kimberley 1960- *167*
Heuston, Kimberley Burton
  See Heuston, Kimberley
Heuvel, Eric 1960- *224*
Hewes, Agnes Danforth 1874-1963 .... *35*
Hewett, Anita 1918-1989 .... *13*
Hewett, Joan 1930- *140*
  Earlier sketch in SATA *81*
Hewett, Richard 1929- *81*
Hewitson, Jennifer 1961- *97*
Hewitt, Margaret 1961- *84*
Hewitt, Sally 1949- *231*
  Earlier sketch in SATA *127*
Hext, Harrington
  See Phillpotts, Eden
Hey, Nigel S(tewart) 1936- *20*
Heyduck-Huth, Hilde 1929- *8*
Heyer, Carol 1950- *130*
  Earlier sketch in SATA *74*
Heyer, Marilee 1942- *102*
  Earlier sketch in SATA *64*
Heyerdahl, Thor 1914-2002 .... *52*
  Earlier sketch in SATA *2*
Heyes, (Nancy) Eileen 1956- *150*
  Earlier sketch in SATA *80*
Heyliger, William 1884-1955
  See YABC *1*
Heyman, Ken(neth Louis) 1930- *114*
  Earlier sketch in SATA *34*
Heyward, (Edwin) DuBose 1885-1940 .... *21*
Heywood, Karen 1946- *48*
Hezlep, William (Earl) 1936- *88*
Hiaasen, Carl 1953- *208*
Hiatt, Shelby *226*
Hibbert, Arthur Raymond
  See Hibbert, Christopher
Hibbert, Christopher 1924-2008 .... *4*
  Obituary *201*
Hibbert, Eleanor Alice Burford 1906-1993 .... *2*
  Obituary *74*
Hickman, Estella (Lee) 1942- *111*

Hickman, Janet 1940- *127*
  Earlier sketch in SATA *12*
Hickman, Martha Whitmore 1925- *26*
Hickman, Pamela 1958- *186*
  Earlier sketch in SATA *128*
Hickock, Will
  See Harrison, C(hester) William
Hickok, Lorena A. 1893-1968 .... *20*
Hickox, Rebecca (Ayres) *116*
Hicks, Barbara Jean 1953- *165*
Hicks, Betty *191*
Hicks, Clifford B. 1920- *50*
Hicks, Eleanor B.
  See Coerr, Eleanor (Beatrice)
Hicks, Harvey
  See Stratemeyer, Edward L.
Hicks, Peter 1952- *111*
Hicyilmaz, Gaye 1947- *157*
  Earlier sketch in SATA *77*
Hieatt, Constance B(artlett) 1928- *4*
Hiebert, Ray Eldon 1932- *13*
Hierstein, Judith *212*
Hierstein, Judy
  See Hierstein, Judith
Higdon, Hal 1931- *4*
Higginbottom, David 1923- *87*
  Earlier sketch in SATA *25*
Higginbottom, J(effrey) Winslow 1945- *29*
Higgins, Dalton *223*
Higgins, F.E. *219*
Higgins, Fiona
  See Higgins, F.E.
Higgins, Joanna 1945- *125*
Higgins, Simon (Richard) 1958- *105*
Higginsen, Vy *79*
High, Linda Oatman 1958- *188*
  Autobiography Feature *188*
  Earlier sketches in SATA *94, 145*
High, Philip E. 1914- *119*
High, Philip Empson
  See High, Philip E.
Higham, David 1949- *50*
Higham, David Michael
  See Higham, David
Higham, Jon Atlas
  See Higham, Jonathan Huw
Higham, Jonathan Huw 1960- *59*
Highet, Helen
  See MacInnes, Helen (Clark)
Hightman, Jason 1971(?)- *189*
Hightman, J.P.
  See Hightman, Jason
Hightower, Florence Cole 1916-1981 .... *4*
  Obituary *27*
Highwater, Jamake (Mamake)
  1942(?)-2001 .... *69*
  Brief entry *30*
  Earlier sketch in SATA *32*
  See also CLR *17*
Hilb, Nora 1953- *178*
Hildebrandt, Greg, Jr. 1970- *228*
Hildebrandt, Greg 1939- *172*
  Brief entry *33*
  Earlier sketch in SATA *55*
Hildebrandt, Tim 1939-2006 .... *55*
  Brief entry *33*
Hildebrandt, Timothy
  See Hildebrandt, Tim
Hildebrandts, The
  See Hildebrandt, Greg
  and Hildebrandt, Tim
Hilder, Rowland 1905-1993 .... *36*
  Obituary *77*
Hildick, E. W.
  See Hildick, Wallace
Hildick, Wallace 1925-2001 .... *68*
  Earlier sketch in SATA *2*
  See also SAAS *6*
Hilgartner, Beth 1957- *58*

Hill, Alexis
   See Craig, Mary (Francis) Shura
   and Glick, Ruth
Hill, Anthony R. 1942- *164*
   Earlier sketch in SATA *91*
Hill, Anthony Robert
   See Hill, Anthony R.
Hill, David 1942- *152*
   Earlier sketch in SATA *103*
Hill, Donna (Marie) 1921- *124*
   Earlier sketch in SATA *24*
Hill, Douglas 1935-2007 .... *78*
   Earlier sketch in SATA *39*
Hill, Douglas Arthur
   See Hill, Douglas
Hill, Elizabeth Starr 1925- *143*
   Earlier sketch in SATA *24*
Hill, Eric 1927- *133*
   Brief entry *53*
   Earlier sketch in SATA *66*
   See also CLR *13*
Hill, Gordon
   See Eldin, Peter
Hill, Grace Brooks *67*
   Earlier sketch in SATA *1*
Hill, Grace Livingston 1865-1947
   See YABC *2*
Hill, Helen M(orey) 1915- *27*
Hill, Isabel *225*
Hill, Isabel T.
   See Hill, Isabel
Hill, John
   See Koontz, Dean
Hill, Johnson
   See Kunhardt, Edith
Hill, Judy I. R.
   See Roberts, Judy I.
Hill, Kathleen Louise 1917- *4*
Hill, Kay
   See Hill, Kathleen Louise
Hill, Kirkpatrick 1938- *188*
   Earlier sketches in SATA *72, 126*
Hill, Laban
   See Hill, Laban Carrick
Hill, Laban Carrick *170*
Hill, Lee Sullivan 1958- *96*
Hill, Lorna 1902-1991 .... *12*
Hill, Margaret (Ohler) 1915- *36*
Hill, Meg
   See Hill, Margaret (Ohler)
Hill, Meredith
   See Craig, Mary (Francis) Shura
Hill, Monica
   See Watson, Jane Werner
Hill, Pamela Smith 1954- *112*
Hill, Ralph Nading 1917-1987 .... *65*
Hill, Robert W(hite) 1919-1982 .... *12*
   Obituary *31*
Hill, Ruth A.
   See Viguers, Ruth Hill
Hill, Ruth Livingston
   See Munce, Ruth Hill
Hill, Stuart 1958- *186*
Hill, Susan 1942- *183*
Hill, Susan Elizabeth
   See Hill, Susan
Hill, Susanna Leonard 1965- *193*
Hill, Thomas 1960- *82*
Hillcourt, William 1900-1992 .... *27*
Hillenbrand, Will 1960- *210*
   Earlier sketches in SATA *84, 147*
Hiller, Ilo (Ann) 1938- *59*
Hillerman, Anthony Grove
   See Hillerman, Tony
Hillerman, Tony 1925-2008 .... *6*
   Obituary *198*
Hillert, Margaret 1920- *91*
   Earlier sketch in SATA *8*
Hilliard, Richard *183*
Hillman, Ben 1957- *202*
Hillman, Elizabeth 1942- *75*

Hillman, John 1952- *120*
Hillman, Martin
   See Hill, Douglas
Hillman, Priscilla 1940- *48*
   Brief entry *39*
Hillman, Shane *200*
Hills, C.A.R. 1955- *39*
Hills, Charles Albert Reis
   See Hills, C.A.R.
Hills, Tad *173*
Hilton, Irene Pothus -1979 .... *7*
Hilton, James 1900-1954 .... *34*
Hilton, Margaret Lynette 1946- *105*
   Earlier sketch in SATA *68*
   See also CLR *25*
   See also SAAS *21*
Hilton, Nette
   See Hilton, Margaret Lynette
Hilton, Ralph 1907-1982 .... *8*
Hilton, Suzanne 1922- *4*
Hilton-Bruce, Anne
   See Hilton, Margaret Lynette
Him, George 1937-1982
   Obituary *30*
Himelblau, Linda -2005 .... *179*
Himelstein, Shmuel 1940- *83*
Himler, Ann 1946- *8*
Himler, Ronald 1937- *183*
   Earlier sketches in SATA *6, 92, 137*
Himler, Ronald Norbert
   See Himler, Ronald
Himmelman, John 1959- *221*
   Earlier sketches in SATA *47, 94, 159*
Himmelman, John C.
   See Himmelman, John
Hinckley, Helen
   See Jones, Helen Hinckley
Hind, Dolores (Ellen) 1931- *53*
   Brief entry *49*
Hindin, Nathan
   See Bloch, Robert (Albert)
Hindley, Judy 1940- *179*
   Earlier sketch in SATA *120*
Hinds, P. Mignon *98*
Hinds, Patricia Mignon
   See Hinds, P. Mignon
Hine, Sesyle Joslin 1929- *2*
Hines, Anna Grossnickle 1946- *209*
   Brief entry *45*
   Earlier sketches in SATA *51, 95, 141*
   See also SAAS *16*
Hines, Gary (Roger) 1944- *136*
   Earlier sketch in SATA *74*
Hinman, Bonnie 1950- *216*
Hinojosa, Maria (de Lourdes) 1961- *88*
Hinton, Nigel 1941- *166*
Hinton, S. E. 1950- *160*
   Earlier sketches in SATA *19, 58, 115*
   See also CLR *23*
Hinton, Sam 1917-2009 .... *43*
Hinton, Susan Eloise
   See Hinton, S. E.
Hintz, Martin 1945- *128*
   Brief entry *39*
   Earlier sketch in SATA *47*
Hintz, Stephen V. 1975- *129*
Hippopotamus, Eugene H.
   See Kraus, (Herman) Robert
Hirano, Cathy 1957- *68*
Hirao, Amiko *203*
Hirsch, Karen 1941- *61*
Hirsch, Odo *157*
   Earlier sketch in SATA *111*
Hirsch, Phil 1926- *35*
Hirsch, S. Carl 1913-1990 .... *2*
   See also SAAS *7*
Hirschfelder, Arlene B. 1943- *227*
   Earlier sketches in SATA *80, 138*
Hirschi, Ron 1948- *192*
   Earlier sketches in SATA *56, 95*
Hirschmann, Linda (Ann) 1941- *40*

Hirsh, Marilyn 1944-1988 .... *7*
   Obituary *58*
Hirshberg, Al(bert Simon) 1909-1973 .... *38*
Hiscock, Bruce 1940- *204*
   Earlier sketches in SATA *57, 137*
Hiser, Constance 1950- *71*
Hiser, Iona Seibert -1998 .... *4*
Hislop, Julia Rose Catherine 1962- *74*
Hissey, Jane 1952- *130*
   Autobiography Feature *130*
   Earlier sketches in SATA *58, 103*
Hissey, Jane Elizabeth
   See Hissey, Jane
Hitchcock, Alfred (Joseph) 1899-1980 .... *27*
   Obituary *24*
Hite, Sid 1954- *175*
   Earlier sketches in SATA *75, 136*
Hitte, Kathryn 1919- *16*
Hitz, Demi
   See Demi
Hitzeroth, Deborah L. 1961- *78*
Hnizdovsky, Jacques 1915- *32*
Ho, Jannie *226*
Ho, Louise *185*
Ho, Minfong 1951- *151*
   Earlier sketches in SATA *15, 94*
   See also CLR *28*
Hoagland, Edward (Morley) 1932- *51*
Hoare, Robert J(ohn) 1921-1975 .... *38*
Hoban, Julia *217*
Hoban, Lillian 1925-1998 .... *69*
   Obituary *104*
   Earlier sketch in SATA *22*
   See also CLR *67*
Hoban, Russell 1925- *136*
   Earlier sketches in SATA *1, 40, 78*
   See also CLR *139*
Hoban, Russell Conwell
   See Hoban, Russell
Hoban, Tana 1917(?)-2006 .... *104*
   Obituary *173*
   Earlier sketches in SATA *22, 70*
   See also CLR *76*
   See also SAAS *12*
Hobart, Lois (Elaine) *7*
Hobbie, Holly 1942- *225*
   Earlier sketch in SATA *178*
   See also CLR *88*
Hobbie, Jocelyn *190*
Hobbie, Nathaniel *196*
Hobbs, Leigh 1953- *166*
Hobbs, Valerie 1941- *193*
   Autobiography Feature *145*
   Earlier sketches in SATA *93, 145*
   See also CLR *148*
Hobbs, Will 1947- *177*
   Autobiography Feature *127*
   Earlier sketches in SATA *72, 110*
   See also CLR *59*
Hobbs, William Carl
   See Hobbs, Will
Hoberman, Mary Ann 1930- *228*
   Earlier sketches in SATA *5, 72, 111, 158*
   See also CLR *22*
   See also SAAS *18*
Hobson, Bruce 1950- *62*
Hobson, Burton (Harold) 1933- *28*
Hobson, Laura Z(ametkin) 1900-1986 .... *52*
Hobson, Sally 1967- *172*
   Earlier sketch in SATA *84*
Hoce, Charley E. *174*
Hochman, David *202*
Hochschild, Arlie Russell 1940- *11*
Hockaby, Stephen
   See Mitchell, Gladys (Maude Winifred)
Hockenberry, Hope
   See Newell, Hope Hockenberry
Hodge, Deborah 1954- *163*
   Earlier sketch in SATA *122*
Hodge, P. W.
   See Hodge, Paul W(illiam)

Hodge, Paul W(illiam) 1934- *12*
Hodgell, P(atricia) C(hristine) 1951- *42*
Hodges, C. Walter 1909-2004 .... *2*
  Obituary *158*
Hodges, Carl G. 1902-1964 .... *10*
Hodges, Cyril Walter
  See Hodges, C. Walter
Hodges, Elizabeth Jamison *1*
Hodges, Margaret 1911-2005 .... *167*
  Obituary *172*
  Earlier sketches in SATA *1, 33, 75, 117*
  See also SAAS *9*
Hodges, Margaret Moore
  See Hodges, Margaret
Hodgetts, Blake Christopher 1967- *43*
Hodgkins, Fran 1964- *199*
Hodgkinson, Leigh 1975- *202*
Hodgman, Ann 1956- *198*
Hodgson, Harriet (W.) 1935- *84*
Hoehne, Marcia 1951- *89*
Hoellwarth, Cathryn Clinton
  See Clinton, Cathryn
Hoestlandt, Jo 1948- *221*
  Earlier sketch in SATA *94*
Hoestlandt, Jocelyne
  See Hoestlandt, Jo
Hoexter, Corinne K. 1927- *6*
Hoeye, Michael 1947- *136*
Hof, Marjolijn 1956- *226*
Hoff, Carol 1900-1979 .... *11*
Hoff, Mary (King) 1956- *157*
  Earlier sketch in SATA *74*
Hoff, Syd(ney) 1912-2004 .... *138*
  Obituary *154*
  Earlier sketches in SATA *9, 72*
  See also CLR *83*
  See also SAAS *4*
Hoffman, Edwin D. *49*
Hoffman, Elizabeth P(arkinson) 1921-2003
  Obituary *153*
Hoffman, Mary 1945- *211*
  Earlier sketches in SATA *59, 97, 144*
  See also SAAS *24*
Hoffman, Mat 1972- *150*
Hoffman, Nina Kiriki 1955- *160*
Hoffman, Phyllis M. 1944- *4*
Hoffman, Phyllis Miriam
  See Hoffman, Phyllis M.
Hoffman, Rosekrans 1926- *15*
Hoffmann, E(rnst) T(heodor) A(madeus)
  1776-1822 .... *27*
  See also CLR *133*
Hoffmann, Felix 1911-1975 .... *9*
Hoffmann, Heinrich 1809-1894
  See CLR *122*
Hoffmann, Margaret Jones 1910- *48*
Hoffmann, Peggy
  See Hoffmann, Margaret Jones
Hofher, Catherine Baxley 1954- *130*
Hofher, Cathy
  See Hofher, Catherine Baxley
Hofmeyr, Dianne (Louise) *138*
Hofsepian, Sylvia A. 1932- *74*
Hofsinde, Robert 1902-1973 .... *21*
Hogan, Bernice Harris 1929- *12*
Hogan, Inez 1895-1973 .... *2*
Hogan, James P. 1941-2010 .... *81*
Hogan, James Patrick
  See Hogan, James P.
Hogan, Jamie 1956- *192*
Hogan, Linda 1947- *132*
Hogan, Mary 1957- *210*
Hogarth, Burne 1911-1996 .... *89*
  Earlier sketch in SATA *63*
Hogarth, Grace (Weston Allen) 1905-1995 .. *91*
Hogarth, Jr.
  See Kent, Rockwell
Hogarth, (Arthur) Paul 1917-2001 .... *41*
Hogg, Garry 1902-1976 .... *2*
Hogg, Gary 1957- *172*
  Earlier sketch in SATA *105*

Hogner, Dorothy Childs *4*
Hogner, Nils 1893-1970 .... *25*
Hogrogian, Nonny 1932- *74*
  Autobiography Feature *127*
  Earlier sketch in SATA *7*
  See also CLR *95*
  See also SAAS *1*
Hoh, Diane 1937- *102*
  Brief entry *48*
  Earlier sketch in SATA *52*
Hoke, Helen
  See Watts, Helen L. Hoke
Hoke, Helen L.
  See Watts, Helen L. Hoke
Hoke, John 1925-2011 .... *7*
Hoke, John Lindsay
  See Hoke, John
Hokenson, Terry 1948- *193*
Hol, Coby 1943- *126*
Holabird, Katharine 1948- *213*
  Earlier sketches in SATA *62, 135*
Holaday, Bobbie 1922- *153*
Holbeach, Henry
  See Rands, William Brighty
Holberg, Ruth L(angland) 1889-1984 .... *1*
Holbrook, Kathy 1963- *107*
Holbrook, Peter
  See Glick, Carl (Cannon)
Holbrook, Sabra
  See Erickson, Sabra Rollins
Holbrook, Sara *131*
Holbrook, Stewart Hall 1893-1964 .... *2*
Holcomb, Jerry (Leona) Kimble 1927- *113*
Holcomb, Nan
  See McPhee, Norma H.
Holdcroft, Tina *227*
Holden, Elizabeth Rhoda
  See Lawrence, Louise
Holding, James (Clark Carlisle, Jr.)
  1907-1997 .... *3*
Hole, Stian 1969- *204*
Holeman, Linda 1949- *136*
  Autobiography Feature *136*
  Earlier sketch in SATA *102*
Holgate, Doug *225*
Holinger, William (Jacques) 1944- *90*
Holisher, Desider 1901-1972 .... *6*
Holl, Adelaide Hinkle 1910- *8*
Holl, Kristi
  See Holl, Kristi D.
Holl, Kristi D. 1951- *51*
Holl, Kristi Diane
  See Holl, Kristi D.
Holland, Gay W. 1941- *128*
Holland, Isabelle (Christian) 1920-2002 .... *70*
  Autobiography Feature *103*
  Obituary *132*
  Earlier sketch in SATA *8*
  See also CLR *57*
Holland, Janice 1913-1962 .... *18*
Holland, John L(ewis) 1919- *20*
Holland, Joyce
  See Morice, Dave
Holland, Julia 1954- *106*
Holland, Lynda (H.) 1959- *77*
Holland, Lys
  See Gater, Dilys
Holland, Marion 1908-1989 .... *6*
  Obituary *61*
Holland, Richard 1976- *216*
Holland, Trish *221*
Hollander, John 1929- *13*
Hollander, Nicole 1940(?)- *101*
Hollander, Paul
  See Silverberg, Robert
Hollander, Phyllis 1928- *39*
Hollander, Zander 1923- *63*
Holldobler, Turid 1939- *26*
Holliday, Joe
  See Holliday, Joseph
Holliday, Joseph 1910- *11*

Holling, Holling C(lancy) 1900-1973 .... *15*
  Obituary *26*
  See also CLR *50*
Hollingsworth, Alvin C(arl) 1930- *39*
Hollingsworth, Mary 1947- *166*
  Earlier sketch in SATA *91*
Holloway, Teresa (Bragunier) 1906- *26*
Hollyer, Beatrice 1957- *226*
Hollyer, Belinda *204*
Holm, (Else) Anne (Lise) 1922-1998 .... *1*
  See also CLR *75*
  See also SAAS *7*
Holm, Jennifer L. 1968(?)- *183*
  Earlier sketches in SATA *120, 163*
Holm, Matthew 1974- *174*
Holm, Sharon Lane 1955- *114*
  Earlier sketch in SATA *78*
Holman, Felice 1919- *82*
  Earlier sketch in SATA *7*
  See also SAAS *17*
Holm and Hamel
  See Holm, Jennifer L.
Holmberg, Bo R. 1945- *203*
Holme, Bryan 1913-1990 .... *26*
  Obituary *66*
Holmes, Barbara Ware 1945- *127*
  Earlier sketch in SATA *65*
Holmes, Elizabeth 1957- *191*
Holmes, Elizabeth Ann
  See Holmes, Elizabeth
Holmes, John
  See Souster, (Holmes) Raymond
Holmes, Liz
  See Holmes, Elizabeth
Holmes, Marjorie (Rose) 1910-2002 .... *43*
Holmes, Martha 1961- *72*
Holmes, Mary Tavener 1954- *199*
Holmes, Mary Z(astrow) 1943- *80*
Holmes, Oliver Wendell 1809-1894 .... *34*
Holmes, Peggy 1898- *60*
Holmes, Raymond
  See Souster, (Holmes) Raymond
Holmes, Rick
  See Hardwick, Richard Holmes, Jr.
Holmes, Sara Lewis *186*
Holmgren, Helen Jean 1930- *45*
Holmgren, Sister George Ellen
  See Holmgren, Helen Jean
Holmgren, Virginia C(unningham) 1909- *26*
Holmquist, Eve 1921- *11*
Holt, K.A.
  See Roy, Kari Anne
Holt, Kimberly Willis 1960- *223*
  Earlier sketches in SATA *122, 179*
Holt, Margaret 1937- *4*
Holt, Margaret Van Vechten (Saunders)
  1899-1963 .... *32*
Holt, Michael (Paul) 1929- *13*
Holt, Rackham
  See Holt, Margaret Van Vechten (Saunders)
Holt, Rochelle L.
  See DuBois, Rochelle Holt
Holt, Stephen
  See Thompson, Harlan
Holt, Victoria
  See Hibbert, Eleanor Alice Burford
Holtei, Christa 1953- *214*
Holton, Leonard
  See Wibberley, Leonard
Holtz, Thomas R., Jr. 1965- *203*
Holtze, Sally Holmes 1952- *64*
Holtzman, Jerome 1926-2008 .... *57*
  Obituary *194*
Holub, Joan 1956- *229*
  Earlier sketches in SATA *99, 149*
Holub, Josef 1926- *175*
Holubitsky, Katherine 1955- *165*
  Earlier sketch in SATA *121*
Holyer, Erna Maria 1925- *22*
Holyer, Ernie
  See Holyer, Erna Maria

Holyfield, John 1969- *227*
Holz, Loretta 1943- *17*
Holz, Loretta Marie
    See Holz, Loretta
Homel, David 1952- *97*
Homze, Alma C. 1932- *17*
Honey, Elizabeth 1947- *137*
    Autobiography Feature *137*
    Earlier sketch in SATA *112*
Honeycutt, Natalie 1945- *97*
Hong, Lily Toy 1958- *76*
Hong, Maxine Ting Ting
    See Kingston, Maxine Hong
Honig, Donald 1931- *18*
Honig, Donald Martin
    See Honig, Donald
Honness, Elizabeth H. 1904- *2*
Hoobler, Dorothy 1941- *161*
    Earlier sketches in SATA *28, 109*
Hoobler, Thomas *161*
    Earlier sketches in SATA *28, 109*
Hood, Joseph F. 1925- *4*
Hood, Robert E. 1926- *21*
Hood, Sarah
    See Killough, (Karen) Lee
Hook, Brendan 1963- *105*
Hook, Frances 1912-1983 .... *27*
Hook, Geoffrey R(aynor) 1928- *103*
Hook, Jeff
    See Hook, Geoffrey R(aynor)
Hook, Martha 1936- *27*
Hooker, Richard
    See Heinz, W. C.
Hooker, Ruth 1920-1998 .... *21*
hooks, bell 1952(?)- *170*
    Earlier sketch in SATA *115*
Hooks, William H(arris) 1921- *94*
    Earlier sketch in SATA *16*
Hoon, Patricia Easterly 1954- *90*
Hooper, Byrd
    See St. Clair, Byrd Hooper
Hooper, Mary 1948- *205*
    Earlier sketch in SATA *160*
Hooper, Maureen Brett 1927- *76*
Hooper, Meredith 1939- *159*
    Earlier sketches in SATA *28, 101*
Hooper, Meredith Jean
    See Hooper, Meredith
Hooper, Patricia 1941- *95*
Hoopes, Lyn Littlefield 1953- *49*
    Brief entry *44*
Hoopes, Ned E(dward) 1932- *21*
Hoopes, Roy 1922-2009 .... *11*
Hoose, Phillip 1947- *215*
    Earlier sketch in SATA *137*
Hoover, H(elen) M(ary) 1935- *132*
    Brief entry *33*
    Earlier sketches in SATA *44, 83*
    See also SAAS *8*
Hoover, Helen (Drusilla Blackburn)
    1910-1984 .... *12*
    Obituary *39*
Hope, Christopher 1944- *62*
Hope, Christopher David Tully
    See Hope, Christopher
Hope, Laura Lee
    See Goulart, Ron
    and Stanley, George Edward
Hope Simpson, Jacynth 1930- *12*
Hopf, Alice (Martha) L(ightner) 1904-1988 ... *5*
    Obituary *55*
Hopgood, Tim 1961- *224*
Hopkins, A. T.
    See Turngren, Annette
Hopkins, C. M.
    See Hopkins, Cathy
Hopkins, Cathy 1953- *165*
Hopkins, Cathy M.
    See Hopkins, Cathy
Hopkins, Clark 1895-1976
    Obituary *34*

Hopkins, Ellen 1955- *128*
Hopkins, Ellen L.
    See Hopkins, Ellen
Hopkins, Jackie
    See Hopkins, Jackie Mims
Hopkins, Jackie Mims 1952- *178*
    Earlier sketch in SATA *92*
Hopkins, Joseph G(erard) E(dward) 1909- ... *11*
Hopkins, (Hector) Kenneth 1914-1988
    Obituary *58*
Hopkins, Lee Bennett 1938- *215*
    Earlier sketches in SATA *3, 68, 125, 168*
    See also CLR *44*
    See also SAAS *4*
Hopkins, Lyman
    See Folsom, Franklin (Brewster)
Hopkins, Marjorie 1911-1999 .... *9*
Hopkins, Mary R(ice) 1956- *97*
Hopkinson, Amanda 1948- *84*
Hopkinson, Deborah 1952- *216*
    Autobiography Feature *180*
    Earlier sketches in SATA *76, 108, 159, 180*
    See also CLR *118*
Hopman, Philip 1961- *177*
Hoppe, Joanne 1932- *42*
Hoppe, Matthias 1952- *76*
Hoppe, Paul *209*
Hopper, Nancy J. 1937- *38*
    Brief entry *35*
Hoppey, Tim 1958- *225*
Hopping, Lorraine Jean
    See Egan, Lorraine Hopping
Horacek, Judy 1961- *211*
Horaek, Petr *214*
    Earlier sketch in SATA *163*
Horenstein, Henry 1947- *108*
Horgan, Paul (George Vincent O'Shaughnessy)
    1903-1995 .... *13*
    Obituary *84*
Horlak, E.E.
    See Tepper, Sheri S.
Horler, Sydney 1888-1954 .... *102*
Horley, Alex 1970- *229*
Horn, Sandra Ann 1944- *154*
Hornblow, Arthur, Jr. 1893-1976 .... *15*
Hornblow, Leonora 1920-2005 .... *18*
    Obituary *171*
Hornblow, Leonora Schinasi
    See Hornblow, Leonora
Horne, Constance 1927- *149*
Horne, Richard 1960-2007 .... *169*
    Obituary *180*
    Earlier sketch in SATA *111*
Horne, Richard Henry Hengist
    1802(?)-1884 .... *29*
Horner, Althea (Jane) 1926- *36*
Horner, Dave 1934- *12*
Horner, Jack 1946- *106*
Horner, John R.
    See Horner, Jack
Horner, John Robert
    See Horner, Jack
Hornik, Laurie Miller *159*
Horniman, Joanne 1951- *167*
    Earlier sketch in SATA *98*
Hornos, Axel 1907-1994 .... *20*
Hornstein, Reuben Aaron 1912- *64*
Horowitz, Anthony 1955- *195*
    Earlier sketch in SATA *137*
Horowitz, Dave 1970- *204*
    Earlier sketch in SATA *172*
Horowitz, Eli *230*
Horowitz, Ruth 1957- *136*
Horrocks, Anita 1958- *169*
Horse, Harry
    See Horne, Richard
Horsfield, Alan 1939- *153*
Horstman, Lisa 1964- *219*
Hort, Lenny *179*
Horton, James O. 1943- *173*

Horton, James Oliver
    See Horton, James O.
Horton, Joan *217*
Horton, Madelyn (Stacey) 1962- *77*
Horvath, Betty 1927- *4*
Horvath, David 1972(?)- *192*
Horvath, Polly 1957- *194*
    Earlier sketches in SATA *85, 140*
    See also CLR *90*
Horwich, Frances R(appaport) 1908-2001 .... *11*
    Obituary *130*
Horwitz, Elinor Lander *45*
    Brief entry *33*
Horwood, William 1944- *85*
Hosford, Dorothy (Grant) 1900-1952 .... *22*
Hosford, Jessie 1892-1990 .... *5*
Hoshi, Shin'ichi 1926- *101*
Hoshino, Felicia 1968- *189*
Hoskyns-Abrahall, Clare (Constance
    Drury) *13*
Hosler, Danamarie 1978- *184*
Hossack, Sylvia 1939- *83*
Hossack, Sylvie Adams
    See Hossack, Sylvia
Hosseini, Khaled 1965- *156*
Hossell, Karen Price
    See Price, Karen
Hosta, Dar *192*
Hostetler, Marian 1932- *91*
Hostetter, Joyce Moyer 1952- *228*
Houck, Carter 1924- *22*
Hough, Charlotte 1924-2008 .... *9*
    Obituary *202*
Hough, Helen Charlotte
    See Hough, Charlotte
Hough, Judy Taylor 1932- *63*
    Brief entry *51*
    Earlier sketch in SATA *56*
Hough, Richard (Alexander) 1922-1999 .... *17*
Houghton, Eric 1930- *7*
Houk, Randy 1944- *97*
Houlehen, Robert J. 1918- *18*
Houlton, Peggy Mann 1925(?)-1990 .... *6*
Household, Geoffrey 1900-1988 .... *14*
    Obituary *59*
Housman, Laurence 1865-1959 .... *25*
Houston, Dick 1943- *231*
    Earlier sketch in SATA *74*
Houston, Gloria *138*
    Autobiography Feature *138*
    Earlier sketch in SATA *81*
Houston, James A(rchibald) 1921-2005 .... *74*
    Obituary *163*
    Earlier sketch in SATA *13*
    See also CLR *3*
    See also SAAS *17*
Houston, James D. 1933-2009 .... *78*
    Obituary *203*
Houston, James Dudley
    See Houston, James D.
Houston, James Dudley
    See Houston, James D.
Houston, Jeanne Toyo Wakatsuki
    See Houston, Jeanne Wakatsuki
Houston, Jeanne Wakatsuki 1934- *168*
    Autobiography Feature *168*
    Earlier sketch in SATA *78*
Houston, Juanita C. 1921- *129*
Houtman, Jacqueline 1960- *231*
Houtman, Jacqueline Jaeger
    See Houtman, Jacqueline
Houton, Kathleen
    See Kilgore, Kathleen
Houts, Amy F. *164*
Houts, Michelle *219*
Hovey, Kate *158*
Howard, Alan 1922- *45*
Howard, Alyssa
    See Buckholtz, Eileen (Garber)
    and Glick, Ruth
    and Titchener, Louise

Howard, Arthur 1948- 212
  Earlier sketch in SATA 165
Howard, Arthur Charles
  See Howard, Arthur
Howard, Elizabeth Fitzgerald 1927- 119
  Earlier sketch in SATA 74
Howard, Ellen 1943- 184
  Earlier sketches in SATA 67, 99
Howard, Jane R(uble) 1924- 87
Howard, Norman Barry 1949- 90
Howard, P. M.
  See Howard, Pauline Rodriguez
Howard, Paul 1967- 190
  Earlier sketch in SATA 118
Howard, Pauline Rodriguez 1951- 124
Howard, Prosper
  See Hamilton, Charles (Harold St. John)
Howard, Robert West 1908-1988 5
Howard, Todd 1964- 135
Howard, Tristan
  See Currie, Stephen
Howard, Vernon (Linwood) 1918-1992 40
  Obituary 73
Howard, Warren F.
  See Pohl, Frederik
Howarth, Daniel 222
  Earlier sketch in SATA 188
Howarth, David (Armine) 1912-1991 6
  Obituary 68
Howarth, Lesley 1952- 94
Howe, Deborah 1946-1978 29
Howe, James 1946- 224
  Earlier sketches in SATA 29, 71, 111, 161
  See also CLR 9
Howe, John F. 1957- 79
Howe, Norma 1930-2011 126
Howe, Peter 1942- 214
Howell, Pat 1947- 15
Howell, S.
  See Styles, (Frank) Showell
Howell, Simmone 1971- 214
Howell, Virginia
  See Ellison, Virginia H(owell)
Howells, Tania 229
Howes, Barbara 1914-1996 5
Howie, Betsy 1962- 215
Howie, Diana 1945- 122
Howie, Diana Melson
  See Howie, Diana
Howker, Janni 1957- 72
  Brief entry 46
  See also CLR 14
  See also SAAS 13
Howland, Ethan 1963- 131
Hoxter, Holly Nicole 1983- 231
Hoy, Linda 1946- 65
Hoy, Nina
  See Roth, Arthur J(oseph)
Hoyle, Geoffrey 1942- 18
Hoyt, Ard 190
Hoyt, Edwin P(almer), Jr. 1923- 28
Hoyt, Erich 1950- 140
  Earlier sketch in SATA 65
Hoyt, Olga
  See Gruhzit-Hoyt, Olga (Margaret)
Hrdlitschka, Shelley 1956- 167
  Earlier sketch in SATA 111
Hrdlitschka, Shelley Joanne
  See Hrdlitschka, Shelley
Hromic, Alma A.
  See Alexander, Alma
Htin Aung, U.
  See Aung, (Maung) Htin
Hu, Ying-Hwa 173
Huang, Benrei 1959- 86
Huang, Nathan 1982(?)- 228
Hubalek, Linda K. 1954- 111
Hubbard, Crystal 209
Hubbard, Jennifer R. 227
Hubbard, Margaret Ann
  See Priley, Margaret (Ann) Hubbard

Hubbard, Michelle Calabro 1953- 122
Hubbard, Patricia 1945- 124
Hubbard, Woodleigh Marx 160
  Earlier sketch in SATA 98
Hubbell, Patricia 1928- 186
  Earlier sketches in SATA 8, 132
Hubery, Julia 195
Hubley, Faith Elliot 1924-2001 48
  Obituary 133
Hubley, John 1914-1977 48
  Obituary 24
Huck, Charlotte S. 1922- 136
  Earlier sketch in SATA 82
Hucke, Johannes 1966- 218
Hudak, Michal 1956- 143
Hudson, Cheryl Willis 1948- 160
  Earlier sketch in SATA 81
Hudson, Jan 1954-1990 77
  See also CLR 40
Hudson, Jeffery
  See Crichton, Michael
Hudson, Jeffrey
  See Crichton, Michael
Hudson, (Margaret) Kirsty 1947- 32
Hudson, Margaret
  See Shuter, Jane (Margaret)
Hudson, W(illiam) H(enry) 1841-1922 35
Hudson, Wade 1946- 162
  Earlier sketch in SATA 74
Huelsmann, Eva 1928- 16
Huerlimann, Bettina 1909-1983 39
  Obituary 34
Huerlimann, Ruth 1939- 32
  Brief entry 31
Huff, Barbara A. 1929- 67
Huff, Tanya 1957- 171
  Earlier sketch in SATA 85
Huff, Tanya Sue
  See Huff, Tanya
Huff, T.S.
  See Huff, Tanya
Huff, Vivian 1948- 59
Huffaker, Sandy 1943- 10
Huffman, Tom 24
Huggins, Nathan Irvin 1927-1989 63
Huggins, Peter 1951- 178
Hughes, Carol 1955- 217
  Earlier sketch in SATA 108
Hughes, Dean 1943- 139
  Earlier sketches in SATA 33, 77
  See also CLR 76
Hughes, Eden
  See Griffin, W. E. B.
Hughes, Edward James
  See Hughes, Ted
Hughes, James Langston
  See Hughes, Langston
Hughes, Langston 1902-1967 33
  Earlier sketch in SATA 4
  See also CLR 17
Hughes, Libby 71
Hughes, Matilda
  See MacLeod, Charlotte (Matilda)
Hughes, Monica 1925-2003 162
  Earlier sketches in SATA 15, 70, 119
  See also CLR 60
  See also SAAS 11
Hughes, Monica Ince
  See Hughes, Monica
Hughes, Pat 197
Hughes, Richard (Arthur Warren)
  1900-1976 8
  Obituary 25
Hughes, Sara
  See Saunders, Susan
Hughes, Shirley 1927- 159
  Earlier sketches in SATA 16, 70, 110
  See also CLR 15
Hughes, Susan 1960- 216

Hughes, Ted 1930-1998 49
  Brief entry 27
  Obituary 107
  See also CLR 131
Hughes, Thomas 1822-1896 31
  See also CLR 160
Hughes, Virginia
  See Campbell, Hope
Hughes, Walter (Llewellyn) 1910-1993 26
Hughey, Roberta 1942- 61
Hugo, Pierre Brackers de
  See Brackers de Hugo, Pierre
Hugo, Victor 1802-1885 47
Hugo, Victor Marie
  See Hugo, Victor
Huline-Dickens, Frank William 1931- 34
Huling, Jan 172
Huliska-Beith, Laura 175
Hull, Eleanor (Means) 1913- 21
Hull, Eric Traviss
  See Harnan, Terry
Hull, H. Braxton
  See Jacobs, Helen Hull
Hull, Jesse Redding
  See Hull, Jessie Redding
Hull, Jessie Redding 1932- 51
Hull, Katharine 1921-1977 23
Hull, Lise (E.) 1954- 148
Hull, Maureen 1949- 142
Hulme, Joy N. 1922- 161
  Earlier sketches in SATA 74, 112
Hults, Dorothy Niebrugge 1898-2000 6
Humble, Richard 1945- 60
Hume, Lachie 189
Hume, Lotta Carswell 7
Hume, Ruth Fox 1922-1980 26
  Obituary 22
Hume, Stephen Eaton 1947- 136
Hummel, Berta 1909-1946 43
Hummel, Sister Maria Innocentia
  See Hummel, Berta
Hummon, Marcus 1960- 213
Humphrey, Carol Sue 1956- 167
Humphrey, Henry (III) 1930- 16
Humphrey, Kate
  See Forsyth, Kate
Humphrey, Sandra McLeod 1936- 95
Humphreys, Martha 1943- 71
Humphreys, Susan L.
  See Lowell, Susan
Humphries, Tudor 1953- 226
Hundal, Nancy 1957- 128
Huneck, Stephen 1949- 183
  Earlier sketch in SATA 129
Hungerford, Hesba Fay
  See Brinsmead, H(esba) F(ay)
Hungerford, Pixie
  See Brinsmead, H(esba) F(ay)
Hunkin, Tim 1950- 53
Hunkin, Timothy Mark Trelawney
  See Hunkin, Tim
Hunt, Angela Elwell 1957- 159
  Earlier sketch in SATA 75
Hunt, Bernice 1920- 4
Hunt, Charlotte Dumaresq
  See Demi
Hunt, Francesca
  See Holland, Isabelle (Christian)
Hunt, Irene 1907-2001 91
  Earlier sketch in SATA 2
  See also CLR 1
Hunt, Janie Louise 1963- 102
Hunt, Jonathan 1966- 84
Hunt, Joyce 1927- 31
Hunt, Linda 1940- 39
Hunt, Lisa B(ehnke) 1967- 84
Hunt, Mabel Leigh 1892-1971 1
  Obituary 26
Hunt, Morton M(agill) 1920- 22
Hunt, Nigel
  See Greenbank, Anthony Hunt

Hunt, Peter (Leonard) 1945- 76
Hunter, Anne B. 1966- 118
Hunter, Bernice Thurman 1922-2002 85
  Brief entry 45
Hunter, Bobbi Dooley 1945- 89
Hunter, Captain Marcy
  See Ellis, Edward S.
Hunter, Chris
  See Fluke, Joanne
Hunter, Clingham M.D.
  See Adams, William Taylor
Hunter, Edith Fisher 1919- 31
Hunter, Erin
  See Cary, Kate
Hunter, Evan 1926-2005 25
  Obituary 167
Hunter, George E.
  See Ellis, Edward S.
Hunter, Hilda 1921- 7
Hunter, Jana
  See Hunter, Jana Novotny
Hunter, Jana Novotny 190
Hunter, Jim 1939- 65
Hunter, Kristin
  See Lattany, Kristin Hunter
Hunter, Leigh
  See Etchison, Birdie L(ee)
Hunter, Lieutenant Ned
  See Ellis, Edward S.
Hunter, Linzie 1979- 227
Hunter, Mel 1927-2004 39
Hunter, Mollie 1922- 139
  Autobiography Feature 139
  Earlier sketches in SATA 2, 54, 106
  See also CLR 25
  See also SAAS 7
Hunter, Ned
  See Ellis, Edward S.
Hunter, Norman (George Lorimer)
  1899-1995 84
  Earlier sketch in SATA 26
Hunter, Ryan Ann
  See Greenwood, Pamela D.
  and Macalaster, Elizabeth G.
Hunter, Sara Hoagland 1954- 98
Hunter Blair, Pauline
  See Clarke, Pauline
Huntington, Amy 1956- 180
  Earlier sketch in SATA 138
Huntington, Geoffrey 145
Huntington, Harriet E(lizabeth) 1909- 1
Huntley, Amy 225
Huntsberry, William E(mery) 1916- 5
Hurd, Clement (G.) 1908-1988 64
  Obituary 54
  Earlier sketch in SATA 2
  See also CLR 49
Hurd, Edith Thacher 1910-1997 64
  Obituary 95
  Earlier sketch in SATA 2
  See also CLR 49
  See also SAAS 13
Hurd, John Thacher
  See Hurd, Thacher
Hurd, Thacher 1949- 219
  Autobiography Feature 123
  Brief entry 45
  Earlier sketches in SATA 46, 94
Hurley, Jo
  See Dower, Laura
Hurley, Tonya 207
Hurlimann, Bettina
  See Huerlimann, Bettina
Hurlimann, Ruth
  See Huerlimann, Ruth
Hurmence, Belinda 1921- 77
  See also CLR 25
  See also SAAS 20
Hurst, Carol Otis 1933-2007 185
  Earlier sketch in SATA 130
Hurt-Newton, Tania 1968- 84

Hurwin, Davida Wills 1950- 180
Hurwitz, Johanna 1937- 175
  Earlier sketches in SATA 20, 71, 113
  See also SAAS 18
Hurwood, Bernhardt J. 1926-1987 12
  Obituary 50
Husain, Shahrukh 1950- 108
Huser, Glen 1943- 151
Hutchens, Paul 1902-1977 31
Hutchins, Carleen M.
  See Hutchins, Carleen Maley
Hutchins, Carleen Maley 1911-2009 9
  Obituary 206
Hutchins, Hazel J. 1952- 175
  Brief entry 51
  Earlier sketches in SATA 81, 135
  See also SAAS 24
Hutchins, Pat 1942- 178
  Earlier sketches in SATA 15, 70, 111
  See also CLR 20
  See also SAAS 16
Hutchins, Ross Elliott 1906- 4
Hutchison, Linda 1942- 152
Huthmacher, J. Joseph 1929- 5
Hutto, Nelson (Allen) 1904-1985 20
Hutton, Kathryn 1915- 89
Hutton, Sam
  See Jones, Allan Frewin
Hutton, Warwick 1939-1994 20
  Obituary 83
  See also SAAS 17
Huxley, Aldous 1894-1963 63
  See also CLR 151
Huxley, Aldous Leonard
  See Huxley, Aldous
Huxley, Elspeth (Josceline Grant)
  1907-1997 62
  Obituary 95
Hyde, Catherine R.
  See Hyde, Catherine Ryan
Hyde, Catherine Ryan 1955- 224
  Earlier sketch in SATA 141
Hyde, Dayton O(gden) 9
Hyde, Hawk
  See Hyde, Dayton O(gden)
Hyde, Jeannette
  See Eyerly, Jeannette
Hyde, Margaret O. 1917- 139
  Earlier sketches in SATA 1, 42, 76
  See also CLR 23
  See also SAAS 8
Hyde, Margaret Oldroyd
  See Hyde, Margaret O.
Hyde, Shelley
  See Reed, Kit
Hyde, Wayne Frederick 1922- 7
Hylander, Clarence J(ohn) 1897-1964 7
Hyman, Miles 1962- 210
Hyman, Paula Chase
  See Chase, Paula
Hyman, Robin 1931- 12
Hyman, Robin Phiilip
  See Hyman, Robin
Hyman, Trina Schart 1939-2004 95
  Obituary 158
  Earlier sketches in SATA 7, 46
  See also CLR 50
Hymes, Lucia M(anley) 1907-1998 7
Hyndman, Jane Andrews Lee 1912-1978 46
  Obituary 23
  Earlier sketch in SATA 1
Hyndman, Robert Utley 1906-1973 18
Hynes, Pat 98

I

Iannone, Jeanne
  See Balzano, Jeanne (Koppel)
Ibatoulline, Bagram 1965(?)- 225
  Earlier sketch in SATA 174
Ibbitson, John Perrie 1955- 102
Ibbotson, Eva 1925-2010 221
  Earlier sketches in SATA 13, 103, 156
Ibbotson, M. C(hristine) 1930- 5
Icenoggle, Jodi 1967- 168
Icenoggle, Jodi O.
  See Icenoggle, Jodi
Ichikawa, Satomi 1949- 208
  Brief entry 36
  Earlier sketches in SATA 47, 78, 146
  See also CLR 62
Idle, Molly Schaar 223
Iggulden, Hal 1972- 196
Ignoffo, Matthew 1945- 92
Igus, Toyomi 1953- 112
  Earlier sketch in SATA 76
Ihimaera, Witi (Tame) 1944- 148
Ikeda, Daisaku 1928- 77
Ilowite, Sheldon A. 1931- 27
Ilsey, Dent
  See Chapman, John Stanton Higham
Ilsley, Dent
  See Chapman, John Stanton Higham
Ilsley, Velma (Elizabeth) 1918- 12
Imai, Ayano 1980- 190
Imai, Miko 1963- 90
Imershein, Betsy 1953- 62
Immel, Mary Blair 1930- 28
Immell, Myra H. 1941- 92
Impey, Rose 1947- 223
  Earlier sketches in SATA 69, 152
Ingalls, Ann 227
Ingelow, Jean 1820-1897 33
Ingermanson, Randall 1958- 134
Ingermanson, Randy
  See Ingermanson, Randall
Ingersoll, Norman 1928- 79
Ingham, Colonel Frederic
  See Hale, Edward Everett
Ingman, Bruce 1963- 182
  Earlier sketch in SATA 134
Ingman, Nicholas 1948- 52
Ingold, Jeanette 128
Ingpen, Robert 1936- 166
  Earlier sketch in SATA 109
Ingpen, Robert Roger
  See Ingpen, Robert
Ingraham, Erick 1950- 145
Ingraham, Leonard W(illiam) 1913-2003 4
Ingram, Scott 1948- 167
  Earlier sketch in SATA 92
Ingram, W. Scott
  See Ingram, Scott
Ingrams, Doreen 1906-1997 97
  Earlier sketch in SATA 20
Ingrid, Charles
  See Salsitz, Rhondi Vilott
Ingves, Gunilla 1939- 101
Ingves, Gunilla Anna Maria Folkesdotter
  See Ingves, Gunilla
Inkpen, Mick 1952- 154
  Earlier sketch in SATA 99
Innes, (Ralph) Hammond
  See Hammond Innes, Ralph
Innes, Ralph Hammond
  See Hammond Innes, Ralph
Innes, Stephanie 220
Innocenti, Roberto 1940- 159
  Earlier sketch in SATA 96
  See also CLR 126
Innocenti and Gallaz
  See Gallaz, Christophe
  and Innocenti, Roberto
Inns, Chris 212

Inyart, Gene
  See Namovicz, Gene Inyart
Ionesco, Eugene 1909-1994 7
  Obituary 79
Ipcar, Dahlov (Zorach) 1917- 147
  Autobiography Feature 147
  Earlier sketches in SATA *1, 49*
  See also SAAS *8*
Ireland, Karin 151
  Earlier sketch in SATA *101*
Ironside, Jetske 1940- 60
Irvin, Fred 1914- 15
Irvine, Georgeanne 1955- 72
Irvine, Joan 1951- 80
Irving, Alexander
  See Hume, Ruth Fox
Irving, Robert
  See Adler, Irving
Irving, Washington 1783-1859
  See YABC *2*
  See also CLR *97*
Irwin, Ann(abelle Bowen) 1915-1998 89
  Brief entry 38
  Obituary 106
  Earlier sketch in SATA *44*
  See also CLR *40*
  See also SAAS *14*
Irwin, Constance (H.) Frick 1913-1995 6
Irwin, Hadley
  See Hadley, Lee
  and Irwin, Ann(abelle Bowen)
Irwin, Keith Gordon 1885-1964 11
Isaac, Joanne 1934- 21
Isaacs, Anne 1949- 185
  Earlier sketch in SATA *90*
Isaacs, Jacob
  See Kranzler, George G(ershon)
Isaacson, Philip M(arshal) 1924- 87
Isadora, Rachel 1953(?)- 204
  Brief entry 32
  Earlier sketches in SATA *54, 79, 121, 165*
  See also CLR *7*
Isbell, Rebecca T(emple) 1942- 125
Isham, Charlotte H(ickock) 1912- 21
Ishida, Jui 176
Ish-Kishor, Judith 1892-1972 11
Ish-Kishor, Sulamith 1896-1977 17
Ishmael, Woodi 1914-1995 31
  Obituary 109
Isle, Sue 1963- 105
Isol 1972- 220
Israel, Elaine 1945- 12
Israel, Marion Louise 1882-1973
  Obituary 26
Iterson, S(iny) R(ose) Van
  See Van Iterson, S(iny) R(ose)
Ivanko, John D. 1966- 111
Ivanko, John Duane
  See Ivanko, John D.
Iversen, Jeremy 1980(?)- 174
Iversen, Jeremy Watt
  See Iversen, Jeremy
Iverson, Carol (L.) 1941- 145
Iverson, Diane 1950- 122
Iverson, Eric G.
  See Turtledove, Harry
Ivery, Martha M. 1948- 124
Ives, David 1951- 173
Ives, Morgan
  See Bradley, Marion Zimmer
Ives, Penny 1956- 215
Iwai, Melissa 183
Iwamatsu, Jun Atsushi 1908-1994 81
  Earlier sketch in SATA *14*
  See also CLR *4*
Iwamura, Kazuo 1939- 213
Iwasaki (Matsumoto), Chihiro 1918-1974
  See CLR *18*
Iyengar, Malathi Michelle 1954- 220

J

Jabar, Cynthia 210
Jablonski, Carla 184
Jac, Lee
  See Morton, Lee Jack, Jr.
Jacka, Martin 1943- 72
Jackson, Alison 1953- 228
  Earlier sketches in SATA *73, 108, 160*
Jackson, Anne 1896(?)-1984
  Obituary 37
Jackson, Barry
  See Jackson, Barry E.
Jackson, Barry E. 200
Jackson, C(aary) Paul 1902-1991 6
Jackson, Caary
  See Jackson, C(aary) Paul
Jackson, Charlotte E. (Cobden) 1903(?)-1989
  Obituary 62
Jackson, Dave
  See Jackson, J. David
Jackson, Donna M. 1959- 206
Jackson, Ellen 1943- 214
  Earlier sketches in SATA *75, 115, 167*
Jackson, Ellen B.
  See Jackson, Ellen
Jackson, Garnet Nelson 1944- 87
Jackson, Geoffrey (Holt Seymour) 1915-1987
  Obituary 53
Jackson, Gina
  See Fluke, Joanne
Jackson, Guida M. 1930- 71
Jackson, J. David 1944- 91
Jackson, Jacqueline 1928- 65
Jackson, Jacqueline Dougan
  See Jackson, Jacqueline
Jackson, Jesse 1908-1983 29
  Obituary 48
  Earlier sketch in SATA *2*
  See also CLR *28*
Jackson, Marjorie 1928- 127
Jackson, Melanie 1956- 141
Jackson, Mike 1946- 91
Jackson, Neta J. 1944- 91
Jackson, O. B.
  See Jackson, C(aary) Paul
Jackson, Rob 1961- 176
Jackson, Robert B(lake) 1926- 8
Jackson, Robert Bradley
  See Jackson, Rob
Jackson, Sally
  See Kellogg, Jean (Defrees)
Jackson, Shirley 1919-1965 2
Jackson, Woody 1948- 92
Jackson Issa, Kai 205
Jacob, Helen Pierce 1927- 21
Jacobin
  See Bisson, Terry
Jacobs, Deborah Lynn 187
Jacobs, Flora Gill 1918-2006 5
  Obituary 178
Jacobs, Francine 1935- 150
  Brief entry 42
  Earlier sketch in SATA *43*
Jacobs, Frank 1929- 30
Jacobs, Helen Hull 1908-1997 12
Jacobs, Joseph 1854-1916 25
Jacobs, Judy 1952- 69
Jacobs, Laurie A. 1956- 89
Jacobs, Leah
  See Gellis, Roberta
Jacobs, Lee
  See Stone, Tanya Lee
Jacobs, Leland Blair 1907-1992 20
  Obituary 71
Jacobs, Linda
  See Altman, Linda Jacobs
Jacobs, Lou(is), Jr. 1921- 2
Jacobs, Shannon K. 1947- 77
Jacobs, Susan
  See Quinn, Susan

Jacobs, William Jay 1933- 89
  Earlier sketch in SATA *28*
Jacobsen, Laura 177
Jacobson, Daniel 1923- 12
Jacobson, Jennifer
  See Jacobson, Jennifer Richard
Jacobson, Jennifer Richard 1958- 170
Jacobson, Morris K(arl) 1906- 21
Jacobson, Rick 170
Jacopetti, Alexandra
  See Hart, Alexandra
Jacques, Brian 1939-2011 176
  Earlier sketches in SATA *62, 95, 138*
  See also CLR *21*
Jacques, Robin 1920-1995 32
  Brief entry 30
  Obituary 86
  See also SAAS *5*
Jaekel, Susan M. 1948- 89
Jaffe, Michele 179
Jaffe, Michele Sharon
  See Jaffe, Michele
Jaffee, Al(lan) 1921- 66
  Earlier sketch in SATA *37*
Jagendorf, Moritz (Adolf) 1888-1981 2
  Obituary 24
Jago 1979- 216
Jahn, Joseph Michael
  See Jahn, Michael
Jahn, Michael 1943- 28
Jahn, Mike
  See Jahn, Michael
Jahn-Clough, Lisa 1967- 193
  Earlier sketches in SATA *88, 152*
Jahsmann, Allan Hart 1916- 28
Jakes, John 1932- 62
Jakes, John William
  See Jakes, John
James, Andrew
  See Kirkup, James
James, Ann 1952- 168
  Earlier sketches in SATA *82, 117*
James, Betsy 183
James, Bill 1929- 205
James, B.J.
  See James, Brian
James, Brian 1976- 212
  Earlier sketch in SATA *140*
James, Bronte
  See Nash, Renea Denise
James, Captain Lew
  See Stratemeyer, Edward L.
James, Charlie 1961- 185
James, Curtis E. 182
James, Dynely
  See Mayne, William
James, Edwin
  See Gunn, James E.
James, Elizabeth 1942- 97
  Earlier sketches in SATA *39, 45, 52*
James, Emily
  See Standiford, Natalie
James, Gordon C. 1973- 195
James, Harry Clebourne 1896-1978 11
James, J. Alison 1962- 146
  Earlier sketch in SATA *83*
James, Josephine
  See Sterne, Emma Gelders
James, Mary
  See Meaker, Marijane
James, Matt 201
James, Philip
  See del Rey, Lester
  and Moorcock, Michael
James, Robin 1953- 50
James, Robin Irene
  See James, Robin
James, Simon 1961- 202
James, T. F.
  See Fleming, Thomas

James, Tegan
See Odgers, Sally Farrell
James, Will(iam Roderick) 1892-1942 .... *19*
Jameson, W. C. 1942- *93*
Jamieson, Ian R.
See Goulart, Ron
Jamieson, Victoria *218*
Jamiolkowski, Raymond M. 1953- *81*
Jane, Mary Childs 1909-1991 .... *6*
Jane, Pamela *158*
Janeczko, Paul B(ryan) 1945- *155*
Earlier sketches in SATA *53, 98*
See also CLR *47*
See also SAAS *18*
Janes, Edward C. 1908-1984 .... *25*
Janes, Edward Clarence
See Janes, Edward C.
Janes, J(oseph) Robert 1935- *148*
Brief entry *50*
Earlier sketch in SATA *101*
Janeway, Elizabeth (Hall) 1913-2005 .... *19*
Janger, Kathleen N. 1940- *66*
Jango-Cohen, Judith 1955- *208*
Janice
See Brustlein, Janice Tworkov
Janisch, Heinz 1960- *181*
Janni, Rebecca *229*
Janosch
See Eckert, Horst
Janover, Caroline (Davis) 1943- *141*
Earlier sketch in SATA *89*
Janovitz, Marilyn *194*
Jansen, Jared
See Cebulash, Mel
Janson, Dora Jane (Heineberg) 1916- *31*
Janson, H(orst) W(oldemar) 1913-1982 .... *9*
Jansson, Tove (Marika) 1914-2001 .... *41*
Earlier sketch in SATA *3*
See also CLR *125*
Janus, Grete
See Hertz, Grete Janus
Jaques, Faith 1923-1997 .... *97*
Earlier sketches in SATA *21, 69*
Jaquith, Priscilla 1908- *51*
Jaramillo, Mari-Luci 1928- *139*
Jarka, Jeff *221*
Jarman, Julia 1946- *198*
Earlier sketch in SATA *133*
Jarman, Rosemary Hawley 1935- *7*
Jarrell, Mary Von Schrader 1914- *35*
Jarrell, Randall 1914-1965 .... *7*
See also CLR *111*
Jarrett, Clare 1952- *201*
Jarrett, Roxanne
See Werner, Herma
Jarrie, Martin 1953- *219*
Jarrow, Gail 1952- *185*
Earlier sketch in SATA *84*
Jarvis, E.K.
See Ellison, Harlan
and Silverberg, Robert
Jarvis, Robin 1963- *181*
Jarzab, Anna 1984- *227*
Jaskol, Julie 1958- *127*
Jasner, W. K.
See Watson, Jane Werner
Jassem, Kate
See Oppenheim, Joanne
Jauss, Anne Marie 1902(?)-1991 .... *10*
Obituary *69*
Javaherbin, Mina *230*
Javernick, Ellen 1938- *217*
Earlier sketch in SATA *89*
Javins, Marie 1966- *212*
Jay, Alison *196*
Jay, Stacey 1978(?)- *231*
Jayne, Lieutenant R. H.
See Ellis, Edward S.
Jaynes, Clare
See Mayer, Jane Rothschild

Jeake, Samuel, Jr.
See Aiken, Conrad
Jean-Bart, Leslie 1954- *121*
Jeapes, Ben 1965- *174*
Jecan, Gavriel 1962- *200*
Jefferds, Vincent H(arris) 1916- *59*
Brief entry *49*
Jefferies, (John) Richard 1848-1887 .... *16*
Jeffers, Dawn *189*
Jeffers, Oliver 1977- *213*
Earlier sketch in SATA *175*
Jeffers, Susan 1942- *202*
Earlier sketches in SATA *17, 70, 129, 137*
See also CLR *30*
Jefferson, Sarah
See Farjeon, (Eve) Annabel
Jeffries, Roderic 1926- *4*
Jeffries, Roderic Graeme
See Jeffries, Roderic
Jenkin-Pearce, Susie 1943- *80*
Jenkins, A. M. 1961- *174*
Jenkins, Amanda McRaney
See Jenkins, A. M.
Jenkins, Debra Reid
See Reid Jenkins, Debra
Jenkins, Emily 1967- *174*
Earlier sketch in SATA *144*
Jenkins, Jean *98*
Jenkins, Jerry B. 1949- *149*
Jenkins, Jerry Bruce
See Jenkins, Jerry B.
Jenkins, Leonard *189*
Jenkins, Marie M(agdalen) 1909- *7*
Jenkins, Martin 1959- *216*
Jenkins, M.D.
See Jenkins, Martin
Jenkins, Patrick 1955- *72*
Jenkins, Steve 1952- *218*
Earlier sketches in SATA *154, 188*
Jenkins, William A(twell) 1922-1998 .... *9*
Jenkyns, Chris 1924- *51*
Jennewein, James *215*
Jennewein, Jim
See Jennewein, James
Jennings, Christopher S. 1971(?)- *201*
Jennings, Coleman A(lonzo) 1933- *64*
Jennings, C.S.
See Jennings, Christopher S.
Jennings, Dana Andrew 1957- *93*
Jennings, Elizabeth (Joan) 1926-2001 .... *66*
Jennings, Gary 1928-1999 .... *9*
Obituary *117*
Jennings, Gary Gayne
See Jennings, Gary
Jennings, Linda 1937- *211*
Jennings, Linda M.
See Jennings, Linda
Jennings, Patrick 1962- *205*
Earlier sketches in SATA *96, 160*
Jennings, Paul 1943- *165*
Earlier sketch in SATA *88*
See also CLR *40*
Jennings, Richard W. 1945- *185*
Earlier sketch in SATA *136*
Jennings, Robert
See Hamilton, Charles (Harold St. John)
Jennings, S. M.
See Meyer, Jerome Sydney
Jennings, Sharon 1954- *231*
Earlier sketch in SATA *95*
Jennings, Sharon Elizabeth
See Jennings, Sharon
Jennison, C. S.
See Starbird, Kaye
Jennison, Keith Warren 1911-1995 .... *14*
Jensen, Kathryn 1949- *81*
Jensen, Kristine Mary 1961- *78*
Jensen, Niels 1927- *25*
Jensen, Vickie (Dee) 1946- *81*
Jensen, Virginia Allen 1927- *8*
Jenson-Elliott, Cynthia L(ouise) 1962- *143*

Jeram, Anita 1965- *219*
Earlier sketches in SATA *71, 102, 154*
Jerman, Jerry 1949- *89*
Jernigan, E. Wesley 1940- *85*
Jernigan, Gisela (Evelyn) 1948- *85*
Jerome, Elaine *228*
Jeschke, Susan 1942- *42*
Brief entry *27*
Jessel, Camilla (Ruth) 1937- *143*
Earlier sketch in SATA *29*
Jessell, Tim *225*
Earlier sketch in SATA *177*
Jessey, Cornelia
See Sussman, Cornelia Silver
Jewel
See Kilcher, Jewel
Jewell, Nancy 1940- *109*
Brief entry *41*
Jewett, Eleanore Myers 1890-1967 .... *5*
Jewett, Sarah Orne 1849-1909 .... *15*
Jewett, Theodora Sarah Orne
See Jewett, Sarah Orne
Jezard, Alison 1919- *57*
Brief entry *34*
Jiang, Cheng An 1943- *109*
Jiang, Ji-li 1954- *101*
Jiang, Zheng An
See Jiang, Cheng An
Jiler, John 1946- *42*
Brief entry *35*
Jimenez, Francisco 1943- *219*
Earlier sketch in SATA *108*
Jinks, Catherine 1963- *207*
Earlier sketches in SATA *94, 155*
Jobb, Jamie 1945- *29*
Jobling, Curtis *131*
Jocelyn, Ann Henning 1948- *92*
Jocelyn, Marthe 1956- *198*
Earlier sketches in SATA *118, 163*
Joerns, Consuelo *44*
Brief entry *33*
Joey D
See Macaulay, Teresa
Johansen, Krista V.
See Johansen, K.V.
Johansen, K.V 1968- *186*
Johansen, K.V. 1968- *186*
Earlier sketch in SATA *129*
Johansson, Philip *163*
John, Antony 1972- *206*
John, Joyce *59*
Johns, Avery
See Cousins, Margaret
Johns, Elizabeth 1943- *88*
Johns, Janetta
See Quin-Harkin, Janet
Johns, Linda 1945- *173*
Johns, W(illiam) E(arle) 1893-1968 .... *55*
Johns, Captain W. E.
See Johns, W(illiam) E(arle)
Johnson, A.
See Johnson, Annabell
Johnson, A. E.
See Johnson, Annabell
and Johnson, Edgar (Raymond)
Johnson, Angela 1961- *188*
Earlier sketches in SATA *69, 102, 150*
See also CLR *33*
Johnson, Annabel
See Johnson, Annabell
Johnson, Annabell 1921- *72*
Earlier sketch in SATA *2*
Johnson, Art 1946- *123*
Johnson, B. F. 1920- *1*
Johnson, Benjamin F., of Boone
See Riley, James Whitcomb
Johnson, Bettye 1858-1919
See Rogers, Bettye
Johnson, Caryn
See Goldberg, Whoopi

Johnson, Caryn E.
  See Goldberg, Whoopi
Johnson, Caryn Elaine
  See Goldberg, Whoopi
Johnson, Charles R. 1925- *11*
Johnson, Charlotte Buel
  See von Wodtke, Charlotte Buel Johnson
Johnson, Chuck
  See Johnson, Charles R.
Johnson, Crockett
  See Leisk, David (Johnson)
Johnson, D(ana) William 1945- *23*
Johnson, Daniel Shahid 1954- *73*
Johnson, David
  See Johnson, David A.
Johnson, David A. 1951- *191*
Johnson, D.B. 1944- *183*
  Earlier sketch in SATA *146*
Johnson, Dianne 1960- *130*
  See Johnson, Dinah
Johnson, Dinah *231*
  See Johnson, Dianne
Johnson, Dolores 1949- *69*
Johnson, Donald B.
  See Johnson, D.B.
Johnson, Dorothy M(arie) 1905-1984 .... *6*
  Obituary *40*
Johnson, E(ugene) Harper *44*
Johnson, Edgar (Raymond) 1912-1990 .... *72*
  Earlier sketch in SATA *2*
Johnson, Eleanor Murdock 1892-1987
  Obituary *54*
Johnson, Elizabeth 1911-1984 .... *7*
  Obituary *39*
Johnson, Eric W(arner) 1918-1994 ....
  Obituary *82*
  Earlier sketch in SATA *8*
Johnson, Evelyne 1922- *20*
Johnson, Fred 19(?)-1982 .... *63*
Johnson, Gaylord 1884-1972 .... *7*
Johnson, Gerald White 1890-1980 .... *19*
  Obituary *28*
Johnson, Gillian 1963- *215*
Johnson, Harper
  See Johnson, E(ugene) Harper
Johnson, Harriett 1908-1987
  Obituary *53*
Johnson, James Ralph 1922- *1*
Johnson, James Weldon 1871-1938 .... *31*
  See also CLR *32*
Johnson, Jane 1951- *48*
Johnson, Jen Cullerton 1972- *230*
Johnson, Joan J. 1942- *59*
Johnson, John E(mil) 1929- *34*
Johnson, Johnny 1901-1995
  See Johnson, (Walter) Ryerson
Johnson, Kathleen Jeffrie 1950- *186*
Johnson, La Verne B(ravo) 1925- *13*
Johnson, Layne *222*
  Earlier sketch in SATA *187*
Johnson, Lee Kaiser 1962- *78*
Johnson, Lissa H(alls) 1955- *65*
Johnson, Lois Smith 1894-1993 .... *6*
Johnson, Lois Walfrid 1936- *130*
  Earlier sketches in SATA *22, 91*
Johnson, Margaret S(weet) 1893-1964 .... *35*
Johnson, Marguerite Annie
  See Angelou, Maya
Johnson, Mary Frances K. 1929(?)-1979
  Obituary *27*
Johnson, Maud Battle 1918(?)-1985
  Obituary *46*
Johnson, Maureen 1973- *200*
Johnson, Meredith Merrell 1952- *104*
Johnson, Milton 1932- *31*
Johnson, Neil 1954- *135*
  Earlier sketch in SATA *73*
Johnson, Pamela 1949- *71*
Johnson, Patricia Polin 1956- *84*
Johnson, Paul Brett 1947- *132*
  Earlier sketch in SATA *83*

Johnson, Rebecca L. 1956- *147*
  Earlier sketch in SATA *67*
Johnson, Rick L. 1954- *79*
Johnson, (Walter) Ryerson 1901-1995 .... *10*
  Obituary *106*
Johnson, Scott 1952- *119*
  Earlier sketch in SATA *76*
Johnson, Sherrie 1948- *87*
Johnson, Shirley K(ing) 1927- *10*
Johnson, Siddie Joe 1905-1977
  Obituary *20*
Johnson, Spencer 1938- *145*
  Brief entry *38*
Johnson, Stacie
  See Myers, Walter Dean
Johnson, Stephen T. 1964- *189*
  Earlier sketches in SATA *84, 141*
Johnson, Steve 1960- *230*
  Earlier sketch in SATA *177*
Johnson, Sue Kaiser 1963- *78*
Johnson, Sylvia A. *166*
  Brief entry *52*
  Earlier sketch in SATA *104*
Johnson, Varian 1977- *229*
Johnson, William R. *38*
Johnson, William Weber 1909-1992 .... *7*
Johnson-Feelings, Dianne
  See Johnson, Dianne
Johnston, Agnes Christine
  See Dazey, Agnes J(ohnston)
Johnston, Annie Fellows 1863-1931 .... *37*
Johnston, Dorothy Grunbock 1915-1979 ..... *54*
Johnston, Ginny 1946- *60*
Johnston, H(ugh) A(nthony) S(tephen)
  1913-1967 .... *14*
Johnston, Janet 1944- *71*
Johnston, Jeffry W. *188*
Johnston, Johanna 1914(?)-1982 .... *12*
  Obituary *33*
Johnston, Julie 1941- *110*
  Autobiography Feature *128*
  Earlier sketch in SATA *78*
  See also CLR *41*
  See also SAAS *24*
Johnston, Lynn 1947- *216*
  Earlier sketch in SATA *118*
Johnston, Lynn Beverley
  See Johnston, Lynn
Johnston, Mark *194*
Johnston, Norma
  See St. John, Nicole
Johnston, Portia
  See Takakjian, Portia
Johnston, Susan Taylor 1942- *180*
  Earlier sketches in SATA *8, 83, 128*
  See Johnston, Tony
Johnston, Tim(othy Patrick) 1962- *146*
Johnston, Tony *226*
  See Johnston, Susan Taylor
Joinson, Carla *160*
Jolin, Paula *186*
Jolivet, Joelle 1965- *221*
Jonas, Ann 1932- *135*
  Brief entry *42*
  Earlier sketch in SATA *50*
  See also CLR *74*
Jonell, Lynne 1956- *196*
  Earlier sketch in SATA *109*
Jones, Adrienne 1915-2000 .... *82*
  Earlier sketch in SATA *7*
  See also SAAS *10*
Jones, Allan Frewin 1954- *204*
Jones, Annabel
  See Lewis, Mary
Jones, Betty Millsaps 1940- *54*
Jones, Carol 1942- *153*
  Earlier sketch in SATA *79*
Jones, Carrie 1971- *229*
  Earlier sketch in SATA *191*
Jones, Charles M.
  See Jones, Chuck

Jones, Charlotte Foltz 1945- *122*
  Earlier sketch in SATA *77*
Jones, Chuck 1912-2002 .... *53*
  Obituary *133*
Jones, Constance *112*
Jones, Constance A.
  See Jones, Constance
Jones, David 1956- *202*
Jones, Diana Wynne 1934-2011 .... *160*
  Earlier sketches in SATA *9, 70, 108*
  See also CLR *120*
  See also SAAS *7*
Jones, Douglas B. *202*
Jones, Douglas C(lyde) 1924-1998 .... *52*
Jones, Elizabeth McDavid *155*
Jones, Elizabeth Orton 1910-2005 .... *18*
  Obituary *164*
Jones, Evan 1915-1996 .... *3*
Jones, Frewin
  See Jones, Allan Frewin
Jones, Geraldine
  See McCaughrean, Geraldine
Jones, Gillingham
  See Hamilton, Charles (Harold St. John)
Jones, Gwyneth A. 1952- *159*
Jones, Gwyneth Ann
  See Jones, Gwyneth A.
Jones, Harold 1904-1992 .... *14*
  Obituary *72*
Jones, Helen Hinckley 1903-1991 .... *26*
Jones, Helen L(ouise) 1903-1973
  Obituary *22*
Jones, Hettie 1934- *42*
  Brief entry *27*
Jones, Hortense P. 1918- *9*
Jones, J. Sydney 1948- *101*
Jones, Jasmine
  See Papademetriou, Lisa
Jones, Jennifer (Berry) 1947- *90*
Jones, Jessie Mae Orton 1887(?)-1983
  Obituary *37*
Jones, John R(obert) 1926- *76*
Jones, Jon Sydney
  See Jones, J. Sydney
Jones, Judith
  See James, Bill
Jones, Kimberly K. 1957- *187*
Jones, Marcia Thornton 1958- *217*
  Earlier sketches in SATA *73, 115*
Jones, Martha T(annery) 1931- *130*
Jones, Mary Alice 1898(?)-1980 .... *6*
Jones, McClure *34*
Jones, Noah Z. *182*
Jones, Patrick 1961- *210*
  Earlier sketch in SATA *136*
Jones, Penelope 1938- *31*
Jones, Rebecca C(astaldi) 1947- *99*
  Earlier sketch in SATA *33*
Jones, Robin D(orothy) 1959- *80*
Jones, Sanford W.
  See Thorn, John
Jones, Sylvie *185*
Jones, Sylvie Michelle
  See Jones, Sylvie
Jones, Terence Graham Parry 1942- *127*
  Brief entry *51*
  Earlier sketch in SATA *67*
Jones, Terry
  See Jones, Terence Graham Parry
Jones, Tim Wynne
  See Wynne-Jones, Tim
Jones, Traci L. *186*
Jones, V. M. 1958- *147*
Jones, Veda Boyd 1948- *119*
Jones, Victoria Mary
  See Jones, V. M.
Jones, Volcano
  See Mitchell, Adrian
Jones, Weyman (B.) 1928- *4*
  See also SAAS *11*

Jones, William Glynne
　See Glynne-Jones, William
Jonk, Clarence 1906-1987 .... *10*
Jonsberg, Barry 1951- *168*
Joos, Francoise 1956- *78*
Joos, Frederic 1953- *78*
Joosse, Barbara 1949- *220*
　Earlier sketches in SATA *52, 96, 164*
Joosse, Barbara M.
　See Joosse, Barbara
Joosse, Barbara Monnot
　See Joosse, Barbara
Jordan, Alexis Hill
　See Glick, Ruth
　and Titchener, Louise
Jordan, Anne Devereaux 1943- *80*
Jordan, Chris
　See Philbrick, Rodman
Jordan, Deloris *191*
Jordan, Devin *221*
Jordan, Don
　See Howard, Vernon (Linwood)
Jordan, Hope Dahle 1905-1995 .... *15*
Jordan, Jael (Michal) 1949- *30*
Jordan, June 1936-2002 .... *136*
　Earlier sketch in SATA *4*
　See also CLR *10*
Jordan, June Meyer
　See Jordan, June
Jordan, Lee
　See Scholefield, Alan
Jordan, Martin George 1944- *84*
Jordan, Robert 1948-2007 .... *95*
Jordan, Robert K.
　See Jordan, Robert
Jordan, Rosa 1939- *191*
Jordan, Roslyn M. *189*
Jordan, Sherryl 1949- *122*
　Earlier sketch in SATA *71*
　See also SAAS *23*
Jordan, Shirley 1930- *154*
Jordan, Tanis 1946- *84*
Jorgensen, Ivar
　See Ellison, Harlan
　and Garrett, Randall
Jorgensen, Mary Venn -1995 .... *36*
Jorgensen, Norman 1954- *157*
Jorgenson, Ivar
　See Silverberg, Robert
Jorisch, Stephane *178*
Joseph, Anne
　See Coates, Anna
Joseph, James (Herz) 1924- *53*
Joseph, Joan 1939- *34*
Joseph, Joseph M(aron) 1903-1979 .... *22*
Joseph, Patrick
　See O'Malley, Kevin
Josephs, Rebecca
　See Talbot, Toby
Josephson, Judith Pinkerton 1943- *198*
Josh
　See Twain, Mark
Joshua, Peter
　See Stone, Peter
Joslin, Mary 1953- *176*
Joslin, Sesyle
　See Hine, Sesyle Joslin
Joubert, Beverly 1957- *204*
Joubert, Dereck *204*
Journet, Mireille
　See Marokvia, Mireille
Joyce, Bill
　See Joyce, William
Joyce, J(ames) Avery 1902-1987 .... *11*
　Obituary *50*
Joyce, Peter 1937- *127*
Joyce, William 1957- *118*
　Brief entry *46*
　Earlier sketch in SATA *72*
　See also CLR *26*
Joyner, Jerry 1938- *34*

Juan, Ana 1961- *179*
Juarez, Fernando *230*
Juarez, Fernando Lopez
　See Juarez, Fernando
Jubb, Sophie *210*
Jubert, Herve *185*
Juby, Susan 1969- *202*
　Earlier sketch in SATA *156*
Jucker, Sita 1921- *5*
Judah, Aaron 1923- *118*
Judd, Cyril
　See Kornbluth, C(yril) M.
　and Merril, Judith
　and Pohl, Frederik
Judd, Denis (O'Nan) 1938- *33*
Judd, Frances K.
　See Benson, Mildred
Jude, Conny *81*
Judge, Lita *192*
Judson, Clara Ingram 1879-1960 .... *38*
　Brief entry *27*
Judy, Stephen
　See Tchudi, Stephen N.
Judy, Stephen N.
　See Tchudi, Stephen N.
Juhasz, Victor 1954- *177*
Jukes, Mavis 1947- *219*
　Brief entry *43*
　Earlier sketches in SATA *72, 111*
　See also SAAS *12*
Jules, Jacqueline 1956- *218*
　Earlier sketches in SATA *148, 183*
Julesberg, Elizabeth Rider Montgomery
　1902-1985 .... *34*
　Obituary *41*
　Earlier sketch in SATA *3*
Julian, Jane
　See Wiseman, David
Jumpp, Hugo
　See MacPeek, Walter G.
Junco, Martha Aviles
　See Aviles, Martha
Jungman, Ann *165*
Jupo, Frank J. 1904-1981 .... *7*
Jurmain, Suzanne 1945- *169*
　Earlier sketch in SATA *72*
Jurmain, Suzanne Tripp
　See Jurmain, Suzanne
Juster, Norton 1929- *220*
　Earlier sketches in SATA *3, 132*
　See also CLR *112*
Justus, May 1898-1989 .... *1*
　Obituary *106*
Jutte, Jan 1953- *231*
Juvenilia
　See Taylor, Ann

K

Kaaberbol, Lene
　See Kaaberbol, Lene
Kaaberbol, Lene 1960- *159*
Kabdebo, Tamas
　See Kabdebo, Thomas
Kabdebo, Thomas 1934- *10*
Kabibble, Osh
　See Jobb, Jamie
Kacer, Kathy 1954- *184*
　Earlier sketch in SATA *142*
Kaczman, James *156*
Kadair, Deborah Ousley *184*
Kadefors, Sara 1965- *218*
Kadesch, Robert R(udstone) 1922- *31*
Kadohata, Cynthia 1956(?)- *228*
　Earlier sketches in SATA *155, 180*
　See also CLR *121*
Kadohata, Cynthia L.
　See Kadohata, Cynthia

Kaempfert, Wade
　See del Rey, Lester
Kaestner, Erich 1899-1974 .... *14*
　See also CLR *153*
Kagawa, Julie *228*
Kahl, Jonathan (D.) 1959- *77*
Kahl, M(arvin) P(hilip) 1934- *37*
Kahl, Virginia (Caroline) 1919-2004 .... *48*
　Brief entry *38*
　Obituary *158*
Kahn, Joan 1914-1994 .... *48*
　Obituary *82*
Kahn, Katherine Janus 1942- *220*
　Earlier sketches in SATA *90, 167*
Kahn, Peggy
　See Katz, Bobbi
Kahn, Roger 1927- *37*
Kahukiwa, Robyn 1940- *134*
Kains, Josephine
　See Goulart, Ron
Kaizuki, Kiyonori 1950- *72*
Kajikawa, Kimiko *212*
Kakimoto, Kozo 1915- *11*
Kalashnikoff, Nicholas 1888-1961 .... *16*
Kalb, Jonah 1926- *23*
Kalbacken, Joan 1925- *96*
Kalechofsky, Roberta 1931- *92*
Kaler, James Otis 1848-1912 .... *15*
Kalis, Jennifer *207*
Kalish, Claire M. 1947- *92*
Kallen, Stuart A. 1955- *126*
　Earlier sketch in SATA *86*
Kallen, Stuart Arnold
　See Kallen, Stuart A.
Kallevig, Christine Petrell 1955- *164*
Kalman, Bobbie 1947- *63*
Kalman, Maira 1949- *137*
　Earlier sketch in SATA *96*
　See also CLR *32*
Kalnay, Francis 1899-1992 .... *7*
Kaloustian, Rosanne 1955- *93*
Kalow, Gisela 1946- *32*
Kalstein, Dave *175*
Kamara, Mariatu *214*
Kamen, Gloria 1923- *98*
　Earlier sketch in SATA *9*
Kamerman, Sylvia E.
　See Burack, Sylvia K.
Kamm, Josephine (Hart) 1905-1989 .... *24*
Kammerman, Sylvia K.
　See Burack, Sylvia K.
Kandel, Michael 1941- *93*
Kandell, Alice S. 1938- *35*
Kane, Bob 1916-1998 .... *120*
Kane, Henry Bugbee 1902-1971 .... *14*
Kane, Kim 1973(?)- *221*
Kane, L. A.
　See Mannetti, Lisa
Kane, Robert W. 1910- *18*
Kane, Wilson
　See Bloch, Robert (Albert)
Kanefield, Teri 1960- *135*
Kanell, Beth *215*
Kaner, Etta 1947- *198*
　Earlier sketch in SATA *126*
Kanetzke, Howard W(illiam) 1932- *38*
Kangas, Juli 1958- *200*
Kann, Elizabeth *180*
Kann, Victoria *180*
Kanninen, Barbara *196*
Kanninen, Barbara J.
　See Kanninen, Barbara
Kanoza, Muriel Canfield
　See Canfield, Muriel
Kantner, Seth 1965- *179*
Kanzawa, Toshiko
　See Furukawa, Toshi
Kanzler, John 1963- *188*
Kaplan, Andrew 1960- *78*
Kaplan, Anne Bernays
　See Bernays, Anne

Kaplan, Bess 1927- 22
Kaplan, Boche 1926- 24
Kaplan, Elizabeth 1956- 83
Kaplan, Elizabeth A.
    See Kaplan, Elizabeth
Kaplan, Irma 1900- 10
Kaplan, Jean Caryl Korn 1926- 10
Kaplow, Robert 1954- 70
Karageorge, Michael
    See Anderson, Poul
Karas, G. Brian 1957- 222
    Earlier sketch in SATA 178
Karas, George Brian
    See Karas, G. Brian
Karasz, Ilonka 1896-1981
    Obituary 29
Karen, Ruth 1922-1987 9
    Obituary 54
Kark, Nina Mary
    See Bawden, Nina
Karl, Herb 1938- 73
Karl, Jean E(dna) 1927-2000 122
    Earlier sketch in SATA 34
    See also SAAS 10
Karlin, Bernie 1927- 68
Karlin, Eugene 1918- 10
Karlin, Nurit 103
    Earlier sketch in SATA 63
Karlins, Mark 1947- 219
Karnes, Frances A. 1937- 110
Karp, Naomi J. 1926- 16
Karpinski, J. Rick
    See Karpinski, John Eric
Karpinski, John Eric 1952- 81
Karpinski, Rick
    See Karpinski, John Eric
Karr, Kathleen 1946- 212
    Earlier sketches in SATA 82, 127
Karr, Phyllis Ann 1944- 119
Karwoski, Gail 1949- 127
Karwoski, Gail Langer
    See Karwoski, Gail
Kashiwagi, Isami 1925- 10
Kaslik, Ibi
    See Kaslik, Ibolya Emma
Kaslik, Ibolya Emma 1973- 185
Kassem, Lou 1931- 62
    Brief entry 51
Kastel, Warren
    See Silverberg, Robert
Kastner, Erich
    See Kaestner, Erich
Kastner, Jill (Marie) 1964- 117
    Earlier sketch in SATA 70
Kasuya, Masahiro 1937- 51
Kasza, Keiko 1951- 191
    Earlier sketch in SATA 124
Kataphusin
    See Ruskin, John
Katchen, Carole 1944- 9
Katcher, Brian 1975- 203
Kathryn
    See Searle, Kathryn Adrienne
Kato, Aya 1982- 202
Katona, Robert 1949- 21
Katsarakis, Joan Harries
    See Harries, Joan
Katz, Alan 231
    Earlier sketch in SATA 185
Katz, Avi 1949- 199
Katz, Avner 1939- 103
Katz, Bobbi 1933- 217
    Earlier sketches in SATA 12, 179
Katz, Fred(eric Phillip) 1938- 6
Katz, Jane B(resler) 1934- 33
Katz, Karen 1947- 195
    Earlier sketch in SATA 158
Katz, Marjorie P.
    See Weiser, Marjorie P(hillis) K(atz)
Katz, Susan 1945- 156

Katz, Welwyn Wilton 1948- 96
    Autobiography Feature 118
    Earlier sketch in SATA 62
    See also CLR 45
Katz, William 1940- 98
Katz, William Loren 1927- 13
Kaufman, Bel 57
Kaufman, Jeff 1955- 84
Kaufman, Joe 1911-2001 33
Kaufman, Joseph
    See Kaufman, Joe
Kaufman, Mervyn D. 1932- 4
Kaufmann, Angelika 1935- 15
Kaufmann, John 1931- 18
Kaula, Edna Mason 1906-1987 13
Kaur Khalsa, Dayal
    See Khalsa, Dayal Kaur
Kavaler, Lucy 1930- 23
Kavanagh, Jack 1920- 85
Kavanagh, P(atrick) J(oseph Gregory)
    1931- 122
Kavanaugh, Ian
    See Webb, Jean Francis (III)
Kay, Alan N. 1965- 144
Kay, Elizabeth 1949- 165
Kay, Guy Gavriel 1954- 167
    Earlier sketch in SATA 121
Kay, Helen
    See Goldfrank, Helen Colodny
Kay, Jackie 1961- 165
    Earlier sketch in SATA 97
Kay, Jacqueline Margaret
    See Kay, Jackie
Kay, Julia 205
Kay, Mara 13
Kay, Verla 1946- 210
    Earlier sketch in SATA 120
Kaye, Danny 1913-1987
    Obituary 50
Kaye, Geraldine (Hughesdon) 1925- 85
    Earlier sketch in SATA 10
Kaye, Judy
    See Baer, Judy
Kaye, Marilyn 1949- 230
    Earlier sketches in SATA 56, 110
Kaye, Mary Margaret
    See Kaye, M.M.
Kaye, M.M. 1908-2004 62
    Obituary 152
Kaye, Mollie
    See Kaye, M.M.
Kaye, Peggy 1948- 143
Keach, James P. 1950- 125
Keams, Geri 1951- 117
Keane, Bil 1922- 4
Keane, Dave 1965- 216
Keaney, Brian 1954- 188
    Earlier sketch in SATA 106
Kearney, Meg 1964- 178
Kearny, Jillian
    See Goulart, Ron
Keat, Nawuth 1964- 222
Keating, Bern
    See Keating, Leo Bernard
Keating, Frank 1944- 143
Keating, Lawrence A. 1903-1966 23
Keating, Leo Bernard 1915- 10
Keats, Emma 1899(?)-1979(?) 68
Keats, Ezra Jack 1916-1983 57
    Obituary 34
    Earlier sketch in SATA 14
    See also CLR 35
Keefer, Catherine
    See Ogan, George F.
    and Ogan, Margaret E. (Nettles)
Keefer, Janice Kulyk
    See Kulyk Keefer, Janice
Keegan, Marcia 1943- 104
    Earlier sketch in SATA 9
Keehn, Sally M. 1947- 165
    Earlier sketch in SATA 87

Keel, Frank
    See Keeler, Ronald F(ranklin)
Keeler, Patricia 183
Keeler, Patricia A.
    See Keeler, Patricia
Keeler, Ronald F(ranklin) 1913-1983 47
Keely, Jack 1951- 119
Keen, Martin L. 1913-1992 4
Keenan, Sheila 1953- 95
Keene, Ann T. 1940- 86
Keene, Ann Todd
    See Keene, Ann T.
Keene, Carolyn
    See Benson, Mildred
    and Goulart, Ron
    and Lerangis, Peter
    and McFarlane, Leslie
    and Stanley, George Edward
    and Stratemeyer, Edward L.
Keens-Douglas, Richardo 1953- 154
    Earlier sketch in SATA 95
Keep, Linda Lowery
    See Lowery, Linda
Keep, Richard 1949- 170
Keep, Richard Cleminson
    See Keep, Richard
Keeping, Charles (William James)
    1924-1988 69
    Obituary 56
    Earlier sketch in SATA 9
    See also CLR 34
Keeshan, Robert J. 1927-2004 32
    Obituary 151
Kehlenbeck, Angela 1959- 186
Kehoe, Tim 1970- 224
Kehret, Peg 1936- 212
    Autobiography Feature 149
    Earlier sketches in SATA 73, 108, 149
Keillor, Garrison 1942- 58
Keillor, Gary Edward
    See Keillor, Garrison
Keir, Christine
    See Pullein-Thompson, Christine
Keiser, Paige 220
Keister, Douglas 1948- 88
Keith, Doug 1952- 81
Keith, Eros 1942- 52
Keith, Hal 1934- 36
Keith, Harold (Verne) 1903-1998 74
    Earlier sketch in SATA 2
Keith, Robert
    See Applebaum, Stan
Keleinikov, Andrei 1924- 65
Kelemen, Julie 1959- 78
Kelen, Emery 1896-1978 13
    Obituary 26
Kelleam, Joseph E(veridge) 1913-1975 31
Kelleher, Anne 1959- 97
Kelleher, Annette 1950- 122
Kelleher, Daria Valerian 1955- 79
Kelleher, Victor (Michael Kitchener)
    1939- 129
    Brief entry 52
    Earlier sketch in SATA 75
    See also CLR 36
Keller, Beverly L(ou) 91
    Earlier sketch in SATA 13
Keller, Charles 1942- 82
    Earlier sketch in SATA 8
Keller, Debra 1958- 94
Keller, Dick 1923- 36
Keller, Emily 96
Keller, Gail Faithfull
    See Faithfull, Gail
Keller, Holly 1942- 216
    Brief entry 42
    Earlier sketches in SATA 76, 108, 157
    See also CLR 45
Keller, Irene (Barron) 1927-2002 36
    Obituary 139
Keller, Laurie 1961(?)- 196

Kelley, Ann 1941- 217
Kelley, Ellen A. 185
Kelley, Ellen Chavez
  See Kelley, Ellen A.
Kelley, Gary 1945- 217
  Earlier sketch in SATA *183*
Kelley, J.A.
  See Kelley, Jane
Kelley, Jane 1954- 231
Kelley, Leo P(atrick) 1928- 32
  Brief entry 31
Kelley, Marty 1971- 211
Kelley, Patrick (G.) 1963- 129
Kelley, Patte 1947- 93
Kelley, True 1946- 179
Kelley, True (Adelaide) 1946- 130
  Brief entry 39
  Earlier sketches in SATA *41, 92*
Kelley, True Adelaide
  See Kelley, True
Kellin, Sally Moffet 1932- 9
Kelling, Furn L. 1914-2000 37
Kellogg, Gene
  See Kellogg, Jean (Defrees)
Kellogg, Jean (Defrees) 1916-1978 10
Kellogg, Steven 1941- 177
  Earlier sketches in SATA *8, 57, 130*
  See also CLR *6*
Kellogg, Steven Castle
  See Kellogg, Steven
Kellow, Kathleen
  See Hibbert, Eleanor Alice Burford
Kelly, C. M. O.
  See Gibbs, (Cecilia) May
Kelly, Clint 1950- 140
Kelly, Eric P(hilbrook) 1884-1960
  See YABC *1*
Kelly, Fiona
  See Coleman, Michael
    and Hendry, Frances Mary
    and Jones, Allan Frewin
    and Oldfield, Jenny
    and Welford, Sue
Kelly, Irene 1957- 210
  Earlier sketch in SATA *147*
Kelly, Jacqueline 216
Kelly, Jeff
  See Kelly, Jeffrey
Kelly, Jeffrey 1946- 65
Kelly, Joanne (W.) 1934- 87
Kelly, Kate 1958- 91
Kelly, Kathleen M. 1964- 71
Kelly, Katy 1955- 215
  Earlier sketch in SATA *169*
Kelly, Lauren
  See Oates, Joyce Carol
Kelly, Laurene 1954- 123
Kelly, Martha Rose 1914-1983 37
Kelly, Marty
  See Kelly, Martha Rose
Kelly, Mij 166
Kelly, Ralph
  See Geis, Darlene Stern
Kelly, Regina Z(immerman) 1898-1986 5
Kelly, Rosalie (Ruth) 43
Kelly, Tara 230
Kelly, Tom 1961- 191
Kelly, Walt(er Crawford) 1913-1973 18
Kelsey, Alice Geer 1896-1982 1
Kelsey, Elin 1961- 159
Kelsey, Marybeth 216
Kemly, Kathleen 1958- 197
Kemnitz, Thomas Milton, Jr. 1984- 152
Kemnitz, Tom, Jr.
  See Kemnitz, Thomas Milton, Jr.
Kemp, Gene 1926- 75
  Earlier sketch in SATA *25*
  See also CLR *29*
Kempner, Mary Jean 1913-1969 10
Kempter, Christa 1945- 187
Kempton, Jean Welch 1914- 10

Kenah, Katharine 1949- 182
Kenda, Margaret 1942- 71
Kendall, Carol (Seeger) 1917- 74
  Earlier sketch in SATA *11*
  See also SAAS *7*
Kendall, Gideon 1966- 215
Kendall, Katherine
  See Applegate, Katherine
Kendall, Lace
  See Stoutenburg, Adrien (Pearl)
Kendall, Martha E. 87
Kendall, Russ 1957- 83
Kenealy, James P. 1927- 52
  Brief entry 29
Kenealy, Jim
  See Kenealy, James P.
Kennaway, Adrienne 1945- 171
  Earlier sketch in SATA *60*
Kennedy, Anne 1955- 198
Kennedy, Anne Vittur
  See Kennedy, Anne
Kennedy, Brendan 1970- 57
Kennedy, Dana Forrest 1917- 74
Kennedy, Dorothy M(intzlaff) 1931- 53
Kennedy, Doug 1963- 189
  Earlier sketch in SATA *122*
Kennedy, Frances 1937- 192
Kennedy, James 214
Kennedy, John F. 1917-1963 11
Kennedy, John Fitzgerald
  See Kennedy, John F.
Kennedy, Joseph Charles
  See Kennedy, X. J.
Kennedy, Kim 189
Kennedy, Marlane 1962- 210
Kennedy, Pamela (J.) 1946- 87
Kennedy, Paul E(dward) 1929- 113
  Earlier sketch in SATA *33*
Kennedy, Richard (Pitt) 1910-1989
  Obituary 60
Kennedy, (Jerome) Richard 1932- 22
Kennedy, Robert 1938- 63
Kennedy, T.A. 1953- 42
  Brief entry 35
Kennedy, Teresa
  See Kennedy, T.A.
Kennedy, Teresa A.
  See Kennedy, T.A.
Kennedy, William 1928- 57
Kennedy, William Joseph
  See Kennedy, William
Kennedy, X. J. 1929- 130
  Autobiography Feature 130
  Earlier sketches in SATA *14, 86*
  See also CLR *27*
  See also SAAS *22*
Kennell, Ruth Epperson 1893-1977 6
  Obituary 25
Kennemore, Tim 1957- 220
  Earlier sketch in SATA *133*
Kennen, Ally 190
Kennett, David 1959- 206
  Earlier sketch in SATA *121*
Kennison, Ruth 202
Kenny, Ellsworth Newcomb 1909-1971
  Obituary 26
Kenny, Herbert Andrew 1912-2002 13
Kenny, Jude
  See Daly, Jude
Kenny, Kathryn
  See Bowden, Joan Chase
    and Krull, Kathleen
    and Sanderlin, Owenita (Harrah)
    and Stack, Nicolete Meredith
Kenny, Kevin
  See Krull, Kathleen
Kensinger, George
  See Fichter, George S.
Kensington, Kathryn Wesley
  See Rusch, Kristine Kathryn

Kent, Alexander
  See Reeman, Douglas Edward
Kent, David
  See Lambert, David
Kent, Deborah Ann 1948- 155
  Brief entry 41
  Earlier sketches in SATA *47, 104*
Kent, Jack
  See Kent, John Wellington
Kent, John Wellington 1920-1985 24
  Obituary 45
Kent, Lisa 1942- 90
Kent, Mallory
  See Lowndes, Robert A(ugustine) W(ard)
Kent, Margaret 1894- 2
Kent, Rockwell 1882-1971 6
Kent, Rose 188
Kent, Sherman 1903-1986 20
  Obituary 47
Kenward, Jean 1920- 42
Kenworthy, Leonard S. 1912-1991 6
Kenyon, Karen (Smith) 1938- 145
Kenyon, Kate
  See Adorjan, Carol (Madden)
    and Ransom, Candice
Kenyon, Ley 1913-1990 6
Keown, Elizabeth 78
Kepes, Juliet A(ppleby) 1919-1999 13
Kephart, Beth 1960- 196
Kerby, Mona 1951- 202
  Earlier sketch in SATA *75*
Kerigan, Florence 1896-1984 12
Kerley, Barbara 1960- 191
  Earlier sketch in SATA *138*
Kerman, Gertrude
  See Furman, Gertrude Lerner Kerman
Kerns, Thelma 1929- 116
Kerr, Anne Louise
  See Mackey, Weezie Kerr
Kerr, Bob 1951- 120
Kerr, Jessica 1901-1991 13
Kerr, (Anne-)Judith 1923-1970 24
Kerr, M. E.
  See Meaker, Marijane
Kerr, P.B.
  See Kerr, Philip
Kerr, Philip 1956- 168
Kerr, Phyllis Forbes 1942- 72
Kerr, Tom 1950- 77
Kerrin, Jessica Scott 174
Kerry, Frances
  See Kerigan, Florence
Kerry, Lois
  See Duncan, Lois
Kershen, (L.) Michael 1982- 82
Kerven, Rosalind 1954- 83
Ker Wilson, Barbara 1929- 121
  Earlier sketches in SATA *20, 70*
  See also SAAS *18*
Kerz, Anna 1947- 220
Keselman, Gabriela 1953- 128
Kesey, Ken 1935-2001 66
  Obituary 131
Kesey, Ken Elton
  See Kesey, Ken
Kesler, Jay 1935- 65
Kessel, Joyce Karen 1937- 41
Kessler, Cristina 190
Kessler, Ethel 1922- 44
  Brief entry 37
Kessler, Leonard P. 1921- 14
Kessler, Liz 1966- 206
Kest, Kristin 1967- 168
  Earlier sketch in SATA *118*
Kesteven, G. R.
  See Crosher, G. R.
Ketcham, Hank
  See Ketcham, Henry King
Ketcham, Henry King 1920-2001 28
  Brief entry 27
  Obituary 128

Ketcham, Sallie 1963- 124
Ketchum, Liza 1946- 132
  Earlier sketch in SATA 78
Ketner, Mary Grace 1946- 75
Kettelkamp, Larry (Dale) 1933- 2
  See also SAAS 3
Ketteman, Helen 1945- 223
  Earlier sketches in SATA 73, 115, 167
Kettle, Peter
  See Glover, Denis (James Matthews)
Kevles, Bettyann Holtzmann 1938- 23
Key, Alexander (Hill) 1904-1979 8
  Obituary 23
Key, Samuel M.
  See de Lint, Charles
Key, Watt 1970- 189
Keyes, Daniel 1927- 37
Keyes, Diane 207
Keyes, Fenton 1915-1999 34
Keyes, Greg 1963- 116
Keyes, J. Gregory
  See Keyes, Greg
Keyser, Marcia 1933- 42
Keyser, Sarah
  See McGuire, Leslie (Sarah)
Khalid, Mohamed Nor
  See Lat
Khalsa, Dayal Kaur 1943-1989 62
  See also CLR 30
Khan, Hena 214
Khan, Rukhsana 1962- 231
  Earlier sketches in SATA 118, 165
Khanshendel, Chiron
  See Rose, Wendy
Kheirabadi, Masoud 1951- 158
Khemir, Sabiha 87
Kherdian, David 1931- 74
  Autobiography Feature 125
  Earlier sketch in SATA 16
  See also CLR 24
Khing, T.T. 1933- 192
Kibbe, Pat (Hosley) 60
Kidd, Diana 1933-2000 150
Kidd, Richard 1952-2008 152
  Obituary 194
Kidd, Ronald 1948- 173
  Earlier sketches in SATA 42, 92
Kiddell, John 1922- 3
Kiddell-Monroe, Joan 1908-1972 55
Kidwell, Carl 1910- 43
Kiefer, Irene 1926- 21
Kiefer, Kathleen Balmes 1957- 142
Kiepper, Shirley Morgan 1933- 10
Kierstead, Vera M.
  See Kierstead-Farber, Vera M.
Kierstead-Farber, Vera M. 1913- 121
Kierstead-Farber, Vera May
  See Kierstead-Farber, Vera M.
Kiesel, Stanley 1925- 35
Kiesler, Kate (A.) 1971- 152
  Earlier sketch in SATA 90
Kihn, Greg 1952- 110
Kikukawa, Cecily H(arder) 1919- 44
  Brief entry 35
Kilaka, John 1966- 223
Kilcher, Jewel 1974- 109
Kile, Joan 1940- 78
Kilgore, Kathleen 1946- 42
Kilian, Crawford 1941- 35
Killdeer, John
  See Mayhar, Ardath
Killien, Christi 1956- 73
Killilea, Marie (Lyons) 1913-1991 2
Killingback, Julia 1944- 63
Killough, (Karen) Lee 1942- 64
Kilpatrick, Don 206
Kilreon, Beth
  See Walker, Barbara (Jeanne) K(erlin)
Kilworth, Garry 1941- 216
  Earlier sketch in SATA 94

Kilworth, Garry D.
  See Kilworth, Garry
Kilworth, Garry Douglas
  See Kilworth, Garry
Kim, David 1977- 201
Kim, Dong-hwa 1950- 225
Kim, Helen 1899-1970 98
Kim, Joung Un 1970- 205
Kimball, Gayle 1943- 90
Kimball, Violet T(ew) 1932- 126
Kimball, Yeffe 1914-1978 37
Kimber, Murray 1964- 171
Kimble, Warren 176
Kimbrough, Emily 1899-1989 2
  Obituary 59
Kimeldorf, Martin 1948- 121
Kimeldorf, Martin R.
  See Kimeldorf, Martin
Kimenye, Barbara 1940(?)- 121
Kimmel, Elizabeth Cody 209
  Earlier sketch in SATA 170
Kimmel, Eric A. 1946- 208
  Earlier sketches in SATA 13, 80, 125, 176
Kimmel, Margaret Mary 1938- 43
  Brief entry 33
Kimmelman, Burt 1947- 180
Kimmelman, Leslie 1958- 211
  Earlier sketches in SATA 85, 156
Kincaid, Jamaica 1949-
  See CLR 63
Kincher, Jonni 1949- 79
Kindl, Patrice 1951- 128
  Earlier sketch in SATA 82
  See also CLR 132
Kindred, Wendy (Good) 1937- 7
Kinerk, Robert 199
Kines, Pat Decker 1937- 12
King, Adam
  See Hoare, Robert J(ohn)
King, Alison
  See Martini, Teri
King, (Maria) Anna 1964- 72
King, A.S. 1970- 217
King, Billie Jean 1943- 12
King, Christine
  See Farris, Christine King
King, Christopher (L.) 1945- 84
King, (David) Clive 1924- 144
  Earlier sketch in SATA 28
King, Colin 1943- 76
King, Cynthia 1925- 7
King, Daniel (John) 1963- 130
King, Daren 1972- 197
King, Elizabeth 1953- 83
King, Frank O. 1883-1969
  Obituary 22
King, Frank R. 1904-1999 127
King, Jane
  See Currie, Stephen
King, Jeanette (Margaret) 1959- 105
King, Larry L. 1929- 66
King, Laurie R. 1952- 88
King, Marian 1900(?)-1986 23
  Obituary 47
King, Martin Luther, Jr. 1929-1968 14
King, Mary Ellen 1958- 93
King, Paul
  See Drackett, Phil(ip Arthur)
King, Paula
  See Downing, Paula E.
King, Stephen 1947- 161
  Earlier sketches in SATA 9, 55
  See also CLR 124
King, Stephen Edwin
  See King, Stephen
King, Stephen Michael 218
  Earlier sketch in SATA 157
King, Steve
  See King, Stephen
King, Thomas 1943- 96

King, Thomas Hunt
  See King, Thomas
King, Tony 1947- 39
King, Willie Christine
  See Farris, Christine King
Kingfisher, Rupert 209
Kingman, Dong (Moy Shu) 1911-2000 44
Kingman, Lee
  See Natti, Lee
Kingsbury, Evan
  See Walker, Robert W.
Kingsland, Leslie William 1912- 13
Kingsley, Charles 1819-1875
  See YABC 2
  See also CLR 167
Kingsley, Emily Perl 1940- 33
Kingsley, Kaza 193
King-Smith, Dick 1922-2011 192
  Brief entry 38
  Earlier sketches in SATA 47, 80, 135
  See also CLR 40
Kingston, Maxine Hong 1940- 53
Kingston, Maxine Ting Ting Hong
  See Kingston, Maxine Hong
Kinkade, Sheila 1962- 229
Kinney, C. Cle(land) 1915- 6
Kinney, Harrison 1921- 13
Kinney, Jean Stout 1912- 12
Kinney, Jeff 1971- 187
Kinsey, Elizabeth
  See Clymer, Eleanor
Kinsey, Helen 1948- 82
Kinsey-Warnock, Natalie 1956- 167
  Earlier sketches in SATA 71, 116
Kinzel, Dorothy 1950- 57
Kinzel, Dottie
  See Kinzel, Dorothy
Kipling, Joseph Rudyard
  See Kipling, Rudyard
Kipling, Rudyard 1865-1936 100
  See also YABC 2
  See also CLR 65
Kippax, Frank
  See Needle, Jan
Kirby, David 1944- 78
Kirby, David K.
  See Kirby, David
Kirby, David Kirk
  See Kirby, David
Kirby, Margaret
  See Bingley, Margaret (Jane Kirby)
Kirby, Pamela F. 1952- 220
Kirby, Susan E. 1949- 62
Kirk, Connie Ann 1957- 167
Kirk, Daniel 1952- 196
  Earlier sketches in SATA 107, 153
Kirk, David 1955- 161
  Earlier sketch in SATA 117
Kirk, Heather 1949- 166
Kirk, Ruth (Kratz) 1925- 5
Kirkham, Dinah
  See Card, Orson Scott
Kirkland, Will
  See Hale, Arlene
Kirkpatrick, Katherine (Anne) 1964- 113
Kirkup, James 1918-2009 12
Kirkus, Virginia
  See Glick, Virginia Kirkus
Kirkwood, Kathryn
  See Fluke, Joanne
Kirsch, Vincent X. 211
Kirshenbaum, Binnie 79
Kirshner, David S. 1958- 123
Kirtland, G. B.
  See Hine, Sesyle Joslin
  and Hine, Al(fred Blakelee)
Kirwan, Wednesday 198
Kish, Eleanor M(ary) 1924- 73
Kish, Ely
  See Kish, Eleanor M(ary)
Kishida, Eriko 1929- 12

Kisinger, Grace Gelvin (Maze) 1913-1965 .. *10*
Kissel, Richard *209*
Kissin, Eva H. 1923- *10*
Kissinger, Rosemary K.
 See Updyke, Rosemary K.
Kistler, John M. 1967- *160*
Kitamura, Satoshi 1956- *201*
 Earlier sketches in SATA *62, 98, 143*
 See also CLR *60*
Kitanidis, Phoebe 1977- *230*
Kitchen, Bert
 See Kitchen, Herbert Thomas
Kitchen, Herbert Thomas 1940- *70*
Kite, L. Patricia
 See Kite, Pat
Kite, Pat 1940- *78*
Kitt, Tamara
 See de Regniers, Beatrice Schenk (Freedman)
Kittinger, Jo S(usenbach) 1955- *148*
 Earlier sketch in SATA *96*
Kituomba
 See Odaga, Asenath (Bole)
Kitzinger, Sheila 1929- *57*
Kiwak, Barbara 1966- *103*
Kjelgaard, James Arthur 1910-1959 .... *17*
 See also CLR *81*
Kjelgaard, Jim
 See Kjelgaard, James Arthur
Kjelle, Marylou Morano 1954- *146*
Klages, Ellen 1954- *196*
Klagsbrun, Francine (Lifton) *36*
Klaits, Barrie 1944- *52*
Klam, Cheryl *191*
Klaperman, Gilbert 1921- *33*
Klaperman, Libby Mindlin 1921-1982 .... *33*
 Obituary *31*
Klass, David 1960- *207*
 Earlier sketches in SATA *88, 142*
Klass, Morton 1927-2001 .... *11*
Klass, Sheila Solomon 1927- *219*
 Autobiography Feature *126*
 Earlier sketches in SATA *45, 99*
 See also SAAS *26*
Klause, Annette Curtis 1953- *175*
 Earlier sketch in SATA *79*
 See also CLR *104*
Klaveness, Jan O'Donnell 1939- *86*
Kleberger, Ilse 1921- *5*
Kleeberg, Irene (Flitner) Cumming 1932- *65*
Klein, Aaron E. 1930-1998 .... *45*
 Brief entry *28*
Klein, Bill 1945- *89*
Klein, David 1919-2001 .... *59*
Klein, Frederick C. 1938- *154*
Klein, Gerda Weissmann 1924- *44*
Klein, H(erbert) Arthur *8*
Klein, James 1932- *115*
Klein, Leonore (Glotzer) 1916- *6*
Klein, Lisa 1958- *211*
Klein, Lisa M.
 See Klein, Lisa
Klein, Mina C(ooper) 1906-1979 .... *8*
Klein, Norma 1938-1989 .... *57*
 Earlier sketch in SATA *7*
 See also CLR *162*
 See also SAAS *1*
Klein, Rachel S. 1953- *105*
Klein, Robin 1936- *164*
 Brief entry *45*
 Earlier sketches in SATA *55, 80*
 See also CLR *21*
Klemin, Diana *65*
Klemm, Barry 1945- *104*
Klemm, Edward G., Jr. 1910-2001 .... *30*
Klemm, Roberta K(ohnhorst) 1884-1975 ..... *30*
Kleven, Elisa 1958- *217*
 Earlier sketches in SATA *76, 173*
 See also CLR *85*
Klevin, Jill Ross 1935- *39*
 Brief entry *38*

Kliban, B(ernard) 1935-1990 .... *35*
 Obituary *66*
Klier, Kimberly Wagner *208*
Klimo, Kate *214*
Klimowicz, Barbara 1927- *10*
Kline, Christina Baker 1964- *101*
Kline, James
 See Klein, James
Kline, Jim
 See Kline, Jim
Kline, Lisa Williams 1954- *143*
Kline, Suzy 1943- *193*
 Autobiography Feature *193*
 Brief entry *48*
 Earlier sketches in SATA *67, 99, 152*
Klinger, Shula *230*
Kliros, Thea 1935- *106*
Klise, Kate *221*
 Earlier sketch in SATA *181*
Klise, M. Sarah 1961- *180*
 Earlier sketch in SATA *128*
Klots, Alexander Barrett 1903-1989
 Obituary *62*
Klug, Ron(ald) 1939- *31*
Knaak, Richard A. 1961- *166*
 Earlier sketch in SATA *86*
Knaak, Richard Allen
 See Knaak, Richard A.
Knapman, Timothy *200*
Knapp, Edward
 See Kunhardt, Edith
Knapp, Ron 1952- *34*
Knebel, Fletcher 1911-1993 .... *36*
 Obituary *75*
Kneeland, Linda Clarke 1947- *94*
Kneen, Maggie 1957- *221*
Knickerbocker, Diedrich
 See Irving, Washington
Knifesmith
 See Cutler, Ivor
Knigge, Robert (R.) 1921(?)-1987 .... *50*
Knight, Anne (Katherine) 1946- *34*
Knight, Brenda *112*
Knight, Christopher G. 1943- *96*
Knight, Damon (Francis) 1922-2002 .... *9*
 Obituary *139*
Knight, David C(arpenter) 1925-1984 .... *14*
 See also CLR *38*
Knight, Eric 1897-1943 .... *18*
Knight, Eric Mowbray
 See Knight, Eric
Knight, Francis Edgar 1905- *14*
Knight, Frank
 See Knight, Francis Edgar
Knight, Hilary 1926- *132*
 Earlier sketches in SATA *15, 69*
Knight, Joan
 See Knight, Joan (MacPhail)
Knight, Joan (MacPhail) *159*
 Earlier sketch in SATA *82*
Knight, Kathryn Lasky
 See Lasky, Kathryn
Knight, Mallory T.
 See Hurwood, Bernhardt J.
Knight, Ruth Adams 1898-1974
 Obituary *20*
Knight, Theodore O. 1946- *77*
Knobloch, Dorothea 1951- *88*
Knoepfle, John (Ignatius) 1923- *66*
Knorr, Laura 1971- *200*
Knott, Bill
 See Knott, William C(ecil, Jr.)
Knott, William C(ecil, Jr.) 1927- *3*
Knotts, Howard (Clayton, Jr.) 1922- *25*
Knowles, Anne 1933- *37*
Knowles, Jo 1970- *197*
Knowles, Johanna Beth
 See Knowles, Jo

Knowles, John 1926-2001 .... *89*
 Obituary *134*
 Earlier sketch in SATA *8*
 See also CLR *98*
Knox, Calvin M.
 See Silverberg, Robert
Knox, (Mary) Eleanor Jessie 1909-2000 ...... *59*
 Earlier sketch in SATA *30*
Knox, Elizabeth 1959- *176*
Knox, Elizabeth Fiona
 See Knox, Elizabeth
Knox, James
 See Brittain, William
Knox, Jolyne 1937- *76*
Knudsen, James 1950- *42*
Knudsen, Michelle 1974- *220*
 Earlier sketch in SATA *171*
Knudson, Mike 1965- *209*
Knudson, R. R.
 See Knudson, Rozanne
Knudson, Richard L(ewis) 1930- *34*
Knudson, Rozanne 1932-2008 .... *79*
 Earlier sketch in SATA *7*
 See also SAAS *18*
Knutson, Barbara 1959-2005 .... *166*
Knutson, Kimberley *115*
Knye, Cassandra
 See Disch, Thomas M.
Kobayashi, Masako Matsuno 1935- *6*
Kober, Shahar 1979- *213*
Koch, Dorothy Clarke 1924- *6*
Koch, Kenneth 1925-2002 .... *65*
Koch, Kenneth Jay
 See Koch, Kenneth
Koch, Phyllis (Mae) McCallum 1911- *10*
Kochalka, James 1967- *196*
Kocsis, J. C.
 See Paul, James
Koda-Callan, Elizabeth 1944- *140*
 Earlier sketch in SATA *67*
Kodera, Craig 1956- *222*
Kodman, Stanislawa *201*
Koehler, Phoebe 1955- *85*
Koehler-Pentacoff, Elizabeth 1957- *160*
 Earlier sketch in SATA *96*
Koehn, Ilse
 See Van Zwienen, Ilse Charlotte Koehn
Koeller, Carol *192*
Koenig, Viviane 1950- *80*
Koering, Ursula 1921-1976 .... *64*
Koerner, W(illiam) H(enry) D(avid)
 1878-1938 .... *21*
Koertge, Ron 1940- *209*
 Earlier sketches in SATA *53, 92, 131*
Koestler-Grack, Rachel A. 1973- *156*
Koff, Richard Myram 1926- *62*
Koffinke, Carol 1949- *82*
Kogan, Deborah
 See Kogan Ray, Deborah
Kogan Ray, Deborah 1940- *203*
 Earlier sketches in SATA *8, 50, 161*
Kogawa, Joy 1935- *99*
Kogawa, Joy Nozomi
 See Kogawa, Joy
Kogler, Jennie
 See Kogler, Jennifer Anne
Kogler, Jennifer Anne 1982(?)- *174*
Kohara, Kazuno *207*
Kohl, Herbert 1937- *47*
Kohl, Herbert R.
 See Kohl, Herbert
Kohl, MaryAnn F(aubion) 1947- *144*
 Earlier sketch in SATA *74*
Kohler, Dean Ellis 1947- *226*
Kohler, Julilly H(ouse) 1908-1976
 Obituary *20*
Kohn, Bernice
 See Hunt, Bernice
Kohn, Rita (T.) 1933- *89*
Kohner, Frederick 1905-1986 .... *10*
 Obituary *48*

Koide, Tan 1938-1986 .... *50*
Koike, Kay 1940- *72*
Koja, Kathe 1960- *199*
   Earlier sketch in SATA *155*
Koja, Stephan *198*
Kolar, Bob 1960(?)- *206*
Kolb, Larry J. 1953- *175*
Kolba, St. Tamara *22*
Kolibalova, Marketa
   See Kolibalova, Marketa
Kolibalova, Marketa 1953- *126*
Koller, Jackie French 1948- *157*
   Earlier sketches in SATA *72, 109*
   See also CLR *68*
Kolodny, Nancy J. 1946- *76*
Kolosov, Jacqueline 1967- *199*
Komaiko, Leah 1954- *164*
   Earlier sketch in SATA *97*
Komisar, Lucy 1942- *9*
Komoda, Beverly 1939- *25*
Komoda, Kiyo 1937- *9*
Kompaneyets, Marc 1974- *169*
Komroff, Manuel 1890-1974 .... *2*
   Obituary *20*
Konigsberg, Bill 1970- *207*
Konigsburg, E.L. 1930- *194*
   Earlier sketches in SATA *4, 48, 94, 126*
   See also CLR *81*
Konigsburg, Elaine Lobl
   See Konigsburg, E.L.
Koning, Hans 1921-2007 .... *5*
   Obituary *182*
Koningsberger, Hans
   See Koning, Hans
Konkle, Janet Everest 1917- *12*
Kono, Erin Eitter 1973- *177*
Konrad, Marla Stewart *218*
Konzak, Burt 1946- *151*
Koob, Theodora (J. Foth) 1918- *23*
Kooiker, Leonie
   See Kooyker-Romijn, Johanna Maria
Koons, James
   See Pernu, Dennis
Koontz, Dean 1945- *165*
   Earlier sketch in SATA *92*
   See Koontz, Dean R.
Koontz, Dean R. *225*
   See Koontz, Dean
Koontz, Dean Ray
   See Koontz, Dean
Koontz, Robin Michal 1954- *136*
   Earlier sketch in SATA *70*
Kooyker, Leonie
   See Kooyker-Romijn, Johanna Maria
Kooyker-Romijn, Johanna Maria 1927- *48*
Kooyker-Romyn, Johanna Maria
   See Kooyker-Romijn, Johanna Maria
Kopelke, Lisa 1963- *154*
Kopper, Lisa 1950- *105*
   Brief entry *51*
Kopper, Lisa Esther
   See Kopper, Lisa
Koppes, Steven N. 1957- *169*
Koppes, Steven Nelson
   See Koppes, Steven N.
Korach, Mimi 1922- *9*
Koralek, Jenny 1934- *215*
   Earlier sketches in SATA *71, 140*
Korczak, Janusz
   See Goldszmit, Henryk
Koren, Edward (Benjamin) 1935- *148*
   Earlier sketch in SATA *5*
Koren, Edward 1935- *206*
Korinets, Iurii Iosifovich
   See Korinetz, Yuri (Iosifovich)
Korinetz, Yuri (Iosifovich) 1923- *9*
   See also CLR *4*
Korman, Bernice 1937- *78*

Korman, Gordon 1963- *226*
   Brief entry *41*
   Earlier sketches in SATA *49, 81, 119, 167*
   See also CLR *25*
Korman, Gordon Richard
   See Korman, Gordon
Korman, Justine 1958- *70*
Kornblatt, Marc 1954- *147*
   Earlier sketch in SATA *84*
Kornprobst, Jacques 1937- *177*
Korte, Gene J. 1950- *74*
Korthues, Barbara 1971- *203*
Korty, Carol 1937- *15*
Koscielniak, Bruce 1947- *153*
   Earlier sketches in SATA *67, 99*
Koshin, Alexander (A.) 1952- *86*
Kositsky, Lynne 1947- *158*
Koskenmaki, Rosalie
   See Maggio, Rosalie
Koss, Amy Goldman 1954- *158*
   Earlier sketch in SATA *115*
Kossin, Sandy (Sanford) 1926- *10*
Kossman, Nina 1959- *84*
Kostecki-Shaw, Jenny Sue *203*
Kostick, Conor 1964- *186*
Kotzwinkle, William 1938- *146*
   Earlier sketches in SATA *24, 70*
   See also CLR *6*
Kouhi, Elizabeth 1917- *54*
   Brief entry *49*
Kouts, Anne 1945- *8*
Koutsky, Jan Dale 1955- *146*
Kovacs, Deborah 1954- *132*
   Earlier sketch in SATA *79*
Kovalski, Maryann 1951- *175*
   Earlier sketches in SATA *58, 97*
   See also CLR *34*
   See also SAAS *21*
Kowalski, Kathiann M. 1955- *151*
   Earlier sketch in SATA *96*
Koz, Paula G.
   See Goodman Koz, Paula
Kozjan, Drazen *209*
Kraft, Betsy Harvey 1937- *157*
Kraft, Erik P. *193*
Krahn, Fernando 1935- *49*
   Brief entry *31*
   See also CLR *3*
Krakauer, Hoong Yee Lee 1955- *86*
Krakauer, Jon 1954- *108*
Krall, Dan 1970- *218*
Kramer, George
   See Heuman, William
Kramer, Nora 1896(?)-1984 .... *26*
   Obituary *39*
Kramer, Remi (Thomas) 1935- *90*
Krantz, Hazel (Newman) *12*
Kranzler, George G(ershon) 1916- *28*
Kranzler, Gershon
   See Kranzler, George G(ershon)
Krasilovsky, Phyllis 1926- *38*
   Earlier sketch in SATA *1*
   See also CLR *83*
   See also SAAS *5*
Krasne, Betty
   See Levine, Betty K(rasne)
Krasner, Steven 1953- *154*
Krasnesky, Thad 1969(?)- *224*
Krasno, Rena 1923- *104*
Kratman, Tom *175*
Kraus, Joanna Halpert 1937- *87*
Kraus, (Herman) Robert 1925-2001 .... *93*
   Obituary *130*
   Earlier sketches in SATA *4, 65*
   See also SAAS *11*
Krauss, Ruth 1911-1993 .... *30*
   Obituary *75*
   Earlier sketch in SATA *1*
   See also CLR *42*
Krauss, Ruth Ida
   See Krauss, Ruth

Krautter, Elisa (Bialk) 1912(?)-1990 .... *1*
   Obituary *65*
Krautwurst, Terry 1946- *79*
Kray, Robert Clement 1930- *82*
Krech, Bob 1956- *185*
Krech, Robert
   See Krech, Bob
Kredel, Fritz 1900-1973 .... *17*
Kreikemeier, Gregory Scott 1965- *85*
Kreloff, Elliot *189*
Krementz, Jill 1940- *134*
   Earlier sketches in SATA *17, 71*
   See also CLR *5*
   See also SAAS *8*
Kremer, Marcie
   See Sorenson, Margo
Krenina, Katya 1968- *221*
   Earlier sketch in SATA *101*
Krensky, Stephen 1953- *188*
   Brief entry *41*
   Earlier sketches in SATA *47, 93, 136*
Krensky, Stephen Alan
   See Krensky, Stephen
Kresh, Paul 1919-1997 .... *61*
   Obituary *94*
Kress, Nancy 1948- *147*
   Autobiography Feature *147*
   Earlier sketch in SATA *85*
Kricher, John C. 1944- *113*
Krieger, Melanie 1944- *96*
Krinitz, Esther Nisenthal 1927-2001 .... *194*
Kripke, Dorothy Karp *30*
Krisher, Trudy 1946- *160*
   Earlier sketch in SATA *86*
Krisher, Trudy B.
   See Krisher, Trudy
Krishnaswami, Uma 1956- *182*
   Earlier sketch in SATA *144*
Kristiansen, Teddy 1964- *210*
Kristiansen, Teddy H.
   See Kristiansen, Teddy
Kristof, Jane 1932- *8*
Kroeber, Theodora (Kracaw) 1897-1979 .... *1*
Kroeger, Mary Kay 1950- *92*
Krohn, Katherine E(lizabeth) 1961- *125*
   Earlier sketch in SATA *84*
Kroll, Francis Lynde 1904-1973 .... *10*
Kroll, Steven 1941-2011 .... *212*
   Autobiography Feature *135*
   Earlier sketches in SATA *19, 66, 125, 135*
   See also SAAS *7*
Kroll, Virginia L. 1948- *225*
   Earlier sketches in SATA *76, 114, 168*
Kroll, Virginia Louisa
   See Kroll, Virginia L.
Kromhout, Rindert 1958- *189*
Krommes, Beth 1956- *208*
   Earlier sketches in SATA *128, 181*
Kronenwetter, Michael 1943- *62*
Kroniuk, Lisa
   See Berton, Pierre (Francis de Marigny)
Kropp, Paul 1948- *38*
   Brief entry *34*
   See also CLR *96*
Kropp, Paul Stephan
   See Kropp, Paul
Krosoczka, Jarrett J. 1977- *200*
   Earlier sketch in SATA *155*
Krovatin, Christopher 1985- *171*
Krudop, Walter
   See Krudop, Walter Lyon
Krudop, Walter Lyon 1966- *210*
Kruess, James
   See Kruss, James
Kruglik, Gerald *187*
Krull, Kathleen 1952- *229*
   Autobiography Feature *106*
   Brief entry *39*
   Earlier sketches in SATA *52, 80, 149, 184*
   See also CLR *44*

Krumgold, Joseph (Quincy) 1908-1980 48
  Obituary 23
  Earlier sketch in SATA *1*
Krupinski, Loretta 1940- *161*
  Earlier sketches in SATA *67, 102*
Krupnick, Karen 1947- *89*
Krupp, E. C. 1944- *123*
  Earlier sketch in SATA *53*
Krupp, Edwin Charles
  See Krupp, E. C.
Krupp, Robin Rector 1946- *53*
Krush, Beth 1918- *18*
Krush, Joe 1918-
  See Krush, Joseph P.
Krush, Joseph P. 1918- *18*
Kruss, James 1926-1997 .... *8*
  See also CLR *9*
Kruusval, Catarina 1951- *201*
Krykorka, Vladyana 1945- *96*
Krystoforski, Andrej 1943- *196*
Kubick, Dana *212*
Kubie, Eleanor Gottheil
  See Kubie, Nora Gottheil Benjamin
Kubie, Nora Benjamin
  See Kubie, Nora Gottheil Benjamin
Kubie, Nora Gottheil Benjamin 1899-1988 . *39*
  Obituary *59*
Kubinyi, Laszlo 1937- *94*
  Earlier sketch in SATA *17*
Kudlinski, Kathleen V. 1950- *213*
  Earlier sketch in SATA *150*
Kuehnert, Stephanie 1979- *205*
Kuenstler, Morton 1927- *10*
Kuh, Charlotte 1892(?)-1985
  Obituary *43*
Kuharski, Janice 1947- *128*
Kuhn, Dwight *199*
Kuijer, Guus 1942- *179*
Kujoth, Jean Spealman 1935-1975
  Obituary *30*
Kuklin, Susan 1941- *163*
  Earlier sketches in SATA *63, 95*
  See also CLR *51*
Kulak, Jeff 1984(?)- *223*
Kulikov, Boris 1966- *205*
  Earlier sketch in SATA *170*
Kulka, Joe *188*
Kulling, Monica 1952- *89*
Kullman, Harry 1919-1982 .... *35*
Kulyk Keefer, Janice 1952- *132*
Kumin, Maxine 1925- *12*
Kumin, Maxine Winokur
  See Kumin, Maxine
Kunhardt, Dorothy (Meserve) 1901-1979 .... *53*
  Obituary *22*
Kunhardt, Edith 1937- *67*
Kunjufu, Jawanza 1953- *73*
Kunstler, Morton
  See Kuenstler, Morton
Kuntz, J(ohn) L. 1947- *91*
Kuntz, Jerry 1956- *133*
Kupferberg, Herbert 1918-2001 .... *19*
Kuratomi, Chizuko 1939- *12*
  See also CLR *32*
Kurczok, Belinda 1978- *121*
Kurelek, William 1927-1977 .... *8*
  Obituary *27*
  See also CLR *2*
Kurian, George 1928- *65*
Kurilla, Renee 1981- *231*
Kurjian, Judi(th M.) 1944- *127*
Kurland, Gerald 1942- *13*
Kurland, Michael 1938- *118*
  Earlier sketch in SATA *48*
Kurland, Michael Joseph
  See Kurland, Michael
Kuroi, Ken 1947- *120*
Kurokawa, Mitsuhiro 1954- *88*
Kurten, Bjorn (Olof) 1924-1988 .... *64*

Kurtz, Jane 1952- *139*
  Earlier sketch in SATA *91*
  See also CLR *123*
Kurtz, Katherine 1944- *182*
  Earlier sketches in SATA *76, 126*
Kurtz, Katherine Irene
  See Kurtz, Katherine
Kurusa 1942- *226*
Kurz, Rudolf 1952- *95*
Kushner, Donn (J.) 1927- *52*
  See also CLR *55*
Kushner, Ellen 1955- *202*
  Earlier sketch in SATA *98*
Kushner, Ellen Ruth
  See Kushner, Ellen
Kushner, Jill Menkes 1951- *62*
Kushner, Lawrence 1943- *169*
  Earlier sketch in SATA *83*
Kushner, Tony 1956- *160*
Kuskin, Karla 1932-2009 .... *164*
  Obituary *206*
  Earlier sketches in SATA *2, 68, 111*
  See also CLR *4*
  See also SAAS *3*
Kuskin, Karla Seidman
  See Kuskin, Karla
Kusugak, Michael 1948- *143*
Kusugak, Michael Arvaarluk
  See Kusugak, Michael
Kutner, Merrily 1948- *196*
Kuttner, Paul 1922- *18*
Kuyper, Sjoerd 1952- *177*
Kuzma, Kay 1941- *39*
Kvale, Velma R(uth) 1898-1979 .... *8*
Kvasnosky, Laura McGee 1951- *182*
  Earlier sketches in SATA *93, 142*
Kwasney, Michelle D. 1960- *162*
Kyle, Benjamin
  See Gottfried, Theodore Mark
Kyle, Elisabeth
  See Dunlop, Agnes M. R.
Kyte, Kathy S. 1946- *50*
  Brief entry *44*

L

L., Barry
  See Longyear, Barry B(rookes)
L., Tommy
  See Lorkowski, Thomas V(incent)
Labatt, Mary 1944- *215*
Labouisse, Eve Curie
  See Curie, Eve
Labouisse, Eve Denise
  See Curie, Eve
Lace, William W. 1942- *126*
Lacey, Joshua
  See Doder, Josh
Lachenmeyer, Nathaniel 1969- *221*
Lachner, Dorothea
  See Knobloch, Dorothea
Lachtman, Ofelia Dumas 1919- *179*
Lackey, Mercedes
  See Lackey, Mercedes R.
Lackey, Mercedes R. 1950- *127*
  Earlier sketch in SATA *81*
Lackey, Mercedes Ritchie
  See Lackey, Mercedes R.
Lacoe, Addie *78*
Lacombe, Benjamin 1982- *198*
Lacome, Julie 1961- *174*
  Earlier sketch in SATA *80*
LaCour, Nina 1982- *222*
Lacy, Leslie Alexander 1937- *6*
Lacy, Rick *231*
Ladd, Cheryl (Jean) 1951- *113*
Ladd, London 1972(?)- *206*
Ladd, Louise 1943- *97*

Ladd, Veronica
  See Miner, Jane Claypool
Laden, Nina 1962- *148*
  Earlier sketch in SATA *85*
Lader, Lawrence 1919-2006 .... *6*
  Obituary *178*
LaDoux, Rita C. 1951- *74*
Ladwig, Tim 1952- *223*
Ladwig, Timothy
  See Ladwig, Tim
Lady, A
  See Taylor, Ann
Lady Mears
  See Tempest, Margaret Mary
Lady of Quality, A
  See Bagnold, Enid
La Farge, Oliver 1901-1963 .... *19*
La Farge, Oliver Hazard Perry
  See La Farge, Oliver
La Farge, Phyllis *14*
LaFave, Kim *196*
LaFaye, A. 1970- *220*
  Earlier sketches in SATA *105, 156*
LaFaye, Alexandria R.T.
  See LaFaye, A.
LaFevers, R.L. *191*
LaFevers, Robin L.
  See LaFevers, R.L.
Lafferty, Mur 1973- *227*
Laffin, John (Alfred Charles) 1922- *31*
LaFleur, Suzanne 1983- *221*
LaFontaine, Bruce 1948- *176*
  Earlier sketch in SATA *114*
La Fontaine, Jean de 1621-1695 .... *18*
Lafrance, Marie 1955- *197*
Lager, Claude
  See Lapp, Christiane (Germain)
Lager, Marilyn 1939- *52*
Lagercrantz, Rose (Elsa) 1947- *39*
Lagerloef, Selma
  See Lagerlof, Selma
Lagerlof, Selma 1858-1940 .... *15*
  See also CLR *7*
Lagos, Joseph *231*
Laguna, Sofie 1968- *158*
LaHaye, Tim 1926- *149*
LaHaye, Timothy F.
  See LaHaye, Tim
Laidlaw, Rob *205*
Laiken, Deirdre S. 1948- *48*
  Brief entry *40*
Laiken, Deirdre Susan
  See Laiken, Deirdre S.
Laimgruber, Monika 1946- *11*
Lain, Anna
  See Lamb, Nancy
Laing, Alexander (Kinnan) 1903-1976 .... *117*
Laing, Martha 1951- *39*
Laird, Christa 1944- *108*
  Autobiography Feature *120*
  See also SAAS *26*
Laird, Elizabeth 1943- *228*
  Earlier sketches in SATA *77, 114, 159*
  See also CLR *65*
Laird, Elizabeth Mary Risk
  See Laird, Elizabeth
Laird, Jean E(louise) 1930- *38*
Laite, Gordon 1925- *31*
Lake, Harriet
  See Taylor, Paula (Wright)
Lake, Nick *227*
Lakeman, Victoria
  See Forester, Victoria
Lakin, Patricia 1944- *190*
Laklan, Carli 1907-1988 .... *5*
Laliberte, Louise-Andree 1958- *169*
Lalicki, Barbara *61*
Lalicki, Tom 1949- *186*
Lally, Soinbhe 1945- *119*
LaMarche, Jim *162*
Lamb, Albert *187*

Lamb, Beatrice Pitney 1904-1997 .... *21*
Lamb, Charles 1775-1834 .... *17*
Lamb, Elizabeth Searle 1917- *31*
Lamb, G(eoffrey) F(rederick) *10*
Lamb, Harold (Albert) 1892-1962 .... *53*
Lamb, Lynton (Harold) 1907-1977 .... *10*
Lamb, Mary Ann 1764-1847 .... *17*
Lamb, Nancy 1939- *80*
Lamb, Robert (Boyden) 1941- *13*
Lamba, Marie *195*
Lambert, David 1932- *84*
    Brief entry *49*
Lambert, David Compton
    See Lambert, David
Lambert, Janet 1895(?)-1973 .... *25*
Lambert, Martha L. *113*
Lambert, Saul 1928- *23*
Lambert, Stephen *174*
Lamburn, Richmal Crompton 1890-1969 ...... *5*
Lamensdorf, Len 1930- *120*
Lamensdorf, Leonard
    See Lamensdorf, Len
Laminack, Lester L. 1956- *163*
    Earlier sketch in SATA *120*
Lammle, Leslie 1965- *213*
Lamont, Priscilla *200*
Lamorisse, Albert (Emmanuel) 1922-1970 ... *23*
Lampert, Emily 1951- *52*
    Brief entry *49*
Lamplugh, Lois 1921- *17*
Lampman, Evelyn Sibley 1907-1980 .... *87*
    Obituary *23*
    Earlier sketch in SATA *4*
Lamprey, Louise 1869-1951
    See YABC *2*
Lampton, Chris
    See Lampton, Christopher F.
Lampton, Christopher
    See Lampton, Christopher F.
Lampton, Christopher F. *67*
    Brief entry *47*
Lamstein, Sarah 1943- *174*
    Earlier sketch in SATA *126*
Lamstein, Sarah Marwil
    See Lamstein, Sarah
Lanagan, Margo 1960- *201*
    Earlier sketch in SATA *163*
Lancaster, Bruce 1896-1963 .... *9*
Lancaster, Matthew 1973(?)-1983
    Obituary *45*
Lance, Kathryn 1943- *76*
Land, Barbara (Neblett) 1923- *16*
Land, Jane
    See Borland, Kathryn Kilby
    and Speicher, Helen Ross S(mith)
Land, Myrick (Ebben) 1922-1998 .... *15*
Land, Ross
    See Borland, Kathryn Kilby
    and Speicher, Helen Ross S(mith)
Landa, Norbert 1952- *218*
Landau, Elaine 1948- *141*
    Earlier sketches in SATA *10, 94*
Landau, Jacob 1917- *38*
Landeck, Beatrice 1904-1978 .... *15*
Landin, Les 1923- *2*
Landis, J. D. 1942- *60*
    Brief entry *52*
Landis, James D.
    See Landis, J. D.
Landis, James David
    See Landis, J. D.
Landis, Jill Marie 1948- *101*
Landman, Tanya *207*
Landmann, Bimba 1968- *176*
Landon, Dena 1978(?)- *168*
Landon, Lucinda 1950- *56*
    Brief entry *51*
Landon, Margaret (Dorothea Mortenson)
    1903-1993 .... *50*
Landowne, Youme 1970- *211*
Landry, Leo *202*

Landshoff, Ursula 1908-1989 .... *13*
Landstrom, Lena 1943- *206*
    Earlier sketch in SATA *146*
Landstrom, Olof 1943- *146*
Landy, Derek 1974- *210*
Lane, Alison Hoffman *215*
Lane, Carolyn 1926-1993 .... *10*
Lane, Connie
    See Laux, Constance
Lane, Dakota 1959- *166*
    Earlier sketch in SATA *105*
Lane, Jerry
    See Martin, Patricia Miles
Lane, John (Richard) 1932- *15*
Lane, Leena *199*
Lane, Margaret 1907-1994 .... *65*
    Brief entry *38*
    Obituary *79*
Lane, Rose Wilder 1887-1968 .... *29*
    Brief entry *28*
Lanes, Selma G. 1929- *3*
Lanes, Selma Gordon
    See Lanes, Selma G.
Lanfredi, Judy 1964- *83*
Lang, Andrew 1844-1912 .... *16*
    See also CLR *101*
Lang, Aubrey *169*
Lang, Glenna 1951- *221*
Lang, Lang 1982- *208*
Lang, Paul 1948- *83*
Lang, Susan S. 1950- *68*
Lang, T.T.
    See Taylor, Theodore
Langart, Darrell T.
    See Garrett, Randall
Langdo, Bryan 1973- *191*
    Earlier sketch in SATA *138*
Lange, John
    See Crichton, Michael
Lange, Karen E. *190*
Lange, Suzanne 1945- *5*
Langley, Andrew 1949- *166*
    Earlier sketch in SATA *104*
Langley, Charles P(itman) III 1949- *103*
Langley, Jonathan 1952- *122*
Langley, Noel 1911-1980
    Obituary *25*
Langley, Wanda *173*
Langner, Nola
    See Malone, Nola Langner
Langone, John (Michael) 1929- *46*
    Brief entry *38*
Langreuter, Jutta 1944- *122*
Langrish, Katherine *177*
Langsen, Richard C. 1953- *95*
Langstaff, John 1920-2005 .... *68*
    Obituary *172*
    Earlier sketch in SATA *6*
    See also CLR *3*
Langstaff, John Meredith
    See Langstaff, John
Langstaff, Launcelot
    See Irving, Washington
Langston, Laura 1958- *186*
Langton, Jane 1922- *200*
    Autobiography Feature *140*
    Earlier sketches in SATA *3, 68, 129, 140*
    See also CLR *33*
    See also SAAS *5*
Lanier, Sidney 1842-1881 .... *18*
Lanier, Sterling E. 1927-2007 .... *109*
Lanier, Sterling Edmund
    See Lanier, Sterling E.
Lanino, Deborah 1964- *123*
Lankford, Mary D. 1932- *112*
    Earlier sketch in SATA *77*
Lannin, Joanne 1951- *121*
Lannin, Joanne A.
    See Lannin, Joanne
Lansdale, Joe R. 1951- *116*

Lansdale, Joe Richard
    See Lansdale, Joe R.
Lansing, Alfred 1921-1975 .... *35*
Lansing, Karen E. 1954- *71*
Lansky, Vicki 1942- *177*
Lanthier, Jennifer 1964- *204*
Lantier-Sampon, Patricia 1952- *92*
Lantz, Fran
    See Lantz, Francess L(in)
Lantz, Francess L(in) 1952-2004 .... *153*
    Autobiography Feature *153*
    Obituary *159*
    Earlier sketches in SATA *63, 109*
Lantz, Paul 1908- *45*
Lantz, Walter 1900-1994 .... *37*
    Obituary *79*
Lanza, Barbara 1945- *101*
Lapp, Christiane (Germain) 1948- *74*
Lappin, Peter 1911-1999 .... *32*
Larbalestier, Justine *231*
    Earlier sketch in SATA *178*
Lardy, Philippe 1963- *168*
LaReau, Jenna *181*
LaReau, Kara *181*
Larios, Julie 1949- *178*
Larios, Julie Hofstrand
    See Larios, Julie
Larkin, Amy
    See Burns, Olive Ann
Larkin, Maia
    See Wojciechowska, Maia (Teresa)
Larkspur, Penelope
    See Wyatt, Valerie
Laroche, Giles 1956- *221*
    Earlier sketches in SATA *71, 126*
LaRochelle, David 1960- *171*
    Earlier sketch in SATA *115*
Larom, Henry V. 1903(?)-1975
    Obituary *30*
LaRose, Linda *125*
Larrabee, Lisa 1947- *84*
Larranaga, Ana Martin 1969- *229*
Larrecq, John M(aurice) 1926-1980 .... *44*
    Obituary *25*
Larrick (Crosby), Nancy 1910-2004 .... *4*
Larsen, Anita 1942- *78*
Larsen, Egon 1904- *14*
Larsen, Rebecca 1944- *54*
Larson, Eve
    See St. John, Wylly Folk
Larson, Gary 1950- *57*
Larson, Hope 1982- *205*
Larson, Ingrid D(ana) 1965- *92*
Larson, Jean Russell 1930- *121*
Larson, Kirby 1954- *181*
    Earlier sketch in SATA *96*
Larson, Norita D. 1944- *29*
Larson, Norita Dittberner
    See Larson, Norita D.
Larson, William H. 1938- *10*
Larsson, Carl (Olof) 1853-1919 .... *35*
LaSalle, Charles A.
    See Ellis, Edward S.
LaSalle, Charles E.
    See Ellis, Edward S.
Lasell, Elinor H. 1929- *19*
Lasell, Fen H.
    See Lasell, Elinor H.
Lasenby, Jack 1931- *172*
    Earlier sketches in SATA *65, 103*
Laser, Michael 1954- *117*
Lash, Joseph P. 1909-1987 .... *43*
Lasher, Faith B. 1921- *12*
Lasker, David 1950- *38*
Lasker, Joe
    See Lasker, Joseph Leon
Lasker, Joseph Leon 1919- *83*
    Earlier sketch in SATA *9*
    See also SAAS *17*
Laski, Marghanita 1915-1988 .... *55*
Laskin, Pamela L. 1954- *75*

Lasky, Kathryn 1944- *210*
    Earlier sketches in SATA *13, 69, 112, 157*
    See also CLR *140*
Lasky Knight, Kathryn
    See Lasky, Kathryn
Lass, Bonnie *131*
Lassalle, C. E.
    See Ellis, Edward S.
Lassiter, Mary
    See Hoffman, Mary
Lassiter, Rhiannon 1977- *157*
Lat 1951- *196*
Latham, Barbara 1896- *16*
Latham, Frank B(rown) 1910-2000 .... *6*
Latham, Irene 1971- *228*
Latham, Jean Lee 1902-1995 .... *68*
    Earlier sketch in SATA *2*
    See also CLR *50*
Latham, Mavis
    See Clark, Mavis Thorpe
Latham, Philip
    See Richardson, Robert S(hirley)
Lathrop, Dorothy P(ulis) 1891-1980 .... *14*
    Obituary *24*
Lathrop, Francis
    See Leiber, Fritz (Reuter, Jr.)
Latimer, Jim 1943- *80*
Latta, Rich
    See Latta, Richard
Latta, Richard 1946- *113*
Latta, Sara L. 1960- *174*
Lattany, Kristin
    See Lattany, Kristin Hunter
Lattany, Kristin (Eggleston) Hunter 1931- . *154*
    Autobiography Feature *154*
    Earlier sketch in SATA *132*
Lattany, Kristin Hunter 1931-2008 .... *132*
    Earlier sketch in SATA *12*
    See also CLR *3*
    See also SAAS *10*
Lattimore, Eleanor Frances 1904-1986 .... *7*
    Obituary *48*
Lattin, Ann
    See Cole, Lois Dwight
Lauber, Patricia (Grace) 1924- *138*
    Earlier sketches in SATA *1, 33, 75*
    See also CLR *16*
Laugesen, Malene *207*
Laugesen, Malene Reynolds
    See Laugesen, Malene
Laugesen, Mary E(akin) 1906-1995 .... *5*
Laughbaum, Steve 1945- *12*
Laughlin, Florence Young 1910-2001 .... *3*
Laughlin, Rosemary 1941- *123*
Launder, Sally *206*
Laure, Ettagale
    See Blauer, Ettagale
Laure, Jason 1940- *50*
    Brief entry *44*
Laurence, Ester Hauser 1935- *7*
Laurence, Jean Margaret Wemyss
    See Laurence, Margaret
Laurence, Margaret 1926-1987
    Obituary *50*
Laurie, Rona 1916- *55*
Laurie, Victoria *218*
Laurin, Anne
    See McLaurin, Anne
Lauritzen, Jonreed 1902-1979 .... *13*
Lauscher, Hermann
    See Hesse, Hermann
Lauture, Denize 1946- *86*
Laux, Connie
    See Laux, Constance
Laux, Constance 1952- *97*
Laux, Dorothy 1920- *49*
Lavallee, Barbara 1941- *166*
    Earlier sketch in SATA *74*
Lavender, David (Sievert) 1910-2003 .... *97*
    Obituary *145*
    Earlier sketch in SATA *64*

Lavender, William D. 1921- *143*
Laverne, Christine *175*
Lavert, Gwendolyn Battle 1951-
    See Battle-Lavert, Gwendolyn
Laverty, Donald
    See Blish, James
    and Knight, Damon (Francis)
Lavigne, Louis-Dominique 1949- *107*
Lavine, David 1928- *31*
Lavine, Sigmund Arnold 1908-1986 .... *82*
    Earlier sketch in SATA *3*
    See also CLR *35*
Lavis, Steve *225*
Lavond, Paul Dennis
    See Kornbluth, C(yril) M.
    and Lowndes, Robert A(ugustine) W(ard)
    and Pohl, Frederik
Law, Stephen *225*
Law, Stephen
    See Law, Stephen
Lawford, Paula Jane 1960- *57*
    Brief entry *53*
Lawhead, Stephen R. 1950- *109*
Lawhead, Steve
    See Lawhead, Stephen R.
Lawler, Janet *222*
Lawlor, Laurie 1953- *137*
    Earlier sketch in SATA *80*
Lawlor, William
    See Lawlor, William T.
Lawlor, William T. 1951- *183*
Lawrence, Ann (Margaret) 1942-1987 .... *41*
    Obituary *54*
Lawrence, Caroline 1954- *203*
Lawrence, Iain 1955- *183*
    Earlier sketch in SATA *135*
Lawrence, J. T.
    See Rowland-Entwistle, (Arthur) Theodore
    (Henry)
Lawrence, Jerome 1915-2004 .... *65*
Lawrence, John 1933- *30*
Lawrence, Josephine 1890(?)-1978
    Obituary *24*
Lawrence, Louise 1943- *119*
    Earlier sketches in SATA *38, 78*
Lawrence, Louise de Kiriline 1894-1992 ..... *13*
Lawrence, Lynn
    See Garland, Sherry
Lawrence, Margery H. 1889-1969 .... *120*
Lawrence, Michael 1943- *132*
Lawrence, Mildred Elwood 1907-1997 .... *3*
Lawrence, R(onald) D(ouglas) 1921- *55*
Lawrinson, Julia 1969- *141*
Lawson, Amy
    See Gordon, Amy
Lawson, Carol (Antell) 1946- *42*
Lawson, Don(ald Elmer) 1917-1990 .... *9*
Lawson, Joan 1906- *55*
Lawson, Julie 1947- *126*
    Earlier sketch in SATA *79*
    See also CLR *89*
Lawson, Marion Tubbs 1896-1994 .... *22*
Lawson, Robert 1892-1957 .... *100*
    See also YABC *2*
    See also CLR *73*
Lawton, Clive A. 1951- *145*
Laxdal, Vivienne 1962- *112*
Laybourn, Emma *193*
Layburn, Joe *228*
Laycock, George (Edwin) 1921- *5*
Layne, Laura
    See Knott, William C(ecil, Jr.)
Layne, Steven L. *171*
Layson, Annelex Hofstra 1938(?)- *211*
Layton, Neal 1971- *187*
    Earlier sketch in SATA *152*
Layton, Neal Andrew
    See Layton, Neal
Lazare, Gerald John 1927- *44*
Lazare, Jerry
    See Lazare, Gerald John

Lazarevich, Mila 1942- *17*
Lazarus, Keo Felker 1913-1993 .... *21*
    Obituary *129*
Lea, Alec 1907- *19*
Lea, Bob 1952- *203*
Lea, Joan
    See Neufeld, John (Arthur)
Leach, Maria 1892-1977 .... *39*
    Brief entry *28*
Leacock, Elspeth 1946- *131*
Leacroft, Helen (Mabel Beal) 1919- *6*
Leacroft, Richard (Vallance Becher) 1914- *6*
Leaf, Margaret P. 1909(?)-1988
    Obituary *55*
Leaf, (Wilbur) Munro 1905-1976 .... *20*
    See also CLR *25*
Leaf, VaDonna Jean 1929- *26*
Leah, Devorah
    See Devorah-Leah
Leakey, Richard E(rskine Frere) 1944- *42*
Leal, Ann Haywood *216*
Leander, Ed
    See Richelson, Geraldine
Lear, Edward 1812-1888 .... *100*
    Earlier sketch in SATA *18*
    See also CLR *75*
Lears, Laurie 1955- *127*
Leasor, James 1923-2007 .... *54*
Leasor, Thomas James
    See Leasor, James
Leavitt, Jerome E(dward) 1916- *23*
Leavitt, Martine 1953- *170*
LeBar, Mary E(velyn) 1910-1982 .... *35*
LeBlanc, Annette M. 1965- *68*
LeBlanc, L(ee) 1913- *54*
LeBox, Annette 1943- *145*
Lebrun, Claude 1929- *66*
Le Cain, Errol (John) 1941-1989 .... *68*
    Obituary *60*
    Earlier sketch in SATA *6*
Lechner, Jack *201*
Lechner, John 1966- *200*
Leck, James 1973- *229*
Lecourt, Nancy (Hoyt) 1951- *73*
Ledbetter, Suzann 1953- *119*
Leder, Jane Mersky 1945- *61*
    Brief entry *51*
Lederer, Muriel 1929- *48*
Lederer, William J. 1912-2009 .... *62*
Lederer, William Julius
    See Lederer, William J.
Lee, Amanda
    See Baggett, Nancy
    and Buckholtz, Eileen (Garber)
    and Glick, Ruth
Lee, Benjamin 1921- *27*
Lee, Betsy 1949- *37*
Lee, Carol
    See Fletcher, Helen Jill
Lee, Carol Ann 1969- *185*
Lee, Chinlun *182*
Lee, Cora *223*
    See Anderson, Catherine Corley
Lee, Dennis (Beynon) 1939- *102*
    Earlier sketch in SATA *14*
    See also CLR *3*
Lee, Dom 1959- *146*
    Autobiography Feature *121*
    Earlier sketch in SATA *83*
    See also SAAS *26*
Lee, Doris Emrick 1905-1983 .... *44*
    Obituary *35*
Lee, Edward
    See Lee, J. Edward
Lee, Elizabeth Rogers 1940- *90*
Lee, Harper 1926- *11*
Lee, Hector Viveros 1962- *115*
Lee, Howard N.
    See Goulart, Ron
Lee, Huy Voun 1969- *217*
    Earlier sketch in SATA *129*

Lee, Insu 213
Lee, J. Edward 1953- 130
Lee, Jared 1943- 215
Lee, Jared D.
    See Lee, Jared
Lee, Jeanne M. 1943- 138
Lee, John R(obert) 1923-1976 27
Lee, Jordan
    See Scholefield, Alan
Lee, Joseph Edward
    See Lee, J. Edward
Lee, Julian
    See Latham, Jean Lee
Lee, Linda
    See Eyerly, Jeannette
Lee, Liz
    See Lee, Elizabeth Rogers
Lee, Lucy
    See Talbot, Charlene Joy
Lee, Lyn 1953- 128
Lee, Manning de Villeneuve 1894-1980 37
    Obituary 22
Lee, Marian
    See Clish, (Lee) Marian
Lee, Marie G. 1964- 178
    Earlier sketches in SATA *81, 130*
Lee, Marie Myung-Ok
    See Lee, Marie G.
Lee, Mary Price 1934- 82
    Earlier sketch in SATA *8*
Lee, Mildred
    See Scudder, Mildred Lee
Lee, Nelle Harper
    See Lee, Harper
Lee, Richard S. 1927- 82
Lee, Robert C. 1931- 20
Lee, Robert Edwin 1918-1994 65
    Obituary 82
Lee, Robert J. 1921- 10
Lee, Roy
    See Hopkins, Clark
Lee, Sally 1943- 67
Lee, Suzy 193
Lee, Tammie
    See Townsend, Thomas L.
Lee, Tanith 1947- 185
    Earlier sketches in SATA *8, 88, 134*
Lee, Virginia 1976- 208
Leech, Ben
    See Bowkett, Stephen
Leeds, Contance 188
Leedy, Loreen 1959- 175
    Brief entry 50
    Earlier sketches in SATA *54, 84, 128*
Leedy, Loreen Janelle
    See Leedy, Loreen
Lee-Hostetler, Jeri 1940- 63
Leekley, Thomas B(riggs) 1910-2001 23
Leeming, Jo Ann
    See Leeming, Joseph
Leeming, Joseph 1897-1968 26
Leemis, Ralph B. 1954- 72
Leese, Jennifer L.B. 1970- 163
Leeson, Muriel 1920- 54
Leeson, R. A.
    See Leeson, Robert (Arthur)
Leeson, Robert (Arthur) 1928- 76
    Earlier sketch in SATA *42*
Lee Tae-Jun 1904-1956(?) 194
Lee-Tai, Amy 1964- 189
Leffland, Ella 1931- 65
Leffler, Silke 197
Lefler, Irene (Whitney) 1917- 12
LeFrak, Karen 182
Le Gallienne, Eva 1899-1991 9
    Obituary 68
Legg, Gerald 1947- 143
Legg, Sarah Martha Ross Bruggeman (?)-1982
    Obituary 40
LeGrand
    See Henderson, LeGrand

Le Guin, Ursula K. 1929- 194
    Earlier sketches in SATA *4, 52, 99, 149*
    See also CLR 91
Le Guin, Ursula Kroeber
    See Le Guin, Ursula K.
Legum, Colin 1919-2003 10
Lehman, Barbara 1963- 170
    Earlier sketch in SATA *115*
Lehman, Bob 91
Lehman, Elaine 91
Lehmann, Debra Lynn
    See Vanasse, Deb
Lehman-Wilzig, Tami 1950- 224
Lehn, Cornelia 1920- 46
Lehne, Judith Logan 1947- 93
Lehr, Delores 1920- 10
Lehr, Norma 1930- 71
Leiber, Fritz (Reuter, Jr.) 1910-1992 45
    Obituary 73
Leibold, Jay 1957- 57
    Brief entry 52
Leichman, Seymour 1933- 5
Leick, Bonnie 205
Leigh, Nila K. 1981- 81
Leigh, Tom 1947- 46
Leigh-Pemberton, John 1911-1997 35
Leighton, Clare (Veronica Hope)
    1899-1989 37
Leighton, Margaret (Carver) 1896-1987 1
    Obituary 52
Leijten, Aileen 216
Leiner, Al(an) 1938- 83
Leiner, Katherine 1949- 93
Leipold, L. Edmond 1902-1983 16
Leisk, David (Johnson) 1906-1975 30
    Obituary 26
    Earlier sketch in SATA *1*
    See also CLR 98
Leist, Christina 226
Leister, Mary 1917- 29
Leitch, Patricia 1933- 98
    Earlier sketch in SATA *11*
Leitner, Isabella 1924- 86
Lekich, John 202
Leland, Bob 1956- 92
Leland, Robert E.
    See Leland, Bob
Leloup, Genevieve 230
Lematre, Pascal 1967- 225
    Earlier sketch in SATA *176*
Lember, Barbara Hirsch 1941- 92
LeMieux, A.C. 1954- 125
    Earlier sketch in SATA *90*
LeMieux, Anne
    See LeMieux, A.C.
LeMieux, Anne Connelly
    See LeMieux, A.C.
Lemieux, Michele 1955- 139
Lemke, Horst 1922- 38
Lemna, Don 1936- 216
Lenain, Thierry 1959- 201
Lenanton, Carola Mary Anima Oman
    See Oman, Carola (Mary Anima)
Lenard, Alexander 1910-1972
    Obituary 21
Lendroth, Susan 207
L'Engle, Madeleine 1918-2007 128
    Obituary 186
    Earlier sketches in SATA *1, 27, 75*
    See also CLR 57
    See also SAAS 15
L'Engle, Madeleine Camp Franklin
    See L'Engle, Madeleine
Lengyel, Cornel Adam 1915- 27
Lengyel, Emil 1895-1985 3
    Obituary 42
Lennon, John 1940-1980 114
Lennon, John Ono
    See Lennon, John
Leno, Jay 1950- 154
LeNoir, Janice 1941- 89

Lens, Sidney 1912-1986 13
    Obituary 48
Lenski, Lois 1893-1974 100
    Earlier sketches in SATA *1, 26*
    See also CLR 26
Lent, Blair 1930-2009 133
    Obituary 200
    Earlier sketch in SATA *2*
Lent, Henry Bolles 1901-1973 17
Lent, John 1948- 108
Leodhas, Sorche Nic
    See Alger, Leclaire (Gowans)
Leokum, Arkady 1916(?)- 45
Leon, Carol Boyd 212
Leon, Sharon 1959- 79
Leonard, Alison 1944- 70
Leonard, Anna
    See Gilman, Laura Anne
Leonard, Constance (Brink) 1923- 42
    Brief entry 40
Leonard, Dutch
    See Leonard, Elmore
Leonard, Elmore 1925- 163
Leonard, Elmore John, Jr.
    See Leonard, Elmore
Leonard, Jonathan N(orton) 1903-1975 36
Leonard, Laura 1923- 75
Leonard, Tom 1955- 207
Leonetti, Mike 1958- 202
Leong, Gor Yun
    See Ellison, Virginia H(owell)
Leonhard, Herb 217
Leonhardt, Alice 1950- 152
Lerangis, Peter 1955- 171
    Earlier sketch in SATA *72*
Lerman, Josh 215
Lerner, Aaron 1920-2007 35
    Obituary 179
Lerner, Aaron Bunsen
    See Lerner, Aaron
Lerner, Carol 1927- 86
    Earlier sketch in SATA *33*
    See also CLR 34
    See also SAAS 12
Lerner, Gerda 1920- 65
Lerner, Harriet 1944- 101
Lerner, Marguerite Rush 1924-1987 11
    Obituary 51
Lerner, Sharon (Ruth) 1938-1982 11
    Obituary 29
Leroe, Ellen 1949- 99
    Brief entry 51
    Earlier sketch in SATA *61*
Leroe, Ellen W.
    See Leroe, Ellen
Leroe, Ellen Whitney
    See Leroe, Ellen
Leroux, Gaston 1868-1927 65
Leroux-Hugon, Helene 1955- 132
LeRoy, Gen 52
    Brief entry 36
Lerrigo, Marion Olive 1898-1968
    Obituary 29
LeShan, Eda J(oan) 1922-2002 21
    See also CLR 6
Leshem, Yossi 1947- 222
LeSieg, Theo.
    See Dr. Seuss
Lesinski, Jeanne M. 1960- 120
Leslie, Robert Franklin 1911-1990 7
Leslie, Roger 1961- 168
Leslie, Roger James
    See Leslie, Roger
Leslie, Sarah
    See McGuire, Leslie (Sarah)
LeSourd, Catherine
    See Marshall, (Sarah) Catherine (Wood)
Lessac, Frane
    See Lessac, Frane
Lessac, Frane 1954- 209
    Earlier sketches in SATA *61, 148*

Lessem, Dino Don
See Lessem, Don
Lessem, Don 1951- 182
Earlier sketches in SATA *97, 155*
Lesser, Margaret 1899(?)-1979
Obituary 22
Lesser, Rika 1953- 53
Lester, Alison 1952- 218
Earlier sketches in SATA *50, 90, 129*
Lester, Helen 1936- 189
Earlier sketches in SATA *46, 92, 145*
Lester, Julius 1939- 157
Earlier sketches in SATA *12, 74, 112*
See also CLR *143*
Lester, Julius Bernard
See Lester, Julius
Lester, Mike 1955- 206
Earlier sketch in SATA *131*
Le Sueur, Meridel 1900-1996 6
Leszczynski, Diana 211
Lethcoe, Jason 191
Le Tord, Bijou 1945- 95
Earlier sketch in SATA *49*
Letts, Billie 1938- 121
Letts, Elizabeth
See Alalou, Elizabeth
Leuck, Laura 1962- 192
Earlier sketches in SATA *85, 146*
Leung, Hilary 1975- 225
Leutscher, Alfred (George) 1913- 23
Levai, Blaise 1919- 39
Levchuk, Lisa 215
Leveen, Tom 230
Levenkron, Steven 1941- 86
Leverich, Kathleen 1948- 103
LeVert, John 1946- 55
Levert, Mireille 1956- 211
LeVert, William John
See LeVert, John
Levete, Sarah 1961- 153
Levin, Betty 1927- 201
Earlier sketches in SATA *19, 84, 137*
See also SAAS *11*
Levin, Ira 1929-2007 66
Obituary 187
Levin, Ira Marvin
See Levin, Ira
Levin, Marcia Obrasky 1918- 13
Levin, Meyer 1905-1981 21
Obituary 27
Levin, Miriam (Ramsfelder) 1962- 97
Levine, Abby 1943- 54
Brief entry 52
Levine, Anna 212
Levine, Betty K(rasne) 1933- 66
Levine, David 1926-2009 43
Brief entry 35
Levine, Edna S(imon) 35
Levine, Ellen 1939- 190
Levine, Evan 1962- 77
Earlier sketch in SATA *74*
Levine, Gail Carson 1947- 195
Earlier sketches in SATA *98, 161*
See also CLR *85*
Levine, I(srael) E. 1923-2003 12
Obituary 146
Levine, Joan Goldman 11
Levine, Joseph 1910- 33
Levine, Kristin 1974- 213
Levine, Marge 1934- 81
Levine, Rhoda 14
Levine, Sarah 1970- 57
Levine, Shar 1953- 131
Levine-Freidus, Gail
See Provost, Gail Levine
Levinson, Nancy Smiler 1938- 211
Earlier sketches in SATA *33, 80, 140*
Levinson, Riki 99
Brief entry 49
Earlier sketch in SATA *52*
Levithan, David 1972- 166

Levitin, Sonia 1934- 192
Autobiography Feature 131
Earlier sketches in SATA *4, 68, 119, 131*
See also CLR *53*
See also SAAS *2*
Levitt, Sidney (Mark) 1947- 68
Levon, O. U.
See Kesey, Ken
Levoy, Myron 1930- 49
Brief entry 37
Levy, Barrie 112
Levy, Constance 1931- 140
Earlier sketch in SATA *73*
See also SAAS *22*
Levy, Elizabeth 1942- 169
Earlier sketches in SATA *31, 69, 107*
See also SAAS *18*
Levy, Janice 172
Levy, Marilyn 1937- 67
Levy, Nathan 1945- 63
Levy, Robert 1945- 82
Lewees, John
See Stockton, Francis Richard
Lewin, Betsy 1937- 222
Autobiography Feature 115
Earlier sketches in SATA *32, 90, 169*
Lewin, Hugh 1939- 72
Brief entry 40
See also CLR *9*
Lewin, Ted 1935- 226
Autobiography Feature 115
Earlier sketches in SATA *21, 76, 119, 165,
195*
Lewis, Alice C. 1936- 46
Lewis, Alice Hudson 1895(?)-1971
Obituary 29
Lewis, Amanda 1955- 80
Lewis, Anthony 1927- 27
Lewis, Anthony 1966- 227
Earlier sketch in SATA *120*
Lewis, Barbara A. 1943- 73
Lewis, Beverly 1949- 80
Lewis, Brenda Ralph 1932- 72
Lewis, Brian 1963- 128
Lewis, C. S. 1898-1963 100
Earlier sketch in SATA *13*
See also CLR *109*
Lewis, Claudia (Louise) 1907-2001 5
Lewis, Clive Staples
See Lewis, C. S.
Lewis, Cynthia Copeland 1960- 111
Lewis, E. M. 123
Earlier sketch in SATA *20*
Lewis, Earl Bradley
See Lewis, E.B.
Lewis, E.B. 1956- 211
Earlier sketches in SATA *93, 124, 168*
Lewis, Elizabeth Foreman 1892-1958 121
See also YABC *2*
Lewis, Francine
See Wells, Helen
Lewis, Harry Sinclair
See Lewis, Sinclair
Lewis, Hilda (Winifred) 1896-1974
Obituary 20
Lewis, J. Patrick 1942- 205
Earlier sketches in SATA *69, 104, 162*
Lewis, Jack P(earl) 1919- 65
Lewis, Jean 1924- 61
Lewis, Jon Samuel
See Lewis, J.S.
Lewis, Joseph Anthony
See Lewis, Anthony
Lewis, J.S. 1972- 203
Lewis, Julinda
See Lewis-Ferguson, Julinda
Lewis, Kevin 173
Lewis, Kim 1951- 217
Earlier sketches in SATA *84, 136*
Lewis, Linda (Joy) 1946- 67

Lewis, Lucia Z.
See Anderson, Lucia (Lewis)
Lewis, Marjorie 1929- 40
Brief entry 35
Lewis, Mary 1907(?)-1988 64
Obituary 56
Lewis, Mervyn
See Frewer, Glyn (M.)
Lewis, Michael
See Untermeyer, Louis
Lewis, Naomi 1911-2009 144
Earlier sketch in SATA *76*
Lewis, Paeony 1960- 173
Lewis, Paul
See Gerson, Noel Bertram
Lewis, Richard 1935- 3
Lewis, Richard 1956- 209
Lewis, Rob 1962- 72
Lewis, Roger
See Zarchy, Harry
Lewis, Rose 209
Lewis, Rose A.
See Lewis, Rose
Lewis, Shannon
See Llywelyn, Morgan
Lewis, Shari 1934-1998 35
Brief entry 30
Obituary 104
Lewis, Sylvan R.
See Aronson, Virginia
Lewis, Thomas P(arker) 1936- 27
Lewis, Wendy A. 1966- 150
Lewis-Ferguson, Julinda 1955- 85
Lewison, Wendy Cheyette 177
Lewiton, Mina 1904-1970 2
Lew-Vriethoff, Joanne 186
Lexau, Joan M. 130
Earlier sketches in SATA *1, 36*
Ley, Willy 1906-1969 2
Leydon, Rita (Floden) 1949- 21
Leyland, Eric (Arthur) 1911- 37
L'Hommedieu, Dorothy Keasley 1885-1961
Obituary 29
Li, Xiao Jun 1952- 86
Liao, Jimmy 1958- 202
Liatsos, Sandra Olson 1942- 103
Libby, Alisa M. 189
Libby, Barbara M. 153
Libby, Bill
See Libby, William M.
Libby, William M. 1927-1984 5
Obituary 39
Liberty, Gene 1924- 3
Lichtenheld, Tom 208
Earlier sketch in SATA *152*
Lichtman, Wendy 1946- 193
Liddell, Kenneth 1912-1975 63
Liddiment, Carol 224
Lidz, Jane 120
Lieb, Josh 1972- 224
Lieberman, E(dwin) James 1934- 62
Liebers, Arthur 1913-1984 12
Lieblich, Irene 1923- 22
Liers, Emil E(rnest) 1890-1975 37
Lies, Brian 1963- 190
Earlier sketch in SATA *131*
Lieshout, Elle van
See van Lieshout, Elle
Liestman, Vicki 1961- 72
Lietz, Gerald S. 1918- 11
Liew, Sonny 1974- 219
Life, Kay (Guinn) 1930- 83
Lifton, Betty Jean 1926-2010 118
Earlier sketch in SATA *6*
Lifton, Robert Jay 1926- 66
Lightburn, Ron 1954- 91
Lightburn, Sandra 1955- 91
Lightner, A. M.
See Hopf, Alice (Martha) L(ightner)
Lightner, Alice
See Hopf, Alice (Martha) L(ightner)

Lignell, Lois 1911- *37*
Liles, Maurine Walpole 1935- *81*
Lillegard, Dee *184*
Lilley, Stephen R. 1950- *97*
Lilley, Stephen Ray
    See Lilley, Stephen R.
Lillington, Kenneth (James) 1916-1998 .... *39*
Lilly, Nate *182*
Lilly, Ray
    See Curtis, Richard
Lim, John 1932- *43*
Liman, Ellen (Fogelson) 1936- *22*
Limb, Sue 1946- *203*
    Earlier sketch in SATA *158*
Limburg, Peter R(ichard) 1929- *13*
Lin, Grace 1974- *198*
    Earlier sketches in SATA *111, 162*
Lincoln, C(harles) Eric 1924-2000 .... *5*
Lincoln, Christopher 1952- *208*
Lincoln, Hazel *187*
Lincoln, James
    See Bates, Katharine Lee
Lindbergh, Anne
    See Sapieyevski, Anne Lindbergh
Lindbergh, Anne Morrow 1906-2001 .... *33*
    Obituary *125*
Lindbergh, Anne Spencer Morrow
    See Lindbergh, Anne Morrow
Lindbergh, Charles A(ugustus, Jr.)
    1902-1974 .... *33*
Lindbergh, Reeve 1945- *163*
    Earlier sketch in SATA *116*
Lindblom, Steven (Winther) 1946- *94*
    Brief entry *39*
    Earlier sketch in SATA *42*
Linde, Gunnel 1924- *5*
Lindenbaum, Pija 1955- *183*
    Earlier sketches in SATA *77, 144*
Lindgren, Astrid (Anna Emilia Ericsson)
    1907-2002 .... *38*
    Obituary *128*
    Earlier sketch in SATA *2*
    See also CLR *119*
Lindgren, Barbro 1937- *207*
    Brief entry *46*
    Earlier sketches in SATA *63, 120*
    See also CLR *86*
Lindman, Maj (Jan) 1886-1972 .... *43*
Lindo, Elvira 1962- *219*
Lindop, Edmund 1925- *5*
Lindquist, Jennie Dorothea 1899-1977 .... *13*
Lindquist, Rowena Cory 1958- *98*
Lindquist, Willis 1908-1988 .... *20*
Lindsay, Nicholas Vachel
    See Lindsay, Vachel
Lindsay, Norman Alfred William
    1879-1969 .... *67*
    See also CLR *8*
Lindsay, Vachel 1879-1931 .... *40*
Lindsey, Kathleen D(orothy) 1949- *153*
Line, David
    See Davidson, Lionel
Line, Les 1935-2010 .... *27*
Lines, Kathleen Mary 1902-1988
    Obituary *61*
Linfield, Esther *40*
Lingard, Joan (Amelia) 1932- *130*
    Autobiography Feature *130*
    Earlier sketches in SATA *8, 74, 114*
    See also CLR *89*
    See also SAAS *5*
Link, Martin 1934- *28*
Linn, Margot
    See Ziefert, Harriet
Linnea, Sharon 1956- *82*
Lintern, Tom *228*
Lion, Melissa 1976- *176*
Lionni, Leo(nard) 1910-1999 .... *72*
    Obituary *118*
    Earlier sketch in SATA *8*
    See also CLR *71*

Lipinsky de Orlov, Lino S. 1908- *22*
Lipkind, William 1904-1974 .... *15*
Lipman, David 1931-2008 .... *21*
Lipman, Matthew 1923-2010 .... *14*
Lipp, Frederick *204*
Lippincott, Bertram 1898(?)-1985
    Obituary *42*
Lippincott, Gary A. 1953- *220*
    Earlier sketches in SATA *73, 119*
Lippincott, Joseph W(harton) 1887-1976 ..... *17*
Lippincott, Sarah Lee 1920- *22*
Lippman, Peter J. 1936- *31*
Lipsyte, Robert 1938- *198*
    Earlier sketches in SATA *5, 68, 113, 161*
    See also CLR *76*
Lipsyte, Robert Michael
    See Lipsyte, Robert
Lisandrelli, Elaine Slivinski 1951- *94*
Lisker, Sonia O. 1933- *44*
Lisle, Holly 1960- *208*
    Earlier sketch in SATA *98*
Lisle, Janet Taylor 1947- *150*
    Brief entry *47*
    Earlier sketches in SATA *59, 96*
    See also SAAS *14*
Lisle, Rebecca *162*
Lisle, Seward D.
    See Ellis, Edward S.
Lisowski, Gabriel 1946- *47*
    Brief entry *31*
Liss, Howard 1922-1995 .... *4*
    Obituary *84*
Lissiat, Amy
    See Thompson, Colin
Lisson, Deborah 1941- *110*
    Earlier sketch in SATA *71*
List, Ilka Katherine 1935- *6*
Liston, Robert A. 1927- *5*
Litchfield, Ada B(assett) 1916-1999 .... *5*
Litchfield, Jo 1973- *116*
Lithgow, John 1945- *145*
Lithgow, John Arthur
    See Lithgow, John
Litowinsky, Olga 1936- *26*
Litowinsky, Olga Jean
    See Litowinsky, Olga
Littke, Lael J. 1929- *140*
    Earlier sketches in SATA *51, 83*
Little, A. Edward
    See Klein, Aaron E.
Little, Douglas 1942- *96*
Little, (Flora) Jean 1932- *149*
    Earlier sketches in SATA *2, 68, 106*
    See also CLR *4*
    See also SAAS *17*
Little, Lessie Jones 1906-1986 .... *60*
    Obituary *50*
Little, Mary E. 1912-1999 .... *28*
Littlechild, George 1958- *85*
Littledale, Freya (Lota) 1929-1992 .... *74*
    Earlier sketch in SATA *2*
Littlefield, Bill 1948- *83*
Littlefield, Holly 1963- *97*
Littlesugar, Amy 1953- *176*
    Earlier sketch in SATA *122*
Littleton, Mark R. 1950- *142*
    Earlier sketch in SATA *89*
Littlewood, Karin *211*
Littman, Sarah Darer *221*
    Earlier sketch in SATA *175*
Litty, Julie 1971- *181*
Litzinger, Rosanne 1948- *196*
Liu, Cynthea *221*
Lively, Penelope 1933- *164*
    Earlier sketches in SATA *7, 60, 101*
    See also CLR *159*
Lively, Penelope Margaret
    See Lively, Penelope
Liverakos, L. A.
    See Gilman, Laura Anne
Liversidge, (Henry) Douglas 1913- *8*

Livesey, Claire (Warner) 1927- *127*
Livingston, Carole 1941- *42*
Livingston, (M.) Irene 1932- *150*
Livingston, Myra Cohn 1926-1996 .... *68*
    Obituary *92*
    Earlier sketch in SATA *5*
    See also CLR *7*
    See also SAAS *1*
Livingston, Richard R(oland) 1922- *8*
Livo, Norma J. 1929- *76*
Liwska, Renata *199*
Ljungkvist, Laura *180*
Llerena Aguirre, Carlos 1952- *19*
Llerena Aguirre, Carlos Antonio
    See Llerena Aguirre, Carlos
Llewellyn, Claire 1954- *196*
    Earlier sketches in SATA *77, 143*
Llewellyn, Grace 1964- *110*
Llewellyn, Richard
    See Llewellyn Lloyd, Richard Dafydd Vivian
Llewellyn, Sam 1948- *185*
    Earlier sketch in SATA *95*
Llewellyn Lloyd, Richard Dafydd Vivian
    1906-1983 .... *11*
    Obituary *37*
Llewelyn, T. Harcourt
    See Hamilton, Charles (Harold St. John)
Lloyd, Alan
    See Lloyd, A.R.
Lloyd, Alan Richard
    See Lloyd, A.R.
Lloyd, Alison 1966- *231*
Lloyd, A.R. 1927- *168*
    Earlier sketch in SATA *97*
Lloyd, David
    See Lloyd, David T.
Lloyd, David T. 1954- *167*
Lloyd, E. James
    See James, Elizabeth
Lloyd, Errol 1943- *22*
Lloyd, Hugh
    See Fitzhugh, Percy Keese
Lloyd, James
    See James, Elizabeth
Lloyd, Megan 1958- *189*
    Earlier sketches in SATA *77, 117*
Lloyd, Norman 1909-1980
    Obituary *23*
Lloyd, (Mary) Norris 1908-1993 .... *10*
    Obituary *75*
Lloyd, Saci 1967- *220*
Lloyd, Sam *183*
Lloyd-Jones, Sally 1960- *179*
Lloyd Webber, Andrew 1948- *56*
Llywelyn, Morgan 1937- *109*
Lo, Ginnie *165*
Lo, Malinda 1974- *222*
Lo, Virginia M.
    See Lo, Ginnie
Lobato, Jose Bento Monteiro 1882-1948 ... *114*
Lobel, Anita (Kempler) 1934- *162*
    Earlier sketches in SATA *6, 55, 96*
Lobel, Arnold (Stark) 1933-1987 .... *55*
    Obituary *54*
    Earlier sketch in SATA *6*
    See also CLR *5*
Lobel, Gillian *181*
Lobsenz, Amelia *12*
Lobsenz, Norman M(itchell) 1919- *6*
Lochak, Michele 1936- *39*
Lochlons, Colin
    See Jackson, C(aary) Paul
Locke, Clinton W. *1*
Locke, Elsie (Violet) 1912-2001 .... *87*
Locke, Gary 1963- *197*
Locke, Lucie 1904-1989 .... *10*
Locke, Robert 1944- *63*
    See also CLR *39*
Locker, Thomas 1937- *109*
    Earlier sketch in SATA *59*
    See also CLR *14*

Lockhart, E.
  See Jenkins, Emily
Lockridge, Hildegarde (Dolson)
  1908-1981 .... *121*
  Earlier sketch in SATA *5*
Lockwood, Mary
  See Spelman, Mary
Lodge, Bernard 1933- *215*
  Earlier sketches in SATA *33, 107*
Lodge, Jo 1966- *173*
  Earlier sketch in SATA *112*
Loeb, Jeffrey 1946- *57*
Loeb, Robert H., Jr. 1917- *21*
Loefgren, Ulf 1931- *3*
Loehfelm, Bill 1969- *153*
Loehr, Mallory *184*
Loehr, Patrick 1968(?)- *194*
Loeper, John J(oseph) 1929- *118*
  Earlier sketch in SATA *10*
Loescher, Ann Dull 1942- *20*
Loescher, Gil 1945- *20*
Loescher, Gilburt Damian
  See Loescher, Gil
Loewer, Jean Jenkins
  See Jenkins, Jean
Loewer, (Henry) Peter 1934- *98*
LoFaro, Jerry 1959- *77*
Lofo
  See Heimann, Rolf
Lofthouse, Liz *199*
Lofting, Hugh (John) 1886-1947 .... *100*
  Earlier sketch in SATA *15*
  See also CLR *143*
Lofts, Norah (Robinson) 1904-1983 ..... *8*
  Obituary *36*
Logan, Alysia
  See Divine, L.
Logan, Jake
  See Knott, William C(ecil, Jr.)
  and Krepps, Robert W(ilson)
  and Pearl, Jacques Bain
  and Riefe, Alan
  and Rifkin, Shepard
  and Smith, Martin Cruz
Logan, Mark
  See Nicole, Christopher
Logan, Rochelle 1954- *169*
Logsted, Greg *221*
Logston, Anne 1962- *112*
Logue, Christopher 1926- *23*
Logue, Mary 1952- *161*
  Earlier sketch in SATA *112*
Logue, Mary Louise
  See Logue, Mary
Loh, Morag 1935- *73*
Lohans, Alison 1949- *101*
Loizeaux, William *185*
Loken, Newton Clayton 1919- *26*
Lomas, Steve
  See Brennan, Joseph Lomas
Lomask, Milton (Nachman) 1909-1991 ..... *20*
Lombard, Jenny *178*
Lombino, Salvatore
  See Hunter, Evan
LoMonaco, Palmyra 1932- *102*
London, Jack 1876-1916 .... *18*
  See also CLR *108*
London, Jane
  See Geis, Darlene Stern
London, John Griffith
  See London, Jack
London, Jonathan 1947- *221*
  Earlier sketches in SATA *74, 113, 157*
Lonergan, (Pauline) Joy (MacLean) 1909- ... *10*
Lonette, Reisie (Dominee) 1924- *43*
Long, Cathryn J. 1946- *89*
Long, Earlene (Roberta) 1938- *50*
Long, Emmett
  See Leonard, Elmore
Long, Ethan 1968(?)- *223*
  Earlier sketch in SATA *182*

Long, Helen Beecher *1*
Long, Judith Elaine 1953- *20*
Long, Judy
  See Long, Judith Elaine
Long, Kim 1949- *69*
Long, Laura Mooney 1892-1967
  Obituary *29*
Long, Laurel *203*
Long, Loren 1966(?)- *188*
  Earlier sketch in SATA *151*
Long, Melinda 1960- *152*
Long, Sylvia 1948- *179*
  Earlier sketch in SATA *120*
Longbeard, Frederick
  See Longyear, Barry B(rookes)
Longfellow, Henry Wadsworth 1807-1882 ... *19*
  See also CLR *99*
Longfellow, Layne 1937- *102*
Longfellow, Layne A.
  See Longfellow, Layne
Longman, Harold S. 1919- *5*
Longsworth, Polly 1933- *28*
Longtemps, Kenneth 1933- *17*
Longway, A. Hugh
  See Lang, Andrew
Longyear, Barry B(rookes) 1942- *117*
Look, Lenore *180*
Loomans, Diane 1955- *90*
Loomis, Christine *160*
  Earlier sketch in SATA *113*
Loomis, Jennifer A. 1942- *101*
Loomis, Robert D. *5*
Lopez, Angelo (Cayas) 1967- *83*
Lopez, Antonio Castro
  See Castro L., Antonio
Lopez, Barry 1945- *67*
Lopez, Barry Holstun
  See Lopez, Barry
Lopez, Jack 1950- *178*
Lopez, Loretta 1963- *190*
Lopez, Lorraine 1956- *181*
Lopez, Lorraine M.
  See Lopez, Lorraine
Lopez, Mario 1973- *226*
Lopez, Rafael 1961(?)- *198*
Lopshire, Robert M(artin) 1927- *6*
Loraine, Connie
  See Reece, Colleen L.
Lorbiecki, Marybeth 1959- *172*
  Earlier sketch in SATA *121*
Lord, Athena V. 1932- *39*
Lord, Beman 1924-1991 .... *5*
  Obituary *69*
Lord, Bette Bao 1938- *58*
  See also CLR *151*
Lord, Cynthia *182*
Lord, Doreen Mildred Douglas
  See Lord, Douglas
Lord, Douglas 1904-1992 .... *12*
Lord, Janet *204*
Lord, John Vernon 1939- *21*
Lord, Michele *201*
Lord, Nancy J.
  See Titus, Eve
Lord, Patricia C. 1927-1988
  Obituary *58*
Lord, Walter 1917-2002 .... *3*
Lorde, Diana
  See Reno, Dawn E(laine)
Lorenz, Albert 1941- *115*
Lorenzini, Carlo
  See Collodi, Carlo
Lorey, Dean 1967- *193*
Lorimer, Janet 1941- *60*
Loring, Emilie (Baker) 1864(?)-1951 ..... *51*
Lorkowski, Thomas V(incent) 1950- *92*
Lorkowski, Tom
  See Lorkowski, Thomas V(incent)
Lorraine, Walter (Henry) 1929- *16*
Lorrimer, Claire
  See Robins, Patricia

Loss, Joan 1933- *11*
Lothrop, Harriet Mulford Stone 1844-1924 . *20*
Lottridge, Celia Barker 1936- *157*
  Earlier sketch in SATA *112*
LoTurco, Laura 1963- *84*
Lotz, Wolfgang 1912-1981 .... *65*
Loughridge, Stuart 1978- *214*
Louie, Ai-Ling 1949- *40*
  Brief entry *34*
Louis, Catherine 1963- *186*
Louis, Pat
  See Francis, Dorothy
Louisburgh, Sheila Burnford
  See Burnford, Sheila (Philip Cochrane Every)
Louise, Anita
  See Riggio, Anita
Louise, Tina 1934- *191*
Lourie, Helen
  See Storr, Catherine (Cole)
Lourie, Peter 1952- *183*
  Earlier sketches in SATA *82, 142*
Lourie, Peter King
  See Lourie, Peter
Love, Ann 1947- *168*
  Earlier sketch in SATA *79*
Love, D. Anne 1949- *180*
  Earlier sketches in SATA *96, 145*
Love, Douglas 1967- *92*
Love, Judith Dufour
  See Love, Judy
Love, Judy *188*
Love, Katherine (Isabel) 1907- *3*
Love, Kathleen Ann
  See Love, Ann
Love, Maryann Cusimano *223*
Love, Sandra (Weller) 1940- *26*
Lovegrove, James 1965- *216*
Lovegrove, J.M.H.
  See Lovegrove, James
Lovejoy, Jack 1937- *116*
Lovelace, Delos Wheeler 1894-1967 .... *7*
Lovelace, Maud Hart 1892-1980 .... *2*
  Obituary *23*
Lovell, Ingraham
  See Bacon, Josephine Dodge (Daskam)
Lovelock, Brian 1956- *214*
Loverseed, Amanda (Jane) 1965- *75*
Lovett, Margaret (Rose) 1915- *22*
Low, Alice 1926- *156*
  Earlier sketches in SATA *11, 76*
Low, Elizabeth Hammond 1898-1991 .... *5*
Low, Joseph 1911-2007 .... *14*
Low, Penelope Margaret
  See Lively, Penelope
Low, William *177*
Lowe, Helen 1961- *206*
Lowe, Jay, Jr.
  See Loeper, John J(oseph)
Lowell, Pamela *187*
Lowell, Susan 1950- *206*
  Earlier sketches in SATA *81, 127*
Lowenstein, Dyno 1914-1996 .... *6*
Lowenstein, Sallie 1949- *116*
Lowery, Linda 1949- *151*
  Earlier sketch in SATA *74*
Lowery, Mike *227*
Lowitz, Anson C. 1901(?)-1978 .... *18*
Lowitz, Sadyebeth Heath 1901-1969 .... *17*
Lowndes, Robert A(ugustine) W(ard)
  1916-1998 .... *117*
Lowrey, Janette Sebring 1892-1986 .... *43*
Lowry, Lois 1937- *230*
  Autobiography Feature *127*
  Earlier sketches in SATA *23, 70, 111, 177*
  See also CLR *72*
  See also SAAS *3*
Lowry, Lois Hammersberg
  See Lowry, Lois
Lowry, Peter 1953- *7*
Lowther, George F. 1913-1975
  Obituary *30*

Loxton, Daniel 1975- 229
Loyie, Larry 1933- 150
Lozansky, Edward D. 1941- 62
Lozier, Herbert 1915- 26
Lubar, David 1954- 190
   Earlier sketch in SATA *133*
Lubell, Cecil 1912-2000 6
Lubell, Winifred (A. Milius) 1914- 6
Lubin, Leonard
   See Lubin, Leonard B.
Lubin, Leonard B. 1943-1994 45
   Brief entry 37
Lubka, S. Ruth 1948- 154
Lubner, Susan 185
Luby, Thia 1954- 124
Lucado, Max (Lee) 1955- 104
Lucas, Cedric 1962- 101
Lucas, David 1966- 208
Lucas, E(dward) V(errall) 1868-1938 20
Lucas, Eileen 1956- 113
   Earlier sketch in SATA *76*
Lucas, George 1944- 56
Lucas, Jerry 1940- 33
Lucas, Margeaux 186
Lucas, Victoria
   See Plath, Sylvia
Lucashenko, Melissa 1967- 104
Luccarelli, Vincent 1923- 90
Luce, Celia (Geneva Larsen) 1914- 38
Luce, Willard (Ray) 1914-1990 38
Lucht, Irmgard 1937- 82
Lucke, Deb 202
Luckett, Dave 1951- 220
   Earlier sketches in SATA *106, 167*
Luckhardt, Mildred Corell 1898-1990 5
Ludden, Allen (Ellsworth) 1918(?)-1981
   Obituary 27
Ludel, Jacqueline 1945- 64
Ludlow, Geoffrey
   See Meynell, Laurence Walter
Ludlum, Mabel Cleland
   See Widdemer, Mabel Cleland
Ludwig, Helen 33
Ludwig, Lyndell 1923- 63
Ludwig, Trudy 1959- 209
   Earlier sketch in SATA *166*
Luebs, Robin 1949- 212
Lueders, Edward (George) 1923- 14
Luenn, Nancy 1954- 79
   Earlier sketch in SATA *51*
Lufkin, Raymond H. 1897- 38
Lugard, Flora Louisa Shaw 1852-1929 21
Luger, Harriett Mandelay 1914- 23
Luhrmann, Winifred B(ruce) 1934- 11
Luis, Earlene W. 1929- 11
Lujan, Jorge 201
Lukas, Catherine
   See Albee, Sarah
Luke, Pauline 178
Luke, Pauline R.
   See Luke, Pauline
Lum, Bernice 230
Lum, Kate 229
Lum, Peter
   See Crowe, (Bettina) Peter Lum
Lumry, Amanda (R.) 159
Lund, Deb 157
Lund, Doris Herold 1919- 12
Lunde, Darrin 202
Lundebrek, Amy 1975- 213
Lung, Chang
   See Jordan, Robert
Lunge-Larsen, Lise 1955- 184
   Earlier sketch in SATA *138*
Lunn, Carolyn (Kowalczyk) 1960- 67
Lunn, Janet (Louise Swoboda) 1928- 110
   Earlier sketches in SATA *4, 68*
   See also CLR *18*
   See also SAAS *12*
Lunsford, Cin Forshay
   See Forshay-Lunsford, Cin

Lupica, Michael
   See Lupica, Mike
Lupica, Michael Thomas
   See Lupica, Mike
Lupica, Mike 1952- 177
Lupoff, Dick
   See Lupoff, Richard A(llen)
Lupoff, Richard A(llen) 1935- 60
Lurie, Alison 1926- 112
   Earlier sketch in SATA *46*
Lurie, Morris 1938- 72
Lussert, Anneliese 1929- 101
Lusted, Marcia Amidon 1962- 143
Lustig, Arnost 1926-2011 56
Lustig, Loretta 1944- 46
Lutes, Jason 1967- 210
Luthardt, Kevin 1973- 172
Luther, Frank 1905-1980
   Obituary 25
Luther, Rebekah (Lyn) S(tiles) 1960- 90
Luttmann, Gail
   See Damerow, Gail
Luttrell, Guy L. 1938- 22
Luttrell, Ida (Alleene) 1934- 91
   Brief entry 35
   Earlier sketch in SATA *40*
Luttrell, William (J. III) 1954- 149
Lutz, John 1939- 180
Lutz, John Thomas
   See Lutz, John
Lutz, Norma Jean 1943- 122
Lutzeier, Elizabeth 1952- 72
Lutzker, Edythe 1904-1991 5
Luxbacher, Irene 1970- 219
   Earlier sketch in SATA *153*
Luzadder, Patrick 1954- 89
Luzzati, Emanuele 1921-2007 7
Luzzatto, Paola Caboara 1938- 38
Ly, Many 1977- 208
Lybbert, Tyler 1970- 88
Lydon, Michael 1942- 11
Lyfick, Warren
   See Reeves, Lawrence F.
Lyle, Katie Letcher 1938- 8
Lynch, Chris 1962- 209
   Earlier sketches in SATA *95, 131, 171*
   See also CLR *58*
Lynch, Janet Nichols 1952- 221
Lynch, Jay 1945- 204
Lynch, Lorenzo 1932- 7
Lynch, Marietta 1947- 29
Lynch, Patricia (Nora) 1898-1972 9
   See also CLR *167*
Lynch, Patrick James
   See Lynch, P.J.
Lynch, P.J. 1962- 213
   Earlier sketches in SATA *79, 122*
Lynds, Dennis 1924-2005 47
   Brief entry 37
Lyne, Alison Davis 188
Lyngseth, Joan
   See Davies, Joan
Lynn, Elizabeth A(nne) 1946- 99
Lynn, Mary
   See Brokamp, Marilyn
Lynn, Patricia
   See Watts, Mabel Pizzey
Lynn, Tracy 175
Lyon, Elinor 1921-2008 6
   Obituary 192
Lyon, Elinor Bruce
   See Lyon, Elinor
Lyon, George Ella 1949- 207
   Autobiography Feature 148
   Earlier sketches in SATA *68, 119, 148*
Lyon, Lea 1945- 212
Lyon, Lyman R.
   See de Camp, L. Sprague
Lyons, Dorothy M(arawee) 1907-1997 3
Lyons, Grant 1941- 30
Lyons, Jayne 226

Lyons, Marcus
   See Blish, James
Lyons, Mary E. 1947- 195
   Autobiography Feature 195
   Earlier sketches in SATA *93, 142*
Lyons, Mary Evelyn
   See Lyons, Mary E.
Lystad, Mary (Hanemann) 1928- 11
Lytle, Elizabeth Stewart 1949- 79
Lytle, Robert A. 1944- 119
Lyttle, Richard B(ard) 1927- 23
Lytton, Deborah 1966- 218
Lytton, Edward G.E.L. Bulwer-Lytton Baron
   See Bulwer-Lytton, Edward
Lytton of Knebworth, Baron
   See Bulwer-Lytton, Edward

M

Ma, Wenhai 1954- 84
Maar, Leonard (Frank, Jr.) 1927- 30
Maartens, Maretha 1945- 73
Maas, Selve -1997 14
Maass, Robert 195
Mabie, Grace
   See Mattern, Joanne
Mac
   See MacManus, Seumas
   and Maccari, Ruggero
Macalaster, Elizabeth G. 1951- 115
MacAlister, Katie 159
MacAlister, V. A.
   See McKernan, Victoria
MacAllan, Andrew
   See Leasor, James
MacAodhagain, Eamon
   See Egan, E. W.
MacArthur-Onslow, Annette Rosemary
  1933- 26
Macaulay, David (Alexander) 1946- 137
   Brief entry 27
   Earlier sketches in SATA *46, 72*
   See also CLR *14*
Macaulay, Teresa 1947- 95
Macauley, Theresa E.
   See Macaulay, Teresa
Macavinta, Courtney 176
MacBeth, George (Mann) 1932-1992 4
   Obituary 70
MacBride, Roger Lea 1929-1995 85
MacCarter, Don 1944- 91
MacClintock, Dorcas 1932- 8
MacCready, Robin Merrow 1959(?)- 190
MacCullough, Carolyn 174
MacDonald, Alan 1958- 192
MacDonald, Amy 1951- 156
   Autobiography Feature 156
   Earlier sketches in SATA *76, 136*
MacDonald, Anne Elizabeth Campbell Bard
  -1958
   See MacDonald, Betty
MacDonald, Anne Louise 1955- 217
MacDonald, Anson
   See Heinlein, Robert A.
MacDonald, Betty 1908-1958
   See YABC *1*
Macdonald, Blackie
   See Emrich, Duncan (Black Macdonald)
Macdonald, Caroline 1948- 86
   Obituary 111
   See also CLR *60*
Macdonald, Dwight 1906-1982 29
   Obituary 33
MacDonald, George 1824-1905 100
   Earlier sketch in SATA *33*
   See also CLR *67*
MacDonald, Golden
   See Brown, Margaret Wise
Macdonald, Guy 195

Macdonald, James D. 1954- 67
    Earlier sketches in SATA *81, 114, 165, 1*
Macdonald, Marcia
    See Hill, Grace Livingston
MacDonald, Margaret Read 1940- 194
    Earlier sketches in SATA *94, 164*
Macdonald, Marianne 1934- 113
Macdonald, Mary
    See Gifford, Griselda
Macdonald, Maryann 1947- 189
    Earlier sketch in SATA *72*
MacDonald, Ross 1957- 201
Macdonald, Shelagh 1937- 25
MacDonald, Suse 1940- 193
    Brief entry 52
    Earlier sketches in SATA *54, 109*
Macdonald, Wendy 217
Macdonald, Wendy M.
    See Macdonald, Wendy
Macdonald, Zillah K(atherine) 1885-1979 ... *11*
MacDonnell, Megan
    See Stevens, Serita
MacDougal, John
    See Blish, James
Mace, Elisabeth 1933- 27
Mace, Varian 1938- 49
MacEachern, Stephen 206
MacEwen, Gwendolyn (Margaret)
    1941-1987 50
    Obituary 55
Macfarlan, Allan A. 1892-1982 35
MacFarlane, Iris 1922- *11*
MacGill-Callahan, Sheila 1926-2000 78
MacGregor, Carol Lynn 153
MacGregor, Ellen 1906-1954 39
    Brief entry 27
MacGregor-Hastie, Roy (Alasdhair Niall)
    1929- 3
MacGrory, Yvonne 1948- 142
Machado, Ana Maria 1941- 150
MacHale, D.J. 1956- 175
MacHale, Donald James
    See MacHale, D.J.
Machetanz, Frederick 1908- 34
Machin, Sue
    See Williams, Sue
Machin Goodall, Daphne (Edith) 37
Macht, Norm
    See Macht, Norman L.
Macht, Norman L. 1929- 122
Macht, Norman Lee
    See Macht, Norman L.
Macht, Norman Lee
    See Macht, Norman L.
MacInnes, Helen (Clark) 1907-1985 22
    Obituary 44
Macintosh, Brownie 1950- 98
MacIntyre, Elisabeth 1916- 17
MacIntyre, Rod
    See MacIntyre, R.P.
MacIntyre, R.P. 1947- 203
MacIntyre, R.P. 1947- 203
MacIntyre, Wendy 1947- 196
Mack, Jeff 194
Mack, L.V.
    See Kimmelman, Burt
Mack, Stan(ley) 17
Mack, Todd 168
Mack, Tracy 1968- 183
    Earlier sketch in SATA *128*
Mackall, Dandi D.
    See Mackall, Dandi Daley
Mackall, Dandi Daley 1949- 218
    Earlier sketches in SATA *118, 177, 182*
Mackay, Claire 1930- 97
    Autobiography Feature 124
    Earlier sketch in SATA *40*
    See also CLR *43*
Mackay, Constance D'Arcy (?)-1966 125
Mackay, Donald 1914-2005 81
    Obituary 173

Mackay, Donald Alexander
    See Mackay, Donald
MacKaye, Percy (Wallace) 1875-1956 32
Mackel, Kathryn 1950- 162
Mackel, Kathy
    See Mackel, Kathryn
MacKellar, William 1914- 4
Macken, JoAnn Early 1953- 201
Macken, Walter 1915-1967 36
Mackenzie, Anna 1963- 212
MacKenzie, Jill (Kelly) 1947- 75
Mackenzie, Robert 1974- 204
Mackey, Ernan
    See McInerny, Ralph
Mackey, Weezie Kerr 188
Mackie, Maron
    See McNeely, Jeannette
Mackin, Edward
    See McInerny, Ralph
MacKinnon, Bernie 1957- 69
MacKinnon Groomer, Vera 1915- 57
MacKinstry, Elizabeth 1879-1956 42
Mackler, Carolyn 1973- 231
    Earlier sketch in SATA *156*
MacLachlan, Emily
    See Charest, Emily MacLachlan
MacLachlan, Patricia 1938- 229
    Brief entry 42
    Earlier sketches in SATA *62, 107, 168*
    See also CLR *14*
MacLane, Jack
    See Crider, Bill
MacLean, Alistair 1922(?)-1987 23
    Obituary 50
MacLean, Alistair Stuart
    See MacLean, Alistair
Maclean, Art
    See Shirreffs, Gordon D(onald)
MacLean, Christine Kole 1962- 177
MacLean, Glynne 1964- 150
MacLean, Jill 1941- 211
MacLeod, Beatrice 1910- 162
    Earlier sketch in SATA *10*
MacLeod, Beatrice Beach
    See MacLeod, Beatrice
MacLeod, Charlotte (Matilda) 1922-2005 28
    Obituary 160
MacLeod, Doug 1959- 201
    Earlier sketch in SATA *60*
MacLeod, Elizabeth 184
    Earlier sketch in SATA *158*
MacLeod, Ellen Jane (Anderson) 1916- 14
MacManus, James
    See MacManus, Seumas
MacManus, Seumas 1869-1960 25
MacMaster, Eve (Ruth) B(owers) 1942- 46
MacMillan, Annabelle
    See Quick, Annabelle
MacMillan, Dianne M(arie) 1943- 125
    Earlier sketch in SATA *84*
Macnaughton, Tina 218
    Earlier sketch in SATA *182*
Macneill, Janet
    See McNeely, Jeannette
MacPeek, Walter G. 1902-1973 4
    Obituary 25
MacPhail, Catherine 1946- 197
    Earlier sketch in SATA *130*
MacPherson, Margaret 1908-2001 9
    See also SAAS *4*
MacPherson, Thomas George 1915-1976
    Obituary 30
MacPherson, Winnie 1930- 107
MacRae, Tom 1980- 181
Macrae, Travis
    See Feagles, Anita MacRae
MacRaois, Cormac 1944- 72
Macumber, Mari
    See Sandoz, Mari(e Susette)
Macy, Sue 1954- 227
    Earlier sketches in SATA *88, 134*

Madaras, Lynda 1947- *151*
Madden, Colleen 228
Madden, Colleen M.
    See Madden, Colleen
Madden, Don 1927- *3*
Madden, Kerry 1961- 168
Madden-Lunsford, Kerry
    See Madden, Kerry
Maddern, Eric 1950- 166
Maddigan, Beth 1967- 174
Maddison, Angela Mary 1923- 10
    See also CLR *24*
Maddock, Reginald (Bertram) 1912-1994 15
Maddox, Jake
    See Trumbauer, Lisa
Madenski, Melissa (Ann) 1949- 77
Madian, Jon 1941- 9
Madigan, Lisa Kay
    See Madigan, L.K.
Madigan, L.K. (?)-2011 224
Madison, Alan 182
Madison, Arnold 1937- 6
Madison, Bennett 220
Madison, Winifred 5
Madonna 1958- 149
Madsen, Gunnar 171
Madsen, Jim 1964- 202
Madsen, Ross Martin 1946- 82
Madsen, Susan A. 1954- 90
Madsen, Susan Arrington
    See Madsen, Susan A.
Maehlqvist, Stefan 1943- 30
Maestro, Betsy (Crippen) 1944- 106
    Brief entry 30
    Earlier sketch in SATA *59*
    See also CLR *45*
Maestro, Giulio 1942- 106
    Earlier sketches in SATA *8, 59*
    See also CLR *45*
Maeterlinck, Maurice 1862-1949 66
Magee, Doug 1947- 78
Magee, Wes 1939- 64
Maggio, Rosalie 1943- 69
Magid, Ken(neth Marshall) 65
Magnus, Erica 1946- 77
Magoon, Kekla 1980- 213
Magoon, Scott 222
    Earlier sketch in SATA *182*
Magorian, James 1942- 92
    Earlier sketch in SATA *32*
Magorian, Michelle 1947- 128
    Earlier sketch in SATA *67*
Magorian, Michelle Jane
    See Magorian, Michelle
Magovern, Peg 103
Magsamen, Sandra 1959- 213
Maguire, Anne
    See Nearing, Penny
Maguire, Gregory 1954- 200
    Autobiography Feature 200
    Earlier sketches in SATA *28, 84, 129*
    See also SAAS *22*
Maguire, Gregory Peter
    See Maguire, Gregory
Maguire, Jack 1920-2000 74
Maguire, Jesse
    See Smith, Sherwood
Maguire, Jessie
    See Smith, Sherwood
Maher, Ramona 1934- 13
Mahlqvist, Stefan
    See Maehlqvist, Stefan
Mahon, Julia C(unha) 1916- 11
Mahony, Elizabeth Winthrop
    See Winthrop, Elizabeth
Mahood, Kenneth 1930- 24
Mahy, Margaret 1936- 171
    Earlier sketches in SATA *14, 69, 119*
    See also CLR *155*
Mahy, Margaret May
    See Mahy, Margaret

Maiden, Cecil (Edward) 1902-1981 52
Maidoff, Ilka
    See List, Ilka Katherine
Maifair, Linda Lee 1947- 83
Maik, Henri
    See Hecht, Henri Joseph
Maillu, David G(ian) 1939- 111
Maine, Trevor
    See Catherall, Arthur
Mains, Randolph P. 1946- 80
Maione, Heather 189
Maiorano, Robert 1946- 43
Maisner, Heather 1947- 89
Maison, Della
    See Katz, Bobbi
Maitland, Antony Jasper 1935- 25
Maitland, Barbara 102
Mai-Wyss, Tatjana 1972- 187
Maizels, Jennie 210
Major, Kevin (Gerald) 1949- 134
    Earlier sketches in SATA *32, 82*
    See also CLR *11*
Majure, Janet 1954- 96
Makhijani, Pooja 188
Makie, Pam 1943- 37
Makowski, Silk
    See Sullivan, Silky
Makowski, Silvia Ann
    See Sullivan, Silky
Malam, John 1957- 152
    Earlier sketch in SATA *89*
Maland, Nick 195
Malaspina, Ann 1957- 222
Malcolm, Dan
    See Silverberg, Robert
Malcolm, Jahnna N.
    See Beecham, Jahnna
Malcolmson, Anne
    See von Storch, Anne B.
Malcolmson, David 1899-1978 6
Maletta, Dr. Arlene
    See Feltenstein, Arlene
Maley, Carleen
    See Hutchins, Carleen Maley
Mali, Jane Lawrence 1937-1995 51
    Brief entry 44
    Obituary 86
Malkin, Nina 1959(?)- 179
Mallett, Jerry J. 1939- 76
Malley, Gemma 198
Malley, G.R.
    See Malley, Gemma
Mallory, Kenneth 1945- 185
    Earlier sketch in SATA *128*
Mallowan, Agatha Christie
    See Christie, Agatha
Malmberg, Carl 1904-1979 9
Malmgren, Dallin 1949- 65
Malo, John W. 1911-2000 4
Malone, James Hiram 1930- 84
Malone, Marianne 229
Malone, Nola Langner 1930-2003 8
    Obituary 151
Malone, Patricia 1932- 155
Malone, Peter 1953- 191
Maloney, Pat
    See Markun, Patricia Maloney
Malory, Sir Thomas 1410(?)-1471(?) 59
    Brief entry 33
Maltese, Michael 1909(?)-1981
    Obituary 24
Malvasi, Meg Greene 143
Malvern, Corinne 1905-1956 34
Malvern, Gladys (?)-1962 23
Mama G.
    See Davis, Grania
Mammano, Julie 1962- 202
    Earlier sketch in SATA *107*
Mamonova, Tatyana 1943- 93
Manchel, Frank 1935- 10
Manchess, Gregory 1955- 203

Manchester, William (Raymond)
    1922-2004 65
Mandabach, Brian 1962(?)- 197
Mandel, Brett H. 1969- 108
Mandel, Peter 1957- 87
Mandel, Sally (Elizabeth) 1944- 64
Mandell, Muriel (Hortense Levin) 1921- 63
Manders, John 1957- 219
    Earlier sketch in SATA *175*
Mandine, Selma 1973- 228
Manes, Stephen 1949- 99
    Brief entry 40
    Earlier sketch in SATA *42*
Manfred, Frederick (Feikema) 1912-1994 30
Mangin, Marie France 1940- 59
Mangione, Gerlando 1909-1998 6
    Obituary 104
Mangione, Jerre
    See Mangione, Gerlando
Mango, Karin N. 1936- 52
Mangurian, David 1938- 14
Mania, Cathy 1950- 102
Mania, Robert 1952- 102
Mania, Robert C., Jr.
    See Mania, Robert
Maniatty, Taramesha 1978- 92
Maniscalco, Joseph 1926- 10
Manivong, Laura 1967- 229
Manley, Deborah 1932- 28
Manley, Seon 1921- 15
    See also CLR *3*
    See also SAAS *2*
Mann, Elizabeth 1948- 153
Mann, Josephine
    See Pullein-Thompson, Josephine (Mary
    Wedderburn)
Mann, Kenny 1946- 91
Mann, Pamela 1946- 91
Mann, Patrick
    See Waller, Leslie
Mann, Peggy
    See Houlton, Peggy Mann
Mannetti, Lisa 1953- 57
    Brief entry 51
Mannheim, Grete (Salomon) 1909-1986 10
Manniche, Lise 1943- 31
Manning, Jane K. 185
Manning, Maurie
    See Manning, Maurie J.
Manning, Maurie J. 211
Manning, Maurie Jo
    See Manning, Maurie J.
Manning, Mick 1959- 176
Manning, Rosemary 1911-1988 10
Manning, Sarra 162
Manning-Sanders, Ruth (Vernon)
    1895(?)-1988 73
    Obituary 57
    Earlier sketch in SATA *15*
Mannion, Diane
    See Paterson, Diane
Mannis, Celeste Davidson 173
Mannon, Warwick
    See Hopkins, (Hector) Kenneth
Manos, Helen 199
Mansir, A. Richard 1932- 170
Manson, Ainslie Kertland 1938- 115
Manson, Beverlie 1945- 57
    Brief entry 44
Mantchev, Lisa 221
Mantha, John 1960- 217
Manthorpe, Helen 1958- 122
Mantinband, Gerda (B.) 1917- 74
Manton, Jo
    See Gittings, Jo (Grenville) Manton
Manuel, Lynn 1948- 179
    Earlier sketch in SATA *99*
Manushkin, Fran 1942- 205
    Earlier sketches in SATA *7, 54, 93, 166*
Manushkin, Frances
    See Manushkin, Fran

Man Without a Spleen, A
    See Chekhov, Anton
Many, Paul 1947- 210
Many, Paul A.
    See Many, Paul
Manzano, Sonia 1950- 167
Mapes, Mary A.
    See Ellison, Virginia H(owell)
Maple, Marilyn 1931- 80
Mappin, Strephyn 1956- 109
Mara, Barney
    See Roth, Arthur J(oseph)
Mara, Jeanette
    See Cebulash, Mel
Mara, Rachna
    See Gilmore, Rachna
Marais, Josef 1905-1978
    Obituary 24
Marasmus, Seymour
    See Rivoli, Mario
Marbach, Ethel
    See Pochocki, Ethel (Frances)
Marcal, Annette B.
    See Callaway, Bernice (Anne)
Marcelino
    See Agnew, Edith J(osephine)
Marcellino, Fred 1939-2001 118
    Obituary 127
    Earlier sketch in SATA *68*
March, Carl
    See Fleischman, Sid
Marchant, Bessie 1862-1941
    See YABC *2*
Marchant, Catherine
    See Cookson, Catherine (McMullen)
Marcher, Marion Walden 1890-1987 10
Marchesi, Stephen 1951- 114
Marchesi, Steve
    See Marchesi, Stephen
    and Older, Effin
    and Older, Jules
Marchetta, Melina 1965- 170
Marciano, John Bemelmans 1970- 167
    Earlier sketch in SATA *118*
    See also CLR *93*
Marco, Lou
    See Gottfried, Theodore Mark
Marcus, Leonard S. 1950- 187
    Earlier sketch in SATA *133*
Marcus, Paul 1953- 82
Marcus, Rebecca B(rian) 1907- 9
Marcuse, Aida E. 1934- 89
Marek, Margot L. 1934(?)-1987
    Obituary 54
Maren, Julie 1970- 199
Margaret, Karla
    See Andersdatter, Karla M.
Margolin, Harriet
    See Ziefert, Harriet
Margolis, Jeffrey A. 1948- 108
Margolis, Leslie 187
Margolis, Richard J(ules) 1929-1991 86
    Obituary 67
    Earlier sketch in SATA *4*
Margolis, Vivienne 1922- 46
Mariana
    See Foster, Marian Curtis
Marie, Geraldine 1949- 61
Mariner, Scott
    See Pohl, Frederik
Marino, Dorothy Bronson 1912- 14
Marino, Gianna 231
Marino, Jan 1936- 114
Marino, Nan 216
Marino, Nick
    See Deming, Richard
Marino, Peter 1960- 179
Marinsky, Jane 227
Mario, Anna
    See Odgers, Sally Farrell

Marion, Henry
  See del Rey, Lester
Maris, Ron 71
  Brief entry 45
Mark, Jan 1943-2006 164
  Obituary 173
  Earlier sketches in SATA 22, 69, 114
  See also CLR 11
Mark, Janet Marjorie
  See Mark, Jan
Mark, Joan T. 1937- 122
Mark, Pauline (Dahlin) 1913-1997 14
Mark, Polly
  See Mark, Pauline (Dahlin)
Mark, Ted
  See Gottfried, Theodore Mark
Markel, Michelle 169
Marker, Sherry 1941- 76
Markert, Jennifer 1965- 83
Markert, Jenny
  See Markert, Jennifer
Markey, Kevin 1965- 215
Markham, Lynne 1947- 102
Markham, Marion M. 1929- 60
Markham, Wendy
  See Staub, Wendy Corsi
Markins, W. S.
  See Jenkins, Marie M(agdalen)
Markle, Sandra 1946- 218
  Brief entry 41
  Earlier sketches in SATA 57, 92, 148, 185
Markle, Sandra L.
  See Markle, Sandra
Marklew, Gilly 211
Marko, Katherine D(olores) 28
Markoosie
  See Patsauq, Markoosie
Marks, Alan 1957- 187
  Earlier sketches in SATA 77, 151
Marks, Burton 1930- 47
  Brief entry 43
Marks, Graham 158
Marks, Hannah K.
  See Trivelpiece, Laurel
Marks, J.
  See Highwater, Jamake (Mamake)
Marks, J(ames) M(acdonald) 1921- 13
Marks, Laurie J. 1957- 68
Marks, Margaret L. 1911(?)-1980
  Obituary 23
Marks, Mickey Klar -1986 12
Marks, Peter
  See Smith, Robert Kimmel
Marks, Rita 1938- 47
Marks, Stan(ley) 14
Marks-Highwater, J.
  See Highwater, Jamake (Mamake)
Markun, Patricia Maloney 1924- 15
Markusen, Bruce (Stanley Rodriguez)
  1965- 141
Marley, Louise 1952- 173
  Earlier sketch in SATA 120
Marlin, Hilda
  See Van Stockum, Hilda
Marlow, Layne 204
Marlow, Max
  See Nicole, Christopher
Marlow, Susan K. 1953- 178
Marlowe, Amy Bell 67
  Earlier sketch in SATA 1
Marlowe, Jack
  See Deary, Terry
Marlowe, Tess
  See Glick, Ruth
Marney, Dean 1952- 90
Marokvia, Artur 1909- 31
Marokvia, Mireille 1908-2008 5
  Obituary 197
Marokvia, Mireille Journet
  See Marokvia, Mireille
Marol, Jean-Claude 1946- 125

Marr, John S(tuart) 1940- 48
Marr, Melissa 1972- 189
Marric, J. J.
  See Butler, William Vivian
  and Creasey, John
Marrin, Albert 1936- 193
  Brief entry 43
  Earlier sketches in SATA 53, 90, 126
  See also CLR 53
Marriott, Alice Lee 1910-1992 31
  Obituary 71
Marriott, Janice 1946- 134
Marriott, Pat(ricia) 1920- 35
Marriott, Zoe 1982- 216
Marriott, Zoe Davina
  See Marriott, Zoe
Marroquin, Patricio
  See Markun, Patricia Maloney
Mars, W. T.
  See Mars, Witold Tadeusz J.
Mars, Witold Tadeusz J. 1912-1985 3
Marsden, Carolyn 1950- 212
  Autobiography Feature 212
  Earlier sketches in SATA 140, 175
Marsden, John 1950- 146
  Earlier sketches in SATA 66, 97
  See also CLR 34
  See also SAAS 22
Marsh, Carole 1946- 127
Marsh, Dave 1950- 66
Marsh, J. E.
  See Marshall, Evelyn
Marsh, James 1946- 73
Marsh, Jean
  See Marshall, Evelyn
Marsh, Joan F. 1923- 83
Marsh, Katherine 1974- 220
Marsh, Paul
  See Hopkins, (Hector) Kenneth
Marsh, Valerie 1954- 89
Marshall, Anthony D(ryden) 1924- 18
Marshall, Bonnie C. 1941- 141
  Earlier sketch in SATA 18
Marshall, Bridget M(ary) 1974- 103
Marshall, (Sarah) Catherine (Wood)
  1914-1983 2
  Obituary 34
Marshall, Douglas
  See McClintock, Marshall
Marshall, Edmund
  See Hopkins, (Hector) Kenneth
Marshall, Edward
  See Marshall, James
Marshall, Evelyn 1897-1991 11
Marshall, Felicity 1950- 116
Marshall, Garry 1934- 60
Marshall, H. H.
  See Jahn, Michael
Marshall, James 1942-1992 75
  Earlier sketches in SATA 6, 51
  See also CLR 21
Marshall, James Edward
  See Marshall, James
Marshall, James Vance
  See Payne, Donald Gordon
Marshall, Janet (Perry) 1938- 97
Marshall, Jeff
  See Laycock, George (Edwin)
Marshall, Kim
  See Marshall, Michael (Kimbrough)
Marshall, Michael (Kimbrough) 1948- 37
Marshall, Percy
  See Young, Percy M(arshall)
Marshall, S(amuel) L(yman) A(twood)
  1900-1977 21
Marsoli, Lisa Ann 1958- 101
  Brief entry 53
Marsten, Richard
  See Hunter, Evan
Marston, Elsa 1933- 156

Marston, Hope Irvin 1935- 127
  Earlier sketch in SATA 31
Marszalek, John F. 1939- 167
Marszalek, John Francis, Jr.
  See Marszalek, John F.
Marszalek, John Francis 1939-
  See Marszalek, John F.
Martchenko, Michael 1942- 154
  Earlier sketches in SATA 50, 95
Martel, Aimee
  See Thurlo, Aimee
  and Thurlo, David
Martel, Suzanne 1924- 99
Martignoni, Margaret E. 1908(?)-1974
  Obituary 27
Martin, Ann M. 1955- 192
  Brief entry 41
  Earlier sketches in SATA 44, 70, 126
  See also CLR 32
Martin, Bill, Jr. 1916-2004 145
  Brief entry 40
  Earlier sketches in SATA 40, 67
  See also CLR 97
Martin, Charles E(lmer)
  See Mastrangelo, Charles E(lmer)
Martin, Christopher
  See Hoyt, Edwin P(almer), Jr.
Martin, C.K. Kelly 207
Martin, Claire 1933- 76
Martin, Courtney Autumn 1984- 205
Martin, David Stone 1913-1992 39
Martin, Donald
  See Honig, Donald
Martin, Dorothy 1921- 47
Martin, Dorothy McKay
  See Martin, Dorothy
Martin, Eugene 1
Martin, Eva M. 1939- 65
Martin, Frances M(cEntee) 1906-1998 36
Martin, Francesca 1947- 101
Martin, Fred 1948- 119
Martin, Fredric
  See Christopher, Matt(hew Frederick)
Martin, George Raymond Richard
  See Martin, George R.R.
Martin, George R.R. 1948- 118
Martin, J(ohn) P(ercival) 1880(?)-1966 15
Martin, Jacqueline Briggs 1945- 188
  Earlier sketches in SATA 98, 149
Martin, Jane Read 1957- 84
Martin, Jeremy
  See Levin, Marcia Obrasky
Martin, Les
  See Schulman, L(ester) M(artin)
Martin, Linda 1961- 82
Martin, Lynne 1923- 21
Martin, Marcia
  See Levin, Marcia Obrasky
Martin, Marvin 1926- 126
Martin, Melanie
  See Pellowski, Michael (Joseph)
Martin, Nancy
  See Salmon, Annie Elizabeth
Martin, Patricia 200
Martin, Patricia A.
  See Martin, Patricia
Martin, Patricia Miles 1899-1986 43
  Obituary 48
  Earlier sketch in SATA 1
Martin, Peter
  See Chaundler, Christine
Martin, Rafe 1946- 175
Martin, Rene 1891-1977 42
  Obituary 20
Martin, Rupert (Claude) 1905- 31
Martin, S. R.
  See Mappin, Strephyn
Martin, Stefan 1936- 32
Martin, Vicky
  See Storey, Victoria Carolyn

Martin, Webber
See Silverberg, Robert
Martin, Wendy
See Martini, Teri
Martin, William Ivan, Jr.
See Martin, Bill, Jr.
Martineau, Diane 1940- 178
Martineau, Harriet 1802-1876
See YABC 2
Martinet, Jeanne 1958- 80
Martinez, Agnes 167
Martinez, Arturo O. 1933- 192
Martinez, Claudia Guadalupe 1978- 214
Martinez, Ed(ward) 1954- 98
Martinez, Elizabeth Coonrod 1954- 85
Martinez, Victor 1954-2011 95
Martini, Angela 1972(?)- 223
Martini, Teri 1930- 3
Martini, Therese
See Martini, Teri
Martino, Alfred C. 1964- 174
Martinson, Janis
See Herbert, Janis
Martinusen, Cindy
See Martinusen-Coloma, Cindy
Martinusen, Cindy McCormick
See Martinusen-Coloma, Cindy
Martinusen-Coloma, Cindy 1970- 218
Marton, Jirina 1946- 230
Earlier sketches in SATA 95, 144
Marton, Pierre
See Stone, Peter
Martson, Del
See Lupoff, Richard A(llen)
Martyr, Paula (Jane)
See Lawford, Paula Jane
Maruki, Toshi 1912-2000 112
See also CLR 19
Marvin, Isabel R(idout) 1924- 84
Marx, Patricia Windschill
See Marx, Trish
Marx, Robert F(rank) 1936- 24
Marx, Trish 1948- 202
Earlier sketches in SATA 112, 160
Marzani, Carl (Aldo) 1912-1994 12
Marzollo, Jean 1942- 190
Autobiography Feature 190
Earlier sketches in SATA 29, 77, 130
See also SAAS 15
Masefield, John (Edward) 1878-1967 19
See also CLR 164
Masiello, Ralph 1961- 214
Masoff, Joy 1951- 118
Mason, Adrienne 1962- 163
Mason, Cherie 170
Mason, Edwin A. 1905-1979
Obituary 32
Mason, Ernst
See Pohl, Frederik
Mason, F(rancis) van Wyck 1901-1978 3
Obituary 26
Mason, Frank W.
See Mason, F(rancis) van Wyck
Mason, George Frederick 1904-2000 14
Mason, Miriam E(vangeline) 1900-1973 2
Obituary 26
Mason, Prue 195
Mason, Simon 1962- 178
Mason, Tally
See Derleth, August (William)
Mason, Van Wyck
See Mason, F(rancis) van Wyck
Mass, Wendy 1967- 196
Earlier sketch in SATA 158
Mass, William
See Gibson, William
Masse, Josee 221
Masselman, George 1897-1971 19
Massey, Misty 212
Massie, Dianne Redfield 1938- 125
Earlier sketch in SATA 16

Massie, Elizabeth 108
Massini, Sarah 213
Masson, Sophie 1959- 179
Earlier sketch in SATA 133
Masters, Anthony (Richard) 1940-2003 112
Obituary 145
Masters, Kelly R(ay) 1897-1987 3
Masters, Mildred 1932- 42
Masters, William
See Cousins, Margaret
Masters, Zeke
See Bensen, Donald R.
and Goulart, Ron
Mastrangelo, Charles E(lmer) 1910-1995 70
Earlier sketch in SATA 69
Masuda, Takeshi 1944- 56
Matas, Carol 1949- 194
Autobiography Feature 112
Earlier sketch in SATA 93
See also CLR 52
Matchette, Katharine E. 1941- 38
Math, Irwin 1940- 42
Mathabane, Mark 1960- 123
Mather, Kirtley F(letcher) 1888-1978 65
Mathers, Petra 1945- 176
Earlier sketch in SATA 119
See also CLR 76
Matheson, Richard (Christian) 1953- 119
Matheson, Shirlee Smith 1942- 155
Mathews, Eleanor
See Mathews, Ellie
Mathews, Ellie 1946(?)- 193
Mathews, Janet 1914-1992 41
Mathews, Judith
See Goldberger, Judith M.
Mathews, Louise
See Tooke, Louise Mathews
Mathiesen, Egon 1907-1976
Obituary 28
Mathieu, Joe 1949- 185
Brief entry 36
Earlier sketches in SATA 43, 94
Mathieu, Joseph P.
See Mathieu, Joe
Mathis, Sharon Bell 1937- 58
Earlier sketch in SATA 7
See also CLR 147
See also SAAS 3
Matlin, Marlee 1965- 181
Matlin, Marlee Beth
See Matlin, Marlee
Matloff, Gregory 1945- 73
Matott, Justin 1961- 109
Matranga, Frances Carfi 1922- 78
Matray, James I. 1948- 161
Matray, James Irving
See Matray, James I.
Matson, Emerson N(els) 1926- 12
Matson, Morgan 230
Matsui, Tadashi 1926- 8
Matsuno, Masako
See Kobayashi, Masako Matsuno
Matsuoka, Mei 1981- 192
Matte, (Encarnacion) L'Enc 1936- 22
Mattern, Joanne 1963- 122
Mattheson, Jenny 180
Matthew, James
See Barrie, J. M.
Matthews, Aline
See De Wire, Elinor
Matthews, Andrew 1948- 138
Matthews, Caitlin 1952- 122
Matthews, Cecily 1945- 221
Matthews, Downs 1925- 71
Matthews, Elizabeth 1978- 194
Matthews, Ellen
See Bache, Ellyn
Matthews, Ellen 1950- 28
Matthews, Harold Downs
See Matthews, Downs

Matthews, Jacklyn Meek
See Meek, Jacklyn O'Hanlon
Matthews, John (Kentigern) 1948- 116
Matthews, L. S. 183
Matthews, Laura S.
See Matthews, L. S.
Matthews, Liz
See Pellowski, Michael (Joseph)
Matthews, Morgan
See Pellowski, Michael (Joseph)
Matthews, Nicola
See Browne, N.M.
Matthews, Patricia 1927-2006 28
Matthews, Patricia Anne
See Matthews, Patricia
Matthews, Tina 1961- 190
Matthews, Tom L.
See Lalicki, Tom
Matthews, William Henry III 1919- 45
Brief entry 28
Matthiessen, Peter 1927- 27
Mattingley, Christobel (Rosemary) 1931- 85
Earlier sketch in SATA 37
See also CLR 24
See also SAAS 18
Matulay, Laszlo 1912- 43
Matus, Greta 1938- 12
Matzigkeit, Philip 220
Maugham, W. S.
See Maugham, W. Somerset
Maugham, W. Somerset 1874-1965 54
Maugham, William S.
See Maugham, W. Somerset
Maugham, William Somerset
See Maugham, W. Somerset
Maurer, Diane Philippoff
See Maurer-Mathison, Diane V(ogel)
Maurer, Diane Vogel
See Maurer-Mathison, Diane V(ogel)
Maurer-Mathison, Diane V(ogel) 1944- 89
Mauser, Pat Rhoads
See McCord, Patricia
Mauser, Patricia Rhoads
See McCord, Patricia
Maves, Mary Carolyn 1916- 10
Maves, Paul B(enjamin) 1913-1994 10
Mavor, Salley 1955- 125
Mawicke, Tran 1911- 15
Max 1906-1989
See Diop, Birago (Ismael)
Max, Jill
See Bennett, Kelly
Max, Peter 1939- 45
Maxon, Anne
See Best, (Evangel) Allena Champlin
Maxwell, Arthur S. 1896-1970 11
Maxwell, B.E. 1957- 211
Maxwell, Bruce E.
See Maxwell, B.E.
Maxwell, Edith 1923- 7
Maxwell, Gavin 1914-1969 65
Maxwell, Katie
See MacAlister, Katie
Maxwell, William (Keepers, Jr.) 1908-2000
Obituary 128
Maxwell-Hyslop, Miranda 1968- 154
May, Charles Paul 1920- 4
May, Elaine Tyler 1947- 120
May, J. C.
See May, Julian
May, Julian 1931- 11
May, Katie 225
May, Robert Lewis 1905-1976
Obituary 27
May, Robert Stephen 1929-1996 46
May, Robin
See May, Robert Stephen
Mayall, Beth 171
Mayberry, Florence V(irginia) Wilson 10
Maybury, Richard J. 1946- 72

Maybury, Rick
 See Maybury, Richard J.
Maydak, Michael S. 1952- 220
Mayer, Agatha
 See Maher, Ramona
Mayer, Albert Ignatius, Jr. 1906-1994
 Obituary 29
Mayer, Ann M(argaret) 1938- 14
Mayer, Bill 200
Mayer, Danuta 1958- 117
Mayer, Hannelore Valencak 1929- 42
Mayer, Jane Rothschild 1903-2001 38
Mayer, Marianna 1945- 132
 Earlier sketches in SATA *32, 83*
Mayer, Mercer 1943- 137
 Earlier sketches in SATA *16, 32, 73, 129*
 See also CLR *11*
Mayerson, Charlotte Leon 36
Mayerson, Evelyn Wilde 1935- 55
Mayfield, Katherine 1958- 118
Mayfield, Sue 1963- 146
 Earlier sketch in SATA *72*
Mayhar, Ardath 1930- 38
Mayhew, James 1964- 204
 Earlier sketches in SATA *85, 149*
Maynard, Olga 1920- 40
Mayne, William 1928-2010 122
 Earlier sketches in SATA *6, 68*
 See also CLR *123*
 See also SAAS *11*
Mayne, William James Carter
 See Mayne, William
Maynes, J. O. Rocky, Jr.
 See Maynes, J. Oscar, Jr.
Maynes, J. Oscar, Jr. 1929- 38
Mayo, Gretchen Will 1936- 163
 Earlier sketch in SATA *84*
Mayo, Margaret 1935- 165
 Earlier sketches in SATA *38, 96*
Mayo, Margaret Mary
 See Mayo, Margaret
Mayr, Diane 1949- 197
Mays, Lucinda L(a Bella) 1924- 49
Mays, (Lewis) Victor (Jr.) 1927- 5
Mazellan, Ron 210
Mazer, Anne 1953- 192
 Earlier sketches in SATA *67, 105*
Mazer, Harry 1925- 167
 Earlier sketches in SATA *31, 67, 105*
 See also CLR *16*
 See also SAAS *11*
Mazer, Norma Fox 1931-2009 198
 Earlier sketches in SATA *24, 67, 105, 168*
 See also CLR *23*
 See also SAAS *1*
Mazille, Capucine 1953- 96
Mazo, Michael 223
Mazza, Adriana 1928- 19
Mazzio, Joann 1926- 74
Mbugua, Kioi Wa 1962- 83
McAfee, Carol 1955- 81
McAllister, Amanda
 See Dowdell, Dorothy (Florence) Karns
 and Hager, Jean
 and Meaker, Eloise
McAllister, Angela 225
 Earlier sketch in SATA *182*
McAllister, Margaret I. 1956- 169
 Earlier sketch in SATA *117*
McAllister, M.I.
 See McAllister, Margaret I.
McArdle, Paula 1971- 198
McArthur, Nancy 96
McAvoy, Jim 1972- 142
McBain, Ed
 See Hunter, Evan
McBain, Georgina 189
McBratney, Sam 1943- 203
 Earlier sketches in SATA *89, 164*
 See also CLR *44*

McBrier, Michael
 See Older, Effin
 and Older, Jules
McCafferty, Jim 1954- 84
McCaffery, Janet 1936- 38
McCaffrey, Anne 1926- 152
 Autobiography Feature 152
 Earlier sketches in SATA *8, 70, 116*
 See also CLR *130*
 See also SAAS *11*
McCaffrey, Anne Inez
 See McCaffrey, Anne
McCaffrey, Kate 1970- 228
McCaffrey, Mary
 See Szudek, Agnes S(usan) P(hilomena)
McCain, Becky Ray 1954- 138
McCain, Murray (David, Jr.) 1926-1981 7
 Obituary 29
McCall, Bruce 1935(?)- 209
McCall, Edith (Sansom) 1911- 6
McCall, Virginia Nielsen 1909-2000 13
McCall, Wendell
 See Pearson, Ridley
McCall Smith, Alexander
 See Smith, Alexander McCall
McCallum, Phyllis
 See Koch, Phyllis (Mae) McCallum
McCallum, Stephen 1960- 91
McCampbell, Darlene Z. 1942- 83
McCann, Edson
 See del Rey, Lester
 and Pohl, Frederik
McCann, Gerald 1916- 41
McCann, Helen 1948- 75
McCannon, Dindga 41
McCants, William D. 1961- 82
McCarter, Neely Dixon 1929- 47
McCarthy, Agnes 1933- 4
McCarthy, Colin (John) 1951- 77
McCarthy, Mary 1951- 203
McCarthy, Meghan 199
 Earlier sketch in SATA *168*
McCarthy, Ralph F. 1950- 139
McCarthy-Tucker, Sherri N. 1958- 83
McCarty, Peter 1966- 182
McCarty, Rega Kramer 1904-1986 10
McCaslin, Nellie 1914-2005 12
McCaughrean, Geraldine 1951- 173
 Earlier sketches in SATA *87, 139*
 See also CLR *38*
McCaughren, Tom 1936- 75
McCauley, Adam 1965- 209
 Earlier sketch in SATA *128*
McCay, (Zenas) Winsor 1869-1934 134
 Earlier sketch in SATA *41*
McClafferty, Carla Killough 1958- 137
McClary, Jane Stevenson 1919-1990
 Obituary 64
McCleery, Patsy R. 1925- 133
 Earlier sketch in SATA *88*
McClelland, Susan 214
McClements, George 196
McClintock, Barbara 1955- 213
 Earlier sketches in SATA *57, 95, 146*
McClintock, Marshall 1906-1967 3
McClintock, May Garelick
 See Garelick, May
McClintock, Mike
 See McClintock, Marshall
McClintock, Norah 226
 Earlier sketch in SATA *178*
McClintock, Theodore 1902-1971 14
McClinton, Leon 1933- 11
McCloskey, Kevin 1951- 79
McCloskey, (John) Robert 1914-2003 100
 Obituary 146
 Earlier sketches in SATA *2, 39*
 See also CLR *7*
McCloy, James F(loyd) 1941- 59

McClung, Robert M(arshall) 1916- 135
 Earlier sketches in SATA *2, 68*
 See also CLR *11*
 See also SAAS *15*
McClure, Gillian Mary 1948- 31
McClure, Nikki 218
McColley, Kevin 1961- 80
 See also SAAS *23*
McConduit, Denise Walter 1950- 89
McConnell, James Douglas Rutherford
 1915-1988 40
 Obituary 56
McCord, Anne 1942- 41
McCord, David (Thompson Watson)
 1897-1997 18
 Obituary 96
 See also CLR *9*
McCord, Jean 1924- 34
McCord, Pat Mauser
 See McCord, Patricia
McCord, Patricia 1943- 159
 Earlier sketch in SATA *37*
McCord, Patricia Sue Rhoads Mauser
 See McCord, Patricia
McCormack, Caren McNelly 217
McCormick, Brooks
 See Adams, William Taylor
McCormick, Dell J. 1892-1949 19
McCormick, (George) Donald (King)
 1911-1998 14
McCormick, Edith (Joan) 1934- 30
McCormick, Kimberly A. 1960- 153
McCormick, Patricia 1956- 181
 Earlier sketch in SATA *128*
McCourt, Edward (Alexander) 1907-1972
 Obituary 28
McCourt, Lisa 1964- 214
 Earlier sketches in SATA *117, 159*
McCourt, Malachy 1931- 126
McCoy, Glenn 1965- 212
McCoy, Iola Fuller 3
McCoy, J(oseph) J(erome) 1917- 8
McCoy, Karen Kawamoto 1953- 82
McCoy, Lois (Rich) 1941- 38
McCrady, Lady 1951- 16
McCrea, James (Craig, Jr.) 1920- 3
McCrea, Ruth (Pirman) 1921- 3
McCreigh, James
 See Pohl, Frederik
McCrumb, Sharyn 1948- 109
McCue, Lisa 1959- 212
 Earlier sketches in SATA *65, 177*
McCue, Lisa Emiline
 See McCue, Lisa
McCullen, Andrew
 See Arthur, Robert, (Jr.)
McCullers, Carson 1917-1967 27
McCullers, Lula Carson Smith
 See McCullers, Carson
McCulloch, Derek (Ivor Breashur) 1897-1967
 Obituary 29
McCulloch, John Tyler
 See Burroughs, Edgar Rice
McCulloch, Sarah
 See Ure, Jean
McCullough, David 1933- 62
McCullough, David Gaub
 See McCullough, David
McCullough, Frances Monson 1938- 8
McCullough, Sharon Pierce 1943- 131
McCully, Emily Arnold
 See Arnold, Emily
McCune, Dan
 See Haas, Dorothy F.
McCunn, Ruthanne Lum 1946- 63
McCurdy, Michael (Charles) 1942- 147
 Earlier sketches in SATA *13, 82*
McCusker, Paul 1958- 220
McCutcheon, Elsie (Mary Jackson) 1937- ... 60
McCutcheon, John 1952- 97
McDaniel, Becky Bring 1953- 61

McDaniel, Lurlene 1944- 218
    Earlier sketches in SATA 71, 146
McDaniels, Pellom III 1968- 121
McDaniels, Preston 1952- 192
McDearmon, Kay 20
McDermott, Beverly Brodsky 1941- 11
McDermott, Eleni 156
McDermott, Gerald (Edward) 1941- 163
    Earlier sketches in SATA 16, 74
    See also CLR 9
McDermott, Michael 1962- 76
McDevitt, Jack 1935- 155
    Earlier sketch in SATA 94
McDevitt, John Charles
    See McDevitt, Jack
McDole, Carol
    See Farley, Carol (J.)
McDonald, Candice Hartsough 1982- 225
McDonald, Collin 1943- 79
McDonald, Gerald D(oan) 1905-1970 3
McDonald, Jamie
    See Heide, Florence Parry
McDonald, Janet 1953-2007 204
    Earlier sketch in SATA 148
McDonald, Jill (Masefield) 1927-1982 13
    Obituary 29
McDonald, Joyce 1946- 164
    Earlier sketch in SATA 101
McDonald, Lucile Saunders 1898-1992 10
McDonald, Mary Ann 1956- 84
McDonald, Megan 1958- 202
    Autobiography Feature 151
    Earlier sketches in SATA 67, 99, 148, 151
    See also CLR 94
McDonald, Meme 1954- 112
McDonald, Mercedes 1956- 169
    Earlier sketch in SATA 97
McDonal, Rae A. 1952- 201
McDonell, Chris 1960- 138
McDonnell, Christine 1949- 225
    Earlier sketches in SATA 34, 115
McDonnell, Flora (Mary) 1963- 146
    Earlier sketch in SATA 90
McDonnell, Kathleen 1947- 186
McDonnell, Lois Eddy 1914-2001 10
McDonnell, Patrick 1956- 221
    Earlier sketch in SATA 179
McDonough, Yona Zeldis 1957- 73
McDowell, Marilyn Taylor 217
McElligott, Matt 1968- 196
    Earlier sketch in SATA 135
McElligott, Matthew
    See McElligott, Matt
McElmeel, Sharron L. 1942- 128
McElmurry, Jill 198
    Earlier sketch in SATA 159
McElrath, William N. 1932- 65
McElrath-Eslick, Lori 1960- 204
    Earlier sketch in SATA 96
McEntee, Dorothy (Layng) 1902- 37
McEvoy, Anne 214
McEwen, Katharine 183
McEwen, Robert (Lindley) 1926-1980
    Obituary 23
McFadden, Kevin Christopher
    See Pike, Christopher
McFall, Christie 1918- 12
McFall, Gardner 1952- 183
McFarlan, Donald M(aitland) 1915- 59
McFarland, Henry "Hammer"
    See McFarland, Henry O.
McFarland, Henry O. 1934- 143
McFarland, Kenton D(ean) 1920- 11
McFarland, Martha
    See Smith-Ankrom, M. E.
McFarlane, Leslie 1902-1977 100
    Earlier sketches in SATA 31, 1, 65, 67
    See also CLR 118
McFarlane, Leslie Charles
    See McFarlane, Leslie
McFarlane, Peter 1940- 95

McFarlane, Peter William
    See McFarlane, Peter
McFarlane, Sheryl P. 1954- 86
McFarlane, Todd 1961- 117
McGaw, Jessie Brewer 1913-1997 10
McGee, Barbara 1943- 6
McGee, Marni 163
McGhee, Alison 1960- 231
    Earlier sketch in SATA 196
McGhee, Alison R.
    See McGhee, Alison
McGhee, Holly M.
    See Durand, Hallie
McGiffin, (Lewis) Lee (Shaffer) 1908-1978 ... 1
McGill, Alice 159
McGill, Marci
    See Balterman, Marcia Ridlon
McGill, Marci Ridlon
    See Balterman, Marcia Ridlon
McGill, Ormond 1913- 92
McGinley, Jerry 1948- 116
McGinley, Phyllis 1905-1978 44
    Obituary 24
    Earlier sketch in SATA 2
McGinnis, Lila S(prague) 1924- 44
McGinty, Alice B. 1963- 202
    Earlier sketch in SATA 134
McGivern, Justin 1985- 129
McGivern, Maureen Daly
    See Daly, Maureen
McGivern, Maureen Patricia Daly
    See Daly, Maureen
McGough, Elizabeth (Hemmes) 1934- 33
McGovern, Ann 1930- 132
    Earlier sketches in SATA 8, 69, 70
    See also CLR 50
    See also SAAS 17
McGowen, Thomas E. 1927- 109
    Earlier sketch in SATA 2
McGowen, Tom
    See McGowen, Thomas E.
McGrady, Mike 1933- 6
McGrath, Barbara Barbieri 1953- 230
    Earlier sketches in SATA 108, 169
McGrath, Robin 1949- 121
McGrath, Thomas (Matthew) 1916-1990 41
    Obituary 66
McGraw, Eloise Jarvis 1915-2000 67
    Obituary 123
    Earlier sketch in SATA 1
    See also SAAS 6
McGraw, William Corbin 1916-1999 3
McGreal, Elizabeth
    See Yates, Elizabeth
McGregor, Barbara 1959- 82
McGregor, Craig 1933- 8
McGregor, Iona 1929- 25
McGrory, Anik 193
McGuffey, Alexander Hamilton 1816-1896 . 60
McGuigan, Mary Ann 1949- 228
    Earlier sketch in SATA 106
McGuire, Edna 1899- 13
McGuire, Leslie (Sarah) 1945- 94
    Brief entry 45
    Earlier sketch in SATA 52
McGuire, Robert 187
McGuirk, Leslie (A.) 1960- 152
McGurk, Slater
    See Roth, Arthur J(oseph)
McHargue, Georgess 1941- 77
    Earlier sketch in SATA 4
    See also CLR 2
    See also SAAS 5
McHenry, E.B. 1963(?)- 193
McHugh, (Berit) Elisabet 1941- 55
    Brief entry 44
McIlvaine, Jane
    See McClary, Jane Stevenson
McIlwraith, Maureen Mollie Hunter
    See Hunter, Mollie

McInerney, Judith W(hitelock) 1945- 49
    Brief entry 46
McInerny, Ralph 1929-2010 93
McInerny, Ralph Matthew
    See McInerny, Ralph
McKaughan, Larry (Scott) 1941- 75
McKay, Donald 1895- 45
McKay, Hilary 1959- 208
    Earlier sketches in SATA 92, 145
    See also SAAS 23
McKay, Hilary Jane
    See McKay, Hilary
McKay, Lawrence, Jr. 1948- 114
McKay, Robert W. 1921- 15
McKay, Sharon E. 1954- 165
McKay, Simon
    See Nicole, Christopher
McKean, Dave 1963- 197
McKean, David Jeff
    See McKean, Dave
McKeating, Eileen 1957- 81
McKee, David (John) 1935- 158
    Earlier sketches in SATA 70, 107
    See also CLR 38
McKee, Tim 1970- 111
McKeever, Marcia
    See Laird, Jean E(louise)
McKellar, Danica 1975- 213
McKelvey, Carole A. 1942- 78
McKelvy, Charles 1950- 124
McKendrick, Melveena (Christine) 1941- 55
McKendry, Joe 1972- 170
McKenna, Colleen O'Shaughnessy 1948- .. 136
    Earlier sketch in SATA 76
McKenzie, Dorothy Clayton 1910-1981
    Obituary 28
McKenzie, Ellen Kindt 1928- 80
McKernan, Victoria 1957- 171
McKie, Robin 112
McKillip, Patricia A. 1948- 174
    Earlier sketches in SATA 30, 80, 126
McKillip, Patricia Anne
    See McKillip, Patricia A.
McKim, Audrey Margaret 1909-1999 47
McKimmie, Chris 194
McKinley, Jennifer Carolyn Robin
    See McKinley, Robin
McKinley, Robin 1952- 229
    Brief entry 32
    Earlier sketches in SATA 50, 89, 130, 195
    See also CLR 127
McKinney, Barbara Shaw 1951- 116
McKinney, Nadine 1938- 91
McKinty, Adrian 186
McKissack, Fredrick L. 1939- 162
    Brief entry 53
    Earlier sketches in SATA 73, 117
    See also CLR 55
McKissack, Fredrick Lemuel
    See McKissack, Fredrick L.
McKissack, Patricia C. 1944- 195
    Earlier sketches in SATA 51, 73, 117, 162
    See also CLR 129
McKissack, Patricia L'Ann Carwell
    See McKissack, Patricia C.
McKissack and McKissack
    See McKissack, Fredrick L.
    and McKissack, Patricia C.
McKown, Robin (?)-1976 6
McKy, Katie 1956- 184
McLaren, Chesley 213
McLaren, Clemence 1938- 158
    Earlier sketch in SATA 105
McLaughlin, Frank 1934- 73
McLaughlin, Julie 1984- 226
McLaughlin, Lauren 209
McLaurin, Anne 1953- 27
McLean, Andrew 1946- 172
    Earlier sketch in SATA 113

McLean, J. Sloan
  See Gillette, Virginia M(ary)
  and Wunsch, Josephine (McLean)
McLean, Jacqueline
  See Kolosov, Jacqueline
McLean, Janet 1946- 113
McLean, Kathryn (Anderson) 1909-1966 9
McLean, Virginia Overton 1946- 90
McLean-Carr, Carol 1948- 122
McLeish, Kenneth 1940-1997 35
McLenighan, Valjean 1947- 46
  Brief entry 40
McLennan, Connie 171
McLennan, Will
  See Wisler, G(ary) Clifton
McLeod, Bob 1951- 173
McLeod, Chum 1955- 95
McLeod, Emilie Warren 1926-1982 23
  Obituary 31
McLeod, Kirsty
  See Hudson, (Margaret) Kirsty
McLeod, Margaret Vail
  See Holloway, Teresa (Bragunier)
McLerran, Alice 1933- 137
  Earlier sketch in SATA 68
McLimans, David 1949- 182
McLoughlin, John C. 1949- 47
McMahon, Bob 1956- 208
McManus, Patrick F. 1933- 46
McManus, Patrick Francis
  See McManus, Patrick F.
McMeekin, Clark
  See McMeekin, Isabel McLennan
McMeekin, Isabel McLennan 1895-1973 3
McMenemy, Sarah 1965- 226
  Earlier sketch in SATA 156
McMillan, Bruce 1947- 192
  Earlier sketches in SATA 22, 70, 129
  See also CLR 47
McMillan, Naomi
  See Grimes, Nikki
McMorey, James L.
  See Moyer, Terry J.
McMorrow, Annalisa 1969- 104
McMullan, Jim 1934- 150
  Earlier sketch in SATA 87
McMullan, K. H.
  See McMullan, Kate
McMullan, Kate 1947- 189
  Brief entry 48
  Earlier sketches in SATA 52, 87, 132
McMullan, Kate Hall
  See McMullan, Kate
McMullan, Margaret 1960- 203
McMurtrey, Martin A(loysias) 1921- 21
McNabb, Linda 1963- 147
McNair, Kate 3
McNair, Sylvia 1924-2002 74
McNamara, Margaret C(raig) 1915-1981
  Obituary 24
McNaught, Harry 32
McNaughton, Colin 1951- 211
  Earlier sketches in SATA 39, 92, 134
  See also CLR 54
McNaughton, Janet 1953- 162
  Earlier sketch in SATA 110
McNeal, Laura 194
McNeal, Tom 194
McNeely, Jeannette 1918- 25
McNeer, May (Yonge) 1902-1994 81
  Earlier sketch in SATA 1
McNeese, Tim 1953- 139
McNeill, Janet
  See Alexander, Janet
McNicholas, Shelagh 191
McNickle, D'Arcy 1904-1977
  Obituary 22
McNickle, William D'Arcy
  See McNickle, D'Arcy
McNicoll, Sylvia (Marilyn) 1954- 113
  See also CLR 99

McNulty, Faith 1918-2005 168
  Earlier sketches in SATA 12, 84, 139
McPhail, David 1940- 219
  Brief entry 32
  Earlier sketches in SATA 47, 81, 140, 183
McPhail, David M.
  See McPhail, David
McPhail, David Michael
  See McPhail, David
McPhee, Norma H. 1928- 95
McPhee, Peter 1957- 214
McPhee, Richard B(yron) 1934- 41
McPherson, James M. 1936- 141
  Earlier sketch in SATA 16
McPherson, James Munro
  See McPherson, James M.
McQueen, Lucinda 1950- 58
  Brief entry 48
McQueen, Mildred Hark 1908-1978 12
McQuillan, Mary 200
McRae, Russell (William) 1934- 63
McShean, Gordon 1936- 41
Mc Swigan, Marie 1907-1962 24
McTavish, Sandy
  See Eyerly, Jeannette
McVeity, Jen 148
McVey, Vicki 1946- 80
McVicker, Charles (Taggart) 1930- 39
McVicker, Chuck
  See McVicker, Charles (Taggart)
McVoy, Terra Elan 220
McWhirter, A(lan) Ross 1925-1975 37
  Obituary 31
McWhirter, Norris (Dewar) 1925-2004 37
McWilliam, Howard 1977- 219
McWilliams, Karen 1943- 65
Mdurvwa, Hajara E. 1962- 92
Meacham, Margaret 1952- 203
  Earlier sketch in SATA 95
Meachum, Virginia 1918- 133
  Earlier sketch in SATA 87
Mead, Alice 1952- 146
  Earlier sketch in SATA 94
Mead, Margaret 1901-1978
  Obituary 20
Mead, Russell (M., Jr.) 1935- 10
Mead, Stella (?)-1981
  Obituary 27
Meade, Elizabeth Thomasina 1854(?)-1914(?)
  See CLR 163
Meade, Ellen
  See Roddick, Ellen
Meade, Holly 207
Meade, L. T.
  See Meade, Elizabeth Thomasina
Meade, Marion 1934- 127
  Earlier sketch in SATA 23
Meader, Stephen W(arren) 1892-1977 1
Meadmore, Susan
  See Sallis, Susan (Diana)
Meadow, Charles T(roub) 1929- 23
Meadowcroft, Enid LaMonte
  See Wright, Enid Meadowcroft (LaMonte)
Meadows, Daisy
  See Chapman, Linda
Meadows, Graham (W.) 1934- 161
Meadows, Michelle 202
Meaker, M. J.
  See Meaker, Marijane
Meaker, Marijane 1927- 160
  Autobiography Feature 111
  Earlier sketches in SATA 20, 61, 99
  See also CLR 29
  See also SAAS 1
Meaker, Marijane Agnes
  See Meaker, Marijane
Means, Florence Crannell 1891-1980 1
  Obituary 25
  See also CLR 56
Mearian, Judy Frank 1936- 49
Mebus, Scott 1974- 216

Mecca, Judy Truesdell 1955- 127
Mechling, Lauren 1978(?)- 194
Mechling, Lauren 1978(?)- 194
Mechner, Jordan 1964- 205
Medary, Marjorie 1890-1980 14
Meddaugh, Susan 1944- 176
  Earlier sketches in SATA 29, 84, 125
Medearis, Angela Shelf 1956- 123
  Earlier sketch in SATA 72
Medearis, Mary 1915- 5
Medina, Jane 1953- 167
  Earlier sketch in SATA 122
Medina, Meg 1963- 212
Medina, Nico 1982- 193
Medlicott, Mary 1946- 88
Mee, Charles L., Jr. 1938- 72
  Earlier sketch in SATA 8
Meehan, Kierin 218
Meehl, Brian 204
Meek, Jacklyn O'Hanlon 1933- 51
  Brief entry 34
Meek, S(terner St.) P(aul) 1894-1972
  Obituary 28
Meeker, Clare Hodgson 1952- 96
Meeker, Oden 1919(?)-1976 14
Meeker, Richard
  See Brown, Fornan
Meeks, Esther MacBain 1
Meggs, Libby Phillips 1943- 130
Mehdevi, Alexander (Sinclair) 1947- 7
Mehdevi, Anne (Marie) Sinclair 1947- 8
Meidell, Sherry 1951- 73
Meier, Minta 1906- 55
Meighan, Donald Charles 1929- 30
Meigs, Cornelia Lynde 1884-1973 6
  See also CLR 55
Meilach, Dona Z(weigoron) 1926- 34
Meilman, Philip W(arren) 1951- 79
Meinstereifel, Ronald L. 1960- 134
Meisel, Paul 224
  Earlier sketch in SATA 184
Meister, Cari 204
Melanson, Luc 198
Melcher, Daniel 1912-1985
  Obituary 43
Melcher, Frederic Gershom 1879-1963
  Obituary 22
Melcher, Marguerite Fellows 1879-1969 10
Meldrum, Christina 206
Melendez, Francisco 1964- 72
Melhuish, Eva 199
Melin, Grace Hathaway 1892-1973 10
Mellersh, H(arold) E(dward) L(eslie)
  1897- 10
Melling, David 186
Melmed, Laura Krauss 212
Melmoth, Sebastian
  See Wilde, Oscar
Melnikoff, Pamela (Rita) 97
Meltzer, Amy 1968- 202
Meltzer, Milton 1915-2009 201
  Autobiography Feature 124
  Earlier sketches in SATA 1, 50, 80, 128
  See also CLR 13
  See also SAAS 1
Melville, Anne
  See Potter, Margaret
Melville, Herman 1819-1891 59
Melwood, Mary
  See Lewis, E. M.
Melzack, Ronald 1929- 5
Memling, Carl 1918-1969 6
Menchin, Scott 188
Mendel, Jo
  See Bond, Gladys Baker
  and Gilbertson, Mildred Geiger
Mendelson, Steven T. 1958-1995 86
Mendelson-Stevens, Serita Deborah
  See Stevens, Serita
Mendes, Valerie 1939- 157
Mendez, Raymond A. 1947- 66

Mendez, Simon 1975- 215
Mendonca, Susan
    See Smith, Susan Vernon
Mendoza, George 1934- 41
    Brief entry 39
    See also SAAS 7
Menendez, Shirley (C.) 1937- 146
Meng, Cece 194
Meng, Heinz (Karl) 1924- 13
Mennen, Ingrid 1954- 85
Menotti, Gian Carlo 1911-2007 29
    Obituary 180
Menuhin, Sir Yehudi 1916-1999 40
    Obituary 113
Menville, Douglas 1935- 64
Menzel, Barbara Jean 1946- 63
Menzel, Peter 1948- 207
Mercati, Cynthia 164
Mercati, Cynthia J.
    See Mercati, Cynthia
Mercer, Charles (Edward) 1917-1988 16
    Obituary 61
Mercer, Jessie 21
Mercer, Sienna 192
Meredith, Arnold
    See Hopkins, (Hector) Kenneth
Meredith, David William
    See Miers, Earl Schenck
Meringoff, Laurene Krasny
    See Brown, Laurene Krasny
Meriwether, Louise 1923- 52
    Brief entry 31
Merlin, Arthur
    See Blish, James
Merlin, Christina
    See Heaven, Constance (Christina)
Merrell, Billy 1982- 222
Merriam, Eve 1916-1992 73
    Earlier sketches in SATA *3, 40*
    See also CLR *14*
Merrill, Jane 1946- 42
Merrill, Jane Merrill
    See Merrill, Jane
Merrill, Jean (Fairbanks) 1923- 82
    Earlier sketch in SATA *1*
    See also CLR *52*
Merrill, Phil
    See Merrill, Jane
Merriman, Alex
    See Silverberg, Robert
Merriman, Rachel 1971- 149
    Earlier sketch in SATA *98*
Merrit, Elizabeth
    See Goudge, Eileen
Merski, Patricia K.
    See Merski, P.K.
Merski, P.K. 172
Mertz, Barbara
    See Peters, Elizabeth
Mertz, Barbara Gross
    See Peters, Elizabeth
Merveille, David 200
Merz, Jennifer J. 196
Meschel, Susan V. 1936- 83
Meschenmoser, Sebastian 1980- 229
Meserve, Jessica 211
Messenger, Charles (Rynd Milles) 1942- 59
Messer, Stephen 1972- 231
Messick, Dale 1906-2005 64
    Brief entry 48
Messier, Claire 1956- 103
Messieres, Nicole de
    See de Messieres, Nicole
Messinger, Carla 198
Messmer, Otto 1892(?)-1983 37
Messner, Kate 224
Mesta, Gabriel
    See Moesta, Rebecca
Metaxas, Eric 1963- 211
Metcalf, Doris H(unter) 91

Metcalf, Suzanne
    See Baum, L. Frank
Metos, Thomas H(arry) 1932- 37
Metter, Bert(ram Milton) 1927- 56
Metzenthen, David 1958- 167
    Earlier sketch in SATA *106*
Meunier, Brian 1954- 195
Meyer, Barbara 1939- 77
Meyer, Carolyn 1935- 142
    Autobiography Feature 142
    Earlier sketches in SATA *9, 70, 118*
    See also SAAS *9*
Meyer, Carolyn Mae
    See Meyer, Carolyn
Meyer, Edith Patterson 1895-1993 5
Meyer, F(ranklyn) E(dward) 1932- 9
Meyer, Jean Shepherd 11
Meyer, Jerome Sydney 1895-1975 3
    Obituary 25
Meyer, June
    See Jordan, June
Meyer, Kerstin 1966- 190
Meyer, L.A. 1942- 221
    Earlier sketches in SATA *12, 144*
Meyer, Louis A.
    See Meyer, L.A.
Meyer, Renate 1930- 6
Meyer, Stephenie 1973- 193
    See also CLR *142*
Meyer, Susan E. 1940- 64
Meyerhoff, Jenny 1972- 208
Meyers, Susan 1942- 164
    Earlier sketches in SATA *19, 108*
Meynell, Laurence Walter 1899-1989
    Obituary 61
Meynier, Yvonne (Pollet) 1908- 14
Mezey, Robert 1935- 33
Micale, Albert 1913- 22
Michael, James
    See Scagnetti, Jack
Michael, Jan 1947- 216
Michael, Livi 1960- 172
Michael, Manfred
    See Winterfeld, Henry
Michael, Olivia
    See Michael, Livi
Michaelis, Antonia 1979- 215
Michaels, Barbara
    See Peters, Elizabeth
Michaels, Jamie 195
Michaels, Joanne Louise
    See Teitelbaum, Michael
Michaels, Kristin
    See Williams, Jeanne
Michaels, Molly
    See Untermeyer, Louis
Michaels, Neal
    See Teitelbaum, Michael
Michaels, Rune 194
Michaels, Ski
    See Pellowski, Michael (Joseph)
Michaels, Steve 1955- 71
Michaels, William M. 1917- 77
Michalak, Jamie 1973- 217
Michel, Anna 1943- 49
    Brief entry 40
Michel, Francois 1948- 82
Michelin, Linda 183
Michelson, Richard 198
    Earlier sketch in SATA *173*
Micich, Paul 74
Mickelson, Scott 1963- 213
Micklish, Rita 1931- 12
Micklos, John, Jr. 1956- 173
    Earlier sketch in SATA *129*
Micklos J., John, Jr. 1956-
    See Micklos, John, Jr.
Micucci, Charles (Patrick, Jr.) 1959- 144
    Earlier sketch in SATA *82*
Middleton, Charlotte 230

Middleton, Haydn 1955- 152
    Earlier sketch in SATA *85*
Miers, Earl Schenck 1910-1972 1
    Obituary 26
Migdale, Lawrence 1951- 89
Miglio, Paige 1966- 201
Mikaelsen, Ben 1952- 173
    Earlier sketches in SATA *73, 107*
Mikaelsen, Benjamin John
    See Mikaelsen, Ben
Miklowitz, Gloria D. 1927- 129
    Earlier sketches in SATA *4, 68*
    See also SAAS *17*
Mikolaycak, Charles 1937-1993 78
    Obituary 75
    Earlier sketch in SATA *9*
    See also SAAS *4*
Mild, Warren (Paul) 1922- 41
Milelli, Pascal 1965- 135
Miles, Betty 1928- 78
    Earlier sketch in SATA *8*
    See also SAAS *9*
Miles, Miska
    See Martin, Patricia Miles
Miles, (Mary) Patricia 1930- 29
Miles, Patricia A.
    See Martin, Patricia Miles
Miles, Victoria 1966- 188
Milgrim, David 223
    Earlier sketches in SATA *158, 187*
Milgrom, Harry 1912-1978 25
Milhous, Katherine 1894-1977 15
Milich, Zoran 174
Milios, Rita 1949- 79
Militant
    See Sandburg, Carl
Millais, Raoul 1901- 77
Millar, Barbara F. 1924- 12
Millar, Margaret (Ellis Sturm) 1915-1994 61
    Obituary 79
Millard, Glenda 203
Millard, Kerry 204
Millbank, Captain H. R.
    See Ellis, Edward S.
Millen, C(ynthia) M. 1955- 114
Miller, Albert G(riffith) 1905-1982 12
    Obituary 31
Miller, Alice Ann 1958- 150
Miller, Alice P(atricia McCarthy) 22
Miller, Allan 1978- 216
Miller, Christopher 1976- 215
Miller, Debbie 1951- 160
    Earlier sketch in SATA *103*
Miller, Debbie S.
    See Miller, Debbie
Miller, Deborah Uchill 1944- 61
Miller, Don 1923- 15
Miller, Doris R.
    See Mosesson, Gloria R(ubin)
Miller, Eddie
    See Miller, Edward
Miller, Edna Anita 1920- 29
Miller, Edward 1905-1974 8
Miller, Edward 1964- 218
    Earlier sketch in SATA *183*
Miller, Elizabeth 1933- 41
Miller, Ellanita 1957- 87
Miller, Eugene 1925- 33
Miller, Frances A. 1937- 52
    Brief entry 46
Miller, Heather Lynn 1971- 214
Miller, Helen M(arkley) -1984 5
Miller, Helen Topping 1884-1960
    Obituary 29
Miller, Jane (Judith) 1925-1989 15
Miller, Jewel 1956- 73
Miller, John
    See Samachson, Joseph
Miller, Judi 117
Miller, Karen 1949- 210

Miller, Karen Hokanson
  See Miller, Karen
Miller, Kate 1948- 193
Miller, Kirsten 1973- 185
Miller, Louise (Rolfe) 1940- 76
Miller, M. L. 85
Miller, Madge 1918- 63
Miller, Margaret J.
  See Dale, Margaret J(essy) Miller
Miller, Marilyn (Jean) 1925- 33
Miller, Marvin 65
Miller, Mary
  See Northcott, (William) Cecil
Miller, Mary Beth 1942- 9
Miller, Mary Beth 1964- 185
Miller, Maryann 1943- 73
Miller, Natalie 1917-1976 35
Miller, Pat 1951- 214
Miller, Robert H. 1944- 91
Miller, Ron 1947- 185
Miller, Ruth White
  See White, Ruth
Miller, Sandra
  See Miller, Sandy
Miller, Sandra Peden
  See Miller, Sandy
Miller, Sandy 1948- 41
  Brief entry 35
Miller, Sarah 1969- 175
Miller, Virginia
  See Austin, Virginia
Miller, William R. 1959- 116
Miller Brothers
  See Miller, Allan
Milligan, Bryce 1953- 170
Milligan, Spike
  See Milligan, Terence Alan
Milligan, Terence Alan 1918-2002 29
  Obituary 134
  See also CLR 92
Millington, Ada
  See Deyneka, Anita
Millman, Isaac 1933- 140
Mills, Adam
  See Stanley, George Edward
Mills, Claudia 1954- 191
  Brief entry 41
  Earlier sketches in SATA 44, 89, 145
Mills, Elaine (Rosemary) 1941- 72
Mills, G. Riley 196
Mills, Joyce C. 1944- 102
Mills, Judith Christine 1956- 130
Mills, Yaroslava Surmach 1925-2008 35
Millspaugh, Ben P. 1936- 77
Millstead, Thomas E. 30
Millward, Gwen 202
Milne, A. A. 1882-1956 100
  See also YABC 1
  See also CLR 108
Milne, Alan Alexander
  See Milne, A. A.
Milne, Lorus J. 5
  See also CLR 22
  See also SAAS 18
Milne, Margery 5
  See also CLR 22
  See also SAAS 18
Milne, Terry
  See Milne, Theresa Ann
Milne, Theresa Ann 1964- 84
Milnes, Irma McDonough 1924- 101
Milonas, Rolf
  See Myller, Rolf
Milone, Karen
  See Dugan, Karen
Milone-Dugan, Karen
  See Dugan, Karen
Milord, Susan 1954- 200
  Earlier sketches in SATA 74, 147
Milotte, Alfred G(eorge) 1904-1989 11
  Obituary 62

Milstein, Linda 1954- 80
Milton, Ann 134
Milton, Hilary (Herbert) 1920- 23
Milton, John R(onald) 1924- 24
Milton, Joyce 1946- 101
  Brief entry 41
  Earlier sketch in SATA 52
Milusich, Janice 216
Milverton, Charles A.
  See Penzler, Otto
Milway, Alex 1978- 215
Milway, Katie Smith 1960- 203
Minahan, John A. 1956- 92
Minar, Barbra (Goodyear) 1940- 79
Minard, Rosemary 1939- 63
Minarik, Else Holmelund 1920- 127
  Earlier sketch in SATA 15
  See also CLR 33
Miner, Jane Claypool 1933- 103
  Brief entry 37
  Earlier sketch in SATA 38
Miner, Lewis S. 1909-1971 11
Mines, Jeanette 1948- 61
Mines, Jeanette Marie
  See Mines, Jeanette
Minier, Nelson
  See Stoutenburg, Adrien (Pearl)
Minnitt, Ronda Jacqueline
  See Armitage, David
Minor, Wendell 1944- 199
  Earlier sketches in SATA 78, 109, 164
Minter, Daniel 1961- 176
Mintonye, Grace 4
Miranda, Anne 1954- 109
  Earlier sketch in SATA 71
Miranda, Inaki 1983(?)- 207
Mirocha, Paul 192
Mirsky, Jeannette 1903-1987 8
  Obituary 51
Mirsky, Reba Paeff 1902-1966 1
Misako Rocks! 192
Misenta, Marisol
  See Innes, Stephanie
Mishica, Clare 1960- 91
Miskovits, Christine 1939- 10
Miss Frances
  See Horwich, Frances R(appaport)
Miss Read
  See Saint, Dora Jessie
Mister Rogers
  See Rogers, Fred McFeely
Mitchard, Jacquelyn 1956- 219
  Earlier sketches in SATA 98, 168
Mitchell, Adrian 1932-2008 166
  Obituary 200
  Earlier sketch in SATA 104
Mitchell, Allison
  See Griffin, W. E. B.
Mitchell, Betty Jo
  See Mitchell, B.J.
Mitchell, B.J. 1931- 120
Mitchell, Clyde
  See Ellison, Harlan
  and Silverberg, Robert
Mitchell, Cynthia 1922- 29
Mitchell, (Sibyl) Elyne (Keith) 1913- 10
Mitchell, Gladys (Maude Winifred)
  1901-1983 46
  Obituary 35
Mitchell, Jay
  See Roberson, Jennifer
Mitchell, Joyce Slayton 1933- 142
  Brief entry 43
  Earlier sketch in SATA 46
Mitchell, K. L.
  See Lamb, Elizabeth Searle
Mitchell, Kathy 1948- 59
Mitchell, Lori 1961- 128
Mitchell, Margaree King 1953- 84
Mitchell, Marianne 1947- 145
Mitchell, Rhonda 89

Mitchell, Saundra 1974(?)- 217
Mitchell, Stephen 1943- 199
Mitchell, Susan
  See Mitchell, Susan K.
Mitchell, Susan K. 1972- 210
Mitchell, Todd 1974- 191
Mitchell, Yvonne 1925-1979
  Obituary 24
Mitchelson, Mitch
  See Mitchelson, Peter Richard
Mitchelson, Peter Richard 1950- 104
Mitchison, Naomi (Margaret Haldane)
  1897-1999 24
  Obituary 112
Mitchnik, Helen 1901-1982 41
  Brief entry 35
Mitchum, Hank
  See Knott, William C(ecil, Jr.)
  and Murray, Stuart A. P.
  and Newton, D(wight) B(ennett)
  and Sherman, Jory (Tecumseh)
Mitgutsch, Ali 1935- 76
Mitsuhashi, Yoko 45
  Brief entry 33
Mitton, Jacqueline 1948- 162
  Earlier sketches in SATA 66, 115
Mitton, Simon 1946- 66
Mitton, Tony 1951- 203
  Earlier sketches in SATA 104, 149
Miura, Taro 1968- 181
Mizner, Elizabeth Howard 1907- 27
Mizumura, Kazue 18
Mlynowski, Sarah 1977(?)- 180
Mobin-Uddin, Asma 216
  Earlier sketch in SATA 172
Mobley, Joe A. 1945- 91
Moche, Dinah (Rachel) L(evine) 1936- 44
  Brief entry 40
Mochi, Ugo (A.) 1889-1977 38
Mochizuki, Ken 1954- 146
  Earlier sketch in SATA 81
  See also SAAS 22
Modarressi, Mitra 1967- 200
  Earlier sketch in SATA 126
Modell, Frank B. 1917- 39
  Brief entry 36
Modesitt, Jeanne 1953- 217
  Earlier sketches in SATA 92, 143
Modesitt, L.E., Jr. 1943- 164
  Earlier sketch in SATA 91
Modesitt, Leland Exton, Jr.
  See Modesitt, L.E., Jr.
Modrell, Dolores 1933- 72
Moe, Barbara 1937- 20
Moe, Jorgen (Ingebretsen) 1813-1882
  See CLR 104
Moed-Kass, Pnina 169
Moerbeek, Kees 1955- 98
Moeri, Louise 1924- 93
  Earlier sketch in SATA 24
  See also SAAS 10
Moesta, Rebecca 1956- 182
Moffett, Jami 1952- 84
Moffett, Mark W. 1957(?)- 203
Moffett, Martha (Leatherwood) 1934- 8
Mogensen, Suzanne A(ncher) 1946- 129
Mohammed, Khadra 197
Mohanty, Raja 223
Mohn, Peter B(urnet) 1934- 28
Mohn, Viola Kohl 1914- 8
Mohr, Nicholasa 1938- 97
  Autobiography Feature 113
  Earlier sketch in SATA 8
  See also CLR 22
  See also SAAS 8
Mok, Esther 1953- 93
Molan, Christine 1943- 84
Molarsky, Osmond 1909- 16
Moldon, Peter L(eonard) 1937- 49

Mole, John 1941- *103*
  Earlier sketch in SATA *36*
  See also CLR *61*
Molesworth, Mary Louisa 1839-1921 .... *98*
  See also CLR *166*
Molin, Charles
  See Mayne, William
Molina, Silvia 1946- *97*
Molk, Laurel 1957- *162*
  Earlier sketch in SATA *92*
Mollel, Tololwa M. 1952- *88*
Molloy, Anne Baker 1907-1999 .... *32*
Molloy, Michael (John) 1940- *162*
Molloy, Paul (George) 1924- *5*
Molnar, Haya Leah 1951(?)- *230*
Moloney, James 1954- *202*
  Autobiography Feature *144*
  Earlier sketches in SATA *94, 144*
Molski, Carol *215*
Momaday, N. Scott 1934- *48*
  Brief entry *30*
Momaday, Navarre Scott
  See Momaday, N. Scott
Monaco, Octavia 1963- *169*
Monagle, Bernie 1957- *121*
Moncure, Jane Belk 1926- *23*
Monjo, F(erdinand) N(icholas III)
  1924-1978 .... *16*
  See also CLR *2*
Monk, Isabell 1952- *136*
Monks, Lydia *189*
Monroe, Chris 1962- *219*
Monroe, Christine
  See Monroe, Chris
Monroe, Lyle
  See Heinlein, Robert A.
Monroe, Marion
  See Cox, Marion Monroe
Monroy, Manuel 1970- *196*
Monsell, Helen Albee 1895-1971 .... *24*
Monson-Burton, Marianne 1975- *139*
Montalbano, Andrea *231*
Montana, Bob 1920-1975
  Obituary *21*
Montanari, Eva 1977- *209*
Montecalvo, Janet *177*
Montenegro, Laura Nyman 1953- *95*
Montero, Gloria 1933- *109*
Montes, Marisa 1951- *144*
Montgomerie, Norah (Mary) 1913- *26*
Montgomery, Constance
  See Cappel, Constance
Montgomery, Elizabeth
  See Julesberg, Elizabeth Rider Montgomery
Montgomery, Elizabeth Rider
  See Julesberg, Elizabeth Rider Montgomery
Montgomery, Hugh (Edward) 1962- *146*
Montgomery, L. M. 1874-1942 .... *100*
  See also YABC *1*
  See also CLR *145*
Montgomery, Lucy Maud
  See Montgomery, L. M.
Montgomery, Michael G. 1952- *208*
Montgomery, Raymond A. (Jr.) 1936- *39*
Montgomery, Rutherford George 1894-1985 . *3*
Montgomery, Sy 1958- *184*
  Autobiography Feature *132*
  Earlier sketches in SATA *114, 132*
Montgomery, Vivian *36*
Monthei, Betty *179*
Montijo, Rhode *179*
Montileaux, Donald F. 1948- *183*
Montpetit, Charles 1958- *101*
Montresor, Beni 1926-2001 .... *38*
  Earlier sketch in SATA *3*
  See also SAAS *4*
Montserrat, Pep *181*

Monty Python
  See Chapman, Graham
  and Cleese, John (Marwood)
  and Gilliam, Terry
  and Idle, Eric
  and Jones, Terence Graham Parry
  and Palin, Michael
Moodie, Craig 1956- *172*
Moodie, Fiona 1952- *133*
Moody, Minerva
  See Alcott, Louisa May
Moody, Ralph Owen 1898-1982 .... *1*
Moon, Carl 1879(?)-1948 .... *25*
Moon, Grace (Purdie) 1877(?)-1947 .... *25*
Moon, Lily
  See Warnes, Tim
Moon, Nicola 1952- *147*
  Earlier sketch in SATA *96*
Moon, Pat 1946- *113*
Moon, Sheila 1910-1991 .... *5*
  Obituary *114*
Moon, Sheila Elizabeth
  See Moon, Sheila
Mooney, Bel 1946- *95*
Mooney, Bill 1936- *122*
Mooney, Elizabeth C(omstock) 1918-1986
  Obituary *48*
Mooney, William
  See Mooney, Bill
Moor, Emily
  See Deming, Richard
Moorcock, Michael 1939- *166*
  Earlier sketch in SATA *93*
Moorcock, Michael John
  See Moorcock, Michael
Moorcock, Michael John
  See Moorcock, Michael
Moore, Anne Carroll 1871-1961 .... *13*
Moore, Cheri
  See Ladd, Cheryl (Jean)
Moore, Clement Clarke 1779-1863 .... *18*
Moore, Cyd 1957- *186*
  Earlier sketches in SATA *83, 133*
Moore, Don W. 1905(?)-1986
  Obituary *48*
Moore, Elaine 1944- *86*
Moore, Eva 1942- *103*
  Earlier sketch in SATA *20*
Moore, Ishbel (Lindsay) 1954- *140*
Moore, Jack (William) 1941- *46*
  Brief entry *32*
Moore, Janet Gaylord 1905-1992 .... *18*
Moore, Jim 1946- *42*
Moore, John Travers 1908- *12*
Moore, Lilian 1909-2004 .... *137*
  Obituary *155*
  Earlier sketch in SATA *52*
  See also CLR *15*
Moore, Liz
  See Moore, M. Elizabeth
Moore, M. Elizabeth 1959- *156*
Moore, Margaret R(umberger) 1903- *12*
Moore, Margie *224*
  Earlier sketch in SATA *176*
Moore, Marianne 1887-1972 .... *20*
Moore, Marianne Craig
  See Moore, Marianne
Moore, Patrick (Alfred Caldwell) 1923- *49*
  Brief entry *39*
  See also SAAS *8*
Moore, Patrick 1959- *184*
Moore, Perry 1971-2011 .... *193*
Moore, Peter 1963- *175*
Moore, Peter G.
  See Moore, Peter
Moore, Raina 1970- *212*
Moore, Ray (S.) 1905(?)-1984
  Obituary *37*
Moore, Regina
  See Dunne, Mary Collins
Moore, Rosalie (Gertrude) 1910-2001 .... *9*

Moore, Ruth (Ellen) 1908-1989 .... *23*
Moore, Ruth Nulton 1923- *38*
Moore, S(arah) E. *23*
Moore, Sarah Margaret
  See Hodges, Margaret
Moore, Stephanie Perry 1969(?)- *214*
Moore, Tara 1950- *61*
Moore, Yvette 1958- *154*
  Earlier sketches in SATA *69, 70*
Moores, Dick
  See Moores, Richard (Arnold)
Moores, Richard (Arnold) 1909-1986
  Obituary *48*
Mooser, Stephen 1941- *75*
  Earlier sketch in SATA *28*
Mora, Francisco X(avier) 1952- *90*
Mora, Pat 1942- *186*
  Earlier sketches in SATA *92, 134*
  See also CLR *58*
Mora, Patricia
  See Mora, Pat
Morais, Flavio *207*
Morales, Magaly *225*
Morales, Yuyi *180*
  Earlier sketch in SATA *154*
Moran, Tom 1943- *60*
Moranville, Sharelle Byars *196*
  Earlier sketch in SATA *152*
Moray Williams, Ursula 1911-2006 .... *3*
  Obituary *177*
  See also SAAS *9*
Mordecai, Martin *220*
Morden, Simon 1966(?)- *211*
Mordhorst, Heidi 1964- *222*
Mordvinoff, Nicolas 1911-1973 .... *17*
More, Caroline
  See Cone, Molly (Lamken)
  and Strachan, Margaret Pitcairn
Moreau, Jean-Pierre
  See Jarrie, Martin
Moreno, Rene King *190*
Moreton, Andrew Esq.
  See Defoe, Daniel
Morey, Charles
  See Fletcher, Helen Jill
Morey, Walt(er Nelson) 1907-1992 .... *51*
  Obituary *70*
  Earlier sketch in SATA *3*
  See also SAAS *9*
Morgan, Alfred P(owell) 1889-1972 .... *33*
Morgan, Alison (Mary) 1930- *85*
  Earlier sketch in SATA *30*
Morgan, Anne 1954- *121*
Morgan, Christopher 1956- *199*
Morgan, Clay 1950- *198*
Morgan, Douglas
  See Macdonald, James D.
Morgan, Ellen
  See Bumstead, Kathleen Mary
Morgan, Geoffrey 1916- *46*
Morgan, Helen (Gertrude Louise)
  1921-1990 .... *29*
Morgan, Jane
  See Cooper, James Fenimore
  and Franklin, Jane (Morgan)
  and Moren, Sally M(oore)
Morgan, Lenore H. 1908-1976 .... *8*
Morgan, Mary 1957- *213*
  Earlier sketches in SATA *81, 114*
Morgan, McKayla
  See Basile, Gloria Vitanza
Morgan, Michaela
  See Basile, Gloria Vitanza
Morgan, Nicola 1961- *161*
Morgan, Nina 1953- *110*
Morgan, Pierr 1952- *122*
  Earlier sketch in SATA *77*
Morgan, Robin (Evonne) 1941- *80*
Morgan, Roxanne
  See Gentle, Mary
Morgan, Sarah (Nicola) 1959- *68*

Morgan, Shirley
  See Kiepper, Shirley Morgan
Morgan, Stacy T(owle) 1959- 104
Morgan, Stevie
  See Davies, Nicola
Morgan, Tom 1942- 42
Morgan, Wendy
  See Staub, Wendy Corsi
Morgan-Vanroyen, Mary
  See Morgan, Mary
Morgenstern, Susie Hoch 1945- 133
Mori, Hana 1909-1990(?) 88
Mori, Kyoko 1957- 122
  Autobiography Feature 126
  See also CLR 64
  See also SAAS 26
Moriarty, Jaclyn 1968- 162
Moriarty, William J. 1930- 127
Morice, Dave 1946- 93
Morin, Isobel V. 1928- 110
Morine, Hoder
  See Conroy, John Wesley
Morley, Ben 228
Morley, Taia 199
Morley, Wilfred Owen
  See Lowndes, Robert A(ugustine) W(ard)
Morningstar, Mildred (Whaley) 1912-1997 .. 61
  Obituary 114
Morozumi, Atsuko 217
  Earlier sketch in SATA 110
Morpurgo, Michael 1943- 225
  Earlier sketches in SATA 93, 143, 184
  See also CLR 51
Morrah, Dave
  See Morrah, David Wardlaw, Jr.
Morrah, David Wardlaw, Jr. 1914-1991 10
Morreale-de la Garza, Phyllis
  See De la Garza, Phyllis
Morressy, John 1930-2006 23
Morrill, Leslie H(olt) 1934-2003 48
  Brief entry 33
  Obituary 148
  See also SAAS 22
Morris, Carla 210
Morris, Carla D.
  See Morris, Carla
Morris, Chris(topher Crosby) 1946- 66
Morris, Deborah 1956- 91
Morris, Desmond 1928- 14
Morris, Desmond John
  See Morris, Desmond
Morris, Don 1954- 83
Morris, Gerald 1963- 207
  Earlier sketches in SATA 107, 150
Morris, Gerald Paul
  See Morris, Gerald
Morris, Gilbert (Leslie) 1929- 104
Morris, Jackie 202
  Earlier sketch in SATA 151
Morris, Janet (Ellen) 1946- 66
Morris, Jay
  See Tatham, Julie Campbell
Morris, (Margaret) Jean 1924- 98
Morris, Jeffrey
  See Morris, Jeffrey Brandon
Morris, Jeffrey B.
  See Morris, Jeffrey Brandon
Morris, Jeffrey Brandon 1941- 92
Morris, Jennifer E. 1969- 179
Morris, Jill 1936- 165
  Earlier sketch in SATA 119
Morris, Juddi 85
Morris, Judy K. 1936- 61
Morris, Oradel Nolen 128
Morris, Richard 1969- 224
Morris, Robert A(da) 1933- 7
Morris, William 1913-1994 29
Morrison, Angela 218
Morrison, Bill 1935- 66
  Brief entry 37

Morrison, Chloe Anthony Wofford
  See Morrison, Toni
Morrison, Dorothy Nafus 29
Morrison, Frank 1971- 226
  Earlier sketch in SATA 185
Morrison, Gordon 1944- 183
  Earlier sketches in SATA 87, 128
Morrison, Joan 1922- 65
Morrison, Lillian 1917- 108
  Earlier sketch in SATA 3
Morrison, Lucile Phillips 1896- 17
Morrison, Martha A. 1948- 77
Morrison, Meighan 1966- 90
Morrison, P.R. 196
Morrison, Richard
  See Lowndes, Robert A(ugustine) W(ard)
Morrison, Robert
  See Lowndes, Robert A(ugustine) W(ard)
Morrison, Roberta
  See Webb, Jean Francis (III)
Morrison, Slade 1964-2010 228
Morrison, Susan Dudley
  See Gold, Susan Dudley
Morrison, Taylor 1971- 187
  Earlier sketches in SATA 95, 159
Morrison, Toni 1931- 144
  Earlier sketch in SATA 57
  See also CLR 99
Morrison, Velma Ford 1909- 21
Morrison, Wilbur Howard 1915- 64
Morrison, William
  See Samachson, Joseph
Morriss, James E(dward) 1932- 8
Morrissey, Dean 183
Morrow, Barbara Olenyik 1952- 167
Morrow, Betty
  See Bacon, Elizabeth
Morrow, Sue Anne 1966- 218
Morse, C. Scott
  See Morse, Scott
Morse, Carol
  See Yeakley, Marjory Hall
Morse, C.S.
  See Morse, Scott
Morse, Dorothy B(ayley) 1906-1979
  Obituary 24
Morse, Flo 1921- 30
Morse, Scott 1973- 200
Morse, Tony 1953- 129
Mort, Vivian
  See Cromie, Alice Hamilton
Mortensen, Denise Dowling 179
Mortensen, Lori 1955- 221
Mortimer, Anne 1958- 206
  Earlier sketch in SATA 116
Mortimer, Mary H.
  See Coury, Louise Andree
Morton, Alexandra (Hubbard) 1957- 144
Morton, Anthony
  See Arthur, Robert, (Jr.)
Morton, Christine
  See Morton-Shaw, Christine
Morton, Jane 1931- 50
Morton, Joseph C. 1932- 156
Morton, Lee Jack, Jr. 1928- 32
Morton, Miriam 1918(?)-1985 9
  Obituary 46
Morton-Shaw, Christine 1957- 211
Mosatche, Harriet 1949- 122
Mosatche, Harriet S.
  See Mosatche, Harriet
Moscow, Alvin 1925- 3
Mosel, Arlene (Tichy) 1921-1996 7
Moseley, James W(illett) 1931- 139
Moseng, Elisabeth 1967- 90
Moser, Barry 1940- 185
  Earlier sketches in SATA 56, 79, 138
  See also CLR 49
  See also SAAS 15
Moser, Don(ald Bruce) 1932- 31
Moser, Laura 194

Moser, Lisa 192
Moses, Sheila P. 1961- 168
Moses, Will 1956- 178
  Earlier sketch in SATA 120
Mosesson, Gloria R(ubin) 24
Mosher, Richard 1949- 120
Moskin, Marietta D(unston) 1928- 23
Moskof, Martin Stephen 1930- 27
Mosley, Francis 1957- 57
Moss, Don(ald) 1920- 11
Moss, Elaine (Dora) 1924- 57
  Brief entry 31
Moss, Jeff(rey) 1942-1998 73
  Obituary 106
Moss, Marissa 1959- 216
  Earlier sketches in SATA 71, 104, 163
  See also CLR 134
Moss, Miriam 1955- 202
  Earlier sketches in SATA 76, 140
Moss, Thylias 1954- 108
Moss, Thylias Rebecca Brasier
  See Moss, Thylias
Most, Bernard 1937- 134
  Brief entry 40
  Earlier sketches in SATA 48, 91
Mosz, Gosia 1972- 194
Mott, Evelyn Clarke 1962- 133
  Earlier sketch in SATA 75
Motz, Lloyd 1909-2004 20
Mould, Chris 205
Mould, Edwin
  See Whitlock, Ralph
Moulton, Mark Kimball 212
Mouly, Francoise 155
Mountain, Robert
  See Montgomery, Raymond A. (Jr.)
Mountfield, David
  See Grant, Neil
Mourlevat, Jean-Claude 1952- 187
Mourning, Tuesday 206
Moussard, Jacqueline 1924- 24
Mowat, Claire 1933- 123
Mowat, Claire Angel Wheeler
  See Mowat, Claire
Mowat, Farley 1921- 55
  Earlier sketch in SATA 3
  See also CLR 20
Mowat, Farley McGill
  See Mowat, Farley
Mowll, Joshua 1970(?)- 188
Mowry, Jess 1960- 131
  Autobiography Feature 131
  Earlier sketch in SATA 109
  See also CLR 65
Moxley, Sheila 1966- 96
Moyer, Terry J. 1937- 94
Moyes, Patricia
  See Haszard, Patricia Moyes
Moyler, Alan (Frank Powell) 1926- 36
Mozelle, Shirley 179
Mozley, Charles 1915- 43
  Brief entry 32
Mphahlele, Es'kia 1919-2008 119
  Obituary 198
Mphahlele, Ezekiel
  See Mphahlele, Es'kia
Mphahlele, Zeke
  See Mphahlele, Es'kia
Mr. McGillicuddy
  See Abisch, Roslyn Kroop
Mr. Sniff
  See Abisch, Roslyn Kroop
Mr. Tivil
  See Lorkowski, Thomas V(incent)
Mr. Wizard
  See Herbert, Don
Mraz, David 1947- 219
Mrs. Fairstar
  See Horne, Richard Henry Hengist
Muchamore, Robert 1972- 175
Muchmore, Jo Ann 1937- 103

Mude, O.
  See Gorey, Edward (St. John)
Mudgeon, Apeman
  See Mitchell, Adrian
Mueller, Jorg 1942- 67
  See also CLR 43
Mueller, Miranda R. 201
Mueller, Virginia 1924- 28
Muggs
  See Watkins, Lois
Muir, Diana
  See Appelbaum, Diana Muir Karter
Muir, Frank (Herbert) 1920-1998 30
Muir, Helen 1937- 65
Muirhead, Margaret 220
Mukerji, Dhan Gopal 1890-1936 40
  See also CLR 10
Mulcahy, Lucille Burnett 12
Muldrow, Diane 229
Mulford, Philippa G. 1948- 112
  Earlier sketch in SATA 43
Mulford, Philippa Greene
  See Mulford, Philippa G.
Mulgan, Catherine 1931- 24
Mulila, Vigad G.
  See Maillu, David G(ian)
Mull, Brandon 1974- 190
Mullen, Michael 1937- 122
Muller, Billex
  See Ellis, Edward S.
Muller, Birte 1973- 214
Muller, Jorg
  See Mueller, Jorg
Muller, (Lester) Robin 1953- 86
Mullin, Caryl Cude 1969- 130
Mullins, Edward S(wift) 1922- 10
Mullins, Hilary 1962- 84
Mulock, Dinah Maria
  See Craik, Dinah Maria (Mulock)
Mulvihill, William Patrick 1923- 8
Mumford, Ruth
  See Dallas, Ruth
Mumy, Bill 1954- 112
Mun
  See Leaf, (Wilbur) Munro
Munari, Bruno 1907-1998 15
  See also CLR 9
Munce, Ruth Hill 1898- 12
Mundy, Simon 1954- 64
Mundy, Simon Andrew James Hainault
  See Mundy, Simon
Munger, Nancy 170
Munowitz, Ken 1935-1977 14
Munoz, Claudio 208
Munoz, William 1949- 92
  Earlier sketch in SATA 42
Munro, Alice 1931- 29
Munro, Alice Anne
  See Munro, Alice
Munro, Eleanor 1928- 37
Munro, Roxie 1945- 223
  Earlier sketches in SATA 58, 136, 184
Munsch, Bob
  See Munsch, Robert (Norman)
Munsch, Robert (Norman) 1945- 120
  Brief entry 48
  Earlier sketches in SATA 50, 83
  See also CLR 19
Munsinger, Lynn 1951- 221
  Earlier sketches in SATA 33, 94, 177
Munson, Derek 1970- 139
Munson, R. W.
  See Karl, Jean E(dna)
Munson-Benson, Tunie 1946- 15
Munsterberg, Peggy 1921- 102
Muntean, Michaela 182
Munthe, Nelly 1947- 53
Munves, James (Albert) 1922- 30
Munzer, Martha E. 1899-1999 4
Murawski, Darlyne A. 193

Murch, Mel
  See Manes, Stephen
Murdoch, David H(amilton) 1937- 96
Murdoch, Patricia 1957- 192
Murdock, Catherine Gilbert 185
Murhall, J(acqueline) J(ane) 1964- 143
Murphy, Barbara Beasley 1933- 130
  Earlier sketch in SATA 5
Murphy, Claire Rudolf 1951- 137
  Earlier sketch in SATA 76
Murphy, E(mmett) Jefferson 1926- 4
Murphy, Elizabeth Ann Maureen
  See Murphy, Liz
Murphy, Jill 1949- 214
  Earlier sketches in SATA 37, 70, 142
  See also CLR 39
Murphy, Jill Frances
  See Murphy, Jill
Murphy, Jim 1947- 224
  Brief entry 32
  Earlier sketches in SATA 37, 77, 124, 185
  See also CLR 53
Murphy, Joseph E., Jr. 1930- 65
Murphy, Kelly 1977- 190
  Earlier sketch in SATA 143
Murphy, Liz 1964- 210
Murphy, Louise 1943- 155
Murphy, Mary 1961- 196
Murphy, Pat
  See Murphy, E(mmett) Jefferson
Murphy, Patricia J. 1963- 132
Murphy, Rita 180
Murphy, Robert (William) 1902-1971 10
Murphy, Shirley Rousseau 1928- 126
  Earlier sketches in SATA 36, 71
  See also SAAS 18
Murphy, Stuart J. 1942- 157
  Earlier sketch in SATA 115
Murphy, Thomas Basil, Jr. 1935- 191
Murphy, Tim
  See Murphy, Jim
Murphy, Tom
  See Murphy, Thomas Basil, Jr.
Murray, John 1923- 39
Murray, Kirsty 1960- 165
  Earlier sketch in SATA 108
Murray, Marguerite 1917- 63
Murray, Marian 5
Murray, Martine 1965- 125
Murray, (Judith) Michele (Freedman)
  1933-1974 7
Murray, Ossie 1938- 43
Murray, Peter
  See Hautman, Pete
Murrow, Liza Ketchum
  See Ketchum, Liza
Musgrave, Florence 1902-1999 3
Musgrove, Margaret W(ynkoop) 1943- 124
  Earlier sketch in SATA 26
Musgrove, Marianne 207
Mussey, Virginia Howell
  See Ellison, Virginia H(owell)
Mussey, Virginia T.H.
  See Ellison, Virginia H(owell)
Mussi, Sarah 206
Mutel, Cornelia F. 1947- 74
Muth, Jon J. 206
  Earlier sketch in SATA 165
Mutz
  See Kuenstler, Morton
Mwangi, Meja 1948- 174
My Brother's Brother
  See Chekhov, Anton
Myers, Anna 220
  Earlier sketch in SATA 160
Myers, Arthur 1917- 91
  Earlier sketch in SATA 35
Myers, Bernice 81
  Earlier sketch in SATA 9
Myers, Caroline Elizabeth Clark
  1887-1980 28

Myers, Christopher 1975- 183
  See also CLR 97
Myers, Edward 1950- 227
  Earlier sketches in SATA 96, 172
Myers, Elisabeth P(erkins) 1918- 36
Myers, (Mary) Hortense (Powner)
  1913-1987 10
Myers, Jack 1913-2006 83
  Obituary 178
Myers, Jack Edgar
  See Myers, Jack
Myers, Lou 1915-2005 81
  Obituary 171
Myers, Louis
  See Myers, Lou
Myers, R.E. 1924- 119
Myers, Robert Eugene
  See Myers, R.E.
Myers, Tim 1953- 176
  Earlier sketch in SATA 147
Myers, Timothy Joseph
  See Myers, Tim
Myers, Walter Dean 1937- 229
  Brief entry 27
  Earlier sketches in SATA 41, 71, 109, 157,
  193
  See also CLR 110
  See also SAAS 2
Myers, Walter M.
  See Myers, Walter Dean
Myller, Rolf 1926-2006 27
  Obituary 175
Myra, Harold L(awrence) 1939- 46
  Brief entry 42
Myracle, Lauren 1969- 204
  Earlier sketch in SATA 162
Myrus, Donald (Richard) 1927- 23
Mysterious Traveler, The
  See Arthur, Robert, (Jr.)

N

Na, An 149
Na, Il Sung 231
Naaslund, Goorel Kristina 1940- 170
Nadel, Laurie 1948- 74
Naden, Corinne J. 1930- 166
  Earlier sketch in SATA 79
Nadimi, Suzan 188
Nadol, Jen 228
Nagda, Ann Whitehead 199
Nagel, Andreas Fischer
  See Fischer-Nagel, Andreas
Nagel, Heiderose Fischer
  See Fischer-Nagel, Heiderose
Nagle, Shane 176
Nahoko, Uehashi
  See Uehashi, Nahoko
Naidoo, Beverley 1943- 180
  Earlier sketches in SATA 63, 135
  See also CLR 29
Nails, Jennifer 213
Naiyomah, Wilson Kimeli 1977- 226
Nakae, Noriko 1940- 59
Nakata, Hiroe 205
Nakatani, Chiyoko 1930-1981 55
  Brief entry 40
  See also CLR 30
Nally, Susan W. 1947- 90
Namioka, Lensey 1929- 157
  Autobiography Feature 116
  Earlier sketches in SATA 27, 89
  See also CLR 48
  See also SAAS 24
Namovicz, Gene Inyart 1927- 6
Nance, Andrew 210
Nanji, Shenaaz 1954- 204
  Earlier sketch in SATA 131
Nanogak Agnes 1925- 61

Napier, Mark
  See Laffin, John (Alfred Charles)
Napoli, Donna Jo 1948- 230
  Autobiography Feature 230
  Earlier sketches in SATA *92, 137, 190*
  See also CLR *51*
  See also SAAS *23*
Napp, Daniel 1974- 204
Narahashi, Keiko 1959- *115*
  Earlier sketch in SATA *79*
Narayan, R. K. 1906-2001 62
Narayan, Rasipuram Krishnaswami
  See Narayan, R. K.
Nascimbene, Yan 1949- 173
  Earlier sketch in SATA *133*
Nash, Bruce M(itchell) 1947- 34
Nash, Fredric Ogden
  See Nash, Ogden
Nash, Linell
  See Smith, Linell Nash
Nash, Mary (Hughes) 1925- 41
Nash, Ogden 1902-1971 46
  Earlier sketch in SATA *2*
Nash, Renea Denise 1963- 81
Nast, Elsa Ruth
  See Watson, Jane Werner
Nast, Thomas 1840-1902 51
  Brief entry 33
Nastick, Sharon 1954- 41
Natale, Vince 196
Natalini, Sandro 1970- 222
Natarajan, Srividya 187
Nathan, Adele (Gutman) 1900(?)-1986
  Obituary 48
Nathan, Amy 155
  Earlier sketch in SATA *104*
Nathan, Dorothy (Goldeen) (?)-1966 15
Nathan, Robert (Gruntal) 1894-1985 6
  Obituary 43
Nathanson, Laura Walther 1941- 57
Nation, Kaleb 1988- 222
Natti, Lee 1919- 67
  Earlier sketch in SATA *1*
  See also SAAS *3*
Natti, Susanna 1948- 125
  Earlier sketch in SATA *32*
Nau, Thomas 186
Naughtie, Eleanor
  See Updale, Eleanor
Naughton, Bill
  See Naughton, William John (Francis)
Naughton, James Franklin 1957- 85
Naughton, Jim
  See Naughton, James Franklin
Naughton, William John (Francis)
  1910-1992 86
Navarra, John Gabriel 1927- 8
Nayeri, Dina 226
Naylor, Penelope 1941- 10
Naylor, Phyllis 1933-
  See Naylor, Phyllis Reynolds
Naylor, Phyllis Reynolds 1933- 209
  Autobiography Feature 152
  See also CLR *135*
  See also SAAS *10*
Nazarian, Nikki
  See Nichols, Cecilia Fawn
Nazaroff, Alexander I(vanovich) 1898-1981 .. 4
Nazoa, Aquiles 1920-1976 198
Neal, Harry Edward 1906-1993 5
  Obituary 76
Neal, Michael
  See Teitelbaum, Michael
Nearing, Penny 1916- 47
  Brief entry 42
Nebel, Gustave E. 45
  Brief entry 33
Nebel, Mimouca
  See Nebel, Gustave E.
Nee, Kay Bonner 10
Needham, Kate 1962- 95

Needle, Jan 1943- 98
  Earlier sketch in SATA *30*
  See also CLR *43*
  See also SAAS *23*
Needleman, Jacob 1934- 6
Neel, David 1960- 82
Neel, Preston 1959- 93
Neff, Henry H. 1973- 221
Negri, Rocco 1932- *12*
Negrin, Fabian 1963- 189
Neidigh, Sherry 1956- 204
Neier, Aryeh 1937- 59
Neigoff, Anne *13*
Neigoff, Mike 1920- *13*
Neilan, Eujin Kim 1969- 200
Neilson, Frances Fullerton (Jones)
  1910-2001 .... *14*
Neimark, Anne E. 1935- 145
  Earlier sketch in SATA *4*
Neimark, Paul G. 1934- 80
  Brief entry 37
Neitzel, Shirley 1941- *134*
  Earlier sketch in SATA *77*
Nell
  See Hanna, Nell(ie L.)
Nelscott, Kris
  See Rusch, Kristine Kathryn
Nelson, Blake 1960- *177*
Nelson, Catherine Chadwick 1926- 87
Nelson, Cordner 1918-2009 54
  Brief entry 29
Nelson, Cordner Bruce
  See Nelson, Cordner
Nelson, D.A. 1970- 215
Nelson, Dawn Ann
  See Nelson, D.A.
Nelson, Drew 1952- 77
Nelson, Esther L. 1928- *13*
Nelson, Jandy 229
Nelson, Jim A.
  See Stotter, Mike
Nelson, Julie L. 1970- *117*
Nelson, Kadir 213
  Earlier sketches in SATA *154, 181*
Nelson, Kris
  See Rusch, Kristine Kathryn
Nelson, Lawrence E(rnest) 1928-1977
  Obituary 28
Nelson, Marilyn 1946- 60
  Autobiography Feature 180
Nelson, Mary Carroll 1929- 23
Nelson, O. Terry 1941- 62
Nelson, Peter 1953- 73
Nelson, Peter N.
  See Nelson, Peter
Nelson, R. A. 197
Nelson, Richard K(ing) 1941- 65
Nelson, Robin Laura 1971- 141
Nelson, Roy Paul 1923- 59
Nelson, S.D. *181*
Nelson, Sharlene (P.) 1933- 96
Nelson, Suzanne 1976- 184
Nelson, Ted (W.) 1931- 96
Nelson, Theresa 1948- 143
  Autobiography Feature 143
  Earlier sketch in SATA *79*
Nelson, Vaunda Micheaux 1953- 220
Nemeth, Sally 187
Neri, G. 197
Neri, Greg
  See Neri, G.
Neri, Gregory
  See Neri, G.
Nerlove, Miriam 1959- 53
  Brief entry 49
Nesbit, E. 1858-1924 100
  See also YABC *1*
  See also CLR *70*
Nesbit, Edith
  See Nesbit, E.

Nesbit, Troy
  See Folsom, Franklin (Brewster)
Nespojohn, Katherine V(eronica) 1912-1975 . 7
Ness, Evaline (Michelow) 1911-1986 26
  Obituary 49
  Earlier sketch in SATA *1*
  See also CLR *6*
  See also SAAS *1*
Ness, Patrick 1971- 207
Nestor, Larry 1940- 149
Nestor, William P(rodromos) 1947- 49
Nethery, Mary 93
Neubecker, Robert 214
  Earlier sketch in SATA *170*
Neuberger, Julia (Babette Sarah) 1950- 142
  Earlier sketch in SATA *78*
Neufeld, John (Arthur) 1938- *131*
  Autobiography Feature *131*
  Earlier sketches in SATA *6, 81*
  See also CLR *52*
  See also SAAS *3*
Neuhaus, David 1958- 83
Neumeyer, Peter F(lorian) 1929- *13*
Neurath, Marie (Reidemeister) 1898-1986 ..... *1*
Neuschwander, Cindy 1953- 157
  Earlier sketch in SATA *107*
Neusner, Jacob 1932- 38
Neville, Charles
  See Bodsworth, (Charles) Fred(erick)
Neville, Emily Cheney 1919- *1*
  See also SAAS *2*
Neville, Mary
  See Woodrich, Mary Neville
Nevins, Albert (Francis) J(erome)
  1915-1997 20
Nevius, Carol 1955- 186
Newberger, Devra
  See Speregen, Devra Newberger
Newberry, Clare Turlay 1903-1970 .... *1*
  Obituary 26
Newbery, John 1713-1767 20
  See also CLR *147*
Newbery, Linda 1952- 184
  Earlier sketch in SATA *142*
Newbigging, Martha 198
Newbold, Greg 199
Newcomb, Ellsworth
  See Kenny, Ellsworth Newcomb
Newcombe, Eugene A. 1923-1990 45
  Brief entry 33
Newcombe, Jack
  See Newcombe, Eugene A.
Newcome, Robert 1955- 91
Newcome, Zita 1959- 88
Newell, Crosby
  See Bonsall, Crosby Barbara (Newell)
Newell, Edythe W(eatherford) 1910-1989 .... *11*
Newell, Hope Hockenberry 1896-1965 24
Newfeld, Frank 1928- 26
Newgarden, Mark 1959- 194
Newland, Gillian 220
Newlon, (Frank) Clarke 1905(?)-1982 6
  Obituary 33
Newman, Barbara Johansen 191
Newman, C.J.
  See Newman, Coleman J.
Newman, Coleman J. 1935- 82
Newman, Daisy 1904-1994 27
  Obituary 78
Newman, Gerald 1939- 46
  Brief entry 42
Newman, Jeff 1976- 228
Newman, Jerry
  See Newman, Coleman J.
Newman, Leslea 1955- *134*
  Earlier sketches in SATA *71, 128*
Newman, Margaret
  See Potter, Margaret
Newman, Marjorie 146
Newman, Matthew (Harrison) 1955- 56
Newman, Nanette 1934- *162*

Newman, Robert (Howard) 1909-1988 87
   Obituary 60
   Earlier sketch in SATA 4
Newman, Shirlee P(etkin) 144
   Earlier sketches in SATA 10, 90
Newsom, Carol 1948- 92
   Earlier sketch in SATA 40
Newsom, Tom 1944- 80
Newth, Mette 1942- 140
Newton, David E(dward) 1933- 67
Newton, James R(obert) 1935- 23
Newton, Jill 1964- 200
Newton, Robert 1965- 191
Newton, Suzanne 1936- 77
   Earlier sketch in SATA 5
Newton, Vanessa
   See Newton, Vanessa Brantley
Newton, Vanessa Brantley 1962(?)- 206
Ney, John 1923- 43
   Brief entry 33
Nez, John 218
   Earlier sketch in SATA 155
Nez, John Abbott
   See Nez, John
Ng, Franklin 82
Ngui, Marc 1972- 229
Nguyen, Vincent 226
   Earlier sketch in SATA 187
Nichol, B(arrie) P(hillip) 1944-1988 66
Nicholas, Louise D.
   See Watkins, Dawn L.
Nicholls, Judith (Ann) 1941- 61
Nicholls, Sally 1983- 209
Nichols, Cecilia Fawn 1906-1987 12
Nichols, Grace 1950- 164
   Earlier sketch in SATA 98
Nichols, Janet (Louise) 1952- 67
Nichols, Judy 1947- 124
Nichols, Leigh
   See Koontz, Dean
Nichols, Michael 1952- 215
Nichols, Nick
   See Nichols, Michael
Nichols, Paul
   See Hawks, Robert
Nichols, Peter
   See Youd, Samuel
Nichols, (Joanna) Ruth 1948- 15
   See also CLR 149
Nichols, Travis 206
Nicholson, C. R.
   See Nicole, Christopher
Nicholson, Christina
   See Nicole, Christopher
Nicholson, Joyce Thorpe 1919-2011 35
Nicholson, Lois P. 1949- 88
Nicholson, Robin
   See Nicole, Christopher
Nicholson, William 180
Nicholson, William 1872-1949
   See CLR 76
Nickel, Barbara 1966- 188
Nickell, Joe 1944- 167
   Earlier sketch in SATA 73
Nickelsburg, Janet 1893-1983 11
Nickerson, Betty 1922- 14
Nickerson, Elizabeth
   See Nickerson, Betty
Nickl, Barbara (Elisabeth) 1939- 56
Nicklaus, Carol 62
   Brief entry 33
Nickle, John 181
Nickless, Will 1902-1979(?) 66
Nic Leodhas, Sorche
   See Alger, Leclaire (Gowans)
Nicol, Ann
   See Turnbull, Ann
Nicolas
   See Mordvinoff, Nicolas
Nicolay, Helen 1866-1954
   See YABC 1

Nicole, Christopher 1930- 5
Nicole, Christopher Robin
   See Nicole, Christopher
Nicoll, Helen 1937- 87
Nicolson, Cynthia Pratt 1949- 141
Ni Dhuibhne, Eilis 1954- 91
Niehaus, Paddy Bouma
   See Bouma, Paddy
Nields, Nerissa 1967- 166
Nielsen, Kay (Rasmus) 1886-1957 16
   See also CLR 16
Nielsen, Laura F. 1960- 93
Nielsen, Laura Farnsworth
   See Nielsen, Laura F.
Nielsen, Nancy J. 1951- 77
Nielsen, Susin 1964- 195
Nielsen, Virginia
   See McCall, Virginia Nielsen
Nielsen-Fernlund, Susin
   See Nielsen, Susin
Niemann, Christoph 1970- 191
Nieuwsma, Milton J(ohn) 1941- 142
Nightingale, Sandy 1953- 76
Nikolajeva, Maria 1952- 127
Nikola-Lisa, W. 1951- 180
   Earlier sketch in SATA 71
Niland, Deborah 1951- 172
   Earlier sketch in SATA 27
Niland, Kilmeny 75
Nilsen, Anna 1948- 174
   Earlier sketch in SATA 96
Nilsson, Eleanor 1939- 117
   Earlier sketch in SATA 81
   See also SAAS 23
Nilsson, Per 1954- 159
Nimmo, Jenny 1944- 144
   Earlier sketch in SATA 87
   See also CLR 44
Nishimura, Kae 196
Niven, Larry 1938- 171
   Earlier sketch in SATA 95
Niven, Laurence Van Cott
   See Niven, Larry
Niven, Laurence VanCott
   See Niven, Larry
Nivola, Claire A. 1947- 208
   Earlier sketches in SATA 84, 140
Nix, Garth 1963- 210
   Earlier sketches in SATA 97, 143
   See also CLR 68
Nixon, Hershell Howard 1923- 42
Nixon, Joan Lowery 1927-2003 115
   Obituary 146
   Earlier sketches in SATA 8, 44, 78
   See also CLR 24
   See also SAAS 9
Nixon, K.
   See Nixon, Kathleen Irene (Blundell)
Nixon, Kathleen Irene (Blundell)
   1894-1988(?) 14
   Obituary 59
Nobati, Eugenia 1968- 201
Nobisso, Josephine 1953- 121
   Earlier sketch in SATA 78
Noble, Iris (Davis) 1922-1986 5
   Obituary 49
Noble, Marty 1947- 125
   Earlier sketch in SATA 97
Noble, Trinka Hakes 1944- 197
   Brief entry 37
   Earlier sketch in SATA 123
Nobleman, Marc Tyler 1972- 203
Noda, Takayo 1961- 168
Nodelman, Perry 1942- 101
Nodset, Joan L.
   See Lexau, Joan M.
Noel Hume, Ivor 1927- 65
Noestlinger, Christine
   See Nostlinger, Christine
Noguere, Suzanne 1947- 34

Nolan, Dennis 1945- 166
   Brief entry 34
   Earlier sketches in SATA 42, 92
Nolan, Han 1956- 157
   Earlier sketch in SATA 109
Nolan, Janet 1956- 191
   Earlier sketch in SATA 145
Nolan, Jeannette Covert 1897-1974 2
   Obituary 27
Nolan, Lucy 215
Nolan, Paul T(homas) 1919- 48
Nolan, William F. 1928- 88
   Brief entry 28
Nolan, William Francis
   See Nolan, William F.
Nolen, Jerdine 1953- 157
   Earlier sketch in SATA 105
Noll, Amanda 219
Noll, Sally 1946- 82
Nolte, Jack
   See Carter, Scott William
Noonan, Brandon 1979- 184
Noonan, Diana 1960- 146
Noonan, Julia 1946- 148
   Earlier sketches in SATA 4, 95
Norac, Carl 1960- 166
Norcross, John
   See Conroy, John Wesley
Nordan, Robert W(arren) 1934-2004 133
Nordhoff, Charles Bernard 1887-1947 23
Nordlicht, Lillian 29
Nordstrom, Ursula 1910-1988 3
   Obituary 57
Nordtvedt, Matilda 1926- 67
Norling, Beth 1969- 149
Norman, Charles 1904-1996 38
   Obituary 92
Norman, Geoffrey 223
Norman, Howard
   See Norman, Howard A.
Norman, Howard A. 1949- 81
Norman, James
   See Schmidt, James Norman
Norman, Jay
   See Arthur, Robert, (Jr.)
Norman, Lilith 1927- 120
   Earlier sketch in SATA 86
Norman, Mary 1931- 36
Norman, Steve
   See Pashko, Stanley
Norment, Lisa 1966- 91
Norris, Gunilla Brodde 1939- 20
North, Andrew
   See Norton, Andre
North, Anthony
   See Koontz, Dean
North, Captain George
   See Stevenson, Robert Louis
North, Captain George
   See Stevenson, Robert Louis
North, Howard
   See Trevor, Elleston
North, Joan 1920- 16
North, Milou
   See Erdrich, Louise
North, Robert
   See Withers, Carl A.
North, Sara
   See Bonham, Barbara Thomas
   and Hager, Jean
North, Sherry 201
North, Sterling 1906-1974 45
   Obituary 26
   Earlier sketch in SATA 1
Northcott, (William) Cecil 1902-1987
   Obituary 55
Northeast, Brenda V(ictoria) 1948- 106
Northmore, Elizabeth Florence 1906-1974 . 122
Norton, Alice Mary
   See Norton, Andre

Norton, Andre 1912-2005 91
  Earlier sketches in SATA *1, 43*
  See also CLR *50*
Norton, Browning
  See Norton, Frank R. B(rowning)
Norton, Frank R. B(rowning) 1909-1989 10
Norton, Mary 1903-1992 60
  Obituary 72
  Earlier sketch in SATA *18*
  See also CLR *140*
Nosredna, Trebor
  See Anderson, Bob
Nostlinger, Christine 1936- 162
  Brief entry 37
  Earlier sketch in SATA *64*
  See also CLR *12*
Nourse, Alan E(dward) 1928-1992 48
  See also CLR *33*
Novak, Matt 1962- 204
  Brief entry 52
  Earlier sketches in SATA *60, 104, 165*
Novelli, Luca 1947- 61
Novgorodoff, Danica 1982(?)- 215
Nowell, Elizabeth Cameron 12
Noyes, Deborah 1965- 194
  Earlier sketch in SATA *145*
Nugent, Cynthia 1954- 205
Nugent, Nicholas 1949- 73
Numberman, Neil 1981(?)- 220
Numeroff, Laura 1953- 206
  Earlier sketches in SATA *28, 90, 142*
  See also CLR *85*
Numeroff Joffe, Laura
  See Numeroff, Laura
Nunes, Lygia Bojunga 1932- 154
  Earlier sketch in SATA *75*
Nunn, Laura (Donna) Silverstein 1968- 124
Nurenberg, Thelma
  See Greenhaus, Thelma Nurenberg
Nurnberg, Maxwell 1897-1984 27
  Obituary 41
Nussbaumer, Paul (Edmund) 1934- 16
Nutt, Ken 1951- 163
  Earlier sketch in SATA *97*
Nuttall-Smith, Margaret Emily Noel 1919- .. 26
Nuygen, Mathieu 1967- 80
Nuzum, K. A. 195
Nuzum, Kathy A.
  See Nuzum, K. A.
Nwapa, Flora (Nwanzuruaha) 1931-1993
  See CLR *162*
Nyberg, (Everett Wayne) Morgan 1944- 87
Nyce, (Nellie) Helene von Strecker
  1885-1969 19
Nyce, Vera 1862-1925 19
Nye, Naomi Shihab 1952- 198
  Earlier sketches in SATA *86, 147*
  See also CLR *59*
Nye, Robert 1939- 6
Nyeu, Tao 206
Nyikos, Stacy A. 1969- 164
Nystrom, Carolyn 1940- 130
  Earlier sketch in SATA *67*

O

O. Henry
  See Henry, O.
Oakes, Elizabeth H. 1964- 132
Oakes, Vanya 1909-1983 6
  Obituary 37
Oakley, Don(ald G.) 1927- 8
Oakley, Graham 1929- 84
  Earlier sketch in SATA *30*
  See also CLR *7*
Oakley, Helen (McKelvey) 1906- 10
Oaks, J. Adams 220
Oana, Katherine 1929- 53
  Brief entry 37

Oates, Eddie H. 1943- 88
Oates, Joyce Carol 1938- 159
Oates, Stephen B(aery) 1936- 59
Obed, Ellen Bryan 1944- 74
Oberdieck, Bernhard 1949- 230
Oberle, Joseph 1958- 69
Oberman, Sheldon 1949-2004 85
  Autobiography Feature 114
  Obituary 153
  See also CLR *54*
  See also SAAS *26*
Obligado, Lilian (Isabel) 1931- 61
  Brief entry 45
Obrant, Susan 1946- 11
O'Brian, E.G.
  See Clarke, Arthur C.
O'Brien, Anne Sibley 1952- 213
  Brief entry 48
  Earlier sketches in SATA *53, 80*
O'Brien, E.G.
  See Clarke, Arthur C.
O'Brien, Esse Forrester 1895(?)-1975
  Obituary 30
O'Brien, Johnny 222
O'Brien, Patrick 1960- 193
O'Brien, Robert C.
  See Conly, Robert Leslie
O'Brien, Thomas C. 1938-2010 29
O'Brien, Thomas Clement
  See O'Brien, Thomas C.
O'Callaghan, Julie 1954- 113
O'Callahan, Jay 1938- 88
O'Carroll, Ryan
  See Markun, Patricia Maloney
Ochiltree, Dianne 1953- 117
Ockham, Joan Price
  See Price, Joan
O'Connell, Margaret F(orster) 1935-1977 30
  Obituary 30
O'Connell, Peg
  See Ahern, Margaret McCrohan
O'Connell, Rebecca 1968- 212
  Earlier sketch in SATA *130*
O'Connor, Barbara 1950- 193
  Earlier sketch in SATA *154*
O'Connor, Francine M(arie) 1930- 90
O'Connor, Genevieve A. 1914- 75
O'Connor, George 228
  Earlier sketch in SATA *183*
O'Connor, Ian 1965- 188
O'Connor, Jane 1947- 186
  Brief entry 47
  Earlier sketches in SATA *59, 103, 150*
O'Connor, Karen 1938- 89
  Earlier sketch in SATA *34*
O'Connor, Patrick
  See Wibberley, Leonard
O'Connor, Richard 1915-1975
  Obituary 21
O'Conor, Jane 1958- 78
Odaga, Asenath (Bole) 1937- 130
  Earlier sketch in SATA *67*
  See also SAAS *19*
O Danachair, Caoimhin
  See Danaher, Kevin
Odanaka, Barbara 159
O'Daniel, Janet 1921- 24
O'Day, Cathy
  See Crane, Barbara (Joyce)
O'Dell, Scott 1898-1989 134
  Earlier sketches in SATA *12, 60*
  See also CLR *126*
Odenwald, Robert P(aul) 1899-1965 11
Odgers, Sally
  See Odgers, Sally Farrell
Odgers, Sally Farrell 1957- 139
  Earlier sketch in SATA *72*
Odone, Jamison 1980- 209
O'Donnell, Dick
  See Lupoff, Richard A(llen)
  and Thompson, Don(ald Arthur)

O'Donnell, Liam 1970- 209
Odriozola, Elena 186
Oechsli, Kelly 1918-1999 5
Oertel, Andreas 1966- 230
Oesterle, Virginia Rorby
  See Rorby, Ginny
Ofek, Uriel 1926- 36
  See also CLR *28*
Ofer, Avi 1975- 207
Offenbacher, Ami 1958- 91
Offermann, Andrea 231
Offill, Jenny 1968- 211
Offit, Sidney 1928- 10
Ofosu-Appiah, L(awrence) H(enry) 1920- ... 13
Ogan, George F. 1912-1983 13
Ogan, M. G.
  See Ogan, George F.
  and Ogan, Margaret E. (Nettles)
Ogan, Margaret E. (Nettles) 1923-1979 13
Ogburn, Charlton (Jr.) 1911-1998 3
  Obituary 109
Ogburn, Jacqueline K. 162
Ogilvie, Elisabeth May 1917-2006 40
  Brief entry 29
  Obituary 176
Ogilvy, Gavin
  See Barrie, J. M.
Ogilvy, Ian 1943- 177
Ogilvy, Ian Raymond
  See Ogilvy, Ian
Ogle, Lucille Edith 1904-1988
  Obituary 59
Ogletree, Charles J. 1952- 175
O'Green, Jennifer
  See Roberson, Jennifer
O'Green, Jennifer Roberson
  See Roberson, Jennifer
O'Hagan, Caroline 1946- 38
O'Hanlon, Jacklyn
  See Meek, Jacklyn O'Hanlon
O'Hara, Elizabeth
  See Ni Dhuibhne, Eilis
O'Hara, Kenneth
  See Morris, (Margaret) Jean
O'Hara, Mary
  See Alsop, Mary O'Hara
O'Hara (Alsop), Mary
  See Alsop, Mary O'Hara
O'Hare, Jeff(rey A.) 1958- 105
O'hearn, Kate 225
Ohi, Ruth 1964- 95
Ohiyesa
  See Eastman, Charles A(lexander)
Ohlsson, Ib 1935- 7
Ohmi, Ayano 1959- 115
Ohtomo, Yasuo 1946- 37
o huigin, sean 1942- 138
  See also CLR *75*
Oiseau
  See Moseley, James W(illett)
Oke, Janette 1935- 97
O'Keefe, Susan Heyboer 176
  Earlier sketch in SATA *133*
O'Keeffe, Frank 1938- 99
O'Kelley, Mattie Lou 1908-1997 97
  Earlier sketch in SATA *36*
Okimoto, Jean Davies 1942- 103
  Earlier sketch in SATA *34*
Okomfo, Amasewa
  See Cousins, Linda
olafsdottir, Gudrun Elin
  See Gunnella
Olaleye, Isaac O. 1941- 96
  See also SAAS *23*
Olander, Johan 1967- 231
Olcott, Frances Jenkins 1872(?)-1963 19
Old, Wendie C(orbin) 1943- 154
Old Boy
  See Hughes, Thomas
Oldenburg, E(gbert) William 1936-1974 35
Older, Effin 1942- 114

Older, Jules 1940- 156
Earlier sketch in SATA *114*
Oldfield, Jenny 1949- 140
Oldfield, Margaret J(ean) 1932- 56
Oldfield, Pamela 1931- 86
Oldham, June 70
Oldham, Mary 1944- 65
Oldland, Nicholas 1972- 223
Olds, Elizabeth 1896-1991 3
Obituary 66
Olds, Helen Diehl 1895-1981 9
Obituary 25
Oldstyle, Jonathan
See Irving, Washington
O'Leary, Brian (Todd) 1940- 6
O'Leary, Chris 208
O'Leary, Patsy B. 1937- 97
O'Leary, Patsy Baker
See O'Leary, Patsy B.
Oleynikov, Igor 1953- 202
Oliphant, B.J.
See Tepper, Sheri S.
Oliver, Burton
See Burt, Olive Woolley
Oliver, Chad
See Oliver, Symmes C.
Oliver, John Edward 1933- 21
Oliver, Lauren 1982- 228
Oliver, Lin 202
Oliver, Marilyn Tower 1935- 89
Oliver, Mark 1960- 214
Oliver, Narelle 1960- 197
Earlier sketch in SATA *152*
Oliver, Shirley (Louise Dawkins) 1958- 74
Oliver, Symmes C. 1928-1993 101
Oliviero, Jamie 1950- 84
Olmsted, Lorena Ann 1890-1989 13
Olney, Ross R. 1929- 13
Olschewski, Alfred (Erich) 1920- 7
Olsen, Barbara 148
Olsen, Carol 1945- 89
Olsen, Ib Spang 1921- 81
Earlier sketch in SATA *6*
Olsen, Violet (Mae) 1922-1991 58
Olson, Arielle North 1932- 67
Olson, David J. 1974- 198
Olson, Gene 1922- 32
Olson, Gretchen 187
Olson, Helen Kronberg 48
Olson, Kay Melchisedech 1948- 175
Olson, Marianne
See Mitchell, Marianne
Olson-Brown, Ellen 1967- 183
Olten, Manuela 1970- 197
Olugebefola, Ademole 1941- 15
Oluonye, Mary N(kechi) 1955- 111
Om
See Gorey, Edward (St. John)
O'Malley, Donough 208
O'Malley, Kevin 1961- 230
Earlier sketches in SATA *157, 191*
Oman, Carola (Mary Anima) 1897-1978 35
O'Mara, Carmel 1965- 166
O'Mara-Horwitz, Carmel
See O'Mara, Carmel
O'Meara, Walter (Andrew) 1897-1989 65
Ommanney, F(rancis) D(ownes) 1903-1980 . 23
Omololu, Cynthia Jaynes 222
O Mude
See Gorey, Edward (St. John)
Oneal, Elizabeth 1934- 82
Earlier sketch in SATA *30*
See also CLR *13*
O'Neal, Katherine Pebley 1957- 204
O'Neal, Reagan
See Jordan, Robert
O'Neal, Regan
See Jordan, Robert
Oneal, Zibby
See Oneal, Elizabeth
O'neill, Alexis 1949- 220

O'Neill, Amanda 1951- 111
O'Neill, Catharine 203
O'Neill, Gerard K(itchen) 1927-1992 65
O'Neill, Judith (Beatrice) 1930- 34
O'Neill, Mary L(e Duc) 1908(?)-1990 2
Obituary 64
O'Neill, Reagan
See Jordan, Robert
Onslow, Annette Rosemary MacArthur
See MacArthur-Onslow, Annette Rosemary
Onslow, John 1906-1985
Obituary 47
Onyefulu, Ifeoma 1959- 157
Earlier sketches in SATA *81, 115*
Opie, Iona (Margaret Balfour) 1923- 118
Earlier sketches in SATA *3, 63*
See also SAAS *6*
Opie, Peter (Mason) 1918-1982 118
Obituary 28
Earlier sketches in SATA *3, 63*
Oppel, Kenneth 1967- 199
Earlier sketches in SATA *99, 153*
Oppel, Kenneth Kerry
See Oppel, Kenneth
Oppenheim, Joanne 1934- 174
Earlier sketches in SATA *5, 82, 136*
Oppenheim, Shulamith Levey 1928- 177
Oppenheimer, Joan L(etson) 1925- 28
Oppong, Joseph Ransford 1953- 160
Optic, Oliver
See Adams, William Taylor
and Stratemeyer, Edward L.
Oram, Hiawyn 1946- 101
Earlier sketch in SATA *56*
Orbach, Ruth Gary 1941- 21
Orback, Craig 197
Orczy, Emma
See Orczy, Baroness Emmuska
Orczy, Emma Magdalena Rosalia Maria Josefa
See Orczy, Baroness Emmuska
Orczy, Emmuska
See Orczy, Baroness Emmuska
Orczy, Baroness Emmuska 1865-1947 40
Orde, A.J.
See Tepper, Sheri S.
O'Reilly, Jackson
See Jordan, Robert
Orenstein, Denise Gosliner 1950- 157
Orgad, Dorit 1936- 199
Orgel, Doris 1929- 148
Earlier sketches in SATA *7, 85*
See also CLR *48*
See also SAAS *19*
Orgill, Roxane 198
Oriolo, Joe
See Oriolo, Joseph D.
Oriolo, Joseph D. 1913-1985
Obituary 46
Orlandelli, Alessandro
See Horley, Alex
Orlean, Susan 1955- 209
Orleans, Ilo 1897-1962 10
Orlev, Uri 1931- 135
Earlier sketch in SATA *58*
See also CLR *30*
See also SAAS *19*
Ormai, Stella 57
Brief entry 48
Ormerod, Jan 1946- 210
Brief entry 44
Earlier sketches in SATA *55, 70, 132*
See also CLR *20*
Ormerod, Janette Louise
See Ormerod, Jan
Ormes, Jackie
See Ormes, Zelda J.
Ormes, Zelda J. 1914-1986
Obituary 47
Ormondroyd, Edward 1925- 14
Ormsby, Virginia H(aire) 1906-1990 11
Orona-Ramirez, Kristy 1964- 189

Orozco, Jose-Luis 1948- 179
Orr, Katherine S(helley) 1950- 72
Orr, Wendy 1953- 206
Earlier sketches in SATA *90, 141*
Orris
See Ingelow, Jean
Orth, Richard
See Gardner, Richard (M.)
Ortiz Cofer, Judith
See Cofer, Judith Ortiz
Orwell, George 1903-1950 29
See also CLR *68*
Orwin, Joanna 1944- 141
Os, Eric van
See van Os, Erik
Osborn, Elinor 1939- 145
Osborn, Jacob 1981(?)- 215
Osborn, Kathy 1955(?)- 199
Osborn, Lois D(orothy) 1915- 61
Osborne, Charles 1927- 59
Osborne, Chester G(orham) 1915-1987 11
Osborne, David
See Silverberg, Robert
Osborne, George
See Silverberg, Robert
Osborne, Leone Neal 1914-1996 2
Osborne, Linda Barrett 1949- 215
Osborne, Mary Pope 1949- 144
Earlier sketches in SATA *41, 55, 98*
See also CLR *88*
Osceola
See Blixen, Karen
Osgood, William E(dward) 1926- 37
O'Shaughnessy, Darren
See Shan, Darren
O'Shaughnessy, Ellen Cassels 1937- 78
O'shaughnessy, Tam 1951- 221
O'Shea, Catherine Patricia Shiels
See O'Shea, Pat
O'Shea, Pat 1931-2007 87
See also CLR *18*
Osmond, Edward 1900- 10
Ossoli, Sarah Margaret
See Fuller, Margaret
Ostendorf, (Arthur) Lloyd, (Jr.) 1921-2000 .. 65
Obituary 125
Osterweil, Adam 1972- 217
Ostow, Micol 1976- 223
Earlier sketch in SATA *170*
Otfinoski, Steven 1949- 116
Earlier sketch in SATA *56*
Otis, James
See Kaler, James Otis
O'Toole, Thomas 1941- 71
O'Trigger, Sir Lucius
See Horne, Richard Henry Hengist
Otten, Charlotte
See Otten, Charlotte F.
Otten, Charlotte F. 1926- 98
Otten, Charlotte Fennema
See Otten, Charlotte F.
Ottley, Matt 1962- 171
Earlier sketch in SATA *102*
Ottley, Reginald Leslie 1909-1985 26
See also CLR *16*
Otto, Margaret Glover 1909-1976
Obituary 30
Otto, Svend
See Soerensen, Svend Otto
Ouellet, Debbie 1954- 219
Oughton, Jerrie (Preston) 1937- 131
Earlier sketch in SATA *76*
Oughton, (William) Taylor 1925- 104
Ouida
See De La Ramee, Marie Louise
Ousley, Odille 1896-1976 10
Outcalt, Todd 1960- 123
Overmyer, James E. 1946- 88
Overton, Jenny (Margaret Mary) 1942- 52
Brief entry 36

Owen, Ann
  See Qualey, Marsha
Owen, Annie 1949- 75
Owen, Caroline Dale
  See Snedeker, Caroline Dale (Parke)
Owen, Clifford
  See Hamilton, Charles (Harold St. John)
Owen, Dilys
  See Gater, Dilys
Owen, (Benjamin) Evan 1918-1984 38
Owen, (John) Gareth 1936-2002 162
  Earlier sketch in SATA 83
  See also CLR 31
  See also SAAS 14
Owen, James A. 185
Owens, Bryant 1968- 116
Owens, Dana Elaine
  See Queen Latifah
Owens, Gail 1939- 54
Owens, Mary Beth 191
Owens, Thomas S(heldon) 1960- 86
Owens, Tom
  See Owens, Thomas S(heldon)
Oxenbury, Helen 1938- 149
  Earlier sketches in SATA 3, 68
  See also CLR 70
Oxendine, Bess Holland 1933- 90
Oz, Frank (Richard) 1944- 60
Ozer, Jerome S. 1927- 59

P

Paananen, Eloise (Katherine) 1923-1993 9
Pace, Lorenzo 1943- 131
Pace, Mildred Mastin 1907- 46
  Brief entry 29
Pachter, Hedwig (?)-1988 63
Pack, Janet 1952- 77
Pack, Robert 1929- 118
Packard, Edward 1931- 148
  Earlier sketches in SATA 47, 90
Packer, Kenneth L. 1946- 116
Packer, Vin
  See Meaker, Marijane
Pad, Peter
  See Stratemeyer, Edward L.
Page, Eileen
  See Heal, Edith
Page, Eleanor
  See Coerr, Eleanor (Beatrice)
Page, Gail 1950- 205
Page, Jake 1936- 81
Page, James Keena, Jr.
  See Page, Jake
Page, Lou Williams 1912-1997 38
Page, Mary
  See Heal, Edith
Page, Robin 1943- 154
Pagliarulo, Antonio 1977(?)- 212
Pagnucci, Susan 1944- 90
Pahlen, Kurt 1907-2003
  Obituary 147
Pahz, Cheryl
  See Pahz, Cheryl Suzanne
Pahz, Cheryl Suzanne 1949- 11
Pahz, James Alon 1943- 11
Paice, Margaret 1920- 10
Paige, Harry W(orthington) 1922- 41
  Brief entry 35
Paige, Richard
  See Koontz, Dean
Paige, Robin
  See Albert, Susan Wittig
Paillot, Jim 230
Paine, Penelope Colville 1946- 87
Paine, Roberta M. 1925- 13
Paisley, Tom 1932- 11
  See also CLR 3

Palatini, Margie 207
  Earlier sketches in SATA 134, 174
Palazzo, Anthony D.
  See Palazzo, Tony
Palazzo, Tony 1905-1970 3
Palder, Edward L. 1922- 5
Palecek, Josef 1932- 56
Palecek, Libuse 1937- 89
Palen, Debbie 195
Palin, Michael 1943- 67
Palin, Michael Edward
  See Palin, Michael
Palladini, David (Mario) 1946- 40
  Brief entry 32
Pallas, Norvin 1918-1983 23
Pallister, John C(lare) 1891-1980
  Obituary 26
Pallotta, Gerard Larry
  See Pallotta, Jerry
Pallotta, Jerry 1953- 186
Pallotta-Chiarolli, Maria 1960- 117
Palmer, Bernard (Alvin) 1914-1998 26
Palmer, C. Everard 1930- 14
Palmer, (Ruth) Candida 1926- 11
Palmer, Cyril Everard
  See Palmer, C. Everard
Palmer, Don
  See Benson, Mildred
Palmer, Gary 1968- 231
Palmer, Hap 1942- 68
Palmer, Heidi 1948- 15
Palmer, Helen Marion
  See Geisel, Helen
Palmer, Jessica 1953- 120
Palmer, Judd 1972- 153
Palmer, Juliette 1930- 15
Palmer, Kate Salley 1946- 97
Palmer, Maria
  See Strachan, Ian
Palmer, Maria
  See Brennan, Herbie
Palmer, Robin 1909-2000 43
Palmero Caceres, Ana 198
Palmisciano, Diane 202
Paltrowitz, Donna 1950- 61
  Brief entry 50
Paltrowitz, Donna Milman
  See Paltrowitz, Donna
Paltrowitz, Stuart 1946- 61
  Brief entry 50
Pamela, Todd 1950- 124
Pamintuan, Macky 214
  Earlier sketch in SATA 178
Panagopoulos, Janie Lynn 149
Panati, Charles 1943- 65
Panchyk, Richard 1970- 138
Panetta, George 1915-1969 15
Panetta, Joseph N. 1953- 96
Pang, YaWen Ariel 206
Panik, Sharon 1952- 82
Panowski, Eileen Thompson 1920- 49
Pansy
  See Alden, Isabella (Macdonald)
Pantell, Dora (Fuchs) 39
Panter, Carol 1936- 9
Paolini, Christopher 1983- 157
  See also CLR 102
Papademetriou, Lisa 175
Paparone, Pam 185
Paparone, Pamela
  See Paparone, Pam
Papas, Bill
  See Papas, William
Papas, William 1927-2000 50
Papashvily, George 1898-1978 17
Papashvily, Helen (Waite) 1906-1996 17
Pape, D. L.
  See Pape, Donna (Lugg)
Pape, Donna (Lugg) 1930- 82
  Earlier sketch in SATA 2

Paperny, Myra (Green) 1932- 51
  Brief entry 33
Papineau, Lucie 1962- 224
Papp, Robert 1967- 205
Paradis, Adrian A(lexis) 1912- 67
  Earlier sketch in SATA 1
  See also SAAS 8
Paradis, Marjorie Bartholomew
  1886(?)-1970 17
Paradiz, Valerie 1963- 176
Paratore, Coleen
  See Paratore, Coleen Murtagh
Paratore, Coleen Murtagh 1958- 200
Pardo DeLange, Alex 211
Parenteau, Shirley 1935- 199
  Brief entry 40
  Earlier sketch in SATA 47
Parish, Margaret 1927-1988 73
  Obituary 59
  Earlier sketch in SATA 17
  See also CLR 22
Parish, Margaret Holt
  See Holt, Margaret
Parish, Peggy
  See Parish, Margaret
Park, Barbara 1947- 123
  Brief entry 35
  Earlier sketches in SATA 40, 78
  See also CLR 34
Park, Bill
  See Park, W(illiam) B(ryan)
Park, Frances 1955- 171
Park, Ginger 173
Park, Janie Jaehyun 150
Park, Jordan
  See Kornbluth, C(yril) M.
  and Pohl, Frederik
Park, Linda Sue 1960- 200
  Earlier sketches in SATA 127, 173
  See also CLR 84
Park, Nick 1958- 113
Park, Rosina Ruth Lucia
  See Park, Ruth
Park, Ruth 1917(?)-2010 93
  Earlier sketch in SATA 25
  See also CLR 51
Park, W(illiam) B(ryan) 1936- 22
Parke, Marilyn 1928- 82
Parker, Barbara Keevil 1938- 157
Parker, Daniel
  See Ehrenhaft, Daniel
Parker, Elinor Milnor 1906- 3
Parker, Jake 1977- 227
Parker, Julie F. 1961- 92
Parker, Kim 1963- 174
Parker, Kristy 1957- 59
Parker, Lois M(ay) 1912-1996 30
Parker, Margot M. 1937- 52
Parker, Marjorie Blain 1960- 205
  Earlier sketch in SATA 145
Parker, Mary Jessie 1948- 71
Parker, Nancy Winslow 1930- 132
  Earlier sketches in SATA 10, 69
  See also SAAS 20
Parker, Richard 1915-1990 14
Parker, Robert
  See Boyd, Waldo T.
  and Parker, Robert Andrew
Parker, Robert Andrew 1927- 200
Parker, Steve 1954- 213
Parker, Tom S. 215
Parker, Toni Trent 1947-2005 142
  Obituary 169
Parker-Rees, Guy 193
Parker-Rock, Michelle 214
Parkes, Lucas
  See Harris, John (Wyndham Parkes Lucas)
  Beynon
Parkhill, John
  See Cox, William R(obert)

Parkins, David 1955- 218
Earlier sketch in SATA 176
Parkinson, Curtis 219
Parkinson, Ethelyn M(inerva) 1906-1999 11
Parkinson, Kathryn N. 1954- 71
Parkinson, Kathy
See Parkinson, Kathryn N.
Parkinson, Siobhan
See Parkinson, Siobhan
Parkinson, Siobhan 1954- 178
Parks, Deborah A. 1948- 133
Earlier sketch in SATA 91
Parks, Edd Winfield 1906-1968 10
Parks, Gordon 1912-2006 108
Obituary 175
Earlier sketch in SATA 8
Parks, Gordon Roger Alexander
See Parks, Gordon
Parks, Peggy J. 1951- 143
Parks, PJ
See Parks, Peggy J.
Parks, Rosa 1913-2005 83
Obituary 169
Parks, Rosa Louise Lee
See Parks, Rosa
Parks, Van Dyke 1943- 62
Parlato, Stephen 1954- 222
Parley, Peter
See Goodrich, Samuel Griswold
Parlin, John
See Graves, Charles Parlin
Parme, Fabrice 1966- 191
Parnall, Peter 1936- 69
Earlier sketch in SATA 16
See also SAAS 11
Paros, Jennifer 210
Parotti, Phillip (Elliott) 1941- 109
Parr, Ann 1943- 144
Parr, Danny
See Parr, Ann
Parr, Letitia (Evelyn) 1906-1985(?) 37
Parr, Lucy 1924- 10
Parr, Todd 179
Earlier sketch in SATA 134
Parra, John 1972- 225
Parrish, Anne 1888-1957 27
Parrish, Mary
See Cousins, Margaret
Parrish, Maxfield
See Parrish, (Frederick) Maxfield
Parrish, (Frederick) Maxfield 1870-1966 14
Parry, Marian 1924- 13
Parry, Rosanne 212
Parson Lot
See Kingsley, Charles
Parsons, Alexandra 1947- 92
Parsons, Ellen
See Dragonwagon, Crescent
Parsons, Garry 197
Parsons, Martin 1951- 116
Parsons, Martin Leslie
See Parsons, Martin
Parsons, Tom
See MacPherson, Thomas George
Parsons-Yazzi, Evangeline 172
Partch, Virgil Franklin II 1916-1984 39
Obituary 39
Parton, Dolly 1946- 94
Parton, Dolly Rebecca
See Parton, Dolly
Partridge, Benjamin W., Jr. 1915-2005 28
Obituary 163
Partridge, Benjamin Waring, Jr.
See Partridge, Benjamin W., Jr.
Partridge, Cora Cheney
See Cheney, Cora
Partridge, Elizabeth 216
Earlier sketch in SATA 134
Partridge, Jenny (Lilian) 1947- 52
Brief entry 37
Pasachoff, Naomi 1947- 147

Pascal, David 1918- 14
Pascal, Francine 1938- 143
Brief entry 37
Earlier sketches in SATA 51, 80
See also CLR 25
Paschal, Nancy
See Trotter, Grace V(iolet)
Paschkis, Julie 1957- 220
Earlier sketch in SATA 177
Pascudniak, Pascal
See Lupoff, Richard A(llen)
Pashko, Stanley 1913-1982 29
Pasqualotto, Chiara 1976- 228
Passailaigue, Thomas E.
See Paisley, Tom
Pastel, Elyse 201
Pateman, Robert 1954- 84
Patent, Dorothy Hinshaw 1940- 162
Autobiography Feature 162
Earlier sketches in SATA 22, 69, 120
See also CLR 19
See also SAAS 13
Paterson, A(ndrew) B(arton) 1864-1941 97
Paterson, Banjo
See Paterson, A(ndrew) B(arton)
Paterson, Diane 1946- 177
Brief entry 33
Earlier sketch in SATA 59
Paterson, John (Barstow) 1932- 114
Paterson, Katherine 1932- 204
Earlier sketches in SATA 13, 53, 92, 133
See also CLR 127
Paterson, Katherine Womeldorf
See Paterson, Katherine
Patience, John 1949- 90
Patneaude, David 1944- 159
Earlier sketch in SATA 85
Paton, Alan 1903-1988 11
Obituary 56
Paton, Alan Stewart
See Paton, Alan
Paton, Jane (Elizabeth) 1934- 35
Paton, Priscilla 1952- 98
Paton Walsh, Gillian
See Paton Walsh, Jill
Paton Walsh, Jill 1937- 190
Autobiography Feature 190
Earlier sketches in SATA 4, 72, 109
See also CLR 128
See also SAAS 3
Patricelli, Leslie 207
Patrick, Susan
See Robins, Patricia
Patron, Susan 1948- 182
Earlier sketch in SATA 76
Patsauq, Markoosie 1942-
See CLR 23
Patschke, Steve 1955- 125
Patt, Beverly 231
Patten, Brian 1946- 152
Earlier sketch in SATA 29
Patterson, Charles 1935- 59
Patterson, Geoffrey 1943- 54
Brief entry 44
Patterson, James 1947- 197
Earlier sketch in SATA 164
Patterson, James B.
See Patterson, James
Patterson, Lillie G. -1999 88
Earlier sketch in SATA 14
Patterson, Nancy Ruth 1944- 148
Earlier sketch in SATA 72
Patterson, Valerie O. 223
Pattison, Darcy (S.) 1954- 126
Earlier sketch in SATA 72
Pattou, Edith 164
Patz (Blaustein), Nancy 154
Paul, Aileen 1917- 12
Paul, Alison 196
Paul, Ann Whitford 1941- 209
Earlier sketches in SATA 76, 110, 168

Paul, Chris 1985- 224
Paul, David (Tyler) 1934-1988
Obituary 56
Paul, Dominique 1973- 184
Paul, Elizabeth
See Crow, Donna Fletcher
Paul, Hamish Vigne Christie 1951- 151
See also CLR 87
Paul, James 1936- 23
Paul, Korky
See Paul, Hamish Vigne Christie
Paul, Robert
See Roberts, John G(aither)
Paul, Tessa 1944- 103
Pauley, Kimberly 1973- 208
Pauli, Hertha (Ernestine) 1909-1973 3
Obituary 26
Paull, Grace A. 1898- 24
Paulsen, Gary 1939- 231
Earlier sketches in SATA 22, 50, 54, 79, 111,
158, 189
See also CLR 82
Paulson, Jack
See Jackson, C(aary) Paul
Pauquet, Gina Ruck
See Ruck-Pauquet, Gina
Pausacker, Jenny 1948- 72
See also SAAS 23
Pausewang, Gudrun 1928- 165
Earlier sketch in SATA 104
Pavel, Frances 1907- 10
Paver, Michelle 215
Earlier sketch in SATA 170
Paxton
See Barr, Nevada
Paxton, Thomas R. 1937- 70
Paxton, Tom
See Paxton, Thomas R.
Paye, Won-Ldy 185
Payne, Alan
See Jakes, John
Payne, Bernal C., Jr. 1941- 60
Payne, C. Douglas
See Payne, C.D.
Payne, C.D. 1949- 133
Payne, C.F. 1956- 179
Payne, Chris Fox
See Payne, C.F.
Payne, Donald Gordon 1924- 37
Payne, Emmy
See West, Emily Govan
Payne, Nina 135
Payne, Rachel Ann
See Jakes, John
Payson, Dale 1943- 9
Payzant, Charles 18
Paz, A.
See Pahz, James Alon
Paz, Natalia Toledo
See Toledo, Natalia
Paz, Zan
See Pahz, Cheryl Suzanne
Peace, Mary
See Finley, Mary Peace
Peacock, Louise 210
Peacock, Phyllis Hornung 1977- 230
Peacock, Shane 1957- 192
Peake, Mervyn 1911-1968 23
Peale, Norman Vincent 1898-1993 20
Obituary 78
Pearce, Ann Philippa
See Pearce, Philippa
Pearce, Carl 229
Pearce, Emily Smith 1975- 199
Pearce, Jacqueline 1962- 146
Pearce, Margaret 104
Pearce, Philippa 1920-2006 129
Obituary 179
Earlier sketches in SATA 1, 67
See also CLR 9
Peare, Catherine Owens 1911- 9

Pearle, Ida 207
Pearsall, Shelley 1966- 190
Pearson, Gayle 1947- 119
　Earlier sketch in SATA 53
Pearson, Jean Mary
　See Gardam, Jane
Pearson, Kit 1947- 77
　Autobiography Feature 117
　See also CLR 26
Pearson, Mary E. 1955- 211
　Earlier sketch in SATA 134
Pearson, Michael Parker
　See Pearson, Mike Parker
Pearson, Mike Parker 1957- 228
Pearson, Ridley 1953- 182
Pearson, Susan 1946- 166
　Brief entry 27
　Earlier sketches in SATA 39, 91
Pearson, Tracey Campbell 1956- 219
　Earlier sketches in SATA 64, 155
Pease, (Clarence) Howard 1894-1974 2
　Obituary 25
Peavy, Linda 1943- 54
Peck, Anne Merriman 1884-1976 18
Peck, Beth 1957- 190
　Earlier sketch in SATA 79
Peck, Jan 159
Peck, Jeanie J. 1967- 147
Peck, Marshall III 1951- 92
Peck, Richard 1934- 228
　Autobiography Feature 110
　Earlier sketches in SATA 18, 55, 97, 110, 158,
　190
　See also CLR 142
　See also SAAS 2
Peck, Richard Wayne
　See Peck, Richard
Peck, Robert Newton 1928- 156
　Autobiography Feature 108
　Earlier sketches in SATA 21, 62, 111
　See also CLR 163
　See also SAAS 1
Peck, Sylvia 1953- 133
Peck-Whiting, Jeanie J.
　See Peck, Jeanie J.
Peddicord, Jane Ann 199
Pedersen, Janet 193
Pederson, Sharleen
　See Collicott, Sharleen
Pedler, Caroline 197
Peebles, Anne
　See Galloway, Priscilla
Peek, Merle 1938- 39
Peel, John 1954- 79
Peel, Norman Lemon
　See Hirsch, Phil
Peeples, Edwin A(ugustus, Jr.) 1915-1994 6
Peers, Judi 1956- 119
Peers, Judith May West
　See Peers, Judi
Peet, Bill
　See Peet, William Bartlett
Peet, Creighton B. 1899-1977 30
Peet, Mal 227
　Earlier sketch in SATA 171
Peet, Malcolm
　See Peet, Mal
Peet, William Bartlett 1915-2002 78
　Obituary 137
　Earlier sketches in SATA 2, 41
　See also CLR 12
Peete, Holly Robinson 1964- 229
Peguero, Leone 116
Pelaez, Jill 1924- 12
Pelham, David 1938- 70
Pelikan, Judy 1941- 219
Pell, Ed(ward) 1950- 157
Pelletier, Andrew T. 195
Pelletier, Andrew Thomas
　See Pelletier, Andrew T.
Pellowski, Anne 1933- 20

Pellowski, Michael (Joseph) 1949- 151
　Brief entry 48
　Earlier sketch in SATA 88
Pellowski, Michael Morgan
　See Pellowski, Michael (Joseph)
Pelta, Kathy 1928- 18
Peltier, Leslie C(opus) 1900-1980 13
Pemberton, Bonnie 191
Pemberton, John Leigh
　See Leigh-Pemberton, John
Pembury, Bill
　See Groom, Arthur William
Pemsteen, Hans
　See Manes, Stephen
Pendennis, Arthur Esquir
　See Thackeray, William Makepeace
Pender, Lydia Podger 1907- 61
Pendery, Rosemary (Schmitz) 7
Pendle, Alexy 1943- 29
Pendle, George 1906-1977
　Obituary 28
Pendleton, Don
　See Cunningham, Chet
　and Garside, Jack
　and Jagninski, Tom
　and Krauzer, Steven M(ark)
　and Obstfeld, Raymond
Pendleton, Thomas 1965- 206
Pendziwol, Jean E. 1965- 177
Pene du Bois, William (Sherman)
　1916-1993 68
　Obituary 74
　Earlier sketch in SATA 4
　See also CLR 1
Penn, Audrey 1947- 212
Penn, Audrey 1950- 22
Penn, Ruth Bonn
　See Rosenberg, Eth Clifford
Pennac, Daniel 1944- 155
Pennage, E. M.
　See Finkel, George (Irvine)
Penner, Fred 1946- 169
　Earlier sketch in SATA 67
Penner, Frederick Ralph Cornelius
　See Penner, Fred
Penner, Lucille Recht 1942- 226
Penney, Grace Jackson 1904-2000 35
Penney, Ian 1960- 76
Penney, Sue 1957- 152
　Earlier sketch in SATA 102
Pennington, Eunice 1923- 27
Pennington, Lillian Boyer 1904-2003 45
Pennypacker, Sara 1951- 187
Penrose, Gordon 1925- 66
Penson, Mary E. 1917- 78
Penzler, Otto 1942- 38
Pepe, Phil 1935- 20
Pepe, Philip
　See Pepe, Phil
Peppe, Rodney (Darrell) 1934- 74
　Earlier sketch in SATA 4
　See also SAAS 10
Pepper, Frank S. 1910-1988
　Obituary 61
Percy, Charles Henry
　See Smith, Dorothy Gladys
Percy, Rachel 1930- 63
Perdomo, Willie 228
Perdrizet, Marie-Pierre 1952- 79
Perenyi, Constance 1954- 93
Perenyi, Constance Marie
　See Perenyi, Constance
Perera, Hilda 1926- 105
Perera, Thomas Biddle 1938- 13
Peretti, Frank E. 1951- 141
　Earlier sketch in SATA 80
Perez, L. King 1940- 199
Perez, Lana
　See Perez, Marlene
Perez, Lucia Angela 1973- 182
Perez, Marlene 170

Pericoli, Matteo 1968- 178
Perkins, Al(bert Rogers) 1904-1975 30
Perkins, Dan
　See Tomorrow, Tom
Perkins, Lucy Fitch 1865-1937 72
Perkins, Lynne Rae 1956- 212
　Earlier sketches in SATA 131, 172
Perkins, (Richard) Marlin 1905-1986 21
　Obituary 48
Perkins, Mitali 1963- 188
　Earlier sketch in SATA 88
Perks, Anne-Marie 1955- 122
Perl, Erica S. 222
　Earlier sketch in SATA 188
Perl, Lila 72
　Earlier sketch in SATA 6
Perl, Susan 1922-1983 22
　Obituary 34
Perlman, Janet 1954- 222
Perlman, Rhea 1948- 183
Perlmutter, O(scar) William 1920-1975 8
Pernu, Dennis 1970- 87
Perrault, Charles 1628-1703 25
　See also CLR 134
Perret, Delphine 1980- 190
Perret, Gene (Richard) 1937- 76
Perriman, Cole
　See Perrin, Pat
Perriman, Cole
　See Coleman, Wim
　and Perrin, Pat
Perrin, Pat 212
Perrine, Mary 1913-1976 2
Perrins, Lesley 1953- 56
Perrow, Angeli 1954- 121
Perry, Andrea 1956- 190
　Earlier sketch in SATA 148
Perry, Barbara Fisher
　See Fisher, Barbara
Perry, Elizabeth 1959- 174
Perry, Elizabeth Goodwin
　See Perry, Elizabeth
Perry, John 1967- 223
Perry, Marie Fritz 165
Perry, Patricia 1949- 30
Perry, Phyllis J(ean) 1933- 152
　Earlier sketches in SATA 60, 101
Perry, Ritchie (John Allen) 1942- 105
Perry, Roger 1933- 27
Perry, Steve(n Carl) 1947- 76
Pershall, Mary K. 1951- 172
　Earlier sketch in SATA 70
Pershing, Marie
　See Schultz, Pearle Henriksen
Perske, Robert 1927- 57
Persun, Morgan Reed
　See Watkins, Dawn L.
Perversi, Margaret 213
Petach, Heidi 149
Peter
　See Stratemeyer, Edward L.
Peters, Alexander
　See Hollander, Zander
Peters, Andrew Fusek 1965- 169
　Earlier sketch in SATA 107
Peters, Bernadette 1948- 212
Peters, Caroline
　See Betz, Eva Kelly
Peters, David
　See David, Peter
Peters, Elizabeth 1927- 49
Peters, Emma
　See Price, Karen
Peters, Gabriel
　See Matott, Justin
Peters, Julie Anne 1952- 197
　Earlier sketches in SATA 82, 128
Peters, Linda
　See Catherall, Arthur
Peters, Lisa Westberg 1951- 161
　Earlier sketches in SATA 74, 115

Peters, Patricia 1953- 84
Peters, Russell M. 1929- 78
Peters, S. H.
    See Henry, O.
    and Proffitt, Nicholas
Peters, Stephanie True 1965- 224
Petersen, David 1946- 109
    Earlier sketch in SATA 62
Petersen, Gwenn Boardman 1924- 12
Petersen, P(eter) J(ames) 1941- 118
    Brief entry 43
    Earlier sketches in SATA 48, 83
Petersen, Palle 1943- 85
Petersham, Maud 1890-1971 17
    See also CLR 24
Petersham, Maud Sylvia Fuller
    See Petersham, Maud
Petersham, Miska 1888-1960 17
    See also CLR 24
Peterson, Cris 1952- 174
    Earlier sketches in SATA 84, 145
Peterson, Dawn 1934- 86
Peterson, Esther (Allen) 1934- 35
Peterson, Hans 1922- 8
Peterson, Harold L(eslie) 1922-1978 8
Peterson, Helen Stone 1910- 8
Peterson, Jean Sunde 1941- 108
Peterson, Jeanne Whitehouse 1939- 159
    Earlier sketch in SATA 29
Peterson, Kathleen B. 1951- 119
Peterson, Lorraine 1940- 56
    Brief entry 44
Peterson, Mary 215
Peterson, Shelley 1952- 146
Peterson, Will
    See Cocks, Peter
Petie, Haris
    See Petty, Roberta
Petricic, Dusan 1946- 176
Petrides, Heidrun 1944- 19
Petrie, Catherine 1947- 52
    Brief entry 41
Petrone, Valeria 186
Petrosino, Tamara 193
Petroski, Catherine (Ann Groom) 1939- 48
Petrovich, Michael B(oro) 1922- 40
Petrovskaya, Kyra
    See Wayne, Kyra Petrovskaya
Petruccio, Steven James 1961- 67
Petrucha, Stefan 1959- 213
Petry, Ann 1908-1997 5
    Obituary 94
    See also CLR 12
Petry, Ann Lane
    See Petry, Ann
Pettit, Jayne 1932- 108
Petty, J.T. 1977- 189
Petty, Kate 1951-2007 204
Petty, Roberta 1915- 10
Pevsner, Stella 131
    Earlier sketches in SATA 8, 77
    See also SAAS 14
Peyo
    See Culliford, Pierre
Peyton, K. M.
    See Peyton, Kathleen Wendy
Peyton, Kathleen Wendy 1929- 157
    Earlier sketches in SATA 15, 62
    See also CLR 3
    See also SAAS 17
Pfanner, (Anne) Louise 1955- 68
Pfeffer, Susan Beth 1948- 180
    Earlier sketches in SATA 4, 83
    See also CLR 11
    See also SAAS 17
Pfeffer, Wendy 1929- 204
    Earlier sketches in SATA 78, 142
Pfeiffer, Janet (B.) 1949- 96
Pfister, Marcus 207
    Earlier sketches in SATA 83, 150
    See also CLR 42

Pfitsch, Patricia Curtis 1948- 148
Pfitzenmaier, Audrey 1959- 220
Pflieger, Pat 1955- 84
Pham, LeUyen 1973- 201
    Earlier sketch in SATA 175
Phelan, Mary Kay 1914- 3
Phelan, Matt 1970- 215
    Earlier sketch in SATA 172
Phelan, Terry Wolfe 1941- 56
Phelps, Ethel Johnston 1914-1984 35
Philbrick, Rodman 1951- 163
Philbrick, W. Rodman
    See Philbrick, Rodman
Philbrick, W.R.
    See Philbrick, Rodman
Philbrook, Clem(ent E.) 1917- 24
Phillipps, J.C. 218
Phillipps, Julie Christine
    See Phillipps, J.C.
Phillips, Aileen Paul
    See Paul, Aileen
Phillips, Betty Lou
    See Phillips, Elizabeth Louise
Phillips, Bob 1940- 95
Phillips, Douglas A. 1949- 161
Phillips, Elizabeth Louise 58
    Brief entry 48
Phillips, Gary R. 225
Phillips, Irv(ing W.) 1905-2000 11
    Obituary 125
Phillips, Jack
    See Sandburg, Carl
Phillips, Leon
    See Gerson, Noel Bertram
Phillips, Loretta (Hosey) 1893-1987 10
Phillips, Louis 1942- 102
    Earlier sketch in SATA 8
Phillips, Mark
    See Garrett, Randall
    and Janifer, Laurence M(ark)
Phillips, Mary Geisler 1881-1964 10
Phillips, Michael
    See Nolan, William F.
Phillips, (Woodward) Prentice 1894-1981 10
Phillpotts, Eden 1862-1960 24
Phin
    See Thayer, Ernest Lawrence
Phipson, Joan
    See Fitzhardinge, Joan Margaret
Phiz
    See Browne, Hablot Knight
Phleger, Fred B. 1909-1993 34
Phleger, Marjorie Temple 1908(?)-1986 1
    Obituary 47
Piaget, Jean 1896-1980
    Obituary 23
Piatti, Celestino 1922- 16
Picard, Barbara Leonie 1917- 89
    Earlier sketch in SATA 2
    See also SAAS 10
Pichon, Liz 174
Pickard, Charles 1932- 36
Pickering, James Sayre 1897-1969 36
    Obituary 28
Pickering, Jimmy 195
Pickering, Robert B. 1950- 93
Pielichaty, Helena 1955- 142
Pien, Lark 222
Pienkowski, Jan (Michal) 1936- 131
    Earlier sketches in SATA 6, 58
    See also CLR 6
Pierce, Edith Gray 1893-1977 45
Pierce, Katherine
    See St. John, Wylly Folk
Pierce, Meredith Ann 1958- 127
    Brief entry 48
    Earlier sketch in SATA 67
    See also CLR 20
Pierce, Ruth (Ireland) 1936- 5
Pierce, Sharon
    See McCullough, Sharon Pierce

Pierce, Tamora 1954- 187
    Brief entry 49
    Earlier sketches in SATA 51, 96, 153
Pierce, Terry 178
Pierik, Robert 1921- 13
Piernas-Davenport, Gail 199
Piers, Robert
    See Anthony, Piers
Pig, Edward
    See Gorey, Edward (St. John)
Pignataro, Anna 1965- 223
Pike, Aprilynne 218
Pike, Bob
    See Pike, Robert W.
Pike, Christopher 1954(?)- 156
    Earlier sketch in SATA 68
    See also CLR 29
Pike, Deborah 1951- 89
Pike, E(dgar) Royston 1896-1980 22
    Obituary 56
Pike, R. William 1956- 92
Pike, Robert
    See Pike, Robert W.
Pike, Robert W. 1931- 102
Pike, Robert Wilson
    See Pike, Robert W.
Pilarski, Laura 1926- 13
Pilgrim, Anne
    See Allan, Mabel Esther
Pilkey, Dav 1966- 166
    Earlier sketches in SATA 68, 115
    See also CLR 160
Pilkey, David Murray, Jr.
    See Pilkey, Dav
Pilkington, Francis Meredyth 1907-1993 4
Pilkington, Roger (Windle) 1915-2003 10
    Obituary 144
Pilutti, Deb 208
Pin, Isabel 1975- 183
Pinchot, David 1914(?)-1983
    Obituary 34
Pincus, Harriet 1938- 27
Pinczes, Elinor J(ane) 1940- 81
Pine, Nicholas 1951- 91
Pine, Tillie S(chloss) 1896-1999 13
Pini, Richard (Alan) 1950- 89
Pini, Wendy 1951- 89
Pinkerton, Kathrene Sutherland (Gedney)
    1887-1967
    Obituary 26
Pinkett, Jada
    See Smith, Jada Pinkett
Pinkney, Andrea Davis 1963- 160
    Earlier sketch in SATA 113
Pinkney, Brian 1961- 206
    Earlier sketches in SATA 74, 148
    See also CLR 54
Pinkney, Gloria Jean 1941- 212
    Earlier sketch in SATA 85
Pinkney, J. Brian
    See Pinkney, Brian
Pinkney, Jerry 1939- 198
    Autobiography Feature 198
    Brief entry 32
    Earlier sketches in SATA 41, 71, 107, 151
    See also CLR 43
    See also SAAS 12
Pinkney, John 97
Pinkney, Sandra L. 193
    Earlier sketch in SATA 128
Pinkwater, D. Manus
    See Pinkwater, Daniel
Pinkwater, Daniel 1941- 210
    Earlier sketches in SATA 8, 46, 76, 114, 158
    See also CLR 4
    See also SAAS 3
Pinkwater, Daniel M.
    See Pinkwater, Daniel
Pinkwater, Daniel Manus
    See Pinkwater, Daniel
Pinkwater, Jill 188

Pinkwater, Manus
   See Pinkwater, Daniel
Pinner, Joma
   See Werner, Herma
Pinto, Sara .... _200_
Pioneer
   See Yates, Raymond F(rancis)
Piowaty, Kim Kennelly 1957- .... _49_
Piper, Roger
   See Fisher, John
Pirner, Connie White 1955- .... _72_
Piro, Richard 1934- .... _7_
Pirot, Alison Lohans
   See Lohans, Alison
Pirotta, Saviour .... _184_
Pirsig, Robert M(aynard) 1928- .... _39_
Pita
   See Rendon, Maria
Pitcher, C.
   See Pitcher, Caroline
Pitcher, Caroline 1948- .... _214_
   Earlier sketch in SATA _128_
Pitcher, Caroline Nell
   See Pitcher, Caroline
Pitman, (Isaac) James 1901-1985
   Obituary .... _46_
Pitre, Felix 1949- .... _84_
Pitrone, Jean Maddern 1920- .... _4_
Pittman, Helena Clare 1945- .... _71_
Pitz, Henry C(larence) 1895-1976 .... _4_
   Obituary .... _24_
Pitzer, Susanna 1958- .... _181_
Piven, Hanoch 1963- .... _173_
Pixley, Marcella .... _194_
Pizer, Vernon 1918- .... _21_
Place, Marian T(empleton) 1910- .... _3_
Place, Robin (Mary) 1926- .... _71_
Plaidy, Jean
   See Hibbert, Eleanor Alice Burford
Plain, Belva 1919-2010 .... _62_
Plaine, Alfred R. 1898(?)-1981
   Obituary .... _29_
Plant, Andrew .... _214_
Plath, Sylvia 1932-1963 .... _96_
Platt, Chris 1959- .... _185_
Platt, Kin 1911- .... _86_
   Earlier sketch in SATA _21_
   See also SAAS _17_
Platt, Randall 1948- .... _95_
Platt, Randall Beth
   See Platt, Randall
Platt, Richard 1953- .... _218_
   Earlier sketches in SATA _120, 166_
Playfellow, Robin
   See Ellis, Edward S.
Playsted, James
   See Wood, James Playsted
Plecas, Jennifer 1966- .... _229_
   Earlier sketches in SATA _84, 149_
Plimpton, George 1927-2003 .... _10_
   Obituary .... _150_
Plimpton, George Ames
   See Plimpton, George
Plomer, William Charles Franklin
   1903-1973 .... _24_
Plotz, Helen Ratnoff 1913-2000 .... _38_
Plourde, Lynn 1955- .... _218_
   Earlier sketches in SATA _122, 168_
Plowden, David 1932- .... _52_
Plowden, Martha Ward 1948- .... _98_
Plowhead, Ruth Gipson 1877-1967 .... _43_
Plowman, Stephanie 1922- .... _6_
Pluckrose, Henry 1931-2011 .... _141_
   Earlier sketch in SATA _13_
Pluckrose, Henry Arthur
   See Pluckrose, Henry
Plum, J.
   See Wodehouse, P. G.
Plum, Jennifer
   See Kurland, Michael

Plumb, Charles P. 1900(?)-1982
   Obituary .... _29_
Plume, Ilse .... _170_
   Brief entry .... _43_
Plumme, Don E.
   See Katz, Bobbi
Plummer, Margaret 1911- .... _2_
Plum-Ucci, Carol 1957- .... _184_
Poblocki, Dan 1981- .... _224_
Pochocki, Ethel (Frances) 1925- .... _76_
Podendorf, Illa (E.) 1903(?)-1983 .... _18_
   Obituary .... _35_
Podwal, Mark 1945- .... _224_
   Earlier sketches in SATA _101, 160_
Podwal, Mark H.
   See Podwal, Mark
Poe, Edgar Allan 1809-1849 .... _23_
Poe, Ty (Christopher) 1975- .... _94_
Pogany, William Andrew 1882-1955 .... _44_
   Brief entry .... _30_
Pogany, Willy
   See Pogany, William Andrew
Pogue, Carolyn 1948- .... _223_
Pogue, David 1963- .... _231_
Pohl, Frederik 1919- .... _24_
Pohlmann, Lillian (Grenfell) 1902-1997 ...... _11_
Pohrt, Tom 1953- .... _195_
   Earlier sketches in SATA _67, 152_
Pointon, Robert
   See Rooke, Daphne
Points, Larry G. 1945- .... _177_
   Earlier sketch in SATA _133_
Points, Larry Gene
   See Points, Larry G.
Pokeberry, P.J.
   See Mitchell, B.J.
POLA
   See Watson, Pauline
Polacco, Patricia 1944- .... _212_
   Earlier sketches in SATA _74, 123, 180_
   See also CLR _40_
Polacco, Patricia Ann
   See Polacco, Patricia
Polak, Monique 1960- .... _230_
   Earlier sketch in SATA _178_
Polatnick, Florence T. 1923- .... _5_
Polcovar, Jane 1948- .... _211_
Polder, Markus
   See Kruss, James
Polenghi, Evan 1961- .... _225_
Polese, Carolyn 1947- .... _58_
Polese, James 1914- .... _87_
Polette, Nancy (Jane) 1930- .... _42_
Polhamus, Jean Burt 1928- .... _21_
Polhemus, Coleman .... _210_
Policoff, Stephen Phillip 1948- .... _77_
Polikoff, Barbara G. 1929- .... _162_
   Earlier sketch in SATA _77_
Polikoff, Barbara Garland
   See Polikoff, Barbara G.
Polisar, Barry Louis 1954- .... _134_
   Earlier sketch in SATA _77_
Politi, Leo 1908-1996 .... _47_
   Obituary .... _88_
   Earlier sketch in SATA _1_
   See also CLR _29_
Polking, Kirk 1925- .... _5_
Pollack, Jill S. 1963- .... _88_
Pollack, Merrill S. 1924-1988
   Obituary .... _55_
Polland, Barbara K(ay) 1939- .... _44_
Polland, Madeleine A(ngela Cahill) 1918- ... _68_
   Earlier sketch in SATA _6_
   See also SAAS _8_
Pollema-Cahill, Phyllis 1958- .... _123_
Pollock, Bruce 1945- .... _46_
Pollock, Mary
   See Blyton, Enid
Pollock, Penny 1935- .... _137_
   Brief entry .... _42_
   Earlier sketch in SATA _44_

Pollowitz, Melinda Kilborn 1944- .... _26_
Polner, Murray 1928- .... _64_
Polonsky, Arthur 1925- .... _34_
Polseno, Jo .... _17_
Pomaska, Anna 1946- .... _117_
Pomerantz, Charlotte 1930- .... _177_
   Earlier sketches in SATA _20, 80_
Pomeroy, Pete
   See Roth, Arthur J(oseph)
Pon, Cindy 1973- .... _216_
Pon, Cynthia .... _229_
Pond, Alonzo W(illiam) 1894-1986 .... _5_
Pontiflet, Ted 1932- .... _32_
Poole, Gray Johnson 1906- .... _1_
Poole, Josephine
   See Helyar, Jane Penelope Josephine
Poole, (Jane Penelope) Josephine
   See Helyar, Jane Penelope Josephine
Poole, Lynn 1910-1969 .... _1_
Poole, Peggy 1925- .... _39_
Poon, Janice .... _228_
Poortvliet, Rien 1932- .... _65_
   Brief entry .... _37_
Pope, Elizabeth Marie 1917-1992 .... _38_
   Brief entry .... _36_
Pope, Kevin 1958- .... _183_
Popescu, Christine
   See Pullein-Thompson, Christine
Poploff, Michelle 1956- .... _67_
Popp, K. Wendy .... _91_
Poppel, Hans 1942- .... _71_
Porfirio, Guy 1958- .... _197_
Portal, Colette 1936- .... _6_
Porte, Barbara Ann 1943- .... _152_
   Brief entry .... _45_
   Earlier sketches in SATA _57, 93_
Porter, A(nthony) P(eyton) 1945- .... _68_
Porter, Connie (Rose) 1959(?)- .... _129_
   Earlier sketch in SATA _81_
Porter, Donald Clayton
   See Gerson, Noel Bertram
Porter, Eleanor H(odgman) 1868-1920
   See CLR _110_
Porter, Gene Stratton
   See Stratton-Porter, Gene
Porter, Janice Lee 1953- .... _108_
   Earlier sketch in SATA _68_
Porter, Katherine Anne 1890-1980 .... _39_
   Obituary .... _23_
Porter, Kathryn
   See Swinford, Betty (June Wells)
Porter, Pamela 1956- .... _193_
Porter, Sheena 1935- .... _24_
   See also SAAS _10_
Porter, Sue
   See Limb, Sue
Porter, Sue 1951- .... _213_
   Earlier sketch in SATA _76_
Porter, Tracey .... _191_
Porter, William Sydney
   See Henry, O.
Portis, Antoinette .... _189_
Porto, Tony 1960- .... _153_
Portteus, Eleanora Marie Manthei (?)-1983
   Obituary .... _36_
Posada, Mia .... _187_
Posell, Elsa Z(eigerman) -1995 .... _3_
Posesorski, Sherie .... _216_
Posten, Margaret L(ois) 1915- .... _10_
Postgate, Daniel 1964- .... _216_
Posthuma, Sieb 1960- .... _150_
Postier, Jim 1965- .... _202_
Potok, Chaim 1929-2002 .... _106_
   Obituary .... _134_
   Earlier sketch in SATA _33_
   See also CLR _92_
Potok, Herbert Harold
   See Potok, Chaim
Potok, Herman Harold
   See Potok, Chaim
Potter, Alicia .... _216_

Potter, Beatrix 1866-1943 .... *132*
  Earlier sketch in SATA *100*
  See also YABC *1*
  See also CLR *165*
Potter, Ellen 1973- *218*
Potter, Giselle *187*
  Earlier sketch in SATA *150*
Potter, Helen Beatrix
  See Potter, Beatrix
Potter, Katherine *217*
Potter, Margaret 1926-1998 .... *21*
  Obituary *104*
Potter, Marian 1915- *9*
Potter, Miriam Clark 1886-1965 .... *3*
Potter, Ryan *230*
Poulin, Stephane 1961- *98*
  See also CLR *28*
Poulton, Kimberly 1957(?)- *136*
Pournelle, Jerry 1933- *161*
  Earlier sketches in SATA *26, 91*
Pournelle, Jerry Eugene
  See Pournelle, Jerry
Povelite, Kay 1955- *102*
Pow, Tom 1950- *163*
Powe-Allred, Alexandra
  See Allred, Alexandra Powe
Powell, A. M.
  See Morgan, Alfred P(owell)
Powell, Consie *174*
Powell, E. Sandy 1947- *72*
Powell, E.S.
  See Powell, E. Sandy
Powell, Pamela 1960- *78*
Powell, Patricia Hruby 1951- *136*
Powell, Randy 1956- *118*
Powell, Richard Stillman
  See Barbour, Ralph Henry
Powell, Robert (Stephenson Smyth) Baden
  See Baden-Powell, Robert (Stephenson Smyth)
Powell, Stephanie 1953- *93*
Power, Margaret (M.) 1945- *125*
  Earlier sketch in SATA *75*
Powers, Anne
  See Schwartz, Anne Powers
Powers, Bill 1931- *52*
  Brief entry *31*
Powers, Daniel 1959- *164*
Powers, J. L. *195*
Powers, Jessica
  See Powers, J. L.
Powers, Jessica Lynn
  See Powers, J. L.
Powers, Margaret
  See Heal, Edith
Powers, Tim 1952- *107*
Powers, Timothy Thomas
  See Powers, Tim
Powledge, Fred 1935- *37*
Poydar, Nancy *190*
Poynter, Margaret 1927- *27*
Prachaticka, Marketa
  See Kolibalova, Marketa
Prachatika, Marketa
  See Kolibalova, Marketa
Prager, Arthur *44*
Prager, Ellen J. 1962- *136*
Prange, Beckie *172*
Prap, Lila 1955- *177*
Praprotnik-Zupancic, Lilijana
  See Prap, Lila
Pratchett, Terence David John
  See Pratchett, Terry
Pratchett, Terry 1948- *185*
  Earlier sketches in SATA *82, 139*
  See also CLR *64*
Prater, John 1947- *149*
  Earlier sketches in SATA *72, 103*
Prato, Rodica *184*
Pratt, Christine Joy *214*
Pratt, (Murray) Fletcher 1897-1956 .... *102*

Pratt, Kristin Joy 1976- *87*
Pratt, Pierre 1962- *208*
  Earlier sketches in SATA *95, 166*
Preiss, Byron 1953-2005 .... *166*
  Brief entry *42*
  Earlier sketch in SATA *47*
Preiss, Byron Cary
  See Preiss, Byron
Preller, James 1961- *209*
  Earlier sketch in SATA *88*
Prelutsky, Jack 1940- *171*
  Earlier sketches in SATA *22, 66, 118*
  See also CLR *115*
Prentice, Amy
  See Kaler, James Otis
Prescott, Casey
  See Morris, Chris(topher Crosby)
Presnall, Judith (Ann) Janda 1943- *96*
Pressler, Mirjam 1940- *155*
Preston, Douglas 1956- *113*
Preston, Edna Mitchell *40*
Preston, Lillian Elvira 1918- *47*
Preus, Margi *209*
Preussler, Otfried 1923- *24*
Prevert, Jacques 1900-1977
  Obituary *30*
Prevert, Jacques Henri Marie
  See Prevert, Jacques
Prevost, Guillaume 1964- *192*
Prevost, Mikela *203*
Price, Beverley Joan 1931- *98*
Price, Charlie *187*
Price, Christine (Hilda) 1928-1980 .... *3*
  Obituary *23*
Price, Garrett 1896-1979
  Obituary *22*
Price, Jennifer
  See Hoover, Helen (Drusilla Blackburn)
Price, Joan 1931- *124*
Price, Jonathan (Reeve) 1941- *46*
Price, Karen 1957- *125*
Price, Kathy Z. 1957- *172*
Price, Lucie Locke
  See Locke, Lucie
Price, Olive 1903-1991 .... *8*
Price, Susan 1955- *128*
  Earlier sketches in SATA *25, 85*
Price, Willard 1887-1983 .... *48*
  Brief entry *38*
Price-Groff, Claire *127*
Priceman, Marjorie 1958- *168*
  Earlier sketches in SATA *81, 120*
Prichard, Katharine Susannah 1883-1969 ..... *66*
Priddy, Roger *227*
Prideaux, Tom 1908-1993 .... *37*
  Obituary *76*
Priestley, Alice 1962- *227*
  Earlier sketch in SATA *95*
Priestley, Chris 1958- *198*
Priestley, Lee (Shore) 1904-1999 .... *27*
Priestly, Doug 1954- *122*
Priestly, Douglas Michael
  See Priestly, Doug
Prieto, Mariana Beeching 1912-1999 .... *8*
Priley, Margaret (Ann) Hubbard 1909-1992
  Obituary *130*
Primavera, Elise 1954- *230*
  Brief entry *48*
  Earlier sketches in SATA *58, 109, 185*
Prime, Derek (James) 1931- *34*
Prince, Alison (Mary) 1931- *86*
  Earlier sketch in SATA *28*
Prince, April Jones 1975- *180*
Prince, J(ack) H(arvey) 1908- *17*
Prince, Joshua *188*
Prince, Maggie *102*
Prineas, Sarah *204*
Pringle, Eric *138*

Pringle, Laurence 1935- *201*
  Autobiography Feature *201*
  Earlier sketches in SATA *4, 68, 104, 154*
  See also CLR *57*
  See also SAAS *6*
Pringle, Laurence Patrick
  See Pringle, Laurence
Prinz, Yvonne 1960- *175*
Prior, Natalie Jane 1963- *106*
Pritchett, Elaine H(illyer) 1920- *36*
Pritchett, Laura 1971- *178*
Pritchett, Laura Rose
  See Pritchett, Laura
Pritts, Kim Derek 1953- *83*
Prochazkova, Iva 1953- *68*
Proctor, Everitt
  See Montgomery, Rutherford George
Proeysen, Alf 1914-1970 .... *67*
  See also CLR *24*
Professor Scribbler
  See Hollingsworth, Mary
Proimos, James 1955- *217*
  Earlier sketch in SATA *173*
Promitzer, Rebecca *229*
Prose, Francine 1947- *198*
  Earlier sketches in SATA *101, 149*
Prosek, James 1975- *216*
Protopopescu, Orel *186*
Protopopescu, Orel Odinov
  See Protopopescu, Orel
Provensen, Alice 1918- *147*
  Earlier sketches in SATA *9, 70*
  See also CLR *11*
Provensen, Martin 1916-1987 .... *70*
  Obituary *51*
  Earlier sketch in SATA *9*
  See also CLR *11*
Provensen, Martin Elias
  See Provensen, Martin
Provenzo, Eugene (F., Jr.) 1949- *142*
  Earlier sketch in SATA *78*
Provist, d'Alain 1906-1989
  See Diop, Birago (Ismael)
Provost, Gail Levine 1944- *65*
Provost, Gary (Richard) 1944-1995 .... *66*
Proysen, Alf
  See Proeysen, Alf
Pruett, Candace (J.) 1968- *157*
Pryor, Bonnie H. 1942- *69*
Pryor, Boori (Monty) 1950- *112*
Pryor, Helen Brenton 1897-1972 .... *4*
Pryor, Michael 1957- *153*
Pucci, Albert John 1920- *44*
Pudney, John (Sleigh) 1909-1977 .... *24*
Pugh, Ellen (Tiffany) 1920- *7*
Pullein-Thompson, Christine 1925-2005 ...... *82*
  Obituary *172*
  Earlier sketch in SATA *3*
Pullein-Thompson, Diana
  See Farr, Diana
Pullein-Thompson, Joanna Maxwell
  1898-1961 .... *82*
Pullein-Thompson, Josephine (Mary
  Wedderburn) *82*
  Earlier sketch in SATA *3*
Pullen, Zachary *189*
Pullman, Philip 1946- *198*
  Earlier sketches in SATA *65, 103, 150*
  See also CLR *84*
  See also SAAS *17*
Pullman, Philip Nicholas
  See Pullman, Philip
Pulver, Harry, Jr. 1960- *129*
Pulver, Robin 1945- *208*
  Earlier sketches in SATA *76, 133*
Puner, Helen W(alker) 1915-1989 .... *37*
  Obituary *63*
Purdy, Carol 1943- *120*
  Earlier sketch in SATA *66*
Purdy, Susan G(old) 1939- *8*
Purkiss, Diane 1961- *194*

Purmell, Ann 1953- 206
  Earlier sketch in SATA *147*
Purnell, Idella 1901-1982 120
Purscell, Phyllis 1934- 7
Purtill, Richard L. 1931- 53
Pushker, Gloria 1927- 162
  Earlier sketch in SATA *75*
Pushker, Gloria Teles
  See Pushker, Gloria
Pushkin, Aleksandr Sergeevich
  See Pushkin, Alexander
Pushkin, Alexander 1799-1837 61
Putnam, Alice 1916- 61
Putnam, Arthur Lee
  See Alger, Horatio, Jr.
Putnam, Peter B(rock) 1920-1998 30
  Obituary 106
Puttapipat, Niroot 199
Puttock, Simon 178
Puvilland, Alex 205
Puvilland, Alexandre
  See Puvilland, Alex
Puybaret, Eric 1976- 299
  Earlier sketch in SATA *195*
Pyle, Charles S. 1954(?)- 229
Pyle, Chuck
  See Pyle, Charles S.
Pyle, Howard 1853-1911 100
  Earlier sketch in SATA *16*
  See also CLR *117*
Pyle, Katharine 1863-1938 66
Pyne, Mable Mandeville 1903-1969 9
Pyrnelle, Louise-Clarke 1850-1907 114

Q

Quackenbush, Robert M(ead) 1929- 133
  Autobiography Feature 133
  Earlier sketches in SATA *7, 70*
  See also CLR *122*
  See also SAAS *7*
Qualey, Marsha 1953- 124
  Earlier sketch in SATA *79*
Qualls, Sean 177
Quammen, David 1948- 7
Quark, Jason
  See Eldin, Peter
Quarles, Benjamin 1904-1996 12
Quarles, Benjamin Arthur
  See Quarles, Benjamin
Quatermass, Martin
  See Carpenter, John
Quattlebaum, Mary 1958- 185
  Earlier sketches in SATA *88, 134*
Quay, Emma 173
  Earlier sketch in SATA *119*
Queen, Ellery
  See Deming, Richard
  and Dannay, Frederic
  and Davidson, Avram (James)
  and Fairman, Paul W.
  and Flora, Fletcher
  and Holding, James (Clark Carlisle, Jr.)
  and Hoch, Edward D.
  and Kane, Henry
  and Lee, Manfred B.
  and Marlowe, Stephen
  and Powell, (Oval) Talmage
  and Sheldon, Walter J(ames)
  and Sturgeon, Theodore (Hamilton)
  and Tracy, Don(ald Fiske)
  and Vance, Jack
Queen Latifah 1970- 185
Queen Raina
  See al Abdullah, Rania
Quennell, Marjorie Courtney 1884-1972 29
Quentin
  See Sheldon, David

Quentin, Brad
  See Bisson, Terry
Quest, (Edna) Olga W(ilbourne) Hall
  See Hall-Quest, (Edna) Olga W(ilbourne)
Quick, Annabelle 1922-1986 2
Quigg, Jane (Hulda) (?)-1986
  Obituary 49
Quigley, Sarah 1976- 220
Quill, Monica
  See McInerny, Ralph
Quin-Harkin, Janet 1941- 165
  Earlier sketches in SATA *18, 90, 119*
Quin-Harkin, Janet Elizabeth
  See Quin-Harkin, Janet
Quinlan, Susan E. 1954- 88
Quinlan, Susan Elizabeth
  See Quinlan, Susan E.
Quinn, Elisabeth 1881-1962 22
Quinn, Pat 1947- 130
Quinn, Patrick 1950- 73
Quinn, Rob 1972- 138
Quinn, Susan 1940- 30
Quinn, Susan Taft
  See Quinn, Susan
Quinn, Theodora K.
  See Kroeber, Theodora (Kracaw)
Quinn, Vernon
  See Quinn, Elisabeth
Quirk, Anne (E.) 1956- 99
Quixley, Jim 1931- 56
Quyth, Gabriel
  See Jennings, Gary

R

Ra, Carol F. 1939- 76
Raab, Evelyn 1951- 129
Rabb, Margo 1972- 188
Rabb, M.E.
  See Rabb, Margo
Rabe, Berniece (Louise) 1928- 148
  Autobiography Feature 148
  Earlier sketches in SATA *7, 77*
  See also SAAS *10*
Rabe, Olive H(anson) (?)-1968 13
Rabin, Staton 1958- 162
  Earlier sketch in SATA *84*
Rabinowich, Ellen 1946- 29
Rabinowitz, Sandy 1954- 52
  Brief entry 39
Rachlin, Carol K(ing) 1919- 64
Rachlin, Harvey 1951- 47
Rachlin, Harvey Brant
  See Rachlin, Harvey
Rachlin, Nahid 64
Rachlis, Eugene (Jacob) 1920-1986
  Obituary 50
Rackham, Arthur 1867-1939 100
  Earlier sketch in SATA *15*
  See also CLR *57*
Racoma, Robin Yoko 1953- 207
Raczka, Bob 1963- 228
  Earlier sketches in SATA *163, 191*
Radencich, Marguerite C. 1952-1998 79
Rader, Laura 197
Radford, Ruby L(orraine) 1891-1971 6
Radin, Ruth Yaffe 1938- 107
  Brief entry 52
  Earlier sketch in SATA *56*
Radlauer, David 1952- 28
Radlauer, Edward 1921- 15
Radlauer, Ruth Shaw 1926- 98
  Earlier sketch in SATA *15*
Radley, Gail 1951- 112
  Earlier sketch in SATA *25*
Radunsky, Vladimir 177
Radzinski, Kandy 1948- 212
Rae, Gwynedd 1892-1977 37
Raebeck, Lois 1921- 5

Rael, Elsa Okon 1927-
  See CLR *84*
Raffi
  See Cavoukian, Raffi
Raftery, Gerald (Bransfield) 1905-1986 11
Ragan-Reid, Gale 1956- 90
Rahaman, Vashanti 1953- 98
Rahn, Joan Elma 1929- 27
Rai, Bali 1971- 152
Raible, Alton (Robert) 1918- 35
Raiff, Stan 1930- 11
Railsback, Lisa 230
Raines, Shirley C(arol) 1945- 128
Rainey, W. B.
  See Blassingame, Wyatt Rainey
Rake, Jody 1961- 157
Rallison, Janette 1966- 183
Ralston, Jan
  See Dunlop, Agnes M. R.
Rama, Sue 190
Ramal, Walter
  See de la Mare, Walter (John)
Ramanujan, A(ttipat) K(rishnaswami)
  1929-1993 86
Rame, David
  See Divine, Arthur Durham
Ramirez, Jose 1967- 198
Ramirez, Orlando L. 1972- 194
Ramos, Jorge 1958- 205
Ramstad, Ralph L. 1919- 115
Ramthun, Bonnie 214
Rana, Indi
  See Rana, Indira Higham
Rana, Indira Higham 1944- 82
Rana, J.
  See Bhatia, Jamunadevi
Ranadive, Gail 1944- 10
Rand, Ann (Binkley) 30
Rand, Gloria 1925- 156
  Earlier sketch in SATA *101*
Rand, Paul 1914-1996 6
Randall, Carrie
  See Ransom, Candice
Randall, David 1972- 167
Randall, Florence Engel 1917-1997 5
Randall, Janet
  See Young, Janet Randall
  and Young, Robert W(illiam)
Randall, Robert
  See Garrett, Randall
  and Silverberg, Robert
Randall, Ruth (Elaine) Painter 1892-1971 3
Randell, Beverley
  See Price, Beverley Joan
Randle, Kristen D. 1952- 92
  Autobiography Feature 119
  See also SAAS *24*
Randle, Kristen Downey
  See Randle, Kristen D.
Randolph, Boynton M.D.
  See Ellis, Edward S.
Randolph, Ellen
  See Rawn, Melanie
Randolph, Geoffrey
  See Ellis, Edward S.
Randolph, J. H.
  See Ellis, Edward S.
Randolph, Lieutenant J. H.
  See Ellis, Edward S.
Rands, William Brighty 1823-1882 17
Raney, Ken 1953- 74
Rankin, Joan 1940- 212
  Earlier sketches in SATA *88, 148*
Rankin, Laura 1953(?)- 176
Ranney, Agnes V. 1916-1985 6
Ransom, Candice 1952- 222
  Brief entry 49
  Earlier sketches in SATA *52, 89, 135, 183*
Ransom, Jeanie Franz 1957- 187
Ransome, Arthur (Michell) 1884-1967 22
  See also CLR *8*

Ransome, James E. 1961- 227
Earlier sketches in SATA *76, 123, 178*
See also CLR *86*
Rant, Tol E.
See Longyear, Barry B(rookes)
Rao, Rohitash 218
Raphael, Elaine
See Bolognese, Elaine
Raposo, Joseph Guilherme 1938-1989
Obituary 61
Rapp, Adam 1968- 148
Rappaport, Doreen 211
Earlier sketch in SATA *151*
Rappaport, Eva 1924- 6
Rappoport, Ken 1935- 167
Earlier sketch in SATA *89*
Rarick, Carrie 1911-2002 41
Raschka, Chris 1959- 207
Earlier sketches in SATA *80, 117, 166*
Raschka, Christopher
See Raschka, Chris
Rascol, Sabina I. 159
Rash, Andy 219
Earlier sketch in SATA *162*
Raskin, Edith Lefkowitz 1908-1987 9
Raskin, Ellen 1928-1984 139
Earlier sketches in SATA *2, 38*
See also CLR *12*
Raskin, Joseph 1897-1982 12
Obituary 29
Rathjen, Carl Henry 1909-1984 11
Rathmann, Peggy 1953- 157
Earlier sketch in SATA *94*
See also CLR *77*
Ratliff, Thomas M. 1948- 118
Ratner, Sue Lynn
See Alexander, Sue
Rattigan, Jama Kim 1951- 99
Ratto, Linda Lee 1952- 79
Rattray, Simon
See Trevor, Elleston
Ratz de Tagyos, Paul 1958- 198
Earlier sketch in SATA *76*
Rau, Dana Meachen 1971- 218
Earlier sketches in SATA *94, 167*
Rau, Margaret 1913- 168
Earlier sketch in SATA *9*
See also CLR *8*
Rauch, Mabel Thompson 1888-1972
Obituary 26
Raucher, Herman 1928- 8
Raude, Karina 199
Rauh, Sherry
See North, Sherry
Raum, Elizabeth 1949- 155
Raut, Radhashyam 222
Rave, Friederike 1970- 231
Raven, Margot Theis 184
RavenWolf, Silver 1956- 155
Ravielli, Anthony 1916-1997 3
Obituary 95
Ravilious, Robin 1944- 77
Ravishankar, Anushka 1961- 200
Rawding, F(rederick) W(illiam) 1930- 55
Rawlings, Marjorie Kinnan 1896-1953 100
See also YABC *1*
See also CLR *63*
Rawlins, Donna 1956- 206
Rawlinson, Julia 212
Earlier sketch in SATA *175*
Rawls, (Woodrow) Wilson 1913-1984 22
See also CLR *81*
Rawlyk, George Alexander 1935- 64
Rawn, Melanie 1954- 98
Rawn, Melanie Robin
See Rawn, Melanie
Rawson, Katherine 1955- 190
Ray, Carl 1943-1978 63
Ray, Deborah
See Kogan Ray, Deborah

Ray, Delia 1963- 179
Earlier sketch in SATA *70*
Ray, Irene
See Sutton, Margaret Beebe
Ray, Jane 1960- 196
Earlier sketches in SATA *72, 152*
Ray, JoAnne 1935- 9
Ray, Mary (Eva Pedder) 1932- 127
Earlier sketch in SATA *2*
Ray, Mary Lyn 1946- 154
Earlier sketch in SATA *90*
Rayban, Chloe 1944- 167
Rayevsky, Robert 1955- 190
Earlier sketch in SATA *81*
Raymond, James Crossley 1917-1981
Obituary 29
Raymond, Robert
See Alter, Robert Edmond
Rayner, Catherine 204
Rayner, Hugh 151
Rayner, Mary 1933- 87
Earlier sketch in SATA *22*
See also CLR *41*
Rayner, Shoo
See Rayner, Hugh
Rayner, William 1929- 55
Brief entry 36
Raynor, Dorka 28
Raynor, Gemma 1985- 216
Rayson, Steven 1932- 30
Rayyan, Omar 1968- 216
Razzell, Arthur (George) 1925- 11
Razzell, Mary (Catherine) 1930- 102
Razzi, James 1931- 10
Read, Elfreida 1920- 2
Read, Nicholas 1956- 146
Read, Piers Paul 1941- 21
Reade, Deborah 1949- 69
Reader, Dennis 1929- 71
Reading, Richard P(atrick) 1962- 161
Readman, Jo 1958- 89
Ready, Kirk L(ewis) 1943- 39
Reaney, James 1926-2008 43
Reaney, James Crerar
See Reaney, James
Reardon, Joyce
See Pearson, Ridley
Reaver, Chap 1935-1993 69
Obituary 77
Reaver, Herbert R.
See Reaver, Chap
Reaves, J. Michael
See Reaves, (James) Michael
Reaves, (James) Michael 1950- 99
Reber, Deborah 189
Recorvits, Helen 191
Redding, Robert Hull 1919- 2
Redekopp, Elsa 61
Redlich, Ben 1977- 181
Redsand, Anna 1948- 184
Redway, Ralph
See Hamilton, Charles (Harold St. John)
Redway, Ridley
See Hamilton, Charles (Harold St. John)
Reece, Colleen L. 1935- 116
Reece, Gabrielle 1970- 108
Reed, Amy 1979- 223
Reed, Betty Jane 1921- 4
Reed, Dallas
See Pendleton, Thomas
Reed, E.
See Evans, Mari
Reed, Gwendolyn E(lizabeth) 1932- 21
Reed, Kit 1932- 184
Autobiography Feature 184
Earlier sketches in SATA *34, 116*
Reed, Lynn Rowe 215
Earlier sketch in SATA *171*
Reed, Mike 1951- 211
Reed, Neil 1961- 99

Reed, Talbot Baines 1852-1893
See CLR *76*
Reed, Thomas (James) 1947- 34
Reed, William Maxwell 1871-1962 15
Reeder, Carolyn 1937- 97
Earlier sketch in SATA *66*
See also CLR *69*
Reeder, Colin (Dawson) 1938- 74
Reeder, Colonel Red
See Reeder, Russell P(otter), Jr.
Reeder, Russell P(otter), Jr. 1902-1998 4
Obituary 101
Reeder, Stephanie Owen 1951- 102
Reed-Jones, Carol 1955- 112
Reef, Catherine 1951- 223
Earlier sketches in SATA *73, 128, 189*
Reekie, Jocelyn (Margaret) 1947- 145
Reeman, Douglas Edward 1924- 63
Brief entry 28
Rees, Celia 1949- 124
Rees, David (Bartlett) 1936-1993 69
Obituary 76
Earlier sketch in SATA *36*
See also SAAS *5*
Rees, Douglas 1947- 169
Rees, Ennis (Samuel, Jr.) 1925-2009 3
Rees, (George) Leslie (Clarence)
1905-2000 105
Obituary 135
Reese, Bob
See Reese, Robert A.
Reese, Carolyn Johnson 1938- 64
Reese, Della 1931(?)- 114
Reese, Lyn
See Reese, Carolyn Johnson
Reese, Robert A. 1938- 60
Brief entry 53
Reese, (John) Terence 1913-1996 59
Reeve, Joel
See Cox, William R(obert)
Reeve, Kirk 1934- 117
Reeve, Philip 201
Earlier sketch in SATA *170*
Reeve, Rosie 188
Earlier sketch in SATA *186*
Reeves, Dia 1977- 227
Reeves, Faye Couch 1953- 76
Reeves, James
See Reeves, John Morris
Reeves, Jeni 1947- 111
Reeves, John Morris 1909-1978 87
Earlier sketch in SATA *15*
Reeves, Joyce 1911- 17
Reeves, Lawrence F. 1926- 29
Reeves, Ruth Ellen
See Ranney, Agnes V.
Regan, Dian Curtis 1950- 224
Autobiography Feature 149
Earlier sketches in SATA *75, 133, 149*
Regehr, Lydia 1903-1991 37
Reger, James P. 1952- 106
Reger, Rob 1969- 227
Reggiani, Renee 1925- 18
Rehm, Karl M. 1935- 72
Reibstein, Mark 211
Reich, Ali
See Katz, Bobbi
Reich, Susanna 1954- 214
Earlier sketch in SATA *113*
Reiche, Dietlof 1941- 159
Reichert, Edwin C(lark) 1909-1988
Obituary 57
Reichert, Mickey Zucker
See Reichert, Miriam Zucker
Reichert, Miriam Zucker 1962- 85
Reichert, Renee 172
Reichhold, Jane(t E.) 1937- 147
Reid, Alastair 1926- 46
Reid, Barbara 1922- 21
Reid, Barbara (Jane) 1957- 93
See also CLR *64*

Reid, Desmond
  See Moorcock, Michael
  and McNeilly, Wilfred (Glassford)
Reid, Eugenie Chazal 1924- *12*
Reid, John Calvin *21*
Reid, (Thomas) Mayne 1818-1883 .... *24*
Reid, Meta Mayne 1905-1991 .... *58*
  Brief entry *36*
Reid, Robin (Nicole) 1969- *145*
Reid Banks, Lynne 1929- *165*
  Earlier sketches in SATA *22, 75, 111*
  See also CLR *86*
Reider, Katja 1960- *126*
Reid Jenkins, Debra 1955- *87*
Reidy, Jean *228*
Reiff, Stephanie Ann 1948- *47*
  Brief entry *28*
Reig, June 1933- *30*
Reigot, Betty Polisar 1924- *55*
  Brief entry *41*
Reilly, Joan *195*
Reim, Melanie (K.) 1956- *104*
Reinach, Jacquelyn (Krasne) 1930-2000 ...... *28*
Reiner, Carl 1922- *151*
Reiner, William B(uck) 1910-1976 .... *46*
  Obituary *30*
Reinfeld, Fred 1910-1964 .... *3*
Reinhardt, Dana 1971- *175*
Reinhart, Matthew 1971- *197*
  Earlier sketch in SATA *161*
Reiniger, Lotte 1899-1981 .... *40*
  Obituary *33*
Reinsma, Carol 1949- *91*
Reinstedt, Randall A. 1935- *101*
Reinstedt, Randy
  See Reinstedt, Randall A.
Reisberg, Mira 1955- *82*
Reisberg, Veg
  See Reisberg, Mira
Reiser, Lynn 1944- *180*
  Earlier sketches in SATA *81, 138*
Reiser, Lynn Whisnant
  See Reiser, Lynn
Reisgies, Teresa (Maria) 1966- *74*
Reiss, Johanna 1929(?)- *18*
  See also CLR *19*
Reiss, Johanna de Leeuw
  See Reiss, Johanna
Reiss, John J. *23*
Reiss, Kathryn 1957- *144*
  Earlier sketch in SATA *76*
Reit, Seymour Victory 1918-2001 .... *21*
  Obituary *133*
Reit, Sy
  See Reit, Seymour Victory
Relf, Patricia 1954- *134*
  Earlier sketch in SATA *71*
Remark, Erich Paul
  See Remarque, Erich Maria
Remarque, Erich Maria 1898-1970
  See CLR *159*
Remi, Georges 1907-1983 .... *13*
  Obituary *32*
  See also CLR *114*
Remington, Frederic S(ackrider)
  1861-1909 .... *41*
Remkiewicz, Frank 1939- *217*
  Earlier sketches in SATA *77, 152*
Rempt, Fiona 1973- *198*
Remy, Georges
  See Remi, Georges
Renaud, Anne 1957- *211*
Renaud, Bernadette 1945- *66*
Renault, Mary 1905-1983 .... *23*
  Obituary *36*
Rendell, Joan *28*
Rendina, Laura (Jones) Cooper 1902- *10*
Rendon, Marcie R. 1952- *97*
Rendon, Maria 1965- *116*
Renee, Janina 1956- *140*
Renfro, Ed 1924- *79*

Renick, Marion (Lewis) 1905-1983 .... *1*
Renier, Aaron 1977- *202*
Renken, Aleda 1907- *27*
Renlie, Frank H. 1936- *11*
Rennert, Laura Joy *224*
Rennert, Richard Scott 1956- *67*
Rennison, Louise 1951- *149*
Reno, Dawn E(laine) 1953- *130*
Rensie, Willis
  See Eisner, Will
Renton, Cam
  See Armstrong, Richard
Renvoize, Jean *5*
Resau, Laura 1973- *230*
  Earlier sketch in SATA *190*
Resciniti, Angelo G. 1952- *75*
Resnick, Michael David
  See Resnick, Mike
Resnick, Mike 1942- *159*
  Earlier sketches in SATA *38, 106*
Resnick, Seymour 1920- *23*
Retla, Robert
  See Alter, Robert Edmond
Rettig, Liz *199*
Rettstatt, Chris
  See Ashland, Monk
Reuter, Bjarne (B.) 1950- *142*
  Earlier sketch in SATA *68*
Reuter, Carol (Joan) 1931- *2*
Revena
  See Wright, Betty Ren
Revsbech, Vicki
  See Liestman, Vicki
Rex, Adam *225*
  Earlier sketch in SATA *186*
Rex, Michael *191*
Rey, H. A. 1898-1977 .... *100*
  Earlier sketches in SATA *1, 26, 69*
  See also CLR *93*
Rey, Hans Augusto
  See Rey, H. A.
Rey, Luis V. 1955- *201*
Rey, Margret 1906-1996 .... *86*
  Obituary *93*
  Earlier sketch in SATA *26*
  See also CLR *93*
Rey, Margret Elisabeth
  See Rey, Margret
Reyher, Becky
  See Reyher, Rebecca Hourwich
Reyher, Rebecca Hourwich 1897-1987 .... *18*
  Obituary *50*
Reynish, Jenny *222*
Reynold, Ann
  See Bernardo, Anilu
Reynolds, Aaron 1970- *197*
Reynolds, Adrian 1963- *192*
Reynolds, C. Buck 1957- *107*
Reynolds, Dickson
  See Reynolds, Helen Mary Greenwood Campbell
Reynolds, Helen Mary Greenwood Campbell
  1884-1969
  Obituary *26*
Reynolds, Jan 1956- *180*
Reynolds, John
  See Whitlock, Ralph
Reynolds, Madge
  See Whitlock, Ralph
Reynolds, Malvina 1900-1978 .... *44*
  Obituary *24*
Reynolds, Marilyn 1935- *121*
  See also SAAS *23*
Reynolds, Marilyn M.
  See Reynolds, Marilyn
Reynolds, Marilynn 1940- *141*
  Earlier sketch in SATA *80*
Reynolds, Pamela 1923- *34*
Reynolds, Peter H. 1961- *226*
  Earlier sketch in SATA *128*
Reynolds, Peter J. 1961- *179*

Reynolds, Susan *179*
Rhine, Richard
  See Silverstein, Alvin
  and Silverstein, Virginia B.
Rhoades, Diane 1952- *90*
Rhodes, Bennie (Loran) 1927- *35*
Rhodes, Donna McKee 1962- *87*
Rhodes, Frank Harold Trevor 1926- *37*
Rhuday-Perkovich, Olugbemisola *227*
Rhue, Morton
  See Strasser, Todd
Rhyne, Nancy 1926- *66*
Rhynes, Martha E. 1939- *141*
Ribbons, Ian 1924- *37*
  Brief entry *30*
  See also SAAS *3*
Ricciuti, Edward R(aphael) 1938- *10*
Rice, Alice (Caldwell) Hegan 1870-1942 ..... *63*
Rice, Bebe Faas 1932- *89*
Rice, Charles D(uane) 1910-1971
  Obituary *27*
Rice, Dale R. 1948- *42*
Rice, Dale Richard
  See Rice, Dale R.
Rice, Dick
  See Rice, R. Hugh
Rice, Earle (Wilmont), Jr. 1928- *151*
  Earlier sketch in SATA *92*
Rice, Edward 1918-2001 .... *47*
  Brief entry *42*
Rice, Elizabeth 1913-1976 .... *2*
Rice, Eve 1951- *91*
  Earlier sketch in SATA *34*
Rice, Eve Hart
  See Rice, Eve
Rice, Inez 1907- *13*
Rice, James 1934- *93*
  Earlier sketch in SATA *22*
Rice, John F. 1958- *82*
Rice, R. Hugh 1929- *115*
Rice, Richard H.
  See Rice, R. Hugh
Rich, Anna 1956- *212*
Rich, Barbara
  See Graves, Robert
Rich, Elaine Sommers 1926- *6*
Rich, Josephine Bouchard 1912- *10*
Rich, Louise Dickinson 1903-1991 .... *54*
  Obituary *67*
Rich, Naomi *217*
Richard, Adrienne 1921- *5*
  See also SAAS *9*
Richard, James Robert
  See Bowen, Robert Sydney
Richards, Chuck 1957- *170*
Richards, Frank
  See Hamilton, Charles (Harold St. John)
Richards, Hilda
  See Hamilton, Charles (Harold St. John)
Richards, Jackie 1925- *102*
Richards, Jame *230*
Richards, Jean 1940- *135*
Richards, Justin *169*
Richards, Kay
  See Baker, Susan (Catherine)
Richards, Laura E(lizabeth Howe) 1850-1943
  See YABC *1*
  See also CLR *54*
Richards, Leigh
  See King, Laurie R.
Richards, Marlee
  See Brill, Marlene Targ
Richards, Norman 1932- *48*
Richards, R(onald) C(harles) W(illiam)
  1923- *59*
  Brief entry *43*
Richards, Walter Alden (Jr.) 1907-1988
  Obituary *56*
Richardson, Andrew (William) 1986- *120*
Richardson, Carol 1932- *58*

Richardson, Frank Howard 1882-1970
  Obituary 27
Richardson, Grace Lee
  See Dickson, Naida
Richardson, Jean (Mary) 59
Richardson, Judith Benet 1941- 77
Richardson, Nigel 1957- 187
Richardson, Robert S(hirley) 1902-1981 8
Richardson, Sandy 1949- 116
Richardson, V.A. 189
Richardson, Willis 1889-1977 60
Richelson, Geraldine 1922- 29
Richemont, Enid 1940- 82
Richler, Mordecai 1931-2001 98
  Brief entry 27
  Earlier sketch in SATA *44*
  See also CLR *17*
Richman, Sophia 1941- 142
Rich-McCoy, Lois
  See McCoy, Lois (Rich)
Richmond, Robin 1951- 75
Richoux, Pat(ricia) 1927- 7
Richter, Alice 1941- 30
Richter, Conrad (Michael) 1890-1968 3
Richter, Hans Peter 1925-1993 6
  See also CLR *21*
  See also SAAS *11*
Richter, Jutta 1955- 184
Rickard, Graham 1949- 71
Rico, Don(ato) 1917-1985
  Obituary 43
Riddell, Chris 1962- 219
  Earlier sketches in SATA *114, 166*
Riddell, Christopher Barry
  See Riddell, Chris
Riddell, Edwina 1955- 82
Ridden, Brian 1934- 123
  See Ridden, Brian John
Riddle, Tohby 1965- 223
  Earlier sketches in SATA *74, 151*
Riddleburger, Sam 202
Riddles, Libby 1956- 140
Ride, Sally 1951- 219
Ride, Sally Kristen
  See Ride, Sally
Rideout, Sandy 194
Rider, D. F.
  See Perrin, Pat
Rider, David F.
  See Perrin, Pat
Ridge, Antonia (Florence) (?)-1981 7
  Obituary 27
Ridge, Martin 1923-2003 43
Ridley, Philip 171
  Earlier sketch in SATA *88*
Ridlon, Marci
  See Balterman, Marcia Ridlon
Riedman, Sarah R(egal) 1902-1995 1
Riehecky, Janet 1953- 164
Ries, Lori 185
Riesenberg, Felix, Jr. 1913-1962 23
Rieu, E(mile) V(ictor) 1887-1972 46
  Obituary 26
Riffenburgh, Beau 1955- 175
Rigg, Sharon
  See Creech, Sharon
Riggenbach, Holly
  See Black, Holly
Riggio, Anita 1952- 148
  Earlier sketch in SATA *73*
Riggs, Shannon 190
Riggs, Sidney Noyes 1892-1975
  Obituary 28
Riggs, Stephanie 1964- 138
Riglietti, Serena 1969- 189
Rigney, James Oliver, Jr.
  See Jordan, Robert
Rikhoff, Jean 1928- 9
Rikki
  See Ducornet, Erica
Riley, James A. 1939- 97

Riley, James Whitcomb 1849-1916 17
Riley, Jocelyn 1949- 60
  Brief entry 50
Riley, Jocelyn Carol
  See Riley, Jocelyn
Riley, Linda Capus 1950- 85
Riley, Martin 1948- 81
Rim, Sujean 225
Rimbauer, Steven
  See Pearson, Ridley
Rimes, (Margaret) LeAnn 1982- 154
Rinaldi, Ann 1934- 202
  Brief entry 50
  Earlier sketches in SATA *51, 78, 117, 161*
  See also CLR *46*
Rinard, Judith E(llen) 1947- 140
  Earlier sketch in SATA *44*
Rinck, Maranke 1976- 214
Rinder, Lenore 1949- 92
Ring, Elizabeth 1920- 79
Ringdahl, Mark
  See Longyear, Barry B(rookes)
Ringgold, Faith 1930- 187
  Earlier sketches in SATA *71, 114*
  See also CLR *30*
Ringi, Kjell (Arne Soerensen) 1939- 12
Rinkoff, Barbara Jean (Rich) 1923-1975 4
  Obituary 27
Rinn, Miriam 1946- 127
Riordan, James 1936- 95
Riordan, Rick 208
  Earlier sketch in SATA *174*
Rios, Tere
  See Versace, Marie Teresa Rios
Rioux, Jo 226
Rioux, Jo-Anne
  See Rioux, Jo
Ripken, Cal, Jr. 1960- 215
  Earlier sketch in SATA *114*
Ripken, Calvin Edward, Jr.
  See Ripken, Cal, Jr.
Ripley, Catherine 1957- 82
Ripley, Elizabeth Blake 1906-1969 5
Ripper, Charles L(ewis) 1929- 3
Ripper, Chuck
  See Ripper, Charles L(ewis)
Rippin, Sally 220
Riq
  See Atwater, Richard
Rish, David 1955- 110
Riskind, Mary 1944- 60
Rissinger, Matt 1956- 93
Rissman, Art
  See Sussman, Susan
Rissman, Susan
  See Sussman, Susan
Ritchie, Barbara Gibbons 14
Ritchie, Scot 1954- 217
Ritter, Felix
  See Kruss, James
Ritter, John H. 1951- 215
  Earlier sketches in SATA *129, 137*
Ritter, Lawrence S(tanley) 1922-2004 58
  Obituary 152
Ritthaler, Shelly 1955- 91
Ritts, Paul 1920(?)-1980
  Obituary 25
Ritz, Karen 1957- 202
  Earlier sketch in SATA *80*
Riu, Isabel Ferrer 1969- 222
Rivera, Geraldo (Miguel) 1943- 54
  Brief entry 28
Rivera, Guadalupe
  See Rivera Marin, Guadalupe
Rivera Marin, Guadalupe 1924- 224
Rivers, Elfrida
  See Bradley, Marion Zimmer
Rivers, Karen 1970- 131
Riverside, John
  See Heinlein, Robert A.
Rivkin, Ann 1920- 41

Rivoli, Mario 1943- 10
Roach, Marilynne K. 1946- 9
Roach, Marilynne Kathleen
  See Roach, Marilynne K.
Roach, Portia
  See Takakjian, Portia
Robb, Don 1937- 194
Robb, Laura 1937- 95
Robberecht, Thierry 1960- 182
Robbins, Frank 1917-1994(?) 42
  Brief entry 32
Robbins, Jacqui 221
Robbins, Ken 1945- 219
  Brief entry 53
  Earlier sketches in SATA *94, 147*
Robbins, Raleigh
  See Hamilton, Charles (Harold St. John)
Robbins, Ruth 1917(?)- 14
Robbins, Tony
  See Pashko, Stanley
Robbins, Wayne
  See Cox, William R(obert)
Robel, S. L.
  See Fraustino, Lisa Rowe
Roberson, Jennifer 1953- 72
Roberson, John R(oyster) 1930- 53
Robert, Adrian
  See St. John, Nicole
Roberton, Fiona 230
Roberts, Bethany 202
  Earlier sketch in SATA *133*
Roberts, Bruce (Stuart) 1930- 47
  Brief entry 39
Roberts, Charles G(eorge) D(ouglas)
  1860-1943 88
  Brief entry 29
  See also CLR *33*
Roberts, David
  See Cox, John Roberts
Roberts, David 1970- 191
Roberts, Diane 1937- 184
Roberts, Elizabeth 1944- 80
Roberts, Elizabeth Madox 1886-1941 33
  Brief entry 27
  See also CLR *100*
Roberts, Jim
  See Bates, Barbara S(nedeker)
Roberts, Jody 218
Roberts, John G(aither) 1913-1993 27
Roberts, Judy I. 1957- 93
Roberts, Katherine 1962- 152
Roberts, Ken 223
  See Lake, Kenneth R(obert)
Roberts, M. L.
  See Mattern, Joanne
Roberts, Marion 1966- 212
Roberts, Nancy Correll 1924- 52
  Brief entry 28
Roberts, Priscilla 1955- 184
Roberts, Terence
  See Sanderson, Ivan T(erence)
Roberts, Willo Davis 1928-2004 150
  Autobiography Feature 150
  Obituary 160
  Earlier sketches in SATA *21, 70, 133*
  See also CLR *95*
  See also SAAS *8*
Robertson, Barbara (Anne) 1931- 12
Robertson, Don 1929-1999 8
  Obituary 113
Robertson, Dorothy Lewis 1912- 12
Robertson, Ellis
  See Ellison, Harlan
  and Silverberg, Robert
Robertson, James I., Jr. 1930- 182
Robertson, James Irvin
  See Robertson, James I., Jr.
Robertson, Janet (E.) 1935- 68
Robertson, Jennifer Sinclair 1942-1998 12
Robertson, Jenny
  See Robertson, Jennifer Sinclair

Robertson, Keith (Carlton) 1914-1991 85
　Obituary 69
　Earlier sketch in SATA *1*
　See also SAAS *15*
Robertson, Mark
　See Robertson, M.P.
Robertson, M.P. 1965- 197
Robertson, Stephen
　See Walker, Robert W.
Robertus, Polly M. 1948- 212
　Earlier sketch in SATA *73*
Robeson, Kenneth
　See Dent, Lester
　and Goulart, Ron
Robeson, Kenneth
　See Johnson, (Walter) Ryerson
Robinet, Harriette Gillem 1931- 104
　Earlier sketch in SATA *27*
　See also CLR *64*
Robins, Deri 1958- 166
　Earlier sketch in SATA *117*
Robins, Patricia 1921- 117
Robins, Rollo, Jr.
　See Ellis, Edward S.
Robins, Seelin
　See Ellis, Edward S.
Robinson, Adjai 1932- 8
Robinson, Aminah Brenda Lynn 1940- 159
　Earlier sketch in SATA *77*
Robinson, Barbara (Webb) 1927- 84
　Earlier sketch in SATA *8*
Robinson, C(harles) A(lexander), Jr.
　1900-1965 36
Robinson, Charles 1870-1937 17
Robinson, Charles 1931- 6
Robinson, Dorothy W. 1929- 54
Robinson, Elizabeth Keeler 1959- 204
Robinson, Eve
　See Tanselle, Eve
Robinson, Fiona 1965- 225
Robinson, Glen 1953- 92
Robinson, Glendal P.
　See Robinson, Glen
Robinson, Jan M. 1933- 6
Robinson, Jean O. 1934- 7
Robinson, Joan (Mary) G(ale Thomas)
　1910-1988 7
Robinson, Kim Stanley 1952- 109
Robinson, Lee 1948- 110
Robinson, Lloyd
　See Silverberg, Robert
Robinson, Lynda S(uzanne) 1951- 107
Robinson, Marileta 1942- 32
Robinson, Maudie Millian Oller 1914- 11
Robinson, Maurice R(ichard) 1895-1982
　Obituary 29
Robinson, Nancy K(onheim) 1942-1994 91
　Brief entry 31
　Obituary 79
　Earlier sketch in SATA *32*
Robinson, Ray 1920- 23
Robinson, Raymond Kenneth
　See Robinson, Ray
Robinson, Shari
　See McGuire, Leslie (Sarah)
Robinson, Sharon 1950- 197
　Earlier sketch in SATA *162*
Robinson, Spider 1948- 118
Robinson, Sue
　See Robinson, Susan Maria
Robinson, Susan Maria 1955- 105
Robinson, Susan Patricia
　See Gates, Susan
Robinson, Suzanne
　See Robinson, Lynda S(uzanne)
Robinson, T(homas) H(eath) 1869-1950 17
Robinson, Tim 1963- 205
Robinson, (Wanda) Veronica 1926- 30
Robinson, W(illiam) Heath 1872-1944 17
Robison, Bonnie 1924- 12
Robison, Nancy L(ouise) 1934- 32

Robles, Harold E. 1948- 87
Robottom, John 1934- 7
Robson, Eric 1939- 82
Roca, Francois 1971- 200
Rocco, John 1967- 188
Roche, A. K.
　See Abisch, Roslyn Kroop
　and Kaplan, Boche
Roche, Denis 1967- 196
　Earlier sketch in SATA *99*
Roche, Denis Mary
　See Roche, Denis
Roche, Luane 1937- 170
Roche, P(atricia) K. 1935- 57
　Brief entry 34
Roche, Terry
　See Poole, Peggy
Rochman, Hazel 1938- 105
Rock, Lois
　See Joslin, Mary
Rock, Maxine 1940- 108
Rocker, Fermin 1907- 40
Rockliff, Mara 224
Rocklin, Joanne 1946- 134
　Earlier sketch in SATA *86*
Rockwell, Anne F. 1934- 194
　Earlier sketches in SATA *33, 71, 114, 162*
　See also SAAS *19*
Rockwell, Anne Foote
　See Rockwell, Anne F.
Rockwell, Bart
　See Pellowski, Michael (Joseph)
Rockwell, Harlow 1910-1988 33
　Obituary 56
Rockwell, Lizzy 1961- 185
Rockwell, Norman (Percevel) 1894-1978 23
Rockwell, Thomas 1933- 231
　Earlier sketches in SATA *7, 70*
　See also CLR *6*
Rockwood, Joyce 1947- 39
Rockwood, Roy
　See McFarlane, Leslie
　and Stratemeyer, Edward L.
Rodanas, Kristina 1952- 155
Rodari, Gianni 1920-1980
　See CLR *24*
Rodd, Kathleen Tennant
　See Rodd, Kylie Tennant
Rodd, Kylie Tennant 1912-1988 57
　Obituary 55
　Earlier sketch in SATA *6*
Rodda, Emily 1948- 230
　Earlier sketches in SATA *97, 146*
　See also CLR *32*
Roddenberry, Eugene Wesley 1921-1991 45
　Obituary 69
Roddenberry, Gene
　See Roddenberry, Eugene Wesley
Roddick, Ellen 1936- 5
Roddie, Shen 153
Roddy, Lee 1921- 57
Rodenas, Paula 73
Rodgers, Frank 1944- 69
Rodgers, Mary 1931- 130
　Earlier sketch in SATA *8*
　See also CLR *20*
Rodman, Emerson
　See Ellis, Edward S.
Rodman, Eric
　See Silverberg, Robert
Rodman, Maia
　See Wojciechowska, Maia (Teresa)
Rodman, Mary Ann 185
Rodman, (Cary) Selden 1909-2002 9
Rodowsky, Colby 1932- 164
　Earlier sketches in SATA *21, 77, 120*
　See also SAAS *22*
Rodowsky, Colby F.
　See Rodowsky, Colby
Rodriguez, Alejo 1941- 83
Rodriguez, Alex 1975- 189

Rodriguez, Beatrice 1969- 230
Rodriguez, Christina 1981- 177
Rodriguez, Edel 1971- 196
Rodriguez, Luis J. 1954- 125
Rodriguez, Rachel 180
Rodriguez, Rachel Victoria
　See Rodriguez, Rachel
Roeder, Virginia Marsh 1926- 98
Roehrig, Catharine H. 1949- 67
Roennfeldt, Robert 1953- 78
Roessel-Waugh, C. C.
　See Waugh, Carol-Lynn Rossel
　and Waugh, Charles G(ordon)
Roets, Lois F. 1937- 91
Roever, J(oan) M(arilyn) 1935- 26
Rofes, Eric 1954-2006 52
Rofes, Eric Edward 1954-2006
　See Rofes, Eric
Roffey, Maureen 1936- 33
Rogak, Lisa 1962- 80
Rogak, Lisa Angowski
　See Rogak, Lisa
Rogan, S. Jones 199
Rogan, Sally Jones
　See Rogan, S. Jones
Rogasky, Barbara 1933- 144
　Earlier sketch in SATA *86*
Rogers, (Thomas) Alan (Stinchcombe)
　1937- 81
　Earlier sketch in SATA *2*
Rogers, Bettye 1858-1919 103
Rogers, Cindy 1950- 89
Rogers, Emma 1951- 74
Rogers, Frances 1888-1974 10
Rogers, Fred McFeely 1928-2003 33
　Obituary 138
Rogers, Gregory 1957- 211
Rogers, Hal
　See Sirimarco, Elizabeth
Rogers, Jacqueline 1958- 213
Rogers, Jean 1919- 55
　Brief entry 47
Rogers, Matilda 1894-1976 5
　Obituary 34
Rogers, Pamela 1927- 9
Rogers, Paul 1950- 98
　Earlier sketch in SATA *54*
Rogers, Robert
　See Hamilton, Charles (Harold St. John)
Rogers, Sherry 193
Rogers, W(illiam) G(arland) 1896-1978 23
Rohan, M. S.
　See Rohan, Michael Scott
Rohan, Michael Scott 1951- 98
Rohan, Mike Scott
　See Rohan, Michael Scott
Rohmann, Eric 1957- 171
　See also CLR *100*
Rohmer, Harriet 1938- 56
Rohrer, Doug 1962- 89
Rojan
　See Rojankovsky, Feodor (Stepanovich)
Rojankovsky, Feodor (Stepanovich)
　1891-1970 21
Rojany, Lisa 94
Rokeby-Thomas, Anna E(lma) 1911- 15
Roland, Albert 1925-2002 11
Roland, Mary
　See Lewis, Mary
Roleff, Tamara L. 1959- 143
Rolerson, Darrell A(llen) 1946- 8
Roll, Winifred 1909-1998 6
Rollins, Charlemae Hill 1897-1979 3
　Obituary 26
Rollins, James 1961- 216
Rollock, Barbara T(herese) 1924- 64
Rolston, Steve 1978- 209
Romack, Janice Reed
　See LeNoir, Janice
Romain, Trevor 134
Romanenko, Vitaliy 1962- 101

Romano, Christy
  See Romano, Christy Carlson
Romano, Christy Carlson 1984- 210
Romano, Clare 1922- 111
  Earlier sketch in SATA 48
Romano, Louis G. 1921- 35
Romano, Melora A. 1966- 118
Romano, Ray 1957- 170
Romano, Raymond
  See Romano, Ray
Romijn, Johanna Maria Kooyker
  See Kooyker-Romijn, Johanna Maria
Romyn, Johanna Maria Kooyker
  See Kooyker-Romijn, Johanna Maria
Rong, Yu 1970- 174
Rongen, Bjoern 1906- 10
Rongen, Bjorn
  See Rongen, Bjoern
Ronson, Mark
  See Alexander, Marc
Rood, Ronald (N.) 1920- 12
Rook, Sebastian
  See Jeapes, Ben
Rooke, Daphne 1914-2009 12
Rooke, Daphne Marie
  See Rooke, Daphne
Rooney, Ronnie 1970- 212
Roop, Connie 1951- 167
  Brief entry 49
  Earlier sketches in SATA 54, 116
Roop, Constance Betzer
  See Roop, Connie
Roop, Peter 1951- 167
  Brief entry 49
  Earlier sketches in SATA 54, 116
Roop, Peter G.
  See Roop, Peter
Roop, Peter Geiger
  See Roop, Peter
Roos, Maryn 225
Roos, Stephen 1945- 128
  Brief entry 41
  Earlier sketches in SATA 47, 77
Roosa, Karen 1961- 218
Roose-Evans, James 1927- 65
Roosevelt, Eleanor 1884-1962 50
Root, Barry 182
Root, Betty 84
Root, Kimberly Bulcken 192
Root, Phyllis 1949- 224
  Brief entry 48
  Earlier sketches in SATA 55, 94, 145, 184
Root, Shelton L., Jr. 1923-1986
  Obituary 51
Roper, Laura (Newbold) Wood 1911-2003 .. 34
  Obituary 150
Roper, Robert 1946- 142
  Earlier sketch in SATA 78
Roraback, Robin (Ellan) 1964- 111
Rorby, Ginny 1944- 94
Rorer, Abigail 1949- 85
Rosaler, Maxine 208
Rosamel, Godeleine de 1968- 151
Roscoe, D(onald) T(homas) 1934- 42
Rose, Anne 8
Rose, Deborah Lee 1955- 185
  Earlier sketches in SATA 71, 124
Rose, Elizabeth (Jane Pretty) 1933- 68
  Brief entry 28
Rose, Florella
  See Carlson, Vada F.
Rose, Gerald (Hembdon Seymour) 1935- 68
  Brief entry 30
Rose, Malcolm 1953- 168
  Earlier sketch in SATA 107
Rose, Nancy A.
  See Sweetland, Nancy A(nn)
Rose, Naomi C. 228
Rose, Ted 1940- 93
Rose, Wendy 1948- 12
Rosen, Elizabeth 1961- 205

Rosen, Lillian (Diamond) 1928- 63
Rosen, Marvin 1933- 161
Rosen, Michael 1946- 229
  Brief entry 40
  Earlier sketches in SATA 48, 84, 137, 181
  See also CLR 45
Rosen, Michael J. 1954- 199
  Earlier sketch in SATA 86
Rosen, Michael Wayne
  See Rosen, Michael
Rosen, Sidney 1916- 1
Rosen, Winifred 1943- 8
Rosenbaum, Maurice 1907-1987 6
Rosenberg, Amye 1950- 74
Rosenberg, Dorothy 1906- 40
Rosenberg, Eth Clifford 1915- 92
  See also SAAS 22
Rosenberg, Jane 1949- 58
Rosenberg, Liz 1958- 129
  Earlier sketch in SATA 75
Rosenberg, Maxine B(erta) 1939- 93
  Brief entry 47
  Earlier sketch in SATA 55
Rosenberg, Nancy 1931- 4
Rosenberg, Sharon 1942- 8
Rosenberry, Vera 1948- 219
  Earlier sketches in SATA 83, 144
Rosenblatt, Arthur
  See Rosenblatt, Arthur S.
Rosenblatt, Arthur S. 1938- 68
  Brief entry 45
Rosenblatt, Lily 1956- 90
Rosenbloom, Joseph 1928- 21
Rosenblum, Richard 1928- 11
Rosenburg, John M. 1918- 6
Rosenfeld, Dina 1962- 99
Rosenstiehl, Agnes 1941- 203
Rosenthal, Amy Krouse 1965- 222
  Earlier sketch in SATA 177
Rosenthal, Betsy R. 1957- 178
Rosenthal, Harold 1914-1999 35
Rosenthal, M(acha) L(ouis) 1917-1996 59
Rosenthal, Marc 1949- 193
Rosenthal, Mark A(lan) 1946- 64
Rosing, Norbert 1953- 196
Rosman, Steven M 1956- 81
Rosman, Steven Michael
  See Rosman, Steven M
Rosoff, Meg 1956- 209
  Earlier sketch in SATA 160
Ross, Alan
  See Warwick, Alan R(oss)
Ross, Christine 1950- 172
  Earlier sketch in SATA 83
Ross, Clare
  See Romano, Clare
Ross, Dana Fuller
  See Cockrell, Amanda
  and Gerson, Noel Bertram
Ross, Dave
  See Ross, David
Ross, David 1896-1975 49
  Obituary 20
Ross, David 1949- 133
  Earlier sketch in SATA 32
Ross, Deborah J.
  See Wheeler, Deborah
Ross, Diana
  See Denney, Diana
Ross, Edward S(hearman) 1915- 85
Ross, Eileen 1950- 115
Ross, Frank (Xavier), Jr. 1914- 28
Ross, Jane 1961- 79
Ross, John 1921- 45
Ross, Judy 1942- 54
Ross, Katharine Reynolds
  See Ross, Kathy
Ross, Kathy 1948- 169
  Earlier sketch in SATA 89
Ross, Kent 1956- 91
Ross, Lillian Hammer 1925- 72

Ross, Michael Elsohn 1952- 170
  Earlier sketches in SATA 80, 127
Ross, Pat(ricia Kienzle) 1943- 53
  Brief entry 48
Ross, Ramon R(oyal) 1930- 62
Ross, Stewart 1947- 134
  Earlier sketch in SATA 92
  See also SAAS 23
Ross, Sylvia 1937- 231
Ross, Tom 1958- 84
Ross, Tony 1938- 225
  Earlier sketches in SATA 17, 65, 130, 176
Ross, Wilda 1915- 51
  Brief entry 39
Rossel, Seymour 1945- 28
Rossell, Judith 1953- 187
Rossel-Waugh, C. C.
  See Waugh, Carol-Lynn Rossel
Rossetti, Christina 1830-1894 20
  See also CLR 115
Rossetti, Christina Georgina
  See Rossetti, Christina
Rossi, Joyce 1943- 116
Rossotti, Hazel Swaine 1930- 95
Rostkowski, Margaret I. 1945- 59
Rostoker-Gruber, Karen 229
Roth, Arnold 1929- 21
Roth, Arthur J(oseph) 1925-1993 43
  Brief entry 28
  Obituary 75
  See also SAAS 11
Roth, Carol 222
Roth, David 1940- 36
Roth, Julie Jersild 180
Roth, Matthue 1978(?)- 174
Roth, R.G.
  See Roth, Robert
Roth, Rob
  See Roth, Robert
Roth, Robert 1965- 230
Roth, Roger 190
Roth, Ruby 1983(?)- 216
Roth, Stephanie 202
Roth, Susan L. 181
  Earlier sketch in SATA 134
Rothberg, Abraham 1922-2011 59
Roth-Hano, Renee 1931- 85
Rothkopf, Carol Z. 1929- 4
Rothman, Joel 1938- 7
Rotner, Shelley 1951- 169
  Earlier sketch in SATA 76
Rottman, S.L. 1970- 157
  Earlier sketch in SATA 106
Rottman, Susan Lynn
  See Rottman, S.L.
Roueche, Berton 1911-1994 28
Roughsey, Dick 1921(?)-1985 35
  See also CLR 41
Roughsey, Goobalathaldin
  See Roughsey, Dick
Rounds, Glen (Harold) 1906-2002 112
  Obituary 141
  Earlier sketches in SATA 8, 70
Rourke, Constance Mayfield 1885-1941
  See YABC 1
Rouss, Sylvia 211
Rovetch, Gerda 1925(?)- 202
Rovetch, L. Bob
  See Rovetch, Lissa
Rovetch, Lissa 201
Rowan, Deirdre
  See Williams, Jeanne
Rowe, Jennifer
  See Rodda, Emily
Rowe, John A. 1949- 198
  Earlier sketch in SATA 146
Rowe, Viola Carson 1903-1969
  Obituary 26
Rowh, Mark 1952- 90
Rowland, Florence Wightman 1900-1997 8
  Obituary 108

Rowland-Entwistle, (Arthur) Theodore (Henry)
1925- *94*
   Earlier sketch in SATA *31*
Rowling, J.K. 1965- *174*
   Earlier sketch in SATA *109*
   See also CLR *112*
Rowling, Joanne Kathleen
   See Rowling, J.K.
Rowsome, Frank (Howard), Jr. 1914-1983 .. *36*
Roy, Gabrielle 1909-1983 .... *104*
Roy, Jacqueline 1954- *74*
Roy, James 1968- *218*
Roy, Jennifer
   See Roy, Jennifer Rozines
Roy, Jennifer Rozines 1967- *178*
Roy, Jessie Hailstalk 1895-1986
   Obituary *51*
Roy, Kari Anne 1977(?)- *221*
Roy, Liam
   See Scarry, Patricia (Murphy)
Roy, Ron 1940- *228*
   Brief entry *35*
   Earlier sketches in SATA *40, 110*
Roybal, Laura 1956- *85*
Roybal, Laura Husby
   See Roybal, Laura
Royds, Caroline 1953- *55*
Royston, Angela 1945- *230*
   Earlier sketches in SATA *120, 169*
Rozakis, Laurie E. 1952- *84*
Rozen, Anna 1960- *206*
Rubbino, Salvatore 1970- *220*
Rubel, David 1961- *223*
Rubel, Nicole 1953- *181*
   Earlier sketches in SATA *18, 95, 135*
Rubin, Eva Johanna 1925- *38*
Rubin, Susan Goldman 1939- *182*
   Earlier sketches in SATA *84, 132*
Rubin, Vicky 1964- *193*
Rubinetti, Donald 1947- *92*
Rubinger, Ami 1953- *225*
Rubinstein, Gillian 1942- *158*
   Autobiography Feature *116*
   Earlier sketches in SATA *68, 105*
   See also CLR *35*
   See also SAAS *25*
Rubinstein, Gillian Margaret
   See Rubinstein, Gillian
Rubinstein, Patricia -2003
   See Forest, Antonia
Rubinstein, Patricia Giulia Caulfield Kate
   See Forest, Antonia
Rubinstein, Robert E(dward) 1943- *49*
Rublowsky, John M(artin) 1928- *62*
Rubright, Lynn 1936- *171*
Ruby, Laura *227*
   Earlier sketches in SATA *155, 181*
Ruby, Lois 1942- *184*
   Autobiography Feature *105*
   Brief entry *34*
   Earlier sketches in SATA *35, 95*
Ruby, Lois F.
   See Ruby, Lois
Ruchlis, Hy(man) 1913-1992 .... *3*
   Obituary *72*
Ruckdeschel, Liz *214*
Rucker, Mike 1940- *91*
Ruckman, Ivy 1931- *93*
   Earlier sketch in SATA *37*
Ruck-Pauquet, Gina 1931- *40*
   Brief entry *37*
Ruddell, Deborah 1949- *210*
Ruditis, Paul *190*
Rudley, Stephen 1946- *30*
Rudolph, Marguerite 1908- *21*
Rudomin, Esther
   See Hautzig, Esther Rudomin
Rue, Leonard Lee III 1926- *142*
   Earlier sketch in SATA *37*
Rueda, Claudia *183*

Ruedi, Norma Paul
   See Ainsworth, Norma
Ruelle, Karen Gray 1957- *209*
   Earlier sketches in SATA *84, 126*
Ruemmler, John D(avid) 1948- *78*
Ruepp, Krista 1947- *143*
Ruffell, Ann 1941- *30*
Ruffins, Reynold 1930- *125*
   Earlier sketch in SATA *41*
Rugg, Jim *206*
Ruggles, Lucy
   See Williams, Kathryn
Rugoff, Milton 1913- *30*
Ruhen, Olaf 1911-1989 .... *17*
Rui, Paolo 1962- *217*
Rukeyser, Muriel 1913-1980
   Obituary *22*
Rumbaut, Hendle 1949- *84*
Rumford, James 1948- *193*
   Earlier sketch in SATA *116*
Rumsey, Marian (Barritt) 1928- *16*
Rumstuckle, Cornelius
   See Brennan, Herbie
Runholt, Susan *216*
Runnerstroem, Bengt Arne 1944- *75*
Runyan, John
   See Palmer, Bernard (Alvin)
Runyon, Brent *217*
Runyon, Catherine 1947- *62*
Ruoff, A. LaVonne Brown 1930- *76*
Rupp, Rebecca *185*
Rusch, Elizabeth 1966- *198*
Rusch, Kris
   See Rusch, Kristine Kathryn
Rusch, Kristine Kathryn 1960- *113*
Rush, Alison 1951- *41*
Rush, Peter 1937- *32*
Rushdie, Ahmed Salman
   See Rushdie, Salman
Rushdie, Salman 1947-
   See CLR *125*
Rushford, Patricia H(elen) 1943- *134*
Rushmore, Helen 1898-1994 .... *3*
Rushmore, Robert (William) 1926-1986 .... *8*
   Obituary *49*
Ruskin, Ariane
   See Batterberry, Ariane Ruskin
Ruskin, John 1819-1900 .... *24*
Russ, Lavinia (Faxon) 1904-1992 .... *74*
Russell, Charlotte
   See Rathjen, Carl Henry
Russell, Ching Yeung 1946- *107*
Russell, Don(ald Bert) 1899-1986
   Obituary *47*
Russell, Franklin (Alexander) 1926- *11*
Russell, Gertrude Barrer
   See Barrer-Russell, Gertrude
Russell, Helen Ross 1915- *8*
Russell, James 1933- *53*
Russell, Jim
   See Russell, James
Russell, Joan Plummer 1930- *139*
Russell, Natalie 1972- *218*
Russell, P(hilip) Craig 1951- *162*
   Earlier sketch in SATA *80*
Russell, Patrick
   See Sammis, John
Russell, Paul (Gary) 1942- *57*
Russell, Sarah
   See Laski, Marghanita
Russell, Sharman Apt 1954- *123*
Russell, Solveig Paulson 1904-1985 .... *3*
Russo, Marisabina 1950- *188*
   Earlier sketches in SATA *106, 151*
Russo, Monica J. 1950- *83*
Russo, Susan 1947- *30*
Russon, Penni 1974- *179*
Rutgers van der Loeff, An
   See Rutgers van der Loeff-Basenau, An(na)
   Maria Margaretha

Rutgers van der Loeff-Basenau, An(na) Maria
   Margaretha 1910- *22*
Ruth, Rod 1912-1987 .... *9*
Rutherford, Douglas
   See McConnell, James Douglas Rutherford
Rutherford, Meg 1932- *34*
Ruthin, Margaret
   See Catherall, Arthur
Rutkoski, Marie 1977- *219*
Rutledge, Jill Zimmerman 1951- *155*
Rutz, Viola Larkin 1932- *12*
Ruurs, Margriet 1952- *215*
   Earlier sketches in SATA *97, 147*
Ruzicka, Rudolph 1883-1978
   Obituary *24*
Ruzzier, Sergio 1966- *210*
   Earlier sketch in SATA *159*
Ryan, Betsy
   See Ryan, Elizabeth (Anne)
Ryan, Cheli Duran *20*
Ryan, Darlene 1958- *176*
Ryan, Elizabeth (Anne) 1943- *30*
Ryan, Jeanette
   See Mines, Jeanette
Ryan, John 1921-2009 .... *22*
Ryan, John Gerald Christopher
   See Ryan, John
Ryan, Margaret 1950- *166*
   Earlier sketch in SATA *78*
Ryan, Mary E. 1953- *61*
Ryan, Mary Elizabeth
   See Ryan, Mary E.
Ryan, Pam Munoz 1951- *197*
   Earlier sketch in SATA *134*
Ryan, Patrick 1957- *138*
Ryan, Peter (Charles) 1939- *15*
Ryan-Lush, Geraldine 1949- *89*
Rybakov, Anatoli (Naumovich) 1911-1998 .. *79*
   Obituary *108*
Rybakov, Anatolii (Naumovich)
   See Rybakov, Anatoli (Naumovich)
Rybolt, Thomas R. 1954- *62*
Rybolt, Thomas Roy
   See Rybolt, Thomas R.
Rybolt, Tom
   See Rybolt, Thomas R.
Rycroft, Nina *228*
Rydberg, Ernest E(mil) 1901-1993 .... *21*
Rydberg, Lou(isa Hampton) 1908- *27*
Rydell, Katy 1942- *91*
Rydell, Wendell
   See Rydell, Wendy
Rydell, Wendy *4*
Ryden, Hope *91*
   Earlier sketch in SATA *8*
Ryder, Joanne 1946- *226*
   Brief entry *34*
   Earlier sketches in SATA *65, 122, 163*
   See also CLR *37*
Ryder, Pamela
   See Lamb, Nancy
Rye, Anthony
   See Youd, Samuel
Rylant, Cynthia 1954- *195*
   Brief entry *44*
   Earlier sketches in SATA *50, 76, 112, 160*
   See also CLR *86*
   See also SAAS *13*
Rymer, Alta May 1925- *34*
Rymond, Lynda Gene *199*

S

S. L. C.
   See Twain, Mark
S., Svend Otto
   See Soerensen, Svend Otto
Saaf, Donald W(illiam) 1961- *124*

Saal, Jocelyn
    See Sachs, Judith
Sabbeth, Carol (Landstrom) 1957- *125*
Saberhagen, Fred 1930-2007 .... *89*
    Obituary *184*
    Earlier sketch in SATA *37*
Saberhagen, Fred T.
    See Saberhagen, Fred
Saberhagen, Fred Thomas
    See Saberhagen, Fred
Saberhagen, Frederick Thomas
    See Saberhagen, Fred
Sabin, Edwin L(egrand) 1870-1952
    See YABC *2*
Sabin, Francene *27*
Sabin, Lou
    See Sabin, Louis
Sabin, Louis 1930- *27*
Sabre, Dirk
    See Laffin, John (Alfred Charles)
Sabuda, Robert (James) 1965- *120*
    Earlier sketch in SATA *81*
Sabuda, Robert 1965- *170*
Sabuda, Robert James
    See Sabuda, Robert
Sachar, Louis 1954- *154*
    Brief entry *50*
    Earlier sketches in SATA *63, 104*
    See also CLR *161*
Sachs, Elizabeth-Ann 1946- *48*
Sachs, Judith 1947- *52*
    Brief entry *51*
Sachs, Marilyn 1927- *164*
    Autobiography Feature *110*
    Earlier sketches in SATA *3, 68*
    See also CLR *2*
    See also SAAS *2*
Sachs, Marilyn Stickle
    See Sachs, Marilyn
Sackett, S(amuel) J(ohn) 1928- *12*
Sackson, Sid 1920- *16*
Sacre, Antonio 1968- *152*
Saddler, Allen
    See Richards, R(onald) C(harles) W(illiam)
Saddler, K. Allen
    See Richards, R(onald) C(harles) W(illiam)
Sadie, Stanley 1930-2005 .... *14*
Sadie, Stanley John
    See Sadie, Stanley
Sadiq, Nazneen
    See Sheikh, Nazneen
Sadler, Catherine Edwards 1952- *60*
    Brief entry *45*
Sadler, Marilyn (June) 1950- *79*
Sadler, Mark
    See Lynds, Dennis
Sadler, Sonia Lynn *230*
Saffer, Barbara *144*
Sagan, Carl 1934-1996 .... *58*
    Obituary *94*
Sagan, Carl Edward
    See Sagan, Carl
Sage, Angie 1952- *197*
Sage, Juniper
    See Brown, Margaret Wise
    and Hurd, Edith Thacher
Sagsoorian, Paul 1923- *12*
Said, S.F. 1967- *174*
Saidman, Anne 1952- *75*
Saint, Dora Jessie 1913- *10*
St. Anthony, Jane *175*
St. Antoine, Sara L. 1966- *84*
St. Clair, Byrd Hooper 1905-1976
    Obituary *28*
St. Crow, Lili
    See Saintcrow, Lilith
Saintcrow, Lilith 1976- *221*
Saint-Exupery, Antoine de 1900-1944 .... *20*
    See also CLR *142*

Saint-Exupery, Antoine Jean Baptiste Marie
        Roger de
    See Saint-Exupery, Antoine de
St. George, Judith 1931- *161*
    Earlier sketches in SATA *13, 99*
    See also CLR *57*
    See also SAAS *12*
St. George, Judith Alexander
    See St. George, Judith
St. James, Blakely
    See Gottfried, Theodore Mark
    and Platt, Charles
St. James, Blakely
    See Griffin, W. E. B.
St. James, Sierra
    See Rallison, Janette
Saint James, Synthia 1949- *152*
    Earlier sketch in SATA *84*
St. John, Lauren 1966- *214*
St. John, Nicole *143*
    Autobiography Feature *143*
    Earlier sketches in SATA *29, 89*
    See also CLR *46*
    See also SAAS *7*
St. John, Patricia Mary 1919-1993
    Obituary *79*
St. John, Philip
    See del Rey, Lester
St. John, Wylly Folk 1908-1985 .... *10*
    Obituary *45*
St. Max, E. S.
    See Ellis, Edward S.
St. Meyer, Ned
    See Stratemeyer, Edward L.
St. Mox, E. A.
    See Ellis, Edward S.
St. Myer, Ned
    See Stratemeyer, Edward L.
St. Tamara
    See Kolba, St. Tamara
Saito, Michiko
    See Fujiwara, Michiko
Sakai, Komako 1966- *213*
Sakaki, Ichiro 1969- *192*
Sakamoto, Miki *198*
Sakers, Don 1958- *72*
Sakharnov, S.
    See Sakharnov, Svyatoslav
Sakharnov, Svyatoslav 1923- *65*
Sakharnov, Svyatoslav Vladimirovich
    See Sakharnov, Svyatoslav
Saksena, Kate *148*
Sakurai, Gail 1952- *153*
    Earlier sketch in SATA *87*
Salamanca, Lucy
    See del Barco, Lucy Salamanca
Salas, Laura Purdie 1966- *216*
Salassi, Otto R(ussell) 1939-1993 .... *38*
    Obituary *77*
Salat, Cristina *82*
Saldana, Rene, Jr. *186*
Saldutti, Denise 1953- *39*
Sale, Tim 1956- *153*
Salem, Kay 1952- *92*
Salerni, Dianne K. *231*
Salerno, Steven *176*
Salinger, J.D. 1919-2010 .... *67*
    See also CLR *18*
Salinger, Jerome David
    See Salinger, J.D.
Salisbury, Graham 1944- *195*
    Earlier sketches in SATA *76, 108, 161*
Salisbury, Joyce E(llen) 1944- *138*
Salkey, (Felix) Andrew (Alexander)
        1928-1995 .... *118*
    Earlier sketch in SATA *35*
Salley, Coleen *166*
Sallis, Susan (Diana) 1929- *55*
Salmieri, Daniel 1983- *208*
Salmon, Annie Elizabeth 1899- *13*
Salmon, Dena K. 1959(?)- *219*

Salonen, Roxane Beauclair 1968- *184*
Salsi, Lynn 1947- *130*
Salsitz, R. A. V.
    See Salsitz, Rhondi Vilott
Salsitz, Rhondi Vilott *115*
Salten, Felix
    See Salzmann, Siegmund
Salter, Cedric
    See Knight, Francis Edgar
Salter, Sydney *220*
Saltman, Judith 1947- *64*
Saltzberg, Barney 1955- *194*
    Earlier sketch in SATA *135*
Saltzman, David (Charles Laertes)
        1967-1990 .... *86*
Salvadori, Mario (George) 1907-1997 .... *97*
    Earlier sketch in SATA *40*
Salwood, F.K.
    See Kilworth, Garry
Salzer, L. E.
    See Wilson, Lionel
Salzman, Marian 1959- *77*
Salzmann, Siegmund 1869-1945 .... *25*
Samachson, Dorothy (Mirkin) 1914-1997 ...... *3*
Samachson, Joseph 1906-1980 .... *3*
    Obituary *52*
Sammis, John 1942- *4*
Sampson, Emma (Keats) Speed 1868-1947 . *68*
Sampson, Fay 1935- *151*
    Brief entry *40*
    Earlier sketch in SATA *42*
Sampson, Fay Elizabeth
    See Sampson, Fay
Sampson, Michael 1952- *143*
    Earlier sketch in SATA *95*
Samson, Anne S(tringer) 1933- *2*
Samson, Joan 1937-1976 .... *13*
Samson, Suzanne M. 1959- *91*
Samuels, Barbara *199*
Samuels, Charles 1902-1982 .... *12*
Samuels, Cynthia K(alish) 1946- *79*
Samuels, Gertrude 1910(?)-2003 .... *17*
    Obituary *147*
Sanborn, Duane 1914-1996 .... *38*
Sancha, Sheila 1924- *38*
Sanchez, Alex 1957- *151*
Sanchez, Anita 1956- *209*
Sanchez, Sonia 1934- *136*
    Earlier sketch in SATA *22*
    See also CLR *18*
Sanchez-Silva, Jose Maria 1911- *132*
    Earlier sketch in SATA *16*
    See also CLR *12*
Sand, George X. *45*
Sandak, Cass R(obert) 1950-2001 .... *51*
    Brief entry *37*
Sandberg, (Karin) Inger 1930- *15*
Sandberg, Karl C. 1931- *35*
Sandberg, Lasse (E. M.) 1924- *15*
Sandburg, Carl 1878-1967 .... *8*
    See also CLR *67*
Sandburg, Carl August
    See Sandburg, Carl
Sandburg, Charles
    See Sandburg, Carl
Sandburg, Charles A.
    See Sandburg, Carl
Sandburg, Helga 1918- *3*
    See also SAAS *10*
Sandell, Lisa Ann 1977- *175*
Sandemose, Iben 1950- *211*
Sander, Heather L. 1947- *157*
Sanderlin, George 1915- *4*
Sanderlin, Owenita (Harrah) 1916- *11*
Sanders, Betty Jane
    See Monthei, Betty
Sanders, Nancy I. 1960- *141*
    Earlier sketch in SATA *90*
Sanders, Scott Russell 1945- *109*
    Earlier sketch in SATA *56*

Sanders, Winston P.
  See Anderson, Poul
Sanderson, Irma 1912- 66
Sanderson, Ivan T(erence) 1911-1973 6
Sanderson, Margaret Love
  See Keats, Emma
  and Sampson, Emma (Keats) Speed
Sanderson, Ruth 1951- 224
  Earlier sketches in SATA *41, 109, 172*
Sanderson, Ruth L.
  See Sanderson, Ruth
Sanders-Wells, Linda 220
Sand-Eveland, Cyndi 211
Sandin, Joan 1942- 197
  Earlier sketches in SATA *12, 94, 153*
Sandison, Janet
  See Cameron, Elizabeth Jane
Sandler, Martin W. 216
  Earlier sketch in SATA *160*
Sandom, J. Gregory
  See Welsh, T.K.
Sandom, J.G.
  See Welsh, T.K.
Sandoz, Mari(e Susette) 1900-1966 5
Sanford, Agnes (White) 1897-1976 61
Sanford, Doris 1937- 69
Sanford, Rose
  See Simmonds, Posy
Sanger, Amy Wilson 1967- 205
Sanger, Marjory Bartlett 1920- 8
San Jose, Christine 1929- 167
Sankey, Alice (Ann-Susan) 1910- 27
Sansone, Adele 1953- 230
San Souci, Daniel 192
  Earlier sketch in SATA *96*
San Souci, Robert D. 1946- 220
  Earlier sketches in SATA *40, 81, 117, 158*
  See also CLR *43*
Santamaria, Benjamin 1955- 184
Santat, Dan 224
  Earlier sketch in SATA *188*
Santesson, Hans Stefan 1914(?)-1975
  Obituary 30
Santiago, Esmeralda 1948- 129
Santopolo, Jill 214
Santore, Charles 1935- 200
Santoro, C.
  See Santoro, Christopher
Santoro, Christopher 218
Santos, Helen
  See Griffiths, Helen
Santrey, Louis
  See Sabin, Louis
Santucci, Barbara 1948- 130
Sapergia, Barbara 1943- 181
Sapet, Kerrily 1972- 214
Sapieyevski, Anne Lindbergh 1940-1993 81
  Brief entry 32
  Earlier sketches in SATA *35, 78*
Saport, Linda 1954- 123
Sapp, Allen 1929- 151
Sarac, Roger
  See Caras, Roger A(ndrew)
Sarah, Duchess of York
  See Ferguson, Sarah
Sarasin, Jennifer
  See Sachs, Judith
Sarcone-Roach, Julia 215
Sardinha, Rick 192
Sarg, Anthony Frederick
  See Sarg, Tony
Sarg, Tony 1882-1942
  See YABC *1*
Sargent, Pamela 1948- 78
  Earlier sketch in SATA *29*
Sargent, Robert 1933- 2
Sargent, Sarah 1937- 44
  Brief entry 41
Sargent, Shirley 1927-2004 11
Sarnoff, Jane 1937- 10
Saroff, Phyllis V. 202

Saroyan, William 1908-1981 23
  Obituary 24
Sartell, Debra 229
Sarton, Eleanor May
  See Sarton, May
Sarton, May 1912-1995 36
  Obituary 86
Sasaki, Chris 182
Sasaki, Ellen Joy 206
Saseen, Sharon (Dillon) 1949- 59
Sasek, Miroslav 1916-1980 16
  Obituary 23
  See also CLR *4*
Sasso, Sandy Eisenberg 1947- 162
  Earlier sketches in SATA *86, 116*
Sathre, Vivian 1952- 133
  Earlier sketch in SATA *79*
Satterfield, Charles
  See del Rey, Lester
  and Pohl, Frederik
Sattgast, L. J.
  See Sattgast, Linda J.
Sattgast, Linda J. 1953- 91
Sattler, Helen Roney 1921-1992 74
  Earlier sketch in SATA *4*
  See also CLR *24*
Sattler, Jennifer
  See Sattler, Jennifer Gordon
Sattler, Jennifer Gordon 218
Sauer, Julia Lina 1891-1983 32
  Obituary 36
Sauer, Tammi 1972- 223
Sauerwein, Leigh 1944- 155
Saul, Carol P. 1947- 117
  Earlier sketch in SATA *78*
Saul, John 1942- 98
Saul, John W.
  See Saul, John
Saul, John Woodruff III
  See Saul, John
Saul, (Ellen) Wendy 1946- 42
Saulnier, Karen Luczak 1940- 80
Saunders, Caleb
  See Heinlein, Robert A.
Saunders, Dave 1939- 85
Saunders, Julie 1939- 85
Saunders, (William) Keith 1910-1994 12
Saunders, Rubie (Agnes) 1929- 21
Saunders, Steven
  See Jones, Allan Frewin
Saunders, Susan 1945- 96
  Brief entry 41
  Earlier sketch in SATA *46*
Saunders-Smith, Gail 1952- 169
Sauvain, Philip Arthur 1933- 111
Savadier, Elivia 1950- 228
  Earlier sketches in SATA *79, 164*
Savage, Alan
  See Nicole, Christopher
Savage, Blake
  See Goodwin, Harold L(eland)
Savage, Candace 1949- 142
Savage, Deborah 1955- 76
Savage, Jeff 1961- 97
Savage, Katharine James 1905-1989
  Obituary 61
Savage, Stephen 1965- 194
Savage, Thomas 1915-2003
  Obituary 147
Savageau, Cheryl 1950- 96
Savery, Constance (Winifred) 1897-1999 1
Saville, Andrew
  See Taylor, Andrew
Saville, (Leonard) Malcolm 1901-1982 23
  Obituary 31
Saviozzi, Adriana
  See Mazza, Adriana
Savitt, Sam 1917-2000 8
  Obituary 126

Savitz, Harriet May 1933-2008 72
  Earlier sketch in SATA *5*
  See also SAAS *26*
Sawicki, Mary 1950- 90
Sawyer, (Frederick) Don(ald) 1947- 72
Sawyer, Kem Knapp 1953- 84
Sawyer, Robert J. 1960- 149
  Earlier sketch in SATA *81*
Sawyer, Robert James
  See Sawyer, Robert J.
Sawyer, Ruth 1880-1970 17
  See also CLR *36*
Saxby, H.M.
  See Saxby, (Henry) Maurice
Saxby, (Henry) Maurice 1924- 71
Saxon, Andrew
  See Arthur, Robert, (Jr.)
Saxon, Antonia
  See Sachs, Judith
Say, Allen 1937- 161
  Earlier sketches in SATA *28, 69, 110*
  See also CLR *135*
Sayers, Frances Clarke 1897-1989 3
  Obituary 62
Sayles, Elizabeth 1956- 220
  Earlier sketches in SATA *108, 163*
Saylor-Marchant, Linda 1963- 82
Sayre, April Pulley 1966- 191
  Earlier sketches in SATA *88, 131*
Sazer, Nina 1949- 13
Scabrini, Janet 1953- 13
Scagell, Robin 1946- 107
Scagnetti, Jack 1924- 7
Scaletta, Kurtis 1968- 215
Scalora, Suza 224
Scamander, Newt
  See Rowling, J.K.
Scamell, Ragnhild 1940- 180
  Earlier sketch in SATA *77*
Scandiffio, Laura 227
Scanlon, Elizabeth Garton
  See Scanlon, Liz Garton
Scanlon, Liz Garton 226
Scanlon, Marion Stephany 11
Scannel, John Vernon
  See Scannell, Vernon
Scannell, Vernon 1922-2007 59
  Obituary 188
Scarborough, Elizabeth
  See Scarborough, Elizabeth Ann
Scarborough, Elizabeth Ann 1947- 171
  Earlier sketch in SATA *98*
Scarf, Maggi
  See Scarf, Maggie
Scarf, Maggie 1932- 5
Scariano, Margaret M. 1924- 86
Scarlett, Susan
  See Streatfeild, Noel
Scarry, Huck
  See Scarry, Richard McClure, Jr.
Scarry, Patricia (Murphy) 1924- 2
Scarry, Patsy
  See Scarry, Patricia (Murphy)
Scarry, Richard (McClure) 1919-1994 75
  Obituary 90
  Earlier sketches in SATA *2, 35*
  See also CLR *41*
Scarry, Richard McClure, Jr. 1953- 35
Schachner, Judith Byron 1951- 178
  Earlier sketch in SATA *88*
Schachner, Judy
  See Schachner, Judith Byron
Schachtel, Roger 1949- 38
Schachtel, Roger Bernard
  See Schachtel, Roger
Schade, Susan 189
Schaedler, Sally 116
Schaefer, Carole Lexa 173
Schaefer, Jack (Warner) 1907-1991 66
  Obituary 65
  Earlier sketch in SATA *3*

Schaefer, Lola M. 1950- *183*
Earlier sketches in SATA *91, 144*
Schaeffer, Mead 1898- *21*
Schaeffer, Susan Fromberg 1941- *22*
Schaer, Brigitte 1958- *112*
Schallau, Daniel 1966- *222*
Schaller, George
See Schaller, George B.
Schaller, George B. 1933- *30*
Schaller, George Beals
See Schaller, George B.
Schanzer, Rosalyn (Good) 1942- *138*
Earlier sketch in SATA *77*
Schatell, Brian *66*
Brief entry *47*
Schechter, Betty (Goodstein) 1921- *5*
Schechter, Simone
See Elkeles, Simone
Schecter, Ellen 1944- *85*
Scheeder, Louis 1946- *141*
Scheer, Julian (Weisel) 1926-2001 .... *8*
Scheffer, Victor B(lanchard) 1906- *6*
Scheffler, Axel 1957- *230*
Earlier sketch in SATA *180*
Scheffler, Ursel 1938- *81*
Scheffrin-Falk, Gladys 1928- *76*
Scheidl, Gerda Marie 1913- *85*
Scheier, Michael 1943- *40*
Brief entry *36*
Schell, Mildred 1922- *41*
Schell, Orville (Hickok) 1940- *10*
Scheller, Melanie 1953- *77*
Schellie, Don 1932- *29*
Schembri, Jim 1962- *124*
Schembri, Pamela 1969- *195*
Schemm, Mildred Walker 1905-1998 .... *21*
Obituary *103*
Schenker, Dona 1947- *133*
Earlier sketch in SATA *68*
Scher, Paula 1948- *47*
Scherer, Jeffrey *194*
Scherf, Margaret 1908-1979 .... *10*
Schermer, Judith (Denise) 1941- *30*
Schertle, Alice 1941- *231*
Earlier sketches in SATA *36, 90, 145, 192*
Schick, Alice 1946- *27*
Schick, Eleanor 1942- *144*
Earlier sketch in SATA *9, 82*
Schick, Joel 1945- *31*
Brief entry *30*
Schields, Gretchen 1948- *75*
Schiff, Ken(neth Roy) 1942- *7*
Schiller, Andrew 1919- *21*
Schiller, Barbara (Heyman) 1928- *21*
Schiller, Pamela (Byrne) *127*
Schindel, John 1955- *213*
Earlier sketches in SATA *77, 115*
Schindelman, Joseph 1923- *67*
Brief entry *32*
Schindler, S.D. 1952- *198*
Brief entry *50*
Earlier sketches in SATA *75, 118, 171*
Schindler, Steven D.
See Schindler, S.D.
Schinto, Jeanne 1951- *93*
Schisgall, Oscar 1901-1984 .... *12*
Obituary *38*
Schlaepfer, Gloria G. 1931- *154*
Schlee, Ann 1934- *44*
Brief entry *36*
Schleichert, Elizabeth 1945- *77*
Schlein, Miriam 1926-2004 .... *130*
Obituary *159*
Earlier sketches in SATA *2, 87*
See also CLR *41*
Schlesinger, Arthur M., Jr. 1917-2007 .... *61*
Obituary *181*
See Schlesinger, Arthur Meier
Schlesinger, Arthur Meier 1888-1965
Schlessinger, Laura (Catherine) 1947- *160*
Earlier sketch in SATA *110*

Schlitz, Laura Amy *184*
Schloat, G. Warren, Jr. 1914-2000 .... *4*
Schlossberg, Elisabeth *221*
Schmais, Libby *227*
Schmatz, Pat *197*
Schmid, Eleonore 1939- *126*
Earlier sketches in SATA *12, 84*
Schmid, Paul *231*
Schmid, Susan Maupin *208*
Schmiderer, Dorothy 1940- *19*
Schmidt, Annie M. G. 1911-1995 .... *67*
Obituary *91*
See also CLR *22*
Schmidt, C.A. *196*
Schmidt, Diane 1953- *70*
Schmidt, Elizabeth 1915- *15*
Schmidt, Gary D. 1957- *193*
Earlier sketches in SATA *93, 135*
Schmidt, James Norman 1912-1983 .... *21*
Schmidt, Karen Lee 1953- *185*
Earlier sketch in SATA *94*
Schmidt, Lynette 1952- *76*
Schmitz, Tamara *207*
Schneider, Antonie 1954- *167*
Earlier sketch in SATA *89*
Schneider, Christine M. 1972(?)- *171*
Earlier sketch in SATA *120*
Schneider, Dick
See Schneider, Richard H.
Schneider, Elisa
See Kleven, Elisa
Schneider, Herman 1905-2003 .... *7*
Obituary *148*
Schneider, Howie -2007 .... *181*
Schneider, Josh 1980- *196*
Schneider, Laurie
See Adams, Laurie
Schneider, Nina 1913-2007 .... *2*
Obituary *186*
Schneider, Nina Zimet
See Schneider, Nina
Schneider, Rex 1937- *44*
Schneider, Richard H. 1922- *171*
Schneider, Richard Henry
See Schneider, Richard H.
Schneider, Robyn 1986- *187*
Schnirel, James R. 1931- *14*
Schnitter, Jane T. 1958- *88*
Schnitzlein, Danny *134*
Schnur, Steven 1952- *144*
Earlier sketch in SATA *95*
Schnurre, Wolfdietrich 1920-1989
Obituary *63*
Schoberle, Cecile 1949- *80*
Schock, Pauline 1928- *45*
Schoell, William 1951- *160*
Schoen, Barbara (Taylor) 1924-1993 .... *13*
Schoenherr, Ian *177*
Schoenherr, John 1935-2010 .... *66*
Earlier sketch in SATA *37*
See also SAAS *13*
Schoenherr, John Carl
See Schoenherr, John
Schofield, Sandy
See Rusch, Kristine Kathryn
Scholastica, Sister Mary
See Jenkins, Marie M(agdalen)
Scholefield, A. T.
See Scholefield, Alan
Scholefield, Alan 1931- *66*
Scholefield, Edmund O.
See Griffin, W. E. B.
Scholey, Arthur 1932- *28*
Scholz, Jackson Volney 1897-1986
Obituary *49*
Schon, Nick 1955- *223*
Schone, Virginia *22*
Schongut, Emanuel 1936- *184*
Brief entry *36*
Earlier sketch in SATA *52*
Schoonover, Frank (Earle) 1877-1972 .... *24*

Schoor, Gene 1921- *3*
Schories, Pat 1952- *164*
Earlier sketch in SATA *116*
Schorr, Melissa 1972- *194*
Schorr, Melissa Robin
See Schorr, Melissa
Schott, Jane A. 1946- *172*
Schotter, Roni *190*
Earlier sketches in SATA *105, 149*
Schrader, Dave 1967(?)- *225*
Schraff, Anne E(laine) 1939- *92*
Earlier sketch in SATA *27*
Schram, Penninah 1934- *219*
Earlier sketch in SATA *119*
Schrank, Joseph 1900-1984
Obituary *38*
Schrecengost, Maity 1938- *118*
Schrecengost, S. Maitland
See Schrecengost, Maity
Schreck, Karen
See Schreck, Karen Halvorsen
Schreck, Karen Halvorsen 1962- *185*
Schrecker, Judie 1954- *90*
Schreiber, Elizabeth Anne (Ferguson)
1947- *13*
Schreiber, Ralph W(alter) 1942- *13*
Schreiner, Samuel A(gnew), Jr. 1921- *70*
Schroades, John *214*
Schroder, Monika 1965- *229*
Schroeder, Alan 1961- *98*
Earlier sketch in SATA *66*
Schroeder, Binette
See Nickl, Barbara (Elisabeth)
Schroeder, Russell (K.) 1943- *146*
Schroeder, Ted 1931(?)-1973
Obituary *20*
Schubert, Dieter 1947- *217*
Earlier sketches in SATA *62, 101*
Schubert, Ingrid 1953- *217*
Schubert, Leda 1950(?)- *181*
Schubert-Gabrys, Ingrid 1953- *101*
Earlier sketch in SATA *62*
Schuelein-Steel, Danielle
See Steel, Danielle
Schuelein-Steel, Danielle Fernande
See Steel, Danielle
Schuerger, Michele R. *110*
Schuett, Stacey 1960- *168*
Earlier sketch in SATA *75*
Schulke, Flip Phelps Graeme 1930- *57*
Schulman, Arlene 1961- *105*
Schulman, Janet 1933- *208*
Earlier sketches in SATA *22, 137*
Schulman, L(ester) M(artin) 1934- *13*
Schulte, Elaine L(ouise) 1934- *36*
Schultz, Betty K(epka) 1932- *125*
Schultz, Gwendolyn *21*
Schultz, James Willard 1859-1947
See YABC *1*
Schultz, Pearle Henriksen 1918- *21*
Schulz, Charles M. 1922-2000 .... *10*
Obituary *118*
Schulz, Charles Monroe
See Schulz, Charles M.
Schumacher, Julie 1958- *191*
Schumaker, Ward 1943- *96*
Schuman, Michael A. 1953- *134*
Earlier sketch in SATA *85*
Schur, Maxine
See Schur, Maxine Rose
Schur, Maxine Rose 1948- *135*
Autobiography Feature *135*
Brief entry *49*
Earlier sketches in SATA *53, 98*
Schurfranz, Vivian 1925- *13*
Schutzer, A. I. 1922- *13*
Schuyler, Pamela R. 1948- *30*
Schwabach, Karen *185*
Schwager, Tina 1964- *110*
Schwandt, Stephen (William) 1947- *61*
Schwark, Mary Beth 1954- *51*

Schwartz, Alvin 1927-1992 .... *56*
    Obituary *71*
    Earlier sketch in SATA *4*
    See also CLR *89*
Schwartz, Amy 1954- *189*
    Brief entry *41*
    Earlier sketches in SATA *47, 83, 131*
    See also CLR *25*
    See also SAAS *18*
Schwartz, Anne Powers 1913-1987 .... *10*
Schwartz, Carol 1954- *77*
Schwartz, Charles W(alsh) 1914- *8*
Schwartz, David M. 1951- *110*
    Earlier sketch in SATA *59*
Schwartz, David Martin
    See Schwartz, David M.
Schwartz, Elizabeth Reeder 1912- *8*
Schwartz, Ellen 1949- *117*
Schwartz, Jerome L.
    See Lawrence, Jerome
Schwartz, Joanne 1960- *220*
Schwartz, Joel L. 1940- *54*
    Brief entry *51*
Schwartz, Joyce R. 1950- *93*
Schwartz, Julius 1907-2004 .... *45*
Schwartz, Perry 1942- *75*
Schwartz, Sheila (Ruth) 1929- *27*
Schwartz, Stephen (Lawrence) 1948- *19*
Schwartz, Virginia Frances 1950- *184*
    Earlier sketch in SATA *131*
Schwarz, Silvia Tessa Viviane
    See Schwarz, Viviane
Schwarz, Viviane 1977- *204*
Schwarz, (Silvia Tessa) Viviane 1977- *141*
Schweitzer, Byrd Baylor
    See Baylor, Byrd
Schweitzer, Iris *59*
    Brief entry *36*
Schweninger, Ann 1951- *168*
    Earlier sketches in SATA *29, 98*
Schwerin, Doris H(alpern) 1922- *64*
Schy, Yael *197*
Scieszka, Jon 1954- *199*
    Earlier sketches in SATA *68, 105, 160*
    See also CLR *107*
Scillian, Devin *199*
    Earlier sketch in SATA *128*
Scioscia, Mary (Hershey) 1926- *63*
Sciurba, Katie 1957- *196*
Scofield, Penrod 1933- *62*
    Obituary *78*
Scoggin, Margaret C(lara) 1905-1968 .... *47*
    Brief entry *28*
Scoltock, Jack 1942- *141*
    Earlier sketch in SATA *72*
Scoppettone, Sandra 1936- *92*
    Earlier sketch in SATA *9*
Scot, Michael
    See Rohan, Michael Scott
Scot-Bernard, P.
    See Bernard, Patricia
Scotland, Jay
    See Jakes, John
Scott, Alastair
    See Allen, Kenneth S.
Scott, Ann Herbert 1926- *140*
    Autobiography Feature *140*
    Brief entry *29*
    Earlier sketches in SATA *56, 94*
Scott, Bill
    See Scott, William N(eville)
Scott, Bill 1920(?)-1985
    Obituary *46*
Scott, Cora Annett (Pipitone) 1931- *11*
Scott, Dan
    See Barker, S. Omar
Scott, Elaine 1940- *198*
    Earlier sketches in SATA *36, 90, 164*
Scott, Elizabeth 1972- *194*

Scott, Jack Denton 1915-1995 .... *83*
    Earlier sketch in SATA *31*
    See also CLR *20*
    See also SAAS *14*
Scott, Jane (Harrington) 1931- *55*
Scott, Jane Wooster 1939- *226*
Scott, Jennifer Power 1968- *230*
Scott, Jessica
    See De Wire, Elinor
Scott, John 1912-1976 .... *14*
Scott, John Anthony 1916- *23*
Scott, John M(artin) 1913- *12*
Scott, Mary
    See Mattern, Joanne
Scott, Melissa 1960- *109*
Scott, Michael 1959- *211*
Scott, Michael Peter
    See Scott, Michael
Scott, Mike
    See Scott, Michael
Scott, Richard
    See Rennert, Richard Scott
Scott, Roney
    See Gault, William Campbell
Scott, Sally 1909-1978 .... *43*
Scott, Sally 1948- *44*
Scott, Sally Elisabeth
    See Scott, Sally
Scott, W. N.
    See Scott, William N(eville)
Scott, Sir Walter 1771-1832
    See YABC *2*
    See also CLR *154*
Scott, Warwick
    See Trevor, Elleston
Scott, William N(eville) 1923- *87*
Scotti, Anna
    See Coates, Anna
Scotton, Rob 1960- *214*
    Earlier sketch in SATA *177*
Scribner, Charles, Jr. 1921-1995 .... *13*
    Obituary *87*
Scribner, Joanne L. 1949- *33*
Scribner, Kimball 1917- *63*
Scrimger, Richard 1957- *164*
    Earlier sketch in SATA *119*
Scrimsher, Lila Gravatt 1897-1974
    Obituary *28*
Scroder, Walter K. 1928- *82*
Scroggs, Kirk *187*
Scruggs, Sandy 1961- *89*
Scudder, Brooke 1959- *154*
Scudder, Mildred Lee 1908- *6*
    See also SAAS *12*
Scull, Marie-Louise 1943-1993 .... *77*
Scuro, Vincent 1951- *21*
Seabrooke, Brenda 1941- *148*
    Earlier sketches in SATA *30, 88*
Seagraves, D.B.
    See Seagraves, Donny Bailey
Seagraves, Donny
    See Seagraves, Donny Bailey
Seagraves, Donny Bailey 1951- *224*
Seaman, Augusta Huiell 1879-1950 .... *31*
Seamands, Ruth 1916- *9*
Searcy, Margaret Zehmer 1926- *54*
    Brief entry *39*
Searight, Mary W(illiams) 1918- *17*
Searle, Kathryn Adrienne 1942- *10*
Searle, Ronald (William Fordham) 1920- *70*
    Earlier sketch in SATA *42*
Sears, Stephen W. 1932- *4*
Seaskull, Cecil
    See Castellucci, Cecil
Sebastian, Lee
    See Silverberg, Robert
Sebestyen, Igen
    See Sebestyen, Ouida

Sebestyen, Ouida 1924- *140*
    Earlier sketch in SATA *39*
    See also CLR *17*
    See also SAAS *10*
Sebrey, Mary Ann 1951- *62*
Sechrist, Elizabeth Hough 1903-1991 .... *2*
Sederman, Marty *211*
Sedges, John
    See Buck, Pearl S.
Sedgwick, Marcus 1968- *197*
    Earlier sketch in SATA *160*
Seed, Cecile Eugenie 1930- *86*
    Earlier sketch in SATA *8*
    See also CLR *76*
Seed, Jenny
    See Seed, Cecile Eugenie
Seed, Sheila Turner 1937(?)-1979
    Obituary *23*
Seeger, Elizabeth 1889-1973
    Obituary *20*
Seeger, Laura Vaccaro *200*
    Earlier sketch in SATA *172*
Seeger, Pete 1919- *139*
    Earlier sketch in SATA *13*
Seeger, Peter R.
    See Seeger, Pete
Seeley, Laura L. 1958- *71*
Seever, R.
    See Reeves, Lawrence F.
Sefozo, Mary 1925- *82*
Sefton, Catherine
    See Waddell, Martin
Segal, John *178*
Segal, Joyce 1940- *35*
Segal, Lore 1928- *228*
    Autobiography Feature *228*
    Earlier sketches in SATA *4, 66, 163*
    See also SAAS *11*
Segal, Lore Groszmann
    See Segal, Lore
Segar, E(lzie) C(risler) 1894-1938 .... *61*
Segovia, Andres 1893(?)-1987
    Obituary *52*
Seguin, Marilyn W(eymouth) 1951- *91*
Seguin-Fontes, Marthe 1924- *109*
Seibold, J. Otto 1960- *196*
    Earlier sketches in SATA *83, 149*
    See also SAAS *22*
Seidel, Ross *95*
Seidelman, James Edward 1926- *6*
Seiden, Art(hur) *107*
    Brief entry *42*
Seidensticker, John 1944- *200*
Seidler, Ann (G.) 1925- *131*
Seidler, Tor 1952- *149*
    Brief entry *46*
    Earlier sketches in SATA *52, 98*
Seidman, Karla
    See Kuskin, Karla
Seidman, Laurence Ivan 1925- *15*
Seigel, Kalman 1917-1998 .... *12*
    Obituary *103*
Seignobosc, Francoise 1897-1961 .... *21*
Seinfeld, Jerry 1954- *146*
Seitz, Jacqueline 1931- *50*
Seixas, Judith S. 1922- *17*
Sejima, Yoshimasa 1913- *8*
Selberg, Ingrid (Maria) 1950- *68*
Selden, George
    See Thompson, George Selden
Selden, Neil R(oy) 1931- *61*
Self, Margaret Cabell 1902-1996 .... *24*
Selfors, Suzanne 1963- *193*
Selick, Henry 1952- *183*
Selig, Sylvie 1942- *13*
Selkirk, Jane
    See Chapman, John Stanton Higham
Sellers, Naomi
    See Flack, Naomi John White
Sellier, Marie 1953- *212*
Selman, LaRue W. 1927- *55*

Selsam, Millicent E(llis) 1912-1996 .... *29*
  Obituary *92*
  Earlier sketch in SATA *1*
  See also CLR *1*
Seltzer, Meyer 1932- *17*
Seltzer, Richard 1946- *41*
Seltzer, Richard Warren, Jr.
  See Seltzer, Richard
Selvadurai, Shyam 1965(?)- *171*
Selway, Martina 1940- *169*
  Earlier sketch in SATA *74*
Selzer, Adam 1980- *229*
  Earlier sketch in SATA *192*
Selznick, Brian 1966- *210*
  Earlier sketches in SATA *79, 117, 171*
Semel, Nava 1954- *107*
Semloh
  See Holmes, Peggy
Sendak, Jack 1924(?)-1995 .... *28*
Sendak, Maurice 1928- *165*
  Earlier sketches in SATA *1, 27, 113*
  See also CLR *131*
Sendak, Maurice Bernard
  See Sendak, Maurice
Sender, Ruth M(insky) 1926- *62*
Sengler, Johanna 1924- *18*
Senir, Mirik
  See Snir, Mirik
Senisi, Ellen B. 1951- *116*
Senisi, Ellen Babinec
  See Senisi, Ellen B.
Senn, J(oyce) A(nn) 1941- *115*
Senn, Steve 1950- *60*
  Brief entry *48*
Sensel, Joni 1962- *204*
Serafini, Frank *201*
Serage, Nancy 1924- *10*
Seredy, Kate 1899-1975 .... *1*
  Obituary *24*
  See also CLR *10*
Serfozo, Mary 1925- *194*
Seroff, Victor I(lyitch) 1902-1979 .... *12*
  Obituary *26*
Serra, Sebastia 1966- *202*
Serraillier, Ian (Lucien) 1912-1994 .... *73*
  Obituary *83*
  Earlier sketch in SATA *1*
  See also CLR *2*
  See also SAAS *3*
Serros, Michele *175*
Serros, Michele M.
  See Serros, Michele
Servello, Joe 1932- *10*
Service, Pamela F. 1945- *222*
  Earlier sketch in SATA *64*
Service, Robert
  See Service, Robert W.
Service, Robert W. 1874(?)-1958 .... *20*
Serwadda, W(illiam) Moses 1931- *27*
Serwer-Bernstein, Blanche L(uria)
  1910-1997 .... *10*
Sescoe, Vincent E. 1938- *123*
Seskin, Steve 1953- *211*
Seth, Mary
  See Lexau, Joan M.
Seton, Anya 1904(?)-1990 .... *3*
  Obituary *66*
Seton, Ernest (Evan) Thompson 1860-1946 . *18*
  See also CLR *59*
Seton-Thompson, Ernest
  See Seton, Ernest (Evan) Thompson
Seuling, Barbara 1937- *220*
  Autobiography Feature *220*
  Earlier sketches in SATA *10, 98, 145, 193*
  See also SAAS *24*
Seuss, Dr.
  See Dr. Seuss
Severn, Bill
  See Severn, William Irving
Severn, David
  See Unwin, David S.

Severn, William Irving 1914- *1*
Sewall, Marcia 1935- *119*
  Earlier sketches in SATA *37, 69*
Seward, Prudence 1926- *16*
Sewell, Anna 1820-1878 .... *100*
  Earlier sketch in SATA *24*
  See also CLR *17*
Sewell, Helen (Moore) 1896-1957 .... *38*
Sexton, Anne 1928-1974 .... *10*
Sexton, Anne Harvey
  See Sexton, Anne
Seymour, Alta Halverson *10*
Seymour, Jane 1951- *139*
Seymour, Tres 1966- *164*
  Earlier sketch in SATA *82*
Sfar, Joann 1971- *182*
Shachtman, Tom 1942- *49*
Shackleton, C.C.
  See Aldiss, Brian W.
Shader, Rachel
  See Sofer, Barbara
Shadow, Jak
  See Sutherland, Jon
Shadyland, Sal
  See Cooper, Louise
Shafer, Audrey *183*
Shafer, Robert E(ugene) 1925- *9*
Shaffer, Terea 1968- *79*
Shahan, Sherry 1949- *216*
  Earlier sketches in SATA *92, 134*
Shahn, Ben(jamin) 1898-1969
  Obituary *21*
Shahn, Bernarda Bryson
  See Bryson, Bernarda
Shaik, Fatima *114*
Shalant, Phyllis 1949- *150*
Shan, Darren 1972- *199*
  Earlier sketches in SATA *129, 168*
Shan, D.B.
  See Shan, Darren
Shanahan, Lisa *199*
Shanberg, Karen
  See Shragg, Karen (I.)
Shane, Harold Gray 1914-1993 .... *36*
  Obituary *76*
Shange, Ntozake 1948- *157*
Shanks, Ann Zane (Kushner) *10*
Shannon, David 1959- *228*
  Earlier sketches in SATA *107, 152*
  See also CLR *87*
Shannon, George 1952- *202*
  Earlier sketches in SATA *35, 94, 143*
Shannon, George William Bones
  See Shannon, George
Shannon, Jacqueline *63*
Shannon, Margaret
  See Silverwood, Margaret Shannon
Shannon, Monica 1905(?)-1965 .... *28*
Shannon, Terry
  See Mercer, Jessie
Shannon, Terry Miller 1951- *148*
Shapiro, Irwin 1911-1981 .... *32*
Shapiro, Jody Fickes 1940- *193*
Shapiro, Karen Jo 1964- *186*
Shapiro, Michelle 1961- *196*
Shapiro, Milton J. 1926- *32*
Shapiro, Tricia
  See Andryszewski, Tricia
Shapiro, Zachary 1970- *213*
Shapp, Charles M(orris) 1906-1989
  Obituary *61*
Shapp, Martha Glauber 1910- *3*
Sharenow, Robert *193*
Sharfman, Amalie *14*
Sharkey, Niamh *213*
Sharma, Partap 1939- *15*
Sharma, Rashmi
  See Singh, Rashmi Sharma
Sharman, Alison
  See Leonard, Alison

Sharmat, Marjorie Weinman 1928- *133*
  Earlier sketches in SATA *4, 33, 74*
Sharmat, Mitchell 1927- *127*
  Earlier sketch in SATA *33*
Sharp, Anne Wallace 1947- *144*
Sharp, Luke
  See Alkiviades, Alkis
Sharp, Margery 1905-1991 .... *29*
  Obituary *67*
  Earlier sketch in SATA *1*
  See also CLR *27*
Sharp, Zerna A. 1889-1981
  Obituary *27*
Sharpe, Jon
  See Duncan, Alice
  and Knott, William C(ecil, Jr.)
  and Messman, Jon
Sharpe, Mitchell R(aymond) 1924- *12*
Sharpe, Susan 1946- *71*
Sharratt, Nick 1962- *199*
  Earlier sketches in SATA *104, 153*
Shasha, Mark 1961- *80*
Shattuck, Roger 1923-2005 .... *64*
  Obituary *174*
Shattuck, Roger Whitney
  See Shattuck, Roger
Shaw, Arnold 1909-1989 .... *4*
  Obituary *63*
Shaw, Carolyn V. 1934- *91*
Shaw, Charles (Green) 1892-1974 .... *13*
Shaw, Evelyn S. 1927- *28*
Shaw, Flora Louisa
  See Lugard, Flora Louisa Shaw
Shaw, Hannah 1982(?)- *227*
Shaw, Janet 1937- *146*
  Earlier sketch in SATA *61*
  See also CLR *96*
Shaw, Janet Beeler
  See Shaw, Janet
Shaw, Liane 1959- *222*
Shaw, Lisa
  See Rogak, Lisa
Shaw, Margret 1940- *68*
Shaw, Mary 1965- *180*
Shaw, Nancy 1946- *162*
  Earlier sketch in SATA *71*
Shaw, Ray *7*
Shaw, Richard 1923- *12*
Shawn, Frank S.
  See Goulart, Ron
Shay, Art
  See Shay, Arthur
Shay, Arthur 1922- *4*
Shay, Lacey
  See Shebar, Sharon Sigmond
Shea, Bob *231*
  Earlier sketch in SATA *188*
Shea, George 1940- *54*
  Brief entry *42*
Shea, Pegi Deitz 1960- *172*
  Earlier sketches in SATA *77, 137*
Shearer, Alex 1949- *204*
Shearer, John 1947- *43*
  Brief entry *27*
  See also CLR *34*
Shearer, Ted 1919- *43*
Shearing, Leonie 1972- *184*
Sheban, Chris *182*
Shebar, Sharon Sigmond 1945- *36*
Shecter, Ben 1935- *16*
Shedd, Warner 1934- *147*
  Earlier sketch in SATA *87*
Sheedy, Alexandra Elizabeth 1962- *39*
  Earlier sketch in SATA *19*
Sheehan, Ethna 1908-2000 .... *9*
Sheehan, Patty 1945- *77*
Sheehan, Sean 1951- *154*
  Earlier sketch in SATA *86*
Sheen, Barbara 1949- *143*
Shefelman, Janice 1930- *205*
  Earlier sketches in SATA *58, 129*

Shefelman, Janice Jordan
   See Shefelman, Janice
Shefelman, Tom 1927- 204
   Earlier sketch in SATA 58
Sheffer, H. R.
   See Abels, Harriette S(heffer)
Sheffield, Charles 1935-2002 109
Sheffield, Janet N. 1926- 26
Sheikh, Nazneen 1944- 101
Sheinkin, Steve 1968- 204
Sheinmel, Courtney 1977- 211
Shekerjian, Regina Tor 16
Shelby, Anne 1948- 85
   Autobiography Feature 121
   See also SAAS 26
Sheldon, Ann
   See Antle, Nancy
Sheldon, Ann 67
   Earlier sketch in SATA 1
Sheldon, Aure 1917-1976 12
Sheldon, David 185
Sheldon, Deyan 181
Sheldon, John
   See Bloch, Robert (Albert)
Sheldon, Muriel 1926- 45
   Brief entry 39
Shell, Barry 1951- 176
Shelley, Frances
   See Wees, Frances Shelley
Shelley, John 1959- 202
Shelley, Mary
   See Shelley, Mary Wollstonecraft
Shelley, Mary Wollstonecraft 1797-1851 29
   See also CLR 133
Shelton, Paula Young 1961- 227
Shelton, William Roy 1919-1995 5
   Obituary 129
Shemie, Bonnie (Jean Brenner) 1949- 96
Shemin, Margaretha (Hoeneveld) 1928- 4
Shen, Michele 1953- 173
Shenker, Michele
   See Shen, Michele
Shenton, Edward 1895-1977 45
Shepard, Aaron 1950- 187
   Earlier sketches in SATA 75, 113
Shepard, Ernest Howard 1879-1976 100
   Obituary 24
   Earlier sketches in SATA 3, 33
   See also CLR 27
Shepard, James R.
   See Shepard, Jim
Shepard, Jim 1956- 164
   Earlier sketch in SATA 90
Shepard, Mary
   See Knox, (Mary) Eleanor Jessie
Shephard, Esther 1891-1975 5
   Obituary 26
Shepherd, Amanda 201
Shepherd, Donna Walsh
   See Walsh Shepherd, Donna
Shepherd, Elizabeth 4
Shepherd, Irana 173
Shepherd, Roni
   See Shepherd, Irana
Sheppard, Kate 195
Shepperson, Rob 178
Sherburne, Zoa (Lillian Morin) 1912-1995 3
   See also SAAS 18
Sherk-Savage, Candace
   See Savage, Candace
Sherlock, Patti 71
Sherman, D(enis) R(onald) 1934- 48
   Brief entry 29
Sherman, Diane (Finn) 1928- 12
Sherman, Elizabeth
   See Friskey, Margaret (Richards)
Sherman, Harold (Morrow) 1898-1987 37
   Obituary 137
Sherman, Josepha 163
   Earlier sketch in SATA 75

Sherman, Michael
   See Lowndes, Robert A(ugustine) W(ard)
Sherman, Nancy
   See Rosenberg, Nancy
Sherman, Pat 174
Sherman, Peter Michael
   See Lowndes, Robert A(ugustine) W(ard)
Sherrard, Valerie (Anne) 1957- 141
Sherrod, Jane
   See Singer, Jane Sherrod
Sherry, Clifford J. 1943- 84
Sherry, (Dulcie) Sylvia 1932- 122
   Earlier sketch in SATA 8
Sherwan, Earl 1917- 3
Sherwood, Jonathan
   See London, Jonathan
Sheth, Kashmira 186
Shetterly, Will 1955- 78
   Autobiography Feature 106
Shetterly, William Howard
   See Shetterly, Will
Shiefman, Vicky 1942- 22
Shields, Brenda Desmond (Armstrong)
   1914- 37
Shields, Carol Diggory 174
Shields, Charles 1944- 10
Shields, Gillian 203
Shiels, Barbara
   See Adams, Barbara Johnston
Shiffman, Lena 1957- 101
Shiga, Jason 1976- 228
Shiina, Makoto 1944- 83
Shimin, Symeon 1902-1984 13
Shimko, Bonnie 1941- 191
Shine, Andrea 1955- 104
Shine, Deborah 1932- 71
Shinn, Everett 1876-1953 21
Shinn, Sharon 1957- 229
   Earlier sketches in SATA 110, 164
Shippen, Katherine B(inney) 1892-1980 1
   Obituary 23
   See also CLR 36
Shippey, T. A. 1943- 143
Shippey, Thomas Alan
   See Shippey, T. A.
Shipton, Eric Earle 1907-1977 10
Shipton, Jonathan 1948- 215
Shipton, Paul 1963- 196
Shiraz, Yasmin 173
Shirer, William L(awrence) 1904-1993 45
   Obituary 78
Shirley, Debra 203
Shirley, Gayle C 1955- 96
Shirley, Gayle Corbett
   See Shirley, Gayle C
Shirley, Jean 1919- 70
Shirreffs, Gordon D(onald) 1914-1996 11
Shirts, Morris A(lpine) 1922- 63
Shlichta, Joe 1968- 84
Shmurak, Carole B. 1944- 118
Sholokhov, Mikhail 1905-1984
   Obituary 36
Sholokhov, Mikhail Aleksandrovich
   See Sholokhov, Mikhail
Shore, Diane Z. 215
   Earlier sketch in SATA 179
Shore, Diane ZuHone
   See Shore, Diane Z.
Shore, June Lewis 30
Shore, Nancy 1960- 124
Shore, Robert 1924- 39
Short, Michael 1937- 65
Short, Roger
   See Arkin, Alan
Shortall, Leonard W. 19
Shortt, Tim(othy Donald) 1961- 96
Shotwell, Louisa Rossiter 1902-1993 3
Shoulders, Michael 1954- 216
Shoup, Barbara 1947- 156
   Earlier sketch in SATA 86
   See also SAAS 24

Shoveller, Herb 184
Showalter, Jean B(reckinridge) 12
Showell, Ellen Harvey 1934- 33
Showers, Paul C. 1910-1999 92
   Obituary 114
   Earlier sketch in SATA 21
   See also CLR 6
   See also SAAS 7
Shpakow, Tanya 1959(?)- 94
Shpitalnik, Vladimir 1964- 83
Shragg, Karen (I.) 1954- 142
Shreeve, Elizabeth 1956- 156
Shreve, Susan
   See Shreve, Susan Richards
Shreve, Susan Richards 1939- 152
   Brief entry 41
   Earlier sketches in SATA 46, 95
Shriver, Jean Adair 1932- 75
Shriver, Maria 1955- 134
Shriver, Maria Owings
   See Shriver, Maria
Shrode, Mary
   See Hollingsworth, Mary
Shtainmets, Leon 32
Shub, Elizabeth 1915(?)-2004 5
Shuken, Julia 1948- 84
Shulevitz, Uri 1935- 165
   Earlier sketches in SATA 3, 50, 106
   See also CLR 61
Shulman, Alix Kates 1932- 7
Shulman, Dee 1957- 146
Shulman, Irving 1913-1995 13
Shulman, Lisa 202
Shulman, Mark 1962- 184
Shulman, Max 1919-1988
   Obituary 59
Shulman, Milton 1913-2004
   Obituary 154
Shulman, Neil B(arnett) 1945- 89
Shumsky, Zena
   See Collier, Zena
Shura, Mary Francis
   See Craig, Mary (Francis) Shura
Shusterman, Neal 1962- 201
   Autobiography Feature 140
   Earlier sketches in SATA 85, 121, 140
Shuter, Jane (Margaret) 1955- 151
   Earlier sketch in SATA 90
Shuttlesworth, Dorothy Edwards 3
Shwartz, Susan (Martha) 1949- 94
Shyer, Christopher 1961- 98
Shyer, Marlene Fanta 13
Siberell, Anne 29
Sibley, Don 1922- 12
Siburt, Ruth 1951- 121
Siculan, Daniel 1922- 12
Siddon, Barbara
   See Bradford, Barbara Taylor
Sidgwick, Ethel 1877-1970 116
Sidjakov, Nicolas 1924- 18
Sidman, Joyce 1956- 181
   Earlier sketch in SATA 145
Sidney, Frank
   See Warwick, Alan R(oss)
Sidney, Margaret
   See Lothrop, Harriet Mulford Stone
Siebert, Diane 1948- 189
Siegal, Aranka 1930- 88
   Brief entry 37
Siegel, Beatrice 36
Siegel, Helen
   See Siegl, Helen
Siegel, Robert 1939- 39
Siegel, Robert Harold
   See Siegel, Robert
Siegel, Siena Cherson 1967(?)- 185
Siegelson, Kim L. 1962- 114
Sieger, Ted 1958- 189
Siegl, Helen 1924- 34
Siepmann, Mary Aline
   See Wesley, Mary (Aline)

Sierra, Judy 1945- *195*
    Earlier sketches in SATA *104, 162*
Sieswerda, Paul L. 1942- *147*
Sievert, Terri
    See Dougherty, Terri (L.)
Sigsawa, Keiichi 1972- *211*
Silas
    See McCay, (Zenas) Winsor
Silcock, Sara Lesley 1947- *12*
Silin-Palmer, Pamela *184*
Sill, Cathryn 1953- *221*
    Earlier sketches in SATA *74, 141*
Sill, John 1947- *222*
    Earlier sketches in SATA *74, 140*
Sillitoe, Alan 1928-2010 .... *61*
Sills, Leslie (Elka) 1948- *129*
Silly, E. S.
    See Kraus, (Herman) Robert
Silsbe, Brenda 1953- *73*
Silva, Joseph
    See Goulart, Ron
Silvano, Wendi 1962- *223*
Silver, Jago
    See Jago
Silver, Maggie *216*
Silver, Ruth
    See Chew, Ruth
Silverberg, Robert 1935- *91*
    Autobiography Feature *104*
    Earlier sketch in SATA *13*
    See also CLR *59*
Silverman, Erica 1955- *222*
    Earlier sketches in SATA *78, 112, 165*
Silverman, Janis L. 1946- *127*
Silverman, Mel(vin Frank) 1931-1966 .... *9*
Silverman, Robin L. 1954- *96*
Silverman, Robin Landew
    See Silverman, Robin L.
Silverstein, Alvin 1933- *124*
    Earlier sketches in SATA *8, 69*
    See also CLR *25*
Silverstein, Herma 1945- *106*
Silverstein, Robert Alan 1959- *124*
    Earlier sketch in SATA *77*
Silverstein, Shel 1932-1999 .... *92*
    Brief entry *27*
    Obituary *116*
    Earlier sketch in SATA *33*
    See also CLR *96*
Silverstein, Sheldon Allan
    See Silverstein, Shel
Silverstein, Virginia B. 1937- *124*
    Earlier sketches in SATA *8, 69*
    See also CLR *25*
Silverstein, Virginia Barbara Opshelor
    See Silverstein, Virginia B.
Silverthorne, Elizabeth 1930- *35*
Silverwood, Margaret Shannon 1966- *137*
    Earlier sketch in SATA *83*
Silvey, Diane F. 1946- *135*
Sim, David 1953- *162*
Sim, Dorrith M. 1931- *96*
Simak, Clifford D(onald) 1904-1988
    Obituary *56*
Simard, Remy 1959- *168*
Siminovich, Lorena 1976(?)- *219*
Simmie, Lois (Ann) 1932- *106*
Simmonds, Posy 1945- *130*
    See also CLR *23*
Simmonds, Rosemary Elizabeth
    See Simmonds, Posy
Simmons, Andra 1939- *141*
Simmons, Elly 1955- *134*
Simmons, Michael 1970- *185*
Simms, Laura 1947- *117*
Simner, Janni Lee *113*
Simon, Charlie May
    See Fletcher, Charlie May Hogue
Simon, Francesca 1955- *111*
Simon, Gabriel 1972- *118*

Simon, Hilda Rita 1921- *28*
    See also CLR *39*
Simon, Howard 1903-1979 .... *32*
    Obituary *21*
Simon, Joe
    See Simon, Joseph H.
Simon, Joseph H. 1913- *7*
Simon, Martin P(aul William) 1903-1969 .... *12*
Simon, Mina Lewiton
    See Lewiton, Mina
Simon, Norma (Feldstein) 1927- *129*
    Earlier sketches in SATA *3, 68*
Simon, Seymour 1931- *202*
    Earlier sketches in SATA *4, 73, 138*
    See also CLR *63*
Simon, Shirley (Schwartz) 1921- *11*
Simon, Solomon 1895-1970 .... *40*
Simonetta, Linda 1948- *14*
Simonetta, Sam 1936- *14*
Simons, Barbara B(rooks) 1934- *41*
Simont, Marc 1915- *126*
    Earlier sketches in SATA *9, 73*
Simpson, Colin 1908-1983 .... *14*
Simpson, Harriette
    See Arnow, Harriette (Louisa) Simpson
Simpson, Jacynth Hope
    See Hope Simpson, Jacynth
Simpson, Lesley 1963- *150*
Simpson, Margaret 1943- *128*
Simpson, Myrtle L(illias) 1931- *14*
Sims, Blanche *168*
    Earlier sketch in SATA *75*
Sims, Blanche L.
    See Sims, Blanche
Sims, Rudine
    See Bishop, Rudine Sims
Simundsson, Elva 1950- *63*
Sinclair, Clover
    See Gater, Dilys
Sinclair, Emil
    See Hesse, Hermann
Sinclair, Jeff 1958- *77*
Sinclair, Olga 1923- *121*
Sinclair, Rose
    See Smith, Susan Vernon
Sinclair, Upton 1878-1968 .... *9*
Sinclair, Upton Beall
    See Sinclair, Upton
Singer, A.L.
    See Lerangis, Peter
Singer, Arthur 1917-1990 .... *64*
Singer, Isaac
    See Singer, Isaac Bashevis
Singer, Isaac Bashevis 1904-1991 .... *27*
    Obituary *68*
    Earlier sketch in SATA *3*
    See also CLR *1*
Singer, Jane Sherrod 1917-1985 .... *4*
    Obituary *42*
Singer, Julia 1917- *28*
Singer, Kurt D. 1911-2005 .... *38*
    Obituary *172*
Singer, Marilyn 1948- *201*
    Autobiography Feature *158*
    Brief entry *38*
    Earlier sketches in SATA *48, 80, 125, 158*
    See also CLR *48*
    See also SAAS *13*
Singer, Muff 1942-2005 .... *104*
    Obituary *160*
Singer, Nicky 1956- *194*
Singer, Susan (Mahler) 1941- *9*
Singh, Rashmi Sharma 1952- *90*
Singleton, Linda Joy 1957- *166*
    Earlier sketch in SATA *88*
Singleton, L.J.
    See Singleton, Linda Joy
Singleton, Sarah 1966- *214*
Sinykin, Sheri
    See Sinykin, Sheri Cooper

Sinykin, Sheri Cooper 1950- *142*
    Autobiography Feature *142*
    Earlier sketches in SATA *72, 133*
Sinykin, Sheril Terri Cooper
    See Sinykin, Sheri Cooper
Siomades, Lorianne *217*
Sipiera, Paul P., (Jr.) 1948- *144*
    Earlier sketch in SATA *89*
Siracusa, Catherine (Jane) 1947- *82*
Sirett, Dawn (Karen) 1966- *88*
Sirimarco, Elizabeth 1966- *158*
Sirof, Harriet 1930- *94*
    Earlier sketch in SATA *37*
Sirois, Allen L. 1950- *76*
Sirvaitis (Chernyaev), Karen (Ann) 1961- ... *79*
Sis, Peter 1949- *192*
    Earlier sketch in SATA *149*
    See also CLR *110*
Sisson, Rosemary Anne 1923- *11*
Sister Mary Terese
    See Donze, Mary Terese
Sita, Lisa 1962- *87*
Sitarski, Anita *200*
Sitomer, Alan Lawrence *174*
Sitomer, Harry 1903-1985 .... *31*
Sitomer, Mindel 1903-1987 .... *31*
Sittenfeld, Curtis 1975(?)- *164*
Sive, Helen R(obinson) 1951- *30*
Sivulich, Sandra (Jeanne) Stroner 1941- *9*
Siy, Alexandra *193*
Skarmeta, Antonio 1940- *57*
Skeers, Linda 1958- *207*
Skelly, James R(ichard) 1927- *17*
Skelton, Matthew 1971- *185*
Skinner, Constance Lindsay 1877-1939
    See YABC *1*
Skinner, Cornelia Otis 1901-1979 .... *2*
Skipper, G. C. 1939- *46*
    Brief entry *38*
Sklansky, Amy E(dgar) 1971- *145*
Sklansky, Amy E. 1971- *204*
Skofield, James *95*
    Brief entry *44*
Skold, Betty Westrom 1923- *41*
Skorpen, Liesel Moak 1935- *3*
Skott, Maria
    See Nikolajeva, Maria
Skovron, Jon 1976- *229*
Skrypuch, Marsha Forchuk 1954- *134*
Skultety, Nancy Laney 1960- *175*
Skurzynski, Gloria 1930- *145*
    Autobiography Feature *145*
    Earlier sketches in SATA *8, 74, 122*
    See also SAAS *9*
Skurzynski, Gloria Joan
    See Skurzynski, Gloria
Skutch, Robert 1925- *89*
Skye, Maggie
    See Werner, Herma
Skye, Obert *200*
    Earlier sketch in SATA *170*
Slack, Michael 1969- *189*
Slackman, Charles B. 1934- *12*
Slade, Arthur G. 1967- *221*
    Earlier sketches in SATA *106, 149*
Slade, Arthur Gregory
    See Slade, Arthur G.
Slade, Christian 1974- *193*
Slade, Richard 1910-1971 .... *9*
Slade, Suzanne 1964- *226*
Slangerup, Erik Jon 1969- *130*
Slate, Joseph 1928- *174*
    Earlier sketches in SATA *38, 122*
Slate, Joseph Frank
    See Slate, Joseph
Slater, Dashka 1963- *179*
Slater, David Michael 1970- *212*
Slater, Ray
    See Lansdale, Joe R.
Slaughter, Hope 1940- *84*

Slaughter, Jean
    See Doty, Jean Slaughter
Slaughter, Tom 1955- *152*
Slavicek, Louise Chipley 1956- *144*
Slavin, Bill 1959- *199*
    Earlier sketches in SATA *76, 148*
Slaymaker, Melissa Eskridge 1958- *158*
Slayton, Fran Cannon *221*
Sleator, William 1945- *208*
    Earlier sketches in SATA *3, 68, 118, 161*
    See also CLR *128*
Sleator, William Warner III
    See Sleator, William
Slegers, Liesbet 1975- *154*
Sleigh, Barbara 1906-1982 .... *86*
    Obituary *30*
    Earlier sketch in SATA *3*
Slepian, Jan 1921- *85*
    Brief entry *45*
    Earlier sketch in SATA *51*
    See also SAAS *8*
Slepian, Janice B.
    See Slepian, Jan
Slicer, Margaret O. 1920- *4*
Slier, Debby
    See Shine, Deborah
Sloan, Brian 1966- *172*
Sloan, Carolyn 1937- *116*
    Earlier sketch in SATA *58*
Sloan, Glenna 1930- *120*
Sloan, Glenna Davis
    See Sloan, Glenna
Sloane, Eric 1910(?)-1985 .... *52*
    Obituary *42*
Sloane, Todd 1955- *88*
Sloat, Teri 1948- *164*
    Earlier sketches in SATA *70, 106*
Slobodkin, Florence Gersh 1905-1994 .... *5*
    Obituary *107*
Slobodkin, Louis 1903-1975 .... *26*
    Earlier sketch in SATA *1*
Slobodkina, Esphyr 1908-2002 .... *1*
    Obituary *135*
    See also SAAS *8*
Sloggett, Nellie 1851-1923 .... *44*
Slonim, David 1966- *207*
Sloss, Lesley Lord 1965- *72*
Slote, Alfred 1926- *72*
    Earlier sketch in SATA *8*
    See also CLR *4*
    See also SAAS *21*
Slote, Elizabeth 1956- *80*
Small, Charlie
    See Ward, Nick
Small, David 1945- *216*
    Brief entry *46*
    Earlier sketches in SATA *50, 95, 126, 183*
    See also CLR *53*
Small, Ernest
    See Lent, Blair
Small, Mary 1932- *165*
Small, Terry 1942- *75*
Smallcomb, Pam 1954- *159*
Smallman, Steve *227*
    Earlier sketch in SATA *197*
Smalls, Irene
    See Smalls-Hector, Irene
Smalls-Hector, Irene 1950- *146*
    Earlier sketch in SATA *73*
    See also CLR *103*
Smallwood, Norah (Evelyn) 1910(?)-1984
    Obituary *41*
Smaridge, Norah (Antoinette) 1903-1994 ...... *6*
Smath, Jerry 1933- *198*
Smee, Nicola 1948- *167*
    Earlier sketch in SATA *76*
Smiley, Virginia Kester 1923- *2*
Smit, Noelle 1972- *199*
Smith, Alexander McCall 1948- *179*
    Earlier sketch in SATA *73*
Smith, Andrew 1959- *209*

Smith, Andrew Anselmo
    See Smith, Andrew
Smith, Andy J. 1975- *207*
Smith, Anne Warren 1938- *41*
    Brief entry *34*
Smith, Barry (Edward Jervis) 1943- *75*
Smith, Beatrice S(chillinger) *12*
Smith, Betsy Covington 1937- *55*
    Earlier sketch in SATA *43*
Smith, Betty (Wehner) 1904-1972 .... *6*
Smith, Bradford 1909-1964 .... *5*
Smith, Brenda 1946- *82*
Smith, C. Pritchard
    See Hoyt, Edwin P(almer), Jr.
Smith, Caesar
    See Trevor, Elleston
Smith, Cat Bowman 1939- *201*
Smith, Charles R., Jr. 1969- *203*
    Earlier sketch in SATA *159*
Smith, Craig 1955- *172*
    Earlier sketches in SATA *81, 117*
Smith, Cynthia Leitich 1967- *215*
    Earlier sketch in SATA *152*
Smith, D. James 1955- *176*
Smith, Danna *216*
Smith, Danna Kessimakis
    See Smith, Danna
Smith, Datus C(lifford), Jr. 1907-1999 .... *13*
    Obituary *116*
Smith, Debra 1955- *89*
Smith, Derek 1943- *141*
Smith, Dick King
    See King-Smith, Dick
Smith, D.J.
    See Smith, D. James
Smith, Dodie
    See Smith, Dorothy Gladys
Smith, Doris Buchanan 1934-2002 .... *75*
    Obituary *140*
    Earlier sketch in SATA *28*
    See also SAAS *10*
Smith, Dorothy Gladys 1896-1990 .... *82*
    Obituary *65*
Smith, Dorothy Stafford 1905- *6*
Smith, Duane 1974- *202*
Smith, E(lmer) Boyd 1860-1943
    See YABC *1*
Smith, E(dric) Brooks 1917- *40*
Smith, Elwood H. 1941- *203*
Smith, Emily Wing 1980- *215*
Smith, Emma 1923- *52*
    Brief entry *36*
Smith, (Katherine) Eunice (Young)
    1902-1993 .... *5*
Smith, Frances C(hristine) 1904-1986 .... *3*
Smith, Gary R. 1932- *14*
Smith, Geof 1969- *102*
Smith, George Harmon 1920- *5*
Smith, Gordon 1951- *184*
Smith, Greg Leitch *152*
Smith, H(arry) Allen 1907-1976
    Obituary *20*
Smith, Helene 1937- *142*
Smith, Hope Anita *202*
Smith, Howard E(verett), Jr. 1927- *12*
Smith, Hugh L(etcher) 1921-1968 .... *5*
Smith, Icy 1966- *228*
Smith, Imogene Henderson 1922- *12*
Smith, Jacqueline B. 1937- *39*
Smith, Jada Pinkett 1971- *161*
Smith, James Noel 1950- *193*
Smith, Janet (Buchanan) Adam
    See Adam Smith, Janet (Buchanan)
Smith, Janice Lee 1949- *155*
    Earlier sketch in SATA *54*
Smith, Jean
    See Smith, Frances C(hristine)
Smith, Jean Pajot 1945- *10*
Smith, Jeff 1958- *161*
    Earlier sketch in SATA *93*

Smith, Jeff Allen
    See Smith, Jeff
Smith, Jeffrey Alan
    See Smith, Jeff
Smith, Jenny 1963- *90*
Smith, Jessie
    See Kunhardt, Edith
Smith, Jessie Willcox 1863-1935 .... *21*
    See also CLR *59*
Smith, Jim W.W. *231*
Smith, Joan (Mary) 1933- *54*
    Brief entry *46*
Smith, Johnston
    See Crane, Stephen
Smith, Jos A. 1936- *181*
    Earlier sketches in SATA *73, 120*
Smith, Joseph Arthur
    See Smith, Jos A.
Smith, Judie R. 1936- *80*
Smith, Kirsten 1970- *210*
Smith, Lafayette
    See Higdon, Hal
Smith, Lane 1959- *224*
    Earlier sketches in SATA *76, 131, 179*
    See also CLR *47*
Smith, Lee
    See Albion, Lee Smith
Smith, Lendon H(oward) 1921- *64*
Smith, Lillian H(elena) 1887-1983
    Obituary *32*
Smith, Linda 1949- *177*
Smith, Linell Nash 1932- *2*
Smith, Lucia B. 1943- *30*
Smith, Maggie 1965- *190*
Smith, Margaret Emily Noel Nuttall
    See Nuttall-Smith, Margaret Emily Noel
Smith, Marion Hagens 1913- *12*
Smith, Marion Jaques 1899-1987 .... *13*
Smith, Mary Ellen *10*
Smith, Marya 1945- *78*
Smith, Mike
    See Smith, Mary Ellen
Smith, Nancy Covert 1935- *12*
Smith, Norman F. 1920- *70*
    Earlier sketch in SATA *5*
Smith, Patricia Clark 1943- *96*
Smith, Pauline C.
    See Arthur, Robert, (Jr.)
Smith, Pauline C(oggeshall) 1908-1994 .... *27*
Smith, Philip Warren 1936- *46*
Smith, R. Alexander McCall
    See Smith, Alexander McCall
Smith, Rebecca 1946- *123*
Smith, Robert Kimmel 1930- *77*
    Earlier sketch in SATA *12*
Smith, Robert Paul 1915-1977 .... *52*
    Obituary *30*
Smith, Roland 1951- *193*
    Earlier sketches in SATA *115, 161*
Smith, Rosamond
    See Oates, Joyce Carol
Smith, Ruth Leslie 1902- *2*
Smith, Samantha 1972-1985
    Obituary *45*
Smith, Sandra Lee 1945- *75*
Smith, Sarah Stafford
    See Smith, Dorothy Stafford
Smith, Sharon 1947- *82*
Smith, Sherri L. 1971- *156*
Smith, Sherwood 1951- *206*
    Autobiography Feature *206*
    Earlier sketches in SATA *82, 140*
Smith, Shirley Raines
    See Raines, Shirley C(arol)
Smith, Susan Carlton 1923- *12*
Smith, Susan Mathias 1950- *43*
    Brief entry *35*
Smith, Susan Vernon 1950- *48*
    Brief entry *45*
Smith, Tim(othy R.) 1945- *151*
Smith, Ursula 1934- *54*

Smith, Vian (Crocker) 1920-1969 11
Smith, Wanda VanHoy 1926- 65
Smith, Ward
    See Goldsmith, Howard
Smith, William A. 1918- 10
Smith, William Jay 1918- 154
    Autobiography Feature 154
    Earlier sketches in SATA 2, 68
    See also SAAS 22
Smith, Winsome 1935- 45
Smith, Z.Z.
    See Westheimer, David
Smith-Ankrom, M. E. 1942- 130
Smith-Griswold, Wendy 1955- 88
Smith Hernandez, Duncan Tonatiuh
    See Tonatiuh, Duncan
Smith-Rex, Susan J. 1950- 94
Smithsen, Richard
    See Pellowski, Michael (Joseph)
Smithson, Ryan 1985- 216
Smits, Teo
    See Smits, Theodore R(ichard)
Smits, Theodore R(ichard) 1905-1996 45
    Brief entry 28
Smolinski, Dick 1932- 86
Smothers, Ethel Footman 1944- 149
    Earlier sketch in SATA 76
Smucker, Anna Egan 1948- 209
Smucker, Barbara 1915-2003 130
    Earlier sketches in SATA 29, 76
    See also CLR 10
    See also SAAS 11
Smucker, Barbara Claassen
    See Smucker, Barbara
Smyth, Iain 1959- 105
Snedeker, Caroline Dale (Parke) 1871-1956
    See YABC 2
Sneed, Brad 191
Sneider, Marian 1932-2005 197
Snell, Gordon 1933(?)- 228
Snell, Nigel (Edward Creagh) 1936- 57
    Brief entry 40
Snellgrove, L(aurence) E(rnest) 1928- 53
Snelling, Dennis (Wayne) 1958- 84
Sneve, Virginia Driving Hawk 1933- 95
    Earlier sketch in SATA 8
    See also CLR 2
Snicket, Lemony 1970- 215
    Earlier sketches in SATA 126, 187
    See also CLR 79
Sniegoski, Thomas E. 195
Sniegoski, Tom
    See Sniegoski, Thomas E.
Snir, Eleyor 225
Snir, Mirik 1948- 226
Snodgrass, Mary Ellen 1944- 75
Snodgrass, Quentin Curtius
    See Twain, Mark
Snodgrass, Thomas Jefferson
    See Twain, Mark
Snook, Barbara (Lillian) 1913-1976 34
Snow, Alan 1959- 190
Snow, Carol 1965- 208
Snow, Donald Clifford 1917-1979 16
Snow, Dorothea J(ohnston) 1909- 9
Snow, Richard F. 1947- 52
    Brief entry 37
Snow, Richard Folger
    See Snow, Richard F.
Snow, Sarah 229
Snyder, Anne 1922-2001 4
    Obituary 125
Snyder, Bernadette McCarver 1930- 97
Snyder, Betsy 230
Snyder, Carol 1941- 35
Snyder, Gerald S(eymour) 1933- 48
    Brief entry 34
Snyder, Jerome 1916-1976
    Obituary 20
Snyder, Laurel 1974- 209
Snyder, Midori 1954- 106

Snyder, Paul A. 1946- 125
Snyder, Zilpha Keatley 1927- 226
    Autobiography Feature 163
    Earlier sketches in SATA 1, 28, 75, 110, 163
    See also CLR 121
    See also SAAS 2
Snyderman, Reuven K. 1922- 5
So, Meilo 162
Sobel, June 1950- 149
Soble, Jennie
    See Cavin, Ruth
Sobol, Donald J. 1924- 132
    Earlier sketches in SATA 1, 31, 73
    See also CLR 4
Sobol, Harriet Langsam 1936- 47
    Brief entry 34
Sobol, Richard 211
Sobol, Rose 1931- 76
Sobott-Mogwe, Gaele 1956- 97
Soderlind, Arthur E(dwin) 1920- 14
Soentpiet, Chris K. 1970- 159
    Earlier sketch in SATA 97
Soerensen, Svend Otto 1916- 67
Sofer, Barbara 1949- 109
Sofer, Rachel
    See Sofer, Barbara
Softly, Barbara Frewin 1924- 12
Sogabe, Aki 207
Soglow, Otto 1900-1975
    Obituary 30
Sohl, Frederic J(ohn) 1916- 10
Sohr, Daniel 1973- 190
Sokol, Bill
    See Sokol, William
Sokol, William 1923- 37
Sokolov, Kirill 1930- 34
Solbert, Romaine G. 1925- 2
Solbert, Ronni
    See Solbert, Romaine G.
Solheim, James 133
Solomon, Heather M. 188
Solomon, Joan 1930- 51
    Brief entry 40
Solomons, Ikey Esquir
    See Thackeray, William Makepeace
Solonevich, George 1915-2003 15
Solot, Mary Lynn 1939- 12
Solov'ev, Mikhail
    See Soloviov, Michael
Soloviov, Michael 1972- 222
Soman, David 1965- 200
Somerlott, Robert 1928-2001 62
Somers, Kevin 205
Somervill, Barbara A(nn) 1948- 140
Sommer, Angela
    See Sommer-Bodenburg, Angela
Sommer, Carl 1930- 175
    Earlier sketch in SATA 126
Sommer, Elyse 1929- 7
Sommer, Robert 1929- 12
Sommer-Bodenburg, Angela 1948- 113
    Earlier sketch in SATA 63
Sommerdorf, Norma 1926- 131
Sommerdorf, Norma Jean
    See Sommerdorf, Norma
Sommerfelt, Aimee 1892-1975 5
Son, John 160
Sones, Sonya 131
Sonneborn, Ruth (Cantor) 1899-1974 4
    Obituary 27
Sonnenblick, Jordan 1969- 223
    Earlier sketch in SATA 185
    See also CLR 144
Sonnenmark, Laura A. 1958- 73
Soo, Kean 201
Sopko, Eugen 1949- 58
Sorel, Edward 1929- 126
    Brief entry 37
    Earlier sketch in SATA 65
Sorensen, Henri 1950- 115
    Earlier sketch in SATA 77

Sorensen, Svend Otto
    See Soerensen, Svend Otto
Sorensen, Virginia 1912-1991 2
    Obituary 72
    See also SAAS 15
Sorenson, Jane 1926- 63
Sorenson, Margo 1946- 96
Sorley Walker, Kathrine 41
Sorra, Kristin 185
Sorrells, Walter 177
Sorrentino, Joseph N. 1937- 6
Sortor, June Elizabeth 1939- 12
Sortor, Toni
    See Sortor, June Elizabeth
Sosa, Hernan 1977- 203
Soskin, V. H.
    See Ellison, Virginia H(owell)
Soto, Gary 1952- 174
    Earlier sketches in SATA 80, 120
    See also CLR 38
Sotomayor, Antonio 1902-1985 11
Souci, Robert D. San
    See San Souci, Robert D.
Soudley, Henry
    See Wood, James Playsted
Souhami, Jessica 176
Soule, Gardner (Bosworth) 1913-2000 14
Soule, Jean Conder 1919- 10
Soup, Cuthbert
    See Swallow, Gerry
Souster, (Holmes) Raymond 1921- 63
South, Sheri Cobb 1959- 82
Southall, Ivan 1921-2008 134
    Autobiography Feature 134
    Earlier sketches in SATA 3, 68
    See also CLR 165
    See also SAAS 3
Southall, Ivan Francis
    See Southall, Ivan
Southey, Robert 1774-1843 54
Southgate, Vera 54
Souza, Janet
    See Tashjian, Janet
Sovak, Jan 1953- 115
Sowden, Celeste
    See Walters, Celeste
Sowter, Nita 69
Spafford, Suzy 1945- 160
Spagnoli, Cathy 1950- 134
    Earlier sketch in SATA 79
Spain, Sahara Sunday 1991- 133
Spain, Susan Rosson 185
Spalding, Andrea 1944- 150
    Earlier sketch in SATA 101
Spalenka, Greg 1958- 198
Spanfeller, James J. 1930- 19
    See also SAAS 8
Spanfeller, Jim
    See Spanfeller, James J.
Spangenberg, Judith Dunn 1942- 5
Spangler, Brie 212
Spanyol, Jessica 1965- 206
    Earlier sketch in SATA 137
Spar, Jerome 1918- 10
Sparks, Barbara 1942- 78
Sparks, Beatrice (Mathews) 1918- 44
    Brief entry 28
    See also CLR 139
Sparks, Mary W. 1920- 15
Spaulding, Douglas
    See Bradbury, Ray
Spaulding, Leonard
    See Bradbury, Ray
Spaulding, Norma 107
Speare, Elizabeth George 1908-1994 62
    Obituary 83
    Earlier sketch in SATA 5
    See also CLR 8
Spearing, Craig J. 228
Spearing, Judith (Mary Harlow) 1922- 9
Spears, Rick 182

Speck, Katie *196*
Speck, Nancy 1959- *104*
Specking, Inez 1890-1960(?) *11*
Speed, Nell
  See Keats, Emma
  and Sampson, Emma (Keats) Speed
Speed, Nell (Ewing) 1878-1913 .... *68*
Speer, Bonnie Stahlman 1929- *113*
Speer-Lyon, Tammie L. 1965- *89*
Speicher, Helen Ross S(mith) 1915- *8*
Speir, Nancy 1958- *210*
  Earlier sketch in SATA *81*
Spellman, John W(illard) 1934- *14*
Spellman, Roger G.
  See Cox, William R(obert)
Spelman, Cornelia Maude 1946- *144*
  Earlier sketch in SATA *96*
Spelman, Mary 1934- *28*
Spelvin, George
  See Lerangis, Peter
  and Phillips, David Atlee
Spence, Cynthia
  See Eble, Diane
Spence, Eleanor (Rachel) 1928- *21*
  See also CLR *26*
Spence, Geraldine 1931- *47*
Spencer, Ann 1918- *10*
Spencer, Britt *206*
Spencer, Cornelia
  See Yaukey, Grace S(ydenstricker)
Spencer, Donald D(ean) 1931- *41*
Spencer, Elizabeth 1921- *14*
Spencer, Leonard G.
  See Garrett, Randall
  and Silverberg, Robert
Spencer, William 1922- *9*
Spencer, Zane A(nn) 1935- *35*
Spengler, Margaret *223*
Sper, Emily 1957- *142*
Speregen, Devra Newberger 1964- *84*
Sperling, Dan(iel Lee) 1949- *65*
Sperry, Armstrong W. 1897-1976 .... *1*
  Obituary *27*
Sperry, Raymond
  See Garis, Howard R.
Sperry, Raymond, Jr. *1*
Spetter, Jung-Hee 1969- *134*
Spicer, Dorothy Gladys -1975 .... *32*
Spiegel, Beth *184*
Spiegelman, Art 1948- *158*
  Earlier sketch in SATA *109*
Spiegelman, Judith M. *5*
Spielberg, Steven 1947- *32*
Spier, Peter (Edward) 1927- *54*
  Earlier sketch in SATA *4*
  See also CLR *5*
Spilhaus, Athelstan (Frederick) 1911-1998 .. *13*
  Obituary *102*
Spilka, Arnold 1917- *6*
Spillane, Frank Morrison
  See Spillane, Mickey
Spillane, Mickey 1918-2006 .... *66*
  Obituary *176*
Spillebeen, Geert 1956- *225*
Spinelli, Eileen 1942- *225*
  Earlier sketches in SATA *38, 101, 150, 186*
Spinelli, Jerry 1941- *195*
  Earlier sketches in SATA *39, 71, 110, 158*
  See also CLR *82*
Spink, Reginald (William) 1905-1994 .... *11*
Spinka, Penina Keen 1945- *72*
Spinner, Stephanie 1943- *132*
  Earlier sketches in SATA *38, 91*
Spinossimus
  See White, William, Jr.
Spiotta-DiMare, Loren *173*
Spires, Ashley 1978- *183*
Spires, Elizabeth 1952- *215*
  Earlier sketches in SATA *71, 111*
Spiridellis, Gregg 1971(?)- *199*

Spirin, Gennadii
  See Spirin, Gennady
Spirin, Gennadij
  See Spirin, Gennady
Spirin, Gennady 1948- *204*
  Earlier sketches in SATA *95, 134*
  See also CLR *88*
Spiro, Ruth *208*
Spivak, Dawnine *101*
Spizman, Robyn Freedman *194*
Spohn, David 1948- *72*
Spohn, Kate 1962- *147*
  Earlier sketch in SATA *87*
Spollen, Christopher 1952- *12*
Spooner, Michael (Tim) 1954- *92*
Spoor, Mike *218*
Spowart, Robin 1947- *177*
  Earlier sketch in SATA *82*
Spradlin, Michael P. *204*
Sprague, Gretchen 1926-2003 .... *27*
Spranger, Nina 1969- *203*
Sprengel, Artie
  See Lerangis, Peter
Sprigge, Elizabeth (Miriam Squire)
  1900-1974 .... *10*
Spring, (Robert) Howard 1889-1965 .... *28*
Springer, Kristina *226*
Springer, Margaret 1941- *78*
Springer, Marilyn Harris 1931- *47*
Springer, Nancy 1948- *222*
  Earlier sketches in SATA *65, 110, 172*
Springstubb, Tricia 1950- *78*
  Brief entry *40*
  Earlier sketch in SATA *46*
Spudvilas, Anne 1951- *199*
  Earlier sketch in SATA *94*
Spurll, Barbara 1952- *78*
Spurr, Elizabeth *172*
Spykman, E(lizabeth) C(hoate) 1896-1965 .. *10*
  See also CLR *35*
Spyri, Johanna (Heusser) 1827-1901 .... *100*
  Earlier sketch in SATA *19*
  See also CLR *115*
Squires, Janet *215*
Squires, Phil
  See Barker, S. Omar
Srba, Lynne *98*
Sreenivasan, Jyotsna 1964- *101*
S-Ringi, Kjell
  See Ringi, Kjell (Arne Soerensen)
Staake, Bob 1957- *209*
Stacey, Cherylyn 1945- *96*
Stacy, Donald
  See Pohl, Frederik
Stadler, John *204*
Stadtler, Bea 1921- *17*
Stafford, Jean 1915-1979
  Obituary *22*
Stafford, Liliana 1950- *141*
Stafford, Paul 1966- *116*
Stahl, Ben(jamin) 1910-1987 .... *5*
  Obituary *54*
Stahl, Hilda 1938-1993 .... *48*
  Obituary *77*
Stahler, David, Jr. *218*
  Earlier sketch in SATA *162*
Staines, Bill 1949- *213*
Stainton, Sue *187*
Stair, Gobin (John) 1912- *35*
Stalder, Valerie *27*
Stamaty, Mark Alan 1947- *230*
  Earlier sketch in SATA *12*
Stambler, Irwin 1924- *5*
Stamp, Jorgen 1969- *225*
Stampler, Ann Redisch *209*
Standiford, Natalie 1961- *169*
  Earlier sketch in SATA *81*
Stanek, Lou Willett 1931- *63*
Stang, Judit 1921-1977 .... *29*
Stang, Judy
  See Stang, Judit

Stangl, (Mary) Jean 1928- *67*
Stanhope, Eric
  See Hamilton, Charles (Harold St. John)
Stankevich, Boris 1928- *2*
Stanley, Diane 1943- *213*
  Brief entry *32*
  Earlier sketches in SATA *37, 80, 115, 164*
  See also CLR *46*
  See also SAAS *15*
Stanley, Elizabeth 1947- *206*
Stanley, George Edward 1942-2011 .... *228*
  Earlier sketches in SATA *53, 111, 157, 1, 67*
Stanley, Jerry 1941- *127*
  Earlier sketch in SATA *79*
Stanley, Mandy *165*
Stanley, Robert
  See Hamilton, Charles (Harold St. John)
Stanley, Sanna 1962- *145*
Stanli, Sue
  See Meilach, Dona Z(weigoron)
Stanstead, John
  See Groom, Arthur William
Stanton, Karen 1960- *190*
Stanton, Schuyler
  See Baum, L. Frank
Staples, Suzanne Fisher 1945- *207*
  Earlier sketches in SATA *70, 105, 151*
  See also CLR *137*
Stapleton, Marjorie (Winifred) 1932- *28*
Stapp, Arthur D(onald) 1906-1972 .... *4*
Starbird, Kaye 1916- *6*
  See also CLR *60*
Stark, Evan 1942- *78*
Stark, James
  See Goldston, Robert (Conroy)
Stark, Ken 1943- *199*
Stark, Ulf 1944- *124*
Starke, Ruth (Elaine) 1946- *129*
Starkey, Marion L(ena) 1901-1991 .... *13*
Starmer, Aaron 1976- *226*
Starr, Ward
  See Manes, Stephen
Starret, William
  See McClintock, Marshall
Starr Taylor, Bridget 1959- *99*
Stasiak, Krystyna *49*
Staub, Frank 1949- *116*
Staub, Frank Jacob
  See Staub, Frank
Staub, Wendy Corsi 1964- *114*
Stauffacher, Sue 1961- *199*
  Earlier sketch in SATA *155*
Stauffer, Don
  See Berkebile, Fred D(onovan)
Staunton, Schuyler
  See Baum, L. Frank
Staunton, Ted 1956- *167*
  Earlier sketch in SATA *112*
Stead, Judy *210*
Stead, Philip C.
  See Stringer, Helen
Stead, Philip Christian *225*
Stead, Rebecca 1968(?)- *228*
  Earlier sketch in SATA *188*
Steadman, Ralph 1936- *123*
  Earlier sketch in SATA *32*
Steadman, Ralph Idris
  See Steadman, Ralph
Stearman, Kaye 1951- *118*
Stearn, Ted 1961- *218*
Stearns, Monroe (Mather) 1913-1987 .... *5*
  Obituary *55*
Steckler, Arthur 1921-1985 .... *65*
Steding, Laurie 1953- *119*
Steel, Danielle 1947- *66*
Steel, Danielle Fernande
  See Steel, Danielle
Steele, Addison II
  See Lupoff, Richard A(llen)
Steele, Alexander 1958- *116*

Steele, Henry Maxwell
    See Steele, Max
Steele, Mary 1930- 94
Steele, Mary Q(uintard Govan) 1922-1992 .. 51
    Obituary 72
    Earlier sketch in SATA 3
Steele, Max 1922-2005 168
    Earlier sketch in SATA 10
Steele, Philip 1948- 140
    Earlier sketch in SATA 81
Steele, William O(wen) 1917-1979 51
    Obituary 27
    Earlier sketch in SATA 1
Steelhammer, Ilona 1952- 98
Steelsmith, Shari 1962- 72
Stefanik, Alfred T. 1939- 55
Steffanson, Con
    See Cassiday, Bruce (Bingham)
    and Goulart, Ron
Steffens, Bradley 1955- 166
    Earlier sketch in SATA 77
Steffensmeier, Alexander 1977- 195
Stegeman, Janet Allais 1923- 49
    Brief entry 49
Steggall, Susan 1967- 182
Steig, William 1907-2003 111
    Obituary 149
    Earlier sketches in SATA 18, 70
    See also CLR 103
Steig, William H.
    See Steig, William
Stein, David Ezra 211
    Earlier sketch in SATA 180
Stein, Janet 1955- 218
Stein, M(eyer) L(ewis) 1920- 6
Stein, Mathilde 1969- 195
Stein, Mini 2
Stein, R(ichard) Conrad 1937- 154
    Earlier sketches in SATA 31, 82
Stein, Wendy 1951- 77
Steinbeck, John 1902-1968 9
Steinbeck, John Ernst
    See Steinbeck, John
Steinberg, Alfred 1917-1995 9
Steinberg, David 1962- 200
Steinberg, D.J.
    See Steinberg, David
Steinberg, Fannie 1899-1990 43
Steinberg, Fred J. 1933- 4
Steinberg, Phillip Orso 1921- 34
Steinberg, Rafael (Mark) 1927- 45
Steinberg, Saul 1914-1999 67
Steincrohn, Maggie
    See Davis, Maggie S.
Steiner, Barbara A(nnette) 1934- 83
    Earlier sketch in SATA 13
    See also SAAS 13
Steiner, Charlotte 1900-1981 45
Steiner, George 1929- 62
Steiner, Joan 199
    Earlier sketch in SATA 110
Steiner, Jorg
    See Steiner, Jorg
Steiner, Jorg 1930- 35
Steiner, K. Leslie
    See Delany, Samuel R., Jr.
Steiner, Stan(ley) 1925-1987 14
    Obituary 50
Steins, Richard 1942- 79
Stem, Jacqueline 1931- 110
Stemple, Heidi E.Y. 1966- 214
Stemple, Jason 179
Steneman, Shep 1945- 132
Stengel, Joyce A. 1938- 158
Stephanie, Gordon
    See Gordon, Stephanie Jacob
Stephens, Alice Barber 1858-1932 66
Stephens, Casey
    See Wagner, Sharon B.
Stephens, Henrietta Henkle 1909-1993 6

Stephens, J.B.
    See Lynn, Tracy
Stephens, Mary Jo 1935- 8
Stephens, Rebecca 1961- 141
Stephens, Reed
    See Donaldson, Stephen R.
Stephens, Suzanne
    See Kirby, Susan E.
Stephens, William M(cLain) 1925- 21
Stephensen, A. M.
    See Manes, Stephen
Stephenson, Kristina 224
Stephenson, Lynda 1941- 179
Stephenson, Lynda A.
    See Stephenson, Lynda
Stepp, Ann 1935- 29
Stepto, Michele 1946- 61
Steptoe, Javaka 1971- 213
    Earlier sketch in SATA 151
Steptoe, John (Lewis) 1950-1989 63
    Earlier sketch in SATA 8
    See also CLR 12
Sterling, Brett
    See Bradbury, Ray
    and Hamilton, Edmond
    and Samachson, Joseph
Sterling, Dorothy 1913-2008 83
    Autobiography Feature 127
    Obituary 200
    Earlier sketch in SATA 1
    See also CLR 1
    See also SAAS 2
Sterling, Helen
    See Watts, Helen L. Hoke
Sterling, Philip 1907-1989 8
    Obituary 63
Sterling, Shirley (Anne) 1948- 101
Stern, Ellen Norman 1927- 26
Stern, Judith M. 1951- 75
Stern, Madeleine
    See Stern, Madeleine B.
Stern, Madeleine B. 1912-2007 14
Stern, Madeleine Bettina
    See Stern, Madeleine B.
Stern, Maggie 1953- 156
Stern, Philip Van Doren 1900-1984 13
    Obituary 39
Stern, Simon 1943- 15
Sterne, Emma Gelders 1894- 6
Steurt, Marjorie Rankin 1888-1978 10
Stevens, April 1963- 208
Stevens, Bryna 1924- 65
Stevens, Carla M(cBride) 1928- 13
Stevens, Chambers 1968- 128
Stevens, Diane 1939- 94
Stevens, Franklin 1933- 6
Stevens, Greg
    See Cook, Glen
Stevens, Gwendolyn 1944- 33
Stevens, Helen 209
Stevens, Jan Romero 1953- 95
Stevens, Janet 1953- 193
    Earlier sketches in SATA 90, 148
Stevens, Kathleen 1936- 49
Stevens, Leonard A. 1920- 67
Stevens, Lucile Vernon 1899-1994 59
Stevens, Margaret Dean
    See Aldrich, Bess Streeter
Stevens, Patricia Bunning 1931- 27
Stevens, Peter
    See Geis, Darlene Stern
Stevens, Serita 1949- 70
Stevens, Serita Deborah
    See Stevens, Serita
Stevens, Serita Mendelson
    See Stevens, Serita
Stevens, Shira
    See Stevens, Serita
Stevenson, Anna (M.) 1905- 12
Stevenson, Augusta 1869(?)-1976 2
    Obituary 26

Stevenson, Burton Egbert 1872-1962 25
Stevenson, Drew 1947- 60
Stevenson, Emma 207
Stevenson, Harvey 1960- 148
    Earlier sketch in SATA 80
Stevenson, James 1929- 195
    Brief entry 34
    Earlier sketches in SATA 42, 71, 113, 161
    See also CLR 17
Stevenson, Janet 1913- 8
Stevenson, Robert Louis 1850-1894 100
    See also YABC 2
    See also CLR 107
Stevenson, Robert Louis Balfour
    See Stevenson, Robert Louis
Stevenson, Sucie
    See Stevenson, Sucie
Stevenson, Sucie 1956- 194
    Earlier sketch in SATA 104
Stewart, A(gnes) C(harlotte) 15
Stewart, Amber 181
Stewart, Chantal 1945- 173
    Earlier sketch in SATA 121
Stewart, Charles
    See Zurhorst, Charles (Stewart, Jr.)
Stewart, Eleanor
    See Porter, Eleanor H(odgman)
Stewart, Elisabeth J(ane) 1927- 93
Stewart, Elizabeth Laing 1907- 6
Stewart, Gail B. 1949- 141
Stewart, George Rippey 1895-1980 3
    Obituary 23
Stewart, Jennifer J. 1960- 128
Stewart, Jennifer Jenkins
    See Stewart, Jennifer J.
Stewart, Joel 211
    Earlier sketch in SATA 151
Stewart, John 1920- 14
Stewart, Mary (Florence Elinor) 1916- 12
Stewart, Mary Rainbow
    See Stewart, Mary (Florence Elinor)
Stewart, Melissa 1968- 209
    Earlier sketches in SATA 111, 167
Stewart, Paul 1955- 199
    Earlier sketches in SATA 114, 163
Stewart, Robert Neil 1891-1972 7
Stewart, Sarah 143
Stewart, Scott
    See Zaffo, George J.
Stewart, Trenton Lee 1970- 216
Stewart, W(alter) P. 1924- 53
Stewart, Whitney 1959- 167
    Earlier sketch in SATA 92
Stewig, John Warren 1937- 162
    Earlier sketches in SATA 26, 110
Stickler, Soma Han 1942- 128
Stidworthy, John 1943- 63
Stiegemeyer, Julie 180
Stier, Catherine 198
Stiles, Martha Bennett 108
    Earlier sketch in SATA 6
Still, James 1906-2001 29
    Obituary 127
Stille, Darlene R. 1942- 170
    Earlier sketch in SATA 126
Stille, Darlene Ruth
    See Stille, Darlene R.
Stillerman, Marci 104
Stillerman, Robbie 1947- 12
Stilley, Frank 1918- 29
Stilton, Geronimo 158
Stimpson, Gerald
    See Mitchell, Adrian
Stimson, James 1964- 213
Stine, Catherine 165
Stine, G(eorge) Harry 1928-1997 136
    Earlier sketch in SATA 10
Stine, Jovial Bob
    See Stine, R.L.

Stine, R.L. 1943- *194*
  Earlier sketches in SATA *31, 76, 129*
  See also CLR *111*
Stine, Robert Lawrence
  See Stine, R.L.
Stinetorf, Louise (Allender) 1900-1992 .... *10*
Stinson, Kathy 1952- *98*
Stirling, Arthur
  See Sinclair, Upton
Stirling, Ian 1941- *77*
Stirling, Nora B(romley) 1900-1997 .... *3*
Stirnweis, Shannon 1931- *10*
Stobbs, William 1914-2000 .... *17*
  Obituary *120*
Stock, Carolmarie 1951- *75*
Stock, Catherine 1952- *214*
  Earlier sketches in SATA *65, 114, 158*
Stockdale, Susan 1954- *206*
  Earlier sketch in SATA *98*
Stockham, Peter (Alan) 1928- *57*
Stockton, Francis Richard 1834-1902 .... *44*
  Brief entry *32*
Stockton, Frank R.
  See Stockton, Francis Richard
Stockwell-Moniz, Marc J. 1954- *164*
Stoddard, Edward G. 1923- *10*
Stoddard, Hope 1900-1987 .... *6*
Stoddard, Sandol 1927- *98*
  Earlier sketch in SATA *14*
Stoehr, Shelley 1969- *107*
Stoeke, Janet Morgan 1957- *202*
  Earlier sketches in SATA *90, 136*
Stohl, Margaret *227*
Stohner, Anu 1952- *179*
Stoiko, Michael 1919- *14*
Stojic, Manya 1967- *156*
Stoker, Abraham
  See Stoker, Bram
Stoker, Bram 1847-1912 .... *29*
Stokes, Cedric
  See Beardmore, George
Stokes, Jack (Tilden) 1923- *13*
Stokes, Olivia Pearl 1916- *32*
Stolarz, Laurie Faria 1972- *203*
Stolz, Mary 1920-2006 .... *133*
  Obituary *180*
  Earlier sketches in SATA *10, 71*
  See also SAAS *3*
Stolz, Mary Slattery
  See Stolz, Mary
Stone, Alan
  See Svenson, Andrew E(dward)
Stone, David K(arl) 1922- *9*
Stone, David Lee 1978- *166*
Stone, Eugenia 1879-1971 .... *7*
Stone, Gene
  See Stone, Eugenia
Stone, Helen V(irginia) *6*
Stone, Idella Purnell
  See Purnell, Idella
Stone, Ikey
  See Purnell, Idella
Stone, Irving 1903-1989 .... *3*
  Obituary *64*
Stone, Jeff *178*
Stone, Jon 1931-1997 .... *39*
  Obituary *95*
Stone, Josephine Rector
  See Dixon, Jeanne
Stone, Kyle M. 1972- *202*
Stone, Lesley
  See Trevor, Elleston
Stone, Mary Hanlon *231*
Stone, Peter 1930-2003 .... *65*
  Obituary *143*
Stone, Phoebe *205*
  Earlier sketch in SATA *134*
Stone, Raymond *1*
Stone, Rosetta
  See Dr. Seuss

Stone, Tanya Lee 1965- *217*
  Earlier sketch in SATA *182*
Stonehouse, Bernard 1926- *140*
  Earlier sketches in SATA *13, 80*
Stones, (Cyril) Anthony 1934- *72*
Stong, Phil(ip Duffield) 1899-1957 .... *32*
Stoops, Erik D(aniel) 1966- *142*
  Earlier sketch in SATA *78*
Stoppelmoore, Cheryl Jean
  See Ladd, Cheryl (Jean)
Stops, Sue 1936- *86*
Storace, Patricia *193*
Storad, Conrad J. 1957- *119*
Storey, Margaret 1926- *9*
Storey, Victoria Carolyn 1945- *16*
Stork, Francisco
  See Stork, Francisco X.
Stork, Francisco X. 1953- *210*
Storme, Peter
  See Stern, Philip Van Doren
Storms, Patricia 1963- *217*
Storr, Catherine (Cole) 1913-2001 .... *87*
  Obituary *122*
  Earlier sketch in SATA *9*
Story, Josephine
  See Loring, Emilie (Baker)
Stotko, Mary-Ann 1960- *154*
Stott, Ann *219*
Stott, Dorothy (M.) 1958- *99*
  Earlier sketch in SATA *67*
Stott, Dot
  See Stott, Dorothy (M.)
Stotter, Mike 1957- *108*
Stotts, Stuart *227*
Stout, Shawn K. *226*
Stout, William 1949- *132*
Stoutenburg, Adrien (Pearl) 1916-1982 .... *3*
Stoutland, Allison 1963- *130*
Stover, Allan C(arl) 1938- *14*
Stover, Jill (Griffin) 1958- *82*
Stover, Marjorie Filley 1914- *9*
Stowe, Harriet Beecher 1811-1896
  See YABC *1*
  See also CLR *131*
Stowe, Harriet Elizabeth Beecher
  See Stowe, Harriet Beecher
Stowe, Leland 1899-1994 .... *60*
  Obituary *78*
Stowe, Rosetta
  See Ogan, George F.
  and Ogan, Margaret E. (Nettles)
Stower, Adam *229*
  Earlier sketch in SATA *195*
Strachan, Bruce 1959- *205*
Strachan, Ian 1938- *85*
Strachan, Linda *167*
Strachan, Margaret Pitcairn 1908-1998 .... *14*
Strahinich, H. C.
  See Strahinich, Helen C.
Strahinich, Helen C. 1949- *78*
Strait, Treva Adams 1909-2002 .... *35*
Strand, Mark 1934- *41*
Strange, Philippa
  See Coury, Louise Andree
Stranger, Joyce
  See Wilson, Joyce M.
Strangis, Joel 1948- *124*
Strannigan, Shawn 1956- *93*
Strannigan, Shawn Alyne
  See Strannigan, Shawn
Strasnick, Lauren *222*
Strasser, Todd 1950- *215*
  Earlier sketches in SATA *41, 45, 71, 107, 153*
  See also CLR *11*
Stratemeyer, Edward L. 1862-1930 .... *100*
  Earlier sketches in SATA *1, 67*
  See also CLR *166*
  See Adams, Harrison
Stratford, Philip 1927- *47*
Stratton, Allan 1951- *178*

Stratton, J. M.
  See Whitlock, Ralph
Stratton, Thomas
  See Coulson, Robert S(tratton)
  and DeWeese, Thomas Eugene
Stratton-Porter, Gene 1863-1924 .... *15*
  See also CLR *87*
Strauss, Gwen 1963- *77*
Strauss, Joyce 1936- *53*
Strauss, Linda Leopold 1942- *127*
Strauss, Susan (Elizabeth) 1954- *75*
Strayer, E. Ward
  See Stratemeyer, Edward L.
Streano, Vince(nt Catello) 1945- *20*
Streatfeild, Mary Noel
  See Streatfeild, Noel
Streatfeild, Noel 1897(?)-1986 .... *20*
  Obituary *48*
  See also CLR *83*
Street, Janet Travell 1959- *84*
Street, Julia Montgomery 1898-1993 .... *11*
Streissguth, Thomas 1958- *116*
Strelkoff, Tatiana 1957- *89*
Stren, Patti 1949- *88*
  Brief entry *41*
  See also CLR *5*
Strete, Craig Kee 1950- *96*
  Earlier sketch in SATA *44*
Stretton, Barbara (Humphrey) 1936- *43*
  Brief entry *35*
Strickland, Brad 1947- *200*
  Earlier sketches in SATA *83, 137, 142*
Strickland, Craig (A.) 1956- *102*
Strickland, Dorothy S(alley) 1933- *89*
Strickland, Michael R. 1965- *144*
  Earlier sketch in SATA *83*
Strickland, Shadra *209*
Strickland, Tessa *173*
Strickland, William Bradley
  See Strickland, Brad
Striegel, Jana 1955- *140*
Striegel-Wilson, Jana
  See Striegel, Jana
Striker, Lee
  See Clark, Margaret (D.)
Striker, Susan 1942- *63*
Stringer, Helen *225*
Stringer, Lauren 1957- *183*
  Earlier sketch in SATA *129*
Stroeyer, Poul 1923- *13*
Stromoski, Rick 1958- *111*
Strong, Charles
  See Epstein, Beryl
  and Epstein, Samuel
Strong, David
  See McGuire, Leslie (Sarah)
Strong, Jeremy 1949- *175*
  Earlier sketches in SATA *36, 105*
Strong, J.J.
  See Strong, Jeremy
Strong, Pat
  See Hough, Richard (Alexander)
Strong, Stacie 1965- *74*
Stroud, Bettye 1939- *165*
  Earlier sketch in SATA *96*
Stroud, Jonathan 1970- *213*
  Earlier sketches in SATA *102, 159*
  See also CLR *134*
Stroyer, Poul
  See Stroeyer, Poul
Strug, Kerri 1977- *108*
Stryer, Andrea Stenn 1938- *192*
Stryker, Daniel
  See Morris, Chris(topher Crosby)
  and Stump, Jane Barr
Stuart, David
  See Hoyt, Edwin P(almer), Jr.
Stuart, Derek
  See Foster, John L(ouis)
Stuart, Forbes 1924- *13*

Stuart, Ian
  See MacLean, Alistair
Stuart, Jesse (Hilton) 1906-1984 2
  Obituary 36
Stuart, Ruth McEnery 1849(?)-1917 116
Stuart, Sheila
  See Baker, Mary Gladys Steel
Stuart-Clark, Christopher (Anthony) 1940- .. 32
Stubis, Talivaldis 1926- 5
Stubley, Trevor (Hugh) 1932- 22
Stuchner, Joan Betty 209
Stucky, Naomi R. 1922- 72
Stucley, Elizabeth
  See Northmore, Elizabeth Florence
Stultifer, Morton
  See Curtis, Richard
Sture-Vasa, Mary
  See Alsop, Mary O'Hara
Sturges, Philemon 174
Sturtevant, Katherine 1950- 180
  Earlier sketch in SATA *130*
Sturton, Hugh
  See Johnston, H(ugh) A(nthony) S(tephen)
Sturtzel, Howard A(llison) 1894-1985 1
Sturtzel, Jane Levington 1903-1996 1
Stutley, D(oris) J(ean) 1959- 142
Stutson, Caroline 1940- 104
Stuve-Bodeen, Stephanie
  See Bodeen, S. A.
Stux, Erica 1929- 140
Styles, (Frank) Showell 1908- 10
Stynes, Barbara White 133
Suarez, Maribel 1952- 201
Suba, Susanne 4
Suber, Melissa 213
Subond, Valerie
  See Grayland, Valerie (Merle Spanner)
Sudbery, Rodie 1943- 42
Sudyka, Diana 208
Sue, Majella Lue 209
Suen, Anastasia 1956(?)- 157
Sufrin, Mark 1925- 76
Sugarman, Joan G. 1917- 64
Sugarman, Tracy 1921- 37
Sugita, Yutaka 1930- 36
Suhl, Yuri (Menachem) 1908-1986 8
  Obituary 50
  See also CLR 2
  See also SAAS 1
Suhr, Joanne 129
Suid, Murray 1942- 27
Sullivan, Edward T. 206
Sullivan, George (Edward) 1927- 147
  Earlier sketches in SATA *4, 89*
Sullivan, Jacqueline Levering 203
Sullivan, Jody
  See Rake, Jody
Sullivan, Kathryn A. 1954- 141
Sullivan, Mary Ann 1954- 63
Sullivan, Mary W(ilson) 1907- 13
Sullivan, Pat
  See Messmer, Otto
Sullivan, Paul 1939- 106
Sullivan, Sarah G. 1953- 179
Sullivan, Silky 1940- 101
Sullivan, Sue
  See Sullivan, Susan E.
Sullivan, Susan E. 1962- 123
Sullivan, Thomas Joseph, Jr. 1947- 16
Sullivan, Tom
  See Sullivan, Thomas Joseph, Jr.
Sully, Tom 1959- 104
Suma, Nova Ren 223
Sumichrast, Jozef 1948- 29
Sumiko
  See Davies, Sumiko
Summerforest, Ivy B.
  See Kirkup, James
Summers, Barbara 1944- 182
Summers, Cassia Joy
  See Cowley, Joy

Summers, James L(evingston) 1910-1973 57
  Brief entry 28
Summertree, Katonah
  See Windsor, Patricia
Summy, Barrie 208
Sumner, William 1971- 229
Sun, Chyng Feng 1959- 90
Sunderlin, Sylvia (S.) 1911-1997 28
  Obituary 99
Sung, Betty Lee 26
Supeene, Shelagh Lynne 1952- 153
Supplee, Suzanne 204
Supraner, Robyn 1930- 101
  Earlier sketch in SATA *20*
Supree, Burt(on) 1941-1992 73
Surface, Mary Hall 1958- 126
Surge, Frank 1931- 13
Susac, Andrew 1929- 5
Susi, Geraldine Lee 1942- 98
Sussman, Cornelia Silver 1914-1999 59
Sussman, Irving 1908-1996 59
Sussman, Michael 1953- 217
Sussman, Michael B.
  See Sussman, Michael
Sussman, Susan 1942- 48
Sutcliff, Rosemary 1920-1992 78
  Obituary 73
  Earlier sketches in SATA *6, 44*
  See also CLR 138
Sutcliffe, Jane 1957- 138
Sutherland, Colleen 1944- 79
Sutherland, Efua (Theodora Morgue)
  1924-1996 25
Sutherland, Jon 1958- 167
Sutherland, Jonathan D.
  See Sutherland, Jon
Sutherland, Jonathan David
  See Sutherland, Jon
Sutherland, Margaret 1941- 15
Sutherland, Zena Bailey 1915-2002 37
  Obituary 137
Suttles, Shirley (Smith) 1922- 21
Sutton, Ann (Livesay) 1923- 31
Sutton, Eve(lyn Mary) 1906-1992 26
Sutton, Felix 1910(?)-1973 31
Sutton, Jane 1950- 52
  Brief entry 43
Sutton, Larry M(atthew) 1931- 29
Sutton, Margaret Beebe 1903-2001 1
  Obituary 131
Sutton, Myron Daniel 1925- 31
Sutton, Roger 1956- 93
Sutton, Sally 1973- 214
Suzanne, Jamie
  See Hawes, Louise
  and Lantz, Francess L(in)
  and Singleton, Linda Joy
  and Zach, Cheryl (Byrd)
Suzuki, David 1936- 138
Suzuki, David Takayoshi
  See Suzuki, David
Svendsen, Mark 1962- 181
  Earlier sketch in SATA *120*
Svendsen, Mark Nestor
  See Svendsen, Mark
Svenson, Andrew E(dward) 1910-1975 2
  Obituary 26
Swaab, Neil 1978- 191
Swaim, Jessica 1950- 202
Swain, Carol 1962- 172
Swain, Gwenyth 1961- 134
  Earlier sketch in SATA *84*
Swain, Ruth
  See Swain, Ruth Freeman
Swain, Ruth Freeman 1951- 161
  Earlier sketch in SATA *119*
Swain, Su Zan (Noguchi) 1916- 21
Swain, Wilson 1976- 225
Swallow, Gerry 227
Swallow, Pamela Curtis 178
Swamp, Jake 1941- 98

Swan, Susan 1944- 108
  Earlier sketch in SATA *22*
Swann, Brian (Stanley Frank) 1940- 116
Swann, E.L.
  See Lasky, Kathryn
Swann, Ruth Rice 1920- 84
Swanson, Diane 1944- 203
Swanson, Helen M(cKendry) 1919- 94
Swanson, June 1931- 76
Swanson, Susan Marie 209
Swanson, Wayne 1942- 167
Swarner, Kristina 1965- 215
Swarthout, Glendon (Fred) 1918-1992 26
Swarthout, Kathryn 1919- 7
Swayne, Sam(uel F.) 1907- 53
Swayne, Zoa (Lourana) 1905- 53
Swearingen, Greg 1976- 225
Sweat, Lynn 1934- 168
  Earlier sketch in SATA *57*
Swede, George 1940- 67
Sweeney, James B(artholomew) 1910-1999 . 21
Sweeney, Joyce 1955- 167
  Earlier sketches in SATA *65, 68, 108*
Sweeney, Joyce Kay
  See Sweeney, Joyce
Sweeney, Karen O'Connor
  See O'Connor, Karen
Sweeney, Matthew (Gerard) 1952- 156
Sweet, Melissa 1956- 211
  Earlier sketch in SATA *172*
Sweet, Sarah C.
  See Jewett, Sarah Orne
Sweetland, Nancy A(nn) 1934- 48
Swenson, Allan A(rmstrong) 1933- 21
Swenson, May 1919-1989 15
Swentzell, Rina 1939- 79
Swiatkowska, Gabi 1971(?)- 180
Swift, Bryan
  See Knott, William C(ecil, Jr.)
Swift, David
  See Kaufmann, John
Swift, Hildegarde Hoyt 1890(?)-1977
  Obituary 20
Swift, Jonathan 1667-1745 19
  See also CLR 161
Swift, Merlin
  See Leeming, Joseph
Swiger, Elinor Porter 1927- 8
Swinburne, Laurence (Joseph) 1924- 9
Swinburne, Stephen R. 1952- 231
  Earlier sketches in SATA *150, 188*
Swinburne, Steve
  See Swinburne, Stephen R.
Swindells, Robert (Edward) 1939- 150
  Brief entry 34
  Earlier sketches in SATA *50, 80*
  See also SAAS 14
Swinford, Betty (June Wells) 1927- 58
Swinford, Bob
  See Swinford, Betty (June Wells)
Swithen, John
  See King, Stephen
Switzer, Ellen 1923- 48
Swope, Sam 156
Swope, Samuel
  See Swope, Sam
Sybesma, Jetske
  See Ironside, Jetske
Sydney, Frank
  See Warwick, Alan R(oss)
Sydor, Colleen 1960- 207
Sykes, Julie 1963- 202
Sylvada, Peter 1964- 202
Sylver, Adrienne 230
Sylvester, Natalie G(abry) 1922- 22
Syme, (Neville) Ronald 1913-1992 87
  Earlier sketch in SATA *2*
Symes, R. F. 77
Symes, Ruth Louise 1962- 179
Symons, (Dorothy) Geraldine 1909- 33

Symons, Stuart
  See Stanley, George Edward
Symynkywicz, Jeffrey B. 1954- 87
Symynkywicz, Jeffrey Bruce
  See Symynkywicz, Jeffrey B.
Synge, (Phyllis) Ursula 1930- 9
Sypher, Lucy Johnston 1907- 7
Szasz, Suzanne (Shorr) 1915-1997 13
  Obituary 99
Szekeres, Cyndy 1933- 157
  Autobiography Feature 157
  Earlier sketches in SATA 5, 60, 131
  See also SAAS 13
Szekessy, Tanja 98
Szpura, Beata 1961- 93
Szuc, Jeff 1975- 220
Szudek, Agnes S(usan) P(hilomena) 57
  Brief entry 49
Szulc, Tad 1926-2001 26
Szydlow, Jarl
  See Szydlowski, Mary Vigliante
Szydlowski, Mary Vigliante 1946- 94
Szymanski, Lois 1957- 91

T

Taback, Simms 1932- 170
  Brief entry 36
  Earlier sketches in SATA 40, 104
  See also CLR 100
Taber, Gladys (Bagg) 1899-1980
  Obituary 22
Tabor, Nancy Maria Grande 1949- 161
  Earlier sketch in SATA 89
Tabrah, Ruth Milander 1921- 14
Tacang, Brian 213
Tackach, James 1953- 123
Tackach, James M.
  See Tackach, James
Tadgell, Nicole 1969- 220
  Earlier sketch in SATA 177
Tafolla, Carmen 1951- 220
Tafolla, Mary Carmen
  See Tafolla, Carmen
Tafuri, Nancy 1946- 192
  Autobiography Feature 192
  Earlier sketches in SATA 39, 75, 130
  See also CLR 74
  See also SAAS 14
Tagg, Christine Elizabeth 1962- 138
Tagliaferro, Linda 173
Taha, Karen T(erry) 1942- 156
  Earlier sketch in SATA 71
Tai, Sharon O. 1963- 153
Tait, Douglas 1944- 12
Takabayashi, Mari 1960- 156
  Earlier sketch in SATA 115
Takahashi, Hideko 209
Takahashi, Rumiko 1957- 163
Takakjian, Portia 1930- 15
Takashima, Misako
  See Misako Rocks!
Takashima, Shizuye 1928- 13
Takayama, Sandi 1962- 106
Takeda, Pete(r M.) 1964- 148
Tal, Eve 1947- 176
Talbert, Marc (Alan) 1953- 154
  Autobiography Feature 154
  Earlier sketches in SATA 68, 99
Talbot, Charlene Joy 1928- 10
Talbot, Toby 1928- 14
Talbott, Hudson 1949- 212
  Earlier sketches in SATA 84, 131
Talifero, Gerald 1950- 75
Talker, T.
  See Rands, William Brighty
Tallarico, Tony 1933- 116
Tallcott, Emogene 10
Tallec, Olivier 1970- 197

Tallis, Robyn
  See Smith, Sherwood
Tallon, Robert 1939- 43
  Brief entry 28
Talmadge, Marian 14
Tamaki, Jillian 1980- 201
Tamar, Erika 1934- 150
  Earlier sketches in SATA 62, 101
Tamarin, Alfred H. 1913-1980 13
Tamburine, Jean 1930- 12
Tames, Richard (Lawrence) 1946- 102
  Earlier sketch in SATA 67
Tamminga, Frederick W(illiam) 1934- 66
Tammuz, Benjamin 1919-1989
  Obituary 63
Tan, Amy 1952- 75
Tan, Amy Ruth
  See Tan, Amy
Tan, Shaun 1974- 198
Tanaka, Beatrice 1932- 76
Tanaka, Shelley 214
  Earlier sketch in SATA 136
Tanaka, Yoko 1947- 215
Tang, Charles 1948- 81
Tang, Greg 172
Tang, You-Shan 1946- 53
Tania B.
  See Blixen, Karen
Tankard, Jeremy 1973- 191
Tannen, Mary 1943- 37
Tannenbaum, Beulah Goldstein 1916- 3
Tannenbaum, D(onald) Leb 1948- 42
Tanner, Jane 1946- 74
Tanner, Louise S(tickney) 1922-2000 9
Tanobe, Miyuki 1937- 23
Tanselle, Eve 1933- 125
Tapio, Pat Decker
  See Kines, Pat Decker
Tapp, Kathy Kennedy 1949- 88
  Brief entry 50
Tarbescu, Edith 1939- 107
Tarkington, (Newton) Booth 1869-1946 17
Tarpley, Natasha A(nastasia) 1971- 147
Tarr, Judith 1955- 149
  Earlier sketch in SATA 64
Tarry, Ellen 1906-2008 16
  See also CLR 26
  See also SAAS 16
Tarshis, Jerome 1936- 9
Tarshis, Lauren 187
Tarsky, Sue 1946- 41
Taschek, Karen 1956- 185
Tashjian, Janet 1956- 151
  Earlier sketch in SATA 102
Tashjian, Virginia A. 1921-2008 3
Tasker, James 1908- 9
Tate, Don(ald E.) 159
Tate, Eleanora E. 1948- 191
  Earlier sketches in SATA 38, 94
  See also CLR 37
Tate, Eleanora Elaine
  See Tate, Eleanora E.
Tate, Ellalice
  See Hibbert, Eleanor Alice Burford
Tate, Joan 1922- 86
  Earlier sketch in SATA 9
  See also SAAS 20
Tate, Mary Anne
  See Hale, Arlene
Tate, Nikki 134
Tate, Richard
  See Masters, Anthony (Richard)
Tate, Suzanne 1930- 91
Tatham, Betty 142
Tatham, Campbell
  See Elting, Mary
Tatham, Julie
  See Tatham, Julie Campbell
Tatham, Julie Campbell 1908-1999 80
Tavares, Matt 198
  Earlier sketch in SATA 159

Tavares, Victor 1971- 176
Taves, Isabella 1915- 27
Tayleur, Karen 1961- 213
Taylor, Alastair 1959- 130
Taylor, Andrew 1951- 70
Taylor, Andrew John Robert
  See Taylor, Andrew
Taylor, Ann 1782-1866 41
  Brief entry 35
Taylor, Audilee Boyd 1931- 59
Taylor, Barbara J. 1927- 10
Taylor, Ben
  See Strachan, Ian
Taylor, Brooke 205
Taylor, Carl 1937-2010 14
Taylor, Carrie-Jo
  See Taylor, C.J.
Taylor, Cheryl Munro 1957- 96
Taylor, C.J. 1952- 224
Taylor, Cora (Lorraine) 1936- 103
  Earlier sketch in SATA 64
  See also CLR 63
Taylor, Dave 1948- 78
Taylor, David
  See Taylor, Dave
Taylor, David 1900-1965 10
Taylor, Debbie A. 1955- 169
Taylor, Eleanor 1969- 206
Taylor, Elizabeth 1912-1975 13
Taylor, Florance Walton 9
Taylor, Florence M(arian Tompkins)
  1892-1983 9
Taylor, Gage 1942-2000 87
Taylor, Geoff 1946- 204
Taylor, G.P. 1958(?)- 216
  Earlier sketch in SATA 156
Taylor, Graham Peter
  See Taylor, G.P.
Taylor, Greg 1951- 221
Taylor, Herb(ert Norman, Jr.) 1942-1987 22
  Obituary 54
Taylor, J. David
  See Taylor, Dave
Taylor, Jane 1783-1824 41
  Brief entry 35
Taylor, Jerry D(uncan) 1938- 47
Taylor, John Robert
  See Taylor, Andrew
Taylor, Judy
  See Hough, Judy Taylor
Taylor, Kenneth N. 1917-2005 26
Taylor, Kenneth Nathaniel
  See Taylor, Kenneth N.
Taylor, Kim 180
Taylor, L(ester) B(arbour), Jr. 1932- 27
Taylor, Lois Dwight Cole
  See Cole, Lois Dwight
Taylor, Louise Todd 1939- 47
Taylor, Margaret 1950- 106
Taylor, Mark 1927- 32
  Brief entry 28
Taylor, Mildred D. 1943- 135
  See also CLR 144
  See also SAAS 5
Taylor, Mildred Delois
  See Taylor, Mildred D.
Taylor, Paula (Wright) 1942- 48
  Brief entry 33
Taylor, Peter Lane 210
Taylor, Robert Lewis 1912-1998 10
Taylor, Sean 1965- 192
Taylor, Susan Champlin
  See Champlin, Susan
Taylor, Sydney (Brenner) 1904(?)-1978 28
  Obituary 26
  Earlier sketch in SATA 1
Taylor, Theodore 1921-2006 128
  Obituary 177
  Earlier sketches in SATA 5, 54, 83
  See also CLR 30
  See also SAAS 4

Taylor, William 1938- 164
 Earlier sketches in SATA 78, 113
 See also CLR 63
Taylor-Butler, Christine 1959- 218
Tazewell, Charles 1900-1972 74
Tchana, Katrin
 See Tchana, Katrin Hyman
Tchana, Katrin H.
 See Tchana, Katrin Hyman
Tchana, Katrin Hyman 1963- 177
 Earlier sketch in SATA 125
Tchekhov, Anton
 See Chekhov, Anton
Tchen, Richard 120
Tchudi, Stephen N. 1942- 55
Teague, Bob
 See Teague, Robert
Teague, Mark 1963- 205
 Earlier sketches in SATA 68, 99, 170
Teague, Mark Christopher
 See Teague, Mark
Teague, Robert 1929- 32
 Brief entry 31
Teal, Val 1902-1997 10
 Obituary 114
Teal, Valentine M.
 See Teal, Val
Teale, Edwin Way 1899-1980 7
 Obituary 25
Teasdale, Sara 1884-1933 32
Tebbel, John (William) 1912-2004 26
Teckentrup, Britta 1969- 200
Tedesco, P.R.
 See Naylor, Phyllis Reynolds
Teensma, Lynne Bertrand
 See Bertrand, Lynne
Tee-Van, Helen Damrosch 1893-1976 10
 Obituary 27
Teevee, Ningeokuluk 1963- 223
Tegner, Bruce 1928- 62
Teitelbaum, Michael 1953- 116
 Earlier sketch in SATA 59
Tejima
 See Tejima, Keizaburo
Tejima, Keizaburo 1931- 139
 See also CLR 20
Telander, Todd (G.) 1967- 88
Teleki, Geza 1943- 45
Telemaque, Eleanor Wong 1934- 43
Telescope, Tom
 See Newbery, John
Telgemeier, Raina 1977- 228
Tellegen, Toon 1941- 229
Teller, Janne 1964- 230
Tellis, Annabel 1967- 191
Temkin, Sara Anne Schlossberg 1913-1996 . 26
Temko, Florence 13
Tempest, Margaret Mary 1892-1982
 Obituary 33
Templar, Maurice
 See Groom, Arthur William
Temple, Arthur
 See Northcott, (William) Cecil
Temple, Charles 1947- 79
Temple, Frances (Nolting) 1945-1995 85
Temple, Herbert 1919- 45
Temple, Paul
 See McConnell, James Douglas Rutherford
Temple, William F(rederick) 1914-1989 107
Tenggren, Gustaf 1896-1970 18
 Obituary 26
Tennant, Kylie
 See Rodd, Kylie Tennant
Tennant, Veronica 1947- 36
Tenneshaw, S.M.
 See Beaumont, Charles
 and Garrett, Randall
 and Silverberg, Robert
Tenniel, John 1820-1914 74
 Brief entry 27
 See also CLR 146

Teplin, Scott 231
Tepper, Sheri S. 1929- 113
Tepper, Yona 1941- 228
Terada, Alice M. 1928- 90
Terban, Marvin 1940- 54
 Brief entry 45
Teresi, Judith M.
 See Goldberger, Judith M.
ter Haar, Jaap 1922- 6
 See also CLR 15
Terhune, Albert Payson 1872-1942 15
Terkel, Susan N(eiburg) 1948- 103
 Earlier sketch in SATA 59
Terlouw, Jan (Cornelis) 1931- 30
Terrazzini, Daniela Jaglenka 218
Terrell, John Upton 1900-1988
 Obituary 60
Terrill, Beth 198
Terrill, Elizabeth
 See Terrill, Beth
Terris, Susan 1937- 77
 Earlier sketch in SATA 3
Terry, Luther L(eonidas) 1911-1985 11
 Obituary 42
Terry, Margaret
 See Dunnahoo, Terry Janson
Terry, Walter 1913-1982 14
Terry, Will 1966- 205
Terzian, James P. 1915- 14
Tessendorf, K(enneth) C(harles) 1925-2003 . 75
 Obituary 142
Tessler, Manya 200
Tessler, Stephanie Gordon
 See Gordon, Stephanie Jacob
Testa, Dom 208
Tester, Sylvia Root 1939- 64
 Brief entry 37
Tether, (Cynthia) Graham 1950- 46
 Brief entry 36
Tetzner, Lisa 1894-1963 169
Thach, James Otis 1969- 195
Thacher, Mary McGrath 1933- 9
Thackeray, William Makepeace 1811-1863 .. 23
Thaler, Michael C.
 See Thaler, Mike
Thaler, Mike 1936- 215
 Brief entry 47
 Earlier sketches in SATA 56, 93
Thaler, Shmuel 1958- 126
 Earlier sketch in SATA 72
Thamer, Katie 1955- 42
Thane, Elswyth 1900-1984(?) 32
Tharp, Louise (Marshall) Hall 1898-1992 3
 Obituary 129
Tharp, Tim 1957- 189
Thayer, Ernest Lawrence 1863-1940 60
Thayer, Jane
 See Woolley, Catherine
Thayer, Marjorie 1908-1992 74
 Brief entry 37
Thayer, Peter
 See Wyler, Rose
Thelwell, Norman 1923-2004 14
Themerson, Stefan 1910-1988 65
Thermes, Jennifer 1966- 155
Theroux, Paul 1941- 109
 Earlier sketch in SATA 44
Theroux, Paul Edward
 See Theroux, Paul
Thesman, Jean 124
 Earlier sketch in SATA 74
The Tjong-Khing
 See Khing, T.T.
Thieda, Shirley Ann 1943- 13
Thiele, Colin 1920-2006 125
 Earlier sketches in SATA 14, 72
 See also CLR 27
 See also SAAS 2
Thiele, Colin Milton
 See Thiele, Colin

Thiesing, Lisa 1958- 159
 Earlier sketch in SATA 95
Thimmesh, Catherine 189
Thiry, Joan (Marie) 1926- 45
Thisdale, Francois 1964- 222
Thistlethwaite, Miles 1945- 12
Thollander, Earl 1922- 22
Thomas, Abigail 1941- 112
Thomas, Andrea
 See Hill, Margaret (Ohler)
Thomas, Art(hur Lawrence) 1952- 48
 Brief entry 38
Thomas, Carroll
 See Ratliff, Thomas M.
 and Shmurak, Carole B.
Thomas, Dylan 1914-1953 60
Thomas, Dylan Marlais
 See Thomas, Dylan
Thomas, Egbert S.
 See Ellis, Edward S.
Thomas, Estelle Webb 1899-1982 26
Thomas, Frances 1943- 171
 Earlier sketch in SATA 92
Thomas, Garen 213
Thomas, H. C.
 See Keating, Lawrence A.
Thomas, Ianthe 1951- 139
 Brief entry 42
 See also CLR 8
Thomas, J. F.
 See Fleming, Thomas
Thomas, Jan 1958- 226
 Earlier sketch in SATA 197
Thomas, Jane Resh 1936- 171
 Earlier sketches in SATA 38, 90
Thomas, Jerry D. 1959- 91
Thomas, Joan Gale
 See Robinson, Joan (Mary) G(ale Thomas)
Thomas, Joyce Carol 1938- 210
 Autobiography Feature 137
 Earlier sketches in SATA 40, 78, 123, 137
 See also CLR 19
 See also SAAS 7
Thomas, Lee
 See Floren, Lee
 and Pendleton, Thomas
Thomas, Lowell Jackson, Jr. 1923- 15
Thomas, Margaret
 See Thomas, Peggy
Thomas, Meredith 1963- 119
Thomas, Michael
 See Wilks, Michael Thomas
Thomas, Middy 1931- 191
Thomas, Patricia 1934- 199
 Earlier sketch in SATA 51
Thomas, Peggy 174
Thomas, Rob 1965- 97
Thomas, Scott 1959- 147
Thomas, Velma Maia 1955- 171
Thomas, Vernon (Arthur) 1934- 56
Thomas, Victoria
 See DeWeese, Thomas Eugene
 and Kugi, Constance Todd
Thomasma, Kenneth R. 1930- 90
Thomason, Mark 215
Thomassie, Tynia 1959- 92
Thompson, Alicia 1984- 224
Thompson, Brenda 1935- 34
Thompson, Carol 1951- 189
 Earlier sketch in SATA 85
Thompson, China
 See Lewis, Mary
Thompson, Colin 1942- 198
 Earlier sketches in SATA 95, 163
Thompson, David H(ugh) 1941- 17
Thompson, Eileen
 See Panowski, Eileen Thompson
Thompson, George Selden 1929-1989 73
 Obituary 63
 Earlier sketch in SATA 4
 See also CLR 8

Thompson, Harlan 1894-1987 .... *10*
  Obituary *53*
Thompson, Hilary 1943- *56*
  Brief entry *49*
Thompson, Joanna Maxwell Pullein
  See Pullein-Thompson, Joanna Maxwell
Thompson, Julian F(rancis) 1927- *155*
  Brief entry *40*
  Earlier sketches in SATA *55, 99*
  See also CLR *24*
  See also SAAS *13*
Thompson, K(athryn Carolyn) Dyble
  1952- *82*
Thompson, Kate 1956- *204*
Thompson, Kay 1912(?)-1998 .... *16*
  See also CLR *22*
Thompson, Lauren 1962- *200*
  Earlier sketches in SATA *132, 174*
Thompson, Lauren Stevens
  See Thompson, Lauren
Thompson, Megan Lloyd
  See Lloyd, Megan
Thompson, Richard 1951- *184*
Thompson, Ruth Plumly 1891-1976 .... *66*
Thompson, Sharon 1952- *119*
Thompson, Sharon Elaine
  See Thompson, Sharon
Thompson, Stith 1885-1976 .... *57*
  Obituary *20*
Thompson, Vivian L(aubach) 1911- *3*
Thomson, Bill 1963- *187*
Thomson, Celia
  See Lynn, Tracy
Thomson, David (Robert Alexander)
  1914-1988 .... *40*
  Obituary *55*
Thomson, Melissa 1979- *205*
Thomson, Pat 1939- *122*
  Earlier sketch in SATA *77*
Thomson, Peggy 1922- *31*
Thomson, Sarah L. *212*
  Earlier sketch in SATA *178*
Thon, Melanie Rae 1957- *132*
Thong, Roseanne *174*
Thor, Annika 1950- *222*
Thorburn, John
  See Goldsmith, John Herman Thorburn
Thorn, John 1947- *59*
Thorndyke, Helen Louise
  See Benson, Mildred
Thorne, Ian
  See May, Julian
Thorne, Jean Wright
  See May, Julian
Thornhill, Jan 1955- *148*
  Earlier sketch in SATA *77*
Thornton, Hall
  See Silverberg, Robert
Thornton, W. B.
  See Burgess, Thornton Waldo
Thornton, Yvonne S. 1947- *96*
Thornton, Yvonne Shirley
  See Thornton, Yvonne S.
Thorpe, E(ustace) G(eorge) 1916- *21*
Thorpe, J. K.
  See Nathanson, Laura Walther
Thorvall, Kerstin 1925- *13*
Thorvall-Falk, Kerstin
  See Thorvall, Kerstin
Thrasher, Crystal (Faye) 1921- *27*
Threadgall, Colin 1941- *77*
Three Little Pigs
  See Lantz, Francess L(in)
Thum, Gladys 1920- *26*
Thum, Marcella *28*
  Earlier sketch in SATA *3*
Thundercloud, Katherine
  See Witt, Shirley Hill
Thurber, James 1894-1961 .... *13*
Thurber, James Grover
  See Thurber, James

Thurlo, Aimee *161*
Thurlo, David *161*
Thurman, Judith 1946- *33*
Thurman, Mark (Gordon Ian) 1948- *63*
Thwaite, Ann (Barbara Harrop) 1932- *14*
Tibbetts, Peggy *127*
Tibbles, Jean-Paul 1958- *115*
Tibo, Gilles 1951- *107*
  Earlier sketch in SATA *67*
Tiburzi, Bonnie 1948- *65*
Ticheburn, Cheviot
  See Ainsworth, William Harrison
Tichenor, Tom 1923-1992 .... *14*
Tichnor, Richard 1959- *90*
Tichy, William 1924- *31*
Tickle, Jack
  See Chapman, Jane
Tidholm, Anna-Clara 1946- *223*
Tiegreen, Alan F. 1935- *94*
  Brief entry *36*
Tierney, Fiona *229*
Tierney, Frank M. 1930- *54*
Tierney, Tom 1928- *113*
Tiffault, Benette W. 1955- *77*
Tildes, Phyllis Limbacher 1945- *210*
Tiller, Ruth L. 1949- *83*
Tilley, Debbie *190*
Tillman, Nancy *211*
Tillotson, Katherine *224*
Tilly, Nancy 1935- *62*
Tilton, Madonna Elaine 1929- *41*
Tilton, Rafael
  See Tilton, Madonna Elaine
Timberlake, Amy *156*
Timberlake, Carolyn
  See Dresang, Eliza (Carolyn Timberlake)
Timmers, Leo 1970- *190*
Timmins, Jeffrey Stewart 1979- *227*
Timmins, William F(rederick) *10*
Tinbergen, Niko(laas) 1907-1988
  Obituary *60*
Tincknell, Cathy *194*
Tiner, John Hudson 1944- *32*
Tingle, Dolli (?)-
  See Brackett, Dolli Tingle
Tingle, Rebecca *174*
Tingle, Tim *208*
Tingum, Janice 1958- *91*
Tinkelman, Murray 1933- *12*
Tinkham, Kelly A. *188*
Tinkle, (Julien) Lon 1906-1980 .... *36*
Tinling, Marion (Rose) 1904- *140*
Tipene, Tim 1972- *141*
Tippett, James S(terling) 1885-1958 .... *66*
Tirone Smith, Mary-Ann 1944- *143*
Titlebaum, Ellen *195*
Titler, Dale M(ilton) 1926- *35*
  Brief entry *28*
Titmarsh, Michael Angelo
  See Thackeray, William Makepeace
Titus, Eve 1922- *2*
Tjia, Sherwin 1975- *204*
Tjong Khing, The 1933- *76*
Tobias, Katherine
  See Gottfried, Theodore Mark
Tobias, Tobi 1938- *82*
  Earlier sketch in SATA *5*
  See also CLR *4*
Tobin, James *226*
Tocci, C. Lee 1958- *220*
Tocci, Cynthia Lee
  See Tocci, C. Lee
Tocher, Timothy *228*
Todd, Anne Ophelia
  See Dowden, Anne Ophelia Todd
Todd, Barbara 1961- *173*
Todd, Barbara K(eith) 1917- *10*
Todd, Chuck *195*
Todd, H(erbert) E(atton) 1908-1988 .... *84*
  Earlier sketch in SATA *11*
Todd, Loreto 1942- *30*

Todd, Pamela *212*
Todd, Peter
  See Hamilton, Charles (Harold St. John)
Toews, Miriam 1964- *165*
Tofel, Richard J. 1957- *140*
Toft, Kim Michelle 1960- *170*
Tokunbo, Dimitrea *187*
Tolan, Stephanie S. 1942- *142*
  Earlier sketches in SATA *38, 78*
Toland, John (Willard) 1912-2004 .... *38*
Tolbert, Steve 1944- *143*
Toledo, Francisco 1940- *198*
Toledo, Natalia 1967- *197*
Tolkien, J. R. R. 1892-1973 .... *100*
  Obituary *24*
  Earlier sketches in SATA *2, 32*
  See also CLR *152*
Tolkien, John Ronald Reuel
  See Tolkien, J. R. R.
Toll, Emily
  See Cannon, Eileen E(mily)
Toll, Nelly S. 1935- *78*
Tolland, W. R.
  See Heitzmann, William Ray
Tolles, Martha 1921- *76*
  Earlier sketch in SATA *8*
Tolliver, Ruby C(hangos) 1922- *110*
  Brief entry *41*
  Earlier sketch in SATA *55*
Tolmie, Kenneth Donald 1941- *15*
Tolstoi, Lev
  See Tolstoy, Leo
Tolstoy, Leo 1828-1910 .... *26*
Tolstoy, Count Leo
  See Tolstoy, Leo
Tolstoy, Leo Nikolaevich
  See Tolstoy, Leo
Tomalin, Ruth *29*
Tomaselli, Rosa
  See Pausacker, Jenny
Tomecek, Steve *172*
Tomes, Margot (Ladd) 1917-1991 .... *70*
  Brief entry *27*
  Obituary *69*
  Earlier sketch in SATA *36*
Tomey, Ingrid 1943- *77*
Tomfool
  See Farjeon, Eleanor
Tomic, Tomislav 1977- *202*
Tomkins, Jasper
  See Batey, Tom
Tomline, F. Latour
  See Gilbert, W(illiam) S(chwenck)
Tomlinson, Heather *192*
Tomlinson, Jill 1931-1976 .... *3*
  Obituary *24*
Tomlinson, Reginald R(obert) 1885-1979(?)
  Obituary *27*
Tomlinson, Theresa 1946- *165*
  Earlier sketch in SATA *103*
  See also CLR *60*
Tommaso, Rich 1970(?)- *200*
Tomorrow, Tom 1961- *223*
Tompert, Ann 1918- *139*
  Earlier sketches in SATA *14, 89*
Tompkins, Troy
  See Cle, Troy
Tonatiuh, Duncan *231*
Toner, Raymond John 1908-1986 .... *10*
Tong, Gary S. 1942- *66*
Tong, Paul *188*
Took, Belladonna
  See Chapman, Vera (Ivy May)
Tooke, Louise Mathews 1950- *38*
Tooke, Susan *173*
Toonder, Martin
  See Groom, Arthur William
Toothaker, Roy Eugene 1928- *18*
Tooze, Ruth (Anderson) 1892-1972 .... *4*
Topaz, Ksenia *212*
Topek, Susan Remick 1955- *78*

Topping, Audrey R(onning) 1928- *14*
Tor, Regina
  See Shekerjian, Regina Tor
Torbert, Floyd James 1922- *22*
Torgersen, Don Arthur 1934- *55*
  Brief entry *41*
Torley, Luke
  See Blish, James
Torrecilla, Pablo 1967- *206*
Torres, Andres Segovia
  See Segovia, Andres
Torres, Daniel 1958- *102*
Torres, J. 1969- *230*
Torres, John A. 1965- *163*
  Earlier sketch in SATA *94*
Torres, John Albert
  See Torres, John A.
Torres, Joseph
  See Torres, J.
Torres, Laura 1967- *146*
  Earlier sketch in SATA *87*
Torres, Leyla 1960- *155*
Torrey, Rich
  See Torrey, Richard
Torrey, Richard *189*
Torrie, Malcolm
  See Mitchell, Gladys (Maude Winifred)
Toten, Teresa 1955- *99*
Totham, Mary
  See Breinburg, Petronella
Touponce, William F. 1948- *114*
Tournier, Michel 1924- *23*
Tournier, Michel Edouard
  See Tournier, Michel
Towle, Ben 1970- *228*
Towle, Wendy 1963- *79*
Towne, Mary
  See Spelman, Mary
Townley, Rod
  See Townley, Roderick
Townley, Roderick 1942- *177*
Townsend, Brad W. 1962- *91*
Townsend, John Rowe 1922- *132*
  Autobiography Feature *132*
  Earlier sketches in SATA *4, 68*
  See also CLR *2*
  See also SAAS *2*
Townsend, Michael 1981- *231*
  Earlier sketch in SATA *194*
Townsend, Sue 1946- *93*
  Brief entry *48*
  Earlier sketch in SATA *55*
Townsend, Susan Lilian
  See Townsend, Sue
Townsend, Thomas L. 1944- *59*
Townsend, Tom
  See Townsend, Thomas L.
Townsend, Wendy 1962- *201*
Townson, Hazel *134*
Toye, William Eldred 1926- *8*
Traherne, Michael
  See Watkins-Pitchford, Denys James
Trahey, Jane 1923-2000 .... *36*
  Obituary *120*
Trapani, Iza 1954- *214*
  Earlier sketches in SATA *80, 116*
Trapp, Maria Augusta von
  See von Trapp, Maria Augusta
Travers, P(amela) L(yndon) 1899-1996 ...... *100*
  Obituary *90*
  Earlier sketches in SATA *4, 54*
  See also CLR *93*
  See also SAAS *2*
Travis, Lucille *133*
  Earlier sketch in SATA *88*
Treadgold, Mary 1910-2005 .... *49*
Trease, (Robert) Geoffrey 1909-1998 .... *60*
  Obituary *101*
  Earlier sketch in SATA *2*
  See also CLR *42*
  See also SAAS *6*

Treat, Lawrence 1903-1998 .... *59*
Tredez, Alain 1926- *17*
Tredez, Denise 1930- *50*
Treece, Henry 1912-1966 .... *2*
  See also CLR *2*
Tregarthen, Enys
  See Sloggett, Nellie
Tregaskis, Richard 1916-1973 .... *3*
  Obituary *26*
Treherne, Katie Thamer 1955- *76*
Trell, Max 1900-1996 .... *14*
  Obituary *108*
Tremain, Ruthven 1922- *17*
Trembath, Don 1963- *168*
  Earlier sketch in SATA *96*
Tremens, Del
  See MacDonald, Amy
Trent, Robbie 1894-1988 .... *26*
Trent, Timothy
  See Malmberg, Carl
Treseder, Terry Walton 1956- *68*
Tresilian, (Cecil) Stuart 1891-(?) *40*
Tresselt, Alvin 1916-2000 .... *7*
  See also CLR *30*
Trevino, Elizabeth B(orton) de 1904- *29*
  Earlier sketch in SATA *1*
  See also SAAS *5*
Trevor, Elleston 1920-1995 .... *28*
Trevor, Frances
  See Teasdale, Sara
Trevor, Glen
  See Hilton, James
Trevor, (Lucy) Meriol 1919-2000 .... *113*
  Obituary *122*
  Earlier sketch in SATA *10*
Trewellard, J.M. *195*
Trewellard, Juliet
  See Trewellard, J.M.
Trez, Alain
  See Tredez, Alain
Trez, Denise
  See Tredez, Denise
Trezise, Percy 1923-
  See CLR *41*
Trezise, Percy James
  See Trezise, Percy
Triggs, Tony D. 1946- *70*
Trimble, Marshall I(ra) 1939- *93*
Trimby, Elisa 1948- *47*
  Brief entry *40*
Tring, A. Stephen
  See Meynell, Laurence Walter
Triplett, Gina *229*
Tripp, Eleanor B(aldwin) 1936- *4*
Tripp, Janet 1942- *108*
Tripp, Jenny *188*
Tripp, John
  See Moore, John Travers
Tripp, Nathaniel 1944- *101*
Tripp, Paul 1916-2002 .... *8*
  Obituary *139*
Tripp, Valerie 1951- *168*
  Earlier sketch in SATA *78*
Tripp, Wallace (Whitney) 1940- *31*
Trivelpiece, Laurel 1926- *56*
  Brief entry *46*
Trivett, Daphne Harwood 1940- *22*
Trivizas, Eugene 1946- *84*
Trnka, Jiri 1912-1969 .... *43*
  Brief entry *32*
Trollope, Anthony 1815-1882 .... *22*
Trost, Lucille W(ood) 1938- *149*
  Earlier sketch in SATA *12*
Trott, Betty 1933- *91*
Trotter, Deborah W. *184*
Trotter, Grace V(iolet) 1900-1991 .... *10*
Trottier, Maxine 1950- *175*
  Earlier sketch in SATA *131*
Troughton, Joanna (Margaret) 1947- *37*
Trout, Kilgore
  See Farmer, Philip Jose

Trout, Richard E. *123*
Trudeau, Garretson Beekman
  See Trudeau, G.B.
Trudeau, Garry
  See Trudeau, G.B.
Trudeau, Garry B.
  See Trudeau, G.B.
Trudeau, G.B. 1948- *168*
  Earlier sketch in SATA *35*
Trueit, Trudi
  See Trueit, Trudi Strain
Trueit, Trudi Strain 1963- *179*
Trueman, Matthew *183*
Trueman, Terry 1947- *178*
  Earlier sketch in SATA *132*
Truesdell, Judy
  See Mecca, Judy Truesdell
Truesdell, Sue
  See Truesdell, Susan G.
Truesdell, Susan G. *212*
  Brief entry *45*
  Earlier sketch in SATA *108*
Trumbauer, Lisa 1963- *228*
  Earlier sketch in SATA *149*
Trumbauer, Lisa Trutkoff
  See Trumbauer, Lisa
Truss, Jan 1925- *35*
Truss, Lynne 1955(?)- *194*
Tryon, Leslie *194*
  Earlier sketch in SATA *139*
Tubb, Jonathan N. 1951- *78*
Tubb, Kristin O'Donnell 1971- *209*
Tubby, I. M.
  See Kraus, (Herman) Robert
Tucker, Allan James
  See James, Bill
Tucker, Caroline
  See Nolan, Jeannette Covert
Tucker, James
  See James, Bill
Tudor, Edward
  See Browne, Anthony
Tudor, Tasha 1915-2008 .... *160*
  Obituary *205*
  Earlier sketches in SATA *20, 69*
  See also CLR *13*
Tuerk, Hanne 1951- *71*
Tugeau, Jeremy *199*
Tulloch, Richard 1949- *180*
  Earlier sketch in SATA *76*
Tulloch, Richard George
  See Tulloch, Richard
Tulloch, Shirley *169*
Tully, John (Kimberley) 1923- *14*
Tumanov, Vladimir A. 1961- *138*
Tung, Angela 1972- *109*
Tunis, Edwin (Burdett) 1897-1973 .... *28*
  Obituary *24*
  Earlier sketch in SATA *1*
  See also CLR *2*
Tunis, John R(oberts) 1889-1975 .... *37*
  Brief entry *30*
Tunnell, Michael
  See Tunnell, Michael O.
Tunnell, Michael O. 1950- *157*
  Earlier sketch in SATA *103*
Tunnell, Michael O'Grady
  See Tunnell, Michael O.
Tunnicliffe, C(harles) F(rederick)
  1901-1979 .... *62*
Turck, Mary C. 1950- *144*
Turk, Hanne
  See Tuerk, Hanne
Turk, Ruth 1917- *82*
Turkle, Brinton 1915- *79*
  Earlier sketch in SATA *2*
Turlington, Bayly 1919-1977 .... *5*
  Obituary *52*
Turnbull, Agnes Sligh 1888-1982 .... *14*
Turnbull, Ann 1943- *160*
  Earlier sketch in SATA *18*

Turnbull, Ann Christine
  See Turnbull, Ann
Turnbull, Susan 222
Turner, Alice K. 1940- 10
Turner, Ann 1945- 188
  Autobiography Feature 188
  Earlier sketches in SATA *14, 77, 113, 178*
Turner, Ann Warren
  See Turner, Ann
Turner, Bonnie 1932- 75
Turner, Elizabeth 1774-1846
  See YABC 2
Turner, Glennette Tilley 1933- 183
  Earlier sketch in SATA *71*
Turner, Josie
  See Crawford, Phyllis
Turner, Megan Whalen 1965- 174
  Earlier sketch in SATA *94*
Turner, Pamela S. 1957- 211
Turner, Philip (William) 1925- 83
  Earlier sketch in SATA *11*
  See also CLR 89
  See also SAAS 6
Turner, Robyn 1947- 77
Turner, Sheila R.
  See Seed, Sheila Turner
Turngren, Annette 1902(?)-1980
  Obituary 23
Turngren, Ellen (?)-1964 3
Turska, Krystyna (Zofia) 1933- 31
  Brief entry 27
Turteltaub, H. N.
  See Turtledove, Harry
Turtledove, Harry 1949- 166
  Earlier sketch in SATA *116*
Turtledove, Harry Norman
  See Turtledove, Harry
Tusa, Tricia 1960- 207
  Earlier sketches in SATA *72, 111*
Tusiani, Joseph 1924- 45
Twain, Mark 1835-1910 100
  See also YABC 2
  See also CLR 156
Tweit, Susan J 1956- 94
Tweit, Susan Joan
  See Tweit, Susan J
Tweton, D. Jerome 1933- 48
Twinem, Neecy 1958- 92
Twohill, Maggie
  See Angell, Judie
Tworkov, Jack 1900-1982 47
  Obituary 31
Tyche
  See Papademetriou, Lisa
Tyers, Jenny 1969- 89
Tyers, Kathy 1952- 82
Tyler, Anne 1941- 173
  Earlier sketches in SATA *7, 90*
Tyler, Linda
  See Tyler, Linda W(agner)
Tyler, Linda W(agner) 1952- 65
Tyler, Vicki 1952- 64
Tyne, Joel
  See Schembri, Jim
Tyrrell, Frances 1959- 107

U

Ubell, Earl 1926-2007 4
  Obituary 182
Uchida, Yoshiko 1921-1992 53
  Obituary 72
  Earlier sketch in SATA *1*
  See also CLR 56
  See also SAAS 1
Udall, Jan Beaney 1938- 10
Uden, (Bernard Gilbert) Grant 1910- 26
Uderzo, Albert 1927-
  See CLR 37

Udovic, David 1950- 189
Udovic, Jane Morris 1947- 224
Udry, Janice May 1928- 152
  Earlier sketch in SATA *4*
Uegaki, Chieri 1969- 211
  Earlier sketch in SATA *153*
Uehashi, Nahoko 1962- 215
Ueno, Noriko
  See Nakae, Noriko
Ugliano, Natascia 196
Uhlberg, Myron 174
Uhlig, Richard 1970- 195
Uhlig, Susan 1955- 129
Ulam, S(tanislaw) M(arcin) 1909-1984 51
Ullman, Barb Bentler 210
Ullman, James Ramsey 1907-1971 7
Ulm, Robert 1934-1977 17
Ulmer, Louise 1943- 53
Ulmer, Wendy K. 1950- 201
Ulrich, Maureen 1958- 206
Ulriksen, Mark 1957- 210
Ulyatt, Kenneth 1920- 14
Umansky, Kaye 1946- 224
  Earlier sketches in SATA *158, 188*
Unada
  See Gliewe, Unada (Grace)
Uncle Carter
  See Boucher, (Clarence) Carter
Uncle Eric
  See Maybury, Richard J.
Uncle Gus
  See Rey, H. A.
Uncle Mac
  See McCulloch, Derek (Ivor Breashur)
Uncle Ray
  See Coffman, Ramon Peyton
Uncle Shelby
  See Silverstein, Shel
Underhill, Alice Mertie (Waterman)
  1900-1971 10
Underhill, Liz 1948- 53
  Brief entry 49
Underwood, Deborah 1962- 206
Unger, Harlow G. 1931- 75
Unger, Harlow Giles
  See Unger, Harlow G.
Unger, Jim 1937- 67
Ungerer, (Jean) Thomas 1931- 106
  Earlier sketches in SATA *5, 33*
  See also CLR 77
Ungerer, Tomi 1931-
  See Ungerer, (Jean) Thomas
Unkelbach, Kurt 1913-1992 4
Unnerstad, Edith (Totterman) 1900-1982 3
  See also CLR 36
Unobagha, Uzo 139
Unrau, Ruth 1922- 9
Unstead, R(obert) J(ohn) 1915-1988 12
  Obituary 56
Unsworth, Walt(er) 1928- 4
Untermeyer, Bryna Ivens 1909-1985 61
Untermeyer, Louis 1885-1977 37
  Obituary 26
  Earlier sketch in SATA *2*
Unwin, David S. 1918-2010 14
Unwin, David Storr
  See Unwin, David S.
Unwin, Nora S(picer) 1907-1982 3
  Obituary 49
Unzner, Christa 1958- 230
  Earlier sketches in SATA *80, 141*
Unzner-Fischer, Christa
  See Unzner, Christa
Updale, Eleanor 1953- 175
Updyke, Rosemary K. 1924- 103
Upitis, Alvis 109
Urbain, Cat 1956- 211
Urbain, Catherine
  See Urbain, Cat
Urban, Helle (Denise) 1957- 149
Urban, Linda 199

Urbanovic, Jackie 189
Urberuaga, Emilio 1954- 219
Urbigkit, Cat 1965- 196
Urdahl, Catherine 215
Ure, Jean 1943- 192
  Autobiography Feature 192
  Earlier sketches in SATA *48, 78, 129*
  See also CLR 34
  See also SAAS 14
U'Ren, Andrea 1968- 213
  Earlier sketch in SATA *142*
Uris, Leon 1924-2003 49
  Obituary 146
Uris, Leon Marcus
  See Uris, Leon
Ursu, Anne 177
Ury, Allen B. 1954- 98
Uschan, Michael V. 1948- 129
Usher, Margo Scegge
  See McHargue, Georgess
Usher, Mark David
  See Usher, M.D.
Usher, M.D. 1966- 221
Uslan, Michael E. 1951- 169
Uston, Ken(neth Senzo) 1935-1987 65
Uttley, Alice Jane 1884-1976 88
  Obituary 26
  Earlier sketch in SATA *3*
Uttley, Alison
  See Uttley, Alice Jane
Utz, Lois (Marie) 1932-1986 5
  Obituary 50

V

Vaeth, J. Gordon 1921- 17
Vaeth, Joseph Gordon
  See Vaeth, J. Gordon
Vagin, Vladimir (Vasilevich) 1937- 142
Vail, Rachel 1966- 201
  Earlier sketches in SATA *94, 163*
Vainio, Pirkko 1957- 123
  Earlier sketch in SATA *76*
Valen, Nanine 1950- 21
Valencak, Hannelore
  See Mayer, Hannelore Valencak
Valens, Amy 1946- 70
Valens, E(vans) G(ladstone), Jr. 1920-1992 ... 1
Valentine, Johnny 72
Valerio, Geraldo 1970- 180
Valgardson, W. D. 1939- 151
  Earlier sketch in SATA *101*
Valgardson, William Dempsey
  See Valgardson, W. D.
Valleau, Emily 1925- 51
Vamos, Samantha R. 215
Van Abbe, Salaman 1883-1955 18
Van Allsburg, Chris 1949- 156
  Earlier sketches in SATA *37, 53, 105*
  See also CLR 113
Van Anrooy, Francine 1924- 2
Van Anrooy, Frans
  See Van Anrooy, Francine
Vanasse, Deb 1957- 170
Van Buren, David 203
Van Camp, Katie 1981- 222
Vance, Cynthia 207
Vance, Eleanor Graham 1908-1985 11
Vance, Gerald
  See Garrett, Randall
  and Silverberg, Robert
Vance, Marguerite 1889-1965 29
Vance-Abrams, Cynthia
  See Vance, Cynthia
VanCleave, Janice 1942- 116
  Autobiography Feature 123
  Earlier sketch in SATA *75*
Vandenburg, Mary Lou 1943- 17
Vander Boom, Mae M. 14

Vander-Els, Betty 1936- *63*
van der Heide, Iris 1970- *183*
van der Linde, Laurel 1952- *78*
van der Linden, Martijn 1979- *214*
van der Meer, Ron 1945- *98*
van de Ruit, John 1975- *199*
Van der Veer, Judy 1912-1982 .... *4*
    Obituary *33*
Vanderwal, Andrew H. 1956- *219*
Vanderwerff, Corrine 1939- *117*
Vander Zee, Ruth *199*
    Earlier sketch in SATA *159*
Vande Velde, Vivian 1951- *211*
    Earlier sketches in SATA *62, 95, 141*
    See also CLR *145*
Vandivert, Rita (Andre) 1905-1986 .... *21*
Van Draanen, Wendelin *207*
    Earlier sketch in SATA *122*
Van Dusen, Chris *228*
    Earlier sketch in SATA *173*
Van Duyn, Janet 1910- *18*
Van Dyne, Edith
    See Baum, L. Frank
    and Sampson, Emma (Keats) Speed
    and van Zantwijk, Rudolf (Alexander
    Marinus)
Vane, Mitch
    See Vane, Mitchelle
Vane, Mitchelle *176*
van Frankenhuyzen, Gijsbert 1951- *132*
Van Genechten, Guido 1957- *165*
van Haeringen, Annemarie *193*
Van Hook, Beverly 1941- *99*
Van Hook, Beverly H.
    See Van Hook, Beverly
Van Hook, Beverly Hennen
    See Van Hook, Beverly
Van Horn, William 1939- *43*
van Hout, Mies 1962- *178*
Van Iterson, S(iny) R(ose) *26*
Van Kampen, Vlasta 1943- *163*
    Earlier sketch in SATA *54*
Van Laan, Nancy 1939- *214*
    Earlier sketch in SATA *105*
van Lawick-Goodall, Jane
    See Goodall, Jane
Van Leeuwen, Jean 1937- *211*
    Autobiography Feature *141*
    Earlier sketches in SATA *6, 82, 132, 141*
    See also SAAS *8*
van Lhin, Erik
    See del Rey, Lester
van Lieshout, Elle 1963- *217*
van Lieshout, Maria *201*
Van Loon, Hendrik Willem 1882-1944 .... *18*
van Ommen, Sylvia 1978- *186*
VanOosting, James 1951- *170*
Van Orden, M(erton) D(ick) 1921- *4*
van Os, Erik 1963- *217*
Van Patter, Bruce *183*
Van Reek, Wouter *204*
Van Rensselaer, Alexander (Taylor Mason)
    1892-1962 .... *14*
Van Riper, Guernsey, Jr. 1909-1995 .... *3*
van Rossum, Heleen 1962- *174*
Van Rynbach, Iris 1952- *102*
Vansant, Rhonda Joy Edwards 1950- *92*
Van Steenwyk, Elizabeth (Ann) 1928- *89*
    Earlier sketch in SATA *34*
Van Stockum, Hilda 1908-2006 .... *5*
    Obituary *179*
van Straaten, Harmen 1961- *218*
    Earlier sketch in SATA *195*
Van Tuyl, Barbara 1940- *11*
van Vogt, A(lfred) E(lton) 1912-2000 .... *14*
    Obituary *124*
Van Wassenhove, Sue 1951- *202*
Van Woerkom, Dorothy (O'Brien)
    1924-1996 .... *21*
Van Wormer, Joe
    See Van Wormer, Joseph Edward

Van Wormer, Joseph Edward 1913-1998 ...... *35*
Van Wright, Cornelius *173*
Van Zwienen, Ilse Charlotte Koehn
    1929-1991 .... *34*
    Brief entry *28*
    Obituary *67*
Van Zyle, Jon 1942- *176*
    Earlier sketch in SATA *84*
Varela, Barry *180*
Varga, Judy
    See Stang, Judit
Varley, Dimitry V. 1906-1984 .... *10*
Varley, Susan 1961- *134*
    Earlier sketch in SATA *63*
Varon, Sara *195*
Vasileva, Tatiana
    See Wassiljewa, Tatjana
Vasiliev, Valery 1949- *80*
Vasilieva, Tatiana
    See Wassiljewa, Tatjana
Vasiliu, Mircea 1920- *2*
Vass, George 1927- *57*
    Brief entry *31*
Vaughan, Carter A.
    See Gerson, Noel Bertram
Vaughan, Harold Cecil 1923- *14*
Vaughan, Marcia (K.) 1951- *159*
    Earlier sketches in SATA *60, 95*
Vaughan, Richard 1947- *87*
Vaughan, Sam(uel) 1928- *14*
Vaughn, Ruth 1935- *14*
Vaught, Susan 1965- *195*
Vaupel, Robin *198*
Vautier, Ghislaine 1932- *53*
Vavra, Robert James 1935- *8*
Vecsey, George Spencer 1939- *9*
Vedral, Joyce L(auretta) 1943- *65*
Vega, Denise *216*
    Earlier sketch in SATA *174*
Vega, Denise B.
    See Vega, Denise
Vega, Diego
    See Adkins, Jan
Veglahn, Nancy (Crary) 1937- *5*
Vejjajiva, Jane 1963- *189*
Velasquez, Crystal *228*
Velasquez, Eric *226*
    Earlier sketch in SATA *192*
Velasquez, Gloria 1949- *229*
    Earlier sketch in SATA *113*
Velthuijs, Max 1923-2005 .... *110*
    Obituary *160*
    Earlier sketch in SATA *53*
Venable, Alan (Hudson) 1944- *8*
Venezia, Mike 1945- *150*
Venner, Grace Chang
    See Chang, Grace
Ventura, Anthony
    See Pellowski, Michael (Joseph)
Ventura, Piero (Luigi) 1937- *61*
    Brief entry *43*
    See also CLR *16*
Vequin, Capini
    See Quinn, Elisabeth
Verba, Joan Marie 1953- *78*
Verboven, Agnes 1951- *103*
verDorn, Bethea (Stewart) 1952- *76*
Vere, Ed *197*
Verissimo, Erico (Lopes) 1905-1975 .... *113*
Verne, Jules 1828-1905 .... *21*
    See also CLR *88*
Verne, Jules Gabriel
    See Verne, Jules
Verner, Gerald 1897(?)-1980
    Obituary *25*
Verney, John 1913-1993 .... *14*
    Obituary *75*
Verniero, Joan C. 1949- *181*
Vernon, (Elda) Louise A(nderson) 1914- *14*
Vernon, Rosemary
    See Smith, Susan Vernon

Vernon, Ursula *204*
Vernor, D.
    See Casewit, Curtis W(erner)
Verr, Harry Coe
    See Kunhardt, Edith
Verral, Charles Spain 1904-1990 .... *11*
    Obituary *65*
Verrillo, Erica 1953- *199*
Verrillo, Erica F.
    See Verrillo, Erica
Verroken, Sarah 1982- *223*
Verrone, Robert J. 1935(?)-1984
    Obituary *39*
Versace, Marie Teresa Rios 1917- *2*
Vertreace, Martha M(odena) 1945- *78*
Vesey, A(manda) 1939- *62*
Vesey, Mark (David) 1958- *123*
Vesey, Paul
    See Allen, Samuel W(ashington)
Vess, Charles 1951- *215*
Vestergaard, Hope *178*
Vestly, Anne-Cath(arina) 1920-2008 .... *14*
    See also CLR *99*
Vevers, (Henry) Gwynne 1916-1988 .... *45*
    Obituary *57*
Viator, Vacuus
    See Hughes, Thomas
Viau, Nancy *208*
Vicar, Henry
    See Felsen, Henry Gregor
Vick, Helen Hughes 1950- *88*
Vicker, Angus
    See Felsen, Henry Gregor
Vickers, Sheena 1960- *94*
Vickery, Kate
    See Kennedy, T.A.
Victor, Edward 1914- *3*
Victor, Joan Berg 1942- *30*
Vidrine, Beverly Barras 1938- *188*
    Earlier sketch in SATA *103*
Vieceli, Emma 1979- *210*
Viereck, Ellen K. 1928- *14*
Viereck, Phillip 1925- *3*
Viergutz, Dina Nayeri
    See Nayeri, Dina
Viertel, Janet 1915- *10*
Vigliante, Mary
    See Szydlowski, Mary Vigliante
Vigna, Judith 1936- *102*
    Earlier sketch in SATA *15*
Viguers, Ruth Hill 1903-1971 .... *6*
Vila, Laura *207*
Vilela, Fernando 1973- *216*
Villareal, Ray *187*
Villasenor, Edmund
    See Villasenor, Victor E.
Villasenor, Edmundo
    See Villasenor, Victor E.
Villasenor, Victor
    See Villasenor, Victor E.
Villasenor, Victor E. 1940- *171*
Villasenor, Victor Edmundo
    See Villasenor, Victor E.
Villeneuve, Anne *230*
Villiard, Paul 1910-1974 .... *51*
    Obituary *20*
Villiers, Alan (John) 1903-1982 .... *10*
Vilott, Rhondi
    See Salsitz, Rhondi Vilott
Vincent, Amy
    See Gray, Claudia
Vincent, Eric Douglas 1953- *40*
Vincent, Erin 1969- *188*
Vincent, Felix 1946- *41*
Vincent, Gabrielle 1928-2000 .... *121*
    Earlier sketch in SATA *61*
    See also CLR *13*
Vincent, Mary Keith
    See St. John, Wylly Folk
Vincent, Rachel 1978- *222*

Vincent, William R.
   See Heitzmann, William Ray
Vinegar, Tom
   See Gregg, Andrew K.
Vinest, Shaw
   See Longyear, Barry B(rookes)
Vinge, Joan (Carol) D(ennison) 1948- *113*
   Earlier sketch in SATA *36*
Vining, Elizabeth Gray 1902-1999 .... *6*
   Obituary *117*
Vinson, Kathryn 1911-1995 .... *21*
Vinton, Iris 1906(?)-1988 .... *24*
   Obituary *55*
Viola, Herman J(oseph) 1938- *126*
Viorst, Judith 1931- *172*
   Earlier sketches in SATA *7, 70, 123*
   See also CLR *90*
Vip
   See Partch, Virgil Franklin II
Vipont, Charles
   See Foulds, Elfrida Vipont
Vipont, Elfrida
   See Foulds, Elfrida Vipont
Viramontes, Helena Maria 1954-
   See CLR *285*
Viscott, David S(teven) 1938-1996 .... *65*
Visser, W(illem) F(rederik) H(endrik)
   1900-1968 .... *10*
Vitale, Stefano 1958- *225*
   Earlier sketches in SATA *114, 180*
Vivas, Julie 1947- *96*
Vivelo, Jackie 1943- *63*
Vivelo, Jacqueline J.
   See Vivelo, Jackie
Vivelo, Jacqueline Jean
   See Vivelo, Jackie
Vivian, Siobhan 1979(?)- *215*
Vizzini, Ned 1981- *179*
   Earlier sketch in SATA *125*
Vlahos, Olivia 1924- *31*
Vlasic, Bob
   See Hirsch, Phil
Voake, Charlotte *180*
   Earlier sketch in SATA *114*
Voake, Steve 1961- *178*
Vo-Dinh, Mai 1933- *16*
Vogel, Carole Garbuny 1951- *231*
   Earlier sketches in SATA *70, 105*
Vogel, Ilse-Margret 1918- *14*
Vogel, John H., Jr. 1950- *18*
Vogt, Esther Loewen 1915-1999 .... *14*
Vogt, Gregory L. *94*
Vogt, Marie Bollinger 1921- *45*
Vohwinkel, Astrid 1969- *207*
Voight, Virginia Frances 1909-1989 .... *8*
Voigt, Cynthia 1942- *160*
   Brief entry *33*
   Earlier sketches in SATA *48, 79, 116*
   See also CLR *141*
Voigt, Erna 1925- *35*
Voigt-Rother, Erna
   See Voigt, Erna
Vojtech, Anna 1946- *108*
   Earlier sketch in SATA *42*
Vollstadt, Elizabeth Weiss 1942- *121*
Volponi, Paul *228*
   Earlier sketch in SATA *175*
Volting, Dr. R.E.
   See Lerangis, Peter
Von Ahnen, Katherine 1922- *93*
von Buhler, Cynthia *185*
Vondra, J. Gert
   See Vondra, Josef
Vondra, Josef 1941- *121*
Vondra, Josef Gert
   See Vondra, Josef
Von Gunden, Kenneth 1946- *113*
Von Hagen, Victor Wolfgang 1908-1985 ...... *29*
von Klopp, Vahrah
   See Malvern, Gladys

von Schmidt, Eric 1931-2007 .... *50*
   Brief entry *36*
   Obituary *181*
von Storch, Anne B. 1910- *1*
von Trapp, Maria Augusta 1905-1987 .... *16*
von Wodtke, Charlotte Buel Johnson
   1918-1982 .... *46*
von Ziegesar, Cecily 1970- *161*
Vos, Ida 1931-2006 .... *121*
   Earlier sketch in SATA *69*
   See also CLR *85*
Vosburgh, Leonard (W.) 1912- *15*
Votaw, Carol 1961- *201*
Voyle, Mary
   See Manning, Rosemary
Vrettos, Adrienne Maria *187*
Vriens, Jacques 1946- *151*
Vugteveen, Verna Aardema
   See Aardema, Verna
Vulture, Elizabeth T.
   See Gilbert, Suzie
Vuong, Lynette Dyer 1938- *110*
   Earlier sketch in SATA *60*
Vyner, Tim 1963- *228*

                            W

Waas, Uli
   See Waas-Pommer, Ulrike
Waas-Pommer, Ulrike 1949- *85*
Waber, Bernard 1924- *155*
   Brief entry *40*
   Earlier sketches in SATA *47, 95*
   See also CLR *55*
Waber, Paulis *231*
Wachtel, Shirley Russak 1951- *88*
Wachter, Oralee (Roberts) 1935- *61*
   Brief entry *51*
Waddell, Evelyn Margaret 1918- *10*
Waddell, Martin 1941- *129*
   Autobiography Feature *129*
   Earlier sketches in SATA *43, 81, 127*
   See also CLR *31*
   See also SAAS *15*
Waddy, Lawrence 1912-2010 .... *91*
Waddy, Lawrence Heber
   See Waddy, Lawrence
Wade, Mary Dodson 1930- *151*
   Earlier sketch in SATA *79*
Wade, Suzanne
   See Kirby, Susan E.
Wade, Theodore E., Jr. 1936- *37*
Wademan, Peter John 1946- *122*
Wademan, Spike
   See Wademan, Peter John
Wadsworth, Ginger 1945- *223*
   Earlier sketches in SATA *103, 157*
Wagenheim, Kal 1935- *21*
Wagner, Michele R. 1975- *157*
Wagner, Sharon B. 1936- *4*
Wagoner, David (Russell) 1926- *14*
Wahl, Jan (Boyer) 1933- *132*
   Earlier sketches in SATA *2, 34, 73*
   See also SAAS *3*
Wahl, Mats 1945- *186*
Wahman, Wendy *218*
Waide, Jan 1952- *29*
Wainscott, John Milton 1910-1981 .... *53*
Wainwright, Debra *218*
Wainwright, Richard M. 1935- *91*
Wainwright, Ruth
   See Symes, Ruth Louise
Wait, Lea 1946- *137*
Waite, Judy *174*
Waite, Judy Bernard
   See Bernard, Patricia
Waite, Michael
   See Waite, Michael P.
Waite, Michael P. 1960- *101*

Waite, P(eter) B(usby) 1922- *64*
Waites, Joan C. *187*
Waitley, Douglas 1927- *30*
Wakefield, Jean L.
   See Laird, Jean E(louise)
Wakin, Daniel (Joseph) 1961- *84*
Wakin, Edward 1927- *37*
Wakiyama, Hanako 1966- *192*
Walck, Henry Z. 1908(?)-1984
   Obituary *40*
Walden, Amelia Elizabeth *3*
Walden, Mark *188*
Waldherr, Kris 1963- *76*
Waldman, Bruce 1949- *15*
Waldman, Neil 1947- *203*
   Earlier sketches in SATA *51, 94, 142*
Waldrep, Richard *198*
Waldron, Ann Wood 1924-2010 .... *16*
Waldron, Kathleen Cook *176*
Waldron, Kevin 1979- *230*
Wales, Dirk 1931- *205*
Walgren, Judy 1963- *118*
Walker, Addison
   See Walker, Mort
Walker, Addison Mort
   See Walker, Mort
Walker, Alice 1944- *31*
Walker, Alice Malsenior
   See Walker, Alice
Walker, Anna *223*
Walker, Barbara (Jeanne) K(erlin) 1921- *80*
   Earlier sketch in SATA *4*
Walker, Barbara M(uhs) 1928- *57*
Walker, (James) Braz(elton) 1934-1983 .... *45*
Walker, David 1965- *197*
Walker, David G(ordon) 1926- *60*
Walker, David Harry 1911-1992 .... *8*
   Obituary *71*
Walker, Diana 1925- *9*
Walker, Diane Marie Catherine
   See Walker, Kate
Walker, Dick
   See Pellowski, Michael (Joseph)
Walker, Frank 1931-2000 .... *36*
Walker, Holly Beth
   See Bond, Gladys Baker
Walker, Kate 1950- *165*
   Earlier sketch in SATA *82*
Walker, Kathrine Sorley
   See Sorley Walker, Kathrine
Walker, Kristin *228*
Walker, Lou Ann 1952- *66*
   Brief entry *53*
Walker, Louise Jean 1891-1976
   Obituary *35*
Walker, Mary Alexander 1927- *61*
Walker, Mildred
   See Schemm, Mildred Walker
Walker, Mort 1923- *8*
Walker, Pamela 1948- *142*
   Earlier sketch in SATA *24*
Walker, Paul Robert 1953- *154*
Walker, Robert W. 1948- *66*
Walker, Robert Wayne
   See Walker, Robert W.
Walker, Sally M. 1954- *221*
   Earlier sketch in SATA *135*
Walker, Stephen J. 1951- *12*
Walker-Blondell, Becky 1951- *89*
Wallace, Barbara Brooks 1922- *136*
   Earlier sketches in SATA *4, 78*
   See also CLR *150*
   See also SAAS *17*
Wallace, Beverly Dobrin 1921- *19*
Wallace, Bill 1947- *169*
   Brief entry *47*
   Earlier sketches in SATA *53, 101*
Wallace, Carol 1948- *218*
Wallace, Chad *229*
Wallace, Daisy
   See Cuyler, Margery

Wallace, Ian 1950- 219
  Earlier sketches in SATA *53, 56, 141*
  See also CLR *37*
Wallace, John 1966- 155
  Earlier sketch in SATA *105*
Wallace, John A(dam) 1915-2004 3
  Obituary 155
Wallace, Karen 1951- 188
  Earlier sketches in SATA *83, 139*
Wallace, Nancy Elizabeth 1948- 222
  Earlier sketches in SATA *141, 186*
Wallace, Nigel
  See Hamilton, Charles (Harold St. John)
Wallace, Paula S. 153
Wallace, Rich 1957- 196
  Earlier sketches in SATA *117, 158*
Wallace, Robert 1932-1999 47
  Brief entry 37
Wallace, Ruby Ann 1923(?)- 77
Wallace, William Keith
  See Wallace, Bill
Wallace-Brodeur, Ruth 1941- 169
  Brief entry 41
  Earlier sketches in SATA *51, 88*
Wallenta, Adam 1974- 123
Waller, Leslie 1923-2007 20
Walley, Byron
  See Card, Orson Scott
Walliams, David 1971- 227
Wallis, Diz 1949- 77
Wallis, G. McDonald
  See Campbell, Hope
Wallner, Alexandra 1946- 156
  Brief entry 41
  Earlier sketches in SATA *51, 98*
Wallner, John C. 1945- 133
  Earlier sketches in SATA *10, 51*
Wallower, Lucille 11
Walrod, Amy 1973(?)- 182
Walsh, Ann 1942- 176
  Earlier sketch in SATA *62*
Walsh, Ellen Stoll 1942- 194
  Earlier sketches in SATA *49, 99, 147*
Walsh, George Johnston 1889-1981 53
Walsh, Gillian Paton
  See Paton Walsh, Jill
Walsh, Jill Paton
  See Paton Walsh, Jill
Walsh, Joanna 1970- 182
Walsh, Lawrence 1942- 170
Walsh, Marissa 1972- 195
Walsh, Mary Caswell 1949- 118
Walsh, Mitzy
  See Walsh, Marissa
Walsh, Rebecca 217
Walsh, Suella 170
Walsh, V. L.
  See Walsh, Vivian
Walsh, Vivian 1960- 120
Walsh Shepherd, Donna 1948- 78
Walter, Frances V. 1923- 71
Walter, Mildred Pitts 1922- 133
  Brief entry 45
  Earlier sketch in SATA *69*
  See also CLR *61*
  See also SAAS *12*
Walter, Villiam Christian
  See Andersen, Hans Christian
Walter, Virginia
  See Walter, Virginia A.
Walter, Virginia A. 134
Walters, Audrey 1929- 18
Walters, Celeste 1938- 126
Walters, Eric 1957- 205
  Earlier sketches in SATA *99, 155*
Walters, Eric Robert
  See Walters, Eric
Walters, Gregory 1964- 213
Walters, Helen B. (?)-1987
  Obituary 50

Walters, Hugh
  See Hughes, Walter (Llewellyn)
Walther, Thomas A. 1950- 31
Walther, Tom
  See Walther, Thomas A.
Waltner, Elma 1912-1987 40
Waltner, Willard H. 1909- 40
Walton, Darwin McBeth 1926- 119
Walton, Fiona L. M. 1959- 89
Walton, Richard J. 1928- 4
Walton, Rick 1957- 204
  Earlier sketches in SATA *101, 151*
Waltrip, Lela (Kingston) 1904-1995 9
Waltrip, Mildred 1911- 37
Waltrip, Rufus (Charles) 1898-1988 9
Walworth, Nancy Zinsser 1917- 14
Wang, Gabrielle 212
Wang, Lin 1973- 221
Wang, Shaoli 216
Wangerin, Walter, Jr. 1944- 98
  Brief entry 37
  Earlier sketch in SATA *45*
Waniek, Marilyn
  See Nelson, Marilyn
Waniek, Marilyn Nelson 1946-
  See Nelson, Marilyn
Wannamaker, Bruce
  See Moncure, Jane Belk
Warbler, J. M.
  See Cocagnac, Augustin Maurice(-Jean)
Warburg, Sandol Stoddard
  See Stoddard, Sandol
Warburton, Tom 1968(?)- 218
Ward, David 1967- 213
Ward, E. D.
  See Gorey, Edward (St. John)
  and Lucas, E(dward) V(errall)
Ward, Ed
  See Stratemeyer, Edward L.
Ward, Helen 1962- 206
  Earlier sketches in SATA *72, 144*
Ward, Jay 1920-1989
  Obituary 63
Ward, Jennifer 1963- 226
  Earlier sketch in SATA *146*
Ward, John (Stanton) 1917- 42
Ward, Jonas
  See Ard, William
  and Cox, William R(obert)
  and Garfield, Brian (Francis Wynne)
Ward, Lynd (Kendall) 1905-1985 36
  Obituary 42
  Earlier sketch in SATA *2*
Ward, Martha (Eads) 5
Ward, Melanie
  See Curtis, Richard
  and Lynch, Marilyn
Ward, Nicholas John
  See Ward, Nick
Ward, Nick 1955- 190
Ward, Rachel 1964- 229
Ward, Tom
  See Stratemeyer, Edward L.
Wardell, Dean
  See Prince, J(ack) H(arvey)
Wardlaw, Lee 1955- 115
  Earlier sketch in SATA *79*
Ware, Cheryl 1963- 101
Ware, Chris 1967- 140
Ware, Leon (Vernon) 1909-1976 4
Wargin, Kathy-jo 1964- 210
  Earlier sketch in SATA *145*
Warhola, James 1955- 187
Warman, Jessica 1981- 225
Warner, Frank A. 67
  Earlier sketch in SATA *1*
Warner, Gertrude Chandler 1890-1979 9
  Obituary 73
Warner, J(ohn) F. 1929- 75
Warner, Lucille Schulberg 30

Warner, Matt
  See Fichter, George S.
Warner, Oliver (Martin Wilson) 1903-1976 . 29
Warner, Sally 1946- 214
  Earlier sketch in SATA *131*
Warner, Sunny (B.) 1931- 108
Warnes, Tim 1971- 216
  Earlier sketches in SATA *116, 166*
Warnes, Timothy
  See Warnes, Tim
Warnick, Elsa 1942- 113
Warren, Andrea 1946- 98
Warren, Betsy
  See Warren, Elizabeth Avery
Warren, Billy
  See Warren, William Stephen
Warren, Cathy 1951- 62
  Brief entry 46
Warren, Elizabeth
  See Supraner, Robyn
Warren, Elizabeth Avery 1916- 46
  Brief entry 38
Warren, Jackie M. 1953- 135
Warren, Joshua P(aul) 1976- 107
Warren, Joyce W(illiams) 1935- 18
Warren, Mary Phraner 1929- 10
Warren, Robert Penn 1905-1989 46
  Obituary 63
Warren, Scott S. 1957- 79
Warren, William Stephen 1882-1968 9
Warrick, Patricia Scott 1925- 35
Warriner, John 1907(?)-1987
  Obituary 53
Warsh
  See Warshaw, Jerry
Warshaw, Jerry 1929- 30
Warshaw, Mary 1931- 89
Warshofsky, Fred 1931- 24
Warshofsky, Isaac
  See Singer, Isaac Bashevis
Wartski, Maureen (Ann Crane) 1940- 50
  Brief entry 37
Warwick, Alan R(oss) 1900-1973 42
Wa-Sha-Quon-Asin
  See Belaney, Archibald Stansfeld
Wa-sha-quon-asin
  See Belaney, Archibald Stansfeld
Washburn, Bradford 1910-2007 38
  Obituary 181
Washburn, Henry Bradford, Jr.
  See Washburn, Bradford
Washburn, Jan(ice) 1926- 63
Washburn, Lucia 193
Washburne, Carolyn Kott 1944- 86
Washburne, Heluiz Chandler 1892-1970 10
  Obituary 26
Washington, Booker T. 1856-1915 28
Washington, Donna L. 1967- 159
  Earlier sketch in SATA *98*
Wasserman, Robin 1978- 207
Wasserstein, Wendy 1950-2006 94
  Obituary 174
Wassiljewa, Tatjana 1928- 106
Watanabe, Etsuko 1968- 219
Watanabe, Shigeo 1928- 131
  Brief entry 32
  Earlier sketch in SATA *39*
  See also CLR *8*
Waters, John F(rederick) 1930- 4
Waters, Summer
  See Sykes, Julie
Waters, Tony 1958- 75
Waterton, Betty 1923- 99
  Brief entry 34
  Earlier sketch in SATA *37*
Waterton, Betty Marie
  See Waterton, Betty
Watkins, Dawn L. 126
Watkins, Gloria Jean
  See hooks, bell

Watkins, Lis
See Watkins, Liselotte
Watkins, Liselotte 1971- 215
Watkins, Lois 1930- 88
Watkins, Peter 1934- 66
Watkins, Yoko Kawashima 1933- 93
Watkins-Pitchford, Denys James
1905-1990 87
Obituary 66
Earlier sketch in SATA 6
See also SAAS 4
Watling, James 1933- 117
Earlier sketch in SATA 67
Watson, Aldren A(uld) 1917- 42
Brief entry 36
Watson, Amy Zakrzewski 1965- 76
Watson, B. S.
See Teitelbaum, Michael
Watson, Carol 1949- 78
Watson, C.G. 193
Watson, Clyde 1947- 68
Earlier sketch in SATA 5
See also CLR 3
Watson, Helen Orr 1892-1978
Obituary 24
Watson, James 1936- 106
Earlier sketch in SATA 10
Watson, Jane Werner 1915- 54
Earlier sketch in SATA 3
Watson, Jesse Joshua 199
Watson, John H.
See Farmer, Philip Jose
Watson, Mary 1953- 117
Watson, N. Cameron 1955- 81
Watson, Nancy Dingman 32
Watson, Pauline 1925- 14
Watson, Richard F.
See Silverberg, Robert
Watson, Richard Jesse 1951- 211
Earlier sketch in SATA 62
Watson, Sally (Lou) 1924- 3
Watson, Sasha 211
Watson, Wendy (McLeod) 1942- 142
Earlier sketches in SATA 5, 74
Watson Taylor, Elizabeth 1915- 41
Watt, Melanie 1975- 193
Earlier sketch in SATA 136
Watt, Thomas 1935- 4
Wattenberg, Jane 174
Watterson, Bill 1958- 66
Watt-Evans, Lawrence 1954- 121
Watts, Bernadette 1942- 230
Earlier sketches in SATA 4, 103
Watts, Ephraim
See Horne, Richard Henry Hengist
Watts, Franklin (Mowry) 1904-1978 46
Obituary 21
Watts, Helen L. Hoke 1903-1990
Obituary 65
Watts, Irene N(aemi) 1931- 111
Earlier sketch in SATA 56
Watts, Isaac 1674-1748 52
Watts, James K(ennedy) M(offitt) 1955- 59
Watts, Jeri Hanel 1957- 170
Watts, Julia 1969- 103
Watts, Leander 1956- 146
Watts, Leslie Elizabeth 1961- 168
Watts, Mabel Pizzey 1906-1994 11
Watts, Nigel 1957-1999 121
Waugh, C. C. Roessel
See Waugh, Carol-Lynn Rossel
and Waugh, Charles G(ordon)
Waugh, Carol-Lynn Rossel 1947- 41
Waugh, Dorothy -1996 11
Waugh, Sylvia 1935- 169
Waugh, Virginia
See Sorensen, Virginia
Wax, Wendy A. 1963- 219
Earlier sketches in SATA 73, 163

Wayland, April Halprin 1954- 143
Earlier sketch in SATA 78
See also SAAS 26
Wayland, Patrick
See O'Connor, Richard
Wayne, (Anne) Jenifer 1917-1982 32
Wayne, Kyra Petrovskaya 1918- 8
Wayne, Richard
See Decker, Duane
Wayshak, Deborah Noyes
See Noyes, Deborah
Waystaff, Simon
See Swift, Jonathan
Weales, Gerald (Clifford) 1925- 11
Weary, Ogdred
See Gorey, Edward (St. John)
Weatherford, Carole Boston 1956- 226
Earlier sketches in SATA 138, 181
Weatherill, Cat 203
Weatherly, Lee 1967- 192
Weatherly, Myra 1926- 130
Weatherly, Myra S.
See Weatherly, Myra
Weaver, Brian M.
See Numberman, Neil
Weaver, Harriett E. 1908-1993 65
Weaver, John L. 1949- 42
Weaver, Robyn
See Conley, Robyn
Weaver, Robyn M.
See Conley, Robyn
Weaver, Tess 197
Weaver, Ward
See Mason, F(rancis) van Wyck
Weaver, Will 1950- 217
Earlier sketches in SATA 88, 109, 161
Weaver, William Weller
See Weaver, Will
Weaver-Gelzer, Charlotte 1950- 79
Webb, Christopher
See Wibberley, Leonard
Webb, Jacqueline
See Pearce, Margaret
Webb, Jacquelyn
See Pearce, Margaret
and Pearce, Margaret
Webb, Jean Francis (III) 1910-1991 35
Webb, Kaye 1914- 60
Webb, Lois Sinaiko 1922- 82
Webb, Margot 1934- 67
Webb, Sharon 1936-2010 41
Webb, Sophie 1958- 135
Webber, Andrew Lloyd
See Lloyd Webber, Andrew
Webber, Desiree Morrison 1956- 170
Webber, Irma E(leanor Schmidt)
1904-1995 14
Weber, Alfons 1921- 8
Weber, Bruce 1942- 120
Earlier sketch in SATA 73
Weber, Debora 1955- 58
Weber, EdNah New Rider 1919(?)- 168
Weber, Elka 1968- 219
Weber, Jill 1950- 209
Earlier sketch in SATA 127
Weber, Judith E(ichler) 1938- 64
Weber, Ken(neth J.) 1940- 90
Weber, Lenora Mattingly 1895-1971 2
Obituary 26
Weber, Lisa K. 217
Weber, Lori 1959- 220
Weber, Michael 1945- 87
Weber, Sandra 1961- 158
Weber, William J(ohn) 1927- 14
Webster, Alice Jane Chandler 1876-1916 17
Webster, David 1930- 11
Webster, Frank V. 67
Earlier sketch in SATA 1
Webster, Gary
See Garrison, Webb B(lack)

Webster, James 1925-1981 17
Obituary 27
Webster, Jean
See Webster, Alice Jane Chandler
Wechsler, Doug 189
Wechsler, Herman J. 1904-1976
Obituary 20
Wechter, Nell (Carolyn) Wise 1913-1989 .. 127
Earlier sketch in SATA 60
Weck, Thomas L. 1942- 62
Wedd, Kate
See Gregory, Philippa
Weddle, Ethel Harshbarger 1897-1996 11
Wedekind, Annie 204
Weeks, Sarah 194
Earlier sketch in SATA 158
Weems, David B(urnola) 1922- 80
Wees, Frances Shelley 1902-1982 58
Weevers, Peter 1944- 59
Wegen, Ronald 1946-1985 99
Wegman, William (George) 1943- 135
Earlier sketches in SATA 78, 129
Wegner, Fritz 1924- 20
Wehrman, Vicki 223
Weidhorn, Manfred 1931- 60
Weidt, Maryann N. 1944- 85
Weigel, Jeff 1958- 170
Weigelt, Udo 1960- 201
Earlier sketch in SATA 168
Weihs, Erika 1917-2010 107
Earlier sketch in SATA 15
Weik, Mary Hays 1898(?)-1979 3
Obituary 23
Weil, Ann Yezner 1908-1969 9
Weil, Lisl 1910- 7
Weilerstein, Sadie Rose 1894-1993 3
Obituary 75
Weill, Cynthia 1959- 167
Wein, Elizabeth E. 1964- 151
Earlier sketch in SATA 82
Wein, Elizabeth Eve
See Wein, Elizabeth E.
Wein, Hallie
See Zobel Nolan, Allia
Weinberg, Larry
See Weinberg, Lawrence (E.)
Weinberg, Lawrence (E.) 92
Brief entry 48
Weinberger, Tanya 1939- 84
Weiner, Sandra 1922- 14
Weingarten, Lynn 217
Weingarten, Violet (Brown) 1915-1976 3
Obituary 27
Weingartner, Charles 1922- 5
Weinheimer, Beckie 1958- 186
Weinstein, Bruce 1960- 220
Weinstein, Bruce M.
See Weinstein, Bruce
Weinstein, Ellen Slusky 1959- 200
Weinstein, Muriel Harris 215
Weinstein, Nina 1951- 73
Weinstock, Robert 1967- 204
Weir, Bob 1947- 76
Weir, Diana (R.) Loiewski 1958- 111
Weir, Joan S(herman) 1928- 99
Weir, LaVada 2
Weir, Rosemary (Green) 1905-1994 21
Weir, Wendy 1949- 76
Weis, Margaret 1948- 164
Earlier sketches in SATA 38, 92
Weisberger, Bernard A(llen) 1922- 21
Weisburd, Stefi 1957- 202
Weiser, Marjorie P(hillis) K(atz) 1934- 33
Weisgard, Leonard (Joseph) 1916-2000 85
Obituary 122
Earlier sketches in SATA 2, 30
See also SAAS 19
Weiss, Adelle 1920- 18
Weiss, Ann E(dwards) 1943- 69
Earlier sketch in SATA 30
See also SAAS 13

Weiss, Edna
  See Barth, Edna
Weiss, Ellen 1953- 44
Weiss, Harvey 1922- 76
  Earlier sketches in SATA *1, 27*
  See also CLR *4*
  See also SAAS *19*
Weiss, Jaqueline Shachter 1926- 65
Weiss, Malcolm E. 1928- 3
Weiss, Margaret Edith
  See Weis, Margaret
Weiss, Miriam
  See Schlein, Miriam
Weiss, Mitch 1951- 183
  Earlier sketch in SATA *123*
Weiss, Nicki 1954- 86
  Earlier sketch in SATA *33*
Weiss, Renee Karol 1923- 5
Weissberger, Ela 1930- 181
Weissberger, Ela Stein
  See Weissberger, Ela
Weissenborn, Hellmuth 1898-1982
  Obituary 31
Weissman, Elissa Brent 217
Weitzman, David L. 1936- 172
  Earlier sketch in SATA *122*
Wekesser, Carol A. 1963- 76
Welber, Robert 26
Welch, Amanda (Jane) 1945- 75
Welch, D'Alte Aldridge 1907-1970
  Obituary 27
Welch, Holly 206
Welch, Jean-Louise
  See Kempton, Jean Welch
Welch, Pauline
  See Bodenham, Hilda Morris
Welch, Ronald
  See Felton, Ronald Oliver
Welch, Sheila Kelly 1945- 130
Welch, Willy 1952- 93
Weldin, Frauke 1969- 188
Welford, Sue 1942- 75
Weller, George 1907-2002 31
  Obituary 140
Weller, George Anthony
  See Weller, George
Welling, Peter J. 1947- 135
Wellington, Monica 1957- 222
  Earlier sketches in SATA *67, 99, 157*
Wellman, Alice 1900-1984 51
  Brief entry 36
Wellman, Manly Wade 1903-1986 6
  Obituary 47
Wellman, Paul I. 1898-1966 3
Wellman, Paul Iselin
  See Wellman, Paul I.
Wellman, Sam 1939- 122
Wellman, Samuel
  See Wellman, Sam
Wells, H. G. 1866-1946 20
  See also CLR *133*
Wells, Helen
  See Campbell, Hope
Wells, Helen 1910-1986 49
  Earlier sketch in SATA *2*
Wells, Herbert George
  See Wells, H. G.
Wells, J. Wellington
  See de Camp, L. Sprague
Wells, June
  See Swinford, Betty (June Wells)
Wells, Robert
  See Welsch, Roger L(ee)
Wells, Robert E. 184
Wells, Rosemary 1943- 207
  Earlier sketches in SATA *18, 69, 114, 156*
  See also CLR *69*
  See also SAAS *1*
Wells, Susan (Mary) 1951- 78
Wels, Byron G(erald) 1924-1993 9
Welsbacher, Anne 1955- 89

Welsch, Roger L(ee) 1936- 82
Welsh, David
  See Hills, C.A.R.
Welsh, Mary Flynn 1910(?)-1984
  Obituary 38
Welsh, T.K. 1956- 184
Weltevrede, Pieter 1957- 228
Weltner, Linda R(iverly) 1938- 38
Welton, Jude 1955- 143
  Earlier sketch in SATA *79*
Welty, S. F.
  See Welty, Susan F.
Welty, Susan F. 1905- 9
Wemmlinger, Raymond 190
Wendelin, Rudolph 1910-2000 23
Weninger, Brigitte 1960- 189
Wensell, Ulises 1945- 229
Wentworth, Robert
  See Hamilton, Edmond
Werlin, Nancy 1961- 161
  Earlier sketches in SATA *87, 119*
Werner, Elsa Jane
  See Watson, Jane Werner
Werner, Herma 1926- 47
  Brief entry 41
Werner, Jane
  See Watson, Jane Werner
Werner, K.
  See Casewit, Curtis W(erner)
Wersba, Barbara 1932- 58
  Autobiography Feature 103
  Earlier sketch in SATA *1*
  See also CLR *78*
  See also SAAS *2*
Werstein, Irving 1914(?)-1971 14
Werth, Kurt 1896-1983 20
Wesley, Alison
  See Barnes, Michael
Wesley, Kathryn
  See Rusch, Kristine Kathryn
Wesley, Mary (Aline) 1912-2002 66
Wesley, Valerie Wilson 1947- 168
  Earlier sketch in SATA *106*
West, Andrew
  See Arthur, Robert, (Jr.)
West, Anna 1938- 40
West, Barbara
  See Price, Olive
West, Betty 1921- 11
West, Bruce 1951- 63
West, C. P.
  See Wodehouse, P. G.
West, Dorothy
  See Benson, Mildred
West, Emily Govan 1919- 38
West, Emmy
  See West, Emily Govan
West, James
  See Withers, Carl A.
West, Jerry
  See Svenson, Andrew E(dward)
West, (Mary) Jessamyn 1902-1984
  Obituary 37
West, John
  See Arthur, Robert, (Jr.)
West, Owen
  See Koontz, Dean
West, Ward
  See Borland, Harold Glen
Westall, Robert (Atkinson) 1929-1993 69
  Obituary 75
  Earlier sketch in SATA *23*
  See also CLR *13*
  See also SAAS *2*
Westaway, Jane 1948- 121
Westcott, Nadine Bernard 1949- 130
Westera, Marleen 1962- 187
Westerberg, Christine 1950- 29
Westerduin, Anne 1945- 105
Westerfeld, Scott 1963- 230
  Earlier sketch in SATA *161*

Westervelt, Virginia Veeder 1914-2005 10
Westheimer, David 1917-2005 14
  Obituary 170
Westheimer, David Kaplan
  See Westheimer, David
Westmacott, Mary
  See Christie, Agatha
Westman, Barbara 70
Westman, Paul (Wendell) 1956- 39
Westmoreland, William C. 1914-2005 63
Westmoreland, William Childs
  See Westmoreland, William C.
Weston, Allen
  See Hogarth, Grace (Weston Allen)
  and Norton, Andre
Weston, Carol 1956- 135
Weston, Carrie 190
Weston, John (Harrison) 1932- 21
Weston, Martha 1947- 119
  Earlier sketch in SATA *53*
Weston, Robert Paul 209
Westphal, Arnold Carl 1897- 57
Westrup, Hugh 102
Westwood, Jennifer 1940-2008 10
  Obituary 192
Wexler, Jerome (LeRoy) 1923- 14
Weyland, Jack 1940- 81
Weyn, Suzanne 1955- 220
  Earlier sketches in SATA *63, 101, 164*
Weyr, Garret
  See Freymann-Weyr, Garret
Wezyk, Joanna 1966- 82
Whaley, Joyce Irene 1923- 61
Whalin, W. Terry 1953- 93
Whamond, Dave 222
Wharf, Michael
  See Weller, George
Wharmby, Margot 63
Wharton, Edith 1862-1937
  See CLR *136*
Wharton, Edith Newbold Jones
  See Wharton, Edith
Wharton, Thomas 1963- 223
Whatley, Bruce 1954- 213
  Earlier sketch in SATA *177*
Wheatley, Arabelle 1921- 16
Wheatley, Nadia 1949- 147
Wheeler, Cindy 1955- 49
  Brief entry 40
Wheeler, Deborah 1947- 83
Wheeler, Janet D. 1
Wheeler, Jill C. 1964- 136
  Earlier sketch in SATA *86*
Wheeler, Jody 1952- 148
  Earlier sketch in SATA *84*
Wheeler, Lisa 1963- 200
  Earlier sketch in SATA *162*
Wheeler, Opal 1898- 23
Whelan, Elizabeth M(urphy) 1943- 14
Whelan, Gloria 1923- 224
  Earlier sketches in SATA *85, 128, 178*
  See also CLR *90*
Whelan, Gloria Ann
  See Whelan, Gloria
Whinnem, Reade Scott 224
Whipple, A(ddison) B(eecher) C(olvin)
  1918- 64
Whipple, Cal
  See Whipple, A(ddison) B(eecher) C(olvin)
Whisp, Kennilworthy
  See Rowling, J.K.
Whistler, Reginald John 1905-1944 30
Whistler, Rex
  See Whistler, Reginald John
Whitaker, Zai 183
Whitcher, Susan (Godsil) 1952- 96
Whitcomb, Jon 1906-1988 10
  Obituary 56
Whitcomb, Laura 1958- 214
  Earlier sketch in SATA *171*
White, Amy Brecount 228

White, Anne Terry 1896-1980 2
White, Bessie (Felstiner) 1892(?)-1986
   Obituary 50
White, Carolyn 1948- 130
White, Dale
   See Place, Marian T(empleton)
White, Dori 1919- 10
White, E. B. 1899-1985 100
   Obituary 44
   Earlier sketches in SATA *2, 29*
   See also CLR *107*
White, Eliza Orne 1856-1947
   See YABC *2*
White, Elwyn Brooks
   See White, E. B.
White, Florence M(eiman) 1910- 14
White, Laurence B(arton), Jr. 1935- 10
White, Lee 223
   Earlier sketch in SATA *176*
White, Martin 1943- 51
White, Nancy 1942- 126
White, Ramy Allison 67
   Earlier sketch in SATA *1*
White, Robb 1909-1990 83
   Earlier sketch in SATA *1*
   See also CLR *3*
   See also SAAS *1*
White, Ruth 1942- 186
   Autobiography Feature 186
   Earlier sketches in SATA *39, 117, 165*
White, Ruth C.
   See White, Ruth
White, T(erence) H(anbury) 1906-1964 12
   See also CLR *139*
White, Tekla N. 1934- 115
White, Timothy (Thomas Anthony)
   1952-2002 60
White, Tom 1923- 148
White, William, Jr. 1934- 16
Whitehead, Don(ald) F. 1908-1981 4
Whitehead, Jenny 1964- 191
Whitehead, Kathy 1957- 176
Whitehouse, Arch
   See Whitehouse, Arthur George Joseph
Whitehouse, Arthur George Joseph
   1895-1979 14
   Obituary 23
Whitehouse, Elizabeth S(cott) 1893-1968 35
Whitehouse, Jeanne
   See Peterson, Jeanne Whitehouse
Whitelaw, Nancy 1933- 166
   Earlier sketch in SATA *76*
Whitesel, Cheryl Aylward 162
Whiting, Sue 1960- 205
Whiting, Susan Allana
   See Whiting, Sue
Whitinger, R. D.
   See Place, Marian T(empleton)
Whitley, David 1984- 225
Whitley, Mary Ann
   See Sebrey, Mary Ann
Whitley, Peggy 1938- 140
Whitlock, Pamela 1921(?)-1982
   Obituary 31
Whitlock, Ralph 1914-1995 35
Whitman, Alice
   See Marker, Sherry
Whitman, Candace 1958- 208
Whitman, Sylvia (Choate) 1961- 135
   Earlier sketch in SATA *85*
Whitman, Walt 1819-1892 20
Whitman, Walter
   See Whitman, Walt
Whitmore, Arvella 1922- 125
Whitmore, Benette 1955- 203
Whitney, Alex(andra) 1922- 14
Whitney, David C(harles) 1921- 48
   Brief entry 29
Whitney, Kim Ablon 162

Whitney, Phyllis A. 1903-2008 30
   Obituary 189
   Earlier sketch in SATA *1*
   See also CLR *59*
Whitney, Phyllis Ayame
   See Whitney, Phyllis A.
Whitney, Sharon 1937- 63
Whitney, Thomas P. 1917-2007 25
   Obituary 189
Whitney, Thomas Porter
   See Whitney, Thomas P.
Whittington, Mary K(athrine) 1941- 75
Whitworth, John 1945- 123
Whybrow, Ian 202
   Earlier sketch in SATA *132*
Whyte, Mal(colm Kenneth, Jr.) 1933- 62
Whyte, Mary 1953- 148
   Earlier sketch in SATA *94*
Whyte, Ron 1942(?)-1989
   Obituary 63
Whytock, Cherry 177
Wiater, Stanley 1953- 84
Wibbelsman, Charles J(oseph) 1945- 59
Wibberley, Leonard 1915-1983 45
   Obituary 36
   Earlier sketch in SATA *2*
   See also CLR *3*
Wibberley, Leonard Patrick O'Connor
   See Wibberley, Leonard
Wiberg, Harald (Albin) 1908- 93
   Brief entry 40
Wick, Walter 1953- 148
Wickberg, Susan
   See Rottman, S.L.
Wickens, Elaine 86
Wicker, Ireene 1905(?)-1987
   Obituary 55
Wickstrom, Sylvie 1960- 169
Wickstrom, Thor 1960- 200
Widdemer, Mabel Cleland 1902-1964 5
Widener, Terry 1950- 209
   Earlier sketch in SATA *105*
Widerberg, Siv 1931- 10
Wiebe, Rudy 1934- 156
Wiebe, Rudy Henry
   See Wiebe, Rudy
Wieler, Diana (Jean) 1961- 109
Wiener, Lori 1956- 84
Wier, Ester (Alberti) 1910-2000 3
Wiese, Kurt 1887-1974 36
   Obituary 24
   Earlier sketch in SATA *3*
   See also CLR *86*
Wiesel, Elie 1928- 56
Wiesel, Eliezer
   See Wiesel, Elie
Wiesner, David 1956- 181
   Earlier sketches in SATA *72, 117, 139*
   See also CLR *84*
Wiesner, Portia
   See Takakjian, Portia
Wiesner, William 1899-1984 5
Wiewandt, Thomas 1945- 231
Wiggers, Raymond 1952- 82
Wiggin, Eric E. 1939- 167
   Earlier sketch in SATA *88*
Wiggin, Eric Ellsworth 1939-
   See Wiggin, Eric E.
Wiggin (Riggs), Kate Douglas (Smith)
   1856-1923
   See YABC *1*
   See also CLR *52*
Wiggins, VeraLee (Chesnut) 1928-1995 89
Wight, Eric 1974- 218
Wight, James Alfred
   See Herriot, James
Wignell, Edel 1936- 69
Wijnberg, Ellen 85
Wijngaard, Juan 1951- 230
Wikland, Ilon 1930- 93
   Brief entry 32

Wikler, Madeline 1943- 114
Wilber, Donald N(ewton) 1907-1997 35
Wilbur, C. Keith 1923- 27
Wilbur, Frances 1921- 107
Wilbur, Helen L. 1948- 204
Wilbur, Richard 1921- 108
   Earlier sketch in SATA *9*
Wilbur, Richard Purdy
   See Wilbur, Richard
Wilburn, Kathy 1948- 68
Wilcox, Charlotte 1948- 72
Wilcox, Leah 1975(?)- 207
Wilcox, R(uth) Turner 1888-1970 36
Wilcox, Roger
   See Collins, Paul
Wild, Jocelyn 1941- 46
Wild, Kate 1954- 192
Wild, Margaret 1948- 197
   Earlier sketch in SATA *151*
Wild, Robin (Evans) 1936- 46
Wild, Robyn 1947- 117
Wilde, D. Gunther
   See Hurwood, Bernhardt J.
Wilde, Oscar 1854(?)-1900 24
   See also CLR *114*
Wilde, Oscar Fingal O'Flahertie Willis
   See Wilde, Oscar
Wilder, Buck
   See Smith, Tim(othy R.)
Wilder, Laura Elizabeth Ingalls
   See Wilder, Laura Ingalls
Wilder, Laura Ingalls 1867-1957 100
   Earlier sketches in SATA *15, 29*
   See also CLR *111*
Wildish, Lee 231
Wildsmith, Brian 1930- 124
   Earlier sketches in SATA *16, 69*
   See also CLR *52*
   See also SAAS *5*
Wiles, Deborah 171
Wilhelm, Doug 1952- 190
Wilhelm, Hans 1945- 196
   Autobiography Feature 196
   Earlier sketches in SATA *58, 135*
   See also CLR *46*
   See also SAAS *21*
Wilkie, Katharine E(lliott) 1904-1980 31
Wilkin, Eloise 1904-1987 49
   Obituary 54
Wilkins, Frances 1923- 14
Wilkins, Kim 147
Wilkins, Marilyn (Ruth) 1926- 30
Wilkins, Marne
   See Wilkins, Marilyn (Ruth)
Wilkins, Mary Huiskamp 1926- 2
   See also CLR *42*
Wilkins, Mary Huiskamp Calhoun
   See Wilkins, Mary Huiskamp
Wilkins, Rose 180
Wilkinson, (Thomas) Barry 1923- 50
   Brief entry 32
Wilkinson, Beth 1925- 80
Wilkinson, Brenda 1946- 91
   Earlier sketch in SATA *14*
   See also CLR *20*
Wilkinson, (John) Burke 1913-2000 4
Wilkinson, Carole 1950- 210
Wilkinson, Sylvia 1940- 56
   Brief entry 39
Wilkon, Jozef 1930- 133
   Earlier sketches in SATA *31, 71*
Wilkowski, Sue 193
Wilks, Michael Thomas 1947- 44
   See Wilks, Mike
Wilks, Mike 224
   See Wilks, Michael Thomas
Will
   See Lipkind, William

Willard, Barbara (Mary) 1909-1994 74
  Earlier sketch in SATA 17
  See also CLR 2
  See also SAAS 5
Willard, Elizabeth Kimmel
  See Kimmel, Elizabeth Cody
Willard, Mildred Wilds 1911-1978 14
Willard, Nancy 1936- 191
  Brief entry 30
  Earlier sketches in SATA 37, 71, 127
  See also CLR 5
Willcox, Isobel 1907-1996 42
Willems, Mo 228
  Earlier sketches in SATA 154, 180
  See also CLR 114
Willett, Edward 1959- 115
Willett, Edward C.
  See Willett, Edward
Willey, Bee 184
Willey, Margaret 1950- 226
  Earlier sketch in SATA 86
Willey, Robert
  See Ley, Willy
Willhoite, Michael A. 1946- 71
William, Kate
  See Armstrong, Jennifer
Williams, Alex 1969- 209
Williams, Arlene 171
Williams, Barbara 1925- 107
  Earlier sketch in SATA 11
  See also CLR 48
  See also SAAS 16
Williams, Barbara 1937- 62
Williams, Beryl
  See Epstein, Beryl
Williams, Brian (Peter) 1943- 54
Williams, Carol Lynch 1959- 212
  Earlier sketch in SATA 110
Williams, Charles
  See Collier, James Lincoln
Williams, Clyde C. 1881-1974 8
  Obituary 27
Williams, Coe
  See Harrison, C(hester) William
Williams, Colleen Madonna Flood 1963- .. 156
Williams, Cynthia G. 1958- 123
Williams, Dar 1967- 168
Williams, Donna Reilly 1945- 83
Williams, Dorothy
  See Williams, Marcia
Williams, Dorothy Snowden
  See Williams, Dar
Williams, Eric (Ernest) 1911-1983 14
  Obituary 38
Williams, Ferelith Eccles
  See Eccles Williams, Ferelith
Williams, Frances B.
  See Browin, Frances Williams
Williams, Garth (Montgomery) 1912-1996 .. 66
  Obituary 90
  Earlier sketch in SATA 18
  See also CLR 57
  See also SAAS 7
Williams, Guy R(ichard) 1920- 11
Williams, Hawley
  See Heyliger, William
Williams, Helen 1948- 77
Williams, J. R.
  See Williams, Jeanne
Williams, J. Walker
  See Wodehouse, P. G.
Williams, Jay 1914-1978 41
  Obituary 24
  Earlier sketch in SATA 3
  See also CLR 8
Williams, Jeanne 1930- 5
Williams, Jenny 1939- 60
Williams, Karen Lynn 1952- 224
  Earlier sketches in SATA 66, 99
Williams, Kathryn 1981- 222

Williams, Kit 1946(?)- 44
  See also CLR 4
Williams, L. E.
  See Williams, Laura E.
Williams, Laura E.
  See Williams, Laura Ellen
Williams, Laura Ellen 180
Williams, Leslie 1941- 42
Williams, Linda 1948- 59
Williams, Louise Bonino 1904(?)-1984
  Obituary 39
Williams, Lynn
  See Hale, Arlene
Williams, Maiya 1962- 230
Williams, Marcia 1945- 159
  Earlier sketches in SATA 71, 97
Williams, Marcia Dorothy
  See Williams, Marcia
Williams, Margery
  See Bianco, Margery Williams
Williams, Mark
  See Arthur, Robert, (Jr.)
Williams, Mark London 1959- 140
Williams, Maureen 1951- 12
Williams, Michael
  See St. John, Wylly Folk
Williams, Patrick J.
  See Griffin, W. E. B.
Williams, Paulette Linda
  See Shange, Ntozake
Williams, Pete
  See Faulknor, Cliff(ord Vernon)
Williams, S. P.
  See Hart, Virginia
Williams, Sam 177
  Earlier sketch in SATA 124
Williams, Selma R(uth) 1925- 14
Williams, Sherley Anne 1944-1999 78
  Obituary 116
Williams, Sheron 1955- 77
Williams, Shirley
  See Williams, Sherley Anne
Williams, Slim
  See Williams, Clyde C.
Williams, Sophy 1965- 135
Williams, Sue 1948-2007 208
Williams, Susan
  See Beckhorn, Susan Williams
Williams, Suzanne
  See Williams, Suzanne Morgan
Williams, Suzanne 1953- 202
  Earlier sketch in SATA 71
Williams, Suzanne M.
  See Williams, Suzanne Morgan
Williams, Suzanne Morgan 1949- 207
Williams, Ursula Moray
  See Moray Williams, Ursula
Williams, Vera B(aker) 1927- 102
  Brief entry 33
  Earlier sketch in SATA 53
  See also CLR 9
Williams-Andriani, Renee 1963- 98
Williams-Ellis, (Mary) Amabel (Nassau
  Strachey) 1894-1984 29
  Obituary 41
Williams-Garcia, Rita 1957- 160
  Earlier sketch in SATA 98
  See also CLR 36
Williamson, Gwyneth 1965- 109
Williamson, Henry (William) 1895-1977 37
  Obituary 30
Williamson, Joanne S(mall) 1926- 122
  Earlier sketch in SATA 3
Williamson, Kate T. 1979- 215
Williamson, Melanie 196
Willis, Charles
  See Clarke, Arthur C.
Willis, Connie 1945- 110
  See also CLR 66
Willis, Cynthia Chapman 215

Willis, Jeanne 1959- 195
  Earlier sketches in SATA 61, 123
Willis, Jeanne Mary
  See Willis, Jeanne
Willis, Meredith Sue 1946- 101
Willis, Nancy Carol 1952- 139
  Earlier sketch in SATA 93
Willis, Paul J. 1955- 113
Willms, Russ 95
Willoughby, Lee Davis
  See Avallone, Michael (Angelo, Jr.)
  and Brandner, Gary (Phil)
  and Deming, Richard
  and DeAndrea, William L(ouis)
  and Laymon, Richard (Carl)
  and Streib, Dan(iel Thomas)
  and Toombs, John
  and Webb, Jean Francis (III)
Willson, Robina Beckles
  See Beckles Willson, Robina
Willson, Sarah
  See Albee, Sarah
Wilma, Dana
  See Faralla, Dana
Wilsdorf, Anne 1954- 191
Wilson, Anne 1974- 224
Wilson, April 80
Wilson, Barbara Ker
  See Ker Wilson, Barbara
Wilson, Beth P(ierre) 8
Wilson, Budge 1927- 55
  Brief entry 51
Wilson, Carletta 1951- 81
Wilson, Carter 1941- 6
Wilson, Charles Morrow 1905-1977 30
Wilson, Christopher B. 1910(?)-1985
  Obituary 46
Wilson, Darryl B(abe) 1939- 90
Wilson, Diane Lee 172
Wilson, Dirk
  See Pohl, Frederick
Wilson, Dorothy Clarke 1904-2003 16
Wilson, Edward A(rthur) 1886-1970 38
Wilson, Ellen (Janet Cameron) (?)-1976 9
  Obituary 26
Wilson, Eric (H.) 1940- 34
  Brief entry 32
Wilson, Erica 51
Wilson, Forrest 1918- 27
Wilson, Gahan 1930- 35
  Brief entry 27
Wilson, Gina 1943- 85
  Brief entry 34
  Earlier sketch in SATA 36
Wilson, (Leslie) Granville 1912- 14
Wilson, Hazel (Hutchins) 1898-1992 3
  Obituary 73
Wilson, J(erry) M. 1964- 121
Wilson, Jacqueline 1945- 199
  Brief entry 52
  Earlier sketches in SATA 61, 102, 153
Wilson, John 1922- 22
Wilson, John 1951- 227
  Earlier sketch in SATA 182
Wilson, John Alexander
  See Wilson, John
Wilson, Johnniece Marshall 1944- 75
Wilson, Jonathan 1950- 181
Wilson, Joyce M. 84
  Earlier sketch in SATA 21
  See also SAAS 24
Wilson, Karma 221
  Earlier sketch in SATA 174
Wilson, Leslie 1952- 166
Wilson, Linda Miller 1936- 116
Wilson, Lionel 1924-2003 33
  Brief entry 31
  Obituary 144
Wilson, Marjorie
  See Wilson, Budge
Wilson, Martin 1973- 205

Wilson, Maurice (Charles John) 1914- 46
Wilson, Nancy Hope 1947- 138
  Earlier sketch in SATA 81
Wilson, Nathan D.
  See Wilson, N.D.
Wilson, N.D. 1978- 194
Wilson, Nick
  See Ellis, Edward S.
Wilson, Phil 1948- 181
Wilson, Ron(ald William) 1941- 38
Wilson, Sarah 1934- 208
  Earlier sketches in SATA 50, 142
Wilson, Tom 1931- 33
  Brief entry 30
Wilson, Troy 1970- 169
Wilson, Walt(er N.) 1939- 14
Wilson-Max, Ken 1965- 170
  Earlier sketch in SATA 93
Wilton, Elizabeth 1937- 14
Wilton, Hal
  See Pepper, Frank S.
Wilwerding, Walter Joseph 1891-1966 9
Wimmer, Mike 1961- 194
  Earlier sketch in SATA 70
Winborn, Marsha (Lynn) 1947- 75
Winch, John 1944- 165
  Earlier sketch in SATA 117
Winchester, James H(ugh) 1917-1985 30
  Obituary 45
Winchester, Stanley
  See Youd, Samuel
Windawi, Thura al- 1983(?)- 165
Winders, Gertrude Hecker -1987 3
Windham, Basil
  See Wodehouse, P. G.
Windham, Kathryn T. 1918-2011 14
Windham, Kathryn Tucker
  See Windham, Kathryn T.
Windham, Sophie 184
Windling, Terri 1958- 151
Windrow, Martin
  See Windrow, Martin Clive
Windrow, Martin C.
  See Windrow, Martin Clive
Windrow, Martin Clive 1944- 68
Windsor, Claire
  See Hamerstrom, Frances
Windsor, Linda 1950- 124
Windsor, Patricia 1938- 78
  Earlier sketch in SATA 30
  See also SAAS 19
Wineman-Marcus, Irene 1952- 81
Winer, Yvonne 1934- 120
Winerip, Michael 175
Winfield, Arthur M.
  See Stratemeyer, Edward L.
Winfield, Edna
  See Stratemeyer, Edward L.
Winfield, Julia
  See Armstrong, Jennifer
Wing, Natasha 1960- 200
  Earlier sketch in SATA 82
Wingerter, Linda S. 1973(?)- 207
Winget, Susan 211
Winick, Judd 1970- 124
Winks, Robin William 1930-2003 61
Winn, Alison
  See Wharmby, Margot
Winn, Chris 1952- 42
Winn, Janet Bruce 1928- 43
Winn, Marie 1936(?)- 38
Winnick, Karen B. 1946- 211
Winnick, Karen B(eth) B(inkoff) 1946- 51
Winn-Lederer, Ilene 198
Winslow, Barbara 1947- 91
Winstead, Rosie 180
Winston, Clara 1921-1983 54
  Obituary 39
Winston, Richard 1917-1979 54
Winston, Sherri 1964(?)- 201
Winter, Janet 1926- 126

Winter, Jeanette 1939- 184
  Earlier sketch in SATA 151
Winter, Jonah 1962- 225
  Earlier sketch in SATA 179
Winter, Milo (Kendall) 1888-1956 21
Winter, Paula Cecelia 1929- 48
Winter, R. R.
  See Winterbotham, R(ussell) R(obert)
Winter, Susan 182
Winterbotham, R(ussell) R(obert)
  1904-1971 10
Winterbotham, Russ
  See Winterbotham, R(ussell) R(obert)
Winterfeld, Henry 1901-1990 55
Winters, J. C.
  See Cross, Gilbert B.
Winters, Jon
  See Cross, Gilbert B.
Winters, Katherine
  See Winters, Kay
Winters, Kay 1936- 153
  Earlier sketch in SATA 103
Winters, Nina 1944- 62
Winters, Paul A. 1965- 106
Winterson, Jeanette 1959- 190
Winterton, Gayle
  See Adams, William Taylor
Winthrop, Elizabeth 1948- 164
  Autobiography Feature 116
  Earlier sketches in SATA 8, 76
  See also CLR 89
Winton, Ian (Kenneth) 1960- 76
Winton, Tim 1960- 98
Wintz-Litty, Julie
  See Litty, Julie
Wirt, Ann
  See Benson, Mildred
Wirt, Mildred A.
  See Benson, Mildred
Wirtenberg, Patricia Z. 1932-2007 10
Wirtenberg, Patricia Zarrella
  See Wirtenberg, Patricia Z.
Wirth, Beverly 1938- 63
Wirths, Claudine (Turner) G(ibson)
  1926-2000 104
  Earlier sketch in SATA 64
Wise, Bill 1958- 191
Wise, Lenny
  See Wise, Leonard
Wise, Leonard 1940- 167
Wise, Leonard A.
  See Wise, Leonard
Wise, Leonard Allan
  See Wise, Leonard
Wise, William 1923- 163
  Earlier sketch in SATA 4
Wise, Winifred E. 2
Wiseman, Ann (Sayre) 1926- 31
Wiseman, B(ernard) 1922-1995 4
Wiseman, David 1916- 43
  Brief entry 40
Wiseman, Eva 1947- 210
Wishinsky, Frieda 1948- 166
  Earlier sketches in SATA 70, 112
Wisler, G(ary) Clifton 1950- 103
  Brief entry 46
  Earlier sketch in SATA 58
Wismer, Donald (Richard) 1946- 59
Wisner, Bill
  See Wisner, William L.
Wisner, William L. 1914(?)-1983 42
Wisnewski, David 1953-2002
  See Wisniewski, David
Wisniewski, David 1953-2002 95
  Obituary 139
  See also CLR 51
Wister, Owen 1860-1938 62
Witham, (Phillip) Ross 1917- 37
Withers, Carl A. 1900-1970 14
Withers, Pam 1956- 182

Withrow, Sarah 1966- 199
  Earlier sketch in SATA 124
Witt, Dick 1948- 80
Witt, Shirley Hill 1934- 17
Wittanen, Etolin 1907- 55
Wittels, Harriet Joan 1938- 31
Wittenstein, Vicki Oransky 1954- 228
Wittig, Susan
  See Albert, Susan Wittig
Wittlinger, Ellen 1948- 189
  Autobiography Feature 128
  Earlier sketches in SATA 83, 122
Wittman, Sally (Anne Christensen) 1941- 30
Witty, Paul 1898-1976 50
  Obituary 30
Wodehouse, P. G. 1881-1975 22
Wodehouse, Pelham Grenville
  See Wodehouse, P. G.
Wodge, Dreary
  See Gorey, Edward (St. John)
Woelfle, Gretchen 1945- 145
Wohlberg, Meg 1905-1990 41
  Obituary 66
Wohlrabe, Raymond A. 1900-1977 4
Wohnoutka, Mike 230
  Earlier sketch in SATA 195
Wojciechowska, Maia (Teresa) 1927-2002 ... 83
  Autobiography Feature 104
  Obituary 134
  Earlier sketches in SATA 1, 28
  See also CLR 1
  See also SAAS 1
Wojciechowski, Susan 126
  Earlier sketch in SATA 78
Wojnarowski, Adrian 1970- 190
Wojtusik, Elizabeth 208
Wolcott, Patty 1929- 14
Wold, Allen L. 1943- 64
Wold, Jo Anne 1938- 30
Woldin, Beth Weiner 1955- 34
Wolf, Allan 1963- 192
Wolf, Bernard 1930- 102
  Brief entry 37
Wolf, Erica (Van Varick) 1978- 156
Wolf, Gita 1956- 101
Wolf, J. M.
  See Wolf, Joan M.
Wolf, Janet 1957- 78
Wolf, Joan M. 1966- 193
Wolf, Sallie 1950- 205
  Earlier sketch in SATA 80
Wolfe, Art 1952- 76
Wolfe, Burton H. 1932- 5
Wolfe, Frances 216
Wolfe, Gene 1931- 165
  Earlier sketch in SATA 118
Wolfe, Gene Rodman
  See Wolfe, Gene
Wolfe, Gillian 199
Wolfe, Louis 1905-1985 8
  Obituary 133
Wolfe, Rinna (Evelyn) 1925- 38
Wolfenden, George
  See Beardmore, George
Wolfer, Dianne 1961- 167
  Autobiography Feature 117
  Earlier sketch in SATA 104
Wolff, Alexander (Nikolaus) 1957- 137
  Earlier sketch in SATA 63
Wolff, Ashley 1956- 203
  Earlier sketches in SATA 50, 81, 155
Wolff, Diane 1945- 27
Wolff, Ferida 1946- 164
  Earlier sketch in SATA 79
Wolff, Jason 1972- 213
Wolff, Jennifer Ashley
  See Wolff, Ashley
Wolff, Nancy 202
Wolff, Robert Jay 1905-1977 10
Wolff, Sonia
  See Levitin, Sonia

Wolff, Virginia Euwer 1937- *137*
Earlier sketch in SATA *78*
See also CLR *62*
Wolfman, Judy 1933- *138*
Wolfson, Evelyn 1937- *62*
Wolitzer, Hilma 1930- *31*
Wolkoff, Judie (Edwards) *93*
Brief entry *37*
Wolkstein, Diane 1942- *138*
Earlier sketches in SATA *7, 82*
Wollheim, Donald A(llen) 1914-1990
Obituary *69*
Wolny, P.
See Janeczko, Paul B(ryan)
Wolters, Richard A. 1920-1993 .... *35*
Wondriska, William 1931- *6*
Wong, Jade Snow 1922-2006 .... *112*
Obituary *175*
Wong, Janet S. 1962- *210*
Earlier sketches in SATA *98, 148*
See also CLR *94*
Wong, Marissa Lopez *226*
Wong, Nicole *214*
Woo, Howie 1974- *207*
Wood, Addie Robinson
See Wiggin, Eric E.
Wood, Anne (Savage) 1937- *64*
Wood, Audrey *198*
Brief entry *44*
Earlier sketches in SATA *50, 81, 139*
See also CLR *26*
Wood, Catherine
See Etchison, Birdie L(ee)
Wood, David 1944- *212*
Earlier sketch in SATA *87*
Wood, Don 1945- *50*
Brief entry *44*
See also CLR *26*
Wood, Douglas 1951- *180*
Earlier sketches in SATA *81, 132*
Wood, Douglas Eric
See Wood, Douglas
Wood, Edgar A(llardyce) 1907-1998 .... *14*
Wood, Esther
See Brady, Esther Wood
Wood, Frances Elizabeth *34*
Wood, Frances M. 1951- *97*
Wood, Jacqueline
See Wood, Jakki
Wood, Jakki 1957- *211*
Wood, James Playsted 1905- *1*
Wood, Jenny 1955- *88*
Wood, John Norris 1930- *85*
Wood, June Rae 1946- *120*
Earlier sketch in SATA *79*
See also CLR *82*
Wood, Kerry
See Wood, Edgar A(llardyce)
Wood, Kim Marie *134*
Wood, Laura N.
See Roper, Laura (Newbold) Wood
Wood, Linda C(arol) 1945- *59*
Wood, Marcia 1956- *80*
Wood, Marcia Mae
See Wood, Marcia
Wood, Nancy
See Wood, Nancy C.
Wood, Nancy C. 1936- *178*
Earlier sketch in SATA *6*
Wood, Nuria
See Nobisso, Josephine
Wood, Owen 1929- *64*
Wood, Phyllis Anderson 1923- *33*
Brief entry *30*
Wood, Richard 1949- *110*
Wood, Tim(othy William Russell) 1946- *88*
Wood, Wallace 1927-1981
Obituary *33*
Woodard, Carol 1929- *14*

Woodburn, John Henry 1914- *11*
Woodbury, David Oakes 1896-1981 .... *62*
Woodford, Peggy 1937- *25*
Woodhouse, Barbara (Blackburn)
1910-1988 .... *63*
Woodhull, Ann Love *194*
Wooding, Chris 1977- *166*
Wooding, Sharon
See Wooding, Sharon L(ouise)
Wooding, Sharon L(ouise) 1943- *66*
Woodman, Allen 1954- *76*
Woodrich, Mary Neville 1915- *2*
Woodruff, Elvira 1951- *211*
Earlier sketches in SATA *70, 106, 162*
Woodruff, Joan Leslie 1953- *104*
Woodruff, Liza 1971(?)- *182*
Woodruff, Marian
See Goudge, Eileen
Woodruff, Noah 1977- *86*
Woods, George A(llan) 1926-1988 .... *30*
Obituary *57*
Woods, Geraldine 1948- *111*
Brief entry *42*
Earlier sketch in SATA *56*
Woods, Harold 1945- *56*
Brief entry *42*
Woods, Lawrence
See Lowndes, Robert A(ugustine) W(ard)
Woods, Margaret 1921- *2*
Woods, Nat
See Stratemeyer, Edward L.
Woods, Titania
See Weatherly, Lee
Woodson, Jack
See Woodson, John Waddie Jr.
Woodson, Jacqueline 1964- *189*
Earlier sketches in SATA *94, 139*
See also CLR *49*
Woodson, Jacqueline Amanda
See Woodson, Jacqueline
Woodson, John Waddie Jr. 1913- *10*
Woodtor, Dee
See Woodtor, Delores Parmer
Woodtor, Dee Parmer 1945(?)-2002
See Woodtor, Delores Parmer
Woodtor, Delores Parmer 1945-2002 .... *93*
Wood-Trost, Lucille
See Trost, Lucille W(ood)
Woodward, (Landon) Cleveland 1900-1986 . *10*
Obituary *48*
Woodworth, Chris 1957- *168*
Woodworth, Viki 1952- *127*
Woody, Regina Jones 1894-1983 .... *3*
Woodyadd, Charlotte
See Hough, Charlotte
Woog, Adam 1953- *125*
Earlier sketch in SATA *84*
Wooldridge, Connie Nordhielm 1950- *143*
Earlier sketch in SATA *92*
Wooldridge, Frosty 1947- *140*
Wooldridge, Rhoda 1906-1988 .... *22*
Wooley, Susan Frelick 1945- *113*
Woolf, Paula 1950- *104*
Woolfe, Angela 1976- *169*
Woolley, Catherine 1904-2005 .... *3*
Obituary *166*
Woolman, Steven 1969-2004 .... *163*
Earlier sketch in SATA *90*
Woolsey, Janette 1904-1989 .... *3*
Obituary *131*
Worcester, Donald E(mmet) 1915- *18*
Word, Reagan 1944- *103*
Work, Virginia 1946- *57*
Brief entry *45*
Worline, Bonnie Bess 1914- *14*
Wormell, Christopher 1955- *154*
Earlier sketch in SATA *103*
Wormell, Mary 1959- *96*

Wormser, Richard 1933- *106*
Autobiography Feature *118*
See also SAAS *26*
Wormser, Sophie 1897-1979 .... *22*
Worth, Richard
See Wiggin, Eric E.
Worth, Richard 1945- *59*
Brief entry *46*
Worth, Valerie 1933-1994 .... *81*
Earlier sketches in SATA *8, 70*
See also CLR *21*
Worthington, Leonie 1956- *200*
Wortis, Avi
See Avi
Wortis, Edward Irving
See Avi
Wosmek, Frances 1917- *29*
Woychuk, Denis 1953- *71*
Wrede, Patricia C(ollins) 1953- *146*
Earlier sketch in SATA *67*
Wriggins, Sally Hovey 1922- *17*
Wright, Alexandra 1979- *103*
Wright, Betty Ren 1927- *109*
Brief entry *48*
Earlier sketch in SATA *63*
Wright, Cliff 1963- *168*
Earlier sketch in SATA *76*
Wright, Courtni
See Wright, Courtni C(rump)
Wright, Courtni C(rump) 1950- *84*
Wright, Courtni Crump
See Wright, Courtni C(rump)
Wright, Dare 1914(?)-2001 .... *21*
Obituary *124*
Wright, David K. 1943- *112*
Earlier sketch in SATA *73*
Wright, Elinor
See Lyon, Elinor
Wright, Enid Meadowcroft (LaMonte)
1898-1966 .... *3*
Wright, Esmond 1915-2003 .... *10*
Wright, Frances Fitzpatrick 1897-1982 .... *10*
Wright, J. B.
See Barkan, Joanne
Wright, Johanna *220*
Wright, Judith 1915-2000 .... *14*
Obituary *121*
Wright, Judith Arundell
See Wright, Judith
Wright, Katrina
See Gater, Dilys
Wright, Kenneth
See del Rey, Lester
Wright, Kit 1944- *87*
Wright, Leslie B(ailey) 1959- *91*
Wright, Michael 1954- *198*
Wright, Nancy Means *38*
Wright, R(obert) H(amilton) 1906- *6*
Wright, Rachel *220*
Earlier sketch in SATA *134*
Wright, Susan Kimmel 1950- *97*
Wrightfrierson
See Wright-Frierson, Virginia (Marguerite)
Wright-Frierson, Virginia (Marguerite)
1949- *110*
Earlier sketch in SATA *58*
Wrightson, Alice Patricia
See Wrightson, Patricia
Wrightson, Patricia 1921-2010 .... *112*
Obituary *215*
Earlier sketches in SATA *8, 66*
See also CLR *154*
See also SAAS *4*
Wroble, Lisa A. 1963- *134*
Wrongo, I.B.
See Katz, Alan
Wronker, Lili
See Wronker, Lili Cassel
Wronker, Lili Cassel 1924- *10*

Wryde, Dogear
    See Gorey, Edward (St. John)
Wu, Donald 212
Wu, Elizabeth
    See Wu, Liz
Wu, Liz 184
Wu, Norbert 1961- 155
    Earlier sketch in SATA *101*
Wulf, Linda Press 205
Wulffson, Don 1943- 155
    Earlier sketches in SATA *32, 88*
Wulffson, Don L.
    See Wulffson, Don
Wummer, Amy 1955- 201
Wunderli, Stephen 1958- 79
Wunsch, Josephine (McLean) 1914- 64
Wunsch, Marjory 1942- 220
    Earlier sketch in SATA *82*
Wuorio, Eva-Lis 1918- 34
    Brief entry 28
Wurts, Janny 1953- 98
Wyatt, B. D.
    See Robinson, Spider
Wyatt, David 1968- 185
Wyatt, Jane
    See Bradbury, Bianca (Ryley)
Wyatt, Melissa 1963- 177
Wyatt, Valerie 209
Wyeth, Betsy James 1921- 41
Wyeth, N(ewell) C(onvers) 1882-1945 17
    See also CLR *106*
Wyler, Rose 1909-2000 18
    Obituary 121
Wylie, Betty Jane 48
Wylie, Laura
    See Matthews, Patricia
Wylie, Laurie
    See Matthews, Patricia
Wyllie, Stephen 86
Wyman, Andrea 75
Wyman, Carolyn 1956- 83
Wymer, Norman (George) 1911- 25
Wynard, Talbot
    See Hamilton, Charles (Harold St. John)
Wyndham, John
    See Harris, John (Wyndham Parkes Lucas)
    Beynon
Wyndham, Lee
    See Hyndman, Jane Andrews Lee
Wyndham, Robert
    See Hyndman, Robert Utley
Wynne, Patricia J. 210
Wynne-Jones, Tim 1948- 186
    Autobiography Feature 136
    Earlier sketches in SATA *67, 96, 136*
    See also CLR *58*
Wynne-Jones, Timothy
    See Wynne-Jones, Tim
Wynter, Edward (John) 1914- 14
Wynyard, Talbot
    See Hamilton, Charles (Harold St. John)
Wyss, Johann David Von 1743-1818 29
    Brief entry 27
    See also CLR *92*
Wyss, Thelma Hatch 1934- 202
    Earlier sketches in SATA *10, 140*

X

Xavier, Father
    See Hurwood, Bernhardt J.
Xuan, YongSheng 1952- 226
    Autobiography Feature 226
    Earlier sketch in SATA *116*

Y

Yaccarino, Dan 192
    Earlier sketch in SATA *141*
Yadin, (Rav-Aloof) Yigael 1917-1984 55
Yaffe, Alan
    See Yorinks, Arthur
Yagher, Kevin 1962- 143
Yakovetic, (Joseph Sandy) 1952- 59
Yakovetic, Joe
    See Yakovetic, (Joseph Sandy)
Yamada, Utako 1963- 188
Yamaguchi, Marianne (Illenberger) 1936- 7
Yamaka, Sara 1978- 92
Yamanaka, Lois-Ann 1961- 166
Yamasaki, Katie 206
Yancey, Diane 1951- 138
    Earlier sketch in SATA *81*
Yancey, Richard 193
Yancey, Rick
    See Yancey, Richard
Yang, Belle 1960- 170
Yang, James 1960- 190
Yang, Jay 1941- 12
Yang, Mingyi 1943- 72
Yarbrough, Camille 1938- 79
    See also CLR *29*
Yarbrough, Ira 1910(?)-1983
    Obituary 35
Yaroslava
    See Mills, Yaroslava Surmach
Yarrow, Peter 1938- 195
Yashima, Taro
    See Iwamatsu, Jun Atsushi
Yates, Elizabeth 1905-2001 68
    Obituary 128
    Earlier sketch in SATA *4*
    See also SAAS *6*
Yates, Janelle K(aye) 1957- 77
Yates, John 1939- 74
Yates, Kelly 1971- 208
Yates, Louise 1983(?)- 218
Yates, Philip 1956- 212
    Earlier sketches in SATA *92, 149*
Yates, Raymond F(rancis) 1895-1966 31
Yaukey, Grace S(ydenstricker) 1899-1994 ... 80
    Earlier sketch in SATA *5*
Yayo 1961- 226
Yazzie, Johnson 1946- 205
Ye, Ting-xing 1952- 106
Yeahpau, Thomas M. 1975- 187
Yeakley, Marjory Hall 1908- 21
Yeates, Thomas 1955- 230
Yeatman, Linda 1938- 42
Yeatts, Tabatha 1970- 215
Yee, Brenda Shannon 133
Yee, Lisa 1959- 218
    Earlier sketch in SATA *160*
Yee, Paul 1956- 211
    Earlier sketches in SATA *67, 96, 143*
    See also CLR *44*
Yee, Tammy 206
Yee, Wong Herbert 1953- 172
    Earlier sketches in SATA *78, 115*
Yeh, Chun-Chan 1914- 79
Ye Junjian
    See Yeh, Chun-Chan
Yelchin, Eugene 1956- 196
Yenawine, Philip 1942- 85
Yensid, Retlaw
    See Disney, Walt(er Elias)
Yeo, Wilma (Lethem) 1918-1994 81
    Earlier sketch in SATA *24*
Yeoman, John 1934- 80
    Earlier sketch in SATA *28*
    See also CLR *46*
Yep, Kathleen S. 203

Yep, Laurence 1948- 213
    Earlier sketches in SATA *7, 69, 123, 176*
    See also CLR *132*
Yep, Laurence Michael
    See Yep, Laurence
Yepsen, Roger B(ennet), Jr. 1947- 59
Yerian, Cameron John 21
Yerian, Margaret A. 21
Yerxa, Leo 1947- 181
Yetska
    See Ironside, Jetske
Yezerski, Thomas F. 1969- 190
Yin 194
Ylvisaker, Anne 1965(?)- 172
Yoder, Carolyn P. 1953- 149
Yoder, Carolyn Patricia
    See Yoder, Carolyn P.
Yoder, Dorothy Meenen 1921- 96
Yoder, Dot
    See Yoder, Dorothy Meenen
Yoder, Walter D. 1933- 88
Yohalem, Eve 219
Yolen, Jane 1939- 230
    Autobiography Feature 111
    Earlier sketches in SATA *4, 40, 75, 112, 158,
    194*
    See also CLR *149*
    See also SAAS *1*
Yolen, Jane Hyatt
    See Yolen, Jane
Yonezu, Yusuke 196
Yonge, Charlotte 1823-1901 17
Yonge, Charlotte Mary
    See Yonge, Charlotte
Yoo, Paula 1969(?)- 174
Yoo, Taeeun 191
Yoon, Salina 1972- 204
Yorinks, Adrienne 1956- 171
Yorinks, Arthur 1953- 200
    Earlier sketches in SATA *33, 49, 85, 144*
    See also CLR *20*
York, Alison
    See Nicole, Christopher
York, Andrew
    See Nicole, Christopher
York, Carol Beach 1928- 77
    Earlier sketch in SATA *6*
York, Rebecca
    See Buckholtz, Eileen (Garber)
    and Glick, Ruth
York, Simon
    See Heinlein, Robert A.
Yoshida, Toshi 1911- 77
Yoshikawa, Sachiko 181
Yost, Edna 1889-1971
    Obituary 26
Youd, C. S.
    See Youd, Samuel
Youd, Samuel 1922- 135
    Brief entry 30
    Earlier sketch in SATA *47*
    See also CLR *2*
    See also SAAS *6*
Youme
    See Landowne, Youme
Young, Amy L. 185
Young, Anne Mortimer
    See Mortimer, Anne
Young, Bob
    See Young, Robert W(illiam)
    and Young, James Robert
Young, Carol 1945- 102
Young, Catherine
    See Olds, Helen Diehl
Young, Clarence
    See Garis, Howard R.
    and Stratemeyer, Edward L.
Young, Collier
    See Bloch, Robert (Albert)

Young, Dan 1952- 126
Young, Dianne 1959- 88
Young, Dorothea Bennett 1924- 31
Young, Ed 1931- 211
Earlier sketches in SATA 10, 74, 122, 173
See also CLR 27
Young, Ed Tse-chun
See Young, Ed
Young, Edward
See Reinfeld, Fred
Young, E.L. 1973- 219
Young, Elaine L.
See Schulte, Elaine L(ouise)
Young, Emma L.
See Young, E.L.
Young, James
See Graham, Ian
Young, Jan
See Young, Janet Randall
Young, Janet 1957- 188
Young, Janet Randall 1919-1994 3
Young, Janet Ruth
See Young, Janet
Young, Jeff C. 1948- 132
Young, John
See Macintosh, Brownie
Young, Judy 1956- 207
Earlier sketch in SATA 155
Young, Judy (Elaine) Dockrey 1949- 72
Young, Karen Romano 1959- 168
Earlier sketch in SATA 116
Young, Ken 1956- 86
Young, Lois Horton 1911-1981 26
Young, Louisa 161
Young, Louise B. 1919- 64
Young, Margaret B. 1922-2009 2
Young, Margaret Buckner
See Young, Margaret B.
Young, Mary 1940- 89
Young, Miriam 1913-1974 7
Young, Noela 1930- 89
Young, (Rodney Lee) Patrick (Jr.) 1937- 22
Young, Percy M(arshall) 1912-2004 31
Obituary 154
Young, Richard Alan 1946- 72
Young, Robert W(illiam) 1916-1969 3
Young, Ross B. 1955- 150
Young, Ruth 1946- 67
Young, Sara
See Pennypacker, Sara
Young, Scott A. 1918-2005 5
Young, Scott Alexander
See Young, Scott A.
Young, Selina 1971-2006 201
Young, Vivien
See Gater, Dilys
Younger, Barbara 1954- 108
Youngs, Betty 1934-1985 53
Obituary 42
Younkin, Paula 1942- 77
Yount, Lisa (Ann) 1944- 124
Earlier sketch in SATA 74
Yourgrau, Barry 179
Yuditskaya, Tatyana 1964- 75
Yue, Stephanie 1984- 231
Yum, Hyewon 211
Yumoto, Kazumi 1959- 153

Z

Zach, Cheryl (Byrd) 1947- 98
Brief entry 51
Earlier sketch in SATA 58
See also SAAS 24
Zacharias, Gary L. 1946- 153
Zadoff, Allen 1967- 224
Zaffo, George J. (?)-1984 42

Zagarenski, Pamela 1969(?)- 183
Zagwyn, Deborah Turney 1953- 138
Earlier sketch in SATA 78
Zahares, Wade 193
Zahler, Diane 228
Zahn, Timothy 1951- 156
Earlier sketch in SATA 91
Zaid, Barry 1938- 51
Zaidenberg, Arthur 1908(?)-1990 34
Obituary 66
Zakanitch, Robert Rahway 1935- 231
Zakanitch, Robert S.
See Zakanitch, Robert Rahway
Zalben, Jane Breskin 1950- 170
Earlier sketches in SATA 7, 79, 120
See also CLR 84
Zallinger, Jean (Day) 1918- 115
Earlier sketches in SATA 14, 80
Zallinger, Peter Franz 1943- 49
Zambreno, Mary Frances 1954- 140
Earlier sketch in SATA 75
Zanderbergen, George
See May, Julian
Zappa, Ahmet 1974- 180
Zappa, Ahmet Emuukha Rodan
See Zappa, Ahmet
Zappler, Lisbeth 1930- 10
Zarchy, Harry 1912-1987 34
Zarin, Cynthia 1959- 192
Earlier sketch in SATA 108
Zaring, Jane (Thomas) 1936- 40
Zarins, Joyce Audy
See dos Santos, Joyce Audy
Zaslavsky, Claudia 1917- 36
Zaugg, Sandra L. 1938- 118
Zaugg, Sandy
See Zaugg, Sandra L.
Zaunders, Bo 1939- 137
Zawadzki, Marek 1958- 97
Zebra, A.
See Scoltock, Jack
Zebrowski, George 1945- 67
Zebrowski, George T.
See Zebrowski, George
Zecca, Katherine 207
Zeck, Gerald Anthony 1939- 40
Zeck, Gerry
See Zeck, Gerald Anthony
Zed, Dr.
See Penrose, Gordon
Zei, Alki 1925- 24
See also CLR 6
Zeier, Joan T(heresa) 1931- 81
Zeinert, Karen 1942-2002 137
Earlier sketch in SATA 79
Zeises, Lara M. 1976- 184
Earlier sketch in SATA 145
Zelazny, Roger 1937-1995 57
Brief entry 39
Zelazny, Roger Joseph
See Zelazny, Roger
Zeldis, Malcah 1931- 146
Earlier sketch in SATA 86
Zelinsky, Paul O. 1953- 154
Brief entry 33
Earlier sketches in SATA 49, 102
See also CLR 55
Zellan, Audrey Penn
See Penn, Audrey
Zemach, Harve
See Fischtrom, Harvey
Zemach, Kaethe 1958- 149
Brief entry 39
Earlier sketch in SATA 49
Zemach, Margot 1931-1989 70
Obituary 59
Earlier sketch in SATA 21
Zemach-Bersin, Kaethe
See Zemach, Kaethe

Zeman, Ludmila 1947- 153
Zepeda, Gwendolyn 1971- 206
Zephaniah, Benjamin 1958- 189
Earlier sketches in SATA 86, 140
Zephaniah, Benjamin Obadiah Iqbal
See Zephaniah, Benjamin
Zephaniah, Benjamin Pbadiah Iqubal
See Zephaniah, Benjamin
Zerman, Melvyn Bernard 1930-2010 46
Zettner, Pat 1940- 70
Zevin, Gabrielle 1977- 176
Zhang, Christopher Zhong-Yuan 1954- 91
Zhang, Song Nan 1942- 170
Earlier sketch in SATA 85
Ziefert, Harriet 1941- 205
Earlier sketches in SATA 101, 154
Ziegler, Jack (Denmore) 1942- 60
Ziemienski, Dennis (Theodore) 1947- 10
Ziliox, Marc
See Fichter, George S.
Zillah
See Macdonald, Zillah K(atherine)
Zim, Herbert S(pencer) 1909-1994 30
Obituary 85
Earlier sketch in SATA 1
See also CLR 2
See also SAAS 2
Zim, Sonia Bleeker 1909-1971 2
Obituary 26
Zima, Gordon 1920- 90
Zimelman, Nathan 1921- 65
Brief entry 37
Zimmer, Dirk 1943- 147
Earlier sketch in SATA 65
Zimmer, Tracie Vaughn 169
Zimmerman, Andrea 1950- 192
Earlier sketch in SATA 123
Zimmerman, Andrea Griffing
See Zimmerman, Andrea
Zimmerman, H. Werner 1951- 101
Zimmerman, Heinz Werner
See Zimmerman, H. Werner
Zimmerman, Naoma 1914-2004 10
Zimmermann, Arnold E. 1909- 58
Zimmermann, Karl 1943- 211
Zimmermann, Karl R.
See Zimmermann, Karl
Zimmett, Debbie
See Becker, Deborah Zimmett
Zimmy
See Stratemeyer, Edward L.
Zimnik, Reiner 1930- 36
See also CLR 3
Zindel, Bonnie 1943- 34
Zindel, Lizabeth 187
Zindel, Paul 1936-2003 102
Obituary 142
Earlier sketches in SATA 16, 58
See also CLR 85
Ziner, Feenie
See Ziner, Florence
Ziner, Florence 1921- 5
Zingara, Professor
See Leeming, Joseph
Zinger, Yitskhok
See Singer, Isaac Bashevis
Zink, Michelle 1969- 220
Zion, Eugene 1913-1975 18
Zion, Gene
See Zion, Eugene
Zobel, Allia
See Zobel Nolan, Allia
Zobel Nolan, Allia 218
Zoehfeld, Kathleen Weidner 1954- 193
Zohorsky, Janet R. 1958- 148
Zolkower, Edie Stoltz 171
Zolkowski, Cathy (A.) 1969- 121
Zollars, Jaime 191

Zolotow, Charlotte 1915- *138*
    Earlier sketches in SATA *1, 35, 78*
    See also CLR *77*
Zolotow, Charlotte Gertrude Shapiro
    See Zolotow, Charlotte
Zolotow, Ellen
    See Dragonwagon, Crescent
Zonderman, Jon 1957- *92*
Zonia, Dhimitri 1921- *20*
Zonta, Pat 1951- *143*
Zubrowski, Bernard 1939- *90*
    Earlier sketch in SATA *35*
Zubrowski, Bernie
    See Zubrowski, Bernard
Zucker, Jonny *228*

Zucker, Miriam S.
    See Reichert, Miriam Zucker
Zuckerman, Amy *217*
Zuckerman, Andrew 1977- *224*
Zuckerman, Linda *190*
Zudeck, Darryl 1961- *61*
Zug, Mark *204*
Zulkey, Claire 1979- *225*
Zupa, G. Anthony
    See Zeck, Gerald Anthony
Zupancic, Lilijana Praprotnik
    See Prap, Lila
Zurbo, Matt(hew) 1967- *98*
Zurhorst, Charles (Stewart, Jr.) 1913-1989 .. *12*
Zurlo, Tony 1941- *145*

Zuromskis, Diane
    See Stanley, Diane
Zuromskis, Diane Stanley
    See Stanley, Diane
Zusak, Markus 1975- *149*
Zwahlen, Diana 1947- *88*
Zweifel, Frances W. 1931- *14*
Zwerger, Lisbeth 1954- *194*
    Earlier sketches in SATA *66, 130*
    See also CLR *46*
    See also SAAS *13*
Zwinger, Ann (H.) 1925- *46*
Zymet, Cathy Alter 1965- *121*